x Mallers Laubhütte.

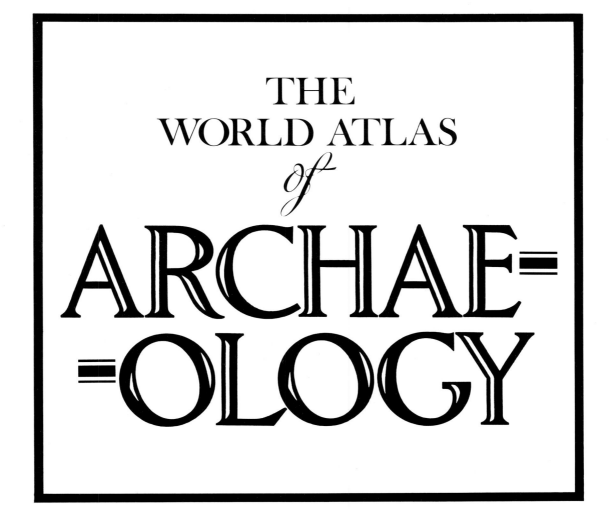

THE
WORLD ATLAS
of
ARCHAE-
-OLOGY

Foreword by
Michael Wood

THE WORLD ATLAS
of
ARCHAE=
=OLOGY

PORTLAND HOUSE
New York

Edited by Mitchell Beazley International Ltd.,
and published in the United Kingdom by Mitchell Beazley,
Artists House, 14–15 Manette Street, London W1V 5LB

Translations in association with First Edition, Cambridge

Original French edition *Le Grand Atlas de l'archéologie*
© Encyclopædia Universalis, 1985
English translation © Mitchell Beazley Publishers 1985
Filmset in Eastleigh, England by Vantage Photosetting Co. Ltd.
Printed and bound in Spain by Printer Industria Grafica S.A., Barcelona
DLB 5649–1988

This 1988 edition published by Portland House, a division of dilithium Press, Ltd.
distributed by Crown Publishers, Inc., 225 Park Avenue South,
New York, New York 10003.

ISBN 0–517–66876–9

hgfedcba

The World Atlas of Archaeology

is the English edition of

Le Grand Atlas de l'archéologie

created by Encyclopædia Universalis

Contributors:
Christine Flon (editor)
**Louis Allaire, Jean Andreau, Daniel Arnaud, Olivier Aurenche,
Dominique Baffier, Ida Baldassarre, François Berthier,
Thierry Berthoud, Dominique Beyer, Jean-François Bouchard,
Françoise Boudon, Jacques Cauvin, Claude Chapdelaine,
Jean Chapelot, Jean Chavaillon, Norman Clermont, Serge Cleuziou,
Jean Devisse, Colette Diény, Dinh Trong Hieu, Marcel Durliat,
Danielle Elisseeff, Vadime Elisseeff, Jean-Yves Empereur,
Catherine Farizy, Jean-Daniel Forest, Henri-Paul Francfort,
José Garanger, Jean-Claude Gardin, René Ginouvès,
Maud Girard-Geslan, Frantz Grenet, Bernard Philippe Groslier,
NIède Guidon, Jean Guilaine, Jean Guillaume, Caroline Gyss-Vermande,
Françoise Hamon, Bernard Holtzmann, Francis Hours, Jean-Louis Huot,
Jean-François Jarrige, Michèle Julien, Michel Kazanski,
Susan Keech McIntosh, Jean-Baptiste Kiethega, Danièle Lavallée,
Jean Leclant, Jacques Lefort, Marie Le Mière, Eliane Lenoir,
Maurice Lenoir, Pierre Leriche, Arlette Leroi-Gourhan,
Philippe Leveau, François Rodriguez Loubet, François Loyer,
Claudine Maréchal, Jean-Claude Margueron,
Roderick James McIntosh, Evelyne Mesnil, Dominique Michelet,
Jean-Pierre Mohen, Jean-François Moreau, Carole Morgan,
Cécile Morrisson, Antoinette Nelken-Terner,
Christine Niederberger Betton, Jean-Pierre Olivier, Michel Orliac,
Madeleine Paul-David, Nicole Périn, Patrick Périn, Olivier Picard,
Michèle Pirazzoli-t'Serstevens, Patrick Plumet,
Jean-François Reynaud, Eric Rieth, Denise Robert-Chaleix,
Agnès Rouveret, Richard P. Schaedel, Véronique Schiltz,
Christian Seignobos, Christine Shimizu, Samuel Sidibé,
Jean-Pierre Sodini, Per Sørensen, Jean-Michel Spieser,
Gilles Tassé, Michel Terrasse, Alain Thote, René Treuil**

Executive Editor: **James Hughes**
Designer: **Zoë Davenport**
Editors: **Margaret Crowther, Elizabeth Pichon**
Editorial Assistant: **Barbara Gish**
Production: **Philip Collyer**

Contents

Foreword

The archaeological excavator is not digging up *things*, he is digging up *people* . . . the life of the past and the present are diverse but indivisible.
Sir Mortimer Wheeler
Archaeology from the Earth (1954)

Time present and time past
Are both perhaps present in time future,
And time future contained in time past.
T.S. Eliot
Four Quartets (1943)

History is a dialogue between past and present in which the present takes and keeps the initiative. The historian cannot be expected to see a society in the same way it saw itself. . . . Only by relating the past to the present can we make it reveal secrets which it has so far kept from even the most careful investigators.

Raymond Aron
Dimensions de la conscience historique (1961)

The poet and the scientist for once agree in their goals: with archaeology we confront a deep need in humankind. In a sense historical thought is the first, the mother of the sciences.

For most people today the archaeologist conjures up a romantic image: a person who searches for lost cities in the depths of the jungle, uncovers ancient tombs buried in the desert, investigates myths and legends, and "proves" the old stories true. This image has provided Hollywood with box-office hits from the beginning of the movies to the present day when, fedora on head, bullwhip in hand, Dr Indiana Jones goes in search of the Lost Ark or the Temple of Doom, divining the secrets of mysterious civilizations from ancient texts and arcane inscriptions. We acknowledge the portrayal as a fantasy; like all fantasies it contains a tiny element of truth, but reality is another matter entirely.

We live in troubled times. From the privileged vantage point of Western civilization in the 1980s it is almost a commonplace that the religious and philosophical systems of the ancient world, on which our own culture has relied, have become increasingly distanced from the needs of the majority of humankind. The world religions which arose during the decline of the Classical world, Christianity and Islam, are now variously in lassitude or turmoil. Western parliamentary democracy has suddenly come to be seen as a fragile, idiosyncratic, and not necessarily permanent growth in world history. Capitalism is frequently spoken of as being in crisis—and yet the utopian communist political systems which hoped to supplant it, beginning in the Soviet Union in 1917, are already economically feeble or morally bankrupt, and have shown themselves no less ruthless as imperialists. More important still, in the 1980s it is now clear that throughout the so-called Third World people are faced with vast and tragic problems which mankind has never previously experienced, namely underdevelopment: this condition, in which two-thirds of the population of the world now live, appears to be a modern phenomenon, unknown in previous epochs of human history. Finally, over it all, there hangs the threat that mankind could obliterate itself in a nuclear war. That is where the human race stands, 6,000 short years after it began to keep records of its civilization.

In such times the reconstruction of the past is not an end in itself. It is a matter of contemporary interest and importance, even of urgency, requiring constant exploration and reinterpretation in order to help us understand the times in which we live. It is natural that appeal should be made to the past for the cultural identity seemingly lost in modern industrial and colonial transformations. Hence archaeology recently has made such headway in China after Mao; in parts of post-colonial black Africa (where black history was frequently suppressed by the white colonials); in Southeast Asia, or for that matter in Britain—now heading to become the first "post-industrial" nation. We are all in search of the past. No longer is there such confidence in the future, but in the past there is at least an identity, a sense of belonging.

Such an attitude to the past has been common in all periods of history. Frequently, it has taken the form of golden age myths—that somehow the past was always "better". Rulers from Rameses II to Ronald Reagan have appealed to it for corroboration of their aims. There is, it would seem, no culture which has not taken pains to record its history in whatever way it thought appropriate, whether in oral tradition, manuscript, print or computer bank. (Every culture, we might add, has also taken *pleasure* in contemplating past time, as well as deeming it a duty to record its traditions and to bear historical witness, albeit of an often selective kind.)

The ancestors of archaeology

For this reason, although we often date the "birth" of archaeology either to the Renaissance or to the 19th century, depending on what we mean by "birth", the deliberate search for the antiquities of former ages goes far back in history. An early example is in the 13th century BC, when Khaemwaset, son of Pharaoh Rameses II of Egypt, instituted a systematic campaign to clear the ancient monuments of Egypt and even physically to restore buildings going back as far as the 3rd Dynasty Step Pyramid of Djoser, "greatly desiring to restore the monuments of the kings of Upper and Lower Egypt *because of what they had achieved* and because the monuments were falling into decay". Khaemwaset, who has been dubbed the "Egyptologist prince", was at pains to emphasize that the accurate recording of the date and architect was important for posterity, not only for the gods.

Similar examples could be cited, from Babylon to China—of kings who collected antiquities, engaged in antiquarian research, and even dug on ancient sites to obtain artifacts. In the first century AD in Rome it was apparently possible to see ancient paintings and artifacts in a kind of museum or art gallery, according to Petronius's *Satyricon*. But it seems safe to assume, on the basis of surviving texts, that no work of comparative classification and chronology was done in the ancient world, despite their ability to relate artifacts found in the ground to a general perception of the three "metal ages" of prehistoric mankind, namely the Stone, Bronze and Iron Ages, an idea found alike in Greek texts from the 7th century BC onwards and in a Chinese compilation of the 1st century AD.

However, it was in ancient Greece that the basis of modern ideas about archaeology developed. Earlier cultures had produced literary works which can loosely be called historical. For example, there was a long tradition of royal annals in Babylon and Egypt. The more factual, reasoned and even objective royal "biographies" of the Hittites strike us today as remarkably contemporary in tone; and the historical books of the Old Testament in a sense provide a model for a "universal history". But it was the Greeks who began the practice of studying all the observable remains of a society. It was Greek travellers and historians, men like Hecataeus and Herodotus, who indulged in anthropology and ethnology, who observed "barbarian" peoples and recorded a vast amount of information about humankind. Unfortunately, an "anthropology and ethnology of the ancient world", which would be of immense value to us today, was never systematized even by the geographers and scholars of Alexandria, and most of the raw material is now lost. The kind of information it might have given us can be judged by a late descendant of the tradition, Tacitus's "anthropological" work on Britain and Germany, the *Germania*.

Some ancient scholars even mooted the idea that the original cradle of mankind was Africa. The continent had first been circumnavigated around 600BC, and Greek scholars in Egypt in Herodotus's day (5th century BC) probably realized that before the invention of fire, and the introduction of organized agriculture, primitive peoples were more likely to have lived in the tropics where systematic cultivation has never been vital for survival, where storage of food is unnecessary, and clothes need not be worn. In such simple anthropological ideas, the germ of archaeology lay.

The Greeks, then, appear to have been alone among the ancient inhabitants of our planet in reaching the stage of rational reflection on the development of primitive man: the first step before knowledge can be employed in the service of science. The next step was almost taken in the medieval Arab world, although the Arab historiographical development had no descendants. The Arab historian Ibn Khaldun

(1337–1406) is now considered a greater historian than any of the ancients, with his penetrating analysis of social structures, his anthropological observations, and his stress on the relevance of environment and climate (*Introduction to History, History of the Berbers*). Especially interesting is Khaldun's proposal that the reasons for change and decline in a society may be traced to its own internal organization rather than to external causes—an idea very much on the lines of today's "new archaeology", as we shall see. But Khaldun had no intellectual disciples until the present century: rather surprising considering that historical thought had a more important role in the Arab world than in any other pre-industrial society.

Instead, the crucial step towards the science of archaeology was not taken until the Renaissance in Western Europe. We can point to certain catalysts: the rediscovery of the Classical world through texts and inscriptions; the fragmentation of the Christian world view with its determinist historiography; finally, the discovery of the New World—a very important development in the origins of archaeology. The discovery of the Americas, and then Polynesia, threw an entirely new light on the comparative stages of civilization at different times and places on earth. We are familiar now with the powerful effect of this on the imaginations of artists and thinkers of the Renaissance and the Enlightenment, from Shakespeare to Rousseau. In those two centuries, as thinkers freed themselves from metaphysical explanations of human history, a scientific view of our pre-classical past was gradually shaped: where had "naked unaccommodated man" or the "noble savage" come from? What were the stages from barbarism to civilization?

Antiquarians groped towards these ideas in the two centuries 1550–1750, years which might be termed the prelude to scientific archaeology. The first occurrence of the word in the English language, simply meaning a record of antiquities, comes in 1607, and for most of the period until the 18th century "Archiology" retained the narrow meaning of the study of monuments, or rather, inscriptions. However, something like archaeology in the modern sense *was* being practised and written about, especially by British antiquarians such as Camden, Aubrey and Stukeley. John Aubrey's books, written in the 1650s and 1660s, reveal a strikingly "modern" approach to the sources. In his attempt to write an account of the ancient Britons (the word prehistory had not yet been invented) Aubrey uses the evidence of topography (even noting cropmarks); artifacts (corroborating the tradition of the metal ages from personal fieldwork); language (making parallels between the Celtic languages of Britain and Brittany); texts (for instance, Julius Caesar's observations on ancient British society) and "archaeology", that is monumental inscriptions; he describes the monuments themselves, whether Stonehenge, Avebury or Offa's Dyke (which he compares with the Great Wall of China at the other end of the scale of fortified boundary works); he makes pertinent deductions from comparative ethnology, remarking for example on the survival of the coracle in Wales and, in a most interesting comparison, suggests that the pre-Roman Britons were "two or three degrees I suppose less savage than the Americans"—in other words the Indians: a contemporary note which underlines how the discovery of the New World excited antiquarians as well as, say, the author of *The Tempest*.

The development of archaeology

There was, then, a consistent development in archaeological ideas from the Renaissance onwards. But archaeology as we understand it is the product of the last 200 years. It now embraces a much wider meaning and may perhaps be defined, in the words of S.J. de Laet, as an auxiliary science to history whose "essential task is to construct the different stages of the material civilization of mankind since the earliest times". Since 99 per cent of human history lies before man learned to keep written records, it will be seen that only through archaeology can we make sense of what was made and done in most of the past.

The landmarks of the modern development are on two levels. First there was the intellectual achievement of formal classification: for instance, the work of Danish and Norwegian scholars from the 1770s onwards who laid the basis for prehistoric research; and then there was the more glamorous practical side—the excavations themselves: Herculaneum and Pompeii in the late 18th century, then Olympia and Samothrace, Babylon and Nineveh, Thebes and Abydos, Troy, Mycenae and Knossos from the mid 19th century onwards.

In this pioneeering, "heroic" age of scientific archaeology, fabulous treasures were found by larger than life characters—Belzoni, Layard, Botta, Schliemann. The public imagination was fired by an image of the archaeologist complementing that of the adventurers and explorers who were even then opening up "dark continents" of the present rather than the past, and sharing with them an absolute assurance of their right to plunder these cultures, dead or living.

But sensational discoveries, gratifying as they are, have never been an end in themselves for archaeologists. The real foundations of scientific archaeology were laid not by diggers but by scholars and thinkers. We should remember here that the mid 19th century was one of the most revolutionary periods in the history of science. Darwin's *On the Origin of Species* (1859) and Lyall's *Antiquity of Man* (1863) are generally regarded as the landmarks for prehistoric research—though Boucher de Perthes' stratigraphic work in the Somme Valley had already been published (see p. 20). By then many scholars, such as Taylor, Lubbock and John Evans were working in this area and by 1859 thinking was already advanced on the chronological classification of "prehistory" (a word apparently first used in France in 1833, but which found wide dissemination in Taylor's publication of 1851). In those few years the basis of all present-day thinking in this area was established, both in Europe and in America, where Lewis Morgan's work on the customs of the Iroquois preceded his major attempt to classify world prehistory (a work which greatly impressed Marx and Engels, and which is still quoted approvingly by some Soviet prehistorians). By 1880 it could fairly be said that "the archaeologists have raised the study of antiquities to the rank of a science" (R. Dawkins, *Early Man*).

The assumption of all these thinkers was that archaeology should illuminate the life of the people as a whole, that it should be "proletarian", and this is how the science is seen today. It is a view matched in the main field of historical writing, where recent historians and sociologists like Braudel and Foucault have encouraged us to understand archaeology in the wider sense, using the tools of sociology, anthropology and environmental geography to explore the long term, the "deep structures", rather than the relatively superficial traditional historiography of events (battles, king lists and so on). This is the emphasis of *The World Atlas of Archaeology*, an approach which has always been popular in America where traditional historiography cannot unlock all the mysteries of pre-Columbian history.

The "new archaeology" is thus in tune with our times in attempting a true people's history of the world, as it is seen at present. It offers the raw materials and shows us the problems involved in interpreting them. The *Atlas* has been described as a "dossier"—a collection of papers on the numerous civilizations that have so far existed on our planet. It is a dossier of a scope wider than any general survey of archaeology so far attempted, and as such is a summation of the state of the art in modern science. It is full of new ideas and intriguing surprises. It offers completely fresh interpretations of events we thought we all knew well. It contains detailed accounts of the latest exciting discoveries in China and Mesoamerica. It brings us right up to date with contemporary problems, as in "Archaeology and Apartheid" (p. 320). It opens up fascinating questions such as the role of women in prehistoric society: when in history did today's sex roles develop (p. 30)? In sum, the *Atlas* is a truly exciting and thought-provoking compilation with something for everyone. If it is each generation's duty to "bear historical witness", it is nonetheless an exquisite pleasure to contemplate the past—not "backlooking curiosity" as Camden wrote in the 1550s, for "in the study of Antiquity (which hath a certaine resemblance with eternity) there is a sweet food of the mind well befitting such as are of honest and noble disposition."

The reason is not hard to see, for true historical inquiry tends not towards abstractions but, as Fernand Braudel has written, "towards the very sources of life, in its most concrete, everyday, indestructible and anonymously human expression".

Michael Wood

Introduction

Archaeology and Mankind

For many years now, archaeologists have been looking not so much for artifacts as for information on the people of the past. The archaeology of artifacts cannot be the ultimate goal, for perhaps even more important is the research that aims to integrate material objects, whatever their nature, into the cultural systems of the past. But any attempt to understand the functioning, for each period, of different social and cultural systems, requires an understanding not only of history but also of the general laws of their development, that is to say, an understanding of human behaviour itself. Archaeology is a means of recognizing the nature of humanity, in all its variety.

René Ginouvès

Archaeology is a subject that provokes widely different and sometimes passionate reactions in today's world. On the one hand it is clearly—as its name implies—the study of ancient things, an occupation which may appear obsolete, useless and even suspect in a world which seems to trust largely in the promises of technological or social innovation. Archaeology can indeed give the impression of a return to the past as a sort of conservative reaction, combining rejection of the present with anxiety about the future. On the other hand, interest in archaeology has become widespread, sometimes amounting almost to a vogue, and its coverage in books has also been extensive. These factors, coupled with the support it receives from numerous governments, suggests that the subject seems to meet a deeply felt need, as if Western civilization was increasingly interested in discovering material evidence of its past (the quest for which began in the Renaissance), and as if, in a broader sense, people all over the world were progressively discovering the same need. So there seems to be a firmly established connection between some of mankind's fundamental demands, whether they are new or have been revived, which we should try to understand better, and the discipline of archaeology, whose scope and methods we must define, so that they can be more accurately related to those demands.

Extensions of the field of archaeology

The meaning of the word archaeology, as already mentioned, assigns to it the objective of studying the past and, in a narrower but widely accepted definition, the physical remains of the past, which may be made to yield information on situations and events involving man. In the historical reality of its development this study was at first very restricted in space, time and subject matter. It is a remarkable fact that these restrictions have gradually fallen away, so that today the field of archaeology includes all cultures, for almost the whole period of their development, investigated through the sum total of their material remains.

...in space

The geographical extension of archaeology with the passing of time is perhaps the easiest area to establish. When the subject first arose, effectively in the Renaissance, its earliest interest was Rome: the first excavations; in the 16th century, were of the Roman Forum and the Villa Hadriana, extending in the 18th century to Campania with work at Herculaneum, and then, towards the middle of the century, to Pompeii* and Stabiae. The 18th century also saw the beginning of exploration in Etruria. In the first half of the 19th century, intensive exploitation of Etruscan burial grounds took place, as well as the opening of field sites in southern Italy and Sicily, but it was also at this time that work began in Greece, at Aegina, Olympia and Athens (liberated after 1835). It was then, too, that the first great missions to Egypt began, associated with Bonaparte's expedition, and the first explorations in the Near and Middle East (at Petra, Khorsabad and Nineveh), which thereafter joined the biblical with the classical world. Meanwhile, in a quite different field, sites were opened in Scandinavia. In the second half of the 19th century, all these regions underwent a considerable increase in the number of sites explored. Asia Minor was very widely studied, but methodical work also began in England, France, Germany, Austria, Spain and the Slav countries, while American anthropology ushered in the archaeology of the New World. With the beginning of the 20th century, sites in these same geographical areas multiplied, with new developments in Crete, Palestine, Cyprus, on the Indus, throughout the Islamic world, in many parts of Asia, in Africa and in Central and South America. Today there is no region in the world where archaeological work does not exist in some form and with more or less ambitious aims. Even in countries like Greece, where research activity has traditionally been intensive, neglected geographical zones such as Macedonia are now the subject of special interest (see fig. 1). In most cases, individual initiative long ago yielded to the organization of research on a national scale, sometimes calling for international collaboration. These international associations form a highly diversified, worldwide information network with many regular and occasional publications, meetings and congresses.

... in time

Parallel to the extension of the geographical area of archaeology from the centre of Italy to the whole world, its expansion in time has been equally significant. As we have seen, archaeology started with Rome, and essentially with imperial Rome. The 18th century began to extend the timescale with the discovery of the Romano-Hellenistic civilization of Campania and the much older civilizations of Etruria. But it was the 19th century which saw the largest chronological extensions, first with the Greek and Roman world, where the main interest in the first half of the century was the "Classical period" (roughly the 5th and 4th centuries BC) and in the "Archaic period" of the 6th century. The second half of the 19th century chose to go back to earlier times with the discovery of Troy in 1870, and of the whole Mycenaean civilization of the 15th–12th centuries BC. We have to wait until the turn of the 19th century for the discovery of still older periods, the civilization of Crete (which flourished in the first half of the second millennium BC) and the Aegean world (third millennium BC). This was the start of "Pre-Hellenic archaeology", whereby the relations between Greek protohistory and the archaeology of Egypt and the Near East were established. These non-classical worlds, too,

* Asterisks throughout the text indicate words or terms found in the Glossary.

11

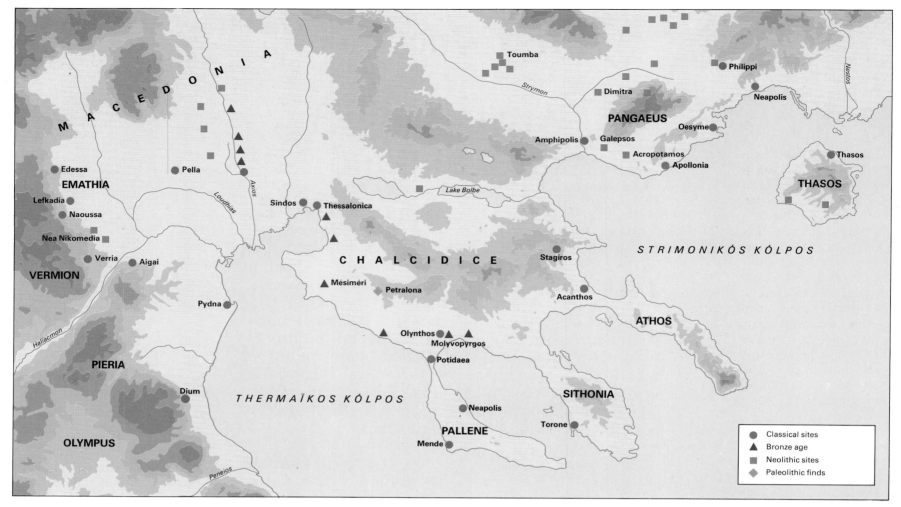

1 Excavations in Greek Macedonia

In the early 1950s archaeological work in Macedonia still consisted largely of exploiting chance finds on known sites, but the end of the decade saw the start of large methodical excavations which subsequently developed not only on the towns of historical Greece (blue circles), but also on the sites from the Bronze Age (violet triangles) and the Neolithic (red squares), and even on finds from the Paleolithic, (yellow lozenge).

received an impulse in the early 19th century, when the first finds from the great sites led scholars to study the two millennia preceding the classical period. At the same time research into European protohistory and prehistory began in the Scandinavian countries. Towards the middle of the same century, these researches culminated in Europe with the celebrated discoveries of Hallstatt, La Tène, Villanova and Altamira, which formed the basis for the astonishing development of protohistoric and prehistoric archaeology.

Towards the last quarter of the century a similar achievement characterized the archaeology of Egypt and the Near East, and it seemed too as if research was going back to human origins, as in Greece, where the existence of Paleolithic deposits was not confirmed until comparatively recently. In the other direction, an archaeology of early Christian times had to wait until the mid-19th century before it became established and extended with the addition of Byzantine archaeology; Islamic and Slavic archaeology widened the area still further. Soon the possibility of a medieval archaeology was discussed, and then of "industrial archaeology" (a term that had already been used in Britain and France during the last quarter of the 19th century, but did not really develop until after World War II). Today there is even discussion of a "modern and contemporary archaeology". And if archaeology really is the study of the material products of the past, it should logically be applied to the study of artifacts of the most recent past, provided that these pieces of evidence really belong to the past, i.e. that they no longer form part (except possibly as survivals) of the system of objects by which our civilization functions here and now. In present-day industrialized countries, first-generation computers are already regarded as archaeological museum pieces. From this point of view, we see that the field of archaeology has spread progressively from the first centuries of our era to the whole history of mankind. Thus a "general archaeology" becomes possible, freed from historicity, and basically concerned with comparing and checking problems and methods.

The content of archaeology

To these two expansions of archaeology in time and space a third must be added, the consequences of which are at least as great. Archaeology was at first almost exclusively a search for works of art. In the Renaissance (and long afterwards), excavations were made to find masterpieces of classical antiquity which were looked on as objects of aesthetic pleasure by connoisseurs and simultaneously served as models for the creation of art. This pursuit of the exceptional object or work of art, which made excavation a source of supply for museums and collections, had many consequences. Until comparatively

recently, departments of archaeology in many universities were in reality departments of the history of antique art, preferably Greek or Roman. However it was gradually realized that excavations could offer much more, namely direct information about the material life of mankind. This was already a reversal of old attitudes, when the removal of the finest sections of mosaics and paintings from the walls and floors of Pompeii came to an end, so as to preserve the decorative unity of the entire area of inhabited space. It was also a time when classical archaeologists began to assemble ceramic fragments in groups, even when they carried representations long regarded as "barbaric" (for example those of the 9th and 8th centuries BC, called "geometric" art) and even more so in the case of undecorated everyday wares. Archaeologists now also began to excavate humbler dwellings with the same care as temples and palaces. By thus moving from the art object to everyday material, our view of the past has been greatly enlarged, and cultural products as a whole have been integrated into the archaeological domain.

New approaches

Underwater archaeology has restored to classical art, often as the result of chance finds, some of its most prestigious masterpieces (notably the great bronze pieces whose paradoxical destiny was to be saved by their shipwreck). This is now an area of intensive exploration which takes into account the totality of the sunken vessel, its equipment as well as its most commonplace merchandise. Furthermore, archaeological investigation is now no longer confined to manmade objects, better known as artifacts. Experts working on graves and their material contents are equally interested in the bones they contain, which can tell us so much about the people, their diseases and mortality rates. Also of interest are animal remains, which provide information about domestication, stockbreeding and diet; pollen traces, which reveal the types of vegetation and their cultures; geological formations, and soils, and finally an "archaeology of the landscape" with its ecological systems which clarify cultural phenomena by way of natural phenomena. Thus the object of archaeology is no longer the totality of material objects produced by human labour, but also the totality of the transformations mankind has imposed on plants and animals in geographical environments, and the totality of the reciprocal relations of mankind with its environment. In view of this triple extension of the archaeological field, it is easier to understand a parallel expansion of social groups interested in archaeology. Confined at first to a few "antiquaries", men of leisure and collectors of curios, (who even called themselves "Dilettanti" in 18th century England), the attraction of archaeology has widened, together with the widening of its terms of reference, to include a much greater public, where the work of professionals (specialist investigators, usually from universities) is associated with that of increasingly well-trained amateurs, both groups being often passionately devoted to their subject. All the more so as the refinement and diversification of methods to solve new problems also tend to bring into detail an archaeology of mankind.

Excavation and archaeology

Excavation in itself clearly implies the most rigorous possible use of stratigraphy*, which by distinguishing the various strata and the different levels separating them (occupation levels, destruction levels, foundation trenches, pockets of inclusion, etc.) establishes the distribution of objects and the associations fundamental to the reconstruction of cultures. But excavation has to be adapted to the needs of each particular case. The formal regularity of excavation by a grid of small squares, a legacy of the teaching of the celebrated English archaeologist Sir Mortimer Wheeler, may no longer be the most effective method when working on buildings and constructions, where it may be better to make stratigraphical sections at points specially chosen by the excavator for their significance, and always perpendicularly to the walls. However, the comparison of shallow and deep soundings produced by this technique tends to encourage a somewhat abstract view of the history of the site (what Wheeler himself called a "timetable without a train"), as opposed to the large-scale open area excavations which alone enable us to grasp the concrete functioning of cultural systems (but which themselves are in danger of being "trains without a timetable" unless constantly checked by stratigraphy).

Nor should it be forgotten that the excavation is carried out by people who are themselves part of history, so that the results can only be relative. In the past the destruction entailed by excavation was excused by the argument that the archaeologist could read the pages of the book at the same time that he was tearing it up, and by requiring him to transcribe the material as fully and faithfully as possible; but we now know that archaeological truth is not a text decipherable once and for all, because the gathering of information can never be entirely exhaustive nor entirely objective. At best, the excavator takes into account everything available to him through the means at his disposal, and everything that has a bearing on the questions he is asking. This means that consciously, or more often unconsciously, choices are made which will not necessarily be compensated for by the drawings and photographs on which we must rely for a permanent record of all the remaining material.

The development of methods of analysis and recording, and the constant raising of new questions, ensure that research can be indefinitely repeated. It is thus well said that, whereas there are countless ways of excavating badly, there is no good method, or rather, the best method is only good in relation to the requirements of a particular period in the development of the research. Furthermore, it seems unreasonable to open up new sites which would only duplicate results already obtained elsewhere. Excavation is too serious an operation to be left to the responsibility of archaeologists who are only attracted by the obvious pleasures of exploration and discovery. Today it is definitely much more useful to give priority to urgent excavations, where modern development threatens to destroy the past for ever, and even more to establish "archaeology reservations" in order to preserve the possibility of studying past mankind according to the successive requirements of the future, in accordance with programmes themselves progressively determined by the raising of new questions.

Archaeology and surveying

In this context there is a clear contribution from the development of scientific survey techniques, such as aerial reconnaissance; to reveal hydrographic indications, for example the dark colours produced by the humidity of ancient ditches or indications of plant life, or differences in the height or colour of vegetation in relation to buried remains. Also valuable are analyses of light and shadow, when light catches revelatory shadows on micro-reliefs at an acute angle, or soil indications, when traces made in the ground by ancient activity are returned to the surface by deep ploughing. Topographical indications are also useful, as when a vanished ancient way is identified through an alignment of elements which themselves lack individual significance. The use of scientific apparatus in the soil based on the principles of electrical resistivity (see fig. 2), magnetic anomalies, the transmission of shock waves in the earth, or chemical phenomena, all these also provide a valuable contribution. By establishing zones where the preservation of the remains seems most desirable, these techniques give the archaeologist a chance to anticipate destruction instead of intervening when it is too late—the chance to propose rather than to oppose. Large-scale earth-moving operations, urban development and the transformations caused by agriculture only too often seem to demand the sacrifice of the past to the entirely legitimate interests of the present. Only a dialogue between the archaeologist and the

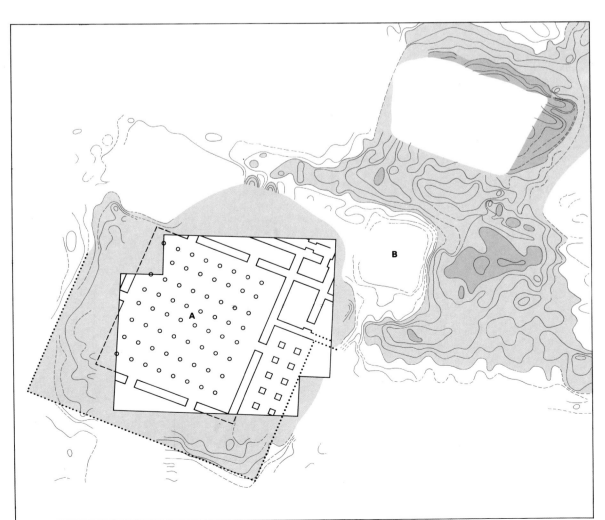

2 Palace of Chaour at Susa

Next to the excavation of a hypostyle hall from the Achaemenid period (A), electrical resistivity measurements enabled archaeologists to identify the alignments and angles of buried constructions, as well as the empty space of an interior court (B). These indications gave direction to the further development of research. After A. Hesse, Dijon, 1978.

town planner, based on a prior examination of the subsoil, can lead to the preservation of areas reserved for future excavations, while they await harmonious integration into the urban fabric and, more generally, into the living milieu which forms the framework for human activity.

Conservation and presentation

It is obvious that after excavation the archaeologist should continue to take an interest in the site he has dug as well as the artifacts he has discovered there; such conservation and presentation should form part of his basic task. It is too often the case that a specialist seems satisfied simply to extract from the site sufficient material for a scholarly publication intended for other specialists, and then leaves the site in a semi-abandoned state, a place where the ruins themselves will perish, or a dumping ground, if the site is in a town or a place where the ancient walls will go on deteriorating even if they escape re-use as building material, or where vegetation will smother them, making the stones crack and causing subsidence in the stratigraphy. The upkeep and organization of a site may be expensive, sometimes as expensive as the excavation itself, but they are absolute duties if the site is to be naturally integrated into the environment, rather than to appear as a dead zone incapable of expressing the living reality of which it forms part. Thus an "archaeological park" may be organized to display ruins that are preserved and explained to the public.

Some buildings require what classical archaeology has called "anastylosis", literally the re-erection of fallen columns, here used in a more general sense of replacing architectural details as far as possible. Such work may extend no further than the kind of preservative measures necessary because the exposed building is no longer supported by the accumulation of centuries; but it may also sometimes involve a complete reconstruction, of which the Portico of Attalus on the Agora at Athens is a magnificent example, where present-day visitors can find the same enjoyment as the people of the past in the beauty of the forms and decorations, the surroundings and the cool shade. In this particular case, part of the building has been turned into a museum, but there is nothing to stop the re-installation of an ancient theatre that would attract the same audiences as in the past, provided that a preliminary study were made; is it not a fact that the pleasantest towns to live in are those which have managed to integrate into their modern fabric the resonance of the past?

In the same way, objects taken from the earth must be cleaned and preserved: metal objects, for example, may have slowly established during the period of their burial an equilibrium with their environment which will be disturbed by exhumation, so that it is important to stop the corrosion which would return them to their original mineral state. The restoration of objects is also sometimes necessary, but always with a concern to demonstrate their meaning and significance as much as their forms. It would be inappropriate to straighten a sword found in a tomb if it had been deliberately twisted during a burial rite, for the human activity or action is of more interest than the object itself. Museums where objects are to be kept and displayed may also contribute to this communication between the present and the past, if, while facilitating the work of the specialists (which implies large "reserves") they are arranged in a way that is both instructive and vividly alive, so as to engage the largest public interest. More generally, it is clear that the work of the archaeologist should not be confined to a narrow circle of specialists. He has a social responsibility to give an account of the results of his actions to the group or society that offered him the project and the means to accomplish it, and he should explain in comprehensible form how the discoveries contribute to our knowledge of past mankind. Popularization, in the correct sense of the word, is a duty that is all the more urgent as our disciplines become more specialized and our methods adopt more components from the physical and mathematical sciences. This requirement leads into the second phase of archaeological work, which is that of developing results once the fieldwork has been completed.

The limits of excavation

It is evident that archaeological research is not confined to excavation, even though a rather simplistic view makes the archaeologist an excavator first and foremost. Furthermore, the archaeologist himself, carried away by the excitement of the finds, is sometimes in danger of forgetting how many days of study are implied for each hour spent on the site, and that he should ration his discoveries according to the time available for drawing conclusions from them. The uncovering of objects is not a result but a point of departure. It is also inadmissible for a fieldworker to reserve for himself the right, sometimes for decades, to publish what he has discovered using public funds, and so deprive the scientific community of information intended for it. Discovery does not confer a right but a duty to publish as soon as possible or leave publication to a more qualified specialist, or one whose work schedule allows

3 Church of St Médard at Chalo-Saint-Mars
This longitudinal section of the nave with left-hand elevation, and the plan of the vaulting of three bays, show how photogrammetry achieves a precise pictorial statement, clearly revealing distortions in the architecture. These records are of equal quality and considerably cheaper than those obtained by traditional techniques. After *Les Relevés photogrammétriques d'architecture de l'Inventaire général*, Château de Chambord, 1977.

him to do so more quickly. It is a fact that the most sensational discovery, even though it may bring a certain notoriety, does not in itself constitute the proof of any particular quality of work, except in exceptional cases where it comes as the reward of patient waiting or through the subtlety of an intuition nourished by reasoning and knowledge. Basic archaeological research may be built on sometimes impressive discoveries, but it depends even more on the mass of artifacts found, possibly over a long period of time, particularly in view of the fact that much modern and contemporary archaeology deals with objects which have never been excavated from a site because they have never been buried. Moreover, the objects themselves may be less important to the archaeologist than their locations, positions and stratigraphy, their environment, configurations and associations, if ancient civilizations are to be reconstructed as completely as possible. For many years now, archaeologists have no longer been looking for artifacts so much as for information on the people of the past.

Archeography and archeometry

The task of the archaeologist consists of a number of stages which need to be itemized separately, even if they are closely linked in practice. The first is undoubtedly description, and today we understand that, far from being a mechanical operation, a sort of photograph of the original artifact (which incidentally an actual photograph or drawing may eventually replace) it is very much dependent on the individual who does the describing (but even the "objective photograph" is much less objective than its name implies). We have already mentioned in connection with work on the site, the impossibility of taking everything into account with complete impartiality. Similarly, the archaeologist inevitably makes choices when confronted with the object to be described, and it is essential to check whether it is indeed a true description or whether it is a construction based on often implied premises, leading to comparative work developed from selected features.

This is not too serious in traditional areas, where the illustrated publication of results often allows, through the provision of images, a chance for others to make evaluations of the material; but it is unacceptable when the results of the operation are subjected, as we shall see, to automated procedures. The creation of a new term, archeography, to designate this work of transposing the object to its linguistic equivalent, does at least exhibit the new concern with this area. On the other hand, descriptions of the archaeological object in terms of organic materials and sediments tend increasingly to incorporate the results of measurements and analyses often obtained by very complex scientific apparatus. The term archeometry emphasizes this use of numerical values. Some types of photogrammetric images (see fig. 3) also supply the equivalents of numerical descriptions, the values of which can be extracted automatically. But in none of these operations should the archaeologist lose control of the representation made of the original artifact. The adoption of a linguistic system to standardize and formalize descriptions, or of a scientific technique to achieve analyses, is the result of a rational decision on the part of the archaeologist. Thus the fundamental novelty is not in the use of an impressive apparatus or the mastering of computer language, but in the explicit and regular character of the operations.

Publication and data banks

In these conditions the publication of material has tended to change its nature. Originally a kind of "correspondence" between scholars, publication of results later developed various forms, from the preliminary report to the definitive publication, expressed in terms that have varied from literary dissertations to simple catalogues. For some 20 years a means has been sought to solve the problems arising from the inadequacy of these formulas in the face of an exponential growth of information, which can no longer be controlled even by specialists working in increasingly narrow fields, and the irregular presentation of which makes it unsuitable for comparative research. Under these conditions, the computer seems to be an ideal tool because it can record in data large masses of standardized information (see fig. 4) which then becomes very widely accessible, particularly for the documentary research of the archaeologist, which is traditionally based on a comparative approach, in the quest for parallel examples which the machine can retrieve instantly according to the most complex formulas. Thus data processing should help to replace lengthy individual research, constantly repeated, with an immediate supply of relevant information, always provided that the information was first assembled not by extraneous sources but by the researchers themselves. The latter, by agreeing to devote their irreplaceable competence as specialists to this task, and a part of the time which they would in any case have had to spend on the personal assembling of information, would in return have the right to use a communal source of supply infinitely richer in information.

Data banks can also be seen to assist not only documentation, but also the calculation of structural forms, which, by the use of algorithms, enable one to recognise in the totality of the material patterns which were not apparent before—sequences, serials, classifications, etc. In effect, the application of statistics at many levels, made possible by the computer, enables archaeologists to identify numerous characteristics found in numerous artifacts and data

(that frequently repetitive mass of information that now comes from excavations) so as to reveal phenomena that would scarcely be apprehended otherwise. Thus the computer plays a role that both subserves and transcends the traditional tasks of the archaeologist, subserving them to the extent that mechanization should contribute to easing the mechanical tasks of documentation, and transcending them by means of synthetic operations exceeding the normal potentialities of our understanding; but in both cases, the computer is under the control of human intelligence, whose field of application it will enlarge, while freeing it for the later stages of research.

There is no reason to fear that when these techniques are generalized (and their introduction assumes that many institutional, technical and psychological obstacles will be removed) they will put an end to the printed publication. What they may put an end to is the type of publication which is not read because it was never really intended to be read, being an accumulation of data, measurements, and stratigraphies whose contribution to our knowledge of humanity the author sometimes seems to have forgotten to explain, and which is not even easy to consult with its mass of unsystematic statements that are often impossible to compare. On the contrary, when it is no longer burdened with material that rightly belongs in the public archives (which does not necessarily mean published), or with information suitable for comparative purposes (which will now exist in a data bank in standardized and immediately accessible form, where it can always be added to or modified depending on developments in research), books can once again become a medium for reasoning and argument about all aspects of archaeological reconstruction other than simple description.

The archaeology of artifacts

This archaeological reconstruction develops on two different levels. There is no doubt that it must first deal with the material itself, each item of which raises certain essential questions: What is it? What is its date? What is its place of origin or its author? An archaeological object inevitably loses a part of what it has to tell us, greater or less depending on the length of time separating its manufacture and use (or possibly successive uses) from the present day. Archaeologists must therefore first try to restore it to its original form (which may have been altered) and function (which perhaps can only be recognized by relying on texts, images or similar but more informative artifacts). It must be dated with an accuracy that may vary from years to centuries, depending on the period and type of object. It must be traced to the geographical area where it was made and if possible attributed to an artist or a school, if it is a work of art, or a workshop if it is an everyday object. In order to answer these questions, indispensable because they can give the object its exact place in the various social and cultural systems of the past, the archaeologist uses complex methods, obtaining the maximum information from the find itself and comparing this with the enormous quantity of knowledge already accumulated, possibly also working from descriptive or critical texts belonging to the same culture. The archaeologist will increasingly use a whole range of scientific techniques, for example the dating of artifacts based on radioactive isotopes (Carbon 14* being the best known) or thermoluminescence*, or variations in the earth's magnetic field, and techniques for localizing these objects by means of certain analyses which make possible, for example, the linking of a particular ceramic product with a correctly identified claypit. But here again we must not succumb to the mirage of technical means. The relevance of an analysis is not necessarily dependent on the delicacy and sophistication of the apparatus, but on the quality of reasoning which conditions that of the conclusions. The scientific method implies, both for the human sciences to which archaeology belongs and for the natural sciences, a process controlled by reasoning that starts from explicit postulates, testing hypotheses and their consequences and seeking for proof and verification—a rigorous procedure that contrasts with the intuitive, if not "impressionistic" approach typical of many archaeologists in the past. But should we not speak of complementarity rather than contrast? The entire section of research that concerns art objects, personalities and craftsmen still requires a personal sensibility and flair which a formal approach could only emulate at the cost of an unacceptable heaviness, as was appreciated by the pioneers of "systems archaeology". Our understanding would be diminished if we ignored the kind of contribution that comes from long familiarity with artifacts which makes them close to us and, as it were, old friends. So it is better to imagine a dual approach for the archaeology of artifacts: formal reasoning which alone can control intuition and give it scientific value, and intuition which alone can give life to research by making us participate through the artifacts and their relation to the existence of past humanity.

The archaeology of cultural systems

However, the archaeology of artifacts cannot be the ultimate aim of archaeological work. How could it be, given that the most recent archaeological period deals with objects for which we know the date, place of manufacture, functioning and use in every case? In addition to the kind of research that aims to restore to an artifact the identity it has lost, there is also research that aims to integrate the artifacts, whatever their nature, into the

École française d'Athènes

```
415  ************************************************************************
     MOSAIQUE = PERGAME / INCOMPLET
     NUMERO = 4
     COMMENTAIRE = MOSAIQUE D'HEPHAISTION
     SIGNATURE = HEPHAISTION
     LIEU DE DECOUVERTE = PERGAME / PALAIS / V / PIECE N 1
     LIEU DE CONSERVATION = BERLIN / MUSEE
     DATATION = -199 A -150
     DIMENSION 1 = 850
     TECHNIQUE = OPUS TESSELLATUM / FIN
     NOMBRE DE COULEURS = 99
     NOMBRE DE TAPIS = 1
        ( PARTIE = RACCORD / LARGE
          DECOR = MONOCHROME
          COULEUR = BLANC / INCERTAIN
        ( PARTIE = TAPIS
          FORME = CARRE
          DIMENSION 1 = 650
          NOMBRE DE PANNEAUX = 2

     ************************************************************************
        ( PARTIE = BORDURE
          NOMBRE DE PARTIES = 20
          NOMBRE DE BANDES DECOREES = 7
          COMMENTAIRE = 1 BANDE DISPARUE
          TECHNIQUE = LAMES DE PLOMB / INCERTAIN
             ( PARTIE = BANDE

     ************************************************************************
             ( PARTIE = BANDE
               POSITION = CENTRE / EXTERIEUR
               DECOR = COMPOSITION / LINEAIRE / TRESSE / 3
               TRAITEMENT = DEGRADE
               COULEUR = NOIR / BLANC / ROUGE / BLEU / BEIGE
               COULEUR FOND = NOIR
             ( PARTIE = BANDE
               POSITION = CENTRE
               DECOR = COMPOSITION / LINEAIRE / ANIME / RINCEAU
               TRAITEMENT = RENDU NATURALISTE
               CHANGEMENT D'ORIENTATION = 8
               POSITION = MILIEU / COTE / ANGLE
               ORIENTATION = MULTIPLE / VU EXTERIEUR
                  ( DECOR = FEUILLE / FEUILLE ENGAINANTE / VIGNE / CORNET / VRILLE /
                            CROISE / FRUIT / RAISIN
                  ( DECOR = FLEUR / COMPOSITE / PERSPECTIVE / VU DESSOUS / VU DESSUS
                  ( DECOR = CULOT / FEUILLE / ACANTHE
                    POSITION = ANGLE
                  ( ANIMAL = SAUTERELLE
                  ( PERSONNAGE = EROS
                    NOMBRE = 3
                    PRESENTATION = VOLANT / NU / AILES
             ( PARTIE = BANDE
               POSITION = CENTRE / INTERIEUR
```

4 Hellenistic mosaic from a palace at Pergamum

A data bank on Greek mosaics, containing standard descriptions of hitherto widely dispersed material, makes possible the immediate retrieval of the information sought, based on a statement of the characteristics desired and their combinations. After A.-M. Guimier-Sorbets.

cultural systems of the past. These systems may sometimes seem rather artificially determined for the convenience of their study, but nevertheless, in terms of their combined functioning and constant interaction, they may represent both cause and consequence, stimulus and response, relating to the life of the people in their environment.

The study of material culture is one area in which archaeological artifacts have contributed much, revealing the technical capacities of manufacture in a given place and a period in terms of technologies of agriculture and stock-breeding, of provisioning and transport (both of food and materials), of building, clothing and decoration. Economic life yields details about which the texts, when they exist, are discreet, with finds of monetary treasures, assessments of the proportion of local and imported pottery of each site, and contents of shipwrecks. Aerial survey identifies across broad sweeps of landscape the sites, plans and densities of antique villas, road systems (see fig. 5), even the holes (in certain examples in North Africa) marking the

positions of olive trees in antiquity, together with their irrigation systems. Techniques of optical filtering make it possible to rediscover, under the confusion of the present-day landscape, ancient systems of land use, in particular Roman centuriations* (see fig. 6), sometimes even when superimposed. Thus there emerge relations of adaptation by human groups to their environment in what is called historical ecology.

Spatial archaeology

Social life is attested by the arrangement and distribution of dwellings, their dimensions and decoration, the disposition of agricultural land use, the organization of cemeteries, the distribution in towns of areas of public buildings and gardens. In English-speaking countries archaeology has brought together under the term "spatial archaeology" a whole complex of studies situating these social phenomena and the economic phenomena from which they are inseparable in a geographical context (see fig. 7), evaluating their importance as had been done before for the temporal dimension.

Political, intellectual and religious concerns and ideology also yield information to archaeologists through the architecture of sanctuaries, temples and libraries, and through imagery and iconography, both as a result of what is revealed and also the way it is revealed, the choice of forms and means of expression reflecting mental attitudes (see fig. 8). Artistic life too is involved, for if the notion of art belongs to relatively limited sections of history, aesthetic quality is a fundamental component of human creation. Opening itself to these dimensions of research, archaeology cannot be reduced to an auxiliary discipline of history, as has sometimes been said. It is history itself, for all the periods and all the places in which literary sources are lacking, and also for all the areas where the texts give no answers or only incomplete answers. And even when the texts provide plenty of information, archaeology can enrich them further by offering, not the simple illustrations for which archaeological material has for too long been used, but a counter-balancing reality of materials and techniques conditioned by, and condition-ing, a whole range of human cultural facts. Nor is archaeology confined to history, trying to reconstruct an organized development in a temporal dimension. The importance of the spatial dimension, already referred to, now becomes apparent, for archaeology is required, no less than anthropology, to try to comprehend the functioning, for each period, of different social and cultural systems, by striving to recognize the general laws of their develop-ment, that is to say by studying human behaviour itself.

Thus archaeology appears as a privileged means of rediscovering the past of humanity through the way that its technical creations express certain aptitudes and fundamental needs; of rediscovering the past in a search that itself depends on the techniques and values of the present. For a quest for the past of mankind involves our own conception of the past that we carry inside ourselves. This alone may explain the enthusiasm for archaeology referred to at the beginning of the Introduction. From this point of view the earliest origins are perhaps the most significant. How can we better judge the specific nature of the human species than by looking at mankind in the first dawn of its development, by examining how those beings whose distant descendants we are were able to adapt themselves to the world by using tools to extend and strengthen their natural capacities and by making images to embody their imaginative worlds, ultimately affecting the real world by means of imagina-tion, long before they began to modify their natural environment by agricultural and stockbreeding?

The cultural heritage

But it is also remarkable that different countries are taking a constantly increasing interest in the preservation and possible recovery of their cultural heritage. This concern is seen in legislation restricting or forbidding export of antiquities, and in the struggle against clandestine excavators who supply the trade in antiquities. The latter are responsible for a considerable loss to science, with the disappearance of objects which, even if they may eventually be recovered, have lost all connection with their stratigraphy and sometimes their place of origin. Also characteristic is the passion with which countries such as Greece may officially demand the return of certain masterpieces that were taken from them. Whatever the sympathy we may feel for such claims, it

5 Map of the ancient habitat in the region of Amiens
Aerial surveys enable identification of Roman roads (red lines), the administration units called *oppida* (red circles), Gallo-Roman foundations (red triangles) and villas of the same period (red squares), as well as medieval foundations (green triangles) often superimposed on older structures.

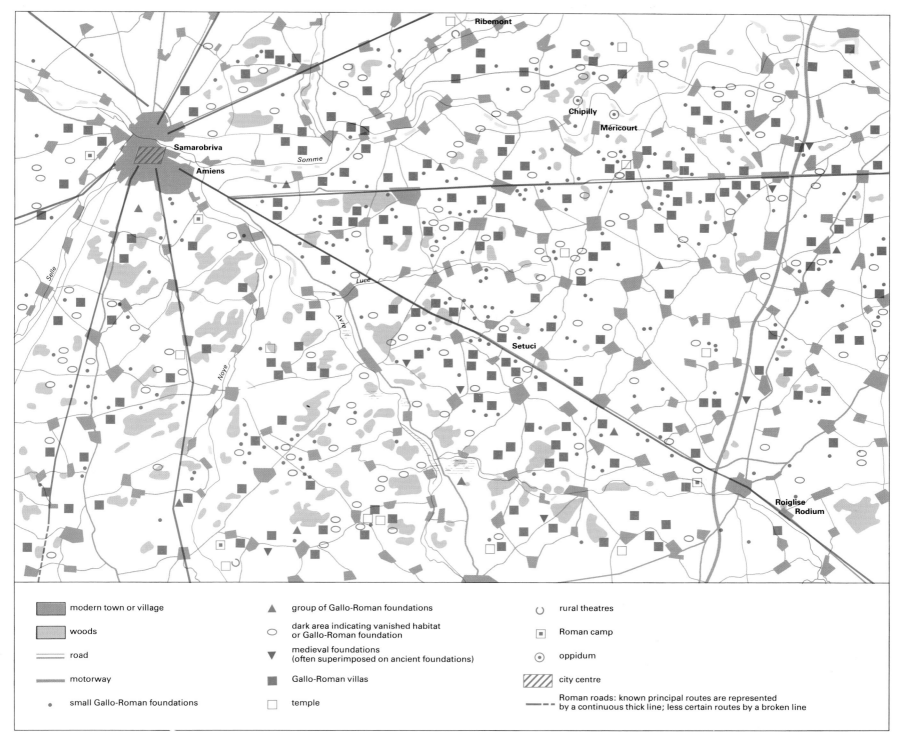

modern town or village	group of Gallo-Roman foundations	rural theatres
woods	dark area indicating vanished habitat or Gallo-Roman foundation	Roman camp
road	medieval foundations (often superimposed on ancient foundations)	oppidum
motorway	Gallo-Roman villas	city centre
small Gallo-Roman foundations	temple	Roman roads: known principal routes are represented by a continuous thick line; less certain routes by a broken line

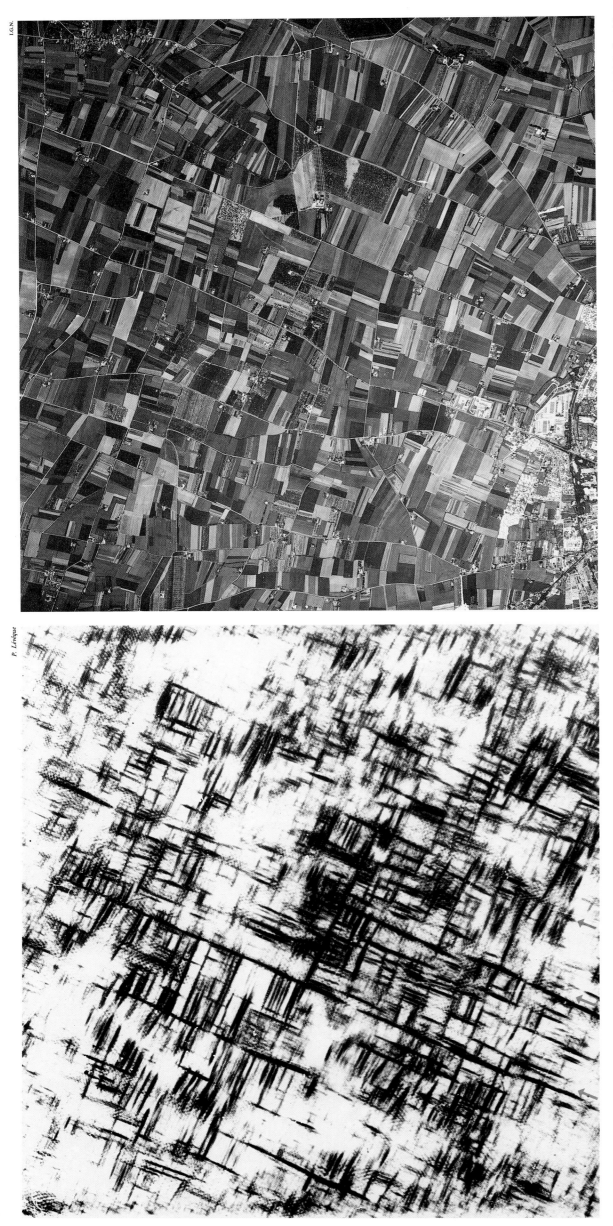

I.G.N.

P. Lévêque

6 Traces of centuriation (Roman land division) at Valence

The technique of optical filtering into an intense beam of coherent light (i.e. the light supplied by a laser) enables us to rediscover beneath the confusion of the actual landscape as it appears in an aerial photograph (see photograph at top) the equidistant parallels and perpendiculars (see arrows at the top bottom and right of the photograph below) corresponding to the Roman division of the land, which continues to structure rural space in the form of more or less evanescent traces (paths, alignments of stones, ditches), but revealing a certain regularity. Thus it becomes possible to reconstruct the ancient landscape, essential for an understanding of rural history.

should not be forgotten that the Cloister of Saint-Guilhem-le-Désert, if it was not today in the Cloisters Museum of New York, would not be anywhere except in the form of building stones in the walls of a few farms; nor that the arrival in London of the marbles brought from the Parthenon by Lord Elgin opened up a new vision of Greek art for the whole of the West; nor, more generally, that certain museums assembling works which have become the common heritage of mankind have played an exceptional part in the creation of a universal culture. But it is also true that archaeology has helped to support claims of a nationalist type: examples include the archaeology of Central Europe and the Balkans after World War I, that of Macedonia, currently divided between three countries, that of the Bible Lands, that of India and Pakistan, and even that of Roman colonization, which some scholars tend to judge by reference to their opinions of 19th-century colonizations. Thus people and nations, particularly those recently emerging into existence or independence, can be tempted to seek confirmation in archaeology of their legitimacy and their rights.

But people may wish to attach themselves to their past for other, more personal reasons. The technological world in which we live, whose achievements and successes cannot be denied, tends of necessity to reduce differences. The same architectural forms are found in Iraq and in Canada, in defiance of the most obvious climatic and psychological contrasts. Our ways of dressing and our diet, and also our amusements and our music tend to become increasingly uniform. The standardization of teaching systems and of machines threatens to abolish the last survivals of craftsmanship, of oral traditions and original creativity, in favour of cultural consumer products. At the same time, large-scale building works and agricultural transformation are seriously modifying landscapes that have been stable for centuries, and thus destroy the remains of the past which they once preserved. Those who feel threatened by this imposition of uniformity and this kind of collective amnesia, as they would be by a loss of their own individuality, may take recourse to a return to the past, to the continuity of a material history into which each person can integrate himself. For to work on an archaeological site is not only to reconstruct the life of the past (not only of the rich and powerful, but also of ordinary people in their everyday existence), it is also to enter into a sympathetic relationship with the landscape, and with the people who continue to live there and who bear its imprint.

8 Fountain at Neschers, France, representing "Marianne" (symbol of French Republic)
Whatever its aesthetic value, the manufactured object with its numerous surrounding features indicates how an area of recent archaeology, in this case an "archaeology of the French Republic", can be based on specialized symbolic material that may be used to reconstruct political attitudes in terms of representations as they existed even in the most distant groups.

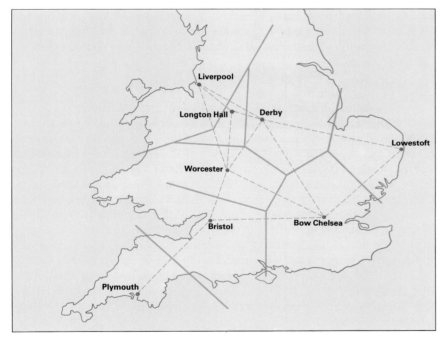

7 Areas of trade for English porcelain factories, c.1776
This diagram proposes a hypothetical demarcation of the areas of sale for each of the principal manufacturing centres. After David L. Clarke, ed., *Spatial Archaeology*, London, 1977.

Thus, for the people of the ancient West and for all those who participate in its culture, Classical and Near Eastern archaeology are a means of rediscovering in their actuality the sources of a heritage on which this culture is still very largely based. And for everybody archaeology is a means of recognizing on the one hand the nature of humanity, in all its generality, and also of rediscovering, from the standpoint of a civilization in the course of becoming universal, a closer community, better suited to individual needs and activities, enriched with an original heritage transmitted by time, a heritage which the individual may feel a vocation to preserve and understand. Thus the frequently impassioned quest for the past also expresses rejection of a reduced and trivialized present, and reflects, above all, the urgent needs of the future of mankind.

Paleolithic Europe:
the archaeological background

Modern ideas about prehistory developed in the 18th century;
its archaeological recovery is the continuing product of the last 150 years.
The achievement of prehistoric humans can now be seen as the
foundation of later civilizations.

The history of prehistoric research is also a history of mental attitudes. Until the 18th century the problem of mankind's origins did not arise since the matter was considered settled by the Book of Genesis. Here it was recorded that all traces of the first humans had disappeared in the Flood, and the only survivors were Noah and his sons, whose descendants formed the various nations of the world. In 1650, Archbishop James Ussher, basing his researches on the genealogies of biblical figures, had proposed the date of 4004BC for the creation of mankind. This date was considered for many years to be as inviolate and as sacred as the Scriptures themselves.

Polished axes and dressed flint points have constantly turned up in freshly dug or storm-washed fields, but these were originally thought to be of supernatural origin, or to be objects whose regular shapes had been fashioned by lightning. As late as the end of the 19th century these "thunderbolts" were carefully collected for their magical and curative properties. Yet even in the 16th century some scholars had the idea of comparing them with the stone tools of the American Indians. Among these M. Mercati* (1541–1593) was the first to suggest that flint arrowheads had been made by men in an age before metal was known.

This opinion was not taken up again until the 18th century, when scholars such as A. de Jussieu suggested that comparison of the customs and tools of "savages" might lead to a better understanding of the "peoples of France, Germany and other northern countries" before the use of iron. Certain philosophers began to assert that man had not been created as he then was, but had evolved from a state of primitive barbarism to the age of civilization.

The rise of Romanticism and the development of nationalism led every country in Europe to search for traces of ancestral Celts, Germans or ancient Britons. The excavations then undertaken still concentrated only on collections of objects, without chronological reference, but it became clear that Genesis provided too cramped a framework to include the Romans, the Greeks, the Egyptians and the European Barbarians as well. As yet there was no attempt to organize a system of dating and arranging all the discoveries, but in 1819 the Danish antiquarian C.J. Thomsen (1788–1865) suggested classifying them in three "ages" related to the materials in which they were made: the Stone Age, Bronze Age and Iron Age. This system, which had hitherto existed more or less implicitly, was confirmed by excavations carried out in Denmark by J.J.A. Worsaae, Thomsen's assistant.

Early investigations into the antiquity of mankind

At about the same period, studies of the formation of the earth and of the fossils contained in its various layers began to challenge "diluvialist" theories that explained fossils as products of the biblical Flood. In 1822, Baron Georges Cuvier, speaking of extinct animal species, observed that "the differences that exist between fossil animals and living animals increase in relation to the age of the layers which hide them."

From the 1820s onwards, various geologists and paleontologists discovered, especially in caves, the bones of vanished species of animals in conjunction with stone and bone tools, and sometimes human remains. However, the discoverers came up against the scepticism of the "Catastrophists", and it was not until the publication in 1846 of the first volume of *Antiquités Celtiques et Antédiluviennes* by a French customs officer, Jacques Boucher de Perthes*, that the question of the existence of an "antediluvian" man was tackled seriously. Starting from a false premise (the Flood could not have wiped out all traces of man living before the cataclysm), Boucher de

Perthes affirmed that the chipped flints he had discovered with the remains of fossil animals in the gravel pits of the Somme (supposedly dating to the Flood) were indeed the work of men contemporary with the great antediluvian animals. His conclusions unleashed a controversy, but one of his bitterest opponents, Dr Rigollot, had to yield to the evidence when he himself discovered similar remains in 1853 in a quarry at Saint-Acheul near Amiens. In 1857 the remains of a man clearly different from modern man were found at Neanderthal, West Germany, and in 1858 the excavation, by William Pengelly, of chipped flints sealed beneath a sheet of stalagmite at Brixham, England, satisfactorily demonstrated the antiquity of mankind.

In 1859, several English scholars, on a visit to Boucher de Perthes, confirmed his conclusions. The existence of fossil man was officially recognized in 1859 with the reading of two papers, one to the Royal Society of London, the other to the Académie des Sciences in Paris. *The Origin of Species* by Charles Darwin appeared in the same year. From then on human history was integrated into the geological scale and measured by the standard of biological evolution.

The establishment of archaeological classifications

In 1865 John Lubbock suggested the terms Paleolithic (Old Stone) for the earlier period of flaked stone tools, and Neolithic (New Stone) for the later period of polished stone axes. The years that followed were marked by intensive research throughout Europe, especially in southeast France, where the work of Edouard Lartet* and the English banker Henry Christy in Périgord soon became a point of reference. Unfortunately, enthusiasm often replaced scientific accuracy and many Paleolithic deposits were emptied without any attempts at preserving the traces of the stratigraphic, layer-by-layer, origin of the thousands of objects exhumed. Some scholars, however, were already trying to establish chronologies, and as early as 1860, Lartet, stating that "the disappearance of animal species considered as characteristic of the last geological period was successive and not simultaneous", proposed a division of Paleolithic periods based on animal life. In 1869 Gabriel de Mortillet* rejected Lartet's classification, putting forward another system based on the actual tools. He identified the Mousterian*, Solutrean*, Aurignacian* and Magdalenian* periods with various assemblages, naming them after the sites where each was found, and this classification was completed by the Acheulian*, preceding the Mousterian*. Other researchers later suggested various divisions which more or less recapitulated the paleontological and typological classifications of Lartet and Mortillet, and it was the system established by Mortillet which, with slight modifications, became orthodox prehistory until the end of the century.

Nevertheless, between 1880 and 1890, an intermediate period was added between the Paleolithic and the Neolithic. Archaeologists generally accepted that a gap existed between these two periods: the last reindeer hunters had travelled northwards in search of herds when the climate became warmer, so that the first farmers who came from Asia afterwards must have found a completely depopulated Europe. However the work of the French archaeologist Piette* in the Pyrenees, notably at Mas d'Azil, showed that levels existed in which temperate-climate animals such as deer predominated, and flat antler harpoons and pebbles painted with ochre were found, these levels occurring just after the levels of the "Reindeer Age". This so-called Azilian* period was clearly post-glacial but lay immediately under the

Excavation at the foot of a dressed stone on the Isle of Lewis, Scotland. Illustration by William Daniel from *A Voyage round Great Britain*, 1819.

The first excavations, undertaken in the 18th century, concerned megalithic monuments — dressed stones and dolmens — which were usually attributed to the Celts or to the Druids. In 1797 John Frere identified shaped flints at Hoxne, Suffolk, dating from "a very remote period indeed". In France, François-Benit Jouannet excavated the first Paleolithic caves, 1815–16, at Combe-Grenal and Pech-de-l'Aze, Périgord.

Neolithic levels. Then other pre-Neolithic deposits were found in the rest of Europe, from Portugal to Norway, always characterized by tools of a very small size, including microliths* and arrowheads. The term Mesolithic was suggested for this transitional period in 1892.

Excavations also revealed Paleolithic bodies, as well as tools and weapons. The first burials recognized as such were discovered in 1868. Five skeletons wearing ornaments made of seashells were uncovered in the rock shelter of Cromagnon near Les Eyzies in southern France. A little later, other burials were found in the Dordogne (Laugerie-Basse), the Landes region (Duruthy) and in the caves of Baoussé-Roussé near Mentone on the French Riviera. Although there were some sceptics, researchers finally came to admit that Upper Paleolithic humans did formally bury their dead.

The end of the 19th century also saw the acceptance of Paleolithic art. In 1864 scholars had had to admit the existence of "mobiliary" art (portable objects such as figurines produced by Paleolithic artists), when Lartet and Christy extracted from the shelter of La Madeleine a fragment of ivory engraved with a delicate representation of a mammoth, irrefutable proof of the age of the piece. But when M. de Sautuola claimed in 1879 that the bisons painted on the wall of the cave of Altamira were the work of Paleolithic humans, very few prehistorians supported him. Between 1890 and 1900, however, the discoveries of decorated caves multiplied in the southwest of France and the finding of Font-de-Gaume and Les Combarelles, explored in 1901 by H. Breuil*, L. Capitan and D. Peyrony*, finally convinced them.

The vision of prehistoric man then prevalent reflected the philosophical doctrines of the day. It was thought that man had progressed steadily from his origins and that Mortillet's periods corresponded more to a logic of technological development than to a genuine temporal stratigraphy*. The use of ethnographical comparisons helped to go beyond the simple description of material traces in order to evoke social and cultural aspects. In this, scholars followed the theories of E. Tylor and L.H. Morgan about the origins and development of societies from the ages of "Savagery" and "Barbarism" to the age of "Civilization".

From the beginning of the 20th century these somewhat theoretical conceptions were completely abandoned in favour of intensive excavation programmes that concentrated exclusively on the typology of tools and the geological structure of archaeological levels. Tools were collected inside visible stratigraphical units representing major stages in the history of the deposits. The aim was to define the similarities and differences in bone and stone assemblages and, by comparing stratigraphies, to organize them in regional sequences and if possible to relate them to each other. Basing himself on the work of Peyrony in Perigord, Breuil published in 1912 *Les Subdivisions du Paléolithique Supérieur* in which he distinguished three phases in the Magdalenian. About the same time, V. Commont worked on the division of the Lower and Middle Paleolithic on the terraces of the Somme. These classifications were re-arranged and improved by Breuil and Peyrony up to 1933. Mortillet's terminology is still in use, but the concept of ages or epochs following each other in an immutable order was replaced by the idea of cultures characterized by assemblages of typical tools called type fossils. Some of them may have developed simultaneously in different regions, as Breuil proved in 1932 with the Lower Paleolithic flake and bifacial industries. However these methods of analysis, though fundamental to the construction of a coherent chronological framework, overemphasized the concept of the type fossil at the expense of other kinds of remains. It is strange to note that

the people themselves—as opposed to their implements—are hardly ever mentioned in the publications of the period, except in a few rare syntheses.

New techniques of archaeological investigation

This tendency was reversed after World War II, and there was a move to put man back in his natural setting. The methods of relative dating*, previously based on geology and typological sequences, were complemented by methods of absolute dating*, the best known of which is Carbon 14 (C^{14}) or radiocarbon* introduced by W.P. Libby in 1949. In 1950, F. Bordes* proposed a methodological analysis of tool kits considered as a whole. The establishment of type lists, and then of percentages for various kinds of tools inside a given level, enabled archaeologists to compare typological series in a much wider cultural framework.

The last 20 years have seen a veritable explosion in the techniques for investigating prehistoric remains. Excavation is no longer looked on as the simplest way to obtain tools in a stratigraphy, but as an essential prerequisite for understanding prehistoric life. The uncovering of prehistoric ground over large areas, already carried out in 1930 on open-air sites in the USSR, has encouraged research into the "structures of the habitat". The scrupulous recording of all remains is the starting point for multiple interdisciplinary laboratory studies of the spatial organization of encampments, the behaviour and technical skills of their occupants, and the choices they made among their environmental resources. Sediments, analyses of plants (fossil pollens and vegetable remains) and animals help not only to place cultural assemblages in a chronological scale, but also to reconstruct the climate and environment in which men lived. Technological analyses, allied to reconstructions of methods of manufacture, the establishment of traces of use on tools (trace-element analysis), research into the sources of raw materials, and the rational use of ethnographical analogies have completely renewed the approach to prehistoric remains. Artifacts have at last come to be seen as evidence of movements and activities. Prehistoric life no longer needs philosophers to describe it; prehistoric humans themselves are beginning to reveal it to us.

The first inhabitants of Europe

The presence of the *Homo erectus* variety of early man in Europe is now known to go back far beyond one million years. As *Homo sapiens*, the intelligent fire-using ancestor of modern man is well over 100,000 years old.

Early varieties of man began to stray out of Africa in pursuit of the wild animals that were their food resource, and entered Europe right at the beginning of the Pleistocene*. Bone-bearing deposits in the Massif Central, France, dated to about 1,800,000 years ago, are perhaps the first indications of their presence: and at the Chilhac III site in the Upper Loire region, some pebbles show signs of flaking that certainly appears intentional. The vast period of almost one million years covered by the Early Pleistocene, followed by the Middle Pleistocene (600,000–130,000BC), saw the spread of mankind over the whole of southern Europe—Spain, France, Italy and Yugoslavia—and its extension during the phases of warmer climate into Britain, Belgium, Germany, Czechoslovakia, and the southern part of the USSR as well.

Until 1983 no human remains had been found at Early Pleistocene levels, but the discovery at Venta Micena, near Granada in Spain, of a skull 1,200,000 years old then confirmed what scholars had suspected; the oldest European hunters were members of the species of mankind called *Homo erectus*. Tools and kitchen debris indicated the presence of these hunters in many places, but no whole skeletons dating to before the Middle Pleistocene have been found, only fragments such as skulls, jaw-bones, pelvises, long bones and teeth, mixed with the bones of animals eaten in the habitations.

The dead were apparently not buried at this period, but left on the floor of the caves. Their bones became scattered and intermingled with the remains of other animal debris, to be gradually buried in the early floors of the habitations. Some 100 fragments of human remains from the Middle Pleistocene have been discovered so far, making it possible to identify about 20 adults, including 7 women and 3 men between 20 and 50 years old, and a dozen children. Thus these scanty fossils represent our only evidence for the thousands of generations which succeeded each other over more than a million years.

The cranial capacity of *Homo erectus* seems to have varied between 1100cc and 1300cc, and the best preserved skulls, such as those from Arago XXI (France) and Petralona (Greece) reveal a thick ridge surmounting deep and wide eye sockets. The forehead is receding and the cranial vault low and elongated. There are great similarities between the characteristics of these two skulls and those of the more fragmentary remains of other Europeans from this period, but none of them can be dated with certainty. Various methods of dating are used, but the results are patchy and it is hard to make them agree: the spectrum of dates proposed for certain fossils may vary from 200,000 to 500,000 years. The most reasonable estimates based on both absolute* and relative* methods of dating give the skulls from Arago and Petralona, and those from Vértesszölös, Hungary, and Bilzingsleben, East Germany, an age between 450,000 and 250,000 years. Anthropologists are currently debating whether these Middle Pleistocene humans are European variations of *Homo erectus* or whether, as descendants of that species, they already represent archaic forms of *Homo sapiens*.

Judging by a certain number of characteristics, the most complete fossils belong to the type *erectus*, but they also exhibit more developed features such as increased brain size which bring them closer to the Neanderthalian type. Some fossils such as those of Swanscombe, England and Steinheim, France, which are probably a little more recent than those previously mentioned, may have been "pre-Neanderthalians", like those from La Ghaise and Biache-Saint-Vaast, France, or Ehringsdorf, West Germany which are from 170,000 to 90,000 years old. Acceptance of the direct connection between *Homo erectus* and *Homo sapiens neanderthalensis* would eliminate the need to look for "pre-sapiens" ancestors in Africa, as some specialists have suggested.

The microscopic study of the enamel-covered crowns of some teeth has shown that the very early hunters of the Pleistocene mainly lived on meat. The animals they hunted were of many kinds, and according to the evidence found in habitations they varied as to both the period and the climate. Pursuit of deer, horses and other medium-sized mammals may not have presented particular problems, whereas the elephants, rhinoceros, hippopotamus and large bovines that were also hunted must certainly have been a dangerous business. The hunters apparently attacked animals that were either very young or very old, being easier to isolate and overcome, and they also were prepared to eat dead animals that they had found.

Tools, buildings, and the use of fire

Throughout the Early Pleistocene, the habitations characteristically yield only a few concentrations of flaked stone tools mingled, it would seem, with more or less shattered animal bones. For example, the cave of Vallonnet, France, inhabited about 950,000 to 900,000 years ago, was no more than a simple den where a few stone tools lay among the bones. Between 900,000 and 800,000 years ago, some people had installed themselves on the shores of a lake of volcanic origin at Soleilhac, France, where tools and broken bones were found in an area about 100 sq m (320 sq ft) demarcated by basalt blocks. The types of habitation apparently remained very rudimentary until about 400,000 years ago. In the open-air encampments of Isernia and Venosa in Italy, or the cave of Arago in France, certain concentrations of bones and flakes from tool-making begin to be discerned, but it is still difficult to see in them a genuine organization of inhabited space.

No trace of fire has been discovered in deposits from this period, with the exception of the cave of Escale in France where, in the levels dated to around 700,000 years ago a few burnt pebbles were found among charcoal debris. However, this apparently precocious use of fire may have been accidental, for another 300,000 years elapse before genuinely purpose-built hearths appear. Small fires were lit on the actual ground or in hollowed out cavities at Vértesszölös in Hungary towards 400,000BC and at Terra Amata in France towards 380,000BC. It was also at this time that genuine areas of habitation, marked off by a border of blocks, low drystone walls or even the insertion of posts, begin to appear. Nevertheless, the encampments of this period are rarely preserved and little is known about their original layout today.

In spite of these gaps in our knowledge, it is clear that the mastery of fire and a concentration of inhabited space would have contributed to the development of social structures. The evolution and diversification of stone tools gave birth to several large regional cultural traditions consisting of various types of the so-called Acheulian* handaxe tradition. It was during this period that the Acheulians developed the Levallois* technique of working stone. Henceforth flakes of a predetermined shape were obtained from a carefully prepared core. These techniques bear witness to the flowering of human intelligence at the end of the Middle Pleistocene (130,000BC). Thus the physical development of these hunters of the Upper Acheulian was accompanied by a corresponding mental development. The later representations were very close to the *Homo sapiens* who was to appear in Europe in the form of *Homo sapiens neanderthalensis* around 100,000BC.

The first Europeans

The head of a Middle Pleistocene man (left) reconstructed from the "Arago XXI" skull of Tautavel, France. This skull and the one found at Petralona (right) are the best preserved of Middle Pleistocene human remains. Both present a large facial area and a clearly marked brow ridge. Archaeologists have identified characteristics indicating that they seem more developed than *Homo erectus*.

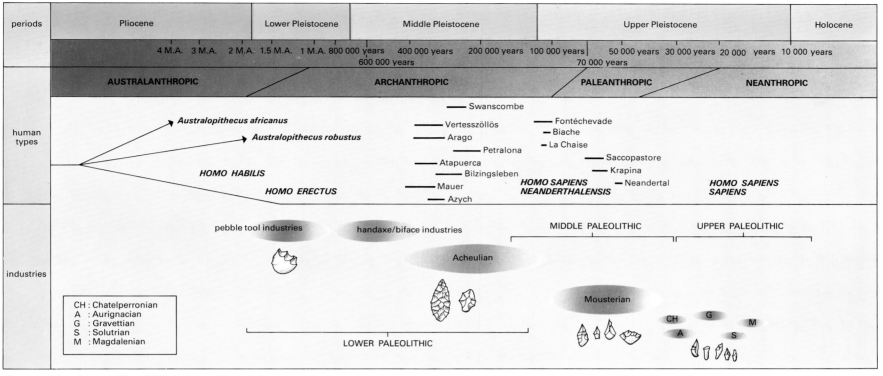

periods	Pliocene		Lower Pleistocene	Middle Pleistocene	Upper Pleistocene	Holocene

4 M.A. 3 M.A. 2 M.A. 1.5 M.A. 1 M.A. 800 000 years 400 000 years 200 000 years 100 000 years 50 000 years 30 000 years 20 000 years 10 000 years
600 000 years 70 000 years

AUSTRALANTHROPIC **ARCHANTHROPIC** **PALEANTHROPIC** **NEANTHROPIC**

human types

Swanscombe
Australopithecus africanus
Vertesszöllös — Fontéchevade
Australopithecus robustus
Arago — Biache
Petralona — La Chaise
Atapuerca — Saccopastore
HOMO HABILIS — Bilzingsleben — Krapina
Mauer **HOMO SAPIENS** — Neandertal **HOMO SAPIENS**
HOMO ERECTUS Azych **NEANDERTHALENSIS** **SAPIENS**

industries

pebble tool industries | handaxe/biface industries | MIDDLE PALEOLITHIC | UPPER PALEOLITHIC

Acheulian

Mousterian

CH | G | M
A | S

CH : Chatelperronian
A : Aurignacian
G : Gravettian
S : Solutrian
M : Magdalenian

LOWER PALEOLITHIC

Chart showing the evolution of industries and human types

Bifaces and chopper (below)

The heart-shaped biface of blueish flint (top, left) measures 145mm × 80mm (5in × 3in). It is less thick than the biface with a yellow patina of the Micoquian type. These two finely fashioned tools have a very regular cutting edge. The chopper, which may have been used as a core, was made on a quartzite pebble and is 80mm (3in) in diameter, 50mm (1.9in) in thickness. Bifaces from Rosny-sur-Seine (France), chopper from Mauran, Nemours Museum (France). Patte collection.

La Caune de l'Arago, Tautavel, France

Opening on the high ground overlooking a river, the cave is situated at a meeting point of different types of natural environment, and often served as a hunting base in the Middle Pleistocene. Through pollen analysis and animal remains, archaeologists can reconstruct the setting, showing the hunters returning with a prehistoric wild sheep, and bison of the steppes grazing in the plain.

Remains from the Acheulian (Lower Paleolithic) level at Castel di Guido, Italy

In the Acheulian period, an organized use of space is rarely discernible. This ground level yielded broken bones of large mammals, hammerstones and cutting tools, suggesting that it may have been a space reserved for eating.

Acheulian hearth (right) from La Roche Gélétan, France

Eleven hearths were found, one above the other, in a hollow in the rock on a beach near Cotentin. Lined with granite pebbles and associated with stone chippings, these hearths are among the oldest in Europe.

The Middle Paleolithic cultures in Europe

For a period of 100,000 years nomadic Paleolithic hunters make up the slow ascent of mankind: a low-level culture roughly working stone, perhaps not even cooking their food with fire, but already exhibiting a care for ancestors in the first formal burials.

The Paleolithic or "Old Stone" age has traditionally been divided into three parts—Upper, Middle and Lower—according to a system based on climatic changes that only approximates to the cultural realities. The Middle Paleolithic first appeared in western Europe towards the end of the ice age known as the Riss glaciation, perhaps as early as 165,000 years ago, and continued until about 40,000 years ago. The dry, cold climate of the Riss period was followed by the warm humidity of the last "interglaciation", a warm interlude between glaciations, which left very few deposits. After a comparatively brief deterioration in the climate at the beginning of the final Würm glaciation (before 70,000BC) a temperate and humid period was followed by a long stretch of some 60,000 years when the climate was again cold and dry. These periods saw the appearance of a human type, *Homo sapiens neanderthalensis**, and a technique of making stone tools by flint flaking, called the Mousterian*. This industry, characterized by assemblages of flake tools dominated by scrapers, is usually contrasted in western Europe with the Acheulian* technique which preceded it and which is characterized by a much greater number of bifaces*.

Until recently, the term Mousterian only applied to complex and varied assemblages dating to the beginning of the last, or Würm, glaciation. But recent excavations have confirmed the presence of identical techniques in the glaciation that came before, and which were until now often regarded as pre-Mousterian. By widening the period covered by the Mousterian, we allow for the existence of a much more complex situation, in which Acheulian and Mousterian techniques could co-exist.

The large number of remains from the Würm period, compared to those from the Riss or Riss-Würm periods, has enabled a detailed comparison between techniques which appear to be more homogeneous than those which came before. In France, a clear difference between fairly homogeneous assemblages has been demonstrated by a method perfected in the 1950s by F. Bordes*. This method has considerably improved our understanding of Mousterian industries but it has also, paradoxically, revealed the limits of our capacity to understand the cultures to which they belong.

The identification of the various groups still relies exclusively on the evidence of the stone tools: the proportions of tools to groups are noted—scrapers, serrated flakes, bifaces, foliated tools, and pebble tools—and the presence of the Levallois technique* of tool-making or other flaking techniques. But it is still unusual to find tools typical of only one group.

A certain number of tool-making techniques of the Middle Paleolithic are clearly defined. Some of them are characterized by bifaces, such as the Epi-Acheulian and the Acheulian-influenced Mousterian in Great Britain and France; or the "Micoquian" of central Europe with its prevalence of bifaces with thick bases and sharp points, foliated convex awls (a pointed hand tool) and foliated scrapers; the Jung-Acheulian of central Europe, contemporary with the Epi-Acheulian, includes, in addition to large, thick-based bifaces and foliate scrapers, retouched blades and numerous awls made in a Levallois technique. In other cultures bifaces are absent and scrapers predominate, as in the "Charentian" industries of southern France, northern Italy, Yugoslavia, Austria and Romania, and the Pontine area of Italy. Other groups are characterized by an absence of their own particular tool types and by the presence of a balanced or "blended" proportion of different objects: serrated flakes, knives, sharp points and scrapers appear in the same quantities. This is the standard or typical Mousterian as it has been defined in France, and it is found over the whole of Europe, from Spain to the Caucasus. But the Caucasus techniques have more in common with those of Western Europe than with the Danube or Rhine valleys. Some include such a large number of flakes showing a Levallois technique that they have been called Levalloiso-Mousterian*.

It has not been possible to demonstrate any degree of interdependence between these tool groups and the contemporary climate, period, environment or even any particular activity. Some kind of cultural correlation has been proposed, but it is not easy to deduce or identify cultural groups from stone assemblages, particularly in view of the great geographical and chronological disparities. Regional variations have been identified, but they are sometimes so fine that each deposit could represent a particular local group. The map of Europe during the Middle Paleolithic shows that regions containing many different industries or techniques, such as south western France, are far rarer than those with a single type of industry. Isolated cultural areas certainly existed, where the same techniques continued in the same place for millennia. But there are many reasons why identical sites may not have come down to us in the same condition, for the levels of conservation differed greatly.

The simplest chronology is provided by the stratigraphical, layer-by-layer, sequences of a sediment, for these certainly show that the higher levels are more recent than the lower ones. However, neither the thickness of the layers nor the identification of the divisions between layers tells us how long a period is covered. Evidence for the evolution of some industries has been proposed as a chronological yardstick. But, indications of an evolutionary process in one area may be reversed in another. As soon as we leave a precise geographical area, we lose touch almost completely with the chronological data.

The overriding need to establish a chronology for these industries meant that archaeologists working during the first half of the 20th century often overlooked the environments of Middle Paleolithic peoples, and any other evidence relating to them apart from stone tools. Animal life, for instance, was seen merely as a means of indicating climate and chronology until it was finally understood that animals were a food source and could as such throw light on contemporary human activity. Also ignored was the spatial distribution of the remains. So what do we really know today about the 100,000-year existence of Middle Paleolithic humanity?

Habitats, hunting and the first burials

First, the people of the Middle Paleolithic were more numerous than their predecessors and followed an exclusively nomadic existence as hunters. Concentrations of habitats over long periods of time, both at open sites and in caves, suggest that they had definite preferences for living in particular places. The size of their communities is completely unknown except that they were large enough and well-organized enough to hunt big animals such as mammoth and aurochs. Given the opportunity, they preferred to hunt large grass-eating animals over any other. Some authorities have made a connection between the locations of the habitats and the kind of game that was hunted and eaten. The presence of burned bones in the hearths does not prove that these were cooked, but the conditions of the bones suggests that large ones were often crushed to extract the marrow.

We know their tools but not their weapons; the fact that they often lived in a wooded environment, together with the abundance of Middle Paleolithic serrated tools, implies a large woodworking capacity, even though the wood is no more. No paintings or drawings from this period have come down to us, but a number of burials prove that certain communities buried their dead.

A linear and partial interpretation of the discoveries of the Middle Paleolithic has slowly been replaced by a more lateral and universal method, an approach that is more selective but also more conducive to an understanding of the living environments and life styles.

Rather than a proper transitional period, the Middle Paleolithic represents, in Western Europe, the point of arrival of tendencies which had been in progress for many years and which seem suddenly to become more homogeneous. These were then replaced by something quite different: the Upper Paleolithic, characterized by fine stone tools as well as by utensils made out of bone and by individual implements. The same may not be applicable to central Europe, where certain industries (Szeletian*, Jerzmanowician*) could represent a transitional stage towards the Upper Paleolithic.

Middle Paleolithic habitat, Mauran, Haute-Garonne, France

The principal level of this open-air deposit, buried beneath 4m (13ft) of sediment, contains many bones of large bovines (aurochs and bison) and some remains of horses. The food debris here consists of jawbones, foot bones, ribs and ends of long bones broken to extract the marrow, and this accompanies a collection of stone objects. Small flint flakes and tools lie beside quartzite pebbles, some unworked and others shaped into choppers. Many fragments of burnt bone have been found in this deposit, but as yet no hearth.

Biache-Saint-Vaast, Pas-de-Calais, France

Clearing of the upper part of level IIa (the level where a Middle Paleolithic skull was found) revealed a number of print marks preserved in the soft tufa rock from the Riss glaciation. These included hooves of bovines and a small horse, and possibly the mark of a human foot. The abundant stone tool industry is of black flint.

The interior of the Guattari cave at Monte Circeo, Latium, Italy (left)

A landslide closed the mouth of the cave at the time of the Würm II glaciation, and the surface of level I, made up of pebbles and blocks of limestone conglomerate, mixed with bones of deer, bovines and horses, and traces of tool-working industry, is just as it was when the Mousterians abandoned it.

Stratigraphic section of Carihuela, Granada, Spain

The sequence of layers in this cave runs from the Middle Paleolithic to the Bronze Age. With its 61 levels, the Mousterian filling—going back to the Würm II glaciation—is one of the most important in Spain. Study of the sediments of these deposits enable us to understand their development and the climate in which they were formed.

Stone tools of the Mousterian, Champlost, France

These scrapers (one convergent, three transversal, two simple) are fashioned on flint flakes showing patination or signs of wear. Their maximum size is 10cm (4in). Several rows of retouching provide a sharp convex working edge.

The principal deposits of the European Middle Paleolithic

The geography of the Middle Paleolithic reflects the present state of archaeological knowledge, and covers a time span of more than 100,000 years. It is therefore only an imaginatively reconstructed picture, but gives some insight into the reality of populations concentrated along big valleys and in certain sheltered regions. It is difficult to trace cultural movements from stone tool industries alone, and methods of study vary from one end of Europe to the other. However, we do note that affinities between different types of industry generally move from west to east. Bifacial industries abound from England to Germany, passing through the north of France. Industries of the Quina type move from southern Hungary to southwest France.

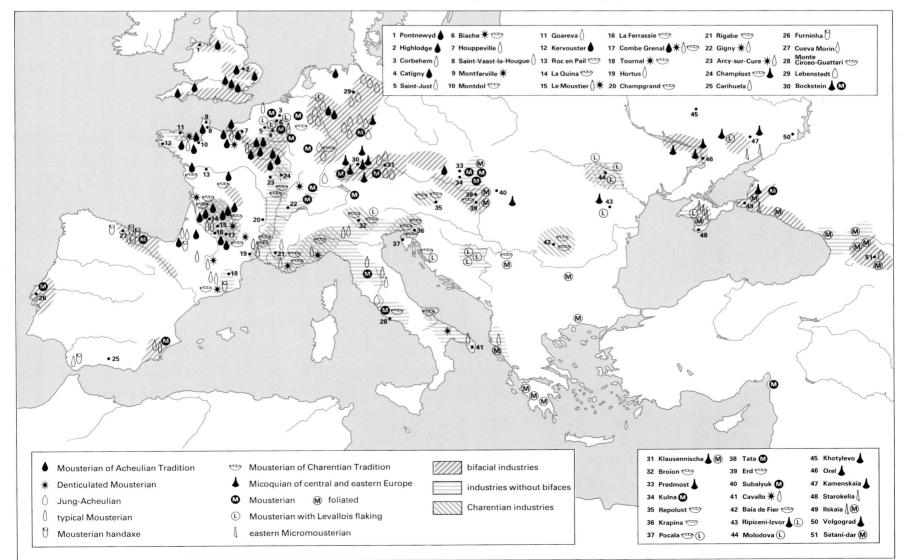

1 Pontnewyd	6 Biache	11 Goareva	16 La Ferrassie	21 Rigabe	26 Furninha
2 Highlodge	7 Houppeville	12 Kervouster	17 Combe Grenal	22 Gigny	27 Cueva Morin
3 Corbehem	8 Saint-Vaast-la-Hougue	13 Roc en Pail	18 Tournal	23 Arcy-sur-Cure	28 Monte Circeo-Guattari
4 Catigny	9 Montfarville	14 La Quina	19 Hortus	24 Champlost	29 Lebenstedt
5 Saint-Just	10 Montdol	15 Le Moustier	20 Champgrand	25 Carihuela	30 Bockstein

31 Klausennische	38 Tata	45 Khotylevo
32 Broion	39 Erd	46 Orel
33 Predmost	40 Subalyuk	47 Kamenskaia
34 Kulna	41 Cavallo	48 Starokelia
35 Repolust	42 Baia de Fier	49 Ilskaïa
36 Krapina	43 Ripiceni-Izvor	50 Volgograd
37 Pocala	44 Molodova	51 Satani-dar

Legend:
- Mousterian of Acheulian Tradition
- Denticulated Mousterian
- Jung-Acheulian
- typical Mousterian
- Mousterian handaxe
- Mousterian of Charentian Tradition
- Micoquian of central and eastern Europe
- (M) Mousterian — (M) foliated
- (L) Mousterian with Levallois flaking
- eastern Micromousterian
- bifacial industries
- industries without bifaces
- Charentian industries

From Neanderthal man to *Homo sapiens sapiens*

The arrival of "modern" man in Western Europe marked a decisive break with the past, in terms of stone tools, utensils and made objects. Did Neanderthal man fall victim to the rule formulated by Darwin that only the fittest survive?

In 1856 a cave in the little valley of Neanderthal near Dusseldorf, West Germany, was the site of a discovery of some bones, among which was the fragment of a cranium, and this was to occupy a key position in the history of the evolution of the human race. Many other discoveries followed in western Europe: remains from Spy and the Trou de la Naulette in Belgium, skulls from Saccopastore and Monte Circeo in Italy, 200 human fragments from Krapina in Croatia representing the remains of more than 15 people, others in Spain, and numerous discoveries in France, the best known being those of La Ferrassie, La Chapelle aux Saints, Arcy-sur-Cure and L'Hortus.

The principal anatomical features shared by these people consisted of a flattened skull with receding forehead, (although brain capacity was high), a thick and continuous brow ridge, massive jaws and a sharply receding chin. As regards their place in human evolution, the Neanderthal people may have descended from *Homo erectus** and they are now classified as representing a sub-species of *Homo sapiens**, *Homo sapiens neanderthalensis**, leaving the term *Homo sapiens sapiens** for modern man.

A few years ago, a sharp distinction was made between the two types. Neanderthals, who made their implements according to the so-called Mousterian* technique or industry, were regarded as beings who were still primitive and obtuse. But as excavations have proceeded and developed, so has their image evolved and improved. Some of their habitations are seen to be very well structured and even to be partly built around hearths. Neither jewels nor art are in evidence, but funeral rites and practices were certainly observed by these early humans with their low foreheads. Six burials at La Ferrassie in France showed the deliberate arrangement of carefully chosen stones; at Teshik Tash in Uzbekistan (USSR) the skull of a young child was crowned by five pairs of ibex horns; and the burial at Shanidar in Iraq, where the body had been placed on a bed of flowers, clearly shows the importance attached to mortuary practices at that time.

Modern humans with high skulls, straight and unridged foreheads and developed chins, then began to appear in Western Europe. They are associated with a more developed industry known as the Upper Paleolithic and mainly characterized by a new range of flint tools. The first culture associated with this industry is the Lower Perigordian or Chatelperronian*. This was followed by the Aurignacian*, a culture that had evolved to include bone tools and works of art. The Middle Paleolithic, characterized as it was by the Mousterian industry, was therefore considered to refer to the Neanderthal people, while the Upper Paleolithic, beginning with the Chatelperronian and the Aurignacian, linked up with modern humans, *Homo sapiens sapiens*. Dates are uncertain for such remote periods of time. They must have been separated, perhaps by 5,000 or 10,000 years, which has led some scholars to form the barely tenable hypothesis that one of the groups descended from the other.

Conflicting evidence

Thus the boundary between the Middle and Upper Paleolithic seems quite clear cut, even though a certain number of tools of the Mousterian type have been found on Chatelperronian sites. But as new excavations have proceeded, the matter has become altogether more complicated. About twenty years ago, an early and disconcerting discovery made at Arcy-sur-Cure, France, revealed human teeth at Chatelperronian levels that shared certain similarities with those of an early human jaw discovered at an older, Mousterian, level. Such teeth could not easily be attributed without reserve to modern man. More recently, Carbon 14* dating, although lacking precision beyond a period of more than 35,000 years, has provided a chronological framework that seems to eliminate the gap between Mousterian and Chatelperronian. In addition, a number of sediment and pollen analyses, indicating a warmer climate that began with the deposit of Mousterian layers and ended in the Chatelperronian, has confirmed the connection between them. In spite of troubled climatic phases, with intervals of heavy rainfall that washed out deposits, the chronology has become much clearer. Then a discovery was made at St Césaire, France, that upset some accepted ideas, but clarified inconsistencies.

Discovered in 1977, the deposit at St Césaire, near Saintes, reveals a stratigraphy* so clear that there could be no argument about it. The lower portion consisted of three Mousterian layers lying beneath three layers of Chatelperronian industries. In the middle layer, tools with the "backed points" typical of the industry were found together with human remains of a clearly Neanderthal type. The skeleton was incomplete, but consisted of the right half of the body and most of the bones. A massive brow ridge, a long jaw and an absence of chin, as well as parts of the shoulder blade and the lower arm, revealed distinctively Neanderthalian characteristics.

Obviously, this discovery has considerably altered existing ideas about the disappearance of the Neanderthalians and the transition to modern man. First of all, we now know that the former continued much longer than had been thought, until at least 30,000BC. Yet modern humans of the Aurignacian period were already in evidence, especially in the south of France. So the two populations must have been contemporaneous 3,000 years before Neanderthal man disappeared without descendants, for reasons that remain mysterious.

Thus the split between the human types is no longer seen to occur between the Middle Paleolithic and the Upper Paleolithic, but between the Chatelperronian and the Aurignacian. And the fact that there was so much Mousterian flint in the Chatelperronian period becomes intelligible, as does the ensuing evolution in the various industries, if we extend it about 3,000 years. But many questions still remain. For example, the bone industry, unknown to the Mousterians, was practised at Arcy-sur-Cure where bone rings, points and pendants as well as pierced animal teeth were found. It seems highly probable that some form of exchange or copying took place, given the frequency of such processes.

A study of pollens giving a finely graduated chronology leads to a better understanding of the retreat of the Neanderthalians and the advance of the Aurignacians by situating them in time in relation to their geographical position. Two prehistoric stations have already shown two cultures alternating on the same site. Undoubtedly, interdisciplinary research will provide new explanations for interactions between the industries. Nevertheless, the evidence is still too scarce and new discoveries will have to be made before it is possible to reconstruct this phase of human evolution.

Tomb of Shanidar IV

In Iraqi Kurdistan, the tomb of Shanidar IV contained a Neanderthal human buried on a carpet of flowers in a kind of niche made of large stone blocks. Earth samples nos. 326, 315 and 271 from a deposit later than the burial gave much the same pollens as other samples taken from the cave; but three samples from the earth on which the corpse had been laid (nos. 313, 314, 304) contained numerous stamens from 8 species of flowers. Natural causes could not possibly have carried this group of whole flowers deep inside a cave, so this deliberate offering proves the existence of certain mortuary rites some 50,000 years ago.

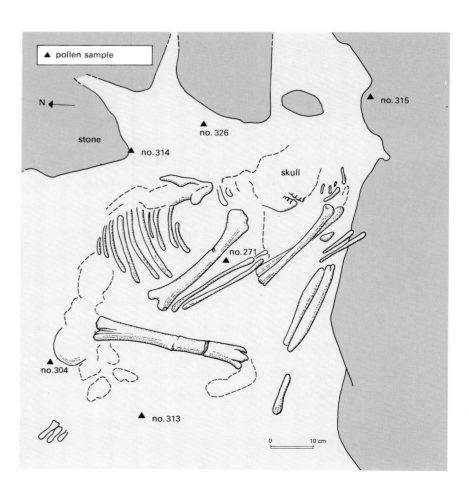

Comparison of human fossil and modern man

Jawbone of a modern man (below, right), and jawbone from Arcy-sur-Cure (France) found in Mousterian levels (below, left). The teeth of these fossils are very similar to those found individually in the overlying Chatelperronian levels. The latter were of a type associated with tool-making industries of the Upper Paleolithic, not the Middle Paleolithic people. This has posed a problem for 30 years. Musée de l'Homme, Paris.

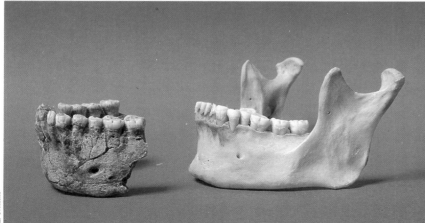

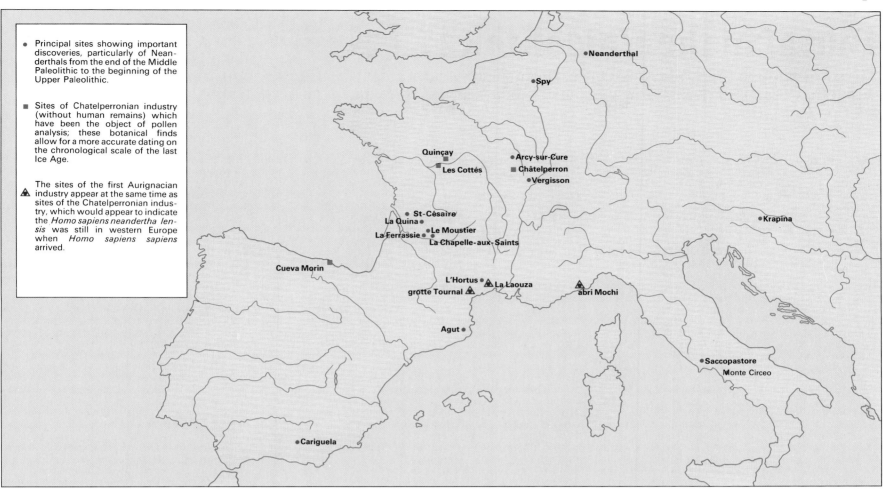

- Principal sites showing important discoveries, particularly of Neanderthals from the end of the Middle Paleolithic to the beginning of the Upper Paleolithic.

- Sites of Chatelperronian industry (without human remains) which have been the object of pollen analysis; these botanical finds allow for a more accurate dating on the chronological scale of the last Ice Age.

- The sites of the first Aurignacian industry appear at the same time as sites of the Chatelperronian industry, which would appear to indicate the *Homo sapiens neanderthalensis* was still in western Europe when *Homo sapiens sapiens* arrived.

Chatelperronian tools

Although it preserves some archaic traits, such as the persistence of Mousterian side scrapers (a) and Mousterian points, the Chatelperronian stone tool industry differs greatly from those which preceded it. Apart from the manufacture of genuine blades, researchers have observed the widespread use of burins (b) and end-scrapers (c). The Chatelperronian point (d, e, f) is the characteristic tool of this industry. The knife (f) with an unpolished cutting edge and a curved back was probably fixed to a haft or handle.

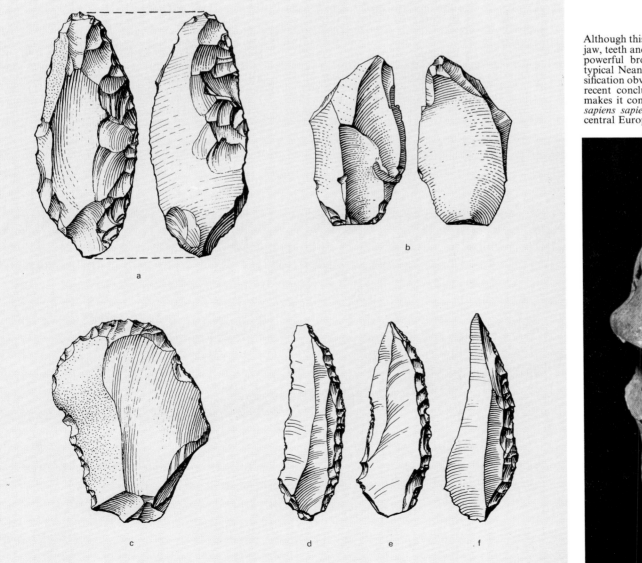

The St-Césaire skull

Although this object is in fragments and incomplete, the lower jaw, teeth and upper jaw, as well as the receding forehead and powerful brow ridge, are sufficiently characteristic of the typical Neanderthalians of western Europe to make its classification obvious to an anthropologist. According to the most recent conclusions, the chronology of this Neanderthalian makes it contemporary with our own direct ancestor *Homo sapiens sapiens*, who, at the same period already occupied central Europe and the south of France.

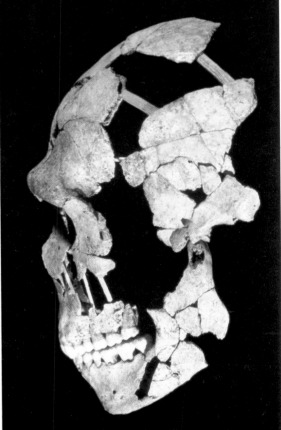

Burial in the Paleolithic

The spirituality of the Stone Age? One of the most important recent discoveries about our prehistoric ancestors is that they practised ritual burial customs: 75,000 years ago men and women contemplated life, death and its relation to afterlife.

When, between 1868 and 1872, skeletons wearing ornaments were exhumed in various Upper Paleolithic deposits, many prehistorians believed that they were the remains of people killed in accidents, perhaps crushed by rock falls or carried away by floods. At the end of the 19th century the idea of burial was still linked with that of religion, and scholars found it hard to believe that these "primitive" men could have had spiritual preoccupations. Nevertheless, the fact that the people of the Upper Paleolithic buried their dead was eventually accepted. Then came the discoveries in 1908 and 1909 of burials dating to the Mousterian* at La Chapelle-aux-Saints and La Ferrassie in the Dordogne, and scholars were forced to accept the inconceivable fact that even the Neanderthalian "brutes" buried their dead. There followed a period when the romantic description of Paleolithic funerary rituals went far beyond objective observation of the facts. Provisions for the journey into the hereafter, funerary meals, hearths to provide warmth for the dead and a cult of skulls were the favourite themes of many specialists for decades. Today critical syntheses, elaborated for some 15 years, enable us to evaluate the facts more accurately.

Deliberate burial in these very ancient times is mainly assumed from the fact that the bones of a skeleton were all found together in the same place. A skeleton left in the open air is in fact unlikely to have survived except in the form of scattered bones. So there is nothing to confirm that Lower Paleolithic men observed funerary rites. At the other extreme, they could even have eaten their fellow men on certain occasions.

Middle Paleolithic burial features

Among the burials known to date, some 140 in quantity, not all yield the same amount of information, either because they are not always well preserved or because they have not been excavated with the necessary care. Nevertheless, we can establish certain general features. They are all found in habitations, mostly caves or shelters, and isolated inhumations are at present unknown. There appears to have been no segregation by sex or age: men, women and children (and even unborn children) were buried in approximately the same circumstances. In nearly half the cases, the skeletons lie at the bottom of specially dug pits, but the traces of other pits may have disappeared or escaped the attention of excavators at the time.

The practice of burial appears in the Middle Paleolithic, probably from 75,000BC. The Mousterian burials of this period, involving Neanderthal peoples, are mostly concentrated in the Périgord and Israel, but they have also been found in Belgium and the Crimea. With two exceptions (a child and a foetus at La Ferrassie

in France and a woman and child at Qafzeh in Israel), the burials are of single individuals. The bodies are generally bent, and their orientation show no particular preference of direction.

On the whole, the construction of the tombs is uncomplicated, but some graves are surrounded or covered with stones. One of the tombs of children at La Ferrassie was covered by a large slab with cup-marks on the lower face. Finally, deliberate deposits such as "offerings" or "grave goods", are extremely rare, in spite of the assertions of early excavators who claimed to identify some "beautiful tools" or "quarters of venison" among the flints and bones contained in the surrounding sediments. A rare exception is the child burial at Qafzeh, where the body was found with the antlers of a deer and an ostrich egg. Outside Europe, there is the burial of a child covered with ibex horns at Teshik Tash, Uzbekistan (USSR); at Shanidar, Iraq, analysis of fossil pollens has shown that a man and a child were lain in graves strewn with flowers.

The Neanderthal people seem to have had other customs besides these when confronted with death. At Monte Circeo, Italy, an isolated skull was found inside a circle of stones. The occipital hole at the back of the skull had been artifically enlarged—possibly in order to eat the brain, in the opinion of the discoverer, A. C. Blanc. It is still difficult to prove that flesh was eaten, but there is no doubt that a skull stripped of flesh was deliberately placed in this remote cave. Finally, broken human bones mixed with the kitchen debris of Mousterian habitations have been found on various sites. At Krapina, Yugoslavia, the bones of 13 individuals had clearly been crushed so as to extract the marrow. Without going so far as to suggest "ritual cannibalism", everything indicates that Neanderthal man did not disdain the chance to eat his fellow men on occasion.

Variations in burial styles

In the Upper Paleolithic, burial becomes more numerous and more varied. The main centres are the Périgord in France, Liguria and Moravia in Central Europe and the USSR. Individual burials are still the most common, but double and triple examples occur, and even one collective burial. At Predmost in Moravia, 18 individuals were buried one after the other in the same structure. The orientation and position of the bodies may vary: sometimes bent to the left (Périgord), stretched out (Italy), bent to the right (Moravia), and sometimes crouched or bent double, as if the body had been bound. In Western Europe, some burials contain stones "pillows" for the deceased, or stone coverings. The well-known grave of a woman at Saint-Germain-La-Rivière was even placed beneath a small dolmen*

made of two horizontal slabs supported by vertical stones. In eastern Europe mammoth bones replaced the slabs. At Pavlov and Dolní Věstonice in Moravia, painted or incised shoulder blades were placed on the bodies, and at Kostienki XVIII, USSR, a child's body was found beneath a pile of mammoth bones and appeared to have been laid in a deliberately constructed burial vault.

People of the Upper Paleolithic practised a wide range of burial customs unknown before. In half the cases, so far discovered, the bodies lie on a layer of red ochre* or are covered with it. This has been interpreted in many ways; for instance, red is the colour of blood and therefore the colour of life. But recent experiments have shown that ochre has the property of preserving human tissue, and may possibly have been used to keep the bodies from decomposition. Men, women and children seem to have been interred with tools and weapons and without distinction of sex or age. Flint cutting blades, points and scrapers, bone points and pierced antler sticks were generally placed near the head, in the hand or near the hips—possibly in the pocket of a long vanished garment. In nearly three-quarters of the cases, an ornament of some kind accompanied the dead person. The wear on some pieces suggests that these must have been worn in life and preserved in the tomb. Shell ornaments feature largely in western Europe, with round and elongated forms often combined with the teeth of foxes and deer. These same round or elongated shapes are also found in eastern Europe, where they are carved out of mammoth ivory, and these too are accompanied by teeth of the blue fox. The bodies of men and children appear to be the most decorated. In Liguria, at Combe-Capelle and La Madeleine in France, and at Sungir' in the USSR, the dead were apparently dressed in a kind of bonnet, to which shells were fixed to form a hairnet. Elongated pendants were attached to the edge of the headdress to hang down to the shoulders.

Perishable clothing has vanished, of course, with the exception of a "loin-cloth" of round shells worn by the woman of Saint-Germain-la-Rivière and the two children found at Baoussé-Roussé, Liguria; its former presence in European graves is suggested only by isolated objects fixed at hip, knee or ankle level. At Sungir', on the other hand, hundreds of ivory beads which outlined the legs and chest of an adult male must have been sewn on to his trousers and skin shirt. Other kinds of grave apparel consist of numerous necklaces and bracelets, made from fish vertebrae and shells in the west and mammoth ivory beads and rings cut in the east.

It is through their deaths that the hunter peoples of the Upper Paleolithic have provided us with a picture of the refinement attained by their cultures.

Homo II, Qafzeh, Israel

This Mousterian (Neanderthal) child of 13 was buried with deer's antlers in his hands, which were bent back towards the neck. This is one of the rare but irrefutable examples of grave offerings from the Middle Paleolithic. Excavations by B. Vandermeersch.

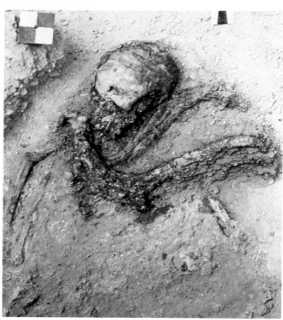

Double burial at Sungir', USSR

Two children of 8 and 13 rested in a narrow, ochre-painted pit 3m (10ft) long. Their heads were covered with ivory beads and foxes' teeth, their wrists and fingers bore ivory rings. Two very long lances, some 15 javelins and daggers, 2 perforated discs and 2 pierced sticks make this the most remarkable burial from the Upper Paleolithic. Excavations by O. Bader.

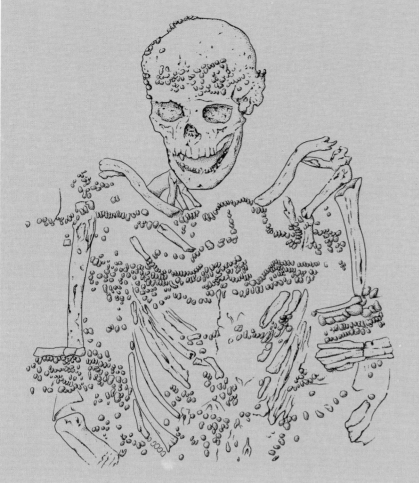

Man from Sungir', USSR

This 55-year old man was covered with garments decorated with 1500 ivory beads. Traces of fire discovered on the bones of his feet and some of the beads indicate that he was placed on embers, the remains of which were laid in the pit. Excavations by O. Bader.

Cave of Cavillon, Liguria (*above*)

A bone awl was placed near the forehead of this Aurignacian wearing a "cap" of 200 netted whelk shells with a border of 22 deer's teeth. A line of red ochre 18cm (7in) long was extended from the face into the ground. Excavations by E. Rivière.

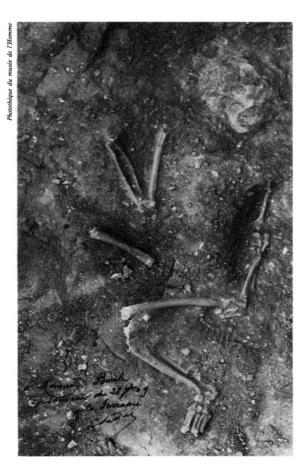

The first Mousterian skeleton from La Ferrassie

Peyrony's discovery in 1909 of the first Neanderthal skeleton at La Ferrassie in the Dordogne provided H. Breuil with material for his report (right) suggesting the deliberate nature of the burial. However, prehistorians were not convinced until 1912, after three more burials had been uncovered in the same shelter. Breuil, in the presence of several prehistorians, then drafted a statement affirming the existence of funerary rituals in the Middle Paleolithic. Musée de l'Homme, Paris.

Woman in the Paleolithic age

Influenced by feminism, modern archaeologists have argued fiercely over the role of woman in prehistory. Has man always been the hunter, or were women the first toolmakers? When did women seek men's protection?

Until quite recently, anthropologists and prehistorians believed that the process of human development was related to the development of hunting skills, and therefore that the first man-made objects were weapons, or tools for making weapons. But in 1981 American anthropologists rejected this theory, which seemed to reflect a typically Western mode of thought whereby the man played a dominant role at the expense of "the other half of humanity". N. Tanner, for instance, claimed that it was not "man the hunter", but "woman the gatherer" who was responsible for the emergence of humanity. Basing his theory on the study of modern hunter-gatherer societies and, even more, on observation of the behaviour of the large apes, N. Tanner proposed that the first hominids to use tools regularly were females accompanied by their young. These used sticks to extract roots from the soil of the African savanna, to trap insects, and to pull down fruit and eggs into some kind of container. Unlike the chimpanzees (which have been observed to use some of these techniques), the hominid females did not eat the food at the place where it had been collected, but carried it off to safer locations protected from large predators. Preparation of sharpened sticks and of effective containers required tools that were invented and maintained over a gradual period of time. Furthermore, food-sharing in communal lairs would have led to the development of new kinds of social behaviour between the females and young of the same group.

According to H. Fisher, the upright posture found in the earliest humans would have affected the structure and anatomy of pregnant females in such a way that giving birth may have been difficult. But premature delivery may have ensured the better survival of pregnant females. Prematurely born young required a longer period of care, and the restriction that this imposed on the mothers' mobility meant that they sought the protection of the males. The latter remained close to the females as the monthly period of heat, or sexual attraction (and consequently of copulation) grew progressively longer through natural selection. Thus, the mother–child bond, sexuality and the production of tools for food-gathering were at the origin of the new social structuring of these hominids.

These theories sometimes appear strained and are obviously the product of the feminist tendency that has developed since the 1960s. They cannot be easily verified, and, like earlier theories, take into account only a part of the total reality; but they do have the merit of putting an emphasis on the role of women in the development of human societies.

For the more recent periods of the development of early mankind, in the Middle and Upper Paleolithic, it is even more difficult to make use of the behaviour of the large primates as a means of establishing the role of human females, and the only methods of investigation here are ethnographic comparison with "primitive" communities and the evidence revealed by fieldwork.

Recent theories

Since the end of the 19th century, prehistorians have assumed that in a mixed economy based on hunting and gathering, women collected the fruits and roots, gathered the shellfish and possibly caught small animals, whereas men undertook the pursuit of large mammals. These hypotheses may remain likely in general terms, but it should be remembered that in the course of this very long period the relative importance of animal and vegetable resources would have varied considerably according to climate and region. The respective role of masculine and feminine tasks would therefore have undergone innumerable changes, and there would undoubtedly have been many different solutions to the problems of a lifestyle shared in common.

Archaeological conclusions and evidence regarding the distribution of activities between the sexes remains very scanty. Although it is now possible to reconstruct the actions of the users and their modes of operation through study of the way tools display signs of wear, the sex of the individual who handled the tools is unknown.

Another approach is to study the distribution of the different tools in the habitation. It is possible that in prehistoric societies,, as in some present-day societies, one space may have been reserved for men and another for women. This is the view of the Soviet prehistorian M. Gerassimov in relation to two Upper Paleolithic habitations discovered at Mal'ta in Siberia. Here, the two areas are distinguished respectively by the presence of "masculine" objects (knives, daggers, statuettes of birds) and "feminine" objects (needles, awls, scrapers, necklaces, female statuettes). This is the only example of such differentiation to have been discovered to date, but it could in any case be interpreted differently. The place where the knives and daggers were found may simply have been a butchery area, and the site where needles and awls were found a sewing location, without any implication of a sexual division of labour.

Moreover, nothing proves that the necklaces from the second sector at Mal'ta belonged to women. Upper Paleolithic burials indicate that the wearing of ornaments was not confined to women but that, on the contrary, men and children wore them to a greater extent. No difference is apparent when we compare the burials of males or females, or the grave goods accompanying the dead. The flint and bone tools placed near the bodies seem to be the same for both men and women.

Lack of information has sometimes led prehistorians to rely on their imagination in order to fill the gaps in our knowledge, and they have tended to project onto prehistoric woman the role assigned to woman in their own society. Thus to them prehistoric women were essentially passive, child-bearing nurturers ill-equipped to work flint or make tools, of little use in active life, but nevertheless regarded as divine in terms of the cults of fertility that were then practised.

Certainly, numerous feminine figures with exaggerated sexual characteristics were fashioned during the Upper Paleolithic. "If the evidence of humans and cave paintings is to be taken at face value, the Paleolithic woman was an uncomplicated creature, naked and with curling hair, who kept her hands folded over her chest, holding her minute head serenely above the dreadfully sagging shape of her breasts and hips," André Leroi-Gourhan has written. He is referring to the stone and ivory "Venus" figures of the Gravettian period (between 25,000 and 20,000BC) which certainly present an obese or heavily pregnant appearance and which are found from the Pyrenees to the USSR. Later, between 15,000 and 10,000BC, another and more gracefully slim type of female figure appears, frequently depicted in profile in engravings or paintings, and sometimes appearing as a statuette. The occasional representations of women in association with animals may indicate that they participated in the symbolism and religious thinking of the Paleolithic period, but had only distant connections with everyday hunter's life.

Nevertheless, deliberate stylization did not always exclude some more realistic details: half-length wavy hair on the Siberian statuettes, a chignon rolled into a knot on the so-called Grimaldi "negroid head", tight curls or a hairnet on the Willendorf Venus, hood or plaits on the Lady of Brassempouy. Sometimes the clothing too is suggested: limited in western Europe to bracelets, necklaces or loincloths, in Siberia the clothing seems to envelop closely the whole body except the face. Some details even suggest that the garment might be lined or tipped with fur.

Finally at Gönnersdorf, Germany, an engraving of a woman in profile seems to be carrying on her back a smaller figure which suggests that the Paleolithic woman need not have remained home-bound when she had a child. But it must be admitted that our knowledge of the activities of the Paleolithic hunters themselves is scarcely more detailed, and that, at the time of writing, the sexual roles of our remote ancestors are still obscure.

Women in single file, Gönnersdorf, Germany

The stylized depiction of these women, represented without heads or feet, was incised on a small schist block and is typical of the Magdalenian period. According to G. Bosinski, the horizontal and vertical incisions may indicate clothing. It is also possible that the smaller silhouette could represent a child carried on its mother's back.

Image of prehistoric woman

This illustration from the end of the 19th century is one of the very few representations of a woman shaping stone. Many prehistorians believed that this difficult and delicate work could only be done by men.

G. Fischer, Institut de protohistoire et de préhistoire

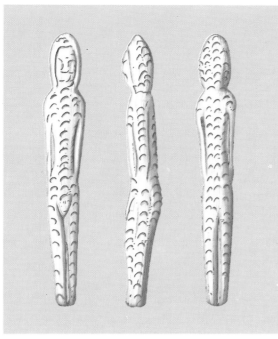

Ivory statuette from Bouret, Siberia

The feminine sex of this statuette with its fine outline is indicated by the pubic triangle. Note that the back of the head is treated in the same way as the rest of the body; this may indicate that this woman was wearing a garment with a hood.

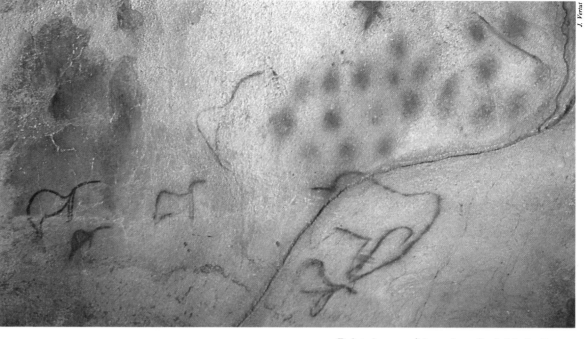

Painted women/bisons from Pech-Merle, France

André Leroi-Gourhan has suggested that these highly stylized silhouettes of women could also have been seen as silhouettes of bison: the head and low-slung breasts corresponding to the hindquarters and upraised tail, and the curve of the buttocks defining the withers.

La Madeleine, France

The two women carved in low relief at the entrance to this cave are shown lying in a relaxed position exceptional in the Paleolithic. The woman most clearly visible here is stretched out on her back with one leg bent and one arm supporting her head, which is only roughly sketched out.

The Venus of Věstonice, Czechoslovakia

This corpulent "Venus" is typical of the female figures of the Gravettian culture. A feature most unusual for the Paleolithic is the use of a mixture of clay and powdered bone to model the object. The horizontal groove on the hips may indicate a belt.

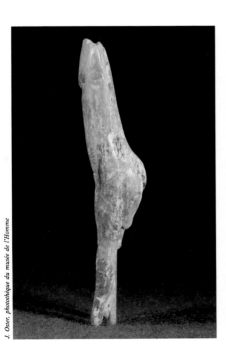

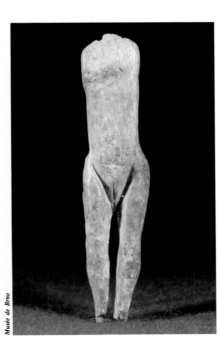

The "immodest Venus" from Laugerie-Basse, Dordogne, France

Like many Magdalenian female figures, this ivory statuette with its thin silhouette has no head, arms or breasts. However, the precise depiction of the pubic triangle and the vulva leaves no doubt about its sexual attribution.

31

Everyday life 12,000 years ago

What was it like to live before History? After 150 years of prehistoric research archaeologists can begin tentatively to give us a human picture going back twelve millennia.

Every archaeologist must have dreamed at least once in his life, that he returned in time to a period when he could observe in real life the people whose worn-out utensils and kitchen debris formed his study. Here is a story that is set about 12,000 years ago, and perhaps it represents the beginning of reality for this dream.

One misty morning in the late spring, an "observer" lies concealed a short distance from a small seasonal encampment sited near a river. The mist prevents him from seeing the whole scene distinctly, but sometimes clears enough for him to make out some details. Several figures are at work not far from the dark bulk of a dwelling that he can just see is of a round shape. One of the individuals has picked up two flint pebblestones from the river bank and has just sat down on a large rock some distance away. After carefully looking at one of the stones he makes himself more comfortable, bending his left leg and stretching out his right, then strikes the flint with a hammerstone. Removing a series of alternate flakes he makes a ridge lengthways along the side of the flint, and then, with a precise stroke, knocks out a long and narrow blade, followed by others. The work continues for about a quarter of an hour. During this time, another figure is busy near a large hearth. The observer cannot make this out clearly, but he assumes that it is a woman cleaning out the hollow that contains the fire. She uses the shoulder blade of a reindeer to collect the ashes and calcined stone in a receptacle, and then scrapes clean the edges of the hearth covered with bits of flint and bone. After throwing all this onto the refuse tip a few yards away, she comes back, puts some stones in the hollow, and quickly relights the fire. The observer fails to see how this was done, but assumes she must have kept some live embers from the night before. Then she sits down by a reindeer skin which is drying, and begins to clean it with a flint scraper. She scrapes the skin carefully for two hours, then starts to impregnate it with a greasy red substance. ("That must be ochre," the observer says to himself.)

While watching this operation, the observer also tries to keep an eye on what the man who was chipping out the stone is doing. First, he goes back to the camp with some roughed-out blades, and sits down by the hearth next to another figure who has appeared there. Now he quickly shapes one of the blades into a cutting tool, and saws through a fairly thick reindeer antler. Chatting away to his companion, he taps a hole in the thick part of the antler. The observer notices that he is left-handed and, seeing fragments of a similar implement some distance away, he realizes that the man is making an arrow straightener. His companion, kneeling by the fire, is repairing a spear barbed with small flint blades. Using the heat of the fire he melts the resin which keeps the blades in place along the shaft, throws away the blades that are broken, and inserts new ones. Now the observer understands why there are so many small blades near the fire.

Finishing work on the skin, the third individual now comes back to the fireside and begins to grill meat on hot stones set in the hollow. "That must be the woman," thinks the archaeological observer.

Methods of reconstruction

Whatever one might think, this story is not romantic fiction. It is just one example of a description of the actions and activities of Paleolithic people that prehistorians are now able to reconstruct. To this end, they adopt several methods of approach, the first being excavation of archaeological sites over large areas. The result is to reveal and restore, in almost living and working form, the long abandoned encampment; only the perishable materials, such as wood, leather or meat are missing. Plans and photos meticulously record all remains, down to the tiniest splinters, so that, when they have been removed and catalogued, we can more easily study their spatial organization. In the laboratory, the systematic search for connections between the fragments that the original inhabitants had scattered on the ground aims to reconstruct the initial blocks of flint, the stones used in the hearths, and even the bones broken to extract the marrow. Thus it becomes possible to reconstruct the series of operations which led to the discarding of these fragments.

The transfer of these related fragments to a plan then shows how movement went on inside the habitation. That is how scholars were able to show, starting from splinters left on the ground, the place where the stone-chipping individual was sitting when he worked on his piece of flint, even though the largest bits of waste were thrown onto a refuse tip and the finished tools were found in the area where they were used.

The replacement of flint flakes on a nucleus or core helps to reconstruct the chain of technical movements made to obtain these tools. On the basis of these observations, some specialists can chip flint in the same way as the prehistoric chippers of a particular site. Practical experiments enable not only the technical hypotheses to be checked, but also the exact position of the flint worker at the time of the operation to be ascertained by observing the arrangement of waste.

For more than a 100 years, prehistorians have tried to guess the function of flint tools from the shape of their edges and by comparing them with other tools used by "primitive" peoples. The introduction some 10 years ago of a new process sometimes called traceology*, has helped increase understanding of how these tools were in fact used. Examination of their worn edges under various magnifications reveals different traces of wear which can be reproduced by experimenting with the same tools on different materials. With a 200–400 magnification we can infer not only the direction of the movement made by the tool—lengthwise, crosswise or circular—but also the precise nature of the materials worked: bone, antler, wood, dry skin, meat, and so on. When the surface of the tools has not been damaged, the results are extraordinarily illuminating. For example, traces of fish scales have been revealed on objects from sites where no fish bones have been preserved; the marks of the circular movement of a piercer show whether it was held by a right-handed or a left-handed person; the extent and strength of the shine due to wear indicates how long the tool might have been used. Ten years ago, such accuracy was impossible.

Even so, the "observer" in our story was baffled by a fictional mist, because even with modern techniques many questions are still unanswered. For instance prehistorians know little about the temporary shelters of Paleolithic people. The ground plan of these dwellings can sometimes be made out by arranging the remains; but how can we tell whether the structure above was a conical skin hut or a semicircular bark hut? Examples from modern societies show that many superstructures can be erected above the same ground plan. In the same way, it is still difficult to evaluate the importance of a group in a given encampment or to know how the various tasks were allotted. Existing examples of hunter-gatherer communities do little to fill the gaps in this field, and the mechanical interpretations advanced by prehistorians are often a travesty of a reality that still cannot be captured. So what can we say about social structures, rites or religion?

Nevertheless, the research that has been going on for some years encourages optimism. Thanks to the hundreds of apparently insignificant details that have been collected, prehistorians are on the way to establishing a genuine ethnology of the past.

Mammoth bone hut USSR

Only through the painstaking removal of remains buried in the ground can prehistorians approximate a Paleolithic hunter's view of his abandoned camp. At Mezhirich in the Ukraine, several huts made of mammoth bones, with collapsed roofs, have been uncovered in this way. Excavations by M. I. Gladkikh.

Le Vigne-Brun, Villerest, France

A central hearth and a floor hollowed out into a slight saucer-like depression characterize the Gravettian habitations of Villerest. A ridge of earth reinforced by large blocks would have formed a foundation for these circular huts, which probably represent a long-term encampment. Excavations by J. Combier.

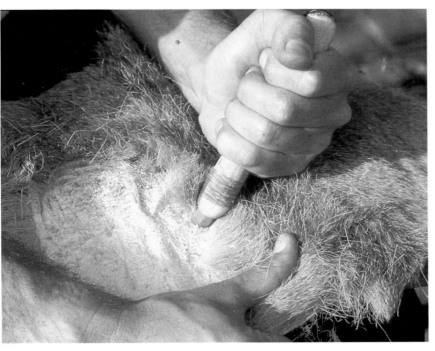

M. Newcomer

H. Plisson

Traces of utilization (*right*)

Under the microscope, the "traceologist" can recognize from the worn edges of stone tools the characteristic signs of work on a given piece of material. This microphotograph (magnified 200 times) shows the shine resulting from working on dried skin.

Experimental reconstruction (*left*)

Modern replicas of prehistoric tools enable archaeologists to reconstruct, through various technical experiments, the nature of the movements made and the function of the tools. A hafted flint scraper fixed to a wooden haft is used here to remove the hair from a skin.

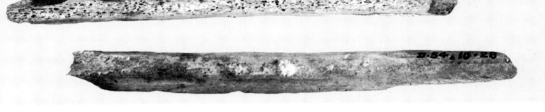

J. Oster, photothèque du musée de l'Homme

Unfinished harpoon from the Magdalenian period

Implements abandoned in the course of manufacture are very useful to the prehistorian in reconstructing methods of fabrication. On this object from Laugerie-Basse, Dordogne (France) it is apparent that the rectangular part of a reindeer antler has first been thinned down on one edge before the next stage of cutting out the barbs. Musée de l'Homme, Paris.

F. Audouze

The reassembly of flint blades

Starting with flint fragments scattered on the ground, specialists can reconstitute the original block of stone and the process of cutting it up. On this Magdalenian example from Étiolles, the form of the nucleus, which has not been found, is indicated by the blades and flakes which were struck off from it and have now been reassembled. Excavations by Y. Taborin, assemblage by N. Pigeot. Institut d'Art et d'Archéologie, Paris.

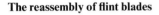

Butchery

Without trace analysis, it would have been impossible to know that this group of blades, recovered in an empty space near a Magdalenian hearth, had been used for cutting up meat. Verberie, Oise, France. Excavations by F. Audouze.

N. Pigeot

Fire and cooking

Many Paleolithic hearths are full of stones showing traces of fire. These stones, which stored heat, were used among other things to separate the food from the flames during cooking. The Magdalenians of Pincevent (France) apparently also brought liquids to the boil by plunging heated stones into the containers, circular imprints of which have been found near hearths. Excavations by A. Leroi-Gourhan.

A. Leroi-Gourhan

Paleolithic rock art and its meaning

Prehistoric cave painting and rock art are one of the glories of Stone Age culture, reflecting the intimate relations with the natural world on which early man depended. The paintings also reveal the complexity of prehistoric thought and their ability to use symbolism.

The discovery in 1879 of prehistoric paintings of bison on the ceilings of caves in Altamira, Spain, came as a revelation, greeted by the specialists with amazement. But when other decorated caves came to light in the south of France, both the authenticity and the age of the painted images could no longer be questioned, for some of them were still covered at prehistoric levels.

A few caves have been discovered with the original occupation areas intact, particularly the Tour Blanche cave (discovered in the Dordogne in 1983), but most of the decorated caves were identified at the beginning of the 20th century, an era when, unfortunately, digs were treated more as treasure hunts than as scientific investigations. It has since been found that excavation of the earth surrounding remains reveals much about the activities of prehistoric humans in their sanctuaries, which is why the more recent discoveries are important.

Any survey of prehistoric art can only be partial, since preservation is dependent on physical and chemical factors, and much of the work has disappeared. Erosion has damaged exterior images exposed to the weather and sited beneath a shelter of rocks, or at the entrance of caves. These works were mainly engraved bas-reliefs, for which an extended period of natural light and sufficient space for the artists were required. Surviving traces of red ochre* pigment suggest that these large works were painted in a naturalistic style. The deep sanctuaries are better preserved. Here the engraved or painted images are in total darkness, being situated a considerable distance from the entrance. Their position indicates that lights were used and it is not unusual to find "lamps"—lumps of stone with natural or artificial hollows in them—which burned animal fat and provided enough light to illuminate the wall.

Prehistoric man was an accomplished master of artistic techniques, from the simplest to the most elaborate. In some of the caves, fingers are outlined by pigments, or finger drawings over the clay of the wall have left undulating lines. These images were once regarded, wrongly, as the most ancient of the art products, because of the simplicity of the means employed. Engraving is now thought to be the technique that probably came first. Using flint implements, the earliest artists cut deeply and irregularly, but progressively improved their techniques until precise and supple contours were achieved. Engraving and painting were frequently used in conjunction to define a contour or stress a detail. Painting was also practised very early on, as the abundance of ochre found in the habitations seems to prove. Mineral pigments were crushed and applied with tufts of hairs or vegetable fibres, and actual "crayons" of ochre have also been found. The outlines of the images are linear, or formed from juxtaposed dots. Colours applied as flat or shaded tints, and the use of hatching, give an impression of volume and relief.

Clay models are rarer, but the preservation of such objects is so uncertain that we may assume that they were more numerous in prehistory. Low relief carvings on stone, which took longer to complete, are only to be found in outdoor sites, and have often been retouched and altered in subsequent periods.

Cave art themes

The favourite subjects of the cave artists were animals, often depicted in association with abstract symbols. The larger grass-eating animals make up the majority—the bison, the aurochs (an ancestor of modern cattle), the horse—together with a lesser number of deer-type animals and reindeer, ibex (wild goats) and mammoths. Dangerous beasts, such as lions, bears and rhinoceros, are much rarer. It is worth stressing that these images do not merely record the animals that were a source of food at that time, since a large number of species hunted for food by prehistoric man are scarcely represented, and even excluded altogether. For example, at the caves at Lascaux in south western France, 90 percent of the food remnants consist of reindeer fragments, yet there is only one representation of this animal in the cave.

Some of the carnivores—the wolf, fox or hyena—appear only in exceptional circumstances, as do reptiles, amphibians, fishes, birds and insects. The cave artists never depicted their physical surroundings and vegetation. Human figures are also rare and, in comparison with the animals, inaccurately rendered, but they are nevertheless characterized by certain stylistic conventions which ensure that they are not just portraits.

There are also certain mysterious figures that combine human and animal forms, animals without heads and impressions of hands. These complete the catalogue of cave art themes, and suggest that the prehistoric artists were less concerned with everyday realism than with symbolic representation. The work surfaces were chosen with care by the artists, who often made skillful use of a mark in the rock to delineate part of the image, and cleverly exploited natural formations to add to the effect. The images themselves are sometimes visible in the centre of the illustrated areas, and sometimes tucked away in a crevice or behind an outcrop.

The restriction of mural art to particular localities makes it difficult to date, for the sites rarely relate to a wider archaeological context. So indirect methods have to be applied, based essentially on the style of the images. At the beginning of the century, Henri Breuil* built up a chronology based on the way images were superimposed on one another, and the representations in perspective of hoofs and horns. One weakness of this system was its failure to take into account the possibility of deliberate superimpositions of images.

Since 1959, André Leroi-Gourhan, basing his theory on evidence that can be securely dated through stratigraphy*, or the study of geological layers, has taken as his guideline the varying representations of horses and bisons (which amount to over half the animals depicted) in order to construct a chronological study of prehistoric art. He has established that in certain periods the graphic style of the animal depictions followed the same compositional rules, and the same conventions governed the details. He identified four styles, each representing an evolutionary stage.

At the same time, the meaning of Paleolithic art is further obscured by the discovery of the organized compositions inside the caves. At the beginning of this century, crude ethnological comparisons had produced theories based on hunting and fertility, and these theories, though outdated, are still applied by some prehistorians. Annette Laming-Empéraire has shown that the animals which cover the walls are not the result of superimpositions carried out over the centuries; rather they represent meaningful representations which form the basis of a now lost ideology.

The arrangement of motifs

Leroi-Gourhan also studied the arrangement of the various motifs inside the caves and demonstrated that the organization of cave art, far from being haphazard, follows a strictly structured scheme which remains basically identical in all cases. These statistical studies have brought to light the existence of a constant main theme, that is, groupings of horses and groupings of bovines are put in juxtaposition with similar groupings of "full signs" (such as vulvae, feminine figures, hands and wombs) and "thin signs" (such as male figures, harpoons and arrows). This basic theme may undergo regional variations, with bovines yielding to female deer or mammoth. Each image occupies a clearly defined place in relation to the layout of the cave and to the other elements surrounding it. The proximity of the position of the bovines to that of the "full signs" led Leroi-Gourhan to believe that these animals were invested with a female potential. The "thin signs" and the horses also followed a similar distribution: they occupy a central position in association with their complementary images but are also found in marginal and end situations—hence the equation between the horses and the male principle. To these groupings are added a number of peripheral animals, placed around the edges of the painted areas and varying according to the period and the region; these include ibex, deer, reindeer and sometimes mammoth.

The decorations of the cave walls therefore form, according to Leroi-Gourhan, a single system made up of associations between animals and semi-abstract signs, consisting essentially of an opposing duality or complementarity. Thus the caves may have been sanctuaries painted with symbolic motifs that reveal the complexity of prehistoric thought. The application of sciences such as zoology and ethnology has further extended the analysis of mural paintings, but their contribution is to the study of the form, not to the meaning of the subject. Leroi-Gourhan's important analytical work still provides a useful base, despite some controversies.

Abri Cellier, Dordogne, France

The deeply incised head of a grass-eating animal, probably a horse, appears on a stone block with sides of 45cm (17in) found at Abri Cellier, Dordogne, France. With it is a possible female sexual representation or symbol.

Figurative art first appears in the Aurignacian period, towards 27,000BC. The works from this period are not many; about 20 have been found, mostly in the Dordogne (Abri Cellier, Castanet, La Ferrassie), in well dated levels. In most cases, the crude and still clumsy treatment of animal figures, often limited to the head and neck, does not permit identification of the species. But from the very beginning the fundamental themes of Paleolithic art were already established, and the association of animal figures and sexual representations remained constant.

La Grèze at Marquay, Dordogne, France

This incised bison is the only well-preserved figure in the little cave of La Grèze. In the Gravettian period (25,000–18,000BC) significant works of mural art appeared. These were basically engravings and low reliefs situated on the walls near the entrance. In the so-called Style II depicted here, the animals are represented in their entirety and follow the same graphic conventions. All the species display a sinuous line for neck and back, roughly in the shape of the letter S on its side, and exaggerating the hindquarters. Specific details, few in number, indicate mane or horns, and thus identify the species. The animal is seen in profile and the legs, which are mostly shown without their extremities, are only sketched in and quite often juxtaposed. Antlers and horns are shown in frontal view. Sexual signs start to become stylized.

The spread of mural art in France and Spain

The most important focus of Franco-Cantabrian mural art, which alone numbers more than 100 decorated caves, is located in a radius of 30km (18 miles) around Les Eyzies de Tayac in the Dordogne. The geographical distribution of mural art is largely dependent on the geology of the limestone areas where erosion has hollowed out caves. However, prehistoric occupation is not associated solely with the presence of caves; in the regions to the north of the Loire river there is an almost total absence of decorated caves, but traces of habitations prove that Paleolithic settlements did exist there.

The Franco-Cantabrian zone forms a homogeneous whole, employing the same means of expression, the same techniques and the same conventional styles for the same periods. Some caves experienced different periods of occupation. Figures added later may either appear on already decorated areas, through modification or addition of subject matter, or on untouched parts of the cave.

The different styles defined by A. Leroi-Gourhan each represent a stage in the development of this art and the acquisition of a certain mastery of the techniques used, but not a change in the meaning of the message expressed.

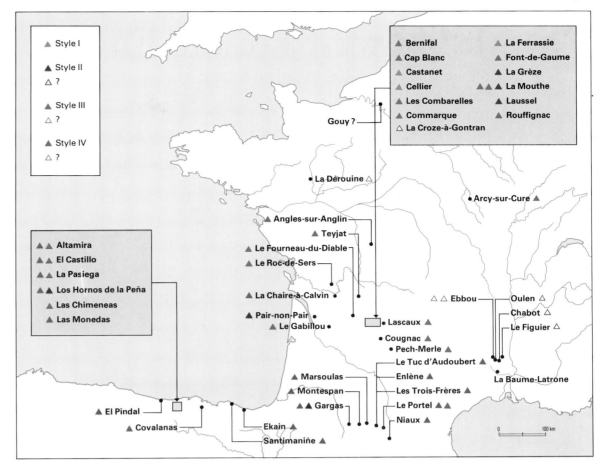

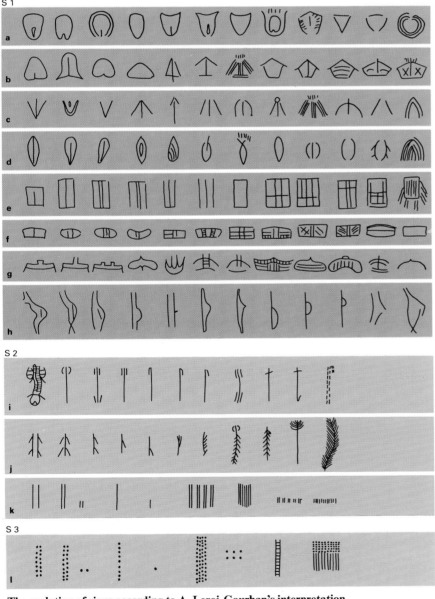

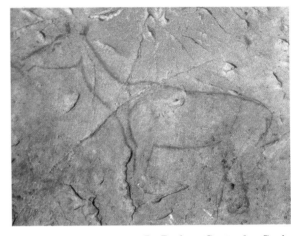

La Pasiega, Santander, Spain

Outline of a deer painted in red ochre from La Pasiega, Santander (Spain). This is a very common theme in Spain. In the so-called Style III of the Solutrean and Lower Magdalenian, 17,000–13,000BC, a sinuous line is still used to depict the neck and back, but more conventional details are added. In France, the appearance of the animals is characterized by an enormous "swollen" body, an exaggeratedly small head, and a slender neck. The legs are short and spread apart, and seem not to touch the ground. Horns and antlers are often shown from an oblique angle. In Spain Style III is a little less archaic and tends to resemble early Style IV, the high point of prehistoric mural art.

Cave at Niaux, Ariege, France

Natural formations in the caves seem to have played an important part in deciding where the figures were to be placed. The cave itself must have been invested with a sexual symbolism which sometimes appears quite clearly. Thus certain oval cavities or fissures have been covered with red ochre, and so-called "thin signs", indicating a masculine connotation, were very often depicted on their edges. The choice of this location cannot be accidental.

The evolution of signs according to A. Leroi-Gourhan's interpretation

S1: "Full" signs with a feminine connotation. These derive from representations of the vulva or stylized female figures in profile. They soon become schematic.

S2: "thin" signs with a masculine connotation. These derive from realistic phallic representations which may develop into single or double lines, as well as branched, hooked or barbed signs.

S3: dots, dotted lines and short rods or sticks may be assimilated to S2 (above). They seem to be specially related to certain natural features in the caves which were themselves endowed with a feminine potential, such as the fissures with which they are often associated.

"Full" signs and "thin" signs are often coupled together. Their original significance may have been sexual, but prehistoric art has not to this day yielded a single example of sexual intercourse. Often associated with animals, the significance of these signs still remains problematical, as does their connection with the other figures. A comparison of forms and shapes indicates that certain signs are characteristic of a particular region. The variety of the forms emphasizes the individuality of each of their elements, and cultural or ethnic uniformities.

The first bowmen of the European forests

Paleolithic Europe was covered in primeval forest: its clearance was one of the revolutions of European history achieved by Neolithic cultivators. Till then it was the preserve of the Paleolithic and Mesolithic hunters.

Europe as we know it was formed during the period which succeeded the intense cold of the last glaciation and preceded the great forest clearance of the Neolithic. This situation clarified between 10,000 and 5000BC, with the submersion of the continental plateau and the progressive isolation of Ireland and England, the disappearance of low-lying glaciers, the extension of the North Sea and formation of the Baltic, and the birth of a multitude of lakes and marshes. The northern tundra then made room for conifers and birches, elms and hazel trees. The foliage of the mixed oak forests covered Central Europe, and Mediterranean species spread from their regions to colonize the hinterlands. This period saw the end of the paradoxical coexistence of reindeer and stag, arctic fox and saiga antelope, bison and chamois. Each found the ecological niche familiar to us today. So the reindeer hunters of the Upper Paleolithic were forced to seek a different type of game. In western and northern Europe they lost the submerged territories, but they gained the lands freed from the ice and benefited from the considerable increase in coastlines and environments where food resources were rich and varied (fjords, marshes and lakes).

Situated between the hunting Paleolithic and the farming Neolithic, this slow change in the landscape corresponds to the Mesolithic period, to use the term employed in the ternary (tripartite) classification. Independently of climatic changes, there was an innovation in hunting techniques at the end of the Upper Paleolithic when small flint points, sometimes with geometric shapes (microliths*), were used to arm arrows that were undoubtedly fired by a bow. The unobtrusive means of firing the missile, the accuracy and force of penetration of the projectile, gave the bow an obvious superiority over the spear-thrower*, which required a more violent movement capable of frightening the game. The growth of the dense forests might have encouraged the use of the bow, which needs less free space around the hunter than the spear-thrower. However, its innovation, appearing c.10,000BC, received a varied reception, even in geographically close cultures, but after a final and severe cold phase, between 9000 and 8000BC, it was adopted wholeheartedly.

Throughout Europe, flint tool kits are characterized by various types of arrowhead; these tended to become increasingly microlithic and geometric, with triangular, rhomboid, trapezoid and partly circular forms; the trapezoidal form appeared broadly to predominate in the Mesolithic, except in England. All these points were fashioned by splitting the thin layers or lamellae of stone, often according to the so-called technique of the microburin*. The diversity of their forms allows archaeologists to single out a multitude of regional cultures, the range of which is much more limited than that of the cultures of preceding millennia. From Lithuania to England these small arrowheads are associated with large stone tools used for working wood such as blades of adzes, shaped or studded, and heavy-duty knives. In southwestern Europe, the heavy tools were made of antlers, sandstone and sometimes stones or rocks fashioned to serve as picks. The equipment of the Mesolithic archers is better known than that of the reindeer hunters as a result of discoveries made in the peat bog sites of northern Europe which yielded bows and arrows of various kinds, canoes, paddles, skis, sledge runners, traps, nets and bark receptacles.

Mesolithic diet

The contrast which has long been made between the Paleolithic artist, hunter of reindeer and mammoths, and the "decadent" archer, is a travesty of the facts. Possibly accompanied by dogs, he hunted the horse, antelope, stag, wild boar, deer, sheep, beaver and many other small mammals. With the bow his range included more birds than in the Paleolithic, especially aquatic birds. In addition to these resources, which were much the same as in the Paleolithic, gathering of shellfish and fishing developed on a large scale. The shells of terrestrial and marine molluscs formed accumulations sometimes several metres deep in rock shelters and hundreds of metres long by the seashores. Neolithic peoples improved fishing techniques with the use of bone hooks. They were the first to venture away from the coast, where dolphins and grampus were fished, as well as small sharks, monk-fish, mackerel and such fish as cod, haddock or hake. Deep-sea navigation now enabled man to settle in Corsica.

Vegetation has left little trace and its part in the Mesolithic diet remains conjectural; but there is no doubt that the temperate forests were richer in edible species than were the cooler regions. In western and northern Europe, the seeds of lilies and water chestnuts, and the shells of hazelnuts have been found in occupation sites, often in great numbers. In the Mediterranean countries, apart from gathering wild cereals such as barley and oats, the distribution of which did not extend to the west of Greece, there is also evidence for the harvesting of lentils, vetches (beanlike vegetables), pistachio nuts and almonds from the final Paleolithic. In the Mesolithic peas and pears, walnuts and grapes were added to the diet.

Mesolithic dwellings, in the open or in rock shelters, have been studied from data drawn from some 50 sites. Their traces on the ground are often very varied: wood or stone platforms, post-holes, alignments of closely set stones. These structures are curved or rectangular in shape and their area, which may cover 5–110 sq m (53–1184 sq ft), is usually between 5–20 sq m (53–215 sq ft). The hearths, in the centre or outside the dwelling, are sometimes surrounded by slabs or stones. Food was cooked on hot stones or by stewing, as in "Polynesian ovens".

The Mesolithic way of life, regulated by seasonal movements within a limited territory, does not mark a break with that of the Upper Paleolithic. On the other hand, art and burials reflect a conception of the world and the hereafter that is increasingly distanced from that of the reindeer hunters. The figurative and highly animated rock art of eastern Spain features human subjects to replace the relentless repetition of animals decorating caves in the ice age.

In Central Europe, works of art are comparatively rare; figurative works coexist for a time with abstract lines of bars and dots, painted or engraved on pebbles, bones or the walls of sandstone shelters. This schematic art had long asserted itself in the Mediterranean cultures. In northern Europe, by contrast, there are hundreds of works of art, including figurines and pendants in amber, but mostly geometric decoration: lozenges, triangles, chevrons, checkerboard patterns, organized in skilful compositions on objects made of antlers, on the cores of flints, and on wooden artifacts. Human and animal representations treated schematically are rare. Among the latter, the antelope is a theme common to Mesolithic cultures from Sweden to the Urals.

Burials were much more numerous than in the Upper Paleolithic and, in a new development, could now be grouped in burial grounds with several dozen tombs. The tombs contained one or several individuals, buried simultaneously or successively, extended or flexed. The most elaborate graves were edged with a border of stones and covered by a small mound or tumulus. Interlacings of stag's antlers sometimes crown the skulls. The burials are often associated with red ochre and accompanied by offerings of venison, ornaments such as shells or animals' teeth, and a deposit of tools or weapons – arrows, awls, flint tools. An estimate of the size of the Mesolithic population established on the basis of the number of known sites shows a regular demographic increase, and a large increase in comparison with the Upper Paleolithic. The archers do not seem to have suffered from malnutrition or tribal wars. They were well placed to receive and assimilate the destroyers of the forests of the Neolithic Revolution, or at least to accept peaceful co-existence with them.

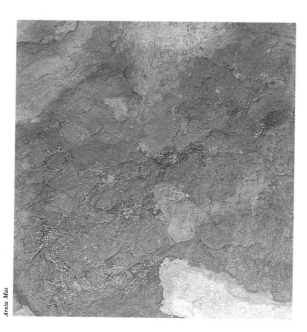

Deer hunt. Cueva de las Caballos. Barranco de la Valltorta, Castellón, eastern Spain

A sketch (right) of 1919 by Hugo Obermaier and P. Wernert before the wall deteriorated (represented by hatching in the drawing) shows a group of 4 archers firing arrows at a herd of 6 hinds, 2 fawns, 1 small deer and 1 tined stag. The scene is some 50cm (19in) in height.

Arrows from Holmegaard, Denmark: 6500–6000BC

With a diameter of 1cm (0.3in), the fragments of these wooden arrows measured (left) 26 and 8cm (10 and 3in), and (right) 28 and 29cm (11 and 11.3in). Their total length was about 90cm (35in). Mostly made of wood from the heart of slow-growing pines, the shafts were beautifully polished. The base, notched to take the bowstring, was probably feathered. The pointed tip was armed with flint microliths embedded in a groove (visible on the right-hand arrows) and fixed by a natural pitch obtained by heating birch bark. There were also arrows with soft tips (left) like those once used by Eskimos and Siberian peoples to hunt birds and small animals, whose plumage and fur they did not want to damage. National Museum, Copenhagen

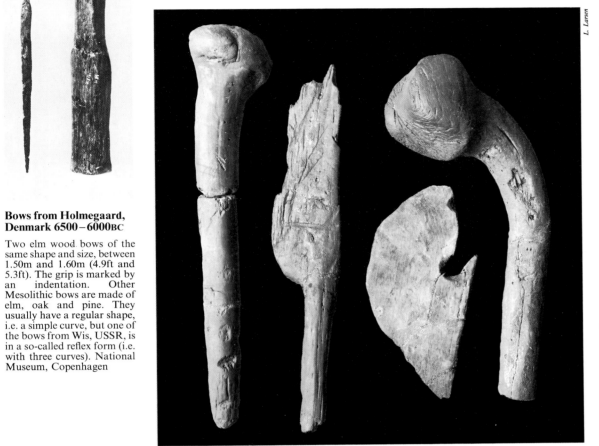

Bows from Holmegaard, Denmark 6500–6000BC

Two elm wood bows of the same shape and size, between 1.50m and 1.60m (4.9ft and 5.3ft). The grip is marked by an indentation. Other Mesolithic bows are made of elm, oak and pine. They usually have a regular shape, i.e. a simple curve, but one of the bows from Wis, USSR, is in a so-called reflex form (i.e. with three curves). National Museum, Copenhagen

Canoe from Pesse, Drente province, Netherlands

Dated to c.6500BC this canoe, 3m (9.6ft) long by 0.45m (1.4ft) wide, was hollowed out of the trunk of a pine tree by burning and scraping. In the 8th millennium vessels of unknown shape and size (but certainly larger than this canoe) were used to import obsidian from the island of Melos into mainland Greece. They also helped to populate Corsica (before 6500BC) and Ireland (early 6th millennium). Deep-sea fishing, attested in northern Europe between 5500 and 5000BC, also required boats more stable than this one. Assen, Netherlands

Wooden paddle and clubs

These objects from the Maglemosian peat bogs of Holmegaard, Denmark, are dated to between 6500 and 6000BC. The club on the left measures 35cm (13.7in), the paddle to its right 32cm (12.5in) and the right-hand club 31cm (12.1in). Mesolithic clubs have been discovered at Braband, Denmark, and Wis, USSR, 500km (310 miles) to the east of Archangel. An older paddle found at Starr Carr, Yorkshire, dates to 7600BC. Other Mesolithic paddles are known in several sites in Denmark, West Germany and the USSR. National Museum, Copenhagen

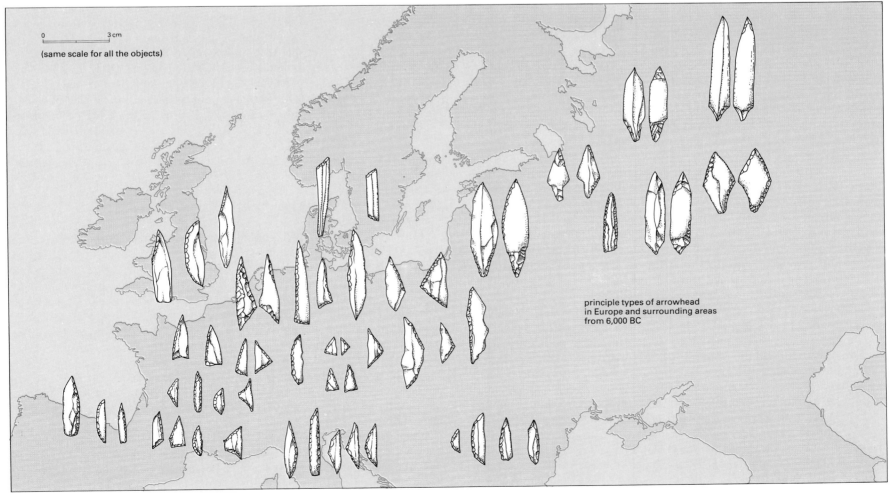

0   3 cm

(same scale for all the objects)

principle types of arrowhead
in Europe and surrounding areas
from 6,000 BC

Neolithic Europe:
the archaeological background

One of the fundamental changes in prehistory was from nomadism to
settled civilization, from hunter to farmer. But how did this come about?
Europe can now be seen to have developed distinctive patterns
as far back as Neolithic times.

The Neolithic ("New Stone" in Greek) was first conceived as a phase in the
evolution of prehistory characterized by polished stone tools, as opposed to
the earlier Paleolithic ("Old Stone") age of flaked (or chipped) stone tools.
This emphasis on techniques proved to be unsuitable, and the term Neolithic,
which appeared in 1865, was deemed satisfactory not because it related to a
particular technique (for stone was still chipped in the Neolithic if not later),
but because it evoked a more general historical phase during which the first
agricultural societies were formed.

European prehistorians first assumed the transition from an exclusively
hunting society to a farming society would naturally have expressed itself in
terms of economic opposition and thus of rupture. Consequently, prehistorians concluded that there must have been a gap or hiatus. The increase of
evidence relating to late Paleolithic and Mesolithic cultures, which existed
elsewhere between the great hunting civilizations and the first farming
civilizations, closed this gap to some extent but did not change the problem in
Europe. For there, from the beginning, the Neolithic appeared as an
economic model breaking away from earlier ways of life. It was thought that
new immigrant populations must have been responsible for the diffusion of
alien techniques of stockbreeding and agriculture, because wild cereals
scarcely existed in Europe. In this debate the so-called Fertile Crescent
(from Israel to the Persian Gulf) monopolized attention as the source and
origin of numerous "inventions" such as the development of village
communities, the domestication of plants and animals, and the origin of
writing. "Civilization" must have emerged in the East.

V. Gordon Childe* was the archaeologist who most successfully upheld
these diffusionist ideas, and two of his works, *The Dawn of European
Civilization* (1925) and *The Danube in Prehistory* (1929), and the concepts they
put forward, were central to archaeological thinking until the 1960s. The
methods used by archaeologists of the time to some extent confirmed these
concepts, with the construction of regional chronological systems linked
together by means of selected comparative remains.

Autonomous development or intercultural borrowing

Nevertheless some problems remained. The different cultural expressions
apparent in the very earliest phases of the Neolithic contributed to the
questioning of the validity of this standard economic model. The idea that
distinct cultural systems existed in different ecological contexts led to a better
understanding of the role of local populations in the formation of the first
agricultural societies. From this followed the concept of acculturation or
intercultural borrowing, which did not deny innovations attributable to
certain outside groups, but stressed the evolution and development of
indigenous populations, whose status gradually altered with the acquisition
of alien techniques such as stockbreeding, agriculture or pottery. This concept
applied particularly to regions with a large Mesolithic population and an
environment rich in natural resources (the Mediterranean, northern Europe),
and thus more able to resist new economic systems. Central Europe, on the
other hand, being well supplied with forests and less populated in the
Mesolithic era than western or northern Europe, was thought to have
developed in ways clearly caused by colonization.

As from the 1950s, attempts to explain the European Neolithic were
balanced between the respective role of indigenous populations and the
influence of cultural and technical innovations introduced by more advanced
populations. Scholars were looking for nuances between the late Paleolithic

and the primitive Neolithic. They also tried to clarify the role of the
environment in the emergence of rural civilizations that were practically free
from any exterior pressure. The work of J.G.D. Clark on Star Carr in
England, and that of D. Srejovic and A. Benac on Lepenski Vir and the Red
Shelter in Yugoslavia, among others that could be mentioned, represent
fieldwork based on these speculations.

These ideas have had an interesting effect insofar as they have tried to
eradicate the categorical break supposedly occurring between the Mesolithic
and Neolithic, and to stress the inevitable indigenous evolution of societies.
They have helped to awaken scholars to the possibilities of fairly advanced
settlements among the late Paleolithic or Mesolithic societies, capable of a
sophisticated exploitation of their environment, the use of storage methods
long before the appearance of agriculture, and the existence of economic
systems that struck a balance between production of food and hunting.

Archaeology and new dating systems

Since the 1960s researchers have no longer regarded European lands as being
closely dependent on the Near Eastern or Aegean world, but as having
undergone a distinctive evolution of their own. The dating of organic evidence
by radioactive carbon (C^{14}*), now widely practised, has supported these
conclusions with irrefutable arguments. Carbon 14 dating has contributed to
pushing certain phenomena considerably further back in time and also to
negating the theory of eastern influence. It has also emphasized the precocity,
vigour and originality of certain European cultural features, such as the
widespread practice of megalith building.

In the 1950s megalith building was still looked on as a legacy from the Near
East (Palestine, Jordan); brilliant architects were supposed to have reached
the south of France and the Iberian peninsula via the staging post of Malta,
before spreading to northwest Europe. It now seems that the Neolithic
communities of the Atlantic area (Portugal, western France) at an early stage
in their development opted for collective tombs built of massive blocks with a
very varied architecture. Megalith building in the Mediterranean expressed
itself in numerous forms such as the Maltese temples, the "giants' tombs" in
Sardinia, the Megalithic chamber tombs in the south of France, and the
Iberian "tholos" tombs, which have been impossible to reduce to a single
common denominator.

Carbon 14 has also made possible the improved correlation of European
civilizations, and the replacement of overly compact systems by lengthier
chronologies more suited to the long development of the first rural
civilizations. In southeast Europe, especially, this reclassification swept away
the traditional scheme which had made the Aegean Early Bronze Age
contemporary with the Balkan copper-producing cultures. Datings going
steadily further back have completely refuted the relative method. The
primary Neolithic groups ("Early" Greek Neolithic, Proto- and Pre-Sesklo,
Starčevo, Karanovo) appeared in the 6th millennium according to C^{14}
chronology. The civilizations of the final Neolithic, or "Chalcolithic," (Vinča,
Gulmenita, Cucuteni) experienced their full flowering in the 4th millennium,
i.e. before the Early Bronze Age of the Aegean, a region where metallurgy
was, moreover, introduced later.

Though less frequently used, other methods of dating (for example,
thermoluminescence*) have confirmed the pushing back of chronologies with
still greater accuracy, so that the first Portuguese passage graves (Poco da
Gateira, Gorginos) have been dated to the 5th millennium. The development

The Pierre-Levée of Poitiers, after a 16th-century engraving

Megalithic monuments have always haunted the human imagination. In 1532 Rabelais attributed the erection of the Poitiers dolmen to Pantagruel. The capstone came to be used as a dining table by students, who carved their names on it. Generally considered in popular tradition to be the home of mythical creatures such as fairies, goblins or witches, dolmens only gradually gained recognition as prehistoric tombs. The excavation of the dolmen of Cocherel in northern France, 1685, which recovered several burials, constitutes one of the oldest explorations of megaliths in Europe. In Alexandre Bertrand, *Archéologie celtique et gauloise*, 1889.

of dendrochronology* (the science of dating by tree-ring analysis) has given an even more exact idea of the unfolding of time. This has shown that radiocarbon data often tend to underestimate the true age, sometimes by several centuries, so that the dates have to be corrected, or "calibrated"*, to give a better idea of real time. So methods of absolute dating have played an essential part in our understanding of the European Neolithic. But today physicists have shown the limitations of the method, and have somewhat disillusioned some prehistorians who had hoped that they could solve certain delicate chronological questions.

In the field: excavations and new techniques

Research in the field has also undergone appreciable modifications since its beginnings. In various European cultural areas, certain projects have proved to be landmarks in the history of these field operations because of their scope, the means employed, or their originality. As regards man-made mounds or "tells", we may mention the excavations by C. Tsountas at Sesklo (from 1901) and Dimini (1903) in Greece, by M. Vasic at Vinča (from 1908), and Kavanovo by V. Mikov and G.I. Georgiev (from 1936 to 1957) in Yugoslavia. There are also the more recent Neolithic excavations of J.D. Evans at Knossos (1957–1960) in Crete. Several terraces and promontories datable to the 4th millennium have been uncovered in Rumania and the Ukraine (Cucuteni from 1901, Vladimirovka from 1927, Habasesti in 1949, Trusesti in 1951, etc.). In the region of the Danube there is the work of Butler and Haberey (1929–30), and at Bylani in Czechoslovakia the excavations by B. Soudsky (1953–61) at Köln-Lindenthal in Germany. The evolution of the Neolithic in the western Mediterranean was first clarified by L. Bernabo-Brea's researches which took place in the cave of Arene Candide near Genoa (published 1946–56).

Studies of Neolithic villages built on piles over peat bogs, or on the edge of lakes, have been revised since the excavation of Ehrenstein and the theories of O. Paret, suggesting that dwellings were mostly built on dry land and only rarely on raised platforms. Connected with this is a whole group of recent works on sites in submerged environments in northern Italy, Switzerland and eastern France.

On the Atlantic coast, research has concentrated on the study of megalithic monuments: dolmens* in the south and west of the Iberian peninsula revealed in the last century by the Siret brothers, mounds with numerous passage graves in the west of France, British long barrows, and "henges", to name but a few examples. In northwestern Europe pollen analyses of the peat bogs have developed interesting methods of reconstructing ancient vegetation. The combined action of several techniques has led to an archaeology of the landscape which tries to perceive the development of vegetation in the Neolithic. In addition, surveys of terrain have benefited from new techniques: aerial photography, used for several decades is complemented on the ground by soil resistivity* and by magnetometry, or the measurement of the intensity and direction of the earth's magnetic field.

In the laboratory: new methods of analysis

Progress in the physico-chemical sciences has provided European Neolithic research with a surer framework. Analyses of organic materials offer a more realistic picture of certain areas, notably the origin and distribution of materials. Archaeologists can concentrate with far greater precision on the whole area of economic and social life now that petrographical analyses have made possible identification of trace elements in mineral compounds. They can now study in greater depth the exploitation of materials, preparation of unworked or finished products, circulation of goods, interpenetration and fluidity of markets, frontier zones, systems of exchange, and so on. Examples include the export of Aegean spondylus shells to the Danube basin, and the use of hard Alpine and Armorican rocks to make polished axes or cult objects, the diffusion of flint (Le Grand Pressigny) or obsidian pieces (Melos, Lipari, Monte Arci, Bukk) from their original deposits, or the analysis of ceramic pastes to determine the provenance of the clay.

Laboratory researches have for some years formed an increasingly large part of disciplines aiming at a better comprehension of the ancient environment, including studies of sediments, pollens, cereals, and the atomic composition of carbonates. The study of Neolithic fauna is also diversified: morphology, quantification of species, curves showing population swings, meat diets and weights of meat, butchery techniques, etc. Long disdained, the study of molluscs and of microfauna now provides precious information about man's impact on the environment.

Lastly, the very size of the sites and the mass of material to be dealt with explain the use of information techniques and statistics in Neolithic archaeology. These methods enable archaeologists to master the increasing flow of information in a more rigorous fashion and, at least in principle, to achieve more trustworthy interpretations.

Current tendencies are moving towards a diversification of approaches. Laboratory reconstruction of ancient ecosystems has suggested to archaeologists such as Eric Higgs the value of detailed examination of the resources accessible from the site. This implies a closer evaluation of the actual potentialities of a living area and its territory by analysis of the soil, the vegetation and the characteristics of the fauna. The results have emphasized the progressive nature of the beginnings of the exploitation of the environment and have again questioned the break between the Paleolithic and the Neolithic, favouring the notion of gradual evolution, and have encouraged further discussion of the concept of domestication.

Experimental archaeology* is also flourishing. The chipping and polishing of stone and bone, the modelling of pottery, the construction of life-size cabins from models or plans of excavations, the erection of menhirs and dolmens, and the sowing of ancient cereals to evaluate their yields; all these provide evidence of past behaviour.

The demands made on ethno-archaeology* are no less important. The verification of certain hypotheses about funeral rites, and the social analysis of cemeteries and dwellings have led some European Neolithic experts to visit Africa and elsewhere. Ethnology is also applicable when it is a case of establishing models for the first European farming societies, taking into account their level of development.

Perhaps the most speculative, but undoubtedly the most exciting approach to the mechanisms of the functioning of societies is so-called "social" archaeology, which has appeared in the last 20 years. To some archaeologists the internal dynamic, assisted by interactions between production, trade, hierarchical systems, symbolism and other factors plays an essential role in the progression of European Neolithic societies.

The triumph of agriculture

The introduction of organized agriculture has been called the greatest revolution in history. From the advanced Neolithic culture of Anatolia the new techniques spread swiftly through Greece and the Balkans into western and northern Europe.

Agricultural communities first appear in Europe as part of a process that started in the southeast and spread progressively throughout most of the continent. It is generally thought that the factors which inaugurated the first peasant societies in the Aegean had their origin in Anatolia (Asia Minor). However, this did not involve a simple transfer of cultures from one place to the other, for by 6,000BC, the probable date for the beginning of the Neolithic in southeastern Europe, Anatolia already possessed a Neolithic culture that was very advanced and entirely original (Çatal Hüyük). We may instead assume the possibility of contacts taking place that would act as a stimulus on peoples mature enough to make the transition to the wholly agricultural stage.

In this way, many regions of southeastern Europe, such as Thessaly, Crete and Cyprus, came to develop a pre-pottery Neolithic culture on the pattern of the Near East but considerably later, involving the growing of cereals and the raising of goats, cattle and pigs. Techniques may have been introduced from outside, but such a situation implies an almost independent development of the early Neolithic in these regions. Moreover, the presence on certain Mediterranean Mesolithic sites, such as Franchthi, Greece, and Abeurador, France, of leguminous (pod-bearing) plants that could have been, if not cultivated, at least "exploited" before the arrival of a true cereal economy does raise certain questions. A diffusion of these species from the Near East implies very early maritime communications, the evidence for which is now recognized. Alternatively, perhaps the maps showing the spontaneous distribution of leguminous plants should be extended to include the western Mediterranean. If the diffusion was the result of human activity, to what extent were people in the Mesolithic age in control of the vegetable world? Equally, what was the role of native species, such as the aurochs or wild boar, in the domestication of animals? Many authorities consider that sheep, goats, pigs and cattle were first domesticated in the Anatolian and Mesopotamian area. Others believe that the peoples of southeastern Europe could have played a part in the mastery of the animal world: the ox in Thessaly, for example.

The question seems much clearer as regards the basic cereals which do not grow naturally in Europe, with the possible exception of millet and a variety of wheat from the Balkan area. Europe's contribution was probably being limited to the relatively late domestication of rye, (1st millennium BC). Many varieties of wheat (einkorn, emmer, soft wheat) and barley (Polystichum, naked or hulled) are already to be found, in addition to legumes, in the earliest levels of various European Neolithic sites.

From the oldest phase of the Neolithic we find, in spite of the circulation of materials over distances of several hundreds of miles, certain cultural enclosures whose traditions were to endure. From the second half of the 6th millennium, permanent farming villages were installed in Greece and Crete, where sheep and goats were the most widely spread species; but cattle already provided most of the meat, as was generally true of the rest of the European Neolithic. From a phase of undecorated pottery at Argissa Magula, Greece, there developed a period of painted pottery at Sesklo and Dimini characteristic of the 5th and 4th millennia.

Almost as old as the agricultural colonization of the Aegean was the colonization of the Balkan countries, and this was accomplished through the intermediary of the Starčevo-Karanovo complex, as evidenced in permanent settlements (tells) or transient localities depending on the region and a solid cereal agriculture. The pottery shows little variation of form but may sometimes be decorated with a series of impressions, and sometimes with a trail of thick slip, (the so-called Barbotine) and occasionally with painted ornamentation of high quality especially in the Bulgarian region.

In central Europe we can attribute the formation of an agricultural economy to the so-called Danubian groups, whose very wide dispersion extended from the Dniestr and the Vistula rivers to the mouth of the Rhine and the Paris basin, from Hungary to central Poland. This vast territory saw the growth of a homogeneous assembly of villages with rectangular wooden houses, built in the 5th millennium on the rich loess (wind-blown silt) lands of river terraces, by people who brought cereal agriculture and cattle-based stockbreeding to the forested land that they had helped to clear.

In the central Mediterranean (the countries fringing the Adriatic) and the western Mediterranean (south of France, Spain and Portugal), the economy of agricultural production developed through a pre-existing maritime network indicated by the pottery groups of the so-called Impressed Ware type from the end of the 6th and 5th millennia. In the 4th millennium, peoples who made a different, smooth type of pottery took over from the original agriculturists of the Mediterranean and Danubian regions and even extended the agricultural economy into new lands, as shown by the Windmill Hill culture in Great Britain.

Northern Europe (north Germany, Poland, Czechoslovakia, the Netherlands, Denmark, Sweden) did not achieve the Neolithic stage of development until the second half of the 4th millennium, according to radiocarbon* chronology. The agricultural advance from the Danube was halted here because conditions favoured living off natural resources, with fish-rich maritime regions and lakes, whereas the soil was sandy, without loess, and less suitable for cultivation. So there was a certain delay before the well-established local Mesolithic culture yielded to the Funnel-beaker culture, so named because of its characteristic pottery with flared rims. These people introduced cereal crops, stockbreeding (often based on pigs) and the construction of rectangular houses. In the north of the temperate zone, in the coniferous forest area, a hunting and fishing economy continued to be followed by the original cultures, sometimes making use of pottery as a result of contact with the farmers settled further south.

Towards the Bronze Age

Towards 4,000BC Europe had fully entered into the cycle of food production, except on its northern fringes. The implantation of cultivated land was wholly selective at first, and it was only with the improvement of techniques and the introduction of the plough that less favourable land was cleared and won over for cultivation. This progressive development of cultivated territories was combined in certain regions with a greater attachment to the soil and increased demographic pressure.

The rich plains of eastern central Europe provide, from the Early Neolithic onwards, the best examples of prosperous village communities making maximum use of fertile land. Technical development was faster here than elsewhere, and from the end of the 5th millennium copper working began in Rumania (Boian) and Yugoslavia (Vinča). In the 4th millennium, a group of brilliant civilizations had achieved a mastery of metallurgical techniques, with Salcuta in the Balkans, Gumelnita in Rumania, Cucuteni-Tripolye in the Ukraine, and Lengyel in Hungary.

Metallurgy did not emerge in the Aegean, Italy and Spain before the first half of the 3rd millennium. In the rest of the European continent, the advent of metallurgy which put an end to the Neolithic period did not come until about 2,000BC.

In the 3rd millennium, the abandonment of some large habitations in the rich lands of eastern Central Europe, their dwindling number, the rise and greater mobility of cattle-grazing, and a decline in metal production, have led some scholars to assume a crisis caused in these regions by exhaustion of the soil following 3,000 years of intensive cultivation. Others suggest a deterioration of the climate. Yet others attribute this state to invasions parallel to other population movements that have been noted in western Europe. Whatever the causes and effects, a study of burials and grave goods reveal new social structures indicating hierarchical organization and individual specialization of professions, which put an end to the first European agricultural world.

Cultivated wheats

From the beginnings of the 5th millennium (uncalibrated chronology) the Neolithic farmers of Europe cultivated several species of wheat. In a favourable environment, these grains, if previously scorched, have been well preserved. On the site of Cova de l'Or, near Valencia, Spain, in an early Neolithic context, several species of domestic wheat have been recognized: einkorn (*triticum monococcum*) with narrow grains, emmer (*triticum dicoccum*) with bigger and wider grains, and hard and soft wheats (*triticum aestivo-compactum, triticum aestivum*) with short rounded grains.

Cultivated barley

Barley was cultivated in Europe at the same period as wheat. At the Cova de l'Or, Spain, two varieties of barley (*hordeum vulgare L.*) with several rows of grains have been identified, one with naked grains, the other with hulled grains. Naked grain barleys were dominant at first, but were gradually overtaken and then supplanted by hulled grain barleys in the Bronze Age. Drawings after M. Hopf.

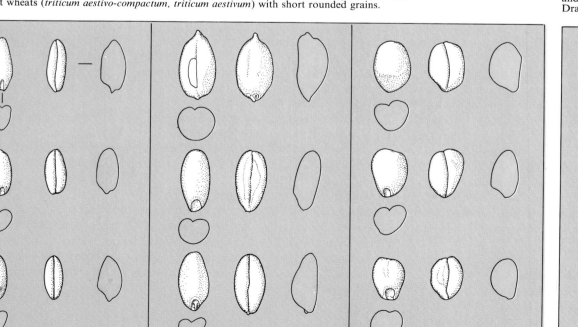

Triticum monococcum   Triticum dicoccum   Triticum aestivo compactum

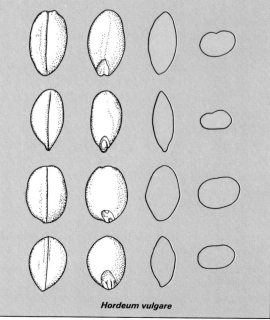

Hordeum vulgare

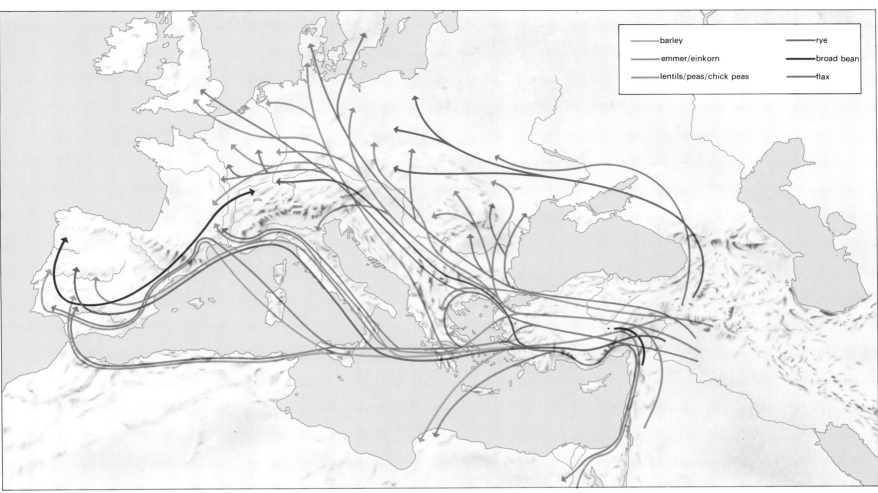

Diffusion of cultivated plants in Europe

It was from the Near East, where their domestication had taken place, that cultivated cereals and certain primitive agricultural techniques were diffused. Indeed, there were hardly any wild cereals in Europe that could be domesticated on the scene. It is accepted that the same was true of vegetables, although the discovery of specimens in some very late Paleolithic sites of the western Mediterranean may suggest the existence of species growing naturally beyond the eastern Mediterranean basin. The correctly dated sites in which botanical remains occur make possible the drawing of accurate maps establishing the appearance of cultivated species. Map after M. Hopf.

Wild and domestic oxen

The illustration shows how the massive horns of a wild ox (aurochs) compare with the smaller horns of a domestic ox from the Neolithic south of France. The intervention of man and the selection of species, together with other evolutionary factors, led to certain morphological changes in the domestic variety, such as a reduction in size of body and horns. Deposits of excavations of Fort Saint-Jean, Marseille.

Decorated pottery, Mediterranean Neolithic

In most of the coastal Mediterranean areas, the first farmers fashioned containers which they decorated with impressed ornamentation. The illustration shows a vase with a neck, hollow handles and flat bottom from the early Neolithic in southern Italy (region of Matera). 6th millennium, uncalibrated.

Decorated pottery, Central European Neolithic

The first farming communities in the Danubian area frequently decorated their vases with spirals or meanders. Here we see a vase with a round bottom and punched indentations belonging to the Bandkeramik culture (5th millennium, uncalibrated). Vase from the habitation site of Vaux-et-Borset, Liège, Belgium. Musées royaux d'art et d'histoire, Bruxelles.

Neolithic dwellings

With stone-built villages, mound sites and lake settlements, a dynamic Neolithic civilization prepared the ground for subsequent epochs of the European Bronze Age.

In Europe, Neolithic building depended on certain cultural factors, such as existing traditions or innovatory construction techniques; on the natural environment and readily available materials; on social, economic or defensive concerns; and, finally, on factors specifically related to the evolution of the individual cultures themselves.

Although the range of building materials was restricted, European Neolithic habitations were far from being uniform. They varied according to the kind of area chosen, the layouts of the huts, the arrangement of the various structures, the systems of boundaries or entrenchments, and so on.

In limestone regions caves continued to be inhabited throughout the Neolithic, but these probably served merely as temporary shelters for people following a nomadic way of life. Open-air Paleolithic habitations of the "hut" type did not vanish immediately. Some of these had features found only in particular sites, just as the "Proto-Neolithic" of Lepenski Vir, Yugoslavia, where trapezoidal huts with wooden frames and assemblages enclosed carefully constructed hearths. Huts built over hollows in the ground have also been reported, for example in the Late Neolithic Starčevo culture, Hungary, where archaeologists have inferred the existence of cabins consisting of roofs with a ridge and two gables resting on the ground and covering a hollowed-out area. The crude nature of these constructions may be due to the fact that the inhabitants were partially nomadic or that the influence of tradition was strong in this particular settlement.

Traditional sites

At first, the use of stone seems to have been confined to the eastern Mediterranean, where it appears in the foundations, although these may rise to a height of 2m (6ft) in, for instance, the circular domed houses of Khirokitia in Cyprus. Except in the north, rectangular mud brick houses predominate in the Aegean region, sometimes with entrance porches, and becoming increasingly complicated with internal subdivisions. Transition to the Bronze Age was marked by increasing use of stone, occasional development of circular or semicircular buildings, and by a greater tendency to bring separate huts together into single constructions. In the western Mediterranean, construction in stone did not really spread until the 3rd millennium, except in isolated cases. The most representative examples are the Portuguese "castros", small fortresses surrounded by several protective walls and by bastions. The huts could have been either round or four-sided, and wood was probably used for the framework and the upper parts. Similar cases exist in southeast Spain (Los Millares).

Round, oval and elongated cabins terminating in an apse characterize the group of buildings at Fontbouisse in the eastern Languedoc, France. In some cases, as at Boussargues, small circular rooms have been given a dome-shaped vault with the addition of flat stones.

Another type of stone village has come to light at Rinyo and Skara Brae in the Orkneys, Scotland, where square or oblong houses had rounded corners. The walls were built with corbelling to a certain height and the top was covered with wood or whalebone. These dwellings were low, partitioned, or separated by narrow covered passages, a type of architecture well suited to their windswept surroundings. The interiors contained a hearth, a (clay-domed) oven, beds, and storage recesses in the walls.

In Balkan Europe, (Bulgaria, Rumania, Hungary, Yugoslavia) the "tell" habitation was very common. In the rich agricultural plains of those countries the first agriculturists originally settled on flat or low ground. The abundance of debris and the construction of new establishments on the same place, one on top of the other, finally created permanent sites several metres higher than the surrounding countryside: in Thrace, Karanovo is more than 12m (38ft) above normal ground level and Diadovo about 18m (58ft). Wood and cob (clay soaked in water mixed with chopped straw and gravel) played an essential part in the construction of houses. Buildings were square, rectangular or trapezoid with double-sloping roofs. In the Bulgarian Late Neolithic, one-roomed houses might be only 5m (16ft) square, but could exceed 19m (61ft) in length. Generally, interiors would include an oven, vases or silos for storage purposes, a hearth, a refuse pit and benches. Rectangular houses with several rooms appeared early in the Balkans (Nikomedia, Azmak). These rectangular Balkan houses persisted without great changes at least until the Bronze Age.

From the so-called Danubian culture extending from Poland or the Ukraine to the Netherlands and the Paris basin archaeologists have identified a typical style of dwelling based on elongated rectangular layout. The length of these houses could vary from 10 to 40m (30 to 128ft) with a width of 6 to 8m (19 to 26ft). The largest may have housed several families. The firmly established structure consisted of five longitudinal rows of posts: the tallest in the centre, two interior rows on each side, and two exterior lateral rows forming a wall of closely-fitting posts. The wooden framework might be completed by a thatch of branches, reeds or straw. The roofs were saddle-backed, with a ridge pole and two gables. Built along the line of the prevailing wind, these houses were sited to face the more protected side. The interior may have been divided. A development of this

primitive type is seen in the houses of the Rössen group, Germany, corresponding to an advanced stage of the Danubian culture. (c.3500BC).

Dwellings by the side of lakes or rivers and bogs occur mainly in central Europe. They are numerous in Alpine regions, as in Switzerland, Germany, northern Italy and eastern France. Reconstruction of the plans of the houses and their layouts has not always been easy, because of the continuous use of the habitations and successive re-building, but a rectangular type seems to have been basic. It was long thought that these wooden dwellings, built on piles, were raised above the water. But recent research has shown that, except in special cases, the majority of the villages were erected on land near the shore, although sometimes in a raised position.

Systems of defence and social organization

Archaeologists are also studying the systems of defence and demarcation employed by these prehistoric villages. The practice of surrounding a village by a rampart or ditch did not spread until the advent of advanced Neolithic societies, although some precocious examples are known. There were various arrangements; a stone enclosure (as at Dimini in Greece), ditches hollowed out of the rock (as at Passo di Corvo and hundreds of other sites in Italy) and wooden enclosures in the lakeside villages. The so-called causewayed camps in Great Britain, the Paris basin and the Charentes provide an interesting example. Here the sites are surrounded by one or more concentric ditches which may be completed by banks of earth, ramparts or palisades, while raised paths (causeways) cut through the ditches. Equally classic are the high sites protected by a fortification or a ditch; often concentrated at nodal points, this type was to continue well into the Neolithic.

The precise organization of these Neolithic villages, their size and lay-out, continue to raise questions. Only extensive research will be able to solve a number of queries relating to Neolithic society: the cattle sheds sited beside human habitations, the specialization of activity among some families or individuals in a function that benefited the community, the presence of prestigious monuments for cult purposes or communal use, the size of the settlements, and so on. However, excavation of entire villages has rarely been achieved and our understanding is in general limited. The eastern part of central Europe has invested most heavily in the field of extensive excavation, with extensive fieldwork at Bylani (Czechoslovakia), Trusesti, Cascioarele, Habasesti (Rumania) and Vlademirovska (Ukraine). The largest early agricultural villages of Europe may have had 100–200 houses, but those are exceptional cases. In the Neolithic era, small villages were the rule.

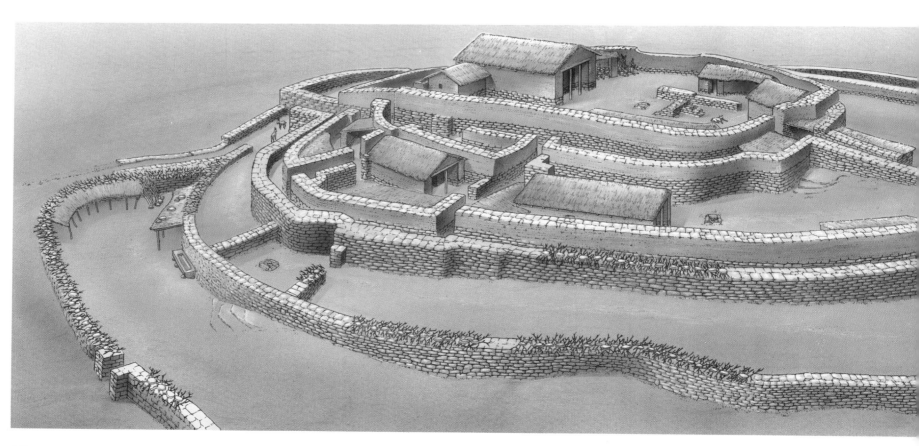

Habitat of Habasesti, Rumania

The exhaustive excavation of Neolithic sites is the only method for a correct understanding of the arrangement of the houses, the overall plan and organization of the villages, in short the systems of protection and demarcation. The practice of extensive excavation was common in Central European countries. Their large villages were the mark of prosperous communities. The site of Habasesti, enclosed by two successive ditches, belonged to the Cucuteni culture (4th millennium, uncalibrated). Reconstruction by V. Dumitrescu.

Fortified site with bastions at Vila Nova de São Pedro, Portugal

As from the 3rd millennium (uncalibrated), the use of stone became general in the western Mediterranean. Fortified sites with walls flanked by semi-circular bastions were built throughout the southern half of the Iberian peninsula.

Reconstructed Danubian house, Cuiry-les-Chaudardes, France

The walls are made of short posts 2m (6.6ft) long, placed close together supporting willow wattling smeared with cob. The central posts support the ridge-pole, the intermediary posts, the rafters and battens. The roof had a double slope. (5th millennium, uncalibrated).

Neolithic habitat of Dimini, Greece

The farmers of southeast Europe very early resorted to stone (ashlar) for building the foundations of walls of unbaked brick. Here we see the abundant use of this material in the lay-out of a series of walls (the exact purpose of which is not known) surrounding the "acropolis" of Dimini (4th millennium, uncalibrated). Reconstruction by M. Korres

Stratigraphy of the Tell of Karanovo, Bulgaria

In the rich lands of Thrace, Neolithic villages were often built on the plain close to their farmland. Progressively rebuilt on the same locations for several millennia, their remains finally created great mounds (tells) where the archaeologist can distinguish the remains of successive occupations superimposed on each other.

The farmer's tools

Archaeologists can now suggest answers to some of the crucial questions of western prehistory: when were specialized tools first introduced for clearance, husbandry and irrigation? Most important, when did the plough and the wheel come to Europe?

Given a territory as vast as Europe, it is possible that diversified agricultural techniques may have existed in the area from the beginning of the Neolithic. Not enough is yet known for archaeologists to be sure. But the transmission of cereal agriculture from the southeast of the continent to its western boundaries in two millennia at the most suggests the spread of simple techniques and their progressive adaptation to different ecological and cultural conditions.

The question of how trees were felled with stone axes has sometimes led to controversy about the capabilities of prehistoric implements. But experiments carried out in Denmark and, more recently, in Oceania, have not only shown the great potentialities of such tools but also how their effectiveness is linked to the specific movement and action of the user. The continual need for hard rock gave rise to a trade both in rough blanks and in finished products that covered an area of several hundred miles. Cutting down the forests led to the cultivation of new fields and also provided wood necessary for building.

Clearing by fire must have been a generally practised method, although we know little about how it actually took place. Grubbing up roots to clear the ground was another technique used to clear large areas of the post-glacial forest of temperate Europe. The colonization by Danubian groups of loess terrain, which extended from the Ukraine to the lower Rhine, formed one of the most remarkable Neolithic examples of temporary agriculture on forest land recovered by burning. The Mediterranean vegetable region with more fragile plant life and more severe erosion was easier to clear.

Digging sticks were probably used for sowing but this remains conjectural. Perforated stone balls have been found which may have been used to weigh such implements but these may have been "clod-breakers" of a type still used in Africa. These "weights" (the wear on the perforation shows that they revolved on the haft) are rare and appear to be confined to certain primary Neolithic groups, for example at Pasardjik in the Karanovo civilization in Bulgaria, or some Franco-Iberian Impressed Ware* sites. In other words, they did not continue to be used for long, and should not be confused with other perforated balls known as maces, often polished and made of fine stone, which were symbols of social status in the 4th and 3rd millennia.

Axes and adzes were probably the principal tools used for preparing the soil. The polished stone blades could have been attached at right angles to handles with curved tips, making a type of tool suitable for digging and hoeing the ground. These stone blades sometimes had an asymmetrical profile. Each region would soon have evolved specific shapes; for instance, the Portuguese megalithic culture appears to have developed blades sometimes with a slightly curved profile. Some authorities consider that "boot-shaped" implements

from the Danubian area may have been the blades for mattocks. Neolithic dwellings from Switzerland, built on piles, contain well-preserved wooden remains which fill out our knowledge of prehistoric adzes. At Egolzwill, for example, a wooden handle terminates in an oblique branch to which a stone or bone blade could be attached. Wooden spades have been found in Denmark. Curved sticks discovered in a lakeside environment could have been used to trace straight furrows and for weeding between rows already planted. Other implements may have been made of deer antlers. This is true of the large tools used to work the soil of eastern Central Europe. The civilizations of Gumelniṭa and Cucuteni in the 4th millennium have yielded numerous "blades" comprising two ends—one with a bevelled polished cutting edge and the other a vertical socket on which a handle could be hafted. There are even spades entirely made of stone (S. Martinho, Portugal, 3rd millennium) but the quality of the material in these very rare cases suggests that they were ceremonial tools, possibly connected with agrarian cults.

The plough

Archaeologists are still uncertain about the date of the introduction of the plough into Europe. Its existence in the Early Bronze Age (beginning of the 2nd millennium) is certain: rock scribings of Mont Bego (Alpes Maritimes) of this period show teams of cattle pulling a plough steered by a farmer. The Swedish Bronze Age has provided engravings of scenes of tillage in which two kinds of plough have been identified (the ard plough and the spade plough). The oldest ploughs, like that from Ledro, Italy, go back beyond the 2nd millennium while others, attributed to the Iron Age, come from Jutland (Hvorslev, Vebbestrup, Sejbaek). Some authorities, however, place the appearance of the plough long before these actual discoveries. Scenes of tillage using a plough are reported in Val Camonica (northern Italy) in association with representations of daggers of the so-called Remedellian type (3rd millennium). Numerous deposits concentrated in the north of Europe show traces of cross-ploughing before the 2nd millennium, as evidenced by the fact that they lie below tumuli tombs from the Lower Bronze Age. Datings to the 3rd millennium are probable in several cases, given that the signs of tillage are not traces of ritual tillings made before the construction of tombs. Such dates appear to be confirmed by actual ploughmarks. The same phenomenon was recently attested in the western Alps beneath a late Neolithic site in the Graubünden, Switzerland, and earlier in Britain, beneath 3rd millennium tombs. Basing themselves on these observations and on more general economic and demographic considerations, some authorities even suggest that the plough may have been introduced into Europe as early as the 4th millennium, if not before.

The sickles of the early agriculturalists are of many varieties. In the primary groups of southwest Europe (Karanovo), curved antlers were used as handles, with incisions into which flint flakes or fragments of blades could be inserted. The cutting edges of these tools could be straight or serrated. In lake-dwelling sites where some handles are preserved, the farmers used straight wooden hafts into which a flint blade was fixed obliquely (Egolzwill, 4th millennium). Another variety of reaping knife had a straight handle and a hook at the other end, with a flint cutting edge inserted in the straight section. The hook may have been used to pull a number of ears of corn together, and these were then cut with the sharp edge (south Burgaschisee). Flint blades sometimes more than 20cm (8in) in length were frequently used as knives in the 3rd millennium. They were probably fitted to mainly straight handles, judging by the fact that one side has been worn shiny through usage, while the other is stained with a tarry substance. In Portugal, a type of hafted sickle with a slightly convex edge was found at Carenque.

The general development towards curved handles, first found in the Neolithic of southeast Europe (Karanovo, Bulgaria) and in the Danubian area (Köln-Lindenthal, Germany) may have stemmed from the need to combine the two purposes of catching and cutting in a single gesture. Sickles from Barche di Solferino, Italy, may be considered as Bronze Age prototypes.

Neolithic millstones were nearly always flat or concave stones of various dimensions, sometimes pitted to increase their "bite". Grinders were used to crush the grain. Pestles and mortars were also used.

It is not clear whether animals were used to till the soil before the invention of the plough, but they were probably put to work in clearing fields, removing felled trees, and so on. Structural changes in the body, due to strain caused by dragging heavy objects, have been observed in cattle remains from the 4th millennium in Vadastra, Rumania, and yokes dating from the 3rd millennium have been found in Vinelz, Switzerland.

The appearance of carts and chariots is connected with the discovery of the wheel. The oldest wheeled vehicles appeared in Mesopotamia in the 4th millennium. Through Anatolia and the Caucasion regions these techniques reached Europe, where they spread very quickly. Chariots with solid wheels are found in 3rd millennium Georgian ditch tombs, and in the Danubian regions (perhaps even before 3,000BC). The most beautiful example is the little ritual chariot of Budakalász, Hungary, from the Baden civilization (c.2700–2400BC). The chariot appeared in Crete at the same period, and solid wheels have been found on Dutch and Swiss sites as early as the second half of the 3rd millennium.

Chariot from Budakálász, Hungary

The construction of chariots reveals details of the carpentry techniques of the Neolithic farmers. Wheeled transport encouraged a much wider circulation of materials, foodstuffs and people. This terracotta miniature chariot gives an idea of these early vehicles. 3rd millennium (uncalibrated). Hungarian National Museum, Budapest.

Wheel from Eese, Copper Age (Netherlands)

Starting from south-eastern Europe, knowledge of the wheel was rapidly diffused throughout the continent. Its presence in the Netherlands is attested by several discoveries, found in a context of the final Neolithic or the Copper Age, in the second half of the 3rd millennium (uncalibrated). After J.-D. Van der Waals.

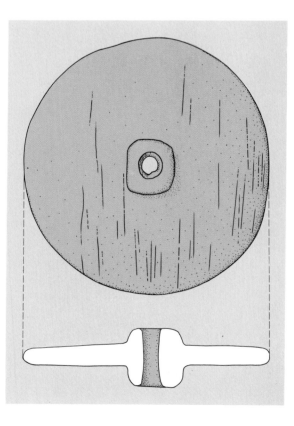

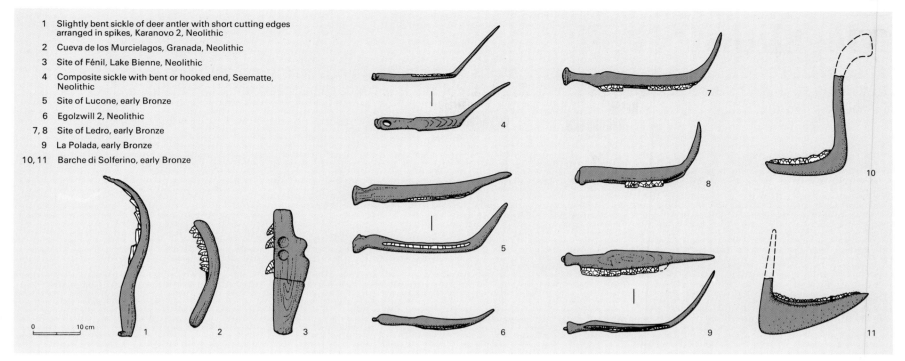

1. Slightly bent sickle of deer antler with short cutting edges arranged in spikes, Karanovo 2, Neolithic
2. Cueva de los Murcielagos, Granada, Neolithic
3. Site of Fénil, Lake Bienne, Neolithic
4. Composite sickle with bent or hooked end, Seematte, Neolithic
5. Site of Lucone, early Bronze
6. Egolzwill 2, Neolithic
7, 8. Site of Ledro, early Bronze
9. La Polada, early Bronze
10, 11. Barche di Solferino, early Bronze

0 ____ 10 cm

Neolithic and Early Bronze Age sickles

Many types of sickles characterize the beginnings of the Metal Ages. All include isolated or juxtaposed flint elements set in wood, antler or bone handles. The most sharply curved models served as prototypes for the sickles of the Bronze Age proper. Types of Neolithic sickles: 1, 2, 3, 4, 6. Model from the Early Bronze Age: 5, 7, 9, 10. After H. Camps, J. Courtin, R. Tringham.

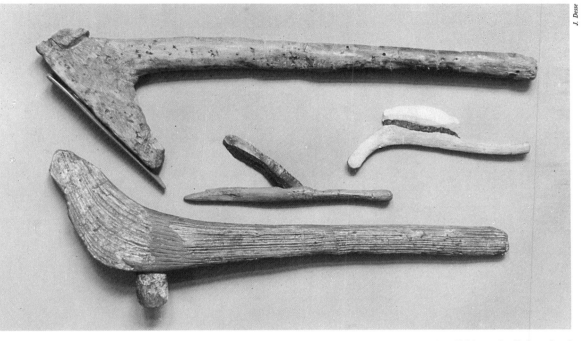

Neolithic tools, Switzerland

Prehistoric implements found in lakeside deposits have frequently been well preserved. Here we see, from bottom to top, a hafted stone axe for felling trees (site of Wetzikon); a sickle consisting of a flint blade inserted into a straight handle (station 3 of Egolzwil, Lucerne, Switzerland); a sickle with a curved handle (Egolzwil, station 1); a reconstructed hoe comprising a handle (Egolzwil, station 4) to which a bone blade was fixed (site of Hitzkirch "Seematte"). Swiss National Museum, Zurich.

Perforated ball, Grotte Gazel, France

On some of the oldest Neolithic sites in the western Mediterranean, archaeologists have found perforated calcite balls that had been slipped along the length of the handle of some tool. It is thought that they may have been weights used to balance digging sticks. Pointed sticks of this kind were certainly used in early Mediterranean agriculture.

Ploughing scene, Val Camonica, Italy

Today there is still controversy about the period when the ard plough, ancestor of the plough with a mould-board, appeared. The oldest remains of ard ploughs date to just before the Bronze Age. However, traces of cross-ploughing going back to at least the 3rd millennium are known. Similarly, rock drawings from some Alpine locations, as at Val Camonica, show cattle teams drawing an ard plough guided by a man. The style of this work and others in the vicinity place this scene in the Copper Age, 3rd millennium (uncalibrated). After E. Anati.

Megaliths

From Ireland to Palestine, the impressive monuments of the megalith builders indicate the existence of not one but many such architectural traditions; scientific archaeology has revealed that megalith building is older, and lasted for longer, than was once believed possible.

There are thousands of megaliths in Europe, large, mostly undressed stones arranged by man for a religious purpose in which spiritual and social concerns were mingled. The period when these monuments were built and used runs from the 5th to the 2nd millennium BC (the Neolithic period and the early Bronze Age). Certain dressed monoliths or menhirs are sometimes found in isolation in the landscape. Others may be assembled in alignments, the most famous being those at Carnac, Brittany, or in circles, sometimes known as cromlechs, which are common in the British Isles. Burial chambers, or dolmens, form the most widespread category of megalithic monument in Europe. The archaeologist Glyn Daniel has calculated that there are 40,000 to 50,000 examples, a figure undoubtedly lower than the number of monuments actually built. The covering of the chamber may be corbelled, as at Newgrange in Ireland, or consist of a large slab weighing as much as 100 tonnes, as at Mount Browne in the same country. Some of these dolmens are extremely large. The Grand Dolmen of Bagneux, in the Loire Valley of France, is nearly 20m (66ft) long and 5m (16.5ft) wide. Dolmens were generally covered with a tumulus or cairn, which transformed a collective burial into a sanctuary.

We now know from carbon 14* datings that the megalithic phenomenon lasted for a long time (three to four millennia) and that the first monuments are much older than was thought. The establishment of these two facts has challenged diffusionist theories (that of Gordon Childe*, for example) which claimed that "the megalithic religion" came from the East.

Megaliths in Europe

In Europe, two megalithic groups stand out for their importance: the first occupies the north and west of the continent, the second the Mediterranean world. The practice of collective burial seems to be indicated in the mesolithic casings, surrounded by small slabs, seen at Téviec, Brittany. These casings have been dated to the middle of the 5th millennium BC by C^{14}. Other similar but more recent burial forms show a ritual tradition which may suggest a local origin for western megaliths in Portugal, west-central France and Brittany. The oldest passage dolmens are round burial chambers covered with drystone corbelling and having an access frequently oriented to the east. Several of these chambers are often assembled under the same structured tumulus. This is the case with the monuments La Hogue at Fontenay-le-Marmion. The C^{14} dating of these is 3850BC (4500 in actual dating*). Chambers with a circular design seem to have been in fashion until the middle of the 4th millennium, but a smaller megalithic passage dolmen with a polygonal, square or rectangular plan may exist side by side with the round type, as at Barnenez. In the 4th millennium, the rectangular passage dolmen increased in Portugal, the west of France, the British Isles, northern Germany and southern Scandinavia. Several regional groups are noteworthy, for example that of Alentejo, Portugal, of Angoulème, west-central France, and of the Severn-Cotswold area, Great Britain. Some of the slabs of these dolmens are decorated with painted motifs (Portugal) or pecked motifs (Brittany and west-central France).

Starting from this simple form, development led to the transept dolmens of Brittany, Ireland (Newgrange) and the Orkney Islands (Maes Howe), or the "funnel" dolmens with a less differentiated passage (Gavrinis Morbihan, Brittany). The slabs of the dolmens or those of the external walls are sometimes richly decorated with stellar motifs or schematized anthropomorphic representations. Brittany (Gavrinis, the Table des Marchands) and Ireland (Boyne valley with Newgrange and Knowth) are the principal centres of this abstract art. Studies and experiments have shown the high level of technical skill achieved by the builders of megalithic dolmens. An experiment in 1979 involved 200 people in dragging and erecting a block weighing 32 tonnes, far less than the 100-tonne slabs of some monuments. The social importance of these collective works must therefore have been considerable, and a count of burials showing comparatively few in each structure, suggests that in some regions a social and probably religious hierarchy must have existed; this emerges clearly in certain burial grounds (Bougon in France and Knowth in Ireland). In the west of France, the south and west of Great Britain, Denmark, northern Germany and Poland there are rectangular and trapezoidal monuments large size, 20 to 120m long (66–400 ft) called long barrows and demarcated by an external drystone facing, sometimes including large blocks; a rectilinear or concave façade is often found on one of the short sides. They generally cover the remains of a burial, and may contain traces of a wooden construction, as seen in recent excavations at Lochhill and Slewcairn in the British Isles. These long barrows may be built adjoining existing tumuli (Bougon C and F in France) or may cover and unite small earlier tumuli with an internal megalithic chamber (Mid Gleniron I and II).

During the 3rd millennium the burial chamber had an elongated design in northern Europe, Brittany, the Paris basin, Belgium and even Hesse. These monuments are either covered by a tumulus or buried in the ground. The burials are generally very numerous. Motifs evoking the "Mother Goddess" or the axe are sometimes incised or sculpted on some slabs. Concurrently, other forms appear, such as hypogea (underground vaults) in the Marne, equivalent to the passage graves and the simple dolmens with vents, of eastern France and Switzerland.

Menhirs are very numerous in the north and west of Europe. To this day they are found either as single individual stones or grouped in alignments or circles. In Brittany offerings found at the base of some isolated menhirs, and the decoration on some others, confirm that these monoliths are mostly Neolithic. Recent excavations of the alignment at Saint-Just, France, have revealed complementary structures such as post holes, and some archaeological remains which date the complex to the Upper Neolithic. Accurate diagrams of the three groups of alignments at Carnac, Brittany, prove the deliberate organization of these upright stones around the great broken menhir of Locmariaquer. We possess little information about the stone circles (cromlechs or henges). Some are spectacular, for example the one at Avebury which is completed by a large circular ditch, dug at the end of the Neolithic. The monumental complex (concentric circles and avenue) of Stonehenge, not far from Avebury, is spectacular and even more famous. It was built in several stages. The first phase is Neolithic (as from 2800BC) and the others date to the early Bronze Age (2000BC and 1500BC). Much has been written about this strange monument, which shows great technical skill and seems to be organized in relation to the position of the sun at the time of the solstice. Other positions of the sun and moon were probably observed there, but it is difficult to pursue these interpretations in the absence of reliable evidence. The role of the sun has often been evoked in connection with the orientation of dolmen passages, at Newgrange in particular, but also in connection with circles containing sighting stones, for example in Scotland.

Megaliths in the Mediterranean

The Mediterranean civilizations produced various kinds of megaliths in certain regions. The fact that monuments developed according to different forms in the Mediterranean basin constitutes a serious obstacle to simplistic diffusionist theories. The considerable gaps recorded in chronological sequences challenge the idea of an architectural form transmitted by way of a clearly defined route.

Chronological differences, the diversity of architectural expression and the play of influences must all be taken into account in tracing the complicated development of Mediterranean megalithism. It seems likely that the phenomenon appeared at the two extremities of the Mediterranean. In the Near East, a nucleus of monuments began from the 4th millennium in Palestine and Syria. At Ala Safat, Jordan valley, small monuments such as round or rectangular burial chambers, mounds and stone circles were built by Copper Age peoples together with large passage dolmens inside circular stone tumuli. At the same period, Neolithic peoples in the southern half of Portugal and the southeast of the Iberian peninsula were moving gradually from the single or double burial to collective burials. In Portugal, analysis of grave goods clearly shows the development from small individual cists (burial chambers), as at Caldas de Monchique, to the first monuments with a circular "aerial" chamber and a short passage, such as those in the region of Beguengos de Monsaraz (dolmen I of Poco de Gateira, dolmens of Gorginos). This change is dated to about the beginning of the 4th millennium by radiocarbon* chronology. The same change occurs at Almeria, where several small circular constructions with ditches bordered by low walls were found to contain bodies. Later, increasingly large ditches were dug and encircled with stone slabs; finally, entry passages began to be built. In the region of Granada, the same evolution took place, beginning with small stone chests, the prototypes for rectangular or polygonal chambers built of flat slabs and containing a short passage. The evolution of the architecture then consisted of alterations in the details, such as the form of chamber or passage, or reinforcement of the protective mound enclosing the central structure. The construction of large elongated trapezoidal monuments in which passage and chamber are combined, as at Cueva de Menga and the dolmen of Soto, already points to an advanced stage of development. The final stage of this southern Iberian megalithic architecture is assigned to the 3rd millennium, a period that saw the brilliant beginnings of the Copper Age. It is characterized by a *tholos* (beehive-shaped chamber) with walls carefully composed of prepared and assembled pillars or made by means of a drystone technique. In both cases, a stone vault arranged as a false dome formed the roof of the chamber. Sometimes a central stone or wood pillar ensured the edifice's stability. A passage gave access to the burial chamber, as at Los Millares. Finally, the whole structure was covered with a protective mound. Monuments of this kind, made of bonded stones or of standing stones, are known in Almeria, in Malaga (Antequera, El Romeral), in the Seville region, in the Algarve, and as far as central Portugal.

Dolmens occur in other sectors of the western Mediterranean, for example in the south of France and the Pyrenees. Some original varieties emerge from this large geographical cluster of several thousand monuments, for example the long rectangular monuments of the Pyrenees and the Aude with notched slabs (Llanera, Artajona, Pépieux, Saint-Eugène), the passage dolmens of eastern Languedoc which sometimes have an antechamber (Lamalou), and the dolmens of the lower Rhône with drystone walls (Coutinargues). Simple rectangular chambers predominate from the Ardèche to Quercy, as well as in the Pyrenees. Among the islands of Corsica, Sardinia and the Balearics, the tombs consist mostly of chests encircled with stones, and suggest a more Mediterranean sub-megalithic culture, such as at Arzachena.

In the southeast of Italy some remarkable examples occur, such as the dolmen of Bisceglia. But the dating of these monuments is uncertain and sometimes appears to be late. The same is true of the "dolmens" from the region of Otranto or Malta, chambers delimited by roughly bonded blocks which have not yielded grave goods earlier than the beginning of the Bronze Age. The same dating difficulty exists for the North African dolmens, mainly concentrated in the east of Algeria and western Tunisia. In addition to some large coastal dolmens, we mainly find small tombs with a base, sometimes assembled in their thousands (Bou Nuara), probably of a pre-Carthaginian date (*c.*800BC).

Maltese megaliths

Apart from the phenomenon of the dolmen itself, highly original monuments appear in the Mediterranean. Thus at Malta trifoliate temples, mostly with three or five chambers, combine shaped pillars and firm masonry. They date to the 3rd millennium (Ggantija, Tarxien). A later date (beginning of 2nd millennium) is generally suggested for the "tombs of the giants" in Sardinia. These long narrow passages built of pillars or blocks of stone, are preceded by a curved façade, sometimes heightened by a monumental arched pediment and flanked by a low door. In the same style are the *navetas* of the Balearics, elongated chambers built of massive blocks and characterized by a semi-circular apse facing a rectilinear façade. They presumably date to the 2nd millennium. As for the Cretan *tholoi* (Platanos, Lebena, Koumasa, Krasi), which were long considered as possible prototypes for much western architecture, these are not earlier than the 3rd millennium.

Hypogea or underground chambers are not necessarily related to megalithic architecture. Nevertheless, some of them are frequently subterranean replicas of collective tombs built at ground level; moreover, their burial functions appear to have been the same. Just like the megaliths, the development of these artificial caves is closely linked to the internal development of Neolithic societies. The evolution from the artificial shaft tombs of the Middle and Upper Neolithic to collective tombs with larger chambers emerges clearly in the Italian peninsula, Sardinia and Malta. Before the full arrival of metallurgy, monuments appearing in Greece (Athens), Sardinia (Su Cuccurru Arrius), Italy, (Serra Alto and Diana), Malta (tombs of Zebbug), France (Laudun) and Portugal (Carenque) consist of tombs that experienced their greatest development in the Copper Age. Various types exist: tombs with lobed chambers (Malta), with many small radiating cells (Sardinia), or elongated chambers with façades (Balearics). The refined internal decoration, such as carved or painted walls and ceilings, clearly indicates that some of these monuments were used for cult practices.

Legend:
- megalith
- □ hypogeum

Megalithic monuments and hypogea of Neolithic Europe

Large stones or megaliths, used in religious monuments varying from dolmens to alignments of standing stones, were widespread in Europe between 4000 and 2000BC. The oldest monuments are recorded in Brittany, in the midwest of France and in Portugal. Southern Scandinavia, the west of England and Ireland are other centres of the development of these structures.

Megalithic architecture in the Mediterranean took many forms: stone "tables" in southern Italy and Malta, *sesi* in Pantellaria, elongated monuments in Andalusia and the Pyrenees, *tholoi* in southeast Iberia, etc. The Mediterranean megalithic world is also characterized by hypogea, great tombs cut out of the rock. The most remarkable examples of these are to be found in the islands (Malta, Sicily, Sardinia and the Balearics).

Interior of chamber A of the megalithic burial ground of Bougon, France

This chamber, built *c.*3500BC, consists of a capstone weighing 90 tonnes, walls made of pillars and drystone walling, and two central pillars 2.35m (7.75ft) high, seen here in the foreground. An entrance passage 10m (33ft) long led to this chamber covered by a large tumulus structured with concentric stones. 200 skeletons were buried there in 2 phases separated by about 1000 years.

Southern Temple of Ggantija Island of Gozo, Malta

One of the greatest original achievements of Mediterranean megalithic architecture is found in the erection of monuments in the Maltese islands built of massive blocks and pillars. These cult buildings had an impressive curved façade, as is the case here, and trifoliate designs with 3 or 5 chambers. 3rd millennium (uncalibrated).

Religious cults and concepts

The beginnings of organized religion are to be sought as far back as c.10,000BC. It is likely that earlier beliefs and practices were often adapted by subsequent cultures, from the Bronze Age to the classical worlds, and hence exist in the great world religions of today.

It is not known for certain whether the religious ideas which inspired the hunter-gatherer peoples were adopted by the first agriculturists. But the evidence suggests that in the regions where a food producing economy developed, the gradual nature of its emergence would not have entailed a sharp break with previous beliefs, rather a progressive adaptation of the old beliefs under the influence of new socio-economic structures.

What we do know of Paleolithic religion strongly suggests an already complicated cosmogony with a marked symbolic element. If woman is the symbol of life and the reproduction of the species, the celebrated Paleolithic Venuses with their deliberately exaggerated shapes may have been the artistic expression of the concepts of woman, mother and humanity. The typological similarities between these and many Neolithic figurines are irrefutable. The corpulence, the large size of breasts and hips, are in both cases magnified to celebrate the productive and food-providing nature of the female body transformed into a symbol of fertility, creation and life. In this sense, it is sometimes proposed that the mother goddess, or goddess of life, may have been a possible legacy handed down from Paleolithic times and reanimated by the agriculturists' vision of reality, as seen in many Neolithic figurines. However, archaeologists agree that the stages of this shift in belief are speculative, and are complicated in Europe by the scarcity of Mesolithic figurative works, although a certain continuity can be discerned.

There are difficulties in the actual recognition of religious concepts in the case of Neolithic deities. At Çatal Hüyük, Turkey, where cult locations have been studied closely, models and paintings emphasize a feminine principle more or less identified with the mother goddess by certain prehistorians. There is an interesting parallel development here of the stone and terracotta figurines intended to represent the goddess in her physical plentitude, together with her more abstract modelled, painted and carved representations. In Anatolia the former often have a thick, bulky expression, whereas the latter are frequently stiff linear figures with arms in a praying position, legs apart and sometimes with a swelling signifying maternity.

Another religious belief may be seen in the carved or modelled heads of cattle (ox-skulls). The symbols of power and vitality could be the extension of a cult that may have begun at Mureybet, Syria, in the 9th millennium and continued to be practised in southeastern Europe throughout the Neolithic and Protohistoric periods, as seen in the horns of consecration at Vinča and, later, in the Minoan period at Crete. It is also found in the western Mediterranean in the 3rd millennium where the Sardinian vaults display carved ox-skulls.

The apparently rich and diversified symbolism and abundant statuary of the first European farming communities, has suggested to most authorities the existence of a relatively complicated religious system. But discussion has arisen over the interpretation of the material evidence found widely in the Mediterranean and Balkan regions, but only scantily in northwest Europe. Some consider that the numerous feminine, masculine and even androgynous figurines are representations of goddesses or gods, with the greater number of feminine statuettes indicating the central importance of the theme of fecundity. But do the feminine figures represent a single goddess or several divinities?

Symbols of the great goddess

The most daring explanations have been formulated by Marija Gimbutas, who interprets the statuary and symbols identified in southeast Europe as representing a bird goddess and a snake goddess, sometimes combined, being divinities of the waters, rain and air, with whom certain signs are associated (spirals, meanders, chevrons, water). Such a great goddess would incorporate the myths of life, death and regeneration and would naturally be connected with the theme of the egg and pregnancy and with signs such as the crescent and concentric circles. Her power would be embodied through the intermediary of insects and animals of Europe (quite unlike the companions of the Anatolian goddess): the dog, the deer, the bear, the tortoise, the frog, the butterfly and the bee. A divinity of vegetation and agriculture would be in direct contrast to the preceding deity, a specifically Neolithic creation. Masculine themes are less common: phallic motifs, bulls with human heads, a masked ithyphallic (upright penis) god prefiguring Dionysos, etc. Masculine divinities may also have been connected with agriculture if we interpret as a god the Szegvar-Tuzkoves statuette of a person holding a reaping tool on his shoulder (unless it is really a sceptre or symbol of power, which could still confirm that he had a supernatural function). According to Gimbutas, the first agricultural societies worshipped a group of divinities that could have carried over into Protohistoric and then Graeco-Roman Europe.

Such an explanation raises several questions. Some authorities claim that the religious function of the figurines has not been entirely proved, although they have sometimes been found in what were probably buildings designed for worship. According to these authors, such objects merely represent realistic or approximate versions of the everyday reality—in other words, they are simply toys. Similar difficulties of interpretation confront attempts to explain the numerous symbols which appear on pottery or other objects, such as the famous tablets of Tartaria from the Early Neolithic of southeast Europe: ideograms, pre-writing or symbols of religious import. These epigramic scribings seem to defy analysis.

Archaeologists also debate the meaning of terracotta models of small buildings, regarded by some as temples and by others as ordinary houses. Nevertheless, we know that models of temples did in fact exist, as in Malta. Figurines and modelled constructions may give rise to conflicting interpretations, but there seems less room for doubt when we are faced with actual cult edifices. It seems hard to explain the Maltese model edifices known as "temples" as simple dwelling houses, in view of their small number, great size and careful construction, their original trifoliate architecture and certain details such as oracle holes, altars, cells. Moreover, the curved façades fronted by courtyards suggest an emphasis on the subtle difference between profane space for the multitude and sacred space for the select few. At the end of the Neolithic these societies apparently revered certain figures responsible for their spiritual needs and beliefs, such as deities, ancestors, or such like. It seems equally difficult not to suppose that some of the statues set up inside the sacred spaces were seen as divinities, impressive as they must have been. The statue at Hal Tarxien in Malta, for example, was nearly 3m (10ft) high. The carved stelae or menhir statues of the 3rd or 2nd millennium, which are found from Bulgaria to Brittany, but mainly appear in the western Mediterranean, may also be interpreted in different ways depending on one's theory.

Ancestor cults, or the expression of being part of a region or a community through the erection of special structures, is a characteristic feature of the Megalithic culture in western Europe. The proportions of some monuments, the physical and material investment needed by such edifices, and their internal decoration, suggest their probable function as temples, in parallel with their funerary functions. The honour accorded to the dead by the living cannot have been negligible in view of the size of wooden structures such as those erected near the settlements or sometimes above stone cellars, as with the houses of the dead in Denmark.

Cults of fertility, of the dead, of natural elements, such are some of the religious concepts which archaeologists identify as the metaphysical preoccupations of Neolithic man. But it is still very difficult to go beyond these basic statements. Nor is it easy to trace the development of these concepts down the various millennia of the Neolithic and Protohistoric periods. Was the disappearance of figurines towards the 3rd millennium connected, as some authors have thought, with the end of an agricultural world dominated by a matriarchal society? This is far from clear. Judging by statuary alone, an appreciable masculinization made itself felt as from the 2nd millennium. The Bronze Age seems to people its material and spiritual world with heroes or male divinities. Some scholars see in this the rise of a patriarchal system. But these mutations may only be the reflection of the social transformations which affect populations. When it comes to religion, the archaeologist is far too dependent on speculation.

Bull symbol from the hypogeum of Anghelu Ruju, Sardinia

In several Sardinian hypogea—underground vaults often associated with burials—heads of cattle appear in carved or painted form, sometimes simplified to an outline of the horns. A certain number of these tombs suggest, by their size and their architectural details, that they were also cult places. The bull, symbol of strength and the male principle, seems to have played an important part in the religious ideas of Neolithic Sardinia. Fourth or third millennium BC (uncalibrated). Museo Archeologico Nazionale, Cagliari.

Menhir-statue from St-Sernin, France

Menhir-statues appear frequently in southern France, especially at Rouergue. They are incised or carved, and represent in stylized form divinities or hero figures, shown with such attributes as sceptre and axe. Interesting features of this example include the marks on the face, the necklace of five rows, the Y-shaped feature or attribute down the front, the pleated dress, the belt with double folds, and the legs set apart. Third millennium BC (uncalibrated). Musée Fenaille, Rodez, France.

"The God of the Sickle", Szegvar-Tüzkoves, Hungary

Despite the title given to this probably male figurine, archaeologists do not really know whether it holds a sickle or a sceptre. However, the attribute appears to confer a particular status on the character represented. Tisza culture, fourth millennium BC (uncalibrated). Szentes museum.

Statuette from Golovita, Romania

A stylized treatment, probably reflecting fertility concepts, characterizes certain Neolithic figurines. This is expressed through an exaggeration of the genital regions or the breasts, while the limbs are attenuated and the head reduced to a cylindrical appendage, as in the Hamangia culture of the fourth millennium BC (uncalibrated). Museum of Romanian History, Bucharest.

"The Thinker of Cernavoda", Romania

Found in a tomb with a female statuette, this figurine of a man with hands resting on either side of his face is famed for its pose. To some the aim of the artist is to express a calm, peaceful and reflective state. Others see it, in common with many Balkan idols, as the wearing of a mask, associated with the need to conceal the face of a possible divinity. Fourth millennium BC.

"Altar" of Divostin, Kragujevac, Yugoslavia

Three-legged "altar" with a cylindrical container. The legs are curved and pierced with a hole in the upper part. The original purpose of these vases is generally considered to have been ritual, but this cannot be established with certainty. Vinça civilization, fourth millennium BC (uncalibrated). National Museum, Kragujevac.

"Altar" of Fafos I, Kosovska, Yugoslavia

This container shows a part-human (upper half) and part-animal (lower half) figure holding a vase in its arms. Vinça civilization, early period, fifth millennium BC (uncalibrated). Kosovo Museum, Pristina.

The Trundholm Chariot, Denmark

This work is .6m (1.9ft) long, and consists of a central pole to which three pairs of wheels are attached. The front two pairs support a horse shown groomed and ready for a procession. The chariot displays a bronze disk covered with gold plate, on which spirals and concentric circles have been traced. Archaeologists interpret the material as a solar symbol, stressing the role played in Bronze Age mythology by a natural element, the sun, and an animal, the horse, that is often associated with it. Middle Bronze Age, c.1200BC. Copenhagen Museum.

49

Protohistory: the archaeological background

Modern advances in scientific techniques have enabled archaeologists to show the originality and creativity of Bronze Age societies in western Europe where no historical records exist. The once fashionable view that "light came from the east" is no longer tenable, for scientific dating techniques show that these brilliant cultures arose independently.

The term "protohistory" was first used at the end of the 19th century by scholars like Gabriel de Mortillet*, a founding member of the International Union of Prehistoric and Proto-historical Sciences (U.I.S.P.P.) which still meets regularly throughout the world. The concept covers a period at the end of prehistory and the beginning of history, and has been adopted by many countries with slight variations in meaning. The English language tends to use "protohistoric" as an adjective rather than noun; in German, there is a clear distinction between protohistory (*Frühgeschichte*) and prehistory (*Vorgeschichte*), but the chronological limits of protohistory are wide and can stretch as late as Charlemagne's period.

Protohistory, it is said, concerns peoples without writing, who existed at the same time as the first historical civilizations. But this negative and conventional definition should not conceal the profound originality of this phase of human evolution, which corresponds to the metal ages in Europe (between 3000–2500BC) and the birth of Christianity or a little later in the northern countries. It now seems clear that the search for native metals and later for mineral ores, and the exploitation of gold, copper and silver which appeared at the end of the Neolithic, corresponded to a change in society. This change was marked by a more emphatic specialization of craftsmanship, trade at greater distances, war techniques better suited to the defence of a more stable hierarchical system, and a specific artistic expression linked to a new male-dominated religious belief. All these are constituent factors of the economic, social and spiritual worlds of protohistory.

Early in the 19th century, some spectacular discoveries drew archaeologists' attention to the ancient cities of Greek and Roman legend, and to the people whom Herodotus called "barbaric" in contrast with the Greek-speaking and classical world. In 1824 K.P. Pollhammer found at Hallstatt, Austria, tombs richly endowed with grave goods. Between 1846 and 1863 J. Ramsauer explored a necropolis, at the same site, that extended over 9000 sq m (97,000 sq ft): 980 tombs containing 19,500 objects made of pottery, bronze, iron and other materials such as amber and ivory. In 1830 the *kurgan* (burial mound) of Kul Oba, USSR, yielded further treasures.

Bronze Age warriors transported by boat

Wooden figurines with quartz inlays for eyes were found near Ross Carr, Holderness, England. They recall rock drawings from Scandinavia. Length of boat, 51cm (20.4in). Hull museum.

After the harsh winter of 1853–54 the level of several Swiss lakes dropped and the stilts of many lakeside villages were revealed. F. Keller began to study these remains and discovered, among others, the La Tène settlement on the shores of Lake Neuchâtel, which contained 2500 objects dating from the end of the second Iron Age. In 1861 a Bronze Age wooden coffin, which had been found in the mount of Trindhoj, was opened in the presence of King Frederik VII of Denmark; and in 1891, the famous cauldron of Gundestrup, decorated with scenes from Celtic mythology, was discovered in the same country. In the meantime Heinrich Schliemann*, working in Greece and Asia Minor from 1870 onwards, excavated on the sites of the cities of Troy and Mycenae. It was then shown that archaeological remains could supply real information of an exciting kind in cases where the written documentation was only allusive (as in the *Iliad*), or even absent. Other great discoveries took place at the same time in the fields of prehistory and classical archaeology. They all aroused much enthusiasm, and frequently led to hasty interpretations which are now regarded as "romantic". This initial phase of protohistory was nevertheless very important in the development of this discipline.

Growth and development of museums

Large archaeological museums were founded to preserve and study these abundant remains, which became a "heritage", providing a new cultural identity for the nations that were forming in Europe at this time. In 1852 the Römisch-Germanisches Zentralmuseum of Mainz, West Germany, was opened; in 1862, Napoleon III took a personal interest in the creation of the Musée des Antiquités Nationales at Saint-Germain-en-Laye, France, and supported the excavations of the Gallic settlement of Alesia. In 1866 the Lisbon archaeological museum was founded, and in 1867 the National Archaeological Museum of Madrid. In 1876, the Museo Pigorini, Rome's archaeological museum, was founded, and research began into the legendary origins of the eternal city; in 1890 the Zurich Schweizerisches Landesmuseum was set up to preserve the often fragile remains salvaged from Swiss lakes. All these museums included laboratories and libraries, together with archives of excavations and archaeological publications which were to be used in the first classifications of protohistorical objects.

The three-period classification

These classifications were actually based on museum collections. In 1836 Thomsen formulated the three-period system (stone, bronze and iron) on the basis of Danish antiquities in the Copenhagen museum, a system that was refined in 1865 by his assistant, Worsaae. In the new museum at Mainz, L. Lindenschmit first applied Thomsen's classification in 1852. At Saint-Germain-en-Laye, de Mortillet's reorganization of the collections, completed in 1881, defined the large subdivisions of the Paleolithic (which are still in use), a Neolithic period, and two phases on the Bronze Age, the so-called Morgian and Larnaudian periods. In 1914, J. Déchelette* brought out his influential *Manual*, which devoted one volume to the Bronze Age, another to the first Iron Age or Hallstatt period, and a third to the second Iron age or La Tène period. Déchelette applied the chronological system of P. Reinecke*, curator of the archaeological museum in Munich, to the Bronze Age and to the two Iron Ages of southern Germany and central Europe in general. D. Viollier, of the Zurich museum, subdivided the second Iron Age in Switzerland at about the same time, while two Swedish scholars, Montelius and Aberg, applied the typological methods to elaborate the chronology of northern protohistory,

Drink for the master: detail from the Vessel of Kuffarn, Lower Austria, *c.*350BC

An important individual, wearing an elegant robe and a broad-brimmed hat, sits comfortably on a low-backed couch. He holds out his cup to a servant, who uses a ladle to draw wine from a vessel. To the left, another servant carries two empty vessels, while on the right a child, standing before a rack of vessels, watches the scene. The decoration and composition on this container reveal the influence of the classical world, but the bronze support, the treatment of the figures, and the theme of drinking in a possibly funerary context, are typical of the protohistoric world which so amazed the Greek historians of antiquity. Museum of Natural History, Vienna.

and then widened their research to cover the whole of Europe and particularly Italy. Montelius's six periods of the Bronze Age (I to VI), are still considered relevant. Other authorities, such as F. Holste, W. Dehn, W. Kimmig, and H. Müller-Karpe in Germany, G. Childe* and C. Hawkes in Great Britain, and J.-J. Hatt in France, suggested various systems of relative chronology which have formed the basis for advanced research into protohistorical lifestyles.

Increasingly detailed excavations and investigative methods, both in the field and in the laboratory, underlay these systems, and recent research has led to the elaboration of protohistory as a discipline in its own right. Further development of this area became possible through the "C^{14}* revolution", as Colin Renfrew has called it, the method that since 1950 has formed the basis for the general chronological scheme of late prehistory and protohistory. By pushing back to an earlier period dates which had till then been commonly accepted, the C^{14} method has shaken the theory of a common Near Eastern origin for complex contemporary civilizations. As a consequence, the Wessex culture, for example, has now to be regarded as outside the sphere of influence of Mycenae. European protohistorical periods assessed by the C^{14} method are now defined more precisely according to a dendrochronological* (tree-ring analysis) scale perfected in Switzerland on material taken from the stilts of the lakeside villages.

Exploring large sites

Protohistorical excavations, like prehistorical ones, have to include an understanding of unusual geological features in the soil and their relation to such natural phenomena as rainy periods, volcanic eruptions, etc., or to manmade features such as ditches or terraces, but the size of most protohistorical sites implies the coordination of data often obtained from an area of considerable extent. Spatial archaeology covers entire settlements, such as a main fortified building, scattered secondary dwellings, burial grounds, mining and extraction areas, and even embanked fields. Such studies are typical of protohistorical archaeology. Underwater exploration has also been widely used, as in the study of a village on Lake Neuchâtel, Switzerland, or on Lake Charavines, France, or a settlement flooded by the Saône, France, or a Mediterranean wreck loaded with bronzes and amphorae. Here the methodology has been greatly developed over the past few years.

Field surveying* has become indispensable to any research of large sites; surface work is often accompanied by aerial photography, which provides information on the topography of ancient villages and often reveals hundreds of protohistorical remains—old plots, isolated dwellings, cemeteries and various funerary structures, stilts of submerged villages, wrecks, and so on. Geophysical surveying methods, using such techniques as soil resistivity, are also very effective in detecting filled-in ditches, silos and other earthworks, as well as the foundations of walls. Thus complete plans of villages, cemeteries and field systems have been discovered.

The conservation and study of protohistorical objects take into account the material from which they were made, as for instance the special methods used to preserve wood soaked with water. Paleometallurgy*, the science of ancient metal-working, is first of all used to identify any trace of metallurgical activity on the site, from remains of ovens, piles of fragments of earthenware moulds and slags, to utensils used by jewellers or craftsmen in copper and iron. Later, metallographical methods identify the composition of the metals by means of chemical analysis and spectrography, and the development of the various technologies through radiography and micrography. An ecological approach investigates the various soils, the animal and human bones, and the pollen and carbonized grains.

Much more information comes through various analyses, for instance petrographical examination (study of rock classification) and identification of the clays of various ceramics and utensils from, say, a Greek potter's workshop, or the elements used to produce glass. Many analyses are based on measurable data furnished by archaeometry*. Computers are now used to monitor the vast amount of information gathered, and specific programmes have been evolved to record and classify vases according to their shape, to group metal objects according to composition or function, to establish a chronology of their individual types, and to distribute to various sites the data supplied by a particular excavation.

The wealth of material, reflected in the abundance of specialized literature, is so great, and at the same time so incomplete, that protohistorians, like archaeologists in general, have to face the problems of putting if together to form a coherent picture. Since the 1960s theoreticians like L.R. Binford, D.L. Clarke and J.C. Gardin have shown that the era of mere classification and research into new excavation techniques is over, and that "models" need to be invented to apply the data to the economic, social and cultural reconstructions of ancient societies. Gordon Childe had already foreseen this in 1930, but the relevance of analytical archaeology* has only been made clear in recent years with spectacular applications to protohistory, an area particularly suited to this type of investigation because of the variety of documentation and the actual spatial dimensions it implies.

Protohistory is no longer purely descriptive; it examines above all the processes of evolution and change. We can now reconstruct the Aegean world during the third millennium BC (C. Renfrew, 1972); follow the development of the Iron Age in Aquitaine during the first millennium BC (J.P. Mohen, 1982); study the life of protohistorical communities of southern Scandinavia (J. Jensen, 1983), and so on. At the same time, we can tackle many themes typical of protohistory: urbanization and proto-urbanization, specialized crafts such as jewellery and metallurgy, the peaceful or hostile relationships between peoples, or religions sharing certain symbols, such as the sun, migratory birds, or deer. The emergence of writing also deserves particular attention, together with the appearance of an historical awareness in a people or nation, the appearance of first names, and the formation of linguistic families, such as the Indo-European.

The metal ages

The ancient idea of the successive metal ages of copper, bronze and iron reflects the importance which all the later prehistoric civilizations attached to the ability to work metals.

Metals have played a basic role in human development, as was recognized by the Danish antiquarian Christian Jurgensen Thomsen in 1819, when he classified prehistory according to three ages: stone, bronze and iron. Archaeologists concerned with the study of paleometallurgy* have noted that the effects vary to some degree from region to region, but there is little doubt that the discovery and use of different metals has often greatly affected the relations between various human groups. This has been particularly apparent in the case of Europe.

Metallurgy greatly encouraged the accumulation of material wealth. Copper, gold and iron can all be recycled for, unlike a flint tool or a ceramic pot which, once broken, cannot be re-used, a broken metal object either retains its worth as metal weight or else can be repaired by welding or hammering. The expansion of a craftsmanship specializing in metals grew up in areas often at a distance from the sites where ores were mined and ingots produced, and this created, in certain countries such as southern Scandinavia, Normandy or southern Germany, centres of technological innovation, and even whole technologies.

Important sites
Remains of the first metallurgical centres in Europe are now known, and have been dated to a period slightly later than the oldest traces found in the Near and Middle East (beginning of the 4th millennium BC). It appears that commercial contacts may have existed between Anatolia (Troy I, II and III) and the Balkans, which in the middle of the 4th millennium saw the development of centres for the extraction and smelting of copper ores at sites such as Rudna Glava in Yugoslavia. Copper mining tools such as sledgehammers and pickaxes have been found in Hungary in the copper-rich mountains of Transylvania.

Further east, at Aibunar in Bulgaria, copper extraction and exploitation provided wealth and power for the princes buried in the necropolis near Varna, where ornaments and cult objects are made of copper and gold. North of the Caucasus, the kurgans (circular burial mounds) of Maikop provide further evidence for the rise of a social order or hierarchy. Here the chief's tomb contained several objects in copper, gold and silver dating from the middle of the 3rd millennium BC.

Copper slags abandoned at Diana on the island of Lipari, Italy, around 3000BC reveal contacts with the Balkan metal industries. The following centuries saw the emergence of local centres of metalwork in several areas of western Europe: at Cabrières, France, copper ores were mined and smelted; in the Iberian peninsula the copper mine of Mola Alta de Serelles contained the moulds of flat axes, and at Zambujal in the west a small fort was perhaps a means of controlling and supervising the activity of the nearby copper mines. Exploitation of copper ores also occurred as far north as Ireland (Gabriel Mount, Cork).

These natural resources gave rise to the formation of cultural groups known as Early Bronze Age: Tiszapolgar and Unütice in central Europe; Remedello, Rinaldone and Gaudo in Italy; Montagne Noire in France; El Argar and Tagus in the Iberian peninsula. The British Isles and western France also participated in the establishment of a metal age with the increasing production of objects in copper and gold such as ornaments (beads and brooches), tools (awls and axes) and weapons (battle axes, halberds and daggers).

Copper alloyed with arsenic is stronger than copper by itself, and this natural alloy as exploited by craftsmen and even artificially induced in regions as separated as the Caucasus and Brittany (where sword blades dating from 1700BC were found at Carnoet). Bronze, which is an alloy of copper and tin, made its appearance in the Early Bronze Age first in the Near East, about 2800BC in the royal tombs at Ur; and sometime later, about 1800BC in the tin-rich areas of Europe such as Bohemia, Wessex or Brittany.

The supply of tin to the large protohistoric workshops of bronzesmiths, particularly in Greece, Italy and Scandinavia, depended on long-distance commercial networks. The precious mineral of the "Isles of the Cassiterides" came from Cornwall or Brittany, and quite a few wrecks loaded with bronze objects probably lie along the maritime "tin roads": English Channel, Huelva in Spain, and Rochelongue in southern France. In Western Europe the greatest period of bronze, with a tin alloy of 15 percent to 20 percent, is the so-called Middle Bronze Age (1500–1200BC). Numerous products from the Atlantic area include axes, swords, lance heads and bracelets, and rival those of central Europe with its axes, swords, brooches, bracelets and greaves as well as northern Europe, where a rich silver and gold industry also developed with many items of plate and jewellery. With the Late Bronze Age (1200–700BC) lead was increasingly introduced into the alloy as a partial substitution for tin.

The high standard of expertise in the bronze industry enabled craftsmen to make great technological advances in the production of numerous objects, such as horns and musical instruments, moulded items from Scandinavia, cuirasses, helmets, shields, cauldrons, and pieces made by hammering or repoussé work. The organization of the bronzesmith's craft can now be examined in detail as a result of excavations in such centres as Fort Harrenard at Sarel-Moussel, France, where remains of furnaces, nozzles, crucibles, moulds and a whole range of tools have been found.

The Iron Age
Iron brought to earth by meteors was seldom used during the Bronze Age. The extraction and separation of iron ores and the exploitation of the new metal required more sophisticated techniques than those used for copper. The great advantages of carbon-rich iron were not fully exploited until the so-called Iron Age, which began in different European regions at dates ranging from 1100 to 700BC. The new techniques probably began in Anatolia, but iron-working centres soon developed throughout Europe under the combined influence of the horse-riding peoples who spread over central Europe and the Mediterranean farmers who moved to the west. Ironworking drastically altered the human geography of protohistoric Europe. All the so-called "barbarian" peoples mentioned in the earliest texts of antiquity made their appearance at this point.

Archaeologists normally distinguish two phases of the Iron Age: the first period known as the Hallstatt phase, lasted until the 5th century BC. The iron objects found in the Hallstatt necropolis in Austria, include mainly weapons, long sword blades and lance heads, occasionally daggers. Certain areas adopted the new metal more easily than others, for instance Aquitaine and Lorraine (France) and Bohemia. Generally speaking, bronze was then confined to vessels, ornaments or statuettes, such as in princely tombs of the 6th and 5th centuries BC. Iron became fully integrated into the sphere of everyday life only during the second, or La Tène, phase: millions of nails were then used in the construction of city walls with nailed beams (*murus gallicus*) *oppida**, as well as private dwellings. The weldings on some of the swords found at La Tène in Switzerland, display techniques that anticipate the technological achievements of the Middle Ages.

Bronze mould, axe and ingot from the deposit of Petit-Villate, France

These objects found at Petit-Villate date from the end of the Bronze Age (9th century BC). It is not unusual to find a bronze working from this period, comprising fragments of bronze objects (sometimes thousands) that were kept for re-casting. Some of these, like the one below, include traces directly linked to metallurgy: these are copper or bronze ingots of various shapes, and two-piece bronze moulds used, like this one, for the smelting of axes. Some archaeologists have suggested that these metal moulds might either have been intended for the preparation of wax models, which would then have been used to construct an earthenware mould, or were employed directly for the casting. Experiments have proved that it would have been possible to use them for casting and perhaps for recasting. The possibility of developing a metallurgy based on recasting enabled metal-working sites to be established away from areas where the ores were mined.

Musées nationaux

Gold lunula from Saint-Potan, France

Goldsmithing began in Europe at the same time as copper metallurgy. Gold, unreactive but very ductile, could be found in its natural state, and was reserved for the manufacture of jewellery and luxury vessels probably associated with libations. These precious objects were sometimes deposited in the tombs of high-ranking individuals, or were hoarded for their intrinsic value. The deposits we find today had either been hidden or else used as offerings. The Saint-Potan lunula, which had been hidden within a crack in a rock, would have been worn like a large collar. This ornament is typical of the early Bronze Age of Ireland, Great Britain and Brittany.

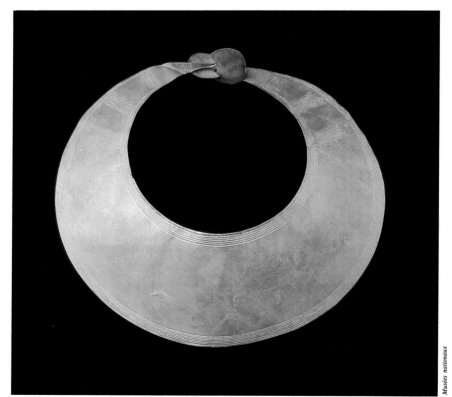

Musées nationaux

Mineral wealth of Europe

Geological variations within the European continent and the existence of several ancient outcrops of mineral ore explain the relative wealth of metals which enabled prehistoric metallurgy to grow so vigorously. The latter industry seems to have benefited from intensive prospecting and from the exploitation of the main deposits then in existence, with only a few exceptions: copper had not yet been found in Sweden, and the tin of northern Spain was probably used in large quantities only during the Iron Age. Local copper and its various mineral ores were mined very early on in the Caucasus, in central Europe, in the south of France, in the Iberian peninsula and in Great Britain. Gold nuggets found in these areas formed the basis of a dynamic jewellery production. Tin was much rarer; it could only be found as an alluvial mineral, cassiterite, large deposits of which were found in Brittany and in Cornwall as well as, to a lesser extent, in Bohemia. The tin trade is one of the main problems posed by protohistoric bronze metallurgy. Silver requires the special technology of cupellation* (extraction from lead). Deposits of iron ore are not shown on this map because they were so widespread.

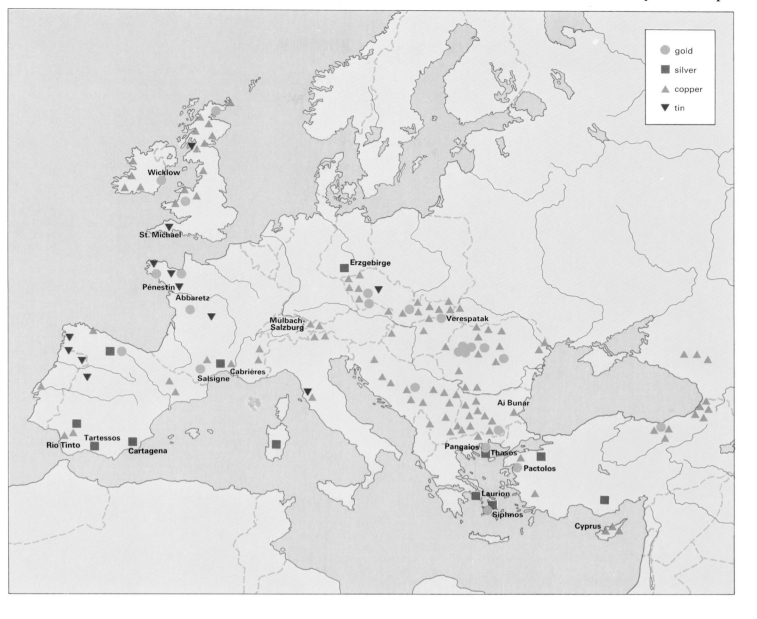

Legend:
- ● gold
- ■ silver
- ▲ copper
- ▼ tin

Map labels: Wicklow, St. Michael, Pénestin, Abbaretz, Salsigne, Cabrières, Erzgebirge, Mülbach-Salzburg, Verespatak, Ai Bunar, Pangaios, Thasos, Pactolos, Laurion, Siphnos, Cyprus, Rio Tinto, Tartessos, Cartagena

Comparative chronology of the various phases of European protohistory

dates	climate	northern zone	temperate zone	Mediterranean zone	historic events
3000	sub-boreal	**Late Neolithic**	**Chalcolithic**	**Early Bronze**	
		megaliths	Tiszapolgar	Cyclades	
2500			Bodrogkeresztur	Lerna	
		Chalcolithic battleaxes	**Early Bronze** Unetice	**Middle Bronze** Knossos	
2000		**Early Bronze**	El Argar		
			Wessex		
1500		**Middle Bronze** Sögel-Wohlde	**Middle Bronze** tumulus Norman group	**Late Bronze** Mycenae	
					1240 Trojan War
1000		**Late Bronze** height of Northern Bronze	**Late Bronze** urns Atlantic metallurgy lakeside sites	**Iron Age** Geometric period	850? Homer?
	sub-Atlantic	peat-bog sacrifices	**First Iron Age** Hallstatt	Orientalizing period	753 foundation of Rome 8thC Hesiod
				Archaic period	600 foundation of Marseille
500		**Iron Age** Jutland	Vix **Second Iron Age**	Classical period	495-429 Pericles 390 sack of Rome by the Celts
				Hellenistic period	356-323 Alexander
0			La Tène		52 fall of Alesia 44 death of Caesar 27 Augustus and the Roman Empire 54-68 Nero 98-117 Trajan
		Gundestrup Roman influence	**Roman period**	**Roman Empire**	
		period of migrations	**period of migrations**		306-337 Constantine
500					465-511 Clovis

▨ rainy and/or cold period

Deposits from Mareisminde bog at Kirchspiel Rönninge, Denmark

This find, dating from the beginning of the Iron Age (8th century BC), included a large decorated bronze vessel containing 11 gold vases with horse-head handles. The solar motif in association with birds, which can be seen on the bronze vessel, was a religious theme very common in Europe at this period. The first objects in iron were produced at about the same time, and consist entirely of weapons and utensils.
Archaeological Museum, Copenhagen.

L. Larsen

Burial customs

From burial sites all over Europe, archaeologists can draw a picture of Bronze Age societies, and attitudes to life and death — including human sacrifice.

An etching of the Danish King Frederic VII at the opening of a coffin discovered in a Bronze Age tumulus at Trindhoj (1861), perfectly captures the activity of the first excavators at a time of spectacular discoveries. Such was the interest of the public in the more or less well-preserved bodies of their ancestors. Protohistorical archaeology has long been concerned mainly with tombs, and certain funerary practices have provided names for archaeological periods, such as the period of the tumuli, or period of the urn fields (Urnfield period). Several burial grounds have characterized cultural groups: Straubing group (also known as Unětice), Kisapostag group, and so on. Death and the various cultural manifestations connected with it are present in all protohistorical societies. The tombs often contain ornaments, weapons of the deceased, and also offerings and sacred vessels — grave goods that represent a "self-contained" collection of objects dated to the same time, enabling archaeologists to determine a cultural level and a comparative chronology. Examination of personal possessions and their position on the skeleton reveals fashions in clothing, as in the case of the costumes of women buried in the Schwarza tumulus in Thuringia. Actual items of clothing, such as capes, skirts, belts, gowns and bonnets, in cloth and leather, have also been found in exceptionally well-preserved Danish burials, usually in humid conditions, as at Egtved. Variations in these clothing styles and in the various grave offerings have enabled archaeologists to distinguish, within the same period and the same territory, rich and poor collections. This has led to a social interpretation of the finds; wealthy graves may be called "princely burials" by archaeologists. The discovery of vast fortified settlements corresponding with princely chariot burials at the end of the first Iron Age in Burgundy at Vix, or along the Rhine at Hochdorf, supports the likelihood that such a social hierarchy did exist.

Two main funerary practices are known: burial and cremation. The buried body was laid out, either stretched full length or crouched, in a "flat grave", a simply dug trench or a tomb surmounted by a tumulus (mound), called a kurgan in eastern Europe. The copper-age kurgan of Maikop in the northern Caucasus covered a huge pit divided into three compartments, each containing a skeleton and, in one case, rich offerings in gold, silver and copper. In the steppes of eastern Europe the evolution of the kurgan consisted, first, of burials in a stone coffin, during the Early Bronze Age, then of a sort of catacomb with a shaft leading to a small side chamber, in the Middle Bronze Age, and finally, at the end of the Bronze and the beginning of the Iron Age, of a wooden superstructure above a large pit containing the coffin.

In central Europe, large cemeteries of flat graves containing crouched skeletons are characteristic of the Early Bronze Age, as at Straubing. Skeletons dating from the Iron Age are usually stretched out, as at Hallstatt. In this same area, a few mounds with rich grave goods, such as those of Leubingen and Helmsdorf, anticipate the tumuli typical of the Middle Bronze Age. During the Iron Age, large tumuli covered the princely chariot burials, some of which were also indicated by stelae or statues, such as the Hirschlanden warrior in Baden-Wurttemberg. In western Europe, the single-burial tumulus of the Early Bronze Age contrasts with the collective-burial tumulus of the Neolithic, in Brittany and western England, the only feature in common being the use of megaliths in the construction of the tomb. Some of these burials, such as Bush Barrow in Britain and Kernonen in Finisterre, contained rich tombs. In the Iberian peninsula during the Early Bronze Age, for instance at El Argar, the bodies were placed in a crouched position inside an urn and buried in a pit. In mid-western France, c.1200BC, burial was practised inside caves, as at Duffaits. At the same time, Mycenaean princes were being buried in the celebrated circular tombs lined with stone slabs. Burial in flat graves was still practised during the Iron Age, as in Champagne and Switzerland.

Cremation practices

Cremation is an ancient practice, but was apparently not very common during the Neolithic, the megalithic burials of Ireland being an exception. From the Early Bronze Age onwards, the ashes of the dead were placed with personal objects inside an urn covered with a lid and surrounded by other vessels containing offerings. In some of the Early Bronze Age burial sites, such as the one at Mokrin in Hungary, some graves have been found to contain burials as well as cremations; the same applies to some contemporary tumuli, such as that at Tarnava in Bulgaria, where several burials and cremations are contained within the same mound. During the Middle Bronze Age in central Europe, cremation was usually accompanied by vases and bronze objects in a new style, which was further developed in the course of the last period. This complex, relatively homogeneous culture is best known from the so-called "urn fields" where cremation burials have been found inside pits often dug in the centre of stone circles (Trepcianske Teplice in Slovakia) or inside a circular barrow (Broussy-Le-Grand in France). The cabin-urns of Italy or northern Europe as well as the face-urns reflect the world of the living. This funerary custom was very widespread and brings to mind the funeral organized for Patroclus by Achilles and described in Homer's *Iliad*. The custom was still practised during the Iron Age in some parts of western Europe.

Protohistorical funerary rites had a religious context, as can be seen in the relation between the megalithic site of Stonehenge and the numerous Early Bronze Age barrows in the neighbourhood. From the same period, the disarticulated (dismembered) skeleton of a young boy has been found in a well near the temple of Salacea in Rumania. Is such child burial a sign of ritual sacrifice? The recent (1980) discovery of the disarticulated skeletons of two children at Knossos has suggested this to Aegean archaeologists: perhaps a memory of such sacrifices is preserved in Greek myths such as those of Medea, and Thyestes. This was certainly practised at the beginning of the Iron Age in the cave of Byciskala ("the cave of the bull"), in Moravia, where some of the 40 piled-up skeletons are without heads, while both hands and skull-caps are separated from the rest. A recent discovery at Ribemont-sur-Ancre in Picardy has yielded a pile of human long bones dating from the Celtic period. In the south of France, the pre-Roman sanctuaries of Provence (Roquepertuse, Entremont) provide the basis for a study of the human skulls cult. Human sacrifice also explains the presence of Iron Age bodies of strangled men in the peat bogs of Tollund and Grauballe, Denmark.

Animals were also apparently killed as offerings (cattle, pigs and horses are sometimes found in the burials); sometimes they are found in their entirety, sometimes represented by large pieces of flesh—in which case they are probably the remains of funerary banquets, traces of which are also to be seen in the wine vessels of the Iron Age. The religion had an iconography represented by earthenware statuettes and small bronze sculptures found in the tombs: the figurine of a water bird, probably a swan, occurs frequently, together with the bull, the deer and the horse. The solar disk is found in association with horse-drawn chariots, boats, and processions of the faithful on the decorated slabs of the barrow at Kivik, Denmark. These Bronze Age themes often occur on the rocks of the large open-air sanctuaries of the north and perhaps in the Mediterranean mythologies.

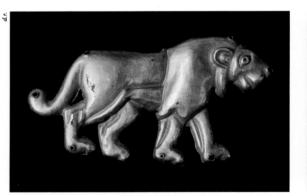

Gold decorations in the tomb of Maïkop, northern Caucasus, USSR

Excavated in 1897, the mound of Maikop was 10m (33ft) high and covered a tomb divided into three compartments, each containing a skeleton reclining on its side with its knees drawn up. The most important of the bodies was surrounded by a rich array of funerary objects: jewellery of gold and precious stones, weapons of stone, gold, silver and copper, utensils of gold and silver, and the components of a canopy including gold ornaments representing a bull and a lion. These funerary objects are typical of the heyday of early metallurgy, during the second half of the 3rd millennium BC. Hermitage, Leningrad.

Elevation and plan of the tomb of Leubingen, Germany

Beneath a large stone mound 34m (108ft) in diameter and 8m (26ft) high, a structure of oak trunks formed a double-sloped roof protecting a princely double burial dated to the end of the early Bronze Age (1700–1500BC). The skeleton of an elderly man was stretched on the soil and was surrounded by two axes, three burins, one halberd, three copper and bronze daggers and a polished axe of serpentine. A ten-year-old girl had been laid over the first body: she had been adorned with two brooches, a bracelet, two rings of hair (?) and a cylinder of wound wire, all in gold.

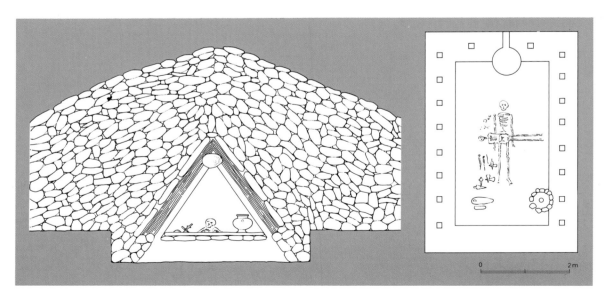

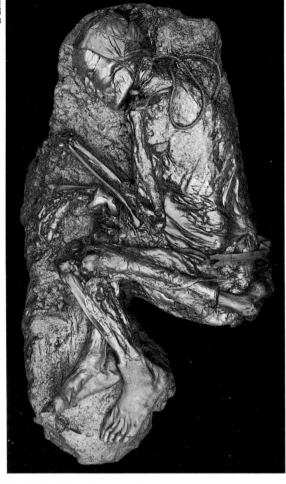

The Egtved woman, Denmark

This young woman, aged about 20, was found inside her oak coffin in the middle of a tumulus dated to the end of the Early Bronze Age (middle of the 2nd millennium BC). The organic matter within the burial was exceptionally well preserved. The body, fully dressed and with jewels (bracelets, bronze earring, bone comb), had been laid on the skin of a cow or bull and covered with a thick woollen cloth. The woman was wearing a blouse and a short string skirt. A bronze disk decorated her belt. A box containing a hair net had been placed at her feet. Copenhagen Archaeological Museum.

The Tollund man, Denmark

The discovery, in 1950, of this "peat-bog man", with his leather cap, created a sensation all over the world: the body was exceptionally well preserved and still bore round the neck a rope which had been used to strangle him. What is the meaning of this tragic event of the northern Iron Age (probably contemporary with the Roman era)? Was it punishment for a vicious crime, or sacrifice to a bog divinity? The latter hypothesis seems to be the more likely, bearing in mind that among the several protohistorical offerings found in Danish bogs there were other human victims. Silkeborg Museum, Denmark.

Cremation tomb of Mailhac, France

Excavated by Jean and Odette Taffanel, the rich burial grounds of Mailhac are an example of the cremation rites so widespread during the early Iron Age. The ashes of the deceased were placed within an urn which was then laid in a pit together with metallic or organic offerings; occasionally they were kept in several vases.

Reconstruction of the princely chariot tomb of Hochdorf, near Stuttgart, Germany

Discovered in 1978, this intact tomb was protected by a partly levelled mound 60m (192ft) across. The tomb itself was a large square casement, each side 5m (16ft) long, 1m (3ft) high, containing the grave goods. The slow process of fieldwork study, consolidation and restoration, undertaken by the staff of the Stuttgart Museum, has produced this reconstruction suggestive of the pomp which surrounded a prince of the early 6th century BC. The offerings are plentiful and some of the objects are quite exceptional, whether made of gold (fibulae, bracelets, belt, the decoration of the dagger and breeches), iron (the large drinking horn over 1m long) or bronze (the litter and the cauldron imported from south of the Alps). After Jorg Biel.

1 drinking horns
2 material with gold fibulae
3 chariot
4 ceramic vases
5 bronze litter
6 bronze cauldron
7 chain mail garment with gold appliqué
8 dagger with gold decoration
9 quiver

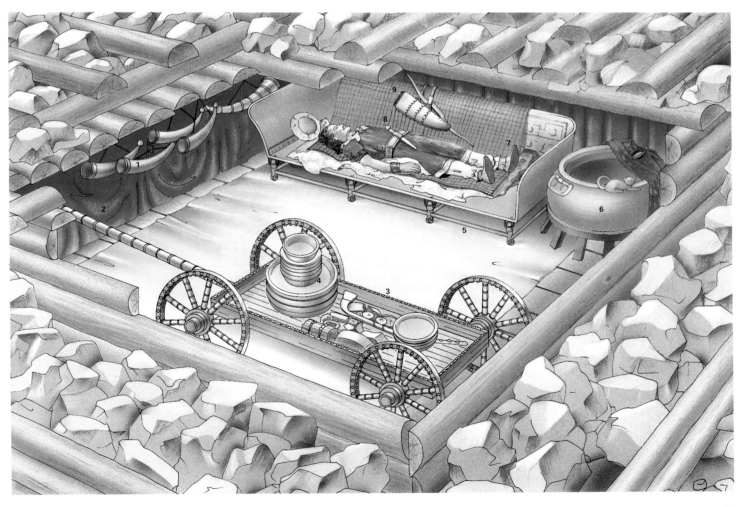

Trade routes

Long distance commercial networks reach far back into the 2nd millennium BC in Western Europe, with some contacts going from west to east, as with the amber trade and weapons technology. By 1200BC much of Europe shared common cultural ideas.

Yellow amber is a fossil resin used from the earliest times for jewellery and ornaments, and mainly found in north Germany (Schleswig-Holstein), Denmark (Jutland) and on the southern shores of the Baltic (Poland). Northern amber has a high content of succinic acid, whereas the smaller deposits noted in southern France, Spain, Italy, Syria and Rumania have considerably less. Chemical analysis can therefore establish that, from the third millennium BC, northern amber was much sought after, and spread throughout Europe, including Greece, where even in the classical period it was reserved for the cult of Zeus and valued for its medicinal and magical properties. So, over 4,000 years ago, there was considerable traffic between northern and southern Europe, and this continued through the Bronze Age (second millennium BC), as we can see from the distribution of several types of archaeological objects and of certain recurrent decorative motifs (suns and birds). The example of Late Bronze Age defensive weapons is particularly important for a better understanding of the nature of the exchange between the Mediterranean and the northern countries (the "Hyperboreans" referred to in Greek mythology). In the 5th century BC Herodotus, and later Pliny, again commented on the trade in amber coming from the north.

Amber was collected as long ago as the Old Stone Age (Isturitz in the Pyrenees and Mezirich in the USSR) but it is especially abundant in the Neolithic sites, for example Danish dolmen* tombs and hypogaea (underground structures) in the Marne. During the Bronze Age, amber was distributed all over Europe, and thousands of amber beads and earrings have been found in northern countries. In addition to its use as an element in necklaces, amber was carved into animal statuettes in Denmark and Poland.

In northern Russia, amber has been found on the lake site of Medlona, and, further south in central Russia, it abounds in the burial sites of Saktych: buttons, beads and small plates appear to have been sewn on to the clothing of the dead as early as the beginning of the second millennium. Turning westwards, we find amber beads both in the megalithic graves of Los Millares in Spain and in the tumuli of Wessex in England, as well as small objects such as the polished gold-bound discs—those at Manton, Amesbury and Normanton (Wiltshire)—which archaeologists have compared to a Minoan ornament found at Isopata in Crete.

The skeleton of a girl aged about seven, and wearing ornaments of bronze, glass and amber was found at Lastours, France, and confirms that relations were established, c.1600–1500BC, between the Baltic (the country of origin of the amber analysed) and the eastern Mediterranean. For in both places we find the same shape of eye engraved on the pendant and the same type of small plate, with many perforations, identified with Kakovatos, a Greek site from the Mycenaean age.

Kakovatos, situated on the west coast of Greece at the end of the Adriatic route mentioned by Pliny, is especially rich in amber. A single grave yielded 500 grains. The small multiperforated plate may be part of a belt, as examples from the "omicron" tomb of circle B at Mycenae would tend to suggest, or a spacer plate on a necklace. These small multiperforated plates are numerous in central Europe and have even been found in Wessex. They may be of Greek origin, as was once thought, or they may come from central Europe where they are numerous, or even from western Europe where they are very old, being dated to before 1600BC according to recent C^{14}* datings—therefore earlier than the earliest Mycenaeans.

In France, amber ornaments appear in the Early Bronze Age in the Armorican tumuli of Brittany (beads and small plates at Lesconil), but even more in the Middle and the beginning of the Late Bronze Age (1500–1200BC) in the funerary grotto of Duffaits (Charente). It is also well represented in the burial places of the Aube, the tumuli of the Haguenau forest (Upper Rhine) and the Hasard cave at Tharaux (Gard).

Other links between north and south Europe

These examples emphasize the wide diffusion of Baltic amber throughout Europe, along the maritime shores of the west or the banks of the big central European rivers flowing into the Adriatic. Central Germany was presumably the scene of busy trading in amber. Scholars have also asked whether Greece was not in certain cases a manufacturing stage point for some ornaments (the Lastours pendant, for example) that subsequently spread westwards. Amber is rare beyond mainland Greece. It has been found at Amira and Isopata in Crete, and in Rhodes, but only at Ialysos.

Consequently, we can only think of the diffusion of Baltic and Danish amber in the context of direct or more often indirect relations between the north and south. The blue segmented faïence beads are another good example of these relations. Some of them may have been of Egyptian origin, but others were produced locally in central Europe and Britain at the beginning of the Bronze Age.

The wearing of armour is also a cultural phenomenon which can be followed from the Baltic to the Mediterranean. The *Iliad*, dating from the end of the Bronze Age, describes Achilles' armour consisting of helmet, breastplate, greaves and shield, together with lance and sword. Warriors wearing this kind of armour are represented on a painted vase found at Mycenae and dated to the 12th century BC. All they lack is the short sword depicted on some Mycenaean seals. A short bronze sword is prevalent in Denmark, and archaeologists have traced its movement as far as Mycenae. Other examples come from Crete, Cyprus and Egypt.

Among defensive armour, several types of objects are found in such widely separated sites that we are entitled to think that warriors had the same arms in both Scandinavia and Greece, in spite of obvious gaps in the archaeological evidence. For example, no shields have been found on French sites, which does not mean that they did not exist. Shields could be made of perishable materials such as leather or wood, like those found in Britain, and the Substantion stele at Castelnau-le-Lez, near Aups, provides a good French example. In the same way, the small number of authentic defensive weapons found in the Iberian peninsula is balanced by the group of stelae found in the south-west of that territory. Each one depicts a fairly complete set of warrior's equipment, generally associated with a horse-drawn chariot, as in the Homeric tradition. Drawings of these chariots are engraved on pottery or rocks as far north as Scandinavia. Small-scale models of chariots are known, for example the famous chariot from Trundholm, Denmark, which bears the sun disk. Bronze breastplates are mainly known in a zone running from Crete to central Europe, but leather types, probably adorned with bronze studs, must also have been used as far as the northern countries. The iconography of stylized birds associated with the sun, recognized *inter alia* on breastplates, greaves and helmets, spread throughout Europe between the 12th and 7th centuries BC.

Gold-bound amber disk

This ornament was found in a Bronze Age tumulus at Manton, Wiltshire, and has often been compared with a similar object from the Tomb of the Double Axes at Isopata in Crete. Chemical analyses of amber pieces in Greece, especially those at Mycenae, strongly indicate a Baltic origin for this precious substance. The diffusion of amber over ancient Europe shows that trade links between northern Europe and the Mediterranean developed in the first half of the second millennium BC and reached their highest point in the Mycenaean period (1600–1100BC).

The Paris Helmet and the Marmesse breastplate

Archaeologists have identified different types of bronze helmets and breastplates. The helmet found in the Seine at Paris (left) belongs to the round crested type, dated to c.1000BC. This type, with two frontal studs suggestive of eyes, is widely distributed from northern Germany to Italy. One of the six decorative breastplates (right) from Marmesse (France) belongs to a type known in the east of France during the 9th and 8th centuries BC, but similar, sometimes older specimens exist in central and Mediterranean Europe.

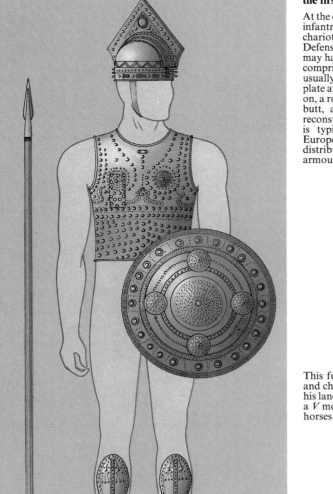

Weapons of a warrior chief at the beginning of the first millennium BC

At the end of the Bronze Age, warriors were armed for infantry warfare and transported to battle in a chariot, as depicted in the Cabañas stele (right). Defensive armour was made of leather or bronze, and may have been as much for display as for function. It comprised a helmet held on by a chinstrap, a cuirass, usually quite short, formed of a front plate and a back plate attached to each other, greaves which were laced on, a round shield, a long lance with a metal point and butt, and a sword mainly used for slashing. The reconstruction suggested here, based on actual pieces, is typical of the warrior's armature throughout Europe at that time. The map (below) shows the distribution of the main finds of bronze defensive armour.

Musée archéologique de Madrid

Engraved stele (9th-8th centuries BC) from Solana de Cabañas, Spain

This funerary stele represents a warrior, his armour and chariot. Viewed from top to bottom, you can see his lance, sword, a gourd(?) a helmet and a shield with a *V* motif. The four-wheeled chariot is drawn by two horses.

Relations between northern and southern Europe in protohistoric times

Links between northern Europe and the Mediterranean world existed over 4,000 years ago. They took different forms depending on the period concerned, but archaeologists have identified many similarities between different objects, burial rites, clothing and warfare practices. The map shows sites where arms dating from the end of the Bronze Age to the beginning of the Iron Age (12th-7th centuries BC) have been found, and also shows how Baltic amber spread southwards along certain routes from at least the Early Bronze Age to the beginning of the Iron Age. The weaponry was not necessarily used in battle. But these bronze parade arms, such as helmets, breastplates, shields, and greaves, indicate similar conceptions of warfare and, probably, of the system of chiefs. Such arms are often decorated with symbolic motifs, such as stylized birds and suns, a common feature of religious thought.

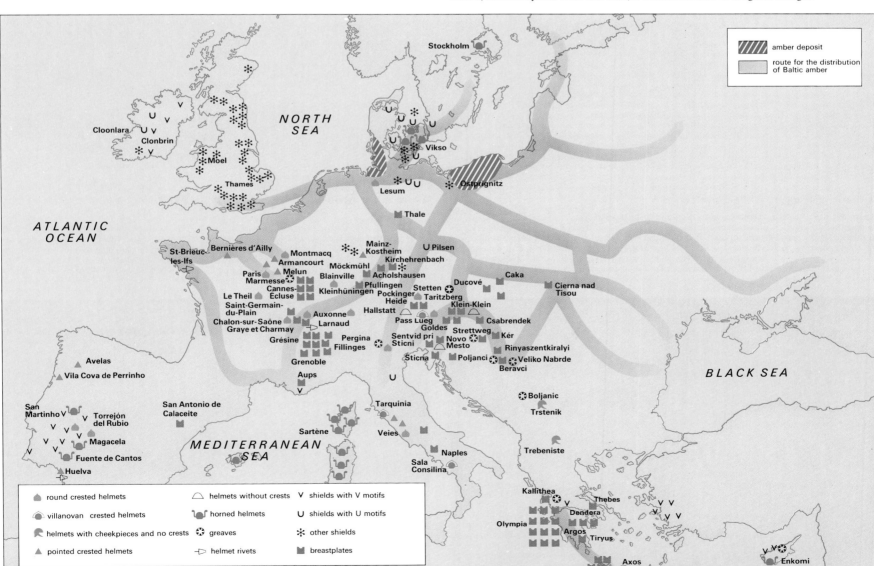

Wine and horses: symbols of prestige

In most early cultures the horse is a noble animal, reserved for the élite, because of the high investment involved in breeding, training and equipment: its spread into southern Europe can often be connected with the wine trade.

Archaeologists investigating chariot burials of the Iron Age (6th century BC) have found traces of horses and of wine in the same tombs, characterizing a society of mounted chieftains with sophisticated tastes. The horse first appeared as a domesticated animal during the 4th millennium BC in the Ukraine and probably further south in Iran and Antolia; horse bits made with antlers discovered at Dereivka (Ukraine) date from this period. However, it is possible that in western and central Europe (Hungary), a comparatively small number of horses descending from paleolithic breeds were also domesticated. The domestic horse, together with types of harness, became more widespread at the beginning of the 3rd millennium in Europe, shortly after the diffusion of copper and gold metallurgy.

The horse became increasingly frequent in the course of the Bronze Age; bits and cheek-straps are commonly found from the Causasus to the British Isles. The animal is usually represented as harnessed to a chariot; the solar chariot of Trundholm, Denmark, is drawn by a horse and dates from the Middle Bronze Age. Stylized representations of the Late Bronze Age, showing horses in harness, include carvings on rock (rock 47 of the Val Camonica, Italy), on the Spanish stelae of Cabeza de Buey and Torrejon del Rubio, and on the stone slabs of Begby in Norway and Frannarp in Sweden. Ceramics are also decorated with chariots, the figures incised on the bodies of certain vases (Saratov in the USSR, Vel'ke Raskovce in Slovakia, the cave of Queroy in Charente, France), while on the vase of Sublaines, France, the theme was created by sticking thin tin scales on the clay of the vessel. The chariots have four, or sometimes two, wheels: the former were used during parades, the latter in war; others still, like those painted on the Greek vases of Dipylon, seem to have been used during funerals.

The panoply of the knight

Horseman with large bronze or iron swords appear in representations slightly later than 1000BC in a large part of continental Europe. Traces of them are found among the furnishings of burials which include pieces of harnessing meant for horses without chariots, for instance in the tombs of Beilngries and Gernlinden in Germany, of Chaveria and Mailhac in France, and of Court-St-Etienne in Belgium. In the British Isles, objects found at Llyn Fawr provide good examples of the panoply of a knight. Individual pieces, such as the bronze fastener with a double sling which allows for two straps to be crossed, have been found from Iran to southwest Europe. Similarly, the custom of burying the horse, though rare, was practised from Scythia to Spain. Because of the timescale, some authorities have confidently identified this broad diffusion as reflecting invasions of horsemen from east to west at the beginning of the Iron Age. They have referred to Thracian-Cimmerian horsemen and have tried to connect these signs of war-induced unrest with the movements of the peoples who migrated as far as Egypt, with their horses, at the end of the 2nd millennium BC.

The role of these horsemen, who used iron for the first time on a large scale, seems to have been important. Their effect was still apparent among the chieftains of the 6th and 5th centuries BC, who built their forts all over Europe and who were sometimes buried with their chariots. The bronze situlae (bucket-shaped vessels) found at Tessin represent men on two-wheeled chariots drawn by two horses. On the chariot of Strettweg, Austria, a goddess figure is accompanied by horsemen in the course of what may be sacred rites associated with the deer. The chariot of Mérida, in Spain, shows a horseman of the same date hunting wild boars with a lance, a weapon which replaced the sword in some areas. The horse as a mount was thus a noble animal.

The spread of wine

The swiftness and agility of the horse, as opposed to the ox, almost certainly encouraged commercial exchanges between the Mediterranean regions and the rest of Europe, particularly when the Alps had to be crossed (Brenner Pass). Strabo wrote in the 1st century that the people of the Danube provinces loaded their carts with the products of Aguileia, in Etruria, such as wine and olive oil in wooden barrels, in exchange for slaves, cattle and hides. There is no doubt that salt and amber should also be added to this list. The Alpine passes were essential to the contacts between Etruria and three areas thirsting for Italian wine: the region of middle Burgundy and the Rhine, the area between Salzburg and Prague, and the north including Denmark and southern Sweden. We know very little about the wine itself, apart from the remains in the flask and vessel found at Durrnberg. On the other hand, Greek and Etruscan bronze vessels (or their imitations) such as craters, stamnos, situlae, baskets, basins, ladles and cups, all of which have been found in tombs more often than in dwellings, are clearly linked with the wine trade.

In western Europe, these common objects are mainly Etruscan although a few Greek imports seem to have travelled via Etruria. The earliest date from the 8th and 7th centuries BC, while the majority belong to the 6th and 5th centuries BC. They come from large princely tombs such as those at Hochdorf or Klein Aspergle in the vicinity of the fortified settlement of Hohenasperg near Stuttgart, Germany; or that of Sainte-Colombe, France, or at Vix near the settlement of Mont Lassois in Burgundy. These often important bronze vessels, like the crater (mixing bowl) of Vix, were valuable in themselves, quite apart from the wine stored or prepared in them. They may have been used as diplomatic gifts or as merchandise for new customers. Bernard Boulomie has suggested they may have represented the means of exchange in an economy based on a "chain" circulation of goods in the absence of a properly organized trade. The first link in this chain, after Etruria, was Tessin; the Burgundy-Rhine region was probably a second important link. The east-central link was the Salzburg area, with the large burial ground of Hallein, representing a later trading post (5th–4th century BC) probably related to the previous one. Also connected with the Burgundy-Rhine area, and even later, was the northern area.

What is certain is that Etruscan wine played an important role in the funerary rites of those chieftains, who were also in touch with the Greek trading outposts on the shores of the Mediterranean. Fragments of archaic Ionian and Massalian amphorae have been found at Mont Lassois and Camp du Château in France as well as at Heuneburg in Germany, where a strange wall built of mud bricks shows Mediterranean influence. The Mediterranean trading posts on the French and Spanish coasts were in touch with the indigenous populations of the hinterland, as shown by the orientalized sanctuary of Pozo Moro, regarded as the birthplace of Iberian art. The situation in western Europe was similar to that found in the eastern regions along the shores of the Black Sea, where contacts between Greeks and Scythians, for instance, were extremely intensive.

A warrior knight at rest: Siberian belt plaque

This gold plaque, dating from the second half of the first millennium BC, was once part of the collection of Peter the Great. It indicates the importance of the cavalry of the Euro-Asiatic steppes. The warrior, his quiver containing bow and arrows hanging from a tree, is stretched out on the ground; his head rests on the knees of a young woman who caresses him with a gesture symbolizing marriage. The equerry holds the reins of the two harnessed horses. This may be one of the first representations of the chivalric legends so widespread in medieval Europe. Hermitage, Leningrad.

Greek auriga (charioteer) and hoplite (heavy-armed infantry): frieze on the Vix crater, France

Discovered in 1953, the princely tomb of Vix contained, among other status objects, a bronze crater (mixing bowl) made in Greece at the end of the 6th century BC. The frieze which surrounds the neck of the crater is comprised of a series of vignettes depicting alternately a helmeted auriga on his chariot drawn by four horses and a hoplite, also helmeted, carrying a shield and probably a lance. They are idealized images of Greek soldiers exported to the "barbarians". Musée Châtillon-sur-Seine, France.

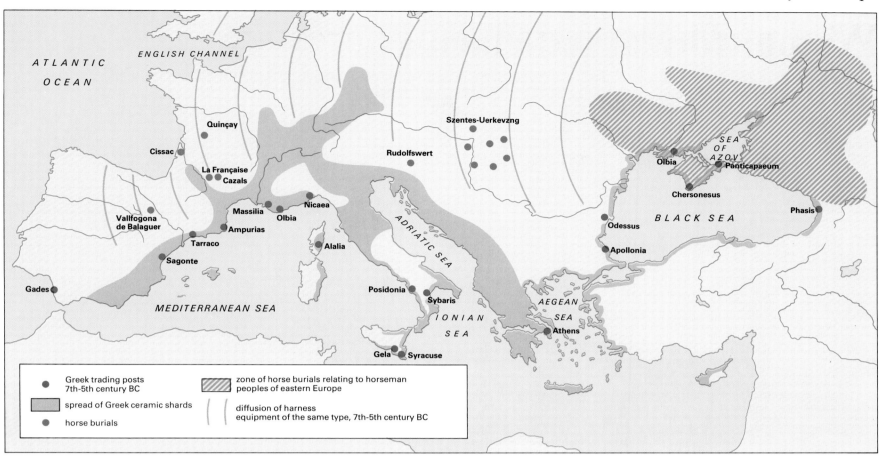

Horse burial and diffusion of Attic black-figure vases (5th century BC)

During the early Iron Age the horse and black-figure ceramics were invested with the same economic and social value: both can be found in particular among the funerary offerings of important figures. But while horse burials seem to have been a typically "barbaric" custom, the diffusion of Attic ceramics shows the coastal expansion of Magna Graecia as well as the attraction which the chieftains of the "barbaric" hinterland felt for such luxury products.

The chariot of Mérida, Spain

Dated by archaeologists to the end of the 6th century, this votive bronze chariot represents a boar hunt. The platform carries small bells and stands on four wheels identical to those which have been found in the chariot burials of the same period. The boar is being pursued by two dogs and by a horseman armed with a lance. This iconographical theme is often depicted in Iberian art: it must have had a precise religious significance. The mounted horse holds an important place in the Iron Age civilization of south-western Europe. Musée des Antiquités Nationales, Saint-Germain-en-Laye.

Plate from a decorated belt originating from Vače, Yugoslavia

Discovered in 1883 in a flat burial tomb dating from the 5th century BC, this plate of sheet bronze shows two horsemen face to face; they are attacking each other with lances and one of them, wearing a helmet, is brandishing a hatchet. On either side are two foot soldiers, protected by crested helmets and large shields, each armed with two lances and one with a hatchet. To the right is a civilian wearing a large robe and a large hat with upturned brim. Natural History Museum, Vienna.

59

Protohistorical settlements

How did Iron Age Europeans live? Julius Caesar described them as living in *urbes* – towns. Now archaeology is showing us what he meant.

Protohistorical agricultural settlements are characterized by a skilful architecture encompassing isolated farms, villages and hillforts. In the larger and more important settlements we can see the beginnings of the first European towns, a phenomenon not only of the classical Mediterranean countries but also of the areas further north. The range of materials used, earth, wood, thatch and stone, and the variety of architectural styles reveal a variety and originality in the protohistorical habitat. Some of the houses were round, as they had been during the Neolithic period: such were the stone dwellings of Filicudi (Aeolian islands) and Porto Perone, near Taranto, which date from the Early Bronze Age. In the British Isles, the round plan was adopted for stone dwellings with very thick walls (Gruting, Shetland) and especially for houses built with posts sunk into the ground, supporting a skilfully constructed framework in thatch. Isolated farms of this type, which date from the Late Bronze Age, have been found at Gwithian, Cornwall, complete with drainage channels and field enclosures, and on the Cheviot hills, where they are situated within rectangular enclosures. At Stayle Howe, another round house built in the middle of the 1st millennium BC had rectangular raised granaries supported by four, six or nine posts, work areas built below ground level and silos; the whole was enclosed by a palisade. At Itford Hill, Sussex, several such farms were gathered to form a small hamlet. On the basis of these remains, an Iron Age farm has been reconstructed at Butser, near Petersfield, Hampshire, and a whole programme of experimental archaeology* has been worked out to study protohistorical rural life.

In the temperate areas of Europe rectangular houses are more commonly found; posts sunk into the soil or fixed to a wooden frame provided a skeleton for the wattle and daub walls, and supported the framework of the thatched roof. As we know from the submerged wooden structures of lakeside settlements building techniques developed very early on. While tenon and mortice joints were already used during the Neolithic period, dovetailed joints seem to have appeared during the Bronze Age. The tools used were hatchets, adzes or axes, wedges, chisels and planes. Iron nails only appear at the end of the Iron Age when they are used to fix the cross-pieces of ramparts. Houses were sparsely furnished: shelf units, benches in the sleeping area, a ladder made from a tree trunk indented at regular intervals, and various tools and utensils. Houses could be locked up, as demonstrated by the keys dating from the end of the Bronze Age found at Morges, Switzerland.

Rectangular houses with a central partition, recognizable by the presence of three rows of post holes, built to a simple plan were quite common during the Neolithic period: the stronger axial posts supported a ridge upon which the rafters were fixed. The stone-flagged houses of Arbon Bleiche, Switzerland, dating from the Early Bronze Age, were built along these lines, as were the house at Aiterhofen and the long buildings of Manching, Bavaria, dating from the end of the Iron Age. The single-room house became more common after the end of the Bronze Age: the lateral posts were linked with tie-beams in order to support the weight of a larger roof, while the rafters rested upon a ridge which no longer carried the weight.

Two exceptional houses dating from the second Iron Age combined the principles of the round plan with those of the rectangular one: both from France, they are the buildings at Verberie (Oise) of some 270 sq m (2,906 sq ft), and that of Antran (Vienne) of 750 sq m (8,073 sq ft).

The Alps and central Europe were characterized by buildings made almost entirely of wood, the walls being constructed of horizontal beams intersecting at the corners: one such building was discovered at Hallstatt in the last century. The houses of the lakeside settlements, built on stilts during the Bronze Age, were also made completely of wood, and had one or more rooms; in the bog village fortified with a palisade at Wasserburg, near Buchau, Germany, which was inhabited during the Late Bronze Age, the buildings of the early phase were square one-room houses, while the later phase is characterized by U-shaped buildings with more than one room. Good examples of other similar fortified sites are those at Piave, in Italy, from the Middle Bronze Age; the sites of Cortaillod, on lake Neuchâtel, Switzerland, and Biskupin in Poland, dating from the Late Bronze Age.

Fortified settlements

Fortification was an important characteristic of some protohistorical settlements. Fortified enclosures are usually found on hilltops, more rarely on the plains, and have moats and ramparts built of wood, stone and earth, or stone alone. Eight hundred such enclosures have been found in France, most of them protohistorical, though some were built during the Neolithic period and, often, re-occupied in later periods. A few of these enclosures were probably simple shelters, but several show traces of permanent occupation, including areas devoted to craft activities: the succession of bastions at Zambujal, Portugal, housed a population which controlled the earliest exploitation of copper. The fortified settlements of Almeria (El Officio and Ifre, near Murcia) were occupied by the rural populations of the Early Bronze Age. The numerous Iberian forts of the Late Bronze Age are a reflection of the nature, both rural and warlike, of their inhabitants. The *talayots* of Majorca (Ses Paisses) and Minorca (San Augusti Vell) were built as shelters and watchtowers. The Sardinian equivalent, the *nuraghe*, probably played the same role (Sant'Antina, near Torralba). Towns, which brought together manufacturing, commercial, religious and political activities, existed from the beginning of the protohistorical period in Greece and Crete, and probably also in central and western Europe. Similar buildings to the Cretan palaces have been found at Thapsos and at Pantalica, in Sicily; while the large fortified sites of central Europe, such as that of Nitriansky-Hradok in western Slovakia, dating from the Early Bronze Age, or that of Fort Harrouard at Sorel-Moussel, France, show that there was a degree of urbanization in these areas as well, dating from the Bronze Age. The origins of Rome can be dated back to around the 12th century BC, and the legendary founding of Rome as a city is dated to the 8th century BC. More and more cities were founded under Greek influence on the shores of the Black Sea and the western Mediterranean from 600BC (Marseille) onwards; this influence was felt as far as Heuneburg, with its brick walls, and Saint-Blaise with its Hellenistic bastions. Julius Caesar used the term *urbes*, i.e. cities, for the fortified enclosures of the Bituriges. Recent excavations in France (Alesia and Mont-Beuvray), Germany (Manching, Kelheim), Czechoslovakia (Tavist, Trisov) have brought to light the urban civilization of the Celts: the town of Grabenstetten, in the Swabian Jura, covers an area of 1,600 hectares (3,953 acres).

The citadel of Zambujal, Portugal

This site, excavated between 1964 and 1973, tells us much about the warring societies which flourished in Portugal from 2400 to 1800BC, when copper mines were first exploited and gold nuggets first discovered. The successive stages of the citadel show an increasing need to reinforce its defences: the walls get thicker and thicker, the entrances are well guarded, drystone towers and ramparts are built, courtyards are replaced by towers. After E. Sangmeister and H. Shubart.

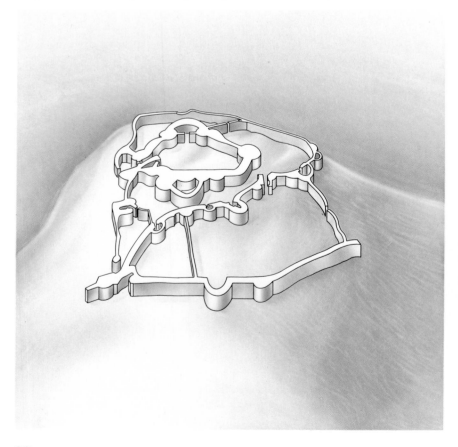

The village of Unterhuldingen on Lake Constance, Germany

This reconstructed village gives us a good idea of what a pile-built lake-hamlet might have looked like. The type of construction was dictated by economic and defensive needs. Archaeological remains reveal that a Neolithic village preceded the Bronze Age one.

60

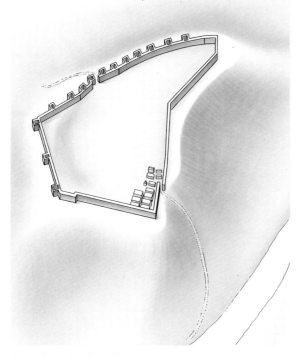

Plan of the fortified site of Heuneburg, Baden-Wurtemberg, Germany

This site overlooking the Danube was built in the 6th century BC on a triangular plateau, the longer sides of which extend to some 300m (960ft). A rampart surrounds the promontory consisting of a dry brick wall between 3 and 4m (9.6 and 12.8ft) high on a stone base; this technique, of Mediterranean origin, was the work of a local ruler who admired classical civilization.

Reconstruction of the dry brick rampart and of the houses of Heuneburg

Excavations carried out at Heuneburg have enabled experts to reconstruct part of the site. On the basis of the objects found, archaeologists have confirmed a Mediterranean influence (Greek black figure pottery, wine jars) on the local culture. The rulers were buried not far from Heuneburg, at Hohmichele and Hundersingen, within tumuli furnished with rich offerings.

The fortified site of Saint-Blaise, South France

This site has a complex system of ramparts and towers, the first courses of which date from the 7th century BC, when Saint-Blaise began to develop as a result of the production industry in the salt-water marshes of the area. The Hellenistic ramparts of the 4th century BC are from Saint-Blaise's most important period, when it was frequented by Celts, Etruscans and Greeks.

The *oppidum* ("town") of Chaussée-Tirancourt, France

This *oppidum* occupies the triangular edge of a plateau towering over the valley of the Somme. A great moat and rampart bar the spur. The *oppidum* was founded and flourished during the 1st century BC, in a part of Europe dominated by the Celts. The exact function of these huge sites is still far from clear.

The protohistorical peoples of Europe

Controversy surrounds the origin of the early inhabitants of Europe, some of whom – like the Celts of Great Britain and Ireland – still live in their prehistoric heartland.

The names of some of the European protohistorical peoples are known to us through the writings of Greek and Roman authors such as Herodotus (5th century BC), Aristotle (4th century BC), Polybius (2nd century BC) and Posidonius (1st century BC), as well as later ones such as Cicero, Caesar, Strabo and Pliny. These texts are often allusive but sometimes throw an amazing amount of light on what would otherwise have been rather enigmatic archaeological discoveries; one instance of this is the princely burials of the Scythians, north of the Black Sea, about whose funerary rites, which involved human and animal sacrifices (mainly of horses), Herodotus has left a detailed description.

The Thracians, to the west of the Balkans, are first mentioned in Greek texts of the 8th–6th century BC. Herodotus tells us that they were extremely powerful and Bulgarian archaeology has confirmed the strong personality of these horsemen living at first in villages and then in fortified towns like Seuthopolis. These towns maintained diplomatic and commercial relations with the Greek trading posts on the Black Sea (Apollonia-Sozopol, Odessos-Varna). Their highly hierarchical society was prosperous around 500BC, as demonstrated by the thousands of burial mounds of Brezovo near Plovdiv, of Duvanlii, Kazanlak and Seuthopolis. The accoutrements of some of the rich tombs and the pieces of jewellery found in hoards like those of Panagurisce and Valci Tran point to a Greek-inspired art largely supported by an aristocratic class. By the 4th century BC, some of the Thracians fell under the rule of the Macedonians, but succeeded in preserving their own culture until the days of the Roman empire. Further to the north, in modern Rumania, one of these peoples emerged as an independent cultural entity during the second half of the first millennium BC: the Geto-Dacians. Their iron products and their jewellery (silver wares of Sincraeni), their architecture (Sarmizegetusa and Piatra Craivei), their ceramics and their coins are all expressions of this identity which was left unaltered by the impact of the Celts in the 3rd century BC.

In Yugoslavia, along the Adriatic coast, the Illyrians formed a federation of peoples intermingled with the Thracians and in constant contact with the Etruscans, whose influence is apparent in the decorated vessels, or *situlae*, of Vace, and with the Greeks, whose proximity explains the gold mask and the crater (a wine-mixing bowl) found in one of the tombs at Trebeniste which

dates from the 6th century BC. Large necropolises, like the 7,000 tombs of Santa Lucia and the hundreds of mounds at Stricna-Novo Mesto, reveal the strength of this culture. Here again, the Celts were unable to impose their rule, and when in 148BC, the Romans founded the province of Illyricum it was in full recognition of local customs and language.

Celtic occupation and art styles

The Celts occupied Gaul and Bohemia, Great Britain and Ireland, northern Italy and the middle Danube area in the second half of the first millennium BC. They plundered Greece, and some of their number founded the kingdom of Galatia in Asia Minor. What unified their rural and warfaring world were to a certain extent linguistic, and above all artistic rather than political bonds. The Celtic style first appeared in the second Iron Age, around 450BC, and was at first inspired by Mediterranean art, but soon became a style of its own. The Attic goblet (5th century BC) found in the tomb at Klein Aspergle (Germany), covered in gold leaf cut into s-shapes, volutes and palmettes exemplifies the new style. Gold bands have also been found at Eygenbilsen and Waldgallscheid in Germany, and the same metal was used for the openwork decoration of the bowl found at Schwarzenbach. Several small bronze objects, such as a brooch and a belt buckle from Weiskirchen in Saarland, and gold objects such as a bracelet from Rodenbach in Germany and another from Reinhein in Saarland, the torques and bracelets of Ersfeld in Switzerland, are all decorated with human heads in relief surrounded by animal and floral motifs. The circular phalerae, in gold like those of Auvers (Val d'Oise) or in openwork bronze like those of Cuperly (Marne) show the Celtic predilection for the curving line which appears again, painted or engraved, on their bulging vases. Celtic art reached its high point at the end of the 4th and during the 3rd centuries BC with the gold, bronze and iron helmets of Agris (Charente) and Amfreville (Eure). The style known as Waldalgesheim, after a bracelet and a torque, both in gold, found on that site, was characterized by curving lines and milling in relief; it was applied to bronze objects such as ornaments or parts of harnessing or even on stones such as the sacred stones of Pfalzfeld (Germany), Kermaria (Finisterre) and Turoe (Ireland). Even more exuberant decoration is found on bracelets with hollow ovoli, on harnessing pieces decorated with faces with globular

eyes, on bronze sword sheaths and on the torques and gold bracelets found in the area around Toulouse. Celtic coins appeared at the same time as the insular art which developed at the beginning of the Christian era: the gold torque of Broighter (Ireland), the bronze buckle found in the Thames at Battersea (London). Celtic society was highly hierarchic as we can see from the descriptions of its lifestyle, its religion and its art which appear in the first Celtic texts of the later Celtic period.

The Ligurians were in contact with the Greeks and the Etruscans of the Mediterranean trading posts, and with the Celts; they have left stone sculptures usually from sanctuaries, such as those at Entremont and Roquepertuse (Rhine estuary).

The Aquitaines, in areas to the south of the Garonne extending to the Pyrenees, resisted all Celtic pressures, traces of which have been identified in the northwest of the Iberian peninsula. Iberian culture reached its peak during the 4th century BC with a degree of sophistication shown by their fortified towns and large sanctuaries (Despanaperros and Serrata de Alcoy).

The customs of the Germanic tribes in the north have been related to us by Tacitus. These peoples had various origins but became unified by very strong cultural traditions, particularly religious ones, and played a crucial role at the end of protohistory in the formation of modern Europe.

Linguistic links

The philologists of the early 19th century were struck by the similarities between Greek, Latin and Sanskrit, and propounded the theory of the Indo-European languages, a group to which it was gradually seen that the old Celtic and Germanic tongues also belong. Only a few languages do not belong to this group: Basque, perhaps spoken by the Aquitaines and related to the language of the Iberians; Hungarian and Finnish. While the philological links between the Indo-European languages are undeniable, the problem of their origins remains to be solved. G. Dumezil has studied the various mythologies to try and find common denominators in social organizations and formulated the theory of Indo-European "trifunctionality": the rulers, the warriors and the producers. The search for the anthropological roots of the Indo-Europeans, however, is still going on and archaeologists are still attempting to identify protohistorical ethnical identities behind the linguistic groups.

Two Scythian archers, kurgan of Kul Oba, USSR

This plaque from the 4th century BC, which was probably sewn onto an item of clothing, depicts two men back to back about to shoot their arrows. The two figures can be identified as Scythian archers from the steppes, by the place where the plaque was found (near Kerch, in the Crimea, on the shores of the Black Sea), by the shape of the bow, which is rather small, and by their clothing consisting of a kaftan held in at the waist and wide pantaloons tucked into soft leather boots. Scythian archers were famous in antiquity for their speed and ability. Only the bun hairstyle was, according to Herodotus, more typical of the Thracians. Height: 2.8cm (1.1in). Hermitage, Leningrad.

A greave from the tumulus of Mogilanska, at Wraza, Bulgaria

This greave (piece of leg armour), found in a rich burial, is decorated with a face reminiscent of the Gorgon in Greek art. Made of gold and silver, this greave illustrates how the native Thracian art was influenced by Hellenistic models. Height: 46cm (18in). Wraza Historical Museum, Bulgaria.

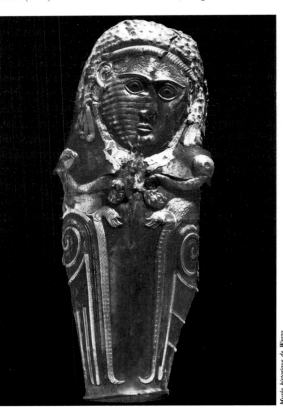

Celtic head from Msecké Zehrovice, near Prague, Czechoslovakia

This stone head, probably from a sanctuary, is typical of the art of the eastern Celts of the 2nd or 1st century BC: the shapes of the forehead, cheeks and chin are simplified and rounded; the bands of hair, the ears, the neck, the globular eyes are sculpted in relief; the eyebrows and the moustache end in curls. The torque around the neck, with its ball-shaped ends, is a feature to be found throughout the Celtic world: this ornament has been considered to be in tribute to a hero or a divinity. Height: 25cm (9.8in). Prague Museum.

The lady from Elche, near Alicante, Spain

This stone sculpture, which still shows traces of polychrome decoration, is regarded as one of the masterpieces of Iberian art in the 4th century BC. It combines an oriental inspiration, discernible in the abundance of jewellery, with a classical treatment of facial features. Iberian stone sculpture varies considerably: there are seated women such as the Lady of Baza (Granada), bearers of offerings like the one from Cerro de los Santos (Albacete), warriors and a flute player, as at Osuna (Seville), as well as variously stylized animals. Height: 56cm (22in). Madrid National Archaeological Museum.

Gallic gold stater coin of the Ambiani people, Picardy

Gallic coins are invaluable to the study of certain aspects of the economy of the various peoples who began to strike coins in the 2nd century BC, taking as a model the stater of Philip of Macedonia. These coins also demonstrate the originality of Celtic art: this gold stater from 30BC is an important example. To the left, on the front, the head of Philip is represented in a very free, decorative style; to the right, on the back, a galloping horse occupies most of the space, while its chariot is reduced to one wheel and the driver is represented by his fibula. Diameter: 2cm (.7in). Musée des Antiquités Nationales de Saint-Germain-en-Laye.

The protohistorical peoples of Europe

Writing first appeared in Greece at the end of the 2nd millennium BC, and from the middle of the first millennium it was used to record historical events or describe neighbouring peoples who had no writing at that time – the "barbarians". The names of some of these peoples are thus known to us at second-hand, through the accounts of Greek, and later Roman, geographers and historians. Through frequent economic and cultural contacts, the protohistorical peoples gradually acquired a knowledge of writing and became part of history. We can partly follow this evolution by comparing the results of archaeological investigation with the (sometimes scant) information supplied by the first ancient texts.

The classical world:
The archaeological background

The rediscovery of the classical world since the beginning of scientific archaeology in the 19th century was preceded by four centuries of exploration and study of the texts.

Since the end of the Middle Ages classical archaeology has gone through several periods, each marked by the predominance of one type of information: literary texts, works of art, sites and "material culture" have all had their day, entailing in every case a change in the approach to and perception of Graeco-Roman antiquity. As a result various disciplines were formed—philology and political history, the history of art and architecture, history of periods rather than events—and their coexistence was not always easy.

Apart from a few monuments that were still visible, and some artifacts found by chance, classical antiquity survived during the Middle Ages thanks to manuscripts. The work of Dante and Petrarch is evidence of this humanism which has always been a living feature of Italian culture. The fall of Constantinople in 1453 led to the exile in Italy of Greek intellectuals who brought manuscripts by classical authors with them. The great Greek authors, previously known only by partial and poor translations, were then restored to the front rank of culture. In Florence, Marsilio Ficino devoted his life to editing and commenting on Plato. In Venice the learned printer Aldus Manutius (Aldo Manuzio) embarked on the systematic publication of the Greek authors in 1494. His *Academia aldina*, the aim of which was to establish the best possible text from the manuscripts available to him, marked the birth of philological criticism.

The spread of humanism

From the beginning of the 16th century, the humanist movement spread to the rest of Europe. In France, François I, at the instigation of G. Budé, founded the Collège de France in 1530, its purpose being the study of antique texts. The literary movement of the *Pléiade* and Montaigne's *Essays* bear witness to the intensity of this humanism, which laid the foundations of subsequent classicism; for some three centuries culture was to be based on the knowledge of ancient texts that were constantly re-edited and commented on. From the 18th century the word philology was introduced to designate this technique of editing and commenting. At the same time a work of vulgarization destined to have a lasting success, *Voyage du jeune Anacharsis en Grèce* by the Abbé Barthelemy (1788) showed the benefit that could be drawn from literary sources for the knowledge of history, ideas and institutions, not to mention geography, mores and practical life. The fruit of 30 years of compilation, this work represents the peak of literary archaeology, although it was already being superseded by the study of works of art and monuments which began to give classical archaeology a more aesthetic and more concrete orientation.

With the upsurge of philological archaeology in the Quattrocento, the first collections of antique objects were not slow in making their appearance in Italy. For example, Pope Paul II (1464–71) assembled a collection of small objects, while Poggio Bracciolini (1380–1459) laid his hands on antiquities from as far afield as Greece and, like a modern Cicero, installed them in his Tuscan villa to decorate what he called his "Academy". Thus Italy was the first country to exhibit two types of collection which were to develop and spread throughout Europe before the appearance of the great museums, each giving birth to a different kind of architecture: on the one hand, the cabinet, successor of the 14th-century *studiolo*, in which small valuable objects were installed, as in the Medici Palace at Florence, in 1492. On the other, the villa where sculptures were an essential feature of the "antique" atmosphere, as at Rome with the Villa Madama, the work of Raphael. A more ambitious treatment, reserved for the great, was the sculpture gallery, the prototype of

which was created at Fontainebleau (1528–40) and imitated in the Farnese Palace in Rome, the Uffizi in Florence, the ducal palace of Mantua, and other places etc. All these "atmospheric" collections (the most celebrated is in the Belvedere in the Vatican) were accessible to connoisseurs. Thus Flavio Biondo was able to embark on the reconstruction of antiquity from collected objects in his *Roma Triumphans* (1457–59). In 1510 Francesco Albertini published (in Latin) the first guide to the antiquities of Rome *Opusculum de Mirabilibus novae et veteris Urbis Romae*, the second volume of which was devoted to statues and paintings. But the first real catalogue did not appear until the 17th century, that of the Giustiniani collection at Rome (1628–31). At the same time, the Earl of Arundel, an English aristocrat, assembled the first collection of objects coming exclusively from Greece (now in the Ashmolean Museum, Oxford).

The importance of Winckelmann

The zenith of this dilettante consumption of "antiques" collected in a haphazard way was at the end of the 17th and in the 18th century, with a series of great compilations such as the *Thesaurus antiquitatum graecarum* by J. Gronovius (13 volumes, Leyden, 1696–1701) and its Roman counterpart by G. Graevius (12 volumes, Utrecht, 1694–99). Between 1716 and 1724 the Benedictine monk Bernard de Montfaucon (1655–1741), who lived in Italy from 1698 to 1701, published *L'Antiquité expliquée et représentée en figures* (10 volumes, 40,000 illustrations) which sold 1,800 copies in two months. Similarly, the Comte de Caylus (1692–1765), a "cantankerous and abrupt antiquary" according to Diderot, published his *Recueil d'Antiquités* in seven volumes (1752–67). Curious rather than scholarly, more interested in methods of manufacture than aesthetic ideas, Caylus, whose enormous collection enriched the Cabinet de Medailles in the Bibliothèque nationale (Paris), was the antithesis of J.J. Winckelmann* (1717–68), who sought to put an end to the chaos caused by the confusing zeal and myopia of the "antiquaries". Even if he had no influence on the establishment of the collection of Cardinal A. Albani (1692–1779), nor its installation in the famous Villa Albani (1746–58) which was the culmination of pre-museum architecture, it was mainly in contact with the 677 sculptures collected there that Winckelmann worked out the aesthetic system he put forward in his *History of Ancient Art (Geschichte der Kunst des Alterthums)*, 1764, a work of capital importance because it marked the emergence of a genuine history of antique art with the first attempt at a chronology *raisonné* and a principle of iconographic interpretation: the mythological significance of every antique work. Winckelmann's work was to have great influence on 19th century thinkers on history, anthropology and archaeology, summarized in his famous doctrine that the phases of "art" in the broadest sense could be divided into the necessary, the beautiful and the decadent: civilization itself was often made to fall into this pattern.

Winckelmann was the reason why the German school, predominant until World War II, favoured for 150 years an aesthetic approach to Graeco-Roman civilization based mainly on the study of sculpture which was considered as the major art of antiquity. The refinement of stylistic criticism, encouraged by finds made in Greece from the mid-19th century, put an end to the neoclassical, idealistic point of view which made Athenian classicism the high point of Greek art. Thus the different periods of Greek and Roman art appeared in all their individuality, and from then on the originality of regional styles in all periods was recognized. Since World War II, the new appreciation

Bibliothèque nationale, Paris

View of the "Temple of Ilissos" at Athens

An engraving illustrating the *Antiquities of Athens* (Vol. 1, 1761; chap. II, pl. I). The extremely accurate drawings made by J. Stuart and N. Revett between 1751 and 1753 are the only documents enabling us to study this small Ionic temple, probably dedicated to Artemis Agrotera *c.*435BC. It was destroyed in 1778 to provide materials for building, as was the bridge (built between AD140 and AD144) visible in the background on the right.

of the 7th century and the Hellenistic period owes much to the consideration of social and technical factors which has anchored aesthetic criticism in history. Thus the history of ancient art, far from being fossilized, continues to develop when stimulated by the increase in fieldwork.

Naturally enough, the enthusiasm for antique objects led to their systematic research, firstly in Italy and then in Greece and the Near East. As the result of chance finds, some limited excavations took place in Italy, starting in the 16th century, but it was with the discovery of the classical villas, buried in the eruption of Vesuvius in AD79, that the era of excavation really began. Herculaneum was explored from 1738 to 1766 and Pompeii from 1748. Here again the main concern was to find artifacts, because the excavations were filled in as soon as the buildings had been stripped of their paintings and furniture. The Museo Ercolanese (1750) of Portici was the first museum associated with an archaeological site; and the eight volumes of the *Antichità di Ercolano* (1757–92), which played a decisive part in the formation of the neoclassical style, was the first publication of an excavation, although still confined to artifacts.

In the Ottoman empire, to which the whole of the Greek sphere belonged until 1830, excavations were preceded by a long period of exploration and rediscovery. Many travellers who passed through the classical east from medieval times to the 19th century, were curious about antiquities. Among these the earliest was an Italian businessman, the Pope's agent in the Aegean, Cyriacus of Ancona (1391–1455) who described and drew the antiquities he came across during his travels. As from the end of the 17th century travel books became more numerous, but the inadequacy of their illustrations reduced their value. As a result, the Dilettante Society, an aristocratic club founded in London in 1733, financed a team of architects and draughtsmen to compile the complete graphic dossier of a major site in the Orient. In this way, the excellent volumes of the *Antiquities of Athens* appeared from 1761 to 1816. They were the work of J. Stuart and N. Revett, who stayed in Greece from 1751 to 1754. A similar though less accurate work was done by Piranesi for the Greek temples of Paestum (1777), followed by W. Wilkins, *Antiquities of Magna Grecia* (1807), and extended to Sicily by J.I. Hittorff (1827). At a time when, following Winckelmann, the distinction between the art of Greece and of Rome was being established in detail, European scholars found that they had a repertory of still visible Greek buildings at their disposal. Thanks to this resurgence of Greek architecture, neoclassicism, originally neo-Roman (or, rather, neo-Campanian), became neo-Greek.

Archaeological plunderers

The curiosity thus aroused could no longer be satisfied with ruins that were still visible. The first excavations of the Forum were carried out in Rome from 1803 to 1817; in Athens from 1801 to 1803 Lord Elgin, British ambassador in Constantinople, removed sculptures and blocks of architecture from the Acropolis, and these were bought by the British Museum in 1816. A little later, a group of English, German and Danish philhellenes, excavating at their own expense, discovered and removed the pediments of the temple of Aphaia at Aegina in 1811, and in 1812 the frieze of the temple of Apollo at Phigalia (Bassae). The pediments, restored by the neoclassical sculptor Thorwaldsen, were bought by King Ludwig I of Bavaria, who was then engaged in founding the Glyptothek at Munich, and the Bassae frieze came into the possession of the British Museum. This predatory archaeology, encouraged in Greece by the indifference of the Turkish authorities, was matched in Etruria by the

unscrupulous exploration of Etruscan burial grounds (Tarquinia in 1827, Vulci in 1828) which brought to light tens of thousands of Greek, mainly Attic vases from the 6th and 5th centuries BC, thus revealing a new field of Greek art. The transfer of artifacts and even whole monuments to the great European museums, such as the monument of the Nereids of Xanthos to the British Museum, or the great altar of Pergamum to Berlin, only came to a halt with the formation of national states in Greece (1832), Italy (1860) and Turkey (1920).

During the last third of the 19th century, the excavations of the burial ground of Ceramica at Athens (1863–1913) and the sanctuary of Olympia by E. Curtius (1875–81) marked the beginning of stratigraphy.* Thus site archaeology ceased to be a search for objects, or the disclosure of monumental ruins to become a historical discipline. The acquisition and mastery of this new dimension were very slow. The excavations by H. Schliemann* at Troy and Mycenae, and even those of Evans at Knossos, which pushed the history of the Aegean back a thousand years by revealing the Mycenaean and Cretan civilizations, suffered from not having, or not satisfactorily applying, this method. As a result there were big chronological mistakes and enigmas that were almost impossible to resolve. The excavation of the *agora* at Athens by the American School of Archaeology from 1931, on the other hand, shows in an exemplary way the historical knowledge that stratigraphy helps to win from a site whose monumental interest is limited because of its dereliction.

New approaches to classical archaeology

The increasingly detailed work of excavation has gradually turned public interest towards social and economic history. Since World War II the archaeology of culture has given way to an archaeology of society in which the study of the habitat, everyday objects, coinage, etc., is of prime importance. To deal with these new categories of frequently repetitive and abundant material, during the last 15 years techniques of documentary analysis have appeared, making use of the latest developments in data processing. At the same time new methods of investigation (aerial photography, magnetic or resistivity surveys) make possible a preliminary X-ray of the ground. In addition, various physico-chemical methods of analysis identify the place of origin of raw materials and hence commercial trends. Lastly, recourse to disciplines such as anthropology or palynology,* long used by prehistoric archaeology, is beginning to reveal the ecology of the Graeco-Roman civilization. Thus there is a fourth phase, serial and technological, which is now beginning in the evolution of classical archaeology, at a time when the traditional primacy of the latter is challenged by the success of other archaeologies. These, exploring as they do other spaces and other times with new methods, seem more attractive and fertile to contempory culture.

Challenged from without, Graeco-Roman archaeology is also challenged from within. There are lively polemics between the supporters of the new social quantitative archaeology and the upholders of traditional archaeology, oriented to literary sources, artifacts and monuments. If this dissension causes a lasting separation it would be a symptom of decline. However the way in which classical archaeology has succeeded in the past in absorbing new methods and points of view suggests that the current dispute can be overcome, provided that the classical archaeologists try to live up to the status of their privilege—that of studying a civilization, which in richness of artifacts, texts, images, sites and monuments, as well as commercial and industrial products, remains unequalled.

Neolithic figurines: idols or toys?

The problem of interpreting the function of any object from a prehistoric society becomes all the more acute when archaeologists and anthropologists suspect a "ritual" use. But how do they come to such a conclusion?

Fertility idols? Images of divinity? Primitive means of communication? Or simply children's toys like our dolls? The role played by Neolithic figurines in primitive society is not easily understood and old controversies about their purpose keep recurring. Recent discoveries at the palace of Knossos in Crete and new arguments make it a topical issue once again, and bring into question our whole conception of prehistoric peoples. Are these figurines expressions of early metaphysical concepts or simply representations based on everyday life?

The records themselves are numerous. Throughout the Neolithic period, from the Near East to Central Europe, excavations over the years have revealed thousands of anthropomorphic terracotta figurines, all of a height rarely exceeding 15cm (6in). This is also the case in Greece and the Balkans: the external appearance of the figurines, with painted and incised designs sometimes depicting anatomical details and clothing, or sometimes purely decorative, echo motifs found on ceramics and other objects discovered in these regions.

Two definite tendencies emerge. In many cases a naturalistic technique predominates with the masculine or feminine figure clearly recognizable. He or she is standing, with legs apart, arms folded on the chest and the facial features shown. In other examples, the subject is treated stylistically. The figure is still standing, but its sexual characteristics are not apparent, the legs are not distinguished, the limbs are sometimes atrophied and the facial features are missing. Often the figurine combines stylistic and naturalistic characteristics. Finally, the posture sometimes varies, especially when the figure is portrayed seated, perhaps the sign of an already established sexual discrimination, since the use of a stool or chair is generally reserved for men, whereas women are usually seated modestly on the ground.

The case for the Mother Goddess

According to a theory originating in the last century and strongly supported for some 50 years, these figurines had a religious significance. They represented the Mother Goddess, a divinity revered, it is thought, by prehistoric peoples over a wide area from the Paleolithic era onwards, and effectively demonstrated historically in Mesopotamia, Anatolia and Greece. There are two essential arguments in support of this: the sexual characteristics of the figurines are very strongly emphasized, and the majority of them are female. Thus the extreme importance attached to fertility found expression, whether it was the fertility of men, cattle or the soil. In some cases, it might even be possible to identify a complete collection of gods, a veritable pantheon, based on the diversity of the figurines.

But today, constant repetition of the theory and the systematic reference to authority no longer suffice to conceal the lack of archaeological confirmation. In fact, the most recent and most accurate studies, at Knossos in particular, have shown that the religious interpretation was based on incomplete observations and hasty conclusions. The exaggeration of sexual characteristics may have an explanation other than religious, for example, the basic desire to designate certain figurines as feminine (or masculine) with the utmost clarity, and to distinguish them from the others. Moreover, it is not true that the majority of figurines are feminine. In Crete, for example, they represent only 37 percent of the total, whereas masculine figurines make up 9 percent, asexual figurines 41 percent and unidentifiable figurines 13 percent. It is possible to claim that the male figurine is the exception, or to consider that it represents the *paredros* or companion of the Mother Goddess, or simply to ignore it; but it is harder to ignore the asexual figurines, or class them with the feminine figurines. But the most obvious weakness of the religous theory is that no positive argument really requires us to adopt it. It is often claimed that the figurines were found in cult sites, but as cult sites are defined by the presence of the figurines, this argument is circular.

The toy theory

In reality, most observations lead in a quite different direction. If we regroup the anthropomorphic figurines with the zoomorphic figurines, the miniature buildings and miniature objects, we see that they form a whole with homogeneous characteristics. All these objects are distinguished by a summary and rapid method of manufacture. They represent, in miniature, objects and beings that are not only real but familiar, and they offer the same diversity as the real world. Nevertheless, they are often difficult to identify with precision. Significant details are missing, animal species are poorly distinguished from each other, the sex of anthropomorphic figurines is often indistinguishable. But since the sex is very clearly indicated in others, we must conclude that where it is not, it was because the maker did not want to do so. In other words, he sought to make the figurine ambiguous by allowing it to represent either sex. Finally, all these objects were found in dwellings or in their immediate vicinity. They are usually quite well preserved; moreover, in Thessaly, Macedonia and the Balkans, they are often found on a platform built near a kiln. They are always accompanied by everyday objects such as millstones, grinders and crockery. When they are found outside houses, it is usually in refuse tips. Then they are often broken and that is obviously why they had been thrown away.

Miniature depictions of various familiar realities, reduced to essentials so that they remain ambiguous, placed on the floor of houses in the midst of evidence of everyday life—all this suggests children's toys. This idea is certainly not new, but it is time to take it seriously, for other arguments support it. Children's toys have always drawn their inspiration from the adult world—utensils, furniture, houses and people are transposed to a reduced scale. Moreover, toys are not all imbued with a specific significance. Even when there are more feminine than masculine figurines, as in the Neolithic period, there are an equally large number of ambivalent examples. Other archaeological and historical evidence confirms the probability of the toy theory: the presence of figurines and models in children's tombs of the Bronze Age and historical periods, ancient texts describing Greek and Roman children's games, and so on. Finally, comparative ethnological studies suggest that, even if not all the figurines were toys, the majority of them fulfilled that function.

Nevertheless, not all the problems are solved. We do not know who made the figurines or on what occasion. We know nothing about other functions they may have fulfilled—and there seems to be no doubt that they did so. It is also hard to explain why they virtually disappear after the Late Bronze Age. But the hypothesis now under consideration seems to tally better with archaeological observations than does the religious interpretation. It gives us a glimpse of the daily life of prehistoric peoples—and suggests that fundamentally their way of life already bore some points of resemblance to our own.

Masculine figurine from Sesklo, Thessaly. Middle Neolithic

From the beginning of the Neolithic period, a minority of masculine figurines existed alongside the asexual, indeterminate, but probably feminine figurines. Difficult to interpret in the framework of a religious theory, they are clearly distinguishable from the other groups. Their sexual characteristics are unmistakable and some of them are, in addition, ithyphallic. The Sesklo figurine is an example of the latter and represents a personage seated on a stool, with hands on knees. His abdomen exhibits a broad fold and his legs are conjoined with the front legs of the stool. The feminine figurines are generally represented seated on the ground (see opposite page).

Head of figurine from Dikili Tash, eastern Macedonia. Late Neolithic

Facial features are in general understated on such figurines, and may often be barely suggested. Sometimes, by contrast, the eyes, nose, mouth and ears are indicated. But apparently they were never intended as realistic portraits. However, some heads, like this one, are of a particular type: almond-shaped eyes, flattened head and pierced ears, probably to hold a ring. It is conceivable that they represent a specific divinity or a clearly defined human type. More probably they reflect aesthetic conventions of the period.

House at Sabatinovka, Soviet Moldavia. Late Neolithic (Scale approximately 1/50.)

This model of a house, from the Cucuteni-Tripolye culture, was recovered at Sabatinovka in the valley of the southern Bug. It comprises a certain number of characteristic elements which figure on the diagram, right: 1) a stone pavement serving as a threshold; 2) a circular earthen hearth; 3) a rectangular earthen platform; 4) an earthen seat; 5) a series of terracotta figurines.

There are about 20 figurines, mostly grouped on the platform, only a few being scattered on the ground or even outside the entrance. This suggests that a sanctuary is represented, with the natural conclusion that the seat and the hearth have a ritual function. However, if we except the figurines, the building differs little from normal dwellings. It is built in the same way, of cob on a framework of wooden posts and wattling; it has a similar floor of beaten earth; it is of a similar rectangular shape and contains the usual fixtures such as hearth and platform. So it may be more reasonable to regard it as a dwelling like any other, where the household tasks, especially the preparation of food, took place close to the hearth and the platform. The latter could have had many uses during the day, and at night served as a bed. If this is so, the figurines may simply be toys and their presence inside a dwelling hardly needs justification. In that case, one would expect to find them on the floor and in the places where children play. In this respect, the platform, close to the source of heat and the zone of maternal activity, offers a particularly striking example. After M. Gimbutas, "Figurines of Old Europe (6500–3500BC)" in *The Religions of Prehistory*, Edizioni del Centro Camuno, Capo di Ponte, 1975, fig. 60, p. 121.

Female figurine from the region of Ieropetra, eastern Crete. Late Neolithic

Representations of seated personages increase in the last phase of the Neolithic period, but models of women are nearly always seated on the ground. However, this celebrated example exhibits certain peculiarities: small head on a long neck, hands on hips, underdeveloped breasts and abdomen. The whole of the lower part of the body, on the other hand, is characterized by its impressive proportions. This may suggest a cult of fertility, but the relative insignificance of the breasts hardly fits in with that hypothesis. Might it not be the case that the shape of the figurine is due simply to a concern for ensuring its stability? Museum of Iraklion, Giamalkis collection.

TAP Service, Athens

Zoomorphic figurines from Dikili Tash, eastern Macedonia. Late Neolithic

Zoomorphic figurines occur less frequently than anthropomorphic ones, but they are far from rare in Neolithic habitations. Normally they represent familiar animals, such as those reared by the group as well as animals of the chase. But it is generally quite difficult to recognize a particular species, especially in the most numerous group, which consists of quadrupeds. One explanation of this fact might be a supposed inability on the part of the Neolithic peoples to render anatomical details in realistic fashion. But we might equally well ask whether this lack of clarity was not deliberate; one object can thus represent, at will, a number of different creatures, requiring only an identifying accessory or a simple act of imagination to give it form. As for the figurines, which like these, are ambiguous, they may pose an additional problem; but they may equally well have been conceived to be ambiguous from the start.

G. Vassianos

The end of the Minoan civilization

Dramatic discoveries made since 1967 on the volcanic island of Santorini, north of Crete, seemed at one time to confirm the "catastrophic" theory put forward to explain the decline of the mighty Minoan civilization. However, recent scientific work has cast doubt on this, suggesting manmade rather than natural causes.

The destruction of the Cretan palaces has intrigued archaeologists and historians for many years. What cause could have been abrupt and general enough to explain the complete disappearance of a civilization as brilliant as the Minoan* (*c*.3000–1100BC)? Was the last great eruption of the volcano of Santorini the cause, or was it due to a human cause — war, invasion or foreign occupation? The question remains, but recent research has enabled the experts to formulate it more accurately than in the past, and to discern new possibilities.

The starting point of the problem is the observed phase of destruction in Crete. At a certain moment in the Late Bronze Age, generalized destructions seem to have affected not only the secondary palaces in Crete (with the exception of the palace of Knossos), but also the houses on the island as a whole. All the dwellings and palaces in central and eastern Crete, at Phaistos, Amnisos, Mallia, Gournia, Pseira, Mochlos and Zakros were destroyed—less is known about the west. Moreover, these destructions seem to have happened at much the same time. The stylistic development of ceramic decoration, as far as archaeology can retrace it, seems to have reached the same stage in each case. The "Floral" style which marks Late Minoan I and secondary Late Minoan is still present; the "Marine" style which characterizes Late Minoan Ib is much in evidence, and the "Palace" style which defines Late Minoan II is already present. So the destructions are attributed to Late Minoan Ib, and preferably towards the end of that era. That would correspond to an absolute dating* *c*.1470BC. These simultaneous destructions were also followed, it is thought, by the general abandonment of inhabited sites. The Late Minoan II era is entirely unrepresented by architectural remains and indeed is only recognizable in a very few places. It was not until the last phase of the Bronze Age, known as Late Minoan III, that certain sites experienced a limited reoccupation, whereas others remained deserted. At all events, the Minoan civilization disappeared.

The eruption of Santorini

Consequently, scholars have long been seeking an explanation which accounts for the simultaneous destruction and, above all, the abandonment of towns and houses. The eruption of the volcano of Santorini seemed to be a possible cause. The morphology of the islands in the Santorini group, and the stratigraphy* legible in their cliffs, enable scientists to retrace the unfolding of a very violent eruption which, in a short time, literally vaporized a volcanic dome four times larger than that of Krakatoa (Indonesia) in the second half of the 2nd millennium BC. In 1939, the Greek archaeologist Spyridon Marinatos put forward the idea that this eruption was the cause of the catastrophes in Crete. In 1967, while excavating the site of Akrotiri on Santorini, he found confirmation of something his predecessors

had caught a glimpse of in 1870. A large and prosperous town with a brilliant culture had been buried there beneath metre upon metre of pumice stone and ashes produced by the eruption.

But this very discovery led him to modify his original theory. For the destruction of Akrotiri proved to be earlier—in stylistic terms—than the events in Crete. It dated from Late Minoan Ia, and was earlier than the eruption, because the volcanic pumice and ashes had fallen on an already ruined town which "squatters" or teams of debris removers had begun to make habitable. As it was also hard to see how the eruption could have been the *direct* cause of the devastation in Crete, Marinatos suggested the following order of events: a) the destruction of Akrotiri by a preliminary earthquake in Late Minoan Ia (before 1500BC); b) the destruction of Cretan habitations by a second earthquake in Late Minoan Ib (*c*.1470BC); c) the abandonment of these habitations as a result of the eruption (*c*.1470–1450BC).

An explanation for the abandonment still had to be found, and a tidal wave and rain of ashes seemed to be the only possible solutions. As regards the first, observations made in 1883 during the eruption of Krakatoa had shown the reality and far-reaching effects of the phenomenon. So there could be no doubt that on Santorini, too, a formidable tidal wave had been produced and that it had inevitably caused tremendous damage, possibly over a wide area. But a tidal wave moves in a given direction; nothing in any other direction is affected, and even obstacles in the way of its movement are unaffected if the wave finds a way round. A tidal wave starting from Santorini could destroy the dwellings on the north coast of Crete (Amnisos, Mallia, Gournia, Pseira), but it could not possibly have reached Palaikastro or Zakros on the east coast, nor Phaistos on the south coast. It also does not explain the abandonment of inhabited places in the regions where it did cause damage. Even after the eruption of Krakatoa, the grass on the coasts of the Sunda Strait had grown again in a month, and life very quickly resumed.

A rain of volcanic ash, on the other hand, could have interrupted this. Ashes could be carried far away from the volcano by the wind, falling in a thick layer, killing cattle with ash-induced fluorosis, making the land infertile and thus causing famine. This is what happened in Iceland after the eruption of Laki in 1783–84. So a population could be forced to abandon its lands. Volcanic ash similar to that from Santorini has been found in Crete from Knossos to Zagros and on the surrounding seabed, proving that there was definitely an enormous cloud of ash that moved towards the southeast and spread across Crete and the sea around it, and agricultural production must have suffered as a result.

Thus various features seem to support Marinatos's theory. Yet other obstacles remain. First, it is difficult to attribute all the destruction in Crete to one single

earthquake, as it would have had to affect structurally distinct regions at the same time, which is most unlikely. Nor is it obvious that we should accept wholesale the chronological system underlying all the hypotheses. In spite of the authority of Sir Arthur Evans* who imposed it, it has no stratigraphic* foundation. On the contrary, wherever accurate observations are available, it is noted that the three pottery styles are present in the same layers. So we should very probably conclude that they are more or less contemporary. Yet if that is so, it follows that there was no Late Minoan II phase and consequently no abandonment. The occupation of Late Minoan I was followed by that of Late Minoan III. Scientists are also uncertain about the dating of the rain of ash. In effect, the presence of such ash in Late Minoan I levels does not give a date, but a *terminus post quem* or chronological point of departure. They could equally well have been deposited at a later period and then have been carried down by water to the underlying layer where we find them today.

So the problem of the destruction remains unresolved. But if we exclude the hypothesis of an earthquake, a tidal wave or a rain of ash (for this would not destroy buildings), we still have to find a cause which explains the number of destructions by fire at virtually the same time. Some archaeologists have discounted the idea of a war or an invasion because it would presumably have been contrary to the interests of an enemy to have destroyed so many living areas. But what invader is stopped by calculations of that kind? And what do we know of his real interests? In fact, war is still the best explanation of the generalized destruction, and invasion the best explanation of the end of the Minoan culture. Since we know that at the time of the destruction of the secondary palaces, the Mycenaeans had installed themselves at Knossos and exercised their hegemony over the whole of Crete, as archives in Linear B prove, it seems likely that they established that hegemony by an invasion and military occupation of the island. If it really was the Mycenaeans, was it not in their interest to destroy all the rival centres?

So many scholars would now see no direct connection between the Thera eruption and the destruction of Cretan palaces in the late 15th century BC. In fact, it is now increasingly believed that the Minoan decline occurred through internal causes, and Crete was overrun by mainlanders at the end of Late Minoan Ib. New evidence for manmade destruction at the end of Late Minoan Ib, found in 1980 at the site of the stratigraphical museum outside the palace of Knossos, indicates that a group of buildings had been burned down — following what appeared to the excavator to be a child sacrifice. After this, Knossos and a number of other sites in central Crete were occupied, and in some cases partly rebuilt, by mainland conquerors who spoke Greek. Knossos was finally destroyed *c*.1200BC.

Vase with floral decoration found at Akrotiri, Santorini

This vase was found in the ruins of the town of Akrotiri, outside a building. It has been compared to a flowerpot, and has an unusual feature that may indicate a religious function: the upper part is formed as a hollow dish with a convex bottom, closed except for a small opening in the centre. But in fact its exact function is not known. The painted decoration depicts lilies on the point of wilting: the flowers are drooping and beginning to fall. This is an unusual aspect of a common theme, for the respresentation of flowers is common in Cretan pottery. The presence and frequency of floral themes enabled archaeologists to date the destruction of Akrotiri to Late Minoan Ia. National Museum of Athens.

Small basin with marine decoration, found at Akrotiri, Santorini

A series of small basins, long and narrow like this example, have been found in the ruins of Akrotiri. Their function remains completely unknown, but great care was devoted to their brown and red painted decoration. Moreover, on this example the polychrome effect is accentuated by white highlights which emphasize the bodies of the animals and the rim of the receptacle. On one side the decoration consists of dolphins playing together above a conventional marine ground framed by seaweed. On the other side, four-footed beasts are galloping through a landscape full of flowers. The frequency of marine decoration characterizes pottery from the phase of the great destructions in Crete (Late Minoan Ib).

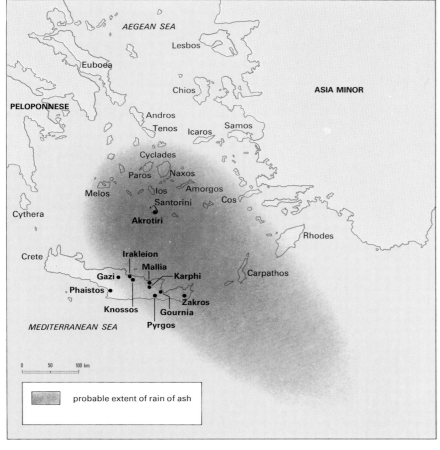

Probable extent of the rain of ash caused by the eruption of the volcano of Santorini

Core samples taken in various parts of Crete and in the surrounding sea have revealed deposits of volcanic ash from one of the great eruptions of the volcano of Santorini, probably the last, datable to the second half of the 2nd millennium BC. By contrast, at other points further away from the volcano the layer of ashes was missing. It has thus been possible to trace the probable extent of the cloud, and consequently the rain of ashes caused by the eruption. If this intepretation is correct, it is apparent that the wind was blowing from the northwest at the time of the eruption, a prevailing direction in the Aegean Sea, but its force must have been rather slight. Apparently the ashes were not carried more than 400 or 500km (248 or 310 miles), whereas in the case of Krakatoa (Indonesia) in 1883, rains of ash were observed 1600km (992 miles) from the volcano. However, the Santorini rain of ash could have been enough to cause a famine in central and eastern Crete.

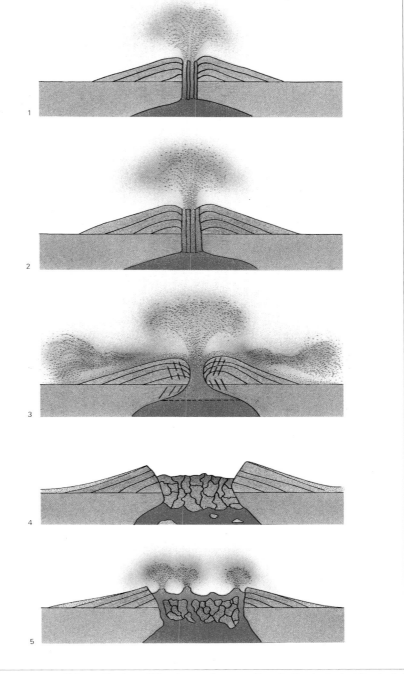

Schematic view of the stages of an eruption similar to that at Santorini

The initial phases (1 and 2) of the eruption have the effect of emptying most of the interior of the volcanic dome: the magma inside is volatilized in the form of very fine vitrified particles, some of which fall back into the volcano itself, while the rest are carried away by the wind (see map). At the same time, however, the walls of the dome lose their support (3). They therefore collapse and form a much larger crater (4), the bottom of which is blocked. As the pressure of the magma begins to build up again, it filters through this blockage and leaps up to the surface (5) in the form of small craters (the Kamenes or burnt islands) in the middle of the great one (the circle outlined by the islands of Thera, Therasia and Aspronisi). Further minor eruptions may then take place. After D. Page, *The Santorini Volcano and the destruction of Minoan Crete*, The Society for the Promotion of Hellenic Studies, London, 1970, fig. 10, p. 17.

The ruins of the town of Gournia, Crete

Situated in eastern Crete on the southern shore of the gulf of Mirabello, the Minoan town of Gournia was almost completely excavated at the beginning of the century. It was located on a low hill, and founded at the end of the Early Minoan or beginning of the Middle Minoan. However, the beginning of the Late Minoan, the period of the second palaces, saw its biggest expansion. Served by an intricate network of alleyways and paved flights of steps, like those of a present day village, the houses clung to the slopes, and the remains indicate that craft activities were practised there. A more important building on top of the hill may well have been a palace. The street which runs alongside it, and which is shown here, is the widest in the town. The destruction, dated as elsewhere to Late Minoan Ib, was due to a fire, clear traces of which have been found.

Female terracotta statuette from Gazi, Crete

This is a type of female statuette characteristic of Late Minoan III. The upper part of the body, treated with comparative realism, contrasts with the lower part, reduced to a cylinder formed by a bell-shaped skirt. Both hands are raised. A small number of similar statuettes at Gazi, Karphi, and Gournia are known, but this example, which is 75cm (30in) high, is one of the only examples with poppy heads attached to the coiffure. It is generally supposed that all these features carry a religious interpretation. They demonstrate, in any case, the changes that Cretan civilization underwent after the destruction of the second palaces. Museum of Iráklion, No. 9305.

Princely burials

Since the sensational finds made by Heinrich Schliemann at Mycenae in 1876, burials have continued to be one of the key sources for early Greek society. Recent discoveries have only emphasized the extraordinary continuity of burial customs.

If the traces of life revealed by archaeology are often tenuous and enigmatic, the traces of death are generally plentiful and eloquent, revealing details of physical appearance, social status, beliefs and preferences. Hence tombs are the great and sometimes the only resource of the archaeologist. This applies equally to Greek civilization, regardless of the variety of documentary sources available. Since World War II, some spectacular finds have confirmed the astonishing persistence in the Greek world of a funerary ritual which for a long time was known only from the text of Homer.

The discovery at Mycenae in 1876 of a group of extraordinarily rich tombs ("Circle A") marked an important stage in our knowledge of early Greek antiquity. In the enthusiasm of his discovery, H. Schliemann,* whose guiding principle was complete reliance on Homer's text, thought he had found the tomb of the most glorious of the Atrides*, Agamemnon, leader of the Achaean coalition at the time of the expedition against Troy (c.1200BC). In fact, continuation of the excavation has shown that "Circle A" is older than this by some four centuries.

The continuing study of a second group of tombs ("Circle B"), found in 1952, has made it possible to complete Schliemann's often inadequate observations. The dead, whose age averaged 38 years, were generally extended on the gravel floor at the bottom of rectangular pits. Their faces were sometimes covered with a gold mask; precious objects and weapons were placed near them; the women wore jewels. Each pit contained two, three or even four dead bodies, men and women. Objects and human remains were sometimes unceremoniously disturbed to make room for a new corpse. These tombs are marked externally by a mound, sometimes bearing a stone stele ornamented with decorative or figurative motifs, carved or painted, foreshadowing the Archaic tombs of a millennium later, although we cannot assume a direct connection between them.

Even if we observe certain constants between the 2nd and 1st millennia, the collapse of Mycenaean civilization c.1150BC marks an important break in Greek history and relegates the previous period to an epic past. Thus, the Trojan War, an episode of which is told in the *Iliad*, is a historical fact of the Mycenaean* period, depicted in the social and material setting of the Geometric* period (1100–700BC). It is surprising that Schliemann did not notice this flagrant distortion when he thought that his finds at Mycenae tallied with the text of Homer, because the aristocratic funerary customs mentioned in the *Iliad* are very different from those he was in a position to observe during his excavations at Mycenae. In Chapter 23 of the *Iliad*, the body of Patroclus is burnt at night on top of a huge pyre on which Achilles sacrificed 4 horses, 2 dogs and 12 Trojan

prisoners; at dawn his ashes are collected in a gold urn which will be buried later under a tumulus. For a long time, experts were unwilling to see more in this grandiose scene than a literary vision having little connection with actual burial practices, but recent archaeological information continues to confirm the practice, at least for the funerals of notables: kings, chiefs of clans and aristocrats from the Geometric period to the beginning of the Hellenistic* period.

Cult of the hero

The extraordinary monument found at Lefkandi in Euboea in August 1981 proved to be a *heróon** or heroic cult site, dating to about 950BC. Two adjoining pits 2.75m (9ft) deep were also found there. The skeletons of four horses rested in one of them, while the other concealed a bronze amphora containing the ashes of the deceased, wrapped in a very well-preserved long linen tunic. Near this cinerary urn lay the extended skeleton of a woman adorned with gold jewellery, her feet and hands crossed as if they had been bound; a dagger with an ivory handle and an iron blade near her head indicated that she might have been ritually sacrificed, perhaps the first archaeologically attested example of human sacrifice in the Greek world. Undoubtedly she was the wife of the chief who had been "heroized"*. For some unknown reason, this cult site was suddenly interrupted and the structure buried under a tumulus.

Another *heróon* discovered in 1965 at Eretria to the south of Lefkandi dates to the beginning of the 7th century BC and exhibits the same ritual. The "hero" of tomb 6 was cremated and his ashes, wrapped in a cloth, were placed in a bronze basin which was buried. The disappearance after barely a century of this aristocratic cult, devoted to a warrior chief around whom certain members of his clan were buried, was possibly due to the decline in feudal society when it was supplanted by new classes of farmer-soldiers and merchants.

At roughly the same period (end of 8th to beginning of 7th century), a tomb of Salamis in Cyprus (No 79) indicates that, at the beginning of the late Archaic period, the local ruling class was still attached to the great Greek feudal ritual, regardless of the strong influence of neighbouring oriental civilizations. The luxury objects buried with the dead are of Egyptian or Syrian origin or inspiration, but the ritual is still "Homeric". The site was a chamber tomb approached by a vast sloping esplanade. The chamber itself was looted in the 19th century, but excavation of the entrance (*dromos*) in 1966 revealed that it had been used twice in succession. The finds included two pairs of bigae,* the horses of which, superbly harnessed in the Assyrian fashion, had been immolated; two large bronze cauldrons, made locally but with marked oriental influence on the decor; and precious objects of

Egyptian type. Amphorae piled in a corner, and fragments of fish and chickens, indicate that a great banquet was held to end the funeral ceremonies, as was the case in the *Iliad* after Hector's obsequies.

Nearly 500 years later, in 311BC, it was still the "Homeric" ritual which dictated the funeral homage paid to the last king of Salamis, Nicocreon, who perished with his family when his palace was burnt during the siege of the town by Ptolemy I (Diodorus XX, 21). All that was found beneath the tumulus was a vast mud brick platform, the centre of which was occupied by a pyre with various offerings lying in the ashes, and the remains of large clay portrait statues, which had been placed in cavities all round the pyre — undoubtedly likenesses of the royal family.

Thus, although the evolution of political institutions towards more representative regimes apparently put an end to such feudal funerary customs in Greece proper, we see them persist on the confines of the Greek world where personal power was retained. The example of Macedonia, now well known from the discoveries made since 1977 at Vergina (the ancient Aigai, first capital of the kingdom before Pella), confirms this in a striking manner. Here the tombs, buried beneath a tumulus, are large vaulted chambers, with stuccoed and painted façades drawing freely on Greek architecture for their inspiration. The ritual, on the other hand, is purely Greek. The members of the royal family were burnt and their ashes, wrapped in a cloth, were placed in a casket or vase around which objects belonging to the deceased were arranged. Above the vault of tomb II, which all the evidence suggests was the grave of Philip II, father of Alexander, were found the remains of a pyre collected there after the cremation of the body. The remains included calcined bones, two iron swords, parts of horses' harnesses and even a few gold tassels belonging to the crown placed in the cinerary urn. Altogether there was enough to show that horses, as well as humans, must have been sacrificed on the funeral pyre. Such burials, which were also provided for the aristocracy, judging by the many tombs with vaulted chambers that have been found, show how the Macedonian ruling class wished to assert its Greek ascendancy over the Greece of the city states, who looked on their northern cousins as country bumpkins.

So a "Homeric" funeral ceremonial, which bestowed a sacred aura on the heroized dead, was perpetuated until the beginning of the Hellenistic period. When we know the concern of these rulers to legitimize a power that had often originated in violence, there is no doubt that a ritual such as this, which sealed the princes' divinity, continued to be favoured by them.

Heróon of Lefkandi

Situated between Chalcis and Eretria, the two great Euboean cities, the settlement of Lefkandi (its classical name remains obscure) played an important role from the 2nd millennium until its disappearance c.700BC. Joint excavations by English and Greek archaeologists have shown its astonishing prosperity during the "Dark Ages" (1100–850BC) which followed the collapse of the Mycenaean civilization. The discovery of this building more than 45m (145ft) long confirmed this in a sensational manner, because it pushed back by some 150 years the date of monumental architecture in Greece, formerly attested only by the badly ruined buildings of Thermos and Samos (which also had an absidal plan). The walls, preserved in some places to a height of 1.50m (5ft), are of unbaked brick on a base of rubble, and faced with plaster internally. The roof was supported by a line of wooden columns resting on stone slabs, the floor being made of clay. With its tripartite division of internal space, this sacred building, soundly dated to 950BC, appears as the direct ancestor of the classical temples.

Tomb No 47 at Salamis Cyprus

This tomb is one of the largest at Salamis. In front of the burial chamber measuring 4 × 2.2m (13 × 7ft), looted in the 19th century, extends a paved esplanade 10.65 × 4.60m (34 × 15ft), reached by three steps from the inclined access ramp (dromos), 13.65m (43.6ft) wide by 20m (64ft) long, with a cemented surface. That is where the two horses harnessed to the burial chariot were sacrificed at the time of the first burial. A generation later, between 700 and 650BC, at the time of the second burial, six horses were sacrificed.

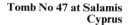

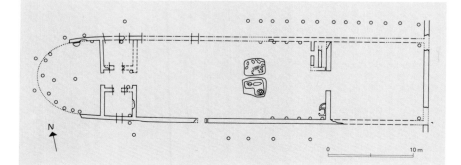

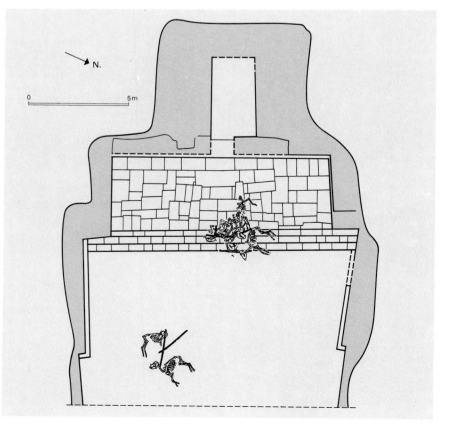

Objects from royal tomb No 2 at Vergina, Macedonia

This tomb with a vaulted chamber, the first to be found intact, contained the ashes of a man in the chamber and of a woman in the antechamber. In the gold coffin (*larnax*) containing the king's remains, archaeologists found a gold crown fashioned like 2 oak branches (above right) the most impressive example known to date, both for its weight (400gr) and the quality of its work. An assortment of the dead man's personal effects were piled up in a corner of the chamber (above): from left to right, a large bronze cauldron on an iron tripod; a magnificent openwork bronze dark lantern; behind it, a bronze tripod with an inscription indicating that it was a prize won at the games in honour of Hera at Argos, where the Macedonian dynasty came from; attached to the wall a bronze cover protecting a prestigious ceremonial buckler with gold, ivory and glass decoration, which took several years to restore; in front of it, three bronze containers with, in front, a sponge that was still supple; and to the right a Macedonian iron helmet with a curved crest resembling a Phrygian cap; resting against the wall a pair of bronze greaves and, further right, a hollow silver-gilt ring, perhaps the royal diadem; in the foreground another pair of greaves. The cinerary casket in the antechamber contained a big surprise: the ashes of the deceased had been wrapped in a very well-preserved fabric (right) on which delicate plant motifs had been woven in purple on a gold ground.

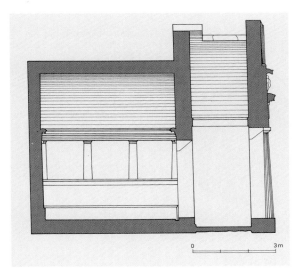

Great tomb of Lefcadia (Macedonia). Restored façade and section

This tomb, discovered in 1954, consists of a barrel-vaulted antechamber 6.50 × 2.12m (20.8 × 6.7ft) wide and *c.* 7.70m (24.6ft) high; and a narrower (4.80 × 4.72m/15.3 × 15.1ft) and lower (5.26m/16.8ft) chamber, the walls being broken up by pilasters marking off panels which are painted red. This early 3rd-centuryBC decoration foreshadows the trompe-l'oeil of Delian and Pompeiian houses, and so it seems that we should seek its origin in Macedonia itself rather than in Alexandria. The eccentricity of Macedonian taste gracefully combines with the functional elements of traditional Greek architecture to produce a striking decorative effect, and proclaims itself in the astonishing articulation of the façade, the superimposed orders of which are separated by a continuous frieze 1.21m (3.8ft) high, ornamented with stucco reliefs depicting a battle. Apart from the personages painted on the upper zone of the groundfloor between the columns (left, Death and Hermes; right, two judges of Hades), there is little to indicate the function of the building. The variegated decoration is a blind.

Scripts and writing in the Aegean world

When prehistoric writing was first found in Crete in the late 19th century, many scholars speculated that the island could be the "missing link" in the development of writing westwards from Sumeria. But how writing appeared in Crete and then Greece is still unclear.

Sumerian writing emerged in Mesopotamia towards the end of the 4th millennium BC. A few decades later Egyptian writing followed. Not until 1,000 years later did the first traces of writing appear in the Aegean world, and, until we have proof to the contrary, we should consider "Cretan hieroglyphic" and "Linear A" as original creations, independent of their predecessors. They were to remain in use for less than 500 years, but the latter was to survive in "Linear B" (which disappeared c.1200BC) and in the classical syllabary of Cyprus, which was used until the 3rd century BC, and coexisted in the last phase of its history with the Greek alphabet.

In conception and usage the Cretan scripts were much less complicated than Oriental ones, for they consisted of syllabaries, each using less than 100 signs to denote simple open syllables such as *ma, me, mi,* in order to form the word. Oriental scripts were logo-syllabic systems which made use of several hundred signs representing entire words or groups of sounds of varying complexity. The Greek script of the 1st millennium, of Phoenician origin, was even simpler: alphabetical, it had only about 20 signs, each representing one sound.

In Crete and on the Greek mainland, the discovery of these scripts goes back only one century, beginning with the work of Arthur Evans, who uncovered Minoan and Mycenaean civilizations. Discovery of scripts had occurred during excavations of the Minoan (Cretan) buildings of Knossos, Khanea, Mallia, Phaestos and Zakros on the one hand, and of the Mycenaean (Greek) palaces of Knossos, Pylos, Mycene, Thebes and Tyrins on the other. They are three in number, and consist of the following:
Cretan hieroglyphic script (traditionally so called with reference to Egyptian hieroglyphics) is attested throughout the period of the first Cretan palaces, c.1900–1625BC.
Linear A script (described as "linear" because the tracing of the signs seems less "graphic" or "realistic" than that of Cretan hieroglyphic) appeared around the 18th century BC and was used during the period of the second Cretan palaces, c.1625–1450BC.

Linear B script (called "B" because it was immediately seen to be closely related to the preceding script) was used in the Mycenaean, Greek-dominated period c.1450–1200BC. However, the first evidence of it goes back only to c.1375BC.

In Cyprus another offshoot of Linear A, Cypro-Minoan, was to develop from about the 16th century BC, although we cannot say exactly where or how it was adopted. This script continued until the 12th century BC, and was then perpetuated in the classical Cypriot syllabary into which the Greek writing was transcribed.

The present state of archaeological knowledge suggests that Linear A did not come from Cretan hieroglyphic, and it seems unlikely that these two systems would have been used to denote a single language. Although independent, they coexisted for about 200 years and they have been found together at least once in the same deposit, at Mallia. So it is more than likely that they had considerable mutual influence on each other.

On the other hand, Linear B certainly grew out of Linear A, becoming separate from the 16th century BC. The cause of this separation seems simple: Linear A, such as it was, did not seem adequate (for reasons unknown to us) to the Mycenaeans in the task of recording their language — which was Greek — so they modified it accordingly.

Surviving scripts and records

All that survives today of Cretan scripts certainly represents a tiny fraction of what must have been actually written. Only what was engraved on resistant materials such as stone, metal or pottery, or painted, mostly on clay vases, was eventually destined to survive. Thus, only 163 inscriptions in Cretan Hieroglyphic script, 86 in Linear A and 150 in Linear B have come down to us.

On the other hand, financial accounts inscribed on unhardened clay were never meant to survive; but many thousands of pieces have come down to us because they were baked during the destruction by fire of the buildings in which they were kept (this was the case with 3,400 tablets in Linear B in the Mycenaean Palace of Knossos and 1,100 in the palace of Pylos). They would

have suffered a different fate if they had not been written a few days or months before the destruction. The oldest tablets had already been eliminated, either because they were no longer useful, or because their contents had been copied onto a less fragile, lighter and less cumbersome material (for example papyrus), which was itself consumed in the flames. If there had been no fire, humidity and successive human occupations would have ensured the destruction of everything, unbaked clay and papyrus. Thus the last Minoan palace of Knossos, where "reoccupation" by the Mycenaeans c.1450BC was more or less peaceful, yielded only 8 clay documents, carrying a total of 53 signs in Linear A.

The destruction of written documentation was almost total. But what civilization really cares to communicate with posterity by handing down the media for communication? Baking has preserved some cuneiform* tablets, the desert climate some Egyptian papyri, stone, some Egyptian, Greek and Latin inscriptions. What will remain of our magnetic tapes?

However that may be, progress in deciphering Cretan scripts depends, logically enough, on their "abundance". The 57,000 occurrences of signs in Linear B enabled Michael Ventris to decipher it in 1952, revealing it to be a form of Greek. The 7,000 occurrences of signs in Linear A are enough to allow the identification of about a dozen signs, out of the 67 in the syllabary that have been identified with some degree of certainty, and some 40 more with varying degrees of probability. That is not enough to make any definitive statement about the written language. We cannot read any of the Cretan hieroglyphic script, two syllabaries of which (one monumental, the other cursive) are still being established. The 1,500 occurrences of known signs give little hope of our achieving really well-founded results.

In the last two examples, only the discovery of hundreds of texts containing thousands of additional signs would help us to make definite progress in reading, and possible progress in deciphering them. The Etruscan language has long been read, because it is written in a slightly modified Greek alphabet, but it still cannot be deciphered because it is in an unknown language.

Cretan hieroglyphic: clay medallion (Knossos: LM 1274)

This medallion, pierced by a hole for hanging, has two groups of signs. Each is preceded by a cross, which often indicates the beginning of hieroglyphic "words", and it should be read from left to right. Signs Nos 02, 813, and 810 (see diagram opposite) can be seen. On the reverse, numbers have been marked. Iraklion Museum.

Cretan hieroglyphic: clay tablet (Phaestos; LM 1)

This financial document, written on clay like all Cretan archives, begins with a "text" of three signs, and then repeats, from left to right, the same sequence of ideograms symbolizing agricultural products: wheat, oil, olives and figs, each followed by an indication of the amount supplied by means of a system of numbers and fractions (the point represents 10 and the vertical stroke a single unit). Iraklion Museum.

Cretan hieroglyphic: imprint of seal on clay (Mallia, Mu quarter; LM 1052)

The inscription imprinted on this small clay ball, 2.20cm (.85in) high, was incised on a round seal that, in view of the precision of the marks, must have been made of metal. The "initial cross" is of no help in deciding in which direction a circular decorative composition like this should be read. Nor do we know what this document was used for, as it gives us absolutely no clue to its function. Iraklion Museum.

Linear A: silver pin (Mavro Spelio; LM 540)

Found in a tomb a few hundred metres to the east of the palace of Knossos, this pin (probably a hairpin) is 15cm (6in) long and bears one of the longest known inscriptions in Linear A: more than 40 signs divided into at least 9 words separated by small vertical strokes. As with most documents in Linear A and all those in Linear B, it was read from left to right. Iraklion Museum.

Linear A: gold ring (Mavro Spelio; LM 530)

From the same tomb as the pin illustrated above, this ring has a bezel only 1cm (.39in) in diameter and bears a spiral inscription reading from outside to inside, with no punctuation marks separating the words. Iraklion Museum.

Linear A: clay tablet (Haghia Triada; LM 1363)

One of 150 tablets from Haghia Triada, west of Phaestos. This is a count of wheat: the ideogram for wheat is preceded by the name of the supplier (or the customer), and followed by numbers from 20 to 74.

Cypro-Minoan: clay cylinder (Enkomi CM 1619)

This terracotta cylinder, 5.2cm (2in) wide and 4cm (1½in) in diameter, was until quite recently the only one of its kind. The incised text consists of 27 lines comprising a total of 179 signs. A horizontal line indicates the beginning, and it reads from left to right. This object, which was deliberately baked, has been compared to Mesopotamian "foundation documents" that commemorated the construction of a building. However, since the script — a syllabary of about 85 signs, obviously of Cretan origin — is still undeciphered, and the language obviously remains unknown, this theory is entirely hypothetical. Nicosia Museum.

Linear B: clay tablets (Knossos; LM 5753, 979 and 906)

The work of a single scribe, these documents, the largest of which is 17.5cm (7in), deal with domestic animals. The first mentions the despatch of 5 cows and 8 bullocks to Knossos. (The variation in colour of two parts of the tablet is due to different oxygenation during firing.) The second records the delivery of a pig in 4 localities in central Crete. The third enumerates 100 rams, 650 ewes, 40 he-goats, 150 she-goats, 80 sows and 6 cows in a canton in the west of Crete. Iraklion Museum.

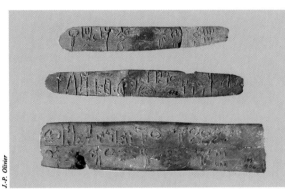

Linear B: ideogram of sheep (Knossos; LM 1147)

This sheep's head (see below, No 106), on a "neck" crossed with two horizontal bars to indicate that it is a castrated wool-producing animal, is followed by a circle representing the number 100. That was the measure of importance for the several thousand flocks of sheep and goats registered in the archives of Knossos. These flocks formed the basis of a highly organized textile industry. Heraklion Museum.

Three Cretan systems of writing: Hieroglyphic (H), Linear A (A) and Linear B (B)

The first two groups of columns show the first 30 *syllabograms* of Linear B (with their phonetic value when it is known); 24 have corresponding signs in Linear A, 10 in hieroglyphic writing. The third group reproduces 15 of the Linear B *ideograms* (with their Latin transcription); 11 have corresponding signs in Linear A, 8 in hieroglyphic. The fourth and fifth groups show the first 15 signs of Linear A which have no parallel in Linear B (but have at least two in hieroglyphic) and the first 15 hieroglyphic signs which have no corresponding signs in either Linear A or Linear B.

n°	value B	H	A	B	n°	value B	H	A	B	n°	value B	H	A	B	n°	H	A	B	n°	H	A	B
01	da				16	qa				100	VIR				301				801			
02	ro				17	za				102	MUL				302				802			
03	pa				18	-				106	OVIS				303				803			
04	te				19	-				107	CAP				304				804			
05	to				20	zo				108	SUS				305				805			
06	na				21	qi				109	BOS				306				806			
07	di				22	-				120	GRA				307				807			
08	a				23	mu				121	HORD				308				808			
09	se				24	ne				122	OLIV				309				809			
10	u				25	a₂				124	PYC				310				810			
11	po				26	ru				125	CYP				311				811			
12	so				27	re				130	OLE				312				812			
13	me				28	i				131	VIN				313				813			
14	do				29	pu₂				159	TELA				314				814			
15	mo				30	ni				180	-				315				815			

Greek expansion in the Mediterranean

Though the Greeks had already planted small settlements in Italy in the Late Bronze Age, the great phases of colonization were in the Dark Age (1100–900BC) and above all in the Archaic period (750–550BC). By 300BC there were Greek cities from the Atlantic to the Indian Ocean.

In very general terms, the establishment of a human enclave outside its original territory—colonization—is a major and recurring feature of Greek history. Ever since the Neolithic, the civilizations which developed in the Aegean had to expand and settle abroad in order to escape from their own cramped home grounds. The Greek civilization, which was originally extremely localized, succeeded in spreading over the whole of the Mediterranean basin, thanks to its vitality and its exceptional ability to adapt and assimilate.

The first phase of enduring colonization to occur in Greek history took place during the "dark centuries" (1100–900BC), when a part of the Greek mainland populations settled the islands and the western coast of Asia Minor. These were the Aeolians in the north, the Ionians in the middle, and the Dorians in the south, and the pattern they produced in the Aegean was to last until the invasions of late antiquity. We still know very little indeed about the reasons for and methods of these migrations, the consequences of which were to be decisive for the evolution of Greek civilization. Nowhere, not even at Smyrna and Miletus, have archaeologists yet found any trace of these settlements from the proto-geometric period. On the other hand, archaeological excavations carried out after World War II have greatly added to our knowledge of the second wave of colonization, that of the historical period, which is still regarded as the Greek colonization *par excellence* (750–550BC). Excavations particularly in southern Italy and Sicily, but also along the coasts of the Black Sea, in Cyrenaica, Spain, Corsica and even in the heart of Marseille, have clarified their objectives and the means employed.

One should not misunderstand the term colonization, normally used to indicate the extraordinary expansion of the Greek world, made possible by maritime exploration that began in the 9th century BC. Unlike the colonies acquired by the European states from the 17th century onwards, when territories inhabited by a large majority of foreign populations were administered by the home country, the Greek colonies of the Archaic period were independent city states founded by groups of citizens who, for various reasons, had left their home towns. (There are a few exceptions to this: for instance, the colonies founded by Corinth along the Adriatic coasts during the 6th century BC.) Far from being motivated by imperialistic aims, the home towns were often relieved to see part of their population leave, since overcrowding led to tensions that undermined their political and social organization. Particular circumstances are revealed in some historical texts: the foundation of Tarentum by dissenting members of ruling families who threatened mainland Sparta's strict oligarchy (Strabo, VI, 3, 2–3); or the foundation of Cyrene by a group of peasants from Thera, chosen by lot in response to a famine after a seven year drought (Herodotus IV,

151–153). This suggests that only the combination of demographic growth (confirmed by modern anthropological study of certain burial grounds), with the seizure of arable lands by powerful families, can explain the extent of the phenomenon.

The hunger for land

The existence from the 8th century BC of well-established commercial routes, extending over long distances in search of the basic products which Greece lacked (metals, wood, cereals), undoubtedly provided a general direction for the colonizing waves, but did not determine them. The traditional distinction between a commercial centre (*emporion*) and an agricultural colony (*apoikia*) is now regarded as artificial: the commercial activity of any given colony was rather an indication of additional success than a determining motive. Even the oldest Chalcidian colonies of the Tyrrhenian Sea (Pithecusa on the island of Ischia, before 750BC, and Cumae in Campania, c.740BC) were from the beginning something more than simple commercial outposts without territorial ambitions. A settled population, however restricted, could not have survived on commerce alone.

The fundamentally agricultural aim of these new towns across the sea is also revealed by the founding ceremonies, which consisted above all of a symbolical and also practical appropriation of the land. The leader of the colonists (*oikistes*) was often appointed by the home town and took care to go to Delphi to seek the advice and protection of the Pythian Apollo, the god of settlement and purification, guarantor of the new civic order. For Apollo himself, after an adventurous journey across the seas, had "colonized" Delphi, driving out the original holder of the site and establishing his own benevolent authority.

Once the exact location of the colony had been chosen, one of the first acts of the *oikistes* was to found a sanctuary to Pythian Apollo, and as soon as relations with the natives allowed it, to establish the topographical definition of the new city state by dividing into equal parts (*cleroi*) the site of the town and the cultivable lands (*chora*). Archaeological research has sometimes revealed traces of these first activities, that of the town at Megara Hyblaea, Naxos and Camarina; that of the countryside at Metapontum and at some of the later Crimean towns such as Heracleia and the unknown city on the peninsula of Majacij. There is no doubt that this regular division of the land into long, usually rectangular plots formed the basis for the rational town planning of Hippodamus of Miletus and for the egalitarian utopias of the classic period. However, it did not prevent several colonies from retaining the oligarchic, even despotic, institutions of their home towns: monarchy survived in Cyrene until 440BC, and tyranny* was the regime common to the Greek towns of Sicily up to the Roman conquest.

Relations with local populations

The groups of colonists were small, often only a few dozen men. This explains how cities like Megara, Chalcis, Miletus or Phocaea were able to found a large number of colonies. Apart from rare exceptions, when groups of different origins merged in the founding of a settlement, these new city states issued from a single metropolis; hence the repetition in this new overseas world of specific characteristics and antagonisms upon which both the cultural wealth and the political weakness of Hellenism were founded. In any case, the permanent settlements, on coastal sites, of small but enterprising groups commanding a more advanced technology than that of the locals, could not have succeeded unless good relations had already been established with the latter, either in the course of precolonial commercial contacts or at the time of the foundation itself. Such relations were often sealed by combining religious beliefs and by intermarriage. Thus Greek civilization not only spread over the coastal areas of several Mediterranean countries but also infiltrated the hinterland by a sort of capillary action. Excavations in the Balkans, Italy, France and Spain enable archaeologists to follow this slow spread of cultural influence which endured until the Roman conquest: the large bronze crater (mixing bowl), manufactured in Magna Graecia (south Italy) and found at Vix, eastern France, in the tomb of a Celtic chieftain, demonstrates the importance of this process from the end of the 6th century BC onwards.

The last colonizing wave of Greek history, beginning with Alexander the Great (336–323BC) and continuing under his successors until stopped at its source by the slow depopulation of Greece itself, was of a totally different nature. This was an interior type of colonization, often military in character, aimed at creating Hellenistic centres within colonial kingdoms. Here a minority of Greek conquerors administered and exploited huge areas which had for centuries been moulded by other civilizations. Although they displayed all the features of traditional Greek cities (institutions, coinage, etc.), these colonial monarchies were far from independent, since their autonomy did not extend beyond the municipal level. In reality, they were totally dependent on the king's protection who, by granting special privileges, particularly of a financial nature, encouraged their growth. Precarious though this situation may seem, it is a fact nonetheless that most of the 300 new cities of the East enjoyed a great success. When Rome conquered, in 30BC, the last of these Greek kingdoms, the eastern Mediterranean was sufficiently Hellenized to retain Greek as its official language.

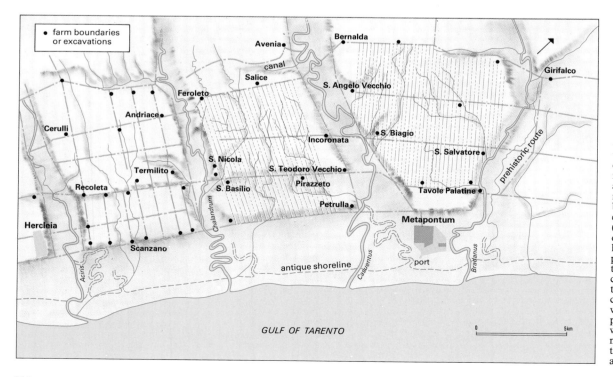

- farm boundaries or excavations

Avenia · Bernalda · canal · Salice · Feroleto · Girifalco · S. Angelo Vecchio · Andriace · Cerulli · S. Biagio · Incoronata · S. Salvatore · Termilito · S. Nicola · S. Teodoro Vecchio · Pirazzeto · Recoleta · S. Basilio · Tavole Palatine · Petrulla · Hercleia · Metapontum · Scanzano · Metapontum · port · antique shoreline · prehistoric route · Acris · Cavone · Bradanus · chalandrum

GULF OF TARENTO   0   5km

Division of land at Metapontum

A city state founded c.630BC by Achaeans from Sybaris and others from the metropolis in mainland Achaea, Metapontum is a typical example of a large colony based on a predominantly agricultural economy. The discovery of the division of this coastal plain into equal lots (*cleroi*) which the colonizers must have disputed keenly with the natives, according to Strabo (VI, 265), is without doubt one of the most spectacular achievements of prospecting by means of aerial photography. The principal lines, at right angles to the sea, are sometimes visible for over 10km (6 miles) and can be found every 210m (672ft). A systematic reconnaissance, in which an international team has been engaged since 1969, has made possible the discovery on the ground of these property boundaries, in the form of partially filled ditches. Some experts believe these to be ancient irrigation canals, but the theory that they were byroads is more plausible. Hundreds of farms, usually by the boundaries of the plots, have also been found; some have been excavated. The date of this general distribution of arable land (*chora*) is still under discussion: most of the excavated farms date from the 4th century BC, but several remains of older habitations have been found, none of which, on the basis of the present state of documentation, is older than 570–560BC. On the other hand, are the two rural plots, differently orientated, contemporary? Might not the one closer to the town be older than the one further away? It is also noticeable that there is a certain continuity between the urban land division, the plots of which are smaller—35 × 90m (112 × 288ft)—and the rural plots; would this space have been left public and undivided with a view to further urban development or to the establishment of a temple or burial ground? Whatever the answer to all these questions, we are faced here with what seems a rational and egalitarian distribution of the land.

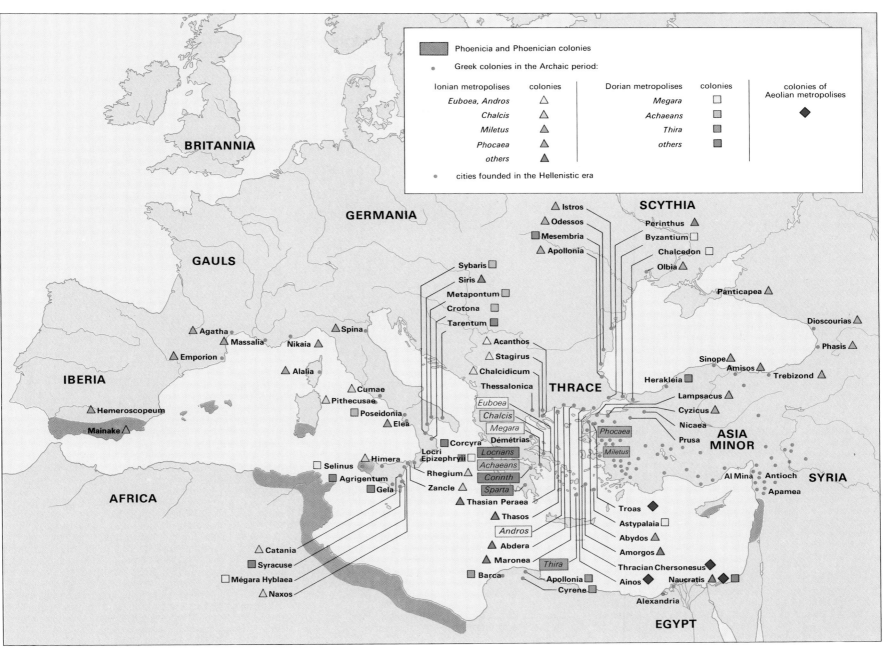

Greek cities and colonies in the Mediterranean

Unlike the civilizations of early antiquity—China, Indus Valley, Mesopotamia, Egypt—Greece did not develop in the valley of a large river, whose fertility and unifying force might have led to the formation of a system administered by a centralized power. The mountain partitions of the Greek peninsula correspond with a microcosm of precipitous islands; the all-pervasive sea provides the only link between these pockets of limited resources. The necessity for overseas trade and the inevitability of political fractionalism are therefore implicit in a geography of enclosed areas where the Indo-European tribes settled during the 2nd millennium BC.

When, after three centuries of bare self-sufficiency (c.1100–800BC), the Greeks ventured outside the Aegean basin, they first turned to the east, where great civilizations offered them superior products and technology; after the beginning of the 8th century, imported objects or objects made from imported materials (metals, ivory) became increasingly frequent in the tombs, and alphabetical writing, borrowed from the Phoenicians, becomes more widespread. By using ports on Crete, Rhodes and Cyprus, the Greek coastal trade retraced, in the opposite direction, the route that had probably already been laid down by Phoenician merchants (whose presence in the Aegean is nevertheless better documented by the texts than by archaeology). Already by 800BC Greek merchants had established at Al Mina (Turkey) at the mouth of the Orontes in northern Syria, a permanent trading outpost, excavated by L. Woolley shortly before World War II. Here the trading routes converged descending, from the neo-Hittite principalities and from Urartu (Armenia) in the north, from Mesopotamia in the east and from Phoenicia in the south, whence came the majority of Egyptian objects to reach Greece before the Nile civilization opened its doors to Greek influence under the 26th Dynasty (664–525BC). Thousands of Greek mercenaries were then stationed in certain garrison towns on the Nile Delta; but, above all, it was at Naucratis that, at the end of the 7th century a real "international concession" grew up, the centre of which was a temple administered by the Ionian towns of Chios, Teos and Phocaea, the Aeolian town of Mytilene and the Dorian towns of Rhodes, Cnidos, Halicarnassus and Phaselis; while Aegina, Samos and Miletus each had their own sanctuary.

Colonization or commerce
This very strong presence explains the importance of the hoards of Greek coins found in Egypt. However, neither Al Mina nor Naucratis were colonies in the Greek sense of the word: they were commercial entrepots without political autonomy, merely tolerated by local authorities. The coastal areas of the eastern Mediterranean, from Egypt to Asia Minor, were then ruled by nations far too powerful to yield up settlements for the Greeks when the need for new land began to be felt. Up to the 5th century, in the eastern Mediterranean, the Greeks

were to play a modest but busy role. They also made for coastlines which were only sporadically occupied by peoples less developed than themselves. Occasionally they would clash with Phoenician competition, as they had already done in Cyprus: after the founding of Carthage (in 814BC according to tradition, but after 750 according to archaeology), the gulf of Syrtes and the coast of northern Africa, the western corner of Sicily, Sardinia, the Balearic islands and the southern coast of Spain became progressively absorbed within the Carthaginian domain—a geographical expansion which the Greeks really tried to contest only in Sicily. Two regions remained open to Greek expansion: in the northeast, the coasts of Thrace and the Black Sea; in the northwest, southern Italy and eastern Sicily with, beyond, the coast between Genoa and Valencia—to which one should add the Libyan coast between Egypt and the Syrtes.

Greek colonization in the Archaic period was everywhere confined to the coastal areas; faced by indigenous populations solidly entrenched in the hinterlands and alert to the dangers of piracy, the Greeks at first owed their superiority to their control of the seas. The sea afforded them direct contact with their metropolis (town of origin) and a possible refuge should the settlement come under threat. Even in those areas where the Greek ascendancy was very strong, such as on the Aegean coast of Thrace or Sicily, the conquest of the hinterland was uncertain for many years and was only achieved at last by negotiation. Thus the Parians, who settled in Thasos, were able to establish a large colony on the coast but could never hold for long the direct control of the gold mines of Pangaeus; they had to come to terms with the turbulent Thracian tribes who occupied the area, and to accept their inability to control the production of the commodity that they distributed in Greece.

Choosing the site
Such being the circumstances, a settlement site had to satisfy certain fundamental necessities: first of all, it had to provide one, or even two, harbours where the ships could be hauled onto a sheltered shore, and a natural defence in the shape of a hill upon which the acropolis, both fortress and sanctuary, could be built. The indented coastline of the Mediterranean offered several such sites of varying size.

The Greeks did not rely on chance when seeking out these sites: geographical specialization, corresponding to definite need, soon became evident. Thus Chalcis, the bronze city (as indicated by its name), was looking for copper: its first settlements by the Tyrrhenian sea mark the great copper route leading to Etruria, while the triple peninsula which juts out into the sea to the east of the Macedonian plain—another mining area—received 30 colonies from Chalcis, thus earning its name of Chalcidike. By the same token, Miletus, a large port and the point of arrival for commercial caravans crossing Asia Minor—and therefore one of the most open and advanced

cities of the Archaic period—turned towards the Black Sea, the Pontus Euxinus of the Greeks. There it first founded Sinope and Trebizond, on the northern coast of Asia Minor, no doubt to secure ease of access to the mines of Urartu (Armenia) and to allow its shipbuilders to take advantage of the vast forests of the interior. But the majority of the 80 or so cities that it founded on the perimeter of this sea, which had become a sort of Milesian lake notwithstanding the competition from Megara (the founder of Byzantium), seem to have been more like implantation colonies. This suggests a real demographic explosion, and perhaps also bad relations with the wheat-producing powers of the interior. As for Phocaea, another large port on the Asiatic coast of the Aegean, the reasons for its interest in the western basin of the Mediterranean are still shrouded in mystery. We can only guess that the search for metals was once again the prime motive, since almost all its colonies were sited either on the route to Tartessus, a mining region in southern Spain, the outlet for land routes which brought southwards the tin of the Cassiterite Islands (Great Britain); or the coast of Languedoc and Provence, where Marseille, founded c.600BC, was to play a vital role in the first contacts between the Gallic tribes and the Mediterranean civilizations.

Hellenistic colonies
The Hellenistic colonization was entirely different, being mainly concerned with the areas which had remained closed to the Greeks of the Archaic period, namely the ancient Persian empire: Asia Minor, the Near East, Egypt. Moreover, the initiative was this time taken by the Greek kings, eager to unify their vast possessions. Each Greek city, often peopled by veteran soldiers, was both a source of strategic support and a centre of Hellenization where local notables were initiated into Greek urban life. This type of colonization was less concerned with the well-worn Mediterranean coastland than with the regions of the interior. Alexander himself had set the example; apart from the two Alexandrias founded on the coasts of Egypt and Syria to open these rich lands to Greek commerce, his other cites were scattered over the eastern outposts of the empire, in Turkestan, Afghanistan, Pakistan. The Seleucid dynasty was to display greater realism by concentrating its colonizing efforts on the central areas of its kingdom: Syria and Mesopotamia. Seleucus I Nicator (301–281BC) founded many cities, several being called Seleucis and 16 Antioch; some of them were to become great centres, like the capital Antioch and its port Seleucis, Apamea on the Orontes, Laodicea on the sea and, above all, Seleucis by the Tigris, the second capital which according to Strabo numbered 600,000 inhabitants during the 1st century BC. In the western part of Asia Minor, the kings of Pergamum founded several cities bearing the names of the royal family: Attaleia, Eumeneia, Apollonia. Such deep Hellenization of the Near East was to be only gradually erased.

Commercial routes and amphorae

The trade routes of the Mediterranean flourished from the Bronze Age to the present. Along them passed the staples of life, transported in the ancient equivalent of mass-produced packaging—the amphora.

Amphorae are the two-handled terracotta transport vases used from the mid 2nd millennium to the end of antiquity (their use still persists in certain regions such as modern Egypt).

With a capacity which varied from 3 or 4 to some 30 litres (0.6–7 gals), averaging about 25 litres (6 gals), their contents were varied: wine, oil, pickled fish, olives, honey, dried fruits (almonds, dates) and so on. Apart from the sacks used to transport cereals (all archaeological traces of which have disappeared), amphorae were the major means of packaging in antiquity, corresponding to our modern bottles, glass jars, tins, jerry cans, etc.

The amphora's shape made its origin and contents instantly recognizable, without any other distinctive sign or label. Each city manufacturing amphorae had one or more types intended for a single product. The wine and oil amphorae of Corinth are known, for example, and the island of Chios confirmed the shape of its wine amphora by depicting it on its coins. On seeing the amphora reproduced opposite, an ancient Greek would immediately recognize it as from Rhodes and containing wine.

Identifying stamps

This universal recognition by shape was often supplemented, especially in the Hellenistic period, by the addition of one or two stamps imprinted on the wet clay of one or both handles, or, more rarely, on the neck. These stamps sometimes bore an official symbol of the city, or an exact reproduction of a type of coin. For Cyrene, it was the palm tree and the silphium, a plant regarded as a veritable panacea in the antique world, which made such a contribution to the celebrity and wealth of the great African city; for Chios the sphinx: for Samos, the head of a bull, and sometimes even an ethnic* sign (as was the case with Thasos, Cnidos, and Samos).

Moreover, these stamps on amphorae often supplied other information, such as the name of the "manufacturer", although this did not indicate whether he was a potter, the owner of a pottery or the owner of the land where the pottery was situated. Amphorae were made by private individuals, but the city exercised some control, as is proved by other indications on the stamp, such as the name of a magistrate or "eponym"* (at Rhodes the priest of the Sun; at Cnidos, the Demiurge; at Thasos the *keramarch*, a magistrate with the task of inspecting the production of amphorae). However, we do not know the precise nature of state control: capacity of the amphorae, export taxes, and so on.

The quantities involved were enormous. The museum of Alexandria has more than 100,000 stamped handles representing almost as many amphorae, and Egyptian papyri have preserved contracts for the location of potteries in which the potters undertake to produce more than 15,000 amphorae a year in their workshops. Moreover, the rubbish tips of antique kilns (see below) still contain tens of thousands of broken amphorae which were either rejects or waste material.

Unsuitable for any kind of land transport (for which skin containers were preferred), amphorae were well suited to maritime freight, and may even have been specifically invented for this purpose. They therefore supply proof of an agriculture rich enough to produce a surplus, and organized enough to find outlets and create exchanges beyond the local areas. The contributions of amphorae to archaeology are remarkable. This ceramic object, which is practically indestructible (although it can be broken into many fragments) makes it possible to establish the commercial routes of antiquity. We can follow the trail of Rhodian amphorae from Spain to Pondicherry in southeast India, and from the Crimea to Upper Egypt. By contrast, the amphorae of Cyrene or Samothrace appear to have had only a restricted distribution, hardly going outside the borders of the region where they were produced.

Certain amphorae have a quite different interest for the archaeologist, since they are datable with extreme precision. As we have seen, Rhodian amphorae bore the name of the eponym, who changed every year, and even indicated the month when he assumed office. Specialists have not yet managed to establish the whole sequence of eponyms (they are still disputing the order of the months), but there can be no doubt that some of these magistrates can be dated to within a few years, or even, in the best cases, to one or two years, which makes the amphora an aid much appreciated by archaeologists when it comes to dating the layers in which they are found.

In conclusion, several shadowy areas persist. A large number of amphora shapes have still not been attributed to specific cities and their place of manufacture remains a mystery. On the other hand, literary sources, inscriptions and coins bearing the symbol of the amphora or grapes, show that some cities produced wine (and consequently amphorae), but give no indication of their type. Whether the amphora is known but the city unknown, or whether the city is known as a wine producer but the amphora unknown, we are generally dealing with unstamped amphorae, and sometimes stamped marks are not explicit enough for their definite identification and attribution to a specific city.

Exposing counterfeit stamps

Recent archaeological research has benefited from the exact sciences: mineralogical analysis (by thin-sectioning) and the identification of traces of metal (by fluorescence* or neutron activation*) have been employed for some 20 years (especially in the USA, Great Britain and France) for determining the origin of amphorae (and of ceramics in general). Archaeologists compare these with reference material whose origin is certain (for example, clay pits) and separate or identify groups of neighbouring amphorae. These analyses play a large part in exposing imitations and counterfeits which are not easily detectable with the naked eye. Thus it has been discovered that the Cypriots tried to pass off their wine as a Rhodian vintage by imitating the amphorae of Rhodes; they did the same with Chios, while the Rhodians, for their part, started imitating the amphorae of Cnidos. Another method which has developed during recent years consists in the systematic study of kilns on the territory of amphora-producing cities. This fieldwork has recently been crowned with success at Thasos, Rhodes and in Egypt (see photos below). First, the archaeologist, by studying ancient texts, travellers' accounts, coins and the amphorae themselves, determines the regions likely to have produced amphorae. Then the geologist, with his maps and readings of different soils, picks out the region most suitable for wine production, and rich enough in clay pits for the manufacture of amphorae. Evidence for the existence of a kiln appears on the surface with the presence of many fragments spoilt and deformed during firing, as well as ashes and large numbers of potsherds of the same kind. In the second phase, a proton magnetometer is used to locate the kiln accurately, to be followed at last by excavation, still the best means of understanding the importance, varied output and duration of production of the workshop.

This search for ancient kilns should be rapidly extended to the eastern Mediterranean as a whole, if we are not to see the irremediable disappearance beneath the bulldozer's scoop of the remains of one of the most prosperous crafts of antiquity, which, though unspectacular, is very instructive for the archaeologist.

Waste tips of amphora kilns in the Alexandria region (Egypt)

The waste tips of amphora kilns were discovered in 1981 on the south shore of Lake Mariut, southwest of Alexandria, where a survey of the region is still going on. This research has located a chain of some 30 workshops datable from the Ptolemaic period to the capture of Alexandria by the Arabs in the mid-7th century AD. They are situated in the actual vineyards a few metres from the shore of the lake. The human figure (below, left) shows the scale of these hillocks, which could be as much as 12m (38ft) high with an area of several hundred square metres. Thousands of amphorae, broken accidentally or deformed during firing, form alternate layers with the ashes from the kiln (below, right). Near these waste tips the potters shaped the amphora on a wheel, dried it, fired it, and coated it with pitch—the inside wall of the amphora was smeared with a coating of natural resin to make it watertight. The container was then filled and closed by means of a cork or a terracotta bung sealed with pozzuolana, or porous volcanic ash. The coastal situation of the site simplified the potter's work for the amphorae could be shipped as soon as they had been filled.

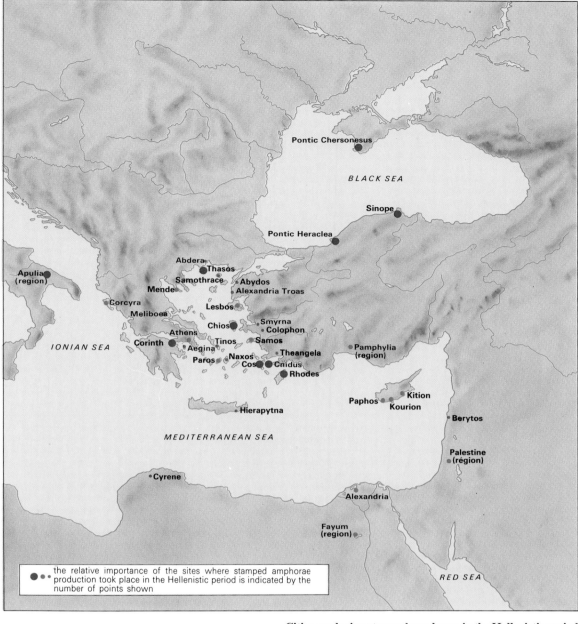

Rhodian amphora (end of 3rd century BC)

This is the most widespread type in the Hellenistic world, recovered in excavations from the Crimea to Egypt, from India to Great Britain. The photograph shows the constituent parts of the Greek amphora: neck with two handles (here stamped), a shoulder and a plump "belly" terminating in a pointed tip which served as a third point for grasping the amphora and made it easier to pour out its contents.

The production of Rhodian amphorae began at the end of the 4th century BC and lasted five centuries, until the second half of the 2nd century BC. From the very end of the 4th to the end of the 1st century BC, each amphora bore two complementary stamps, one giving the name of the "manufacturer", of whom more than 400 are known, and the other the name of the Priest of the Sun, eponym (magistrate) of the city, of whom nearly 200 are known. As from 240BC the name of the month was added, making the Rhodian amphora one of the best dated objects in antiquity.

Cities producing stamped amphorae in the Hellenistic period

The map shows all the sites in the Greek world producing amphorae in the Hellenistic period. To these we should add Ikos, a small island east of Thessalian Meliboea, Acanthus, east of Mende, and Amastris on the southern coast of the Black Sea between Heraclea and Sinope. These 40 odd sites are not all of equal importance (indicated by the relative size of the black circles on the map). For example, although Cnidos flooded the Aegean market, Thasos the Black Sea market, and Rhodes both regions, the products of Colophon, Theangela and Hierapytna had only a regional diffusion. Other cities, such as coastal Laodicea (modern Latakia, to the north of Berytos), are known from the texts as large wine producers, but do not appear on this map because archaeologists have not yet identified their amphorae. A history of the oil and wine trade would also have to take into account the large numbers of unstamped amphorae, which are inevitably harder to interpret and identify. Before studying commercial routes proper, with their distribution and consumption (a project aided considerably by underwater study of shipwrecks with their cargoes, and examination of many amphorae recovered at their ultimate destination through land excavation) archaeologists still have to work on identifying the production sites that must provide solid bases for their theories.

Handle of amphora and coin from Samos

The amphora handle shown on the left bears a stamp (unpublished) with the profile of a bull in a stippled surround accompanied (below the hooves) by the first two letters of the ethnic sign SA for *Sa(miōn)*, "of the Samians". This is the first appearance on an amphora handle of the exact reproduction of the monetary type of the Samian city state. The issue of the coin on the right is dated to the 4th century, which is also the date of our amphora. This example of a more or less faithful depiction of monetary types on amphora handles was widespread in the Greek world, with examples from Chios, Cnidos, Cos, Cyrene, Rhodes, etc. Handle P11033 published by courtesy of Dr El Ghariani, Director General of the Greco-Roman Museum of Alexandria and coin No 130 from the British Museum.

Monetary treasures

Finds of coins throughout the classical world enable archaeologists to trace patterns of exchange, and to show how money movements often cut right across cultural and geopolitical frontiers.

However evocative the term "treasure", to the collector of coins or numismatist this merely denotes a collection of coins deliberately put together (as opposed to pieces asembled by chance, for example in a drain) and lost by their owner, in a war, perhaps, or a shipwreck or any other circumstances. Such hoards provide a very rich source of documentation for the historian.

Whether made to show the distances "travelled" by a city's coinage or, conversely, to map the places where the various coins found in one place were minted, a map of Greek treasures shows a very dense network of exchanges in all directions, throughout the Mediterranean as known to the Greeks, i.e. from Sicily and Cyrenaica to the Gulf of Antioch and from the Straits of Gibraltar to Egypt.

Four examples have been singled out here: two treasures found in Egypt which tell us about the state of monetary circulation at the time of the second Persian war* and just after the conquest of the region by Alexander; and two from cities: Athens, whose navy dominated the Aegean and made Piraeus the main commercial port in the Mediterranean, and Thasos, a humbler town in the north of the Aegean, but one which played an important part in relations between the Greeks and the Thracian world.

Treasures from the Persian wars
In the 1970s workers at Lycopolis, present-day Asyut, discovered about a thousand coins which, unfortunately, went on the market in separate lots. The original treasure had to be reconstructed. On the map, the black circles indicating the sources of these coins extend from Sicily to Cyprus, which marks the eastern limit of mints then active. Pieces such as a tetradrachm of Alexander I of Macedonia show that the treasure was not buried until about 470BC, but the majority date to immediately before 480BC, at the time of the last Greek defence preparations in the face of the Persian invasion. Such is the case for 166 Athenian tetradrachms and 133 staters from Aegina, as well as most of the coins minted in central Greece. Other pieces were issued by cities already subject to the Great King* (title of the Persian monarch) to whom they paid tribute; they included coins from the workshops of the north coast of the Aegean, Asia Minor and Cyprus. Western Greece, Sicily and Magna Graecia (South Italy) hardly took any part in the wars. Their presence here is modest with the exception of Zancle-Messina, where the Samians had come to escape the tyranny imposed by the Persians, and merely shows the vitality of the links of these parts with the rest of the Greek world. In its diversity, this and other treasures show that some parties were able to profit by Xerxes' expeditions in spite of his final catastrophe.

Treasures of Alexander the Great
The 8,000 tetradrachms of the treasure, dating from 150 years later, of Hermopolis Parva, now Damanhur in the Nile Delta, are all those of Alexander the Great, except for 10 tetradrachms of Ptolemy I. Although, like the Great King, he gave allied and subject cities the right to mint coins, he himself created an imperial coinage which was at a premium on the market.

The west, unvisited by Alexander, is not represented in this find and the same is true of ancient Greece, except for Corinth which was occupied by a Macedonian garrison. In contrast, the number of coins from the Macedonian workshops of Pella and Amphipolis clearly shows where the seat of power lay. The places of origin of other coins in the hoard reflect the reorganization of the Persian empire during its periods of shrinking and expansion. They are from regional capitals (Lampsacus for the Straits, Miletus for the coast of Asia Minor, Sardis for ancient Lydia, Sidon, Tarsus, etc.) or issued by the vassal kings who submitted in good time (the princes of Cyprus, Sidon etc.), or lastly from the towns created by Alexander, especially Alexandria itself which was to attach newly conquered Egypt firmly to the Mediterranean.

Apart from the Persian empire, the other great victim of the Macedonian victory was Athens. This makes it all the more interesting to compare the map of the distribution of Athenian "owl" coins (shown in a white circle for 5th-century treasures, a black circle for 4th-century hoards) with that of Alexander's mints. These are found first in the Aegean, dominated by the Athenian fleet in the 5th and to some extent the 4th century. They are rare on the north coast and even more so in the Black Sea straits, where old coinages such as that of Thasos persisted. On the other hand, they abound on the coasts of the Persian empire, and especially in the rich agricultural areas such as the Nile valley or Cilicia around Tarsus. Although usually on bad terms with the Great King and often openly at war with him, throughout the period Athens had traded very actively with the empire, obtaining wheat and slaves, and supplying wine and oil, as well as mercenaries. The number of these owl coins, whose circulation was very little affected by the wars, even the Peloponnesian War, shows above all that they were the great international coinage of the day.

The coins of Thasos (black cantharus on white circle in the 5th, white on black ground in the 4th century)

circulated with far less continuity. The earliest dates from 480BC, the date of the expulsion of the Persians from the region. Thasian staters (fig. 1) were quite numerous in the empire until that time but they are no longer found in treasures after 480. The second, more surprisingly, dates from the end of the Peloponnesian War. In the 5th century, these staters spread widely within the Thracian world, in the heart of present-day Bulgaria, but this movement ceased entirely in the 4th century.

This highlights the fact that no matter how rich in information a map of treasures and monetary circulation may be, there are many gaps in our knowledge. Financial exchanges depended on all kinds of political, military and cultural conditions which disrupted or affected genuine commercial practices, and it is very difficult for us to interpret finds accurately.

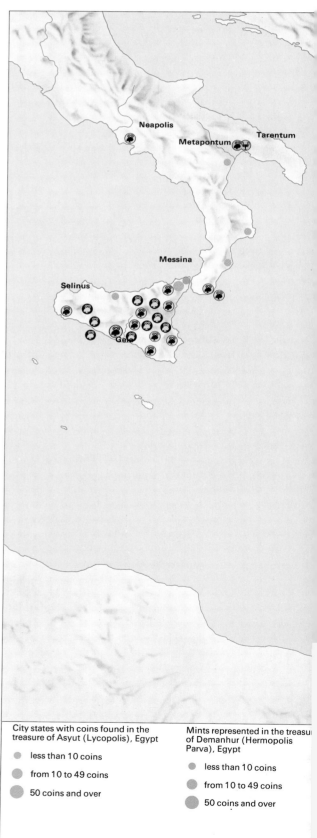

Mints represented in the treasure of Asyut (Lycopolis), Egypt: Quantity of coins per mint (some attributions still uncertain)	
Abdera	15
Abydos	1
Acanthus	38
Aegina	133
Aeneia	1
Alexander I of Macedonia	1
Amathus	1
Athens	166
Barca	4
Boeotia	4
Camirus	9
Caria	25
Carpathos	4
Carystos	3
Chalcis	1
Chios	18
Clazomenae	1
Cnidos	3
Corcyra	4
Corinth	39
Cos	1
Croton	1
Cyprus	9
Cyrenaica	4
Cyrene	18
Cyzicos	1
Delphi	7
Dicaea	4
Eretria	5
Himera	4
Ialysos	4
Idalion	1
Lampsacus	1
Lapethos	5
Lesbos	1
Leucas	1
Lindos	5
Lycia	31
Melos	3
Mende	17
Messina	2
Messina-Zancle (Samians)	14
Metapontum	2
Miletus	5
Naxos	3
Olynthos	1
Paphos	4
Parion	1
Paros	6
Peparethos	1
Phaselis	11
Potidaea	6
Rhegion	1
Salamis	12
Samos	19
Sardis	18
Scione	2
Scyros	
Sermylia	2
Side	1
Sinope	1
Stagirus	1
Tenos	1
Teos	6
Terone	11
Thasos	29
Thracian tribes:	
Derronians	15
Ichnaeans	5
Unidentified tribes:	
Laians	1
Oreskians	36

Mints represented in the treasure of Damanhur (Hermopolis Parva), Egypt: Tetradrachms of Alexander type	
(Acre)	207
Alexandria	217
Amathus	32
Amphipolis	1582
Arados	317
Babylon	630
Berytos	1
Byblos	67
Carne	2
Corinth	27
(Damascus)	369
Hierapolis (?)	1
Kition	122
Lampsacus	72
Macedonian mint (uncertain)	10
Marium/Arsinoe	1
Miletus	68
Myriandros	78
Paphos	16
Pella	56
Phoenician mint (uncertain)	2
Salamis	109
Sardis	3
Side	155
Sidon	113
Soli (?)	3
Tarsus	462

Tetradrachms of Ptolemy I struck at Alexandria	10

Treasures with coins from Athens (A) or Thasos (T): 1. From the Persian wars to the Peloponnesian war

Antioch (Taurus) A/A	28/100
Antiphellos A	3
Athribis T/A	2/10
Bactra A	151 +
Baetocace T/A	1/34
Bubastis T/A	1/34
Caere A	4
Camarina A	3
Chios A	2 +
Cos A	1
Cyprus T	1
Delta T/A	1/3
Drama T	c.100
Ecbatana A	167
Eleusis A	12
Enna A	7
Eretria A	c.25
Euboea A	67
Gela A/A	187/6
(*Hauwran*) T/A	1/31
Hermopolis Magna A	55
Hermopolis Parva T	12
Hippo Diarrhytus A	?
Idalion A	7
Ionia A/T	1/1
(*Kabul*) T/A	1/33
Leontini A	19
Lycopolis T/A	29/166
Megara A	44
Messina A	2 +
Naucratis A/A	6/67
Naxos (Sicily) A	?
Neapolis (Naples) A	?
Nicopolis ad Nestum T	?
Olynthos A	1
Pamphylia A/A	19/2 +
Pautalia T	200 +

Philippopolis A/T/T/T/T	1/51/61/21/?
Phintias A	?
Phocis A	?
Phoenicia A	1
Rhegion A/A/A	1/1/?
Rhodes T	8
Selinus A	4
Serdica T/T	100 + /4 +
Side A	1
Strymon valley T	197 +
Sunion A	4
Syracuse A	?
Tarentum T/A	11/8
Thasos T	27
Xoïs T	2

Treasures with coins from Athens (A) or Thasos (T): 2. From the end of the Peloponnesian War to Alexander's conquest of Asia

(*Al Mina*) A/A	26/18
Athens A/A	2/20
Athribis A	239
Babylonia A/A	6/37
Beroea A	?
Boeotia A/A	3/5
Caria T	12
Catana A/A	3/5
Cilicia A/A/A	3/39/200
Clazomenae A	5 +
Delos A	50
Delta A/A	52/?
Enna A/A/A/A	1/2/2/2
Euboea A	2
(*Figueras*) A	2
Gela A	18
Hieropolis A	1000
Laranda A	5
Larissa A	1
Lesbos A	1
Memphis A	39
(*Mount Athos*) A	100
Naucratis A/A	70/70
Neapolis (Palestine) A/A	1/206
Pautalia A	47
Phintias A	4
Phoenicia A	60
Sidon A	2
Thasos A/T/T/T/T	3/14/36/12 +
Therme A	2

City states with coins found in the treasure of Asyut (Lycopolis), Egypt
- ○ less than 10 coins
- ◎ from 10 to 49 coins
- ● 50 coins and over

Mints represented in the treasure of Demanhur (Hermopolis Parva), Egypt
- ○ less than 10 coins
- ◎ from 10 to 49 coins
- ● 50 coins and over

Stater of Thasos (*c.*500–480BC)

Left: Silenus carrying off a nymph.
Reverse: incuse* square.

Tetradrachm of Thasos (*c.*390–80BC)

Left: profile of bearded Dionysos, crowned with ivy.
Reverse: Herakles kneeling, drawing his bow to the right; left ΘΑΣΙΟΝ; below right, round buckler adorned with a club; all inside an incuse square.

Tetradrachm of Alexander type (*c.*330BC) Amphipolis mint

Left: profile of Herakles, wearing a lion skin.
Reverse: Zeus enthroned, with a large sceptre in his left hand and an eagle in his right; right, ΑΛΕΞΑΝΔΡΟy.

Decadrachm from Athens (*c.*465BC)

Left: profile of Athene.
Reverse: standing owl, wings outspread.

Athenian tetradrachm (*c.*300–295BC)

Left and reverse: profile of Athene, standing owl; ΑΘΕ; olive branch and crescent moon; all in an incuse square.

Tetradrachm of Ptolemy I (*c.*312–305BC) Alexandria mint

Left: profile of Alexander.
Reverse: Athena Alkis; left, ΑΛΞΑΝΔΡΟy; right, an eagle.

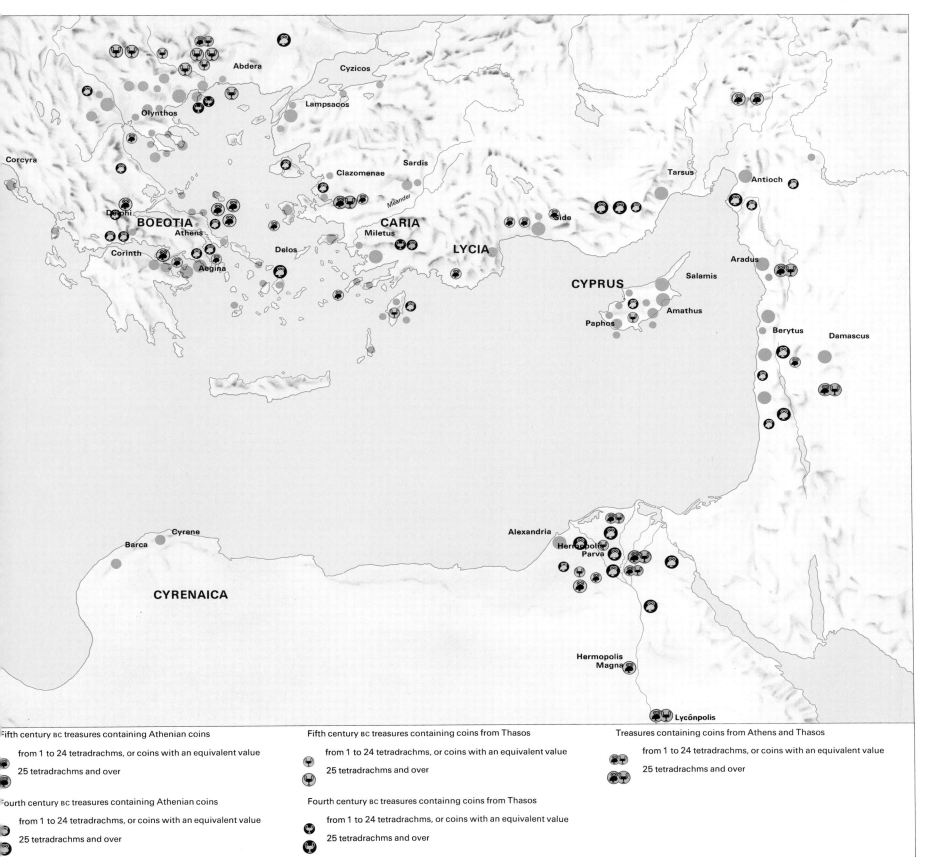

Fifth century BC treasures containing Athenian coins

from 1 to 24 tetradrachms, or coins with an equivalent value

25 tetradrachms and over

Fourth century BC treasures containing Athenian coins

from 1 to 24 tetradrachms, or coins with an equivalent value

25 tetradrachms and over

Fifth century BC treasures containing coins from Thasos

from 1 to 24 tetradrachms, or coins with an equivalent value

25 tetradrachms and over

Fourth century BC treasures containng coins from Thasos

from 1 to 24 tetradrachms, or coins with an equivalent value

25 tetradrachms and over

Treasures containing coins from Athens and Thasos

from 1 to 24 tetradrachms, or coins with an equivalent value

25 tetradrachms and over

Manuscripts and inscriptions

The vast amount of manuscript and epigraphic (inscription) material which has survived, directly or indirectly, from the classical world, provides an indispensable tool for the archaeologist: in these areas exciting discoveries continue to be made.

Until the 19th century our knowledge of Greek civilization was mainly based on the manuscript tradition. Since then the expansion of archaeology has supplied an ever-increasing mass of all kinds of objects revealing a "material civilization" only alluded to in literary sources. Regardless of the historical and aesthetic interest of these objects, which have opened up several new perspectives, the contribution of literary sources is still essential for a deep understanding of ancient Greece, all the more so as none of the three major categories of written Greek documents as yet forms a coherent group.

Because inscriptions and texts on papyrus* did not really enter the field of knowledge until the 19th century, it was the manuscripts on parchment* which ensured the diffusion and survival of Greek civilization for 2,000 years. Thus every so-called "Renaissance" was primarily an attempt to collect, publish and comment on the manuscripts of Greek authors. The first such undertaking was based on the Museum of Alexandria*, a research centre founded by Ptolemy I in the early 3rd century BC to establish and transmit a corpus of Greek knowledge. A large body of textual criticism and selection, based on volumes in circulation at the time, was produced there by generations of eminent philologists, the most famous being Aristarchus (217–145BC) to whom we are indebted for establishing the text of Homer, accompanied by commentaries. It is estimated that this central library of the Greek world must have contained some 500,000 volumes when it burnt down in 47BC — an irreparable catastrophe, even though the rival library founded at Pergamum* by the Attalid kings, and the library of the Gymnasium of Ptolemy at Athens, may have done something to fill the gap. The latter, made up of copies of the originals at the Museum of Alexandria, was magnificently installed by Hadrian in AD131–32 in a building which became the new centre of philology until the library's stocks were transferred to Constantinople by Constantine in the early 4th century.

Meanwhile, the material used for the texts had changed. The more solid and economical parchment book (codex) had replaced the expensive fragile and cumbersome scroll of papyrus (volumen). Regrettably, not all the existing papyrus texts were transcribed, and this unfortunate omission was repeated when the change from so-called "majuscule uncial" script (resembling capital letters) to cursive script occurred in the 9th century. Fortunately this limited transcription took place during the "Byzantine Renaissance" which followed the end of iconoclasm*. Once again, attempts were made to clarify the obscurity of traditional texts by establishing new editions with commentaries which form the basis of our knowledge of Greek literature. None of the 55,000 known Greek manuscripts goes back beyond that period. Of the 900 authors thus preserved, 100 are only represented by a single copy based on an original of that period. The extent of the loss, aggravated by the terrible vicissitudes experienced later by Hellenism, is apparent in the fact that we know only

about 10 percent of attested works. But how many may have disappeared without leaving even a mention of their existence?

Literary papyri

The contribution of papyri found in Egypt is therefore all the more valuable. Some suggest variants, much earlier than the manuscripts, of texts already known; better still, others reveal new texts, sometimes of major interest. That is how the *Constitution of Athens* by Aristotle (British Museum) was discovered in 1890, and the first complete comedy by Menander, the *Dyskolos* (Bodmer Collection, Geneva) in 1957. Without the papyri (unfortunately nearly always fragmentary), other important authors such as Archilochus (7th century) or Bacchylides (5th century) would be reduced to a few insignificant quotations. The great majority of these literary papyri date to the 2nd–3rd century AD, the high point of Graeco-Roman Egypt. In most cases they were papyri thrown on to rubbish tips or re-used as padding for mummies, in other words waste paper regarded as valueless: old books and works by pupils, but also official documents and accounts, private or business correspondence, and technical scripts of all kinds, etc. These tens of thousands of documents, which have only been partially edited and studied to date, reveal unknown aspects of Greek civilization in the Hellenistic and imperial period in the unusual context of an Egypt colonized by the Greeks after Alexander. The administration, economic and everyday life, attitudes and beliefs—all these are illuminated with a detail supplied by no other documents in classical antiquity.

Unfortunately the documents which make up the great European collections (Vienna, London, Berlin, Paris, Florence) were obtained in deplorable conditions. Until the first methodical but cursory excavations by B.P. Grenfell and A.S. Hunt at Oxyrhynchus (1895–1907), the papyri were collected by peasants or unscrupulous traffickers. Documents judged to be unsaleable because they were too fragmentary or too late were simply destroyed. Many others were mutilated deliberately or carelessly at the time of their discovery. Thus groups of documents were dispersed and intact pieces dismembered. Today it is thought that a good half of the papyri discovered in the 19th century disappeared immediately in that way. Even though this fever abated after World War I with the end of the massive finds at Fayum*, official and clandestine discoveries continue sporadically; but the great Aswan dam, which has brought permanent humidity to the soil of Egypt, may well prove fatal to papyri that are still buried. However, that may be, after the "heroic age" of collecting and cleaning up stocks, papyrology has now entered an era of systematic and thematic publication, so making possible, for Graeco-Roman Egypt at least, a social and economic history that is very much a hit or miss affair for the rest of the Greek world in the absence of the corresponding archives.

Archaeological epigraphy

Epigraphy, or the study of incised texts (mainly on marble, but also on bronze and clay), was established much earlier than papyrology. In the 15th century Cyriacus of Ancona copied the Greek inscriptions he came across during his travels in the Aegean Sea. Erudite travellers in the 17th, 18th and 19th centuries often did the same, greatly to our benefit, because the inscriptions have vanished since. Although it may still rely on appreciable finds in some regions of Asia Minor and the Near East, what may be called "descriptive" epigraphy has been eclipsed since the second half of the 19th century by archaeological epigraphy. The excavation of great sanctuaries and public places has led to the discovery of tens of thousands of inscriptions. The end of the exploration of great sites, and the increasing concentration on smaller-scale fieldwork at one time seemed likely to reduce the number of finds, but deep cultivation and the growth of the construction industry in Greece and Turkey since World War II have kept up the momentum of discoveries and continually added new material.

Every year hundreds of new inscriptions appear, the first publications of which are recorded in the *Bulletin Epigraphique* by J. and L. Robert before being taken up again in the *Supplementum Epitaphum Graecum*. These documents on stone are always official texts. Decrees, lists of magistrates, regulations or religious calendars, gifts made to the gods, deeds of emancipation, building accounts or inventories, dedications (often in verse) to benefactors, successful athletes or the dead, these inscriptions provide important information either about the individual or the community that they perpetuate with a guarantee of lasting publicity. Thus although details of private and everyday life are lacking in these inscriptions, unlike the papyri, the effect of reality is nonetheless striking. They reveal the vanity and ambition of individuals, the persistent liveliness of collective life and the obstinate desire of cities for autonomy, first in an unstable world dominated by war, then in the framework of the *Pax Romana*. What we read in them is immediate history, with its petty events and its large constant themes, before it is filtered through the rhetoric of historians. Thus the 200,000 known Greek inscriptions make an essential contribution to our knowledge of Greek history and institutions, all the more so as most of the major categories of inscriptions are organized according to a formula that enables archaeologists to restore, by analogy, some of the gaps in these texts, most of which are fragmentary or badly worn. Moreover, the development and arrangement of the lettering, which is often very elegant and even decorative, indicates an approximate date for a large number of documents, provided we know the regional style, because epigraphy, like all the arts of Greece, followed particular styles and local variations. These anonymous *lapicides** were not only scrupulous scholars; some of them were also artists whose masterly hand is recognizable.

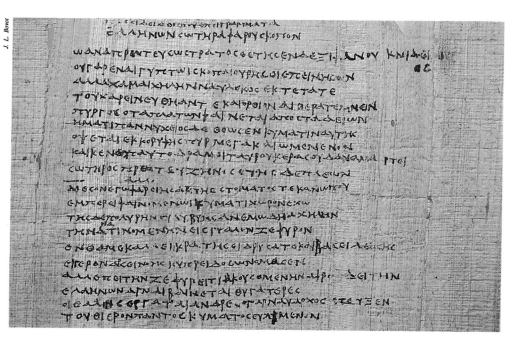

Fragment of the Didot papyrus

This document dating from the 2nd century BC bears, on the right, in its fourth and last column, two epigrams by Poseidippos of Pella, an early 3rd-century BC poet. The first is a dedication in ten verses on the celebrated Pharos (lighthouse) of Alexandria, addressed to Proteus, sea god, guardian of seals, and according to Homer master of the island of Pharos: "This safeguard of the Greeks, this watcher over Pharos, O lord Proteus, was erected by Sostratos, son of Dexiphanes, of Cnidos. In Egypt thou hast provided no high places on the islands as lookout posts: no, the bay which welcomes the ships spreads out at the level of the sea. That is why, standing erect, a tower which during the day can be seen from an infinite distance cleaves the skyline. During the night, soon enough in the midst of the waves the mariner will see the great lamp which blazes on its summit, and he will not fail to reach Zeus the Saviour, O Proteus, he who navigates in these parts." The lighthouse of Alexandria, one of the Seven Wonders of the ancient world, was some 100m (330ft) high. The first storey was a high quadrangular bastion with sides of 60m (192ft). The second was octagonal and 30m (96ft) high and the third, 7m (22ft) high, was round. That was the base of the colossal statue of Zeus the Saviour, protector of mariners. The island of Pharos was joined to the mainland by the Heptastadion, a mole more than 1km long separating two harbours. The Louvre AE/E 7172.

Inscribed vase

The oldest known Greek inscription (*c.*740BC) is inscribed cursively from right to left on the shoulder of this vase found in a tomb of the Dipylon: "Among all who dance at this time, this shows who is the most graceful." It must therefore be a prize for a dancing competition or a dedication at a banquet. The form and position of certain letters—notably the A on its side—are still very close to Phoenician models. National Museum of Athens, Inv. 192.

Inscribed base of a small vase

On the base of this modest Attic goblet for everyday use is inscribed, probably by the hand of the great artist himself, "I belong to Phidias." The vase was found broken into many fragments among the debris of the studio where Phidias executed the colossal ivory and gold cult statue of Zeus throned in majesty, the date of which is not yet established (450 or 430BC). Museum of Olympia.

Fragment of the "Laws of Gortyna", Crete

This text in the Doric dialect, incised on the walls of a public building, is divided into 12 columns, the lines of which read alternately from right to left and from left to right (*boustrophedon*). This archaic arrangement, and the use of an alphabet restricted to 18 letters, illustrates the conservatism of Crete in the 5th century BC. The legal provisions that it codifies are equally archaic, because they mention, in addition to free men and slaves, peasants bound to the land, but able to possess cattle and material objects, a form of serfdom which had disappeared a long time ago outside Crete.

Inscription on the plinth of a statue

"Satyros, son of Eumene, of Samos, the first to stand alone as the sole participant in the contest of the double flute, thanks God and the Greeks for the prize by offering, in the course of the sacrifice following the athletic contest in the Pythian stadium, two extracts from the *Bacchae* by Euripides: Dionysus, chorus, and a piece for the cithara." This illustrious musician, known from other inscriptions, commemorated his uncontested victory in the Pythian Games of 194BC by erecting a statue and playing, or possibly arranging the performance of, two musical sections from the celebrated play by Euripides: a choral passage danced to the accompaniment of the double flute (perhaps the first appearance of the chorus in a hymn of praise to Dionysos, lines 64–169) and a recitative accompanied, not by the double flute as was usual, but by the cithara. If this elliptical text is really saying that he himself played, then it was a transcription for flute of this exceptional score. This recital would have allowed him to show his talents both playing with the chorus and as a virtuoso soloist in the recitative. Sanctuary of Apollo, Delphi.

81

Rome and the development of the city in Latium

How did urban civilization develop in Italy? Archaeological work on "origins" is putting foundation tales such as that of Romulus and Remus in a new context.

As a result of archaeological advances we are now able to form a new understanding of the formation of towns in the area of Latium and to re-assess the influence of external but related phenomena, such as the Greek colonization of southern Italy and Sicily, the structure of Etruscan townships, and relations with the Phoenician and Punic world. Two questions are crucial: the value respectively, of written sources and archaeological documentation, and the validity of the links we may make between the two groups of data. The accounts of the "origins" of these cities are extremely important as they contain a wealth of vital information; their development and elaboration are expressive of the political structure of the societies concerned, although the worship of founding heroes (Aeneas in the case of Lavinium and Romulus in the case of Rome) are examples of a phenomenon which was widespread among the Greek towns of the archaic period. The most complete version of these accounts is the one handed down to us by the writers of the Augustan age: the later history of Rome (particularly that of the last two centuries of the Republic), the analytical approaches of ancient historiography, the legends and the stereotyped traces of ancient rites are all buried in the text like the literary equivalent of sediments and stratifications.

Archaeological research on the other hand has examined sites which are very revealing to the history of the region we are here concerned with: for example the sites at Ischia, Pontecagnano, Pratica di Mare (Lavinium), Castel di Decima (Politorium?), Osteria dell'Osa (Gabii), Pyrgi and Gravisca. The study of archaeological material, especially pottery, has also been useful in establishing chronological sequences. The detailed examination of habitats and burial grounds has facilitated the anthropological analysis of the populations, aided by the results of ethnological research. The formation of the Latium townships, is rooted in prehistory. Our knowledge of the later periods of the Bronze Age (13th–10th century BC) has been revolutionized in recent years. On the basis of much wider documentary information, we now have a much clearer idea of the structural development of various regions between the Late Bronze Age (10th century BC) and the Early Iron Age (9th century BC) and we find that there is a correspondence between areas occupied by different groups as defined by archaeological evidence and territories occupied, in historical times, by the various Italic populations. What has also transpired is the constant importance of Mycenaean imports in southern Italy and Sicily, as well as in Sardinia and in the area north of Rome (Luni sul Mignone, Tolfa mountains).

The later developments which led to the formation of the townships are defined as Phase I (1000–900BC), IIA (900–830), IIB (830–770), III (770–730/20), IVA (730/20–640/30), and IVB (640–580). The definitions of these phases are based on the analysis of documentation and imply that each period be definable by a definite set of characteristics. However, one must recognize that there is bound to be a certain time lag between the evolutionary processes of the various societies and the formalizing of a system of organization (for instance in the planning of the habitat) or an ideology (for example, as expressed in funeral rites), as revealed by the objects and places of everyday life which have been brought fragmentarily to light by archaeological excavations.

In the present state of our knowledge, the phases mentioned above represent the most obvious landmarks of an evolution which is better known for its results than for the various stages of its course. Archaeological analysis has only been able to establish a kind of long-term history, and we know far less about its daily course than we do about its sudden leaps and "crises", such as those which mark the crucial stages in the socio-economic development of the populations under study. The periods I and IIA have yielded traces of extremely fluid and scattered settlements; the shape of the huts has been reconstructed from the few traces left of the remains of posts, and post-holes found and the small earthenware models containing the ashes of the dead. Excavations at Osteria dell'Osa have brought to light a very interesting phenomenon from phase IIA, when it appears that burial was practised together with cremation: the tombs containing ashes, with their hut-like urns and miniature objects (which include weapons) are reserved for males, which seems to indicate the existence of some sort of hierarchy based on the superiority of the "pater familias" which was not apparent before.

Crucial evolutionary stages

The period IIB was characterized by an increase in the population and a redistribution of settlements, now found grouped along the various communication routes (Castel di Decima, for instance, on the road from Veii to Campania). Phase III, which is distinguished by its funerary objects, was characterized by a series of innovations in the agricultural and crafts fields, such as the introduction of viticulture and the production of refined clay pottery, turned on the wheel, of traditional shape but with a painted decoration inspired by the geometric ceramics of Greece, fragments of which have been discovered in Rome itself. These changes coincided with the settling of Ischia by the Euboeans around

775BC and with the founding of Cumae a quarter of a century later. The influx of Greek settlers and the development of commercial relations with Etruria began at this time and placed the lower valley of the Tiber at the heart of economic exchange; this in turn brought about an acceleration and intensification of the process of social differentiation which had already started, and the formation of local aristocracies. This structural evolution was reinforced during phase IVA and spread from Latium to neighbouring Etruria. The most obvious signs have been found in the burial grounds: the underlining of the sex of the dead person (indicating a man by his weapons and a woman by her jewels); the wealth of objects, both imported and manufactured on the spot; the adoption of Greek customs, such as drinking wine during banquets and using perfumed oils. Thanks to the introduction of writing we also know that personal names now consisted of two parts, first name and family name, probably replacing the single name around the second half of the 8th century. This feature, typical of the peoples of central Italy, stresses the importance of the family group. During the last stage of this evolution, phase IVB, the signs that the transition from village to town was now complete can be seen with particular clarity in the plan of Rome, where a public and religious area replaced huts, which themselves were gradually being replaced by houses with tiled roofs. The excavations of the Forum and the Forum Boarium, two areas susceptible to flooding by the Tiber made this transition particularly clear. These sites necessitated effective drainage works, in themselves a proof of sophisticated collective organization. The archaeological evidence of the development of Rome and Latium tallies surprisingly well with what the ancient sources tell us, and it seems to justify the modern tendency to regard the ancient traditions favourably.

The Roman Forum at the beginning of the Republic

The map clearly shows the way the public areas were arranged around an axis formed by the *Via Sacra*, linking the Forum to the citadel (*Arx*). According to the legend of the founding of Rome, this area is where the Romans and Sabines faced each other and where their leaders, Romulus and Titus Tatius, were reconciled—thus uniting the two peoples and leading to the birth of the town. The area is divided into two sections: the first, the likely site of the royal residence, was, under the Republic, subdivided into several buildings united under the symbol of the "common hearth" (the *regia*, the residence of Numa, the second king of Rome, housing the two chapels of Mars and Ops; the *atrium Vestae* consisting of the temple of Vesta and the living quarters of the vestal virgins; the *domus regis*, the house where the "king" of sacrifices lived). The second area, around the *Comitium* (the assembly place), with its sanctuary (*Vulcanalium*), has a black stone (*lapis niger*) among the flagstones which have covered the area from the days of Sulla, and here the most ancient Roman public inscription was found (middle of the 6th century BC). The function of the *Comitium*, linked to the political activities of the king, is related to that of the *Auguraculum*, on the citadel, the place where omens were foretold prior to any political action being taken. After F. Coarelli, *Il Foro Romano*, vol. I, Rome 1983.

1 Palatine Hill
2 Velia mound
3 Carinae (Roman district)
4 Gemoniae (stairs on which victims were dragged)
5 new road
6 Etruscan street
7 Prison
8 Curia
9 temple of Venus Cloacina
10 temple of Jupitor Stator
11 temple of the Penates
12 chapel of Strenia
13 Mugonian Gate
14 fountain of Juturna
15 chapel of Juturna
16 temple of Castor and Pollux
17 Curtius lake
18 temple of Saturn
19 Mundus (Mouth of Hell and city centre, confused later with *Umbilicus Urbis* "navel" of the city)
20 Altar of Saturn
21 Senate's meeting place

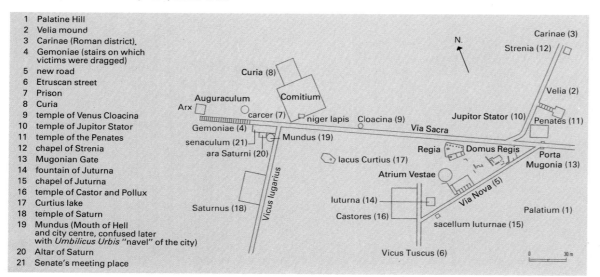

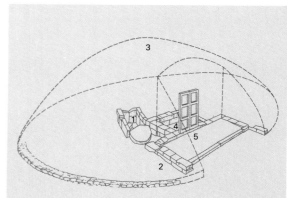

The tomb of Aeneas at Lavinium

The monument, part of the temple to the south of the town known as "thirteen altars", clearly shows three stages: a tumulus tomb dating from the beginning of the 7th century BC (1 and 2), signs of later use of the site (offerings) in the mid-6th century, and a restructuring of the tumulus (3), which added a chamber closed by a false door (4), and preceded by a vestibule (5) at the end of the 4th century. The monument corresponds with the description of the tomb of Aeneas by Dionisius of Halicarnassus (*Roman Antiquities*, I, 64, 4–5). A mid-6th century cult of Aeneas and the changes which took place during the 4th century (the time of the treaty between Rome and Lavinium after the Latin wars, which dates from 338BC) indicate stages in the political and religious exploitation of the legend of Aeneas at Rome.

The Metropolitan Museum of Art. New York

Inkwell (?) with Etruscan alphabet (Viterbo area, end of 7th-beginning of 6th century BC)

The alphabet borrowed by the Etruscans from the Chalcidian colony of Cumae was passed on by them to Rome and the other towns in Latium. Being "lettered" appears, in the tombs of the 7th century, as a sign of distinction and prestige.

Museo archeologico, Firenze. Soprintendenza archeologica della Toscana

Acroterium statue from Poggio Civitate

Thirteen of these life-size statues adorned the roof of one of the buildings of the complex discovered near Murlo (Siena), undoubtedly a palace. Dating from the beginning of the 6th century BC, they are an early example of monumental terracotta sculpture, an art in which, according to Varro (Pliny the Elder, *Natural History*, XXXV, 157), the Etruscans excelled; they probably represent ancestral figures, carrying various attributes in their hands and wearing large hats, characteristic of northern Etruria up to the Po valley.

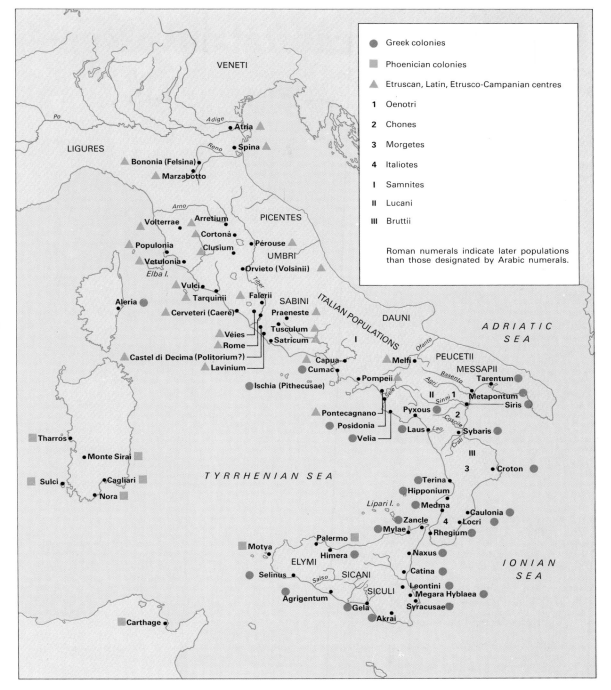

Greek colonization and growth of Etruscan, Latin and Campanian centres

Terracotta relief from temple A at Pyrgi

This relief, with its remarkable pictorial and sculptural rendering, adorned the end of the horizontal beam on the rear façade of temple A at Pyrgi (one of the ports of Caere, modern Cerveteri). The temple probably dates from 480–470BC (although some support a date of *c*.450) and is more recent than the nearby temple B which dates from the end of the 6th century and with which are linked the Etruscan and Phoenico-Punic inscriptions on the gold scales found between the two temples. The relief illustrates an episode from Theban legend: in the background, to the left, the winged Athena, holding in her hand a jug of ambrosia, steps back in horror from the scene shown in the foreground: Tydeus devouring the brain of Melanippus; in the middle ground, to the right, Zeus is about to strike Capaneus.

Hercules and armed female divinity

Like the Forum, the sacred area discovered near the church of Sant'Omobono at the end of the *Vicus Iugarius*, which linked the Forum to the port on the Tiber, shows very clear and harmonious traces of the various stages in the growth of the city. Of the two temples dedicated to Fortuna and Mother Matuta attributed to the king Servius Tullius, only one has been found to date from the archaic phase. This pair of figures, erected on the acroterium, about two-thirds life-size and dating from *c*.530BC, reveals direct links with the sculpture of eastern Greece. Having links with the Etruscan kings, the temple was destroyed at the end of the 6th century with the advent of the Republic. Alterations to temples coincide significantly with the crucial stages in the Roman conquest of Etruria (in 396BC by Camillus, after the fall of Veii, in 264BC by M. Fulvius Flaccus, after the conquest of Volsinii).

B. Malter

De Antonis

The past of a capital city: Republican Rome

Recent "rescue archaeology" has contributed much to our understanding of the elaborate architectural showpiece which was the centre of Rome during its great era of conquests, from the 3rd to the 1st centuries BC.

The growth and organization of modern cities has in recent years led to the development of urban archaeology as an area of great sensitivity, where scientific research, influenced by political and cultural concerns, may lead on to large-scale projects. Such projects aim to recreate in an urban context the density and richness of the past, so that today, in the centre of Rome, an archaeological park can emerge, based on the restoration of the republican and imperial forums of the ancient city. But long before the destructive effects of modern town planning, which have had very serious results for the ancient site, imperial Rome had already largely obliterated the relics of the older city, so that a reconstruction of its stages of development from the beginning of the Republic to Augustus' seizure of power must of necessity be difficult and incomplete.

However, archaeologists can now show that certain methods of urban division which occurred between the end of the 7th and the 6th centuries BC represented a specific political and social organization characteristic of the ancient Graeco-Roman world: the city state. Consequently, whatever can be learned about subsequent alterations of these architectural ensembles, such as religious centres, public centres or residential areas, will reveal a great deal as regards the social and political changes that would have affected the city thereafter. In the case of sites which can only be known through archaeology, these alterations are crucially important. Thus modern research carried out on the urban development of Poseidonia-Paestum has shown how the founding of the Latin colony in 273 BC marked a breach with the Greek and Lucanian periods: a new forum was built in which the Comitium (place of assembly) followed an identical plan to that of the colony founded in the same year in Etruria at Cosa, and both undoubtedly refer to a common Roman model. As for Rome itself, the centre of power, the topographical and archaeological data are confirmed by written records, and by a marble tablet dating from the years of Severus which had been placed in the Forum of Peace near the Basilica of Maxentius.

The importance of the Campus Martius
One area and one period stand out as exemplary in this reconstruction of the urban past of Rome: the Campus Martius in the last two centuries BC. This district was almost entirely inhabited during the Middle Ages, and retains a large part of the ancient network of streets, at the same time boasting some marvellous examples of architectural continuity: the Piazza Navona, for instance, which reproduces the plan of Domitian's stadium, and the square of the Grotta Pinta (painted cave) which preserves that of Pompey's theatre. Research carried out by G. Gatti in 1960 has revolutionized previous understanding of the topography of the southern sector by pinpointing exactly the Circus Flaminius and, since the two buildings were found to be

inverted, the theatre of Balbus. Gatti's previous research had led to correct siting of the Saepta (voting chambers) and of the nearby porticoes in the area immediately to the east of the Pantheon and Agrippa's Thermae (baths). On the basis of these discoveries, which put the pieces of the jigsaw back into the right order, the Campus Martius provides excellent grounds for comparison between the successive ages of Rome; this is particularly clear in the work of F. Coarelli, devoted to the various parts of this area in which the ancient and the new are juxtaposed. At the time when Augustus and his successors had endowed the Campus Martius with superb architectural complexes, Strabo viewed this district as a sort of showpiece which embellished the rest of the town. Dominated by the Mausoleum, the burial place of the imperial family, the area could be described without exaggeration as the earthly embodiment of the Elysian Fields, celebrated in Virgil's *Aeneid*, where heroes gathered after their death. Strabo wrote:

> The size of the campus is remarkable, since it affords space at the same time and without interference, not only for the chariot races and every other equestrian exercise, but also for all that multitude of people who exercise themselves by ball-playing, hoop-trundling, and wrestling; and the works of art situated around the Campus Martius, and the ground, which is covered with grass throughout the year, and the crowns of those hills that are above the river and extend as far as its bed, which present to the eye the appearance of a stage-painting—all this, I say, affords a spectacle that one can hardly draw away from. And near this campus is still another campus [both campuses of course formed a part of the Campus Martius], with colonnades round about it in very great numbers, and sacred precincts, and three theatres, and an amphitheatre, and very costly temples, in close succession to one another, giving you the impression that they are trying, as it were to declare the rest of the city a mere accessory. For this reason, in the belief that this place was holiest of all, the Romans have erected in it the tomb of their most illustrious men and women. The most noteworthy is what is called the Mausoleum, a great mound near the river on a lofty foundation of white marble, thickly covered with evergreen trees to the very summit. Now on top is a bronze image of Augustus Caesar . . . (Strabo, *Geography*, V, 3, 8)

Emblematic image of the new regime, this idyllic picture of a place devoted to religious piety and leisure omits a fundamental aspect of the area under the Republic: the political zone, centred on the Saepta, which formed an appendage of the forum. Here the meetings of the centurions' societies took place, representative of the suffrage system of the corps of

soldier-citizens which tradition attributed to the king Servius Tullius. Connected with the political function of this area, its orientation still determines the central part of a densely populated district. As F. Castagnoli has pointed out, such an orientation was based on the cardinal points, because the Saepta, like the Comitium in the forum, was designed for political assemblies and was included within a space defined as sacred by its orientation (the *templum*). The building programme carried out by Augustus only brought to its conclusion a series of initiatives typical of Roman conquering generals since the 2nd century BC.

Triumphal processions, foreign loot
Placed under the sign of Mars, who had his own altar there, the area maintained the omnipresence of the military function within the scheme of the Roman city. Besides being the place of assembly of the soldier-citizens, it was also used to celebrate and consecrate victories. This practice, probably dating from the town's earliest days, was linked with a northwest-southeast axis, around which the southern part was arranged, and which can be clearly seen in the orientation of the Circus Flaminius, built in 221 BC as the point of departure for the triumphal processions. This explains why, from the beginning of the 2nd century BC onwards, at the time when victories in Asia first caused Rome (according to ancient writers) to be flooded with oriental luxury, the victorious generals chose this sector for their temples and porticoes, simultaneously the fruits and the showpieces of the loot amassed during their campaigns. Artists and craftsmen were called in from Greece and the Hellenistic east to carry out their orders in an unrestrained competition for supremacy in magnificence. Architects like Hermodoros of Salamis, numerous painters, whole families of sculptors like Timarchides and his sons Dionysius and Polycletus, built a core of Hellenistic urbanism in the heart of a Rome still faithful to her old gods. A simple enumeration of the artistic components of this creation shows vividly how the artistic development of Rome as a consequence of her conquests was necessarily drawn from various external sources.

The collection of art as a sign of victory was itself the foundation of Rome's aesthetic expression. Within their architectural settings, works imbued with history by their reference to a prestigious past, whether that of Periclean Athens or of the world of Alexander's conquests, crowded the banks of the Tiber, reaffirming Rome's vocation for universal empire. Thus, once the conquest was achieved, bringing to an end the fratricidal strife which it had encouraged, the Campus Martius of Augustus tried to mitigate, with its white marbles and green fields, the violence of its recent past.

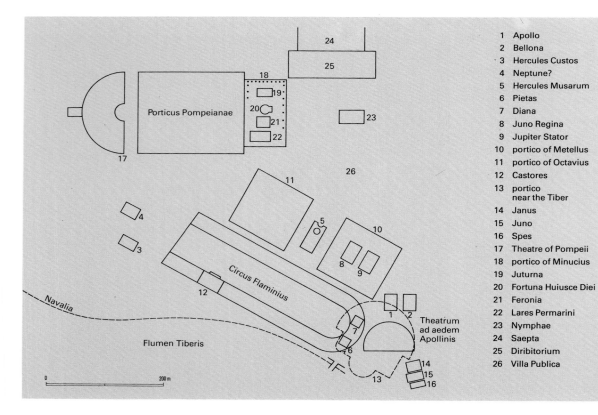

1 Apollo
2 Bellona
3 Hercules Custos
4 Neptune?
5 Hercules Musarum
6 Pietas
7 Diana
8 Juno Regina
9 Jupiter Stator
10 portico of Metellus
11 portico of Octavius
12 Castores
13 portico near the Tiber
14 Janus
15 Juno
16 Spes
17 Theatre of Pompeii
18 portico of Minucius
19 Iuturna
20 Fortuna Huiusce Diei
21 Feronia
22 Lares Permarini
23 Nymphae
24 Saepta
25 Diribitorium
26 Villa Publica

The area around the Circus Flaminius
Arranged in a circle around the Circus Flaminius, as noted by Strabo (*Geography*, V, 3, 8), a series of temples owe their origin in large part to the generals of the conquest (3rd–1st centuries BC). The following list is in chronological order, with names of the politicians and generals responsible for the erection of individual temples:
1. Apollo (341 BC, restored in 179 BC by M. Fulvius Nobilior, completely reconstructed after 34 BC); 2. Bellona (293 BC, Appius Claudius Caecus); 3. Hercules (220 BC); 4. Neptune (end of 3rd century BC) or perhaps, Mars (132 BC, Junius Brutus Callaicus); 5. Hercules Musarum (187 BC, M. Fulvius Nobilior); 6. Pietas (181 BC, M. Acilius Glabrio); 7. Diana (179 BC, M. Aemilius Lepidus); Temples 6 and 7 were covered by the theatre of Marcellus (16) which occupies the site of an earlier temporary theatre (theatrum ad aedem Apollinis). The temple of Juno Regina (no. 8), built 179 BC, by M. Aemilius Lepidus, and the temple of Jupiter Stator (no. 9), built 146 BC by Q. Caecilius Metellus Macedonicus, fit into the portico of Metellus (10) which was built in 146 BC by Metellus Macedonicus and become, under Augustus, the Porticus Octaviae. Nearby is the portico of Octavius (II) built in 168 BC by C. Octavius. No. 12 is the temple of Castor and Pollux (beginning of the 1st century BC). No. 13 reprsents the Arsenals, built by the architect Hermodoros of Salamis; no. 14 "a portico near the Tiber, behind the Temple of Spes [Hope]" nothing of which remains; no. 17, the theatre and the porticoes of Pompey; no. 18, the portico of Minucius; the four republican temples of the sacred area of the Largo Argentina: 19, Iuturna; 20, Fortuna Huiusce Diei [present Fortune]; 21, Feronia; 22, Lares Permarini (protectors of seafarers); 23, the temple of the Nymphs, where the census archives were kept; 24, the voting enclosure; 25, the spoils room; 26, the public villa, a building surrounded by a park where every five years the census officials carried out the *census* (recording and dividing the population into classes). After F. Coarelli, *Roma, Guida Archeologica*, Laterza, p. 271

Fragments of the pediment at Telamon

The terracotta plaques from this pediment (of a type which appeared in Etruria only in Hellenistic times) were discovered at the end of the last century on the hill of Talamonaccio, near the ancient port of Telamon, famous for the victory of the Romans over the Gauls in 225BC. The plaques have only recently been allocated their rightful place in history, as a result of research carried out on the monument after the flooding of Florence in 1966. The central motif of the pediment (right) illustrates the tragic story of the House of Thebes: Oedipus, blind, between the bodies of his two sons, Eteocles and Polyneices, one of them dead, the other dying, supported by Jocasta; on either side, two figures on chariots represent the disastrous end of the expedition of the Seven against Thebes: Adrastus, and the soothsayer Amphiaraos disappearing into hell (above, left and right). Like other monuments close by (the urns of Volterra, Chiusi and Perugia), this pediment is an important product of the artistic movements prevailing in Rome and Italy during the 2nd century BC, with the influx of craftsmen from the eastern shores of the Mediterranean and the increasing number of conquests. Romanization virtually reduced to nothing the southern populations of Lucania, Bruttium (Abruzzi) and Apulia—and finally did so after the war with Hannibal—so that the first expression of Hellenistic art in the west failed to develop; but the Etruscans, thanks to a lasting alliance between their aristocracy and Rome, experienced a relative prosperity of a provincial kind (without sharing in the feverish enrichment of the Campanian region), and thus participated in the artistic development to which Rome held the key from this time onwards. Archaeological Museum, Florence.

Fragment of a statuary group from Lanuvium

Discovered in the last century in the sanctuary of Lanuvium, this group of equestrian statues (seven figures) in Greek marble, is at present divided between the British Museum and the Leeds Museum, except for one statue still in the original location. The group appears to be significant in two ways: F. Coarelli has linked it with a rebuilding of the sanctuary in the middle of the 1st century BC by L. Licinius Murena, the legate of Lucullus during the third war against Mithridates and consul in 62BC; it is also regarded (F. Coarelli, P. Moreno) as a copy of the famous bronze monument by Lysippus showing Alexander and his companions fallen in the battle of the Granicus. The original, brought by Metellus Macedonicus from Dion in Macedonia to Rome, was placed in the Campus Martius in the portico bearing his name. Since one of the main battles in the third war against Mithridates took place near the Granicus, this marble copy can be regarded as one of the examples of *imitatio Alexandri* (imitation of Alexander) which characterized the generals of the late republican times aspiring to a personal power of a monarchic kind.

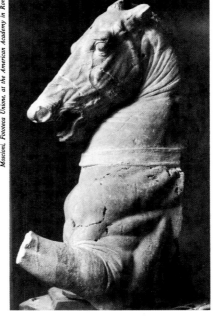

Below: the relief of the "Altar of Domitius Ahenobarbus"

This relief is part of a rectangular base, 5.65 × 1.75m (18.6 × 5.8ft), the other sides of which are now in Munich. It was discovered during works carried out in the church of San Salvatore in Campo, under which was found a marble temple identified by F. Zevi as the temple of Mars connected with the triumph of Brutus Callaicus. Studied in detail by F. Coarelli, this must have formed part of the base of a sculptural group (see Pliny the Elder, *Natural History*, XXXVI, 26) connected with the temple of Neptune which, according to all evidence, is to be placed in the immediate proximity of the temple of Mars (Torelli). The contrast between the reliefs in Munich (the wedding of Amphitrite and Neptune) and this one in the Louvre is not so much of technique (they both came from the same neo-Attic workshop) as diversity of subject. According to a fully recorded Hellenistic tradition, the Louvre relief recently studied by M. Torelli is the oldest "historical" Roman relief. It translates into imagery the rules governing the juridical, political and religious procedures for a census, the symbol of the civic organization of Rome. From left to right: declaration under oath (*professio*) by a citizen wearing a toga and facing a sworn official (*iurator*), who writes the details on the register; assignment to the appropriate class (*descriptio*) of a standing citizen by a seated censor; centre and right: religious ceremony of closure with sacrifice and purification (*lustrum*). Near the altar of Mars, dominated by the statue of the god, the censor proceeds with the *suovetaurilia* (sacrifice of a pig, a sheep and a bull). On either side of the scene are two groups of soldiers: on the left, two infantrymen; on the right, two infantrymen and a mounted soldier, a probable allusion to the classification of the citizen-soldiers. Notwithstanding several still unresolved problems, the relief can be dated to the end of the 2nd century BC. Louvre.

Mediterranean markets and trade

Under the *Pax Romana*, the whole of the Mediterranean became one economic system, imposed on ancient local patterns of exchange which had existed since the Early Bronze Age.

The archaeological study of terracotta crockery, lamps, amphorae, bricks and tiles, as well as of ingots and metal objects, has made considerable progress for a quarter of a century, modifying ideas previously held about trade in the Roman period. In some cases, for example that of "Arretine sigillata", the delicate glossy red pottery produced in Tuscany between the middle of the 1st century BC and the middle of the 1st century AD, or that of "Gallic sigillata", another type of glossy red pottery produced as from the 1st century AD in the Massif Central and then in the east of Gaul and on the banks of the Rhine, the chronology is so well established that the ultimate reversal of the commercial flow can be dated to within one or maybe two decades. New excavations, typological research and chemical analyses of materials (notably terracotta) enable archaeologists to locate the production sites more accurately. Thus we know that Arretine ware, coming at first (as its name implies) from the workshops of Arretium (Arezzo), Tuscany, was later also made at Pisa, Lyon and perhaps in other Gallo-Roman centres.

Yet archaeological knowledge has its own limits. Certain important commercial objects escape attention because they have left virtually no trace for archaeologists to recover. This is the case with cereals and other products of the earth which were not habitually transported in amphorae; it is also the case with wooden objects and all textiles. Secondly, the study of industrial and commercial enterprises, and the identification of their owners, is only possible if the archaeological object bears sufficiently explicit seals or inscriptions (whether they were stamped when the object was made or engraved subsequently during their commercial use). Archaeology, with few exceptions, does not supply information about the commercial politics of the state or the way in which the state treated commercial circles. However, there is no doubt that at the end of the Republic and in the first centuries of the Empire, great commercial freedom existed in the Roman world, even as regards cereals. The state's wheat revenue, destined for supplying Rome (the emperors took great care over this provisioning, for they distributed free wheat every month to a large part of the populace) was conveyed there by private ships; and wheat was also the object of private trade.

Commercial mastery

All recent research takes the view that there was a commercial boom in the 2nd and 1st centuries BC benefiting Roman Italy which then began to sell its products all round the Mediterranean, especially the western end. It was at the beginning of the 2nd century BC after the Second Punic War* (which gave Rome commercial mastery in the Mediterranean) that certain glossy black pottery made in Campania (Campania A) or Tuscany (B) began to be massively sold and used, and then imitated outside Italy.

The glossy black oil lamps known as Esquiline ware, produced at Rome from the 3rd century BC, were exported from 180BC and reached their zenith in the last decades of the 2nd century. At the same period, *c.*130BC amphorae of the so-called Dressel I type (named after a 19th century German scholar) replaced the "Graeco-Italian" receptacles for transporting wine produced on the Tyrrhenian coast of central Italy. Enormous quantities of these were found on certain sites in the Languedoc area of southern France (for example Lagaste), at Toulouse and Vieille-Toulouse, and as far as Chalon-sur-Saône in eastern France.

This impressive flow of Italian exports dried up after the Augustan period. Fine Italian ceramics (Arretine ware and other Italian terra sigillata, goblets and "thin-sided" cups) were copied in the provinces and then gave way to local products. In the middle of the 1st century AD, Arretine ware disappeared, to be replaced by Gallic terra sigillata, manufactured closer to the markets formed by the armies of the Rhine. This in turn was superseded by clear sigillata ware produced in North Africa at a period when urban centres were developing on a large scale in Numidia and Caesarean Mauretania (approximately present-day Algeria). As from the end of the 1st century AD two major types of glossy red pottery developed in parallel: one, the clear sigillata ware, was mainly sold all round the coast of the Mediterranean; the other, Gallic terra sigillata, was sold in Gaul, Britain, Roman Germania and in the regions beyond the Rhine, as far as the banks of the Danube.

Not only does archaeology reveal this long-term development of commercial trends; it also helps to define the specific structures of this ancient commerce. It was primarily a maritime or riverine trade, Gallic terra sigillata being frequently transported by water, even when destined for inland regions. Wrecks have been found to show that ships sailed down the river Allier in France and up the Thames in England with cargoes of terra sigillata. As for Arretine ware, it was transported down the river Arno to Pisa.

When this commerce was carried on with foreign peoples or natives of the Empire, its object was to obtain goods which Rome and Italy needed. Some archaeologists believe, with André Tchernia, that the wines exported to Gaul at the end of the Republican period were probably exchanged for metals and slaves. The success of Italian commerce explains the influx of slaves to Italy, and the celebrated "Agora (market) of the Italians" at Delos was nothing more than a slave market.

In the wrecks recovered, amphorae holding wine, oil and fish sauces predominate. Other manufactured objects were embarked as supplementary freight or home freight. This was obviously true of bricks and tiles, the so-called "Campana" decorative plates made in Italy, and the volcanic stone millstones made in most parts of the Empire, heavy products that did not form part of a regular long-distance trade. This was also the case with ordinary pottery (a shipment has been found in the wreck of Madrague de Giens at Hyères in France, which dates to the 1st century BC). It is also true of fine ceramics, for the wreck of Grand Congloué, in the Rhône, France, contained a ton and a half of glossy black ceramics, and also transported 108 tons of amphorae full of wine.

The state may have intervened hardly at all in this commercial activity, but it was only made possible by the existence of Roman domination. As master of the Mediterranean, Rome made sure that it could be navigated safely. The capital of the Empire was an enormous consumer centre and the geographical distribution of the workshops making terra sigillata shows that the existence of military camps also contributed to stimulating production and commerce.

A coppersmith's shop in Roman Italy

Although some centres of ceramic production (for example Arretine ware) were virtual factories, many artisans worked in small workshops which were also used as shops to sell their wares. That was so with this coppersmith. On the left is a customer with a child clutching his tunic. The objects hanging on the wall (which look like buckets) could be tin ingots like those found some years ago in the Port-Vendres II wreck. National Museum of Naples.

The export of oil lamps in the Mediterranean (1st century BC to 1st century AD)

The majority of these terracotta oil lamps (known as Dressel from the name of a celebrated late 19th-century German scholar) were made in central Italy, some in Rome itself. This map clearly shows that long-distance trade was primarily maritime or along rivers.

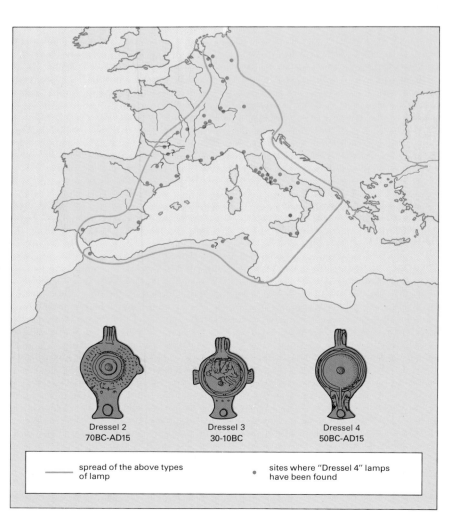

| Dressel 2 | Dressel 3 | Dressel 4 |
| 70BC-AD15 | 30-10BC | 50BC-AD15 |

———— spread of the above types of lamp

• sites where "Dressel 4" lamps have been found

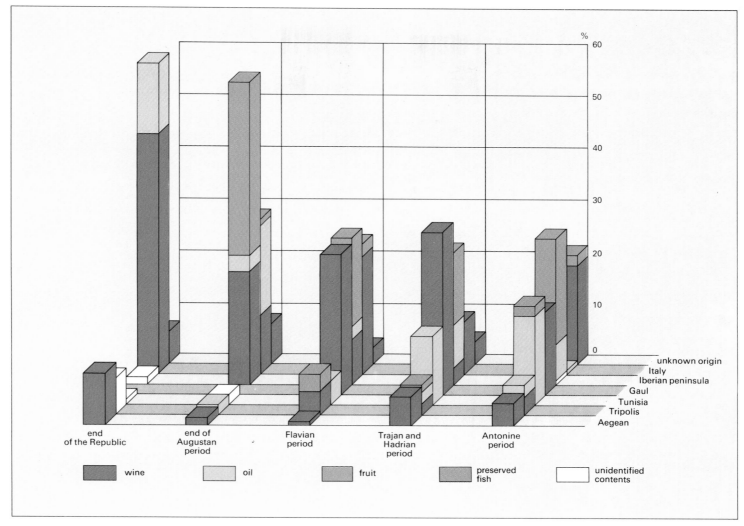

wine	oil
fruit	preserved fish
unidentified contents	

unknown origin
Italy
Iberian peninsula
Gaul
Tunisia
Tripolis
Aegean

end of the Republic — end of Augustan period — Flavian period — Trajan and Hadrian period — Antonine period

Trade in products transported in amphorae: places of origin of amphorae found at Ostia

Between the end of the Republic (1st century BC) and the period of the Antonines (2nd century AD), the places of origin of the amphorae found at Ostia (most of which were intended for provisioning Rome) changed completely. The use of Italian amphorae for oil and even more for wine decreased steadily and was replaced by amphorae from the provinces, especially from Gaul and Spain. African exports increased in the 2nd century AD.

Ostia: mosaic from merchants' office

To ensure that adequate provisions reached Rome, the emperors tended to intervene increasingly in commercial life. From the 2nd century AD, the colonnade of Ostia contained the offices of traders from various Italian and provincial ports. The floor of the office of the "Ship-owners and Merchants of Caralis" (Cagliari in Sardinia) was covered with this mosaic representing a merchant ship and two measures of wheat, thus indicating that the Sardinians mainly transported wheat to this Italian port.

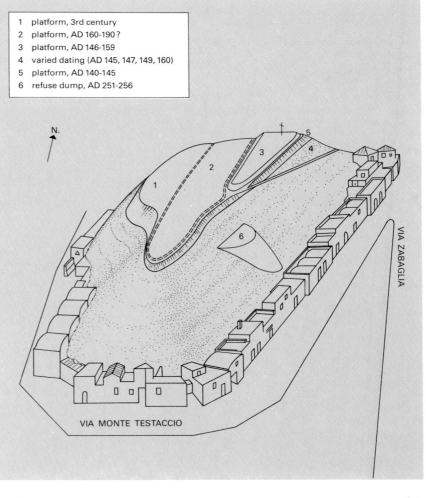

1 platform, 3rd century
2 platform, AD 160-190?
3 platform, AD 146-159
4 varied dating (AD 145, 147, 149, 160)
5 platform, AD 140-145
6 refuse dump, AD 251-256

N.

VIA ZABAGLIA

VIA MONTE TESTACCIO

The public refuse dump of the port of Rome, Monte Testaccio

Neglected by tourists, Monte Testaccio is an artificial hill about 30m (100ft) high, situated near the Tiber to the south of the Aventine, and composed of amphorae fragments. This public refuse dump of the port of Rome has only been superficially excavated. The main finds have been oil amphorae from Baetica (southern Spain) bearing painted inscriptions. These record the weight of the amphorae, the names of the shippers or merchants, and indications of dates, which help to establish how the site gradually increased in height between the 1st and 3rd century AD.

Agricultural and rural life

Quintessential image of privileged Roman life, "villa" is a word that has entered our language: but how did the villa system work? It has left a permanent mark on social structures in the rural West.

Where rural life and agriculture are concerned, archaeologists have, in recent years, tackled problems hitherto neglected, and have developed completely new methods. The medium-sized and large rural properties of the Roman period consisted of extensive buildings, the *villae*, usually in two parts: the *villa urbana*, the often luxurious dwelling of the owner (or, in certain cases, of the farmer), and the *villa rustica*, i.e. the working outhouses. These outhouses were once neglected by archaeologists in favour of the dwellings themselves, but are now being excavated and studied in detail. Good examples of this work are at Francolise and Settefinestre in Italy, and La Garda and Taradeau in France. These excavations have led to a better understanding of farming methods and land use, and of the development of tools and techniques; in certain cases, they also throw some light on the type of labour employed (whether this consisted of slaves*, tenant farmers or owners, or even day labourers). Half a century ago, archaeological sites were studied individually, usually without reference to their environment. On the strength of the work carried out by R. Agache in Picardy, France, and G. Tchalenko in northern Syria, it is now common practice to choose a whole region as the subject of study, and to stress such features as soil development, agricultural structures and the history of the countryside. The land itself is now seen to be as interesting as the architectural details.

Archaeological surveys* rely on the systematic analysis of place-names, maps and other historical documents; they involve a close scrutiny of the terrain, soil tests, and often the use of techniques inspired by the physical sciences. What relics can be found of the peasant habitat are subjected to the same study as the residence itself even when separated from the *villa*.

These new techniques present their own problems. It may happen that nothing can be detected of the flimsier buildings since they have left no trace on the surface. In addition, although some archaeologists may find this contentious, agricultural archaeology seems to supply more information on the size of developments than on the properties themselves. Since a small development could have belonged to a tenant farmer working a section of a larger property, it would be unwise to assume that a dense and widely spread habitat had the status of a system of small properties. Finally, agricultural archaeology tends to favour surveys rather than excavations since it has to study large areas. Surveys however do not yield very detailed information on the chronological evolution of a site, nor are they always possible. As E. Zadora-Rio has pointed out, the results of a survey depend on "the present vegetation, the agricultural history of the area, the nature of the geological substratum, and, to a lesser extent, the condition of the soil at the time of the survey."

Agriculture and slavery

Nevertheless, recent developments in rural archaeology have made some firm conclusions possible, usually based on the work of the most punctilious archaeologists, conscious of the need to understand the soil, and careful to take into account the slightest piece of information; and those who can refer, when this may shed further light, to available documents and all that is known about the period through history.

First among these conclusions is that, at the end of the Republic and during the first century of the Roman Empire (1st century AD), slaves made a crucial contribution to agricultural labour; but not in all parts. Central Italy along the Tyrrhenian, from Etruria to Campania, was the main area in which slaves were used, divided into teams according to the so-called plantation system. A. Carandini believes he has found the cells in which they were housed in the villa at Settefinestre. On the other hand, it is by no means certain that the villas found by R. Agache were farmed by slaves. The villa at Settefinestre, on the territory of the ancient town of Cosa, was built during the second quarter of the 1st century BC and was occupied until the 2nd century AD. The property was not particularly large, perhaps a few hundred hectares. At the height of its prosperity (in the 1st century BC) it was devoted to the cultivation of vines and olive trees. Part of the crops were used by the slaves and perhaps by the owners; what remained was sold. Excavations have brought to light the rooms where wine and oil were made with a press of the endless screw type which is mentioned by Pliny the Elder and which was widely employed at the time.

There were also other, and much larger, working farms which modern scholars call *latifundia* but which they cannot identify with precision. Apart from these *latifundia* and from the villas farmed by slaves (a large number of which belonged to the Emperor), and apart from the collective farms of the natives (about which archaeology has so far been unable to supply any information), several small farms and properties survived, in varying numbers, throughout the whole of the Roman period. It would be wrong to assume that they invariably concentrated on self-sufficiency and highly varied polyculture; the excavations carried out by W. Jashemsky at Pompeii have revealed the existence of small urban vinyards, the wine from which was sold on the spot.

Farming in the provinces

As Roman influence spread, so did the construction of these Roman-style villas, which have often been the object of typological study. G. Tchalenko has shown how the craving for wealth and the spirit of adventure of the urban elite of Antiochia led, in the 1st century AD, to the exploitation of the Belus mountains, which became an important centre for the production of olive oil. And P. Leveau, working in Caesarea and Mauretania, identified two types of countryside: the areas under Roman influence and close to the urban centres, and the areas still in the hands of native farmers; there are many villas in the first area and they are totally absent from the second. Roman influence often manifested itself in a dispersed rural habitat and the absence of large settlements. Work done by A. Leday on Biturigean territory in the south-west part of the Cher area of France has shown at least 100 Gallo-Roman sites. Almost all of them were agricultural centres to varying degrees; the groups of dwellings, the *vici*, were probably not farming villages but centres of commerce and crafts.

However, more ancient groups of dwellings continued to exist in the countryside under Roman occupation, and even to grow in importance. In eastern Languedoc, as shown by J.E. Fiches, protohistorical *oppida** built on hilltops often fell into disuse at the beginning of the empire and were succeeded by widely spread agricultural settlements as well as by new villages built in the valleys: the latter tended to be farming communities, even though they also had buildings of a more residential character. A grouped habitat of this type has been found below the village of Nages in the Gard area of France, at the foot of the *oppidum* of Les Castels; another, in the same area at Saint-Come-et-Naryejols, at the foot of the *oppidum* of Mauressip.

Many other transformations of the provincial countryside were brought about by the Roman presence. An official, so-called "cadastral" registration or "centuriation" was often made, showing full details of the properties in an area. Roman occupation tended to modify the types of cultivation favouring the production of oil and wine (highly profitable at least up to a certain date), which produce was widely sold. It also influenced dietary habits. Thus, while during the 1st century BC, hunting was still important at Nages, France, the supply of meat was coming more and more from domesticated animals (mainly sheep and goats), and a century later the breeding of pigs had spread widely over part of the Narbonne area of Gaul; cattle were better employed and often much stronger than before; and hunting had become a pastime. Neither in Italy nor in the provinces did the Romans confine themselves to ruling and the levying of taxes. Whether knowingly or not, they exercised a deep economical and cultural influence and left an enduring mark on the rural landscape.

An estate from the time of Cicero: the villa at Francolise, Campania

The villa of San Rocco near Capua, Italy, was built shortly after the Sulla period and greatly enlarged towards 30 BC. Notice the importance given to the rainwater tanks, and the residential wing which comprised, around a peristyle or colonnade, the *tablinum* (or reception room for visitors), the *triclinium* (dining room) and the *cubicula* (bedrooms).

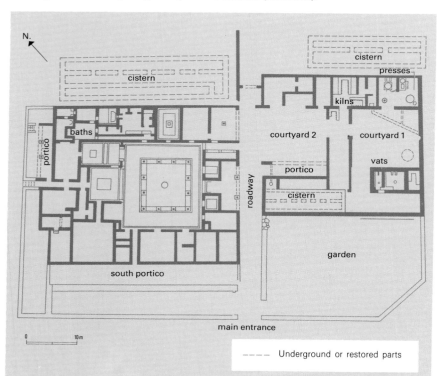

N.

cistern

cistern
presses

baths

kilns

portico

courtyard 2   courtyard 1

vats

roadway

portico

cistern

garden

south portico

main entrance

- - - - Underground or restored parts

0   10m

Reconstruction of a villa in northern Gaul, 1st-3rd century AD

Based on research carried out by R. Agache, this model gives us an idea of the appearance of the Gallo-Roman villas of northern Gaul. Two courtyards are divided by a wall: in the first was the residence of the owner, often having a portico; in the second, the agricultural buildings (and perhaps the dwelling of the *vilicus* or steward). Unlike those in Italy (for instance at Francolise), these dwellings did not, generally speaking, have a peristyle.

R. Agache

Roman settlements in Picardy (Warfusee-Abancourt)

In the areas of Artois and Picardy in France, R. Agache has discovered, through aerial photography, over 1,000 villas (most of which seem to date from the 1st, 2nd and 3rd centuries AD) and has often been able even to trace their plan. From the end of the 3rd century AD, settlements seem to have gathered along the main roads, constituting the origins of villages, some of which still exist. The *locus* is also a rural settlement, albeit a smaller one, more a hamlet than a village.

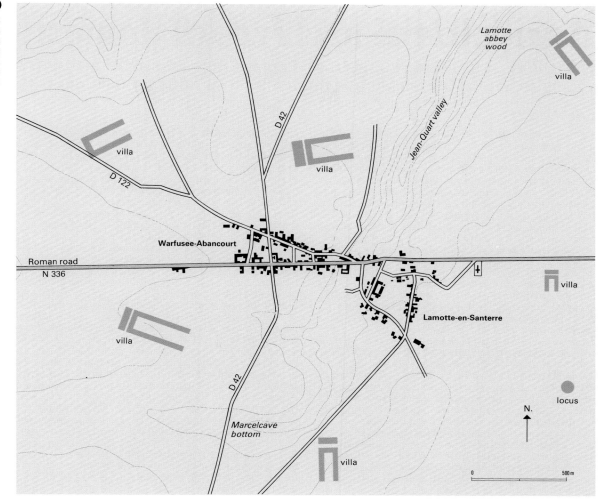

The steward slave and his subordinates, the farmer-slaves of the estate

The farmer-slaves, who worked in teams, were under the leadership of a steward, the *vilicus*, himself the slave of the owner. The *vilicus* Hippocrates was presented, by the slaves he controlled (in Latin, his *familia rustica*), with this modest funerary stele found at the Italian site of Chieti (Abruzzi). It is inscribed: "To Hippocrates, the *vilicus* of Plautius, who ruled over them with clemency, the slaves of the estate offer this funerary stone." National Antiquities Museum of Abruzzi and Molise, Chieti.

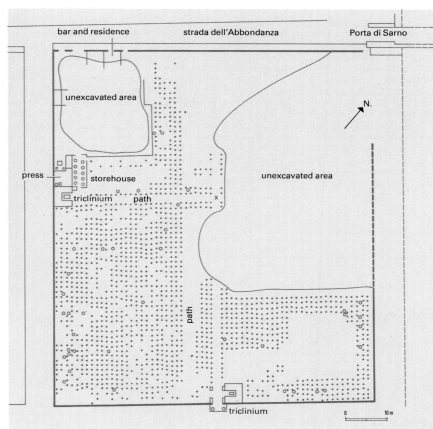

A small "urban" vineyard

From 1966 onwards, W.F. Jashemsky has been excavating in Pompeii, within the city walls, a vineyard of about 7000 sq m, where wine was produced and sold. She has found the holes left in the soil by the roots of trees (about 50 of them; it is not known of what sort) and by vine stocks (over 3000). Along the western wall of the vineyard were three buildings: a press, a storehouse with partly buried jars, and a bar where the wine was sold.

Presents of tenant farmers to their owners

The western face of the famous Igel monument in Germany (2nd century AD?), the mausoleum of the Secundinii, wealthy merchants and landowners, carries this frieze recently reinterpreted by P. Veyne. The frieze shows six rustics, either tenant farmers or sharecroppers, solemnly offering the owner, or rather his representative, presents in kind: a hare, two fishes, a lamb, probably an animal skin, a cockerel, and a basket of fruits. Rheinisches Landesmuseum, Trier.

Pompeii, the archives of domestic decoration

Wall paintings have been known from Pompeii since the sensational finds of the 18th century. But only now has a complete record been made, and this has led to exciting revaluations of this marvellous treasury of Roman art.

The first excavations at Herculaneum took place in 1736 and at Pompeii in 1748, and the gradual unearthing of the towns buried by the eruption of Vesuvius in AD79 which followed had a profound effect on the way modern cultures look upon Graeco-Roman antiquity. The history of these discoveries entails an understanding of the evolution which has taken place in research and archaeological techniques – from the excavation itself to the recording, restoration and conservation of documents, and the applications of scientific methods. Scientific analysis is full of surprises, and by no means suggests a linear and constant progress in the growth of these towns. In the case of wall decorations, present-day research observes requirements which have been in force since the end of the 18th century, when care was taken to record, in those days with drawings and watercolours, the entirety of the walls in order to preserve the whole of the decorative context, in case the paintings were damaged or destroyed. Thanks to works such as *Gli ornati delle pareti delle stanze dell'antica Pompei* (The wall decorations in the rooms of ancient Pompeii) published from 1796, we have sufficient documentation to study figurative works which have since disappeared, although a 1977 inventory of photographs then in existence has revealed that 60 percent of surviving remains had never been recorded. But the effects of such discoveries on the public, which has itself considerably altered between the 18th century, with its tours undertaken by a small cultured elite, to the modern era of mass tourism, provide an interesting study of the influence of antiquity on the taste and sensitivity of the modern age through the ideas of those times which have grown up alongside the discoveries.

First, the shock caused by the earliest explorations of a small Roman town fixed in a moment of its everyday life, an ancient world full of colour, had an impact similar to that exercised by the grotesque painters during the Renaissance. There was great debate about the documentary and aesthetic value of the frescoes, and centuries of idealism were sometimes shattered by their quality. Winckelmann wrote: "These are the paintings of very mediocre artists." When the technique of making moulds developed, during the following century, visitors were fascinated by the sight of the bodies of the people suddenly overtaken by death, which inspired poetic writing too – for instance the young girl found in the Villa of Diomedes was the inspiration for Théophile Gautier when he wrote *Arria Marcella*. But a complete documentation (18,000 photographs) was not achieved until a record of the whole of the archaeological area was undertaken by the Istituto Centrale per il Catalogo e la Documentazione (central institute for cataloguing and documentation) between 1977 and 1980 – a campaign that came to an end only a few days before the earthquake which ravaged much of Campania and Basilicata. The work was carried out systematically, house by house, recording the decorations of the floors and walls; and yet the documentation assembled still represents less than 20 per cent of all that has been revealed on the sites since excavations first began.

Decorative styles and social status

Thanks to such exemplary work, however, we now have a data bank, constituting a valuable archive on the domestic decorations of Pompeii, upon which we can base our study of the conditions under which these decorations were realized, the purposes, means, and taste of the owners, and the workshops and the role they played. The works gathered have been divided into four groups of Pompeiian style*, and by means of a "two-dimensional" analysis, from what the structuralists call "synchronic" and "diachronic" points of view, it is possible to unravel an idea of a hierarchy of decorative schemes which indicates the social status of the owners. Archaeology confirms the distinctions already stressed by Vitruvius in Book VI of his *De Architectura*. Ordinary people did not need sumptuous reception rooms, "as they normally visit other people and are not visited themselves"; but the rulers had to distinguish themselves from the other citizens by the furnishings of their houses, within which state business was transacted. Recent work devoted to the Roman residences of these notables (such as the house of Augustus on the Palatine, or the Villa of the Farnesina probably built for Agrippa), enables us to examine the ways in which the decorative styles elaborated at the highest levels of the social ladder were transposed to more modest dwellings. "Generally speaking, one tries to imitate the ways of the illustrious people," remarked Cicero (*On Duty*, I, 138). "Whoever imitates the virtue of that great man who was Lucullus? And yet how many take as their model the magnificence of his villas!"

A chronological perspective enables us to identify the shifts in the general trends between the 1st century BC and the 1st AD. The beautiful houses of the Republican period – the Villa of the Papyri of Herculaneum, the Villa of Mysteries, the House of the Faun at Pompeii, the Villa of Annius Synistor at Boscoreale, the Villa of Oplontis, to mention only a few of the most famous ones – all show us examples of full-scale decorative schemes and point to the culture of their owners, upon whose intentions detailed iconographical analysis can shed interesting light. The letters written by Cicero, who was himself the owner of magnificent villas in which every one of the smallest decorative details was based on some cultural reference, are an invaluable guide to the deciphering of the pictorial and sculptural decoration found in these houses. Then, during the Julio-Claudian period (27BC–AD68), the new rich who displaced the old ruling classes were not heirs to the latter's refined culture, as is constantly pointed out by the moralists of the 1st century. Trimalchio, in Petronius' *Satyricon*, is a reminder of this. The new development can be seen quite clearly in Pompeii, where it brought about a considerable change in the *modus operandi* of the workshops. Production of decorative themes had already been based on strict formulas, entrusted to craftsmen who specialized in certain types of motif (figurative, architectural, etc.). This now became increasingly standardized; but as the requirements of the patrons became less and less well-defined, so did the workshop assume increasing independence in the choice of motifs, which were sometimes copied from one house to the next. General themes can now be seen to prevail: themes connected with the cult of Dionysus in the dining rooms, erotic scenes or love stories in the bedrooms, marbles, mosaics and stuccoes with marine motifs in the bathrooms. Of course the dwellings had a life and development of their own: with the economic change in the 1st century, widespread in Italy, and with the effects of the earthquake of AD62, profound modifications took place in the way a dwelling was used. The luxurious frescoes of the Republican period eventually formed the background for storerooms for amphorae, fullers' workshops, and bakehouses.

However, apart from helping us to understand the daily life of the people who commissioned them, the now fully documented decorations of Pompeii can at last play an active role in the aesthetic analysis of a decorative art whose roots are embedded in the Hellenistic world, but which, at the time of its disappearance in the cataclysm of AD79, had reached a new point: "A connection between Greek Hellenism and Byzantine neo-Hellenism, that is between the paintings of the ancient world and the first paintings of the modern world." (R. Bianchi Bandinelli, *Storicita dell'arte antica*, Bari, De Donato, 1973).

Storehouse for amphorae

The amphorae or storage jars of a fish sauce factory are stored in a room decorated with frescoes from the Augustan period (house 9, insula 12, region I).

House of Fabius Rufus, details of the decoration of floors and walls (right and opposite)

Two small adjacent rooms in the basement (nos. 13 and 14) had the same mosaic decorative schemes, playing on the inversion of the colours of the background and the squared motifs. In the centre of the pavement of room 13 (opposite) a fine polychrome motif (*emblema*) represents a theatrical mask. The walls have a decorative scheme of red and white panels superimposed on an older design dating from the final phase of style II (end of 1st century BC).

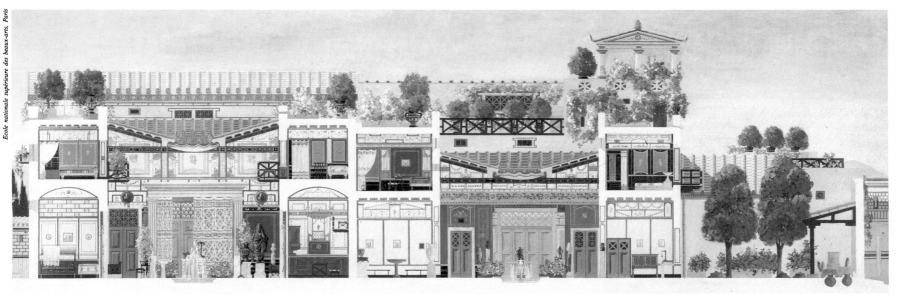

Ecole nationale supérieure des beaux-arts. Paris

Transverse section of the Casa del Centenario (1903)

Archaeological restorations illustrated a purely decorative intention with an emphasis on details of interior decoration (wall decor, hangings, furniture). These principles inspired contemporary (20th century) architects, as, for example, in the extraordinary Villa Kerylos built by Pontremoli for Theodore Reinach and his family at Beaulieu-sur-Mer.

Istituto Centrale per il Catalogo e la Documentazione

Right: composition by A.F. Normand (1885)

The architect A.F. Normand gave an enthusiastic welcome to the contribution which could be made by photography to the documentation of ancient buildings. From 1851 he took a series of photographs at Pompeii, using Talbot's new calotype process (a negative on paper from which positive images could be taken). This composition of reliefs, sculptures, and architectural fragments from various buildings expresses the romantic and rather melancholy vision of an antiquary: a collection of ancient artifacts, detached from their context. This attitude, incidentally, was dominant at the time when our great museums were established and gives the objects displayed an aesthetic rather than a historic significance.

Bakery re-using a dwelling space

A bakery, with oven and millstones, occupies the ancient atrium of house 8 of the 3rd insula of the V region.

Istituto Centrale per il Catalogo e la Documentazione

Arch. Phot. Paris. S.P.A.D.E.M.

The necropolis at Isola Sacra

Excavation of a Roman Empire burial ground near the capital reveals a materialism on the part of the bourgeoisie that seemingly extended to the afterlife. But by the 3rd century a concern with death and destiny had apparently begun to develop.

A number of factors make the Isola Sacra (sacred island) necropolis of the Port of Rome particularly significant: its extent, both spatially and temporally (end of 1st to 4th centuries AD), its state of conservation and the variety and richness of the documentary evidence concerning it. Near to Rome, connected to Ostia and the port, it lay at a point of convergence and dissemination of the great ebb and flow of cultural influences of the Roman empire—which makes it much more valuable to us than a simple necropolis. Discovered by chance, it was excavated by G. Calza between 1925 and 1940. Archaeological soundings, begun in the mid 1970s in the area which had been hurriedly excavated by Calza, are still in progress. They provide a range of extremely interesting data on the chronology and structure of the necropolis and enable archaeologists to understand better the Roman funerary beliefs of imperial times. The area covering approximately 1.5km (1 mile) uncovered by the excavations contains more than 100 graves lying on either side of a two-way road which connects Porto and Ostia. Recent findings make it clear that this road dates from the Flavian period and that it was linked with the port of Claudius even before being connected to that of Trajan. There are two types of tombs: the "chamber" type, with or without an enclosure in front of it and having one or two storeys and a roof covered with either a barrel vault or a terrace; and the "coffin" (cassone) type. There are also burial places in amphorae (narrow-necked jars) or under large tiles which form a roof which slopes both ways. In one place they form a kind of necropolis within the necropolis—the so-called "field of the poor". The first two types of tomb belong—at least in the earliest phase—to family groups. A familia urbana may be identified here, consisting of the owner of the tomb, his children, the freed slaves and their descendants—this being a familia which was defined as a unit of production rather than by the blood relationship connecting its members. It seems possible that certain later tombs which bear no inscriptions were the property of funeral "colleges" or associations. Made first of opus reticulatum (reticulated work), then later of brick, the tombs have a facing which is more carefully executed at the front than on the other sides; but the latter are covered in a thickly glazed red material. The door jambs and architraves at the front are made of travertine stone, and above the door is an inscription on marble, with a skylight window on either side. Often one or two reliefs in terracotta are placed next to the inscription. These give us further information by telling us something which is never mentioned in the inscription, namely the profession of the owner of the tomb.

Outside the monument there are often two benches on either side of the doorway. They raise the question of funerary banquets and how these took place. This was probably in the open air, in public and with some ostentation, but the excavations currently being carried out have not provided a complete answer to this question. The internal arrangement of the chamber tombs is dictated by the nature of the funerary rites. Where this consisted of cremation—which was the general practice in earlier times—a series of aedicules and niches for the terracotta urns (which were walled in for protection) was necessary. Inhumation, which always coexisted with cremation in the Roman world, left its mark only on the architectural structure of the chamber tombs around AD 130–40 when an arcosolium* was inserted in the lower part of each of the walls containing niches, fitting into the overall design, and respecting the principle of symmetry. At the same time, provision began to be made for formae (oblong containers having the dimensions of a body) to be placed inside, under the mosaic-covered floors in two or more layers. This placing of formae under the stone flooring involved the constant destruction and repair of the mosaics, and reveals the lack of functional connection between the tomb and individual burial places, emphasizing the greater significance of the monument, whose purpose was to affirm and make known the identity of the familia of the dead occupants. Inside the chamber tombs, part of the decoration consisted of stucco reliefs on all the architectural elements; the ceilings and the spaces between the niches were painted. These paintings make little reference to the after-life; they simply accentuate the decorative richness of the place as a whole. The paintings, stuccos and mosaics are generally the product of qualified craftsmen meeting the needs of their customers, who belonged to the middle ranks of society and whose aspirations were towards decus (propriety) and social advancement. Other sources confirm this definition of the occupants of the necropolis: middle class people with no members belonging to a higher level of society.

The Roman middle class

An analysis of the necropolis makes it possible to define certain behavioural characteristics of these middle classes, their way of expressing themselves, and how they saw (or chose to represent) themselves. The most important thing was to occupy a position as near as possible to the road (on which there was considerable traffic), and this emphasizes the absence of any strictly religious space proper to the necropolis and the Roman world's lack of interest in questions of the immortality of the soul and the afterlife. Death manifests itself as the disruption of order within the social fabric, but once the burial rites had given the deceased a new status and re-established equilibrium, the tomb became precisely the means by which the dead person retained a place within the framework of social relations and daily life. The funerary monument telling his story carried his image and his ideology and became in its turn a guarantee of the continuity of that image. The monument is a concentration of this ideology. Placed there before the community it is almost independent of its specific function, which is to contain human remains. Thus the funerary monument counted for much more than the space which the dead person occupied. Funerary objects are completely absent from tombs, and the inscription, which is a general statement of ownership, replaces individual inscriptions naming the deceased persons in the tomb. This funerary ideology accords—in a more modest way—with that of the upper classes. There seems to be an absence in the Roman world, at least in the 2nd century, of any marginal ideologies—everything conforms to the dominant model.

But the necropolis covers a sufficiently long period for us to be able to notice in it a change in mental attitudes to death. These changes came about very slowly, at various stages. The new clues found in the 3rd century tombs relate neither to their layout nor to their typology, nor to the richness of the decorations, which are all unchanged (although inhumation is now more common than cremation). But in them their function or purpose—namely to receive the body of the deceased—has been established. The formae are now accessible without damage to the floors because movable slabs of stone were used for the flooring. The main difference however is that the tomb is no longer the place where the individual stated and made known his identity. Groups of tombs of the 3rd century have been identified which were all built at the same time with continuous walls to the rear and at the front. They were divided into medium-sized units with separate entrances and probably belonged to different owners. This phenomenon shows both the diminishing influence of private and individual choice by customers, and the existence of standard funerary monuments whose character was laid down in advance and was primarily functional. All this would seem to justify the hypothesis that a significant change in ideological beliefs had occurred. Death and destiny are now at the centre of a new interest and have become an integral part of everyday experience in a society which has ceased to exorcize them. The tombs of the 3rd century, which are still all pagan, no longer seek to express a privileged relationship with the world of the living and are no longer used as a pretext for the celebration of status. They bear witness to a society which accepted the concept of death.

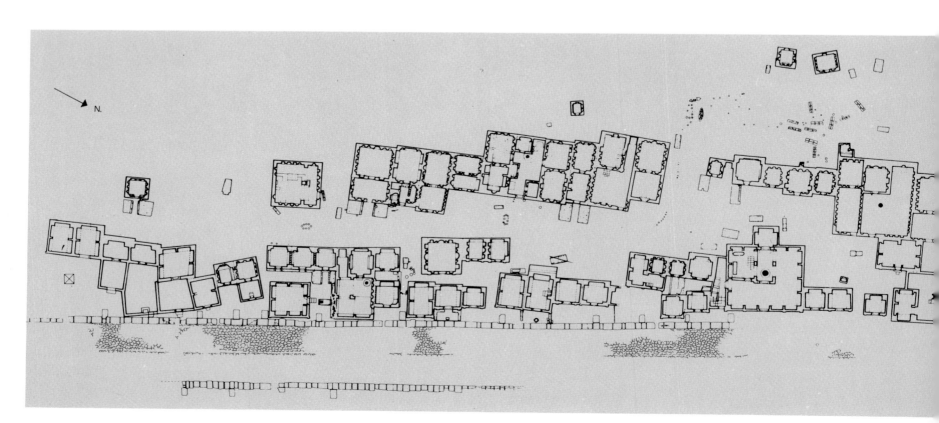

View of the necropolis

On the left, the façades of chamber tombs (Nos. 88–77) in the second row of monuments; on the right, the rear of tombs in the first row (their façades giving on the the road). In the centre, background, two "coffin" (cassone) tombs, and, foreground, burial places where amphorae were used.

Detail of the arrangement of the walls of tomb 92

In the chamber tombs, the aedicules and niches are arranged on the walls observing principles of symmetry which throw the central element into relief with a great richness of detail. This tomb only contains cremations.

Interior of tomb 55

This tomb contained both cremations and inhumations, as is shown by the fact that there are both niches and aedicules for urns as well as arcosolia (one per wall) which show through the surface of the sand covering the flooring. The hierarchy of architectural elements does not seem to indicate a hierarchy of functions: there is nothing—and in particular no inscription—to indicate this, and we shall never know which members of the family group were assigned to the various niches and arcosolia.

Arcosolia* and formae, tomb 34

Arcosolia and formae are typical of the inhumation rite. Sarcophagi were placed in the former and several bodies were placed on top of one another in the latter.

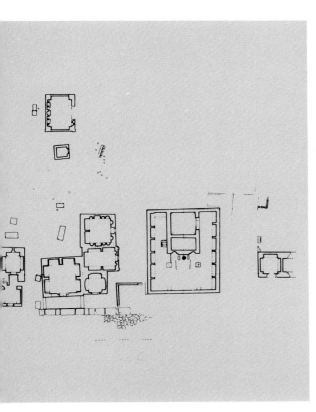

General plan of the necropolis of the Port of Rome at Isola Sacra

The Isola Sacra is a part of the Tiber delta situated between the modern settlements of Ostia Antica and Fiumicino, which was not transformed into an island until 103AD when—with the construction of the port of Trajan (Portus Romae)—it was separated from the mainland to the north by a canal (Fossa Traianea) dug to prevent the port itself from becoming silted up. From very early on, the tombs lined both sides of the road: in the part which has been uncovered—farthest from the port, and where the necropolis began—traces of occupation going back to the end of the first century have been found, but the largest area dates from the 2nd century and the first half of the 3rd century. In the 2nd century, a second line of tombs was built behind the first line, still aligned to the road. In the 3rd century, new tombs grew up in the first row along the road. Because the ground level was, by then, higher, these were able to incorporate the earlier constructions or were built on top of them. From the second half of the 3rd century and the 4th century, all we find are indications of continued use and of repair—no new constructions were built.

Portrait of a woman, detail of central niche in tomb 19

The necropolis at Isola Sacra, together with the houses at Ostia, contains the largest known collection of post-Pompeian Roman paintings.

Town and country in the Roman West

The classical city is one of the great legacies of the Graeco-Roman civilization: for us civilization means life based on the city. But how were these magnificent building projects financed?

Throughout the classical period, philosophers and theoreticians conceived of "the City" as a unity overriding the dual concept of town and country, which we have come to regard as complete opposites since the Industrial Revolution and as a result of the ideas of Marx and Engels. In *The Laws* (V.745), Plato suggested organizing the space of the City so that there would be no distinction between town and country dwellers. In the same way, at Rome, Cicero thought that agriculture was the only occupation "worthy of a free man" (*De Officiis*, 1.151). A century later, the agronomist Columella wrote: "There is only [one way of increasing one's fortune] that can be looked on as honest and noble and that is the cultivation of the land." In the myth of Dionysus, the absence of towns and ignorance of agriculture was equivalent to barbarism. Civilization combined the establishment of the town with an understanding of agriculture. This ideology persists throughout antiquity and recurs in particular in the fourth and fifth centuries, a period that is today seen less and less as a time of irreversible urban decadence, as opposed to an age when the aristocracy still led the semi-urban, semi-rural existence described by intellectual aristocrats like Ausonius and Symmachus. Although conflicts connected with the food shortages and excessive exploitation of the poor rural masses did exist, contemporary historians have ceased to look for the main cause of the fall of the Roman Empire in the revolt of the countryside.

Town development: sources of capital
Since the concept of the classical town as simply feeding off the country cannot really be upheld, we still need to explain the origin of the enormous amounts of capital expended on the monumental adornment of Roman towns. The case of Rome has to be distinguished from that of other imperial towns. The origin of Rome's massive spending lay in war and booty, and the profits from sacking the Mediterranean world—an income arising from its situation as an imperial capital.

In many respects the other major towns were like little Romes, but their prosperity could not have had the same origin. So what was the source of the capital sums spent on the town? The problem is to put the major economic functions in their relative place: handicrafts, industry, trade and agriculture. Generally speaking, crafts are linked with the needs of urban life, necessary products or luxury items, and not with supplying a regional or interregional market. Important industrial activities could even be totally or partially practised outside the town, as in the case of ceramics or even of textile craftsmen, for whom specialized installations were only necessary during a specific phase of production (fulling or dyeing) Even when controlled by town-based merchants, these activities could be sited in the country. Syrian caravan towns, the prosperity of which was connected with desert traffic, or ports such as Alexandria in Egypt, may provide exceptions to this rule. But profits linked with commerce cannot be neglected in the fortunes of notables, provided we do not regard them as an essential feature. The fact remains that most of the wealth consumed by the town came from the country.

Interrelations of town and country
For this reason historians have reacted against the modern conception of a classical town based, like the medieval town, on handicrafts and trade, and have raised the question of the town's role in the Roman world. Studies of classical country areas, and archaeological discoveries deriving from new methods such as photo interpretation, systematic examination on the ground or aerial observation, now provide important evidence challenging the old image of large towns surrounded by cultivated but uninhabited country. There was in fact no single type of countryside, but different types of countryside determined by their relation to the town and valid for specific periods. Land ownership was the foundation of the fortune and reputation of the principal notables, and a necessary condition of their access to positions of power. The organization of rural space by the town was not only expressed by "centuriation"—the allotment of plots of land to colonists organized into urban and civic collectives.

The town was also connected with the *villa*, a term which acquired, first in 2nd century BC Italy and then in the rest of the empire, an increasingly technical sense. It referred to an establishment built of durable materials, comprising certain dimensions and forming a centre of agricultural exploitation. The network of *villae*

geometrically defined the sphere of influence of the classical town at a given moment in its history. Such an organization is a historical phenomenon connected with the development of Roman society corresponding roughly to the period from the 2nd century BC to the 3rd century AD. But even during this period, the Roman empire never displayed an overall uniformity in its land use. Some regions did not experience the complementary aspects of Romanization created by the town and *villa*. Countryside defined by a network of *villae* coexisted with countryside not subject to Romanization and defined negatively by the absence of *villae*, a duality which confirms the cultural opposition felt and expressed by the ancients between the civilized urban Roman world and the indigenous barbaric world.

As from the third century, but sometimes earlier, the relationship between town and country seems to have been modified. The *villa* of the type heavily reliant on slave labour declined, although its regression did not imply the decline of the town, even though the latter would then have been deprived of the ground rent necessary for their survival. The *villa* might be abandoned as an agricultural building without its ownership changing, but the urban rent could be levied directly on the villages which served as stage points in the town's control of the country. In many regions, the decrease in the number of *villae* from the third century AD did not have a proven effect on the wealth of towns. There was a restructuring of the rural space rather than an actual decline. Some scholars have interpreted this reorganization as a "ruralization" of the whole of society. The town may have lost some of its political usefulness, so that the difference became less marked between a countryside where farmers and villages continued to pay ground rent to urban owners, and another which depended directly and completely on the powerful owners of the large *villae*, some of which were veritable palaces, characteristic of the end of antiquity.

Thus, examination of the forms of organization of land use by classical society verifies and renews the idea that at this time there was no real opposition between town and country, except when their relationship was disturbed by other conflicts, in particular by the social and ethnic conflict between Romans and the native population.

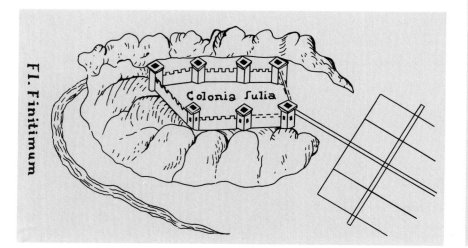

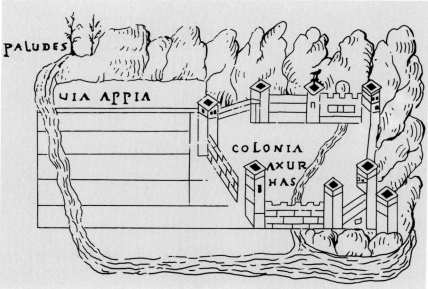

Roman colonies and their rural environment
The manuscripts of *Gromatici Veteres*, a collection of technical texts dealing with surveying problems (the *groma* is an instrument used by surveyors) were illustrated by sketches which give a good idea of how towns were planned in an area of "centuriation" division. Left, a town (Colonia Iulia) located in a geometrically divided area; bottom left, a fortified city (Colonia Iulia Spellatium in Umbria) not divided by centuriation; bottom right, a third town, Anxur (Terracina) located at the edge of an area of centuriation, the *domanus* (east-west axis) of which is formed by the *Via Appia* traversing the town.

The organization of the rural area around a Roman town: ground occupation around Caesarea in Mauritania (Cherchel, Algeria)

A thematic map of a geographically varied area of small plains, valleys, mountains and hills, shows how the distribution of *villae* was not so much dictated by geographical environment as by their proximity to the urban centre. In a geometrical sense, the network of *villae* defines the area of influence of the town at a given moment in its history. The disappearance of the *villae* is linked to their distance away from the town centre, suggesting that high altitudes, mountain valleys or marginal land are not decisive factors. Gradually an agricultural area, consisting of a network of *villae*, gives way to another area without *villae*, where the basic features of the rural landscape consist of the ruins of small and medium-sized holdings.

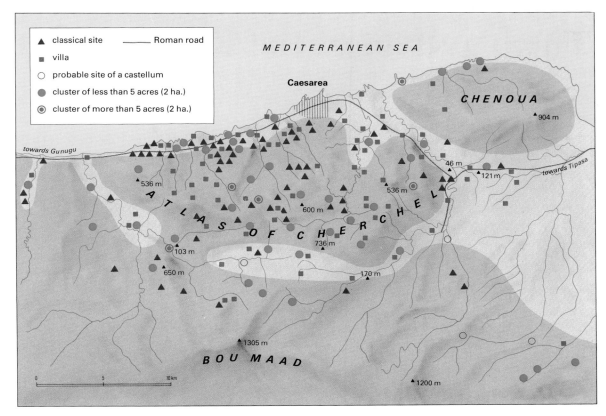

Rural archaeology and industrial development

A striking example of archaeological research operating within an industrial context. Huge excavators clear the wasteland above a vast deposit of lignite, while archaeologists dig up the remains of a rural site. As from 1978, an agreement between the companies involved and the Rhineland State Museum at Bonn has permitted archaeologists to benefit from an industrial project, in spite of the total destruction of archaeological remains covering an area of several hundreds of square miles betweeen Aix-la-Chapelle and Cologne (the Colonia Agrippina of the Romans). A systematical archaeological study of occupation sites from their origins to Merovingian times, (7th century AD) was carried out. The characteristics of habitats in the Roman period was clearly revealed, demonstrating the effects of the Romanization of German rural areas.

The Romanization and urbanization of the country

In Charente-Poitou, France, several sites reveal a complex of public monuments (theatres, forums, baths, religious monuments) although there are no neighbouring residential quarters. Some scholars think these urban centres without residential areas are a legacy of the *conciliabula*, meeting places for Celtic tribes which the government wanted to turn into the centres of Romanization. It is more likely, howener, that the living quarters disappeared because they were not built of durable materials. Nevertheless, these sites ares undoubtedly evidence of generous donations by Gallic noblement financing, in the second century AD, the construction of country monuments similar to those built by their parents at Saintes a century earlier. The photograph shows are aerial view of the Bouchards site in the Angoulème, France.

Monumental evidence of the urban élite's presence in the country

A bridge of the late first century AD situated near Saint-Chamas, southern France. Its monumental character cannot be explained either by the size of the small river, which it spans with a single arch, or its proximity to a crossroad. It was bequeathed by an eminent citizen in the colony of Arles, Lucius Donnius Flavos, who was priest of the cult of Rome and Augustus, as recorded in the inscription engraved on the external face of the arches. Possibly built here to mark the boundary between the colonies of Arles and Aix, or connected with Flavos' own mausoleum, this monumental bridge emphasizes the presence of the urban élite in the countryside. There are several *villae* in the vicinity and one of them at least may have belonged to Flavos.

The frontiers of the Roman Empire

For an empire which extended from Syria to Scotland, Rome had a remarkably tiny army—but it was formidably organized on its frontiers where *Romanitas* confronted the "barbarians".

The Roman army, with its reputation as a solid, well-organized, well-trained and effective fighting force, has always fascinated both soldiers and scholars. Military remains such as camps, fortresses and frontier fortifications were an object of study long before the start of scientific archaeology, and represented a major field of activity among English and German scholars at the end of the last century. New questions and methods (especially aerial survey by visual observation or photography) have served to modify appreciably our concept of the strategic disposition and multiple functions of the army in Roman society and history.

After the battle of Actium (2nd September, 31BC), the territories controlled by Rome—Italy, Dalmatia, Greece, Macedonia, Asia Minor, Cyrenaica and eastern Maghreb—were centred on the Mediterranean, with the exception of Gaul and Spain, which formed two important continental blocks. In the middle of the 2nd century AD, the frontiers of the empire were pushed back to the Danube, with the addition of Dacia in the north, and stabilized on the Euphrates in the east. They incorporated Egypt beyond the First Cataract and North Africa as far as the fringes of the desert, in the western regions (west of present-day Algeria and Morocco), where occupation was concentrated in the northern parts. Britain was occupied as far as Scotland. The territory under direct control had thus been doubled in extent.

Nevertheless, two major setbacks occurred. In spite of repeated and difficult campaigns under Augustus, marked by the disaster of Varus when three legions were wiped out in AD9, the lower Rhine was not permanently crossed. The *agri decumati** (tithe-lands) were only acquired gradually under the Flavians and consolidated under Antoninus. In the east, the provinces finally wrested by Trajan from the Parthian empire—Armenia, Assyria and Mesopotamia—were abandoned two years later by his successor.

These conquests were achieved by a heterogeneous and absurdly small army. Its heterogeneous nature arose from its recruitment: side by side with the legions, which were formed of citizens and represented the elite of the army, auxiliary troops were recruited from the *peregrini* (free men resident in the empire, but without Roman citizenship) and had at first a clearly marked ethnic origin. At least equal in number to the legionary troops, they were less highly regarded, less well paid, and subject to longer service. The army was also heterogeneous in its command structure: whereas the subordinate officers of the legion, the centurions*, had

mostly risen from the ranks and formed a cadre of quality, the senior officers were of senatorial* rank and had no special military training. The leaders of the auxiliary troops were equestrians*, and had often acquired much command experience in the course of their careers, but the highest ranks were closed to them. Above all, the army was small. The number of the legions fluctuated at around 30, or approximately 160,000 men; the auxiliary troops are understood to have numbered about the same. In addition to these troops, we may add the elite corps stationed at Rome, consisting of the praetorian cohorts*, the urban cohorts*, and the emperor's personal guards, as well as the foreign or barbarian contingents, the *numeri**, who served beside the regular troops, and the sailors of the fleets; but even so, the total could scarcely have exceeded a figure of 400,000 men.

Fortifications and mobility

Moreover, the army was widely dispersed. It could be regrouped in the form of *vexillationes** or detachments, for local operations, or as an army corps for large-scale campaigns, such as the 12 legions of Trajan's first Dacian war in AD101, but in ordinary times it covered the whole area of the frontiers. The geographical distribution of the legions followed strategic considerations; they were concentrated along the most threatened or the most coveted frontiers, and the legionary camps acted as bases that were as much offensive as defensive. The task of guarding and holding the frontiers fell mainly to the auxiliaries, divided among many camps and forts. This role increased in the 2nd century with Hadrian and Antoninus, at the time when most of the frontiers were fixed. Even then, the Empire was not a vast entrenched camp surrounded by fortified walls and ditches to be defended every inch of the way. Continuous fortifications such as Hadrian's Wall* and the Antonine Wall in Britain, or the *limes* of Germania, Raetia and the lower Danube, could not be merely defensive lines because of their extent; they were in fact lines of containment and, once crossed, could send rapidly to the threatened region units stationed nearby. Towers disposed at regular intervals facilitated visual control of this border, which was as much economic and psychological as military. Elsewhere in the east, as at Cappadocia, Syria or Arabia, and also in Africa, the *limes* was a border zone sometimes organized around a strategic road enabling the rapid movement of troops. Surveillance of the zone was then ensured by patrols radiating out from their bases to control the area.

Built according to a single plan, apart from variations in detail depending on periods and regions, the camps of the Roman army, legionary *castra* and auxiliary *castella*, have left a deep impression. Staging camps, which sometimes can only be picked out by aerial photography, mark out the campaigns in Britain and Germania. Permanent camps, at first constructed in wood and earth, were built of more durable material from the end of the 1st century. The legionary camp was a town in itself with its own hospital and baths. It was arranged, like the towns, along two right-angled lines based on the headquarters, the *principia*, which formed the administrative and religious centre. Their role as well as their appearance reflect—or anticipate—those of the city centres, the forums. The increasing weight of the army in society thus made itself felt in the bringing together and fusion of civil and military architecture.

Once demobilized, the legionary or auxiliary (who then acquired Roman citizenship) often settled in the region where he had served, sometimes in the village that had grown up near his camp. This might even become a *municipium* (town with charter) or a *colonia* (settlement of retired veterans), such as Carnuntum (Colonia Septimia), near the camp of legio XIII Gemina, today Bad Deutsch Altenberg in Austria. In addition to defending the frontiers, the army thus ensured the urban development and Romanization of the provinces throughout the Empire.

Everything changed with the reign of Marcus Aurelius. In 167, the Quadi and Marcomanni crossed the Danube and threatened Aquileia. Seven years later the situation was re-established, but the impetus had been set in motion and in the 3rd century the barbarians, Alemanni, Goths, Vandals and Persians, swamped the static defences of the Empire. In spite of the energy of the emperors, the army proved unequal to the task. Gallienus tried to establish a new army by splitting up the legions and developing the cavalry; his reforms inaugurated the army of the Lower Empire later organized by Diocletian and Constantine. Numbers were increased, with 500,000 men under Constantine; the distinction between legionaries and auxiliaries was abolished. In addition to a better distribution of frontier troops, a mobile force was created under the orders of two senior officers, the *magistri peditum* and *equitum* (commandants of infantry and cavalry). These generals were often barbarians, such as Stilicho (fifth century AD). Their knowledge of the enemy ensured a number of successes, but that did not stop the capture of Rome by Gaeseric in 455.

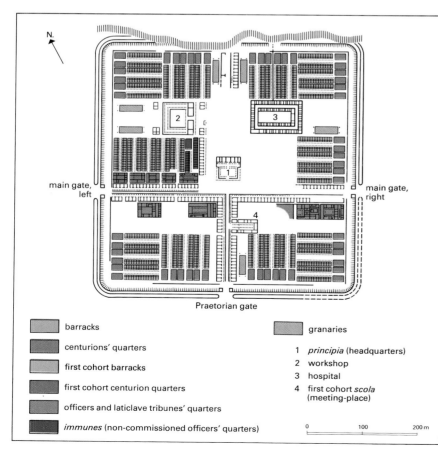

barracks

centurions' quarters

first cohort barracks

first cohort centurion quarters

officers and laticlave tribunes' quarters

immunes (non-commissioned officers' quarters)

granaries

1 *principia* (headquarters)
2 workshop
3 hospital
4 first cohort *scola* (meeting-place)

0   100   200 m

N

main gate, left

main gate, right

Praetorian gate

Plan of the camp of Inchtuthil, Scotland

Probably built in AD83, then abandoned in good condition and systematically destroyed by the army four years later, Inchtuthil in Scotland provides a kind of snapshot of a legionary camp. The rampart, of grass mounds surmounted by a stone wall, duplicated outside by a ditch, enclosed an area of some 21 hectares (13 acres). Set back from the intersection of the two main roads, lined with a portico, are the *principia* or headquarters. The barracks of the cohorts run alongside the rampart and contain the communal buildings: workshop, hospital, granaries, meeting places (*scholae*) and the officers' and non-commissioned officers' (*immunes*) quarters.

The principia of legio X Gemina at Noviomagus, (Nijmegen), Holland

The *principia* combined the functions of headquarters, archives, religious centre and place of assembly. Here a monumental entrance gives access to a court surrounded by porticoes onto which offices open. In the centre of the court is an altar. Set crossways, a basilica occupies the side opposite the entrance. The room where the legion's insignia were kept (the basement of which may have housed a strongroom) projects from the rear of the building. The situation and monumental appearance of the *principia* made them symbolic of imperial authority and power.

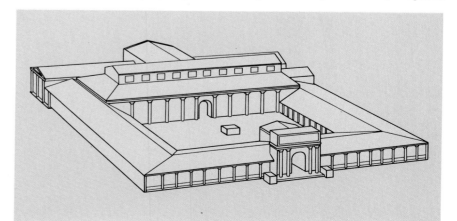

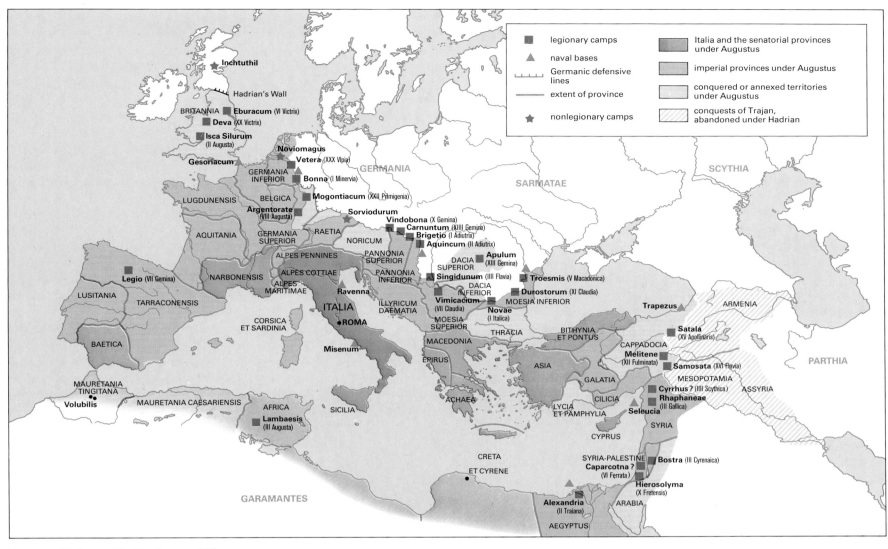

Extent and defence of the Empire *c.* AD135

The provinces administered by the Senate did not contain army units. In the imperial provinces, the distribution of the legions reflected the presence of danger. They were concentrated on the middle and lower Danube (8), where Dacia had just been conquered by Trajan in 107, and in the east (6), opposite the Parthian empire. But Spain, which had 5 legions under Augustus, now had only one. Africa, too, had only one legion, but was held by numerous garrisons of auxiliaries.

Infantry on the frontiers

This soldier, who belonged to a cohort originally recruited from the Tungrian people of Belgium, was garrisoned near Volubilis, Morocco. He himself may have been recruited locally, as was often the rule from the 2nd century. He is wearing his "civilian dress": a short tunic held at the waist by a belt from which hangs a *bulla*, a cape held over the right shoulder by a round fibula or brooch. His weapons include a spear, a short sword worn on the left and a round buckler.

Parade armour of an auxiliary cavalryman, 3rd century AD

Cavalry played a steadily increasing role in tactics and enjoyed a certain prestige, as indicated by the splendour of their parade armour which, despite its rich decoration, had a purely ornamental role. It was worn during special man-oeuvres, prefiguring the armour of medieval tournaments. The visor (right) could be raised; the other items—greaves and knee-pieces (bottom right) and horse's headstall (below)—bear religious motifs, representations of military gods: Mars trampling a giant underfoot, head of Minerva, and Castor and Pollux. Hoard of armour found at Straubing, Sorviodurum, Germany.

The Early Middle Ages:
the archaeological background

Sometimes called the Dark Ages, the period after the decline of Rome can now be seen as one of dynamic transformation in the "Barbarian west", producing such masterpieces as the Sutton Hoo ship burial treasure.

Geographically defined by continental and insular Europe (with the exception of Scandinavia, eastern Europe and the Balkans), the Early Middle Ages in the West lasted from the late 5th to the 10th century, and marked a decisive turning point in European history. The study of this key transitional period between antiquity and the Middle Ages has for many years relied entirely on traditional historical sources. Only recently has our knowledge progressed as a result of the contributions of archaeology.

Historians have traditionally divided the Early Middle Ages into two periods: the Merovingian age, which ended in 751, and the Carolingian age, which in the east ended in 911 and in the west in 987. This division may be useful, but it does present problems. For example, several countries entirely, or in part, avoided domination by the Merovingian and Carolingian dynasties, including the British Isles, Spain and part of Italy. The cultural significance of such a division is also questionable, particularly in view of enduring phenomena only rarely affected by political factors. However, these two chronological divisions do effectively correspond with the sources. Whereas the traditional historical sources covering the 8th–10th centuries have come down to us in greater number (simply because they have been preserved), the archaeological sources covering the 5th–8th centuries are much richer. This unevenness of archaeological sources explains the contradictions which mark the historiography of early medieval archaeology.

The first period (5th–8th centuries)

For several centuries, the archaeology of the first part of the Early Middle Ages (5th–8th centuries) was mainly concerned with burial grounds. One of the most important cultural characteristics of the period appears to be the number of objects connected with everyday life which have been placed in the tombs. The chance discovery at Tournai, in 1653, of the tomb of the Frankish king Childeric I (d. 481 or 482), the father of Clovis, represented an historical point of departure in this research. A few years later, in 1656, the tomb of Childeric II (d. 673) was discovered in Paris, in the church of Saint-Germain des Prés and identified by an inscription engraved on the coffin.

These two discoveries were not at once used as points of reference in dating the tombs of unknown people which contained similar objects. Until the end of the 18th century, the Merovingian tombs were the object of fanciful chronological attribution, having been variously ascribed to Gauls, Romans or even to members of the clergy of the Middle Ages. There are a few exceptions to this rule (in France, J.J. Oberlin, 1775, in England the Rev. James Douglas, 1793).

During the first half of the 19th century, our knowledge of "barbaric" tombs progressed rapidly, thanks to the work of a few farsighted archaeologists: in France, P.J.B. Legrand d'Aussy (1799) and above all Arcisse de Caumont (1830) were prominent; in Germany, the publication of the finding of the Selzen cemetery by W. and L. Lindenschmidt (1848) represents an important stage; in England, Roach Smith (from 1848) played a pioneering role. The correct identification of Merovingian tombs emerged as a result both of better organized excavations and of a critical approach based on comparisons and parallels with the texts.

These assets were refined during the second half of the 19th century and up to World War I. A more precise dating* of Merovingian tombs was the first objective; early classifications of relative chronology were based on study of objects found in the same tomb, their interrelation, and their spatial distribution in the cemetery. Next, absolute chronologies* were attempted, using as a *terminus post quem* (or point of earliest origin) the date on a few Merovingian coins left in the tombs. In France, this line of research gave positive results with J. Pilloy's work from 1880, and C. Boulanger's in 1907; in Germany, it was developed by E. Brenner (1912). In England, R. Smith (1900–12), T. Leeds (1913) and G.B. Brown (1915) determined the chronology of Anglo-Saxon funerary relics.

This period of progress in methodology continued through the inter-war years in various directions, and was centred in Germany. It included syntheses of large regions (Veeck on the Alemanni in Wurttemberg, 1931); a new chronology based on the coin-dated tombs of Austrasia and used until about 1960 (J. Werner, 1935); typologies of funerary objects (G. Thiry, 1939 and H. Kuhn, 1940). Stimulated by the German erudition, a French industrialist, E. Salin, devoted himself to important work and published *Le fer à l'époque merovingienne* together with A. France-Lanord (1943), and as a result the laboratory became an indispensable adjunct of archaeological research.

After World War II, the archaeology of Merovingian tombs continued to develop. E. Salin published a vast work of synthesis, *La civilisation merovingienne*, (1950–59), based on funerary archaeology. The relative and absolute chronology of the tombs was further determined by the work of K. Böhner (1958), followed by Ament (1973 and 1977), and P. Perin and R. Legoux (1980), who both used data-processing techniques. The historical interpretation of the funerary finds greatly benefited from the thorough investigations of large cemeteries, such as Krefeld-Gellep in Germany, Mucking in Great Britain, Rhenen in the Low Countries, Sezegnin in Switzerland, Frénouville, Bulles and Vicq in France, and Duraton in Spain. In this way, a better understanding has developed of the interplay between the barbarians and the local populations in the countries they invaded. An essential role in this study was played by anthropology, a subject too long neglected, both at the ethnic level (M. Buchet, 1978) and in connection with demography (M. Martin, 1976).

The analysis of funerary practices has also found its proper place and has thrown some light on contemporary mental attitudes that have eluded the texts (B.-K. Young, 1975). Other archaeologists have successfully shown that the structural characteristics of the burials have also supplied us with valuable chronological criteria (M. Colardelle, 1983, in the Alps). Finally, one should mention the discovery of several royal and princely tombs which have been the object of particularly detailed study: the royal burial of Sutton Hoo, England, in 1939 (R. Bruce Mitford); the princely tombs of Cologne cathedral in 1959 (O. Doppelfeld); the tomb believed to be that of Queen Aregonda, wife of Clotaire I, discovered in the basilica of Saint Denis (M. Fleury and A. France-Lanord). The excavation of burial grounds today remains an important area for archaeologists, but the study of this particular period is still further diversified owing to recent developments in non-monumental medieval archaeology pioneered by Great Britain and various East European countries.

For a long time, the architecture of the Early Middle Ages was known only by its better preserved monuments, which are rare indeed. Architectural fragments preserved in museums did not help much. A few exceptions apart, such as the "hypogeum" of Dunes, at Poitiers (Père de La Croix, 1887), the contribution of excavations remained of secondary importance in view of the mediocrity of the methods used. Without the aid of stratigraphy*, it was extremely difficult to reconstruct the history of monuments whose only remains were some confused and approximately dated foundations.

Bibliothèque nationale, Paris

Considerable changes have occurred during the last 30 years. Urban archaeology quickly developed and led to the excavation of several churches, some still standing and others in ruins. Thus it has been possible to uncover the remains of primitive sanctuaries and to reconstruct with precision their design and evolution. The remarkable excavations conducted at Trèves, Cologne, Geneva and Lyon have thrown further light on the origin of cathedrals. The same applies to several funerary basilicas on the outskirts of towns, such as La Madeleine in Geneva and Saint Laurent de Choulans in Lyon. This movement spread to the countryside, where the foundations of several churches have been explored, particularly in Belgium, Germany, Switzerland, Italy and, more recently, in France (the French Alps). Other rural churches, the existence of which had not been suspected since they had not survived as places of worship, were discovered during the excavation of burial sites.

Although the development of urban archaeology has led to a better understanding of the topography of towns during the Early Middle Ages, the character of the residential quarters is still little known. In Anglo-Saxon England, however, mention should be made of the very significant excavation made at the royal residence of Yeavering in Northumbria (6th–7th century) by B. Hope-Taylor (published 1977).

Another recent aspect is the study of rural habitations, which could not have developed without elaborate excavation methods prompted by prehistorians. Apart from the southern areas where stone was used, as in the princely buildings of Larina, France, the main building material was wood. The only traces of this to be found in the soil are some coloured patches corresponding to the post-holes and the dug-out foundations. The excavations at Gladbach and Warendorf in Germany, those at West Stow and Mucking in England, or those at Brebières in France, have thus brought to light the layout of several villages of the Merovingian period and have allowed the reconstruction of several types of buildings.

The archaeology of the first part of the Early Middle Ages can also avail itself of other lines of research, so far little exploited, such as artisans' sites (the pottery kilns of Huy, Belgium), or shipwrecks (Fos-sur-mer, off the estuary of the Rhône).

The second period (8th–10th centuries)

Historians of the art of the second part of this period have for a long time restricted their study to existing monuments, mainly of a religious nature. Gradually, however, they have turned to archaeological excavation, as a result of the important discoveries which have shown how archaeology could add to their knowledge. It is enough to mention the excavations at the abbey of Saint-Pierre et Saint-Paul at Flavigny, Burgundy (1890–1905), the bishop's palace and buildings at Metz, Reims cathedral (1919–30), and, in Germany, the abbey at Fulda (1908–29) and Reichenau-Mittelzell (1929–38). To these one should add the excavation of the Carolingian palace of Ingelheim, not far from Mainz (1909–14), which is all the more interesting because it concerns a secular building. In England, a complete excavation of the 9th–10th century royal residence at Cheddar is fully detailed in P. Rahtz's *The Palaces at Cheddar*.

Investigations of this type became more numerous after World War II and were all the more fruitful for being able to benefit from perfected techniques of excavation. The most important discoveries occurred in the church of Corvey-sur-Weser near the cathedral of Paderborn (excavations of the bishop's palace and the imperial palace), in Cologne cathedral, in the basilica of Saint Denis, or, in Italy, at San Salvatore da Brescia, in Belgium (several church excavations have revealed Carolingian buildings) and in Switzerland (Geneva and its canton). In England there have been major excavations at many Anglo-Saxon sites, chief among them Winchester (Biddle, 1961–71) the deserted cathedral site at North Elmham in Norfolk, and a detailed examination of the still extant church at Deerhurst (P. Rahtz, 1976). Studies of Dark Age ecclesiastical architecture have produced a work unrivalled in Europe, a description of all known pre-Conquest church fabrics (H.M. and J. Taylor, *Anglo-Saxon Architecture*, 3 vols., 1965 onwards).

There is a striking contrast between these and the other archaeological areas relevant to the second part of the Early Middle Ages. The situation here is much the same as for the first part, but with the important difference that funerary archaeology is practically non-existent: it was during the 8th century that the custom of burying the dead clothed and accompanied by everyday objects came to an end, and with it a useful means of dating the graves.

The urban habitat of this period is little known, due to the confusion of archaeological layers which, like pottery, could have been useful as guidelines for dating objects of everyday life. Nevertheless, important results have been obtained, for instance with the excavation at Hedeby, in northern Germany, or at Douai, where work has revealed the formative processes of urban cores. Work at Saint Denis, on the other hand, shows how these cores developed; and recent excavations at York have revealed the pre-Viking settlement.

The rural habitat has also been excavated: villages with wooden houses such as Maxey, in Great Britain; Burgheim in Germany (Fehring, 1973); Kootwijk in the Low Countries; and also some stone houses, such as Mondeville, France.

Particular conditions of conservation (a humid environment) and sophisticated excavation methods have led to a better knowledge of wooden architecture, particularly in Germany and Great Britain: private buildings (fortified site of Husterknupp, in Rhenania), coastal sites (Dorestad, in the Low Countries), or churches (several examples in Germany and Great Britain).

Excavations of craft sites are more numerous than those covering the beginning of the Early Middle Ages, but are usually confined to potters' workshops, particularly in Great Britain and the Rhineland (workshops of Badorf and Pingsdorf), more rarely in France (Saran, Loiret). An improvement in this line of research can only contribute to a better knowledge of the archaeological sites of the second part of the Early Middle Ages, if it were possible to identify and date with precision the abundant pottery they yield.

The great invasions and archaeology

The exact nature of the Germanic invasions at the time of the Fall of Rome—including the arrival of the Anglo-Saxons in Britain—is one of the more hotly disputed problems in Western historiography. How do we tell who was "Germanic", and what constituted an invasion?

Written sources from the end of antiquity and the beginning of the Early Middle Ages may have helped us to have a general idea of the history of the "great invasions" but they are not much help when we try to go into the details of what actually took place or their ethnic consequences. So, from the time of the last century, scholars have tried to make up for the short-comings of the texts with archaeological investigation, particularly the examination of "barbarian" tombs.

One of the most striking cultural features of the beginning of the Early Middle Ages, which is found in most parts of western Europe, is the appearance of countless cemeteries with identical characteristics: the alignment in rows of the graves in relation to their predominant orientation and the practice of clothed burial, often accompanied by grave goods (generally confined to crockery). Mistakenly believing the topographical organization of these tombs to be a new feature not found in the Roman period, German archaeologists in the 19th century were led to treat the existence of such burial grounds (*Reihengräberkultur*) as definitive of the "Germanic" culture, since their diffusion coincided perfectly with the historical expansion of the Germans. It was thought that these cemeteries could be seen to belong to different ethnic groups according to their geographical situation within the various "barbarian" kingdoms which took the place of the Roman Empire in these regions, and that the stages of the great invasions and the scope of the "Germanic colonization" that followed could be measured by them.

Although at first sight this ethno-historical interpretation of the *Reihengräber* seemed tenable for those barbarian kingdoms which were stable and clearly defined geographically, for example Anglo-Saxon England or Visigothic Spain, it was a haphazard process without accurate chronological knowledge of the objects placed in the tombs for states which were ephemeral or unstable. Italy, for example, was Ostrogothic and then Lombard; Pannonia was Gepido-Lombard and then Avar. Moreover, how could it be affirmed on the basis of burial practices and grave goods alone, and without resort to anthropology, that all the tombs in the *Reihengräber* were really those of barbarian tribes? Working from the highly complex example of Gaul, French and Belgian archaeologists reacted against these sweeping theories, examining in particular the burial places of the indigenous Romanized populations, in cases where, as they knew from the texts, they had not, on the whole, been eliminated or displaced.

Burial characteristics

Another theory of the ethnic division of the *Reihengräber* was based on an analysis of their characteristics. A predominance of burials in sarcophagi and dry-stone compartments was considered by some archaeologists to indicate an indigenous "Roman" population. Conversely, burials directly in the earth accompanied by a multitude of diverse grave goods were attributed to the Germanic newcomers, in the cases under study, the Franks. The same archaeological criteria also served to differentiate the two populations inside certain so-called "mixed" cemeteries, at least until the 7th century when the completion of the process of "progressive fusion" was deemed to have brought to an end an ethnic distinction in clothing fashions and funerary rites.

Yet these interpretations have not stood up to criticism either. It has been shown (E. James, 1979; P. Périn, 1981) that the alleged criteria could not have had a direct ethnic correspondence, and that they merely expressed a chronological evolution in fashions of dress and burial practices ("Germanic" characteristics to the beginning of the Merovingian period and "indigenous" characteristics to its second phase).

Lastly, turning to anthropology for help, present-day research has moved away from such a literal interpretation of burial customs. The excavation of the cemetery of Frénouville (Calvados, France) is a good example of this. It has been shown that the marked evolution of burial customs between the Late Roman Empire and the Merovingian period took place without any appreciable changes in the ethnic make-up of the population. On the basis of these findings, the historical interpretation of the *Reihengräberkultur* has been reconsidered.

J. Werner has pointed out that archaeological characteristics overhastily qualified as "Germanic", were born not in free Germania (where, incidentally, cremation was the general rule), but in the Roman Empire in northern Gaul. The Germanic auxiliaries (notably of Frankish origin) who became established in this area from the 4th century adopted (and elaborated) the funerary practices of the indigenous Romanized population. The massive influx of Franks in the regions situated between the Somme and the lower Rhine during the first three-quarters of the 5th century served to reinforce the practices which yield the archaeological evidence found, common to both the indigenous population and the newcomers, and gave them their "pre-Merovingian" character. For this reason we now prefer to talk of a "Romano-Germanic" culture. The spectacular diffusion of these funerary practices to the south of the Somme and the east of the Rhine and the Meuse were commensurate with the Frankish expansion from the end of the 5th century, and we are entitled to see it as one of the consequences of this expansion, the repercussions of which were political and social rather than ethnic. Many of the *Reihengräber* began as the rich tombs of "chiefs", and it seems likely that the conquests of Clovis I, king of the Franks, caused the dispersion of the aristocratic "Romano-Frankish" families of northern Gaul. So it is plausible to attribute the diffusion of such northern fashions in clothing and burial customs to these powerful minorities and not to considerable shifts in the population. Moreover, practices were little adopted by the indigenous population in areas where the Frankish influence was weak (especially south of Lyon and the Loire). These practices underwent a general regression during the 7th century, as the progressive cultural assimilation of Frankish minorities was accompanied by the reinstatement of burial customs of the late Roman tradition surviving in the towns and regions that remained the most Romanized.

Cultural contacts and exchanges

This new global interpretation of the *Reihengräber* did not, of course, rule out more detailed research into the ethnic identification of the barbarian migrants and the differences between their cultures. Thus great efforts have been made to make the utmost of the evidence from burials. With the help of cartography an analysis of types of objects found has given us a better understanding of cultural areas corresponding to various barbarian peoples (in the case of the Franks, their special battleaxes, barbed spears and various types of brooch). Attempts have also been made to establish the cultural antecedents of these peoples so as to follow their movements, for example in the work of M. Kazanski on the first Gothic culture in south Russia, which is the key to the study of the subsequent Ostrogothic and Visigothic cultures. The cultural contacts between the barbarian peoples have been studied by the identification and mapping of the objects they exported. This has provided evidence of exchanges which took place between Anglo-Saxon Kent and the Frankish world, thus corroborating the literary sources. At the individual level, persons and groups of persons who settled outside their home country have been identified by their "national" costume.

Alongside these researches based on the study of the movement of artifacts and fashions, there has recently been an emphasis on the contributions which anthropology can make to our knowledge of the great invasions. The application of this discipline had previously been limited to a few spectacular illustrations such as the identification of the primitive Burgundian population in Sapaudia (Swiss and France Jura) after the mid-5th century. Now there is a general recognition of the need for anthropological studies of the "barbarian" cemeteries to determine whether they show the practices of an indigenous population prior to the great invasions or of different Germanic populations before their migration. This area of research seems most likely to yield positive results.

Grave goods from the Merovingian cemetery of Vicq, France, first half of 6th century

A native of Visigothic Spain, the dead woman preserved her "national" Gothic ornaments until her death: a pair of large agate fibulae in sheet-silver, and a gilt and cloisonné belt buckle. She had also complied with the customs of her adoptive country by wearing fibulae of Frankish provenance.

Aerial view of the Gallo-Roman and Merovingian cemetery of Frénouville, France

The study of bone remains found in the cemetery of Frénouville suggests that the population remained stable from the 4th to the 7th century. The significant development of burial practices in the Merovingian period (notably the change in the orientation of tombs on the right of the photograph) is probably due to practices of Barbarian origin rather than to an influx of "Germanic" populations.

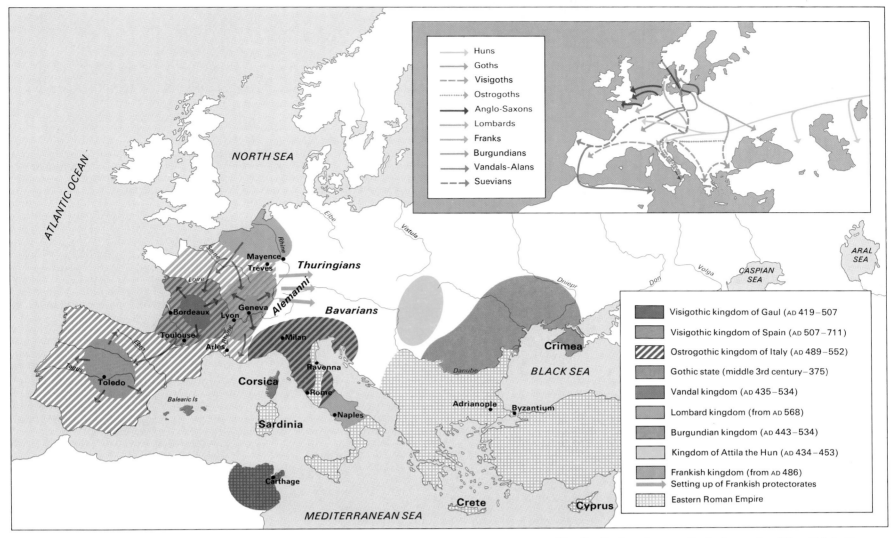

The great Germanic invasions and the birth of the barbarian kingdoms (end 4th – beginning 6th century)

The arrival of the Huns in the West in AD370 set in motion the Germanic peoples who were massed on the frontiers of the Roman world. Whereas the eastern Roman Empire managed to overcome the crisis by diverting the Visigoths to Italy, the western Empire was to collapse in a few decades, to be replaced by a number of barbarian kingdoms, some stable (Anglo-Saxons, Franks, Visigoths), some more or less short-lived (Ostrogoths, Lombards, Burgundians, Suevi, Vandals).

The distribution of angons (barbed spears) and Frankish battle-axes

The study of the geographic distribution of certain types of artifacts supposed to have an ethnic correspondence may give us a better understanding of the history of the great invasions. The Frankish battle-axe (a throwing-axe with a pronounced cutting edge) and "angon" (javelin with a pyramidal point, more than 1m (3.3ft) in length) are considered to have been the Frankish weapons *par excellence* during the second half of the 5th and first half of 6th century. In fact, their zone of distribution coincides exactly with the traditional historical limits of the first Frankish expansion, from the Rhine to the Seine and the frontiers of the Burgundian kingdom. This map also illustrates the practice of burials with arms, transmitted or revived by the Franks.

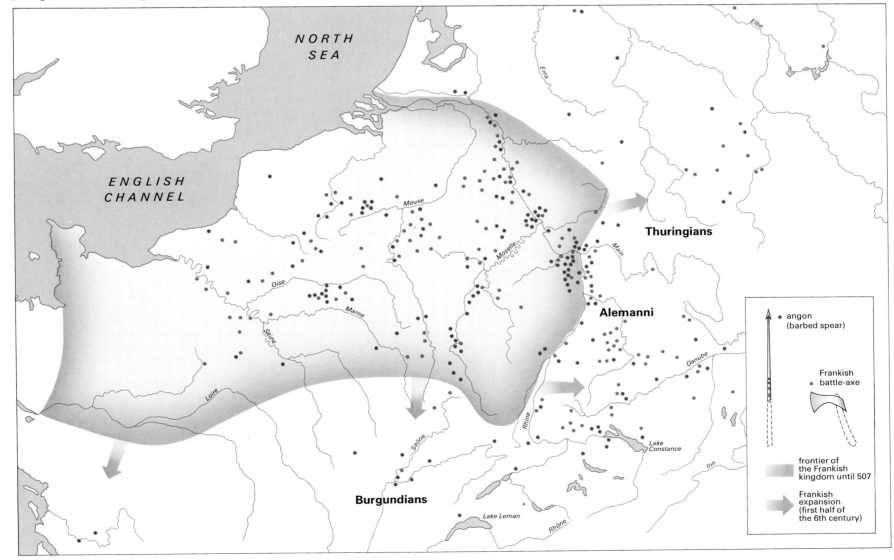

New towns and antique cities

The Late Roman legacy was essential to the new towns of the Early Middle Ages. Though on a tiny scale—Viking York may have numbered only 10,000 people—"urbanization" at this time helped shape the future of Europe.

Our knowledge of Western towns during the Early Middle Ages was for a long time very limited. The generally scanty and rarely descriptive literary sources revealed little about their appearance, for they mainly consist of lists of churches and monasteries, indicating only the broad features of their Christian topography. Archaeology, too, proved disappointing, since all it could provide were a few partial and mediocre excavations of approximately dated religious buildings and burial grounds. Thus there was a great contrast in comparison with the antique and medieval past of cities, which were illustrated by abundant documentation.

The recent spectacular success of urban archaeology has changed this situation. Immediately after World War II, when reconstruction programmes and urban renewal posed a serious threat to the so-called "soil archives", historians and archaeologists did all they could to make public authorities realize the importance of overall historical and archaeological research into the past of towns, studies which might well help to improve the towns' future. The essential point was to seize the opportunity offered by the great increase in public and private works of urbanization, extending to the historical heart of some cities. So experts evaluated the "archaeological risks" of a large number of towns (the City of London and Tours are two of the best examples), by defining the excavations which were essential within a short time limit.

Beginning in Great Britain and northern Europe, and then in other countries like France, a certain number of towns have been the target of coherent historico-archaeological programmes which did not single out any particular period or field. So the traditional concept of archaeology *in* the town (supported more or less strongly depending on the country concerned) gave way to that of archaeology *of* the town, where the town itself became the object of study and no longer simply the location of it. This is the framework within which our knowledge of early medieval towns has made considerable progress for some decades. In order to examine the main benefits of these researches, it is convenient to make a distinction between the towns already in existence in antiquity and those which were only established during the Early Middle Ages.

The legacy of antiquity

From numerous excavations carried out in the former towns, archaeologists can now conclude that they did not undergo a specific urbanization in the Early Middle Ages, but simply an adaptation of the urban fabric inherited from late antiquity. To demonstrate this, we have only to examine the distribution of Christian religious sites, which were nearly all located in relation to the antique road system, or Christian cemeteries, which were mostly situated on the site of Late Empire burial grounds. So the urban space of the Early Middle Ages appears to inherit directly that of late antiquity, whether it is a question of access routes. road systems, reduced city walls, large public monuments (leaving aside their state of preservation and their purpose) or peripheral burial sites.

It is in this perspective that the question of the early medieval urban habitation site should be considered. In fact, excavations have yielded hardly any traces of residential quarters from the Early Middle Ages. So it is possible that urban development at the end of antiquity, the quality of which is known, may have survived to a great extent during the Early Middle Ages (the situation being comparable, taking everything into consideration, to the modern occupation today of buildings dating from the 17th and 18th centuries). Lack of a suitable hypothesis, and comparative neglect of the evidence of material culture (prolongation of the antique pottery tradition, for example), has led to this fact being overlooked by archaeologists, though it deserves to be verified.

Although the appearance of the early medieval town must have been much like that of the cities of late antiquity, it did differ from them by the presence of large numbers of religious sites, which apparently initiated the only major changes in the previous urban fabric. At Cologne, Trier, Geneva and Lyon, the erection within the walls of vast "episcopal groups" (two cathedral churches, a baptistry, as well as adjacent churches and the bishop's palace), and also the construction of other large churches, caused the destruction of ancient residential quarters, as well as the building of new access roads or the laying out of squares.

The example of the Ile de la Cité in Paris is significant. With the exception of the western tip of the island, where the royal Merovingian palace came into being from the transformation of antique administrative buildings, and some residential areas inherited from antiquity, the rest of the island underwent a fundamental change through the installation of the episcopal group and several churches to the east, not to mention the enormous monastery of St Eloi, adjoining the royal palace.

The continuity of funerary topography from late antiquity is still a characteristic feature of early medieval towns. Given that their populations remained stable in spite of the great invasions, it may be understood that funerary customs did not change, both as regards the siting of burial grounds and many of the customs practised there, such as the predominance of burials in sarcophagi and the rarity of deposits of grave goods. As had already been the case from the 4th century, funerary basilicas multiplied during the Early Middle Ages, built over the tombs of martyrs, confessors and saints. However, some towns saw the creation of new cemeteries, which developed around suburban sanctuaries built away from pre-existing burial grounds, for example, Saint-Germain des Prés (formerly Sainte-Croix-et-Saint-Vincent) in Paris.

New towns, old traditions

The methodical excavation of a growing number of urban and suburban sanctuaries has now been applied to many sites: the cathedrals of Trier, Cologne, Geneva and Lyon; the basilicas of La Madeleine at Geneva, Saint Just and Saint Laurent at Lyon, Saint Pierre at Vienne, Saint Laurent at Grenoble, and so on. All this had enabled archaeologists to establish their origin and development, while demonstrating the persistence of antique architectural traditions.

During the Carolingian period (751–987), the topography of these towns, though still strongly influenced by the layout of antique urbanization, seems to have experienced many modifications. This development appears to have been accelerated in many cases by the destruction following the Norse invasions from the beginning of the 9th century. This explains why the majority of medieval towns have often preserved little (apart from their religious topography) from their predecessors of the Early Middle Ages.

It was quite natural for urban archaeology to interest itself in the towns of the west which first appeared during the Early Middle Ages. Some of these gave birth to medieval cities, the example of Douai, France, being one of the most significant, since the excavations carried out in the heart of the city have made it possible to retrace accurately the process which, from the 6th/7th century to the 10th century, enabled the fortified residence of the counts of Flanders to become a medieval town. The example of York, England, is also of great interest, for here remarkable excavations have revealed the role played by the Vikings from 876 onwards. By encouraging the development of the ancient Roman and Anglo-Saxon city, the Vikings were behind the success of the medieval town.

A certain number of port sites in northern Europe, such as Hedeby in West Germany, near the town of Schleswig, and Dorestad, Holland, underwent an urban type of development from the beginning of the Carolingian period, but did not go on to develop into medieval towns. Not possessing a sufficiently ancient historical past, these commercial sites were abandoned fairly quickly in favour of neighbouring towns, when the natural conditions which had encouraged their formation began to deteriorate. Taking into account their ephemeral occupation, such sites constitute remarkable archaeological reserves for our knowledge of the material culture of the Early Middle Ages. This is not the case with the towns, where constant development caused the incessant upheaval of archaeological layers.

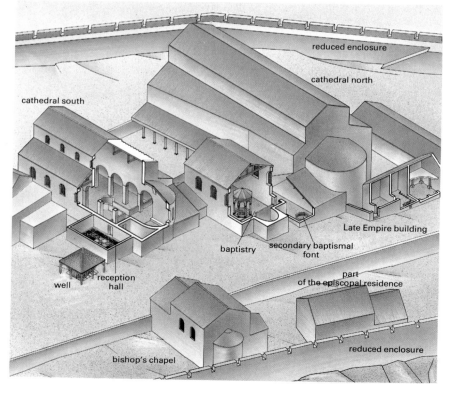

Isometric reconstruction of the episcopal buildings of Geneva, Switzerland (*left*); detail of a mosaic from the episcopal Palace, 5th century (*right*)

Recent excavations at Geneva during the restoration of the cathedral of St Pierre and the adjoining chapel of the Maccabees, complementing earlier research, have completely reorientated our knowledge of the "episcopal group" of the ancient Burgundian capital. On the basis of the foundations already uncovered, it has been possible to propose an isometric reconstruction of the monumental complex formed around two primitive cathedrals framing a baptistry (left). The episcopal residence was luxurious, and the reception hall contained beautiful mosaics in the antique tradition (right). Excavations C. Bonnet, isometric reconstruction G. Deuber.

Paris at the end of the Merovingian period, reconstruction

This reconstructed model of Paris at the end of the Merovingian period (7th–8th centuries) makes the fullest use of the archaeological and written sources available. The main features of the topography of the Late Roman Empire were still visible at the end of the Merovingian period: axial roads, main streets, island blocks consisting of many houses rebuilt to a greater or lesser extent, great monuments transformed or abandoned, the wall of the Ile de la Cité, the main burial grounds. Incidentally, it was in relation to the antique urban network that the many urban and suburban sanctuaries built in Clovis's ancient capital were installed. The persistence of urban life on the left bank is well attested, as well as the development of a suburb on the right bank (top). Concept, P. Périn; executed by L. Renou, Musée Carnavalet, Paris.

An early medieval port on the North Sea: Dorestad, Netherlands, late 6th–9th centuries

Excavations undertaken at Dorestad since 1967 are gradually revealing the appearance of this port, which had a considerable economic importance during the second part of the Early Middle Ages, as attested by numerous historical sources. Besides abundant and varied portable objects (valuable evidence of the material culture), the most significant remains are the dispositions of the harbour. Working from partly preserved stakes (left), carefully re-erected (centre), it has been possible to reconstruct a whole series of wooden pontoons, frequently extended and reorganized as the port silted up (right). Excavations by the Rijksdienst voor het Oudheidkundig Bodemonderzoek, under the direction of W.A. van Es.

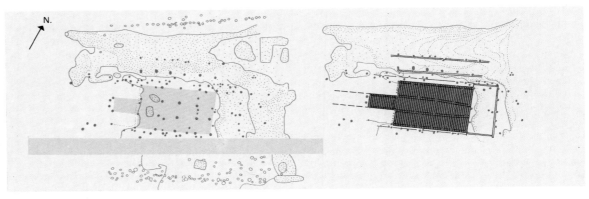

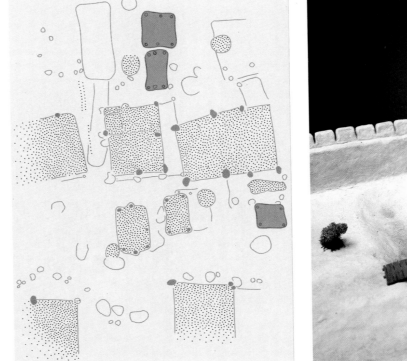

The origins of a town: the excavations of the foundry of Douai, France, 6th–13th centuries

Excavations carried out from 1976 to 1981 in the central area of Douai, in the old royal cannon foundry, have made possible the overall exploration of 1,000sq m (10,000sq ft) of terrain. Thanks to significant finds, archaeologists are able to reconstruct the way in which this town came into being: in the 6th–7th centuries, a modest habitation site with wooden cabins; in the 8th–9th centuries, an impressive pre-urban concentration, due to the density of the wood houses (see left: Period III B–C); during the first half of the 9th century, the site of the residence of the count of Flanders, also of wood, subsequently fortified at the end of the 10th century when it became a wooden keep with a moat surrounded by a stone wall (right). During the 12th century a stone keep replaced the wooden one. Excavations by P. Demolon; model from the Musée de la Chartreuse, Douai.

The making of the medieval countryside

Rural archaeology is a recent development in medieval studies; its impact has been to show the vitality of rural life in the so-called Dark Ages – and frequently to demonstrate remarkable continuities with the late Roman world.

Until a few decades ago our knowledge of the countryside (as opposed to the town) in early medieval western Europe was in practice drawn from written sources and the study of place names, in the absence of significant archaeological discoveries. Although the study of administrative documents supplied valuable information about the organization of the great secular and ecclesiastical domains, it proved very disappointing as regards their physical appearance and told us nothing at all about other types of rural development. As for place names, which are difficult to date accurately, their interpretation was a haphazard affair when it came to land occupation or topographical history. Thanks to the increase in excavations due to the growth of medieval archaeology, it has since been possible to go into traditional historical knowledge in more detail and we now have a more concrete vision of the early medieval countryside.

For a long time archaeologists were limited to investigating older rural remains, because of their nature and situation. Mostly built of stone, the Roman *villae* were easily identifiable and often had the advantage of not being hidden under later dwellings, because later developments in agrarian methods caused a fairly general displacement of habitats. Since World War II the increased use of aerial surveys* has revealed remains which had mostly escaped notice before, because they were built of earth and wood. Investigators have thus identified numerous agricultural, defensive, religious and funerary structures from Prehistory, Protohistory and the Middle Ages proper, but very rarely from the Early Middle Ages. This has led to the conclusion that the rural habitat remained stable in western Europe from the Early Middle Ages on, and that the majority of remains of Merovingian and Carolingian edifices were simply built over by later establishments. As excavation was restricted to villages, hamlets and farms, archaeologists concentrated on habitats which were abandoned during the Early Middle Ages and which had not therefore been obliterated by later construction.

These excavations, when on a sufficiently large scale, have yielded much information about the actual appearance of early medieval villages: in West Germany, Gladbach (7th–8th century) and Warendorf 7th–8th century), situated in the central Rhineland and Westphalia respectively; in the Netherlands, Kootwijk (late 7th–late 10th century), in the province of Gelderland; in Great Britain, Catholme (end 5th/beginning 6th to first half of 10th century) and Church Down at Chalton (6th–7th century) in Staffordshire and Hampshire respectively.

A variety of functions

These sites, which seem to be representative of the habitats of northwestern Europe, all have various types of wooden edifice with quite specific functions. First, we find large hall houses with a rectangular plan, 10 to 30m (33 to 98ft) long. These were built directly on the ground, with a solid framework of posts and the roof timbers either resting directly on the walls or partly supported by buttresses to the ground. These buildings generally had two doors in the middle of the longer side, with a hearth placed close by them, and were obviously dwelling houses, which also sheltered cattle in many regions of northern Europe. Other similar but smaller houses have also been found, sometimes associated with large houses. Used exclusively as dwellings, they may, in some cases, be the dwellings of a lower-class population, or in other cases they may indicate a clear distinction between human habitat and stables. In the vicinity of these houses, there have been frequent finds of small rather makeshift constructions built with the help of a few posts over ditches of varying depth. Some of them, closed by a wooden plank, as at West Stow, had a very cave-like quality. The interpretation of these "cabins" has been the subject of much controversy. At West Stow and Mucking in England (5th – beginning of 8th century), they must have served as houses. However their most common function seems to have been as annexes to the houses around which they were grouped. The discovery of spindle-whorls and balances in the ditches shows that these "cabins" may have been reserved for specific activities, such as spinning and weaving. Their damp interiors could also have been suitable for keeping milk and making cheese. At Leibersheim in France, one such "cabin" was extended by a bread oven. Lastly the majority of these sites have also revealed groups of posts arranged on a circular or polygonal plan. They were supports for granaries in which to store and dry the grain.

The arrangement of buildings

The arrangement of these buildings has shown that early medieval villages, in northwest Europe at least, formed coherent "agricultural units" separated by palisades or enclosures. At Warendorf, for example, each unit comprised a large house, 8 to 10 smaller houses, 3 or 4 "cabins" and 2 granaries in an enclosed space measuring about 70 × 50m (230 × 164ft).

A few rare archaeological examples such as the Merovingian dwelling of Larina at Hières-sur-Amby, (France) show continued use of stone in the Mediterranean West during the Early Middle Ages. We know that stone was also used in other regions as found, for example, in the recent excavations of Mondeville in northwest France. On this site, occupied continuously from the 1st to the 12th century and now methodically explored, Carolingian stone buildings took the place of late Roman and Merovingian wooden buildings (4th–7th centuries).

Today historians accept the decisive contributions made by the rural archaeology of the Early Middle Ages. For example, the discovery of the bases of several "cabins" or outbuildings at the Merovingian site of Brébières in France make the old theory of the total regression of rural life there no longer tenable. As to the image of the Merovingian or Carolingian *villa*, with its wooden buildings, towers and palisades, in fact these *villae* must have consisted of a varying number of "agricultural units", either assembled into villages or dispersed. But the rural residences of the great landed proprietors, (kings, bishops, and members of the aristocracy), although mentioned in literary sources, at present mostly remain undiscovered. Judging by Venantius Fortunatus's description of the domain of Nicetius, bishop of Trier, on the banks of the Moselle (6th century), or the excavation of the celebrated Carolingian palace of Ingelheim in Germany, it seems that these luxurious residences were still firmly in the classical architectural tradition when they did not simply result from the refurbishing of Roman *villae*. As they were important dwellings from their beginning, these buildings have usually been built upon, like the many rural monasteries now covered by the abbeys which succeeded them, and archaeological investigation has therefore been impossible.

The recent development of early medieval rural archaeology has also stimulated other kinds of research centred on land occupation. In West Germany, a fruitful comparison has been made between the distribution of classical and early medieval habitats (the latter mostly identified by their cemeteries), demonstrating profound changes in the organization of the population. Elsewhere, in the Champagne area of France for example, similar studies have led to the conclusion that land occupation was more or less continuous. Intensive archaeological investigations have shown that movement from one habitat to another was frequent between the Roman occupation and the Early Middle Ages. The Roman *villae* and their surrounding buildings were usually succeeded by several "farms" or villages, from many of which the origins of our own villages can often be traced.

From excavation to reconstruction: the Anglo-Saxon villages of West Stow and Church Down (Suffolk and Hampshire, Great Britain), 6th–7th centuries

Nothing was left of the Anglo-Saxon village of Church Down but alignments of post holes and pits corresponding to dwelling houses, as the aerial view of the excavations shows (below). The reconstruction of several Anglo-Saxon pit dwelling, in this case largely submerged, on the site of West Stow, (left) was made possible by the use of archaeological data. Archaeological Park of West Stow (left); excavations P. V. Addyman and P. Leigh, (below).

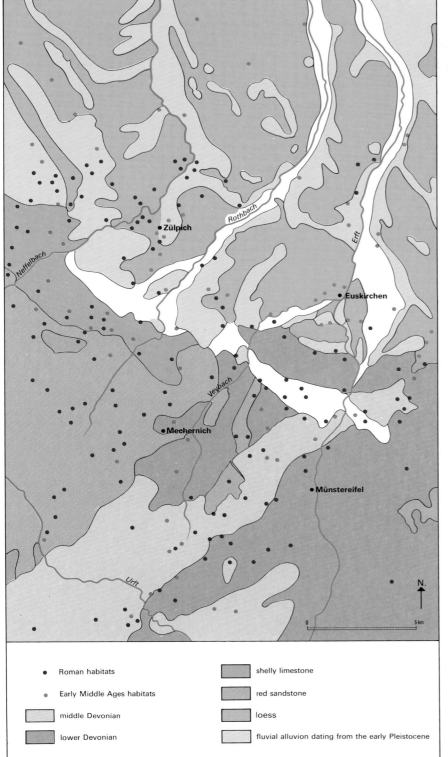

- Roman habitats
- Early Middle Ages habitats
- middle Devonian
- lower Devonian
- shelly limestone
- red sandstone
- loess
- fluvial alluvion dating from the early Pleistocene

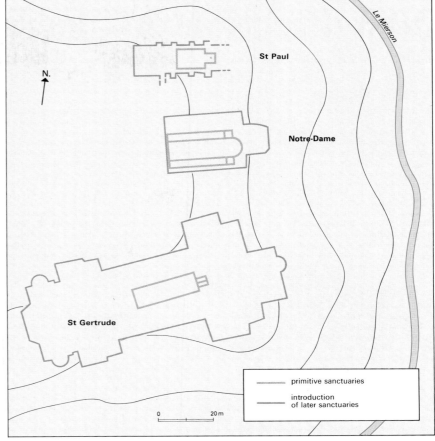

An early medieval rural monastery: Nivelles, Belgium

Excavations carried out at Nivelles shortly after the devastation caused by World War II revealed the plan of this monastery founded in the middle of the 7th century. Apart from monastic buildings, it consisted of three churches with very specific functions: Nôtre Dame, the main church for the nuns; St Paul, reserved for monks and possibly neighbouring laymen; St Gertrude, the funerary church for the nuns. The last-named church was to develop into the celebrated collegiate church of St Gertrude, which eclipsed the neighbouring sancturaries. After J. Mertens.

Land use in the Roman and Frankish periods, northeast Eifel, West Germany

The geographical distribution of Roman and Frankish archaeological finds in the northeast of the Eifel is highly significant for agrarian history, when put into a geological context. The Frankish farmers concentrated on more easily cultivable lands (river floodplains, chalky soil), abandoning sandy soils, loess land and forest regions, none of which had been neglected in the Roman period. After K. Böhner.

Reconstruction of the Frankish village of Gladbach Neuwied, West Germany, 7th–8th centuries

Excavations carried out at Gladbach in 1937, enabled archaeologists for the first time to make a model reconstruction of a Frankish village. Such a village had a number of agricultural units separated by enclosures. Each one consisted of a large dwelling built at ground level with a framework of posts, as well as associated huts for domestic use, built over ditches and using fewer posts. Rheinisches Landesmuseum, Bonn.

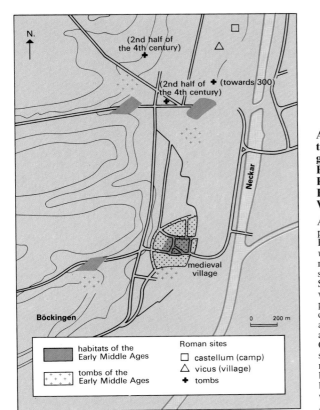

An example of topographical history: the ground of Heilbronn-Böckingen during the Roman period and the Early Middle Ages, West Germany

At the end of the Roman period, the site of Heilbronn-Böckingen consisted of a *vicus* (village), based on the neighbouring *castellum* and served by several cemeteries. Soon after the great invasions, this changed completely. Four Alemannic cemeteries, corresponding to a similar number of land-use areas, then divided the area. Only one of these was to survive, developing into the medieval "burg" of Heilbronn-Böckingen, probably because the parish church was erected on its soil. After K. Weidemann.

- habitats of the Early Middle Ages
- tombs of the Early Middle Ages
- Roman sites
  - □ castellum (camp)
  - △ vicus (village)
  - + tombs

New directions in funerary archaeology

Funerary archaeology has till now tended to concentrate on the spectacular royal sites, such as those from Tournai in France and Sutton Hoo in England. But today it is the rural cemeteries and the middle ranks of society which are the focus of interest.

Funerary archaeology of the Early Middle Ages is mainly confined to the study of the so-called Merovingian period (500–751). In the country regions, the practice of "clothed burial", accompanied by various objects, especially arms and tableware, virtually came to an end in the 8th century. So it becomes difficult to date burials after that period. It was also towards the 8th century that the appearance of rural cemeteries underwent a radical change which, like the disappearance of grave goods deposits, was a result of Christianization and the growing influence of the Church. The large-scale rural burial grounds, where tombs were always placed side by side and clearly individualized, thus facilitating excavation, were replaced by sites covering a limited area in the immediate vicinity of the churches. Burials accumulated there without order and were constantly disturbed by later tombs, sometimes even down to the present. As a result, the archaeological study of rural cemeteries in the Carolingian period (751–987), which were mostly at the origin of medieval cemeteries, has proved disappointing, if not impossible. More or less identical conditions of research apply to the towns, except that the latter experienced this characteristic development of funerary customs much earlier because of their earlier Christianization.

In spite of these obstacles, an effort has been made for some decades to extend the field of funerary archaeology to the Early Middle Ages as a whole. Research has followed two main directions: the general development of burial grounds and the funerary rites which were practised in them.

Country burials

As the question of urban burial grounds has already been dealt with in connection with towns, this section is mainly concerned with what has been learnt about country cemeteries. Thanks to a great increase in methodical excavations covering large areas, researchers now have a more accurate idea of how they were formed. Thus many Merovingian burial sites took the place of pre-existing cemeteries going back at least as far as the end of the Roman period. This fact has been looked on as irrefutable proof of the stability of the population and the permanence of habitation sites (tombs rarely being far away from them). Sometimes it was the arrival of a small number of migrants which caused the introduction of new funerary practices that were quickly adopted by the whole of the community. However, the majority of Merovingian cemeteries seem to have been new creations, which raises complicated questions of historical interpretation. In effect, the discontinuity of funerary styles and layouts between late antiquity and the Early Middle Ages must have been paralleled by a discontinuity of habitation sites, if not of the population as a whole. Depending on the circumstances, different explanations have been put forward: the colonization of virgin or deserted territories (after the Germanic invasions of the 3rd and 5th centuries) by German migrants; the displacement of the habitation sites and hence of the burial grounds as a consequence of the development of an agrarian way of life; or again, in the case of later foundations, a local population increase, the demographic upsurge (well attested from the 7th century) leading to the conquest of new territories.

In the regions where the deposit of grave goods was frequent and abundant, the chronology of burials has been more finely graduated by statistical methods (the comparative study of associations of objects in the tombs) and topographical methods (the study of the topographical distribution of objects in the burial grounds, or "topochronology"). This has made possible an accurate reconstruction of the ways in which such sites developed. The most common progression seems to have been that of growth by way of successive rings, starting from an original core. Nevertheless, the arrangement of tombs in more or less regular rows, as well as the existence of enclosures and stelae at ground level, still leaves open the possibility of more recent burials in the old sectors of the burial grounds, as when family burials were grouped together in the enclosures.

In the regions where grave goods were rare or totally lacking because of the permanence of the traditions of late antiquity, attempts have been made to date tombs by their type, either by the shape of the sarcophagus, decorated or not, or by the shape of the burial chests made of tiles or stone slabs. Quite positive results have been obtained in this way, not only for the Merovingian period, such as the burial ground of Sézegnin in the Canton of Geneva, in Switzerland, but also for the Early Middle Ages as a whole, for example in the plain of the Rhône and the Alpine region.

In the majority of regions considered, an important and hitherto unsuspected fact has been established and has proved decisive for the origin of Merovingian cemeteries: the existence of wooden or stone chapels or churches in rural burial grounds. Although some of these initially had a commemorative function, as was common in towns (one often finds a "privileged" tomb by its situation, without being able to establish the identity of the deceased and the reasons for his veneration), many others were erected by the aristocracy with a funerary purpose. The richness of tombs found is evidence of this.

As such foundations often go back to the beginning of the Merovingian period, it must be accepted that the Christianization of the country was sometimes earlier than had been thought, with the aristocracy playing a decisive role by endowing private mausoleums in imitation of barbarian kings and princes. A large number of these structures were short-lived and disappeared during the 8th century, when the majority of cemeteries were re-sited around the parish churches that had recently been installed in the centre of the habitation sites. However, in many cases these funerary chapels remained in the same place because they marked the cemeteries. This is nearly always the origin of the parish churches that have remained outside villages, or of many cemetery chapels in cases where the installation of a parish church in a village caused neither the transfer of the cemetery nor the abandonment of the chapel.

Excavation of these structures is still very interesting because the ground beneath them conceals traces of earlier wood and stone sanctuaries, enlarged and reconstructed several times between the Merovingian period and modern times. This kind of research is currently being carried on in Belgium, Germany, Switzerland and Italy.

The study of funerary customs has made decisive progress thanks to the improvement of excavation methods and the statistical treatment of information. This has enabled archaeologists to correct a number of accepted ideas. For instance, it is now hardly possible to maintain that the orientation of Merovingian tombs was systematically determined in accordance with the sunrise. As exceptions and variations are numerous, it seems that, on the contrary, topographical factors were decisive for the orientation and alignment of the graves (but the origin of this preferred axis is controversial). Similarly, the presence of stones or nails at the bottom of graves should not be automatically interpreted as the "ritual entourage" of the corpse or as a "funerary stretcher". The experience of recent excavations shows that burials directly in the earth were exceptional, and that the dead body usually rested in a wooden chest built inside the grave and made of planks, nailed or not, and wedged in by stones; thus, they were not coffins.

The detailed excavation of bone remains, covering thousands of burials, has shown the rarity of "deviant" funerary practices, which have too often been exaggerated by archaeologists. Sometimes indeed, their credibility is in doubt, for example when skulls and limbs were supposedly "spiked", or bodies were assumed to be "mutilated", buried "upright" or "seated". The excavation of the topsoil of burial grounds has provided valuable information about the appearance of cemeteries in terms of the layout of paths, stelae and enclosures marking the tombs. It has also sometimes revealed traces of funerary meals or the remains of cremations, which were perhaps more numerous than was thought at the beginning of the Merovingian period.

Reconstruction (below) and excavated area of the Merovingian burial ground at Hordain, North France

During the 6th century, the topographical arrangement of the Merovingian burial ground of Hordain was modified by the installation of a stone funerary chapel for the burials of the local aristocracy (right-hand photograph). Afterwards this carefully orientated building governed the alignment of the tombs and of the quadrangular enclosure of the cemetery (left). Excavations by P. Demolon.

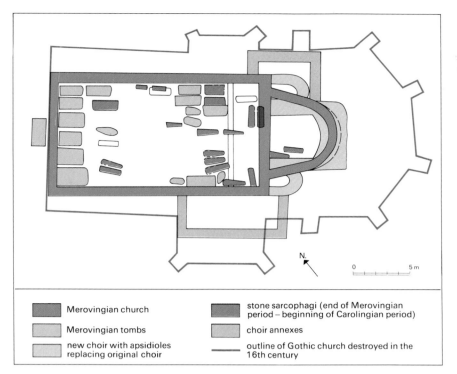

Société historique et scientifique des Deux-Sèvres, J. Boisset

Key

▓ Merovingian church	▒ stone sarcophagi (end of Merovingian period – beginning of Carolingian period)
▒ Merovingian tombs	□ choir annexes
□ new choir with apsidioles replacing original choir	— outline of Gothic church destroyed in the 16th century

From Merovingian funerary chapel to parish church: the example of Saint-Martin d'Arlon, Belgium

Excavations carried out in 1936 and 1938 on the site of the ancient parish church of Saint-Martin d'Arlon, destroyed in the 17th century, have revealed the origin and development of this religious site. The original building, an apsidal funerary chapel, was founded by the local Merovingian aristocracy. It underwent some changes in the pre-Romanesque period (new choir with apsidioles flanked by two annexes), before being entirely rebuilt in the Romanesque period, after which it received only minor alterations. After J. Mertens.

Aerial view of part of the burial ground of Prieuré Saint-Martin at Niort, France

This recently excavated burial ground well illustrates the persistence of antique burial traditions in the urban environment during the first part of the Early Middle Ages. These include extensive development of the cemetery by the juxtaposition of tombs, predominance of burials in stone sarcophagi, scarcity of grave goods. So the Church did not impose specifically Christian burial customs, but simply showed its influence by the installation of sanctuaries in suburban burial grounds. Excavations by C. Papinot.

Ville de Grenoble

Surface appearance of graves, as seen in the Merovingian cemetery of Vorges, France

At Vorges, the rapid in-filling of the Merovingian burial ground soon after its abandonment has preserved the surface appearance of several graves. They were demarcated by rectangular dry-stone compartments and marked by stelae which were sometimes double when they were intended to receive two burials. The stones visible at the bottom of the graves were used to wedge the planks of burial chests, which were much commoner than coffins. Excavations by M. Ballan.

M. Ballan

Excavations (model) of the funerary basilica of Saint-Julien-en-Genevois, France, 5th–8th centuries

Excavations conducted at Saint-Julien-en-Genevois from 1975 to 1977 resulted in the discovery of a Merovingian funerary basilica, hitherto unknown because it had not led to a lasting religious site. A small apsidal church, length 45.6m (146ft), width 8.5m (27ft), was added to the original rectangular building in the second half of the 5th century. This too was enlarged with an L-shaped annex in the 8th century. Excavations by M. Colardelle, model by C. Haudebourg.

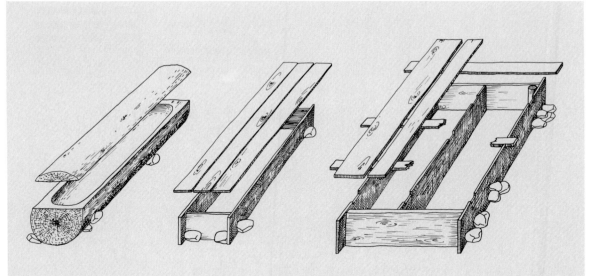

Types of Merovingian tombs uncovered in the burial ground of Soyria, France

Careful examination of wooden remains, traces left by wooden objects, and stones found in the graves, has made possible an accurate reconstruction of the burial practices in use in the Merovingian burial ground of Soyria: coffins made from a single tree trunk (left) and chests for one or two persons made in the graves, using planks wedged by stones. After A.-M. and P. Pétrequin.

Artisan production

The techniques of the craftsmen who made the characteristic products of the Early Middle Ages—swords, fine jewellery, or the glass and metalwork of the great churches—have been revealed by modern archaeology.

Early medieval written sources describe a certain number of artisan activities, but they provide little information about the working methods of these craftsmen and nothing about their techniques of production and ornamentation. Hence archaeology plays a decisive role in the interpretation of existing sites, monuments and objects (when the latter have always formed part of church treasures) or those revealed by excavation.

With the exception of potters' kilns and installations—for example those found at Huy in Belgium in the Merovingian period, at Pingsdorf and Badorf in the Rhineland, and at Saran in France in the Carolingian period—excavations have, until now, hardly exposed any craft sites where metals or glass were worked. Several explanations exist for this gap: installations covered by later workshops or dwellings may be hard to find or inaccessible, and the identification of definitively abandoned craft sites can be problematical because of the scarcity or untypical nature of the remains. Together with Runde Borg, near Urach (West Germany), the site of Batta at Huy is currently one of the rare examples of a multipurpose craft site in the Early Middle Ages. Several potters' kilns and their adjoining installations have been discovered lining the banks of the River Meuse and on the outskirts of the Merovingian settlement, as well as the debris of carved bones and fragments of terracotta fibula moulds, which indicate that craftsmen worked bone there and practised the smelting of metals. But the corresponding furnaces have not been found, doubtless because they were short-term installations, unlike the pottery kilns.

Alongside these permanent establishments, which must have predominated in the suburbs of towns and on the great secular and ecclesiastical estates, there were itinerant craftsmen. Some are mentioned in the texts and they were much in demand for their particular specialities—mosaic-makers, glass-blowers, fountainmakers, sculptors—and some even moved from Italy to England. Others can be identified through archaeology when the personal chattels in some male burials feature assemblages of tools. Since such deposits are exceptional, it has been suggested that they belonged to itinerant craftsmen who died in the course of their wanderings and were buried with their tools in accordance with contemporary custom. As these tool kits are assumed to have been complete, scholars have raised the question of the use to which each of them was put and the artisan's possible areas of specialization. The presence of heavy tools, such as tongs, hammers and files, together with delicate tools such as small hammers,

tweezers, files, pincers, burins, awls and small portable anvils, suggest that such craftsmen may have practised not only the elementary work of smelting metals (dies for stamping clay moulds, bronze scrap), but also goldworking (stamping dies, very small tools, glass beads), and perhaps even damascening (etching and inlaying the metals). As far as we can judge, such craftsmen were probably travelling repairmen in all fields (traces of repairs are visible on several metal objects found in tombs). Tomb 10 in the cemetery at Herouville (Calvados, France), is datable to the 6th century and provides one of the best examples in the west of the burial of an itinerant general smith with goldworking specialization. The presence of armaments, including a long sword, indicates an important rank for this person, which was not always the case with the smith or goldsmith (the *faber ferrarius, faber aerarius, faber argentarius* or *faber aurifex* of the texts).

Production techniques

The study of production techniques has made spectacular progress during recent decades in two different but complementary directions. More and more objects from the excavation sites are finding their way to the laboratory, not only for restoration and preservation, but also for technical examination of the type of materials used, the formulas for alloys, the methods of fabrication and ornamentation, and so on. These analyses have led to attempts at reconstruction which, by faithfully reproducing models, have improved our understanding of the techniques then in use.

Other investigators have turned to experimental archaeology* of another kind, whereby models are reproduced through recreating the original conditions of work and all its stages. In this field, the most spectacular results have involved paleometallurgy*. Close collaboration between a specialist in the restoration of metal objects, J. Ypey of the Netherlands, and a mastersmith, Manfred Sachse of West Germany, has made possible the experimental reconstruction of the extremely complicated process of making damascened sword blades. This not only led to a better understanding of the successive phases of this work, but also made possible the rediscovery of certain organizational forms and procedures: for example, the need to work from a solidly fitted out, and therefore fixed, forge; the indispensable collaboration of several craftsmen, in particular for the twisting of heated damask steel bars, or the reheating of metallic pieces at each stage of the work; and the necessity for a rational

arrangement of the damask bars, since their decoration became visible only during the final phase of forging, when it was revealed by putting the sword into an acid bath. Thus the craftsmen had to pick out the bars with complementary decoration, the result of deliberate alternation between welding and torsion, so that their assembly by soldering would give the sword blade a regular pattern of chevrons.

Similar experiments have involved smelting metals and the "mass production" of moulded objects. Valuable research in this area has been undertaken by P. Andrieux concerning the paleometallurgy of bronze in protohistory, Roman antiquity and the Early Middle Ages. Working from archaeological and ethnographical models, this archaeologist has managed to reconstruct bronze-founders' furnaces and make them work successfully, and in the case of iron, furnaces of a type like those we know from rare early medieval excavations. Thus he has been able to show that the early medieval bronze-founder could have been a mobile craftsman capable of setting up his furnace rapidly and in any place, in a village perhaps, or near a market. He probably travelled with light material, including leather bellows with terracotta nozzles, some crucibles, dies for brooches or belt buckles and a light tool kit.

The activities of early medieval coffin-makers have also been subjected to this kind of archaeological experiment. Thus archaeologists can now answer various questions posed by the mass production of moulded plaster sarcophagi so common in the Paris region. Careful observation of traces of wood and decoration impressed on the walls of many sarcophagi discovered in Paris has enabled researchers at the Carnavalet Museum to reconstruct a double framework of planks which could be dismantled (as was the case in the Merovingian period for the unmoulding and re-use of the mould). Working from samples analysed in the laboratory by a modern plastering company, the plaster product used at the period has been accurately reproduced in a precisely analogous modern material. This invalidated the theory that the plaster sarcophagi were cast and poured at the cemeteries directly into the bottom of graves. Apart from the difficulties of assembling the framework and pouring, it would have been impossible to wait for the finished products to dry if they had to be used rapidly. Archaeologists now assume that the funerary plasterers set up their workshops on the outskirts of the cemetery. The sarcophagi were cast under open shelters which were ventilated and protected from bad weather.

Damascened metalwork: principles and reconstruction

The majority of early medieval sword blades were of damascened structure, that is, they were etched or inlaid with other metals. This was both useful, giving the weapon flexibility and solidity, and also decorative, with patterns traced out by subtle differences in the metal to give a watered effect. Hence the name "damask", referring to the decoration on cloth from Damascus. Conclusions reached in the laboratory were applied at the foundry, resulting in the experimental reconstruction of this sophisticated metallurgy (below left). The smith placed side by side and alternately (below right), (a) four strips of pure iron (shown as white in the drawing) and three strips of steel (black) and he soldered them by hammering under heat (b) to form bars about 0.8cm (0.3in) across. These bars were twisted under heat at regular intervals before recovering their square section by hammering while hot (c, d and right, the damascene being disclosed here by acid for demonstration purposes). The smith then placed side by side three bars with a complementary structure (e), soldered them by hammering while hot (f) and forged them to fashion the sword blade (g). The edges of the steel were then added by soldering (h, i). Finally, the blade was polished on a grindstone, then submerged in an acid bath to bring out its damascened decor (white for the veins of soft iron, dark for the steel veins). Experiments and artifacts J. Ypey.

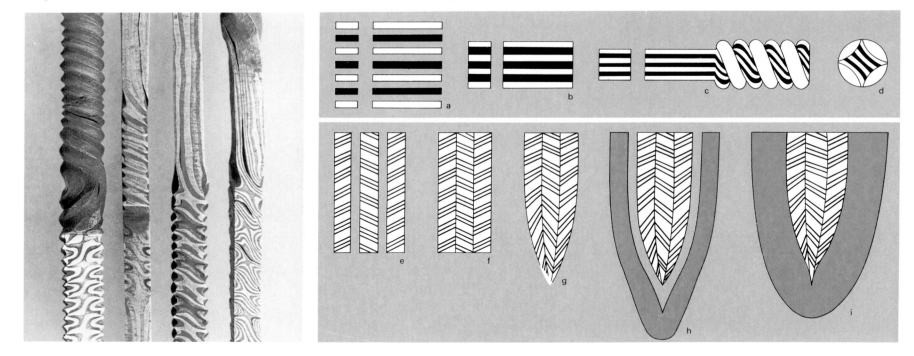

Bibliothèque nationale, Paris

Mould from Gueima, Algeria, 6th century

We only possess half of this mould for the buckle, tongue, boss and prong of a belt. It was cut out of hard stone and had undoubtedly been imported into Vandal Africa from Merovingian Gaul. Originally in two parts, it was not used for casting molten metal, which would have made it burst (there are no ventholes). But it was used to mould easily worked wax "positives", which were then applied in the classic "lost wax" technique. These "positives" were covered with clay. After drying and reheating, the wax was evacuated and metal (gold, bronze or silver) was substituted for it, after installing a funnel for casting and vent holes, fine channels to help the escape of gas from the molten metal.

P. Andrieux

A paleometallurgical experiment: casting a bronze object

By means of a craftsman's furnace activated by hand-worked bellows, the experimenter took several hours to bring to melting point the bronze contained in an earthenware crucible. The hot metal was then poured rapidly into the terracotta two-part moulds, previously reheated near the furnace, then buried close by to prevent deformation. After cooling, the clay mould was broken to free the bronze object which then had to be finished (burring, surfacing, additional ornamentation, etc.) Experiment by P. Andrieux.

Pair of moulded silver gilt fibulae from Trivières, Belgium, 6th century

Many pairs of moulded bronze or silver Merovingian fibulae, apparently identical and from the same mould, actually exhibit slight variations in decoration. The explanation is to be found in the method of casting by the "lost wax" technique, using a "secondary positive". A "primary positive" was used as a matrix to stamp the clay moulds, from which wax "secondary positives" were taken, identical at first. The decoration engraved on the latter inevitably showed variations in detail.

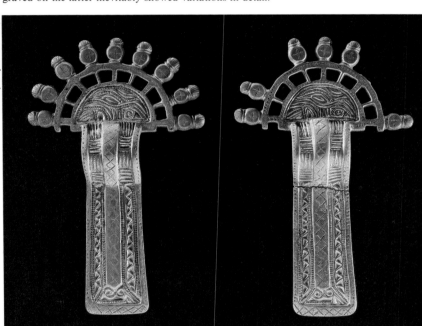

Institut royal du patrimoine artistique

Musée d'Histoire de Berne

Damascened iron belt fastening from Bern-Bümplitz, Switzerland, 7th century

Damascening, a word derived from the town of Damascus and referring to the decoration of the fabrics made there, is the art of inlaying or attaching metals to a base of a different metal. It experienced a remarkable flowering in the Merovingian period. This fine iron belt fastening represents the two main decorative principles used: the inlay of silver and brass wire, and the plating of silver leaf, a "bichrome style" predominant during the 7th century. Historisches Museum, Berne.

Goldsmith's fibula from Rosmeer, Belgium, 7th century

This extremely beautiful fibula illustrates some of the techniques which were widely used by goldsmiths in the Early Middle Ages: cloisonné, the art of inserting flat stones into a geometric and continuous network of metallic compartments soldered to the base of the jewel; stones in relief, given effect by their settings in individual isolated compartments; filigree work, gold wire soldered to the base of the object.

Institut royal du patrimoine artistique

Experimental pouring of a plaster sarcophagus of the Merovingian type

In the Paris region, plaster was widely used for the cheap mass production of sarcophagi, moulded by means of a double encasing of planks. Some of them bore an engraved decoration, which was thus produced in relief on the outside and even sometimes on the inside of the casts. This method of manufacture, very modern in conception, was reconstructed experimentally. After drying for about a month, such sarcophagi were as resistant as those cut out of blocks of soft limestone. (Experiment by P. Périn and C. Collot, Lambert Industrie, in the Músee Carnavalet, Paris.)

M. Tiaumazet

Trade and commerce

Many of the trade routes of the ancient world survived the decline of the Roman empire, but then dynamic commercial centres grew up on the coasts of northern Europe: the beginning of a shift of gravity in the European economy?

Today a profound knowledge of commercial exchanges during the Early Middle Ages in the West is unthinkable without having obligatory recourse to archaeology, not only as a significant illustration of literary sources, but also and primarily as an entirely separate historical source. Texts and excavations complement each other perfectly in this field. Without the former, we should know practically nothing of the administrative, judicial and corporate structures of Merovingian and Carolingian commerce, as well as all the major trading trends which escape archaeological investigation (slaves, exotic foodstuffs, fabrics, perfumes, and so on). In return, excavations can confirm the literary sources, and even supply information that they completely overlook.

Archaeological evidence of the basic commercial structure is not numerous, whether we are dealing with specific quarters of towns, ways of communication and their development, or means of circulation in the real sense of the word. Although early medieval written sources mention numerous commercial towns, especially harbours, few of them are so far accessible to archaeological investigation, either because they have been covered over by later agglomerations (for example, Rouen, Narbonne, Marseille (or Fos-sur-Mer) or because it has not yet been possible to identify them (the Carolingian port of Quentovic, in the Pas-de-Calais, France). So the progressive uncovering of the port of Dorestad, Holland, is a happy exception for the moment. Here the *emporium* (commercial centre) enjoyed prosperity from the end of the 7th to the end of the 8th century as related in the texts, and occupied an area of about 30 hectares (72 acres) on the bank of the Rhine, not far from its mouth. Countless pieces of wood fixed in the old river bed indicate the landing-stages where ships were moored. Behind them were the wooden houses of the boatmen and merchants, and then the town proper. The commercial relations between Gaul and Germania, on the one hand, and the British Isles and Scandinavia, on the other, were largely carried on from this port.

Testimony from the sea
Although often mentioned in written sources, navigation by sea and river has left very few archaeological traces, with the exception of the wrecks discovered in the Scandinavian and Anglo-Saxon countries. An interesting exception is the wreck discovered and explored in 1978 off Fos-sur-Mer, Bouche-du-Rhône, France, by Marie-Pierre Jezegou. Thanks to her research, we possess, for the first time in the western Mediterranean, information about the appearance of an early medieval coaster, dated to the beginning of the 7th century by its

cargo (notably amphorae containing pitch) and by the ship's own material, "fossilized" by the pitch when the amphorae broke during the shipwreck, and consisting of tableware, lamps, metal accessories to clothing. The Fos-sur-Mer wreck also illustrates for the first time in the Mediterranean the method of construction known as "square-framed". The ribs* were first put in place on the keel before receiving the strakes* plank by plank (see p. 130, "From the Viking ship to the three-master"). Although the place of origin for the wheat carried as bulk cargo cannot be determined (we know from literary sources that wheat of Italian, Spanish and African origin was imported through the port of Fos), the pitch was probably of local or regional origin. As for the crew, some of its members must have been orientals, as several graffiti scratched on the ship's pottery attest.

The objects found in the course of excavation also tell us about commercial exchanges in the Early Middle Ages. The study of these exchanges is based on the interpretation of maps showing the distribution of types of objects. Thus archaeologists believe that the zones with the highest density of finds illustrate the areas of their habitual commercial diffusion, centred on the place or places of production. Conversely, less numerous peripheral finds are considered as evidence of exceptional exchanges over longer distances (provided it is not merely the consequence of travel by individuals).

Apart from exotic products such as the Merovingian capitals of Pyrenean marble diffused to the north of the river Loire, stone or terracotta architectural material generally had only a regional or even a local circulation (for example decorated bricks, modillions and antefixes with human faces).

Study of the distribution of stone sarcophagi by type and decoration supplies corresponding results. It has brought to light a certain number of regional "schools" in France (Bordelais, Poitou, Nivernais-Avallonais, Bourgogne-Champagne, Sénonais), more or less centred on the quarries—recent studies having concentrated on the systematic petrographical (rock formation) study of samples taken from sarcophagi and the quarries which might have supplied the stone. The study of ancient Roman roads and river routes has shown their part in the dispatch of these heavy monuments over longer distances, notably towards the urban centres where "luxury" sarcophagi must have been in great demand. Similar research has concentrated on the Merovingian sarcophagi of moulded plaster mass-produced in the Paris region. Study of the geographical distribution of decorations from the same moulds has established that the various products recognized were in strictly local use, and that the rare examples that were

exported demonstrate the circulation of wooden moulds, not the plaster sarcophagi themselves.

Evidence of the graves
Examination of the geographical distribution of grave goods has shown several possible patterns of commercial exchange, the conclusions being based on study of identical objects from the same moulds, partly identical objects from partial mouldings, and identical embossed dies, or similar objects displaying numerous common stylistic, technical and morphological criteria. Thus the diffusion of terracotta vases most often took place on a regional or even local level when, for example, their decorations are found only in a single habitation site or a single burial ground. This was corroborated when the potter's kilns were found at Huy, Belgium. On the other hand, the circulation of personal ornaments and jewellery, as well as metal accessories to garments, generally covered much larger areas. That of luxury objects could be over a very long distance, for example the Coptic vases found in Southern Germany along the Rhine and in England.

Such maps are inevitably based on a provisional and incomplete stage of archaeological research, and are constantly subject to alteration and extension in the light of new information, with a consequent revision at the interpretative level. Nor should it be forgotten that the majority of the Merovingian portable objects studied are from a funerary background and only concern the regions where "clothed burial" was practised. This explains some of the blank areas in the distribution maps. The map of Merovingian mints and scales discovered in tombs of the same period has aroused controversies. Even if the distribution of mints clearly defines the regions where monetary circulation was current, that of scales remains to some extent conjectural. Indeed, the southern boundary of the latter may only correspond to that of the disappearance of burial accompanied by grave goods, but its northern boundary is clearly situated beyond that of the mints in regions where circulation of money must have been episodic, because coins had to be weighed. The reason why scales were placed in tombs, is still under discussion. Was this strange usage originated by currency agents, goldsmiths, money changers, tax collectors or merchants? The question remains open and is evidence of the limitations of the archaeology of the Early Middle Ages when the literary sources are silent. It has been proposed that, since scales appear even in Bronze Age wrecks as part of the merchant's standard equipment, burying the scales in a merchant's grave may be analogous to burying a warrior with his sword.

Wreck from the cove of Saint-Gervais, France: 7th century
The only wreck from the Merovingian period discovered off the coasts of Gaul is that of Fos-sur-Mer, excavated in 1978. As a result, it was possible to put forward the reconstruction (below) of this full-bellied coaster, which was carrying a bulk cargo of wheat and amphorae containing pitch, and has been dated to the 7th century by several objects found in it. This ship, 15 to 18m long (50–60ft), with a beam of 6m (20ft), a hold 2m (6.6ft) deep, and a capacity of about 50 tons, is still of the antique type, but attests for the first time to the medieval technique of "square-frame" construction. This vessel had a bilge pump, parts of which have been preserved, "fossilized" by the pitch which escaped during the shipwreck (centre): pulled by a capstan, leather disks slid inside two wooden posts opening into the bilges (right). Excavations by Marie-Pierre Jezegou.

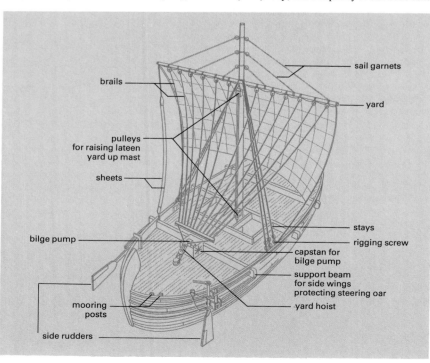

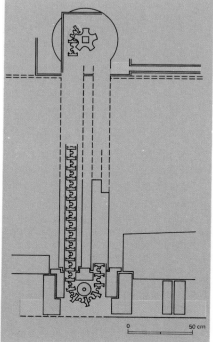

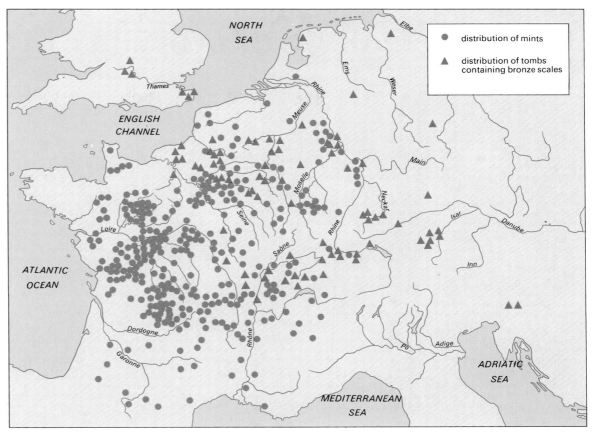

Map of the distribution of Merovingian mints and Merovingian tombs containing bronze scales

It is significant to note that the deposit of small bronze scales with symmetrical dishes in Merovingian tombs was mainly practised on the periphery of the area of distribution of Merovingian mints. In these regions where the mints were rare or non-existent, monetary circulation was heterogeneous and it was necessary to weigh the coins which came from many different places in order to estimate their value. After J. Werner, completed by H. Gaillard de Semainvilley.

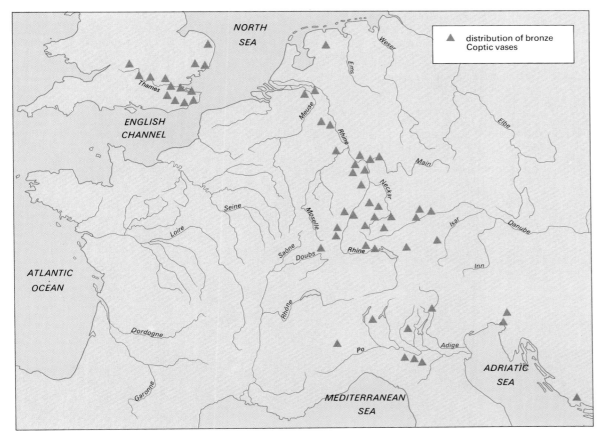

Map of the distribution of Coptic bronze vases discovered in 7th century tombs

The characteristic distribution of 7th-century tombs containing moulded bronze vases of Coptic origin attests to the long-distance circulation of luxury goods, and also the existence of an important commercial route from Italy and England via the Alpine passes, southern Germany and the Rhine. The absence of such vases in Gaul clearly shows that the port of Marseille and the Rhône plain were not involved in this trade in the 7th century. After J. Werner.

Map of the distribution of Merovingian belt plates with human masks and basketwork decoration

The concentration of the sites where these two types of belt plates were found, in France between the central Somme and the Channel, corresponds to the regional scale of their commercial diffusion and enables archaeologists to locate approximately the workshop where they were made. Isolated and peripheral finds are evidence either of occasional trade over longer distances or of the movement of individuals: natives of the west of the Paris basin who had died on a distant journey, or else, having acquired such objects on a journey to those parts took them back to their homeland. After P. Périn, P. Sinon and F. Vallet, C. Lorren.

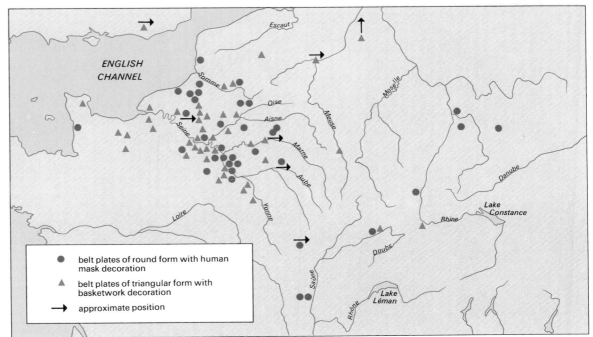

111

The archaeology of everyday life

Recently archaeology has been able to fill many gaps in our knowledge of the lives of ordinary people in the Dark Ages, an area where surviving texts, with their aristocratic and ecclesiastical bias, are invariably silent.

The contribution made by excavations to our knowledge of the Early Middle Ages in the West is not limited to the major themes dealt with in the preceding pages, but concerns equally many other fields which deserve mention here. It is interesting to indicate briefly some of the more specific research trends which concern people and material culture, before emphasizing the role of archaeology as the source of the history of social structures and patterns of thought. Once again it is the excavation of tombs with grave goods that yields most information, unfortunately limited mainly to the Merovingian period, because of the development of the funerary rites already mentioned.

Although urban and rural excavations provide plenty of material for the study of inhabited space, on the other hand they generally prove much more difficult to exploit when it comes to material culture in the real sense of the words. Although habitation areas were fully stocked while they were in use, all they contain when archaeologists explore them is modest evidence of the phase when they were abandoned. Once metal, bone and glass objects have been recovered (almost all the finds), the remainder usually consists of potsherds, which, when they are sufficiently characteristic, can nevertheless supply valuable information about products largely escaping funerary archaeology (tombs generally contain only "tableware" to the exclusion of so-called "common" crockery used for cooking or preserving food). It is quite a different matter with tombs when clothed burial accompanied by the deposit of everyday objects was practised, because intact or archaeologically complete objects are available. If the objects are made of metal, bone, terracotta or glass, they can be studied easily after simple cleaning or restoration, a process of varying complexity (see the remarkable restoration of the objects from the royal tomb of Sutton Hoo in East Anglia).

Conversely, organic materials (wood, leather fabrics, etc.) have usually disappeared, or only survive as fragments if they have been fixed by the oxidation of metals with which they have been in contact. Nevertheless, they have been partially or wholly preserved in certain special cases. This is true of tombs which have never been washed out by the action of water, as with burials placed from the beginning in the interior of religious monuments, such as those in Saint-Denis, Cologne Cathedral, or in Saint Ulrich and Saint Afra in Augsburg, and also of tombs which have benefited from a constant humid environment, such as the site of Oberflacht in West Germany. The importance of such

remains for our knowlege of the material culture of the Early Middle Ages is clearly paramount, whether they be fabrics, embroideries, footwear, almspurses, leather bags or sheaths, receptacles or musical instruments made of wood.

Careful on-site observation of objects preserved in tombs may now extend to their study in the laboratory after removal, which sometimes includes the removal of the whole surrounding archaeological milieu, and its "excavation" in the laboratory itself, as was the case with several tombs from the basilica of Saint-Denis. These activities provide a basis for interesting reconstructions of costumes and details of certain clothing accessories (belt buckles, almspurses, garters, footwear, etc.). The example of the Merovingian tombs in the basilica of Saint-Denis is still the most famous, with the complete reconstruction, in terms of shape, material, colour and embroideries, of garments attributed to Queen Arégonde who died at the end of the 6th century, and was wife of Clotaire I. The recent increase and growing refinement in excavations of burials now make it possible to obtain accurate knowledge of male and especially female clothing fashions according to countries and periods, for the Merovingian period at least (after which iconographical evidence takes the place of archaeological data). The reconstructions of Alemannic costumes on show in the Stuttgart Landesmuseum (West Germany) and the Schweizerisches Landesmuseum in Zurich (Switzerland) are among the most significant.

The importance of anthropology in connection with ethnic questions has already been mentioned, but the subject is also an irreplaceable source of knowledge about early medieval people. When practised systematically, the study of bone remains tells us not only about the physical appearance of individuals (stature, morphology, ethnic type), but also about their way of life (age at the time of death, activities, dietary habits, family links, marks left by accidents or diseases). When such research concentrates on the homogeneous population of a burial ground, where individual burials can be chronologically determined (by the deposits of grave goods), it can sometimes result in spectacular demographic conclusions. A few special archaeological examples also illustrate contemporary medical practices: the setting of broken bones, the use of trepanning and amputation (with artificial limbs), the treatment of hernias with metallic trusses (found in place on the bodies). Finally, recent work on dietary habits, mainly based on the analysis of vegetable remains and animal

bones found at habitation sites, but also of human skeletons, has provided valuable information.

Tombs as "social portraits"

The archaeology of the Early Middle Ages reveals not only the principal aspects of material culture, but also gives an insight into social and intellectual areas. Indeed, the tomb can be considered as a kind of "social portrait" when clothed burial was practised, since the deceased wished to be represented in his last resting place by the material signs of his social status. As a result, comparison of contemporary tombs inside the same burial ground, followed by comparison of one burial ground with another, and finally an examination on a regional or even larger scale, has revealed the social hierarchies mentioned in literary sources. Although some interpretations have been unreliable, for example the identification of "free", "semi-free" and "servile" men in terms of the number or absence of weapons, others seem to be very soundly based.

A perfect illustration of this is the small burial ground, at Basle-Bernerring (Switzerland), of a Frankish aristocratic family installed in Alemannic territory in the 6th century when it became a Merovingian protectorate. Archaeologists could identify, and follow for some decades, the career of a "chief" and his entourage of family and warriors, as well as his household servants. Elsewhere, in regions where clothed burial was not practised, the "privileged" location of tombs in burial grounds or inside religious buildings sometimes reflects the place of individuals in society.

The funerary archaeology of the Early Middle Ages authorizes one last and not the least important historical approach, that of intellectual attitudes and beliefs. The deposit of objects in tombs, connected with the practice of clothed burials, is now no longer considered as evidence of paganism—such burials are common in religious structures and were not condemned by the Church; but some funerary customs do seem to illustrate the survival of pagan beliefs, for example the rare cremations, funerary "obols" (coins placed on the eyes of corpses) and offerings of food. As for Christianization, its progress can be followed both on the collective level by the increase of burials with specifically Christian associations, and on the individual level by the presence of eloquent epitaphs or stelae decorated with Christian symbols, or again by the presence of objects with Christian representations and inscriptions.

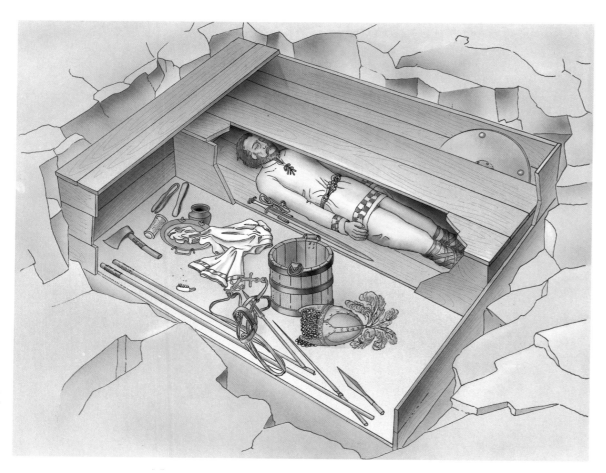

Reconstruction of the tomb of the "chief" of Morken, West Germany, c.600

The tomb of the Frankish "chief" of Morken illustrates the contribution of funerary archaeology to our knowledge of society at the beginning of the Early Middle Ages. The luxury of the burial goods reflects the deceased's high rank. Dressed in his finest garments and girded with his sword, the body rested in a heavy coffin which was placed inside a vast burial chamber of oak planks and beams. The armament of this important personage included lance, hunting spear, axe, helmet and buckler. Also in the grave were his horse's harness and various personal effects, such as a bronze basin, towels, a wooden bucket, glass and earthenware goblets, a comb, knives and shears. All were carefully arranged on the floor of the underground chamber, though the buckler had been slipped between the wall and the coffin. Rheinisches Landesmuseum, Bonn.

Laboratoire d'archéologie des métaux, Jarville

Belt buckle and plate from Ladoix-Serrigny, Cote-d'Or, France, end 6th–7th century

The Latin inscription on the plate reads LANDELIUS FICIT NUMEN QUI ILLA PVSSEDIRAVIT VIVA(T) USQUI ANNUS MILI IN D(EO), which can be translated as: "Landelius represented Divinity. May he who possesses it live for a thousand years in God". So there is no doubt about the identity of this crude representation of a haloed horseman holding a lance: it is clearly Christ (as on one of the faces of the stele of Niederdollendorf).

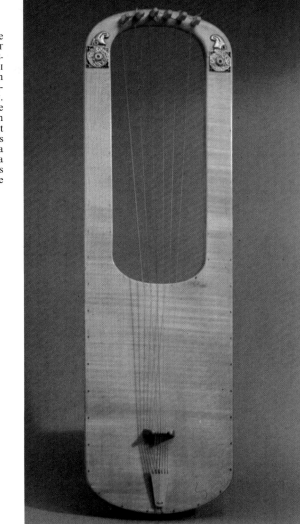

British Museum

Rheinisches Landesmuseum, Bonn

Stele of Niederdollendorf, West Germany, 7th century

On one of the faces of this famous stele (the other side shows Christ triumphant, haloed and armed with a lance), the deceased wanted to establish his status as a free man. He is girded with his sabre and his comb (to the Franks, the hair was the mark of free men and the main seat of the vital force). The two-headed serpent is a standard image, among the Germans, of the underworld and death. As for the flask, it may represent immortality with the water (?) it would have contained. Rheinisches Landesmuseum, Bonn.

Reconstruction of a lyre found in the royal tomb of King Redwald (died c.630) at Sutton Hoo, Great Britain

The extraordinary grave goods found in the royal tomb at Sutton Hoo have benefited from remarkable laboratory work by the British Museum, resulting in spectacular reconstructions like this lyre, 73cm (29in) high. Ornamented with animal motifs in gilded bronze, it was made of maple wood and had six strings. Reconstruction by British Museum.

Musée national suisse

Alemannic clothing accessories, 7th century

The careful on-site observation of metallic objects and organic remains found in tombs from the beginning of the Early Middle Ages enables archaeologists to reconstruct clothing accessories with accuracy. Thus we now know that Alemannic women wore leather almspurses, closed by a bronze ring and attached to their belts. Swiss National Museum, Zurich.

Wooden receptacles from the Alemannic cemetery of Oberflacht, West Germany, 6th century

A favourable climatic environment ensured the exceptional preservation of organic materials, especially wood, in the tombs of Oberflacht. Thus we now have a very good knowledge of the everyday objects which usually evade archaeological investigation, and notably wooden receptacles which were widely used: flasks, kegs, buckets, goblets, etc. Württembergisches Landesmuseum, Stuttgart.

Württembergisches Landesmuseum Stuttgart

Barbarian cultures in the north and east

In the eighth century, Christian Europe faced attack from two new heathen aggressors, Slavs in the east and Vikings in the north; archaeologists can reconstruct the origins of these barbarian peoples.

In the 8th century the Carolingian world was suddenly confronted by two new hostile forces: in the east the Slavs, and in the north the Scandinavians. At that period, the Slavs and the Scandinavians, unlike most other European peoples, were still heathen; they had inherited nothing from the culture of Rome, and the formation of their states owed nothing to Roman law. In the absence of adequate written sources, we have to rely mainly on archaeology to reconstruct the history of these barbarian peoples prior to the 8th century, the period at which they appeared on the frontiers of the western world.

There is little mention of the early Slavs in classical texts. Tacitus, who alludes to them as the Venedi, places them between the Germans and the Sarmatians. All the most recent theories as to the origin of the Slavs have been formulated by archaeologists, but the two main hypotheses are conflicting. One holds that in the Roman period the Slavs were living in the region of Poland and southern Russia, forming part of cultures that were subject to influence from the Roman empire, the Przeworsk and Černjahov cultures. The other locates the earliest Slavs in the forest regions of the upper Dnieper where there was no direct contact with the Roman world, in which case they would form part of the Kiev culture. The debate still continues to this day, but the second hypothesis appears more likely, for later cultures that can be incontrovertibly attributed to the Slavs show no evidence of Roman influence, but do show close links with the Kiev culture.

It is likely that the Slavs advanced from the forests of the upper Dnieper in the course of the 5th century towards the Danube, across territory occupied until then by the Černjahov culture. This culture, which included Germanic and non-Germanic tribes, would have coincided with the Goth confederacy, dismantled at the end of the 4th century by the Huns. The earliest sites that can be definitely ascribed to the Slavs are in this area and do in fact date from the Hunnish period (Kodyn, Teremcy, Hitcy, Pesčanoe, etc). The presence of Slavs at the Danube frontier of the Byzantine empire is attested from the 6th century.

Early Slavic cultures

According to written sources, the Slavs in the 6th century were divided into two tribal groupings, the Sklavenes and the Antes, while archaeology allows us to distinguish three contemporaneous Slav cultures during a period from the 5th to the 7th centuries. The Prague-Korčak culture, attributed to the Sklavenes, was discovered in the western Ukraine, Poland, Czechoslovakia and central Germany; the Pen'kovka culture, associated with the Antes, extended over the forest steppe area, in the Ukraine and Moldavia; finally, the Kiločin culture was found in the upper Dnieper basin.

Archaeologists have noted the homogeneity of these three cultures; they are characterized by a number of similar features. Dwellings were small, usually unfortified, and positioned in valleys formed by rivers or streams. They consisted of small rectangular houses, dug out from the ground or on the same level as it, and having a stone or clay oven, or an open hearth. Burial grounds only yield evidence of incinerations in pits or urns, sometimes beneath kurgans (mounds). There are hardly ever any grave goods. Ceramics, were always hand-modelled, consisting of oval pots for the Prague-Korčak culture, biconical or oval pots for the Pen'kovka culture, and for the Koločin culture cylindro-conical or tulip-shaped pots. Light weaponry consisted of lances, javelins, bows and arrows. Costumes characteristic of the Slavs did not appear until the 7th century, but fibulae (brooches) of the "Danubian" or "Ante" type, worn by women, are notable. The material so far uncovered does not indicate social distinctions inside these cultures.

The Slav cultures of the 5th–7th centuries are thus more archaic than contemporary Germanic cultures, which had been enriched by contact with Roman civilization. This more archaic level of culture probably explains why, unlike the Burgundians, the Franks, the Goths and the Vandals, the Slavs preserved their own ethnic peculiarities after they moved to territory that had been part of the Roman empire, and only became assimilated with the local population with difficulty.

To the east, the Slavs' neighbours were the Turco-Bulgarian nomads whose graves have been found scattered across the Pontic steppes. Of these, "princely" tombs such as those of Pereščepino, Glodosy and Voznesenka contained Byzantine vessels, weapons and jewellery. To the south, Slav lands touched the Danubian *limes* (fortified frontier). To the west were the Germans and to the north the Balts, most nearly related to the Slavs from the linguistic point of view. The Tušemlya, Moščino and probably the "long kurgan" cultures are specific to the Balts of central Russia and Byelorussia.

Farther north and northeast, the forest area was occupied by the Finns (D'jakovo, Muroma and Mordva cultures and a culture characterized by burial grounds surrounded by stone walls). Between 570 and 630, in the Danube basin, the Slavs were subject to the Avars who left numerous burial grounds. (Alatyan, Kiskörös and others). The tombs of warriors found in these have yielded swords, sabres, stirrups (it was with the Avars that sabres and stirrups first appeared in Europe), bows and arrows as well as thonged sword belts. In the 7th century "mixed" Avar-Slav burial grounds are found in this area, such as one at Devinska-Nova Ves in Czechoslovakia.

In the 6th–8th centuries, Slav migrations followed three main directions. To the south, they settled in the former Balkan provinces of the Roman empire, and at the end of the 7th century participated in alliance with the Turco-Bulgars, in the creation of the first Bulgarian state in the lower Danube area; to the west they moved towards the Elbe and the Baltic Sea, reaching the lower Elbe by the 9th century, while the first state of the western Slavs, Great Moravia, dates from the early 9th century; to the north Slav tribes from the Lower Danube area moved along the Dnieper basin, crushing local Slav, Balto-Slav and Baltic communities in the 7th–8th centuries. Traces of fire in the settlements of this area (Koločin, Demidovka, Tušemlya), and the discovery at destruction levels of arrows of the Avar type, as well as javelins with a double hook, weapons in current use by the Slavs of the Danube, are evidence of their advance. Following these migrations, new Slav cultures emerged in the 8th centuries, such as the Luke-Rajkoveckaya or Romny-Borševo cultures, which immediately preceded the culture of medieval Russia.

The history of the Slavs in eastern Europe is also marked at this period by the arrival of two new peoples. At the end of the 7th century and the beginning of the 8th, Slavs of the mid-Dnieper were attacked by Khazars from northern Caucasia, who brought about the end of the Pen'kovka culture in this area, as evidenced by the burial of a number of treasure hoards, known as the "antiquities of the Antes". The Saltov culture, which emerged from the peoples forming the Khazar kingdom, then spread into the steppes of southern Russia, and the neighbouring Slav tribes accepted Khazar dominance. In the 8th century, Varangians from the Baltic area penetrated eastern Europe along the great rivers and came into contact with the Finns, Balts and Slavs. The first proto-urban centres such as Ladoga indicate the fusion of Scandinavian, Slav and Finnish cultural elements, and can be compared with Birka or Hedeby in Scandinavia. In 862, the Slavs of Novgorod and the Finns concluded an alliance with the Varangians, accepting the overlordship of a Scandinavian prince living at Ladoga. This event is generally regarded as marking the birth of Russia.

Thus at the end of the 8th century Slavs were present over a huge territory, extending from Lake Ladoga in the north as far as Greece in the south, and from the Volga in the east as far as the Elbe in the west.

The people of the North

Scandinavia was an almost mythical country to ancient writers; Jordanes, a 6th century Goth author, saw it as the "matrix of the nations". In the first centuries AD, numerous Germanic peoples did in fact come from there: the Vandals, the Burgundians, the Angles, some of the Jutes, and perhaps the Lombards and the Goths. In general, these Nordic peoples of the Early Middle Ages precede historical records, since the earliest Scandinavian texts go no farther back than the 10th century.

In spite of its remote situation, Scandinavia was affected by the upheavals caused by the great migrations. Many treasure hoards were buried in the 4th and 5th centuries; fortresses were built in the countryside on the coast or on islands; votive depositories of weapons and jewels in the coastal swamps were more frequent, as at Skedemosse on the island of Oland. But from the 6th century Scandinavia experienced a period of calm. The departure of most of the Germanic peoples left only Nordic peoples in Scandinavia, gathered into many small kingdoms. The three large states that now form Scandinavia were not in fact unified prior to the Viking period. Excavations from the pre-Viking period enable archaeologists to identify certain characteristics specific to these Nordic societies that would endure well beyond the Viking era. They were rural societies in which three classes of men could be distinguished: slaves and serfs; free men, peasants farming their own land and craftsmen, often living in a village group; and rich rural landowners who were often warlords. They were also trading peoples, as is demonstrated from the time of the Roman empire by the large number of imported items found in the royal tumuli at Vendel: weapons, Frankish glassware, and bronze vessels. Excavations at the merchant town of Helgö on Lake Mälar have yielded imperial gold coins from the 5th–6th centuries, Coptic and Byzantine vases, Syrian glass, a 6th century statuette of Buddha from Turkestan or northwestern India, and an 8th century bishop's crook from Ireland. Also notable is the presence of many craftsmen working with metal. They mass-produced fibulae, but also made all sorts of utilitarian objects, many of which were intended for export. Local products such as furs, leather and amber were dispatched to the south, as well as slaves.

Raiders from the sea

The Nordic peoples were also warriors, participating either in groups (Erules) or as individuals in the great invasions. This resulted in an influx of gold in the 5th–6th centuries, leading to hoards of jewels (bracteates), spirals, or coins. This is demonstrated by the Torslunda treasure (Oland) or the Caldehus drinking horns (Jutland). Burials yield many weapons, including various items of fighting equipment remarkable for the quality of their decoration (helmets, shield bosses and sword handles from Vendel).

Finally, they were sea-going peoples. Even in the first century AD, Tacitus noted their manoeuvrable but sailless boats from Svear. The representational funerary tablets on the island of Gotland show the development of the pre-Viking and Viking ships from the 7th to the 11th centuries, and this knowledge is complemented by excavations carried out on the ship burials at Vendel and Valsgärde. The 7th and 8th centuries marked a turning-point for navigation which benefited from appreciable technical advances: the adoption of the sail, the improvement of the keel, and the clinker-built hull. Expansion in the Viking era owed much to these advances. The drakkars are known to us from Norwegian excavations of the royal ship burials at Oseberg (*c.*850) and Gokstad (*c.*900), as well as from deliberately scuttled boats at Roskilde (Denmark). But there are other reasons for the acceleration of an expansion that started as early as the beginning of the 8th century with the Swedish foundation of trading posts on the eastern shore of the Baltic, and the colonization by Norwegian farmers of groups of islands to the north of Scotland: namely, demographic pressure in Norway and Sweden, the occupation by the Slavs of the shores of the Baltic, and the consolidation of the power of the king in Denmark and in Sweden.

Funerary tablets, particularly those on the island of Gotland, testify to the great deeds claimed by the warriors, both in picture form and increasingly by means of runic* inscriptions. Though the kings and chiefs continued to be buried in boats, the merchants and warriors were surrounded by alignments of stones that suggest the shape of a boat, as in the cemetery of the merchant town of Vendila, near Aalborg (Jutland).

At the beginning of the Viking period, the Nordic countries became richer as the society was altered and modernized itself. Real towns were established in the 9th century and grew rapidly: at Hedeby* in Denmark and Birka* in Sweden archaeologists have found, behind ramparts with wooden towers, wooden houses that were rebuilt every 15 or 30 years. Archaeological remains demonstrate the development of trade. Birka on Lake Mälar, the main town in Sweden until the 10th century, was a huge entrepôt for goods traded with the Arab-Byzantine world: 60,000 Arab coins have been found there as well as countless luxury items from the Rhineland, Slavic and eastern countries. Amber, bone artifacts and all kinds of utilitarian objects made of iron were exported from this trading centre. It was at Hedeby that the first Scandinavian coins were struck at the beginning of the 9th century. Viking military art reached its peak at this period. In Denmark the perimeter wall round Danevirke was reinforced several times; the fortresses of Trelleborg and Aggersborg contained within circular perimeter walls military and other constructions divided into four districts, and at Eketorp (Oland island) there was a fortified country village.

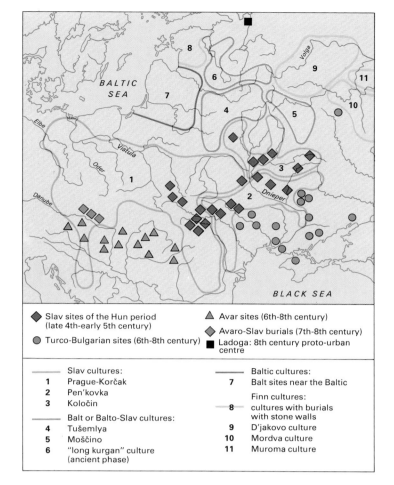

Objects characteristic of 5th–7th century Slav cultures

(1) 7th-century "Ante" fibula (brooch) from the region of Kharkov (Coll. of the Leningrad Institute of Archaeology). (2) Pot of the Pen'kova culture. Surskaja Zabora (excavations by A.V. Bodjanskij). (3) Pot of the Prague-Korčak culture; Kiev-Obolon (excavations by A.M. Šovkopljas).

Fortified Baltic habitat of Tušemlja (5th–8th centuries)

The plan of the habitat shows the social structure of the community. In this case an "extended family" of the patriarchal type lived in buildings arranged in a circle. In the centre are the sanctuary and its idols. After P.N. Tret'jakov, E.A. Šmidt, *Drevnie gorodišča Smolenščiny* (The ancient fortified habitats of the Smolensk region), (Ed. by the Academy of Sciences of the USSR, Moscow-Leningrad, 1963, fig. 5).

Slav sites of the Hun period (late 4th–early 5th century)

Turco-Bulgarian sites (6th-8th century)

Avar sites (6th-8th century)

Avaro-Slav burials (7th-8th century)

Ladoga: 8th century proto-urban centre

Slav cultures:
1 Prague-Korčak
2 Pen'kovka
3 Koločin

Balt or Balto-Slav cultures:
4 Tušemlya
5 Moščino
6 "long kurgan" culture (ancient phase)

Baltic cultures:
7 Balt sites near the Baltic

Finn cultures:
8 cultures with burials with stone walls
9 D'jakovo culture
10 Mordva culture
11 Muroma culture

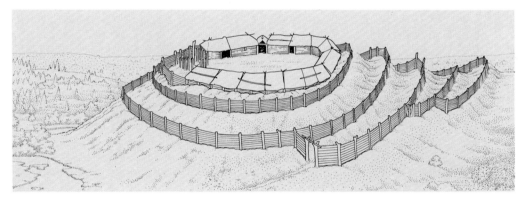

Treasure of Ekero, Uppland, Sweden

A treasure consisting of a gold bracelet and 47 gold *solidi* from the reign of Valentinian III (AD425–455) to the reign of Anastasius (491–518), this find is evidence of the arrival of Roman and Byzantine coins in Scandinavia from the mid-5th century. The treasure may be booty or the pay of Scandinavian warriors. Historiska Museet, Stockholm.

The sword of Snartemo

This sword found in Norway dates to the 6th century. At the top of the silver gilt hilt, two still recognizable animals are symmetrically opposed. Other animals are engraved on the gold panels of the pommel, but these have been reduced to elements so stylized that they are difficult to interpret. B.Y. University Museum of National Antiquities, Oslo.

The Scandinavian world was extremely rural, consisting of small communities living under the authority of a landowner-chieftain and separated as much by forests, marshes and mountains, as by the long harsh winter. However, contacts existed with the rest of Europe throughout the pre-Viking period, as attested by grave goods of objects imported from southern Europe. In this world of peninsulas and islands the sea was the means of contact; the development of marine technology, as seen in the Gokstad ship (*c.*900), and the establishment of commercial centres from the 8th century (Ribe, Hedeby, Kaupang), were to launch the Viking period and end Scandinavia's isolation.

important burial grounds

fortresses or fortified sites

commercial centres

rural habitats

isolated discovery

sacred and royal site

The helmet of Valsgärde, tomb 8, Gamla Uppsala, 650

Tombs dating from the 4th to the 11th centuries have been excavated at Valsgärde (Uppland, Sweden). There were 25 male inhumations in burial chambers or boats and some 50 cremations, apparently of women. Arms played an important role in the male burials. The helmet shown here recalls the helmet from Sutton Hoo, England (*c.*625–635) with its upper crown of decorated rectangular bronze leaves, its crest and its bronze visor, but it differs in the lower part which is made of chain mail. Museum of Nordic Antiquities, University of Uppsala.

The Middle Ages:
the archaeological background

Medieval archaeology as a whole is an expanding area in modern
European archaeology: continuities with our own culture are more
apparent, both in terms of people and in terms of landscape; it is, perhaps,
more "proletarian" than traditional classical archaeology.

In Europe, medieval archaeology is both an old discipline and a very recent form of research. Indeed, the modern archaeological practice of working on medieval sites has only existed for about a quarter of a century. Any description of the history of medieval archaeology should therefore explain why the excavation of medieval churches, cemeteries, castles and villages has been undertaken so late. It is not easy to answer this complicated question, which involves both the history of institutions (universities and scholarly societies, for example) and the history of ideas.

It is remarkable that the 19th century archaeologists did not extend their range to include archaeological objects. Even if the interest in things medieval which became prevalent towards the end of the 19th century was decisive in making the public conscious of the importance of medieval buildings and of preserving them, it has to be admitted that this awareness hardly extended to other evidence of medieval cultures. And the original by-passing of archaeology at the time of the great 19th century institutional developments was followed by other factors which caused the study by archaeology of the Middle Ages to remain in the margins. At this time research was confined to

Vase discovered at Chatenay-Malabry, 1727

The red ochre decoration of this vase is characteristic of production carried out at Paris in the 12th–13th centuries. Bibliothèque nationale, coll. Pierre de Clairambault, Ms 1138, folio 356.

Bibliothèque nationale, Paris

the work of amateurs from a cultivated urban middle class; it remained a poor relation in the field of archaeology and its only support came from private initiatives and a network of scholarly societies. This situation was to remain virtually unchanged until the 1960s.

This is all the more astonishing because the movement of ideas and the institutional reforms which occurred in Europe during the second half of the 19th century could have supplied a solid framework to facilitate a speedier definition and development of medieval archaeology.

Towards the middle of the 19th century, European archaeology was divided into three main currents: the first and possibly best known was exploration involving the discovery of the lost civilizations, mainly of the Middle East. The second was the development, chiefly in Germany, of an academic, university-based approach, with the creation of archaeological departments, the development of the study of philology, and the investigation of monuments of all kinds, albeit concentrated mainly on classical antiquity. The third great current, the Scandinavian tradition, was to have a decisive influence on Germany and, after World War II, on the whole of northwest Europe. An interest in archaeology had begun as early as the 16th century in the Scandinavian countries, which were poorly supplied with medieval archives. Protective legislation was enacted and excavations organized in the 17th century. The Middle Ages occupied a prominent place in this research.

The study of medieval archaeology was still very little undertaken between the two world wars. In France, some aspects of medieval archaeology did exist—there was some study of Merovingian tombs and research into fortification, but this was work of limited scope, carried out by amateurs, who were of a high standard to be sure, but few in number and very much "outsiders". In Europe as a whole, the protection and study of archaeological sites remained secondary, just as it had in the 19th century, and the maintenance and restoration of a few historic, mainly medieval, monuments which was undertaken served to excuse all the crudely executed and poorly organized field investigations made at the time, which destroyed all the archaeological layers. There has been, and still is, a general tendency in Europe to disclaim responsibility for matters of archaeological concern when dealing with the question of historic buildings.

Archaeology in the service of history

During the post-war years the situation has changed and medieval archaeology has at last been properly established. As far back as the 1930s, various English, Danish and German researchers, for example Gudmund Hatt, Axel Steensberg, Gerhard Bersu, Paul Grimm and Herbert Jankuhn, laid the fundations, both in the themes studied (deserted villages, landscapes, urban sites) and in the methods of work (large-scale cleaning and accurate laboratory analysis, emphasizing the importance of the natural sciences) for the approach of archaeologists today. But we had to wait until the 1950s in the British Isles, Holland and Germany, the following decade in France and an even later date in Spain and Italy to witness the appearance of modern medieval archaeology.

At first, and until the 1970s, the main direction of archaeological fieldwork lay in the clarification of historical problems for which excavation played at worst an illustrative, at best a complementary or corroborative role. From this point of view, it is significant that in Great Britain, France and Germany, the essential theme in these founding years was often the excavation of deserted villages, i.e. the study of sites not normally under threat, and where

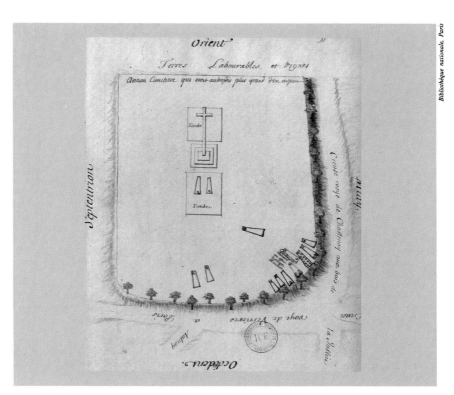

Bibliothèque nationale, Paris

Excavations at Châtenay-Malabry, France in 1727

During the 18th century the first "antiquaries" made their appearance, collecting pictures of monuments, drawing objects and transcribing inscriptions, usually concerning the Roman period and found by chance during building works, rarely in the course of proper excavations. From 1727 onwards, while works were carried out around the church of Chatenay-Malabry, the scholar Pierre de Clairambault recorded the first observations of a medieval churchyard of the 12th–13th century.

the purpose of research was almost always to find out the reasons for their abandonment, a typically historical problem, rather than to seek clues as to the living conditions of the medieval peasant, which would be a specifically archaeological inquiry. The beginnings of modern European medieval archaeology are also marked by the study of earth fortifications and ceramic production.

The importance of "rescue" archaeology

But this state of affairs, characteristic of the 1960s and 1970s, has changed profoundly in less than a decade. Three fundamental and interconnected factors have played a part: wide-spread destruction of sites due to the programme of urban development and refurbishing which followed World War II; the hasty development, from slow beginnings, of an archaeology for rescue operations, with more personnel and financial resources and often working in new fields of study, such as urban archaeology; lastly, the general establishment of national archaeological services based on new or improved legislation, with specialized personnel at their disposal.

This final element is essential. At the culmination of a period of prosperity for research in Europe in the 1960s, through an early awareness of the destruction of sites and the new importance of medieval archaeology, some European countries, notably the British Isles, have greatly enlarged the teaching of medieval archaeology in their universities. This awareness came later in France, where the universities were slower to promote the disciplines that were in full expansion elsewhere: prehistory, protohistory and medieval archaeology. In France and a number of neighbouring countries, two systems tend to emerge, a phenomenon which particularly applies to the Middle Ages. Side by side with the academic sector (universities, various research institutions) mainly oriented towards distant sites, archaeology in one's own country, especially as regards the Middle Ages, is mainly carried out under the auspices of the national archaeological services, in the context of stable or temporary structures, created by national or local government or within the framework of large works requiring immediate rescue excavations. The growing professionalism of archaeology and the existence of some hundreds of specialist investigators in each of the large European countries, including dozens of medievalists, will have very important consequences, because from now on medieval archaeology, like that of other periods, will increasingly be the output of a scientific community conscious of its concerns and its scientific practices.

Modern developments

The problems of working methods in the field and the recording of data have been settled since the 1970s, and now a growing interest is being shown in the practice of taking samples before beginning excavation, laboratory research (analytical archaeology*, dating*) and especially in the study of the ecological environment of the sites excavated. Recent work in America, more easily subsumed under the general designation the "New Archaeology", provides the most obvious illustration of this tendency within the biggest scientific community of archaeologists in the world, consisting of several thousands of researchers. In these investigations the influence of prehistorians, accustomed to relying on archaeological material rather than written sources, is undeniable. Development is less advanced in Europe, but it is beginning to be perceptible. Nevertheless, for the medievalists, the existence of frequently numerous texts poses serious methodological problems that are extremely

difficult to resolve. At the same time, the growing development, mainly through urban excavations, of a post-medieval archaeology is going to play an important role. Through it researchers will increasingly tackle the problems of everyday life, of handicrafts or household equipment, which incidentally are well documented in written sources. An exciting confrontation, already begun in medieval archaeology, between the written and the archaeological sources, is going to develop more and more. In full flower owing to the growing strength of researchers and the financial resources devoted to it throughout Europe, in full intellectual development, able to pose methodological problems concerning archaeology in general, unhampered by the weight of scientific traditions, medieval archaeology occupies and will increasingly occupy a leading place in the development of European archaeology.

Monumental archaeology

The "new archaeology" of early medieval Europe is producing a vast and growing body of evidence to set beside the limited quantity of surviving texts: the history of a building's construction phases can tell us much about the people who planned and built it.

Until recently the term "medieval archaeology" referred to a body of knowledge about Middle Age monuments, based on a serious understanding of architecture but requiring at the same time a command of all the other branches of history as it was then understood.

Over the last few decades, however, archaeologists have applied to the Middle Ages the methods of prehistory, particularly the use of stratigraphic*, or layered, excavations as a basis for research, and this has led to the emergence and rapid development of a new medieval archaeology. For example, funerary archaeology, which combines the study of evidence from tombs with relevant texts and laboratory research, has contributed to the reconstruction of the least known periods of the Middle Ages. Similarly, military archaeology has undergone a complete renewal, as researchers try to place the history of fortifications within a more general context of social history. Rural dwellings have for a long time been ignored, but now form the object of wide-ranging research, particularly with vanished or uprooted villages. Monumental archaeology, or traditional medieval archaeology, has similarly benefited from these new methods.

The nature of the subject has not altered fundamentally, remaining a science of the monument and implying a technically well-informed "archaeology of constructions". Furthermore, the medieval archaeologist cannot today, any more than before, ignore the historical data which constantly emerges. But perhaps the object of research can now be more clearly visualized.

Archaeology and art history
An archaeologist's view of a monument is different from that of an art historian, even though the same person may be familiar with both disciplines. Monumental archaeology considers the monument in its entirety, starting with its ancient origins; thus it is not seen as a harmonious development, designed for a particular objective, and followed through without interruption, but as a series of stages, some of which are no longer visible. The hazards of history have led to the total or partial destruction of many medieval monuments that were later rebuilt or enlarged. An often important part of their history is buried in the ground, and can only be known by being dug up.

An example of this type of monumental archaeology comes from Romainmôtier monastery (Vaud Canton, Switzerland) where systematic research has revealed that four buildings replaced each other on the same spot beside the River Nozon. The original oratory, founded c.450 by St Romanus and his brother Lupicinus, has not been found (it would have been built of earth and wood, and has left no traces). The buildings that have been identified include a very simple chapel, built in the 7th century by the Duke Félix Chramnèlene for a Columban (Iona) monastery; a church consecrated in December 753 by Pope Etienne II on his visit to the kingdom of the Franks to consecrate Pépin, son of Charles Martel, as king; and finally an 11th century church with later enlargements to the east and west. Similar systematic fieldwork, particularly in Germany, has opened up large areas, previously regarded as lost, of the architectural history of the West in the Carolingian and Ottonian periods. Excavations at a number of sites in England have shown the influence of continental ideas on Anglo-Saxon builders, for example at the surviving churches of Deerhurst and Brixworth, and in particular at Winchester, where an important series of excavations have revealed that the builders of the chief church of 10th century England had thoroughly imbibed the architectural practices of the Carolingian renaissance.

Fieldwork is also indispensable in assessing the history of buildings that are still standing, or at least of some of their parts. For example, a dig carried out in 1967 at the large abbey church of La Charité-sur-Loire revealed interesting peculiarities in the building of the choir. Apparently, between 1080 and 1090 the builders had originally intended to follow the Benedictine plan in its largest version, as at Châteaumeillant and Saint-Sever; in such a plan the apse is flanked on either side by three smaller so-called apsidioles of decreasing depth. The choir was consecrated by Pope Pascal II on 9 March 1107. However, at about this time, the choir of the third abbey church of Cluny (Cluny III) was completed. The architect of La Charité-sur-Loire tried to imitate this prestigious model by altering the centre part of his original plan. He made the choir deeper, replacing the central apse and the apsidioles with a deeper, aisled choir and ending in a semicircular ambulatory with five radiating chapels.

The assessment of the successive stages in a monument's history thus begins with stratigraphic excavations. It continues with a study of the building itself, applying a method of archaeological analysis which is a natural continuation of excavation. This phase of research aims to rediscover the progress of the work by identifying those parts on the site of the building sufficiently homogeneous to allow us clearly to determine their extent. These are called "construction campaigns". After comparison with information from surviving texts these are then used to establish both the relative and the absolute chronology of the building. One is also tempted to see some relationship between these phases and the arrival of new masters, but archaeologists are wary of doing this unless documentation is available.

Jean-Pierre Ravaux's recent work on Reims cathedral has identified at least 12 of these campaigns, five of which involve ground plans, while the others affect the upper parts of the building. However, only four architects are illustrated in the celebrated labyrinth of Reims cathedral: these architects include Jean d'Orbais who drew the plan of the apse, Jean le Loup who was the master builder for 16 years, Gaucher de Reims who was in charge of the work for 7 or 8 years, and Bernard de Soissons who built the vaults.

Monumental archaeology is not only a source of knowledge; during the 19th century it played a part—often in spite of itself—in the "restoration" and even re-creation of such archaeological monuments as Saint-Front in Périgueux, rebuilt by Abadie. Restorers claimed their work was solidly based on archaeological knowledge in order to justify their interventions, however crude. Whatever the value of such restorations, they clearly need to be seen as part of the history of the building.

Another kind of intervention shows real respect for the past. This uses archaeological surveys* and excavations to recover fragments of lost buildings in order to produce, not an entire and inevitably conjectural reconstruction, but a presentation which is both honest and evocative. This is the achievement of Léon Pressouyre in his "resurrection" of the cloister of Notre-Dame-en-Vaux at Châlons-sur-Marne.

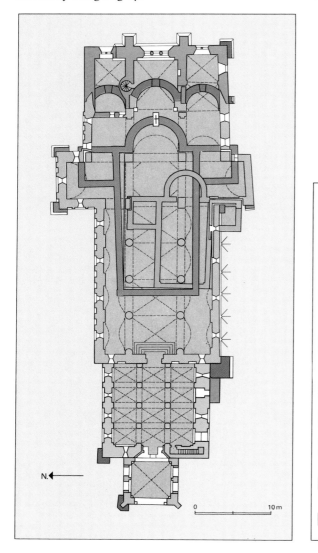

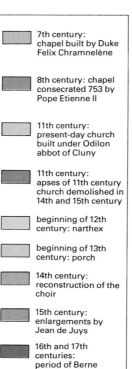

Sequence of churches at Romainmôtier, Vaud, Switzerland

In the seventh century, the monastery was content with a modest church consisting, apart from the nave and a slightly extended apse, of only two annexes. This plan was retained for a later church, consecrated in 753, which merely enlarged the original plan. Under the influence of Cluny, a more complicated construction was undertaken at the beginning of the eleventh century, when there emerged the elements of a Romanesque abbey: jutting transepts, aisles for the nave, and an extended choir crowned with three apses. Shortly afterwards, in accordance with a practice emanating from Burgundy, a large two-storeyed narthex (western portico) was added to the nave. After E. Bach, *Congrés Archéologique de France, Suisse romande*, 1952.

7th century: chapel built by Duke Felix Chramnelène

8th century: chapel consecrated 753 by Pope Etienne II

11th century: present-day church built under Odilon abbot of Cluny

11th century: apses of 11th century church demolished in 14th and 15th century

beginning of 12th century: narthex

beginning of 13th century: porch

14th century: reconstruction of the choir

15th century: enlargements by Jean de Juys

16th and 17th centuries: period of Berne

Romainmôtier from the north east

Contrasts of volume and variations in wall bondings and apertures reveal successive alterations of the chevet (east end of the church). Lombardic bands decorated the transept and choir from the beginning of the eleventh century. The tower above the transept crossing has kept the same decoration, but from a slightly later date. The central apse with its large reticulated window dates from the beginning of the fourteenth century. Two superimposed chapels replaced the northern Romanesque apse between 1433 and 1447.

D. Glauser, *Monuments historiques et archéologie du canton de Vaud, Suisse*

Plan and cross-section of La Charité-sur-Loire church, France

The plan and cross-section of a monument often provide a useful guide to its history. The great church of La Charité-sur-Loire, begun towards 1080, followed the so-called Benedictine system, first seen in the second period of Cluny, with an apse bordered on each side by three equally spaced absidioles, or little apses. On the other side of the transept, the nave was derived from that of the third period of building at Cluny, with its double aisles and its three-story elevation: large arcades, a triforium and high windows. While it was still being constructed, the central apse and the two nearest absidioles were replaced by a choir and ambulatory with five radiating chapels, still on the model of Cluny III. It was at this time that the transept tower went up. The progress of the work can be followed in the variation of decoration on the triforium. However, the church never fully recovered from a terrible fire that destroyed the whole of the western part on July 31, 1559. The six west bays were abandoned and the rest of the nave was crudely restored by the architect Philibert Convers, who removed the double aisles to provide a smooth and bare outline. Construction periods and dates were established by Jean Vallery-Radot. After P.A. Lablaude and M. Duplantier under the direction of P. Lablaude, *Congrès archéologique de France*, Nivernais, 1967.

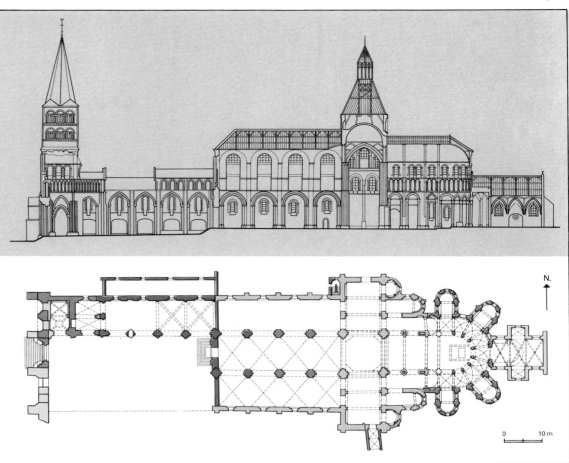

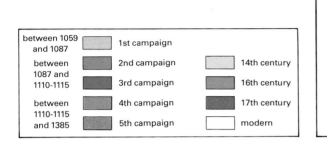

between 1059 and 1087		1st campaign	
between 1087 and 1110-1115		2nd campaign	14th century
		3rd campaign	16th century
between 1110-1115 and 1385		4th campaign	17th century
		5th campaign	modern

The church of St-Front, Périgueux, before and after restoration

The appearance of this church has been much altered in the course of its history. First, large sloping roofs concealed its five cupolas, and the eastern choir was added in 1347. Then in 1855 Paul Abadie, giving as his excuse the poor state of the building, reconstructed it entirely, apart from the belfry. He restored the unity of style by removing the Gothic addition, and modified the layout of the great arches in order, he said, the better to control their thrust. Having uncovered the cupolas, he crowned them with lanterns of his own invention, and these, together with the lanterns on the corner buttresses, give the construction a picturesque appearance in the style and flavour of the "Romano-Byzantine" of the 19th century.

Restoration of the statue-column of St Paul, cloister of Notre-Dame-en-Vaux at Châlons-sur-Marne, France

The cloister was demolished in 1759, but the masons used some of the remains as construction materials. With the help of these fragments, which were often very small and difficult to recover, Léon Pressouyre was able between 1963 and 1977 to carry out a restoration of the monument in successive stages, according to a process that he has himself described. The first task consisted of reconstituting, like pieces in a jigsaw puzzle, the columns' bases, shafts and capitals. These pieces were completed by filling in the missing parts with a substituted material. Since the available evidence was not sufficient for the reconstruction of the whole of the cloister, the final restoration is in a "discontinuous form suitable for museum presentation"

Villages and houses

The period 1050–1250 saw a dramatic upsurge in the rural population of western Europe when the essential character of the village as we know it today was shaped. It is archaeology rather than written texts which has given us the details of the life of the common people.

At the same time as the feudal system was being established, the village in western Europe achieved a form that has survived almost up to the present. The network of rural parishes may often be older than the 11th century, but the great majority of stone-built country churches, which can still be seen in France and elsewhere, were built between 1050 and 1180. We can point to the same pattern in Anglo-Saxon England, where the majority of rural parishes were already old by 1066, but most of the 400 surviving stone churches with Anglo-Saxon fabric are 11th century. It was at about the same period, and after the construction of the first large castles (*c*.1000) and fortified constructions of earth and wood, that the numerous castles of the lesser rural nobility began to proliferate. At this time, also, there emerged around the church and the castle—the classic institutions that virtually determined the medieval rural environment—villages that would become the classic models for rural architecture in Europe.

Europe was then undergoing a phase of population expansion, between 1050 and 1250, the longest then known in the west. Dwellings had to be provided for the increasing population, and villages to be built on lands recently cleared and for the first time opened up to agriculture. The immense effort involved in the building of tens of thousands of religious buildings, both cathedrals and parish churches, directly affected the ordinary everyday building style of the medieval peasants. At about this time, around the 11th to 13th centuries, the typical dwelling of the early Middle Ages, which had been built by its future occupants with rudimentary and often perishable materials such as branches, wooden poles, or bundles of foliage, began to be replaced by real houses, built to last. Such houses incorporated materials acquired through the landlord's foresters or from specialized artisans.

The activity of craftsmen was increasing in the rural world, with tile-makers (from the 12th and 13th centuries), bricklayers in certain parts of Europe, and masons, often brought together for the construction of the religious and military buildings which were now multiplying in rural areas. The presence of craftsmen is one of the essential elements characteristic of this period. The houses were built to be handed down from generation to generation, and not only represented an important part of the village at that time but also created the types of regional architecture which have survived to this day.

The profound transformation of the rural habitation that took place during this important period of the Middle Ages is not easy to trace clearly. Written sources or medieval miniature paintings provide some informa-tion, but not enough, particularly because they do not enable us to follow the process of the emergence of the village and the medieval house. In this area archaeology has made an essential contribution.

Until recently, the research initiated in Great Britain in the 1950s was the major source of accurate information. But during the past 10 or 15 years, the Mediterranean regions of Europe, such as Spain and, particularly, Italy and France, have developed their research in this field so that it is now possible, albeit with gaps, to retrace more easily the evolution of these subjects.

As far as construction methods are concerned, certain techniques which, until a few years ago were only known to exist in the Germanic world of the 7th to 14th centuries, have been found in France in the course of recent excavations. These include the technique of building a wall by *stabbau*, that is, with vertical planks held together by rabbeting (interlocking grooves). In the lord of the manor's motte at Mirville, the evolution of one of the buildings has been traced from the 11th to the 12th century, and this suggests, since there is nothing to indicate that it was different from many other contemporary rural constructions, how widely this technique spread through western Europe.

In this example the walls were still built with perishable materials, but these were carefully treated, and worked with metal tools before being placed in position. The preceding period of wooden poles and roughly hewn tree trunks was over. In southern Europe, the same development in the use of quality materials is apparent in the now frequent construction of rural dwellings in stone and lime mortar. The village of Rougiers was from the start built in this manner on the summit and flanks of the Sainte-Baume range, towards the end of the 12th century, and is entirely typical of the rural settlement throughout the Mediterranean from Spain to Italy, perched high up and spreading fanlike over a slope beneath the lord's castle.

Between these two extremes, stones and lime mortar on one side, rabbeted planks on the other, further materials and techniques can be found on rural sites from the 12th or 13th century, but overall the transition to a permanent dwelling, in various shapes, appears to have been a general process.

The contribution of archaeology

Archaeology, together with analysis of materials and techniques, also permits us to trace the evolution of the ground plans and the use of space in these rural sites. Two problems relate to the place of domestic animals and the means of heating. The mixed dwelling, which included under the same roof, and at either end of the building, humans on one side and cattle or (less commonly) sheep on the other, exemplifies the first issue. Excavations in the British Isles show that this type of construction appeared at the end of the 12th century and became common during the next, before being progressively replaced by other types and finally disappearing, often completely, from several parts of Europe at the end of the Middle Ages. Certain details, such as a sanitary drain at the end of the house reserved for the animals, allow us to identify this type of building, often mentioned in written documents. Its diffusion during the 13th century, its localization in western Europe, and its demise in certain areas, are all interesting indications—though requiring substantiation through further fieldwork—of the expansion of a peasant class of cattle owners, emerging from the less successful and less differentiated rural masses of the preceding periods.

The problem of fire and heating in a medieval rural habitation is another question that only archaeology can clarify, but which is nevertheless of fundamental importance for an understanding of the life and conditions of medieval country people. For over half of the period of the Middle Ages, continuing until the 13th or even 14th century, the only heating system, and at the same time the principal source of lighting, was the open fireplace, usually placed in the centre of the room, far from the wooden walls and other inflammable materials. The chimney fireplace, normally associated with stone walls and having its own flue, first appears in the aristocratic buildings of the Carolingian period, and regularly in the military architecture of the 12th century; but the earliest examples in rural dwellings, for instance in the village of Dracy (eastern France), only date from the 14th century. Yet this is one of the fundamental elements of the traditional old-style country home: the fireplace, the centre of family life, the place for evening gatherings.

This demonstrates the extent to which the Middle Ages, during this central period of the 12th and 13th centuries, was a time of innovations, creating architectural types and construction techniques that would form the basis, up to the present day, of regional differences and traditional styles; it also shows how comparatively late this development came, less than 1,000 years before our time, and how slow it was.

The rural world of pre-revolutionary Europe, with its traditional architecture that even today varies so considerably from region to region, its villages of different ground plans, its disparities in the use of materials, is in fact a medieval creation that later centuries only enriched and refined. This is the world that archaeology, in just a few decades, has brought back to life.

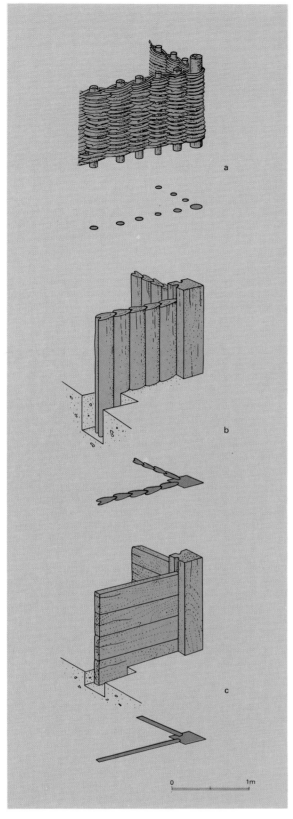

Mirville, France

The site of Mirville, founded in the 11th century, comprised a wall sheltering several buildings; the area was covered with earth and made into a mound at the beginning of the 12th century. There is nothing to indicate that these buildings were different, either in shape or materials, from those found in other contemporary rural sites. Throughout the whole of the 11th century, agricultural buildings were built by the *stabbau* technique of vertical, triangular planks, some 20cm (7in) thick, connected to one another by a series of rabbets or interlocking grooves (B). The marks of these planks (above) were clearly visible during certain stages in the excavations, due to the coloured remains they left in the soil of the trench bottom where they rested.

The same site has shown various other ways of using wood (left), all dating at least from the end of the 11th century: the stacked trunks (C) in a large building erected during the last stage in the occupation of the site, and the wattling (A), a classic technique of fence-making which remained in use in certain areas well beyond the Middle Ages.

Hilltop village of Rougiers, France

Rougiers is a typical example of a hill-top village in Mediterranean Europe. Towards the end of the 12th century a stone castle was built on the edge of the Sainte-Baume range together with a circular wall, inside which superimposed terraces were constructed. Rougiers was inhabited until the beginning of the 15th century and later abandoned in favour of a site lower down on the slope and eventually on the plain, according to a process typical of the history of such a habitat. The houses are characterized by certain features which differentiate them from those built at the same time in the northern half of Europe. They are built with stones and lime mortar, and are covered with hollow tiles of the so-called "Roman" type, still found in southern France today. Other features stress this difference: a very dense exploitation of the area within the walls, without gardens, yards or squares, and the systematic building of upper floors, a feature which is still found in the rural settlements of the Mediterranean. Only much later, towards the end of the Middle Ages and beyond, were a few rural houses in the British Isles and Germany built with an upper floor.

Rougiers shows us how architectural traditions and practices, as well as the criteria governing the use of space, varied considerably from one area to another in the rural world of medieval Europe. At the same time, it exhibits (as at Wharram Percy) the first signs of a type of village and rural habitat which was to characterize the countryside for centuries to come. By kind permission of G. Demians d'Archimbaud

The village of Wharram Percy, Yorkshire, England (opposite)

This village is at the heart of the largest archaeological study ever undertaken on a medieval rural site. Excavations began in 1953 and have not yet come to an end; they have revealed a large proportion of the buildings of this village, which was occupied from the 8th century until about the year 1510. The settlement comprised the lord's manor, built in the centre of the village in the 12th century and, later, replaced by another to the north of the 13th century settlement. The first wooden church, built in Saxon times between the 8th and 10th centuries, was replaced by a stone building; the latter was considerably enlarged at various stages from the middle of the 11th century to the end of the 12th and throughout the 13th: the choir was rebuilt and low sides added. However, from the beginning of the 14th century the church was reduced in size several times, due to the steady depopulation of the village, which was finally abandoned, leaving the church still standing.

Inside the village itself, the area occupied by the houses is distributed along the same lines as many other contemporary rural sites: houses were built lengthwise, parallel or more often at right angles to the pathways, surrounded by small gardens fenced in by stone walls. Fields surrounded the village and were cultivated on the system of ridge and furrow which, due to a particular method of tillage, produced undulations 7–10m (22–32ft) wide, separated by deep furrows.

The houses at Wharram are typical of English medieval dwellings. At first they were all built in wood, but the details of their plans have been obscured by later renovations. During the first half of the 13th century all the houses were gradually rebuilt in harder material, local chalk quarried from gardens and fields. Towards the end of the 14th century a new type of building technique was introduced: the houses were built on a low stone wall, used as a foundation for a type of wooden structure then found in several parts of France, the British Isles and several other European countries, both in towns and in the countryside. All these houses are 4.5 to 6m (14 to 19ft) wide and 15 to 23m (48 to 74ft) long and belong to the mixed type of habitation, which shelters both humans and livestock. There are no outbuildings around these dwellings, which were self-contained units of agricultural production.

In this drawing the village appears as it was at the end of the 14th century. Such villages, however, remained fundamentally the same until the end of the 18th century, a few centuries later, or even in some cases, until as late as the 19th century.

Fortifications

One of the most important aspects of the work of archaeologists since the 1960s has been the discovery of the revolution in fortress-building by 9th and 10th century European rulers, and its central significance in the subsequent development of towns.

Fortified castles are a familiar part of the European landscape, but in their present state most of these buildings are later than the 12th century, and do not provide precise information on the essential nature of earlier medieval fortification architecture. The development of archaeology has now made it possible for us to study military architecture before the 12th century, when building was in stone and wood, and to understand better the stone-built architecture of later periods of the Middle Ages.

Until the end of the 10th century medieval fortifications were for collective use. The massive walls of the old Roman towns, rebuilt during the second half of the 9th century as a response to invasions from Scandinavia, were in many regions the only defence against this type of threat.

However, other forms of collective fortification were also used during the 9th and 10th centuries. The large *oppida** of the protohistorical periods were modified or completely rebuilt, and new constructions of a similar type were put up. In the British Isles the West Saxon kings, Alfred the Great, Edward and Athelstan, built large rectangular enclosures called *burgs*, over 30 of which have survived from the late 9th century, and many more from later years. Most were deliberately planned as centres of town life. In continental Europe circular enclosures were built, ranging in diameter from 100 to 500m (330 to 1650ft), that fulfilled various functions: in parts of Scandinavia, for example at Trelleborg or Fyrkat, they were military encampments; in Normandy or Auvergne, aristocratic residences; in Frisia they protected rural settlements; in other parts of Europe they sheltered religious settlements based on abbeys or episcopal churches as at Trèves or Saint-Martial de Limoges.

Motte fortifications

In all other areas, the response to lawlessness and the raids of the Germanic tribes in the 9th and 10th centuries led to the construction of circular enclosures built on a smaller scale, with diameters less than 100m (330ft) and sometimes only about 20m (65ft). This type of building occurs all over Europe and has a variety of functions. In Germany, for example, they were defensive installations to protect rural populations against Hungarian invasions during the reign of Emperor Henry the Fowler (919–936); in Ireland they were the dwellings of local chiefs, and in France of the lesser nobility. But these buildings, in use until the 12th century and even the 13th century, represent a different form of fortification, designed to protect the private households of minor rural lords. From the end of the 10th century, the "mottes" which were first put up in the valleys of the Loire and the Rhine are the most characteristic expression of this change.

Nothing in earlier fortifications resembled these more or less artificial earthen mounds, with a basal diameter of 30–100m (100–330ft) and a total height of 5–10m (16–32ft). On the level top stood a tower (the keep), or a circular walled enclosure that was eventually combined with the keep. Around this motte or central mound, a wall of variable size protected the other buildings, such as the kitchen and the chapel. This lower courtyard could serve as a refuge for the rural population, but the essential element in this type of fortification was the motte and the keep, which comprised the residence of the lord.

Fortified houses

Motte fortifications were gradually built over all Europe, with the exception of Scandinavia and the Iberian peninsula; in southern Italy and in England they appeared in the middle of the 11th century; in Germany at the end of the 11th or during the 12th century, according to the area; in Denmark at the end of the 12th century; in Poland and Russia during the 13th century. There are two reasons for the spread across Europe of this type of fortification: the progressive diffusion of the feudal system, and the establishment, dating from the 12th century, of knights on land granted by their liege lords. The knights, who represented the lower ranks of the feudal system, had previously lived in the huge castles of the 10th and 11th centuries. This spread of fortifications in earth and wood, and later in stone, then developed in western Europe after the 12th century (when mottes were no longer built) with the construction of fortified houses, the "moated sites" of the British Isles. On a square or more often rectangular foundation of earth, slightly raised, usually by less than 3m (10ft) above ground level, was set a large farmhouse, more or less fortified, where a local rural chief lived. The 13th century saw the widest diffusion of fortified houses in Italy and France, as in Great Britain, and they are normally to be found on the borders of the districts, outside the rural settlements.

Mottes and fortified houses therefore appear to be expressions of the individual fortification. Their appearance coincides with the use of stone—for the keep on top of the motte—which became the standard material in the great castles of the 13th century. But the 12th century is in many ways an essential period in the development of medieval fortifications. It was then that a decisive evolution occurred in the conception of military architecture.

The castles of the 11th century and the first half of the 12th century basically consisted of large rectangular keeps, huge stone buildings surrounded by often inadequately defensible walls. Their function as a residence was more important than their military value. During the 12th century, the confrontations between the Plantagenets and the Capetians in France led to the formation of armies composed of professional soldiers or mercenaries, an improvement in siege techniques, and the need to defend threatened boundaries or to consolidate unstable conquests.

A large part of the major ruler's revenues was employed in building or restoring castles. For example, the French king Philippe Auguste, crowned king in 1180, inherited 22 castles from his father, Louis VII. When he died in 1223 he controlled 144, including 37 that he had had built or rebuilt.

To fulfil its new function as a military building, the castle at the end of the 12th century and during the 13th century was smaller and designed for defence, with protected access, defensive redoubts, and flanking projections on the walls. The needs of defence became paramount and, during the second half of the 12th century (particularly after Philippe Auguste) the design of castles became progressively quadrilateral or rectangular, with a tower in each corner and twin towers defending the entrance.

This tradition continued in the 13th, 14th and particularly the 15th centuries with the extensive building projects of the king and major nobles. But these were not the most numerous. The lower rungs of the aristocracy restored, rebuilt, and often built, a large number of castles of varying size, still to be seen in all European countries. But the most characteristic elements of this whole period are found in the works of kings, armies and important lords, as at Château Gaillard between 1196 and 1198, the Louvre in Paris at about the same time, Coucy between 1225 and 1242, the Krak des Chevaliers in presentday Lebanon, during the 12th and 13th centuries, and, above all, the castles of the English kings in Wales, erected from 1278.

The diverse story of fortifications is therefore to be reconstructed on the basis of archives, existing buildings and archaeological research. The castle, all over Europe, was a place of shelter for rural populations, a centre of rule and fiscal collection, and the residence of the lord and his officers. Fortifications were also very often, particularly with the mottes of the 11th and 12th centuries, the origin of rural settlements. Over and above the picturesque aspect of "feudal" ruins, the medieval fortification in fact represents an essential element in the history of the Middle Ages.

N. D. Roger-Viollet

Loches, Indre-et-Loire, France

These fortifications were built on a rocky plateau, the southern point of which, shown here, was the weakest. The large keep, in the centre, dates from the end of the 11th or beginning of the 12th century, its façade (on left of the illustration) being the earliest. Rectangular in plan, it measures 25m × 13m (82ft × 43ft) at ground level, and it is today still 37m (122ft) high. On the right, a small square yard is visible where the entrance staircase was once situated and which guarded the entrance itself. To the south of the keep, in the foreground, the defensive installations were often altered and carefully looked after. At present they include two walls, here visible, one of which, in the foreground, was reinforced in the 13th century by three large towers (on the left) and several smaller ones (in the centre and to the right).

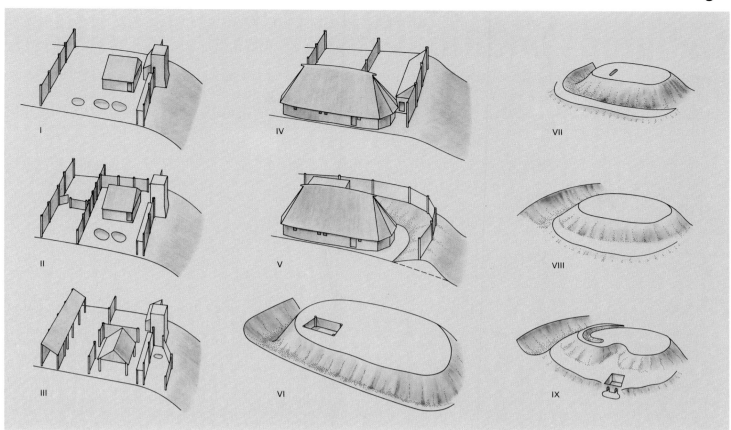

The Seigneural motte at Mirville, France

This example illustrates the way that archaeology can add to our knowledge of earth fortifications, and also how complex was the evolution of military architecture built of wood and soil. Twelve successive stages, summarized here, have been identified during the excavations: apart from a 2nd–3rd century core, of which only a drainage channel remains, archaeologists have found fortifications surrounding a few lean-to sheds and an entrance tower, the whole rebuilt at various stages during the 11th century (I to III). At the end of the 11th century, after a fire, the buildings were replaced by a large house (IV) which was further surrounded by a moat and a palisade (V), suggesting that the whole complex now underwent a change of function (end of the 11th and beginning of the 12th century). Later, this series of early buildings at ground level was replaced by a motte (mound) which totally covered the previous buildings, using soil extracted from a moat. From its establishment at the beginning of the 12th century and its final abandonment, this motte was twice enlarged in the course of the 12th century (VII, VIII) until it became a platform surrounded by a moat 25m (82ft) in diameter and 3m (10ft) deep (VIII). In the 16th century (IX) it formed the base for two brick ovens.

The fortifications of Vismes-au-Mont, France

Ever since 1175, written documentation has indicated the presence, on this site, of a noble family, undoubtedly the same who built the largest of the two mounds. The second must have been built later as a result of a property redistribution. Surrounding these two vital buildings, an enclosure protected the dwellings. The importance of this kind of fortification is demonstrated by the fact that this particular one has given its name to the area.

The keep of Coucy, France

This huge building 31m (102ft) in diameter, had walls 7.5m (25ft) thick at the base, and having a height of 55m (181ft). The largest keep of medieval Europe, it was part of a vast fortified ensemble built between 1225 and 1242 by Enguerrand III of Coucy, one of the most powerful nobles of his day. Its destruction by the German army on 27 March 1917 required 27 tons of explosive.

Beaumaris Castle, Wales

This castle was the eighth and last in a series of fortresses built by the English king Edward I (r.1272–1307) to secure his conquest of north Wales after 20 years of conflict. Building from 1295 until 1330 involved 400 bricklayers, 2,000 labourers, 100 two-wheel carts, 60 four-wheel carts, 30 ships, 200 quarrymen, 30 blacksmiths and several carpenters.

Religious buildings in the early Romanesque

The majesty of Romanesque church buildings is unsurpassed to this day. But what preceded them? Most of the great churches of the 9th–11th century period were subsequently rebuilt or even demolished in favour of later medieval buildings. Archaeology is often the only key to the "prehistory" of the Romanesque.

The archaeology of Romanesque churches came into its own in the period between the two world wars. In France, the main excavations and archaeological studies of the era were carried out at Cluny and St-Denis. Just before the start of World War II, the archaeology of religious buildings received a stimulus when the recommendations of the Charter of Venice, urging an overall study before the restoration of any monument, were rapidly applied in England, Germany and Switzerland. At large sites, such as cathedrals or abbeys, as well as at small buildings, archaeologists became accustomed to working over large areas, to pressing on with excavations and studies of elevation, and to studying structures, soils and burials as carefully as stratigraphical* sequences.

The conclusions from these researches have enriched our knowledge not only of Romanesque buildings, but also of the development of western culture, for of course many churches founded during the early Middle Ages have survived until the present day. The most spectacular results concern buildings that had disappeared completely, or buildings reconstructed over the ages. Thus our image of the episcopal building complex or the single cathedral has been more strictly defined and, in the same way, increased knowledge of rural and urban basilicas and collegiate churches, buildings of no apparent interest, has clearly shown the contribution that can be made by archaeological study of the terrain.

It is evident that, from the Carolingian period, the different functions of the bishop's office, or episcopal group, tended to be concentrated in a single building. For example, in Geneva the central church, built on the axis of the baptistry, took precedence over the others, which soon disappeared. In the 11th century, this church was enlarged eastwards with an impressive chevet, or polygonal extension, which comprised a central rotunda surrounded by side aisles (these eastern structures were partly destroyed by the construction of the Gothic edifice). The 11th century rotunda, the mausoleum of Sigismund, has been replaced as a result of studies still in progress in the group of chevets marking the transition from Carolingian to Romanesque art, of which St Bénigne of Dijon remains the best example.

Recent discoveries in Florence
At Florence, excavations carried out beneath the cathedral since 1965 have uncovered the remains of early Christian, Carolingian and Romanesque churches above Roman structures. In the Romanesque period, the cathedral of Florence adopted a transeptal plan with chapels facing east. The chevet was increased in size and a semicircular apse was attached to the choir with side aisles terminating in small apsidioles. The most remarkable fact was that a vast crypt extended beneath the chevet. The crypt is at ground level, with the nave and side staircases leading to the raised choir. The Romanesque church, influenced by the second Cluny building phase, is dated to the middle 11th century.

At Lyon, on the other hand, an obvious preoccupation with traditionalism contributed to the maintenance of an episcopal group, which was still composed of three churches in the 12th century. These were St Etienne and Ste Croix, which vanished in the French Revolution, and St Jean. Excavations on the north side of the cathedral of St Jean have revealed the church of St Etienne, which replaced the baptistry at the end of the 11th century, as well as the church of Ste Croix, rebuilt in the same period; researches under the cathedral (a resumption of the 1935 excavations) have given us a better idea of the dates of the four apses which succeeded each other on the same site from the 4th century to the beginning of the 12th century.

Excavations at Winchester, England, have been even more spectacular, revealing as they do the Carolingian impulses behind the final development of the late 10th century minster. Excavations at Basle in Switzerland, and Bremen and Ratisbon in Germany, have supplied new information about the Carolingian period.

Among the great monastic and collegiate churches which replaced the basilicas of the early Middle Ages, the church of St Bénigne of Dijon deserves detailed study. Important soundings carried out inside and outside the existing church have shown the precise situation of the transept, and of the crypt which extended not only beneath the transept, but also below a large part of the early 11th century nave. There was a counter-apse with a rotunda at the west end of the building.

An eastern rotunda similar to that at St Bénigne was discovered beneath the apse of the church of St Pierre of Louvain in Belgium, on the west façade of the church of Eichstatt in Germany and, on an older building, the monastic church of St Augustine of Canterbury in England, rebuilt in 1049.

The collegiate churches of St Jean of Geneva, St Just of Lyon, St Michael of Ratisbon and the Abbey of Psalmodi, France, have a classic chronology of buildings succeeding each other, sometimes from the 4th to the 18th century.

At St-Pierre-l'Etrier, Autun and Cruas, studies of elevation have been carried out parallel to the excavations; at La Charité-sur-Loire, Marmoutier, and St Martin of Tours, excavations or soundings have disclosed buildings which had sometimes vanished entirely.

At the Abbey of Novalaise in Italy, recent work undertaken in the church and the neighbouring chapels has shown the evolution of the various buildings and their function between the Carolingian and the Romanesque periods. In particular, the role of the small chapels which still stand close to the monastic church has been discovered: they served as stages in the processions held during the major feasts of the liturgy.

Important work, both in France and elsewhere, has been done on Cistercian abbeys (for example at l'Escale-Dieu in France and Baltinglass in Ireland). The centre of interest has shifted from the now well-known plans of churches to working buildings, such as the water supply system and the kiln for tiles, which were studied recently at Vauclair, France.

The parish church rediscovered
The most spectacular results have sometimes followed the study of parish churches of no great apparent interest. The thorough nature of the excavations and the quality of operations make these studies particularly rewarding, especially when the whole village is excavated, as at Wharram Percy, England.

The excavation of this village in Yorkshire, begun in 1962, concentrated on the peasants' houses (made of wood), the manor, the church and the cemetery. A stone church replaced the original wooden church from the 8th–9th century. This 9th century building was enlarged to the east and west in the 11th century, and in the 15th century it was given a tower on the façade and aisles on the south and north sides. Continental influence is particularly marked in the appearance of the semicircular apse, rare in Saxon buildings (except in certain churches built in Kent). This was replaced in the 13th century by a rectangular apse.

The successive plans of the church at Wharram Percy are well known, but hundreds of other buildings have been excavated with the same scrupulous care, not only in England, but also in Germany, for example at Münstereiffel, as well as in several sites in Switzerland, such as Zurzach, Hermance, Satigny and Ticino. The movement is also gathering force now in Italy (at Val d'Aosta in particular) and France (Viuz-Faverges in the Rhône-Alpes region).

Thematic archaeology has suffered from some misunderstanding in recent years. Nevertheless, there are many archaeologists who think that religious buildings are too important from a cultural point of view for us to allow an essential part of our heritage to disappear. The archaeological study of a church discloses new elements in the evolution of public forms of worship, and therefore in the evolution of the Christian faith; it also expands our knowledge of construction techniques, economic progress and the difficulties experienced in a community, and, lastly, various burial practices. Urban archaeology, like rural archaeology, is enriched by taking into account the study of religious buildings because they still stand as impressive cultural landmarks in the scenery of European towns and villages.

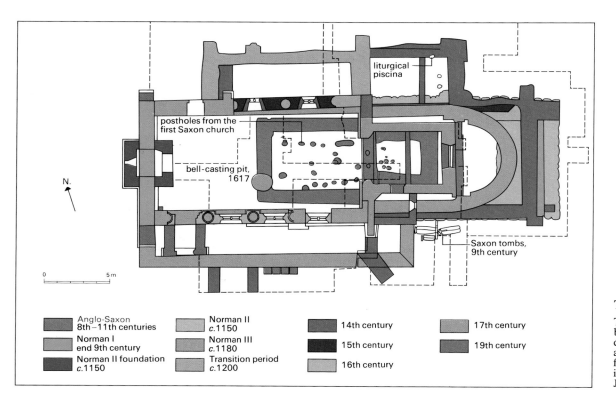

liturgical piscina

postholes from the first Saxon church

bell-casting pit, 1617

N.

0   5 m

Saxon tombs, 9th century

▨ Anglo-Saxon 8th–11th centuries	▨ Norman II c.1150	▨ 14th century	▨ 17th century
▨ Norman I end 9th century	▨ Norman III c.1180	▨ 15th century	▨ 19th century
▨ Norman II foundation c.1150	▨ Transition period c.1200	▨ 16th century	

The church of Wharram Percy, Yorkshire, England

The plan of Wharram Percy is proof that country buildings can be as rich in historical content as city buildings. Here we can discern a historical progression, beginning in the Saxon period and continuing down to our own days, almost like watching a film. Stopping the film in the 12th century, we observe the influence of continental religious architecture. Excavations by J. Hurst.

The cathedral of Geneva

Fieldwork at the cathedral of Geneva is remarkable for its all-inclusive nature. Not only the interior of the building, but also the parvis in front of the cathedral and the neighbouring streets are being uncovered, while work on consolidating the Romano-Gothic building goes on. The 11th-century rotunda appears below the modern dome. Excavations by Charles Bonnet.

St Etienne and Ste Croix, Lyon, France

The archaeological garden laid out north of the cathedral of Saint-Jean contains reconstructions of the churches of St Etienne and Ste Croix: north, the Church of Ste Croix, rebuilt in the 15th century on the foundations of a Roman church; south, a small church with a central plan which replaced the early Christian baptistry (the font at the transept crossing belonged to the baptistry). Excavations J-F. Reynaud.

St Bénigne, Dijon, France

This reconstruction is based on old texts and excavations. Archaeologists can now propose a representation of the church's design with its three aisles, vaulted from the first, as well as a crypt which extended far under the central aisle. An apse probably rounded off the building to the west. Excavations by C. Malone.

Florence cathedral

The cathedral of Florence, rebuilt in the 10th century, has been uncovered in the lower level of the present building. An archaeologically arranged crypt shows the various stages; the Roman construction is well preserved and stands out in this presentation. The photograph shows the chapel aligned from the southern arm of the Roman transept (right), and the staircase leading to the raised choir (left). Excavations by G. Morozzi and N. Bemporad.

125

time schedules. This exceptional enterprise, carried out on one of the most important sites of European urban archaeology, affects a little-known section of western Paris near the city wall, dating from the end of the 12th and the beginning of the 13th century.

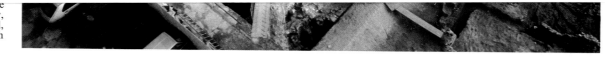

Industry and everyday life

As excavation moves from "capital" centres to lesser habitation sites, the most interesting new evidence yielded to the archaeologist has been of everyday life.

Artisan industries and the daily life of the people are perhaps the areas of study that have changed most in the development of medieval archaeology in Europe during the past 10 or 20 years. The increasing number of excavations has not only greatly added to the objects and information available, but has also shifted the centres of interest and, particularly, the problems demanding solutions. In this field more than in any other, archaeology and traditional history, based entirely on written documents, have most evidently ceased to be complementary and become, if not opposed, at least fundamentally different in their approach. For historians, the two most important industries in terms of capital investment, labour required, value of products, and creation of trade are textiles and building. The textile industry was the cornerstone of the wealth and power of a number of Flemish towns, as well as of the expansion of the adjacent regions. The development of building, particularly in the towns, was responsible for typically urban features such as cathedrals and major public buildings. In the Middle Ages, only war called for the development of capital to the same extent as did urban construction, particularly cathedrals.

However, where it has been applied, archaeology brings little information on these two activities. Finds of textiles are rare and often uninformative, and although the excavation of large buildings is often important in determining dates of construction or modification, or the use of certain techniques, it is still often seen as complementary, though no doubt essential, to the study of the surviving building. In both these areas the fieldwork possibilities remain secondary to studies based on written sources or existing buildings.

It is in the area of artisan production, less valuable commercially and probably also less important in terms of the medieval way of life, that archaeology makes an essential contribution. In three areas of prime importance to the socio-economic study of medieval society, fieldwork has proved irreplaceable, enabling archaeologists to know about the daily life of the people, to determine the conditions of production and exchange, and to establish the pattern of technical development. The progress of medieval archaeology in these areas increasingly allows medieval historians to tackle the

problems which recently seemed insoluble, and not only problems relating to the first centuries of the Middle Ages, when the written sources are rare.

The most decisive contribution of archaeology is in the field of everyday life. Apart from some spectacular or exceptional achievements, such as the discovery of material relating to games, rural or urban environments, or musical instruments, the importance of archaeological finds lies in their quantity and their systematic presence. All medieval excavations yield remains of food, mainly animal bones. Unfortunately, due to a shortage of specialists, these finds are often inadequately examined but the evidence of bones is essential in providing information on the importance of meat in the diet, and of hunting, fishing and raising stock. A careful study of archaeological deposits also provides us with irreplaceable information on the development of agriculture in all periods of the Middle Ages, the kinds of plant that were cultivated, and especially the types of cereal used.

The study of fragments of pottery, leather and wood, particularly from digs on damp or underwater sites, has completely changed our knowledge of tableware and cooking practices, clothing, and so on. The importance of wooden or earthenware utensils, and the scarcity of metal ones in a rural environment, was little known or appreciated from written documents but emerges clearly in the excavations of many rural and urban sites, such as Saint-Denis and Rougiers in France. The study of ceramic styles allows us to establish with certainty the presence or absence of certain practices relating to food or cooking: for example the rarity of open forms of tableware in terracotta, such as plates and saucers, throughout the Middle Ages.

Techniques and social organization

The study of ceramics is central to another contribution that archaeological material can make when properly examined, one that concerns not the quantity and practices of everyday life but its socio-economic organization and history of techniques. Finds of tools, particularly in metal, are infrequent, for metal was rare and expensive at this period, and therefore constantly re-used. But it is still possible to trace out a history of

techniques and, through them, to glimpse the fundamental elements of the socio-economic organization.

The importance of craft activities now becomes clear, for though they may be of little consequence in the context of the medieval economy (unlike the textile and building industries) they are of great value to archaeologists. It is hard to imagine that a weaving loom will be found in the course of a medieval dig. Made of wood, it would have little chance of survival in good condition, and in any case one or two finds would not be very conclusive in the reconstruction of a history of techniques. On the other hand, the craft of pottery has allowed archaeologists all over Europe to study its principal instrument, the kiln. Pottery fragments, found in all medieval excavations and practically indestructible in the soil, are very useful in studies of techniques, both through direct examination and laboratory analysis. It then becomes possible to identify, from domestic objects produced in a family context to systematic and standardized manufacture in specialized urban, and, particularly, rural workshops, the type of product under review, at a given period and in a precise geographical region. As a result, important differences have emerged between different areas of Europe. In some places the potter's wheel and kiln, and production in specialized workshops, are almost totally absent after the Roman period and up to the 11th century, as in several parts of southeast England. In others, specialized workshops using developed techniques reappear as early as the 7th and 8th centuries, as at Eifel in France and around Cologne in Germany.

The development of medieval archaeology has not only enriched museum collections and the representation of crafts and everyday life. By bringing to light a considerable number of objects, and providing often unexpected findings, it has raised new questions, defined original approaches to research, and completely changed our attitude towards whole areas of medieval history. The elaboration of techniques in examining archaeological material, a more systematic and rigorous use of the laboratory for dating, analysis and identification, and the increasing quantity of discoveries and findings, will probably lead to very interesting, original and rewarding work in the years to come.

A potter at his wheel, end 14th century

Excavations have brought to light thousands of pottery fragments but very little information on the potters themselves, about whom archive documents are usually silent. However, a certain number of miniatures depict these craftsmen at work. The wheel that they employed remained in use until the beginning of the 20th century; it resembled a kind of cart wheel, set horizontally and moved by a rod which the potter held against one of the spokes. Detail of a miniature from *Translation et exposition de la Cité de Dieu* (St Augustine) Ms fn. 22912, fol. 227 V°, Bibliothèque Nationale, Paris).

Bibliothèque nationale, Paris

Musées nationaux

O. Meyer, Unité d'archéologie de la ville de Saint-Denis

Medieval ceramics

At the table or in the kitchen, wood and earthenware utensils were widely used in the Middle Ages, but metal less often. Tableware objects like bowls and plates were rare or sometimes absent altogether, whereas the main body of earthenware production consisted of jugs or cooking vessels. Wide variations in shape, texture, quality and decoration enable archaeologists to recognize work from specific pottery workshops, and to date the archaeological layers within which the fragments were found. These wares also tell us much about distribution routes and important commercial activities: the three vases (right) discovered at Saint-Denis, France, were produced locally; the other, manufactured at Saintonge, France, in the 13th–14th century, belongs to a type of production which is widely found in north and northeast Europe.

Fragment of woven material, Amsterdam, Holland

This fragment of woollen material found in Amsterdam can be dated to the first half of the 14th century. In the damp soils of the towns, researchers have found remains of organic matter in a good state of preservation. Textiles, however, are most often found as fragments, more rarely as identifiable parts of clothing. An urban excavation campaign may recover several hundred fragments of cloth, enabling archaeologists to identify raw materials, techniques of weaving and sometimes dyeing substances. Historisch Museum.

Leather shoe, Amsterdam, Holland

This shoe dates from the first half of the 14th century and was found in Amsterdam, Holland. During the Middle Ages this type of footwear consisted of soft leather slippers stitched and fastened by laces, the sole being formed by a single layer of leather. These shoes are sometimes found in large numbers during urban excavations. Their reconstitution and preservation require careful laboratory treatment. Historisch Museum.

The building industry depicted in a 15th century manuscript

The construction of cathedrals and castles was the most important productive activity during the Middle Ages. This miniature, illustrating the life of Girart de Roussillon and of his wife Berthe, founders of 12 abbeys, clearly shows the activity and its various stages of operation: in the foreground, making lime and cutting stones; centre, transporting the materials and using them; background, climbing up the building by means of scaffolding. 15th century miniature, Ms 2549, fo. 164, Österreichische Nationalbibliothek, Vienna.

Objects of everyday life from the village of Rougiers, France

A pair of scissors and an awl to work leather and produce shoes, similar to the one shown above, are among several metal objects found in this village in southern France, occupied from the end of the 12th century to the beginning of the 15th. The bobbins are of clay in this example, and were used to ballast the spindle while spinning; the two sewing thimbles illustrate another aspect of female domestic activity. Centre de documentation archéologique du Var.

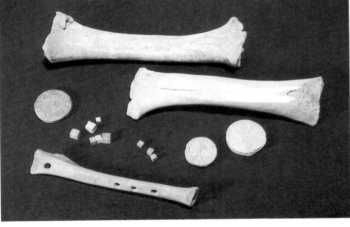

Bone objects found at Saint-Denis

Bone was a material much used in the Middle Ages, often through the recycling of kitchen refuse. These objects are therefore the product either of specialized craftsmen or of household workers, and continued to be made in the rural world until the beginning of the 20th century. The objects shown – a flute cut out of a long bone (foreground), counters, chess pieces and small dice (centre) – are typical of the uses to which bones were put. The two long bones are ice skates, cut expressly for this purpose and attached to the feet by thongs.

From Viking ship to three-master

Marine archaeology, the newest branch of medieval studies, has dramatically transformed our knowledge of early seafaring—from sunken Viking merchantmen to Henry VIII's flagship, the *Mary Rose*, one of the last examples of a Viking shipbuilding technique.

Until the 1950s, all information on medieval ships essentially came from images. Representations of vessels are comparatively numerous in medieval manuscripts, but the information they yield does not easily lend itself to any but an elementary classification in terms of means of propulsion (oared galleys or sails) or number of masts. Some evolution is apparent, such as the development from a square sail and single mast at the start of the period to multiple sails on three masts in the 15th century, as well as regional differences, for instance lateen* sails, triangular and square sails. But this kind of evidence does not really allow us to understand medieval ships. Of all technical systems devised by man, the ship is in fact one of the most complicated in its form, development and operation. But archaeology can give us a clearer understanding of the medieval ship.

At the end of the 19th century the discovery of Viking ships beneath the mounds of Gokstad and of Oseberg, Norway, revealed complete medieval ships for the first time. The reconstructed Gokstad ship crossed the Atlantic in 1892, and this voyage also marked the collaboration of general archaeologists, experimental archaeologists and ethnologists. But naval archaeology just before World War II was primarily concerned with the research and study of wrecks. In addition to wrecks examined under water, river finds, or the boats uncovered in Norway or at Sutton Hoo, England, the study of wrecks in a damp environment—quaysides, mud flats and river banks—has also been very important. Research in these areas has enabled archaeologists to trace the evolution of the ship at least as regards the general area of the North Sea, during the millennium covered by the Middle Ages (AD500–1500). They can also identify a profound break with the tradition of antiquity that occurred during the early medieval period. To construct the hull of a boat, one must either first determine the framework, namely the keel and the ribbing, leaving the planking to later, or one must first assemble the elements which constitute the planking and then put in position, within this shell, the keel and the ribbing. In the first case the shipbuilding technique is called "framework first" and in the second "planking first".

New techniques

All naval construction in antiquity belongs to the second type. But discoveries made comparatively recently in the Mediterranean, notably the so-called wreck of St-Gervais II in the Gulf of Fos, France, show that from the first quarter of the 7th century a "framework first" technique was used in this region. Other discoveries, also in the Mediterranean, indicate the transition from one system to the other, for instance the wreck of Serçe Liman, Turkey, dated to the 11th century. Other wrecks possess a mixed structure, such as the Byzantine wreck of Yassi Ada, Turkey, dating from the 7th century; here the lower part of the hull was constructed according to the "planking first" method, and the hull itself was built almost entirely according to the "framework first" method. The transition from one system to the other, clearly indicated in the Mediterranean region, may have been completely achieved in the period of the Middle Ages, but of all the theories advanced to explain it, whether based on changes in the

modes of production, reduction of maritime trade, or transformation of the structures of armament, none is entirely convincing. The same evolution, though of a later date, has been established for the end of the 15th century in north-western Europe, a region which displayed in addition a special feature: whereas in the Mediterranean the planking was made from conjoined pieces of wood, the strakes being assembled together in a freeboard method, northern Europe made use of another system, the clinker-built technique that certainly derived from a Scandinavian source. Clinker-building is a mode of assembly whereby the boarding (planks for covering the hull) is assembled by a technique of partial overlap, as in the eaves of a roof. This method of construction, for which there is evidence from the first century AD, is a "planking first" type. All the elements of the boarding are fixed by covering one strake over another so as to constitute a kind of homogenous wooden shell. The inner framework, inserted once the boarding has been completed, acts merely as a reinforcement for the structure of the hull. This dominant function of the planking has a bearing on the form of the vessel: the arrangement of the strakes of the planking determines the volume of the lower part of the hull.

The stability of clinker-built construction does not mean there was no technical evolution. Modes of assembly involving planking and interior framework developed between the first centuries AD and the 11th or 12th century, including a flexible assembly by means of cords on the Nydam boat (West Germany) dating to the 4th century, a mixed form of cords and pins on the Gokstad ship burial dating to the 9th century, and rigid assembly by bolting on the ships of Skudelev, Denmark, at the end of the 10th and start of the 11th century. Finally, this technical tradition spread with the Viking expansion of the early Middle Ages far beyond its place of origin.

Our present state of knowledge enables us to identify characteristics of North Sea and Mediterranean ships. However, the intermediate region, represented by the English Channel and the Atlantic, is admittedly less well known as regards the specific character of the vessels. Wrecks found in Great Britain, the Low Countries and Belgium nevertheless suggest what may well be a third tradition. A very characteristic example here is the wreck of Blackfriars I, found in the Thames at London in 1962. This boat, of "Celtic" tradition, dates to the end of the 2nd or the beginning of the third century. The flat bottom which determines its shape belongs neither to the "planking first" system nor to the "framework first" system. The builders used a special method of assembly between the freeboard strakes of the bottom of the keel and the floor timbers: in fact the strakes determine the shape and the floor timbers the cohesion of the structure. The most significant example of this tradition is the wreck of a hull from Bremen, West Germany, dated to the 1380s. It is likely that in addition to these three major groups there existed numerous specific traditions, for example in the Atlantic or in regions of lake or river navigation. But these are areas where research has advanced little. On the other hand, in the area of ocean navigation, at the end of the Middle Ages, a process of unification of the various traditions of naval construction began to develop.

At the end of the 15th century, north and northwest

Europe saw a profound technological change, particularly revealing in the case of England. Here, in the years 1490–95, the principle of clinker-building gradually yielded to the new construction of caravels (freeboard) which, in view of the greater distance between the vessel's deck and the waterline, involved the "framework first" principle. This method of construction was developed primarily for heavy-tonnage ships armed for war. Several written sources from the beginning of the 16th century reveal how clinker-built boats were rebuilt on the caravel principle, the best known being the *Mary Rose*, the wreck of which was recently raised from the Solent near Portsmouth. In Brittany, on the other hand, the appearance of this "framework first" principle of construction is attested from the years 1450–60, although we cannot explain exactly why it developed so much earlier there.

This transition from one system of construction to another raises many questions. For example, did Breton shipyards play a part in the diffusion of this technique, as some documents of the period seem to indicate? And what was the influence of Mediterranean shipbuilders summoned to work in western Europe? In any case, it is very probable that the standardized use of artillery batteries, fired through portholes, was a determining factor in the abandonment of clinker-built warships. So the end of the Middle Ages saw the development, from the Mediterranean to the Baltic, of a freeboard "framework first" construction hitherto limited to the Mediterranean world.

Rudders and rigging

Two other important developments marked the growing importance of north-western Europe in the development of ocean-going ships of medieval naval shipbuilding. One concerns the rudder, the other its propulsion by sails.

A profound change in the steering system took place at the end of the 12th century in north and northwest Europe, when the lateral steering oar gave way to the rudder fixed to the stern post on the line of the hull. This axial rudder was adopted only gradually in the case of Mediterranean ships.

The rigging also underwent major transformations. At the same date, which is difficult to fix accurately (sometime during the 14th century), the square rigging characteristic of northern seas penetrated into the Mediterranean and slowly replaced, on large vessels, lateen rigging.

This interpenetration of two separate technical systems, square rigging in the north, lateen rigging in the south, had many consequences. With the increase in tonnage, particularly in the 14th century, square rigging, originally consisting of a single sail, was modified first by fixing masts to the front and to the rear, and then by placing several sails one above the other.

The end of the Middle Ages saw the appearance of a type of ocean-going sailing ship which exhibited the main characteristics of the three-masters of a much later period. Of course, many details distinguished different types of vessel. Nor should it be forgotten that, alongside the heavy-tonnage ships which had been built since that time on the "framework first" principle, many ships and small boats continued to be built according to regional traditions.

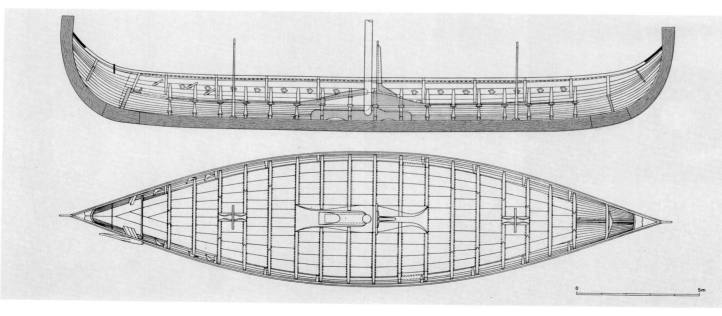

The Gokstad boat (Norway)

The burial boat of Gokstad (mid-9th century) was discovered near Oslo in 1880. Laid in a pit dug out of blue clay — a medium particularly favourable for the preservation of wood — this boat is one of several examples of the clinker-built vessel of the Viking period. The longitudinal section and the plan drawn at deck level emphasize the symmetrical shape of the hull, the lightness of the internal framework serving to reinforce the planking which forms the basic elements of the structure. Drawings after T. Sjövold.

Deutsches Schiffahrtsmuseum

Evolution of planking assembly in the Mediterranean

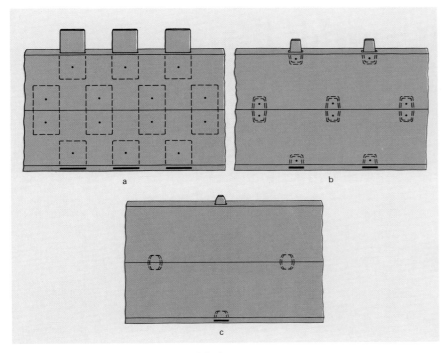

These three diagrams illustrate the evolution of the assembly of planking for ships in the Mediterranean tradition from antiquity to the Middle Ages. The assembly characteristic of antiquity (a) is marked by a very dense system of tenons inserted in mortises cut into the edge of the planking and blocked by pegs. The space between each point of assembly is rarely more than a few centimetres. This multiplicity of connections emphasizes the decisive role played by the planking. This role gradually became less important. Thus, on the 4th-century AD wreck at Yassi Ada in Turkey (b), the space between each point of assembly averages 7–9cm (3–4in) but may often be as much as 24cm (9in). On another Byzantine wreck of Yassi Ada dating from the 7th century (c), the space is often nearly 90cm (36in). In addition, the size of the tenons and the mortises was greatly reduced, and the pegs disappeared. This appreciable development in the method of assembly reveals a profound change in the system of construction by making the interior framework the dominant structural factor. Drawings after F. Van Doorninck.

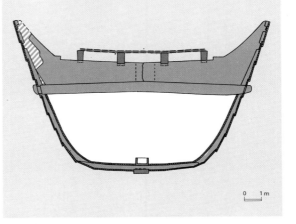

0   1m

The Bremen cog (1380)

The wreck of a cog, the preferred vessel of Hanseatic shipowners, was discovered in 1962 at Bremen, West Germany, in the waters of the Weser. The midships cross-section (left) emphasizes some characteristics of the structure of this type of vessel: flat bottom with freeboard strakes, clinker-built sides, beam with jutting tip, coaming forming a transverse bulkhead. Drawing after D. Ellermers. Deutsches Schiffahrtsmuseum, Bremen.

Vessel from Mataró, Spain (mid-15th century)

This wooden votive model was originally suspended from the vault of the church of Mataró near Barcelona. Now on show in the Maritime Museum of Rotterdam, it provides valuable information about medieval naval construction. The remarkably accurate execution of this model built on a real framework, shows us many technical details, such as the protective walls surrounding the freeboard planking, the extremities of the beam and the light clinker-built covering connecting the forecastle with the central part of the hull.

Maritiem Museum "Prins Hendrik"

Carrack

This late 15th-century German miniature shows a carrack getting under way. This type of ship, in the Mediterranean tradition, is deep-hulled and constructed with freeboard. The structures fore and aft are henceforth integrated with the hull. The increase in tonnage is shown by an increase in the rigging. Here the carrack has four masts: from forward to aft — foremast, mainmast, mizzen-mast and "countermizzen" — the last two being rigged with lateen sails. (*History of the Judaic Wars*, Ms 2538, fo. 109 Österreichische Nationalbibliothek, Vienna).

Österreichische Nationalbibliothek

The seal of Faversham, Kent

The Faversham seal shows a ship in the Scandinavian tradition (clinker-built symmetrical hull, with a lateral steering-oar aft to starboard) fitted out for war. For this purpose, superstructures were placed above the two ends of the hull to allow an overview of the enemy. This is also the purpose of the crow's-nest at the top of the mast, which carries a square sail. On the seal, the yard is hoisted to mid-mast and sailors are furling the sail. Note the modest boom and small inclined mast.

National Maritime Museum

The Byzantine world: the archaeological background

As in other fields of archaeology, the tendency of modern Byzantine research has been to examine not the famous sites but the small ones— rural settlements, small churches and villages. It is these places that are beginning to provide an answer to the important question: What happened to the Eastern Mediterranean and Anatolia after the fall of the Roman empire in the West?

Any description of the development of Byzantine archaeology presupposes a definition of the two words. The term "Byzantine" is apparently simple, but actually covers two worlds separated in time by the "dark centuries" of the Slav and Arab invasions. The term was originally applied to late antiquity in the Mediterranean, especially the eastern part, although it is often difficult and always unsatisfactory to separate a single world and a single culture into two parts. Later, the same term came to define the medieval Orthodox world as opposed to the West and Islam.

As for archaeology, this discipline has as many definitions as it has trends, few of which are straightforward and objective. Moreover, its nature, methods and function vary according to the periods or regions studied, so we should avoid narrow definitions. It is perhaps best described as the study of the development of a site or a region, using surviving structures and their related objects. It may also cover the investigation of a collection of related materials or objects in order to learn about the material culture of a civilization. The demarcation line is often difficult to draw, especially when interpreting data between archaeology and other fields, such as the history of art. It is also necessary to call on other disciplines, such as the study of ceramics, coins, inscriptions, and so on. In the dialogue between disciplines, archaeological research takes on life and form. In its early days Byzantine archaeology was not so much a question of excavation as of a particular method of investigating structures and objects.

In this area, the naturalist Pierre Gylles was an early commentator who anticipated the modern approach of "urban archaeology" through his concern at the daily destructions suffered by old Constantinople, his scientific precision when describing monumental remains, and his understanding of the nature of the urban site. A native of Albi, France, Gylles explored Constantinople from 1544 to 1547 and was responsible for the first publication on the *Topography of Constantinople*, a work which remained the basis for studies of this site for more than three centuries. Much important Turkish archive material remains unexamined in the West; the greatest Turkish topography of Constantinople, produced in the early 17th century, has not yet been translated into English.

Work in the 19th century

We have to wait until the middle or the second half of the 19th century to find anything more than the erudite or devout curiosity of travellers or pilgrims. Then Constantinople was studied by Salzenberg, George, van Millingen and Ebersolt, and Asia Minor by Texier, Strzygowski, Bell and Rott. In Syria, de Voguë attempted the first systematic exploration of the limestone massif in northern Syria and the Hawran. The drawings of the monuments are remarkably good, and the analysis is a serious attempt to identify an art of building native to the region. But the examples chosen seem more like an anthology than a systematic record of a living system. For the latter we must look to the works of H.C. Butler, who went on two long missions in the same regions. In Palestine, the numerous reports made by R.E. Brunnow and A.V. Domaszewski were partly concerned with very early or proto-Byzantine monuments. The profusion of holy places led other scholars to concentrate too exclusively on religious monuments. In Egypt, the collection of V. de Bock and Somers Clarke supplied abundant material, while the researches of J. Clédat at Baouit and Quibbell at Saqqâra concentrated on the painted and carved decoration of large monastic complexes.

The excavation of classical sites expanded at about this same period. In their feverish search for ancient buildings archaeologists neglected or destroyed Byzantine remains, without recording them, except to recover reused antique material such as inscriptions or statuary.

From World War I to the 1950s

The period between World War I and the 1950s was marked by increasing excavation and by a new interest in the material associated with the occupation levels of the buildings excavated. In Constantinople, publications such as that on the City Walls describe all the stages carefully, although no excavation was carried out, except at the Golden Gate. Other works placed more emphasis on excavations, both of monuments (St Sophia, St Euphemia) and sectors (approaches of the Manganes, Hippodrome, Grand Palace, Forum of Theodosius). Collections of ceramics from these areas were made and sometimes published.

In Asia Minor, intensive excavations at Ephesus resulted in the discovery and study of several Byzantine buildings, including the Cathedral of the Virgin, the Basilica of St John and the cemetery of the Seven Sleepers, from which came a large number of lamps. Ground surveys became more accurate. The region of Cilicia revealed a multitude of coastal sites, Meriamlik and Korykos being outstanding. In the adjoining region, the American excavations of Antioch, although they failed to uncover the town itself, revealed

Avec l'aimable autorisation de Harenberg Kommunikation

Tribunes of the church of St Sophia at Constantinople

This watercolour was painted by the Fossati brothers, Swiss architects commissioned by Sultan Abdul Mecid to restore the celebrated building (1847–49). In addition to its fine accuracy, the work undeniably reflects the taste for "Orientalism" prevailing at that time.

Imperial loggia of the palace of Bucoleon at Constantinople

This engraving from a hurried and outmoded sketch is the only record of the main balcony, overlooking the sea, of one of the imperial palaces of Constantinople, the Bucoleon. The engraving formed part of the collection made, c.1870–80, by C.G. Curtis, "curate of the English Commemorative Church", that was published under the title, *Remains of the Queen of Cities*. The development of the Orient Express rail line during the 1870s cut through the Bucoleon at the exact site of the loggia, which may well have dated to the first phase of the palace attributed to Theodosius II (408–50).

peristyle villas decorated with remarkable mosaic pavements in the residential quarter of Daphne. Thus they disclosed a type of urban dwelling very similar to that occupied by the wealthy classes all round the Mediterranean.

Mosaic work appeared to be one of the most widespread crafts, offering an almost new field of investigation between archaeology and the history of art. O. Waagé tackled the first classification of fine pottery from the 4th century to the 6th century. The excavation of Doura Europos on the Euphrates supplied the first information about the religious background of Christian communities before the Edict of Milan (AD313). While J. Lassus and H.C. Butler produced two syntheses on religious architecture in Syria, another specialist, A. Poidebard, used aerial photography to reconstruct the evolution of the Syrian *limes* (or fortified boundary) from Diocletian to Justinian. G. Tchalenko* proposed, without excavations, a genuinely archaeological study of the villages of the limestone massif. Starting from natural geological and geographical conditions, and architectural, epigraphical (inscriptional) and historical data, he explained the origin, functions and abandonment of these sites in masterly fashion. In Palestine, the excavation of Djerash illuminated, as at Ephesus, the transition from pagan city to Christian town.

In Greece and the Balkans a large number of proto-Byzantine basilicas were studied by G.A. Sotiriou, A.K. Orlandos and P. Lemerle, as well as urban sites such as Philippi, Thessalian Thebes and Stobi. Archaeology was thus restoring to history the regions left out by the surviving contemporary textual sources of the capital. At Athens and Corinth, American excavations, conducted with rigorous attention to stratigraphy*, identified homogeneous levels rich in ceramic material. At Corinth, it was possible to retrace the evolution of the Agora (civic centre) up to the Ottoman period. Craft activities such as glass-making were studied in detail, and C.K. Morgan's remarkable publication on medieval ceramics reinforced and complemented the scanty knowledge acquired by examining pieces in collections, or by the excavations of other sites, such as Istanbul.

Recent archaeological research

The progress made by archaeological research since the 1960s has considerably enriched our historical vision of the Byzantine empire. In the capital itself, this progress may have marked time to some extent. Nevertheless, detailed studies of the churches of St Irene and Myrelaion, and especially the excavations carried out at Kalenderhane Camii and St Polyeuctus, have advanced our knowledge of the religious architecture of the town and the changes made in urban space. The forthcoming publication of the last two sites (by C.L. Striker and D. Kuban, and by R.M. Harrison) should supply valuable information about the pottery as well as throwing new light on commercial activity in the capital of the empire. The remarkable topographical lexicon published in 1977 by W. Müller-Wiener shows the advance made in our knowledge of the site since the work of P. Gylles.

In Anatolia, the excavations of Ephesus, Sardis, Aphrodisias, Anamur and Pergamon, have increasingly concentrated on the dwellings, reflecting the prosperity and subsequent decline of the cities in the 7th century and the emergence of the medieval town. As for the countryside, the surveys made by R.M. Harrison in Lycia and G. Dagron and S. Eyice in Cilicia show glimpses of a prosperous agricultural life, even in the mountains, which backs up the conclusions drawn from the study of the villages of northern Syria.

In Syria, excavations of Apamea, Resafa and the *limes* of the Euphrates, and in Palestine those of Caesarea and some Negev towns, have revealed the richness of the eastern basin of the Mediterranean. An astonishing number of churches have been recorded by A. Ovadiah, much greater than that known to J.W. Crowfoot when he published *Early Churches of Palestine* in 1941. In Egypt, Abu Mena, the town created as a result of pilgrimages to St Menas, is gradually emerging from the sands, and the history of the central sanctuary is better known; and archaeology is also revealing the importance of monastic sites like the Kellia, where an exemplary account of the pottery has been published. In Libya, cities that were entirely rebuilt in the time of Justinian (527–565), such as Latrun, Qasr el Lebia and Barce, are being slowly rescued from oblivion.

In the Balkans, the archaeological study of the Danubian *limes* and the auxiliary fortresses, has helped archaeologists to understand the efforts made by Diocletian and Justinian to block invasion, as well as the stages of the *limes'* collapse. The urbanization of the Justinian period, which turned the village of Caričin Grad into an imperial residence, is also found in the cities of the Black Sea now being excavated (Tomis, Callatis). More generally, the urban sites in the course of excavation offer increasingly tangible proofs of the wealth of the Balkans before the Slav invasions. Traces of these invasions, which are discernible in the sudden cessation of monetary circulation at this time, can be read in the metallic and ceramic material yielded in abundance by Yugoslavian, Bulgarian and Romanian sites, and which excavations in Greece are beginning to uncover at Olympia, Demetrias and Argos. The medieval levels that appear from the end of the 9th century are becoming better known throughout this zone, even though there are still large gaps.

Underwater archaeology (the shipwrecked cargoes of Yassi Ada and Alonissos) also supplies a limited quantity of evidence which is very important to our understanding of commercial activity. But here the study of ceramics still provides archaeologists with the best understanding of its intensity throughout the Mediterranean.

The aims and methods of Byzantine archaeology have developed considerably in a few decades. As for the proto-Byzantine period, regional studies of religious buildings provide evidence not only of special rituals, but also of the development of towns and villages, as well as the rapid enrichment of the Church. Archaeologists are also beginning to learn about the material aspect of societies—habitations, craft products, trade—and, with the help of anthropology and the study of plants and animals, to understand their way of life. The obscurity which has long surrounded the abrupt end of proto-Byzantine prosperity is gradually clearing. We should also understand better the emergence of fortified towns in the 9th and 10th centuries, the urban renaissance of the 11th and 12th centuries, and the importance of monastic property ownership in the development of the land.

These preoccupations imply increased archaeological specialization in the techniques of excavation and surveys, and in the study of their results. Investigators themselves are finding it increasingly difficult to master, as in the past, rapidly developing subjects in the fields of architecture, sculpture and, even more, frescoes and manuscripts. They now face a kind of information explosion necessitating the collaboration of different specialists in the service of an enlarged historical vision.

Towns of the early Byzantine period

The latest discoveries concerning towns in the Byzantine world show that "Roman" societies in the Greek east still had wealth and dynamism well into the 6th century AD.

Until archaeological discoveries provided increasing confirmation to the contrary, the very survival beyond the 3rd century of many ancient towns was still questioned comparatively recently, despite the writings of Libanius on Antioch (particularly his *Antiochikos*), descriptions of Justinian's building programme by the historian Procopius, or even the imperial legislation dealing with cities. Moreover, an inscription of the Emperor Constantine (306–37) in the town of Orkistos in Phrygia, proclaims his "ardent desire to build new towns, refurbish the old and restore the dying".

Up to and including the reign of Heraclius (610–41), the urban sites discovered in most regions of the Byzantine empire were well maintained, suggesting a population that remained steady until the middle of the 6th century, and possibly declined after that because of invasions, plagues, and so on. There are even examples of destroyed or abandoned cities being spectacularly refounded, as at Olbia (present-day Qasr el Lebia) in Cyrenaica, which was rebuilt and renamed Theodorias in 539–40 by Justinian, according to an inscription on the mosaic in the church east of this site.

Unlike the Roman towns of the first centuries of the empire, the walled rampart became an essential feature of these Byzantine towns. Constantinople itself was provided with formidable earthworks and walls by Theodosius (408–50). Maintained, restored or completely rebuilt, ramparts can be seen at such places as Thessalonika or Caričin Grad in Yugoslavia, and at Sofia, or Hissar and Mesemvria in Bulgaria. Along the frontiers, particularly on the banks of the Danube and the Euphrates, the towns were established in a network of dense and well-maintained fortifications.

The street pattern was arranged on a grid, with the *decumanus maximus*, or main street, intersected by a transverse way, or *cardo maximus*, demarcating regular "islands" or blocks of buildings, as in the Hellenistic and Roman periods. The main streets were bordered with colonnades from an earlier period, but well maintained, as with the Arcadiane—leading from the theatre to the port of Ephesus—or new ones might be built, as at Jerusalem, Caesarea and Maritima in Palestine. A whole range of "prestige architecture" has been identified, establishing intersections and main squares, which included monumental arches, and tetrastyles—groups of four columns—as at Ephesus, and Ptolemais in Libya, and honorific columns and official statuary lining the colonnades, as at Ephesus and Aphrodisias in Turkey. Sidewalks, decorated with mosaic pavements, as at Ephesus and Apamea in Syria, were lined by booths and workshops where craftsmen and traders, organized in guilds, increasingly concentrated. At Sardis, careful excavation has revealed establishments of dyers, ironmongers and locksmiths, as well as taverns. Major changes have been observed in the function of main roads, as at Apamea, where the central section of the *cardo* was closed to wheeled vehicles and became a pedestrian zone. These large streets were also abundantly provided with fountains, as at Ephesus or, during the reconstructions carried out under Heraclius, at Gortyna in Crete.

Changes to existing public buildings

Public buildings continued to be maintained, apart from temples and places too closely associated with paganism. Thus at Ephesus the *bouleuterion* (the meeting place of the town council) remained in use, but a cross was carved above the eastern entrance, and the *prytaneum* (public hall) associated with it disappeared, as did the building where the sacred fire of Hestia Boulaea was kept. Business premises were also retained, as the previously mentioned development of booths along the main streets has shown. A town in the Negev contained a structure consisting of three rows of shops built along two narrow streets, and adjoining a major building used for cows or horses. The oldest khans or caravanserais—inns with courtyards providing accommodation for caravans—are found in the towns of Syria and Palestine, at Resafa, Kurnub and Nessana.

At Athens, the building of a vast gymnasium in the city centre (the Agora) took place shortly after 400, and was undoubtedly connected with the rapid development of the university of Athens until its closure by Justinian. Thermal baths were preserved, but often with the removal of the palaestra, or athletic training area—an indication of the new contempt for nudity. New baths too, were built by wealthy citizens, for example the baths of Scholastikia at Ephesus towards the end of the 4th century, or even by bishops, such as Plakkos at Jerash in Palestine, towards 454–55. Theatres and hippodromes were much frequented, as at Ptolemais, Aphrodisias, Alexandria or Tyre, and inscriptions on the terraces in some cases reflect the importance of the circus factions in city life.

The private domicile is better known, following excavations of sites at Athens, Argos, Stobi, Histria, Apamea, Apollonia, Cyrene and Ptolemais. Large houses have been found with courtyards surrounded by a peristyle (colonnade) onto which opened a number of rooms, including dining rooms (*triclinia*) with semicircular recesses. The presence of houses of several storeys is well documented, and has been verified in fieldwork carried out at Ephesus.

Churches and urban development

The appearance of churches considerably modified the overall aspect of the towns, as is clearly seen on the plan of Jerash. The bishop's residence was of substantial size, as at Jerash again, at Salone in Yugoslavia, and at Philippi in Greece, where imposing treasuries attest to the wealth of the Church. At Sidon in Asia Minor the episcopal complex encroaches on and breaks up one of the town's main axes, and at Apamea it covers two "island" blocks. Churches dedicated to martyred saints also acted as powerful forces of attraction, thus playing a large part in urban development, and sometimes even inspiring the construction of a whole city, as at Abu Mina, where the site of Egypt's patron saint drew crowds of pilgrims.

The finest example, however, is undoubtedly Jerusalem, where a transformation, begun under the reign of Constantine and continuing into that of Justinian, strikingly reveals the "sacred" urbanization which took complete possession of the former Roman colony of Aelia Capitolia. The close circles of the Imperial court in fact demanded new buildings: churches, hospices, pilgrims' lodging-houses.

Thus not only is archaeology gradually clarifying the typology of the different elements of the town, it is also illuminating the actual life of this urban fabric, the modifications its districts underwent and its relations with more remote areas.

Plan of Gerasa (Jerash) Jordan

A Hellenistic foundation, Gerasa developed in the 1st and 2nd centuries AD with *decumanus* (main street) and *cardo* (cross street) lined with porticoes, forum, temples of Zeus and Artemis, tetrastyles and triumphal arch. Under the Tetrarchy, it was given powerful fortifications. Many churches were fitted harmoniously into this framework until the Arab conquest in 635.

Residential quarter, Stobi, Yugoslavia

This aerial photograph gives an excellent idea of the layout of buildings in a 5th century city. Above the street can be seen, from left to right, a "civil basilica" (public building), a church erected above a synagogue (beyond the apse, baths), a dwelling with its apsidal triclinium, and finally the baths. J.R. Wiseman, Excavations of Stobi.

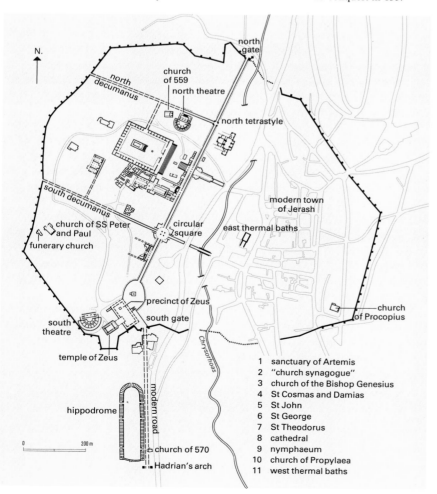

1 sanctuary of Artemis
2 "church synagogue"
3 church of the Bishop Genesius
4 St Cosmas and Damias
5 St John
6 St George
7 St Theodorus
8 cathedral
9 nymphaeum
10 church of Propylaea
11 west thermal baths

The peristyle of the "House with Consoles", Apamea, Syria

The whole house was organized around the peristyle (colonnade). The rooms opened on to it, including a very large reception hall (background), ornamented with a fountain in the centre and comprising an alcove separated by two columns, forerunner of the *diwan* of traditional Syrian houses. Belgian Centre for Archaeological Research, Apamea.

The Academy of Athens

This huge gymnasium was built *c*.400 in the antique Agora; it opens onto a court with four colonnades by way of a monumental porch, decorated with carved giants and tritons. Beyond, a vestibule and an incurved portico lead onto a second court lined with baths and various halls. The building was abandoned when Justinian closed the university of Athens in 529.

Dining-room with horseshoe-shaped bench, Argos, Greece

In this villa, the representation on the mosaic pavement of a semicircular table and the indication of the positioning of sections of the bench surrounding it has enabled archaeologists to make an accurate graphic reconstruction of the layout of the dining room. This semicircular arrangement, which became widespread in the Late Empire, entailed the development of reception halls with many apses. The mosaics displayed before the guests celebrated the pleasures of the table and the performers who enhanced them (here dancers evoked by the Maenads). After G. Akerstrom-Hougen.

Apartment in a prestigious building development, Ephesus, Turkey

The two levels of this dwelling are built round a peristyle. This has a central court with a basin, providing light and ventilation for a collection of rooms with mosaics on the floors and paintings on the walls. Plaster on the wall depicting the Nine Muses has been dated to *c*.400AD. After Strocka.

135

Rural life at the end of antiquity

Recent discoveries have discounted the idea that the end of antiquity was uniformly cataclysmic. Some districts in modern Turkey and Syria enjoyed their greatest prosperity in the 5th century AD.

Archaeological study of marks left by agriculture and digging has progressed considerably, both with the development of aerial photography and with various forms of ground surveying and analysis of organic remains. Nevertheless, in the territories of the Byzantine world, problems arise to prevent application of these proved and successful methods. However, plentiful remains of good quality survive in several regions, such as Lycia, Cilicia, the limestone rock formation of northwest Syria and the Hawran in southern Syria. From these, a picture of rural life in the Byzantine age at the end of antiquity emerges clearly.

Lycia and Cilicia

The abundantly wooded and sparsely populated mountains of Lycia still contain much evidence of rural life active in the Byzantine period: remains of terraces, and an inhabited area with agricultural installations. A few years ago in the valley of Alakilise, R.M. Harrison discovered a whole group of farmers' houses, both connected and detached, with a ground floor and one upper storey, each containing one or two rooms. Floors and roofs were of wood. The ground floor was used for storage or housing the cattle, while the upper storey, which had windows rounded at the edges, was reserved for human habitation. A cistern and a press completed the ensemble.

Lycian villages, with the exception of Arif, which may have been a city where the inhabitants of Arycanda could take refuge, were small, and contained one or two churches. Slightly apart were convents such as that at Karabel, which may perhaps be identified as the Convent of St Sion referred to in traditional sources. This is a remarkably well-built structure with drystone masonry, and contains some fine sculpture.

In the hinterland of the densely populated Cilician coast, a series of remarkably well-preserved villages (kômai) have been discovered. The living areas of these were not densely occupied, and tended to be connected by passages that can still be made out. The churches seem disproportionately large and numerous in relation to the sparse population. Tombs cluster on the outskirts of the villages and are often found with presses for olives or wine. The buildings were mostly on two levels, with arches supporting the wooden floors or structures both at ground and first floor levels. Some buildings opened on to a court, sometimes with a colonnade. The site of Karakabakli has the most complete houses, with one or two storeys, large double windows on the upper storey and sometimes balconies resting on consoles.

Syria: the limestone massif and the Hawran

In northern Syria about 700 villages have been preserved, often close to each other, on the hills of the limestone massif which extends to the east of Antakya (Antioch) for a length of 150km (93 miles) and a width of 40km (25 miles). The corporate areas of the villages can be defined with accuracy in some sectors, not only by a study of the geography, but also by the demarcation established in the records under the Tetrarchy of the Roman Empire. The groupings are of various sizes, ranging from Qirqbize which is one hectare (2.4 acres), to El Bara, which is more than 100 hectares (240 acres). The latter had an area larger than many cities.

These villages did not have proper roads, but lanes of varying width threading between the houses and expanding into irregular open stretches. The villages were not surrounded by town walls, but the houses on the outside often formed a kind of ring with only a few passages through. There were few public buildings, except for a handful of bathhouses spread throughout the area. Churches, on the other hand, were numerous. The public hostelries of Deir Sem'an are exceptional, being required by the large number of pilgrims who came to worship at the place where St Simeon Stylites lived on his column for 40 years. Around the village are presses, tombs and, at some distance, monasteries which may have lent economic importance to the area at the end of the 5th century.

The dwellings consisted of several structures arranged around a courtyard, possessing one or more rooms and an upper storey, and lined with porticoes on the sides. The simple, rectangular drystone masonry in the more sophisticated houses made possible cantilever structures such as balconies and suspended washhouses. A cistern stood in the courtyard, often at the foot of the staircase. The ground floor area was dark, often equipped with troughs, and was reserved for cattle and agricultural activities. On the upper storey lived the farmer and his family. The floor was supported by pillars or arches spanning the ground-floor rooms. The principal crops consisted of vines (essentially in the south), olives, cereals and vegetables. Bone analysis has shown that cows, goats, sheep and poultry were abundant.

The Hawran region of southern Syria contains plentiful remains of agricultural structures: corporate areas demarcated by boundaries dating to the Tetrarchy, and officially registered structures. As in northern Syria, large holdings play little part, the working of the land falling mostly on to the villagers. The villages look much the same as in northern Syria, apart from collective open-air reservoirs (birkeh) and fewer presses. The plan of the houses differs little, with several structures juxtaposed around a court of beaten earth, the ground floor often containing stables and the upper floor the family living room (triclinium).

Nevertheless, the almost total absence of wood and the exclusive use of basalt has given the buildings of Hawran a particular aspect. Arches were used on both upper and ground floors. Floors and roofs were made of carefully dressed basalt slabs resting on these arches. Local traditions also caused their differences. Thus on both upper and ground floors, the large arched room led on to smaller and lower rooms, which doubled the levels in relation to the large rooms and made movement inside much more complicated. Moreover, in some cases, the large arched room was not assigned to agricultural activities, but used as a reception room for guests. Finally, porticoes were much rarer than in northern Syria. It is curious that, although the region was prosperous, the architectural decor that was so striking until the 3rd century declined in the Byzantine period, whereas it was in full flower in northern Syria.

Of the other regions that have been studied, groupings in the Negev such as Nessana, Oboda, Mampsis, Elusa or Sobata were mostly cities, but lacked a grid network of streets and clearly reflected agricultural usage. The houses had a different plan, consisting of a central courtyard with rooms all round, and a different elevation, in spite of the use of slabs much more numerous than were evident in the Hawran for floors, roofs and arches.

Cyrenaica has also yielded villages and large isolated farms, and in Egypt sites of rural houses of mud brick have been found consisting of one or two adjoining rooms. In spite of certain gaps, such as Greece and the Balkans, archaeologists can now reach certain conclusions. Apart from regional peculiarities, these findings indicate the importance of agricultural production in the Byzantine period: the Hawran experienced no decline between the Roman period and the 7th century, while northern Syria, Cilicia and the Negev, according to the evidence, were never so prosperous as they had been between the 4th and 5th centuries.

Village house in Lycia

The village of Alakilise consists of a few dozen houses clinging to the wooded slopes of the massif of Alaca Dǎg. This house comprises two ground-floor rooms partially hollowed out of the rock and various annexes: above, a dwelling level and behind, a court with a cistern and wine press. Wine seems to have been an important product in the region.

House of wealthy farmer in Cilicia

This large house in the village of Karakabakli attests to the wealth of farmers in the region. It is spacious and the upper storey with its balcony and many windows has a sort of monumentality. An impressive gate at the entrance to the village further reinforces this deliberately quasi-urban appearance. Two large basilicas have also been identified in this village.

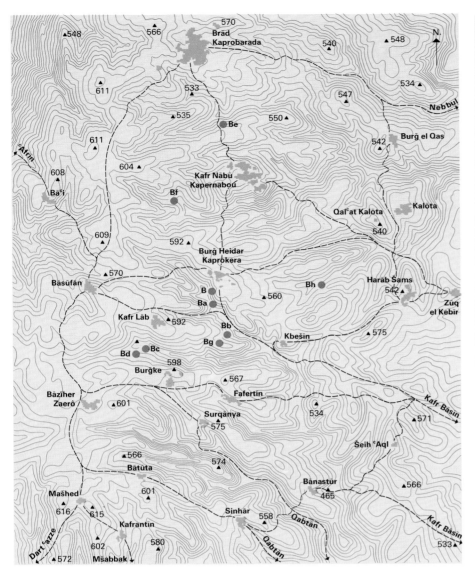

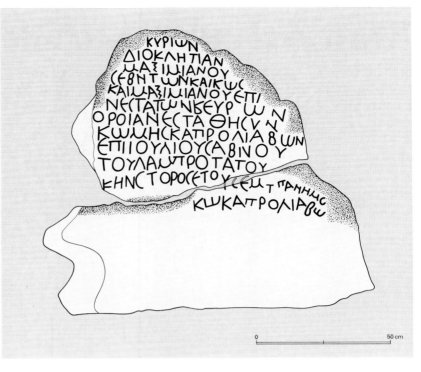

villages
altitudes
tracks and paths
official boundaries

An example of the official boundaries in the Ğebel Sem'an (limestone massif)

The localization of nine boundary limits on the map gives a clear idea of the respective territories of the villages of Brád, Kafr Nábú, Burğ Heidar, Kafr Láb, Kběsín, Fafertin, Burğke and Báziher. Above right the text of one of the inscriptions: "[For the preservation and the victory of our] lords Diocleti[an and] Maximianus Augustus and Const[ans] and Maximianus very brilliant Caesars the boundary limits of the village of Kaprioliaba were erected under Julius Sabinus, the famous surveyor, in the year 345 (AD297), month of Panemos. Village of Kapriolaba."

House of Il Hayâte (578, Hawran)

This house, built by Flavios Seos, is arranged on two levels (sheds, stable and troughs on the ground floor; living quarters in the upper storey) around a small courtyard. It was more compact and more enclosed than previous houses and resembled the fortified farms of Cyrenaica and Byzacene.

Isometric drawing of a hamlet of Dehes (4th–6th century)

This regrouping of three houses is very characteristic of the development of this village which seems mainly to have grown from the 4th century onwards, although a habitat was in existence from the Hellenistic period (ceramics). Each plot was in time completely built over. After J.-L- Biscop.

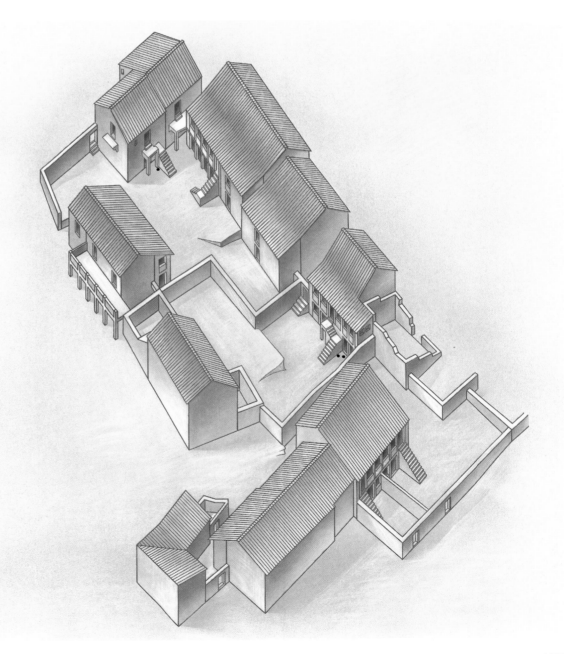

137

Material culture, trade and exchange

At the time of the Arab invasion in the 7th century, the Byzantine commercial network extended as far as northwest Britain and included a vast range of sophisticated products; underwater archaeologists have even found an entire church, lost in process of shipment.

The great upsurge in building activities described in the previous pages led to intensive exploitation of limestone and marble quarries. Coloured breccia and white marbles, which were highly prized, as the lines written by Paul the Silent about Santa Sophia indicate, were exported throughout the eastern part of the Mediterranean basin, as they had been under the Roman empire. Breccia from Thessaly can be found in Syria (Apamea, Resafa), Italy and in Gaul (the thermal baths at Arles); cipolin, a white and green-streaked marble, from Carystos in the Lebanon (Tyre), Libya, and Italy, and marble from Iasos (Caria) at Ravenna.

White marble was mainly exported from quarries near the sea, like Thasos and especially Proconnesus. It was sometimes dispatched in rough blocks as extracted from the quarry for use as slabs to make paving stones and wall facings, building elements (capitals of the basilica of Lechaeon), sarcophagi and foundation stones. But half-finished pieces were also dispatched, with incised decoration not cut completely out of the background; examples include some capitals in Cyrenaica, sarcophagi in Ravenna, and chancel plaques which were subsequently made into openwork as at Ravenna or Thebes in Thessaly; or they were sometimes left more or less as they were, with the decoration cut in high or low relief as at Sicyon, or in southern Italy. Lastly, completed sculptures were also transported (chancel plaques, capitals, columns, ambos (pulpits), or sarcophagi as at Doclea in Yugoslavia). During the 6th century, the number of goods exported in a finished state grew. They were mainly intended for churchbuilding, and to a lesser extent, for embellishing the great city streets. The workmen's marks found in Italy (Ravenna), Yugoslavia (Poreč) and Turkey (Ephesus) can also be found on the masonry blocks of Istanbul. The cargo that was shipwrecked near Marzamemi (Sicily) consisted of a complete church all in pieces which had been loaded at Constantinople. Everything was there, from load-bearing to liturgical elements (bases, columns, capitals), chancel pillars and plaques, the altar, and an ambo made of breccia from Thessaly. A plate in Phocaean ware enables us to date this shipment to the first quarter of the 6th century.

As a result of research carried out on the ceramics of the Early Christian period, archaeologists have been able over the past 10 years to establish a reliable typology for amphorae, and certain key sites have been established for their study, such as Ostia, Carthage, Berenice (Sidi Khrebish), Istanbul (Saint Polyeuctos), and coastal sites in Rumania. We are still not certain about where most of the types found at these sites were manufactured and the nature of the goods transported in them: for the amphora is the only ceramic product to have been exported not in its own right, but for its contents. Of the 14 types catalogued by J.A. Riley, covering virtually all Mediterranean amphorae between the 4th and 7th century, the five most widely diffused come from the eastern basin or the Black Sea, except perhaps for type 8, called *spatheion* (slim-bellied, with a long, tapering foot, a short neck which is distinct from the bulge, ending in a thick, overhanging rim) which may come from North Africa. Type 3, also quite slim, but with a dumpy foot and no neck, short rounded handles and a very irregular surface, was produced in Gaza. It can be found in Spain (Ampurias), Great Britain (Wroxeter and London), France (Tours and Grand Ribaud island), Italy (Ravenna), Greece (Athens, Corinth, Argos, Thasos), Turkey (Bodrum, Tarsus), Palestine (Caesarea, Ashdod), Egypt (Alexandria, Abu Mena, Kellia), Cyrenaica and North Africa (Carthage). Types 1 and 2 may originate from Antioch and the Aegean basin respectively, and the fact that they reached England, Gaul, Italy and North Africa as well as being plentiful throughout the Mediterranean indicates the increasing volume of exports from the East to the West, including England, between the 5th and 7th century. Indeed, the historian P.-A. Février wondered, only partly in jest, whether the military reconquest of North Africa, Spain and Italy undertaken by Justinian had not been preceded by an economic reconquest. This extremely thriving trade seems to have been suddenly broken off at the time of the Arab conquest (c.638). One of the latest known Byzantine shipwrecks relating to this period is that of Yassi Ada I (Turkey, near Bodrum); the date of this is based on 70 coins of Heraclius, the most recent of which, struck in 625/626, must give the date of the shipwreck to within a few years. The cargo included 103 amphorae of Riley's type 1, and 719 of type 2 which must have contained wine. Underwater archaeology provides no further trace of trading in the Aegean area until the 11th century.

The trading of fine ceramics

Fine ceramic tableware, with a slip that was often thick and orange-red in colour, also formed part of this trans-Mediterranean trading. From the 2nd century most of this was stamped (sigillated) North African pottery with a clear glaze which held the whole of the Mediterranean market up until the 7th century, with perhaps a slight decline—though this has still to be verified—in its eastward diffusion during the 5th century at the time of the Vandal occupation of Africa. There is a variety of shapes, imitating not only Italian forms (at the beginning) but also the shapes of metal vessels. The impressed decorations vary greatly, ranging from geometric or floral motifs to representations of animals or human beings (soldiers, emperors, deities, busts) including a great many crosses. Some relatively early (4th century) series have modelled applied slips which are reminiscent of the repoussé techniques used in silversmithing: the motifs may be quite simple and unconnected, they may illustrate a mythological cycle (the life of Achilles), or they may treat subjects from the Old and New Testaments (Jonas, the Sacrifice of Abraham, the Good Shepherd). To the east, a production of comparable scope became established from the second half of the 3rd century, drawing on the traditions of Sinjerli pottery (in the Pergamum district in Turkey). Its workshops and kilns are located, entirely or in part, at Phocaea. The clay is darker and the slip less shiny and often quite thin. There is less variety of shape, and some forms are copies of the North African ones. Certainly the technique of embossing motifs, which was used as well as rollers, seems to have been borrowed from the African ware. This pottery was fairly widely diffused in the east, rivalling African ware. It was also exported to the west, to Italy (southern Italy, Latium, Rome and Ravenna), Provence and Languedoc, Portugal and even as far away as England. Cypriot ceramics, with their characteristic zig-zag edges and roller-applied decoration on the sides, were of more limited quantity, but they too reached the west. Apart from other types of ceramic ware, which were often copies (in Tripolitania, Egypt, and Asia Minor itself), we also find different types of manufacture altogether (plates made of grey paste from Macedonia), some of them quite original (painted ware from Egypt, Athens and Gerasa [Jordan]).

A study of the diffusion of lamps also reveals the superiority in this field of North Africa, as well as the size of the output in Asia Minor and the vigour of some local industries (Antioch area, the Balkans, but above all Palestine and Egypt).

In the field of glassware the east was predominant, but silver was well represented from both west and east, in the form of luxury ware, as items of political propaganda (*Missorium*, Theodosius' silver platter), or of course for liturgical vessels. Though it was often for more aristocratic use and therefore not traded in such quantities as goods in everyday use, silverware is interesting to study in so far as it seems to show a predominance of goods from the end of the 5th century made in the eastern workshops, and consequently the greater wealth of the eastern part of the Mediterranean. The manufacture of Constantinople can be followed most closely because of the stamps with dates, which were impressed on the obverse side of items manufactured between the end of the 5th century and the 7th century. Archaeology can give only a very partial picture of trade relating to goods which do not keep well such as textiles; for these, and even for articles found in good condition, information from written sources continues to be indispensable.

Capitals found in the basilica of Lechaion (port of Corinth)

A rough-hewn block (left) found at the site shows that blocks of (Proconnesian) marble were exported in crudely dressed form and finished on the work site (right) by mixed teams of sculptors from the capital and others recruited on the spot using a local decorative repertory.

J.-P. Sodini

138

African stamped (sigillated ware) dish (form Hayes 53A)

On the inside of this dish are four stamped motifs. The first shows Abraham preparing to sacrifice his son Isaac. It consists of two elements, the second of which, Isaac, is repeated on the right. The third juxtaposes two others, a ram and a tree, recalling the biblical "ram caught in a thicket by his horns". The last, a good shepherd, has no direct connection with the others (second half of the 4th century). Private collection.

Amphora, Thasos, Greece

At the top of the handles is an incised inscription *Valeriou Poritou*. The amphora belongs to Riley's type 2, which appeared during the 5th century and spread widely towards the end of the 6th century. It was probably produced somewhere in the north of the Aegean basin.

Section of the poop of an 8th century ship discovered at Yassi Ada, Turkey

This cross-section shows the main fittings of the ship's galley (notably the stove) and the tiled pitched roof which covered it. 70 coins of Heraclius (the most recent from 526/527), 103 amphorae of Riley's type 1 and 719 amphorae of Riley's type 2 were found on board.

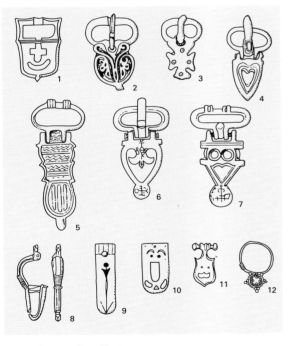

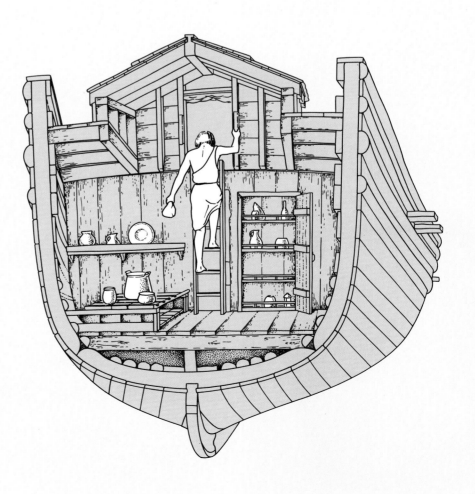

Byzantine metal artifacts

1 to 7, various plaque-buckles: 1. "Sucidava" type; 2. "Syracuse" type; 3. Cruciform plaque-buckles; 4. "Bologna" type; 5. "Trebizond" type; 6. "Bal-gota" type; 7. "Corinth" type. 8. Fibula; 9, 10, 11. Belt accessory plaques; 12. Earring with studded pendant.
Provenance 1. Sucidava (Rumania); 2, 3, 6, 7. Suuk-Su (Crimea); 4. Kertch (Crimea); 5. Igar (Hungary); 8. Goleman-ovo Kale (Bulgaria); 9, 11, 12. Sadovec (Bulgaria); 10. Piatra Precătei (Rumania).
Dating 1, 8, 9, 11, 12: second half of 6th century. 2, 3, 6, 7: 7th–9th century. 4: second half of 7th century–8th century. 5: end of 7th century and beginning of 8th century. 10: probably 7th century.

Invasions and collapse: the dark centuries

After Justinian's brief period of glory, the provinces of the Byzantine empire were inundated by newcomers who forever changed its racial character: Arabs in Africa and the Near East, Slavs in the Balkans. There are still Slav speaking villages within 25 miles of Athens.

The Byzantine empire as Justinian (r.527–65) had precariously reconstituted it, was to collapse before the thrust of assailants from the north (Slavs from the late 6th and early 7th centuries) and south (Arabs from 634). But internal reasons such as an ill-received tax policy and religious dissension also played a part. Nor did the reconquered western provinces (Italy, Africa) recognize the Greek-speaking Byzantine invaders as the liberators of their ancestral lands.

Slavic inroads into the territory of the empire are attested from 527. In the 6th century the Slavs forced the Danubian *limes* (boundary of the empire) on several occasions, using two main routes, by the lower Danube into Thrace and by the central Danube into Illyricum. Two tribal unions took part in these invasions, the Antae, whose territory in the 6th century was situated in the Ukrainian forest steppe, and the Sklavenes, who were located to the north of the Danube and around the Carpathians. In about 560 the Sklavenes were subjugated by the Avars, who settled in the Danubian basin and together with them attacked the Byzantine empire. The Antae allied themselves with Byzantium and fought against the Avars. At the beginning of the 7th century the Danubian *limes* disappeared altogether under the blows of Slavs and Avars. Between 623 and 631 the Slavs freed themselves from the Avar yoke and became masters of the Balkans during the 7th century. At the end of the 8th and beginning of the 9th century the empire gradually recaptured possession of Greece, where elements of Slavic peoples remained until the 15th century and even later.

The traces of destruction and fire in Byzantine towns, as well as the many deposits of 6th and 7th century coinage, signpost the passage of the Avar and Slav invaders during the 6th–7th centuries or at least attest to the panic they provoked. But the discovery of Slavic-type material furnished indubitable proof. Among this material, the 7th century digitated (spread-hand) fibulae of the "Danubian" or "Mazuro-German" type, and the "Ante" or "Dnieper" type, as well as some handmade pottery, are the only real bearers of ethnic significance.

The Slav presence in Byzantine fortresses along the Danubian *limes* is attested from the 7th century and marked by the presence of several cultures. Thus in northern Serbia (Veliki-Gradac, Kladovo) ovoid pots without decoration come from the Slavo-Roman culture of Ipotesti-Cîndesti originally from Wallachia. The culture of Pen'kovka, which covered the zone of the Ukrainian steppe forest and Moldavia, and can be identified by its handmade ovoid and biconical pots (no doubt Ante) was established on the lower Danube (Dinogetia, Piatra Frečatei). Near the mouth of the Danube at Istria 7th century levels have yielded buildings excavated in the ground and pottery of the Prague-Korčak type, ovoid pots with their upper part enlarged. This culture, attributed to the Sklavenes, extended from the 5th to the 7th century over the territory of the western Ukraine, Czechoslovakia, Poland and eastern Germany.

In Thrace the oldest Slav sites are akin to those of the Hlincea I culture (second half of the 8th century to the 9th century), in the territory of present-day Rumania, and probably coinciding with the birth of the first Bulgarian state in the second half of the 7th century.

In the north of Illyricum dug-out Slav habitats of the 6th and 7th centuries have been found, with pottery of the Prague-Korčak type (at Mušići), as well as cremations in urns also of the Prague-Korčak type (at Bakar). At Caričin Grad, a small fibula of the Danubian type and another of "Ante" type, found in levels corresponding to the destruction of the town by the Slavs in 613–14, indicate, according to V. Popovič, the existence of Slav elements in the town. Some Slav sites in Illyricum have furnished turned handmade pottery with an incised decor of horizontal, rectilinear or wavy lines which confirms the massive settlement of Slavs in this region towards the mid-7th century.

In Greece, several small 7th century Danubian fibulae have been uncovered, in particular at Demetrias, Nea Anchialos and Sparta. In the Peloponnese where the Slavs settled after 578, the necropolis of Olympia, the only site irrefutably dated to the 7th century, has yielded cremations with vessels of the late Prague-Korčak type. The Slav occupation at Argos and Demetrias, where excavation has revealed turned handmade pottery decorated with rectilinear and wavy lines, seems to be more recent (650–800). According to M.W. Weithman, Slavs and Greeks lived alongside each other at this date. Recent finds of Byzantine ornaments, dating at the earliest to the second half of the 7th century, and laid in the tombs of a funerary church at Tigani seem to confirm this hypothesis.

So the decline of urban sites throughout the Balkans is obvious, except in Thessalonika. Though little studied, this decline does not seem to be compensated for by the creation of other habitats, for example Karyoupolis in the Peloponnese. Dated inscriptions are rare (some graffiti in the Parthenon from the late 7th to the early 8th century) and there are few monumental remains. Everywhere we find a reduction in the money supply – which does not necessarily imply a return to a natural economy – and a shortage of pottery, little known and scarce, in short a sort of archaeological vacuum.

Invasions of urban sites

In Asia Minor the combined evidence of treasures, isolated finds of bronze coins (*folles** and fractions) and archaeological remains (traces of destruction or abandonment) reveal the impact of Persian and Arab invasions on an essentially urban civilization. On the majority of sites, monetary circulation stopped c.614–16 (Persian attack) and resumed under Constantine II (641–68), often associated with fortification or defence works and the presence of garrisons.

The occupation of urban sites contracted markedly at the beginning of the 7th century (Sardis, Ephesus); fortresses were installed in theatres (Miletus, Xanthos), in temples (at Didyma, which became the *kastro* of Hieron) and on citadels (Priene, Ankara). Perhaps the underground towns of Kaymakli and Derinkuvu in Cappadocia were dug out at this time. In the islands close to Asia Minor (Samos), the large number of coins from the reign of Constantine II is probably linked with the influx of populations that came there seeking refuge. As in the Balkans, archaeological objects, such as coins or pottery, are rare.

Further south, the Arab invaders made a definitive

conquest of Syria and Egypt after the battle of Yarmuk (636). Nevertheless we do not observe a complete break in site occupation. Admittedly, buildings are fewer, in spite of work begun on imposing palaces and mosques, and even churches (at Quweismeh, Jordan, in 717). Pottery and coinage illustrate this continuity perfectly, at least until the 800s (Apamea). Doubtless the transfer of the capital of the caliphate from Damascus to Baghdad brought about the decline then observed in Syria. In North Africa, Byzantine treasures buried during the Arab raid of 647–48 demonstrate the panic of the population. The taking of Carthage in 698 put a final end to the Byzantine occupation.

Nevertheless in the Aegean regions, the only ones to remain under definitive Byzantine control, a crisis began to loom towards the end of the 8th and in the 9th century. As regards Greece, an inscription at Siphnos dated to 787, frescoes of the "iconoclastic" period at Naxos, and monetary circulation which resumed from the beginning of that century at Corinth, suggest the economic and cultural renewal of the region. Dated buildings reappeared in Greece around the 870s (St John Mangoutis at Athens, 871; St Gregory of Thebes, 871–72; church of Skiprou, 873–74). But it was not until the 10th century that signs of liberation were generalized throughout the empire. The fundamental reforms of the iconoclastic emperors reorganizing the army and the administration then bore their fruits, while the military victories of their successors, from Romanus I Lecapanus (920–44) to John Tzimisces (969–76), loosened Islam's grip on the Mediterranean.

Slav pot from Demetrias

Turned ovoid pot with decoration of incised wavy lines. This type of vessel is found in all the Slav cultures from the second half of the 7th to the 9th century.

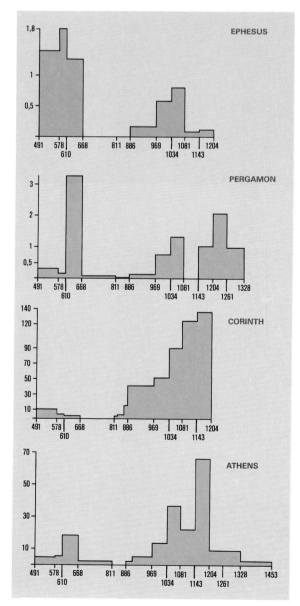

Monetary circulation according to isolated finds of coins (mainly bronze) on the sites of Athens, Corinth, Ephesus and Pergamon

The graphs show the number of coins per year according to the period under consideration. The figures, which vary depending on the importance of the sites and the finds, should be considered in the context of their relative development. The graphs shown for Corinth and Ephesus end in 1204, but circulation did not stop at that date. At Ephesus, the noticeable decline from the 12th century was due to the sanding up of the port and the transfer of activities to another site.

7th century Slav fibulae

These fibulae are characteristic of Slav female costume. The fibulae of the "Dnieper" type (left) are found throughout the territory of the Pen'kovka (Ante) culture, and the small fibulae of the "Danubian" type are mainly found in the region of the Prague-Korčak (Sklavene) culture.

The treasure of Rugga

Discovered during the excavations of Rugga (east of El Djem, Tunisia) in 1972, this treasure of 268 *solidi*, a mixture of pieces from Constantinople and Carthage, was buried in 647 at the time of the first Arab attack in Byzacene. National Institute of Archaeology and Art, Tunis.

Byzantine *solidi* and arab-byzantine half-dinar

After the fall of Carthage in AD698 the Arab victors struck gold coins (dinars and half-dinars) used first in Africa and then in Spain. These coins were based on the Byzantine *solidus* but with the Christian element removed, the cross being replaced by a spear. The inscription, in roman characters, was a condensed form of an exhortation from the Koran: *obverse*, IN Nomine DomiNIs misERICORDIS; *reverse*, NIsi Non EST DeuS NISI SOLVS (In the name of Allah the merciful; there is no god but He). The *solidus*: American Numismatic Society, New York. The half-dinar: Bibliothèque nationale, Paris.

Slav house dug out of the ground (reconstruction)

This type of house is found in different Slav cultures from the 5th to the 10th century. The houses were heated by stoves made of stones or clay. After P.A. Rappoport, *Drevnerusskoe žilišče* (The Houses of Ancient Russia), Leningrad, 1975, pp. 157, 158, fig. 58.

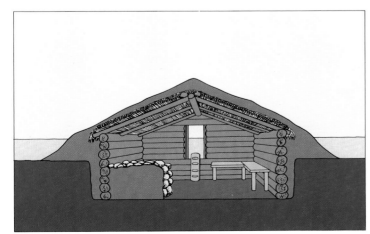

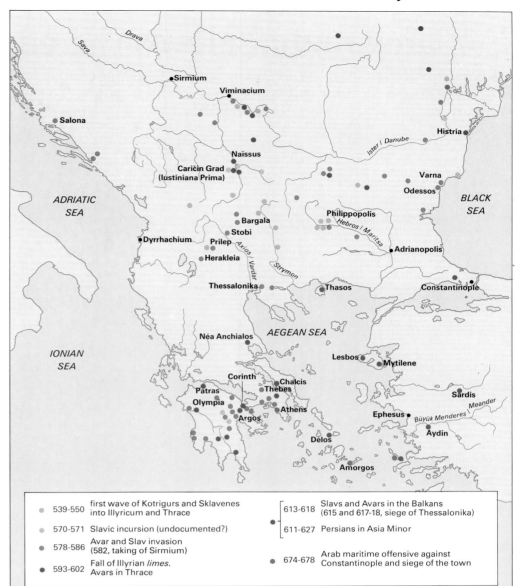

539-550	first wave of Kotrigurs and Sklavenes into Illyricum and Thrace
570-571	Slavic incursion (undocumented?)
578-586	Avar and Slav invasion (582, taking of Sirmium)
593-602	Fall of Illyrian *limes*. Avars in Thrace
613-618	Slavs and Avars in the Balkans (615 and 617-18, siege of Thessalonika)
611-627	Persians in Asia Minor
674-678	Arab maritime offensive against Constantinople and siege of the town

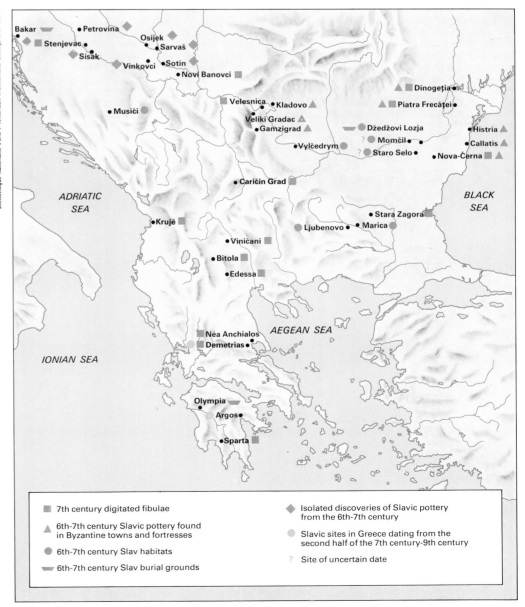

■ 7th century digitated fibulae

▲ 6th-7th century Slavic pottery found in Byzantine towns and fortresses

● 6th-7th century Slav habitats

▬ 6th-7th century Slav burial grounds

◆ Isolated discoveries of Slavic pottery from the 6th-7th century

● Slavic sites in Greece dating from the second half of the 7th century-9th century

? Site of uncertain date

Expansion and crisis: the end of Byzantium

The period from the 9th to the 10th centuries, the Age of Constantine Porphyrogenitus, was the last heyday of the Byzantine state, politically and economically, and it also saw an extraordinary flowering of scholarship and study of ancient texts. From then onwards, the last "Romans" were grimly waiting for the "barbarians".

From the 10th to the mid-14th century, the Byzantine empire underwent a demographic and economic expansion marked by the multiplication of villages and land clearance, and the development of towns. After 1347, an outbreak of the plague put an end to a period of growth that was starting to slow down in the early 14th century. Thus when the Ottoman conquest came it took place in a sombre climate.

Signs of revival appeared in the second half of the 9th century with the reconquest of provinces long occupied by the Arabs, and the establishment of fortifications, both towns and castles, in Asia Minor and Italy. These successes were confirmed in the 10th century, and the long war against the Bulgars was finally won at the beginning of the 11th century. The 10th century and the first half of the 11th century, which correspond to the reign of the Macedonian dynasty, were a period of military power and administrative efficiency. The subsequent changes made in the running of the state tended towards decentralization. In particular, they consisted in subcontracting services of the treasury and the army previously directly administered by the state. These events undoubtedly weakened the central power and hastened the dismemberment of the empire in 1204, with the capture of Constantinople by the Crusaders. But it recovered, albeit with a reduced territorial base, and there is nothing to suggest a decline of civilian society before the middle of the 14th century. At that date the state gave up striking gold coinage, the devaluation of which had revealed the progressive impoverishment of the treasury. Byzantine coins were gradually driven out by western pieces, and the levels of exchange fell below that of the 10th century.

The rebirth of towns

The period of expansion seems to have been indicated first by the reconstruction of the urban network. This could consist either of the restoration of antique cities in decline, the walls of which were rebuilt, or of the establishment of new foundations, in which case the city wall was usually of modest dimensions. Inside the wall there was nearly always a citadel. These towns, which varied widely in importance, had in common the fact of being fortified (which distinguished them from the villages) and the security provided by the presence of a garrison. They were situated at intervals of a day's journey along the major roads, and thus facilitated communications throughout the empire. In addition to traders, artisans and labourers, a bishop was also usually in residence there; there was always a numerous clergy, notables with country estates and, in the largest, officials concerned with revenue and legal affairs.

The town represented a protected area behind its walls, but the dead were not excluded from it, as can be seen at Corinth, Thessalonika or Constantinople. Not many public buildings have been identified, partly because few existed, churches generally taking their place. At Corinth, archaeologists may have identified, by its closeness to a prison indicated by graffiti, the 10th century governor's house. Some baths have been identified in Thessalonika and Lacedemonia. The frequent disappearance of grid-plan street systems resulted in residential quarters being laid out in an anarchic fashion. At Corinth, houses of the 11th and 12th centuries, discovered in the old agora (market), had a series of chambers and storerooms of different shapes and sizes, grouped around courts with wells and ovens. The same was true of Athens, in sites discovered at the Kerameikos, the agora and the precinct of Olympian Zeus. At the same period, Chalkis (Euboea), Thebes, and Argos had similar houses with an interior court and sometimes an external loggia. The Byzantine quarter of Pergamum, built in the 12th century, differs little from the sites previously mentioned. Everywhere the houses were built on an irregular plan, mostly poorly constructed of wood and mud rather than stone and brick, with plain planks acting as internal partitions, as indicated by an unpublished document from the monastery of Iviron (Mount Athos) dated 1104. Often arranged around a courtyard, the house usually consisted of two storeys: on the ground floor storage rooms with many jars embedded in the floor (called *pitharia* in the literary sources); on the first floor, the living room (*triklinos*). The residences of emperors or important dignitaries, such as the palace of Tekfour Saray at Constantinople, or the palace and residences at Mistra, offered a quite different degree of comfort, but they were of course exceptional.

The coins found on the sites, often in their thousands, reflect the contrasting fate of Byzantine towns. But a general pattern emerges, transcending regional or local differences: a progressive recovery is indicated from the end of the 9th century, with prosperity well established in the 11th century, a period in which the use of coinage also extends to the country and sites further away from the sea. Urban crafts industries suggest a revival of activity in the towns: at Corinth, for instance, the workshops of glassblowers and potters have been discovered. The clergy and the leisured classes acquired large quantities of metal objects, precious or otherwise, and archaeologists have recovered evidence to equal that of texts of inventories, *typika* or monastery rules: they include reliquaries, chandeliers, lamps, crosses, and coverings for icons and liturgical books, not forgetting doors covered in bronze, of which a certain number, made in Constantinople by craftsmen sometimes from Syria, were exported to Italy by an Amalfi family. In the case of other products, such as textiles or objects in wood, archaeological evidence is secondary to that of the literary sources.

Many monasteries were situated in the towns. The rural monasteries remained in close contact with the town, which supplied them with overseers and *higoumenoi* (responsible for the convents). Relations between Constantinople, Thessalonika, and the monasteries of Athos are well known, as are those of the monastery of St Luke in Phocis with the Theban aristocracy. The monasteries were practically like small towns behind their walls with numerous cells and often a hospice or an infirmary. The architecture of their churches reflects that of urban churches, even when they were sited in remote places. At St Luke, neither the plans of the church of the Holy Virgin (late 10th century?) and the *Katholikon* (early 11th century), nor the decor of marble sculptures and mosaics, are easily understood unless there was an intervention from Constantinople. This also appears to be the case at Iviron and Vatopedi on Mt Athos (end of 10th century) and Nea Moni at Chios (mid-11th century).

The role of the monasteries

Monasteries fulfilled a charitable function, especially in towns, and some of them contained a scriptorium, but it is their economic role which deserves emphasis. On the one hand, to found a monastery of which their descendants would be the *higoumenoi* seemed to a wealthy laity the surest way of perpetuating their memory and guaranteeing a fortune. On the other hand, the importance of donations and privileges conferred on monasteries by the emperors, sometimes counterbalanced by confiscations, shows that there was close collaboration between the fiscal department and the monasteries, the aim of which was to manage the exploitation of the country from which came the products of the soil and also their taxes.

As regards the Byzantine countryside, the diversity of local conditions and the still incomplete development of archaeological investigations invite caution. The village was usually an unfortified location comprising a few dozen families, but could include as many as 100 or 200 families. The houses, which have been little studied were surrounded by gardens and orchards. Hardly anything remains of these villages apart from heaps of pottery fragments and, possibly, the ground plans of the central parts of some modern villages such as Rodibolos at the foot of Pangaeus. A rudimentary enclosure hidden in the hills, or a neighbouring tower, frequently still standing, served as a refuge in case of raids. Beyond the garden area the village territory included areas of specialist activity. There exist many traces of the organization of space by Byzantine peasant farmers and large landowners: hedges, often grown rising from stone embankments, denote a later land clearance (13th–14th century) of the least advantageous sectors; canals, specially built or hollowed out of the rock diverted streams (sometimes for several kilometres) to drive mills and irrigate land; fortified farms where the manager of a large estate lived. Finally, the deforestation that is now evident in many places is believed to have dated from the end of this long period of expansion in a number of cases.

Achyraous, north tower

A fortress built by John Comnenus (1118–43) in Mysia (Turkey) on a promontory dominating the valley of the Macestos river which flows north–south from the Propontis in Ionia. It has five towers with a handsome decoration of ashlar work surrounded by bricks.

Kastellion Libyzasda, Greece

A wall composed of rubble and mortar closed off the peninsula. It was apparently built by the monastery of Iviron before 1104, providing a refuge for the village of the same name (today Olympiada in eastern Chalcidice).

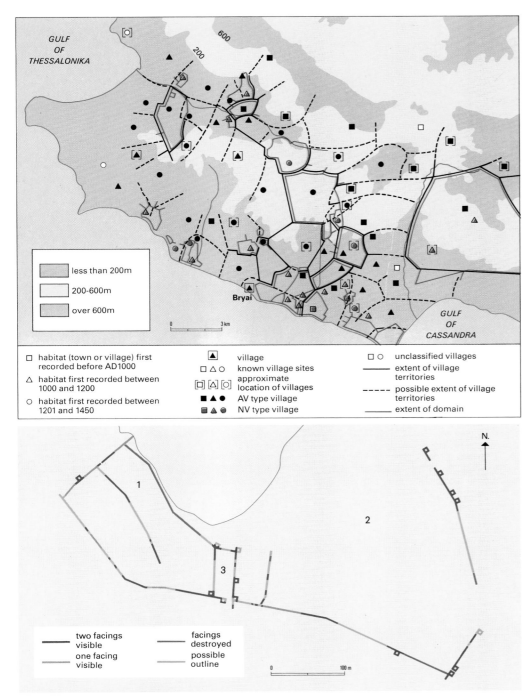

less than 200m

200-600m

over 600m

□ habitat (town or village) first recorded before AD1000

△ habitat first recorded between 1000 and 1200

○ habitat first recorded between 1201 and 1450

▲ village

□ △ ○ known village sites

◨ ◭ ◮ approximate location of villages

■ ▲ ● AV type village

▣ ◮ ◉ NV type village

□ ○ unclassified villages

—— extent of village territories

----- possible extent of village territories

—— extent of domain

Estates and villages in Byzantine western Chalcidicé, Greece

This map illustrates, in a well-documented region, western Chalcidicé, one of the most important aspects of the history of Byzantine rural areas: the creation of new centres of population between the 10th and 14th centuries. Byzantine legislation from the 10th century indicates the fact as general and of recent date. The "powers" (officials, dignitaries, leaders of the church and the monasteries), and then the treasury, acquired estates which they populated with tenants and improved, up to the limits of the village lands. At first this development took place at the expense of the village lands, which contracted, and then of the actual villages, the inhabitants of which, although smallholders, were looked on in the 12th century as tenants of fields in an estate. Thus the old system of village lands was replaced by a system of estates which often tightened their grip, comprising, in addition to the old villages, a number of new ones. With the aid of archives preserved in the monasteries of Athos (published in the *Archives of Athos*), we can estimate the number of these newly created villages in certain regions of Macedonia.

In western Chalcidicé, in the area of 52 modern parishes, Byzantine documents of the 9th–15th century supply the names of 91 villages, 76 of which (shown on the map) can be approximately located. Moreover, some fiscal documents define the boundaries of various monastic domains, mostly inhabited, and also mention, as landmarks, the boundaries of other domains and those of old village territories. The distinction between the two types of boundary is no simple matter, because in the 14th century demarcations (which are the most numerous), the word for village (*chorion*) is used in both cases. Written documentation provides evidence (some older than others) for the various villages, but it does not in general allow us to decide whether a village is "old" or "new".

Old and new villages: criteria for classification

However, thanks to J. Lefort's map of these demarcations (1982), we can classify most of the 76 villages into two types, called AV and NV, so as to indicate the distinction between the old and new villages. Two criteria have been used. First, if we know or can deduce that the property of a village is partially or wholly on the territory of another village, the first is classified as NV and the second as AV (the first probably resulting from the creation of an estate taken from the territory of the second); secondly, in the absence of such information, if the territory of a village is small (with an area of less than 5 sq km), it is classified as NV, otherwise as AV (the estates which do not correspond with old territories are usually less extensive than the latter). These criteria have their shortcomings and we cannot expect the classification obtained by using them to be relevant in every case.

Old villages: conclusions

It seems that we know nearly all the network of old villages (49, in black on the map). Note the absence of any old village on the coast (the apparent exception, Bryai, was a town fortified by the army) and the existence of villages deep in the mountains, suggesting that a lack of security played a part in their siting. Most villages are in the foothills, and their territory combines a level cultivable sector and slopes for pasturage and forest. On the coastal plain there is a second line of villages, below the first. The territories of these are very large, being nearly always more than 10 sq km (4.1 sq miles).

New villages: conclusions

We have a very incomplete knowledge of the network of new villages (in red on the map) based on the monastic archives which have been preserved. On 22 territories of old villages about which we have at least partial information, we find 23 new villages, which suggests that the number of villages in this region increased considerably between the 10th and the middle of the 14th century (when the great plague led to at least 15 sites being abandoned).

The location of the new villages is interesting: they are mostly lower down than the old villages, towards the centre of the valley in the north, near the sea in the south, and more rarely higher up on a slope with a flat terrace under cultivation. We may assume that at first (10th–12th century) the new villages were mainly founded lower down on good land previously left uncultivated because of its distance from the villages, and that other villages were established higher up on poorer ground when demographic pressure increased (around the 13th century).

—— two facings visible

—— one facing visible

—— facings destroyed

—— possible outline

Plan of the town of Chrysoupolis, Greece

The town was founded near the mouth of the Strymon river before the end of the 10th century inside a wall of modest dimensions (1). The eastern part (2), to the east of the citadel (3), is an extension dateable to the 14th century. The site was abandoned at the beginning of the Ottoman period. Archaeologists have identified five types of masonry and four stages in the construction of the walls.

West gate of the town of Zichna, Greece

This town, first mentioned in 1216, occupied a narrow spur on the Serres–Amphipolis road, and was relocated in the Ottoman period. The gate was adorned with an arch of alternating stone and brick vaulting, the bases of which are preserved.

Pergamum, plan of a Byzantine quarter (12th–14th century)

In the reign of Manuel I (1143–80), a period when frontier locations began to be refortified, Pergamum, then perched on the top of the acropolis (citadel), was enlarged. Construction activity continued until the reign of Michael VIII (1259–82). Excavations by the German Archaeological Institute have revealed on the site of the acropolis agricultural buildings that are L-shaped and open on to the valley. Later they were divided by walls of poor quality to cope with the arrival of refugees fleeing the Ottoman advance. After the capture of the town at the beginning of the 14th century, the settlement was moved down into the plain. But a new establishment (not shown on the plan) with a chapel – proof of the existence of a Christian community until the end of the 14th century – was erected on the ruins of the old town. After K. Rheidt.

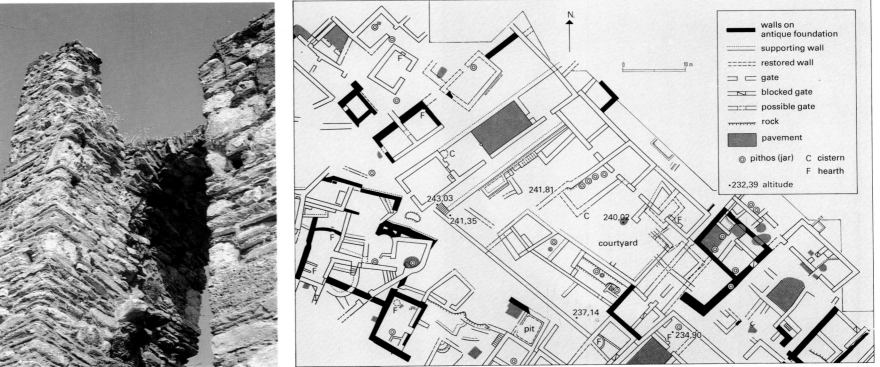

—— walls on antique foundation

.... supporting wall

===== restored wall

gate

blocked gate

possible gate

rock

pavement

◎ pithos (jar)   C cistern   F hearth

•232,39 altitude

Ceramics: a new approach

Pottery is one of the main tools that archaeologists use to date the phases of civilization and to assess their material prosperity and the spread of their contacts.

Byzantine ceramics remains a somewhat backward area of archaeological knowledge in comparison with kindred branches of research. Often neglected during excavations, it scarcely showed in the rapidly developing archaeological studies of the end of the 19th century, and many of the most important sites yielded few examples. Delphi, Olympia and other locations had been almost abandoned during the period under discussion. The earlier publications are consequently dispersed and fragmentary, dealing mainly with high quality wares, generally found in museums and originating from southern Russia, western Asia Minor—particularly Constantinople—and, to a lesser extent, Greece. A synthesis of these first researches was provided in 1930 by D. Talbot Rice in his book *Byzantine Glazed Pottery*, which drew largely on the excavations carried out at Constantinople's Great Palace*. Talbot Rice's classification and conclusions may today seem on the whole outmoded, but they continue to be used, and their author has provided the point of departure for all recent research.

A fuller picture emerges with the publication of excavations carried out at Corinth. These have long provided, and to a certain extent still do provide, the background framework for non-specialist researchers who have come across this type of pottery in their work. Only in the last few years has there been a move away from these well-defined collections with attempts to define new criteria from those previously used. For instance, the composition of the clay is now taken into account when trying to establish the origins of the pottery, and the distribution of shards and characteristic pieces may determine the production of specific centres and their area of influence. But these researches do not of course include wares which, during the first centuries of the Byzantine empire, merely carried on the Roman tradition, particularly the latest examples of the so-called "late ware".

The Byzantine world produced, like other civilizations, ceramic wares in which the clay was left unglazed, as in vessels used to store certain products, cooking utensils, some pitchers and similar objects. Archaeologists have particularly neglected this kind of ware, and so its development is almost unknown. The history of

Byzantine ceramics is often confused with that of glazing, or more precisely, with the rediscovery of this particular technique since, as we shall see, glazing was already practised in antiquity. Glazing is the correct term here, rather than enamelling, varnishing, or faïence, to describe a ceramic ware made of baked clay and covered with a mixture containing silica and, in this case, lead oxide which reduces the melting temperature of silica. Other metallic oxides were added to make colours. This composition had the advantage of other techniques which had been used for centuries, as in Egypt or the Near East, in that it allowed the glaze to adhere perfectly to the clay.

This kind of glazing first appeared in Syria in Hellenistic times and was developed during the Roman period, when it was extensively used to cover pots and make them look, in shape and colour, like metal containers. The technique disappeared during the late empire, but for a shorter period than was thought: it was still used in Athens *c*.AD360, and reappeared, at the latest, at the beginning of the 7th century, as seen in some shards and a small female head in baked clay, found at Caričin Grad*. The glaze was of good quality but its colour was rather dark, due no doubt to too low a baking temperature. Fragments of a similar date (7th century) have recently been found in Istanbul.

Decorative techniques

A number of decorative techniques lend themselves to classification in some chronological order. Apart from a monochromatic glaze without decoration, which survived for centuries, there were several main techniques in use, such as, for instance, printed decoration. An important hoard recently discovered at Istanbul dating from the 10th century contained shards and whole vases with this printed decoration that had been subsequently covered in glaze. A few fragments were painted in various colours, indicating the existence at this time of a type of decoration of exceptional richness in the Byzantine world. The same technique could be used in the production of ceramic icons and of tiles for covering the exterior of buildings.

Roughly contemporary is the ceramic ware painted in brown and green (10th and 11th century). The motifs

vary, sometimes consisting merely of patches of colour, as the pigments tended to run under the lead glaze. From the end of the 11th century and above all during the 12th, the most widespread decoration was the incised or scratched metal called sgraffito with its variations. The vessel was covered with a white slip* and a point or scoop was used to scratch motifs that varied in refinement and complexity. The whole was covered in a coloured, transparent glaze, thus creating a colour contrast between the pale background and the darker motif where the glaze came into contact with the clay. This particular technique survived until the 14th century and beyond. A two-colour effect was sometimes achieved by reversing the techniques, the thick slip being used to draw the motifs on the clay, and the glaze taking on a dark tint against the background.

Problems relating to the origin and spread of ceramic wares are still mainly unresolved. Some facts are beginning to emerge suggesting that two or three systems seem to have existed at the same time. First, the long-distance commercial activities ensured that, apart from wares originating outside the Byzantine world (ceramic wares from the western Mediterranean and also fragments of celadon ware from China), certain types were widespread over large areas of the empire, amongst them a 13th century relatively fine type called "Zeuxippos" ware*. At the other end of the scale, certain locally produced wares are known to have remained near their place of production, even though they sometimes were made to look like foreign wares. Between these two extremes, some varieties were not precisely limited to their area of production, but did not spread very far. Recent analyses have not contradicted these still provisional theories.

One should stress at this point that Byzantine craftsmen never used those techniques which, in the neighbouring world of Islam, led to the production of a thoroughly original ceramic conceived as a luxury product. Byzantine production was in general modest, and its use in the royal court during the 15th century suggests the extreme poverty of the empire.

Cup found at Corinth, 13th century

An example of a decorative technique analogous to *champlevé* (grooves cut into the base and filled with enamelling), where the principle is the same as that of sgraffito (scratched or incised): the colours contrast where the glaze covers the slip and where it comes into contact with the clay. Here, in the medallion, the motif stands out against a darker background. The subject, a princess wearing her crown and seated on the knees of a man, almost certainly refers to a Byzantine epic. Corinth Museum.

Cup showing Islamic influence, Corinth, 11th century

This cup belongs to a kind of ware which seems to have been produced at Corinth in the second half of the 11th century. The type of decoration, such as geometrical motifs, letters in Kufic (early Arabic) script and an unusual addition of birds, shows the influence of the Islamic world. The images are painted in reddish-brown under a glaze of fine quality. The spread of Corinthian products seems to have been limited to the Peloponnese, with fragments found at Sparta. Corinth Museum.

Fouilles de l'Institut archéologique allemand, Istanbul

Drawing of cup fragments, same size. Pergamum, 13th century

This series of drawings, made to size, shows the condition in which ceramic wares are usually found during excavations. These fragments carried representations of people, a comparatively rare form of decoration. Note the stylization of the features, which differs from official Byzantine art as it has reached us in most surviving pictorial monuments. These fragments belong to a group clearly identifiable by other elements of the decoration: a pale yellow to pale green glaze with darker patches which sometimes emphasize the sgraffito (incised) decoration.

Scientific archaeological drawing of a 13th century cup, Pergamum, 13th century

Following the conventions used in drawing archaeological finds, the right side shows the profile in a cutaway style through the vase, while the left shows the exterior. The decoration is shown as seen from above. The linear incisions on the lip are just indicated, whereas the central medallion is virtually complete. The starting point of the lines on the profile shows their actual place on the vase. The drawing should not be considered as an equivalent to photography, but as the first stage in a representation that abstracts and codifies details so as to achieve a precise classification of the object within a series. It enables certain elements to be isolated, analysed and compared so that our perception of the objects is not confused by its complexity.

Fouilles de l'Institut archéologique allemand, Istanbul

Fouilles de l'Institut archéologique allemand, Istanbul

Fragment of cup found at Pergamum, 13th century

The decorative technique is the same as that in the shards showing human faces (illustration at top of page), in spite of differences in the colours of the glaze due to the presence of different oxides. But the existence at the same place of numerous shards with yellow-brown patches, and only occasional examples with green patches, like this one, indicates that the latter were probably manufactured elsewhere.

Fouilles de l'Institut archéologique allemand, Istanbul

A spoiled piece

The bottoms of two pots, stuck together, can clearly be seen, evidence that the baking temperature was too high – as can also be seen by the dark colour of the clay and the deformation of the pieces. Rejects such as this are generally found near the kilns where they were fired. This particular discovery was a very important one because no medieval kilns have been found at Pergamum and this was the only proof of a local production.

Jug found at Pergamum, 13th century

This unglazed vessel shows how such jugs, which are still in use, have changed little in shape over the centuries and are often difficult to date outside their archaeological context. Glazed jugs of the same form also exist. It is not clear why one or the other technique was chosen, but quality would not have been the only consideration: the porosity of an unglazed jug allows the water it contains to remain cooler.

Fouilles de l'Institut archéologique allemand, Istanbul

Jar, 13th century

This large jar was covered with a kind of slip admixed with mica powder, which gives it a slight lustre. This characteristic also appears on a series of lidded vases which are similarly decorated with very simple motifs drawn in red. The very carefully executed relief decoration is exceptional for a vase of this kind. It suggests a connection with certain large glazed goblets, also found at Pergamum.

Fouilles de l'Institut archéologique allemand, Istanbul

Islam:
the archaeological background

Islamic archaeology is a relatively recent phenomenon, but the great tradition of historical writing from the 10th century onwards provides us with documentary evidence unmatched in the West.

A genuine archaeology of Islam only began to emerge in the second quarter of the 20th century, which is very late in comparison with the archaeology of the ancient civilizations and the oriental worlds. But this should not detract from the long history of discoveries relating to material and documents about life in the Islamic world. Of first importance is the question of the interest that Muslims themselves have taken in their heritage, for which we must seek out the evidence of the texts that their ancient authors have bequeathed to us. We also know that the history of Islam has been linked with the history of the Western world for more than 12 centuries. So a Muslim archaeology is likely to reflect the bonds that united Europe and Islam.

Today archaeologists are increasingly interested in the evidence provided by the voluminous works of writers, historians and geographers. Some of these accounts may be cursory or stereotyped, restricted as they often are to almost ritual references to "beautiful" or "well defended" towns, with "beautiful" monuments. Others, however, may contain an especially accurate description or even a simple mention that provides a most valuable guide for the study of a monument or the planning of a survey* programme. For example, in the 11th century al-Bakri* wrote a *Description* of Africa in the form of a collection of itineraries accompanied by accounts of remarkable towns, ethnic groups or emirates. It is from such apparently unpromising sources that the archaeologist learns, for example, that the great mosque of Sabta (Ceuta) was decorated with leaded glass windows, or that there was a palace in the vicinity of Ceuta. These two pieces of information made it possible to locate the place of origin of two important and interesting elements of Moroccan architecture.

But there are also extremely accurate texts. Al-Baidaq, the 12th century Almohade chronicler, gave a detailed list of the fortresses erected by the Almoravides to prevent their successors from penetrating the Atlantic plains of Morocco. In the 14th century, an eastern traveller visiting western Islam described, in his account of Fez, the construction methods and layouts of Hispano-Maghreb houses towards the middle of the century. Such information has been confirmed in every detail by recent archaeological researches at Fez, the Merinid necropolis of Chella, the gates of Rabat or on the sites of the Straits of Gibraltar. The effect of this is to demonstrate the value of such a text, so that we can identify in the Middle Ages the emergence in Islam of a genuine archeography*.

Many other kinds of literature contribute to its development. Thus at the same period, al-Badisi's *Magsad*, a collection of the lives of the saints of the Rif, near the Mediterranean coast, supplies an excellent series of notes about the coast and navigation. This enables archaeologists to compare the arsenals, discovered by research, with the description of the forests, now vanished, which supplied the wood needed by the naval shipyards. Similarly, we know what was exported from ports rediscovered by fieldwork with the aid of these texts. When the archaeologist takes this type of document into account, he can contribute to the economic history of the country he is analysing. Here again ancient texts and contemporary research verify and complement each other. The work of Ibn Khaldun and Ibn Batuta has also proved of great value.

Many other ancient texts invite this kind of study, of which we mention three examples. The *Description of Africa* published in 1550 by John-Léo the African* is an inexhaustibly rich source. For example, it contains an illustration of the spread of settlements, including many sites that disappeared at the end of the Middle Ages. The most modern surveys would be inconceivable without such guides. With regard to a site excavated by the author near Sabta, a contemporary description of the European conquest by al-Ansari provides a detailed description of the region. Comparison of the text's microtopony*of place-names with oral traditions has greatly contributed to the archaeological study of rural structures. But some texts themselves undertake this work of comparison. The *Kitab al-Istiqsa*, by a scholar of Salé (Morocco), written at the beginning of the colonial age, gives details about the Merinid madrasa (institute of learning) of Salé and the fountain at its entrance. A workman who had uncovered the feeder pipe supplying the fountain with water, in order to repair it, had noted that the remains resembled other Merinid works that he had observed. This information, collected by the author, has helped to date this little monument.

So it would be wrong to think that the interest of Islamic countries in their heritage is only a belated consequence of the contributions of western science. These few examples from the Hispano-Maghreb world, and the use that can be made of them, clearly show that valuable documents were written by Muslim authors from the Middle Ages onwards.

The impact of the West

Nevertheless, we cannot deny that there exists an archaeography of Islam arising from the work of Christian travellers, draughtsmen and cartographers. At the end of the 18th century, the Egyptian campaign represented, in the work of scholars accompanying Napoleon, the beginning of a genuinely scientific archaeography. Many of the plates in the resulting *Description de l'Egypte* are documents of rare value. But this undertaking, which marks a transition from the almost accidental recording of information to the systematic work of collection, is only intelligible by reference to the very numerous documents which preceded it.

A recently completed study examines the site of Tyre in terms of the accounts of French travellers in the eastern Mediterranean. The picture they give is in fact dependent on the nature of Islamo-Christian relations. Nevertheless a better picture of the lands traversed does gradually emerge. Pilgrimage to the holy places and the lands of the crusades was the first stimulus to the discovery of the "infidels". The pilgrimage was itself at first a kind of "tour" organized via Venice, but later enlarged its objectives when the envoys of princes and traders travelled widely in the Orient. Their curiosity was aroused and, at the beginning of the contemporary period, led them to the material documents of history. The interest in archaeological remains came late, as did the interest in Islam, which had been eclipsed for so long by that of more ancient civilizations. Nevertheless, westerners exposed to Islam underwent a change in their mental outlook; to them we are indebted for a number of useful accounts, even if they come from amateur archaeologists.

The wealth of deliberate or chance descriptions provided by these travel notes is undeniable. To be sure, we cannot help smiling at the superficial and subjective remarks by visitors to Isfahan; the Safavid capital was apparently both a "large and dirty village" and "a model of attractiveness" (Tavernier and Gobineau). Illustrative documents are often even richer in information: a series of engravings from the *Civitates Orbis Terrarum*, frequently reproduced in the 16th and 17th century, supplies an irreplaceable vision of the towns, especially the ports. Their analysis, in conjunction with the information in the texts, has enabled archaeologists to locate and describe a large number of Islamic strongholds established from the Mediterranean to the Atlantic coast. This abundant series of graphic documents is completed by romantic

Musée archéologique de Madrid

**Bronze deer from the period of the Andalusian Caliphate,
10th century**

The West appears to have been primarily interested in the
"objects" and only later in the architecture of Islam. Perhaps
the time has come to re-examine these and to combine their
evidence with the most recent finds of an archaeology more
concerned with history, for henceforth it will base its conclusions on the totality of texts and material evidence.

An object such as this symbolizes a world linked equally with
the East and West, richer in secular works than was previously
thought, yet finding its unity in the living faith of Islam.

engravings and the drawings of engineers, which are still rather neglected.
Some collections are rich, such as that of the General Archives of Castille or
the collection from the French army: excellent drawings show the existence,
from the 16th to the 20th centuries, of an almost scientific archaeography of
Islam in which the visual image usefully complements the written texts of
reports and enquiries.

As already mentioned, the beginning of the European expansion in the East
marked the emergence of a genuinely scientific archaeography. This continued to develop, even though, in Europe, a science as convinced of its universal
legitimacy as of its truth was asserting itself. Orientalism showed hardly any
interest in the heritage of Islam. Thus Islamic archaeology was born late. No
doubt it benefited from the experience of other archaeological or "Islamiz-
ing" disciplines, but these also transmitted some dogmatic ideas which did
little to help its formation.

Ancient sites, new interpretations

The sites of primitive Islam are rich in remains that recall traditions inherited
from the pre-Islamic age of the conquered lands. The "castles of the desert",
or a royal town like Anjar in Lebanon, were at first regarded as Roman or
Byzantine sites. Moreover, the Islamic town was "defined" according to the
convenient and easily accessible model of contemporary souks (*suqs*); plans
based on *insulae* or street-blocks could only be from antiquity, or so it was
assumed. And yet the use of aerial photography, as applied by Poidebard,
which went on concurrently, marked the opening up of Islamic archaeology
to more modern techniques – a contradiction apparently characteristic of this
growing science.

The so-called "castles of the desert", with foundations standing inside a
walled enclosure flanked by semi-circular towers, were at first associated by
investigators with the pre-Islamic *castella*. However, their actual shape made
them all quite alien to that model. Another explanation was therefore
required: nomadic Arabs had a compulsive need to return to the desert, and so
they erected these enigmatic residences. However, a large number of these
castles were not established on desert sites. They can therefore only be defined
accurately by more modern excavations. In this connection, we should
mention the work of D. Schlumberger, R. W. Hamilton and more recently
Emir Chehab and Oleg Grabar. At Qasr el-Hayr al-Gharbi in Syria and
Lashkari Bazar in Afghanistan, Daniel Schlumberger discovered that these
residences were integrated with vast programmes for developing the territory.
Qasr el-Hayr al-Gharbi formed part of a complex for developing the
Palmyran steppe. Making use of an ancient dam, an irrigation network served
palace, garden and caravanserai. These works confirm, together with Oleg
Grabar's excavation of Qasr el-Hayr al–Sharqi, the role as centres of
colonization of these "castles" which were often groups of different kinds of
buildings. Hamilton has provided an analysis of one, Khirbat al-Mafjar,
which had a bath of enormous dimensions. By his excavation of Anjar, Emir
Chehab has confirmed, following the work of Jean Sauvaget, that the Islamic
construction of towns remained, like its monuments, faithful to the schemes
of Hellenistic town planning and architecture.

Thus, in 50 years, Islamic archaeology has made up for lost time, and
stands revealed as a fascinating subject in its own right. The material it
supplies has eliminated many cliches inherited from the days of orientalism.
Finally, these researches mark the beginning of surveys conceived as part of
much larger programmes. Abandoning the world of palaces, mosques and

towns, they improve our knowledge of the organs of the economy, the
products of craftsmen more concerned with the everyday than with art, and
the structures of the rural world.

Such projects also emerged from a series of remarkable surveys which,
unlike the first excavations, quickly showed a real advance for Islamic
archaeology over its rivals. In the colonial period, nearly all the regions of the
Muslim world were the subject of major systematic undertakings. The studies
devoted to Cairo are the first example of the irreplaceable collection of
monographs born of those surveys. But we should not forget the British
surveys of India, or those made by A. U. Pope in Iran, or A. Gabriel in
Anatolia. The ultimate objective of establishing a mosaic of monographs also
inspired K. A. C. Creswell, whose enormous folio volumes are still consulted
today. His *Early Muslim Architecture* and *Muslim Architecture of Egypt*
remain classics of the archaeology of the Muslim world.

Projects going into finer details marked the development of research in the
western Islamic countries. Leopoldo Torres Balbas, Georges Marçais and
Henri Terrasse* have made vast methodical surveys, both urban and rural,
which rapidly brought to light many documents and artifacts relative to the
Hispano-Maghreb world. But this collecting has always been done with the
aim of achieving genuine historical syntheses by the constant comparison of
archaeological documents and artifacts with the literary sources. Their work,
like Jean Sauvaget's at Aleppo, founded the modern archaeology now
conducted jointly by investigators from Islamic countries and western
archaeologists. This communal programme definitely marks a new stage in
relations between the East and West which are the background for this
research. We shall try to describe the contributions made as a result. But from
the outset they appear as the final form of a centuries-old process.

The Islamic town

Like the Greek and Hellenistic towns of an earlier period, the cities of Islam spread from Spain to India. In most of the intervening countries, their characteristic qualities still define Islam's unique contribution to urban civilization.

Contemporary archaeology may help to renew and modify our image of a particular type of Islamic monument, but its main contribution is the rediscovery of the framework to the rural or urban life of the religious community. However, although the methods used for studying the rural structures of Islam are fairly similar to those used for the archaeology of other civilizations, the approach to Islamic urban life involves original research because it is concerned with a living urban fabric of streets, houses and monuments which have kept their original function. Thus a long evolution can be retraced which, although based on the usual material of the archaeologist, must also take into account the exceptional value represented by perfectly preserved standing buildings; buildings which are still alive, as has been said, and are fulfilling the function that originally brought them into being.

But if one had to make a rapid summary of the most recent archaeological surveys* of Islamic towns, one would first have to go beyond the usual standard image evoked by the madina (the old town) which is generally regarded as a self-contained entity within its setting of the city wall. Today archaeologists must also take into account the diversity of sites, functions and urbanization in Islamic countries. The Islamic town is no longer seen as inflexibly bound in with the notion that Islam, the religion of the city-dweller, decrees a form of town-planning according to an unchangeable model, based around the great mosque and the commercial quarters or official buildings that adjoined it. Moreover, although ancient cities like Fez may exhibit a network of alleyways adapted to a sloping site, a network which is also the reflection of a long history, we also know that town plans with a rectangular layout often existed in reoccupied cities like Damascus, or in newly created towns, as the excavations of Anjar, Lebanon have brilliantly demonstrated. The uncovering of a quarter erected in the 14th century near Rabat, Morocco, in the funerary town of Chella, demonstrates the long survival of these regular layouts and, therefore, the genuine variety of Islamic organization of the urban fabric.

Regional influences
It should also be emphasized that although the town is always dependent on the site it occupies, so that a closed-off spur like Toledo, or a site in flat country like Samarra, determines very different types of town,

nevertheless the effect of regional traditions, like that of interregional exchanges, appears more clearly.

Another standard image, that of the circular Abbasid town of Caliph al-Mansur at Baghdad, may now reclaim its rightful place. Its antecedents, which include a long series of Asiatic circular towns such as Firuzabad, are known to scholars, as is the diffusion of this plan when first Abbasid power, and then Seljuk invasion of the 10th–12th century, strengthened contacts between Mediterranean provinces and Islamic Asia. Recent researches have shown that a round town of about 100 hectares (240 acres), al-Mansuriya, was founded at the gates of Qairwan in the second half of the 10th century by the Ifriqiyan Fatimids. A 12th century town has just been excavated on the south shore of the Straits of Gibraltar; called Qasr al-Saghir, it has the same circular arrangement. A survey conducted in Castilla la Vieja has revealed, at Madrigal de las Altas Torres, a similar plan for the Iberian peninsula when it was reconquered in the 14th century. Thus countries which had best displayed and preserved Hellenistic traditions, from now on appear open to influences from the other half of the Islamic world, that of the Asian lands.

Modern surveys make us aware of another dimension of the town. If on top of it all we compare ancient texts with data provided by aerial observation, photogrammetry and land surveys, a picture of the whole built-up area begins to appear. Thus vast areas of this kind are known at Delhi, India, and Lashkari Bazar, Afghanistan, as well as at Samarra, Cordova and Qairwan. With regard to the latter, we now know that the development of the madina may have left the mosque of the Conquest period and the first commercial artery in a very marginal position, but this was due to three princely towns which developed to the south of the original foundation: Al Abbassiya and Raqqada from the 10th century, and especially the circular town of al-Mansuriya, diverted all the economic activity of Qairwan to new zones. An aqueduct 40km (25 miles) long which linked this built-up area to ancient Roman water supplies is a sign of this: traces of late antiquity on the sites of Qairwan's built-up area suggest that the Tunisian metropolis may have been as much bound to the oldest local traditions as to the most distant Islamic influences. Archaeology proves this, showing how, paradoxically, neither transition to Islam nor the emergence of Fatimid heterodoxy brought about a break.

Everyday life in the city
Much interest has also arisen concerning the framework of the city-dwellers' lives and the variety that is still apparent in them. Archaeologists have studied a whole series of medium-sized towns, from Yazd in Iran to Talavera in Spain or Salé in Morocco, as well as Kuch in Egypt, revealing the actual organization of everyday life. They have shown the value of the city district as an indication of various aspects of the urban economy, as well as of the inhabitants' ethnic origin, or of its union with the suburbs in the history of the town's development. Accurate maps incorporating all the information obtained both in the field and from the texts have recently brought out the importance of the suburbs of Aleppo, especially those of the Turcoman people in the 13th century. At Salé or Fez the structure of neighbourhood life appears in all its richness, with its houses, oratories, baths and schools. At Talavera the same suburb appears to have been reserved from one age to another for minorities or people of humble means. It was successively occupied by Mozarabic Christians under Islam, Mudejar Moslems after the Reconquest, and then increasingly by country folk. Many other examples exist. Archaeological survey of sites as a complement to study of the texts is another approach that also challenges the idea of a static town, based on its great mosque.

Finally, we cannot omit mention of the extraordinary interest that the city-dwellers showed for the neighbouring countryside. Research carried out around Fez has just been published, and clearly shows that country houses and gardens around the towns answered the city-dwellers' needs for light and air in what was often a very dense urban fabric. This density, moreover, required cemeteries to be sited outside towns. Thus archaeological findings confirm the observation of a *hisba* (manual of municipal life), which enjoined that the openings of fortifications should be blocked up so that indiscreet looks would not disturb the promenade of women outside the walls. In terms of hydraulic installations, the countryside could be specially organized for the benefit of city-dwellers, as in the example of Ceuta, Morocco. The towns of Islam were emphatically not unplanned or anarchistic growths: the objective methods of modern archaeology clearly indicate the animation, variety and richness of the material yielded by the Islamic world.

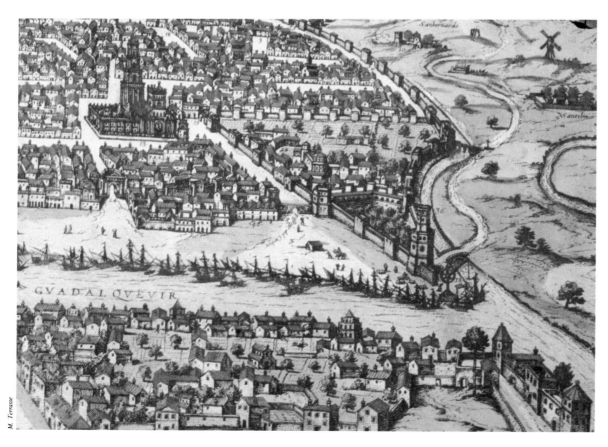

Seville, according to *Civitates Orbis Terrarum* (16th century)

Seville, one of the most important towns in the Hispano-Maghreb world, and 12th century capital of the Almoravides in Andalusia, has partly lost its Islamic heritage, but old engravings help the historian relocate archaeological discoveries. Situated on the banks of the Guadalquivir, it was a port with many naval shipyards. Its medieval wall appears here clearly with its towers and the *Torre de Oro*, the Almohade *albarrana* tower. Some traces of the great mosque are preserved in the cathedral, which owes its plan to the mosque and keeps the minaret as its bell tower, called *La Giralda* and shown here.

Town life and country pursuits

The inhabitants of Islamic towns liked to escape from the overpopulated districts to visit places of leisure in the neighbouring countryside: country houses, villas and pavilions, gardens and hunting grounds. It is this richly varied country life which we see here, confirmed by contemporary agricultural treatises and recent research. Page from an album, end of 16th century, Isfahan. Topkapi Sarayi, Istanbul.

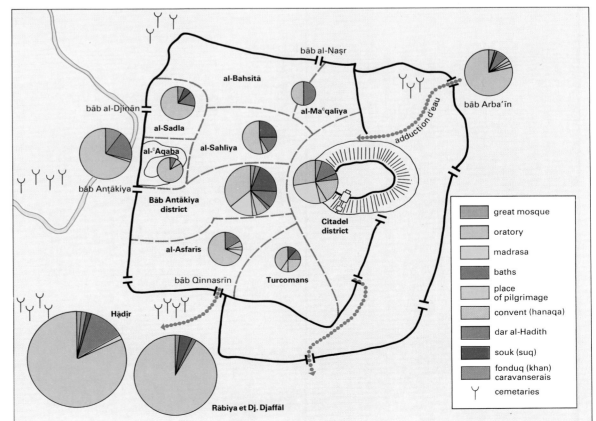

Fez: street leading to the centre of the Qairwan quarter (far left) and aerial view of the old town (left)

After the conquest of Morocco by Islam, which first used towns inherited from the Roman province of Mauretania (Tingitana, Volubilis-Ulili and Tangiers), Fez was the first foundation in the Eastern tradition. Modern study of the urban fabric is often based on photointerpretation and photogrammetric reconstructions using aerial photographs. With their help we can clearly see on either side of the white bed of the Wadi Fez, today covered over and transformed into a street, the two "banks" (*aduat*), the original districts of the town. The bank of the people of Qairwan and that of the Andalusians, settled in the 9th and 10th centuries, were reunited inside one city wall under the Almoravides in the 12th.

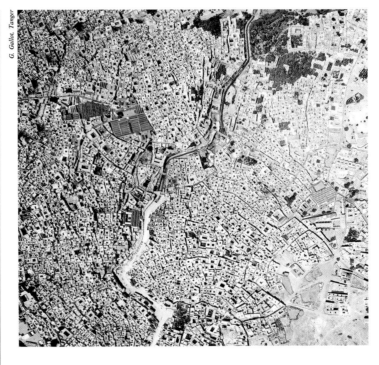

Aleppo in the 13th century: distribution of monuments by district

Statistical maps plotted by computer can fill out and bring to life our knowledge of the town as it emerges from texts and archaeological finds. Thus A.M. Eddé has shown the densities of monumental building complexes in each district, their specific nature, and the importance of the suburbs at that time, especially the southern areas mostly inhabited by Turcomans.

149

"Rediscovery" of the mosque

What are the origins of the mosque, Islam's "building of collective life"? New techniques of research have brought new insights.

In the field of the archaeology of Islam, research devoted to the mosque may at first sight seem thoroughly out of date. The mosque, together with the house of government (the *dar al-imara*) and the palace, was of course one of the first themes to attract the attention of investigators. Thus it became associated with a number of outmoded clichés that followed the Orientalism of an earlier period. The conventional view was of an Islam identified solely in terms of its urban aspect, a theoretical town seen as centred round its mosque which, in this stereotype, was invariably a hall of prayer with a minaret and a court; although we now know that adaptation to the climate, as in Anatolia, or the function of the monument, often entailed the disappearance of such features. Today we have left such excesses behind. We smile at the attempts to "reconstruct", say, the Bab Mardom mosque at Toledo (its real interest will be described later), which many diagrams embellished with a courtyard it never possessed. There was no need at all for this "oratory", associated perhaps with certain funerary rites. Recent research makes it possible to trace out a more accurate picture of this type of monument.

First it is relevant to recall the meaning of the word mosque, since confusion has reigned for so long that, for instance, the Dome of the Rock at Jerusalem was even known as the Mosque of Omar, although it was actually a place of pilgrimage. "Mosque" primarily and correctly designates the great mosque, or Friday mosque, or "cathedral mosque" where the congregation of believers assembled for prayer and prostration at noon on Fridays, the only time when it was indispensable to go there for prayer. We propose to limit the use of the word mosque to this *jami*. It is the "only building of collective life", the centre of the religious, political, legal and even educational life of the community concerned. Nevertheless there were other places for prayer which we also call mosques, although Arabic uses the specific term *masjid*, which should be translated as oratory. This other "mosque" played an important part in the life of the faithful. It was integrated with the other buildings in the quarter and its rediscovery is rich in information that furthers our knowledge of Islamic religious architecture. A simple room for prayer, sometimes in an upper storey, or a luxurious creation, as in the mosque of Sheikh Lutfullah which adjoins the royal palace at Isfahan, the *masjid* has been rescued from the oblivion to which it had been consigned by research projects concerned only with exceptional monuments. The very number of these oratories—the texts sometimes enumerate several hundred in one quarter—confirms the importance of a building that has for too long been considered as minor.

New techniques of research have made possible the discovery or "rereading" of the mosque. Archaeological surveys* have often helped to discover a large number of neglected edifices. Moreover, a general concern for stratigraphy* in fieldwork may be applied to the analysis of monuments with elements that still survive. The remarkable work of Eugenio Galdieri on the Friday mosque at Isfahan is relevant here. He excavated not only the floor but also the walls to establish the successive stages of the monument from the Abbasid Middle Ages to our own day, treating each aspect with an identical concern for accuracy. From the Iranian to the Qairwan mosques, photogrammetry has made it possible to obtain absolutely accurate diagrams—thus the study of an arch and its regulatory outline gives useful information for dating a section of the building. Diagrams composed by more traditional methods can also open the way to discoveries. The appearance in the 12th century in the Hispano-Maghreb world of stalactites in certain parts of mosques has been noted. On the basis of accurate diagrams Michel Ecochard has shown the identity of these *muqarnas* with certain Asiatic models. Similar graphic studies have made it possible to rediscover the method of composition used by architects and decorators. As in our own studies, the work of Christian Ewert on the mosques of the Almohades has established the existence of a modular composition previously unknown. In short, the use of archaeological methods for what previously belonged to the history of architecture or the history of art has made possible the "rediscovery" of the mosque.

Evolution and variation

The evolution of the mosque appears to have followed a line of logical development which constantly adapted the various architectural elements to the use of space available. The Ummayad mosque, first seen at Damascus, made use of the elements of the Roman basilica: an accentuated axial nave marked the direction of prayer, and also of the place where authoritative proclamations were made. The mosque of the Abbasid period enlarged the zone adjoining the *qibla* wall, which provided for the requirements of prayer. This second aisle, together with the axial nave, forms the T-shaped plan which is found from Samarra to Qairwan or Cordova. A dome at the junction of these aisles soon marked the bay before the *mihrab*, which was also where the sovereign or governor took his place. The *maqsura*, a wooden enclosure, which protected him, was accompanied from the Seljuk period at Isfahan by a domed pavilion.

The recent recovery of the Algerian mosque of Mansura makes a hitherto unusual plan intelligible. In the Maghreb, the requirements of internal circulation led to an addition to the T-shaped plan of the mosque in the form of outside and central aisles perpendicular to the enlarged axial nave. Five domes punctuated the structure before the *qibla* at the termination of five noble aisles. Thus there arose a whole range of different solutions. In the mosque of the administrative capital of Marrakesh, the Almohades were to combine this arrangement with a formula referring back to the mosques of the period of the Islamic conquest. Such a borrowing indicated their desire to be the champions of a religion as pure as that of this first Islam. Far from being a rigid and constantly repeated process, the most recent research shows that the mosque was an accurate reflection of the history and tastes of the religious community.

The mosque also shows the influence of regionalism and exchanges between regions: a two-way movement which animated the vast, starshaped network of Islam, continually extending towards the most distant countries of Islam, yet always built with reference to Mecca, towards which the orientation of mosque architecture invited the believer to turn. The mosque became increasingly bound in with the geographical context and the traditions peculiar to the territory where it was erected. From the 16th century to our own time, the Ottoman mosque, based on the model of St Sophia that inspired the greatest architect of the Seljuk dynasty, Sinan (Süleymaniye mosque, Istanbul), continues to perpetuate in its own way the creative work of the Anatolian Seljuks. Analysis of the portals erected by these people reveals an architecture intent on fresh creation while remaining open to lessons learnt from Christianity or neighbouring Syria. The mosque freed itself from models produced at the centre of the empire to create regional models whose flexibility is demonstrated by the example of the Almohades. Thus there was an Indian mosque, just as there had earlier been an Andalusian mosque or an Anatolian mosque. The example of the mosque of Isfahan was valid for the whole of Islam.

Finally, mention should be made of the way that similar elements appeared in a strange synchronism in all the regions of Islam, and in buildings very different from each other. Identical oratories (*masjid*), comprising three times three bays, are found from Toledo (Bab Mardom) to Balkh, as well as in Tunisia (Qairwan and Susa) and in Egypt (Cairo). Each time, the oratory was interpreted in the style of the regional architecture, but it is strange to see how the life of Islam seemed to encourage, everywhere and simultaneously, the building of these edifices on the edge of the townships. Here again, new techniques were adopted to renew the original aims, at once more regional and more "global", thus modifying our conception of the mosque. The latter now seems more than ever the symbol of a constantly threatening explosion, as well as of the lasting strength that from the 9th century marked the life of the Islamic empire and of each of its regions in Europe, Asia and Africa.

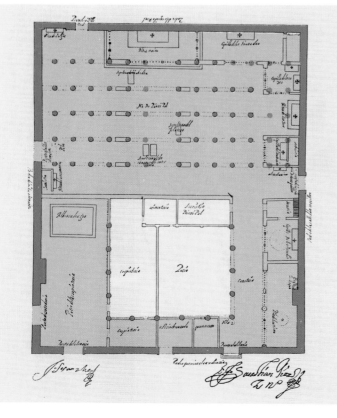

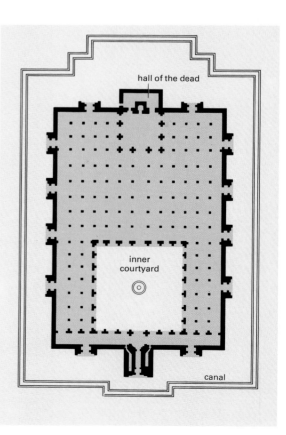

Mosques of Granada, Spain (left) and Mansura, near Tlemcen, Algeria (right), end of 13th century

The great mosque of Granada, now lost, is known from this plan drawn when it was destroyed *c.*1704. A new interpretation of the plan reveals an oratory with 6 aisles parallel to the *qibla* wall. There was also a square court surrounded by enlarged porticoes as in the 12th (Almoravide) century.

The great mosque of Mansura, the seat of the Moroccan Merinids outside Tlemcen (Algeria), has the same court as the mosque of Granada. The plan was inspired by the mosque of the Almohades at Rabat, making a synthesis of the 12th-century Hispano-Maghreb mosque and the Mesopotamian Abbasid mosque. But a new element delimiting a vast space appears before the *mihrab*: the domed pavilion known under Malik Shah at Isfahan (11th century), which took two centuries to reach western Algeria. These two plans show the great similarity between the Andalusian and the Maghrebi mosques.

Mosque of Zafar, Yemen. General view and detail of a ceiling, right

A number of archaeological expeditions, mainly German, French or Russian, have for some years been carrying out surveys of the archaeological heritage of two Yemenite states known chiefly by their capitals, Aden and Sanaa. A raised site of exceptional richness some 150km (243 miles) from Sanaa has been discovered and studied. This shows that at the same time that the Seljuk movement reached the shores of the eastern Mediterranean in the 11th–12th century, and the great Hispano-Maghreb empires developed, the Arabic peninsula possessed an original architecture of great quality. Note the domed tombs in the courtyard of the mosque and the sumptuous ceilings, now undergoing a rescue operation, with the help of UNESCO.

Mosque with nine domes, Balkh, Afghanistan (9th or 10th century)

The district of Balkh (the Bactria of Alexander) contains, not far from the town walls, an oratory with a square plan and nine bays covered by domes. A decor of carved stucco with the ground picked out in colour lightens the heavy masses of this mud-brick edifice. A model known throughout Islam in the 9th century is treated here with regional variations. Spain, Tunisia and Egypt all managed to give this model local characteristics.

Central part of the minaret of Djam, Afghanistan

The triple body, forming a slightly truncated cone, of the minaret of Djam still stands 60m (195ft) high in the high valley of the Hindu Kush, in the centre of the country. The delightful turquoise and brick decor adorning this minaret enable us to date it. It was built in 1194 by the *Ghorid* Ghiath al-Din.

Regional traditions and domestic architecture

Across the vast geographical area of the ancient Islamic civilization, from southern Spain to Central Asia, there is a wide diversity of cultural and ethnic tradition: an interesting example of this is domestic—the house.

From the 9th century the Islamic world reveals clear regional differences in its material remains. Research from the first half of the 20th century has shown how this diversity is apparent in the art associated with the ruling dynasties, whether in Spain, Cairo or Bactriana. But the most recent work, which concentrates more on the Muslim way of life in everyday terms, has shown the growth and energy of local traditions, best symbolized in the development of the house. Whereas craft products often provide evidence of commerce between regions, forms of dwellings seem to emphasize the architects' loyalty to the local heritage.

The first type of house built in Syria in the Umayyad period at Gabal Says has long been familiar to architectural historians. It consisted quite simply of a series of rooms arranged around a court forming an oblong with unequal sides. A group of rooms, or *bayt*, which was long associated, in the case of palaces, with the first Islamic dynasty, has been uncovered in urban remains during the excavation of Anjar in the Lebanon (8th century). Two series of two small rooms flanked the central space. Small bathrooms on hypocausts, decorated with mosaic pavements, doubtless figured among the structures in the quarter. The local origin of these dwellings is obvious; there is nothing to link them with the houses of Arabia, the most famous example of which is still the dwelling of the Prophet Mohammed.

Oleg Grabar's excavation of the Umayyad site of Qasr al-Hayr al-Sharqi, Syria, has led to a new interpretation of the two fortified enclosures found there. The largest of these rectangular complexes contained four entrances, one in the middle of each side. Each of these entrances was framed by two houses opening onto courts with porticoes, and combining simple oblong rooms with Umayyad *bayts*. This confirms clearly the existence of a regional type.

A new element from Asia, the *iwān*, very soon featured in Muslim residential architecture, reaching as far as Egypt. An "Islam of the East", (from Machrek) is thus apparent in this space, which is frequently vaulted, enclosed on three sides, and opening onto a central court. An example of this appears in the Middle Ages in the Cairene group of buildings at Fustat. Sometimes a second *iwān* stood opposite; such an arrangement is also found in Iraq in the apartments of Ukhaidir. A feature of these houses is their comfort, with running water, latrines and in some cases a special room reserved for cooking. Such discoveries, which relate to the entire central zone of the empire, clearly indicate the emphasis on quality that can very early be seen in the framework of Muslim life.

Regional traditions

In this connection, the notion of regional variation deserves a closer look. Concern for variety is first apparent with the development, at Machrek, of a main room where a wide space preceded the *iwān* flanked by other rooms and combined with them to form an inverted T. The word *bayt*, given to this complex discovered in Mesopotamia, is itself of Iranian origin. Its extension to present-day Tunisia from the 10th century reflects the reality of exchanges inside Islam that transcended regional factors. This province of Ifriqiya, where a particular type of house was revealed during the excavation of Raqqada (9th–10th centuries), remained throughout its history a place where such syntheses occurred. In the modern period the Tunisian private house was to draw inspiration from the Ottoman empire and the Hispano-Maghreb world, before acquiring further features from Italy with the approach of the colonial age.

The permanence, as well as the originality, of the house in the Iberian peninsula and the Maghreb is quite remarkable. From the 11th century with the *alcazaba* of Malaga, Spain, an angled entrance gave access to a courtyard of modest dimensions with porticoes. Halls, sometimes preceded by an anteroom, opened on this court which might be adorned with a pool or a fountain. The largest rooms were lined with alcoves, as recently shown in the excavation at Morocco of al-Saghir (12th century) and Belyunech (13th–15th century). Work carried out on this site revealed much about the development of the rooms of the house: two small annexes originally flanked the principal room, and these were not converted into alcoves until the 12th century. These researches further emphasize the similarity between rural and urban houses in the same region of Islam. Studies made at Salé and Fez of houses erected from the 16th to the 18th century have also shown how, in the largest residences, service patios existed alongside the central patio; private baths were then added to the layout of the house, while public baths of the highest quality demonstrate here, as in the east, the relationship of these buildings of everyday life with the most ancient pre-Islamic traditions of these regions.

This plan of the house explains the regionalism throughout Islam of larger buildings, for example the *madrasa* (Islamic religious school). We now know that this oriental institution took over, in North Africa and the Iberian peninsula from the 13th to the 15th century, a strictly local plan derived from the private house. Besides the *madrasas* found by urban survey* we should also mention the *zawiyas*, pious foundations which

offered travellers a hostelry at the gates of towns; one of these has been excavated near Salé. These various monuments have been associated with the *ribats*, monastery-fortresses erected for the holy war, of which Tunisia preserves excellent examples at Sousse, Monastir and Lamta. The similarity of their plans has caused some scholars to propose that they form a regional Maghreb school. But comparison with the *madrasas* built at Cairo, in Syria, at Fez or in Anatolia shows rather that everywhere they stem from a regional tradition to which the private house is surely the key.

The pre-Islamic heritage

Thus a real unity in the framework of local life appears in all domains and all regions. Emergent Islam contributed to the spread of models originating from the centre of the empire as noted in the case of the Iranian *bayt*, but from the end of the Middle Ages the role of regionalism seems to be the decisive factor.

The recent work of Galdieri on the "Friday Mosque" at Isfahan has demonstrated this fact. After Islamization had diffused Syrian and Mesopotamian influences to the outermost regions of the empire, the region of Isfahan developed an innovation derived from its own architectural heritage. In the Middle Ages this monument was originally a porticoed mosque—a feature very close to that of the mosques built by Caliph al-Mutawakkil on the banks of the Tigris at Samarra. Under Malikshah, when the Seljuk power was confirmed, a domed pavilion was placed before the minaret, related to the fire temples of pre-Islamic Iran. Finally, a little later, the mosque was arranged in a layout with four iwāns set in a cross around a central court. The layout of the Iranian or Afghani house is the same as that found in the plan of the apartments of the southern palace of Lashkari Bazar, and which is moreover present in remains preserved over a distance of 10km (6 miles) between this site and the neighbouring village of Bust. A similar arrangement was also adopted in caravanserais, such as that at Ribat i-Sharaf, dated to the 12th century. From now on, regionalism was to feature clearly everywhere.

More intensive and precise research may lead further in the discovery of regional peculiarities. Whereas the design of the Spanish and Moroccan house stems from a single overall element, the part played by a given material (cedar in Morocco) or by slight variations in size or proportions (southern Morocco seems to have much larger houses) makes it possible to discern other local features: a provincialism is perceptible today which will surely be confirmed by future research.

Group of rooms with patio at Qasr al-Hayr al-Sharqui, Syria (left),
House at Fustat, Egypt (centre),
House at Qasr al-Saghir, Morocco, 12th century (right)

Each period of Islam and each region of the empire developed its own tradition of the private house. The Syrian house of the Umayyad type (left) was succeeded by the model shown here in the centre, a 19th century example at Fustat. This Abbasid model, first known in the Mesopotamian world, underwent a rapid expansion in the southern Mediterranean. The Umayyad apartment (*bayt*) yielded to the "Iranian" *bayt*. The Hispano-Maghreb world had its own type—a hall with alcoves arranged round a central court.

	characteristic rooms		other rooms, covered areas
	exposed parts	- - - - extent of existing house	●●●●●● extent of patio ensemble

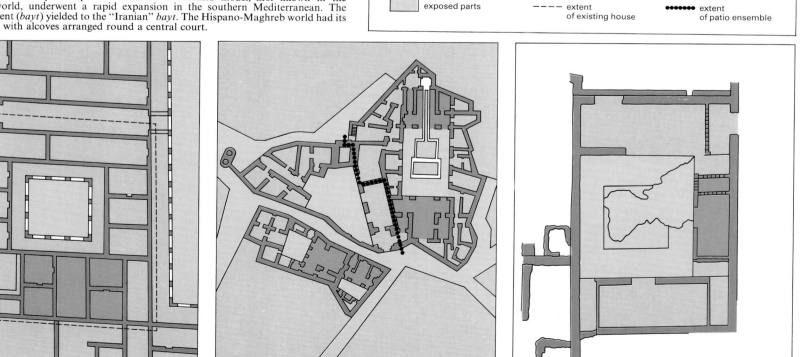

Palace at Belyunech (Morocco), above, and 17th century house at Fez (Morocco), left

These two buildings represent the beginning and end of what is generally known as the Hispano-Maghreb tradition. Belyunech marks the first architectural exchange between Morocco and al-Andalus, the first Andalusian-type monument erected in Morocco, near Ceuta. The view of the house at Fez shows the extent to which Morocco, after the taking of Granada and the expulsion of the Moors from Spain, was able to appropriate this tradition. This house is of the same type as the 12th-century house whose plan appears at the bottom of the left-hand page. A comparatively wealthy structure, it featured galleries ornamented with plaster sculptures surrounding the court; wooden balustrades and the capping of the façades recall the part played by cedar from the neighbouring Middle Atlas in the architecture of Fez since the Middle Ages.

Mosque of Zafar, Yemen: façade of the courtyard

New regional traditions are constantly being revealed. This mosque, recently discovered by a Franco-Yemenite team, reveals, on an extraordinary elevated site, the hitherto almost unknown medieval art of *Arabia felix*. Particularly striking is the quality of the lavish and extremely rich ornament which decorates not only the prayer hall and its ceilings, but also the external façades. Moreover, the form of the arches suggests that this Arabian region of Islam sometimes sought its inspiration in Asia, in the Indo-Iranian world.

Madrasa at Bosra (Syria)

The *ribat* (monastery fortress), the khan and the *madrasa* (religious school) encouraged in every region of Islam the birth of an original type of monument. The development of the *madrasa* proceeded within a regional tradition to which the private house always gives the key. Bosra was located at a strategic position on the originally Roman road which linked Damascus to Amman in the direction of Mecca. The influence of the ancient heritage and the role played by a local material, basalt, explain the unusual architecture of the monument shown here.

Trade routes

The commercial reach of Islam extended from China to Spain, from Zanzibar to Denmark. But Islam could not tap the newly discovered riches of the Americas, the fuel for Europe's new-found energy.

Islam was strongly affected by the changes which took place in the economic life of Europe and the Mediterranean world at the end of the Middle Ages and the beginning of modern times. Islamic cities seem to have failed to share, after the 11th century, in the innovative dynamism of the towns of the Christian West. Moreover, having enjoyed maritime supremacy in the Mediterranean until the 12th century, Islam gradually lost control and after 1492 lacked an outlet to the Atlantic. As a source of wealth America now replaced the two worlds with which Islam was engaged in trade, namely Eastern Asia and Africa south of the Sahara. Archaeologists have attempted to retrace the routes—both recorded and forgotten—followed by this medieval trade, and the objects which were then in circulation.

From the Early Middle Ages, the great cities of Islam were centres of trade and manufacture. Luxurious courts created a demand for rare commodities; for example, in Baghdad and Cordoba from the 9th century, and in Cairo after 1000, the intense activity of local workshops and trade is accurately reflected in the archaeological sections of these cities' museums, with their display of coins, wood, fabrics, glass, pottery, leather, etc. But in addition to the individual items of this trade, archaeologists are beginning to be familiar with the routes which linked these areas of Islam to India, China and the Far East, as well as to Nordic countries or to Africa and the western Mediterranean.

Iraq and Iran were for many years at the centre of these routes. From Baghdad to China, caravans transporting precious woods, spices or ivory crossed Iran from west to east via Hamadan and Nishapur, then to the land beyond the river Oxus (modern Amu Darya) by way of Bukhara and Samarkand or, further south, India; caravanserais providing accommodation for these transports have been studied in Iran and in Turkey. But trade with the Far East could also follow a maritime route. For instance, it is clear that Chinese pottery arrived in the Mediterranean world by way of the Persian Gulf; interesting examples have been found in recent excavations. Paradoxically, the probable existence in Arabia of workshops producing fakes confirms the extent of the demand for Chinese pottery.

Trade with Europe explains the prosperity of cities such as Damascus, Aleppo and Baghdad, and the ports of the eastern Mediterranean such as Antioch, Tripoli, Acre and Tyre, which gave access to the ports of southern Italy. These were connected from the 10th century to Egypt, the Cairo area being itself in contact with Syria and with Spain. Numerous objects found in Italy and Spain indicate the existence of links between Islam and northern Europe: the role of the Slavonians in the 11th-century struggles at the end of the Caliphate of Cordoba is well known; Islamic coins found on the Baltic coast indicate that in the 10th century these regions were linked to the centre of the Islamic empire by trade routes from Azerbaijan, the north of the Caspian Sea and the Volga. There were also routes that connected Africa with Europe, western Islam and the provinces of the Moslem east. Africa could be reached by sea from the Euphrates valley via the Persian Gulf and the Red Sea, or by caravan from Egypt. Trans-Saharan routes served the southern coast of the western Mediterranean. From the "desert ports" in the Maghreb, the way led either towards Qairwan and Tunisia (this route is attested in the 11th century), or towards Melilla and the Moroccan coast. From Fez one route connected the centre of Morocco with the port of Badis whilst another served the ports of the Straits of Gibraltar. This coastline has recently been the subject of reconnaissance work and detailed excavations which provide good information about the maritime life of the region. Furthermore, Ifriqiyan pottery found in excavations at Tegdaoust in Mauritania confirms that, as well as gold, ivory and slaves, craft products played a part in this trade.

The development of ports

Recent research describes how the trade routes were equipped, the port being one of the most important elements. The little boats of the Early Middle Ages needed only simple anchorages from which, when necessary, the boats could be pulled out onto dry land. However, real docks were constructed at an early date, for example at Mahdia, Tunisia, in the 10th century. Throughout the later Middle Ages, towns which were also ports began to install specific equipment; at Malaga, Tangier, Badis and Honian, in Algeria, Tunis, Alexandria and on the Anatolian coast, proper ports developed, sometimes protected by large sea gates as at Salé and Honain. These installations were accompanied by one or more naval shipyards; illustrations from the 16th and 17th centuries give an idea of the original appearance of these ports and arsenals (dar al-sina'a) of Islam.

Each region of Islam had established its own version of the caravanserai, which was half hostelry, half depot: there were the Anatolian khan, the Moroccan fonduq and the Iranian ribat; although they all had a similar function, they were, so to speak, the mirror of local traditions. Urban caravanserais were sometimes designed to accommodate a colony of foreign merchants, such as the "fonduq of the French" in Tunis (which is now in course of restoration), but there were also caravanserais on the established routes, a large number of which have been found in Iran and Anatolia.

The centre of the town also constituted the commercial centre, in the south or the qaysariya, where imported goods were received. The commercial structure of towns is now a subject of archaeological study, and the work of E. Wirth has revealed how economic units moved between the centre and the outlying areas. The productive role played by these outlying districts, where khans were founded in the Middle Ages, can now be evaluated more accurately. At Aleppo, for instance, or Muslim Spain in the 13th century, manufacture involving pollution was relegated to the limit of the town walls. At about the same time, glaziers' and potters' kilns occupied the ruins of the Fatimid palace of al-Mansuriya in the suburbs of Qairwan; fragments of celadon (Chinese) ware have been discovered there, as well as a considerable local production (analysis of the material show that the same clay was used for pottery and for bricks). Trade between east and west, evidenced from the 9th century in the tiles of the mihrab of the Grand Mosque of Qairwan, appears here in all its continuity. The technique of reflected metal, imported from the East, continued in Spain well beyond the reconquest of Granada in the centres of Valencia, Manises and Paterna. From Andalusia, the technique of enamelled clay mosaics reached Portugal. However, Anatolia, which was Ottoman, remained faithful to its own techniques, using facing slabs, and developed them as far as Tunisia. J. Revault's studies of the civic architecture of Tunis clearly illustrate this final encounter between Andalusia and the East.

Ceramic items of various kinds were produced in very large numbers; a medium-sized archaeological expedition can collect up to 40,000 fragments in a month, ranging from simple water pots to water-cooler filters and the moulds used for shaping sugar loaves. Although leather and embroidery are rarely found in excavations, some interesting examples have emerged in the course of surveys. The Moroccan town of Azemmour, on the Atlantic coast, maintained until the 20th century a tradition of embroidery in a very original style, depicting large stylized birds. This was in fact an Italian embroidery adopted by Spain in the Middle Ages and brought to this place by the Moriscos who fled Spain in the 17th century; in the same way, strange similarities of techniques may be seen between those Moroccan embroideries and Palestinian work. Here as elsewhere, trade and manufacture were closely bound together.

The fortified harbour of Mahdiya, Tunisia

Islamic ships made use of most of the maritime routes in the Middle Ages, especially those in the Mediterranean. The Norman invasions, followed by pressure from the Christian crusaders, led them to fortify their coasts and even to create fortified docks such as this one, installed by the Fatimids on the peninsula on the eastern coast of Tunisia, where they had founded their first governing city in the 10th century. A special encircling wall and a chain forming a barrier across the narrows protected access into the harbour.

Plan of the caravanserai at Guilak, Iran

In addition to the Islamic sea lanes, a great many overland routes were set up. Approximately one stage distant from one another, caravanserais afforded shelter to the caravans. In these khans or fonduqs a series of rooms, stables or chambers intended for the merchants and their animals were arranged around a courtyard. A lightly fortified wall enclosed this complex, set in the countryside as shown here. An oratory was sometimes provided as well. After M. Siroux, Caravanserails d'Iran et petites constructions routières, Cairo, 1949.

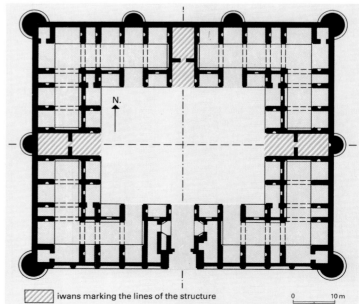

iwans marking the lines of the structure   0   10 m

Construction of a kiln for firing bricks at Rahba-Mayyadin, Syria

Reconstructions of brickmakers' or potters' kilns are frequent. Here three illustrations show how they are still built today in the part of Syria bordering the Euphrates. On the left, bricks are prepared: the fine clay is mixed with water to which a grease-removing agent has been added, and then moulded and dried in the sun. The centre illustration shows the firing chamber of a kiln covered with a dome. On the right we see the kiln almost completed, revealing the way in which the heating system is connected to the kiln. Recent research shows that kilns conceived on identical lines were being built in the late Middle Ages.

Fragments of a vase found at Belyunech, Morocco

This piece with a blue pattern of palms applied to a white background uses a technique that was known in the Hispano-Maghrebi world from the 12th century, but has been found in levels dating from the Merinid dynasty in the Early Middle Ages. It must have come from the southeast coast of the Iberian peninsula, probably from the Malaga area, providing evidence of the trade plied across the Mediterranean.

Fragment of a sculptured stucco head, al-Mansuriya-Sabra, Tunisia

The archaeological team exploring the Fatimid site of al-Mansuriya, founded in the 10th century, found the rubbish dump where the stuccowork from one of the main palaces of the royal town had been thrown. This head proves that anthropomorphic decoration did have its place in the Islamic world. The treatment of this individual's head also demonstrates a continuity with traditions derived from late antiquity to the Islamic forms in medieval Ifriqiya.

Filter of a water-cooler from the Islamic Museum in Cairo (left) and a stucco decoration discovered at al-Mansuriya-Sabra, near Qairwan, Tunisia (right)

These two pieces confirm that realistic decoration held a place in the secular art of the Islamic world. Simple objects were produced by craftsmen in Egypt, as well as pieces for palace decoration at the time of the Fatimids, who expanded from their power base of Ifriqiya but remained faithful to this type of decoration after founding Cairo. The wide range of animals that existed in their art may perhaps have been rejected by the puritan reformers who were responsible for destroying the palace of al-Mansuriya. This type of decoration became rare in the Moslem West after the 12th century.

Hydraulic techniques

Islamic civilization from the 10th century AD was characterized by a high degree of technology – especially for the storage and distribution of water (an essential of Near Eastern civilizations since the Sumerians).

To European travellers, Islam appeared as a world existing apart from the technological advances which ensured the wealth and supremacy of Europe. Islam's technological backwardness in the 19th and 20th centuries is undeniable but from the 7th to the 14th century Islam was constantly expanding, strong in the traditions of Iran and the Byzantine Mediterranean where it had settled, and had developed a remarkable technology. It was already known that in the Middle Ages Arab treatises had helped to transmit to Europe the knowledge of the Greek world. Since 1960 archaeological programmes have found evidence for the impressive development of Islam in the technical field. Hydraulics is an excellent example, together with the art of building, silk-making and the sugar industry. In a climate where heavy rainfall alternates with long dry periods, the regulation of water is indispensable. Undoubtedly Islam also knew how to reclaim marshy regions. The plain of the El Beqa'a in Lebanon is an excellent example of this for the Late Middle Ages, but such undertakings have not yet held the full attention of contemporary investigators. We shall therefore concentrate on the collection, storage and distribution of water, which are now well known.

The crucial problem that Islam had to solve in the field of hydraulics was the canalization of water without evaporation. Thus the system of underground conduits of Iranian origin, the *qanat*, spread rapidly from the east to the west of the empire. The illustration below shows how the conduit was laid out with a gentle slope detectable from the surface by the shafts used for drilling, which served as regulating shafts when the installation was in use. This type of waterwork, known in Algeria by the name of *foggara* and in the Hispano-Maghreb world as *khettara*, appeared in the extreme west of Islam in the Early Middle Ages. It is now clear that these waterworks were very commonly used in Spain from the 10th century, although it was thought for a long time that they were little developed in the western Maghreb before the foundation of Marrakesh in 1070, and then in Spain through the intermediary of the Almoravides. J. Oliver Asin has shown that at this period the Islamic town of Majrit – present-day Madrid – was supplied with water by a system of *khettaras*, many other examples of which have been found in the kingdom of Toledo, for example those of the depopulated town of Calatrava la Vieja in the province of Ciudad Real which the author has studied personally. In Old Castille, not far from the banks of the Duero, we have uncovered an ingenious contrivance in the Castle of Foncastín. A secret passage enabled the defenders to go and draw water from a khettara near the fortress.

This system, linked with a 15th century fortification, shows that in this field as well as in the sphere of defence techniques Christian Spain knew how to adopt the techniques of Al-Andalus. It may be recalled that Muslim Spain had itself developed an Iranian technique in the Umayyad period, an illustration of the scope of the technological exchanges which went on in the medieval world.

Roman influences

Nevertheless, Roman expertise, transmitted by Byzantium, remains the main source of the hydraulic techniques which inspired Islam. A Franco-Tunisian team has just resumed the study of hydraulic installations in the Qairwan region. In the 9th century, the site of the plain where the town was built held huge, generally circular basins. At first these were fed by the neighbouring wadi' which discharged into it by means of a settlement reservoir. But attempts were soon made to fill the reservoirs with purer water. To that end it was necessary to connect them with the ancient Roman catchments of Bir al-Adin, situated some 40km (25 miles) to the east of the town. Archaeologists have traced the method of collecting water by drainage channels driven into the mountain to tap a more abundant supply than was available from the springs. Researches carried out at Belyunech in Morocco have revealed a similar arrangement effected towards the end of the 12th century to supply the neighbouring town of Ceuta with water.

The origin of waterworks installed by the Muslims to ensure the transmission of water is sometimes confirmed by the literary sources. The aqueduct which links Bir al-Adin to Qairwan was repaired in the 10th century by a Fatimid sovereign. An 11th century author, al-Bakri*, relates that this caliph organized a reconnaissance in northern Tunisia to analyse the Roman waterworks and take ideas from their example. Moreover, the Islamic canal relies, in the first part of its course, on the remains of a Roman aqueduct that was already being re-used in the Byzantine period. In the Arabian texts it bears the name of the bishopric of Mems. Here Islamic hydraulics have clearly inherited the hydraulics of late antiquity.

Retention and storage of water

In addition to conduits for supplying water, a hydraulic system needs various installations for retention and storage. The reservoirs of Aden in the Yemen are well known. Surveys carried out in the two Yemeni states since 1970 have revealed others, such as those of Zafar. Near Palmyra, the "engineers" of Qasr el-Hayr al-Gharbi simply re-used the dam bequeathed from the

Roman period. But similar works of very varied size existed everywhere. The first stage of the route of the Holy War, from Marrakesh to Spain, was equipped in the 12th century with a double dam to divert the course of neighbouring rivers to reservoirs where conduits drew water through openings which had stamped ceramic mouths. There again the persistence of models inherited from the classical age is obvious, as well as the original development which Islam managed to give them.

Indeed Islam never ceased to innovate and to choose the solution best adapted to a particular problem. Agriculture made use both of vast irrigation networks and simple contrivances with a counterweight, *shadufs*, or wheels with scoops, *norias*. Irrigation networks are constantly being found in the neighbourhood of Bust and in Seistan on the boundaries of Iran and Afghanistan (11th–12th century), in Syria with the recent excavation of Qasr el-Hayr al-Sharqi, or again in Morocco at Belyunech (10th–15th century), together with the remains of the neighbouring networks of Marrakesh (12th century). As for water-raising wheels, these were sometimes integrated in urban sites with appliances of vast dimensions.

At Hama in Syria the tradition seems to have survived down to our own day. We know that the wheel which supplied the Moroccan palace of Lès Jdid from 1276 was conceived by an engineer from a Seville family trained at Toledo – a Christian town after 1085. Thus Islam, which had adopted and vitalized the ancient techniques, transmitted them to the Christian world of the peninsula, which in turn brought benefit to the Maghreb. Archaeological surveys seem to indicate that in the Late Middle Ages Islam began to give precedence to the West in this field.

Many other examples could be quoted to show the variety of techniques that Islam used, and to qualify previous ideas on the apparent technical decline which seems to mark its history. Here we shall mention only the sugar industry, where original research, carried out in Morocco, has revealed a previously unknown manufacturing centre. A skilful commercial policy led the Sadi sovereigns of the 16th century to instal a remarkable series of sugar works in the country, which have been studied by P. Berthier. At Chichaoua, Morocco, archaeological study can reveal a fact that would otherwise pass unnoticed: the establishment of a "factory" stemmed the slow decline of this town, developed by the Almoravides in the first half of the 12th century with the help of Andalusian technicians and artists. At the same time, the installation of the sugar works entailed the restoration of the water supply system.

The *qanat*, schematic diagram

Qanats (or *khettara*) seem to have originated in Iran, but they were to be found in Spain (*Al-Andalus*) from the early Middle Ages; there were some in use in Madrid at that period. They consisted of a gallery with less of a gradient than that of the water level from which they were supplied, making it possible in an area of foothills to carry water towards a country district or town in need of irrigation. Qanats can be recognized by the line of shaft openings visible on the surface. The use of a natural gradient ensured that water could be conveyed in an especially economical fashion, without any energy requirement.

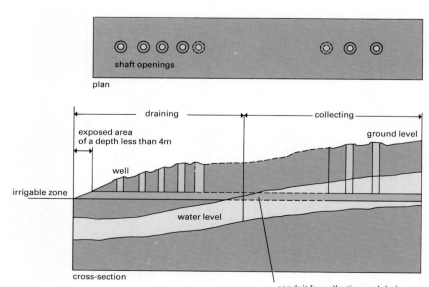

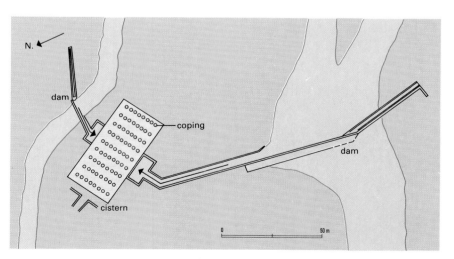

A dam and a cistern at Sidi bou Othman, Morocco

The Almohades in the 12th century established a staging post (*n'zala*) near Marrakesh. The plan shows that the course of two intermittent rivers, held back by two dams, was diverted towards a cistern in which the water was stored. Water was drawn from it via a whole series of copings (marked in blue); these copings were made of clay with an impressed pattern.

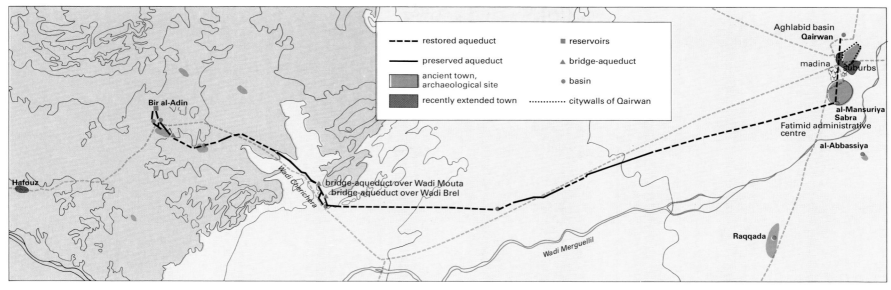

Well with a balance-beam in the region of Konya, Turkey

The well with a balance-beam (*chadouf*) is the simplest Islamic method of drawing water. A balance-beam was placed on a kind of tripod. A rope was used to tie the bucket or water-drawing receptacle to one end while a counterweight at the other assisted in hauling up the bucket. This well is near a caravanserai on the road from Konya to Beysehir.

M. Terrasse

Water-raising wheel at Hama, Syria

Islam made widespread use of water wheels fitted with a series of buckets that picked up water at the bottom of each revolution and tipped it into a higher channel or reservoir. Sometimes, in the case of the Persian wheel for example, the wheel was turned by animals. Here it is the current of the Orontes ('Asi) river that supplies the power necessary to raise the water.

M. Terrasse

Bir al-Adin aqueduct, Qairwan area, Tunisia

The Romans and the Byzantines had built an aqueduct to supply water to one of the mountainous areas 40km (25 miles) away from present-day Qairwan. Possibly in the 9th century, and certainly by the 10th century, the Moslem emirs in charge of the town extended it to carry water to the huge "Aghlabid reservoirs" which had previously collected water from the Merguellil wadi. In the 10th century the Fatimids, who founded the royal city of al-Mansuriya, brought the aqueduct through their palaces, so controlling Qairwan's water supply.

Rural estates and water supply at Belyunech, Morocco

Running through all these properties is a hydraulic system which had been installed on the side of a *thalweg*: this carried spring water to a point where boats anchored, received the water, and conveyed it to the neighbouring town of Ceuta. A private house can be seen to the west of the conduit which serves a watermill at each level of the downward slope.

To the east of the water conduit a large country house supplied with running water extends down the slope. To the southwest, a double door led either to an irrigated garden and a sitting room or, by means of a long ramp, to the centre of the house at a lower level; a group of buildings with a patio and a pool and a fountain-basin can be seen, and adjoining them to the south a private bath. Another ramp with conduits running alongside it led from this first group towards another cluster of buildings overlooking it to the east: three rooms frame a long marble-decorated pool fed from a nearby distribution reservoir; a small private chapel was near them.

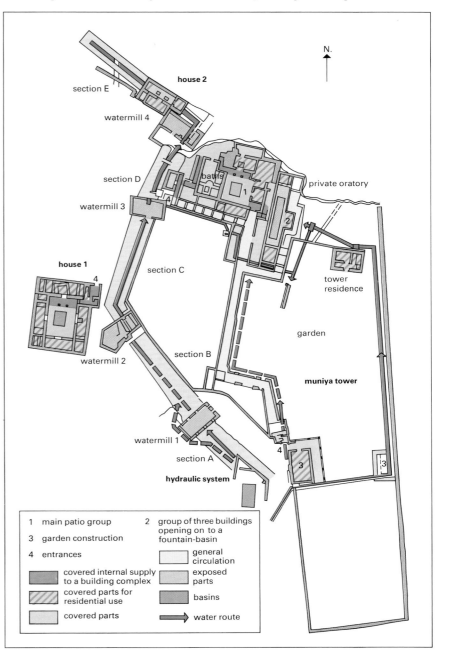

Fortifications and fortified sites

From Afghanistan to Morocco, study of military architecture shows that here too Islam was an innovator, from whom Christianity was quick to borrow.

The study of Islamic fortified sites began in the 19th century, for it coincided with the tastes of a period when the "fortified castle" and the Middle Ages were in general favour. But because Islam covered an enormous area, these works were limited to scattered and isolated sites; due to lack of funds, each researcher had to be satisfied with a particular region. Fortification connected with the crusades was analysed first. It was then abandoned for a time, but has once again captured the interest of researchers, from a new point of view, for its place in the history of trade between provinces or civilizations. The castles discovered early in Spain and the Maghreb also continue to be studied, as do those in Afghanistan. They are one of the most convenient guides for estimating concentrations of population, and analysing the economy of the Islamic lands. A similar series of data thus serves two types of archaeological projects successively; but today more attention is placed on the comparative study of regional styles than on the celebration of the castle.

Fortified sites and fortifications are generally associated with frontier zones. These were often confused in the history of Islam with the zones of the Holy War (*jihad*). This military duty incumbent on the faithful brought about an original form of architecture, the *ribat*, which contributed to the defence of *dar al-islam*, the land of Islam. The Tunisian coast, which had to be protected from Norman attacks, contained many examples. In a recent thesis, complementing A. Lezine's work on Sousse, M. Rumah has shown that this town maintained a fortress of oblong plan, flanked by round towers at the corners and in the middle of the sides. The building was orientated, its entrance being in the centre of the frontage which was turned towards Mecca. A tower in the form of a truncated cone on a square base, simultaneously a watchtower and a minaret, occupied the east corner. This small fort provided the defenders of the faith with two levels of cells arranged around a central porticoed court and, on the first floor, an oratory, the mihrab of which corresponded to the structure at the front of the entrance. On the level of the cultivated terraces, a guiding mark indicated the direction of prayer for the combattants. A type of small fortification common in the Late Empire, the *castellum*, continued to be adapted to the needs of the new civilization.

But this model had many variations. According to the thesis of B. Chabbouh, various studies carried out during restoration work provide information on its evolution in Tunis. On the coast, smaller fortifications, the *Mahrès*, were built to reinforce the defence network. In Spain recent surveys* have concentrated on the towers which completed the system: the *torres atalayas* that the Christians used in their turn. The *ribat* was a new structural type, but marked no break with the traditions preceding the Islamic conquest. South of Sfax, the *ribat* of Yunga undoubtedly made use of a Byzantine installation. A large variety of types

appeared. At Monastir the *ribat*, which was constantly enlarged, became a vast stronghold adjoined by other smaller ribats, one of them for the women.

It appears that the fortification of frontiers or zones threatened by the Christians was often connected with the repopulation and development of a country. The *hisn*, a fortress of large dimensions, held the country against the enemy. If necessary, it offered a refuge to the neighbouring farmers and, once the Christian threat was averted, remained as a sign of the prince's domination over the region. Surveys by M. Terrasse have helped to show that Al-Andalus had such edifices at all periods. Excavations still going on under the direction of J. Zoraya have revived the interest taken in the great fortified hall of Gormaz, erected in the 10th century on the frontier near the Duero in Old Castille. Long curtain walls protected the crest of the spur of an austere stone fortification flanked by towers projecting only slightly. A small cistern was installed there in the 10th century, when Gormaz was on the frontier. It was supplied with a larger reservoir at the end of the Middle Ages. The fortress was therefore still a living structure in the Christian age. It can be compared to Montalban, a splendid castle in the Toledo region. This site was almost deserted in times of peace; when King John II took refuge there in 1420, only two guards made up the whole garrison. This powerful fortification of Islamic tradition served as a refuge for the internal struggles of the kingdom of Castille when it reverted to the Christians and was no longer threatened by an Islamic invasion.

The impact of the crusades

In the east as in the west, the crusades stimulated an abundant and remarkable system of fortifications. The crusader castles of Syria and Lebanon were studied between the two world wars; recent work has resumed on the study of Islamic fortresses in the Ayyubid period; and in the course of excavation at the town of Rahba, M. Paillet, an architect, studied its fortress. Other constructions on the banks of the Euphrates, such as Qal'at Nadjm, have been restored. Many sites in Spain and Portugal reveal the same intensive work of fortification, both at Calatrava la Nueva, seat of the order of the same name, and at all the Andalusian fortresses near the *frontera*. The most recent research has shown that technical advances and intense technological exchanges developed constantly in the very places where Islam and Christianity confronted each other. From the 10th to the 14th century Islam stayed appreciably ahead of the Christian world; conversely it drew inspiration from European discoveries from the 15th century.

In this connection, the development of gates and adjoining structures, contemporary in Islam with the 11th and 12th century Sunnite reaction, deserves attention. Everywhere, the access corridor to the gates was extended and its defences strengthened. The gate of the citadel of Aleppo with its numerous ambush points

matches the winding layout and exposed bays of the Almohade gates of Morocco and Spain. While crusader castles and Ayyubid fortifications developed in the east, Castille, champion of the crusades, was soon showing the influence of the latest developments in Islamic defensive techniques in the west. In the 12th century the latter invented a tower built in front of the wall and connected with it by an arch, the *torre albarrana*. This remarkable advance in adjoining structures was immediately taken up in Christian territory, appearing at sites in New Castille, Talavera, Escalona and Montalban, with the tower forming a kind of keep. Thus connections are revealed everywhere and at all periods. Within the Islamic world one is struck by the similarity of Afghan fortresses to the "qasbas" of south Morocco. This comparative study of such widely separated regions and worlds is, one of the most reliable of recent contributions from Islamic military archaeology.

Fortifications or residences?

At the same time, the role of fortification in history is being defined more accurately. A route from Toledo towards Madrid and the upper frontier of Al-Andalus was fortified from the 9th century, following the valleys. Towns and staging posts made use of natural defences: Toledo was a closed-off spur, with many fortresses erected on outlying hillocks. Then, from the 12th century, peace returned. Towns abandoned elevated positions for flat country in the centre of wheat- or vine-growing regions where water was easier to distribute.

An improved study of the context has restored to their rightful place the Umayyad "castles" of the Syrian provinces from 660 to 750. There fortification was not, as at Anjar, simply to proclaim the rank of the owner, as we shall see further on in connection with the two Qasr el-Hair sites. The location of these structures on sites that were difficult to defend and surrounded by installations for developing the territory, has put in question earlier theories interpreting them as desert castles for nostalgic nomads. In Iraq, work sponsored by the directorate of antiquities has shown that the fortress of Ukhaidir (10th century) was the centre of an important zone with traces of habitation sites. So it is the history of a population and a region that these monuments actually reveal.

Thus a new military archaeology has gradually developed. Starting from regional studies, a genuine classification of types has been established, confirming both the infinite variety and the strange similarities of constructions peculiar to Islam. The comparison of military architecture with other archaeological material yielded by the sites gives them an entirely different significance. Picturesque features no doubt, sometimes regarded as indicating the undeniable technical qualities of medieval and modern master-builders, these structures can now help archaeologists to retrace a history which has a thoroughly global quality.

Gate of the citadel of Aleppo, Syria (left), Bab al-Ronah, Rabat, Morocco (right)

These two illustrations show that the period of the crusades, which was also in the Islamic world the period of Sunnite fundamentalism, can be seen as a time of considerable development in building fortifications. The stone gate of the Aleppo citadel is a formidable structure; inside the bastion, the extension of the entrance corridor, containing portcullises and ambush points, expresses in a Syrian version the same objectives as are found at the main gate into Rabat which the Almohades established in Morocco at about the end of the 12th century: the same difficult approach, with numerous bends and corners, confronted attacking forces. An exposed bay also enabled defenders to fire down from the terraces of the building.

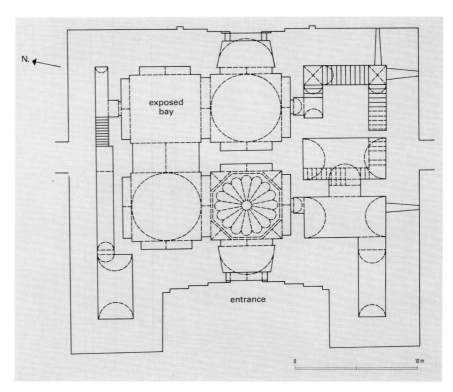

From Marrakesh to Seville: an empire on two coasts

7th century, conquest of the Iberian peninsula by Islam.
10th century, conflict between Umayyads and Fatimids in western Maghreb:
– expeditions from the two sides follow each other at Fez;
– expression of a local art, the *minbar* of the great mosque of the Andalusians commissioned by the Fatimids and re-worked by the Umayyads is the product of a single workshop;
– in Morocco the Andalusians fortify Tangier, Ceuta and Melilla.
11th century, the Mediterranean, an "Islamic lake". Port sites develop, for instance Malaga.
1085-1492, from Toledo to Granada, the advance of the Christian reconquest.
12th century, intervention of Maghrebi peoples in Spain; Almoravides and Almohades:
– Andalusian art penetrates Morocco;
– from Marrakesh to Seville: a major trade route.
13th century, advance of Christian reconquest in Andalusia:
– 1212, Las Navas de Tolosa; 1236, Cordoba retaken; 1248, Seville falls;
– 1260, Castille expedition against Salé in Morocco.
13th-14th centuries, Moroccan intervention in Andalusia and resistance of Granada;
– foundation of al-Biniya, Merinid city near Algeciras;
– development of Granada.
15th and 16th centuries, European bridgeheads on the Moroccan coast: Tangier, Qasr al-Saghir, Ceuta, Velez de la Gomera, Arzila, Safi, then Mazagan (al-Jadida).

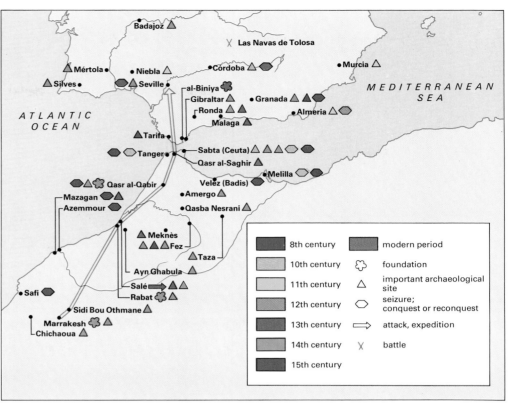

Fortress in the Bamyan region, Afghanistan

The city of Bamyan is mainly famous for its Buddhas, but we should not forget the region's debt to its Islamic period. In addition to the key sites – Ghazni, Herat, Balkh – many other remains are beginning to be explored. To the northeast of the town this fortress, displays, interesting similarities with other buildings of the Islamic world.

Anatolian fortress at Harput, Turkey (right)

Anatolia, which was converted to Islam towards the end of the 11th century owes to the Byzantine period an architectural tradition that can be recognized, for example in its mosques, mingled with eastern additions. But it also preserves an important series of fortifications which have for the most part not yet been studied. The Artuqid town of Harput was the scene of fine building work during the 12th century, showing the extent to which eastern Anatolia developed strong stone fortifications.

Vascos citadel, Spain

The motive for the foundation of this town, situated on the banks of a tributary of the Tagus, west of Toledo, is still uncertain. It may have been a refuge for Nefzo Berbers, or perhaps a mining town. The walled city (*madina*) was overlooked by a citadel (*qasba*). The medium height of the building's walls, occasionally broken by towers which protrude slightly, is typical of the Toledo region. These buildings can be dated to the 9th and 10th centuries.

Montalban castle, Spain (below)

Islamic influences continued to affect Spanish architecture long after Spain had been won back by the Christians. The part of the kingdom of Toledo, reconquered c.1085, where this castle stands, suffered no Muslim incursions after the end of the 12th century. Yet this huge walled refuge, built in the 14th century, has two towers jutting out from the walls, *torres albarranas*, a concept belonging to Almohade fortification. These towers enabled the wall and advanced wall to be defended by a single flanking system; a new advanced wall and, in the foreground, defences intended to protect a water source, show that the site had been adapted to a plan of defence based on firearms. But the purpose of the two *torres albarranas* is evident: that on the left protected the gate, while that on the right was an Islamic-style keep. They are a reminder of the paradoxical fact that, in the very places where Islam and Christianity met as enemies, a long tradition of exchange of ideas was established.

Archaeology and the Islamic garden

Deriving both from religious and from secular inspiration, the Islamic garden reflects spiritual themes and refined sensuality—the latter being perhaps one of the legacies of classical civilization.

A manuscript preserved in the Library of the Escorial, appended to an account of the ransoming of Christian captives, contains a superb view of the Qasba—the palace city adjoining Marrakesh—as it was in the 16th century in the time of the Saadi dynasty. Our own reaction to such a document reflects the wonder that these pleasure gardens inspired in the past, where coolness and fragrance contrasted with the dry heat of the surrounding country. But what was the true nature of these gardens, which have most often disappeared today from their depopulated sites? Were they a normal feature of life, an expression of an aesthetic style restricted to a privileged few, a manifestation of nature in the heart of residential architecture? Archaeology in the last decade has given us a better knowledge of the subject through the discovery of several forgotten gardens.

But perhaps the word itself recalls the actual role of the garden in the Islamic world. *Djanna* in Arabic, or *firdaws* in Persian—the latter from the Greek παράδεισος—evokes paradise, whether it be, as in ancient Arabic poetry, the paradise of the fertile valley as opposed to the desert or, as in the Prophet's home, of an enclosed space. Thus two concepts of the garden assert themselves, the open and the closed garden, as do two conceptions of the role of the garden. On the one hand it is associated, as the most exalted part of paradise, with three themes: light of everlasting brilliance, water flowing from the four rivers of paradise, and nature represented by hills, valleys and orchards. On the other hand, it was the *djanna* of the poets, where the word was regarded as of Christian origin and connected with the theme of the vine. The garden is no doubt represented in the mosaics of the Great Mosque of Damascus only because it is the evocation of paradise. As an inspiration to the miniaturists who, following the poets, depicted the garden for its own sake or as the background for diversions, it obviously carries a more secular connotation.

The examination of ancient gardens

The most ancient gardens of Islam were explored at a comparatively early date, when the Ummayyad "desert castles" of Syria were studied. But they continue to be examined, as seen in the excavations of Oleg Grabar at Qasr al-Hayr al-Sharqi, which usefully complement the earlier discoveries of D. Schlumberger at Qasr al-Hayr al-Gharbi and R.W. Hamilton at Khirbat al-Mafjar. Thus we have an idea of the various types of garden, from natural spaces recreated, irrigated and cultivated over quite large areas—even when the property was enclosed by walls—to orchards and pleasure gardens which developed near residential buildings, as at Khirbat al-Mafjar. These gardens, which needed vast sup-

plies of water for their irrigation and for the fountains which embellished them, were in a way the reward for the great landowner who had thus pursued a policy of enhancing the value of his land.

The layout of a garden often reveals itself to the archaeologist by its water-courses. Nearly all the palaces known from the Abbasid Middle Ages possessed gardens whose sites have been rediscovered. At Samarra, they extended from the most beautiful halls of the palace to the banks of the Tigris; at Ukhaidir archaeologists have traced out enclosed gardens. The Tunisian excavations of Raqqada (9th–11th century) and al-Mansuriya (10th century) show that the gardens must have adjoined enormous ornamental lakes. In 10th century Muslim Andalusia the excavations of Madinat al-Zahra, the royal town near Cordova, provide unusually accurate information. Gardens there have been found composed of four sunken flowerbeds with a cruciform plan. The arrangement of the sectors of these gardens made it easy to water them; it was only necessary to instal in the alleys and on the periphery of the layout small channels from which water flowed easily towards the vegetation. These gardens were not made for walking through. The visitor went round the outside and, looking down on the flower beds, enjoyed the beauty of the colours, the coolness, and the scent of the flowers.

Several recent field sites confirm and complement these discoveries. When the Almoravides had to surrender the seat of their power at Marrakesh to the Almohades in the 12th century, a mosque, the first Kutubiya, partly covered a destroyed residential quarter. The excavations have revealed a garden of just a few square metres with a cruciform plan and an ornamental lake. So even the most humble dwellings had gardens. It was this tradition which was developed on a quite different scale by 12th century Almohade palaces reconstructed in the 16th century by the Saadi and depicted in documents preserved in the Escorial. In this large type of palace, a courtyard, 135m long and 110m wide (445 × 363ft), contained below ground level no less than four orchards planted with orange trees, four ornamental ponds, and pavilions copied from the 14th-century Alhambra. Alleys lined with coloured *zellijs* (enamelled clay mosaics) gave order to this composition. Another garden was situated outside the palace, between it and the surrounding wall. This type of garden was completely made up of large planted spaces, arranged on the outside; examples dating from the 18th century have been found at Meknes. There is also one at Marrakesh, at the Menara, which has a large pond adorned by a pavilion. This oriental theme transmitted via Qairwan, ended up there by way of Algeria, where it inspired the builders of medieval towns such as Qalaa.

Recent studies have revealed similar layouts at the palaces of Fez Jdid, founded by the Merinids in 1276, but the most extraordinary examples remain those of the Alhambra and the Generalife, which dominate the town of Granada. These princely gardens, more than any others, however famous, have contributed to popularizing an entirely false image of the Islamic garden. Indeed we owe these much admired gardens in part to the Christian conquerors of the Alhambra and above all to the Romantics who restored their ruins. In the Alhambra, only the Myrtle Court, with two very elongated flower beds lining the long sides of a rectangular pond, is still in its original state. The Court of Lions was paved like an Islamic cloister. Its sunken flower beds separated by the 11th century lion fountain, have been restored. As regards the Generalife, the fire of 1958 made it possible to excavate the Patio del Acequia and rediscover, in addition to the cruciform plan and the sunken flower beds, the "pots" which indicate the existence of trees. So we are thoroughly familiar with the structure of an internal garden.

During the excavations of Granada and Belyunech (Morocco), the open gardens of the rural *munyas*, Islamic equivalents of the Roman *villae*, were also explored. At the munya of the Tower of Belyunech, two gardens made up the patio gardens. New flotation techniques enable us to form an accurate idea of what was planted: olive trees, fruit trees and aromatic plants. The structures of these properties correspond to those described by a contemporary writer on agriculture, Ibn Luyun. Archaeology and textual study complement each other perfectly in this case.

It is of course regrettable that Asian gardens matching those of Granada and Marrakesh have not been the subject of recent studies. It is known that the funerary city of Gazurgha near Herat in Afghanistan had marvellous gardens in the Timurid Middle Ages. Master landscapists resumed an existing tradition from the 12th century in the palaces of Ghazna and Lashkari Bazar. In the Safawid period, the royal palace of Isfahan or the gardens adjoining the Palace of the Forty Columns confirm that this tradition has stayed alive from the 17th century to our own day. We find it in Mogul India in the Taj Mahal, at Delhi and Lahore, and reflected in the princely complexes of Topkapi Serai at Istanbul or in the small Ottoman palaces of the urban area of Tunis. Lastly floral decorations which developed in all periods on ceramics, ivories and bronzes, and in living rooms and mosques, certainly seem to indicate an extension of the garden theme. Thus archaeology confirms that the Muslims had a taste for a constantly remodelled perception of nature, the search for refined pleasures striving with the more spiritual images that lie at the origin of the *firdaws*.

New Delhi, India. Tomb of Safdar Gang

This monument recalls the Islamic gardens of the modern period of Safavid Iran and Mogul India. A line perpendicular to the monument's façade organizes the symmetrical arrangement of building and gardens. It is reminiscent of the Taj Mahal at Agra, where the cruciform layout suggests the four rivers of Paradise.

The Generalife, Granada: bird's-eye view of the palace

Not far from the Nasrid Alhambra (14th century), the Generalife dominates Granada. This small palace is built amid gardens whose cruciform patio has as its longitudinal axis the *Acequia real* (channel supplying water) and is situated in the middle of vast walled gardens; it was for a long time the only extant example of the *muniya*. Service patios—kitchens, stables and a guest house—adjoined the central court.

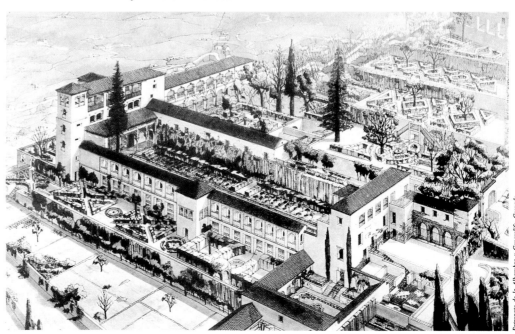

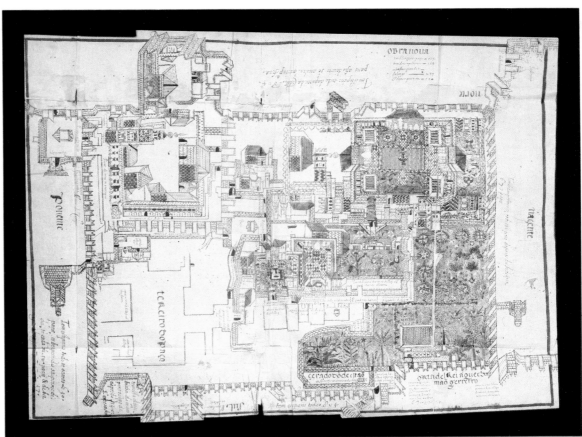

The Marrakesh qasba (right and below) and view of the Court of the Lions in the Alhambra, Granada (above)

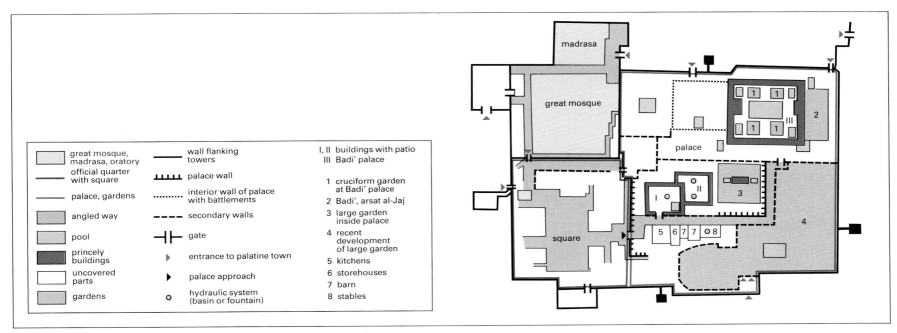

great mosque, madrasa, oratory

official quarter with square

palace, gardens

angled way

pool

princely buildings

uncovered parts

gardens

wall flanking towers

palace wall

interior wall of palace with battlements

secondary walls

gate

entrance to palatine town

palace approach

hydraulic system (basin or fountain)

I, II buildings with patio
III Badi' palace

1 cruciform garden at Badi' palace
2 Badi', arsat al-Jaj
3 large garden inside palace
4 recent development of large garden
5 kitchens
6 storehouses
7 barn
8 stables

The ancient descriptions or, better still, illustrative documents (top, right) preserved in the archives of the Escorial as an appendix to a report on the ransom of prisoners, provide valuable information about Islamic palaces and their gardens. In this case, it concerns a Moroccan royal Almohade town, the qasba of Marrakesh (12th century). The original great mosque is visible to the northwest in the drawing. A Merinid madrasa (institute of learning) adjoins it to the north. The whole palatine city was transformed in the 16th century when the Saadians once again made Marakesh the seat of Moroccan power. Here we see it as it was in 1585.

A square and an official quarter which had just been renovated (to the southwest) preceded the actual palaces. A gate gave access to the angled way which served the main group of buildings. Two patios with pools and gardens were installed in front of the first large enclosed garden, which was connected with the main palace by a monumental double staircase and an arcade. It will be noted that a small edifice opened on to a basin as in the Partal at Granada.

The Badi' to the northeast is the best example of gardens and basins associated with pavilions following the model of the Alhambra, where a sunken cruciform garden was delineated by water channels, the centre of which was marked by the Fountain of Lions. The layout described by the drawing and its caption adapts the Nasrid element to the scale and traditions which Marrakesh apparently owes to its Almohade period. Two large gardens completed the layout of this palace

town to the east of the Badi' and to the southeast. The reproduction of these gardens with their basins and pavilions gives us a faithful reflection of the Hispano-Maghreb tradition. They occupied as much as one-third of the town.

Belyunech, Morocco

The plan of this palace, which is the oldest in Morocco and was built c.1000, is still unpublished. A gate, enlarged by an addition made during alterations, gave access to a court lined to east and west with porticoes fronting the state halls. The rooms to the east opened on to a sunken garden watered by a small channel. Visible to the west of the monument is a group of service buildings consisting of simple rooms laid out around a second court. An ingenious installation, already known from a 15th century text, supplied water to all parts of the palace. It will be noted that all these palaces and gardens are contained within "concrete" enclosures, made of stony earth and lime fixed in casings, with a number of massive oblong towers reinforced by albarrana towers, which communicated with the outside world by typically Almohade gates with multiple bends.

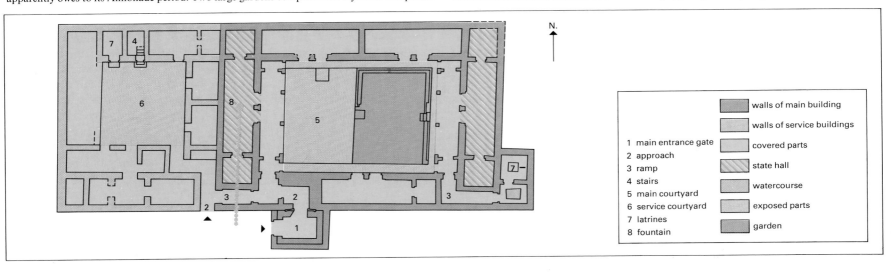

1 main entrance gate
2 approach
3 ramp
4 stairs
5 main courtyard
6 service courtyard
7 latrines
8 fountain

walls of main building

walls of service buildings

covered parts

state hall

watercourse

exposed parts

garden

The Near East:
the archaeological background

It is ironic that although archaeology started with the Bible as its guiding
text in the middle 19th century, within decades it had opened up a very
different view of the chronology of the ancient Near Eastern Bible lands.
Modern dating techniques, combining carbon-14 measurement with tree-ring
chronology (dendrochronology) has pushed dates back even further.

In 1864, four years after Boucher de Perthes's* *Antiquités celtiques et antediluviennes* had proposed a previously unimagined antiquity for mankind, the Jordan valley was explored by the Duke of Luynes with E. Lartet, and the first Near Eastern Paleolithic sites were disclosed at Jiita, Ras el Kelb, Ras Beirut, Adlun, and Hananouiyeh. Two years, later, H.B. Tristram referred to the presence of worked flint tools at Ras Beirut in his short guide for the Palestine Exploration Society. Locally based researchers, who now took up the work started by visiting Europeans, were centred on the higher education colleges opened in Beirut by various missions. From 1890 to 1900, the Swiss Jesuit Father Zumoffen explored the Lebanese caves of Antélias, Nahr el Joz, Adlun and Harajel, and also visited Ras Beirut. At about the same time, the German geologist von Heidenstamm, who was working for the American University and for the water authorities of the town of Beirut, rediscovered Ras el Kelb (1902).

Western influence
The efforts of these pioneers bore fruit after World War I, when so-called mandates were established by European powers in Iraq, Syria, Lebanon and Palestine, and western influence was more or less directly felt in Turkey, Iran and Egypt. Departments of antiquity were then formed to provide prehistoric research with an official framework. Thus the foundations for the study of prehistory in the Near East were laid during these years from 1920 to 1937.

In Palestine, the existence of the British mandate greatly facilitated the work of various archaeologists. The arrival in 1928 of D. Garrod from Cambridge University, and R. Neuville, French Consul in Jerusalem, led to the rapid development of prehistoric studies, with Garrod's systematic excavation on Mount Carmel (El Wad, Tabun, Kebarah), which had already been explored by F. Turville Petre in 1925–26. These excavations supplied researchers with the best stratigraphical foundations, while Neuville's work, published in 1943 and based mainly on his 1931–33 excavations in the desert caves of Abu Sif and Erq el Ahmar, Judaea, supplied a coherent chronology of the Upper Paleolithic in Palestine. Neuville's six phases provided a simple classification that remained operative until about 1970. From 1930 to 1933 the work of the German prehistorian A. Rust at Yabroud, Syria, also brought to light original material marking the transition between the Acheulian period of early man, *Homo erectus*, and the Middle Paleolithic, the so-called "Yabroudian" and "Pre-Aurignacian" periods, but his work was not published until 1951.

Essentially established between 1927 and 1937, the sequence of Paleolithic industries determined by Garrod, Neuville and Rust became the standard model for the Levant, with Late Acheulian forms yielding to those of the Yabroudian, Pre-Aurignacian or Amoudian. Then a Levallois-Mousterian* technique was identified, with elongated points and, later, wide oval blades struck from a core with a wide base. Classification of tools from the Upper Paleolithic followed with a transitional period named the Emirean* after the Emireh grotto excavated by Turville Petre in 1925. After this came a tool industry resembling the European Aurignacian, the Antelian, ending with the microlithic (small-bladed tools) industries of the Natufian and the Kebarian. The Lower Paleolithic was less well known, despite the excavations carried out by Neuville at Umn Katafa in 1928–32 and 1949, and by Stekelis at Gesher Benot Ya'agov in 1936 (published in 1960). As for the Neolithic, Father Vincent had declared that it did not exist in the Near East, and that the chronology should progress from the Upper Paleolithic directly to the

Chalcolithic. This doctrine prevailed, although the excavations carried out by Garstang at Jericho in 1930–36 had already uncovered pre-pottery levels, indicative of a Neolithic culture.

At the same time, prehistoric studies of eastern provinces began with Garrod's expedition to Zarzi and Hazar Merd, Iran, in 1928. There he identified a Mousterian-type tool industry in the Zagros mountains—the "Zagros Mousterian"—that differed from the Levallois-Mousterian of the Levant, and a Zarzian* dated to the end of the Paleolithic.

The prehistoric archaeology of the area entered a new stage just before World War II, with J.F. Ewing's excavation at Ksar Akil, Lebanon, in 1937. This was a rock shelter containing one of the most complete sequences of the Near East, from the end of the Middle Paleolithic through the whole of the Upper Paleolithic. Ewing's fieldwork, although only published in part, constitutes important material evidence. In the same year, the discovery of the sites at Dhobai (Jordan), by D. Kirkbride, V. Seton-Williams and J. Waechter, marked the beginning of desert excavation and the uncovering of a new ecological region.

Investigating the Neolithic
As for the Neolithic, the excavation of the great *tells* (manmade mounds) such as Mersin (1936–39), Tarsus (1937–38) and Tepe Gawra (1932–39), and the reopening of Tell Halaf (1939) indicated the complexity of this period. English-speaking authorities now began the practice of terming "Chalcolithic" (copper-stone) any culture with painted pottery, whether or not it also used metal. Finally, with the exploration of the *tells* of the plain of Antioch by R. Braidwood, of the University of Chicago's Oriental Institute, the first multidisciplinary expedition took place, bringing together in the field specialists on pottery, flints, buildings and wildlife.

World War II precluded major archaeological campaigns, but did not stop work altogether, with local residents carrying on the continuity: M. Stekelis worked at Abu Usba and Iraq el Baroud in Palestine, Father Bergy on the rock shelter in Lebanon that was named after him, J. Haller at Abu Halka and Chekka, also in Lebanon, and at Amrit, Syria, and finally M. Senyürek at Altin Dere near Antioch.

The post-war years saw a period of intensive but dispersed activity. In Turkey, E. Bostanci discovered Dülük near Antioch, and K. Kökten excavated in the cave of Kara'in. J.F. Ewing recommenced work at Ksar Akil and Bergy in Lebanon; M. Stekelis discovered Acheulian (*Homo erectus*) remains at Rephaim Beqaa near Jerusalem; H.E. Wright Jr and B. Howe carried out a probe, also into the Acheulian period, at Barda Balka in Iraq; and C. Coon, working from Iraq to Syria, explored the caves of Belt, Hotu, Bisitun, Khunik, and Jerf Ajla. Newcomers who now joined in the work included H. Fleisch in Lebanon, with his remarkable methodology and rare knowledge of geology, and F. Debono in Egypt. In Iraq, the excavations at Hassuna (1943–44), Eridu (1946–48), and Jarmo (1948–51) led to a preliminary classification of the ancient civilizations of Mesopotamia, which were then thought of as in an almost linear succession of Hassuna*, Samarra*, Halaf* and 'Ubaid*.

The application of modern techniques
The modern approach to prehistory began in the 1950s with the introduction of archaeometry* and an awareness of the importance of spatial archaeology. In fact, it was at about this time that radiometric dating methods, measuring

F. Valla

The cave of Tabun

The cave of Tabun is situated in the Wadi Maghara, a gully on Mount Carmel, and is part of an extraordinary group. The Mount Carmel range, covering several square miles, consists of numerous layers, under excavation since 1925, which supply our basic information on the prehistoric Near East: Abu Usba, Emireh, Iraq el Barud, Kebarah, Nahal Oren, Sheikh Soliman, Skhul, Tabun, Tirat Carmel and El Wad. On the basis of the finds at Tabun, El Wad, Emireh and Kebarah, D. Garrod, together with Rene Neuville, identified a series of Paleolithic cultures, from the Upper Acheulian to the Natufian, all applicable to an area ranging from the Gâvur Dağlari mountains in Turkey to Mount Sinai. No other site in the Near East is so representative of the work carried out over the past 60 years in the field of prehistory.

natural radiation loss in organic objects, came into operation, and the disposition of archaeological remains over a wide area became of greater interest. Maps of sites that showed exactly where the material had been found had previously been few. By contrast, surveys carried out after the war give us today a good idea of the territory occupied by various civilizations. From 1948 to 1955, R. Braidwood applied the C^{14} dating methods; he also worked on several sites in the hills bordering the "Fertile Crescent" to test the theories advanced by G. Childe on how the economy of food production, which marked the transition from the Paleolithic to the Neolithic, may have begun. Meanwhile, the lower levels of the great classic excavations, such as Dunand's at Byblos in the Lebanon, or Schaeffer's and de Cottenson's at Ras Shamra in Syria, yielded Neolithic levels. Following Braidwood's examples, concerted operations were organized, with precise aims and staffed by organized teams. Collections without an overall plan, or speculative excavations by isolated individuals, became things of the past.

To verify the Yabroudian period, in 1958–63 D. Garrod excavated the deposits at Adlun in the Lebanon; Tokyo University initiated a vast programme which led to the excavations at Hamud in 1961, the systematic exploration of Syria and Lebanon in 1967, the fieldwork at Keoue, Lebanon, in 1970, and at Duara and the Syrian basin of Palmyra in 1970–74. W.J. van Liere, a pedologist (soil expert) working with the FAO (Food and Agriculture Organization) also surveyed the entire Syrian territory between 1956 and 1970. To him we owe important discoveries, such as that of a Middle Acheulian occupation at Latamne (excavated by D. Clark in 1964–65) and of the Neolithic sites of Ramad and Bukras. Detailed excavations, planned to take 15–20 years, were started in the Lebanon, with F. Hours' work at Jiita in 1964–75, and J. Tixier's at Ksar Akil in 1969–75. R. Solecki returned to Yabroud in Syria, when he verified the sequences of layers from 1963–1965, and made several probes in the cave of Nahr Ibrahim in the Lebanon, 1969–73.

In Iran, fieldwork included R. Braidwood's work at Warwasi in 1959, and C.M. Burney's at Ali Tappeh in 1962, at Ke Aram in 1963, and at Barde Spid and Humian in 1965. F. Hole and K. Flannery were at Ali Kosh, Khuzistan, in 1961, then at Ghamari and Kunji in 1965; and in the same year P. Smith was working at Ghar i Khar. Meanwhile, R. Solecki worked at Shanidar and Zawi Chemi, Iraq, from 1951 to 1960, and J. Oates at Choga Mami (1967–68). In Turkey, a series of surveys has led to the excavation of the Neolithic sites of Hacilar (1957–60), and Çatal Hüyük (1961–65), carried out by J. Mellaart, as well as work at Can Hasan by D. French, and to the research undertaken by R. Braidwood and H. Cambel at Çayönü, where fieldwork has continued intermittently from 1964 to the present.

However, the most considerable work has been carried out in Israel, first by O. Bar Yosef and his team, with contributions from several foreign expeditions. These include, among many other achievements, the discovery of ancient Acheulian remains at a Ubeidya in 1959; the surveys and excavations in the Negev and the Sinai, refining the general picture of the Paleolithic with the discovery of new cultures; the reopening of fieldwork in the Natufian and the pre-pottery Neolithic levels at Jericho; fieldwork at Malaha, Beisamun and Beidha in Jordan. These discoveries have greatly increased our knowledge of the prehistory of the Near East, particularly in certain vital areas: the transition from the Lower Paleolithic to the Middle Paleolithic, from the Middle to the Upper, from the end of the Paleolithic to the beginning of the productive economy, and the importance of the Natufian* period. The latter has also been the object of particular attention throughout the Near East over the past ten years. The excavations at Mureybet and Cheikh Hasan, Syria, by J. Cauvin, 1971–76, and the surveys carried out in the Hulaylan and the excavations at Tepe Guran in Iran by P. Mortensen, 1973, have demonstrated the importance of the pre-pottery beginnings of the Neolithic throughout the region.

Future directions

Our knowledge of the whole area has recently been the subject of several conferences, held from 1980 to 1982 at Tübingen, Lyon, Haifa and Gronigen, which allow us to forsee the future direction of prehistoric research in the Near East. However, in spite of the contributions of environmental sciences (palynology*, sedimentology, dendrochronology, palaeontology) and the C^{14} datings*, the climatic and ecological picture of the Pleistocene* and Holocene* is still vague and little known.

The years reckoned according to C^{14} are not of the same length as those of our solar calendar. The production of C^{14} from atmospheric nitrogen depends on the intensity of cosmic rays, which is itself subject to variations in the earth's magnetic field. We partially understand these, and consequently know that the quantity of C^{14} produced today differs from that in the past. The net result is that dates supplied by C^{14} for the past 10,000 years are younger than those which would have been calculated in solar years. This presents a problem of calibration which is reduced by dendrochronology, and which is essential to correlate C^{14} dates for the end of prehistory with the calendars of the first urban civilizations, which were based on astronomy.

For the rest, and seen from a traditional perspective, the discovery of new sites and the study of toolmaking industries should not in the short term substantially modify the pattern of prehistory worked out in the course of these last years. But if new directions are confirmed by the study of tool technology and the traces of their utilization (traceology*), as well as by paleoecology, paleoethnology or even paleosociology, a new stage in our knowledge of prehistoric Near Eastern civilizations could be opened up.

Occupation of the Near East in the Paleolithic

The region of Syria, Lebanon, Palestine and Jordan has from the beginning been a crossroads between Africa, Mesopotamia and the Mediterranean world. But when did mankind first settle here?

The first signs of human activity in the Near East go back at least three-quarters of a million years. The most important evidence for this comes from Ubeidiya in the Jordan valley, where several layers date back to the so-called Early Acheulian. As the area's magnetic polarity then was the reverse of ours, its age must be more than 700,000 years (the approximate date of the present phase of magnetic polarity). Acheulian products of a similar age have also been found in riverine deposits at Sitt Markho on the northern Nahr el Kebir, Syria; flint flakes and chopping tools have been taken from a conglomerate on the 'Asi (Orontes) river at Khattab, near Latamne, Syria; and similar objects have been reported in ancient riverine formations at Khurasan in Iran. A fossil beach at the mouth of the Nahr el Kebir has yielded slightly more recent Acheulian material, and simple flakes without shaped edges or bifaces*, have been collected from a similar site at Borj Qinnarit in the Lebanon.

These sites, though few in number, show that humans crossed the region between one million and half a million years ago, and that penetration followed two lines, the first along the central rift, consisting of the Wadi 'Arabah and the Jordan, Litani and 'Asi (Orontes) rivers, and the second along the eastern coast of the Mediterranean. If we accept the view that the African origin of mankind is to be sought in East Africa, this should not come as a surprise, for our knowledge of the distribution of the early Lower Paleolithic in Europe and Asia implies a population movement through the Near East "isthmus".

From 500,000 to about 200,000BC, traces of human presence were still concentrated in the same zones, where two groupings of tool kits characteristic of the Middle Acheulian period stand out. One of these is found from the Jordan to the Litani and on the 'Asi (Orontes), and is characterized by lanceolate (tapering) bifaces, three-sided picks and polyhedrons. The other appears on the coast, at Berzine in northern Syria and Ras Beirut in the Lebanon, and consists of amygdaloid (almond-shaped) and ovate (egg-shaped) bifaces. There are also some assemblages of tools without bifaces, and these raise the question of how such typological variations should be interpreted.

In the Late Acheulian, between 200,000 and 100,000BC, the population spread and the tool kits became more uniform. The inhabited region of Gharmachi on the 'Asi suggests that the Jordanian and Syrian plains were frequently crossed, oases such as Azraq in Jordan and Palmyra in Syria were visited, and the Euphrates valley became an active centre. Human activity is also apparent in the foothill regions of the Taurus—at Altin Dere and Antakya (Antioch) in Turkey—and of the Zagros range at Barda-Balka in Iraq. Tools with the same amygdaloid bifaces, of medium size and beautifully finished, can be found throughout the region.

Diversification of tool-making techniques

Changes that became apparent from about 150,000BC mark the transition from the Lower to the Middle Paleolithic. Flint-working techniques diversified and living conditions changed as the population systematically sought out caves and shelters in addition to open-air settlements. Consequently, the Near East presents a complicated picture during this transitional period. Tool kits characteristic of the Final Acheulian period are found from the foothills of the Taurus to the region around Palmyra. In the central Levant,

archaeologists have identified a coexistence of earlier blade industries (pre-Aurignacian, Amudian and Hummalian) with the so-called "Yabrudian", which is similar to the flint industry known as Mousterian* and associated with Neanderthal man. This coexistence has led some specialists to group all these industries together under a single name, the "Tradition of Wadi Magharah". In the central sector of the coast, tool kits with broad, egg-shaped flakes—a type of Mousterian called Levalloiso-Mousterian*—very soon began to appear, while in the Negev another type of Levalloiso-Mousterian with elongated points marked the beginning of the Middle Paleolithic. Developments further east, beyond the Euphrates, are still unknown.

As from 80,000BC the situation becomes simpler (see map). The western part of the region, from the Mediterranean to the Euphrates, was occupied by groups using a highly developed Levallois technique. Within this basic technology, typological variations reveal different groupings. In the central Levant, for example, from Mount Carmel to Ras el Kelb, tool kits with broad ovate flakes replaced those with elongated points, and they in turn were replaced by points with a wide base. The humid conditions prevailing in the first half of the last "pluvial", or period of high rainfall, made it possible for people to live in regions that are now extremely arid. Our knowledge of the Mesopotamian plain is slight, but we know that the Zagros region was quite densely inhabited by a population ignorant of the Levallois technique. The Zagros Mousterian is known only from cave deposits.

The emergence of modern man

Although the Near East was divided into two cultural zones, the same human type, the so-called Neanderthal man, is found throughout. Ceremonial burials now appear for the first time, sometimes accompanied with offerings; at Shanidar, Iraq, for instance, it has been shown that one body was buried with flowers. In Palestine, findings at Qatzeh indicate that the end of the Middle Paleolithic had already seen the emergence of *Homo sapiens sapiens*.

The second half of the last pluvial, from 40,000BC onwards, saw, with the advent of the Upper Paleolithic, the development of new tools and the spread of a human

type like our own. During this final period of the Paleolithic, the Near East was still divided into two provinces, but occupation was less widespread than in the Middle Paleolithic, a phenomenon undoubtedly connected with drier climatic conditions. As research stands at present, the Upper Paleolithic in the Near East apparently emerged in three separate regions; the Zagros mountains, the central Levant (caves on the Lebanese coast) and the Negev (Boker Tachtit).

Later in the Upper Paleolithic, when it was in full flower, we can observe similar divisions. Throughout the Near East, we find a technique producing thin blades with pocked butts. In the Zagros region this gave rise to the so-called Baradostian, and in the two Levant regions to a variety of Aurignacian (Levant Aurignacian or Antelian) and an industry characterized by pointed blades (Amharian). Sometimes the two types appear on the same site (Ksar Akil), which does not make interpretation any easier.

At an uncertain date which varies according to the region, microlithic tools consisting of bladelets retouched in a variety of ways gradually predominated. Several groupings have been identified: a so-called Lagamian dating to 27,000BC, in the north of Sinai; a Kebaran in the central Levant from 17,000BC, and, towards 12,000BC, a Zarzian in Iraqi Kurdistan which spread as far as the shores of the Caspian, as seen in the caves of Belt, Hotu and Ali Tappeh. Although it is not clear whether the people grouped together under the name Zarzian represented a single civilization, the homogeneity of the Kebaran in the central Levant seems highly probable.

Then, towards the end of the Pleistocene*, we see the first signs of the great changes in civilization that took mankind from a predatory hunter-gatherer economy to one of production, with all the concomitants of that "revolution". The habitat developed from natural shelters to man-made huts, and this was matched by a change in the type of tools, with microliths assuming geometric shapes such as trapezes and trapeze-rectangles (Geometric Kebaran, Mushabian). This would later see the emergence of the so-called Natufian culture, which was to occupy the whole of the Levant from the Amanus to Sinai, from the Mediterranean to the Euphrates between 12,000 and 8300BC.

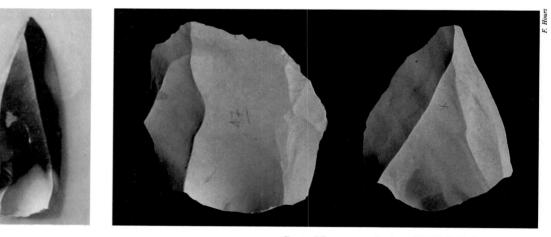

Central Levant: evolution of Middle Paleolithic tools

Stone tools from the Middle Paleolithic period, found in the central Levant, were made from flint flakes according to a technique called Mousterian by archaeologists. The early phase of this technique, the so-called Levalloiso-Mousterian, has been found in the central part of the region, between Mount Carmel and the suburbs of Beirut on the coast, and, in the interior, from the Judaean desert to the foothills of the Anti Lebanon at Yabroud, Syria. It is characterized by tools with elongated points (left), followed by those with broad flakes (centre); finally, points with broad bases (right) make up the bulk of the finds.

The site of Bir Hasan, near Beirut

Solidified dunes extending south from Beirut contain remnants of an important human occupation that lasted from the Middle Paleolithic, some 80,000 years ago, until the Neolithic period, about 5000BC. The Bir Hasan site yielded the first worked flints to be found in the Near East, and was regarded as a key area by prehistorians, but the construction of Beirut airport and refugee camps has removed all traces of it today.

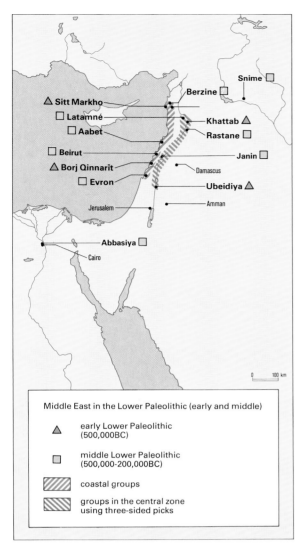

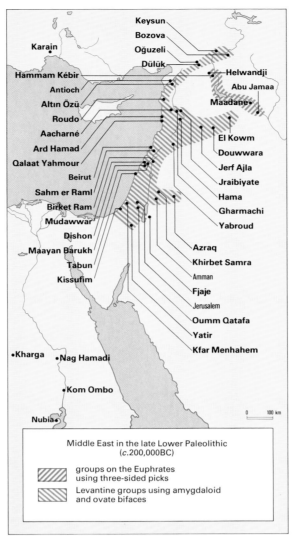

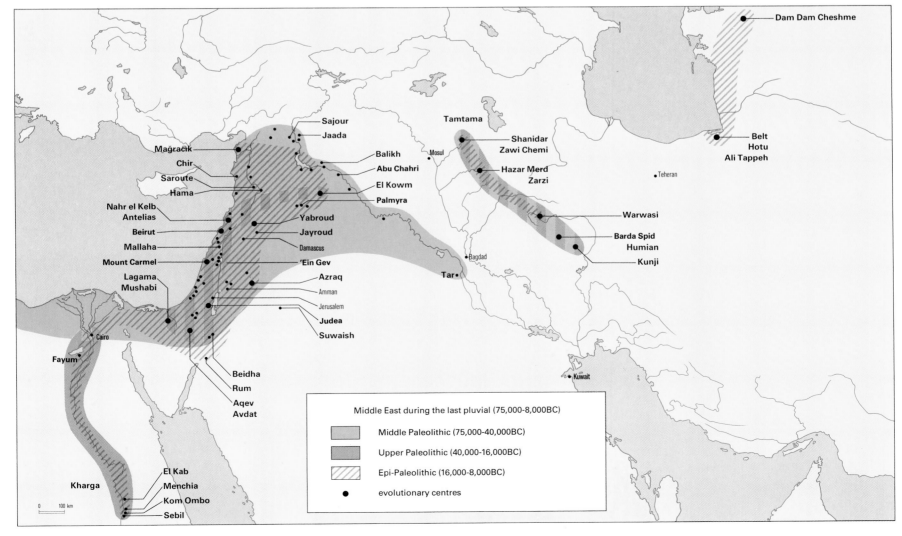

Middle East in the Lower Paleolithic (early and middle)

▲ early Lower Paleolithic (500,000BC)

□ middle Lower Paleolithic (500,000-200,000BC)

▨ coastal groups

▨ groups in the central zone using three-sided picks

Middle East in the late Lower Paleolithic (c.200,000BC)

▨ groups on the Euphrates using three-sided picks

▨ Levantine groups using amygdaloid and ovate bifaces

end of the Acheulian and transition to Middle Paleolithic (150,000 to 80,000BC)

▨ Final Acheulian

▨ Yabroudian

▨ Levalloiso-Mousterian with broad flakes

▨ Levalloiso-Mousterian with elongated points

Throughout the slow development of the Lower and Middle Paleolithic, until about 250,000 years ago, the Near East acted as a transit zone for the spread of humanity from Africa, along the coast on the one hand and a rift consisting of the Dead Sea, the Litani and the 'Asi (Orontes) rivers on the other. This was exemplified in two different groupings of the Acheulian. The eastern part, Iraq and Iran, may have been uninhabited, or is that an illusion owing to our lack of knowledge of the area?

In the Late Acheulian, from 250,000BC onwards, the whole of the western plain was occupied, but Mesopotamia was still a barrier, either because the valleys of the Euphrates and the Tigris actually discouraged habitation, or because the erosions of the last "pluvial", or period of heavy rainfall, and the build-ups of sediment in the Holocene, made access to them difficult.

The transition from the Lower to the Middle Paleolithic, which took place about 80,000BC, was expressed by a mosaic of different industries, the geographical distribution of which once again poses the problem of contacts between civilizations.

With the advent of the last pluvial (rainy period), things became simpler. An independent tradition, as yet largely unknown, reigned to the east of the Taurus-Zagros arc and there is a great deal still to be learnt about it. To the west of the Euphrates, the Levalloiso-Mousterian covered the territory, until there was a decrease in the population in the Upper Paleolithic, countered by a fresh expansion in the so-called Natufian (12,000–8300BC). Climatic variations undoubtedly contributed to the variations in the areas inhabited.

Middle East during the last pluvial (75,000-8,000BC)

▨ Middle Paleolithic (75,000-40,000BC)

▨ Upper Paleolithic (40,000-16,000BC)

▨ Epi-Paleolithic (16,000-8,000BC)

• evolutionary centres

The birth of agriculture

The development of agriculture in the Near East was one of the turning points in the history of the world. It paved the way for the "urban revolution" experienced by Sumeria in the 4th millennium BC.

The Near East played a dual role in the appearance of agriculture: the cultivation of cereals was practised there from the 8th millennium and, moreover, the Levant was the centre for the diffusion of agriculture to the Mediterranean basin and Europe from the 6th millennium onwards.

This capacity was based on a natural phenomenon: a progressively warmer climate between 13,000 and 11,000BC marked the end of the glacial phases and the Pleistocene* and allowed wild cereals (barley, einkorn, emmer wheat) to spread throughout the semi-arid zone. This region, situated in a temperate zone behind the Mediterranean coast of the Levant covers an arc-like area running from the Jordan Rift to the edge of the Iranian plateau, traversing the middle Euphrates and the steppe-like foothills of the Taurus and Zagros. This zone, which R. Braidwood has called "nuclear" because it played an important part in the first agricultural experiments, also contained the wild strains of several legumes (peas, lentils) which were cultivated at the same time as cereals. However, these favourable geographical conditions did not play the decisive part in this formative stage of agriculture, since there was a delay of some two millennia in the domestication of these plants after their first natural appearance.

Human activity was the decisive factor indicating the advent of "productive" societies which had abandoned the hunter-gathering way of life and had gradually learned to control the reproduction of certain species, modify their development and increasingly master their own food supplies through agriculture and careful stockbreeding.

Over the last 25 years, intensive research carried out by international teams in the Near East has helped archaeologists to understand this behaviour. Consequently, the transformation of food "strategies", although only one element in the process, can be placed in their chronological relation to other sociological, technical and cultural aspects of what V. Gordon Childe* names the "Neolithic revolution". This revolution was not as rapid as it was in Europe where developments leading to the Neolithic came from outside. Entirely native to the Near East, it was a progressive development lasting from 10,000 to 5000BC; and it is now possible to analyse its stages and allot the agricultural element its proper place. Indeed, the invention of agriculture itself should not be considered as a sudden phenomenon. After a long preparatory period from the 10th millennium, during which intensified gathering of wild cereals took place, it first appeared in the form of "dry farming" (growing crops in semi-arid conditions without irrigation) in the so-called nuclear zone from the 8th millennium, spreading throughout the Near East and beyond from around 6000BC, when irrigation freed it from climatic constraints and made it possible to control crops in any type of environment.

The first stage, then, was preparatory. Between about 10,000 and 6000BC the semi-arid steppelands of the Levant saw the first Natufian* village-like settlements. The inhabitants were still hunter-gatherers but the exploitation of wild cereals, combined with fishing and hunting small herd animals such as gazelles, as well as water game, formed the basis of a highly diversified economy enabling larger groups of people to settle. At the same time, archaeologists have found the development of tools such as sickles and grinding implements, and storage buildings like the silos at Mallaha, which were long interpreted as "signs" of agriculture, although in fact they considerably preceded it.

The domestication of cereals

The second stage of this evolution to the Neolithic (Neolithization) took place in already established village environments of the Levant, which experimented with cereal culture in the 8th millennium. Emmer wheat was domesticated in the Jordan valley at Jericho in the period known as Pre-Pottery Neolithic A (PPNA). The same thing happened at Tell Aswad in the Damas oasis, where barley, peas and lentils were also cultivated. In the village of Mureybet, founded in the Natufian (c.8500BC) on the Syrian middle Euphrates, the cereals exploited (barley, einkorn) still retained their natural form in the early eighth millennium, but pollen study has shown that certain proto-agricultural practices began to appear at that time, facilitating the denser cultivation of cereal crops near the village. It has been observed that this "proto-agriculture" at Mureybet was accompanied, as at Jericho, by a sudden population increase, for the village grew from a few hundred square metres to three hectares, as well as by a spectacular reduction in the range of wild resources. Fishing virtually disappeared, and hunting was concentrated exclusively on the large herbivores (bovids and wild asses). So the beginnings of agriculture could not have been caused, as was thought for a long time, by a scarcity of natural resources. It was one of the elements in a new strategy aimed at organizing in a different form, and making more profitable, the exploitation of certain species chosen by man.

From about 7000BC, when the whole of the Levant was occupied by the civilization known as Pre-Pottery Neolithic B (PPNB), the agricultural phenomena continued throughout the semi-arid Near East. Agriculture was in effect still confined to the same range of climate, but it now simultaneously spread north toward the Taurus range (Çayönü) and Anatolia (Hacilar), and in the east toward the Zagros foothills as far as present-day Iran. It was in this eastern area that the first steps in the production of a subsistence diet were directed in the 8th millennium to the domestication of animals in a still semi-nomadic context, and real villages grew up in Iran where wheat and barley were cultivated, at Ali Kosh and perhaps at Ganj Dareh.

The third stage, which saw the full expression of agriculture, began c.6000BC and took on a dual aspect, both spatial and technical. It was then that, for the first time, the geographical expansion of the Neolithic farmers of the Levant moved outside the nuclear zone. This expansion began at the end of the 7th millennium, spreading in the direction of the coast, where the wetter Mediterranean climate encouraged domesticated cereals once man had introduced them. Thus, Ras Shamra, on the coast of northern Syria, was founded about 6500BC by farmers of the late Pre-Pottery Neolithic B. There was also expansion into the desert zone, to the banks of the Euphrates (Buqras) and the oases (El Kown) where the rainfall was less than 200mm

a year and basically insufficient to grow crops without irrigation, but where the judicious use of certain low-lying and wetter areas in the immediate vicinity of watercourses or springs at least allowed farmers the possibility of harvests. It seems that, from the beginning, a type of still very primitive irrigation was practised to keep a regular supply of vegetable food, although at first the chief food resources, enabling the exodus of farmers, came from the breeding of goats.

Irrigated agriculture

Irrigation formed the second, technical aspect of the new agriculture. This was not confined to the arid zones, for settlements established in the nuclear zone basically favourable to dry crops, like those on the Anatolian plateau, also discovered its advantages. At Çatal Hüyük and Hacilar the practice of irrigation accounts for the appearance, through mutation, of new domestic species—hybrid cereals—in the 6th millennium, as well as cultivated plants like flax which was certainly not used for food.

From 5500BC, the development of irrigation enabled farmers to conquer new territories in the hitherto neglected desert areas, especially in Iraq and Iran. Although, immediately previously, the small agricultural villages of the Hassuna* culture were still ignorant of it and thus remained confined in Upper Mesopotamia, the succeeding Samarra* culture made the first southward advance in Iraq, even to the edge of the alluvial plain and outside the zone of dry crops. The villages of this culture occupied the banks of the middle Tigris in the region of Mosul, and further east in the region of Mandali, where man-made canals dug across watercourses descending from the Zagros collected the water necessary for crops at Choga Mami. Everywhere irrigation led to the appearance of hybrid cereals and leguminous plants such as peas with larger seeds, as well as flax. Still further east, at the foot of the Iranian Zagros, sites in Khuzistan such as Choga Sefid produced irrigated crops and their attendant new species around 5000BC.

Finally, in the low-lying alluvial plain between the Tigris and the Euphrates, the Ubaid* culture introduced in the 5th millennium another refinement in the mastery of water. In this marshy region the problem was not only to irrigate the crops, but also to clean the soil and drain off excess water by a complicated system of canals.

The cultures of Samarra and Ubaid highlight the social and cultural implications of irrigated agriculture which, by ensuring regular harvests, encouraged denser settlements, more spacious living areas, and the development of more skilful crafts. Moreover, the need to organize distribution of water to a large number of consumers led to new methods of arbitration from which, perhaps during the Ubaid period, a new and from now on hierarchial model of society may have developed.

This evolution, evidenced in the villages of the Ubaid culture by the appearance of new and important public buildings cutting across the existing architectural fabric, directly prepared the way for the emergence of a political power and the "urban revolution" of the 4th millennium, which takes us into the historical period, beginning with Sumer.

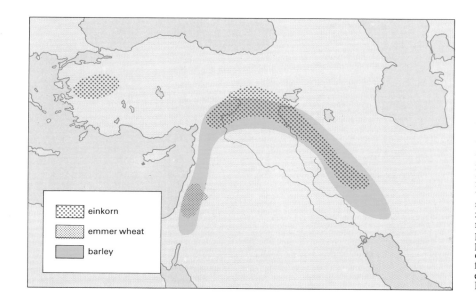

Wild cereals of the Near East

Current distribution of wild cereals in the Near East. This semi-arid climatic zone was the scene of the first attempts at agriculture, in the eighth and seventh millennia BC. However, its boundaries may need to be shifted slightly towards the south to reconstitute the original "nuclear zone", taking into account a more recent increase in temperature in the Anatolian plateau and the effect of this on the Near East. Right, a field of einkorn grown on the experimental farm of Little Butser, Great Britain.

einkorn

emmer wheat

barley

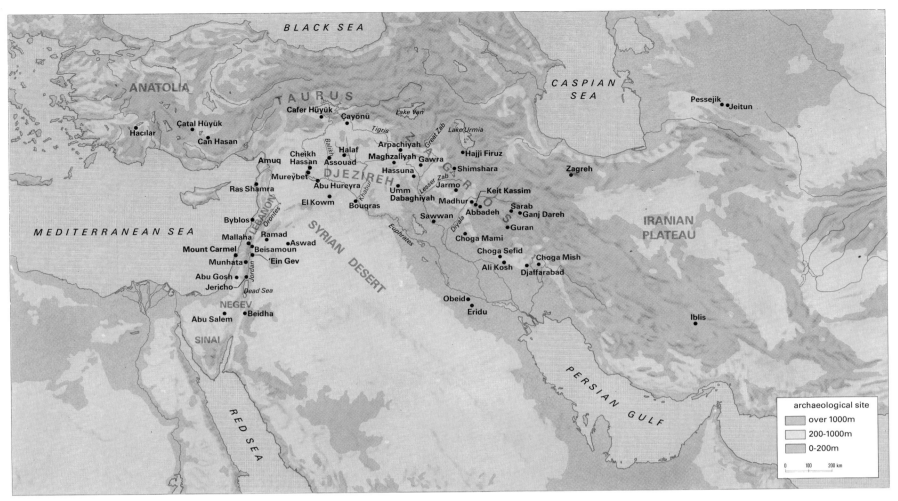

The process of Neolithization in the Near East

The map (above) locates the places, and the chart (below) indicates the times, where the main Neolithic "inventions" appeared in various Near Eastern cultures and sites. We see the first village settlements in the southern Levant by Natufian hunter-gatherers, then the beginning of cereal crops both in Palestine and on the central Euphrates, at the same time that the first rectangular edifices and representations of "goddesses" appear (but these only on the central Euphrates). A little later comes the beginning of pottery, occurring simultaneously in several places in the Zagros, Anatolia and the central Euphrates. Lastly, more complex habitats with upper floors and internal circulation develop in the low alluvial plain of the great rivers. They foretell the great public buildings ("temples") of the 'Ubaid civilization, whose "hierarchized" villages prefigure the urban revolution.

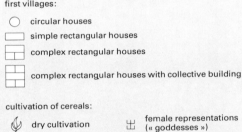

first villages:

○ circular houses

▭ simple rectangular houses

▭ complex rectangular houses

▦ complex rectangular houses with collective building

cultivation of cereals:

🌾 dry cultivation

🌾 irrigated cultivation

⊞ female representations («goddesses»)

⬭ ceramic

(bold symbols correspond to places of first appearance)

Reconstructed harvest, Hacilar, Turkey

An experiment in harvesting primitive cereals with a sickle reconstructed after a prehistoric model from Hacilar, Turkey.

P. Anderson-Gerfaud

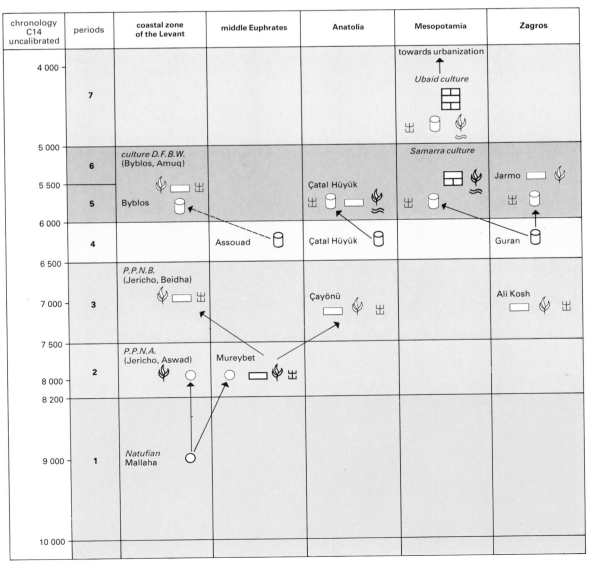

chronology C14 uncalibrated	periods	coastal zone of the Levant	middle Euphrates	Anatolia	Mesopotamia	Zagros
4 000	7				towards urbanization *Ubaid culture* ▦ ⊞ ⬭ 🌾	
5 000	6	*culture D.F.B.W.* (Byblos, Amuq) 🌾 ▭ ⊞			*Samarra culture* ▦ 🌾	Jarmo ▭ 🌾
5 500	5	Byblos ⬭		Çatal Hüyük ⊞ ⬭ ▭ 🌾	⊞ ⬭	⊞ ⬭
6 000	4		Assouad ⬭	Çatal Hüyük ⬭		Guran ⬭
6 500	3	*P.P.N.B.* (Jericho, Beidha) 🌾 ▭ ⊞		Çayönü ▭ 🌾 ⊞		Ali Kosh ▭ 🌾 ⊞
7 000						
7 500	2	*P.P.N.A.* (Jericho, Aswad) 🌾 ○	Mureybet ○ ▭ 🌾 ⊞			
8 000						
8 200						
9 000	1	*Natufian* Mallaha ○				
10 000						

167

From village to town

Mankind's move from the country to the city, one of the great themes in history, today seems to be accelerating fatally in the Third World. This movement began in the Near East, in Mesopotamia, in the 6th millennium BC; and there true city civilization first developed.

Archaeological discoveries in the Near East enable us today to review the earliest stages in mankind's transition from villager to towndweller, or, in other words, the invention and development of architecture. This process can be traced through some ten millennia, from about 14,000BC to 3500BC.

The first stage started in Palestine, where the first people to follow a settled existence required shelters more durable than the flimsy huts erected by their predecessors, the nomadic and constantly mobile Paleolithic populations. The earliest house known to us, at Ein Guev (Kebaran culture, 14,000–12,000BC) resembled a round pit about 4–5m (13–16ft) in diameter, dug into the side of a hill and covered with lightweight materials such as skins and branches. The first Natufian* hamlets came later, about 12,000–10,000BC. These consisted of buildings ranging in diameter from 3–9m (10–29ft), and were grouped together over an area of several hundred square metres. They were constructed according to the same principles, but at Mallaha one of the houses shows traces of a framework resting on wooden posts. These first attempts at housebuilding share a common circular shape and a common dug-out construction method which goes back to the very origins of architecture, and to a time when construction techniques were still unknown.

Originally consisting of a single room, the houses gradually came to be subdivided within so as to enable a more precise usage of the domestic space available. This development occurred at Mureybet during the Neolithic period, c.8000BC, and perhaps also at Jericho. At the same time, basic construction techniques began to emerge, using the same raw materials—stone, wood and moulded earth—and walls began to "rise up" from the ground. The collections of buildings became "real" villages covering some 2–3 hectares (5–7 acres) and the first signs of communal or collective enterprise can be detected, as in the tower at Jericho.

From circular to rectangular buildings

This period saw the first alteration in the form of the house, corresponding to a change in daily activity induced by the progressive development of agriculture. Moreover, the original circular shape implied definite limits on the possibility of further structural expansion, so that the type of building perfected at Mureybet was also something of a dead end. Only a rectangular shape would allow further expansion, but this also required a greater mastery of building technology, particularly in the interconnection of two perpendicular walls. This problem was solved by the invention of the rectangular brick, which was to have a very long future. The transition from the original, or "primitive", architecture to this radically new concept took place around 7700BC at the Mureybet and Sheikh Hassan sites.

The first rectangular buildings, single-unit structures of about 20–30 sq m (215–328 sq ft), were erected either on thick pebble strata or on peripheral foundations which formed a "sanitary gap", as at Çayönü, Cafer Hüyük in Anatolia, or Ganj Dareh in Iran. Çatal Hüyük (6500–5500BC) provides a particularly significant example of this new architecture. Houses built during this second phase of the Neolithic consist either of a single room where all domestic activities took place, or of a main room connected to one or two smaller ones probably used as store rooms. The villages of the farming and cattle-breeding communities of the period, consisting either of detached or conjoined houses, covered areas of up to 10–15 hectares (24–36 acres). This type of settlement, probably originating from the valley of the Euphrates, was adopted over the whole of the Near East, from Palestine (Byblos, Beidha, Jericho, Beisamun, Ramad) to Turkestan (Jeitun, Pessejik) via Iraq (Jarmo) and Iran (Ali Kosh, Zāgheh, Hajji Firuz), and it soon became universal. None of these settlements, however, quite justifies the apellation of town. It was in Mesopotamia, after 5600BC, that this final transition

was achieved, in two stages. First, the interiors of the dwellings were not only substantially enlarged to as much as 100–150 sq m (1,076–1,614 sq ft), and the number of rooms increased (sometimes by as many as ten); they also became much more complex. The arrangement of corridors connecting the rooms indicates that the construction of the house was now carried out according to a preconceived design. One room was no longer added haphazardly to another, but the whole house was planned and built with a precise function in mind. This was also the time when houses began to be built in several stories, connected by external or internal stairs. This new conception of the house probably also originated in the Euphrates valley, as in Buqras, and is clearly evidenced in the Samarra culture (Tell es-Sawwan), at Ubaid* (Gawra, Eridu, Abbadeh, Madhur, Keit Kassim III), and at Susa* (Ja'farābād, Choga Mish, Iblis).

Secondly, this greater complexity of individual living space was accompanied by the first appearance in the settlements of a quite new type of building which stood out from all the others in terms of size, decoration and probably function—perhaps an assembly hall, or the house of the community chief. The first traces of this development appear between 4000 and 3500BC in the settlements of the Ubaid culture (Gawra, Eridu, Abbadeh). Perhaps we can identify in this "exceptional building" the ancestor of what was to become, by the end of the fourth millennium (Uruk culture) and during the third, the temple, and then the palace which, over and above the domestic living spaces, represents in archaeological terms the criterion for a "real" town.

This kind of hierarchical ranking in the architecture of Mesopotamian villages thus anticipates the essential characteristics of the first oriental cities. It is a logical and continuous process, marked with chronologically precise steps, that leads us eventually from the first house to the first town.

An excavated house, Mureybet

This view of a house in the course of excavation shows, in the foreground, the central or "living" area with, on the left, the sleeping platform and, on the right, the entrance. In the middle ground, a low wall, easy to climb over (hence the absence of doorways), surrounds an area probably used for storage. At the back, the internal wall shows traces of the posts which supported the roof and which were burnt when the house was destroyed by fire.

Model of circular house, Mureybet

The site provides evidence from c.8000BC of an architectural scheme comprising a very complex circular design with a 6m (19ft) diameter. The house is partly dug out of the hillside, with only the front emerging into the open air. The flat roof rests on a framework of wooden posts. Low walls divide the interior into areas of different use: a living area, opposite the entrance, has a sleeping bench against the back wall; on the right are the kitchen and the store rooms. Model by G. Deraprahanian.

Village of Mureybet

The houses of this village, grouped together over an area of 2–3 hectares (5–7 acres), fit into their natural surroundings by being terraced on the slope, so that the roof of the lower house forms the terrace of the upper. A paved way leads to a group of sunken hearths, proof that domestic activities took place outside the dwellings. Model by G. Deraprahanian.

A house at Çatal Hüyük

This house (*c.*6000BC) is a fine example of rectangular architecture with a simple plan. The sole room, 20–30 sq m (215–322 sq ft) is built according to a technique very similar to half-timbering: a wooden framework with a filling of mud bricks. The roof is flat. The room includes a hearth, an oven in the wall and benches along the sides. After J. Mellaart.

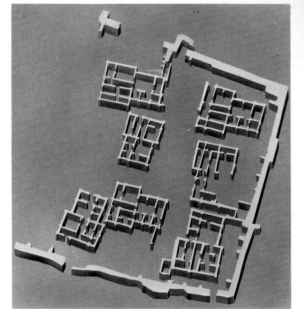

The village of Çatal Hüyük

The houses lack doors, are built close together and, as at Mureybet, are terraced on a slope. Access was through the roof by means of an inner staircase; the opening also allowed the smoke to escape. The canopy which protected the opening is reconstructed from modern Turkish examples. Note the continuous windowless exteriors of the houses, which constituted an uninterrupted wall, probably for security reasons. The village covered some 15 hectares (37 acres). After J. Mellaart.

The village of Sawwan

Built *c.*5600BC, the large farmhouses of Sawwan, covering an area of 100–200 sq m (1,600–2,200 sq ft), were grouped within a surrounding wall. Built of brick, they contained over ten rooms, each communicating with the others by means of doorways. At least part of their surface was covered by an upper floor which was reached via an external staircase. Space between the detached houses was left open for people and animals to move through. After W. Yasin and P. Aniret.

The village of Abbadeh

The Abbadeh houses (*c.*4000BC) also contained several rooms symmetrically arranged around a central hall. An internal staircase led to the upper floor. One of the buildings differed in its size, its decoration (flat pilasters of bricks) and its central position. Such buildings are one of the first indications of "hierarchical" architecture and represent the embryonic precursors of the public buildings characteristic of a township. After S. Aboud.

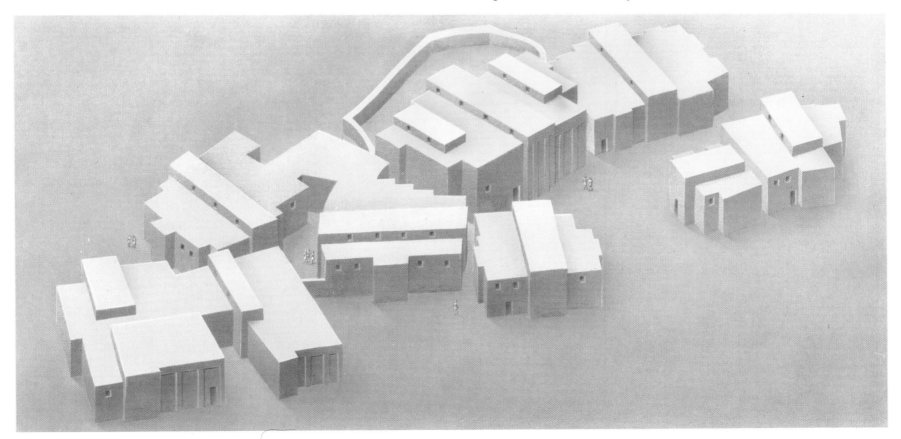

The expansion of the arts of fire

Without fire, as the Prometheus myth says, there can be no civilization. In Neolithic Mesopotamia the most revolutionary advances were made in using fire for pottery, building and metallurgy. The techniques evolved then are still very much in existence.

Techniques of firing, which became of primary importance with the advent of metallurgy at the end of the Stone Age, emerged in the Near East from the beginning of the Neolithic period (c.8000BC) with lime, plaster and pottery. Fire had in fact been used previously to assist in fashioning bone and flint, but in the case of lime, plaster and pottery, the raw material was itself so modified that it acquired completely new qualities and potentialities.

The main difficulty in the formation of these three materials may have been that of the firing temperature. A temperature of 120°C (248°F) is sufficient to obtain plaster, but firing clay requires 500°C (932°F) and lime 800°C (1472°F). However in "open air baking" without the use of kilns, when the objects to be fired are arranged in a heap below the combustible material, such temperatures can easily be reached. It is also interesting to note that lime was made in the Near East before plaster, so the obstacle of the firing temperature could not have played a major role.

Stages in the development of pottery

The term pottery or ceramics is applied to vessels of fired clay (terracotta), even though the production of fired clay preceded its application to vessels or pots. In the Neolithic Near East, where clay was used quite intensively, the idea of baking this material was not altogether surprising. It was utilized in architecture from the Natufian* period (10th–9th millennia) for coatings, for walls of cob or rammed earth, for trenches and ditches, and above all for fire-pits. From the beginning of the 8th millennium, brick appeared in the Jordan valley at Jericho (Pre-Pottery Neolithic A*). Unbaked clay was also used at that period to make figurines and small objects. Thus the principle qualities of clay, its pliability and hardness when dried, have been exploited since the beginning of human settlement.

The origin of pottery is harder to pinpoint because of the presence of small containers of unbaked clay, or clay sometimes fired accidentally, which are found from the 8th millennium. Nevertheless, deliberately fired clay was still only used for figurines and small geometric objects for another 1000 to 500 years. It was only in the second half of the 7th millennium that it really began to develop as material for making utensils. Just as terracotta made its appearance on sites dispersed throughout the Near East, so its application for pots began more or less simultaneously in Anatolia (Çatal Hüyük), in the middle Euphrates (Tell Asswad), and in the Zagros (Tepe Guran). Pottery was to spread rapidly until, by 6000BC, it was found in great quantities on all sites in the Near East, with the exception of Palestine. This region failed to exploit the new technology until the second half of the 6th millennium.

The pottery of the 7th millennium, wherever it came from, was extremely simple and very homogeneous. This similarity may have been due to limited techniques. Regional variations were therefore slight, as opposed to later developments once the technology was more skilled and widespread. In fact, independently of purely local differences, these regional differences very soon began to appear from the beginning of the 6th millennium, as with the so-called "dark-faced" burnished ware of the northern Levant, or the ceramic styles characteristic of Mesopotamia and the Zagros.

The next stage in the development of pottery concerns the export and standardization of the product. With the Halafian* civilization in the second half of the 6th millennium, a sophisticated pottery emerged as regards technical quality, form and decoration. This culture seems to have originated in the region of Djezireh, but the pottery is widely diffused as far as the Mediterranean coast to the west, and the Zagros and the shores of the Persian Gulf to the east. Export implies production beyond the needs of the producers, even a certain degree of specialization and standardization. This evolution is confirmed with Ubaid* pottery, which in the 5th millennium was to have an even larger area of diffusion and a greater degree of homogeneity.

The invention of lime and plaster

The stages in the invention of lime and plaster are much less clear, because these two materials needed a series of more complicated operations. They are formed from the calcination of limestone for lime and of gypsum for plaster, but such baking only produces the basic material, to which water must be added before it can be used; it is only during drying that setting takes place and the material becomes hard. The transition from limestone or gypseous rock to the finished object appears much less clearly than in the case of clay, where baking follows the shaping of the object. Perhaps fires lit in fireplaces made of limestone blocks or hollowed out of gypseous soil first showed the inhabitants how such rocks were transformed under the action of great heat.

Plaster appeared for the first time in Palestine, in the 8th millennium on the site of Beidha. This was also the region where its use was most systematically applied. During the first half of the 7th millennium ground earths coated with lime are a common feature of all the installations of so-called Pre-Pottery Neolithic B*. From the second half of the 8th millennium the use of lime and plaster is evidenced equally in Anatolia (Çayönü), and on the middle Euphrates (Abu Hureyra) and in the Zagros (Ganj Dareh). Although the use of this type of material spread fairly rapidly in Anatolia and the Zagros, it was not quite universal. As from 6500BC, these various materials were adopted on the majority of sites on the middle Euphrates, not only for architectural facings, but also for the manufacture of crockery and objects of geometric shape, such as disks and spheres. This diversification of use reached sites in central and northern Levant such as Ramad and Ras Shamra between 6000BC and 5500BC. In Mesopotamia, plaster and lime appeared in the first settlements in the region, in the 7th millennium (Maghzalieh), and multiplied as from 6000BC (Umm Dabaghiya, Hassuna). Thus, the manufacture of plaster and lime was practised throughout the Near East during the Neolithic period, but with regional variations and sometimes on a different time-scale.

Technical progress made it possible to diversify the uses of these new materials. Lime and plaster began to be used in a wider field of application from the original simple plastering, to the modelling of objects, and in particular of crockery. Thus, they began to compete with terracotta. But the latter rapidly won out as the material for utensils, not least because of its ability to withstand high temperatures. Plaster and lime, on the other hand, predominated in architectural plastering, for which their qualities were perfectly suited. So the materials most appropriate for each function were gradually selected. This process was comparable to the making of terracotta sickles in the Ubaid culture, when better adapted materials such as stone and then metal soon put an end to the experiment.

The first techniques of firing not only served as an area of experimentation for metallurgy, but also gave birth to materials whose respective qualities have been well tested, since they have continued through the millennia and, in spite of innovations offered by modern technology, remain largely in use to this day.

Plaster objects from Buqras, Syria

Dishes, geometrical objects such as the sphere shown here (c.6000BC), coatings for architectural features, basins made from "prefabricated" slabs, slips and coatings for ceramics, plaster coverings for skulls in burials, figurines—these represent some of the many applications of plaster or chalk known in the Near East during the seventh and sixth millennia, when the use of these materials was at its height. Museum of Deir-ez-Zor, Syria.

Plaster vessel, El Kowm, Syria

It appears that, after preliminary analyses, chalk was the preferred medium for the manufacture of objects to the west and north of the Syrian desert, and plaster for objects to the east, whether or not resources of chalk or gypsum were locally available. Both substances served the same purpose in application. Excavations by J. Cauvin.

Wall painting, Buqras, Syria

These birds, which may be ostriches or possibly cranes, were painted in ochre on a mud-brick wall coated with plaster. The model of a human head, also plaster-coated and painted red, was found near the pillar of a house in the area. These decorations are usually badly preserved, but they are in evidence throughout the Neolithic Near East, where they seem to have played a part in daily life. Excavations of the University of Amsterdam and the University of Groningen.

Ceramic fragment, Buqras, Syria

The rapid evolution of form and decoration is a valuable aid to dating pottery in the Near East. In the case of this fragment, however, which dates to c.6000BC, the technical characteristics are still very much like those of the first pottery: hand cast, usually by means of coiling; clay with plant inclusions, fairly thick, and of brown colour, varying in shade; surface simply smoothed or polished, never covered with slip. Museum of Deir-ez-Zor, Syria.

Painted vase, Buqras, Syria

The first pottery was undecorated, but decoration soon appeared, with several regional variations: painted wares to the east of the Euphrates, impressed or incised decoration to the west. Apart from certain geometric designs, such as the chevrons shown here, which are very widespread, painted motifs and their arrangement vary from one region to another and from site to site. Museum of Deir-ez-Zor, Syria.

Clay figurine, Mureybet, Syria

In the Near East, the earliest objects in terracotta, made in the eighth millennium BC, presented few problems of modelling or drying, for they were of very small size. This also explains why their material was never bulked out with plant inclusions of the kind frequently used in clay or cob. Excavations by J. Cauvin.

Early Neolithic pottery from Byblos, Lebanon

These two vessels show the simplicity of form of the oldest ceramics: closed or straight-sided, with flat or round bases, a profile with no break in the curve. Increasingly open shapes, developed bases and sides, necks, ridges and even rudimentary handles, emerged in an order and at a speed that varied according to the region. Excavations by M. Dunand.

Halaf vessel from Tell Arpachiyah, Iraq

The Halaf decoration is very rich. It includes not only, as on this plate from the 6th millennium, polychrome geometric motifs, centred or in bands, but also human or animal figures and decorations in the intervening spaces. A decoration as elegant as this required regular firing by means of a special kiln where the firing chamber was separated from the furnace. The first examples of this process are in fact found on Halaf sites. Excavations by M. Mallowan, British Museum, London.

Neolithic art and ideology

As is usually the case in history, the agrarian and technological revolution in the Neolithic Near East was accompanied by an ideological transformation, a profound rethinking of Man's relation to his environment.

Between 10,000 and 5000BC the peoples of the Near East experienced a set of fundamental changes in the most concrete aspects of their way of life, namely their habitats, food economy and technology. Also worthy of study is the equally important and simultaneous revolution in their spiritual attitudes: art is our main key to understanding their collective imagination.

The Natufians* were the last of the Near Eastern hunter-gatherers, although they were already involved in the process of "Neolithization" in that they lived in primitive villages. Their art of around 10,000BC is the immediate successor to the Franco-Cantabrian art of the western Upper Paleolithic which was already on the road to extinction. Like the latter, its inspiration was still basically zoomorphic, but it was confined to portable objects. Statuettes and carved bone tool handles were decorated with small herbivores treated both realistically and schematically. Their species cannot always be identified, but the gazelle, the favourite game of Natufian hunters, seems to be the most common subject. Human figures appear very rarely and have no sexual characteristics.

A profound revision of the symbolic vocabularly took place at the beginning of the 8th millennium. From 8300BC, the complete skulls of bulls were found embedded in the walls of houses at Mureybet on the middle Euphrates. This was at the end of the Natufian, when the species was as yet very little hunted, the gazelle still being the favourite game. Such deposits were undoubtedly ritual. They were to continue in the 8th millennium with the custom of embedding bulls' horns in walls under construction, even before the specialized hunting of this herbivore began, followed by early stock-raising, c.7500BC. This looks like an example of an initially ideological preference preceding or even forming a change in eating habits.

In the 8th millennium the stone and terracotta figurines of Mureybet become almost wholly anthropomorphic; they are also the first feminine representations in the Near East. The sex is indicated and the buttocks are exaggerated. The head is of normal size, but the face is only suggested. It is worthy of note that this increase in human representation immediately precedes the first recorded traces of early agriculture. From this period, we see the introduction of two dominant symbols, the woman and the bull, both destined to become of major importance.

During the 7th millennium in the Pre-Pottery Neolithic B* (PPNB) period, terracotta female figurines spread rapidly from the Levant (Aswad, Jericho, Beidha) to Cayönü in the north near the Taurus. They are also found at Ali Kosh in Iran. About 6000BC,

figurines from Ramad in Syria introduced a style which, while preserving opulent feminine forms, takes special care in rendering faces, particularly the eyes. This is a new theme peculiar to the Neolithic. The few feminine statuettes (the "Venuses") to have survived from the western Paleolithic exaggerated specifically female features to the virtual exclusion of those parts of the body common to both sexes. The head in particular is nearly always attenuated.

In the Ramad style, by contrast, the head is elongated towards the top and the back, the eyes being rendered by incised clay lozenges. The same characteristics are found in the 6th millennium at Byblos in Lebanon and in the Munhata culture in Palestine. In Iraq and Iran, the same themes may emerge in different styles. Some figurines (Sarab) still have attenuated heads, while the hips and breasts are disproportionately large, but in the Zagros the face alone may occupy a third or even half of the total volume of the schematic T-shaped figurines. Further south, in the Sawarra culture, where the style is more naturalistic, the eyes are emphasized by incised and painted clay lozenges (Choga Mami) or bitumen inlays (Tell Sawwan).

Clay animal figurines are still found everywhere, but their more careless manufacture makes it difficult to identify and consequently to interpret them. The image of woman, on the contrary, treated with care and expressing constant themes through very diversified artistic styles depending on places and cultures, asserts its symbolic character more clearly. Did this image represent a goddess? The answer is surely yes, if Anatolian artifacts from the 6th millennium are taken into account. The exceptional state of preservation of the town of Çatal Hüyük has supplied archaeologists not only with isolated statuettes but also with a group of representations linked with architectural elements (paintings and high reliefs), in which the feminine and animal images are integrated into a network of spatial relations which help to define their meaning. First, the statuettes themselves are more complex, and may connect with several characters. It is surely a "goddess" who is shown giving birth on a throne of panthers, her form portrayed with expressionist exuberance. The same divinity appears on monumental high reliefs dominating the north wall of shrines and giving birth to bulls superimposed below in the form of clay bucrania (skulls with horns). The frequent association of the goddess not only with the panther or leopard, but also with various other carnivorous animals (birds of prey, foxes, etc.), the beaks and teeth of which protrude from the walls near the high reliefs, sometimes enveloped in clay breasts, emphasizes her mastery of wild beasts, in

addition to her maternal aspect. This may well be the oriental Mother Goddess, mistress of wild animals, here appearing for the first time.

A second dominant figure, this time masculine, exists at Çatal Hüyük. Depicted only once in human form (a bearded man sitting astride a bull), the figure is generally confined to its zoomorphic version, the bull itself, the evocation of which is intensified in dwellings where we find bucrania protruding from walls, benches decorated with horns, and so on. Its painted or engraved silhouette appears several times on walls, sometimes in hunting or "armed dance" scenes, in which the animal, out of all proportion to the humans surrounding it, draws its supernatural power from its own vast size.

Thus the ideological evolution appropriate to the neolithization process emerges clearly. First of all, there is the growing importance of human representations, still mainly feminine. Next there is an original manner of handling these representations, undoubtedly reflecting the development of anthropological conceptions themselves. The exaggeration of the female parts of the human body most symbolic of fertility still continues, but the insistence on emphasizing the head and especially the eyes is new. This interest finds a corresponding expression in the funerary rites. The collective burials of the Natufian are replaced throughout the Levant by the "skull cult" which consists in preserving human skulls outside the actual tombs, these skulls sometimes being modelled over in clay in the image of the living, as in the Palestinian PPNB, the eyes being denoted by shells or painting. This cult also existed in Syria, Turkey and as far as Iraq in the 5th millennium during the Halafian civilization.

Finally, very different from the bestiary of the hunter gatherers, which was certainly symbolic, but not hierarchical, we find the new appearance of "divine" personages. At a time when Near Eastern societies were emerging from the Paleolithic "age of abundance" (Sahlins), in which day-to-day hunting and gathering ensured survival for little effort, it is strange to find that the first agricultural "work" and the progressive mastery of the environment by the domestication of animals and plants coincides with a human spirituality now expanded to include both an "above" and a "below", the order of the divinity and that of ordinary humanity. This inner dramatization may not be unrelated to the paradoxical effort to leave the old-established way of life behind and set forth on a new adventure that was not justified ecologically.

Fresco of bull hunt at Çatal Hüyük, Anatolia. 6th millennium BC.

From the 8th millennium, the wild bull played a key symbolic role in the Neolithic Near East, long before the domestication of cattle. At Çatal Hüyük it is represented everywhere, in figurines and as a *bucranium* (horns and skull) protruding from the walls. In this fresco depicting a "hunting scene" the artist's exaggeration of the animal's size contrasts with the reduced dimensions of the hunters.

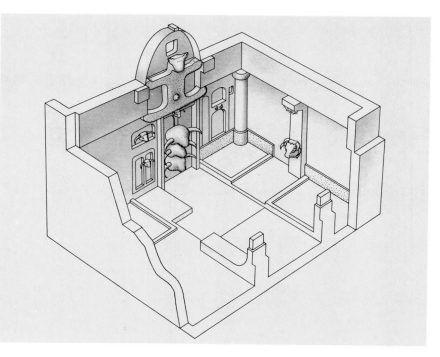

Goddess giving birth to bulls. Reconstruction of a high relief at Çatal Hüyük. 6th millennium BC.

The principal figure in the Neolithic pantheon of divinities, the goddess dominates the north wall of several "domestic sanctuaries" at Çatal Hüyük, where *bucrania* (horns and skull) of bulls seem to proceed from her. The stomach is always emphasized by a prominent navel. Note, too, on the panel reproduced here, protruding from the walls, a ram's head to the right of the goddess and a wild boar's jawbone to her left.

J. Mellaart

Young ruminant carved on a bone handle. Natufian, from Mount Carmel, Israel. 10th millennium BC.

In the Natufian, the last hunter gatherers of the Levant clung to an almost exclusively animal art, using stone and, even more, bone, depicting gazelles and deer. The artifacts are delicately fashioned in the round, like the handle above, or in a more schematic style. Rockefeller Museum, Jerusalem.

Terracotta "goddess' from Munhata, Jordan Valley. 5th millennium BC.

Several features common throughout the Levant from the early 7th millennium are found in this figurine: amplification of the buttocks, elongation of the back of the head, and emphasis of the eyes. The peculiar style of the Munhata culture, which applied clay coils and lozenges, modelled in advance, deliberately gives these feminine representations a frightening appearance. The Bronfman Museum, Jerusalem.

Alabaster female statuette from Tell Sawwan, Iraq. 6th millennium BC

On the statuettes from Tell Sawwan, probably goddesses, the eyes are emphasized by bitumen inlays. They sometimes have a conical bonnet of the same material. Slimmer than the Levant statuettes, they are always represented in an upright position. Iraq Museum.

The goddess with panthers from Çatal Hüyük, Anatolia. 6th millennium BC.

This terracotta statuette shows an obese hieratic woman giving birth in a sitting position, on a throne composed of three panthers. She attests to the cult in the Near East of a Mother Goddess, mistress of wild animals.

The Vulture Fresco at Çatal Hüyük, Anatolia. 6th millennium BC.

Vultures with unfurled wings pounce on headless humans. Sometimes interpreted as evidence of a rite of the de-fleshing of corpses by birds of prey, this scene may simply have a symbolic value. Vultures, jackals and wild boars figure among the "funerary" attributes of the mother goddess at Çatal Hüyük.

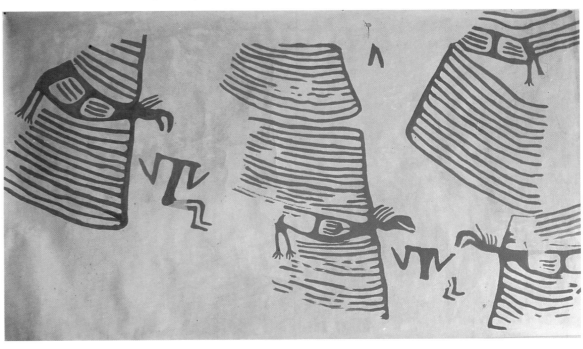

173

The Ancient Near East: the archaeological background

The discovery of the ancient civilizations of the Near East is the product of the "heroic age" of archaeology—the late 19th and early 20th centuries—and of course its "heroic" figures, Botta, Layard, Schliemann, Woolley. More recent discoveries, such as the palace of Ebla at Tell Mardikh, Syria, show that spectacular finds of this type are still possible.

In 1782, the botanist A. Michaux brought back from Persia a "stone", probably originating in Ctesophon, which was acquired by the Cabinet des Antiquités of the Bibliothèque Nationale in Paris. This was the first Babylonian epigraphic document or inscription to reach Europe. The Near East, and particularly the Mediterranean area of Egypt, Turkey, Lebanon and Palestine, received many famous travellers, with Palestine above all attracting a constant stream of pilgrim-visitors, bibles in hand. But more distant regions such as Mesopotamia and Persia were less well known.

The same year that Michaux brought his *Kudurru* back to France, a French astronomer, Abbé Joseph de Beauchamp, sent a description of the major Mesopotamian sites to Paris. His correspondent in Paris, Abbé Barthelemy (who had deciphered the Phoenician script in 1758), guided his enquiries from afar, recommending that he should undertake "the comparison of a large number of monuments which he could see with his own eyes . . ."

Beauchamp had drawn the attention of western scholars to the ruins of Nineveh, Ctesiphon, Babylon and Persepolis, and later on diplomats and agents of the Compagnie des Indes began to publish papers on the great Mesopotamian cities. During the first half of the 19th century, Mesopotamia, Anatolia and Iran were all investigated by keen observers.

Palestine was the subject of detailed descriptions from the beginning of the 19th century. In Anatolia, the ruins of Boghazkoy were reported in 1834. In Persia, Flandin and Coste were officially commissioned in 1839 to make an accurate record of any sculptures and inscriptions they might find.

If ancient Mesopotamia is taken as an example, archaeological exploration began very early, P.E. Botta*, appointed French Consul at Mosul in 1842, recognized the importance of the *tells* which covered the ruins of ancient Nineveh. He began excavating in December 1842, thus inaugurating archaeological research in this country, and then transferred his attentions to Khorsabad, some 20 kilometres (12 miles) to the northwest. He found "figures and inscriptions" almost at once and wrote to the Académie des Inscriptions in April 1843, announcing his discoveries: "I am now continuing my excavations with greater interest, because I believe I am the first to have discovered sculptures that have all the appearance of going back to the age when Nineveh was flourishing." Botta immediately received an official government subsidy to continue his researches.

Political rivalries and archaeology

This began the long story of a political rivalry between France and England that often took precedence over scientific concerns. However, as the result of Botta's discoveries, the Musée Assyrien was inaugurated in the Louvre on 1 May 1847, and 10 years later the collection was arranged in its current form and location. To western museums, where antiquity had previously been only Graeco-Roman or Egyptian, these Neo-Assyrian reliefs were a revelation. The French expeditions of Place and Fresnel, and the English ones of Layard and Rassam, now followed. The Near East was now open to fieldwork, and not just in distant Mesopotamia. In 1860, Napoleon III attached an archaeological mission led by E. Renan to the Syrian expedition, caused by the conflict between Maronites and Druses. The hasty and badly conducted excavation (Renan was no archaeologist) did not have the desired success. A few years later, in 1863, F. de Saulcy, a protégé of the Emperor, returned to the Holy Land accompanied by a cartographer, an architect and a photographer, and with the assistance of these specialists was able to carry out and achieve remarkable descriptive work.

However, there is no doubt that the pursuit of the object often prevailed over real archaeological observation. Throughout the second half of the 19th century, in the case of Mesopotamia alone, ancient mud-brick architecture was the victim of research that was too often random and self-interested. But these undertakings saved from destruction monuments and documents in which the local authorities of the day took little or no interest, and sometimes plans and drawings were scrupulously executed in difficult conditions.

The stratigraphic method

Then came the work of H. Schliemann* at Troy in Asia Minor (1871–1890). An amateur, a businessman, keen on publicity and driven by his desire to establish connections between textual references and field sites, Schliemann devoted his life and fortune to Homeric research, using references in the texts to identify the ancient city of Troy. In the eyes of later archaeologists, he is above all the man who realized that an antique site had developed and that it was made up of successive layers. Even if Schliemann was far out in some of his dates (he attributed to Priam treasures of jewellery actually going back to the third millennium BC), he revealed that an artificial hill such as Troy covered at least seven successive towns. The practice of establishing a site in time (stratigraphy*) had made its appearance.

The stratigraphic method was difficult to apply to Near Eastern sites where mud-brick architecture has often been used exclusively, and where the remains of buildings reduced to fragments are especially difficult to extract and interpret. The contribution of the great German archaeologists of the end of the last century lay in this skilful decipherment of a lost architecture. When the *Deutsche Orient Gesellschaft*, under the patronage of Wilhelm II, decided in 1898 to undertake the methodical excavation of the most prestigious site of all, Babylon, the task was entrusted to an architect, R. Koldeway*, and not to an epigraphist or inscription specialist. In 1903, his pupil W. Andrae began work on the site of Ashur, and Andrae's work from 1903 to World War I was a model of its kind.

Until 1914, although there were difficulties such as lack of understanding by local authorities or peoples, and communication problems, conditions in general were favourable to scientific research. At that time the Orient was basically divided only between the Ottoman and the Persian Empires. Western scientific research enjoyed financial superiority which made large-scale undertakings possible.

The golden age of archaeology?

After World War I, in spite of considerable political changes, the West thought at first that things would go on as usual; excavations were rapidly resumed and major operations successfully carried out. The most striking example is the impressive series of sites opened by the Oriental Institute of Chicago, then directed by the Egyptologist J. Breasted. One or two major sites in every region of the Near East were excavated by the OIC, which aimed at total exploration. They included Alishar in Central Anatolia, Tepe Hissar and Persepolis in Iran, four large tells in Central Mesopotamia (in the lower valley of the Diyala) and Megiddo in Palestine. Even on the last-named site, where excavations took place on a staggering scale, total excavation (which is now considered harmful) was not achieved. The project was humanly impossible and, partly due to the world financial crisis, the great "total" excavation of Megiddo was soon limited to large-scale probes.

From this fertile period dates the exploration of sites important because of

Reliefs from the Royal Palace of Sargon II at Khorsabad

From 1843 to 1844, P.E. Botta (1802–70), French consular agent at Mosul, explored part of the royal palace of Sargon II (721–705BC) at Khorsabad, 16km (10 miles) from Mosul, and uncovered many carved reliefs. Two volumes of engraved plates were meticulously executed by M.E. Flambin at a time when photography was not yet used by archaeologists. This plate (relief 14 from Hall II of the palace) represents a low relief forming part of a long frieze with two sections, one above the other, separated by an inscription. Above, a banquet scene; below, the capture of a mountain town by the Assyrian armies. P.E. Botta and M.E. Flambin, *Monument de Ninive*, Imprimerie Nationale, 1849–50, plate 61.

their size or the diversity of the periods represented, as at Ur, Mari, Alishar, Boghazkoy, Persepolis, Byblos and Ugarit. The aim was to identify major monuments and establish a definite chronology, sometimes corroborated, as in Mesopotamia, by material from Assyrian studies.

For some scholars this was the golden age of Near Eastern archaeology, helped by the system of political mandates in Lebanon, Syria, Jordan, and Iraq or confronted, as in Turkey and Iran, by growing nationalism. Archaeology ensured its means, made use of aerial photography, especially in Syria and Iran, refined certain methods (ceramology), and built up preliminary reports and definitive publications. Sometimes spectacular discoveries aroused public interest, as with the find of the royal tombs of Ur, 1927–29. Sometimes more obviously patient work at a well-chosen site allowed the establishment of a kind of table of reference for a region which later research might improve or amend, but on which it could be relied on for a long time, as was the case with R. Ghirshman's* work at Tepe Sialk near Kashan in Iran, 1933–38. The exploration of important sites such as Mari or Ras Shamra led scholars to reconsider whole sections of the history of the ancient Near East. Closer to our own day, a Syrian site such as Tell Mardikh, the ancient Ebla, suggests that this period has not yet been completely explored, and that great discoveries are still possible.

Post-war problems

However, the resumption of work after World War II was slower. The financial resources needed for the large sites dried up. The rise of young nations, rightfully interested in preserving their heritage, forced the countries traditionally interested in eastern archaeology (Europe, the United States and Japan) to renounce their rights to a part of the antiquities discovered. Archaeology itself underwent deep changes in the east and elsewhere. From now on, fieldwork entailed classifying as well as describing material, understanding as well as cataloguing it. The enormous mass of material has gradually imposed the use of a wide range of scientific methods. Above all, archaeology has tried to widen its field of activity as far as possible, and has sought to explain the pattern of ancient man's daily life and the social structure of ancient societies. A kind of "paleosociology" was born.

This evolution towards an increasingly global archaeology did not take place without sectarian quarrels. Some scholars incline to a tendency which could be called ethnographic. Others take a more anthropological approach and try to discover and establish laws of cultural development through archaeological studies.

The archaeology of the Near East soon felt the urgent need to expand its aims and its means. R. Braidwood's work at Jarmo is an excellent example of this. His *Prehistoric Investigations in Iraqi Kurdistan* was published in 1960, but work on location had begun in 1948 (the project lasted from 1948 to 1955). Thanks to his team, the Near East became "the laboratory of an ecological archaeology sensitive to cultivated species and domestication" (A. Schnapp). Although the hypotheses and interpretations put forward at the time are now mostly out of date, Braidwood's method is still valid. Moreover, this was the first time that the usefulness to archaeology of other sciences was clearly recognized, for Braidwood included amongst others in his team zoologists, botanists and geomorphologists.

Of course these methods inevitably caused contradictions. Modern techniques of excavation require the establishment of very accurate records, which greatly reduces the area covered. At the same time, expeditions are staffed with ever increasing numbers working on limited surfaces. It thus becomes difficult to make progress in areas such as urbanism or the organization of space. To our knowledge there is not one plan of a village going back to the beginnings of cultivation in lower Mesopotamia. The site of Uruk may have given its name to a period, also known as proto-urban, but we do not know a single street or a single house in the overall construction of that period because of the narrowness of the areas excavated.

However, such enlargement of the programme of archaeological investigation is more suited to some periods than to others. The archaeology of historical periods in the Near East often suffers owing to the vast size of the sites. But regardless of the period, a modern investigation will usually involve careful surveying of the surface, the study of aerial photographs and much pedological (soil analysis) and ecological work.

A political situation in constant turmoil is not exactly favourable to long-term undertakings. In our day it is much harder to travel between Istanbul and the Indus than it was 100 years ago. The speed of modern means of transport has been counterbalanced by political partitions which raise many barriers. Administrative formalities now create often insurmountable obstacles. Unhindered investigation of the ground in the form of field surveys is sometimes out of the question, access to aerial photographs is often forbidden, good topographical maps are practically non existent. The catalogue is endless.

Finally, the rapid economic development of some countries may pose a threat to remains of the past which local archaeological authorities are aware of, requiring an increase in rescue operations. These monopolize efforts in the field and concentrate on a region which may be interesting but is sometimes of secondary importance. Most of the time the result is fruitful, but it is necessary to work fast and to have the men and money available at the right time. On the other hand, in Syria, as in Iraq and Turkey, the construction during the last 15 years of large hydroelectric dams, flooding entire valleys, has provided many unexpected opportunities to explore certain less well-known regions, such as the upper and middle Euphrates, Diyala, and the central valley of the Tigris.

For many years now, thanks to these exceptional operations and to the continuous exploration of sites, important questions have been revived, such as the emergence of food cultivation in lower Mesopotamia, Sumerian influence on the middle Euphrates, the first Syrian kingdoms, and so on. The ancient Orient still has much to tell us.

The following pages are far from exhaustive. By means of a few examples, they aim to give an account of recent research, investigations, successes and, sometimes, setbacks. At all events, they definitely testify to the vitality of a field where there is still much to discover and interpret.

The colonization of Lower Mesopotamia

Mesopotamia is the earliest and one of the most influential centres of city civilization in world history. But the origin of human settlement in Lower Mesopotamia (Babylonia) is still the subject of great controversy.

Mesopotamia, the vast lowland area between Iraq and the Syrian desert, is divided into two very different zones on both sides of the 34th parallel. The north, upstream from Samarra* and Anah, is a steppe-like plain where non-irrigated crops are possible; the south, which the people of antiquity called Babylonia, is a non-productive arid zone where agriculture is only possible by bringing in water from outside, taken from the Tigris and the Euphrates. Irrigation techniques were therefore needed in order to exploit the area, as in the central valley of the Indus or in Khorezm in Central Asia.

In Lower Mesopotamia, archaeologists have succeeded in working out how the region could have been peopled. The preliminary stages are all the more interesting because they may explain the subsequent development of a region which later completely overshadowed the neighbouring countries. From the end of the 4th millennium the town of Uruk (level 4) contained vast buildings with sophisticated decorations. Writing on clay tablets was practised there, and the written documents were sealed with cylinder seals. Not far away in Khuzistan, which is merely an extension of the Mesopotamian plain to the foothills of the Zagros, the state of Susa* experienced a more or less parallel development. Lower Mesopotamia, arid but irrigable, may have owed its early success to its hard confrontation with a hostile environment. Between the first human settlements in the region and great urban centres dating to the end of the 4th millennium, only a short time elapsed, not more than 2,000 years, so the archaeological study of the evidence remaining from this period is of the first importance.

There is no shortage of unsolved problems. In the absence of serious geomorphological or soil studies, the exact location of the shore of the Gulf in antiquity is unknown. Five thousand years ago, it was probably some 150km (93 miles) further north than the present-day shore. The quantity of sediments transported and deposited by the Tigris and the Euphrates is considerable, but so too is the wind erosion. The most ancient sites may be buried under a thick layer of sediment. The present ruins may be merely the much eroded remains of sites that were once far more important. The present courses of the Euphrates and the Tigris may be far distant from their beds in antiquity. The questions are seemingly endless.

The first colonists of Lower Mesopotamia

In Lower Mesopotamia the oldest known sites date from the middle of the 6th millennium. Until we are better informed, we may assume that the region was uninhabited before that date. Where did the first colonists come from? They knew how to make terracotta pottery, so if a trustworthy comparison of ceramic styles can be made between the material from two excavated sites (Eridu and Oueili), a few shards found on the surface in the Uruk region, and material from certain sites in central Iraq, at Choga Mami, we may assume that the first farmers in Lower Mesopotamia came from the centre of the country and that they were displaced in the late phase of the so-called Samarra period, during the second half of the 6th millennium. Also relevant is the fact that, according to some authors, the first examples of channel irrigation appeared in central Iraq, at Choga Mami in fact, near Mandali. No doubt the first villages of the future land of Sumer developed only small-scale works to bring the water of the Euphrates to the fields, not vast networks. However, that could have been enough to enable small groups of villagers to settle and grow crops.

Very little is known about these first villages. At Eridu, about 40km (25 miles) from Ur, an Iraqi team revealed some 40 years ago a series of levels from the two millennia which concern us. A succession of buildings from Eridu XVI to VI was uncovered, which divided roughly into four phases of development, the so-called Ubaid* 1 to 4 period, from the middle of the 6th millennium to the beginning of the 4th millennium. Thorough fieldwork covers the end of this period at Ur and Uruk, where research relating to these remote periods has been handicapped by the vast mass of later ruins. At Oueili, near Larsa, a village from the Ubaid 1 to 4 period is still being explored. Finally, there are large cemeteries from the end of the period at Eridu and Tell Ubaid.

Land surveys reveal that the agriculturists inhabited small villages lying some distance from each other and probably distributed along the main irrigation channels, according to material taken from the surface in the Uruk region. Of small size—an average of 4 hectares (10 acres) a village has been suggested—they probably consisted of a few large farms. Barley was the main crop, being well adapted to the local climate. The banks of the channels supplied aquatic plants and reeds which were harvested with terracotta sickles, broken fragments of which abound in sites of that period. Livestock, according to the first estimates at Oueili in the Ubaid 4 period, consisted of cattle (57.9 percent), pigs (36.9 percent) and only 5.2 percent of sheep and goats. Such a distribution is hardly surprising in the ecological context and corresponds roughly with earlier estimates made at Eridu in 1970. Fish played a large part in the inhabitants' diet, which is not surprising in a region irrigated by numerous channels. In addition to a plentiful tool kit of ordinary flint, which nevertheless had to be supplied from distant sources, the farmers of Oueili used finer raw materials such as rock crystal and obsidian, which also were not locally found materials.

Were villages of this type numerous? Surface surveys both in Lower Mesopotamia proper and in the Susian region have made it possible to map a fairly loose network of such settlements, at least for the end of the Ubaid period. But, we must be careful and not infer too much from these results until the publication of a series of monographs about sites explored in depth and over a sufficiently wide area.

The main problem to be solved is that of the transition of these village cultures, which were responsible for initiating the exploitation of a difficult environment, into the subsequent so-called Uruk and Jamdat Nasr cultures. The latter possessed writing, an accounting system, a network of long-distance commercial exchanges based on counting-houses, and a ranked social structure, as we can deduce from certain representations carved on stone found at Uruk. But at present only the last-named site and Susa have supplied a stratigraphic, layer-by-layer sequence from the Ubaid 4 period to the very end of the 4th millennium, thus throwing light on this major development, but only over small areas.

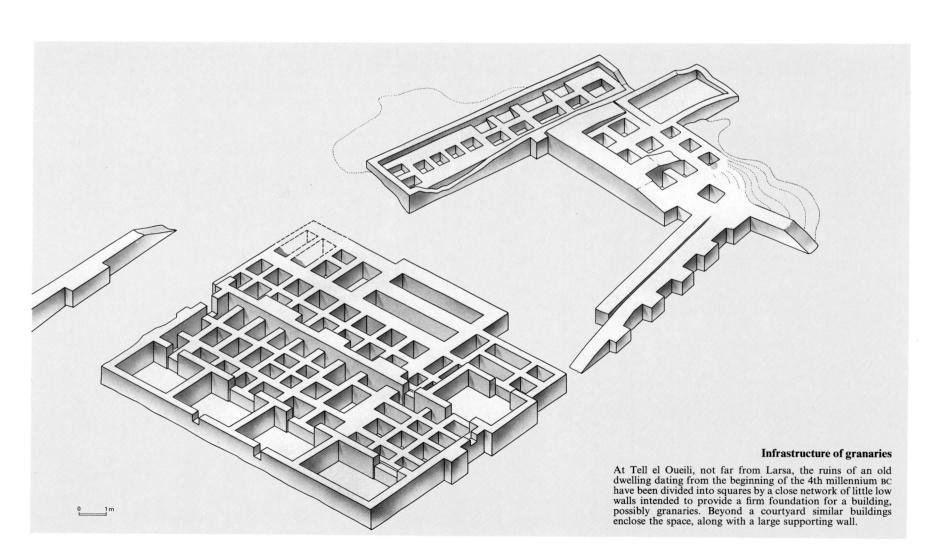

Infrastructure of granaries

At Tell el Oueili, not far from Larsa, the ruins of an old dwelling dating from the beginning of the 4th millennium BC have been divided into squares by a close network of little low walls intended to provide a firm foundation for a building, possibly granaries. Beyond a courtyard similar buildings enclose the space, along with a large supporting wall.

0   1 m

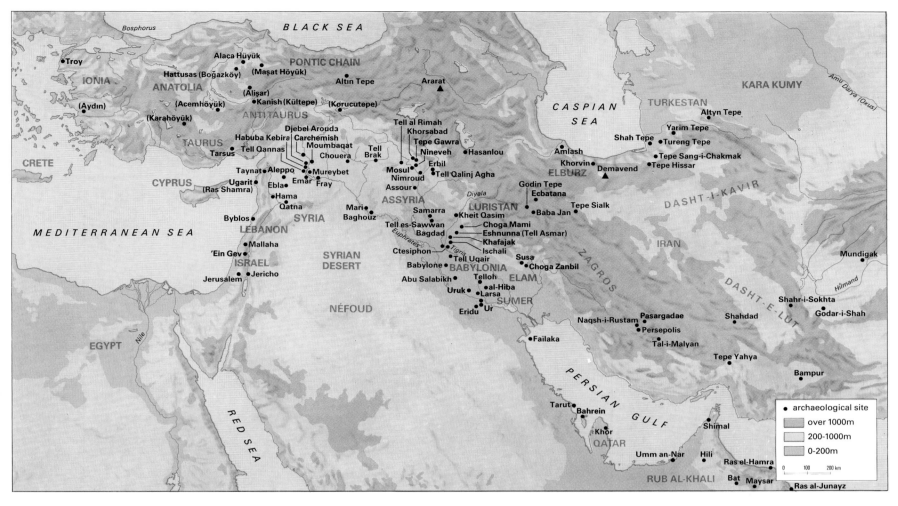

Painted pottery, Tell el Oueili (*c.*4000BC)

At the end of the Ubaid period, certain dishes from Tell el Oueili were decorated with more care than the usual product, but the quality of the decoration was still far removed from that of the first painted ceramics in Lower Mesopotamia (in what is known as the Eridu period, 6th millennium).

Stone hoes, Tell el Oueili (*c.*4000BC)

The farmers of Lower Mesopotamia used stone hoes, worked on both surfaces and made from flint flakes which often still had part of their core. They were intended for working the land, and are found in great numbers on sites from the Ubaid period.

Pottery in common use, Tell el Oueili (*c.*4000BC)

At the end of the Chalcolithic Age, painted pottery became much less common (it represents just 12% of total output) while unpainted pottery increased. Painted decoration was applied quite roughly and quickly. It followed geometric patterns, and often consisted only of parallel bands or lines.

Earthenware sickles, Tello

All sites of the Ubaid period have yielded large numbers of earthenware sickles, moulded in one piece, blade and handle. The paste has inclusions of quartz sand, and was often fired almost to the point of vitrification. These tools really were used, but they may have been intended for cutting reeds rather than harvesting cereals. Musée de Louvre, Paris.

Small terracotta wild boar, Tell el Oueili (*c.*4000BC)

The farming peoples in Lower Mesopotamia fashioned numerous clay figures, often very successfully, representing the animal world that surrounded them. While cattle, sheep and pigs are often depicted, it is worth emphasizing that fish are not found despite the fact that they were plentiful in the waterways that ran through the area.

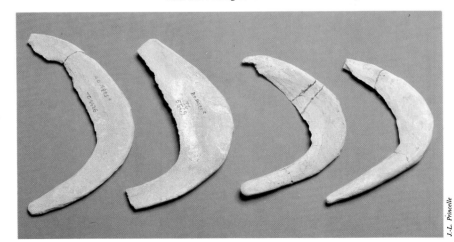

The invention of writing

Writing was invented in the 4th millennium BC in what is now Iraq. The first alphabet followed in the 2nd millennium BC, and only in the 2nd millenium AD have the printing press and the computer improved on it.

A generation has passed since the last important discovery relating to our knowledge of Eastern Mediterranean methods of writing. Specialists have concentrated on improving the translation of known texts without forming more theories about them. Nevertheless such theories, rather than an increase in the already voluminous documentation, will alone enable us to understand the inner working of Near Eastern societies.

This part of the world witnessed the "birth" of writing on three successive but connected occasions. Towards 3200BC, the large cities of Sumer (southern Mesopotamia) enjoyed immense prosperity. This was undoubtedly due to new irrigation techniques. As a result the old methods of administration became inadequate; administrators and stewards needed more effective methods to record and process increasing volumes of complex information. These people may not have invented writing, but for a long time they were the only ones to use it. So it was not surprising that the whole process took place at Uruk, then the metropolis of this world.

The system, invented in its entirety, functioned from the beginning as a self-contained organism: it was not the last stage of a hesitant development nor the product of an unplanned accumulation of independent symbols. Admittedly, some symbols may already have existed before their integration into a new function: for instance, a cross inside a circle came to mean "sheep" for it was habitually used as the brand on animals destined for shearing or slaughtering. Similarly, the choice of moist clay as the "writing paper" only continued an old custom whereby clay was used to seal doors or jars, and then stamped with the mark of the owner.

These early signs are ideograms, that is, they directly represent a concept, idea or thing. Thus their meaning cannot be guessed from their outline. Even if the original relationship between drawing and idea was not arbitrary, it later became, and remained, obscure. Little more than one-fifth of these signs escaped deliberate abstraction, and even these, which depicted exotic but real entities, later disappeared and left no successors. Each sign denoted a single concept, without grammatical qualifications, and the whole worked as a system of rules to aid memory. But the system concealed two fertile possibilities: first, an organized association of ideas meant that "branch", for example, would suggest "staff", then "sceptre" and "chief"; and secondly, a use of the rebus (a kind of word picture) meant that words of similar sound could be denoted by the same sign. Thus a single written shape might simultaneously represent words with an identical pronunciation but a different meaning, and words with a similar meaning but a different pronunciation. Then the number of symbols was restricted and it was no longer necessary to keep on inventing and learning new ones.

Schools became necessary to transmit this knowledge and standardize it so that its practitioners could communicate with each other. An unexpected result of this was to widen the field of what had been a skill reserved for administrators. Literature, which had been oral until then, was used in the exercises for scribes; writing thus slowly became an instrument of intellectual life, though alien to it both in origin and purpose. This development caused a cultural shock throughout the area. Regions such as Syria were content to import it; western Iran and Egypt—cultures with strongly developed personalities—adopted its principles, but recreated their own writing. Of these, Iranian writing soon disappeared, but that of Egypt prospered considerably.

A compromise between two contradictory requirements implicit in writing—the need for rapid ciphering and for reliable deciphering—led to the emergence of the classical system in c.2800BC. The original outline of continuous flowing lines yielded to impressions made by a split reed, the calamus. The signs then became groupings of "angles". Previously, they had been placed at random in cartouches (oblong figures), but these were gradually suppressed. Signs were now aligned logically, and line and sentence tended to merge. A complete element of meaning ran from the left-hand to the right-hand margin of the tablet, so that logical analysis and material arrangement coincided.

This classical cuneiform* (so called because of its "cuneic" or wedgeshaped characters) was used until the first century AD, but it remained extremely complicated even though its 900 signs were reduced to about half that number. Those which were purely ideograms were rare; the majority also simultaneously denoted one or more sounds, generally monosyllabic, without indicating, to those unfamiliar with the system, which sound to choose. But a limit was put on this graphic game: ideograms were used for common words, but the rest were cut up syllable by syllable, each expressed by only one grapheme (or unit of writing). Thus it was possible to transcribe the whole spoken sequence, and not just the essential concepts, as before, so that with minor adjustments Sumerian writing could record all kinds of languages: Semitic ones such as Babylonian and Assyrian, Indo-European ones such as Hittite and Luvite (Anatolia, second millennium) or very differently formed languages such as Hurrian or Urartian (Armenia, second and first millennia BC).

The birth of the alphabet

The oldest alphabet of which we have a record, that of Ugarit, appeared c.1500BC and was connected with earlier developments by its technique, the clay tablet and reed-pen borrowed from Mesopotamia. However, it was based on an original but simple idea: a sign corresponded to each consonant, and a consonant to each sign. There were no vowels, for in the Semitic languages (to which Ugarit belonged) the consonantal skeleton gives the meaning, while the role of the vowel is to specify the grammatical function in the spoken language. The reader has the generally simple task of supplying them mentally in the written text. The reason for this failure to record vowels may have been to preserve Ugaritic words in a fixed form, like cuneiform ideograms.

In fact, these inventors of the alphabet had no intention of making an important technical advance, nor were they aware that they had done so. They were simply trying to imitate the prestigious Babylonian system more economically. Following the example of other peoples at about the same period (the Hittites for example), the people of Ugarit wanted to have their own writing, just as those of Mesopotamia and Egypt had theirs. But they kept it as a local usage, not putting it into direct competition with cuneiform, which they continued to use.

The Byblos alphabet marked a second decisive stage in the evolution of writing. This alphabet was the direct ancestor of our own, but at the beginning of the second millennium BC it was merely the adaptation of Ugarit principles to the instruments of Egyptian scribes: ink and a flexible material, leather or papyrus.*

The consonantal system undoubtedly marks a break with the past, especially in speed of learning, for there are only some 30 graphic forms. The physiology of the human eye may have played a part here, for the eye does not scan by means of continuous movement along the lines, but by stops and starts, taking in whole sections of the text. A long revolution, marked at first by the introduction of vowels by the Greeks, finally restored to the writing known as alphabetical some of the contradictory and encumbering features of the earliest writing, as for instance when the same letter represents different sounds, or signs that are not pronounced are nevertheless written. It almost seems as though the legacy of the Sumerian system, overshadowed for a time by the consonantal alphabet, is once again weighing down some versions of present-day writing.

Mission archéologique française en Iraq

Musées nationaux

Musées nationaux

An archaic tablet

Scholars believe that this document, one of the first ever written (c.3200BC) carries three proper names on its upper left. On the left a "hand", which probably indicates "power", may refer to the personage whose name covers the bottom of the tablet. In order to decipher the meaning a reader must use these remnants as a basis from which to reconstitute omitted words and grammatical marks. Louvre, Paris.

An ancient record of "Rimuch, King of the Universe"

This inscription represents a decisive advance in the development of cuneiform writing in the 23rd century BC. The signs, still in cartouches (oblong boxes) are aligned in the direction of the reading line, and are used on the top line as syllables and not as ideograms. Louvre, Paris

Clay tablet, 18th century BC

Found in the temple of the Sun God at Larsa (Iraq) this inscription is a good example of the standard module as it gradually developed over the centuries. The surface is quite large, but the tablet is not too bulky for use by scribes. Iraqi Museum, Baghdad

An Assyrian manual of ancient scripts

In order to read archaic inscriptions and compose imitations of them, the scribes drew up lists of correspondences between their own and past signs, but here the ancient shapes (on the left of each column) are pure fantasies dreamed up by a scholar in the service of King Assurbanipal (8th century BC).

Stele of King Melichihov (14th century BC)

In Mesopotamia, writing never enjoyed an authority superior to that of word, gesture or drawing. This stele bears divine protecting symbols on one side, and curses on the other. The text of the donation is inscribed on the same surface.

An Ugaritic "alphabet" (13th century BC)

Ugaritic writing comprised 29 consonants, recorded here in an order which was close to that of the Latin alphabet. It was normally written from left to right and much more rarely from right to left. Nevertheless, the latter direction was applied in the use of the Phoenician alphabet, which transmitted it to Arabic and Hebrew. National Museum, Syria.

The development of some cuneiform characters

Up to the 2nd millennium BC, the trend was to graphic simplification. Over-specialized signs (1 and 2) were abandoned; others became silhouettes recalling only vaguely the original signs (9), especially as the latter (3 and 8) had no obvious connection with their meaning, but, in return, each cuneiform sign acquired increasingly rich ideogramatic and phonetic values, hence the progressive complication of the system in practice.

end of 4th millenium BC	towards 2200BC	towards 1800BC	towards 1300BC	towards 650BC	
1					
2		*signs that disappeared*			▨ Northern Mesopotamia ▧ Southern Mesopotamia
3					ideogram "fate" prefix for abstract names (phonetically: *nam, bir*)
4					ideogram "vessel" determinative of names of vases (phonetically: *dug, lud*)
5					ideogram "son", "small" (phonetically: *tur*)
6					ideogram "clothing", "to live", "flour"; determinative of names of clothes (phonetically: *ku, dur*)
7					ideogram "branch", "commander" (phonetically: *pa, had*)
8					ideogram "year", "name" (phonetically: *mu*)
9					ideogram "goddess of fecundity"; Inanna in Sumerian, Ishtar in Assyro-Babylonian

Burial practices and society

How far can we deduce a society's beliefs from its burial practices? Today some archaeologists must also be comparative ethnologists in order to interpret successfully not only the material but also the symbolic evidence of the burial.

The traditional attitude of archaeologists towards research into burial practices consists broadly of two basic and often associated tendencies: on the one hand, they treat the subject like any other cultural feature, and try to determine its place in time and space as a contribution to the definition of the culture; on the other, they are concerned with the exploration of these practices in terms of religious beliefs.

American anthropologists have recently demonstrated, on the basis of carefully selected ethnographical examples, that this double approach is dubious: burial practices are *symbols* arbitrarily chosen by people to express what they regarded as significant characteristics of their society. Each feature, such as the position of the dead, the type of entombment, or the nature and quantity of grave goods, contributes a detail to the definition of the status of the deceased within the social environment: age, sex, important qualities, prestige, and so on. The same physical detail can easily mean something quite different in different cultures or, conversely, similar cultures can express similar laws by means of physical signs that have nothing in common. Therefore, it is the symbolic value of the feature and not the feature itself that one should consider when researching a geographical or chronological distribution. In so far as each society is a structure containing a coherent organization of social strata, the burial practices which express these strata represent a system, or a code, reflecting that social structure. They cannot therefore be arbitrarily linked with religious beliefs.

Such an approach poses considerable problems. The archaeologist must first of all select, from the observations made in the field, those with a symbolic value. He must then try to decipher the code he is faced with, not knowing whether the facts he has gathered are sufficiently numerous and varied to be representative. Inevitably, the effectiveness of this approach varies according to each case, but the effort is very rarely wasted. The funerary site of Kheit Qasim in Mesopotamia is an example of a relatively successful investigation.

The tombs of Kheit Qasim
The site is near the river Diyala, some 150km (93 miles) to the northwest of Baghdad; it was occupied for only one, relatively short, period at the beginning of the third millennium BC. The tombs cover an almost circular area with a diameter of about 80m (256ft), but only the western half has been explored. The dead had been laid in shallow ditches, each protected by a brick structure with a corbelled vault which was originally visible above

ground. The bodies were deliberately folded and lying on their right sides, hands at head height, and facing west. Various objects near them included terracotta vessels and a few wicker baskets to hold food and drink, as well as copper ornaments and weapons. In some cases large jars, together with stacks of smaller bowls, had been left outside the tomb, indicating the remains of a funeral ceremony.

If only a few tombs had been excavated, this brief description would sum up our understanding of the site, which would be very slender indeed. Fortunately the area uncovered was large enough to reveal some remarkable facts in connection with the siting of the tombs, the distribution of certain architectural features, and the arrangement of the grave goods. Some large coffins were ranged in two roughly parallel rows, north to south, and show signs of deliberately planned arrangement, as where a platform and low parallel walls extend the brick construction to the west; smaller coffins were spread over the rest of the area, as well as often being placed side by side with the former. While the larger coffins generally contain weapons and are associated outside with a variety of pots, the smaller ones have only yielded pieces of jewellery. Such a distinction can perhaps be explained by the sex of the dead person, although this theory has not yet been confirmed by bone analysis: women were probably buried without numerous grave goods, at the feet of their husbands.

These are not the only differences; for the "male" tombs also vary in elaboration of detail and grave goods. Two very large coffins stand out from the rest in terms of their conspicuous position in the middle of the western row, their more elaborate supporting structures—the platform is larger and the low walls more numerous—and their larger quantity of goods left outside. The farther one gets from these main tombs the simpler they become. The dead person's age may play a part in the cemetery, as suggested by the absence of children (these were buried in the dwellings), but this still does not explain the grading of the tombs, for the most elaborate are not numerous enough to suggest a status determined by age. A more likely explanation is that these differences indicate a degree of social status carefully preserved by a very hierarchical society.

The settlement near the burial ground, excavated by an Iraqi team, supports such an interpretation. It consists of a small fortress, probably built to control a commercial route running along the Diyala and leading to Iran; such a route would have enabled the large cities

of central Mesopotamia to trade in provisions and basic materials. The general impression conveyed by this site is reminiscent of the small feudal mottes of medieval times, occupied by a member of the nobility, his family and his retainers.

Burial practices and social status
Nevertheless, to get a full picture of Mesopotamian burial practices in the 3rd millennium, we must consider a range of examples, sometimes separated by several centuries. Interment in cemeteries seems to have been the practice everywhere for ordinary people. The dead were endowed with only a few personal objects, such as weapons or ornaments, and were provided with offerings of food in pottery vessels.

On the other hand, in the large cities some of the important individuals were buried under their own houses, sometimes in substantial vaults, as at Khafadje. The goods buried with them were not necessarily particularly sumptuous, but their high status is suggested by the quantity in the tomb of vessels used at the funeral banquet (140 at Abu Salabikh), which testifies to the number of people summoned to attend the obsequies. Nevertheless, "princely" or "royal" tombs were usually grouped in special cemeteries, probably because the construction of large underground chambers, and the laying out of the ramps to let down the harnessed chariot that went with the dead person, were very complicated matters in an urban environment.

The princes of Ur were endowed at their burial with objects of an unprecedented variety and richness. Gold, silver, lapis lazuli and cornelian were the main materials used to make and decorate jewellery, weapons, vases, gaming tables, musical instruments and pieces of furniture. The dead were also accompanied by relatives and servants, who were sacrificed for the occasion (up to 80 people were found at Ur). The victims may well have been not only content but even proud to follow their masters, to judge from similar and better known cases. However surprising we may find this practice, it was relatively widespread and characterizes an evolutionary stage of highly hierarchical societies.

At Mesopotamia, in addition to particular sites such as Kheit Qasim, there were thousands of peasant villages and some enormous urban developments. The observations drawn from Kheit Qasim only partially correspond to a much larger system of burial practices. In spite of the long span of time that separates them, Ur and Kheit Qasim reflect different aspects of an already very complex society.

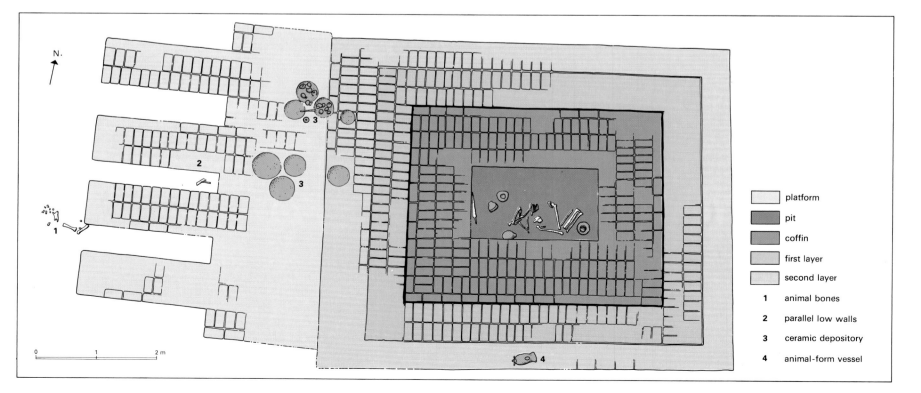

	platform
	pit
	coffin
	first layer
	second layer
1	animal bones
2	parallel low walls
3	ceramic depository
4	animal-form vessel

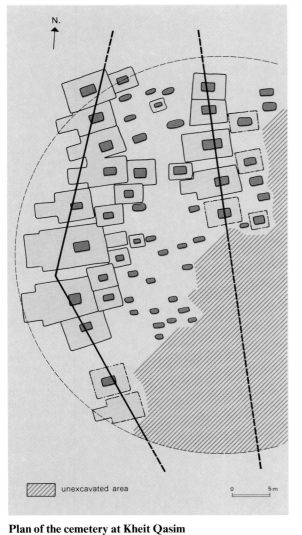

Plan of the cemetery at Kheit Qasim

Inside the cemetery, the tombs containing men were arranged in roughly parallel rows running from north to south, as marked in the plan. The row on the west side has the shape of an open V, and at its tip were two very large tombs, containing personages of exceptional status. The position of the graves precisely reflects the social standing of the dead people during their lives. It seems that, even after death, the chiefs stood at the forefront to lead their community.

Deposit left on the outside bench of a tomb at Kheit Qasim

An accumulation of drinking vessels near certain tombs reflects the fact that the life of archaic communities was punctuated by ceremonies in which banquets had an important place. The decisive events of life (marriage, warlike exploits, death) were an opportunity for each person to put on a show as far as his means allowed, and to proclaim his standing.

Record of a tomb at Kheit Qasim

Inside the cemetery, custom demanded that the deceased be placed in a curled up position on his right side, pointing west, with hands at the same height as the face. In addition to the body lying in this position, evidence for two further bodies is now indicated by nothing more than the skulls and a few bones. The presence of these remains suggests that the tomb was re-used after being cleared of most of the earlier remains.

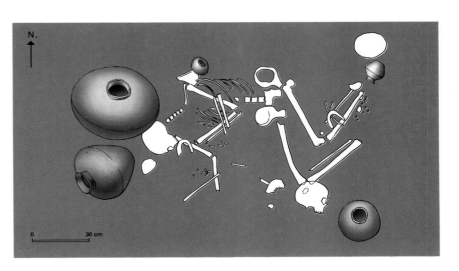

A chief's tomb, Iraq (opposite)

One of the leading figures in the community had been buried with the ceremony due to his rank. His vaulted tomb was surrounded by a double bench extended to the west by a platform and four parallel walls. The deceased was accompanied by receptacles containing food and drink for the world beyond, as well as a copper sword, while a chisel, an axe and a knife were embedded in the masonry of the tomb above him. About 40 goblets piled up in heaps, jars for holding liquids, and animal bones were left outside, indicating that a funeral banquet had followed the death. The fact that there was so much of this material suggests the presence of many guests and the importance of the dead man. A vessel in the form of an ox was placed apart on one of the benches, and probably played a part in the ceremony as well.

Re-used tomb, Kheit Qasim

Some tombs were used again, especially those of humbler people, and these were probably covered over with billets of wood, matting and clay instead of being vaulted. When no opening had been made in the sides of the masonry chamber, such building methods made it possible to re-open the tomb. An extra body could then be deposited where the earlier remains had lain, pushing these along the walls, or simply placed on top of the previous remains.

The Emergence of Syria

Sensational discoveries made since 1974 in the Syrian palace of Ebla have thrown startling light on the early Bronze Age city civilization of Syria, and on its relation to the older Mesopotamian world.

Archaeological research carried out in Syria between the two world wars has revealed the existence of a particularly brilliant urban civilization, the celebrated city of Mari on the Euphrates, in the Early Bronze Age (3rd millennium); inland and coastal Syria yielded the Middle Bronze Age (2000–1600BC) cities of the Amorite dynasties, such as Alep, Carchemish and Qatna; and the resplendent city of Ugarit (Ras Shamra), on the coast, represented the Late Bronze Age (1600–1200BC).

After World War II, further discoveries have thrown light on the major role played by the Syrian region in the process which led from the Paleolithic to the Neolithic way of life between the 12th and 7th millennia. But from the beginning of the 6th millennium and the systematic colonization of Mesopotamia, archaeologists noted that the earlier dynamism appeared to desert Syria. It was in Mesopotamia that the decisive progress took place that led the Neolithic village societies to the urban stage at the beginning of history. The birth of the first cities, particularly of Uruk*, was responsible for placing the Land of the Two Rivers in a dominant position for a long time. Fifty years of fieldwork in Syria had produced hardly any signs of an active local life during the 4th and 3rd millennia: everything suggested that in the age when Sumer was all-powerful, Syria was still struggling to emerge from the Neolithic. However, two discoveries that occurred almost at the same time in the course of the last decade have enabled archaeologists to make a complete revision of this scenario.

In the first case, the discovery of installations of a Sumerian type took place on the bank of the Euphrates in the most westerly part of the curve made by the river as it enters Syria and turns back towards Mesopotamia. On the right bank, a German mission at Habuba Kabira led by E. Heinrich and E. Strommenger, and a Belgian team at Tell Qannas, led by A. Finet, have traced and partially uncovered a town whose close association with the river can be seen in its establishment and general state of organization.

The level uncovered stands on bare earth without traces of previous structures, and the layout suggests that the town was a deliberately planned settlement datable to 3400 or 3300BC. The material found, such as decoration of the temples, groundplans of the buildings, pottery, tools, and symbolic elements, all bear the mark of the city of Uruk. The evidence indicates not merely an influence, but an actual transfer of material. And the presence of cylinder seals and calculi* ("counters") in these houses emphasizes the importance of an economic life based on commercial exchange.

The inevitable conclusion is that Habuba Kabira was a settlement of a colonial type implanted by the Sumerians, the colonists perhaps coming originally from the city of Uruk, and that its principal function was to encourage a river traffic of essential products such as wood and stone, which were in desperately short supply in the land of Sumer. Other commodities may have accompanied these heavy materials, which justified siting the town on a river bank. Moreover, a city of this type could only have been established if the internal situation of Syria allowed it, so that no power comparable to that of Uruk could have developed there. It is also clear, however, that Syria was already playing a part in the economic activity of the Near East. The establishment of a colony indicates the requirements of Sumer and the coming together of different regions into an economic whole to permit the circulation of certain commodities. This situation enabled Syria to become a powerful kingdom in the next millennium. Thus the dynamic role of the Euphrates in the process of Near Eastern development stands out clearly. The colony at Habuba does not appear to have lasted very long—possibly a century before a fire put an end to it. But the current Dutch excavation at Jebel Aruda on the plateau several miles from Habuba shows that it was not an isolated phenomenon.

The archives of Ebla

The second discovery, which was much more sensational, relates to the second half of the 3rd millennium. The ruins of Tell Mardikh, excavated since 1964 by an Italian team under P. Matthiae, from 1974 began to reveal a part of the palace where about 16,000 tablets have been found, proving the exceptional importance of this site in the Early Bronze Age. Thus Ebla (Tell Mardikh) became the most famous archaeological site in the second half of the 20th century, and the status of 3rd millennium Syria began to receive a recognition it had not known earlier.

As regards the site of Ebla, a small part of the monumental palace dating to the second half of the 3rd millennium has been identified on the flank of an acropolis. Finds include walls 2.5–3m (8–10ft) thick; a majestic ceremonial stairway in a massive corner tower; an impressive colonnade to the north containing the dais where the king may have held audiences; and a colonnade to the east, which probably concealed the most private part of the palace. These remains are ample evidence of the power of the city of Ebla.

Nevertheless, in spite of its magnificence, the fame of the site really rests on the discovery of about 16,000 clay tablets, written in cuneiform* script, in two halls along the eastern side of the great audience court. When a fire destroyed the palace, these slipped from their shelves and were rediscovered in the order of their original classification. The archive consists of administrative and economic documents, religious items, dictionary material, and even letters, which give a picture of life in the palace before its destruction. But the importance of the discovery goes beyond the history of Ebla alone. The whole history of the Near East is involved, and it is likely to be extraordinarily enriched by these archives; they are the most comprehensive known in the 3rd millennium and their study has barely begun.

Thus, several centuries before the expansion of the kingdoms of the Amorite period, on which the clay tablets from the palace of Mari are so informative, it seems that Syria had reached a level of development identical to that of Mesopotamia, thanks to Sumerian stimulus. The enterprises of the great Sargon of Akkad and his grandson Naram-Sin, who boasted in their inscriptions of having ravaged or wiped out Ebla, prove that Mesopotamia and Syria were closely associated in the middle of the 3rd millennium.

The uncovering of this possible colonial implantation of the 4th millennium, and of the capital of a powerful kingdom, less than 1,000 years later: these are the two discoveries that have partially filled the gap previously existing in the history of Syria in the 4th and 3rd millennia. Admittedly there are still some lacunae, but now archaeologists are better able to see how Mesopotamian power may have functioned in Syria through the intermediary of colonial settlements, and then continued for a second period, still under the influence of commercial relations. This could have been done by allowing a powerful Syrian kingdom to develop along Mesopotamian lines as the privileged go-between for economic relations between the eastern Mediterranean and the Land of the Two Rivers.

Model of the city of Habuba Kabira

The town extended for 700m (2,240ft) along the bank of the Euphrates and was only 150m (480ft) wide. The defence system, consisting of a rampart with square towers and a simply built outer wall, developed on the three sides away from the river. Two long streets parallel to the river bank gave the town its structure, while to the south an acropolis, on which stood two buildings very similar to the temples of Uruk, represented the official, perhaps religious, sector of the town. By kind permission of E. Strommenger.

Bulla from Habuba Kabira

Hollow spherical vessel of terracotta, containing small modelled objects, usually known as *calculi*, which probably represented a given quantity of items, thus certifying their delivery or preservation. The contents of the *bulla* were guaranteed intact by a cylinder seal impression, the design of which authenticated the origin, person or institution. Here sheep and goats appear in a figurative scene of considerable realism. Aleppo Museum. E. Strommenger.

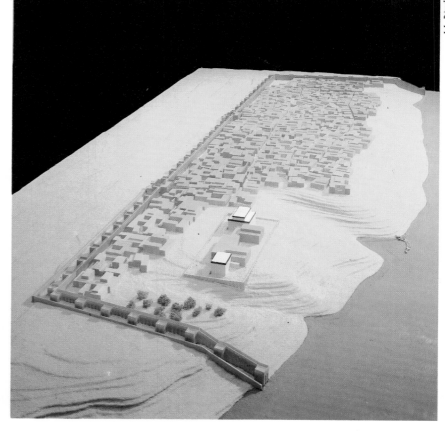

The royal palace of Ebla

This majestic building, though not yet completely excavated, can already be recognized as one of the great monuments of the 3rd millennium BC. The major architectural form is constituted by a vast space lined with porticoes to the north and east. A handsome platform in the centre of the north portico enables us to identify an official court where the king held audiences. The east side of the court is cut off by a second portico, behind which a monumental flight of steps opens up, possibly leading to the private quarters of the palace. Next there is the celebrated hall of the archives, followed by the entrance to an elegant complex, whose purpose is unknown, consisting of two hypostyle halls and an outbuilding with a corner staircase. The importance of the upper storey is strongly suggested by the numerous staircases, and even more by the tower at the northeast corner of the court with its three flights of stairs decorated with mosaics. This tower, which still stands 4m (13ft) high, seems to indicate that the original height of the monument was considerably more than 10–12m (32–38ft). There are affinities between this palace and those of contemporary Mesopotamia (for example Kish), but its pillars, porticoes, staircases and official court suggest that the palace of Ebla may be the first example of an emerging Syrian style of architecture.

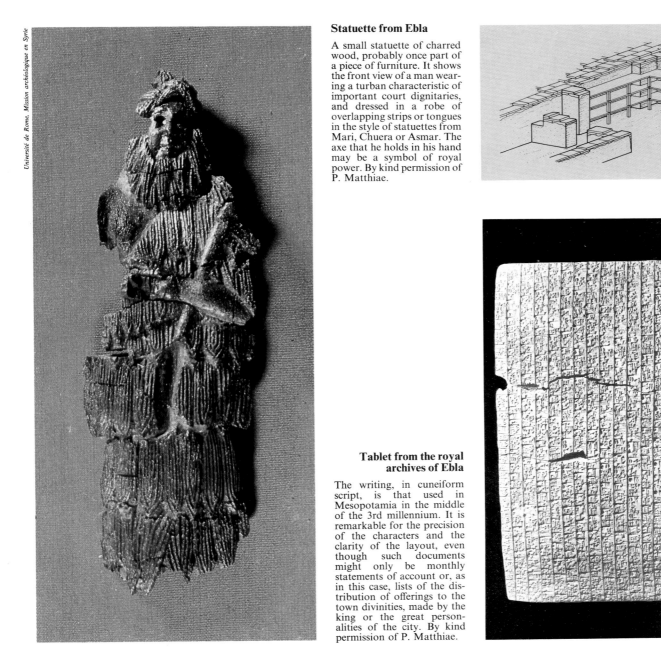

Université de Rome. Mission archéologique en Syrie

Statuette from Ebla

A small statuette of charred wood, probably once part of a piece of furniture. It shows the front view of a man wearing a turban characteristic of important court dignitaries, and dressed in a robe of overlapping strips or tongues in the style of statuettes from Mari, Chuera or Asmar. The axe that he holds in his hand may be a symbol of royal power. By kind permission of P. Matthiae.

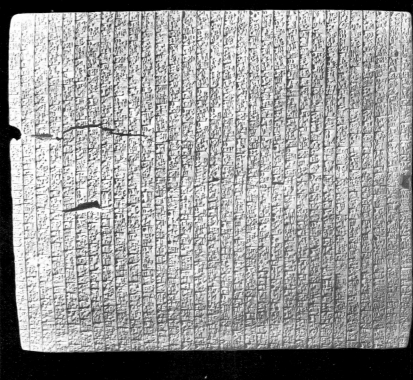

The Hall of Archives, Ebla

This reconstruction of the hall that contained an important find of archives has been drawn up from traces left by structural elements of the shelves on the ground or along the walls. A fire caused all the shelves to collapse, but without appreciably disturbing the order in which the tablets were classified. They were arranged in rows placed one above the other.

Université de Rome. Mission archéologique en Syrie

Tablet from the royal archives of Ebla

The writing, in cuneiform script, is that used in Mesopotamia in the middle of the 3rd millennium. It is remarkable for the precision of the characters and the clarity of the layout, even though such documents might only be monthly statements of account or, as in this case, lists of the distribution of offerings to the town divinities, made by the king or the great personalities of the city. By kind permission of P. Matthiae.

Towns of the Iranian plateau in the 3rd millennium

Persia has been little studied by Western prehistorians, but an important urban civilization existed there from Neolithic times, forming a vital link between the Near East and India. We do not yet know the reason for its mysterious disappearance in the 3rd millennium BC.

The mountain barrier of the Zagros mountains, lying to the east of the Mesopotamian plain, once represented the boundary of that branch of oriental archaeology for which the main points of reference were the Bible and the Tower of Babel. Beyond those mountains lay the desert plateau of Iran, and it was only further east, in the Indus Valley, that a flourishing urban civilization once again became apparent.

The Iranian plateau does not look like an ideal place for human settlement. In the middle of it lies the salt desert of Dasht-e-Kavir and the sand desert of Dasht-e-Lut. But the valleys and the foothills of the Zagros and Elburz mountains, and the interior basins of Seistan and Baluchistan may encourage certain forms of agriculture. The areas suited to cultivation are geographically limited, no more than small islands of greenery separated by immense deserts, and this has led to the development of strong regional characteristics. Beyond this diversity, however, the overall situation retains its own originality and has played a basic role in the contacts between Mesopotamia, the Indus Valley and Central Asia.

Agricultural communities occupied the fertile areas of the foothills in the 7th millennium BC, and Tepe Tang-e-Chakmak, situated between the Elburz and the salt desert, had been inhabited from the Neolithic period before the invention of pottery. From the 6th to the 4th millennium there were numerous villages, characterized by painted pottery, as seen at Tepe Sialk or Tepe Hissar and by the beginnings of metal industry as at Tepe Sialk or Tal-i-Iblis, if copper deposits were near at hand. During the second half of the 4th millennium, this complex of village communities developed certain changes, still little understood, that varied according to the region and led, a few centuries later, to the appearance of genuine towns.

To the north, the plain of Gorgan links the Elburz mountains with the Turkoman steppes. Sites on the narrow fertile band stretching along the foot of the mountains have yielded a polished grey pottery which, towards the last quarter of the 4th millennium BC, had replaced the painted wares at Shah Tepe, Yarim Tepe and Tureng Tepe. The same change occurred at Tepe Hissar, on the southern foothills of the Elburz. For a long time this change was considered as an effect of the arrival in Iran of the Indo-Europeans who would have replaced the painted pottery made by the occupants of the region with their own grey ware. However, it cannot be ruled out that this was a purely local phenomenon, similar to what had happened a little earlier in Mesopotamia when the painted pottery of the Ubaid* period was discarded when towns began to develop in the Uruk period. But irrespective of the possibility of population migrations, a cultural identity now began to form which characterized the region until the beginning of the 2nd millennium.

New systems of economic management

Several regional surveys have shown that important changes in the occupation of the territory took place at about the same time. Only a few big sites remained, and in each area one began to dominate the rest: for example, Tal-i-Malyan in the Kur basin and Tepe Yahya in a valley next to that of Dowlatabad. This may have been due to an increase in climatic aridity—sites in the Kur basin are near easily irrigated areas and that of Tepe Yahya lies in a more humid valley. Equally, it may have been due to economic changes, such as the development of important nomadic herds of small livestock like sheep and goats, in which case the large sites would have acted as markets. The answer to these questions is linked to another phenomenon: the appearance in all the major sites, around 3000BC, of a new system of economic management, which undoubtedly originated in the area of Susa*, in Iranian Khuzistan.

The existence of this system is confirmed by clay tablets inscribed in characters known as "Proto-Elamite"—the writing developed at Susa towards the end of the 4th millennium—as well as by clay seals on jars, baskets and doors which all bear the prints of cylinders identical in style to those of Susa and Mesopotamia. "Proto-Elamite" tablets have been found at Tepe Sialk IV, Godin Tepe V, Tal-i-Malyan ("Banesh" period) and Tepe Yahya IVc. Several centuries earlier, a very particular type of vessel appeared in the same regions: the "coarse bowls" known in Mesopotamia since the Uruk period, which seem somehow to be associated with the economy of urban centres. Tablets and seeds are often found with jars displaying painted geometrical decoration very similar to certain models from Susa and Mesopotamia *c.*3000BC.

These discoveries, and particularly those of Tepe Yahya, have lent weight to the theory of an organized trade association between the already well-developed towns of Mesopotamia and Susa on one side and the village communities of Iran on the other. The aim of the association would have been to enable the towns to tap the mineral wealth they totally lacked. Archeometry* seems to confirm such a theory: we know, for instance, that Susa was then buying her copper in the area of Anarak, near Tepe Sialk, and of Tepe Yahya.

A more careful study has filled in some details of this picture. Some authorities believe that they indicate the adoption by local elites of a system of economic management inspired by the foreign power which dominated the region economically and probably politically. Whatever the case, there had never been so many contacts between relatively distant areas; taken in association with local charges, they represent the beginning of a kind of urbanization in southwest Iran.

The evolution of Shahr-i-Sokhta

To the east, the Sistan basin is a large depression occupied by the lakes and the marshes into which the Hilmand river, springing from the Hindu Kush, debouches. We know nothing of the prehistory of Shahr-i-Sokhta, a major site in the region, which seems to have been inhabited only at the very end of the 4th millennium. Its painted pottery shows affinities with the culture of Namazga III in Soviet Turkmenistan and with that of Mundigak in Afghanistan, several hundreds of miles up the Hilmand. But in Shahr-i-Sokhta a Proto-Elamite tablet and some imprints of cylindrical seals testify to extremely ancient contacts with the west. The site is very well preserved and has even yielded traces of wood and fabrics. Archaeologists have enterprisingly reconstructed the whole area supplying the site, both in the immediate surroundings (fishing, gathering shellfish in the marshes and lakes, irrigated agriculture near channels of water, stockbreeding, where goats and sheep gradually took over from cattle) and the collection of raw materials within a radius of approximately 100km (62 miles). Each of the towns on the Iranian plateau had its own closely defined territory which conditioned its development and its inclusion in exchange networks.

Growth from 3000 to 2300BC

The evolution of Shahr-i-Sokhta is a good illustration of the period which follows. Between 3000 and 2300BC the inhabited area grew from a few hectares to 80 hectares (198 acres). Various crafts also made their appearance, each localized in specific areas: semi-precious stonework (lapis lazuli, cornelian, turquoise) or soft stonework (alabaster, steatite), copperwork, etc. The more polluting crafts, such as metallurgy, pottery, leather work, were restricted to the outskirts, to distinct sites such as that of the pottery kilns of Rud-i-Biyaban. These workshops looked after local supplies, but were also involved in long-distance trade. Lapis lazuli originating from Badakhshan and turquoise from Nishapur were exported to Mesopotamia, either as raw materials or as finished or half-finished objects. Certain products depended directly on local resources: a rich copper industry at Tepe Hissar, the manufacture of alabaster or chalcite vases at Shahr-i-Sokhta, and of steatite vases at Tepe Yahya.

Long-distance trade favoured the exchange of ideas as well as objects. For instance, several authorities see a Mesopotamian influence in the decoration of some of the local gold and silver items of the Asterabad treasure, discovered in the 19th century probably at Tureng Tepe but now lost. A wooden game board found in a tomb at Shahr-i-Sokhta is of a similar shape to the "game of Enmerkar" found in one of the royal tombs at Ur. The most remarkable product from this point of view is the series of steatite vases of Tepe Yahya, upon which Iranian craftsmen reproduced symbolic motifs of Sumerian inspiration; the vases were exported to Mesopotamia and the surrounding areas.

It is not clear whether these symbolic images retained their original significance on the Iranian plateau or whether they were adapted to local beliefs. At Shahdad, Iranian archaeologists have collected objects from a cemetery used in the 3rd millennium and at the beginning of the 2nd, which include stone and clay statuettes similar to Mesopotamian models found in temples and dating from around 2500BC. It is agreed that they represent praying figures, but the change in the context in which they were found may also indicate a change in meaning. On the same site, "banquet" scenes with a Mesopotamian influence comprise a number of local elements which possibly also indicate a change in the significance of the scenes.

Sites like Bampur, in Iranian Baluchistan, seem to have remained marginal to this movement, but this may well be due to insufficient fieldwork. A type of pottery decorated with black motifs on a red ground continues the earlier tradition, just as it does at other areas such as Tepe Yahya or at Shahdad, a vast site where only the very rich necropolis is known.

Large public buildings appeared towards the 23rd century BC at the high point of the urban development with structures such as the "high terrace" of Tureng Tepe, or the "burnt building" of Shahr-i-Sokhta IV. The high terrace of Tureng Tepe IIIc, a building on two levels, about 15m (49ft) high and with a south façade at least 80m (262ft) long, is thought to be a religious building. Its construction is similar to that of other contemporary monuments, such as the "terrace" at Altyn Tepe, in Turkmenistan, or the "stepped building" of Mundigak. This similarity in the construction of what are probably religious buildings is underlined by the presence of a certain number of objects: small stone columns which have been found at the top of the Tureng Tepe terrace, in the tombs of Tepe Hissar, at Altyn Tepe, at Godar-i-Shah in Seistan and as far as Bactria*; long spindle-like stone "sceptres" found in the tombs of Tepe Hissar, Shahdad and Bactria, and others. Such an impressive unity of conception and idea is far ahead of the local characteristics as they are represented by the pottery styles.

The wealth of the Iranian plateau could not fail to attract bands of conquerors. Shortly after 2300BC Manishtushu, the son and successor of Sargon Akkad led an expedition against Anshan (Tal-i-Malyan) and reached far into the east, crossing the Straits of Hormuz in an effort to invade the Oman peninsula. This is recorded in the cuneiform* tablets, but has not been confirmed by any concrete find.

Towards the end of the 3rd millennium, contacts with Bactria became increasingly common, as shown by the presence at Tepe Yahya and Shahdad of pots and other objects similar to those of northern Afghanistan. This could be due to the expansion southwards of the Bactrian cultures, but it is difficult to distinguish this from another expansion about which we still know little, namely that of the western boundaries of the Indus civilization, which took place at about the same time.

Vanished urban cultures

The disappearance of the urban cultures of the Iranian plateau of the 3rd millennium, particularly those of Tepe Hissar, Tureng Tepe and Shahr-i-Sokhta, seems to have taken place shortly after their high point and has long puzzled archaeologists. Explanations based on climatic change have now been rejected. Elsewhere, shortly after the disappearance of the sites of Gorgan, several burial grounds in the area around Teheran (Khurvin), in Gilan (Marlik) and in the Zagros (Tepe Giyan I) still produced a polished type of pottery, either black or grey, based on shapes clearly derived from the painted pottery styles. According to some authors, such pottery would indicate a westward migration of "Indo-Europeans" or "Indo-Iranians", who are believed to be connected with the grey pottery cultures of the Gorgan. But the archaeology of this period is still an extremely complex subject, whether dealing with the Iranian plateau, Central Asia or the Indus Valley; even its chronology is uncertain. It cannot be used to determine the movements of populations to which particular pottery styles cannot be attributed.

One of the most attractive of recent theories postulates social and economic changes. The urban way of life may have been abandoned, as a result of overpowering internal pressures, in favour of either a nomadic or a village existence in new territories and with different crops. But no archaeological traces of this new way of life have yet been found. Only further research will explain these fundamental changes which anticipate a lifestyle that has continued to the present. In the vast area under consideration, extending from the Zagros to central Asia and the Indus Valley, and including the Arabian peninsula, the Iranian plateau towns of the 3rd millennium are only one element. Their study represents a considerable revolution both in its applications, methods and results, in our knowledge of the archaeology of the ancient Near East.

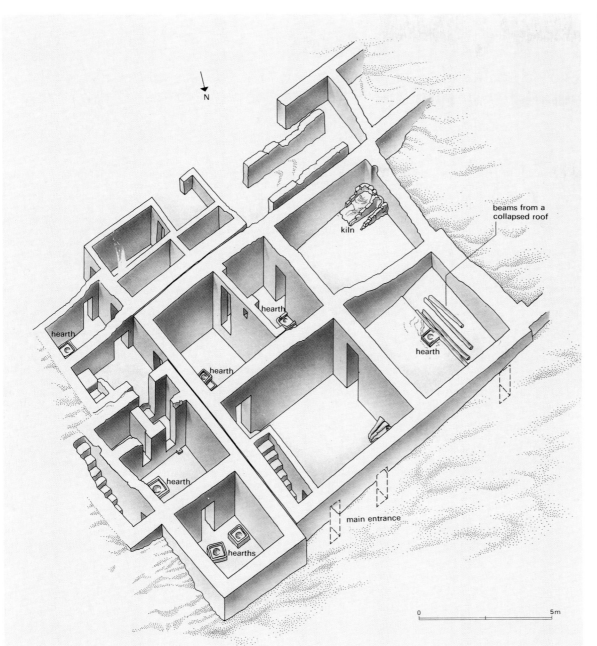

A tomb in the Shahr-i-Sokhta necropolis (c.2300BC)

Two hundred tombs have been excavated, although the necropolis contains over 20,000. These are for the most part individual burials with offerings which point to the social status of the dead person in his lifetime: pieces of jewellery in metal, bone, shell, semi-precious stones; wooden combs; craftsman's tools, etc. By permission of M. Piperno, Istituto Italiano per il Medio ed Estremo Oriente.

A house at Shahr-i-Sokhta (c.2400BC)

Terraced houses were built of mud bricks, as they are still to this day. They comprised several rooms, often with fireplaces and ovens. A staircase led to the flat roof built with layers of reeds and earth supported by poplar beams. By permission of M. Tosi, Istituto Italiano per il Medio ed Estremo Oriente.

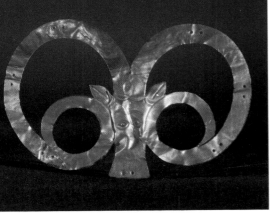

Gold ibex head from Tepe Hissar (left), and earthenware female figure from Tureng Tepe (bottom left)

Both the tombs and a few rich houses at Tepe Hissar have yielded vases, weapons, and ornaments made of copper, silver and gold, such as this pectoral in the shape of a stylized ibex head. Similar objects were found at Tureng Tepe, together with nude, male or female figurines adorned with jewels (bracelets, necklaces, ear pendants). The University Museum, Philadelphia.

Proto-Elamite tablets from Tepe Yahya IV C (c.3000BC)

These tablets were found in the ruins of a large brick building together with similar tablets without inscriptions, some rough bowls and the marks of seals of Susian type. They are thought to represent several animals and objects. By permission of C. C. Lamberg-Karlousky, Peabody Museum, Harvard.

Grey pottery with smooth decoration found at Tureng Tepe (c.2500BC)

The grey pottery of northern Iran, obtained by firing in a reducing atmosphere, is characterized by its angular shapes. The surface has been polished with a hard instrument, apart from certain areas which have been decorated with geometrical motifs (hatching, lattice work, etc). Musée du Louvre, Paris.

185

The prehistory of the Gulf region

A remarkable Bronze Age civilization once flourished in the lands which now form the oil states bordering the Arabian Gulf. Excavations at Bahrain suggest that this may have been the rich and mysterious island known throughout the ancient world as Dilmun.

South of the Lower Mesopotamian marshes, the Gulf area was for a long time an empty space on archaeological maps. Cuneiform* texts assigned to this area the lands of Dilmun and Magan, but their location was much disputed and some authorities even regarded them as legendary. Only since 1954, thanks to the prosperity brought to the area by the oil industry, have archaeologists been able to discover their extraordinarily rich past.

The earliest known sites, dating from the 6th to the 4th millennium, are fishing settlements along the coast of Saudi Arabia, Qatar and the island of Bahrain. Pottery shards found there are painted in the same style as those of the Ubaid* civilization of Mesopotamia, with the result that archaeologists recognize an Ubaid period in the Gulf. Archeometric* research has shown that the pottery was imported and served as containers for the foodstuffs that formed the real objects of exchange. We do not know the nature of these foodstuffs nor of the products that the coastal regions might have exported in return. These could have been fine pearls, which until the 1930s represented the wealth of Bahrain, or flint tools, particularly from Qatar.

Further to the east, the mountain barrier of Oman encloses the Gulf. Numerous settlements of fishermen and shellfish gatherers occupied the most favourable places along the coast of the Indian Ocean. The site at Ras el-Hamra, near Muscat, has revealed the existence of a community whose lives revolved entirely around maritime resources, including funerary rites. The hinterland was then more humid than it is today, and included lakes which gradually evaporated and disappeared during the 3rd millennium. Hunting communities lived there, about whom little is known apart from a range of flint tools.

The first oases, favoured centres of agricultural production in the region, appeared around 3000BC along the narrow band of open grassland which borders the Rub-al-Khali desert at the southern foot of the mountains of Oman. The excavations carried out at Hili provide a good idea of life at that time. Date palms were grown, and under their shade grew various vegetables and fruits, such as melons and grapes, while cereals were cultivated at the edges of the palm groves: several varieties of wheat and barley, together with sorghum. This agriculture relied on irrigation systems of which we know little. Livestock mainly consisted of cattle, the hump-backed oxen called zebu, and sheep and goats.

The resources of the surrounding grasslands were exploited, with the collection of fruit from jujube bushes, but hunting played a very minor part in the food supply. Dwellings were grouped at the edge of the palm groves, round fortified towers of mud bricks or stones.

The origin of this oasis economy is still unknown. Certain elements, such as the date palms, are local, but zebu came from Baluchistan, where they had been domesticated in the 5th millennium, while sorghum is native to Africa. The most likely theory is that the life of the oasis arose from a combination of local and imported resources. Contemporary pottery (c.3000BC) almost certainly testifies to commercial links with Mesopotamia, the equivalent of those of the Iranian plateau, for instance at Tepe Yahya.

These contacts became stronger towards 2600BC, when copper began to be exported in large quantities from the mountains of Oman to Mesopotamia. Analyses of the chemical composition of minerals and metals have proved the existence of such a copper trade: moreover, several copper mines dating from the 3rd millennium have been identified, one very near the site of Maysar, where furnaces for the smelting of mineral ores were found. Texts tell us that this "Magan copper" was taken to Mesopotamia by ship, and the fishing settlement of Umm an-Nar, near what is now Abu Dhabi, seems to have been one of the departure points. We do not know how these loads were brought from the interior to the coast: perhaps the camel was used at this period, but this is pure speculation.

The deep cultural homogeneity of the Oman peninsula is revealed by the study of the collective tombs, dating from 2700 to 2000BC, which have been found in the immediate vicinity of all the sites, both in the interior and on the coast. The monumental character of some of these tombs, like that of the towers, indicates a well organized population, governed by local potentates enriched by the copper trade. Pottery found in these tombs show similarities with that of southern Iran nearby, but the cultural ensemble seems to be solidly rooted in a region which one is tempted to identify with the "land of Magan" mentioned in texts.

About 2000BC the Omani peninsula seems to have been absorbed into the sphere of influence of the Indus civilization. An inscription in characters from the Harappa* civilization, incised on a pottery shard, was recently discovered on the coastal site of Ras al-Junayz, facing the coast of Pakistan.

A sacred island

During the 3rd millennium, the islands of Tarut and Bahrain saw the emergence of an entirely original civilization which is now identified with the land of Dilmun. Its origins are little known, but Tarut appears to have been inhabited from the beginning of the 3rd millennium. The pottery and objects found there testify to a strong Mesopotamian influence. Towards 2400BC Bahrain enjoyed a very rich agricultural phase, due to abundant freshwater springs, and underwent considerable development, culminating between 2100 and 1750BC. The island was then densely inhabited, and had fortified towns, such as Qala'at al-Bahrain, and richly endowed temples like Barbar. It was a commercial centre which gradually monopolized the trade with Magan and the Indus civilization. Thousands of funerary mounds probably reflect the importance of this people at the time, but some archaeologists believe that Bahrain was a sacred land—as such it was often mentioned in religious Sumerian texts—where people came to be buried from Arabia or Mesopotamia. The objects found in the tombs were obviously the products of a very active industry that specialized entirely in this line, but some also came from international trade. Bahrain's influence spread along the entire coast of the Gulf, covering the distance from Qatar to the island of Failaka near Mesopotamia.

Towards the middle of the 18th century BC, this prosperity suddenly vanished, at a time when profound changes affected the Indus civilization, the Iranian plateau and Mesopotamia. Bahrain was still inhabited during the 2nd millennium, in the Kassite period, but in a fairly reduced way. Nothing further is known about the people of the Omani peninsula, who seem to have taken to a nomadic way of life based on the camel, a fundamental feature of Arabian life that yields little in the way of archaeological remains.

Not until the 8th century BC do villages and agricultural economies reappear in Bahrain and in the Omani peninsula. There they survived without noticeable changes up to historical times. But the extremely important transformations which took place between the 3rd millennium and the 8th century BC, are still a matter for conjecture amongst the specialists.

Tomb A at Hili North (2200–2000BC)

This chamber was part of a larger collective tomb; these circular stone monuments were divided into compartments, and often contained the bones of several hundred individuals, laid in a foetal position as and when they died, with various offerings, particularly painted pottery and stone vases specially carved for the purpose.

Mission archéologique française en Abou Dhabi

A fisherman's tomb at Ras el-Hamra (c.3000BC)

Tombs of fishermen were trenches covered with stones, dug in the immediate vicinity of their huts; they sometimes look like turtle's shells. The deceased was often accompanied by the skull of a sea turtle, a fact which stresses the importance of the sea in the life of the fishing communities. From 2700BC onwards, the same collective tombs were used by the fishermen as by the peasants of the interior.

Mission archéologique italienne en Oman

Excavations at Hili (3000–1700BC)

This view shows Hili 8, one of the four or five towers built within the perimeter of the oasis during the 3rd millennium. Mud bricks were used for the buildings. In the upper centre of the excavated area is a square construction with rounded corners subdivided into watertight compartments: this was the base of a tower 16m (53ft) wide and some 12m (40ft) high. In the centre, a well ensured an independent supply of fresh water. Built towards 3000BC, this tower was in use until c.2700; it was then rebuilt on a circular plan and surrounded with a ditch; the latter can be seen in the foreground, covered by later constructions. Identical towers can be found on all the sites in the Omani peninsula dating from the 3rd millennium BC.

Mission archéologique française en Abou Dhabi

Mission archéologique française en Abou Dhabi

Hili: sorghum impression in mud brick (c.2500BC)

First exploited in eastern Africa, the cultivation of sorghum was known at Hili from 3000BC. This drought-resistant plant could be harvested throughout the year and formed a dietary supplement when wheat and oat crops failed in years of drought.

Mission archéologique française en Abou Dhabi

Large tomb at Hili: relief on the south door (c.2250BC)

Some of the large stone slabs, about 3 to 4m (10 to 13ft) high, which form the façade of the monument are decorated with motifs in relief; here two human figures hold hands, flanked by two oryxes (Arabian antelope). It is a symbolic scene, of uncertain meaning.

Bahrain: bronze bull's head (c.2250BC)

Cast with the "lost wax" method, this head is a good example of the accomplishments of the craftsmen of the period. It was found in the foundation deposit of the temple at Barbar and can be compared with similar objects found in Mesopotamia (Ur) or in Central Asia (Altyn Depe).

Bahrain: areas of tumuli (c.2100–1750BC)

It is thought that more than 100,000 tumuli make up the Bahraini burial grounds. Varying in size from 4 to 20m (13 to 66ft) in diameter, they cover a main stone chamber and sometimes a few secondary ones. Each chamber contained one body only, together with offerings: these were sometimes very rich, particularly within the "royal tombs", unfortunately pillaged in antiquity.

Mission archéologique danoise à Bahrein

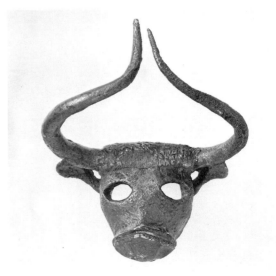

Mission archéologique danoise à Bahrein

Copper metallurgy in the 4th and 3rd millennium BC

Using modern atomic physics and the ancient evidence of cuneiform tablets, scientists can now show how the development and monopoly of metal technology were central to the political success of the great Mesopotamian city states in *c*.3000BC.

Ever since the first excavations, in the mid 19th century, the ancient cities of the so-called Fertile Crescent have yielded evidence of an extremely elaborate metalwork tradition. Many questions are raised by these discoveries with regard to its origins, development and technology. Archaeologists have also sought to establish the part played by the search for metal resources in the development of long-distance trade, and the relationship between the emergence of metal craftsmen and the appearance of politically organized societies.

Physicists, chemists and geologists have from the beginning collaborated with archaeologists in trying to answer such questions. The study of ancient metallurgy is an area where field investigations and laboratory research work have always been linked. At the end of the 19th century, researchers used their knowledge to establish a chronological framework for the whole of protohistory with a sequence of various ages of metal—Chalcolithic (copper), Bronze and Iron—following after the Stone Age. This classification is still partially valid and establishes the essential role that archaeologists have identified in metallurgy as a key to the development of societies. However, it has also proved to be a hindrance to research, since all results which would not fit neatly into the scheme tended to challenge a structure that offered an interpretation of the succession of societies characteristic of the Near East.

The evolution of copper products

Present knowledge of ancient Near Eastern metallurgy affirms a technical evolution from the exploitation of local copper in the 7th millennium to the standardized metallurgy of bronze (an alloy of copper and tin) at the end of the 3rd millennium. However, the most recent research has revealed chronological differences in this evolution, both as regards the different regions under consideration, and certain local variants in the techniques employed.

If techniques evolved in the course of time, so too did the objects produced by the metalworkers of different periods. The most ancient objects are some small tools such as scissors and awls, and above all jewellery such as beads, brooches and rings. These objects have been found all over the Near East, making it difficult to identify a single centre of production for this type of primitive metalwork. Sites where it has been found include Çayönü and Suberde in Turkey, Tell Ramad in Syria and Ali Kosh in Iran. These objects made of local copper are remarkable, dating as they do from the 7th or 6th millennia, but they can only be regarded as the products of an infant industry.

A more elaborate type of metallurgy appeared during the 5th millennium, particularly on the eastern borders of the Zagros, in Iran. Numerous traces of waste material from crucibles have been found at Sialk and Tal-i-Iblis, together with mineral fragments, which testify to a knowledge of copper extraction techniques. The types of object produced are still fairly similar to those of the previous period, although some tools are larger. The most important step forward is represented by the use of stone moulds which, at the beginning of the 4th millennium, led to the manufacture of the first metal axes. The earliest examples of copper casting also came from the Iranian plateau.

Another important factor first appears at the beginning of the 4th millennium: metal objects are now found at some considerable distance from the source of the mineral. For instance, the economic activity of Elam during this period was concentrated around a few large sites, one of which, Susa*, quickly gained dominion over the others. Susa lies some 600km (373 miles) from the nearest mines; and yet excavations which have been carried out almost uninterruptedly since 1884 have revealed a large number of objects, axes in particular, which prove the existence of a transfer of technologies along with long-distance trade contacts. Archaeologists have established that a highly organized economy ensured a constant supply of agricultural produce and raw materials for this large city.

The Mesopotamian plain on the other hand, though lacking mineral resources like its neighbour Elam, was left out of this technical evolution, even though the development of its society was very similar to that of Elam. A significant metalworking activity only developed in Mesopotamia towards the end of the 4th millennium. As in Susa 1,000 years before, the earliest Mesopotamian techniques are also the most elaborate of the time. Craftsmen produced a wide range of objects including weapons, utensils, jewellery, vessels and containers. Sumerian workshops were familiar with the technique of fitting handles through a hole (an important innovation that first appeared at Sialk, *c*.3800BC) as well as the lost-wax technique (moulds in wax that then melts and drains out), which appeared simultaneously in Elam and in Mesopotamia, *c*.3200BC.

Sumerian tablets

For the period beginning at the 3rd millennium, archaeological knowledge was enriched by a large number of clay tablets bearing cuneiform* script that described both the techniques used at the time, the type of objects produced and the source of the ore. Recent excavations, carried out by the French Commission for Atomic Energy in cooperation with several international archaeological teams and museum departments, have shown that the Elam region of the 4th millennium drew its metal from the Iranian plateau but that towards 3200BC all the copper used in Elam and in Mesopotamia began to be imported from the mountains of Oman. Complex techniques have enabled archaeologists to discover, from the metal in an object, the provenance of the copper ore from which it was made. Thus it has been possible to identify the mineral producing countries mentioned on the Sumerian tablets. So "the copper mountain in the land of Magan" has been positively identified with the mountains of the Sultanate of Oman, and the area called Melukhkha by the Sumerians is now known to be a region of eastern Iran and western Afghanistan which supplied the tin necessary for the manufacture of bronze. Archaeological excavations have supported these identifications by discovering traces of an important metallurgic activity in the Omani peninsula at the beginning of the 3rd millennium.

As regards the nature of the alloys made in this period, the standard technology consisted of a systematic use of arsenical copper. This practice only disappeared towards the end of the 3rd millennium when true bronze became more widely employed. This development seems to have been in part connected with the importation into the Near East of tin from Cornwall, England. Arsenic alloys may have predominated, but many other alloys were used; at Susa in particular an alloy of copper and lead was much in use between 3500 and 3200BC. In Mesopotamia, ternary alloys (copper-arsenic-tin) and quaternary alloys (copper-arsenic-tin-lead) were used to produce either objects with particular properties or metals of special colours. This was particularly applicable to mirrors, which the craftsmen made as white as they could in order to increase their power of reflection.

As we have seen, the Iranian plateau played an important role at the beginning of metallurgy as a result of its rich mineral resources. This importance dwindled at the end of the 4th millennium, and during the 3rd millennium the new techniques came from the towns of Mesopotamia. This technological dynamism is linked with the sophisticated techniques employed by palace and temple craftsmen for the benefit of urban elites. It was for these that the long-distance commerce developed in order to obtain the raw materials necessary to the manufacture of precious objects which have been found in such numbers in Mesopotamian burial grounds, especially the royal tombs of Ur. However, the secrets of these techniques remained hidden in the Mesopotamian workshops. Sumer and Elam imported their raw materials from all over the Iranian region as well as from the Arabian peninsula, but there is no evidence to indicate any feedback from Mesopotamian technology to these other cultures. The widespread diffusion of the technology only took place at the beginning of the 2nd millennium, when events transformed the urban societies of Mesopotamia.

Traditional method of washing sand in a trough

In order to reconstitute ancient techniques and trading routes it is necessary to study natural resources using traditional methods. Here washing sand in a trough has enabled archaeologists to verify that the Sarkar valley in west Afghanistan may have been an area in which tin was worked in ancient times. What is more, this is the only area where this is recognized as such throughout the Near East.

Vessel with hiding-place

The "hiding-place vessel" (which in reality possessed two such compartments) was found in Susa in 1908. It contained a hoard which was rediscovered, and included a remarkable collection of weapons, tools, and copper and bronze dishes typical of metalwork in Elam and in southern Mesopotamia around 2500BC. These artifacts have been studied jointly by the Research Laboratory of French Museums and the French Atomic Energy Commission, and they have been able to identify the place of origin of the metal used to make them. It came from deposits in the Sultanate of Oman, more than 1,500km (930 miles) from Susa. Louvre Museum.

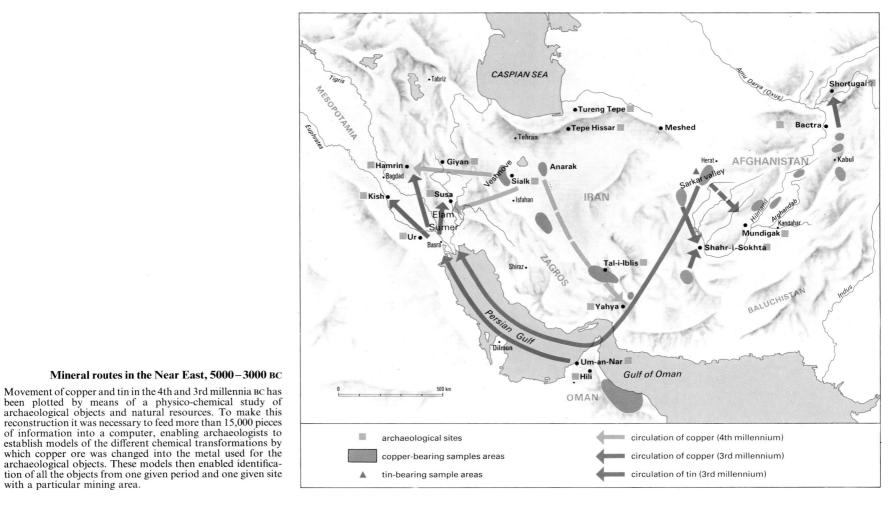

Mineral routes in the Near East, 5000–3000 BC

Movement of copper and tin in the 4th and 3rd millennia BC has been plotted by means of a physico-chemical study of archaeological objects and natural resources. To make this reconstruction it was necessary to feed more than 15,000 pieces of information into a computer, enabling archaeologists to establish models of the different chemical transformations by which copper ore was changed into the metal used for the archaeological objects. These models then enabled identification of all the objects from one given period and one given site with a particular mining area.

Protohistoric copper mine at Veshnove, Iran

In ancient times miners did not excavate shafts or galleries, but extracted the ore by following the lode-carrying seams. Study of the archaeological remains on the site itself has shown that mining was carried on at this place from the 4th millennium BC. Chemical analysis of the ore reveals that it was exported as far as Susa, 600km (372 miles) away, in the 4th millennium BC.

Bronze Age hoe

A bronze hoe was found during clandestine excavations of Bronze Age cemeteries in northern Afghanistan, and appeared on the market at Kabul in 1977. This remarkable artifact demonstrates a technique for making a hole for the handle exactly like that found on a hoe from Sialk (central Iran) dating from the end of the 4th millennium. This hoe illustrates the advanced state of copperworking technology in the Irano-Afghan world in the Bronze Age. Carbonnel collection.

Copper ore, Sultanate of Oman

Copper ore outcropping on the surface, as the miners of antiquity may have found it. The dryness of desert areas (here the Sultanate of Oman) made it easy to identify such deposits, and they were worked from the 5th millennium BC.

Hittite seals

Hittite kings, the most sophisticated formulators of diplomacy and law in the Late Bronze Age, made much use of royal seals. Seal styles and their local variations also illuminate our knowledge of the multinational character of the ancient Hittite empire.

In most ancient Near East civilizations, the making and use of seals has taken on a particular importance. These simple objects, which have been found in their thousands, offer the historian precious evidence on the art, religion and structure of the social and economic systems of antiquity. Square, round or cylindrical in shape, they were sometimes made of precious or semi-precious stones, sometimes of metals such as bronze or silver, or of shell, porcelain, glass or terracotta. The seals were engraved with a more or less elaborate device that, when pressed on soft clay, gave a distinctive impression in relief.

These seals were impressed as a mark of ownership upon certain earthenware jars before firing, or as a mark of "inspection and control" on the clay used to seal various containers, such as clay jars, cloth sacks, baskets, wooden boxes, and even the doors of the premises where access was controlled. Finally, the witnesses of a legal decision, for instance, impressed their seals to the foot of the deed written in cuneiform* characters on a clay tablet.

Hittite engravings of this kind are less impressive than those of Sumer and Babylon because their figurative development was more limited. The importance given to the inscription, whether cuneiform or hieroglyphic, tended to detract from the image, which as a result takes on a relatively austere character.

Up to the present time, the most numerous finds have mainly come from the German excavations of Hattusha, the capital of the Hittite empire, now Boğazköy. In the course of the last decade an abundant new source of material has emerged both from Anatolia and along the borders of the Hittite empire, in northern Syria. In Anatolia, the most important discoveries are from Maşat Hüyük, the first site outside the capital to yield Hittite archives in cuneiform writing. But the most valuable evidence comes from the south-eastern border of the Hittite empire, on the Syrian middle Euphrates. The site of Meskéné, ancient Emar, has been excavated by a French expedition under the direction of J. Margueron and has yielded several hundred seal impressions on clay tablets. Beside the seals in local Mitannian or Syrian style, numerous Hittite or, more precisely, Syro-Hittite documents have been found, characteristic of this pivotal area where different civilizations meet.

Anatolia has always favoured the round or square tablet as a form of seal, whereas the neighbouring regions of Mesopotamia used seals in the shape of small cylinders ever since the Uruk* period, c.3300BC. In Anatolia, from the beginning of the 2nd millennium, the cylindrical seal appeared briefly in connection with the Assyrian trading posts of Cappadocia, to disappear again with the collapse of Assyrian commerce. The cylinder seals of the so-called "Tyskiewicz group" represent an important exception (see illustration below) but their complicated imagery is not particularly easy to interpret.

Gods, kings and hieroglyphs

At the time of the ancient Hittite empire (c.1700–1400BC) stamps with square or polygonal bases predominated. These were often engraved on the sides as well as the base, and were surmounted by a wedge-shaped handle with a head resembling that of a hammer. One of the difficulties of classifying these seals arises from the fact that they were used for a very long time and have often been re-engraved.

The shape of the royal seals of the ancient empire is still unknown, for only their impressions have survived. Their imagery is comparatively slight: at the centre, hieroglyphs translated as *life* and *health*—the looped cross derived from the Egyptian *ankh* symbol of life— are surrounded by concentric circles carrying the cuneiform inscription.

During the New Empire, under the role of Arnuwanda I (c.1400BC) a new type of "kiosk-like" seal appeared: in the centre the name of the sovereign is engraved in hieroglyphic characters, framed by the symmetrical signs for *great king*, the whole being crowned by a winged sun symbolizing the royal title "My Sun" (i.e. "My Majesty"). Since the reign of Muwatalli (c.1300BC) some seals bore the effigy of the king protected by his guardian god, who is often the thunder god and figures largely in the Hittite pantheon.

The south-eastern region of the Hittite empire, northern Syria, conquered by Shuppiluliumà I c.1360BC, generally yields two characteristic forms of seal: the cylinder and the ring seal. The first represents the seal normally used in Syria. By adapting Hittite imagery to the medium they habitually employed, local engravers created a special Syro-Hittite style, examples of which

are known to come from Tarsus, Ugarit (Ras Shamra), Carchemish and especially from Meskéné-Emar, in the 13th century BC. The cylindrical form allowed the development of an imagery where the figures of the Hittite tradition are often presented in a system and with decorative elements belonging to the Syrian tradition. But the most common composition is the simplest: it shows a meeting between two gods, for example, the sun god and the thunder god, separated by a column of hieroglyphs announcing the name of the owner. This name, in the Syrian regions, is generally Semitic, sometimes Hurrian, rarely Anatolian. An interesting feature of the seals found in Meskéné is the fact that there are often two scripts on the seals, cuneiform and hieroglyphic set in transcription. This "digraphic" style enables specialists to decipher obscure Hittite hieroglyphics or, alternatively, Sumerian ideograms found in the cuneiform transcription. This is true of the cylinder seals and also of the numerous ring seals which generally only bear the name of the owner framed by a few decorative or symbolic motifs: palm trees, sphinxes or griffins. This Syro-Hittite style, as seen on the gold ring of Konya, differs from that of other rings used in Anatolia, particularly under the ancient empire. Here the setting is not round but formed by an enlargement of the ring itself, thus creating an oval impression variable in width. This shape is generally considered to be derived from the Egyptian rings of the Amarnian period. Like the cylinder seal, it is rarely found in an Anatolian context.

After the collapse of the Hittite empire (c.1180BC) and the destruction of most of the large centres of Anatolia and northern Syria, a certain number of small principalities, called neo-Hittite, established themselves gradually on either side of the large mountain range of the Taurus. In this new setting, the Hittite art of engraving had little chance to develop further. Some traditional forms, like the two-sided tablet seal, continued to be made without much change. The principalities which established themselves to the south of the Taurus, in northern Syria, were sometimes strongly affected by Aramaean infiltration or by Assyrian influence and occupation. Certain ethnic groups may have retained Hittite traditions, in particular the Hittite system of hieroglyphic writing, but they could do little to prevent the gradual disappearance of the Hittite civilization.

Cylinder seals and impressions of the "Tyskiewicz group"

These two haematite (ironstone) seals represent a compromise between the tablet and the cylinder shape, for they combine the two. This arrangement only reappears with the Urartu Kingdom at the beginning of the 1st millennium BC. The decorative borders of the Boston seal (below, height 5.8cm, diameter 2.2cm) engraved with spirals and interlacings, are characteristic of the Cappadocian period and of the ancient Hittite epoch. On the left a procession of gods pays homage to a seated divinity. They are ushered in by a two-faced god of Babylonian origin. On the right of the procession, the goddess unveiling herself comes from the Syrian tradition. At the side, a warrior god tramples on his adversary near a group of people among whom one, lying on his back, seems to be consumed by flames. Perhaps this is a mythological scene with a defeated god placed on a pyre, or perhaps the exorcism of an evil spirit from an invalid. 17th century BC, Museum of Fine Arts, Boston.

The decoration of the cylinder seal from the Louvre, Paris (bottom, height 4.5cm, diameter 2.2cm) appears more recent, and the seal was undoubtedly re-engraved in the 15th century BC. Under a frieze of human heads of Mitannian appearance, it shows the meeting of the two divine processions. At the head, the great goddess unveils herself and is joined by the thunder god in his chariot. The meeting of these two divine figures may be a pledge of fertility. In the bottom level, a hunting scene may represent certain incidents in the myth of the thunder god. The circular base is engraved with hieroglyphic characters. Musée du Louvre, Paris.

Museum of Fine Arts, Boston

D. Beyer

Seal with hammer-like handle

This type of seal was particularly in favour during the ancient Hittite epoch c.1600BC. The cubic shape allows five faces to be engraved on the same seal, including divine figures, mythological scenes, and the name of the owner in hieroglyphs. Musée du Louvre, Paris.

D. Beyer

Drawings of royal Hittite seals on tablets found at Ras Shamra, ancient Ugarit (Syria)

Left: seal of Suppiluliuma I (1380–1346BC) and his queen Tawananna. Under the winged sun disk (centre) are inscribed the hieroglyphs of the name of Suppiluliuma and of Tawananna, respectively *great king* and *great queen*. The concentric circles of cuneiform writing state: "Seal of Suppiluliuma, great King, king of the Hittite land, favoured by the god of thunder; seal of Tawananna, great Queen, daughter of the king of Babylon." This seal of the royal couple indicates the importance of the queen's role at the Hittite court. Diameter 4.2cm.

Right: seal of Tudhaliya IV (1265–1235BC). Here the image is more elaborate, with particular attention being paid to symmetry: on either side of the royal "pavilion" with the names of the king, stand (left) a goddess, almost certainly the solar goddess Arinna holding the solar symbols, and the god of thunder (right) wearing the horned tiara of the Hittites. With his left arm the god protects the king, whose genealogy is proclaimed by the surrounding cuneiform inscription. Diameter 5.5cm. National Museum of Damascus, Syria.

Some hieroglyphic characters

The Hittites used two systems of writing: hieroglyphics and cuneiform. The former, consisting of a kind of ornamental script, was used only for inscriptions on stone, rock reliefs, stelae (stone slabs) or seals. The latter is normally found on clay tablets, since it was used for texts written in all the languages of the empire. Both in the case of hieroglyphics and of cuneiform, one should distinguish between phonetic (sound form) and ideogrammatic (idea form) values.

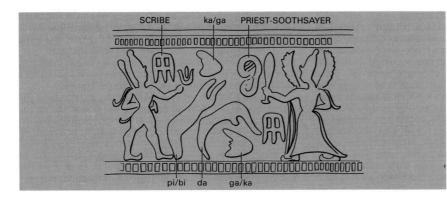

Impression of the seal of the soothsayer Kapi-Dagan, found on several tablets from Meskéné-Emar, 13th century BC

Set between the thunder god and a winged goddess holding a mace (?), the name of the owner is inscribed with his profession in hieroglyphs: the ear represents the "comprehension" of the soothsayer; the glyph for the word *scribe* is the symbol of the top of a cuneiform tablet with incised columns. Aleppo Museum, Syria.

Impression of a Syro-Hittite cylinder seal found on a jar, 14th–13th century BC

On the left, the king pours a libation to the thunder god. The variety of plant elements symbolically indicates both the act of libation and the nature of the god, dispenser of the life-giving rain. On the right an unusual scene shows the thunder god as a triumphant warrior. Museum of The Ancient East, Istanbul.

Various kinds of individual seals

Apart from the silver seal (bottom left) and the bronze ring (top centre), these various seals are double-sided and shaped like disks with or without a mount or a metal handle. They are perforated and could consequently be hung, for example from a belt. The decoration is generally limited: hieroglyphs in the centre give the name of the owner, while decorative or symbolic motifs such as rosettes, symbols of life, heraldic two-headed eagles are incised on the outer edge. Certain seals (bottom left) display an additional band with divine figures or possibly historical scenes. Hittite imperial period, *c.* 15th–13th century BC. Musée du Louvre, Paris. A seal ring from Konya (bottom right) is one of the very few surviving examples of this type of Syro-Hittite seal (although numerous impressions have been found on clay, especially at Meskéné). This is the seal of a prince, showing in the centre the effigy of Shaushga, the Hurrite warrior goddess. 13th century BC, Ashmolean Museum, Oxford.

Cuneiform tablet from Meskéné-Emar

Written in Akkadian cuneiform script, this tablet displays the seals of two witnesses. Left, an impression in Mitannian style; right, a Syro-Hittite type of seal comprising, above the impression, the words "Seal of Matkali-Dagan" incised in cuneiform by the reed pen of a scribe. That same cuneiform phase appears on the cylinder itself, in vertical columns, and is also written in hieroglyphics framed by two divine figures, (left) Jeshub, the thunder god, on his symbolic animal the bull; (right) the Hurrite moon god Kushuk mounted on a lion. Aleppo Museum, Syria.

The Phoenicians in Phoenicia

Inventors of the alphabetic script later adopted by the Greeks, the Phoenicians were the archetypal Mediterranean sea people, merchants and dealers *par excellence*, and their great cities such as Beirut have retained that character ever since.

One of the glories of Phoenicia, according to the epigraphist John Starkey, was her gift to the world of the alphabet. Tradition also records that Phoenician sailors founded a "new town" (*qart-hadasht*, or Carthage) in 814BC under the leadership of Princess Elissa (the Dido of Virgil's *Aeneid*) whence her lover Aeneas fled in order to found Rome.

Yet these celebrated Phoenicians have largely evaded archaeological investigation. Their name (from Φοίνιξ "purple") is Greek. They called themselves Sidonians, as did the Old Testament and Homer. Their country consisted of the Syro–Palestinian coast from the isle of Rouad (Arwad) to Acre, and lay between the sea and the mountains of Lebanon. Phoenician history, strictly speaking, extends from about 1200BC to the conquest of Alexander in 333BC.

The results of archaeological research in this region and for this period are disconcertingly poor. For various reasons, the great Phoenician cities of Tyre, Beirut, Sidon, Byblos and Arvad have supplied hardly any information. At Tyre the ancient town stood on a rocky island near the shore with which it is connected today by a sand spit or bar. Ernest Renan made probes there in 1860, after Napoleon III's expedition to the Levant, but the systematic fieldwork which began in 1947 under M. Chéhab only uncovered the Hellenistic and Roman levels. The ancient site of Beirut is occupied by the modern town, and although archaeological remains have been discovered in the course of urbanization or destruction by war, they hardly date back beyond the Persian period. The islet of Sidon is occupied by a fortress built by the Crusaders and on the shore the ancient city is covered by the modern town. This encloses a tell (mound) under a medieval castle. The genuinely Phoenician levels excavated at Byblos, where the whole of the ancient site has been explored, revealed little of importance: the main monuments discovered are from the Persian period. Rouad, ancient Arvad, is today entirely built up.

Thus, none of these great cities is really known through excavations. That is why the majority of recent books about the Phoenicians are reticent about the archaeology of the period in Phoenicia itself. As one of the outstanding specialists, S. Moscati, noted, "The archaeological material [of this period] is very scanty, at least as regards the material from actual Phoenician towns."

This does not mean that we are totally without information. Material evidence from Phoenician territory itself may be lacking, but it is much more abundant in the neighbouring countries. Phoenicia yields a few, often late, monuments such as the temples of Amrit and Eshmun, and several fragments of statuary and low reliefs. Numerous ivories are found in Iraq, Palestine, Crete and Etruria, which may have come from Phoenician or from Syrian workshops. Metal vases occur in countries which had commercial links with Phoenicia, but never in the country itself. Seals and figurines are also found. Many Phoenician inscriptions exist, and the development of the language and its writing are well known. The origin of the Phoenician* alphabetic script, consisting of 22 letters, and appearing at Byblos at the end of the 2nd millennium, is also well documented. This linear alphabet was well adapted for writing on papyrus, and an invaluable tool for the brilliantly skilful merchants who were the inhabitants of Tyre and Sidon. Diffused as far as Tunisia, Sardinia and Greece, the development of this script was undoubtedly connected with the commercial vocation of the Phoenicians and then the Greeks. But none of the Phoenician literary works written on papyrus has survived. This writing material, made from the stem and pith of the papyrus plant, was too fragile to last in a comparatively humid climate.

Old Testament evidence

Furthermore, we have to admit that archaeologists have failed to describe a single Phoenician city in Phoenicia. The largest and most sumptuous of all the temples built by the Phoenicians, erected at Jerusalem by architects and bronze craftsmen from Tyre at Solomon's behest, is only known thanks to the Old Testament description in 1 *Kings*, 5–7. Archaeologists can form a reasonably accurate idea of the temple of Jerusalem during the time of Herod as a result of recent excavations, and an analysis of contemporary oriental temples such as the temple of Bel at Palmyra, but no trace of the Temple of Solomon has survived. However, comparison of biblical texts with certain religious buildings from Syria leads to the conclusion that Syrian origins underlie the Temple of Solomon and the model for the most famous building in Jerusalem, whose destruction Jeremiah foretold (*Jeremiah* chs. 7 and 26), must be sought in the Syrian cultural context and not in Phoenicia itself. As regards the layout of the districts of a Phoenician town, the harbour installations, the funerary practices, the development of articles in daily use such as pottery, ceramics, metal or glass, the evidence is remarkably slight.

The study of large Phoenician cities has yielded disappointing results, but recent fieldwork has filled out our knowledge. In the Lebanon, of the two excavations interrupted by the war, that of Khalde south of Beirut (excavated 1961–74 by R. Saidah who died in 1979) yielded an important necropolis. The other was at Sarafand, the ancient Sarepta (excavated by J.B. Pritchard from 1968–74) where an area of settlement was explored. The levels exposed were on a modest scale, but nevertheless provide an insight into the daily life of Phoenicians in their own country. This town, where the Old Testament prophet Elijah was hospitably received by a "charitable widow", was almost continuously occupied from the end of the 13th century up to the Hellenistic and Roman period. In a small sanctuary that may well be the earliest temple of Tanit (the great goddess of Carthage) to have been excavated in Phoenicia, the researchers found some 200 votive objects, figurines, ivories, terracotta pieces and a variety of Egyptian amulets.

In Galilee, recent work undertaken at Tell Kaisan—10km (6 miles) east of Acre—has disclosed traces of the Phoenician period from *c.*1100BC to the Persian occupation. At the southern limit of Phoenician territory, the site has supplied abundant documentation about these people. To mention only two categories of object, terracotta wares and engravings, discoveries of terracottas of Phoenician style are very rare, and as regards engravings and carvings, archaeologists have identified numerous symbolic elements of Egyptian, Assyrian or Syrian origin, but authentic Phoenician motifs and stylistic features are almost entirely absent from the catalogue of the excavation. But these various sites suffice to show that it is possible to get round the difficulties and that, even if the great cities have disappeared forever or cannot be excavated, smaller, less famous villages may increase our knowledge of the material culture of the Phoenicians. Then we may find out much more about these rich merchants whom Ezekiel has evoked in these unforgettable words:

> *'O Tyre, you have said,*
> *I am perfect in beauty.*
> *Your frontiers are on the high seas . . .*
> *Men of Sidon and Arvad became your oarsmen*
> *You had skilled men within you, O Tyre,*
> *who served as your helmsmen . . .'*
> 27 *Ezek 1:9*

Arvad under the Phoenicians

The small Syrian island of Rouad (Arwad) is ancient Aradus (Arvad in Genesis). This island, easy to fortify and to defend, is a typical Phoenician site. The Assyrian king Teglath-Phalasar I (1112–1074BC) mentioned it in these terms: "I received tribute from Byblos, Sidon and Arvad. On vessels from Arvad I made the crossing from Arvad which is on the sea coast to Simyra in the land of Amurru." Much later Assurbanipal (668–626BC) proclaimed: "I crushed Yakinlu, king of Arvad, which is in the middle of the sea, for he had not submitted to the kings, my fathers . . .".

The tribute of Tyre

At Balawat, ancient Imgur-Bel, between Nineveh and Nimrud, King Salmanasar III and King Assurnasirpal II erected ceremonial gates covered with decorative metal plaques. Inscriptions, added after the plaques had been set in place, give us precise information about the scenes depicted. In this one the artist has portrayed the king of Tyre, on his rock in the middle of the sea. In the company of his daughter (or his wife) he is looking at the boats bearing towards the land the tribute intended to appease the Assyrian king. The ships have stopped some way from the shore and labourers are carrying the cargo onto the beach. The British Museum.

The sign of Tanit

At Sarafand, ancient Sarepta, 13km (8 miles) south of Sidon, J.B. Pritchard found a glass disk 1cm in diameter which may have been set in a ring or some other ornament. The disk is decorated with a very simple drawing (a triangle and a circle separated by a horizontal bar) which the archaeologist interpreted as a kind of "sign of Tanit", an iconographical motif that subsequently enjoyed great popularity in the Punic (Carthaginian) world.

The sarcophagus of Ahiram

On the sarcophagus of Ahiram, king of Byblos (c.1000BC), there is a long inscription. The scene represents the dead man, holding a lotus head downwards as a token of his death, seated at a table laden with dishes as he receives the homage of his subjects. The inscription uses almost every letter in the alphabet: "Sarcophagus made by Ittobaal, son of Ahiram, king of Byblos, for his father Ahiram when he laid him in his final resting place. And if a king among kings or a governor among governors or an army commander rises against Byblos and opens the sarcophagus, may the sceptre of his dominion be stripped (?) from him, the throne of his royalty overturned, and may peace disappear from Byblos . . ."

The port of Byblos

Byblos – modern Jubail, north of Beirut – was one of the foremost Phoenician ports which throughout its long history was always closely linked with Egypt (according to legend, the body of the Egyptian god, Osiris, was swept ashore by the waves at Byblos). It was excavated by E. Renan, then by P. Montet, but mainly, over a long period, by M. Dunand. The medieval perimeter wall protects a natural bay, the Phoenicians' harbour and the modern port. The medieval castle with a central keep overlooking it dates from the 12th century.

Egypt and Sudan: the archaeological background

It was only in the early 19th century that the Egyptian hieroglyphic script was deciphered, opening a window on a civilization which can show four millennia of recorded history: one of the most successful which has so far existed on earth.

Under the triple blows of Hellenism, Christianity and lastly Islam, the pharaonic civilization died out and hieroglyphic script was abandoned. All that remained of the glory of a great past were many silent monuments. Four millennia of history, however, came back to life, simultaneously with the birth of Egyptology, when Jean-François Champollion* revealed the secret of reading hieroglyphs in his letter to Monsieur Dacier in September 1822. In a few years Champollion was able to compile all the chapters of his history of Egyptian civilization: grammar, pantheon and archaeology. In Italy he worked on the Turin Canon (a list of Egyptian kings) and acquired what was to become the Egyptian collection at the Louvre of which he was appointed Curator in 1826. In 1828, he set off for Egypt at the head of a Franco-Tuscan expedition. In the course of intensive work all down the Nile valley he amassed considerable material which was not published until after his death. On his return in 1831, he was elected member of the Académie des Inscriptions et Belles-lettres and occupied the chair created for him at the Collège de France – for a brief while only, as he died almost immediately.

Richard Lepsius* was to be the second founder of Egyptology. He copied the Egyptian monuments collected at Paris and confirmed the doctrine of Champollion. Appointed to head an important expedition by the King of Prussia, Frederick Wilhelm IV, Lepsius travelled the valley of the Nile as far as the borders of present-day Ethiopia. He assembled a vast mass of material – monuments and objects which are the basis of the Berlin collection, sketches and prints which were published in the 12 volumes of the *Denkmäler*. Through his teachings and publications, Lepsius exercised considerable influence until his death in 1874. He trained the majority of German Egyptologists, except Heinrich Brugsch (1827–94), who became a master of deciphering the late (demotic) script and who settled in Egypt with Auguste Mariette (see below) after he had travelled all over Europe. Throughout the early 19th century, the hunt for treasure was all the rage in Egypt. Whether or not equipped with *firmans* (orders) from the Pasha, adventurers in the service of unscrupulous consuls skimmed off the antiquities which littered the soil of Egypt. Some of them such as Belzoni, Drovetti, Rifuad or Salt won fame, because they supplied the basis for the great collections of the Louvre, the British Museum and the museums of Turin and Florence.

For the scientific study of monuments, research into the Egyptian language was resumed in France by the Vicomte de Rougé (1811–72), who in 1849 presented a translation of the inscription of Ahmes the mariner. Appointed professor at the Collège de France in 1860, he visited Egypt in 1862–63, but he had the additional burden of being a councillor of state and a senator, and delegated his post to his brilliant pupil, Gaston Maspero*. During this time, François Chabas (1817–82) had also become an expert in the study of Egyptian texts, but he never left Chalon-sur-Saône, where he was also engaged in the wine trade.

Practical Egyptology, which sought out the materials for its research in the field, was created by Auguste Mariette* (1821–81). Bitten by the Egyptology bug, he obtained a mission to Cairo to buy Coptic manuscripts. During excavations in the sands of Saqqara, he discovered the Serapeum (temple of Serapis) on 12 November 1851. His four years of research in the field ended with work on the temple of the Sphinx, when he had to return to France owing to shortage of funds. Out of his utter devotion to Egypt, to which he returned in 1857, Mariette took great care that sites were preserved and that the antiquities discovered remained in Egypt. In the area of the pyramids, he discovered several masterpieces of the Memphite dynasties, the tomb of Ti

and the royal list of Saqqara. At Abydos, he found the famous king list in the temple of Sethi I. At San-el-Hagar, antique Tanis, in the Delta, he revealed the monuments of the Hyksos pharaohs. In the Theban region, we have to thank him for the treasure of Queen Aahhotep, the uncovering of the temple of Hatshepsut at Deir el-Bahri and the great temple of Amon at Karnak. Lastly, he freed from the debris accumulated beneath some wretched hovels the great Ptolemaic temples of Edfu and Dendera.

Attracted to Egypt from his youth, Gaston Maspero was elected professor at the Collège de France in 1874. In 1880 he was commissioned to set up a School of Oriental Archaeology, the headquarters of which were to be in Cairo. It was the beginning of what was to become the Institut Français d'Archéologie Orientale. Maspero arrived in Egypt to see Auguste Mariette die in June 1881. He was immediately chosen as director of the Service des Antiquités. Two sensational discoveries followed hard on each other. At Saqqara, excavations revealed the texts vital for an understanding of Egyptian religion which Unas, the last king of the 6th dynasty, and then the Pharaohs Teti, Pepi I, Merenre and Pepi II of the 6th dynasty had had engraved for their afterlife in their funerary apartments. At Deir el-Bahri, a hiding-place revealed a set of mummies of the great conquerors of the New Kingdom and their queens: Amenophis I, Thutmosis II, Queen Nefertiti, Rameses II and Sethi I. From 1881 to 1885, Maspero was extremely active throughout Egypt with fieldwork, excavations and restorations. He reorganized the museum and initiated the publication of a systematic and immense General Catalogue which today comprises more than 100 large volumes. His guide for visitors to Cairo Museum was a veritable manual of Egyptian archaeology. Chasing out clandestine excavators, he personally directed the works at Karnak, Kom Ombo and Saqqara. When Nubia was in danger of being submerged by the building of the first Aswan dam at the end of the century, he personally led an energetic campaign in the world's press and scientific periodicals. A systematic inspection of the threatened region was organized (entrusted first to Firth and then to G.A. Reisner*).

With Maspero, the last of the "all-round Egyptologists" disappeared. By then, Egyptology had grown so much that it required specialization by periods, sites and types of discipline. Nevertheless, such is the part played by hieroglyphics – a kind of monument in themselves – that the role of epigraphy is predominant, more so than in the archaeology of other countries. In Egypt's remarkably dry climate, monuments are usually very well preserved. In the muddy plain, on the other hand, fieldwork is sometimes more delicate, but the inscriptions engraved on the temples, tombs and palaces generally give the name of the builder and the date. That does not mean that we can neglect modern excavation techniques, the methods of stratigraphy*, the use of Carbon[14]* and palynology*, but these have only gradually become an everyday part of archaeology, and may be less effective in the Nile valley than in other areas where they are essential to the operations.

The administrative and scientific framework for the protection of monuments and the surveying of sites was provided in 1857 by the creation of the Service des Antiquités. Egypt was certainly one of the first countries in the world to possess such a body. Beginning with Pierre Lacau, followed by Canon E. Drioton, it was directed by eminent Egyptologists until 1951. Since then, extremely capable Egyptian directors have been in charge. The country is combed by inspectors who supervise chance discoveries and help scientific missions from countries all over the world. For more than a century, not a year has passed without interesting discoveries. At the end of the 19th and

J.-L. Princelle

The temple of Amenophis III at Soleb

A coloured lithograph attributed to Weidenbach and published by R. Lepsius (*Denkmäler* I, pl. 116) shows the state of the ruins of the jubilee temple of Amenophis III at Soleb in July 1844. Eminently romantic, this document nevertheless constitutes important evidence of the history of the monument, thanks to the scrupulous accuracy of the drawing. The view is taken from the southwest. At the foot of the only palmiform column still standing, we see the collapsed drums of the hypostyle hall, celebrated for the representations of the "enchanted peoples" which appeared on them. Beyond stand the clustered columns of the court and the pylon on which the famous scenes of the Sed feast unfold. On the horizon, the course of the Nile behind a curtain of palm trees can be seen.

beginning of the 20th century, the now almost legendary figure of Sir Flinders Petrie* (1853–1942) dominated excavations. There have been reservations about the sometimes precipitate methods of this tireless excavator, but the list of his publications is impressive and their interest undeniable.

The prehistory of Egypt

Although it cannot be compared in brilliance with the pharaonic finds, a study of Egyptian prehistory has developed, though never holding the place it undoubtedly deserves. If scholars have looked on the culture of ancient Egypt as basically African, such a proposition should be properly established by a better knowledge of its prehistory. At the end of the last century, the research of Jacques de Morgan marked a milestone. Then came the investigations in Nubia, which the creation and then the first raising of the Aswan dam threatened with submersion.

The surveys* carried out by Firth and Reisner introduced us to new cultures. So as not to prejudge their nature, the excavators wisely called them by letters – Group A, Group C and Group X cultures. Later, the discoveries of Gerzeh, Nagada and Tasa helped us to learn more about Egypt in the dawn of its history. Nevertheless, the location of the oldest capital of Upper Egypt, Thebes, remains unknown. Its necropolis is Abydos. Excavated somewhat unmethodically, the cemeteries of this site are currently being re-examined.

One would have to cover the whole Nile valley and study each one of its sites and monuments to trace a substantial history of the progress of research and discovery. It is enough to point out that the Delta remained virtually ignored until recent years. A thick layer of alluvium covers the remains. Those which were visible have been used as building materials. Tanis alone, in the northeast of the Delta, was successfully investigated by Mariette and Petrie before Pierre Montet made the great discovery in 1939 of the tombs of the sovereigns of the 21st and 22nd dynasties, the Psusennes and Sheshonk.

Previously, between the two wars, the most astonishing discovery had been the tomb of Tutankhamen. From 1890 the archaeologist Howard Carter continuously investigated the Theban left bank. In 1907 he joined forces with Lord Carnarvon, a passionate art lover. Their association was rewarded by many remarkable finds, including the first tomb of Queen Hatshepsut and then the tomb of Amenophis I in 1910. In 1917 Lord Carnarvon asked for the concession of the Valley of the Kings, having obtained a subsidy from the Metropolitan Museum of New York. Six successive campaigns produced no results. Then in 1922 the excavators returned without high hopes to the area near the tomb of Rameses VI and discovered a staircase at the foot of which was a large wall covered with plastering bearing the seals of the necropolis and Tutankhamen. From it a gently sloping corridor led to a second wall bearing the same seals. In November 1922 Carter managed to make an entrance into the wonderful accumulation of treasures in the small tomb. There was an immediate furore in the international press. Administrative and psychological difficulties did not facilitate the task of uncovering, packing and dispatching the objects. Under the directorship of Pierre Lacau, the Service des Antiquités had made it a rule that not a single piece should leave Egypt; everything had to be assembled in Cairo Museum. Lord Carnarvon, who had always had a weak constitution, died. Howard Carter disappeared in 1939 without writing the long-awaited scientific report on his discovery. Even now we have no overall inventory and scarcely any detailed studies of this exceptional material.

After World War II, which caused an interruption in archaeological activity in Egypt, the large international institutions resumed their work. Alongside the French and German institutes, new research centres from various countries – Poland, Czechoslovakia and the Netherlands – were established. New missions from American universities and museums were based on the traditional House of Chicago at Luxor and an American centre at Cairo. Of course, the English and Italians were also present, among others. New formulas of association between the Egyptian authorities and foreign scholars were developed, for example the Franco-Egyptian Centre for studying the Karnak temples.

The riches of Nubia

In 1958 Gamel Abdel Nasser decided to raise the height of the Aswan dam, submerging the whole of Lower Nubia, but UNESCO succeeded in arousing public opinion. As a result, international funds made it possible to dismantle the two temples of Abu Simbel and rebuild them on top of a cliff, and to move whole temples such as Amada, which was transported nearly 6km (3.7 miles) across the desert. Teams of all nationalities explored both banks of the Nubian Nile, both in Egypt and the Sudan. Egyptologists proper were comparatively few in number, but they were joined by colleagues from the most varied scientific disciplines: paleontologists, prehistorians, ceramologists, even Byzantologists and Arabists. In this way Nubia, a poor country and a mere corridor between Egypt and the rest of Africa, paradoxically became one of the best-known archaeological regions in the world. There were finds of all kinds. The discovery of many rock engravings, for example, has shown that Nubia was one province of the magnificent rock art of the Sahara. New predynastic cultures have been established, but little has been added to our knowledge of the Egyptian colonial period, when the Egyptian pharaohs were dominant far to the south, from about 1560 to 1080BC. On the other hand, the discovery of the cathedral of Faras, in the far north of the Sudan, has brought to light an astonishing collection of superimposed paintings from the 10th to the 13th century AD. Removed from the walls with great care, they are today the glories of the Museums of Khartoum and Warsaw. But it will be many long years before all the scientific material collected from submerged Nubia is published or otherwise made available.

Long neglected, apart from the researches of the British F. Griffith and the American G.A. Reisner, who explored the royal pyramids of Napata and Meroë, the sites in the Sudan (which became independent in 1960) have now begun to attract attention. Considerable discoveries have been made in the field of prehistory. As for Egyptology in the true sense of the word, it can no longer scorn the contribution of finds made in the Sudan.

Egyptology today, 160 years after Champollion's discovery, and 130 years after Mariette's valuable initiative, is still a branch of archaeology full of vitality, in spite of the inevitable destruction caused by agricultural, industrial and demographic growth. In this exciting field, Egyptians, Sudanese, Europeans and Americans are all collaborating to achieve a better knowledge of a great past.

Egypt and the Desert: rock carvings and oases

Archaeological discoveries suggest that the Egyptian civilization of the pharaohs, one of the most sumptuous and sophisticated ever known, derived its origins and many features from African peoples living in the Sahara—then green and filled with wildlife.

In the eastern part of the Sahara Desert, Egypt appears as an oasis stretching along the length of its river, the Nile. This is formed when the waters of the White and the Blue Nile meet at Khartoum, the former constantly supplied by the daily rain of the equatorial forest, the latter swollen in spring by melting snow and the monsoon rains, and flooding Egypt at the beginning of July. The Libyan desert, now one of the harshest in the world, carries a chain of oases parallel to the valley: Siwa, Farafra, Dakhla, Kharga and Selima. From time immemorial to the present day, these have made travel possible through the solitudes of sand and stones.

A few millennia ago the climate of the Sahara was less arid. Lakes and plateaus rich in game spread out at the foot of the mountain massifs of Hoggar, Tibesti and Gelf el-Kebir. Many rock carvings survive from this Sahara of the hunters' period; Nubia is one area containing Saharan rock art that was little known until recently. Elephants, giraffes, ostriches, antelopes and gazelles are depicted in hundreds of images, providing evidence of the great paleo-African wildlife. Then, with the coming of domestication, herders replaced hunters, and thousands of images of cattle have been found, their coats often marked with the check patterns or geometric motifs also found on the vases of some predynastic cultures in Egypt and the Sudan. Dewlaps and distorted horns are also characteristic. This is the environment from which are derived certain original features of the pharaonic civilization. For example, up until the late periods, the pharaoh wore a false pigtail which was a relic of the animal remains donned by the head hunts-man, the great sorcerer and rain-maker.

In the dawn of pharaonic Egypt, about 3000BC, votive schist palettes were engraved with images of the victorious pharaoh, hunting scenes, or triumphs over enemies. The palette of tribute from Libya shows that what is desert today was then rich in trees and animals.

Relations between the valley and the oases continued throughout the millennia of the historical period. Recent research in the regions of Dakhla and Kharga, carried out by the Institut Français d'Archéologie Orientale, has established the presence of Egyptian governors at the end of the Old Kingdom, especially in the burial ground of Balat. In the Persian period (c.500BC) and under the Romans (30BC to c. AD300), the oases were the object of special attention, indicated by the consecration of numerous temples and the building of fortresses, for example at Dush and Qasr el-Gueita. These desert expanses then formed the limits of the "classical" world confronting the threat of the "barbarians": the Meroitic kingdom or the peoples of the desert. The discovery that this area had a *limes*, or fortified frontier, comparable to that of the Rhine or the Danube, is one of the more fascinating outcomes of the archaeology of Egypt and its borders.

The investigation of these remote regions, and the recent excavation of many sites, constitutes one entirely new chapter in Egyptian archaeology; another, as we shall see, is emerging from the development of research in Nubia and the Sudan. These discoveries may not equal the extraordinary wealth of monuments in the Nile valley itself, but they do help to place Egypt more accurately in its African context.

In the Nile valley, towards the end of the 4th and the beginning of the 3rd millennium, a series of very rapid changes helped Egyptian civilization to assert its own originality, while preserving many traces of its deepest roots.

The mystery of the Delta

Among the most interesting archaeological researches, studies recently made in the Delta stand out. Until then, theorists systematically proposed a clear opposition between Upper and Lower Egypt during the prehistoric and protohistoric periods. In Upper Egypt, the discoveries made at the beginning of the century at Nakada were so spectacular that the name of the village was given to one of the particularly brilliant civilizations in the protohistory of the valley. The Nakada craftsmen's choice of forms may have been limited, but their imagination excelled in the decoration of ceramics with stylized animals, as well as geometrical motifs. A concern with simplification is also found in cosmetic palettes, which frequently depict familiar animals in schematic outline: tortoises, fish, ibexes and hippopotamuses. During the same period, by contrast, a great archaeological silence reigned over Lower Egypt. Was the region uninhabited, with vast unhealthy marshes where only wild animals lived? Were the sites buried beneath five millennia of Nile mud, or is this simply a hiatus due to the haphazard nature of finds? Recent discoveries now tend to prove a unity from those early periods between the Delta and the rest of the valley. At Manshet Abu Omar in the eastern Delta, where a team from Munich Museum has been working since 1977, rich finds of votive palettes and hard stone and pottery receptacles, sometimes of Syro-Palestinian importation, have been made.

Fundamental rethinking is also in order for Egyptian sites in the periods which might seem the most "classical", for the archaeology of this area is no longer static or confined to repetitive discoveries. Tourism clings to the great traditional sites, and rightly so, but we should realize that not only are hundreds of expeditions from the Egyptian Antiquities Service at work every year, but also expeditions from the universities and great scientific institutions of all countries. Scholars continue to accumulate the patient inventory of the gigantic monumental and archaeological documentation left by the Old Kingdom (2600–2200BC), the Middle Kingdom (2130–1780BC), the New Kingdom (1560–1070BC) and the various phases of the long cultural twilight experienced by Egypt during the 1st millennium BC, a period which has not yet received the attention it deserves.

Beneath a clear sky, and sharply demarcated by its Libyan and Arabian cliff ranges, the valley provided a disciplined framework, a rigorous model for Egyptian architects and artists. Surely the exemplary geometry of Egyptian art was the product of this environment.

The Roman fortress of Qasr el-Gueita, in the Kharga oasis

In the immensity of the great Libyan desert which flanks the Nile valley to the west, a chain of oases has continued to offer the possibilities of culture and life throughout Egyptian history. These oases also formed staging posts for a major caravan route facilitating exchanges with the west and particularly with the south, modern Sudan and furthest Africa. Archaeological discoveries range from prehistory to the Roman and Byzantine periods. The Persian and Roman conquerors in particular built temples and citadels there, evidence of their interest in trans-Saharan traffic.

Rock carving, Tomas, Egyptian Nubia

Recent researches in various parts of Nubia have resulted in the discovery of thousands of rock carvings, evidence of the hunters and, later, the herders who successively developed their cultures there. At Tomas, in Egyptian Nubia, engravings picked out of the rock depict elephants in various styles; those here have "butterfly wing" ears, indicating a much more humid climatic and paleobotanic environment than today's.

Alabaster vessels from German excavations at Manshet Abu Omar

Although long neglected by archaeologists, the Delta conceals many remains; their disclosure and study are opening up new vistas in Egyptian prehistory and history. The excavations carried out by Munich Museum in the eastern Delta have yielded not only stone pottery and vessels, but also palettes testifying to the cultural unity of the Nile valley from the remotest periods.

The palette of the Libyan tribute: grey schist

Fragment of a votive palette, decorated on both faces, which, if it were complete, would have a small cup-like depression for grinding cosmetics in the centre. On the face not shown, seven fortified towns surmounted by symbolic animals may indicate an Egyptian victory on enemy territories or, more probably, the foundation of cities won from the hostile marshes at the edge of the Delta. On the other face, seen here, four superimposed sections show, from top to bottom, a row of bulls, a row of donkeys, a file of rams, and several trees, possibly olives. Two hieroglyph characters represent the word "Tjehenu", a region to the west of the Delta, and this has led to the identification of this motif as the "Libyan tribute", suggesting that the palette is evidence in the 1st dynasty of commercial or warlike exchanges with the western marshes of the Egyptian Delta.

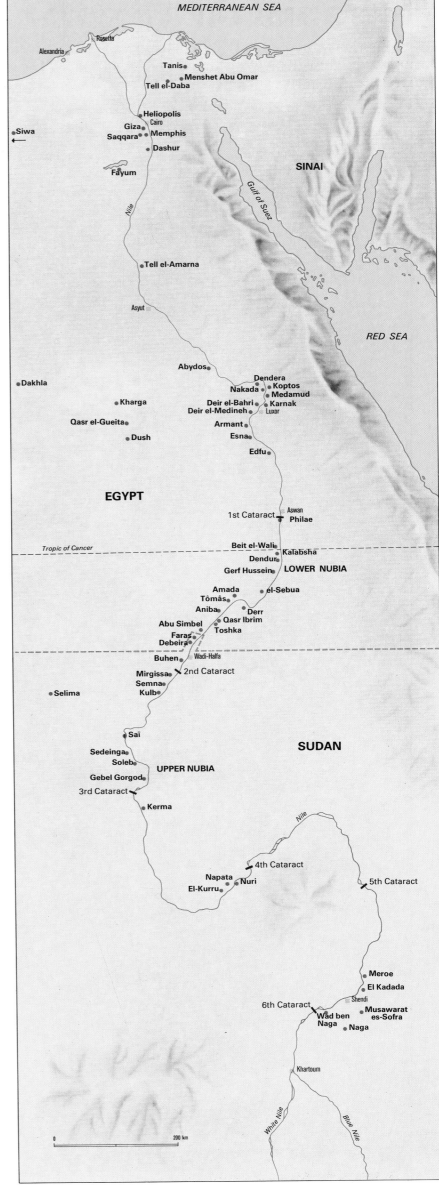

Necropolis of a capital: Memphis and Saqqara

Egyptian history begins around 3100BC when the two lands of Upper and Lower Egypt were united and the country was governed by one master, the equal of the gods, Pharaoh. The seat of power was Memphis, at the junction of the narrow corridor of the river valley and the large alluvial expanse we call the Delta.

No trace has been found of the sites of the Pharaoh's residence, palace and household quarters in the early dynastic period. In the well watered plain, the vast palm groves of Memphis, occupied today by housing and military camps, covers ancient remains, many of them still unexcavated. Several large temples date to the New Kingdom, basically the Ramesid period (c.1300–c.200BC). The principal god, Ptah, is depicted tightly swathed in a mummy-like robe, holding his sceptre in front of him. He was essentially a god of creation and theological texts describe his functions. His wife was the lioness goddess Sekhmet; their son was the god Nefertoum, associated with successful agriculture.

The Cairo region contains many burial grounds: the predynastic tombs of Meadi and Heliopolis, and the vast monumental complexes of Giza, Saqqara and Dahshur, these last three being situated on the edge of the Libyan cliffs. They were dominated by an impressive sequence of pyramids, only some of which survive.

The necropolis of the pharaohs of the first two dynasties was situated at north Saqqara. The tombs were characterized by vast mudbrick superstructures in the form of benches, which were known as *mastabas*, from the Arabic for bench.

Tombs of the early pharaohs

Since the names of the same pharaohs recur in the tombs discovered at Abydos in Upper Egypt, it is assumed that these early sovereigns were given a double "burial" in their capacity as kings of Upper and Lower Egypt, one at Abydos, the other at Saqqara—one of them of course was a cenotaph. At the beginning of the 3rd dynasty the Pharaoh Djoser ordered his architect, the famous Imhotep, to build the prestigious stepped pyramid complex. Dummy buildings were erected on almost 16 hectares (40 acres) inside an enclosure with projections. In these simulacra, simple doors stood open or closed for eternity. The king's sarcophagus was placed at the foot of a deep shaft beneath the six steps of the pyramid. Access to the southern cenotaph was by a long causeway. The vast funerary apartments contained chambers faced with faience tiles of sparkling green, the colour of seasonal renewal and eternal growth.

Then the pyramidal shape was simplified. From a stairway permitting communication between heaven and earth, it became a shape of unrivalled purity, with plane surfaces bounded by ridges like the petrified rays

of the sun. The 4th Dynasty, that of Kheops, Khephren and Mykerinos, is dedicated to Re, the sun god. The proportions of their edifices are impressive: the Great Pyramid, "Kheops belongs to the horizon", was more than 140m (460ft) high. The pharaohs of the 5th Dynasty seemed to attach less importance to their pyramids and more to vast temples consecrated to the sun at Abusir. The cult took place in the open air on an enormous terrace surmounted by a sort of obelisk built of limestone blocks.

With Unas, the last sovereign of the 5th Dynasty, and then the kings Teti, Pepi I, Merenre and Pepi II, the pharaohs again returned to Saqqara. Their pyramids became more modest. They were about 60m (200ft) high and the sides of the base were 75m (275ft) long. Hoping for survival in another world, they had their funerary apartments covered with inscriptions. With variations, these formulae were repeated from one king to another: they are the famous Texts of the Pyramids. The king ardently aspired to continue his existence in the hereafter: "No, not as a dead king did you depart; as a living king you did depart," asserts an introductory formula found in all the pyramids. The cult of the dead king was performed in vast temples attached to the eastern façade of the pyramids. In recent years, the total excavation of the monumental temple of Pepi I has been undertaken. A hall at the top of an ascending causeway led to a court surrounded by a peristyle supported by pillars. The slightly raised inner temple consisted of a chapel with five niches holding statues and, behind, adjoining the pyramid, a hall where offerings were consecrated. A vast complex of storerooms was served by long corridors.

Burials of the New Kingdom

Although the New Kingdom was known mainly for the burials of kings and notables in the Theban region, research shows that Saqqara was by no means abandoned in this period. Admittedly, Thebes did experience an exceptional flowering demonstrated by the magnificence of the sanctuaries and the unparalleled luxury of the royal and private tombs grouped at the foot of the Theban summit. But work undertaken by a French team on the cliff of Bubasteion has revealed an important area of 18th dynasty inhumations. The researchers found the tomb of Resh, a naval officer of foreign extraction, son of Tentiabet ("the Oriental") and in the immediate vicinity was the tomb of Aperia, or Aper-el,

vizier of the Amarnean period. Recent excavations by the Egypt Exploration Society have revealed the site of the tomb of General Horemheb, who later became Pharaoh and had a royal burial in a new tomb in the Theban necropolis. On the walls scenes of victory are complacently depicted with countless vivid details: a scribe beats a recalcitrant prisoner; the faces of dejected prisoners are treated realistically; the horses drawing the chariots of the Egyptian army prance in battle array as they confront the demoralized enemy.

Just to the north of this tomb, English archaeologists have also uncovered the tomb of a sister of Rameses II, Princess Tiya, and her husband, who bore the same name. The quality of the reliefs and paintings is exceptional; they mainly depict mythological scenes with protective genii and divinities from the other world. The special seat of the vizier of the north, Memphis's exceptional geographical position undoubtedly helped it to retain its importance in the New Kingdom. It was to preserve its role as a capital down to the Late Period. The arsenal and port of Memphis benefited from the installation of garrisons setting out to conquer Asiatic provinces. Foreign colonies also settled there and became prosperous: Syrians and Phoenicians, then Greeks and Jews. Chabaka, pharaoh of the 26th dynasty, had the sacred texts of the temples copied there; Taharqua, his successor, was crowned there. The University of Pisa is undertaking the excavation and restoration of the tomb of Bakenrenef, vizier of the 26th dynasty, the sumptuousness and complexity of which are reminiscent of Theban tombs of the period. Thanks to the French researcher Mariette,* we know of the institution of the Apis bulls sacred to the god Ptah which were buried during sumptuous festivities in the Serapeum of Saqqara. In the 1970s English excavations revealed gigantic galleries in which the mummified mothers of the Apis bulls were inhumed in granite sarcophagi in the Late Period. Nearby, other galleries with smaller proportions but an equally complicated layout have yielded hundreds of thousands of mummified falcons swathed in wrappings. These humble *ex voto* offerings witness to the fervour of the Egyptian masses who flocked to Saqqara as pilgrims. They implored the divinities of the pharaonic pantheon whose strength was being asserted at a time when Egypt's traditional values clashed with those of the Greeks and Persians in Egypt as conquerors.

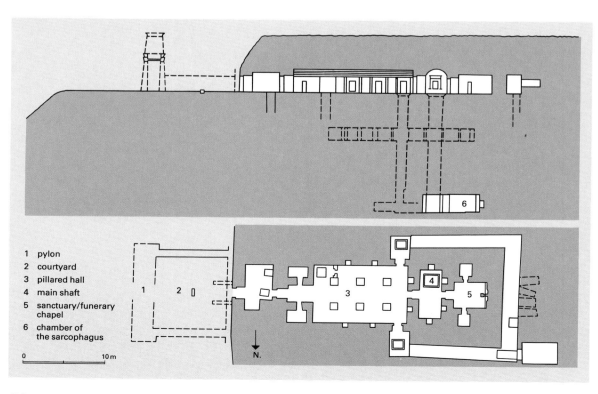

1 pylon
2 courtyard
3 pillared hall
4 main shaft
5 sanctuary/funerary chapel
6 chamber of the sarcophagus

0   10 m

N.

Saqqara, tomb of the Vizier Bocchoris (Bakenrenef), 26th dynasty

Visited and looted abundantly in the 19th century, the tomb of Bocchoris, vizier in the period of Psammetichus I (663–609BC), was a heap of deplorable and dangerous ruins when the Italian University of Pisa undertook methodical excavation and large-scale restoration work in 1974. The tomb assumes the plan of a partially hollowed-out temple and still has its coloured decoration in the Theban style. Religious litanies are engraved on the walls of the great pillared hall, while the hours of the day and night are represented on the vault in a spangle of stars. The ceiling of the sanctuary has a very beautiful low-relief, still bearing its original colours, depicting a group of vultures with wings outspread in protection. The quality and richness of the decor and the scenes preserved have led scholars to look upon this tomb as that of a member of the royal family.

East wall of the horizontal corridor of the Pyramid of Pepi I, Saqqara South

From the time of Pharaoh Unas, last sovereign of the 5th dynasty, a new fashion appeared within the funerary monuments, formerly completely without epigraphs. From then on and throughout the 6th dynasty, the walls of the underground apartments were covered with carefully carved and sometimes painted texts. Doubtless this was to eternalize the ritual which the priests intoned during the funeral ceremony. The litanies preserved are obscure but poetic. In them the king may be likened to an imperishable star or even a bird; the favourable gods are invited to help him to come safely through the traps awaiting him in the hereafter. Frequent alterations to the engravings indicate that the personage named in the text had been changed.

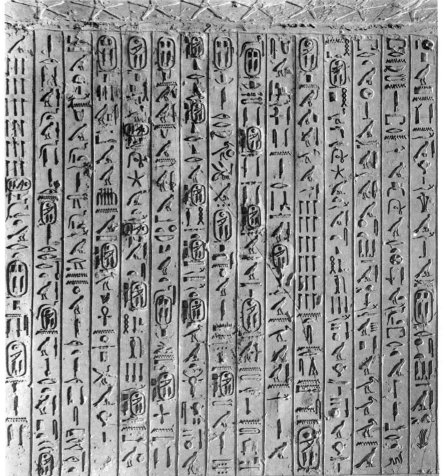

The temple of Pepi I at Saqqara

Since 1968 the temple of Pepi I, pharaoh of the 6th Dynasty, has been excavated and restored by the French Archaeological Mission of Saqqara. It was built on the desert cliff immediately to the east of the pyramid. A long covered causeway leading to the valley connected it with a small reception temple erected on the edge of the canal where the body of the dead pharaoh was brought. Built of limestone and surrounded by a thick enclosure wall, some of this temple's walls were decorated with beautiful coloured reliefs to remind the gods of the hereafter of the pharaoh's power on earth.

Temple of Pepi

On either side of the central line of the temple where, from east to west, an entrance hall, pillared court, chapels and sanctuaries succeeded each other, "shops" or "stores", sometimes of more than one storey, were arranged like the teeth of a comb on both sides of a long corridor. In them was kept the material necessary for the cult: receptacles, jars, valuable objects in chests, fabrics and papyrus scrolls on which temple ritual and details of everyday life were recorded.

Cosmetic spoon from the tomb of Aperia

This spoon in the shape of the *tilapia* fish, of carved and painted ivory, was discovered during the study of the tombs hollowed out of the rock at Bubasteion which was carried out under the auspices of the French Archaeological Mission of Saqqara. In addition to some attractive New Empire material collected in a badly disturbed site, this recent research has yielded a great deal of information about important officials working at Memphis.

The tomb of Princess Tiya

Recent researches by the Egypt Exploration Society to the south of the pyramid of Unas have located at Saqqara an extremely important site from the New Empire. Immediately to the north of the tomb of Horemheb, the tomb of Princess Tiya, sister of Rameses II, and of her husband, opened through a portico on to a vast colonnaded court. An antechamber led to the cult hall flanked by five lateral chapels. A limestone pyramid terminated the tomb to the west. The numerous inscriptions repeat the names and titles of the owners, among outstanding reliefs with themes that are essentially religious, but embellished with picturesque details.

Karnak: a dynastic sanctuary

The power of the pharaohs, expressed in monuments of unsurpassed magnificence, was linked with the cult of Amen, the divine symbol of life and fertility.

The splendour of Thebes, the "city of a hundred portals", sums up the glory of Egypt under the New Kingdom during the 2nd millennium BC. And yet nothing about the site seems to make it a natural choice for this position: some 700km (434 miles) to the south of the Nile Delta, Thebes did not control an important route and the fertility of its valley was no greater than that of the surrounding areas. True, the landscape is impressive and worthy of the enterprising rulers through whose political and military strength the local god, Amen, was raised to the status of "King of the Gods".

The oldest divinity of the *nome** – the fourth *nome* in Upper Egypt – was Montu, the warrior-god with a falcon head who reigned over four sanctuaries: Medamud and Karnak in the north, Armant and Tôd in the south, a sort of "palladium"* for the protection of Thebes. At the beginning of the 2nd millennium, Antef and Mentuhotep of the 11th Dynasty ruled over the whole of the country and founded the Middle Kingdom; Sesostris I (1970–1930BC) was one of the first to build at Karnak, to the glory of Amen-Re. Amen, "the hidden", the cosmic power present in the whole of creation, was identified with Ra, the god of the sun, and brought the kings their victory: the pharaonic establishment and Amenian pre-eminence were thus indissolubly linked.

After the period of foreign occupation under the Hyksos, Egypt regained its independence and glory under the Theban rulers Sekenenra-Taa, Kamosis, Ahmosis, who marked the beginnings of the New Kingdom. For two and a half centuries (1545–1295BC), with the exception of Amenophis IV, Akehenaten and the brief episode of Tell el-Amarna (c.1360–1340BC) the rulers of the 18th Dynasty made Thebes their main residence and their burial ground. Even when, during the 19th and 20th Dynasties, under Sethi and Rameses, the centre of gravity was switched to the eastern Delta, Thebes remained the major town and the pharaohs were still buried in the Valley of the Kings. An inventory from the time of Rameses III (c.1180–1150BC) shows that more than 80,000 men were employed in the service of Amen; the god also owned 65 villages, a herd of half a million cattle, ship-building yards and huge revenues from all the agricultural areas of Egypt.

The Ramesids erected huge buildings in Thebes and held splendid festivals: during the sacred processions, the statue of the god was carried in a special three-masted ship, accompanied by his wife Mut and by the child-god Khonsu and escorted by a crowd of priests, soldiers and followers. The procession would stop at the small chapels on the way, like the "white chapel" of Sesostris now reconstructed with original blocks; hymns would be chanted and the god would be consulted for his oracles. During the Opet festival, the god would travel to Luxor, his southern temple complex; for the festival of the Valley, he would cross the Nile and travel to the "temples of millions of years" on the left bank, halting on the way at Medinet Habu, where the eight gods of Hermopolis, companions of disorder, were buried.

In the course of the 1st millennium Thebes lost its position as the political capital but still retained its status as religious centre. The high priests of the 21st Dynasty were also pharaohs and gave rise to the "Amenian theocracy". More buildings were added to the huge monuments of the New Kingdom, but they were unimportant compared with the colossal temples of Edfu and Dendera built in the Ptolemaic and Roman periods. The wealth of Amen was in decline, although theological thought still linked the power of the monarch to the constant renewal of the power of the god, and the Theban cult survived until the end of the pharaonic civilization. Eventually, at the beginning of the 4th century AD, Karnak was deprived of two of its most beautiful obelisks: one is today in Constantinople, the other, the unique obelisk of Tutmosis III, is in Rome opposite the basilica of St. John Lateran. The year 356 saw the triumph of Christianity with Constantine II and the end of Karnak.

The temple of Amen

Karnak is a vast complex, the investigation of which is still far from complete. Its stone buildings are impressive and perhaps best known: the hypostyle room of the great temple of Amen, measuring 102m × 53m (334 × 173ft) and with its forest of 134 colossal columns best of all. Many buildings, however, are of unbaked bricks, starting with the enclosure walls often 8m (26ft) thick. Religious buildings are mixed with the dwellings of the priests and of the numerous servants of the god, and with the storerooms for the sacred materials, the tributes and the treasures.

The effigy of Amen appears constantly on the walls of the Theban temples: he has a human head and wears a jerkin of white, blue and red feathers; behind his head, a ribbon descends from his headdress, a kind of round cap surmounted by long plumes reaching to the sky. Two animals were associated with him: the ram, god of water, whose origins are to be found in the Sahara, and whose head bears large coiled horns; and the Nile goose, which was kept in aviaries connected by slips to the sacred lake.

The vast quadrangle of the great Temple, some 2,400m (7,874ft) in circumference, was dedicated to Amon. Another enclosure, in Karnak-north, was the domain of the ancient local god Montu whose worship was always kept up. To the south is the precinct dedicated to Mut, Amen's wife, which has only been partially explored; it comprises a construction with a west-east orientation which is now being investigated by a team of American archaeologists, and a temple built by Rameses III; the temple of Mut itself, with its north-south orientation, rises on the shores of the sacred lake, the crescent shape of which recalls female symbolism. Several lion-headed statues of the goddess Sekhmet stand protectively by. In the great precinct, the huge temple of Amen, with its two axes north-south and east-west, is surrounded by a variety of buildings with different functions which are indicated either by the name of the divinity to whom they are dedicated or by that of the most important of the rulers involved in their construction; thus, on either side of the courtyard, there is a "temple of Sethi II" and a "temple of Rameses III", and to the east, between the ninth and tenth columns, is the "building of Amenophis II", while near the sacred lake is the "building of Taharqa". In the south-west corner of the precinct is the temple of the god Khonsu, while the temple of Ptah is near the north gate. Excavations of the north and north-east sectors of the complex have revealed several small chapels where the name of Osiris is inscribed: he was worshipped under several different names, "master of eternity", "ruler of all perpetuity", "master of life", "the one who gives life" and "the one who comforts the afflicted". Thus Osiris, the god of death and cyclic renewal, is omnipresent. Several of these constructions date from the "Ethiopian" period, when Egypt was ruled by a southern dynasty, one of whose native gods was the ram. Osiris gained in popularity during the course of the 1st millennium: he was represented as an understanding god, who had himself known death and resurrection. The goddess Isis, nursing the child Khonsu, enjoyed the same popularity.

Karnak may seem to represent a statement in stone of an official religion: the cult of Amen and of the Pharaoh. But beside the glory of these impressive monuments, and behind the images of power and conquest constantly repeated with such pomp, Osiris's humble chapels testify to a lively faith based on a theme that would later be found in the Christian religion.

Aerial view of the great enclosure of Amen, the central part of the group of sanctuaries at Karnak

Within the sacred enclosure, which defines and protects the holy area, can be seen the main west-east axis along which the main buildings were grouped, pylon alternating with courtyard, hypostyle hall, then sanctuaries proper, crowded together, enlarged, modified over the centuries (basically from the Middle Dynasty to the end of the Egyptian civilization). To the south, the vast Sacred Lake was thought to be representative of the primordial water from which the world emerged. The secondary axis to the south led towards the temple of Mut; an avenue of sphinxes with rams' heads led to the temple of Luxor, belonging to the god Amen, the lord of Karnak. Finally, in the south-west corner (top left) stands the small temple of Khonsu, the child god of the Theban trilogy.

Portrait of the heretic pharaoh Akhenaten (or Amenophis IV) on a talatate

Exceptional conditions of preservation for the blocks found inside the 9th pylon of Karnak explain the freshness of the colours in this portrait. The pharaoh can be recognized immediately by his almost caricature-like features, his pointed chin, thick mouth, a deep wrinkle running from nose to chin, his narrow and elongated eyes. The pierced ear lobe was a frequent feature in Amarnian times.

View of the inside of the western jetty of the 9th pylon being dismantled

Restoration work carried out by the Franco-Egyptian Centre for the study of Karnak temples has brought to light almost 12,000 *talatates* (sandstone construction blocks of constant dimensions, often decorated on one side) which constituted the core of the massive 9th pylon. After the return to Amenian orthodoxy, the monument of the heretic pharaoh Akhenaten had been dismantled to be reused in later buildings: carefully laid in regular courses, these sculpted and painted blocks of sandstone have managed to survive and to retain their freshness. Whole walls can be reconstructed on the basis of the blocks from the 9th pylon; patient piecing together has revealed historical texts of vital importance, as well as details of everyday life in the days of Nefertiti and Akhenaten: a panel of 64 *talatates*, some 12m (39ft) long, shows scenes of dancing and festivities celebrating the royal jubilee.

The chapel-altar of Achoris in course of reconstruction

Immediately outside the enclosure of the temple of Karnak, a small monument of the 29th Dynasty is now being restored. It was used to receive the three-masted ship of the god Achoris during sacred processions. The external walls of the chapel are covered with graffiti made by Cypriot mercenaries in the service of the last of the native pharaohs.

Work in progress to the south of the great axis of the temple of Amen at Karnak, inside a small hall with elegant clustered columns

After the meticulous excavations of the temples of Karnak had been completed, the architectural elements were carefully repositioned and the site restored for the countless people who visit it.

The Theban necropolis

It is no exaggeration to say that the Theban "City of the Dead" is the most famous cemetery in the world. But the Valley of the Kings, where the treasure of Tutankamun was found in 1922, was only one part of an elaborate funerary complex extending over several sites.

Apart from the ancient kings, Antef and Mentuhotep, the pharaohs of the Middle Kingdom, who came originally from Upper Egypt, continued to exert power from Memphis and the surrounding area, where they built their "eternal dwellings". Under the New Kingdom, however, Thebes became the capital of the empire and the kings chose to be buried on the western bank of the Nile, opposite the impressive sanctuaries of Karnak and Luxor.

Changes took place in the royal funeral complex; the pharaohs had obviously realized the futility of their predecessors' efforts to protect their tombs from robbers. After the First Intermediate Period and again during the Second, the pillaging of the royal tombs was organized on a vast scale; even the great pyramids had failed to ensure the repose of the deceased, despite their size and their complex system of internal rooms sealed with heavy sliding gates. From the New Kingdom onwards, no exterior monuments were built for the tombs themselves. At the bottom of a dry river bed in the desert, descending from the Libyan cliffs, they dug out the royal tombs in the hill of Thebes, a natural pyramid. The temples of the funeral cult were now at a distance of several miles from the actual tombs, and stretched along the whole of the valley at the edge of the cultivated area. The temples were built to honour the great gods of the Egyptian pantheon, with whom the pharaoh himself was associated in a divinized form. Prayers and rites were offered to his everlasting presence in these "temples of a million years".

The funerary temple of Amenophis III, described in Egyptian texts as particularly huge and sumptuous, has almost totally disappeared. Standing in the middle of a field, only the two huge statues of Memnon, which once stood at the pylon entrance of the building, now give us some idea of its location and dimensions. Among the funerary temples that are still preserved, Medinet Habu, originally built for Rameses III, still stands imposingly at the foot of the mountain. Scenes of the pharaoh's victory over the Sea Peoples are commemorated, perhaps too insistently, over the main pylon. Other scenes show the numbering of the victims after the battles; severed hands, casually piled up, testify to the valour of Egyptian warriors. But gradually, as one goes on into the deeper interior of the temple, details of worldly life give way to large compositions of a religious nature. The offerings heaped in front of the gods were designed to intercede on behalf of the deceased, and religious texts cover the walls without reliefs.

North of Medinet Habu stands the Ramesseum, dedicated to Rameses II. Within its vast enclosing wall of unbaked bricks are preserved the remains of chapels, colossal statues and vaulted store rooms. Above the scenes of battle a version of the "Poem of Pentaur" is inscribed, a hymn of praise to the victorious pharaoh who defeated at Qadesh the Hittite armies united against Egypt. Still further to the north, excavations recently carried out by the German Archeological Institute have concentrated on the funerary temple of Seti I, the first pharaoh of the 19th Dynasty; here, a particular study has been made of the links between palaces and the funerary temples.

The finest architectural discovery among these temples is undoubtedly the one designed for Queen Hatshepsut by her architect Senenmut during the 18th Dynasty. In the heart of the semicircular space at Deir el-Bahri, Senenmut created a series of superimposed terraces, linked by a monumental ramp and set against the side of the mountain, which encloses the monument like a huge casket. The Egyptians called this "the most sublime of all that is sublime". A woman pharaoh, the queen recorded under the colonnades of the terraces the story of how she had been conceived by the god Amon and recognized as his daughter—a fact which enabled her to sit on the throne of Horus. She has also proudly recorded the great event of her reign, the expedition to the Land of Punt, deep in Africa. Painted reliefs also record the queen's concern in embellishing the dwelling of her father Amon, and the transport of two granite obelisks by boat from Aswan to Karnak. One of these still stands within the Karnak temple, its tip covered with a gold-silver alloy of electrum.

The tombs of the kings

In order to reach the tombs of the kings, one has to leave the fields and the rich temples and cross the desert to a narrow and dry wadi with rocky banks scorched by the sun. Sunk into the side of this are 58 tombs, approached by a sometimes steeply sloping passage occasionally interrupted by a shaft. The funerary apartments are of very different sizes, with added rooms complicating the various plans. The walls are covered in painted scenes, sometimes in relief and always of a mythological nature—the pleasures of earthly life are no longer mentioned here. Infernal spirits and protection-giving prayers follow on each other in weird, disconcerting scenes; they reflect the ancient Egyptians' vision of the otherworld and may have acted as reminders to the dead person to help him on his way to the next world. Their titles are explicit: "Book of the Portals", "Book of the World Beyond", "Book of the Two Paths", "Book of the One who lives in Hades".

Ever since antiquity, these tombs have suffered from numerous robberies and deterioration. Their grave goods have completely disappeared. What extraordinary riches must have been piled up inside the tombs of the most famous pharaohs, if one recalls the treasures of Tutankamun, a minor king of no great fame who died at 18 during a troubled period in Egyptian history. Tutankamun's two modestly sized rooms contained a disorderly array of furniture with gold veneer, sumptuous textiles, costumes, statues, vessels and dismantled chariots, which still amaze us to this day with their luxury and abundance.

The construction of a royal tomb required specialized and expert labour. Under Tutmosis I, c.1550BC, a village reserved for workers was built at the foot of the hill of Thebes in the valley of Deir el Medina. Regular excavations of the site were carried out by the French Institute of Oriental Archaeology between 1921 and 1940, and again from 1945 to 1951, revealing the village itself and the cemetery that bordered it. Since that date the material found in the village and the tombs has been systematically published. The village archives are a very interesting source of information on the economic history of the period. In their leisure hours the craftsmen decorated their own tombs, making a visit to the necropolis of Deir el Medina an enchanting experience. Topped by a small cult chapel and fronted by a pylon opening on a courtyard, the tombs were hollowed out of the sides of the mountain. The underground rooms are most often decorated with sculptures of paintings in vivid colours. The powerful imagination and compositional sense of the artists are apparent in the wall paintings, which reproduce the scenes painted on funerary papyri: mythological themes with fresh colours, to facilitate understanding of the long texts, drawn up in tight columns.

The high functionaries and dignitaries of the court were buried near the tomb of the pharaoh whom they had served in life. The tombs of the nobles of the 18th and 19th Dynasties are beginning to be well known, and have been the subject of important publications. A new sector of the necropolis, the Assasif, has recently attracted attention, with German and Austrian teams recovering the funerary palaces of the dignitaries of the 25th and 26th Dynasties. Archaeologists have discovered huge underground palaces of complex design, enclosed with massive walls of unbaked bricks. In the inscriptions, references to the king and his dignitaries provide a precious contribution to our scanty knowledge of this troubled period.

Underground chambers of the tomb of Pached, Deir el Medina

Theban tomb no. 3, known as that of Pached, is situated in the middle of the necropolis of Deir el Medina. Pached was one of a family of workmen from the village of craftsmen responsible for the construction and the decoration of the royal tombs. He lived under Rameses II and had links with the quarries belonging to the Theban priests of Amen. The sumptuous, richly coloured decoration of his tomb combines mythological representations (falcons with outspread wings, gods and genies) with long columns of text. The eastern wall of the funerary chamber shows the deceased kneeling under a date palm and leaning towards the water which should quench his thirst; the composition testifies to the proficiency of an artist, who transferred to the walls of the tomb the illuminations of funerary papyri.

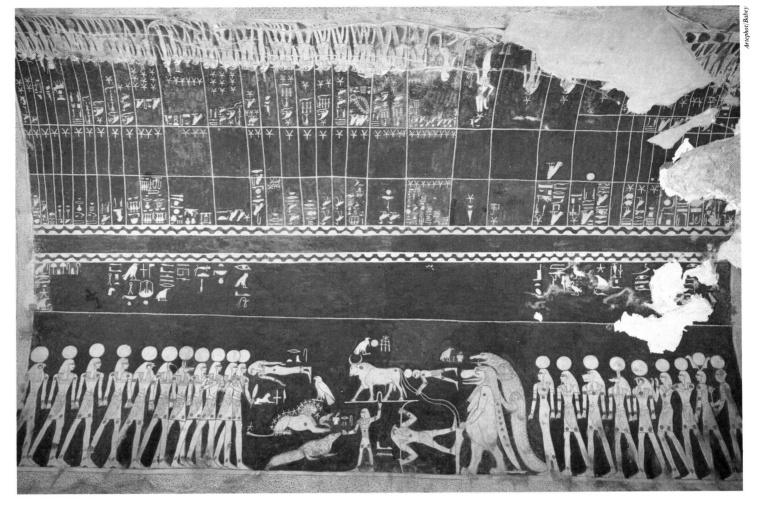

Artephot/Babey

Ceiling of the tomb of Seti I

Among all the splendid sepulchres of the Valley of the Kings, the tomb of Seti I, the founder of the 19th Dynasty, is particularly well known for its extraordinary painted ceiling representing the sky. A varied crowd of human and animal figures in gold stand out against a black background: they symbolize the ancient Egyptian constellations, as well as the Egyptian concept of the calendar and of the hours of day and night. The astronomical theories elaborated by the priests of the end of the 2nd millennium BC are also depicted with an impressive feeling for decoration and aesthetics. They are currently being studied by an American Egyptologist who combines an excellent knowledge of the Egyptian world with sound astronomical information. Another aspect of research, within the wider field of pharaonic architecture, concerns the vaults, the vaulted ceilings of the Theban tombs in particular, their construction techniques and meaning.

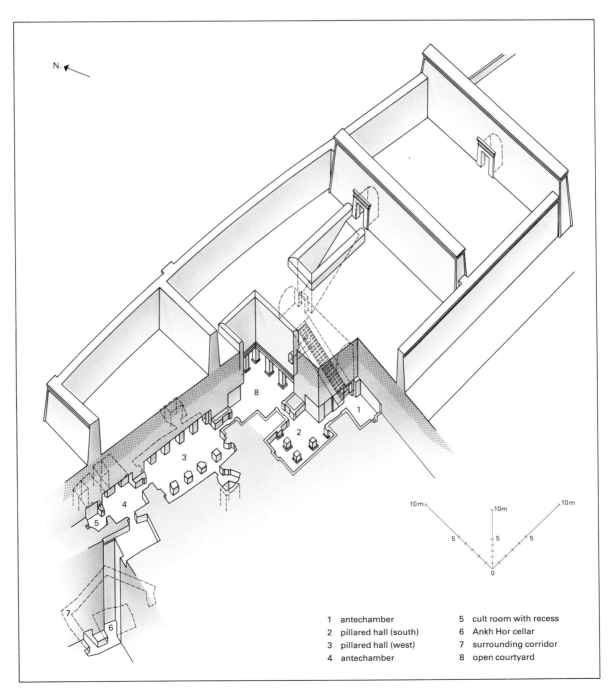

Axonometric view of the tomb of Ankh-Hor, no. 44

The tombs of the great dignitaries of the 26th Dynasty (known as Saite) occupied the sector of the Assasif at the foot of the hill of Thebes, and developed, in the manner of the royal funerary complexes, into veritable underground palaces. Thus, the tomb of Ankh-Hor, excavated and carefully restored by an Austrian team, comprises a series of courtyards, corridors and staircases, underground pillared halls and a deep shaft leading to the vault. During the 7th century BC it was still the custom, as it had been 2,000 years before, to depict, with the same religious concern for survival in the afterlife, funerary texts and scenes from everyday life on the walls of tombs. After M. Bietak.

1 antechamber
2 pillared hall (south)
3 pillared hall (west)
4 antechamber
5 cult room with recess
6 Ankh Hor cellar
7 surrounding corridor
8 open courtyard

Scythia:
the archaeological background

Archaeological knowledge of the Steppe nomads mainly concerns the Scythians, who have fired the imagination of "civilized" writers from Herodotus to Ruskin. Discoveries such as the treasure of the frozen tombs of Tolstaia Mogila (1971) today provide a factual basis for this romantic world.

The Greek historian, Herodotus, provides the point of departure of written history about the Scythians, and even if in doing so he tells us a great deal more about the Greeks themselves, the evidence he provides—mostly confirmed by archaeology—is nevertheless irreplaceable. His account of Scythians whom he actually saw in Olbia in the 5th century BC, as well as the imaginary Scythians whose portrait he has passed on to future generations, continued to carry weight long after all trace of the nomads had been buried.

It was not until the 18th century that the objects buried in the Steppes began to reappear. Perhaps paradoxically, it was Peter the Great, the scourge of the barbarians, who was behind this rediscovery. Very impressed by the pieces of ancient gold plate which he received from Siberia in 1715, the Czar sent for other pieces from the governor, Prince Gagarin. He received 10 from Tobolsk in January, 1716 and over 100 in December, and placed this Siberian collection—which was later to increase—in his chamber of curiosities, the Kunstkamera on the banks of the Neva. Probably neither the Emperor himself nor his entourage in Petersburg was aware of the extent to which the tombs had already been plundered, and when the Czar promulgated edicts

ordering the collection of what is called *raritet* in Russian, and founded the Academy of Sciences in 1725, it was probably almost too late. When expeditions were sent into Siberia to draw up an inventory—in the spirit of the 18th century—of all its resources, they were only able to gather, from the disembowelled tombs, the memory of enormous quantities of gold which was by now dispersed and, alas, generally melted down.

The birth of Siberian archaeology

The first expedition, that of Messerschmidt, a German who was shortly afterwards accompanied by Strahlenberg, a Swedish officer then imprisoned in Siberia, nevertheless marks a decisive step. The date when Siberian archaeology was born may be tentatively put at 6 January 1722, for it was on that day that scholars decided to excavate a kurgan or burial chamber on the Yenisey. It proved to have been plundered, but the inventory made was the first in the history of the Steppes. Two other Germans, Miller and Gmelin, explored many tombs on the Irtysh between 1733 and 1743. Disappointed by their lack of success, they did manage to bring back a few beautiful pieces which were placed in the Kunstkamera. They also had some amazing encounters, such as when they met an old hermit living in a hovel surrounded by gaping kurgans which he had excavated over a period of 30 years, only going out to exchange his finds for vodka. He explained to the two men that the dig had ceased to be profitable, but he gave very precise indications about the structure of the tombs and what had been in them. The consequence of this meeting was that Miller was the first to attempt a classification of the tombs according to their shape, their contents, and the position of the bodies. He suggested as early as 1764 that the use of iron succeeded the use of bronze. Tatishchev, who was the author of the first history of Russia from its origins, preferred to attempt to identify places from the ancient texts. For him, Siberia was Hyperborea, the Urals were the Mountains of Ryphe—rich in gold—and the Samoyeds, whose name in Russian means self-devouring, were none other than the *Androphagi*, Herodotus' man-eaters. Together with the famous historian and man of letters, Lomonosov, he was the inspiration for the creation of an archaeological map of Russia.

In 1770 a German from Berlin, Pallas, spent the year in southern Siberia. He described the wooden framework of the kurgans, noted remains of fabric and fur, "ducks . . . covered in gold leaf", "hemispherical buttons reminiscent of little bells appearing as decorations on the top of figurines representing a wild ram", and many objects on which modern excavations have thrown further light. Another researcher, Radischev, was exiled to Siberia in 1791, but he nevertheless took the time to notice the ancient mines and to study weapons and—40 years before the Dane Thomsen—he suggested a classification system in which stone, bronze and iron followed one another.

Catherine the Great's "Greek project"

During all this time a single kurgan was explored in the western Steppes, the Litoy kurgan, which was excavated in 1763 on the orders of General Melgunov; the precious objects found were taken to the Kunstkamera. But an event of prime importance for Russian archaeology then occurred: the capture from the Turks of the Black Sea coast. Kerch became Russian in 1774; in 1783 it was the turn of the khanate of the Crimea, of the mouths of the Dnieper and the Kuban. Russia was jubilant at annexing in this way an ancient past that had been described in texts and attested by a few visible ruins—a "classical" early history which put her on a par with the West in the

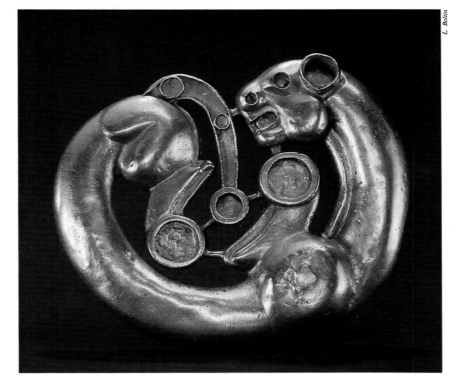

L. Boltin

Panther from the Siberian Collection

This massive gold jewel, 11cm (4in) in diameter and weighing 221gr (7.7oz), was sent to Peter the Great by the governor of Siberia in December 1716, but nothing is known about its origin. The note which accompanied the object described it as "a coiled serpent". The ear, eye and nostril, which are on a single line, and the tail and the paws have round indentations which may have contained inlays. Peculiar to the art of the Steppes where it was very popular and found from a very early date, this feline motif coiled into a circle is, like the stag motif, emblematic of this art. The Hermitage, Leningrad.

period of the Enlightenment. With her ambitious "Greek project", Catherine the Great was keen to restore the empire of Constantinople and as a result renamed such towns as Sevastopol and Kherson with appropriately Greek names. She also took her favourite, Potemkin—whom she made "Prince of Tauri"—with her on a would-be triumphal journey through the region, the first of the voyages into the past which so preoccupied the 19th century. In 1794, Pallas identified the ancient Olbia. In 1820, Pushkin visited the ruins of Kerch. If he expected to see the Athens of the ancient texts rise up before him, or grandiose ruins in the manner of Piranesi, he would have been cruelly disappointed by the piles of stones he saw. But Pushkin may have been less concerned that the ancient kingdom of Pontus existed no more, or that Scythia was an empty shell, preferring to see himself as an Ovid in exile, consigned like the Roman poet to banishment on the orders of a tyrant.

The discovery of the tomb at Kul Oba in 1830, by the Frenchman du Brux, proved a double shock. Inevitably, the researchers were dazzled by the gold they found, but they were also astonished to see the image of Athene in the midst of the barbarian jewels. There was great excitement at the court; funds

Fastener from Tillia Tepe.

Kabul museum

were made available for excavations. After Alexandropol (1853), the kurgans of Chertomlik (1863), Bolshaia Bliznitsa (1864), the Seven Brothers (1875) as well as the Greek town of Tanais (1855) were explored. The Imperial Archaeological Commission was founded in 1859 and from then on published annual reports on excavations. In the same year, the Siberian collection was transferred to the Imperial Museum at the Hermitage, Leningrad. Attaching itself firmly to its past, Russia added to its territorial conquests a kind of "vertical" conquest of its temporal origins, the keynotes being classical culture sharing the same Hellenism as that of the newly independent Greece itself.

Meanwhile, in Siberia, the era of science had succeeded the era of plunder. In the first half of the 19th century, the engineer Frolov gathered a remarkable collection of bronzes, which are today divided between the Hermitage and the Moscow Historical Museum, and founded the Barnaul Museum. The Finnish etymologist Castren was the first to seek an archaeological answer in Siberia to the question of the original source of the Finno-Ugrian languages, and he made some excavations there. But the real father of Siberian archaeology was undoubtedly Radlov, an Orientalist and Turcologist by training. His discovery of clothes, furs and wooden objects in the kurgans at Katanda and Berel, in 1865, anticipated the great finds in the Altai region in the following century. Most importantly, he was the first to publish a comprehensive work on the ancient past of Siberia, a work in which he laid the foundations for a chronological classification based on ethnic groups.

This was followed by an enormous resurgence of interest in the scientific study of Siberia. At Minusinsk, a museum opened in 1877, gathered a whole community of enthusiasts around its founder, Martyanov; these were often exiles like the revolutionary Klementz, who engaged in an enormous amount of archaeological activity. The deported victims of Czarist repression were able to devote the time spent in exile to study. At the same time excavations continued in the west, with kurgans at Kostromskaya (1897), Kelermes (1903), Ulski Ayul (1898 and 1908) in the Kuban, Solokha (1912) on the Dnieper, and also at the Greek city of Olbia (1901). In 1890, Tolstoy and Kondakov published their *Russian Antiquities in Monuments with Figures*—a study which for the first time connected southern Russia, Siberia and Kazakhstan. By the eve of the revolution, it had become accepted that the peoples of the Steppes were of Iranian origin and that Scythian and Siberian cultures shared a basic unity. In those years, Rostovtzev, Borovka and Minns made the art of the Steppes known from Petersburg to Oxford and Princeton. Since then, under the Soviet administration, an enormous amount of archaeological work has been undertaken, co-ordinating—under the aegis of the Academy of Sciences of the USSR—the efforts of the institutes and museums of each republic. Not only have there been particularly spectacular finds, such as the frozen tombs of the Altai (Gryaznov, 1929, and Rudenko* 1947), or Tolstaia Mogila in 1971, but work has been done to illuminate various aspects: the Siberian cultures (Teployukhov, Kisselev, Gratch), the Scythian relations with Urartu at Karmir-Blyur (Pyotrovsky), or animal art (Grakov, Artamonov) represent the earliest work, which we can now judge from a certain distance. More recently, the field of study has been broadened by the discovery in 1977 at Vergina of a Scythian-type quiver, and the discovery by a combined Russian and Afghani team in the autumn of 1978 of a necropolis at Tillia Tepe dating from about the 1st century AD which clearly bears the imprint of the art of the Steppes. The researchers' training as Hellenists or Orientalists at first affected their conclusions, causing them sometimes to concentrate overmuch on what was familiar to them. However, the work is now turning in other directions, showing a concern to provide a better definition of the characteristics of each culture: the Sauromates of the Steppes between the Urals and the Caspian, from whom came the Sarmatians; the Saka (Sacae) of Central Asia and the tribes of the Pamir, the Altai region, Sayan-Tuva and Minusinsk. As archaeologists become more aware of the importance of the centre and east of the continent for the origin and growth of the culture of the Steppes, and as they establish the relevance both for eastern Asia and for the West of what took place there, they are increasingly carrying out research which is leading them to Mongolia and thence to China, thus becoming, as it were, nomads themselves.

Ural

Tobol'sk

Leningrad

Moscow

Orenburg

SAUROMATES

Uigarak
Tagisken

Voronezh
Tchastye Kurgany

MASSAGETAE

*ARAL
SEA*

Dnieper (Borysthenes)

Tolstaia Mogila
Chertomlyk
Dniepropetrovsk
Alexandropol
Solokha
Tsimbalka
Zaporozh'ye
Gaïmanova mogila

Don (Tanais)

CHORASMIA

Kiev

Sula

Jurovka
Martonocha
Melgunov-Litoi
Nemirovskoe

Donetz

Novotcherkassk
Elizavetovskaya

Bug

SCYTHIANS

Melitopol
*SEA
OF AZOV*

Elizavetinski
Krasnodar

Volga

Dniestr

Olbia
Odessa

Kherson

Kuban

Ulsky
Kelermes
Kostromskaya

Terek

CASPIAN SEA

Prut

Kulakovsky

Karagodenashkh

Caucasus

Seven Brothers
Kul Oba
Panticapaeum
(Kertch)

COLCHIDUS

Kura
Lake Sevan

Danube (Ister)

BLACK SEA

URARTU

Yrevan
Aras

Amlach
Marlik

THRACE

ANATOLIA

Lake Van

Tushpa
Toprak

Lake Urmia

Ziwiyé

MACEDONIA

Gordium

PHRYGIA

Hassanlu

IRAN

ASSYRIA

Nineveh

LURISTAN

Vergina

LYDIA

Euphrates

Tigris

Zagros

Athens

Miletus

ELAM

Persepolis

AEGEAN SEA

PERSIAN GULF

Nile

*RED
SEA*

212

modern town
ancient town
tumulus
archaeological site

Ob
Yenisey
Lena
Lake Baikal
●Krasnoyarsk◯
Irkutsk◯
Sayan
●Minusinsk
HIONG-NU
Amur
●Pazyryk⌂
Tuekta⌂
●Bachadar⌂
●Ulan-Bator◯
Irtysh
MONGOLIA
Omsk Kamenogorsk◯
Altai
GOBI
Lake Zaysan
●Tchilikta⌂
ORDOS
CHENSI
Lake Balkash
AZAKHSTAN
Great Wall
Huangho
KANSU
●Alma-Ata◯
Lake Issyk-Kul
CHINA
Daria (Iaxarte)
SACES
Tian Chan
Yangtse
●Samarkand◯
Pamir
Amu Daria (Oxus)
Tillia-tepe ●Bactra◯
TIBET
BACTRIA
●Kabul◯
Indus
Ganges

INDIA

213

The archaeology of a nomadic world

Peoples in constant movement, leaving very little trace behind, present a formidable challenge to the archaeologist. But today much can be deduced from the effects of the nomads on traditional civilizations, both east and west.

A nomadic way of life is the essential factor underlying the cultural unity of the peoples of the Steppes. However, nomadism has not always been the rule in this huge area with its severely continental climate and its wide, bare, windswept spaces. It began to spread at the dawn of the 1st millennium BC with the development of animal husbandry and the use of the horse for riding, and was to endure for centuries. It could consist either of daily wandering in search of grass, or of seasonal migrations of people and their animals towards water supplies or into the high valleys, or it could also take the form of long-distance migrations, which were permanent. Then a group would break up, sometimes causing chain reactions that reverberated from one end of the Steppes to the other, still further destabilizing a world already on the move. Aware of what was happening on the frontiers of China, the nomad peoples were also open to the pull of the great established empires of ancient Asia, as well as of the Mediterranean civilizations. An irresistible current tended to cause a drift of peoples from east to west. It eventually carried the Sarmatians towards the Roman world and the Yue-tche into Bactria*, before a last wave from Asia, the Huns, upset the ethnic and cultural pattern of the continent.

Many of the implications of nomadic life seem self-evident, a simple matter of common sense. In a world without towns, houses, temples or palaces, stone—a rare phenomenon on the steppeland in any case—had no place. Architecture, sculpture, painting, all that comes into the category of "monument", which we as town dwellers call "great art", nothing of this existed in the Steppes. Attention was focused on the essentials: weapons which, in the absence of defensive walls, were the only means of ensuring the defence of the community; and the horse, the prime instrument of mobility, with its gear. But going beyond its practical consequences, the nomadic style had a profound effect on the social behaviour patterns of the communities involved, on their relationship with their environment, their religious life and their art. In this uncentred expanse without territorial limits, the structure of social organization and power were different. For nomadic people there was no civic state, but a flexible system of tribal groupings, of shifting and often ephemeral alliances. Military tactics were also different, and as the Persian king Darius learnt to his cost, a retreat that used distance as a protective barrier could be very effective, or the enemy could be attacked and harried in pitiless guerrilla tactics, or fall victim to a lightning raid.

The economy was fluid, relying on barter and raids, but apart from herds of animals the idea of acquiring possessions and accumulating wealth was unknown. In terms of religious life, lacking cult buildings and monuments, the sacred was dispersed through the natural world, omnipresent. Its mediator was the shaman, a person with multiple powers, and its predominant themes were access to the supernatural, the sacred journey and transformation. In this context we can see how and why their art made animals the major theme of its manifestations. But though the eye of an aesthete might see this differently, the art of the Steppes was essentially as devoid of decorative ornament as it could be. Nothing was there without reason. A practical approach was paramount, with images adapted to, and even constituting, their supports, tending always to concentrate their force, saturating form with meaning.

A world in movement

This dynamic organization was reinforced by a specific sense of space, with the possibility of being interpreted in two ways, and multiple or swirling motifs which result in the decorated object developing its full significance only when in motion. A harness buckle might swing round in a gallop for full effect, a saddlecloth might assume its full meaning only when its sides, edged with horsehair, struck against the horse's flanks. Rendering a Scythian image as static often mutilates it, and in order to understand it, an effort to visualize it in movement is required, thus restoring to it a necessary dimension.

The archaeologist must also acquire familiarity with a new idea of reality. For those accustomed to excavating the sites of settled peoples, exploring time as it has accumulated vertically in an orderly succession, interpreting neatly arranged levels, or deciphering a tangled pattern of walling, the nomadic world may seem confusing. On the Steppes there are no ruins, nowhere do we find those welcome rubbish dumps in which refuse, accumulated daily over the generations, reveals the continuous pattern of the daily round through rejects, broken pottery and food scraps—objects which the archaeologist can use patiently to reconstruct the past. In this "sea of grass" which was their domain, the nomads left almost as few traces of their passage as the boats of the Vikings on the surface of the water. And time too has left no imprint, except of course in their tombs: the swelling of the mounds of the kurgans can be located on the Steppes, and supply the archaeologist with the main part of such direct information as he has.

The archaeologist's task

How then should we set about trying to understand properly what we find, once we have combed the early texts? Ethno-archaeology and the observation of existing societies of mounted nomads, in Asia or elsewhere, can be a great help. But the most fruitful approaches aim to capture the identity of the people of the Steppes by studying the peripheral manifestations, the mixed forms, as a chemist analyses a pure element through its various reactions. And in this respect Scythian contacts with Greek cities on the Black Sea, a thoroughly mongrel civilization, and the process of semi-settlement that these contacts induced, works in a wonderfully revealing way. Or again, just as a physicist deals with particles that lose their characteristics if they are not in movement, so the archaeologist may try to reconstitute movement by considering the force of its impact on the obstacles encountered. The Romans' defence of their eastern *limes* (boundary), and the need of the Chinese to build their Wall, give some indication of the pressure exerted by the barbarians. The archaeologist should also aspire to a psychologist's skill in detecting differences of tone and meaning. Without succumbing to excessive romanticism, or accepting a whole literary tradition which makes the Scythian the metaphorical embodiment of "otherness", we must surely acknowledge the existence, beyond the conditions and facts of nomadism, of a love of space for its own sake, something which may impel people to seek the removal of all that inhibits it, quite independently of any desire for material possession.

Thus it is above all an acute awareness of its specific quality that the archaeologist seeks from the world of the nomad. We have to accept that, beside the temporal dimension embodied by the familiar tool of stratigraphy*, there is another dimension in which the human adventure is inscribed with equal pertinence. We should accept that cultures can flourish and blossom without taking root and germinating in a single spot, but that this unceasing movement and continual transferral of people and objects through space can radically alter them. And we should also accept that time and space can change places and, as far as studying the Steppes is concerned, we have to give the second of these two pride of place.

Wooden waggon from Pazyryk

Four horses, the remains of which have been found, were harnessed to this waggon. Its light structure and the fact that it can be dismantled suggest that it was a ceremonial vehicle. Greek texts give us descriptions of the heavy felt-covered waggons, drawn by oxen, into which the Scythians piled women, children and belongings, and which they used as homes on wheels. Hermitage Museum, Leningrad.

Detail of the silver gilt amphora from Tchertomlyk, USSR

Decorating the side of a vase used for *kumys*, the fermented mare's milk that formed part of the nomads' diet, the scene appropriately illustrates the importance of the horse and the different stages of training, from breaking in to saddling. Hermitage Museum, Leningrad.

Riders from the Kul Oba torc

Two horsemen form the ends of this piece of jewellery, mounted bareback on horses with cropped manes and headgear depicted down to the last detail. This perfect union of man and horse may perhaps explain how the mythical image of the centaur came to be formed in the imagination of settled people. Hermitage Museum, Leningrad.

Badge of fraternity, Kul Oba, USSR

"When the Scythians enter into an oath of alliance, they pour wine into a large pottery cup, and mix with it blood from the parties to the contract who have been pricked with an awl, or a small incision may have been made in their bodies with a knife; they then dip a sabre, arrows, an axe and a javelin into the cup; when that has been done they utter many religious formulas, then drink the contents of the cup" (Herodotus, IV, 70). The two juxtaposed profiles, which can also be read as a single face, convey a remarkably effective expression in plastic terms of the idea of "being at one". Hermitage Museum, Leningrad.

Comb from Solokha, USSR

Found near the helmeted head of the dead man, this comb carries a decorative theme above the teeth in the same way as, in architecture, the entablature rests on columns, with recumbent lions as the base, thus showing a strong Greek influence. But all the combatants on this double relief are barbarians, as is proved by their kaftans, wide trousers and their weapons, notwithstanding the presence of the Corinthian helmet and the greaves worn by the central horseman. Hermitage Museum, Leningrad.

The Scythians and Asia

History and legend date the emergence of the Scythians in Western Asia to the 7th century BC; archaeology enlarges both the chronological and the geographical range of this glamorous people.

Right at the beginning of their history, before they finally settled in the part of the Steppes which would become their territory, the Scythians penetrated into Western Asia in the wake of the Cimmerians*. There they founded a kingdom that lasted 28 years. They then set back off towards the north and returned to the Steppes. So runs the "historical" version of the Scythians' emergence, based on legends of origin, the unanimous tradition of antiquity and the formal evidence of Herodotus. Their name does in fact appear for the first time around 670BC, in the form *ashgusa*, similar to their biblical name Ashkenaz, in the annals of the Assyrian king Assarhadon who saw them as a threat to the north of his empire. As for their brief reign, our knowledge of eastern chronology enables us to date it exactly to between 653 and 625BC.

And yet it is not until the second half of the 7th century, and more particularly the beginning of the 6th century, that the first archaeologically discernible signs of change appear, with the three specific elements that characterize Scythian culture: weapons, harness and animal decoration. Moreover, they seem to appear suddenly without noticeable traces of any earlier development, as if they were immediately endowed with their full powers of expression. Another disconcerting factor is that these displays, even in the earliest tombs, bear the mark of a perceptible Near Eastern influence. This is conveyed by the presence of some imported objects and also, as the example of Kelermes clearly indicates, by the many motifs and techniques known to be associated with the repertory of the east, especially Urartu (Armenia) and Assyria: hybrid beasts, lions with wings or horns, benevolent spirits, trees of life, as well as patterns involving processions or confrontations, not to mention many stylistic conventions in the depiction of the eye or the nose of an animal, or the emphasis on muscles and joints. Does this mean that the culture and art of the Scythians must be understood as a kind of by-product of the Asiatic prototype? What kind of contact did they have with the east and what was its impact? The evidence of archaeology confirms that of the historians' written documents.

Many sites in Western Asia contain lobed arrow-heads characteristic of the Scythians, and it is clear that in about 590BC they attacked and destroyed the Urartu citadel of Teishebaïni, near modern Yerevan (Armenian SSR), after having been their allies, just as in 612BC they had contributed to the fall of Assyria by attacking Nineveh alongside the Medes. The situation in that part of Asia was unstable in the 7th century. Assyria was at war with its great rival, Urartu, while both were under unremitting pressure from smaller peoples that were aspiring towards independence, and even more from newcomers undermining security. Following upon the Cimmerian raids, other Iranian tribes were threatening their frontiers: in the northeast the Medes, a people that would form first a state and then an empire; and in the north the Scythians. The Assyrians attempted a policy of alliance with the latter, and allowed them to establish their kingdom in the country of Manna, northwest of the Iranian plateau, a proper base camp from which they could undertake more distant expeditions towards Syria, Palestine and even to the frontiers of Egypt, where the Pharaoh managed to stop them. Then in 625 they were driven out by the Medes themselves, against whom the Assyrians had hoped they would serve as a rampart, abandoned their lands and crossed back over the Caucasus mountains. Not all of them left, however, since we come across Scythians as allies or vassals of the Medes after that date. We have convincing archaeological evidence of their presence, as at Hassanlu where a tomb containing horses was a first indication, corroborated by the discovery of a typical horse's bit and fragments of a bronze vase bearing a characteristic decoration of a bearded man wearing trousers and carrying an axe.

The evidence of Ziwiyeh

The clearest example, however, is that of the Ziwiyeh treasure. This group of objects was found by chance south of Lake Urmia by local peasants and immediately dispersed, but the fact that it came from a burial is indicated by the presence of a tub-shaped bronze sarcophagus. Elements of the funeral procession and pieces of harness have been found, giving a sufficient indication of the important place occupied by horses in the Ziwiyeh context; items from the hoard reflect a wide variety of artistic traditions – Assyrian, Urartu, Syro-Phoenician as well as Iranian elements. Other objects display motifs well known in the Steppes but were without precedent in the eastern world. Examples of this include the belt shown here (below), a gold headband bordered with heads of predatory birds with a typical eye-beak motif, together with small cats with rounded backs and curled up paws and tails, their eyes and ears inlaid in blue paste; and above all a gold breastplate typical of Urartu in its shape, but displaying a tree of life with hares and small coiled cats of a completely Scythian type, along with creatures borrowed from various Asiatic repertories of images. This tomb is dated to the last quarter of the 7th century, and is certainly not later than the archaic Scythian tombs of the Kuban and Dnieper areas with which it has much in common.

This suggests that Asiatic cultures were not the sole sources of inspiration or civilizing models to which the Scythians owed everything, but rather a stimulus to the growth and blossoming of a seed that was already there or was actually forming. The nomads' period in the East acted as a powerful catalyst by bringing them face to face with what had been built up over many centuries of settled civilization, by affording them the means of self-fulfilment, but also no doubt by giving them some concept of their own difference. On ground that had been nurtured in the oldest Mesopotamian traditions, and was also open to movements from Anatolia, Syria, Egypt and indirectly from the Syro-Phoenician world, they were able to discover materials, new techniques and a whole new world of images on which they drew, borrowing animal forms and motifs where appropriate, making use of a detail, a stylistic convention or a plastic solution to convey more effectively the world that was theirs and which they had brought with them.

It is not easy to follow the history of these borrowings and to determine exactly their origins and dates. Indeed, the direct contribution evidenced by items and motifs that had obviously been imported, or brought back, receives another, indirect, contribution made at the same time by Greek art in Asia Minor, itself very eastern. In addition, the Iranian nomads from the Steppes were in constant contact, admittedly often as adversaries, with their relations in Achaemenid Persia. There is documentary evidence of this in texts and pictures on the Persian side. Tribes living under the Great King* Darius's rule complied with his desire to subdue their turbulent neighbours, whose presence was a permanent threat at the frontiers of the empire. The relief sculpture at Behistun shows the last of the prisoners in chains before the king to be wearing a high pointed hood; he is a Saka captured by the king during his campaign in Central Asia, a few years earlier than the unfortunate expedition against the Scythians mentioned by Herodotus. At Persepolis, the reliefs on the staircases of the Apadana clearly proclaim the nomads' acceptance of the power of the Great King: their delegation moves towards him bearing gifts.

On the Steppes we find archaeological evidence indicating this contact: imported objects such as the sword handle from Tchertomlyk or, right in the heart of Asia, Iranian rugs and cloths from the Altaï tomb, as well as material showing more subtle influences. Real as it may be, the importance of the East at the outset of the Scythian civilization should not obscure the fact that they emerged in a context of changes linked with the rise of pastoral nomadism and the transition from the Bronze Age to the Iron Age – changes which were affecting the whole of the Steppes from the beginning of the 1st millennium BC. The existence in Mongolia of "deer stones", rock drawings displaying pictures that are already almost Scythian, and the discovery at Arjan in the heart of Asia of a large bronze plaque depicting a curled up panther, possibly dating from the 8th century BC, remind us that many crucial events took place to the east of the Steppes. Exclusive attention on what happened west of them may be no more than a form of ethnocentricity.

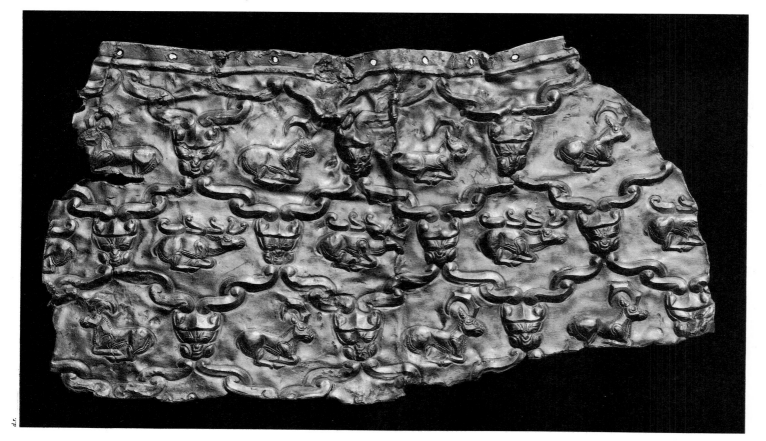

Gold belt cladding, Ziwiyeh

Not only a weapon of defence designed to protect the vital organs, but also, through its shape and decoration, imbued with the magic powers attributed in Caucasian tradition to the circle surrounding the body, this type of high belt, whether it is bronze or simply has metal fasteners, is often found in burials in the Caucasus and Transcaucasia, as well as throughout Urartu. The network of brackets on this one is typical of Urartu, but the use of gold, the animal decorations, and above all the typical attitude of the deer are completely Scythian in taste.

Lion's head, Kelermes

This animal, which forms the end of a complex piece of plate combining the very elaborate techniques of cloisonné and granulation, is from the Kuban area; its mouth is open to show fearsome teeth, the nose is wrinkled, and the eyes are triangular, features showing great stylistic affinity with lions in the Asiatic tradition. Hermitage Museum, Leningrad

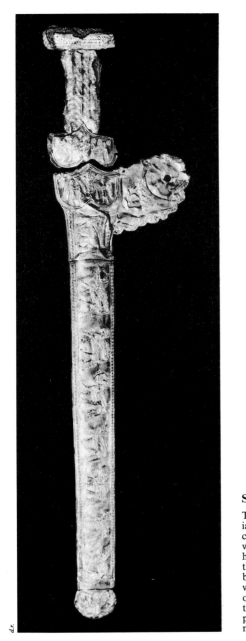

Piece of harness, Pazyryk

Edged with fur enhanced by gold, this coloured woollen braid sewn onto a felt band holding a horse's saddlecloth was imported from Achaemenid Persia. Its tapestry technique and the motif of lions have exact parallels in Susa and Persepolis. An Iranian carpet and Chinese silk were found in the same tomb, clear proof of the existence in Asia of trade on a very far-reaching scale.

Sword from Kelermes

The sheath of this *akinakes*, the short Scythian sword, shows a procession of hybrid creatures, cats drawing the bow and monsters with griffin's heads, scorpion's tails, talons or hooves, and wings in the form of fish biting their shoulders. Towards the hilt, other scenes borrowed from the Assyrian repertory depict winged spirits surrounding a tree of life. But on the side fastening a garland motif repeats the eye-and-beak theme and frames a completely Scythian portrayal of a deer. Hermitage Museum, Leningrad

Saka delegation from Persepolis

The members of the delegation, Sakas from Central Asia rather than western Scythians, have pointed hoods on their heads. Over their trousers they wear a garment pulled in by a belt, and a short sword hangs down in a sheath fixed to the belt with a very prominent fastening. They are bringing as gifts to the Great King a horse in harness, a pair of bracelets worked with an animal motif, two fur-line coats, and a pair of trousers probably made of reversed skin.

Animals in art and religion

By decorating their possessions—and often their own bodies—with depictions of animals, the shamanistic Steppe nomads sought to acquire their qualities of strength, swiftness and power; in the process an entire language of imagery was developed.

In the world of the nomad, where everything is reduced to bare essentials, animals are depicted everywhere and in a wealth of detail; in gold, bone, bronze or wood; on weapons and horses' harnesses, carpets and clothes; in felt, leather, fur and even on human flesh, animals stretch out, curl up, twist and turn or face on another in ferocious attitudes. Although they may often be recognizable, they sometimes appear in the shape of hybrid creatures borrowing disparate elements from the animal kingdom, reconstituted in outlandish combinations; sometimes the animal theme consists simply of a swarm of barely recognizable shapes in which a round eye, a sharp beak or a sinuous spine may be made out.

Of course the art of the steppes has no monopoly in the portrayal of animals – they are to be found from the very beginning of art. But from China to the Danube, animals are constantly—almost obsessively—present, and in particular ways which, many hundreds of miles apart, are strikingly similar. Obviously, this omnipresence is neither accidental nor simply ornamental, but has its *raison d'être* and its laws, which can be rediscovered. Moreover, it constitutes, for the archaeologist, one element of the three (the others being the type of weapons and the harness) which make it possible to define the civilization of the steppes.

This depiction of animals is an essential aspect of Steppes culture, as vital for the nomad as the necessity of self-defence and mobility. Although the animals portrayed largely reflect the fauna of these regions, art, in deciding which animals to portray, is nevertheless very selective. The stag is the animal which appears most frequently, particularly in the western Steppes. It appears in an attitude which, as the example from Kostromskaia shows, evokes in particular the idea of its mobility. In all the traditions of Eurasia the stag is the mobile animal *par excellence*, the guide, the mediator, the animal which finds access to new territories, to the world of the dead and to the divine in particular. We have only to recall the echo of this which our own culture has retained in the story of Saint Hubert, whose hunt became a mystical quest when he saw the cross shining in the antlers of a stag. For the ancient Germans the stag accompanied the soul in death. The people of the Altai region showed a similar belief when they dressed the horses in the funeral cortège at Pazyryk as stags, using masks of felt and leather. The stag has such importance in the art of the steppes, perhaps also because it is, more than any other, the animal with which the nomad can identify. Like man, the stag lives in herds which have a hierarchical system under the rule of an old male. Like the stag, man is subject to the harsh authority of growing things, water and the cycle of the seasons, as well as the need to move around to survive. What better emblem could the nomad have chosen for his own mobility? Besides the stag, other hoofed animals appear—ibexes and wild sheep, antelopes and gazelles and also elks and boar.

In contrast to this world of hunted grass-eaters is the ferocious world of the meat-eating hunters, the wolf, the bear, the many predators and big cats of all types. These creatures, living together in a strong, inextricable relationship—at once blood-brothers, competitors, hunted objects and substitutes in shamanic practice—evoke in man, with his short sight, his slow pace and his soft nails, feelings of admiration and envy. What he admires in them is what makes for their superiority: on the one hand the swift flight which enables them to escape when preyed upon, and on the other the keen eyesight, the clawed foot and the sharp fangs which ensure victory for the predator. By decorating the objects he uses with representations of all these qualities, man seeks—by a kind of magical transfer—to make them his own. The better to do this he isolates them, exaggerates them, multiplies them and ends up combining them in accordance with a law which, despite appearances, is strictly logical because it is based on effectiveness. The eagle, for example, is reduced to a round eye extended from the curve of the beak like an ideogram for rapacity; and the beak in its turn is lodged in the antlers of a stag or at the end of the tail of a big cat, to increase their power. In this manner the Kelermes panther (facing page) displays an increase in its aggressive nature. In practice, the monsters created by the art of the Steppes, when they are not borrowed ready-made from the Orient or Greece, have the minimum amount of fantasy about them. The fantastic, which always inspires a feeling of unease and fear, proceeds from the desire to create a strange, disturbing shape, whereas the art of the Steppes simply captures those meaningful elements which are dispersed in nature and reconstitutes them in a unique whole which is effectively reassuring; this art merely creates quintessential forms whose virtues are all positive.

Art as language

The art of the Steppes is a coherent system of signs and operates like a language. For these peoples with no writing system, it must have occupied the place of written language. Like language it has its vocabulary which consists of details selected from the bestiary, its syntax which operates by juxtapositions, combinations and confrontations, and also its stylistic devices. Besides the constant use of metaphor, there are other linguistic devices, such as: metonymy which reduces the animal to one of its parts; anacoluthon when the front of one animal is joined to the rear of another; expressive pleonasm as in the case of the Kelermes panther; or alliteration giving expression by repetition—like the branches of the stag's antlers. This is indeed a unique and original style. In the course of its formation, it may well have borrowed, but it still remains radically different from the images which the Eurasian continent knew elsewhere or before, even if the "stag stones" (below) constitute a link in a chain of development. This was the specific language of the nomads, and it changed its nature when they changed their way of life—as did Graeco-Scythian art of the 4th century.

It seems moreover to have been the language of one caste, the warring aristocracy. It is particularly abundant in the tombs of the chiefs and may be seen in its purest forms on what constituted the warrior's main attraction, namely his weapons and his horse's harness, as if it were the symbolic language of a kind of chivalry. It is eminently dynamic in the expression of this ideology of combat and shows an exceptional ability to seize the qualities of each species "live" and translate them into undulating lines, curves and spirals—everything that expresses movement or the tension which immediately precedes movement. Many of the artifacts take up an animal shape, and when this is not so, the animal portrayed adapts to the shape designed to it. They appear to us in a space which they make entirely theirs and which expresses the privileged connection with the animal kingdom which is part of the relationship which the nomad maintains with the world which surrounds him, visible or invisible, and his religious beliefs which are basically shamanic.

Shamanism, which is a means of communication with the supernatural, places great importance on animals. The animal is the helper of the shaman, his messenger and his mount; he is his double, into which the shaman transforms himself on his journey into the forces of nature. Archaeology provides other indications of this shamanism, for which evidence has recently been found in Siberia—for example finds at Pazyryk include implements used in the smoking of hemp for the purpose of producing ritual ecstasy. Many objects such as mirrors, charms and animal signs which are part of the modern shaman's equipment seem to echo those found in the tombs of the Steppes. However, these shamanic practices did not exclude the existence of divinities. Herodotus listed the Scythians' divinities, finding for each one an equivalent in the Greek pantheon. Although a historian, he was a representative of the most anthropomorphic of ancient cultures, and did not notice the importance of animals in the Scythian religion. He only noted the elements which, for him, lent themselves—to a greater or lesser extent—to transposition.

Bearing witness to the radical difference which separates two views of the world, the animals in the art of the Steppes would one day be traced to the capitals of churches in the West and around ornamental letters in manuscripts.

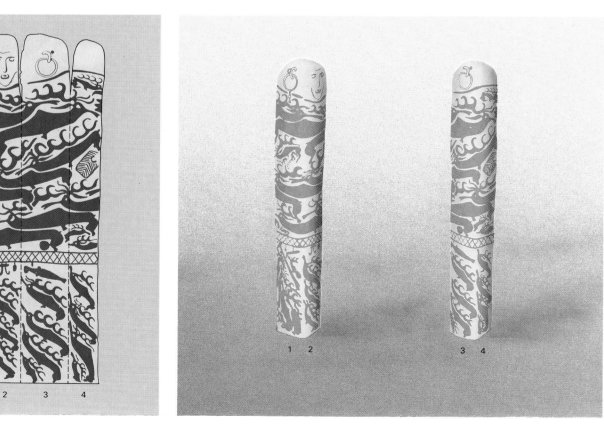

"Stag stone", Mongolia

From this drawing we can see the development of the images of stags which appear all around the upper part of the stele (slab) and above one another on each of the lower faces. The elongated shapes, the large antlers bent back parallel to the spine, the lengthened muzzle, all seem to be the precursors—in the tradition of the rock carvings of the Bronze Age—of the image of the animal as it will appear in the following centuries from one end of the steppes to the other. On the stone is a warrior, whose face is framed by earrings and emphasized by the line of a torc (necklace). An axe and a sword hang from his belt.

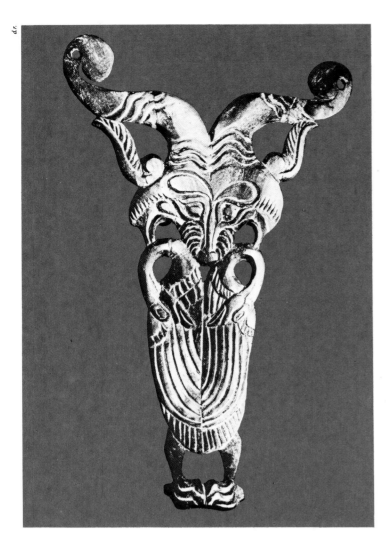

Geese attacked by horned monster. Pazyryk

A single monster appears to be attacking two geese with gracefully curved necks. But the picture is constituted of two halves placed together, each one showing the beast in profile seizing one side of the bird in its gaping jaw. This is a fragmented, multiple image which captures one scene and ensures that its magic is fully effective. Unlike the griffon, the panther and the stag, which are all made of metal and come from the Kuban, this plaque is made of stag horn and was used to decorate the nose of a horse found in a frozen tomb in the Altai region. Hermitage Museum, Leningrad.

Griffon from Ulski Ayul

This object fitted onto the top of a wooden shaft, and consists of a cone-shaped bell surmounted by the head of a horned griffon represented by its enormous hooked beak. Having both a visual and an auditory presence, this type of bronze bell, combined with the depiction of an animal must have served as some sort of sign. It is found in the very oldest Scythian tombs and continued to exist in its traditional form until a very late date. Hermitage Museum, Leningrad.

Kelermes panther

This panther is the same size as the stag (32cm) and probably had the same function. The eye is inlaid with enamel and the ear, which is applied to the surface, is made of pieces of amber. The animal is shown pointing, sniffing out the trail, its nostrils dilated, its lips drawn back on sharp fangs. Ten little panthers are curled up into balls on the tail and the feet, reinforcing the animal's power by the use of a very expressive form of sculptural repetition. Hermitage Museum, Leningrad.

Kostromskaia stag

The leaping attitude, the slender muzzle, the stretched neck, the eye appearing to turn towards the rear, the S-shaped branches of the flattened antlers, the tapered hooves and the many hollow shapes which lighten the outline all suggest speed in a wild chase. The polished ridged surface reminds us of work in bone or wood. This plaque is embossed work and was found with the remains of an iron shield, of which it formed the central boss. Hermitage Museum, Leningrad.

Burial practices – Tolstaia Mogila

Studied by Soviet specialists in 1971, a royal Scythian burial mound of the Dnieper valley has yielded an extraordinary profusion of material and archaeological riches from the 4th century BC.

The burial-places of the kings are in the land of the Gerrhi, which is the end of the navigation of the Berysthenes [Dnieper]. There, whenever their king has died, the Scythians dig a great four-cornered pit in the ground; when this is ready . . . they lay the dead in a tomb on a couch . . .; in the open space which is left in the tomb they bury, after strangling them, one of the king's concubines, his cup-bearer, his cook, his groom, his squire, and his messenger, beside horses and first fruits of all else, and golden cups. Having done this they all build a great barrow of earth, vying zealously with one another to make this as great as may be.

Herodotus, IV, 71.

The great princely tombs of the lower reaches of the Dnieper are the precise archaeological counterpart of Herodotus' account. But most of them were explored in the 19th century by scholars more concerned with the objects themselves than with their context. This was the case at Solokha and Tchertomlyk to which the Hermitage Museum owes many of its most beautiful pieces. We could not get a precise idea of what a 4th century BC Scythian *kurgan* or burial mound consisted of, until Tolstaia Mogila was systematically studied, in 1971. By a fortunate turn of fate, these excavations, which were undertaken principally in order to discover the structure of a kurgan which it was believed had been completely ransacked, have brought to light a harvest of treasures which has been greater than even the most unrestrained of treasure-seekers might have dared to hope.

Situated on the west bank of the Dnieper, on the outskirts of the modern town of Ordzhonikidze, Tolstaia Mogila – or more precisely in Ukrainian, Tovsta Mogila, the Great Tomb – is the highest and most northerly of a chain of 26 kurgans of various heights which stretches over 2km (1.2 miles) The mound is nearly 9m (29ft) high with a diameter of about 60m (197ft). It consists of an enormous mass of 15,000cu m (529,720cu ft) of earth, which had been surrounded by a ditch about 2m (6.5ft) wide and 1.5m (5ft) deep. Pieces of amphorae and the bones of animals (stags, boar and especially horses), the remains of the funeral feast (the site of which has been identified, littered with pieces of broken pottery, near the earth bank which interrupts the ditch to the northeast) have been found here, lying in 11 piles. The mound covered two burial places built deep below ground level. The first, in the centre, was that of a man accompanied by a servant. It had been plundered and partly emptied of its contents.

The layout was as follows. A rectangular shaft 4 × 2m (13 × 6.5ft) in size descended vertically right in the centre of the kurgan. At the bottom, a *dromos* (approach way) continued downwards broadening as it neared the burial chamber, 8.5m (27.8ft) under the surface. At the bottom of this well were two large niches which must have contained objects and provisions. Thieves had dug a tunnel in the side of the kurgan and emerged in the western niche and the access shaft. They had eventually reached the western corner of the chamber and ignored the *dromos* in which they thought they would not find anything, especially as, like the chamber itself, it must already have been in a state of partial collapse. Turning over the crumbling soil they collected what they could, haphazardly abandoning the dislocated skeleton, some animal bones, pieces of amphorae, the remains of a belt and an iron scale-armour breast-plate, some bronze arrow-heads, a gold ring and various embossed gold ornaments and bracts. However, in the *dromos*, which had not been disturbed – its entrance was blocked by the skeleton of a guard – were found a bronze vessel, a little cauldron, its bottom blackened, which must have been used as a lamp, arrow-heads, a Greek amphora and, most notably, besides the gold spiral ribbon around the handle of a *nagaika* whip and the gold pearls decorating its thongs, there was a superb sword – its handle and a sheath covered in gold leaf with an animal motif—and a large breastplate.

To the northeast of this burial place, there were two ditches at ground level, each of which contained the remains of three horses with their trappings: iron bits and bit-straps, breast plates, cheek-pieces, and various ornaments in silvered bronze, silver or gold, all richly decorated. The tombs of the two ostlers, of whom one was a boy aged 10–12 years, were beside the first ditch. Near the second ditch was another ostler wearing a thin gold torque around his neck and an iron bracelet on his wrist. Near were two iron knives with bone handles.

A second burial place

This whole collection of tombs was surrounded by a double row of large stones leaning towards the interior and forming a lining for the base of the first kurgan, which was built immediately after the man's funeral. But a second burial place – that of a woman and a child – was then constructed at the edge of this first kurgan. It was untouched and contained no less than six skeletons. A well, 6m (20ft) deep, had been dug level with the original mound; the clay spoil thus removed has been identified on the slope of the mound and a whole collection of bronze objects – the remains of the funeral procession – had been placed on top of this spoil. A corridor ran from the eastern corner of the well shaft and at the end of this lay – on its right side—the body of a very young girl. To the north, access to the *dromos* was blocked by the wheels of a wooden cart and its tracks were visible in the clay. The *dromos* led to the funerary chamber which was 4.2 by 3.5m (13.7 × 11.4ft). Here was found the skeleton of a woman about 30 years old (at the most) which was literally covered with gold and jewellery. It was surrounded by vessels in silver and clay. Near her lay a small child who had been placed in a wooden sarcophagus which had decomposed. He was wearing a torque, a ring and earrings made of a simple gold thread. His body was covered with pearls and embossed gold bracts. A cup, a rhyton (drinking vessel) and a little vase with a spherical lower section – all made of silver – had been placed near him. At the head of the two deceased was the skeleton of a man armed with a bow with a quiver full of bronze-headed arrows by his side. At their feet lay the skeleton of a woman. Behind was a bronze cauldron containing the remains of a horse, a bronze plate and two iron knives.

The position of the servants' bodies would indicate that they were placed on the ground whilst still warm and perhaps had even been killed there. But not all these inhumations took place at the same time, as demonstrated by the existence of a second access shaft which was also blocked by the wheels of a cart, and the fact that the funerary chamber was obviously enlarged later. The woman was buried first, with the girl and the servant who are adjacent to the first shaft. Then the child died later. For him the second shaft was dug and the chamber was broadened for it was clearly at that time that the armed man and the woman – who was perhaps his nurse – were placed near him. The man in the main burial place, the woman covered with gold and the child were, however, interred within a very short period of time in the middle of the 4th century BC; this is clear when one studies the objects found, in particular the Greek pottery.

The fact that all three of them were closely connected is confirmed both by the arrangement of the kurgan itself and the fact that some of the ornaments, covering the body of the child and the body of the man, are absolutely identical. It is reasonable to suppose that the Scythian chief who lies here was followed swiftly in death first by his partner and then by their child. Judging by the richness of the kurgan and the weight of gold found there, he must certainly have been a man of very high rank and probably a king. Furthermore, a whole series of similarities in structure and grave goods establish correspondences between the kurgan at Tolstaia Mogila and the other great kurgans of the 4th century, particularly those at Solokha and Tchertomlyk, which are very near in both time and space.

Pectoral ornament

This item of male costume (below right), made in gold and weighing 1150 grammes (40 oz.) is a quadruple torque depicting a scene of animal combat, embossed foliage, and a tranquil scene of a shepherd in the midst of his flock, the whole in a Greek style. The two men engaged in sewing a sheepskin Kaftan (detail, below) probably illustrate a well-known episode from Scythian history. Kiev Museum.

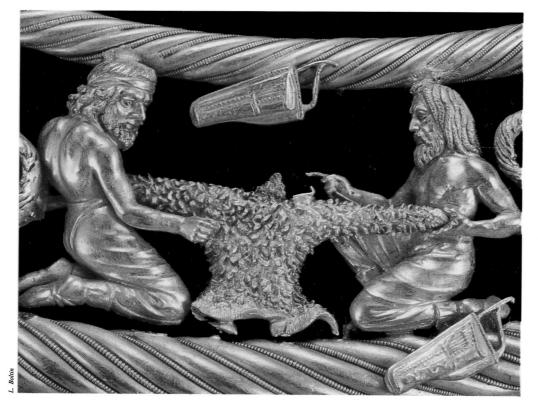

Burial of woman on her side

The ornamented skeleton of the woman and the objects with her were taken as they were found to the Kiev Museum. The embossed gold bracts lying all over the upper part of the body must have been sewn to a veil which was kept in place by a high crown.

L. Boltin

1 gold headband superimposed on a diadem

2 gold pendants

3 ornate torque decorated with animals

4 Greek plate with black varnish

5 silver dish

6 bronze mirror

7 veil with gold bracts

8 gold bracelets

9 gold rings

10 coloured beads and gold-clasped bracelet

11 shoes with bracts

12 shroud hooks

13 fragments of a glass vessel

14 torque

15 earrings

16 bracelet

17 gold bracts

18 silver vase

19 rest of funerary chamber

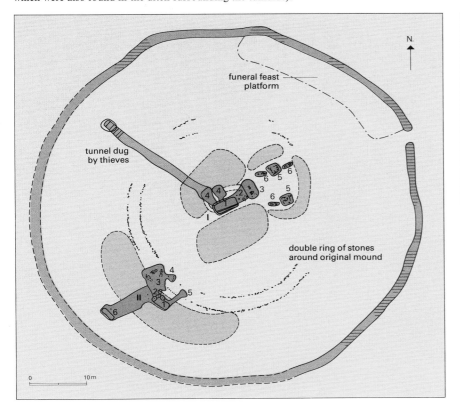

Plan of the Tolstaia Mogila Kurgan

The circular area of the kurgan is arranged around the male burial place, with the access shaft directly lined up with the top. This was the point reached by the tunnel dug by thieves bypassing the horses and ostlers. The female burial place was undamaged. It was constructed at the edge of the original mound, the outline of which is delineated by the double ring of stones. To the northeast, an area covered with fragments of amphorae shows where the funeral feast took place (remains of which were also found in the ditch surrounding the tumulus).

I central burial

1 access shaft

2 dromos approach way

3 burial chamber

4 niches

5 horse burials

6 ostler tombs

II side burial

1 first access shaft

2 dromos approach way

3 burial chamber

4 niche

5 corridor where young girl's body was found

6 second access shaft

pit cross-hatched areas indicate accumulations of broken pottery from the funeral feast

earth debris from dug tombs

Metal tip of a pole

These bronze objects combined the function of bells and animal emblems in the form of a stag or griffin. They represented a very old Scythian tradition and had been piled up – together with the ornaments from the funeral procession (bells, horses' bits, parts of harnesses)—on the rubble removed from the shaft giving access to the female burial place.

L. Boltin

The art of the Steppes, 5th to 3rd centuries BC

Perishable materials—wood, leather, felt, fur—have been miraculously preserved in the ice of the Siberian Altai mountains; from these remains, archaeologists can reconstruct in vivid detail the nomadic lifestyle of the Scythian riders of the Steppes.

In the south of Siberia, a lucky chance has preserved the contents of several tombs by turning them into ice pits. Here the Altai massif had afforded summer pasturage to neighbouring tribes, who buried their dead in the neighbourhood. The valley of Pazyryk alone, situated at a height of 1,500m (4,950ft), contains some 40 tombs (*kurgans*), the five largest of which belonged to high-ranking men and women, and have proved to be extraordinarily interesting. Their disputed date ranges from the 5th to the 3rd century BC, but their structure and the culture they reflect are homogeneous. Immediately below each cairn a pit contained a log burial chamber, outside which horses and harnesses were deposited. All these remains were caught inside the layer of ice formed winter after winter by condensation and infiltrating water. The piled up stones of the cairn screened off the rays of the sun and prevented the summer heat from penetrating the ground to any depth. The process was accelerated by the violation of the tombs, which were robbed at an early date. Rain streamed in through the breach made by the robbers and so did cold air, enveloping everything in a covering of ice. Greedy for metal and jewels, the looters despoiled the dead of their weapons and carried off the precious objects, taking bodies from the half-frozen coffins, cutting off a hand for a bracelet, a finger for a ring, removing a head with its torque. But clothing, cloths, and portable objects, all the small wooden artifacts and humble materials which they disdained to take, were left there, close to the desecrated corpses.

Thus the tombs provide a reverse image of the Scythian burials in which metal is the only or almost the only thing that has survived. A fleshly world where the bodies are present; a tactile world of furs, felt, leather and even silk; above all an astonishingly colourful world. This image is all the more valuable because the nomadic universe is essentially the domain of the perishable, the victory of the soft over the hard, of the organic over the inert. Wood (larch was used in the Altai) took the place of clay and metal for most of the needs of everyday life, and the nomad practised a sort of mobile self-sufficiency which forced him to live off what the animals supplied: milk products and meat for food, skins and wool for clothing, but also leather, horns, bones, tendons, fur and horsehair for a thousand and one uses. Horses, those indispensable aids to nomadic life and sign of wealth, accompanied the deceased. With high withers, larger and more thoroughbred than the stocky horses usual on the steppe, the horses of Pazyryk had their manes trimmed, their tails plaited and the mark of their owner incised on the ear. Their stomachs still contained the grass they had eaten before they were slaughtered by a blow on the head. Each horse had its harness placed next to it. Only the bit was of metal, generally iron. The rest (bars of the bit, headbands, bridles, straps and various pendants with animal decoration) were made of horn, leather and especially carved wood, sometimes plated with a fine sheet of gold. In every tomb, one or two horses, probably those which had headed the funeral procession, wore strange leather and felt headdresses disguising them as reindeer or gryphons.

Testimony of the graves

Inside the chambers, and with their lids raised, sarcophagi hollowed out of the single log of a larch trunk contained the bodies of the dead, whose flesh, hair and features were preserved by the joint action of cold and embalming. The dead man in Kurgan 2 had undoubtedly died in combat from a wound which left its mark on his skull. He had been scalped by his adversary, but had been given a wig and a false beard. But the strangest feature was the skin, which was covered with tattoos. A fantastic lion uncurled his tail on the left shoulder-blade, turning to occupy the exact centre of the chest with his head. A whole bestiary tattooed on the arms of the so-called "Lionheart" must have undulated when his muscles rippled under the skin: ibexes with their hindquarters reversed, deer with large antlers, a feline with sharp teeth. Four wild sheep ran below a fish which occupied the shinbone. Dots all down the backbone and on the ankle apparently corresponded to places used by practitioners of acupuncture. Tattooing, infamous to the Greeks and generally associated in our society with drifters, sailors, prisoners and drop-outs, remained the mark of courage and nobility among the Khirgiz of Central Asia.

But the peoples of the Altai were also masters in another kind of work involving skins. They used a great deal of leather and fur, especially for clothing. Thus the wife from the same Kurgan 2 wore a short ermine kaftan, with dummy sleeves which were thrown back over the shoulder, fur side in. This kaftan was edged with a broad band of dark pony skin and otter skin dyed blue. The outside, dressed like suede, was embroidered all over in the manner of an Afghan fur-lined coat and ornamented with red leather appliqué work set off with gilded copper. The ensemble was completed by a shirt-front of otter skin, pony skin and sable. Over stockings of very fine felt, the woman wore red leather boots, the uppers of which were entirely covered with appliqué work and embroidery using thread wrapped in tin. Even the soles were decorated with small black glass beads and precious pyrite crystals arranged in a lozenge shape, which would only have made sense if the woman frequently sat in the nomadic manner, on a carpet and with her feet turned out.

Here and there lay the artifacts of everyday life: small bronze cauldrons, a few clay vases, and many wood receptacles and objects. Even more were made of leather: bags, flasks, goatskin bottles, pouches containing cheese, seeds, and even hair and nail clippings with magic powers. The limited furniture consisted of small rounded wooden pillows, slightly incurved at a centre, low stools and tables with movable tops resting on carved legs that held the remains of an appetizing saddle of mutton intended for the deceased. But in this life at ground level, the essential feature was the cushions, of felt, leather and fur stuffed with dried grass or animal hair, and especially the hangings and rugs which, while acting as insulators, made up the decoration of the nomads' life. Felt of local manufacture was most commonly used. There have been finds of enormous hangings decorated with coloured motifs, cut out and sewn on, sometimes still affixed to the log walls. A superb velvety carpet, mainly red, measuring 1.83m × 2m (6 × 6.6ft) decorated with a central checkered motif framed by a file of deer grazing and, near the edge, by a procession of horsemen, was found in Kurgan 5. Study of the motifs and technique of this finely knotted and short-napped carpet, the oldest which has come down to us, indicate a foreign provenance, perhaps Persia, or more probably non-nomadic Central Asia. Also imported, but this time from China, was an extremely fine piece of raw silk of which unfolds an exotic universe of embroidered floral arabesques, pheasants or phoenixes. Out of this royal present a saddlecloth had been made, edged with a band of felt inlaid with leather and plated with gold and tin, from which hung six large tufts of yak hair. These two examples among many others illustrate the importance of textiles, an incomparable medium for the diffusion of forms and motifs in long-distance east-west exchanges, long before the establishment of the regular Silk Route which was to pass further south. In more general terms, what the frozen Altai tombs offer us is a striking picture of everything that time normally removes: the vivacity of the colours, contact with skins and fabrics and the art of combining the most varied materials in a single piece. By giving us back this dimension of the perishable, the finds at Pazyryk restore to us in material form what could only be guessed at in the Scythian tombs. So now a broad-scale approach to the nomadic civilizations of the Steppes becomes possible, and the archaeologist's dream of becoming the ethnologist of vanished peoples may be realized.

"Goddess" (left) and horseman (right): detail of a felt hanging from Kurgan 5, Pazyryk

With a bow in his belt, and cape floating in the wind, a horseman advances towards a female form clad in a long dress and a large tiara, whose ear is strangely depicted back to front. Enthroned on a seat with carved legs, she holds a small branch with flowers in her right hand. The theme, repeated several times, decorates a felt hanging, measuring 6.5 × 4.5m (21.5 × 14.8ft). It is exceptional in the art of the Steppes, where women are rarely depicted except in scenes of this type. It may represent an investiture, or perhaps a sacred wedding or the glorification of the deceased. The enthroned figure is probably divine, and the scene assuredly has a religious significance. The Hermitage, Leningrad.

Leather pouch illustrating a fight between winged creatures. Kurgan 2, Pazyryk

Filled with seeds of hemp (cannabis) the pouch was hung from the pole of a leather tent enclosing a cauldron full of pebbles and calcined hemp. Common in Atlai tombs, such ritual accessories are very accurately described by Herodotus (IV, 73), who records that the Scythians purified themselves after funerals by inhaling, under a covering of blankets, the smoke of hemp seeds thrown on to red-hot stones, inducing them to "howl with pleasure". Hermitage, Leningrad.

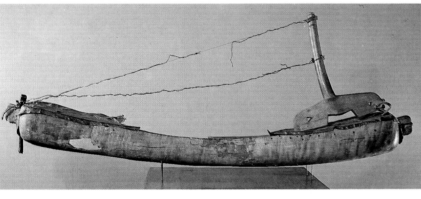

Swan from Kurgan 5

Four similar figures made of felt stuffed with dried grass were fastened at the feet, as if they were perching on the wooden chariot, the body of which was padded with black felt. The first example in the world of "soft sculpture", the figure of the swan reveals remarkable powers of observation. It is very rarely depicted among the Iranian nomads, but the Mongols are known to have regarded the swan as a sacred animal, and Siberian ethnology had a swan woman, ancestor of the Buryat people. The Hermitage, Leningrad.

Wood and leather musical instrument from Kurgan 2, Pazyryk

The instrument comprised several strings (reconstructed here) mounted on a hollow wooden box covered with leather. This kind of harp and small drums, found in all the tombs, strongly suggest that music was played as an accompaniment. Among people with no writing, the richness of the oral, probably epic, tradition is confirmed by analysis of the most archaic substratum of epic poems surviving in Iran and Central Asia. The Hermitage, Leningrad.

Detail of a felt and leather saddle cover from Kurgan 1, Pazyryk

Pieces of coloured felt sewn onto a red ground depict a gryphon with characteristic crest and tuft of hair. It is using its sharp beak and powerful talons to crush an ibex whose hindquarters are up-ended. Muscles and joints are emphasized by the "stops" and "commas" according to a favourite convention in eastern art. On the gryphon's wing and head and the ibex's hooves the remains of leather appliqué work can be seen which may have been covered with a fine sheet of gold. The scene had its counterpart on the other side of the cover from which hung long fringes of red horsehair. This covered a saddle made of two small leather cushions attached to wooden hoops resting on a thick felt cover. The Hermitage, Leningrad.

The Scythians and the Greek world

To the ancient Greeks, Scythia contained not only the strange creatures of myth and fantasy, but also the real wealth of gold; this was to forge an interesting and enduring link between the two cultures in historical times.

Away from the centre and much smaller than the huge areas adjoining it, the coastal edge of the Steppes bordering on the Black Sea, the farthest boundary that could be mastered by Greek ships or Scythian horses, rapidly became a point of contact between these peoples, then a place of permanent exchange and finally the scene of a two-way cultural process. This profoundly changed the Scythians, but also affected certain aspects of Greek life, producing mixed forms which in their turn inspired the world of late antiquity, particularly Sarmatian art.

In this region of Pontus the Greeks located many stories which illustrate all degrees of human knowledge, from the *mythos* concealing germs of truth to the falsely objective *logos* of Herodotus, from imaginary happenings to events experienced, lived through and rationalized. This region contained the unreal boundaries of the known world; the white and happy home of the Hyperboreans where Apollo, god of light, took refuge among the swans in the winter; the black gate of Hades; the land of the Cimmerians enveloped in mist and cold. It was also the country of the Caucasus where Prometheus was chained by the gods for bringing fire to mankind, the country of Colchis, rich in gold, of the one-eyed Arimaspes, who snatched the precious gold nuggets from the gryphons. All of which tell of the real reason which drove the Greeks there: the lure of that precious metal. The voyage of the Argonauts, the victory of Theseus or Hercules over the Amazons of Pontus, Io's wanderings through the Cimmerian Bosphorus, the fate of Iphigenia in Tauris or the story of Pontic Achilles—all these reflect appropriations of territory confirmed by archaeology.

Both on the coast and inland, excavations have yielded fragments of Greek pottery, from the 7th century BC, mostly Rhodo-Ionian. In fact, it was the Asian Greeks, from Miletus, who were the most enterprising, until the Athenians overtook them. Attracted by the resources and commercial outlets which these new lands offered, they settled first at safe ports of call, for example on the islet of Berezan, opposite future Olbia; then, becoming bolder, they installed themselves on shore, preferably near to river mouths, favourite routes for penetrating inland. Thus the Greeks founded Istros on the Danube, Tyras on the Dniester, Olbia at the mouth of the Bug and the Dnieper, and Panticapaeum at the outlet of the Sea of Azov; and lastly Tanais, which gave access to the steppes of the Volga via the Don.

Although the foundation dates of these cities are traditionally attributed to the mid-7th century, it was not until the following century that the settlements proper were established. Even at the end of the 6th century, the Greek *polis* (city state) of Olbia was no more than a large village, not to become genuinely urban until the 5th century.

During this first phase the Greeks and Scythians lived side by side rather than mingling. From these lands the Greeks acquired and exported quantities of wheat, which they themselves cultivated, skins and furs, dried fish, and human beings to be used both as slaves and, above all, as mercenaries, like the Scythian archers who, before the Median wars*, were auxiliaries in the Athenian army and formed one of the contingents of the Athenian police in the 5th century. In exchange they offered the Scythians oil, wine, luxury pottery and manufactured metal objects, acting in every case as intermediaries rather than manufacturers, except that they had skilful craftsmen who could adapt their work to the demands of their barbarian customers. On either side of the Dnieper, as well as in Kuban, Scythian tombs have been found to contain imported bronze bowls, hand mirrors, and typically Greek armour, helmets and greaves. But with other objects, such as the mirror found at Kelermes, it is strikingly clear that they were made by craftsmen trained in the artistic traditions of Asian Greece to meet the demands of a Scythian clientele. A little later, there appear motifs such as palmettes and the lotus, ovolos and pearls, and Greek animal symbols on their coins which strongly suggest the impact of the Greek presence.

New demand for grain

However, these material contributions did not make a deep impression on the nomadic civilization of the people of the Steppes. The Median wars put an end to the privileged relations of Ionian cities with the Black Sea; and even Athens, which had played such an active part in this area, maintained only rather loose relations with the Black Sea during the 5th century, as is shown by the comparative rarity of Athenian imports in that period, although the neighbouring Greek towns on the Strait of Kerch assembled round the town of Panticapaeum for the kingdom of the Bosphorus, which acted as a go-between for the Athenians. Then came a radical change which inaugurated a new phase in relations in the early 4th century BC. Athens, which had seen its agriculture laid waste and its relations with other Greek cities seriously disrupted after the Peloponnesian War*, found it could no longer count on the Bosphorus to supply it with grain. The increase in demand caused by the war led to those who supplied the Greeks with wheat or traded with them in any way to get rich quickly. Indeed, these events produced the wealth of the whole Scythian aristocracy which we can now see in the abundance of luxurious objects found in their princely tombs, especially in the regions of the black lands of the Dnieper: Tohertomlyk, Solokha and the great kurgan of Tolstaia Mogila which has been described earlier.

The Scythians of this generation seem to have wished to live the same nomadic life beyond the grave as their fathers. Yet others seem to have succumbed to the attractions of the town to the point of becoming settled. The tombs of these groups have been found in the necropolis of Panticapaeum and its environs. The kurgan of Kul Oba, 6km (4 miles) from the town, is a perfect example of a Hellenized Scythian tomb. Beneath the traditional mound, the burial chamber is of stone, not wood. Its cantilevered structure and the presence of a majestic *dromos* betray the influence of Greek architecture. The deceased was buried in the Scythian manner with his spouse, a servant and a horse, his cypress sarcophagus was lined with engraved and painted ivory on which are figured an *auriga* (charioteer) as well as Athena, Aphrodite and Eros in a Judgment of Paris. Food was placed in a Scythian bronze cauldron, and wine in four amphorae, one of which bears the stamp of the Greek island of Thasos. The dead man was apparently clothed in a pointed felt hood. Both he and his spouse were covered with gold bracts (gold plates). As well as his bow and quiver, his *nagaika* whip and short sheathed sword, he had a helmet and greaves worthy of a hoplite (Greek infantryman). But most significant of all was the profusion of gold artifacts found near the couple. An abundance of objects—vase, phial, torque, bracelets, diadem, pendants and a wealth of ornamental plaques and bracts attest to an immoderate love of gold and ornaments and a somewhat rapacious wealth. The themes decorating these objects are a blend of the animal images dear to the art of the Steppes, images flowing from everyday Scythian life depicted with ethnographic accuracy, and purely Greek images: Pegasus, Gorgons, dolphins, a sphinx and even the Athena Parthenos of Phidias, as well as purely decorative motifs. The techniques used in all these pieces, and the style of the images, were entirely Greek.

The example of Kul Oba is far from unique and the workshops of the Bosphorus may have catered to a more distant clientele or produced objects which travelled far and wide. That may be the case with the gold-leaf plating discovered in 1977 during the excavation of the royal tumulus of Vergina in Macedonia which was very probably the tomb of Philip, the father of Alexander the Great. This plating ornamented a *goryte*, a Scythian-type quiver, but several very similar examples have been discovered in Scythian tombs. One, on a plaque at Karagodeuachkh in Kuban, is an exact replica of the Vergina example and must have been made from the same mould, perhaps at Panticapeum.

When the Sarmatians came from the Caspian region and replaced the Scythians on the shore of the Black Sea, they brought with them an animal repertoire that came straight from the authentic tradition of the Steppes. But it was the Hellenistic workshops of the Bosphorus which, with all the refinement of their metalworking skills, gave form to these images which were to fertilize the imagination of the west.

Bracelets from Tillia tepe

Backs arched, feet outspread, horns and ears seemingly forced back by the wind, these antelopes inlaid with turquoises, with cornelians for eyes, belong to the purest Steppe tradition. But a ring, also of heavy gold, on the finger of the dead person, bore the image and name of Athena, which shows the importance of the Greek contribution to the art of these nomads, who, after invading Bactria, were to found the Indian empire of the Kushans.

The Kelermes mirror

This silver disk, which once had a central stud, is of a local type, but it was a Greek hand which engraved the gold leaf plated on the reverse side with alternating winged creatures and real animals. This idea of access to the supernatural through the intermediary of animals and flight reflects ideas and practices common to the Steppes as a whole and still much the same in present-day shamanism. The mirror, magical instrument of divination, is also an attribute of power.

L. Bobin

Bracts of the "Seven Brothers"

In accordance with barbarian custom, these small stamped gold leaves were sewn on to clothing. Many of them take their form from images on Greek coins which circulated as far as Scythia. Thus the winged wild boar was the monetary emblem of two Greek towns in Asia Minor, Ialysos and Clazomenae. But the most spectacular example is that of the owl, an animal alien to the Steppe bestiary, but emblem of the drachma of Athens which the Scythians adopted long before they accepted the image of the goddess herself. The Hermitage, Leningrad.

Sword scabbard

The body of this scabbard depicts, instead of the traditional animal figures, a battle scene between the Greeks and the Barbarians. It is fashioned in the purest Greek style, drawing directly from the repertory of monumental sculptural forms. The flared connecting piece, however, which differs from one example to the next, is decorated with animals. The Metropolitan Museum of Art, New York.

Pendant from Kul Oba

On the medallion forming the body of the two gold pendants, set off with enamel, which framed the face of the dead woman appears the helmeted head of Athena Parthenos, conceived by Phidias for the Parthenon. Thus, by an extraordinary paradox, a Scythian tomb and a barbarian jewel are instrumental in handing down to us the most faithful image of this most celebrated statue which was the symbol of classical Greece. The Hermitage, Leningrad.

Stag from Kul Oba

This buckle plaque is apparently the exact equivalent of the one from Kostromskaya. But the Hellenized stag portrayed here is more massive, its antlers stiffened, a third hoof suggesting depth. Yet, coated with irrelevant animals, it loses in suggestive capacity what it gains in realism, giving the measure of the irreducible opposition between two approaches to the world: the rational analysis of the Greeks and the magical vision of the Scythians. The Hermitage, Leningrad.

Central Asia:
the archaeological background

The vast region of Central Asia contains untold archaeological treasures, from the Neanderthal grave offerings of Teshik-Tash to the brilliant Sogdian civilization of the 8th century AD. Most of these finds have been uncovered only recently, through the work of archaeologists from numerous countries, and much remains to be discovered.

There has been no lack of tales over the past 2,000 years about the wonderful people and things to be encountered by travellers from west or east who penetrated the vast area of deserts and mountains from the Caspian Sea to the plains of China. The picture emerging from these tales was of an isolated world that had remained separated from the great civilizations, or at any rate was worthy of attention only at special periods, when one or another of these – Persian, Graeco-Roman, Indo-Buddhist, Moslem – had left its mark on it. We have had to wait until the 20th century for this picture to be replaced by an authentic history, based mainly on the results of explorations that began less than 100 years ago, which today offers us a completely different concept of the links between Central Asia and the civilizations of the Asiatic and Mediterranean worlds.

We must however be careful not to belittle the contribution made to this study by the chroniclers of bygone eras – the *logopoioi* (word-makers) spoken of by Herodotus, himself the most illustrious of them. In his famous work (written in the 5th century BC), the *logoi* dealing with Central Asia mark the beginning of a long series of tales which were for a long time the only available sources of information on the geography of these areas, the peoples who lived there, their customs and their history, insofar as it was possible to re-establish these things from accounts of traditions or monuments given by these chroniclers. The historiography of Central Asia begins with the accumulation of these stories, even if there is a singular variety in the quality of writing of those who recorded them. Some of them we could regard as historians, Ctesias, for example, a little later than Herodotus, or the annalists of Alexander and his successors in Bactria in the Roman era; others were geographers from the same period, such as Strabo and, in particular, Ptolemy, to whom we owe the first description of the trading routes linking Bactra in Central Asia to the capital of the land of silk, in China. However, most of them do not have the status of scholars but were ambassadors sent by the great powers of the day as missionaries or traders. There were embassies from China (Chang-K'ien, 2nd century BC, Fa-hien, 4th century AD); Byzantium (Zemarchus, 6th century); and, later, the Pope (Giovanni da Pian del Carpine), France (Guillaume de Rubrouck), and Venice (Marco Polo and his brothers) in the 13th century, to mention only the earliest and best-known. To the tales of these amazing travellers we must add from the 9th century onwards the accounts of Central Asia given by Arab geographers and historians: the term Arab is accepted as covering a huge collection of works written mainly in Arabic, but often in Persian as well, by authors coming from all parts of the Moslem world, from the Mediterranean to the Pamir Mountains. Even today it is mainly through the systematic study of these texts, set against archaeological evidence, that the historical geography of Central Asia in the early Middle Ages, not to mention ancient times, can be constructed. Another useful group of sources is represented by the chapters devoted to the "western regions" in the dynastic histories and annals of China, collections of which, compiled by scholars of all countries, Chinese and European, have recently appeared.

However, with the modern period, collections of tales relating to Central Asia seem to mark time. From the 15th century onwards, traders and missionaries from the West were more interested in the Far East, which they could by then reach by sea, or in Persia, beyond whose eastern frontiers they did not go; and the first embassies sent by the government in Moscow to Central Asia in the 16th and 17th centuries have left virtually no records of their missions. It was not until the 19th century that the area once more became the site of systematic explorations. These were still mixed up with political considerations: England and Russia were vying with each other to extend their hold on Central Asia through a combination of alliances and military pressures, the former with a view to Afghanistan and eastern Turkestan, the latter concentrating on the Uzbek khanates of Khiva and Bokhara.

Travellers of a new description emerged as a result of these tendencies, and we owe to them the first systematic studies of Central Asia relating to all aspects of the subject: history, geography, archaeology, linguistics, ethnology, religions, and so on. The remarkable descriptions of Afghanistan, rich in historical and archaeological observations and still of value today, which we owe to learned observers who had come there from India, Persia or Russia during the first half of the 19th century are especially worth attention: the observers were mostly English (Elphinstone, Masson, Burnes, Conolly, Wood), but there were some French as well (Ferrier). Next there are the first systematic works devoted to the history and antiquities of the same country or to some of its provinces, published in the second half of the 19th century by a new generation of British explorers serving in India (Raverty, Yates, Robertson, Tate). Parallel observations were undertaken by the Russians in the khanates of Central Asia (Bokhara, Khiva, Khokand) where there were likewise firstly enlightened explorers, who sought out manuscripts and studied monuments while undertaking their practical missions (Muraviev, Khanikov, Lehman, Ignatiev, Veliaminov-Zernov), and then scholars to whom we are indebted for the first systematic studies of epigraphic inscriptions and material remains, in the final quarter of the 19th century, sometimes supported by excavations (in particular, at Samarkand-Afrasiyab and Ferghana). Finally, a considerable body of material was collected in eastern Turkestan (now Sinkiang Province, China) in the late 19th and early 20th centuries by Russian, French, Swedish, English, German, Japanese and American expeditions.

This scientific tendency was consolidated in the first decades of the 20th century, particularly in Turkmenistan, where an American mission under Pumpelly uncovered remains of very early habitation (from the end of the Neolithic and the Bronze Age) on the site of Anau (1904). At the same time historians and philologists were beginning to use the mass of newly discovered material to reconstruct the amazing succession of cultures which have left their imprint to this day on Central Asia, in its languages, monuments, place names and even its beliefs (see the work of Markwart, Nöldeke, and Barthold in particular).

Archaeology in Afghanistan

Afghanistan, on the other hand, had been closed to field study until in 1922, shortly after achieving independence, the government at Kabul decided to entrust archaeological exploration of their country to France. A mission was immediately organized under the leadership of Alfred Foucher and was to continue its work for 60 years, under the name of Délégation Archéologique Française en Afghanistan (D.A.F.A.). At the same time the new Soviet State had just established its authority over the area, from the Caspian Sea to the Pamir Mountains; and new programmes of archaeological exploration were being set up in conjunction with major projects intended to ensure the agricultural and industrial development of the newly formed republics (Turkmenistan, Uzbekistan, Tadjikistan and Kirghizia). From then until World War II, the state of our knowledge about Central Asia tends to reflect progress made in archaeological discovery by the French and Soviet missions

The British Museum

Scale model of a chariot in gold, from the "Oxus Treasure"

In 1877 on the right bank of the Oxus (Amu Darya) not far from its meeting with the River Vakhsh a hoard of treasures were found consisting of about 200 items in gold and silver (jewels, statuettes, vessels, etc) and 1,500 coins. The suggested dating lies betwen the 5th and 3rd century BC. At that period Bactria – which incorporated this section of the Oxus – passed from Persian into Greek rulership, the Greeks being the heirs of Alexander. Those writing about the find have struggled to distinguish the elements that are Oriental or Classical in the inspiration or the manufacture of the objects. The British Museum, London.

respectively south and north of the Amu Darya river. To the French we are mainly indebted for two types of work. On the one hand, there was a series of reconnoitring expeditions led by Alfred Foucher between 1922 and 1925, partly to identify the monuments which would serve as landmarks for *La vieille route de l'Inde, de Bactres à Taxila* (the title of his great work on the subject, the first of some 30 volumes which have so far appeared under the auspices of D.A.F.A.), and partly in search of the remains of Greek settlements in Bactria (this hope was not fulfilled at Bactra itself, but it was elsewhere, 40 years later, at Aï Khanum). Secondly a series of excavations was undertaken on the foremost sites of Graeco-Buddhist or Indo-Buddhist art: at Hadda, with work supervised by J. Barthoux, 1926–28; and at Bamiyan, with work supervised by J. Hackin, 1929–34, to mention only the most famous sites. The ancient town of Begram yielded Indian, Chinese and Mediterranean art treasures indicating the extent of trading relations maintained between the Kushan empire and the great civilizations that existed at the beginning of the Christian era (work supervised by J. Hackin, 1936–39, and continued for some time by R. Ghirshman). During this same period, the first Soviet missions discovered north of the Amu Darya remains which though less spectacular were no less significant for the ancient history of Central Asia, a subject then still in a state of limbo: Bronze and Iron Age burial grounds in the Tashkent area and in Ferghana (work supervised by M.E. Masson, 1928–1939, along with excavations devoted to the study of Buddhist monuments at Airtam-Termez), and Mousterian tools found with the first traces of Neanderthal men in the famous cave at Teshik-Tash (work supervised by A.P. Okladnikov, 1938).

Recent investigations

The full story does not really take shape until many years later, with the large archaeological expeditions mounted by the USSR in Central Asia after World War II, and the increased amount of research set in motion at the same period by the Afghan archaeological services, with the collaboration of numerous foreign missions. It is possible here to do no more than list these briefly, restricting the list to the largest-scale undertakings in terms of area or time. Noteworthy expeditions undertaken by the USSR include those to Khwarezm (Chorasmia), Turkmenistan, Sogdiana, southern Tadjikistan, and Pamir-Ferghana – the various *Trudi* (works) published in the course of the years by the archaeologists concerned add up to an impressive body of work; Russian scholars have also published a number of other outstanding writings relating to all the prehistoric ages – the Stone Age, the Bronze Age, and the Iron Age – and every historic period: Graeco-Bactrian or Graeco-Parthian, and on into Islamic. In the case of Afghanistan missions were active during a number of years between the end of World War II and the Revolution (1978): first of all, the French delegation (D.A.F.A.) resumed its programme of excavations on the great historical sites (D. Schlumberger at Bactra, Lashkari Bazar and Surkh-Kotal; P. Bernard at Aï Khanum). Expeditions from many nations, German, American, English, Indian, Italian, Japanese and Soviet have since then considerably broadened our knowledge of all periods of the history of Central Asia from earliest times to the present day. Finally, there is the important contribution of Afghan teams (S. Mostamandi, Z. Tarzi).

Indeed, if Central Asia has at last won its place in the history of civilizations, it is basically by virtue of the combined research of these many teams of archaeologists and philologists over the course of the last few decades: the following articles tracing its history could not have been written even fifteen years ago. The picture which emerges is that of a permanent historiographical balancing act between two opposite, but not conflicting points of view: a justified insistence on the contribution made by the local communities in the economic and cultural development of Central Asia from its beginnings until the present, but also the uncovering of the considerable influence arising from the links maintained at all periods by these peoples, willy-nilly, with the civilizations that surrounded them, from the Pacific to the Mediterranean, from the Indian peninsula to the Eurasian steppes.

This last factor means that from now on the study of Central Asia must have an international dimension, and this is revealed in a number of recent initiatives. An international association has been established for the study of the history of the cultures of Central Asia under the aegis of UNESCO, which publishes an information bulletin in two languages (Russian and English) and is working on a *History of the Civilizations of Central Asia*, to be published in several volumes. The number of international conferences devoted to the same subject (or bilateral conferences in the context of the agreements reached for example between the USSR and the United States, France and India) has greatly increased in the last few years. Finally, and most important, an increasing share of the research is being taken by the Asian countries most directly concerned – China (work of An Zhimin), India (work of S. Rahula, S.P. Gupta), Pakistan (work of A.H. Dani) and soon, we hope, Iran – all included in *Central'naya Aziya*, as it is called in the Soviet Union, extending beyond the narrower limits of *Srednyaya Aziya* (middle Asia) within which we had hitherto been confined.

Towns in the Bronze Age

The urban revolution of the Bronze Age Mesopotamian and Indus civilizations also spread to Central Asia, where it emerged in its own distinctive form. One striking feature is the long distance trade in lapis lazuli from the mines of Afghanistan.

Between 3000BC and 1500BC, a vast region of the Near East saw the development of large urban settlements. This phenomenon, which was first confirmed during the excavation of the great sites in Mesopotamia and the Indus basin, has been called the "urban revolution". It came after the "Neolithic revolution" which had seen the start of the domestication of plants and animals, and was marked by the formation of vast, densely populated settlements. Some of the population were engaged in non-agricultural activities, such as the priesthood, or craftworking. A central authority governed the cities and brought together the people for the construction of large public monuments. The governing classes were linked with the scribes and astronomers, who were in charge of writing and the calendar, and with the artists and craftsmen, who received commissions for work and raw materials. This definition of the urban phenomenon is entirely appropriate to the civilizations of the great basins of the Nile, Mesopotamia and the Indus, but needs modification if it is to be applied to Central Asia.

The civilizations of Central Asia, known from excavations carried out since the 1950s, did not possess writing and have not yielded artistic works of the same quality as the great Mesopotamian sculpture. So we must use different criteria when deciding whether or not they experienced the "urban revolution". The urban phenomenon may have arisen in Central Asia, but it was on a diminished scale and related to developments in Mesopotamia and the Indus.

Two of the criteria for recognizing urbanization in the region were identifiable even before excavation began, by simple observation of the sites (tepes): the surface area and the positioning of the craftsmen's quarters. The surface area of the sites is the most evident criterion; those of Central Asia are enormous, with Namazga and Gonur covering an area of 120 acres, Altyn 72 acres, Khapuz and Ulug 24 acres, Shahr-i-Sokhta 192 acres and Mundigak nearly as much. Moreover, in Bactria*, establishments of considerable size often surround the most important monuments.

Archaeologists identify the quarters occupied by specialized craftsmen by searching the ground for traces of their activities. The metallurgists' quarters can be identified by the slag left by copper, the potters' quarters by traces of kilns and mis-fired pieces, the lapidaries' quarters by fragments of semi-precious stones such as lapis lazuli, cornelian, or turquoise, scattered on the ground. At Altyn, the potters and metallurgists have been located in this way, and at Shahr-i-Sokhta the areas for the production of copper and flint tools, and a workshop for dressing lapis lazuli. Research carried out at Tepe Hissar and Mohenjo Daro shows an identical specialization of quarters. It is thought likely that the craftsmen working in these districts were exempt from agricultural work and received their means of subsistence from other groups in the city.

The excavation of Central Asian establishments has revealed groups of monuments which have sometimes been identified with the existence of a ruling class. Such are the fortresses or citadels at Dashly, Sapalli and Gonur, and the temples or palaces at Dashly. However, these edifices do not attain the monumental grandeur of the terrace at Altyn, which has been compared not only to the terrace of Tureng Tepe but even to the Mesopotamian ziggurats*. In the area of the terrace, the excavators of Altyn have uncovered a rich collection of buried goods, which they have interpreted as connected with the priesthood. Large-scale public works included the construction of powerful ramparts, as at Mundigak and Altyn, and above all the design, execution and maintenance of the vast irrigation networks necessary for agricultural development in these semi-arid regions. Networks dating to the Bronze Age have been explored in Bactria and Margiana*. Some scholars have linked these vast public works with the existence of a strong central power, in spite of the absence of writing and hence of any kind of bureaucratic administration.

Archaeological analyses have recently added to these two criteria of the "urban revolution" two more characteristic features: a high level of technological development and long-distance trade.

The level of technological development emerges from laboratory analysis, and the analysis in operating chains of the components discovered. Laboratory analyses, for example, have shown that Central Asia was not familiar with real bronze made from tin, but rather with arsenical copper. Analyses of technological operating chains involved in the manufacture of ceramics have shown the existence and skilful use of the potter's wheel in the elaboration of elegant vases. Similar analyses applied to alabaster, cornelian and lapis lazuli objects have revealed a grasp of uniform circular movement operations, such as the lathe or drill with bow, which can only be attributed to genuine craftsmen transmitting their knowledge from generation to generation. Thus it has been possible to distinguish different areas of technological spread, Central Asia appearing on its own and not just an annex of more developed regions.

The trail of lapis lazuli

The term "long-distance contacts" includes many different transactions, from war to barter, whose details are usually unknown. But we can distinguish between those relating to raw materials and those relating to finished products. Central Asia is an ideal place for the study of traffic in raw materials, because at Sar-i Munjan it contains one of the only deposits of lapis lazuli known and exploited at this period. Lapis lazuli acts as a marker, sign-posting a route that traversed Bactria and Margiana, then made for the northeast of Iran and beyond it to the Elamite and Mesopotamian world. Another route went down towards Seistan and passed along the fringes of the desert of Lut before reaching the Elamo-Mesopotamian region.

Turquoise from Kyzyl Kum may have followed similar routes from the region of Lyavlyakan. In addition, the transport of ore and metals, although more difficult to demonstrate from archaeological remains alone, must nevertheless have existed, because Mesopotamia and the Indus have no minerals. The metal trade might explain the Harappan* (Indus) colony settled at Shortughai on the banks of the Amu Darya, as well as the presence of materials from far away at Sarazm in the mineral-rich valley of Zarafshan. Finished products also travelled widely; for example, certain engraved serpentine vases made in Iran are found from Mesopotamia to Bactria.

The traffic described here would have put Central Asia in contact not only with Iran and Mesopotamia, but also with the basins of the Indus and the Tarim, and the regions beyond. Silk has been found in Bactria, and Central Asian seals in China. All these transactions imply the existence over vast territories of systems for the conversion of weights and measures, and processes for translation into different languages. The little we know of the mythology of Central Asia at this time shows that it closely resembles the mythology of Elamite Iran. Examination of these transactions reveals that Central Asia did not stand outside the movement of civilizations of the age of protohistoric cities, but experienced and contributed to it.

In spite of the absence of writing and astronomy, we may assume that the "urban revolution" appeared in Central Asia as a result of human and economic growth, caused by irrigation and the subsequent development of agriculture. Although they cannot compete with Ur or Memphis, the towns of Central Asia were most certainly more than large farming villages.

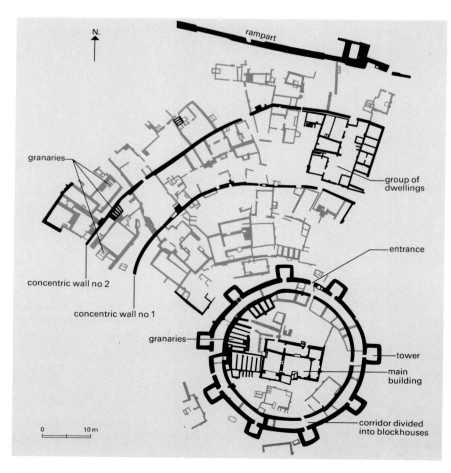

The round "temple", Dashly 3, Afghanistan

This circular monument, which could equally well be a "palace", stands in the middle of a fortified village. Hundreds of such villages occupied the delta oases of Bactria and Margiana.

Craft industries of protohistoric Central Asia, Dashly, Shortughai, Altyn

These open-work copper seals, cruciform beads and the pins come from Bactrian tombs (Dashly). The right of the two stone seals from Shortughai (below right) is of local manufacture, the left is in the Harappan style. The latter represents a rhinoceros and bears two signs in the Indus script. The gold bull's head (below) found in the burial complex at Altyn has been compared with the emblem of the Mesopotamian god of the moon, Sin.

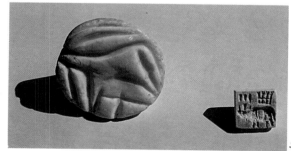

228

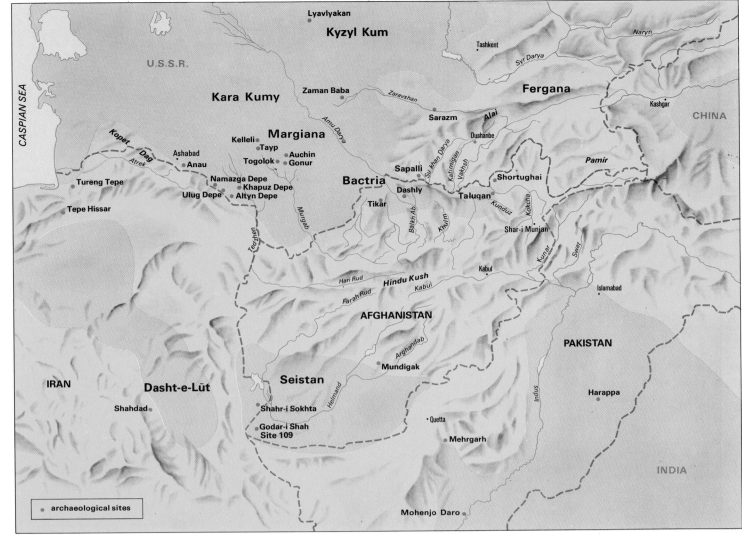

Central Asia is situated in an arid zone. The rivers whose sources are in the Hindu Kush and the Pamir have been used for irrigation since the Bronze Age. The geographical units thus defined by the relief and the river basins were often reflected by the local administration of the satrapies (provinces) of the Achemenid period and their names have come down to us (Bactria, Margiana, for example).

archaeological sites

Collection of funerary material, Altyn, Turkmenistan

This burial chamber contained stone artifacts, beads and a gold bull's head (see opposite page), mingled with the bones. The small ivory rods may have come from the Indus civilization. The burial complex forms part of a larger priestly complex adjoining a monumental stepped terrace. Excavation No 7, piece No 7.

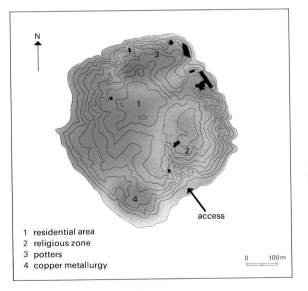

Plan of the location of quarters, Altyn, Turkmenistan

Excavation and clearance of the surface have identified quarters with different functions in this town. The various groups of craftsmen (potters, metallurgists) lived outside the monumental, religious and funerary zones.

1 residential area
2 religious zone
3 potters
4 copper metallurgy

0   100 m

access

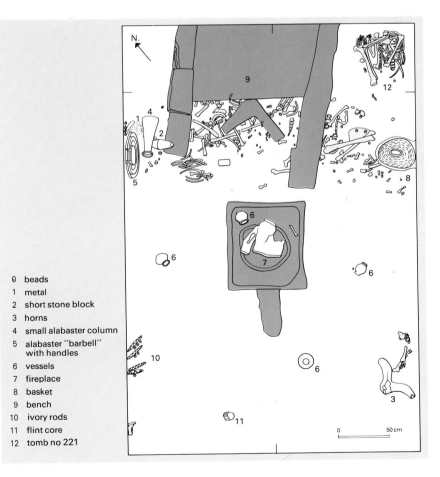

0 beads
1 metal
2 short stone block
3 horns
4 small alabaster column
5 alabaster "barbell" with handles
6 vessels
7 fireplace
8 basket
9 bench
10 ivory rods
11 flint core
12 tomb no 221

0   50 cm

Operative chain

Today meticulous studies of technology such as those carried out by the team of M. Tosi give us a better idea of the structure of protohistoric societies by examining how work was organized.

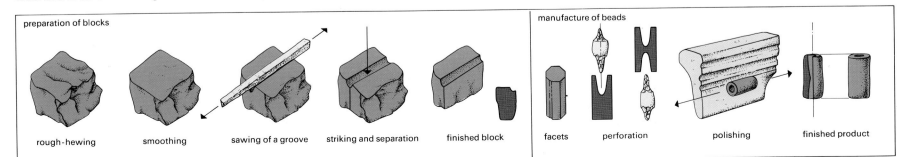

preparation of blocks

rough-hewing   smoothing   sawing of a groove   striking and separation   finished block

manufacture of beads

facets   perforation   polishing   finished product

Early irrigation: a model for archaeologists

Large scale public irrigation projects are characteristic of Bronze Age cultures across the world. Soviet archaeologists have found new evidence of this in Bactria — used right up to modern times.

Central Asia is an ill-defined area geographically: a vast region extending from the Euro-Asian Steppes to the north, the Iranian plateau to the west, the Indo-Baluchi plains to the south, and to the east the Tarim basin or the Gobi desert. Commanding the centre of this area is a mountain range (the Pamirs and the Hindu Kush) from which large rivers such as the Amu Darya and the Syr Darya descend towards the Aral Sea or to the Indian Ocean (the Indus). The first agricultural and pastoral societies developed on the foothills of this range and later spread to the plains, which were more favourable to agricultural activities as long as they could be irrigated with water from local springs and rivers. The semi-arid climate of Central Asia requires that the insufficient rainfall be supplemented with artificial irrigation systems extending from reliable water sources. This environmental constraint, still valid today, was already an important limiting factor in the distant past when the colonization of the plains took place during the Bronze Age. The remains of canals which archaeologists have recently found in the more accessible parts of Central Asia, and which date to remote times, are a more certain proof of this than any demonstration of the stability of the climate over the last few thousand years, a subject still under dispute.

Two Russian archaeologists were responsible for the first systematical research on ancient irrigation in Central Asia, concentrating first on the area near the Aral Sea in Khwarazm. Here, S.P. Tolstov and his colleagues uncovered a network of canals covering the vast region of the Amu Darya delta and dating from the 2nd millennium BC. The archaeological exploration of Turkmenistan, led successively by M.E. and V.M. Masson, then revealed traces of an even older irrigation system in the area surrounding Kopet Dagh: some three or four millennia before our time, the people of this region already practised the art of directing into the plain artificial water courses fed either by springs or by torrents descending from nearby hills. The technique used was one of surface canals: a channel was dug at a chosen point of the river (the outlet or "head" of the canal) and led downstream to the furthest possible lands, following the natural slope of the ground (in modern Persian, the *paï-ab*, or "foot" of the canal). Later on, the more sophisticated technique of underground channels (or *kanat*), of Irano-Mesopotamian origin, was also applied in Central Asia, particularly in Seistan and as far as Chinese Turkestan. But this marks a second development in that part of Asia, where the progress of irrigated agriculture was originally characterized by surface works that were by no means less ingenious than their successors.

One of the most interesting regions in this respect is the central basin of the Amu Darya, on the border of Afghanistan and the Soviet republic of Tadzhikistan. The tributaries of this large river — the Oxus of antiquity — are here numerous on both banks, and with the main river provide numerous sources of water to irrigate the plains which extend either side of the rivers on the ancient plateaux where they have carved their beds over the centuries. Excavations carried out particularly by T.I. Zejmal and M. D'Jakonov have revealed remains of canals in the valleys of the Vakhsh and the Kafirnigan in Tadzhikistan; but modern agricultural and urban development in this region have largely obliterated them. In Afghanistan, where the transformation of the country has been less rapid, a French team led by J.C. Gardin recently (1974–78) studied the better preserved remains of irrigation and human settlements still visible on the surface on the left bank of the Amu Darya, between the Rustaq and Kunduz rivers.

Bronze Age irrigation

In a historical context, these boundaries scarcely make much sense: the hills which surround this area to the east and south rise steadily to the passes of the Hindu Kush and the Pamirs, which have always connected the basin of the Oxus with India and China. However, neither the Amu Darya in the north nor the desolate expanse of the Dasht-i Mir Alam in the west ever hindered communications with Eurasia, Turkmenistan or Iran. This region can therefore be regarded as a model for archaeologists, where the circumstances of archaeological exploration have allowed a fuller reconstruction than elsewhere of the history of irrigation from the Bronze Age to the present, testifying to the early mastery of this technique in Central Asia, to the same degree as in Mesopotamia or in India.

The first irrigation works were no doubt confined to the setting up of rudimentary dams built on the river banks, by the accumulation of bundles of wood and stones, so as to divert the water to natural channels more suitable for the irrigation of the nearest lowlands, in the valleys. For instance, the positioning of settlements of the Chalcolithic period, recovered in the region of Taluqan, seems to suggest that works of this kind might have been necessary from the fourth millennium along the northern branch of the river Taluqan (today called Rud-i Shahrawan).

A more spectacular step forward was taken with what might be called the conquest of the plateaux. The photograph below shows the difficulty of such an undertaking, in view of the considerable differences in altitude between the rivers and the surrounding plateaux. In the area under consideration, the oldest example is the canal built at the end of the 3rd millennium on the right bank of the Kokcha to irrigate the plain of Shortughai; the excavations of this site led by H.P. Francfort have confirmed the existence of such a construction, as predicted by a paleogeographical study, but which had been considered at such an early age unlikely in view of the technical expertise required.

Several such irrigation systems were built on the terraces of our showplace region during the Bronze Age. A new stage began at the start of the 1st millennium BC when the inhabitants started to irrigate the foothills themselves by means of increasingly bold constructions carved out of the side of the hills. The photograph shows one of these channels built in Hellenistic times on the heights above the plateaux of the Amu Darya, between Aï Khanum and Shortughai. The complexity of the system is due to topographical restrictions which are easier to understand than to overcome: since the land to be irrigated lay at the foot of the hills, the canals could reach them only by means of adventurous courses along the contours of the hills for several kilometres.

The land surface thus gained was nevertheless limited, to the extent that the irrigation of these foothills may be regarded as the expression of a policy of intensive agricultural development, where criteria of profitability did not carry much weight. At what period would such a policy have been in force in Central Asia? Within the limits of our showplace area, the answer seems to be, around the year 1000BC. The feudal society described in the *Avesta* (a collection of Zoroastrian writings), where the problem of water was so important, immediately comes to mind. However, the trend continued after the campaigns of Cyrus, under the Achaemenid domination (*c*.550–331BC), the most spectacular project in our area being the canalization of the Rud-i Shahrawan, a long term project, parts of which were only completed after the conquest by Alexander (e.g. the canal of Hazar-Bagh).

The advent of the Kushan dynasty after the expulsion of the Greeks brought new irrigation projects, but these were limited to techniques inherited from earlier times. Traditional knowledge built up over the millennia had by now reached its highest level, and it was on this knowledge that all subsequent works in the area were based whether under the Samanids (10th century), the Timurids (15th century) and even to modern times (*c*.1920); whenever, in short, there has been a need to rebuild canals abandoned through some misfortune.

J.-C. Gardin

The Kokcha and the terraces of the Amu Darya

The plains of eastern Bactria extend over ancient terraces where rivers hollowed out their beds. To irrigate them, it was necessary to build long channels which collected water several kilometres upstream at an altitude higher than that of the terraces. That is the case here. The Kokcha, in the foreground, thrusts into the terraces of the Amu Darya, some 30m (96ft) high. The horizontal line on the side of the cliff in the background marks the passage of a modern channel which takes water from the Kokcha to the top of the terrace, following a course conceived more than 3,000 years ago to irrigate the plain of Shortughai.

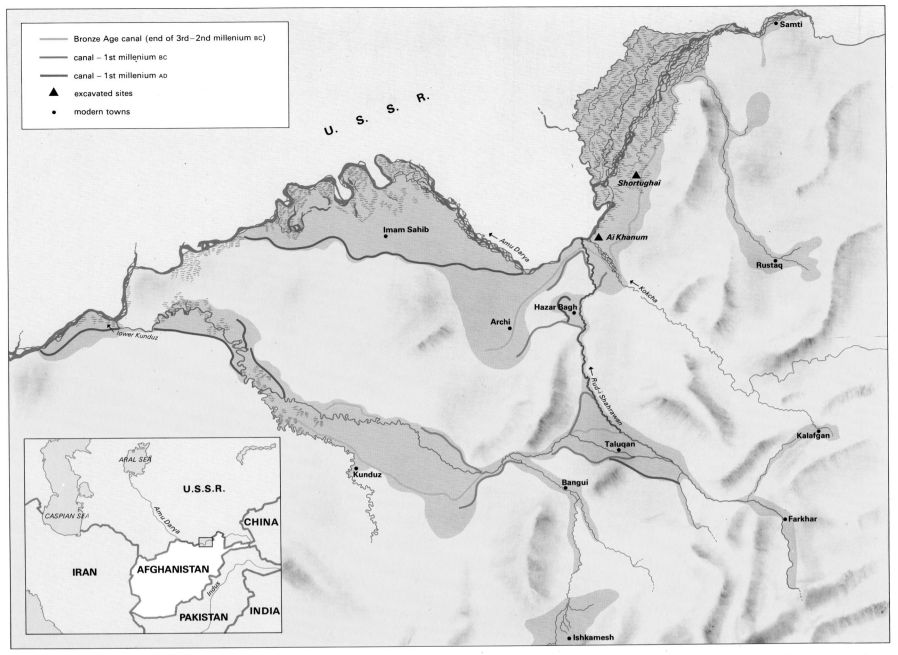

The oldest irrigation works were confined to the eastern sector in the region of Taluqan and the plain of Shortughai from the Bronze Age (until *c*.2200BC). They were completed in the 2nd millennium by the installation of similar channels in the plains situated further west, mainly Archi and Kunduz.

A second phase began early in the 1st millennium BC with the systematic supply of water to lands hitherto judged inaccessible on the heights dominating the plains just mentioned. It was a period when agriculture was intensively developed and there was no hesitation in undertaking difficult works in order to irrigate comparatively small additional areas. This trend seems to have continued under the Persian and Greek dominations until the invasions by the nomadic peoples which put an end to them *c*.130BC.

The Kushan dynasty which followed those invasions resumed the policy of extending cultivated lands. The great plain of Imam Sahib, until then occupied only on the bank of the Amu Darya, was supplied with water under the Kushans, as were the narrower strips of land bordering on the lower Kunduz, whereas the channels in the foothills were abandoned at Kunduz, Hazar Bagh, Archi and Aï Khanum. They were repaired for a short time at the beginning of Islam when the region experienced its greatest prosperity, until the disastrous Mongol invasion of 1220AD put an end for some centuries to the amazing achievements of Bactrian irrigation.

A Hellenistic channel on the heights dominating the Amu Darya

The frequently considerable differences between the altitude of the irrigable plains and the rivers from which the channels started meant that the channels had to run through difficult terrain. Here, on the heights which line the plain of Shortughai to the east, we see the twisting course of an ancient channel, the offtake of which is some 12km (7 miles) away. This long stretch on the hillside was the route invented to irrigate the foothill lands from the 1st millennium BC on.

The Rud-i Shahrawan

The highlands between the basins of the Amu Darya and the River Taluqan were always difficult to irrigate, simply because of their altitude. Nevertheless, the obstacle was overcome long before Alexander's conquest by the cutting of a spectacular channel still in use today, the Rud-i Shahrawan. Here we see the passage of this artificial arm of the River Taluqan across the sill separating the two basins.

The Hellenistic towns of Central Asia

The conquests of Alexander the Great led to the planting of new cities right across the Near East to what is now Soviet Central Asia. Most exciting of recent digs is at Aï Khanum on the Oxus river.

The Hellenistic* period is one of the most important ages in terms of the emergence of urbanism. Using the new ideas that first appeared in the Greek world during the 4th century BC, Alexander the Great and his successors founded a large number of cities in the East named after them, in order to spread Hellenism and to ensure their dominion over the conquered countries.

In Asia Minor, Egypt and the Near East, the characteristics of this urbanism are relatively well known from classical descriptions and archaeology. Until recently, however, almost nothing was known about the cities founded east of the Euphrates and particularly in Central Asia. Over the past 20 years the situation has changed considerably with the development of archaeological research in Afghanistan and in the Soviet territories of Tadzhikistan, Uzbekistan and Turkmenistan. After a few serious setbacks encountered in Bactra, Termez, Samarkand and Merv, where the Greek levels were buried under huge accumulations of more recent strata, this research has revealed a number of sites which have clarified the principal aspects of this particular form of urbanism.

In order to understand the typical features of Hellenistic urbanism* in Central Asia, it is important to remember that the Greeks settled in already inhabited areas, where irrigation had led to the creation of several oases within which numerous towns developed, particularly to the south of the Oxus (Amu Darya), with Bactra as the capital. Greek domination lasted for one and a half centuries, first with the Seleucid* empire and later within the much narrower limits of the kingdom of Bactria*. During this period, irrigation developed strongly, particularly on the other side of the Oxus, and urbanism grew vigorously, so much so that from the 2nd century BC Bactria could be described as the region "of a thousand towns".

The Seleucid rulers who took control of the area did not confine themselves to completing the existing urban network, but considered it in terms of completely different criteria, particularly with reference to the need for better control and a more efficient exploitation of the land. Some of the towns were therefore abandoned, one of them being Kunduz, the capital of eastern Achaemenid Bactria; others were restored and yet others were founded on new sites.

Of the ancient towns, Alexandria-Kandahar and Maracanda-Samarkand were rebuilt exactly as they had been. Elsewhere, the town which grew at the feet of the ancient citadel was surrounded with an irregular wall, as in Bactra, or with a quadrangular one, as in Antioch-Merv. Some of the oases were surrounded with a thick wall, 31km (19 miles) long at Merv and 70km (43 miles) at Bactra.

Very little is known of the internal organization of these ancient towns, but one can assume, in each case, the existence of an important building with the same function as that of the Achaemenid palace, namely administrative, governmental and residential. The network of streets around this central building must have been adapted to a pre-existing system and to the local topography, except where, as at Merv, a principle of streets arranged at right angles existed, as suggested by the tracks of main roads built in later periods.

An unknown capital — Aï Khanum

Among the new foundations dating from the beginning of the Hellenistic period, only Aï Khanum has been properly excavated. Founded at the command of Alexander or of Seleucus I, the name of this large town is still unknown, but may have been another Alexandria according to P. Bernard. It was abandoned by the Greeks after a century and a half and was so completely deserted that no later construction came to change its features, apart from the citadel and the northern rampart. This exceptional situation makes the site extraordinarily well suited to archaeological observation, particularly since, to judge by its size, which is similar to that of Bactra, it was probably one of the capitals of the kingdom.

The choice of site provided first class strategic advantages, for it was at the confluence of the Oxus and its left-bank tributary, the Kokcha, where both rivers are hemmed in between steep banks. A high plateau runs along the Kokcha and dominates the plain and the entire area, and it was here, on the southern tip, that the citadel was built. The town itself was sited on the plain between the plateau and the Oxus.

The lie of the land dictated the arrangement of the lines of defence, which followed the steep banks of the two rivers and the eastern border of the plateau. To the northeast, between the plateau and the Oxus, the absence of natural obstacles was overcome by the erection of a powerful rampart broken by a monumental gate and flanked by several square towers built close to one another. Thus the external features of the city, such as the choice of site, the presence of a citadel on the highest and best defended point, and the adaptation of the defensive system to the natural terrain, clearly connect Aï Khanum with the principles of Hellenistic urbanism. However, the surrounding walls inevitably reflected local conditions, being built entirely of unbaked bricks, but thick and massive enough to withstand siege machinery, and defensible by a small garrison.

The town planning of Aï Khanum therefore shows a real desire for order and regularity; without undue systematization it expresses great flexibility and a remarkable ability to adapt. In this, Aï Khanum clearly belongs in the main stream of Greek thought in the 3rd century, which softened the original (Hippodamian) grid system with adaptation to the natural terrain and finally led to the so-called "Pergamenian urbanism".

In one aspect, however, Aï Khanum shows a certain originality in comparison with contemporary towns in the Mediterranean world, evidenced in the ostentatiousness of its monuments and dwellings. The palace, the exercise ground, the theatre and the mansions are among the largest of all those in the Hellenistic world and are obviously built to impress. Moreover, the interior organization of the buildings clearly establishes the fact that everything must have been calculated to stress the preeminence of the ruling class: the huge size of the palace court, the importance of the reception rooms both in the palace and in the houses, and in the presence of three boxes in the theatre reserved for the aristocracy. All this points to the fundamentally aristocratic character of a colonial society in Central Asia and shows how the Greeks, while introducing the typical features of their own culture, were able to adapt to local conditions and to exploit them whenever it suited them to do so.

During its brief existence, from c.250BC to c.150BC, the Graeco-Bactrian kingdom carried on the town-building activity initiated by the Seleucids, founding a new capital at Termez and a series of small towns of a new type. And when, during the 2nd century, it undertook the conquest of the Indian subcontinent, it founded two important cities: Begram in the Hindu Kush and Taxila near the Indus.

The study of these different foundations raises problems due to the absence or insufficiency of excavation at the Greek levels, or to uncertainty as to their identification. Nevertheless, these sites possess certain individual features which enable archaeologists to follow the development of urbanism in Central Asia up to the end of the Greek period and to evaluate its later phases.

Termez, built in a loop of the Oxus, has not yet been excavated. The present state of knowledge suggests that the town was dominated by a rectangular citadel of about 10 hectares (25 acres), high over the river. Its exact boundaries and internal organization are as yet unknown.

Begram, situated on the southern slopes of the Hindu Kush at the confluence of the Gorband and the Panshir, seems to have been founded as a replacement for the ancient Alexandria of the Caucasus at the beginning of the 2nd century BC. With dimensions of 700 × 450m (224 × 1440ft), it is decidedly smaller than Aï Khanum, but resembles the latter in many respects. Sited on a triangular piece of land, with the citadel in the angle of the rivers, its massive ramparts with square towers follow a straight line on the side of the open country, but on the other two sides follow the curving lines of the plateau. The citadel has not been excavated, and the town, greatly damaged by ploughing, can only be partially recovered and only to the Kushan (post-Greek) levels. But the existence on the south side of a palace integrated into a rectilinear network of streets is probably a relic of the Hellenistic period.

At Taxila, the town that has been excavated lies immediately above the Greek level, which it only partially covers. The Hellenistic town would have been founded further to the north, between the mountain barrier of the Katcha Kot, where the citadel would have been, and the bed of the Tamra Nala which, with one of its tributaries, encloses the site on three sides. This recalls the principles which were already applied in the other sites. The internal organization of the Greek town covering an area 850 × 350m (2720 × 1120ft) has not yet been studied, but it is apparent that the plan of the Arsacid* (or Parthian*) town is organized around a main axis from which radiate rectilinear and evenly spaced streets, with a palace to the south integrated into the plan. All this clearly indicates the influence of new urban theories which strikingly cut through the web of entangled lanes uncovered in the neighbouring pre-Greek town that lay close by.

It seems clear therefore that, as far as the important towns are concerned, the traditional forms continued throughout the period of the Graeco-Bactrian Kingdom, with perhaps a more marked taste for systematic organization, and were perpetuated during the centuries that followed the departure of the Greeks from the region.

The emergence of small fortified towns during the Graeco-Bactrian period marked a new feature, as, under the Seleucids, only important cities appear to have been founded. These towns increased in number within the kingdom, and the collapse of the Greek domination seems to have accelerated rather than to have ended the process. Ceramics dating from the end of the Greek period are very similar to those of the next, so that it is often impossible to establish whether a town was founded before or after the departure of the Greeks. This serious problem is still far from being solved, but has not prevented the study of this new reality which is clearly part of the phenomenon of Hellenistic urbanism.

Common Hellenistic features

An overall examination of the sites soon reveals a certain number of common features. First among them is the importance of the citadel, which is always present and may occupy up to half of the total extent of the town. It may be situated either in the centre of the settlement or, more often, to one side, and displays very different features: at Jiga, for instance, there is a temple, at Dil'bergine an area of dense population, and at Kuhna Kala or Saksanochour a fortified palace. The second factor is the decidedly geometrical design of the enclosure, sometimes circular or square but more often rectangular, which surrounds a surface of not more than 20 hectares (49 acres), as at Key Kobad Sah or Khairabad. The citadel is often circular or even irregular as at Karabag or Dal'verzine.

Inside the walls, the buildings are arranged in a regular grid of streets. The only public buildings to be built beside the palace are the temples. These are richly decorated with paintings and sculptures in stucco, and were built according to two different plans: the Greek plan, as in the temple of Dioscuri at Dil'bergine, and the asymmetrical plan with several inner rooms, as at Dal'verzine. The arrangement of the palaces and houses was directly derived from the Aï Khanum model: the various functions are situated in different sectors, organized around courtyards, with access provided by long corridors bordering the rooms and the courtyards. In the houses of the aristocrats, the usual plan comprised two courtyards and three sets of living quarters: men's apartments and reception rooms, family quarters and servants' quarters.

The character of these new towns also reveals the kind of society in existence at the time. The importance and the siting of the military, aristocratic and religious buildings, and the absence of those which were typical of Greek towns, such as the agora (city centre), the theatre, the gymnasium and the bouleuterion (parliament) point to a highly hierarchical society in which a military aristocracy ruled over a settled population tied to the land by the development of irrigation. The only remaining traces of Greek urban traditions are seen in the taste for severely geometrical plans, a tendency which was often taken to extremes since it was applied even to the boundaries of the new towns, which had never been the case before.

The Greek approach to town-building, which was originally aimed at the harmonious organization of collective and public life, was thus deprived of its spirit, and became nothing more than a technique to embellish the achievements of an oriental society whose foundations had actually been reinforced by the presence of the Greeks. Its mark, however, can be found deeply impressed on the development of the towns of Central Asia, so much so that Alexander's conquest, far from being a mere interlude, can be said to have effectively introduced a new spirit which considerably modified, if not the function, certainly the appearance of Central Asian towns up to the arrival of Islam.

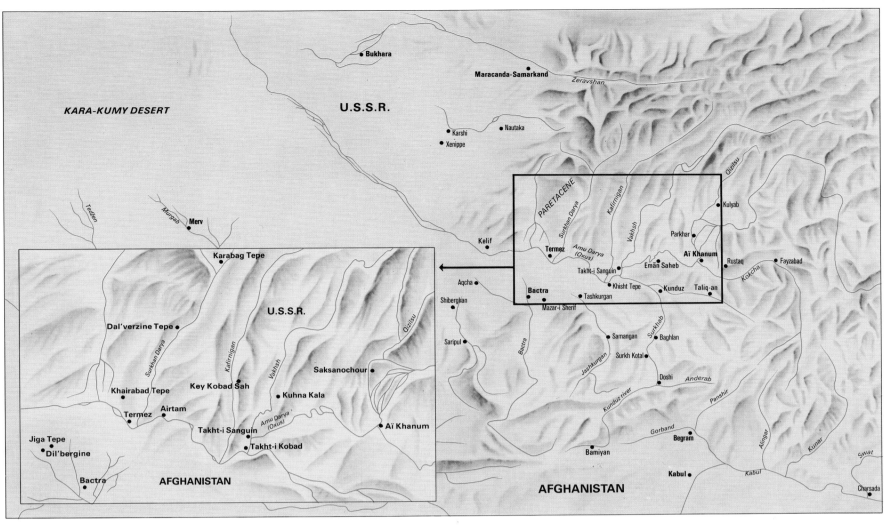

Aï Khanum

The city evidently developed with success on the plain, where three zones have been determined. In the centre, covering half the total area, are grouped the public buildings, including a palace of impressive size 350 × 250m (1120 × 800ft), a great temple with its large sanctuary, a mausoleum, an arsenal, and other features characteristic of Greek cities of the time: the tomb of the founder (herōon), the exercise ground (palaestra) and the theatre. To the south there is a residential quarter with large aristocratic dwellings and a craftsmen's quarter. To the north extends a district that may have been reserved for working-class houses. A few humble houses have been found on the plateau of the upper town, but this part of the site was abandoned in the 3rd century, probably because of provisioning difficulties and the harsh climate. Finally, the burial ground and a series of buildings, including a temple, are outside the town.

The distribution of buildings was conceived according to a very clear regular plan, based on a central axis formed by the main street, which traversed the whole town from city gate to the Kokcha river. The course of this street was determined by the escarpment which runs along the foot of the plateau, slightly above the level of the plain. The secondary streets, the houses and nearly all the monuments are orientated in relation to it, without the least rigidity.

In this complex, the palace, which has a markedly different orientation from that of the main street, constitutes an anomaly, possibly arising from the existence of an earlier building or an original plan centred on the great gate of the city wall (see photograph right).

Délégation archéologique française en Afghanistan

Dil'bergine, a small Graeco-Bactrian town

The geometrical course followed by the walls and the rectangular design suggest a Greek inspiration. The round citadel was established on the site of the Achaemenid town. When the Graeco-Bactrian kingdom came to an end, the town continued to grow outside the walls.

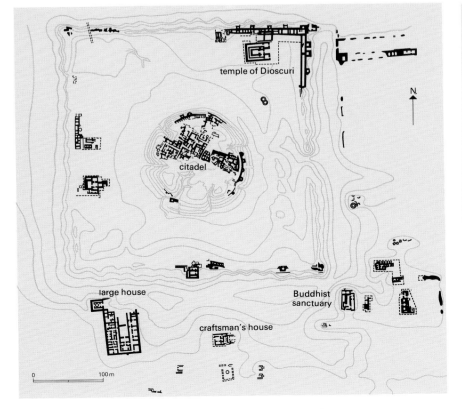

temple of Dioscuri

citadel

large house

Buddhist sanctuary

craftsman's house

100 m

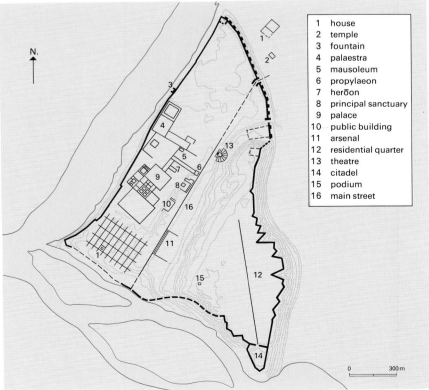

1	house
2	temple
3	fountain
4	palaestra
5	mausoleum
6	propylaeon
7	herōon
8	principal sanctuary
9	palace
10	public building
11	arsenal
12	residential quarter
13	theatre
14	citadel
15	podium
16	main street

300 m

The last days of the Sogdian civilization

Recent Soviet excavations in Uzbekhistan (Sogdiana), at the end of the Golden Road to Samarkand, have brought to vivid life this ancient civilization, destroyed by Arab expansion into Central Asia in the 8th century AD.

Sogdiana, the region centred on the valley of Zarafshan and the towns of Bokhara and Samarkand, was the scene of a civilization which flourished between the 6th and 8th centuries AD. The influence of this brilliant and original civilization extended as far east as T'ang China, but was not achieved by conquest. Divided into principalities, the Sogdians never felt the need for an imperialist state, leaving such concerns to the Central Asian Turks, their theoretical masters. From the Turks they accepted hereditary rule and military contingents, while devoting themselves to the actual administration of the empire and above all to the control of commerce and of the caravans of the silk route. Chinese chronicles and accounts of the Arab conquest have provided detailed information about them, long familiar and translated. Then, in 1937 and 1965 archaeologists discovered the palaces of the rulers of Bokhara and Samarkand and the extraordinary frescoes which adorned their walls. Nevertheless, most of our information on the Sogdian civilization comes essentially from a town of moderate importance, Pendjikent.

This site, 60km (37 miles) to the east of Samarkand, owes its particularly favourable condition to the fact that it had been abandoned shortly after the Arab conquest, and had never been built over in modern times. It came to the archaeologists' attention with the discovery, in a mountain castle, of a bundle of texts in Sogdian (the Iranian language spoken in the area before the Islamic conquest). Translation revealed them to be the archives of Dewāshtich, the last king of Pendjikent, who had taken them with him on his flight from the capital, before being defeated and crucified in AD722 by the Arabs. Paradoxically, excavations of the town undertaken uninterruptedly by Russian archaeologists from the end of World War II onwards, have yielded very few written documents. But they have exceeded expectations in all other ways, and count among the great adventures of recent times in the important rediscovery of the Middle Ages.

The city explored

The city's turbulent history has become more clearly apparent in its various phases now that a stratigraphic, level-by-level approach has replaced extensive clearing operations. Founded at the beginning of the 5th century AD, the town comprised two distinct units: a citadel and a fortified rectangular urban area of moderate size, 330 × 250m (1082 × 820ft) and with a chequerboard network of streets. Soon this became too small, and a new line of city walls had to be added to the east and south. From about 670–80 onwards the town had a king who issued his own coinage. In 712, Dewāshtich, who had recently ascended the throne, received numerous noble families and their military retinues

fleeing from Arab-occupied Samarkand. For ten years a feverish period of building took place in the town and extended to the citadel, where Dewāshtich, now proclaimed king of Sogdiana, built a palace below the castle with audience halls worthy of his new rank. The catastrophe of 722 is clearly indicated by the traces of a big fire, and an Arab garrison then took over the citadel. However, conversion to Islam was very gradual, and many rich dwellings continued to be occupied and decorated in a "pagan" style. Only after 750, under the Abbassid caliphs, did a policy of systematic conversion begin to show its effects, in the transformation of the houses' appearance, before the entire population was finally moved to a nearby site.

The size of the present excavations—about a third of the whole area—gives a precise idea of what the town looked like. Building materials consisted exclusively of mud bricks and clay, and enough wood to form flat roofs (domes were rarely made). The area was densely occupied, with some 4,000 people in a space of 15 hectares (37 acres) within the walls. Detached buildings were few, most houses being built in compact blocks without internal courtyards and comprising two or three floors, sometimes bridging the streets and turning them into passageways. This congestion was partly due to the influx of refugees in 712, making necessary the demolition of the old eastern wall, which previously formed part of the internal defences, in order to erect in its place a long block of aristocrats' dwellings.

Craftsmen and the nobility

The animation and congestion of the streets were compounded by craftsmen's activities. Workshops and stores, often sharing the same space and opening onto the street, existed all over the town but were particularly numerous alongside the houses of the aristocratic quarter. Adjacent to the latter, a metal market had grown where all stages in the manufacture of metal objects took place side by side, from the refining of the ores to the finishing of products such as armour, coins and bronze items. Some craftsmen had begun to set themselves up outside the walls, where a forge and a glazier's shop have been discovered near a wine press. Here we can observe the beginning of that process which, in the Islamic period, led to all commercial activity being transferred from the fortified town (shah-restan*) to the suburbs (rabad*). Although most of their work was carried out near the wealthy houses, the craftsmen had no personal links with them: they lived away from their place of work and managed their own activities (most of the coins found during the excavations were in the shops). It is much more likely that the craftsmen's dependence on the nobility was strictly a matter of economics: the latter rented out the commer-

cial property, controlled the sources of raw materials (as testified by the stock of iron found in their houses) and represented the essential requirement of the market—the demand. For it was this large aristocratic population (particularly after 712), eager to acquire weapons and equipment that explains the unusual number of metal workshops. The industrial production usually associated with the caravan trade seems to have had a limited importance in Pendjikent, although silkworking implements were found in one of the houses.

Social and cultural life mainly took place within private dwellings. Each aristocratic house included a huge reception hall of up to 80 sq m (860 sq ft) equipped with benches around the sides. The frescoes which embellished the walls from top to bottom, and which have contributed more than anything else to the fame of Pendjikent, give an idea of the activities which took place in these halls: banquets apparently restricted to men, libations to the family deity, who was depicted on the wall facing the entrance; concerts, recitals of legends and epic sagas copiously illustrated in wall paintings that call up a literary world which only survives fragmentarily in the Persian texts of the Islamic period. Some researchers have claimed that the smaller rooms were chapels with fire-bearing altars, but they may simply have been heated winter rooms. Domestic life, and perhaps also the social life of the women, was concentrated on the main floor.

The craftsmen's houses, though considerably smaller, often had a reception room and painted walls; the town-dweller, it seems, however modest, enjoyed a different order of existence from the countryman. The various social classes shared a passion for gambling, as evidenced by numerous finds of knucklebones, dice, tric-trac, and probably also chess, pieces of which have been excavated at Samarkand.

The royal archives show that the community had its own identity and its own revenues. The main centre of communal life was provided by the neighbouring enclosures of the two temples, where religious and probably also lay gatherings took place. Decorations on the porches and religious buildings illustrate processions on horseback, banquets, and a collection of deities combining Hindu elements with a Zoroastrian base. Fragments of texts found in the town testify to the existence of other communities including orthodox Zoroastrians, Buddhists and Christians, but their places of worship have not yet been found. Unlike the situation which prevailed in Iran under the Sassanids, and which extended over central Asia, the ordinary life of the people does not seem to have suffered any serious pressure from either a state priesthood or from a sovereign, enthroned in the citadel with his attention concentrated on serious matters of war and diplomacy.

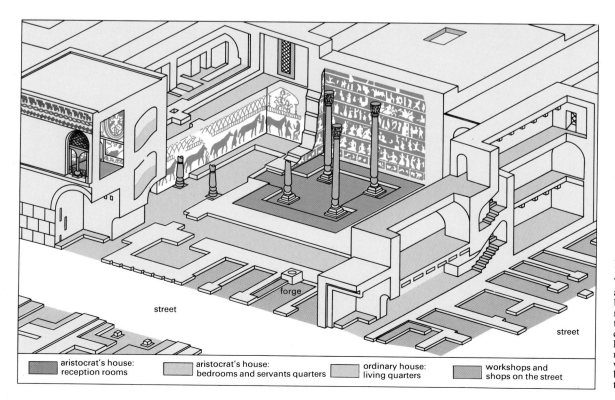

aristocrat's house: reception rooms

aristocrat's house: bedrooms and servants quarters

ordinary house: living quarters

workshops and shops on the street

Reconstruction of a residential quarter

The arched doorway opens on the street beside a row of shops and workshops, established on sites leased by the owner of the big house. The plan of the latter is arranged around a reception room two storeys high and decorated with frescoes, beneath a terrace roof supported by four carved wood columns, in the centre of which a lantern opens. A spiral ramp in a stairwell leads to the upper rooms. These include a small salon, possibly reserved for the women, which opens on the exterior by a window with small columns (the frescoes also show corbelled balconies). Right, an ordinary house with three storeys connected by flights of steps. Reconstruction after L.L. Gurevich.

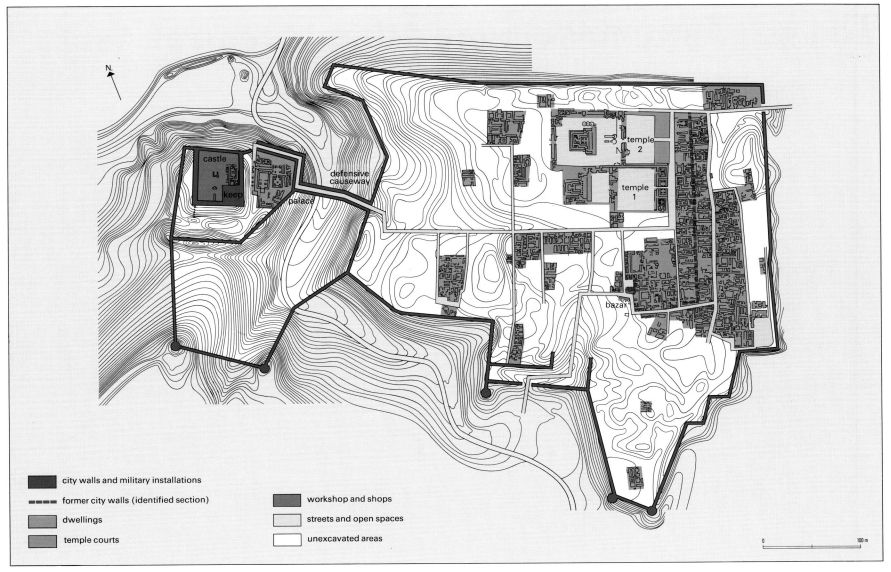

city walls and military installations

- - - former city walls (identified section)

dwellings

temple courts

workshop and shops

streets and open spaces

unexcavated areas

0   100 m

Fresco of a harpist

Stylistic conventions show the influence of Indian art, particularly the swing of the hips and position of the feet. The importance of musical life at Pendjikent is attested not only by the large number of figurative representations, but also by the existence of certain houses with stages for the use of orchestras, which participated in exchanges between Central Asia and the Far East: one fresco shows a concert given by Chinese lute players and dancers.

Topography of Pendjikent, *c.*720

To the west is the citadel, including the castle and the palace, flanked to the south by a forward line of defence. To the east, separated by a natural ditch, lies the lower town. Communication between the two areas was by a causeway built across the ditch. The city walls, made of rammed earth and mud brick, were, like all the town's structures, constantly reinforced until at the citadel they reached a thickness of 16m (51ft) at the base. Another interesting feature is the relative importance of temple courts among the spaces given over to social life.

Group of banqueters

The character in the middle holds a fly whisk, the partly preserved figure on the right is probably raising a cup. The clothes are undoubtedly of silk, and are adorned with beaded medallions inspired by the art of Sassanid Iran. This fresco comes from a house adjoining the metal bazaar and the banqueters may well be merchants, their status being indicated by their purses and their weapons: simple daggers attached to the belt, instead of the long swords reserved for noblemen.

235

Funerary practices in pre-Islamic central Asia

Soviet archaeologists have shown that funeral customs in ancient Central Asia in the ages before the Arab invasion diverged in significant detail from those of prehistoric Europe and the Near East.

Ancient writers have left us lengthy descriptions of the funerary customs of the nomadic Scythians, but they have hardly dealt at all with those of the settled populations of central Asia. Both Greek historians and Chinese writers mention, as a peculiar and incomprehensible practice, the custom of delivering the dead to carnivorous animals. The obvious links with the "Towers of Silence", to this day used by those Zoroastrians who still practise this religion in Iran and India, has long stimulated the curiosity of historians. Archaeology in general, and particularly the work of Russian archaeologists during the past 30 years, have confirmed and largely filled out the accounts of the writers of antiquity.

As far as we know, the first of these "flesh removal" entombments, where the bones had previously been "cleaned" by animals, took place in the 5th century BC in Chorasmia, where the custom may have been borrowed from certain nomadic tribes of the Caspian region. At around the same time, we find this practice among the Magi, the tribal priests of the Persian empire and the champions of the religion founded by Zoroaster*. As a matter of fact, this type of funerary ritual conformed well to the moral rules formulated by that prophet: respect for the whole of creation which was the work of the supreme God Ahuramazda (hence the need to avoid defiling fire or earth with dead matter, which was regarded as the receptacle of evil forces); and a conception of the soul's destiny in the afterworld that was simultaneously ethical and egalitarian, and held that there was no point in a corporeal form or costly grave goods for the dead. According to these principles, the rules governing funeral practices were codified in detail until, under the Parthian kings (2nd century BC–2nd century AD) they appeared in their definitive form in the holy book of the *Vendidád*.

It should be stressed, however, that in both central Asia and Iran this combination of Zoroastrian observance and funerary rites of flesh removal became widespread only as the result of a long process. Monarchs in particular, being often of Scythian origin, continued to embark on the afterlife wearing all their ornaments, as for instance in the stately tombs of the Parthian aristocracy at Nisa, or the tombs of the princes at Tilla-tepe in Bactria*, dating from the 1st century AD. In Chorasmia, the gigantic tomb of the king Koj-Krylgan-Kala is the first of a long tradition of big tomb buildings with military decoration—a tradition which, in this part of Asia, was to last a long time.

On the other hand, while the practice of flesh removal is well attested, there is no clear evidence to link it with Zoroastrian beliefs. In Chorasmia at about this time (4th century BC–3rd century AD) the bones from ordinary tombs were collected in urns, or ossuaries* in the form of hollow statues of the deceased holding a cup for offerings. This may have been a way of prolonging the physical presence of the dead person among the descendants, as was the custom in northern Asia, or, alternatively, a means of preserving the bones until the day of resurrection promised by Zoroaster.

The sacred dog

In Bactria, by contrast, the bones were left scattered on the soil—a fact which, together with use of dogs as scavengers and the rumoured custom of doing away with older people, much scandalized Alexander, who tried to put an end to such customs without concerning himself particularly with their religious significance. As a result, the Bactrians of the Kushan period (1st–3rd centuries AD), influenced as they were by their Greek inheritance, and politically independent of Parthia, habitually buried their dead within monumental tombs. These practices seem to reveal little application of Zoroastrian rules (except perhaps in the care taken to isolate the body from the soil), notwithstanding the theories advanced by Russian archaeologists.

This divergence of custom was gradually replaced, during the 3rd and 4th centuries, by a more widespread uniformity and a more definite effort to conform to the rules set out in the *Vendidád*. One might be tempted to read in this process the growing influence of Iran, which had by now been reorganized by her Sassanian kings. These transformed Zoroastrianism into a hierarchical state based on a unified doctrine. The Sassanian dynasties ruled for a while over the greater part of central Asia and, even after their withdrawal behind the Margian frontiers, they continued to exercise their cultural influence over the principalities which had replaced them. The custom of flesh removal and the preservation of bones within special ossuaries now became widespread all over central Asia; the latter practice indeed indicates a certain independence from Iran, where the preservation of parts of the body was not regarded as an indispensable condition for resurrection.

The dead were placed in collective dog pens tended by "untouchables" or, if the family had the means, on private platforms (a Sogdian bill of sale has been found relating to a structure of this type). Once they had been put in the ossuaries the bones were then deposited in family tombs, simple graves or small tomb houses, which relatives visited each New Year, bringing offerings of food. Dogs were venerated above all other animals, and got the same respect as the dead humans.

Funerary buildings always faced east and the ossuaries were often perforated because, according to the Zoroastrian beliefs, the dead would rise again at the first light of dawn. The ossuaries themselves represent, by their form, their decoration and also their inscriptions, a leading source of information on the lives and religion of the people. The hollow statues of the preceding period gave way to ordinary jars, boxes, and funerary edifices. The dead person was only referred to indirectly, such as by means of doorknobs in the form of human heads, or birds symbolizing the soul, whereas the walls were decorated in more elaborate style, especially in Sogdia. Here the motifs might refer either to a belief in the afterlife or to the rituals of the funeral. Among the latter, it is interesting to note that scenes of lamentation were depicted sometimes showing the practice of voluntary mutilation. This custom was formally condemned by the religious texts, and deemed worthy of damnation both for the participants and for the dead person. Obviously the practice must have been deeply rooted in Central Asia, as it was in the steppes regions, so much so that the local priesthood had neither the means nor the will to put an end to it. This is demonstrated by the fact that, within the same tombs in Chorasmia, some ossuaries show scenes of lamentation and others are inscribed with prayers and blessings that are purely Zoroastrian. The lamentation customs have survived to the present as a traditional practice in certain areas, notwithstanding the influence of Islam.

At the same period, these funerary customs spread to the north-east, to the lands ruled by the first Turkish empire, transversed by the routes of the Asiatic merchants, slowly converted to urban civilization. The new practices were strongly resisted by the Buddhists, who remained loyal to the Indian custom of cremation. This could explain the almost total absence of ossuaries in Bactria, where Buddhism had long been widespread. However, they were present in the Jewish and Christian communities of central Asia—a surprising discovery revealed by recent fieldwork. This may well have been the result, at least in the case of the Christian communities, of the missionary zeal of Nestorian* Christianity, where the mass of new converts remained firmly attached to their local customs.

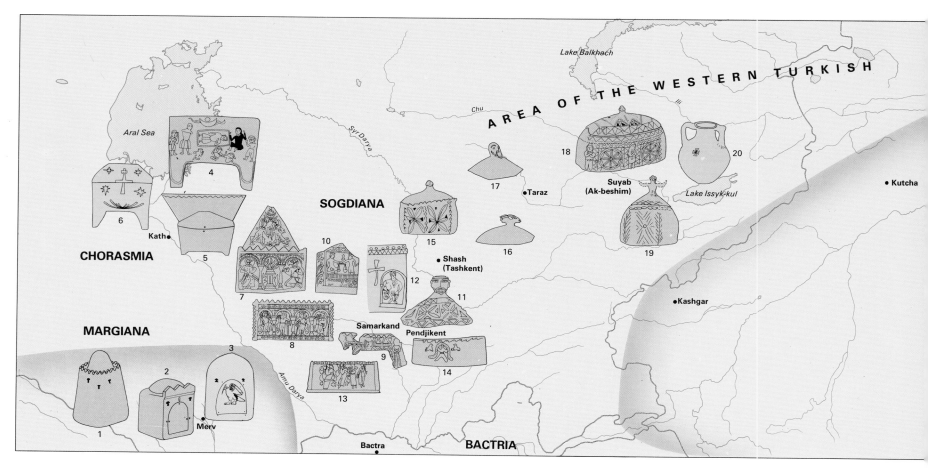

Royal mausoleum of Koj-Krylgan-Kala (Chorasmia, 4th–2nd century BC)

Above: general reconstruction (after M.S. Lapirov-Skoblo)

The construction materials consist of mud brick mixed with cob. The purpose of the upper part of the tower remains uncertain: traces of ash suggest a funerary pyre open to the sky to some specialists, while for others they indicate the destruction by fire of a temple celebrating a cult of dead kings. The space between the tower and the enclosing wall was inhabited, perhaps originally by priests of the cult. Size: exterior wall, diameter 93m (307ft); central tower, diameter 42m (139ft), height 9m (30ft).

Right: plan of Lower storey of the tower

Stairways located at the two ends provided access to the outside and were walled up after the bodies had been arranged for burial. These, a target for tomb robbers from antiquity, had been laid out in rooms lit by high windows, apart from room VIII, which was closed off by a partition and a ditch, and must have contained the most precious burial. The layout, consisting of a rectangular arrangement on a circular background, is characteristic of Scythian funerary architecture from the Syr Darya region.

well

pit

N.

eastern limit of Sassanid Persia

western limit of Tang China

(between them: sovereign principalities under western Turkish hegemony)

Principal types of ossuary just before the Islamic conquest (7th–8th centuries AD)

Zoroastrian ossuaries

Jewish ossuaries

Christian (Nestorian) ossuaries

● Beshbaligh

21

Turfan ●

Tuen Huang

Tarim

Tuen Huang

1   Merv: miniature funeral tower
2   Merv: miniature mausoleum (arched gateway, cupola, battlements)
3   Merv: Jewish cemetery (dove from Noah's ark)
4   Tok-Kala: lamentation scene (dead body stretched out, widow in black, astral symbols)
5   Berkut-Kala: ossuary with fixed canopy for the ritual of adoration (restoration)
6   Mizdakhkan: Nestorian cross, stars, ribbons
7   Mullakurgan (Samarkand region): lower part service for the dead (the priests wear masks in order not to pollute the fire altar); upper part, symbols of stars and dancers.
8   Bija-Najman (Samarkand region): gods and goddesses displaying symbols of the final resurrection of the dead (left to right, post and plant for the ceremonial drink; sacred fire; auspicious gesture; casket and key)
9   Samarkand: lamentation scene
10   Samarkand (incomplete ossuary): weighing the soul. The figure on the right holds the dead person in one hand and with the other a weight symbolizing his acts
11   Samarkand: cover with human head
12   Samarkand (detail): Nestorian cross; David holding a sling and the head of Goliath
13   Uzkishlak (southern Sogdiana): dance scene with harp player
14   Pendjikent: dance scene with birds
15   Tashkent region: floral motifs, cover with human head
16   Pskent (Tashkent region); cover with joined heads of ram and goat
17   Taraz: cover with head of old man
18   Krasnorechenskoe (Suyab region): cover with human head and lamentation scene (the central figure has gashed his cheeks)
19   Ossuary found near the previous site: cover featuring a hooded hunting falcon
20   Suyab: jug with Nestorian cross, used as an ossuary
21   Beshbaligh: Nestorian cross, cover with human head

Ossuaries shown on the map include only the most representative examples, indicated according to their religion and place of discovery. Apart from nos. 1 and 3, which are of stucco, all are terracotta objects, averaging 50–60cm (20–24in) in length and 30–40cm (12–16in) in height or width. The form may refer directly (nos. 1, 2) or indirectly (nos. 3, 8, 9, 14) to funerary buildings with military decoration, such as battlements and archer windows, which anticipate in their appearance the Islamic mausolea of this region.

Decoration is sometimes painted (nos. 3, 4, 5), but more often moulded or modelled in relief. Zoroastrian ossuaries display a very varied iconographic imagery: some refer to end of the world myths known from the texts of this religion (nos. 8,9); others illustrate funerary ceremonies such as the typically Zoroastrian cult of fire (no. 7), and also lamentation rituals condemned by the clergy but shown here in a sometimes violent form (nos. 4, 9) or in a calmer fashion (no. 18). The dance scenes are more difficult to interpret (nos. 7, 13, 14); they may also be part of the funeral ceremony, or they may allude to the happiness of paradise. The dead person is often symbolized by the handle (nos. 11, 15, 17). The nomadic peoples who adopted Zoroastrian funeral practices modified this iconography in accordance with their own beliefs, including protective heads of horned animals (no. 16), or a soul metamorphosed into a hunting falcon (no. 19).

Jewish and Christian ossuaries are characterized by particular symbols (nos. 3, 6, 20, 21); in one example the image of David as conqueror of Goliath is used as a sign of victory over death (no. 12). Ossuary no. 21, the only example so far discovered in China, reflects the role played by Nestorian merchants from Sogdiana in the spread of Christianity to the Far East.

The Indian World:
the archaeological background

From the mighty Bronze Age civilization of the Indus valley to the
Greek-influenced art of Gandhara, the subcontinent of India contains an
archaeological heritage of unparalleled diversity and richness.

From the mid-18th century, officials in the service of the East India Company began to show an interest in the archaeological remains they found in the course of the rapid colonization of the continent. The Asiatic Society of Calcutta was founded in 1784 in order to further the study of Asian history and antiquities. Subsequently, throughout the 19th century, officials, army officers and enlightened amateurs took advantage of their travels and tours of inspection to record the monuments of ancient India, bringing to light its prestigious past, but from the perspective of the romantic climate then current in European thinking. From the middle of the 19th century, studies became more systematic under the direction of General Alexander Cunningham*, whose mission was officially supported by the Governor of India. His research was mainly devoted to identifying the sites mentioned in ancient written sources, such as the texts describing Alexander's campaign and the travel accounts of Chinese Buddhist pilgrims.

The beginning of genuine site archaeology can be dated to 1851 when Colonel Meadow Taylor published a remarkable report of the excavations of megalithic tombs in the Deccan. The accuracy of this study was in happily sharp contrast to the practices of the period, when people commonly destroyed Buddhist stupas with pickaxes in order to steal their reliquaries. In 1856, Cunningham went to visit Harappa* in the Punjab (now part of Pakistan), where workmen had just discovered the ruins of one of the great Bronze Age major cities. Admittedly he did not realize the importance of this discovery, but out of curiosity he sent the British Museum some Harappan antiquities with seals bearing mysterious pictograms. As the west began to take an interest in its remote Stone Age ancestors, Robert Bruce Foot discovered the evidence of the first Indian Paleolithic peoples. This discovery was followed by many others in nearly every region of the subcontinent, yielding rich collections of stone choppers*, chopper tools*, flake tools and blades of various types and shapes.

The Archaeological Survey of India
In 1904, Lord Curzon created the Archaeological Survey of India which centralized many Indian archaeological activities. From 1904 to 1934, its first director, Sir John Marshall*, did excellent work with the aid of numerous British and Indian collaborators.

Priority was still given to excavating the great historical sites. Taxila, the town where, by repute, Alexander stayed before it became a provincial capital of the Mauryan and Kushan empires, was the object of extensive excavations. The great Buddhist sites of Sarnath, where Buddha preached the law, and Sanchi, with its stupas and their splendid sculptured gateways, were uncovered. These excavations and the studies of great cave sanctuaries such as Ajanta and Ellora revealed the richness of the Indian cultural heritage and so contributed to the building up of a national consciousness in the decades preceding independence.

The chance discovery in 1920 of Mohenjo-Daro on the banks of the Indus and the rediscovery in 1921 of Harappa, the site already visited by Cunningham, encouraged Marshall to undertake two vast excavation projects. The excavations of Mohenjo-Daro and Harappa and later of Chanhu-Daro revealed the existence on the river banks of a great civilization, remarkable for the quality of its urban life and its system of private and public hygiene. The interest taken in this civilization with its aura of mystery increased when the discovery of a number of these Indus seals found at various Mesopotamian sites, showed that it had maintained relations with

Sumerian towns at the end of the 3rd millennium BC. Similarly, explorations by Sir Aurel Stein in Baluchistan and by Majumdar in Sind led to the discovery of many Chalcolithic (Copper Age) sites, some older than the Indus civilization, some contemporary with it.

The exploration undertaken by De Terra and Paterson in 1935 in the foothills of the Himalayas made important discoveries. The investigations succeeded in relating the terraces of the Soăn valley, rich in Paleolithic deposits, to the glacial phases of the Himalayas, which they thought they could connect with the European glacial phases. This study still serves as a point of reference for most research into the Paleolithic industries of the north of the Indian subcontinent.

After the war years, which caused a break in archaeological activity, Sir Mortimer Wheeler* was summoned to India in 1944 to reorganize the Archaeological Survey. In three years, he accomplished a remarkable task that has become almost legendary in the world of Indo-Pakistani archaeology. The school of archaeology he set up at the time taught excavation techniques, insisting on the importance of stratigraphy* and the accurate study of material, using strict and clear methods of recording. The Wheeler method was put into practice on the great training digs at Brahmagiri, a megalithic site in the south of India, and Harappa (excavation of the cemetery and the rampart). On these digs the students were trained who were later to become the leading figures in Indian and Pakistani archaeology.

Paleolithic investigations
After independence, the Department of Archaeology of Pakistan was founded at Karachi to complement the Archaeological Survey of India. On-site researches multiplied despite financial difficulties. The field of study devoted to the Paleolithic Age in particular flourished, thanks to work carried out by the Deccan College of Poona (Pune). As regards the Lower Paleolithic period, work centred on the study of collections of comparatively crude bifaces (bifacial, or double-faced tools) which were connected with the European, African and Central Asian phase of the period known as the Acheulian*. Nevertheless, there is nothing enabling us to date these artifacts, most of which come from areas where they have been deposited by floods. Even in the case of deposits where the material is still in place, as at Hungsi in the Karnataka, the absence of organic remains or anything to show the presence of dwellings leaves us without information about the way of life of the Lower Paleolithic people with whom it has been impossible as yet to associate any remains.

There is rather more information about the Middle Paleolithic period, but it is mainly confined to the studies of collections of flake tools which exhibit parallels with the phase known as the Mousterian of western and central Asia. This applies particularly to finds in Nevasa, Maharashtra and Luni at the foot of the Aravalli. Nevertheless, in spite of the discovery of habitats still in place, notably in caves at Bhimbetka in the Vindhya Mountains, it has not yet been possible to make any study of the organic remains at these deposits, some of which have recently been dated by Carbon 14* to between 35,000 and 8000 BC. Several other sites may well be even older. In the north of Pakistan, a mission from Cambridge University, in collaboration with the Department of Archaeology of Pakistan, has resumed the work of De Terra and Paterson in the Soăn valley. Vast areas used as "workshops" for the production of chopper tools supplied important evidence, and the British team dated the deposits found to the Middle Paleolithic period.

J.-L. Princelle

The Buddhist rock sanctuary of Tin Tali at Ellora, India

Illustration by Thomas and William Daniell (after a drawing by J. Wales in 1795), from *A Picturesque Voyage to India by Way of China*, London, 1810

The Buddhist caves of Tin Tali are part of a complex of 7th and 8th century rock sanctuaries carved out of the cliff of Ellora in the Bombay region. In the late 18th and early 19th century, the Daniells' illustrations helped to inform Europe about India's rich cultural heritage and to encourage the enlightened amateurs who undertook the first archaeological and epigraphical researches in this part of the world. Private collection, Paris.

As for the Upper Paleolithic period, the sites, which have yielded a set of stone tools of ever-decreasing size, are few in number. The following phase may have been marked by the advent of a wetter and more favourable climate, which would explain the large number of sites from this period discovered during the last 20 years. These sites are characterized by the presence of very small stone artifacts, in particular geometric microliths (segments, triangles and trapezes), which were used to make arrows and harpoons during a period when hunting and fishing techniques were very much improved. Such pieces resemble the tools of the Near Eastern Mesolithic period (*c*.12,000–10,000 before present or BP), but most of these sites in western India are not so old. Some excavations, notably at Bagor in Rajasthan and Adamghar have brought to light caves decorated with rock paintings, which show that the people often called "Mesolithic" practised a mixed economy combining hunter-gatherer activities with agriculture in a chronological context roughly contemporary with that of the Neolithic and Chalcolithic communities of Baluchistan and Sind from the 7th to the 3rd millennia. Villages have recently been discovered in the valley of the Ganges where hunting and fishing with very small shaped points (geometric microliths) was combined with a still rudimentary agriculture which gradually specialized in rice growing.

The affects of partitioning

Research into the Chalcolithic cultures of Baluchistan and Sind on the one hand and the Indus civilization on the other has inevitably been affected by the division of the Indian subcontinent into two states. The northwestern provinces and the Indus valley became Pakistani territory in 1947. During the 1950s and 1960s Pakistani teams and foreign missions have tried to provide a geographical and chronological framework for a whole group of Chalcolithic cultures in Baluchistan, Sind and the Punjab, roughly preceding the Indus civilization, while seeking to understand their relation to the latter. In Sind, the Pakistani excavations of Kot Diji (1955–1957) and the French excavations of Amri (1959–1962) have helped to establish a chronological grid for cultures more usually defined in a highly artificial way on the basis of different pottery styles. Until very recently, scholars seeing stylistic resemblance in the field of pottery between Iranian and Central Asian sites gave these cultures (or rather pseudo-cultures) very late dates, between 3500 and 2500BC, which made them out to be marginal and backward branches of the civilizations of western Asia. This made it hard to explain how a highly developed civilization like the Indus could have appeared suddenly towards 2300BC out of such a sluggish cultural context. But since 1974 the excavations of Mehgarh, which have revealed the existence in the Indus regions of a rich Neolithic culture from 7000BC and a Chalcolithic sequence marked by an impressive economic organization, enable us to place the Indus civilization in its genuine cultural context.

The "loss" to Pakistan of the great sites of the Indus stimulated research in the Indian provinces bordering on Pakistan. This quickly yielded spectacular results with the discovery and excavation of towns such as Kalibnagan in Rajasthan and Lothal in Gujarat, cities from the mature phase of the Indus civilization, *c*.2000BC. Several hundred sites, influenced in varying degrees by the Harappan civilization, have been discovered throughout the northwest of present-day India, as well as in the region of Delhi.

In peninsular India, thanks especially to the work of the Deccan College of Poona, many sites enabling us to follow the stages of the agricultural exploitation of these regions from 2000BC have been catalogued and studied.

Their pottery styles (black and red ceramics and painted pottery of the Malva and Jorwe styles) also serve to establish the chronological (2000–800BC) and geographical framework of these villages, while the hunter-gatherer economy still thriving in the Iron Age at Langanaj in Gujarat tends to recede, and to continue only in isolated areas, where it still persists today to some extent. Indian archaeologists have also been able to establish relations between Chalcolithic sites in the Deccan and the so-called "Neolithic" establishments of southern India, the oldest of which date to the 2nd millennium. It is now possible to confirm links between the Deccan villages in the Jorwe pottery period, *c*.1000BC, and the oldest sites with megalithic burials in the south of India, which still existed in the historic period when commercial contacts with the Roman empire were established. Thus all the research carried out in peninsular India in recent years has given us a better understanding of the social and economic organization of groups which served as a substratum for the population of India in the historic period.

Another important field of research since independence has involved investigation of on-site traces of the first Indo-Aryan kingdoms, known from the Vedic texts which were reputedly composed between the end of the 2nd and the beginning of the 1st millennium BC. These investigations have resulted in the discovery of many sites, either earlier than or corresponding to the early Bronze Age, throughout the middle valley of the Ganges. But the tendency to identify a pottery style, in this case the painted grey pottery present in many sites of the Ganges valley, with a particular ethnic group, the Indo-Aryan invaders, conceals the need to make a serious and detailed analysis of the material culture of the first great agricultural communities of northern India at the beginning of the Iron Age.

At the level of historical archaeology, the need to preserve the countless monuments discovered before independence has taken up much of the archaeological services' time, although the Italian excavations of Butkara in Pakistani Swat from 1956 to 1962 have made a major contribution to our knowledge of the Graeco-Buddhist civilization of Gandhara. More recently the German excavations of Sonkh place important monuments of Mathura art of the Kushan period (2nd century BC to 2nd century AD) in a sequence going back to the Iron Age (period of painted grey pottery). Indian excavations of Purana Qila, one of the old forts of Delhi, have also pushed back the history of the present-day capital of India to the early Iron Age. For its part, the Department of Archaeology of Pakistan has concentrated on the study of sites from the beginning of the Islamic conquest, in particular Banbhore and Mansurah.

Agricultural origins in the Indian subcontinent

Archaeology has recently pushed back the date of the earliest villages in the subcontinent by some 2,000 years, and has shown that a sophisticated agriculture was established by local peoples.

For a long time archaeologists ascribed the first appearance of settled villages in the north west of the subcontinent to groups originating from Iran, who were thought to have established themselves in the south of Afghanistan, particularly at Mundigak, and then in Baluchistan from 4000BC. However, recent excavations at Mehrgarh in Baluchistan indicate that in a region at the foot of mountains on the edge of the Indus valley peoples were from the beginning of the 7th millennium BC cultivating cereals around a large built-up area consisting of sturdy buildings made of mud bricks.

Groups of hunter-gatherers from the Upper Paleolithic, the predecessors of the first agriculturists in this area, are known to us only through large areas where flints were chipped, and the sites of camps on some hills in the Indus valley. However, the swampy banks of the Indus with their thick jungle cover were better suited to hunting and fishing than to the development of basic agriculture. The Baluchistan foothills, on the other hand, offered a succession of varied ecological zones, ranging in altitude from alluvial floor plains to mountain valleys, supplying a variety of habitats for plant, animal and mineral resources which were easy to exploit with limited mobility. Near the Mehrgarh site the low-lying ground in the Bolan basin, which was prone to flooding, allowed cereals like barley that grew wild in Baluchistan to be cultivated almost spontaneously. But because the harvesting period was short, the first inhabitants of Mehrgarh found it necessary to construct important storage buildings with mud brick walls that have been uncovered, often well-preserved at Neolithic levels. Archaeologists have discovered a large quantity of charred grain and imprints of cereals in the plasterwork and bricks of the buildings, and these, together with a study of the animal life of the region, permits a reconstruction of the subsistence patterns of these communities in the Neolithic. At the beginning of the 7th millennium, barley (*Hordeum vulgare*) was the main crop, whereas wheat (*Triticum monococcum, T. dicoccum, T. Durum*) is found on a much smaller scale; meat as a food source was supplied almost solely by hunting, as indicated by the presence in the earliest levels of the Neolithic of a large number of bones from gazelles, wild goats, wild sheep, wild cattle, nilgais, onagers, barasinghas, wild boar and sometimes buffalo. However, domesticated goats, sometimes found in burial places, were also present in a context where hunting activity in the tradition of the Upper Paleolithic was still dominant. But in the course of the 7th millennium, domestication of a clearly local type took place whereby an increasing number of goats, sheep and cattle altered the economic basis of these first Neolithic communities. Towards 6000BC, hunting ceased to be important and animal-rearing, especially cattle-rearing, almost completely replaced it. New strains of barley and wheat which were hardy and well-suited to flood irrigation (*H.* and *T. Sphaerococcum*) appeared at the time when the big collective mud-brick granaries occupied large areas on the edge of the inhabited areas.

With regard to craft activities, the Neolithic peoples of the 7th millennium did not yet make pottery, but used bitumen-coated baskets. They excelled in making ornaments from stone, sometimes semi-precious ones such as lapis lazuli or turquoise, from sea shells and from bones. Very fine sets of jewellery have been found on skeletons from large cemeteries. Receptacles made of very crude pottery appear after 6000BC.

Hunters and farmers

In the mountains, uninhabited during the very severe winters, the site of Kili Ghul Mohammed, near Quetta, has a stratigraphical sequence with an earliest phase that could go back to the Neolithic. Over a depth of several metres, but in a probe going down only 1.2m (4ft), deposits without pottery have produced flints and bones from wild animals and domesticated goats.

To the east of the Indus, in continental India, Indian archaeologists have found numerous strata relating to hunter-gatherers; many seem to be contemporary with the first agricultural peoples of Baluchistan who, as we have seen, still hunted on a large scale. The tool kit of these crop-growing hunters in Baluchistan and the Indus area included composite arrowheads, made up of geometric microliths* in the tradition of the epi-Paleolithic* of western Asia. It is possible that contacts between these communities in Baluchistan and around the Indus, and the hunting and gathering peoples of continental India, promoted the diffusion of these types of composite arrowheads into hunters' camps in Gujarat, Rajasthan and central India, probably from the 7th millennium. This improvement in hunting methods coincides with the adoption of agricultural practices by the continental Indian hunter-gatherers, in particular goat-rearing, and the appearance of pottery and metal objects (Bagor, Rajasthan, 4th millennium), influenced by the Neolithic and Chalcolithic communities of Baluchistan and the Indus valley.

In the caves in the Vindhya Mountains, overlooking the valley of the Ganges, deposits with a wealth of microliths including composite arrowheads have been found under walls decorated with paintings that depict hunting scenes where bow and arrow are used. These communities, which were also already rearing goats, as can be seen in the Adamgarh caves, spread into the Ganges valley where they founded villages of circular huts near ancient lakes left by the meandering course of the river, like those at Sarai-Nahar-Rai and Mahadaba, near Allahabad, or along tributaries of the Ganges, at Mahagara or Chopani Mando. These first villages, with tombs near the houses containing skeletons lying full-length, sometimes with ornaments and offerings of food, mark the beginning of the exploitation of the natural resources of the Ganges valley, and in particular of the rice which grew wild there. It is difficult to establish precisely the date of these Ganges sites which have been discovered very recently. But most experts tend to place these communities which, along with hunting, fishing and gathering were already involved in rearing zebus and goats, and probably in cultivating rice, in a time scale which would be no earlier than the 5th or 4th millennium.

The sum of this new information from Baluchistan and the Ganges valley enables us to understand the beginnings of the agricultural economy in the Indian sub-continent. In this process the contacts between peoples which, like those of Mehrgarh or Kili Gul Mohammad in Baluchistan, are linked geographically to western Asia, and communities whose ways of life are more specific to southern Asia and in particular to the Ganges valley, have played an important part.

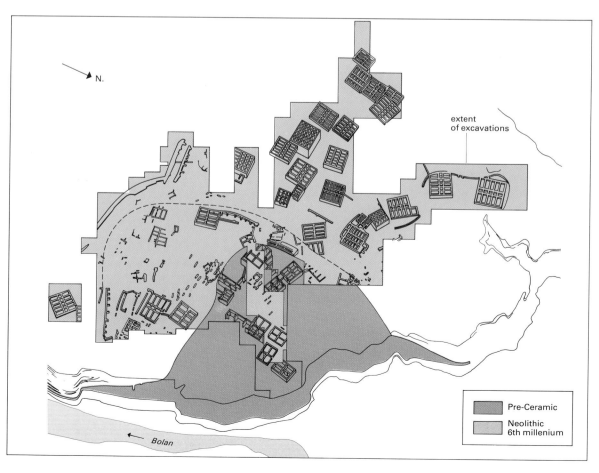

Overall plan of the Neolithic town of Mehrgarh (7th and 6th millennia BC)

Remains from the pre-ceramic period (in black and grey tint), cut through by the river Bolan, form a bank 7m (23ft) high, composed of the mud-brick ruins of rectangular buildings divided into four or six symmetrical rooms. Between the various building levels cemetery areas are interposed. In the part shown in white, on the edge of the pre-ceramic settlement, buildings divided into compartments or boxes form a vast group of storage buildings from the 6th millennium, built on terraces bordered by retaining walls.

N.

extent of excavations

Pre-Ceramic

Neolithic 6th millennium

Bolan

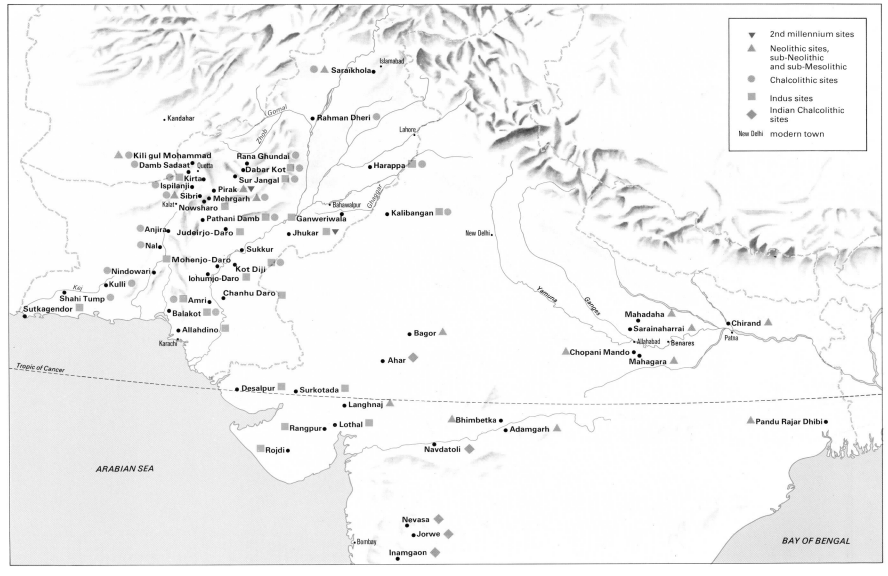

Legend:
- ▽ 2nd millennium sites
- ▲ Neolithic sites, sub-Neolithic and sub-Mesolithic
- ● Chalcolithic sites
- ■ Indus sites
- ◆ Indian Chalcolithic sites
- New Delhi modern town

Principal prehistoric sites in the north of the Indo-Pakistani subcontinent

The earliest sites, Neolithic and Chalcolithic (7th–4th millennium), are mainly concentrated in the valleys and foothills of Baluchistan. In the Harappa period the Indus valley became the centre of economic life, while colonies were founded in the west and southwest of present-day India. The group of sub-Mesolithic or sub-Neolithic sites in the Indian interior and the valley of the Ganges must certainly go back to the 4th millennium, while the Chalcolithic sites in the Deccan date from the 2nd millennium.

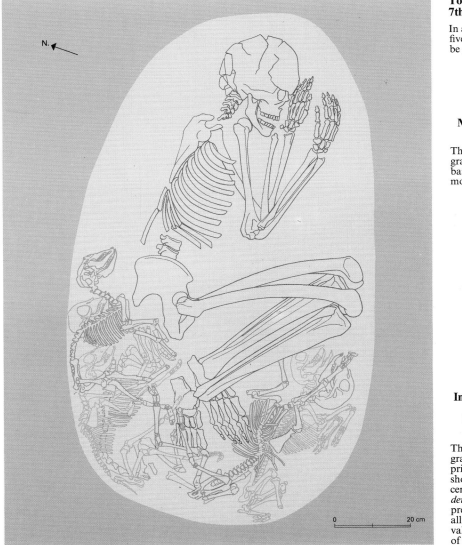

Tomb of an adult male, buried with five young goats, Mehrgarh. Neolithic, beginning of 7th millennium

In a context where meat as a food source was supplied almost solely by hunting, the presence of five kids in this tomb, and in another one nearby, suggests that goat-husbandry was beginning to be practised.

Detail of a grave at Mehrgarh. Neolithic, 7th millennium

The woman buried in this grave was wearing a head-band made of shells and a mother-of-pearl pendant.

Imprint of an ear of wheat (*Triticum dicoccum*), Mehrgarh. Beginning of 7th millennium

The discovery of charred grains and thousands of imprints of barley and wheat shows the importance of cereal-growing; barley (*Hordeum vulgare*) was the preferred crop on the rich alluvial land in the Bolan valley right at the beginning of the Neolithic.

Baluchistan villages and Indus cities

Modern archaeological research has been able to show how the development of agricultural techniques and the spread of Neolithic villages in Baluchistan was to form the prelude to the magnificent city civilization of the Indus in the third millennium BC.

At the end of the 6th millennium and during the 5th millennium BC, the way of life and craft activities of the early Neolithic period underwent a gradual transformation. Rough pottery yielded to glossy red wares of finer quality, and this in turn gave way, during the 5th millennium, to a pottery style initially making use of simple geometric motifs, and later, shortly before 4000BC, developing a more complex decoration associated with animals and birds.

This type of decoration resembles that found on certain sites of the Iranian plateau; it is fairly common in the Baluchistan sites and even further west, in Afghanistan at the time of the foundation of Mundigak. Mehrgarh (eastern Baluchistan) is the only well-known site dating from this period, and here archaeologists have found remains dating from the end of the 5th millennium and extending over almost 70 hectares (168 acres). They include large groups of store rooms very much in the tradition of the compartmentalized buildings of the Neolithic; areas where pots were thrown; stonemasons' workrooms where lathes were operated by belts or bows ending in small green-jasper drills (a system enabling a piece of wood to be turned by pressure on the belt, often attached to a bow which was wound and unwound to generate a regular rotation); and burial grounds with a large concentration of tombs, apparently indicating a considerable population density. By the end of the 5th millennium, too, the cultivation of wheat tended to become more important and to replace, in part, that of barley, which was predominant in the Neolithic. Similarly, sheep and goats became more widely bred, although cattle continued to predominate.

The development of a more diversified agriculture, better suited to the exploitation of new territories, led to an increase in the number of settlements after 4000BC, and a wide network of villages and towns appeared in the valleys of Baluchistan and in the areas bordering the Indus Valley. A few villages were built in the fertile alluvial valley of the Indus, such as Amri, founded before 3500BC, at a time when the banks of the river began to change from marshy jungle to agricultural land. It was the exploitation of this land which later supplied the food resources necessary for the large urban developments of the second half of the 3rd millennium.

The end of the 4th and the beginning of the 3rd millennium correspond with a phase of population increase; in Baluchistan, the number of settlements continued to grow, as they did in the Indus Valley and along its tributaries, particularly the Hakra, near the frontier between Pakistan and India. Ceramic styles, figurines, tablets, and several other objects provide archaeologists with the means to identify vast, relatively homogeneous cultural areas. The art of painted ceramic reached its height at about this time: the grey ceramic with black decoration produced in the Kachi valley, in Baluchistan, was exported as far as eastern Iran. The elegant polychrome pottery in the style of the Nal necropolis, and the Quetta style wares, with their geometrical motifs so similar to those painted by the potters of Turkmenistan in the days of the Namazga III culture, also spread far and wide. The variety of human figurines, sometimes of great artistic quality, are also characteristic of the period from 3000 to 2500BC, a time when numerous contacts were established between the Indus Valley, Baluchistan, the Hilmand culture in Afghanistan (Mundigak III and IV) and Iran (Shahr-i-Sokhta), and southern Central Asia of the Manazga III phase. These contacts and exchanges stimulated economic activities and encouraged the growth of increasingly specialized craft production; and also the formation of social structures upon which the development of the large Indus Valley cities, such as Mohenjo-Daro and Harappa, was based in the second half of the 3rd millennium.

Indus Valley civilization

It seems clear today that the Indus civilization comes directly within a framework of economic and cultural structures found in the same region, whose history can be traced from the Neolithic to the middle of the 3rd millennium. These links with older local cultures undoubtedly explain the originality of this civilization when it is compared, for instance, with Mesopotamia in the same period. Nevertheless, in view of the remarkable expansion of the Indus civilization, characterized not only by the building of large cities like Mohenjo-Daro and Harappa, sometimes over an area of more than 100 hectares (240 acres), but also by the diffusion of a highly standardized material culture over a huge area (from Makran in the west to the Delhi region in the east, and from the site of Shortughai in northern Afghanistan to Gujarat in the south), all this has led several authorities to propose a vast Harappan empire controlled by a rigid political organization.

However, the existence of a political entity, determined to emphasize its presence and power by means of material manifestations, is not suggested by any particular imagery or iconographical representation, any document, or any religious or secular monument, as it is in the case of Mesopotamia or Egypt. A large pool surrounded by a colonnade was found in the citadel of Mohenjo-Daro, and may suggest the existence of ceremonial activities connected with ablution rites, particulary in view of the proximity of a building made up of rows of "bathrooms". In fact, the concern for urban life and for systems of hygiene, both public and private, gives the large Indus Valley cities their exceptional character, unique in the whole of the ancient East. The spacious dwellings of the lower part of Mohenjo-Daro, with their sanitary installations linked to a whole network of sewers, may indicate the existence of a bourgeois merchant oligarchy who would have benefited from the development of commercial exchange routes on a trans-Asiatic scale. The objects typical of this civilization include a whole range of weights and inscribed tablets, examples of which have been found not only in the Indus Valley and neighbouring areas but also in the region of the Persian gulf and in Mesopotamia; and this at a time when the texts mention commercial contacts with "Melukhkha", an important eastern country that can be identified with the Indus Valley. It is to be regretted that, despite several attempts at decipherment, the writing of the Indus, comprising over 400 pictograms, is still unknown.

Other objects, particularly in ivory, testify to the links between the Indus Valley and the cities of the urban phase of the Namazga V culture in southern Turkmenistan. This period (second half of the 3rd millennium) corresponds with the decline of the Hilmand culture in Iran (Shahr-i-Sokhta) and Afghanistan (Mundigak), and also with the development of the brilliant Bronze Age culture of Bactria* and Margiana (Afghanistan, Uzbekistan and eastern Turkmenistan), as well as with a phase of prosperity for sites such as Shahdad in eastern Iran. All these places have yielded tablets, cylinder seals and stone and metal objects belonging to an interregional style which was typical of the area between Susiana and northern Iran (Hissar III) on one side, and Bactria and the Indus valley on the other.

The active role played by Baluchistan in the establishment of these exchange routes and contacts between various cultural groups at the end of the 3rd millennium, is further demonstrated by the discovery of similar objects in the burial ground of Mehrgarh VIII and on the site near Sibri. The latter yielded cylinders obviously derived from Mesopotamia or Iranian prototypes, amulets in the Bactrian and Margian style, and an amulet inscribed with two different characters of Indus writing.

Vessels with polychrome decoration, Nal, Baluchistan, c.3000BC

At the beginning of the 1930s, the Nal burial ground yielded an impressive amount of polychrome pottery, which testifies, together with another contemporary grey pottery decorated with plant, animal or geometrical themes, to the high quality of earthenware products at the start of the 3rd millennium BC.

Painted jar, Nindowari, Baluchistan, c.2200BC

The zebu occupied an important place in the imagery of the Kulli culture, which flourished in southern Baluchistan at the same time as the civilization of the Indus Valley. Paintings of zebus are often accompanied by a whole group of painted signs which relate to a symbol system characteristic of the epoch when writing first appears.

Aerial view of part of the citadel of Mohenjo-Daro, 2nd half of 3rd millennium

The "Great Bath" appears here as a rectangular pit or pool, made of fired bricks and measuring 11.7 × 6.9m (37 × 22ft) and with a depth of 2.4m (7.6ft), into which a stair descended. Surrounded by colonnades, the "Great Bath" was fed by a well which can be seen beside it on the left, near a street where the drains are covered with blocks of limestone. The pool was emptied through a corbelled channel which ran under the colonnades on the right. To the right of the pool, there stands a group of platforms, made of fired bricks. Some authorities have regarded this, without conclusive proof, as the substructure of a warehouse where the ventilation came through the narrow corridors between the blocks.

White stone cylinder and impression—Sibri, Baluchistan, end of 3rd millennium

This complex scene shows a zebu attacked by a lion, and a figure carrying on his shoulders a branch or a lance, one end forming the shape of a fish; other animals are more difficult to identify. This object, stylistically close to the cylinders found in eastern Iran and Central Asia, is a good indication of the commercial exchanges which characterized the second half of the 3rd millennium BC.

The second agricultural revolution

The period after the Indus civilization is a key moment in the subcontinent's history; elements inherited from the Neolithic and Chalcolithic periods were then combined with new phenomena, forming the foundations of ancient India's civilization.

We still do not know the exact causes which brought about the end of the cities of the Indus civilization *c*.1800–1700BC. The city of Mohenjo-Daro went through a period of decline before it was abandoned, thus apparently marking the beginning of some crisis at a period when Harappa* was deserted. There is no shortage of hypotheses to explain these phenomena: impoverishment of over-exploited and salinated soil, natural catastrophes, or the arrival of invaders, the vanguard of the Indo-Aryan* groups which, on the basis of linguistic evidence, seem to have been present at the end of the 2nd millennium on the Indo-Gangetic plains. Some experts combine all these hypotheses, borrowing from each as they see fit. Nonetheless at some point or other in these explanations the theme of invasion comes through. This provides an explanation for the presence of a large number of skeletons which were found in the ruins of Mohenjo-Daro, supposedly the victims of the celebrated "final massacre" of the city. However, it now seems increasingly certain that many of these bodies, which were hastily thrown into pits, in fact correspond to several periods of occupation in the city and could not be considered evidence of a "final massacre" where there is otherwise no evidence of sudden destruction.

The arrival of invaders from Central Asia, usually described as semi-nomadic herdsmen, is given by several researchers as an explanation for the apparent absence of settled urban areas in the Indus area after 1700BC and, by way of contrast, the formation of a great many settlements to the east of the Indus, in Haryana (the Delhi area), and in the south, in Gujurat. The new herding communities must have destroyed the foundations of the settled agricultural economy on the Indus plain, and the inhabitants would have fled towards the eastern areas of the old Harappan empire.

Very recently, more systematic explorations have shown that Baluchistan and the Indus did not become mere areas of pasturage in the 2nd millennium. For example, some 50 late Harappa or post-Harappa sites have just been identified along a tributary of the Indus, the Hakra. Some of these sites are large enough to qualify as real towns, though they do not have the characteristic features of Harappa town-planning. This decline in the great cities of the Indus may perhaps be partly associated with the crisis in inter-Asiatic trade mentioned in Mesopotamian texts of *c*.1800BC, in which references to "Melukhkha" almost disappear; but it does not mean that agricultural production fell, as is shown by excavations at Pirak, at the exit of the Bolan pass onto the Indus plain. Pirak was a large town covering a surface area of about 9 hectares (22 acres), occupied from 1800 to 700BC, with solidly built houses, craftsmen's workshop areas, and agricultural buildings which have revealed not only winter cereals—wheat or barley—which were cultivated in the 3rd millennium, but also summer cereals—rice, millet and sorghum—which were unknown in the Indus valley prior to 2000BC. In Pirak we can see the introduction and establishment of the agrarian system of southern Asia, characterized by its several harvests in each year. Thus in the 2nd millennium there was a genuine agricultural revolution, whereas the 3rd millennium still remained within the general context of the agrarian economy of the Near East.

A new agriculture

If an economic crisis really did erupt on the alluvial plains at the beginning of the 2nd millennium, it was resolved by increasing agricultural production thanks to importing cereals grown in the surrounding areas which were increasingly in contact with the Harappa world, *c*.2000BC. This is particularly true of the Arabian Gulf, especially the Oman peninsula, where sorghum was being grown in the 3rd millennium. Millet, for which there is evidence at the end of the 3rd millennium at Sappali Tepe in Uzbekistan, was in use at Shortughaï, a Harappa settlement in eastern Bactria (northeast of Afghanistan). We also know that rice was an important element for the survival of the communities of fishers and hunters in the mid Ganges valley, and their contacts with the agricultural communities of the Indus valley were strengthened around 2000BC. It is indeed at this period that we find evidence of the foundation in the northwest of the Ganges valley, near present-day Delhi, of a great many villages that were strongly influenced by Harappan culture.

It is becoming increasingly evident that the development of a more diversified agricultural system, including cereals which, like millet and sorghum, are especially well suited to semi-arid conditions, led to the colonization of new territory. In Gujurat in central India and in the Deccan, the hunter-gatherers whose geometric microliths* indicate the sites of temporary camps, thus increasingly changed over to an agricultural way of life, as it shown by the foundation of a great many villages made up of circular huts. These peoples, who continued to manufacture microliths alongside metal objects, in the course of the 2nd millennium produced pottery decorated with a rich variety of motifs in the Malwa style, yielding after 1500BC to the Jorwe style, in villages where rice and different varieties of millet played an important role.

The impact of the horse

As for animal husbandry, the beginning of the 2nd millennium marks the appearance in the Indus area of the horse and the presence of the Bactrian camel, as is shown by a group of figurines found in Pirak at the same time as some statuettes of horsemen. These animals, together with the donkey, whose bones have also been found at Pirak, completely revolutionized the mobility of the peoples and their means of transport, with all that this implies in the economic and political spheres. The development of horseback herding in the Eurasian Steppes, where horses were playing an increasingly important role at the beginning of the 2nd millennium, must be connected with the appearance in the Indus area of an animal to which Vedic literature attached such importance in its earliest texts. Receptacles in the same style as the pottery of the Steppes, as well as horses' bones, have been found from about 2000BC in eastern Turkmenistan, especially in the Kelleki oasis, an area which previously kept up links with the Indus valley by way of sites like those at Sibri and the burial ground of Mehrgarh VIII in Baluchistan. In the valleys of the Himalayas, notably in Swat, agricultural settlements proliferated in the 2nd millennium, cultivating not only wheat but rice too from 1700BC. These sites in the north of modern Pakistan are characterized by rich cemeteries with grave goods that sometimes reveal contacts with central Asia; and some sites, such as Katelai, contain buried horses from the second half of the 2nd millennium.

Grains of charred rice, Pirak, Baluchistan

Rice which was cultivated in the valley of the Ganges from the 3rd millennium, became in the 2nd millennium one of the main crops in the foothills of Baluchistan and of the Himalayas, especially in Swat, from 1700BC. The appearance of rice marks the beginning of new techniques of irrigation.

Built-up area at Pirak, Baluchistan, beginning of the Iron Age (*c*.1100BC)

The buildings, which have mud brick walls containing symmetrical niches, are packed together and form recognizable districts, some of which are characterized by significant remains of craft activity. The town of Pirak, founded *c*.1700BC, covers nearly 9 hectares (22 acres) and is remarkable for the great continuity of its material culture during its period of occupation, until *c*.700BC when it was abandoned.

Reconstruction of a Chalcolithic village at Navdatoli, Deccan (2nd millennium)

The first agricultural settlements in the Ganges valley and the 2nd millennium Chalcolithic villages in peninsular India consist of circular huts, quite distinct from the quadrangular mud brick and baked-brick houses found on sites in Baluchistan and the Indus valley. This type of village with circular huts persisted in the Ganges valley until the historical period, after 500BC. From H.D. Sankhalie.

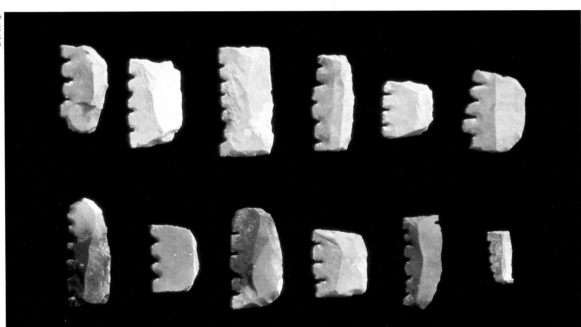

Group of flint sickle parts (c.1000BC)

In the 2nd millennium BC the northwest of the Indian subcontinent saw the appearance of new cereals such as rice, sorghum and millet, but harvests continued to be gathered by means of sickles made up of blades and microliths of geometric shape, probably inserted into a wooden framework. Silicate from the cut plants has left a shiny deposit on the cutting edge of these pieces, which remained in use at Baluchistan well into the Iron Age.

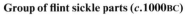

Terracotta figurines of horses and horsemen, Pirak, Baluchistan (1st half of 2nd millennium)

These objects are the first evidence of the appearance of the horse in the Indian world. They are symbols of a new age in which groups of horsemen would start to play an important role in the history of these areas.

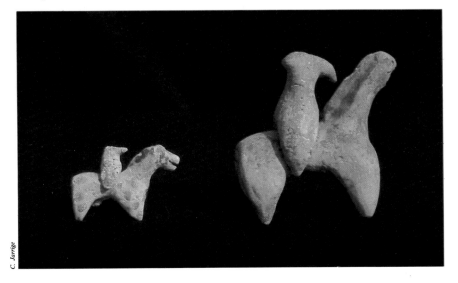

Funerary jar from the late Jorwe culture, Inamgaon, Deccan (c.1100BC)

This unfired clay jar stands on four hollow legs and contains a crouched skeleton and two containers. It is the earliest example of the type of sarcophagus with several feet which was to become general in the Iron Age at megalithic sites in southern India.

The prehistory of Thailand

Recent research has shown that the oldest human culture in Thailand goes back almost one million years.

Prehistoric research in Thailand really began in 1960. Various digs, both Thai and foreign, were carried out from then, but it was not until 1972 that traces of the Early Paleolithic period were discovered in a datable geological context. It had been known for many years that a number of pebble tool cultures existed in South, Southeast and East Asia. It is generally accepted that these fall into two groups: the so-called chopper/chopping tool* cultures of the Lower Paleolithic, mainly dating from the Middle and Late Pleistocene*, and the Hoabinhian* culture, belonging to the Holocene*.

The first of these groups is associated with fossil bones belonging to *Homo erectus**, the second with those of *Homo Sapiens**. Both groups used tools made from pebbles formed from local rock, especially quartzite, collected from river beds. Stones were selected with a view to the shape of the intended tool, so that they needed to be retouched as little as possible. They were almost all worked on one side only, starting from the lower face, usually the flatter one, and working towards the upper, rounder face of the pebble, with work generally confined to only one side of the stone. Sometimes, however, both edges have been worked, and converge to form a point: most of the surface area of the tool remains covered by the core, and the natural section of the stone, whether oval or convex, is preserved. With the passage of time the variety of types increased slightly. The method of shaping improved, and the traces left by removing flakes became finer; but still only one face was worked in almost all cases.

One Lower Paleolithic pebble tool culture is found mainly in the Mae Tha and Mae Mo districts (Lampang province) and the Song, Rong Kwang and Muang districts (Phrae province) in the north of Thailand. This has been given the name of Lannathai culture. Stone tools have been found in laterites forming the deepest, and so oldest, flood terraces of the basins that lie between the mountains of Lampang and Phrae. Geological study has revealed that the tools were buried in the basins during the course of their sedimentation, and they were mostly found covered by later sediments. Subsequently, probably through a change in the balance of the natural water network, the Wang and the Yom rivers became more deeply embedded, allowing the buried objects to appear on the terraces which now stand above the level of the water. The area was then covered by volcanic basalt which extended to the edge of the terraces, but did not overlap them. Paleomagnetic measurements taken on the basalt surrounding or covering the Mae Tha sites indicate that they go back at least to the Matuyama-Brunhes geomagnetic variation (720,000 years ago) or possibly to the Jaramillo period (940,000 years ago). Thus the pebble tools would be earlier, and might date back to from 750,000 to 1,000,000 years ago. The formation of laterite as a result of increased rainfall or a significant fluctuation in the ground water level took place after the basalt had been deposited. This process destroyed all the organic matter which might have given us information about the creators of the tools, their environment or the nature of their diet.

The sites at Mae Mo which lie to the north-east of the area of volcanic activity show no signs of being affected by it. There are other reasons too which allow us to

regard them as more recent than the Mae Tha sites, and probably contemporary with most sites in Phrae, the age of which is thought to be 500,000 years. One of the Phrae sites, Ban Dan Chumpol, has been excavated as a test case. The tools are similar to those of Mae Tha in weight and shape, but a greater number of forms can be recognized, such as elongated picks which are triangular in section. On the other hand the so-called flatiron and horse-hoof types have not yet been found. The proportion of chopping tools to choppers is small and virtually insignificant. We are still dealing essentially with a manufacture based on cores*, and the numerous flakes found were not reworked. However, the excavations have also revealed an advanced technology, widely using anvils and hammers, similar to that prevalent at Zukuodian (Chou Kou Tien) near Peking, after 460,000BP (before present). The tools there were made by *Homo erectus*, and there is also evidence of his presence in Indonesia, at the same period as when the Mae Tha sites were occupied. Thus it appears likely that he was also responsible for the tools belonging to the Lannathai culture.

Changing climates and their effects

The chronological gap between the sites of Mae Tha and most of the others, and then another gap separating these other sites from the subsequent series, are undoubtedly connected with the cyclical variations of climate during the Pleistocene. The alternation of glacial and interglacial periods at a high altitude, especially in the Himalayas, though it never directly affected Southeast Asia, had indirect consequences there. The accumulation of ice at high altitudes led to a drop in sea level, and some variable drying out of the Sunda Sea between the mainland and the groups of islands, so creating a land mass with a continental climate. The snow line came down lower too, pushing vegetation towards the bottom of the slopes and producing a southward migration of the tropical forest, both deciduous and evergreen, which had repercussions on both animals and humans.

The interglacial periods produced the opposite effects, especially the period after the final glaciation. It is known that in Kashmir the ice started to melt in about 18,000BP. Moreover, the peat bogs that were engulfed beneath the Sunda sea provide us with the information that in 11,000BP the water level was 67m (221ft) below its present level; it went on rising and in 9500BP reached a point 2m 40cm (7.9ft) above the present level (measured at high tide). The shoreline was perhaps further inland then, probably 100km (62 miles) north of Bangkok near Lopburi. For such a change to occur, temperatures 6–7°C above present levels were required, and the pollen analysis studies carried out in Taiwan indicate that this was the case. The heat caused the air to expand, enabling it to absorb more moisture, which was restored in the form of increased rainfall during the no doubt prolonged monsoon seasons. This in conjunction with other factors relating to the environment might have led primitive man to seek refuge in caves, and evidence of his dwelling there is present in many caves in Southeast Asia.

At the height of the last glacial period, temperatures were 3° or 4°C lower than they are today, according to the Taiwan pollen analyses. The fact that the weather

was mainly dry meant that it was still possible to live in the open, with rock shelters providing no more than seasonal protection from the winter storms. This is true of the Son Vi culture, found in Vietnam from 30,000BP. It has not yet been found in Thailand, but a comparable cultural phase seems to be represented there in the lower level of the rock shelter at Soi Yok on the River Kwai (Kanchanaburi province). The chopper/chopping tool tradition was still in force there, though the tools were more elaborately worked on than at Phrae. Then tool types with a very convex back started to appear (horse-hoof, flatiron) as well as the distinctively Hoabinhian types: so-called Sumatraliths, short adzes, and discoid scrapers, along with truly bifacial* tools. In the upper levels the same types of tool are still present, but they are less rough technically; and it is this type which forms the Hoabinhian element in the lower levels of the caves at Tam Ongbah (Kanchanaburi), dated 11,180 ± 180BP, and Tam Phii (Spirit Cave: Mae Hogson), dated 11,350 ± 500BP, as well as at all the other dated sites in Southeast Asia. At Tam Phii, the charred remains of nuts and various plant seeds have been found, providing evidence of the type of diet eaten by those dwelling there. The species represented are all known to have grown wild in the area and in Thailand, and there is nothing to prove that these were cultivated forms, which would indicate the existence of the beginnings of primitive agriculture.

It is in any case certain that the Hoabinhian culture and the cultural phases immediately preceding it are the work of *Homo sapiens*. A skeleton of this type, in a foetal position and sprinkled with red ochre*, was found in the rock shelter at Sai Yok. On the basis of the remains found with it, it is known that these people lived on fishing and hunting, by collecting molluscs and shellfish, and gathering plants, berries and nuts.

Site PS 3 at Ban Dan Chumpol

Overall view of one sector of the excavations of the Early Paleolithic site PS 3 at Ban Dan Chumpol (Phrae province, Thailand). Excavations covered an area of 200 sq m (2,150 sq ft), with an average of 9 objects being found per square metre. Every stage of manufacture is represented from raw pebbles and stones to finished tools, including anvils, striking implements and various waste by-products of manufacture. All these objects are buried in laterite on the upper fluvial terrace.

Choppers and scrapers are the most common type of tool on Early Paleolithic sites in Thailand. They are made from stones that are naturally triangular, flat, rectangular or round with straight, inward-curving, crescent-shaped or fan-shaped cutting edges. If the angle between the retouched surface and the main line of the stone is less than 65°, the tool is described as a "chopper", and if this angle is between 70° and 90°, a "scraper". This tabular chopper with a straight cutting edge is the most common type of chopper at Mae Tha II and at PS 3 at Ban Dan Chumpol. With this kind of tool it is easy to cut even quite thick branches or to sharpen a stick so as to make a javelin.

Heavy pointed tools from Mae Tha form 3.4% of all the tools found here, as against 7.5% at PS 3. The increase in the number of heavy tools on this later site may reflect a change either in the environment or in hunting or lifestyle.

P. Sørensen

Small tomb at Ban Kao, Thailand (*c.*4000BC)

Just above the right shoulder of this skeleton dating from the Ban Kao culture is an adze made of polished stone. Its position indicates that it was hafted as an adze and not as an axe. Between the adze and the vase we can see a small pile of animal bones. Another pile can be seen near the left arm and two others were beside the knees. These bones are the toe bones from the front and rear legs of the same pig. It is possible that the body had been wrapped up in or covered by a pig's skin, and that nobody had bothered to remove from it the tiny bones at the end of the trotters.

Short adze (below)

This is one of the key types from the Hoabinhian stone tool kit. It is characterized by a straight heel, and the cutting edge has been retouched to form a "horse-shoe"; this type can easily be distinguished from broken Sumatraliths which have generally been broken off at an oblique angle towards the heel.

Discoidal scraper (bottom)

One of the many types of scraper characteristic of the Hoabinhian culture. Mention should also be made of keeled scrapers and scrapers on flakes. All of these have a cutting edge that has been retouched evenly and skilfully, and often only the heel and the lower face of the main parts of the pebble have not been retouched.

Tomb B.1, Bang site, Ban Kao

This tomb contained the skeleton of a man who had died aged about 40 years and was 1m70 (5.6ft) tall. With him were two black-polished, fairly shallow cups, a jar and two bowls, and a cup with a foot, all placed on his legs. There was a large, heavily barbed bone lance-head beneath his right leg, and the barbed end of another near his elbow. Small disc-shaped shell beads lay on his elbow and on his pelvis. After the burial a black jar, probably containing food for the dead man, had been placed on the tomb near the head.

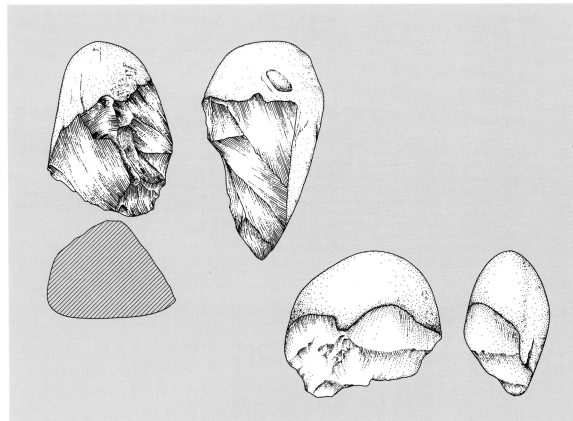

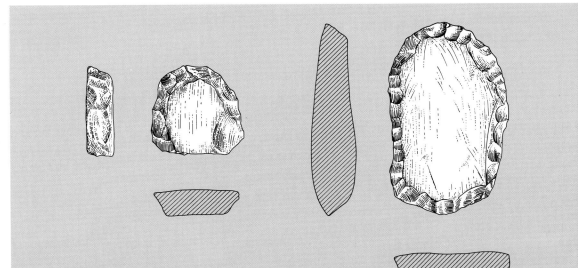

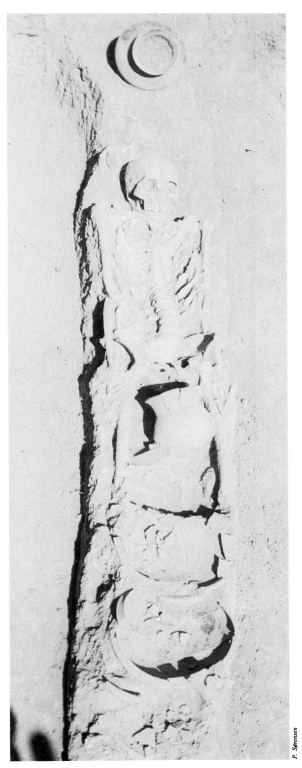

Agricultural civilizations

Archaeologists are beginning to find out more about the intriguing Bronze Age agricultural societies of Thailand, especially their ingenious tools and superb pottery.

The use of caves as a habitat persisted in Southeast Asia for thousands of years, in some cases until the 1st millennium AD. Thus the cave in the Banyan Valley (Mae Hogson, Thailand) where artifacts were found together with charred grains of wild rice, was occupied until 900AD, and the cave at Laang Spean (Cambodia) until 830AD. Ceramics appeared at Laang Spean from at least 2000BC and perhaps from 4300BC, whereas at Gua Kechil 2 (Malaysia) they go back only to 2800BC.

According to pollen analyses in Sumatra, which give results generally in line with those from Taiwan, the climate became drier *c.*5000BP (before the present). From then on an increase in the number of open-air Hoabinhian* sites can be observed, and the appearance of new types of tool: flat stones perforated with a hole in the shape of an hour-glass, slightly sharpened slate knives, square pebbles of a smaller size, retouched to a cutting edge on the narrow side. These finds may indicate the beginnings of agriculture, though sure proof is yet to be found. Indeed, the need to create new tools may equally well have been due to some alteration in the plant life, resulting from the drier climate.

Pottery was made with a bung and a bat. Fibrous materials were twisted, or sometimes braided or plaited, to make ropes, which were fixed onto the bat and have left their imprint on the surfaces of the vases. This corded pottery may have been a local invention. However, if its development did not occur until the 5th millennium, and not in the 6th, then it may result from early contacts with communities that already knew how to make pottery. Thus we find ceramics from the beginning of the 4th millennium in west and northeast Thailand, whereas the central basin of the Chao Phraya does not seem to have been inhabited until later. But recent fieldwork at Kok Phnom Di 70km (44 miles) north-east of Bangkok, has uncovered an important maritime site seasonally occupied from *c.*6500BC, when it was an island, by fishing communities. After 3500BC a drier period converted it into a marshy refuge for a pottery-making culture based on maritime resources. Towards 2000BC forests covered the region. This fieldwork confirms the theory that climate played a key role in the occupation of Thailand's central plain.

The best known Neolithic and Chalcolithic cultures in Thailand are those of Ban Kao and Ban Chiang. The Ban Kao culture, which is represented by habitats with burials and by burials in caves, extended from Kanchanaburi province (central west Thailand) to north Malaysia, crossing over peninsular Thailand. So far archaeologists have found traces of open-air habitats, generally located on the old floor terraces beside present-day rivers, on islands in estuaries, or on the shores of former lakes.

Study of the site at Nong Chae Sao (Chom Bung) has shown that these people lived in houses built on piles, very probably covered with conical thatched roofs. They may have grown rice, as the presence of sickles of a Chinese type (crescent-shaped, and with two holes) seems to indicate, and they reared pigs. We do not know if either the rice or the pigs were wild or domesticated species. In addition to this, they hunted wild animals and birds, collected molluscs from the rivers, and fished for freshwater and marine turtles. Their dead were buried beneath the houses or in caves, lying on their backs and sometimes wrapped in pigskin. No systematic orientation of the tombs can be observed, and no trace has been found of any signs or marks placed on the surface. The dead were supplied with funerary furnishings, sometimes plentiful, sometimes less so, pottery (possibly with food) which had sometimes been deliberately broken and crushed in the tomb, stone adzes, hunting equipment, and personal jewellery; in some cases, the pottery had been placed above the burial places. Life expectancy was short, most people dying at between 25 and 35; but a few lived to the age of 50 and even 70. These peoples had numerous and quite elaborate tools made of clay, stone, bone, antler tine, shell, wood and bamboo. The hand-modelled ceramics are of good qualty; as well as the corded ceramics there is polished red or black pottery, finely executed. The very elegant shapes are usually streamlined, and the bottom, which is generally round, sometimes stands on a pedestal or on three conical hollow feet. In line with the development of this pottery, the Ban Kao culture is divided into several phases, the first (possibly of Chinese origin) beginning *c.*4000BP. Village life continued virtually unchanged until the introduction of metal into the area during the last centuries BC.

Ban Chiang culture

Since the 1960s several sites belonging to the Ban Chiang culture have been discovered in northeast Thailand: first the site of Non Nok Tha (Phu Wiang district, Kon Khaen province), then that of Ban Chiang (Nong Han district, Udon Thani province), as well as a fair number of less important sites.

These two large sites have aroused controversy, for a series of problematic datings seemed to indicate that rice cultivation by means of flooding the fields ("wet" cultivation) and bronze and iron metalwork had been in use there longer than anywhere else in the world. A recent reassessment based partly on the evidence of other sites in the area that were excavated subsequently has enabled us to establish a chronological table for northeast Thailand which puts it in line with the Ban Kao cultural area on the one hand, and on the other with the sequences of cultures in North Vietnam (Phung Nguyen, Dong Dau, Go Mun, Dong Son) which have some features in common with Ban Chiang.

Like most of the sites in northeast Thailand, Ban Chiang is a low knoll with burial places. The small number of post holes found during fieldwork has not enabled archaeologists to reconstruct the plan of the houses. The burial layers at Ban Chiang cover one another or cut across one another – though not so often as at Non Nok Tha. It has nonetheless been possible to classify them into three phases: the early phase, from 2000BC to *c.*1500–1350BC; the middle phase, from 1350BC to 500–400BC; and the late phase, from 400–300BC to 200–300AD.

The funerary customs of the early and recent phases seem quite similar to those of Ban Kao, but there are different types of pottery. During the middle phase, skeletons were laid on their backs as in the early phase, but covered with a bed of broken pottery. The middle and recent phases are well represented at Ban Nadi, a neighbouring site. The average age at death was 29 at Ban Nadi, 31 at Ban Chiang, and 37–48 at Non Nok Tha.

It is not known whether bronze was in use during the early phase, but it certainly was in the middle phase, as at Dong Dau. Crucibles have been found on both sites, and at Ban Nadi furnaces as well. Iron made its appearance *c.*600BC at Ban Nadi. In the recent phase of the Ban Chiang culture we find bronze and iron, often as alloys, and glass beads. From the evidence available, the whole of the sequence reflects an agricultural society, based on pig and chicken husbandry and rice-growing. But here as elsewhere archaeologists do not know if it was a cultivated or wild strain of rice, nor whether dry or wet cultivation was practised. The presence during the middle phase of the bones of water buffalo, which could have been used as draught animals, is not decisive. However it is generally thought that the domestication of the water buffalo, the wet cultivation of rice and the advent of iron all coincided.

The recent phase was very rich culturally. Its pottery, with red painted onto a cream background and complicated curvilinear designs of scrolls and spirals, has made Ban Chiang famous: among the objects made were clay figurines, very elaborate jewellery, and incised terracotta cylinders. It has recently been suggested that this phase could have seen the arrival of a new wave of immigrants. This same theory had already been proposed for the early phase of Ban Chiang, in the absence of any contemporary or earlier sites on which to base comparison. Thus the Ban Chiang culture would represent two waves of immigration into northeast Thailand.

Pottery from the Bang site, Ban Kao

These pieces are typical of the early phase of the Bang site, Ban Kao. Like pottery of the late phase, they have a rounded base and thin walls, but mostly they have some permanent support such as a ring-shaped foot, three hollow feet or a pedestal. The pottery is of fine quality, and is polished, but never has a slip; the colours are not as intense as in late types of pottery. If there is any decoration, it consists simply of applied bands or, less often, of incised lines framing comb marks. National Museum, Bangkok.

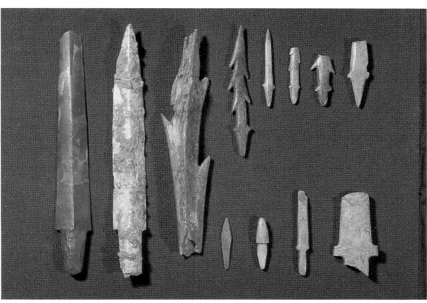

L. Larsen, The National Museum, Copenhague

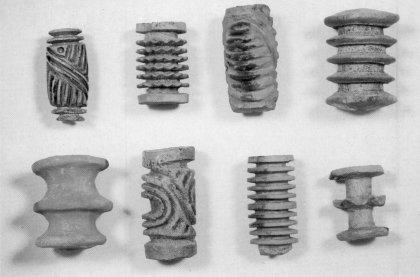

J. Broderick, by kind permission of the University Museum, Philadelphia

Bone lance and arrow heads

These objects are generally the shape of a flat or triangular lens in section. The arrowheads usually have barbs, and most have a "tongue" at the back of the stem which was inserted into the (bamboo?) shaft. Small side protuberances or shoulders prevented the head from being pushed back into the shaft when it struck. Bone was also used to make such implements as harpoons and fish-hooks of various sizes, combs, rings and awls. Shell was used to make spoons, cutting tools, sickles, saws and beads. National Museum, Bangkok.

Clay cylinders

In the upper levels at Ban Chiang and in the graves of children, clay cylinders such as these were found, with deeply incised complex designs, often similar to the most complicated of the patterns encountered on the red-painted pottery with a cream base. They may have been used as rollers to print patterns on textiles or garments made of bark, but their presence in graves could equally well indicate other purposes. Similar rollers have been found at Hao Loc, Tan Hoa, in Vietnam. National Museum, Bangkok.

National Museum, Bangkok

J. Broderick, by kind permission of the University Museum, Philadelphia

Bronze bracelet, Ban Chiang

This bracelet is adorned with little bells decorated with a spiral pattern, which were common in the Dong Son culture, but similar ones can still be found today, for example on the head harness of water buffalo. National Museum, Bangkok.

National Museum, Bangkok

Bronze bracelet, Ban Chiang

This bracelet is decorated with a pattern overlay of plaited cords and an edging of small balls. National Museum, Bangkok.

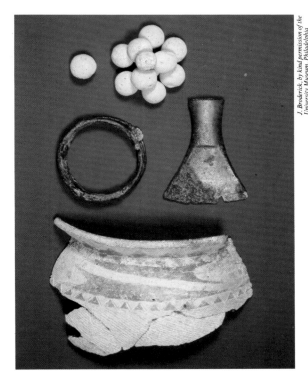

Objects from Ban Chiang grave "Vulcan's Tomb", dating from the early phase (2000–c.1500/1350BC)

As well as four bronze bracelets, this grave contained a bronze axe with a socket, and a painted and engraved eartheware pot. Behind the head there was a pile of 30 small clay balls. This same type of ball is still to be found today, for example among the Song Dam people of Thailand who fire them with special bows. National Museum, Bangkok.

Vase from the late phase of Ban Chiang (400/300BC–AD200/300)

One of the finest vases of the late phase of Ban Chiang. The firmly drawn patterns, painted in red on a cream background, meandering, spiralling or describing some other curve, were the first to make the Ban Chiang site famous. The National Museums Division, Department of Fine Arts, Thailand.

Three receptacles from the early phase of Ban Chiang (2000–c.1500/1350BC)

Characteristics include experiments with red, black or grey pigmentation, a polished surface, not coated with slip, and the use of a permanent support. These are reminiscent of pottery of the Ban Kao phase, but despite these similarities, we are clearly dealing with two different cultures. The National Museums Division, Department of Fine Arts, Thailand.

J. Broderick, by kind permission of the University Museum, Philadelphia

J. Broderick, by kind permission of the University Museum, Philadelphia

The "Indianization" of Southeast Asia

Indian expansion in Southeast Asia, a region rich in spices, gold and precious stones, was in part connected with trade arising from Imperial Rome's taste for luxury products; but modern archaeology suggests a more complex, two-way process.

The civilization of India moulded the countries of the Indo-Chinese peninsula and the Indonesian islands running from Sumatra through Java to Bali. The results of this are still perceptible. We do not know the causes of this influence nor how it spread: only the Hellenization and subsequent Romanization of the Mediterranean and western Europe are comparable in scope. We do know that unlike the spread of Chinese influence down into Vietnam it was not a case of conquest followed by political domination, though it is possible that a few groups of Indians established themselves here and there as masters. Earlier oriental scholars have stressed the missionary zeal of the Buddhists which can be encountered at about the same time in Central Asia. Buddhism certainly was introduced, as archaeology verifies: the earliest Indian remains found in Southeast Asia are bronze Buddhas, either imported or copied from India down to the last detail. However, it must be emphasized that only a dozen of them have been found, scattered from Malaysia to Sulawesi covering a period of at least three centuries. Moreover, Hinduism was also firmly established here at the same period: but archaeologically speaking nothing has been found to indicate this, and we have to wait until the 5th century to see signs of it with the first locally executed inscriptions and monuments. Thus we cannot treat these few sparse, later remains as a basis for deducing the causes of Indian expansion and how it happened.

Looking at the names of the places that the Indians visited overseas, which are mainly names of spices, precious stones and gold, historians have also wondered whether these rare, highly prized commodities might have attracted the Indians who would use them themselves or resell them to the West. This would have created trading posts from which Indian civilization could radiate out. We have a good knowledge of the trading relations between India and the Mediteranean in the Roman era through classical texts which describe them in detail. The finds of Roman currency made in India since the 18th century bear out the textual descriptions. E.H. Warmington has given a detailed account of this trade (1928).

The contribution of Mortimer Wheeler

After being appointed director of the Archaeological Survey of India in 1944, Sir Mortimer Wheeler reorganized the system, introducing strict methods of excavation and establishing a programme; he breathed new life into the service and opened up a new role for it, with particularly brilliant results in the fields of prehistory and protohistory. Putting to good use his knowledge of Roman archaeology, he had all finds of Mediterranean coinage catalogued and entered on maps. This work revealed an exceptional concentration of hoards (57 out of 68) in the south of the country, all dating from the 1st century AD, the precise point in time when the classical texts tell us that trade was going on. Then, looking at the sites, Wheeler noted a collection of intaglios, coins, stamped wares and glass beads: these had been found in 1937 at Virampatnam-Arikamedu near Pondicherry on an estuary that would obviously have made an ideal harbour. He excavated the site himself in 1945, and work on it was resumed by Jean-Marie Casal in 1947–48. It was found to be the site of a vast settlement, remarkable especially for its textile-dyeing workshops and Arretine ceramics dating from the first half of the 1st century. All these discoveries conclusively confirmed the information from written sources. From the reign of Augustus trade between the Mediterranean – mainly via Alexandria – and India grew in volume. Some of the goods purchased by the West (cinnamon, textiles, pearls) came from India itself; the rest (spices, precious stones, Chinese silk) came from beyond the Indian Ocean. Everything was paid for by and large in gold and silver, to the great detriment of the "balance of payments", a fact bitterly bewailed by Pliny the Elder. Basing his proposal on the information supplied by the finds of money, Wheeler maintained that there had been a direct route between Arikamedu – in all likelihood what the author of the *Periplus* (1st century AD) and Ptolemy called Podouke – and the Malabar Coast where it seems reasonable to suppose that Muziris, mentioned in the *Periplus*, was sited, at Cranganore, and, close by, Nelcynda which was also mentioned in the texts. This route went up the Ponnani valley, then through the Pâlghât gap to join the Kāvērī valley on its way to the Coromandel Coast. According to Wheeler this would avoid rounding Cape Comorin, and from time immemorial trade routes cut across land when this proved possible.

A judiciously established programme, investigations systematically carried out, excavations selected and executed to the highest possible standards, and results that cross-check the working hypotheses and information supplied by written texts: the reality of the trade between India and Imperial Rome thus established by Wheeler is a perfect demonstration of the specific application and efficacy of archaeology.

With this contribution as his starting point, Wheeler developed his conclusions using only information relating to the Roman period. He even put forward as an answer to the very difficult problem of Graeco-Buddhist art a solution based on a link between Rome and Buddhism. Remarkably enough, Italian art historians have since shown that this art did have a Roman phase during which the influence of Imperial sculpture was important, arriving via the Red Sea; what is more, archaeologists have recently highlighted the role played by the ports of Berenice and Eilat. But influence was also spread by trade through Syria, Petra and the ancient Gulf routes through Iran or further north from Pontus towards Margiana and Bactria. This "Roman" phase could emerge largely because the ground was prepared for it by the penetration and establishment of Hellenistic traditions in Bactria and Gandhara.

In India itself the southward diffusion of Hindu civilization and the art that expressed it followed the line of the Godavarī basin towards the Kṛṣṇā, then from the Kṛṣṇā delta went towards Tamilnadu and Coḷamandala. The role of the Sâtavâhana dynasty was crucial to this diffusion; they were in control of this line from coast to coast and had contacts with the Bactrian kingdoms through the Scythian satraps (the provincial governors) in the northwest. The next links in the chain were the Iṣvâkus in Ândhra and the Cedîs in Kalinga. From great sites like Amarâvatî and Nâgârjunikoṇḍa Buddhism travelled down along the eastern coast to Ceylon, and went back up part of the way towards the Bay of Bengal. And it was from these centres that Indian influence spread into Southeast Asia. The southern route through the Pâlghât gap, which Wheeler maintains existed, may have appeared relatively late, after the Coḷa and Tamil areas had been incorporated into India, and was perhaps established from east to west. In any case it seems to have been of secondary importance. Moreover, Wheeler put the time limits between which trading took place in too narrow a band. It started earlier and went on later than he suggests. Many factors that were already known when he was working prove this, as does archaeological information from Southeast Asia. Even so, it is greatly to his credit that his discoveries substantiated trade between India and Southeast Asia.

The theory of trade

Another series of finds occurred to corroborate Wheeler's views. The kingdom of Fu Nan, the first Indianized state in Indo-China of which there is evidence from the 1st century AD, had been located by the great Sinologist, Paul Pelliot, in the extreme southwest of Indo-China in 1902. In 1942 Louis Malleret first systematically surveyed the area between the Mekong and the Gulf of Siam, pinpointed a good many sites and then examined one of them: Oc-Eo. As well as the remains of an advanced indigenous culture, he uncovered a number of Indian items – mainly jewellery, as well as Mediterranean objects such as a medal of Antontinus Pius, intaglios, cabochon gemstones, etc., and Chinese items. In spite of the fact that Malleret, an entirely untrained excavator, did not use proper archaeological methods, it was possible for the first time to see in concrete form the earliest proofs of Indian trade, from the 2nd–3rd century, and the odd items from the Mediterranean that had been carried along with it. We now know the destination (at least the oldest yet discovered) of the route for which Wheeler had discovered the departure point, at least so far as the Imperial Roman period is concerned.

On this basis the theory of trade (motivated by the Roman taste for luxury) as the springboard, or cause, of Indian expansion was adopted by most historians. There can be no question that this accounts for a good part of what really took place. But we also know that in the end this trade was episodic. When it ceased, Rome quite simply forgot about it, and India did the same to such an extent that it was nearly 20 centuries later, through the work of Oriental scholars, that its extent was realized. The trading theory was maintained because it rested on tangible "facts", and because economic explanations were fashionable at that time. And if indeed it was the case that Buddhist missionaries and Brahmans boarded the merchant vessels more or less by stealth, it was their effect which was in the long term crucial, and which caused the Indianization of Southeast Asia.

At all events the origins of this trade, which was certainly in existence before the time of Imperial Rome, remain unclear. There is really nothing to enable us to state categorically that it was established from west to east. Chinese texts are abundant and precise, and give clear information. From the early Han period, the 2nd century BC, the Chinese were trading in the southern seas. There is archaeological proof of this in the form of the many items of Han pottery found in Java, predating the first Indian remains by four centuries. Relations between China and the countries on her frontiers like Burma and Vietnam were very volatile, to the point of resulting, in the 3rd century BC, in the conquest of North Vietnam. Using this unquestionable, coherent information as our basis, we might think that the Chinese and the peoples in direct contact with them made overtures to India, offering their spices and silk for sale: we know that Chinese silk reached the south of India by sea. Then the Indians would have needed only to follow the same routes at a later period, but travelling from west to east.

The Chinese texts are quite categorical on another point as well: the native peoples of the south were intrepid sailors so that the traders of the Celestial Empire preferred to use their boats. This implies the existence of technically advanced societies with good social organization. Now, the study of the Bronze Age in this area – by and large the 1st millennium BC – actually proves that these societies existed. Thus it is obvious that very advanced civilizations, or at least centres, were in existence in this area, actively involved in sea trade. Theoretically speaking, the first historians of the Indianization of Southeast Asia made a mistake in neglecting those at the receiving end, or in implicitly regarding them as "primitive". A civilization as complex as that of India could be assimilated and then developed only by societies that were already advanced – especially when there was no conquest with the victorious race establishing its own citizens there. The gap between historians and philologists on the one hand, and that between prehistorians and archaeologists on the other must certainly be the reason for this defect of logic.

Archaeology itself has helped us to renew our ideas. Burmese excavations carried out from 1959 to 1963 at Beikthano and Halin, Pyu cities (proto-Burmese), have uncovered a very elaborate urban civilization going back to at least the very beginning of the 2nd century BC. The first traces of Buddhism, the alphabet and other signs of increasing Indian influence do not appear until the history of these cities is under way. Thus there is no justification for the idea that the Indians "came" to these cities. It is just as logical to argue that the Pyus who were already organized and wealthy went to India to trade their merchandise and brought back with them spiritual leaders from there. Or possibly that the latter, spurred on by their zeal, boarded merchant ships and went on to spread their beliefs. If that were the case trade would have been no more than an aspect of spreading Indian influence.

Mortimer Wheeler's archaeological work enriched our knowledge of the trading transactions between India and Southeast Asia. However, we will begin to understand this trade only when we have information through the excavation of the coastal sites of that area. But it is as difficult to interpret archaeological "facts" as it is to unearth them. When they are all we have to go on, as in prehistory, we have to exercise the greatest caution in reading their significance. In the historical sphere it is appropriate to set them against written sources and other available information. Then there is a risk that they will produce more problems than they resolve. The objectivity people attribute to their own disciplines is an illusion. To be aware of these limits is in no way to belittle archaeology: quite the contrary, it is the best way of practising it.

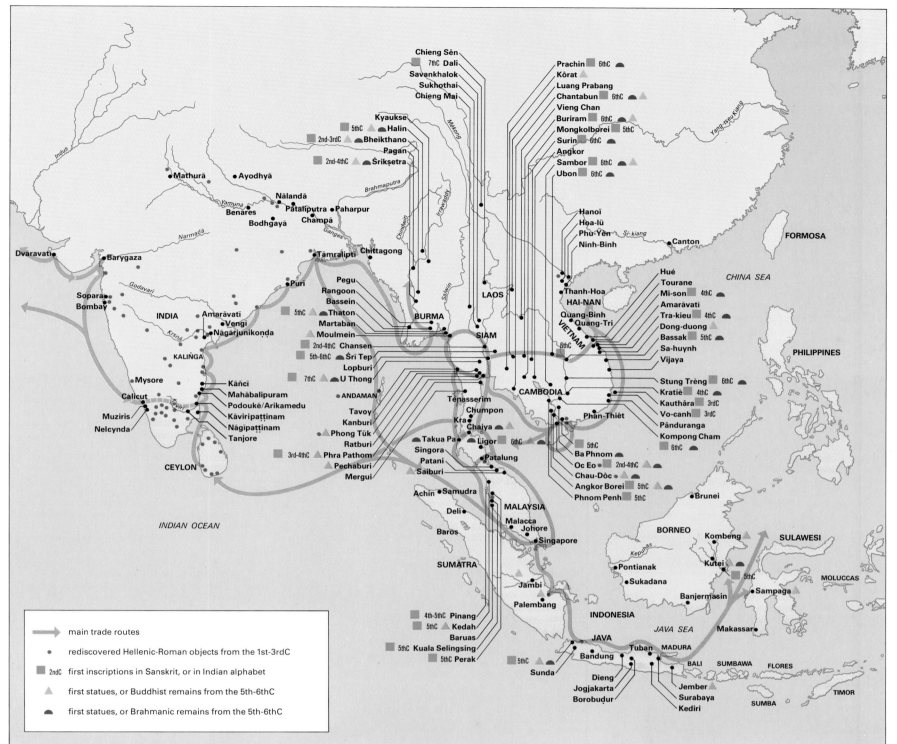

Map labels (India/mainland/islands):

Indus · Mathurā · Ayodhyā · Nālandā · Benares · Pātalīputra · Paharpur · Bodhgayā · Champā · Dvāravatī · Barygaza · Sopara · Bombay · Puri · INDIA · Amarāvatī · Vengi · Nāgārjunikoṇḍa · KALINGA · Godāvarī · Kṛṣṇā · Narmadā · Yamunā · Ganges · Brahmaputra · Mysore · Kāñci · Calicut · Mahābalipuram · Podouké/Arikamedu · Kāviripaṭṭinam · Muziris · Nāgipaṭṭinam · Nelcynda · Tanjore · CEYLON · INDIAN OCEAN

Chittagong · Tāmralipti · Pegu · Rangoon · Bassein · Thaton · Martaban · Moulmein · Chansen · Śri Tep · Lopburi · U Thong · BURMA · Kyaukse · Halin · Bheikthano · Pagan · Śrikṣetra · Chindwin · Irrawaddy · Salween · Mékong · Chieng Sèn · Dali 7thC · Savankhalok · Sukhothai · Chieng Mai · SIAM · LAOS · Ténasserim · Chumpon · Tavoy · Kanburi · Phong Tük · Ratburi · Singora · Phra Pathom · Pechaburi · Mergui · ANDAMAN · Kra · Chaiya · Ligor 6thC · Patalung · Patani · Saïburi · Takua Pa · Achin · Samudra · Deli · Baros · MALAYSIA · Malacca · Johore · Singapore · SUMATRA · Jambi · Palembang · Pinang 4th-5thC · Kedah 5thC · Baruas · Kuala Selingsing 5thC · Perak 5thC · Sunda 5thC

Prachin 6thC · Kôrat · Luang Prabang · Chantabun 6thC · Vieng Chan · Buriram 6thC · Mongkolborei 5thC · Surin · Angkor · Sambor 6thC · Ubon 6thC · Hanoï · Hoa-lû · Phu-Yên · Ninh-Binh · Canton · FORMOSA · CHINA SEA · Thanh-Hoa · HAI-NAN · Quang-Binh · Quang-Tri · VIETNAM 6thC · CAMBODIA · Hué · Tourane · Mi-son 4thC · Amarāvati · Tra-kieu 4thC · Dong-duong · Bassak · Sa-huynh · Vijaya · Stung Trèng 6thC · Kratiè 4thC · Kauthâra 3rdC · Vo-canh 3rdC · Pànduranga · Kompong Cham 6thC · Phan-Thiêt · Ba Phnom 5thC · Oc Eo 2nd-4thC · Chau-Dôc · Angkor Borei 5thC · Phnom Penh 5thC · PHILIPPINES · Brunei · BORNEO · Kombeng · SULAWESI · Kutei 5thC · Sampaga · MOLUCCAS · Pontianak · Sukadana · Banjermasin · Makassar · JAVA SEA · INDONESIA · Bandung · Tuban · MADURA · BALI · SUMBAWA · FLORES · JAVA · Dieng · Jogjakarta · Borobuḍur · Jember · Surabaya · Kediri · SUMBA · TIMOR · Kepulas · Si-kiang · Yang-tseu-kiang

Legend:

→ main trade routes

• rediscovered Hellenic-Roman objects from the 1st-3rdC

■ 2ndC first inscriptions in Sanskrit, or in Indian alphabet

▲ first statues, or Buddhist remains from the 5th-6thC

◗ first statues, or Brahmanic remains from the 5th-6thC

Musée de Djakarta

Face of a ring-seal, Oc-Eo, Vietnam

Found by L. Malleret (*Archéologie du Delta du Mékong*, vol. 3, pl. XXXIX), this gold ring is one of the most significant indications of Indian trade. The Sanskrit inscription (photograph taken from the reverse to facilitate reading) in 2nd/3rd-century *brahmi* script gives a name peculiar to the genitive: *saṅghapottasya*: "property of Saṅgapottha" (or Saṅghpautta). These seals may have been used to authenticate documents, seal consignments of valuable goods – even to identify offerings to the sanctuaries. Museum of Saigon, Ho Chi Minh City.

E.F.E.O.

Imprint of a cornelian intaglio, Oc-Eo, Vietnam

Of Mediterranean (Roman or Alexandrian?) origin and dating to the beginning of our era, this piece, found by L. Malleret (*Archéologie du Delta du Mékong*, vol. 3, pl. LXVII), is a good example of the objects carried to the shores of Southeast Asia by Indian merchants to be exchanged for local products. They may also have been worn by travellers as protective amulets. Museum of Saigon, Ho Chi Minh City.

E.F.E.O.

Buddha found near the river Tamara, Sikendeng, Sulawesi

This type of Buddha, hand raised in the "fear-dispelling" gesture, came originally from Amaravati in the 3rd–4th centuries and was diffused by the Buddhist schools of Ceylon in the 5th–6th centuries. It is one of the oldest effigies of the Buddha found in Southeast Asia and the most oriental, marking the extreme limits of Indianization. Imported or made locally, it provides an essential signpost for following the expansion of Buddhism. Bronze, h., 0.75m (2.96ft). Jakarata Museum.

Angkor: the archaeology of an agricultural empire

The ruined city of Angkor, ancient Khmer capital, has amazed westerners ever since its rediscovery in the 19th century; archaeology has revealed the still more extraordinary irrigation system that provided the wealth for its creation and sustained its prosperity.

Though they were unknown until about a century ago, the Khmer kingdom and the impressive monuments of its capital, Angkor, have become the commonplace stock of textbooks. A handful of epigraphists, art historians and architects were responsible for its rediscovery. But while archaeology should have played an important role, the main part of the work was done at second hand, to such an extent that the most distinguished historian of Khmer art, Philippe Stern*, wrote his thesis without ever having been to Angkor. The excellence of his work, in retrospect, excuses this approach. Nonetheless, it would have been possible to do research on the spot.

Because of the immensity of the task, on-site work tended to be concentrated on Angkor. After the inventory of the sites on ancient Cambodia drawn up in 1900 by Etienne Lunet de Lajonquière which was expanded a little by Henri Parmentier, almost no further work was done virtually throughout the Khmer area. The Geographical Service of Indo-China published a map to a scale of 1:100,000 in the 1920s, which could have formed a solid base for a historical geography, or a toponymy, but it remained unused. As for Angkor itself, until 1960 nobody bothered to produce more than small-scale maps surveyed with a plane table, which were inadequate if not plain wrong. It was not until 1936 that Maurice Glaize made available large-scale plans of the main monuments; they were precise compared with previous material, but really very inadequate, with virtually no cross-sections or isometric projections. With regard to smaller objects other than statuary and bronzes, on rare occasions a few specimens were collected and immediately buried in the reserve stocks of museums. No thought was given to undertaking stratigraphic excavations.

Khmer studies likewise mainly neglect the present, while Angkor goes back roughly to the time when our cathedrals were built. This meant they were deprived of important points of reference, particularly in respect of a close understanding of the language. J. Delvert's human geography of Cambodia was not available until 1961, and the first essays on contemporary Khmer society did not appear until after this date. But still no questions were addressed to the problem of the Khmers' way of life, in particular their agriculture.

During the 1950s a broader view was taken, especially in studying Khmer linguistics, religion and the symbolism of the monuments of Angkor, accompanied by a more thorough analysis of Indian sources, and, although the political situation at that time made it difficult to get to part of the country, thanks to the work of the French Air Force and Fleet Air Arm it was possible to begin a systematic aerial exploration, backed up by the reconnaissance photographs taken during the war by the Royal Air Force which had been given to the Geographical Service of Indo-China.

Khmer sites by air

Aerial observations had already been carried out above Angkor at an earlier date. From as early as 1933 the Fleet Air Arm was making a photographic reconnaissance of the capital, which revealed many sites and canals. Except for identifying an outline of the capital's first boundaries (the date and role of which have since been interpreted differently), these discoveries were not used and the research was not pursued. What is more, while this photographic record showed up the incorrectness of the maps of Angkor, they were not revised. Yet aerial observation is exceptionally easy and fruitful here. The ancient monuments were built alongside one another, and are almost never superimposed. Modern occupation rarely conceals previous occupation, unless it has simply adapted itself to the previous mould. However, recent irrigation schemes and the use of machines in cultivation have altered the situation somewhat. Vegetation masks nothing on the plains; but the undulating and wooded areas remain almost impenetrable, though large sites may be located there. Monsoons and a generally cloudy sky do not make flying easy, but the differences of humidity and vegetation from one season to the next reveal ancient buildings and sites clearly.

The first large-scale records of the Angkor area revealed new sites by the dozen, and gave a new dimension to our knowledge of the monuments already listed in inventories by adding to them a quantity of earthworks. When these results were checked on the ground it was clear that these unknown sites could easily have been detected by a simple land survey. A mound with moats around it and a reservoir in front of it indicates the presence of a Khmer site, even if not a brick or stone is to be seen. The map drawn up to a scale of 1:50,000 (based on aerial surveys) by the US Ordnance Survey confirmed that almost all ancient building work could be read from it. The same results were achieved on the spot by asking the inhabitants themselves. Verification of results in the field is still essential for this enables us to make a rapid identification of the site, and even a rough dating. Then all that remains is for an exhaustive examination to be carried out to trace the extent of Khmer civilization, and if possible to date its various stages. While it is faster, aerial archaeology does not represent a marked step forward at this level in comparison with investigation on the ground. On the other hand, only aerial study shows up the way the ground round the temples has been planned and arranged in order to make cultivation possible; in that respect it revolutionizes our approach.

The temples had moats and reservoirs dug out which would fill when rivers were in spate, or with collected runoff water—contained water diverted from streams or rivers. The dyke-causeways between the waterways were in the rainy season more part of the irrigation system than a means of communication. Canals completed the network and the dykes seemed as often as not to have been formed simply by piling up the earth removed when the canals were dug out. Finally the way in which the paddy fields were divided within these works was designed to improve water distribution, and must thus have been a collective enterprise. Only the community as a whole could have undertaken and then managed work on this scale. The allocation of property to individuals or families is inconceivable in this context. To sum up, seen from the air the land of the Khmers proved to be an "artificial landscape" shaped by men with the objective of obtaining the largest possible number of flooded paddy fields. It was then possible to map this system, so very different from the present-day landscape. Taking an extreme view, the temples could be seen simply as chapels crowning an enormous undertaking in which the hydraulic system represented a far more impressive achievement even than Angkor's pyramid of sculpted and carved stones. Thus the synthetic approach made possible by aerial exploration formed a qualitative change in archaeology.

Khmer sites by land

George Trouvé, who was curator at Angkor from 1931 to 1935, discovered parts of the amazing hydraulic network feeding the cities, and emphasized its importance. In 1936 the engineers working for the public works department noticed that one of the big artificial lakes made by the Khmers, the western Baray (8km × 2km, constructed in the 11th century), was still more than a third full and had the idea of using it to irrigate lower-lying land. While working on the project they partially rediscovered the Khmer methods of irrigation. But research along these lines was not pursued, though it could have elucidated the causes of Angkor's prosperity and the bases of its economic power. This is all the more surprising as the inscriptions in Old Khmer—mainly charts relating to the foundation of the temples—already provided a fair amount of information in that connection.

An aerial exploration to resume this research was not in itself adequate. Verification of the findings had to take place on the ground, at least on one carefully chosen test area. This work was undertaken in 1957–58 for the area round Roluos, ancient Hariharālaya, the capital of Indravarman, 877–89, and one of the oldest Angkorian cities on the plain, built over sites dating from the 7th–8th century. Here archaeologists found the first "hydraulic city", a complex of temples celebrating the faith and power of the king, "master of the Surface here below", and of hydraulic works enabling rice to be grown intensively. The testimony of the first Europeans to visit Angkor in the 16th century when it was still in "working order" provides evidence that Angkor Thom, which was built at the end of the 12th century, was also a "hydraulic city".

When conservator at Angkor, the author limited research in 1959 to the central cities of the complex, which made it possible at least to produce a detailed analysis of certain characteristic points. More particularly a series of excavations and stratigraphic soundings revealed the sections of the ditches, canals and reservoirs, and the agricultural changes obscuring them. A start was also made on assembling the information necessary for palynological* analyses, which will shed light on the study of the plant cover and its evolution. Above all, a map at a scale of 1:10,000 and a series of large-scale detail surveys made it possible at least to put aerial observations into a coherent and reliable context, and to study them on the basis of precise contouring, which is obviously essential in reinstating the pattern of water flow.

It then became possible to sketch out a complete analysis of Khmer agriculture. In the 7th–8th century on the high lands it depended on "natural" exploitation of the terraced paddy fields, arranged so as to take advantage of the rain as it ran away. Around the first great Khmer capital, Sambor Prei Kuk, this system was improved upon: dykes were constructed to form compartments, artificial shelves where rainwater and runoff were used to irrigate larger paddy fields. In the centre of the Mekong basin, a network of dykes and cuts in the high river banks directed the autumn spate towards enclosed shelves where it deposited its fertilizing silt, and was trapped until the seedlings had been planted out. Near living areas and temples, reservoirs positioned between dykes were adequate to ensure supplies until the end of the dry season. This was in a way an "automatic" method of irrigation.

Irrigation and empire

The hydraulic city on the Angkor model constructed at Roluos followed these measures but represented a great step forward technically by increasing water storage facilities and its distribution to the vast outer areas, which were now really being "irrigated". This was true "artificial" irrigation. The system involved further construction, built alongside the earlier system so as to benefit both from that investment and to increase its output. This resulted in more and more land being used up. Given that it was necessary to use permanent rivers which were limited in number, the successive capitals were obliged to be built beside each other from west to east, and to go from south to north, from the shores of the lakes to the foot, or almost to the foot, of the Kulên hills which act as the water tower of the plain of Angkor. Looked at from this point of view, the history of the successive capitals appears in a new light, though the role of the ambition, not to say megalomania, of the Khmer kings, constantly spurred on by the desire to built bigger and better, should not be totally disregarded because of this. We can at least show that their undertakings needed to be backed by corresponding resources. This mastery of the climate and rice cultivation even made it possible towards the end of the 11th century to create real "colonial" cities in areas which, with little natural water supply, were hostile to settlement, but in which the skill of Khmer hydraulic engineers nonetheless succeeded in creating suitable growing conditions. However, this system did have some negative consequences: the silting up of reservoirs, the leaching of the soil, the decanting of water that had lost its fertile silt, and lastly deforestation; these must all have played a part in the impoverishment of the Angkor empire. Works such as these required a strong central power: in fact the most imposing were built during the happiest reigns, which contrast with periods where no "hydraulic investment" was made.

Thus archaeology has supplied some answers to the economic history of the Khmer empire. It has enabled us to understand how growth came about through the development of elaborate production methods. Yet, as always, it raises more questions than it has answered. It is true that the work described was only a beginning and that it would have to be continued for years before the relevant factors emerge clearly. The interpretations suggested here rest on hypotheses, especially that the climate was by and large the same in the 10th–13th centuries as it is in the 20th century, and these assumptions have to be verified. Palynology will enable us to establish a parallel between what was grown and the inscriptions bearing plant names. The inscriptions themselves may also shed some light on the price of land and its variations, despite the fact that the absence of currency or a constant standard of measures makes it impossible to assess land values with any precision or to give figures for output and population density. This economy-based approach should not make us lose sight of the symbolic and religious intentions underlying the temples. It was long ago demonstrated that the moat surrounding the mountain-temple symbolizes the ocean encircling the land. It must be stressed that the Khmers made special use of the myths and symbols celebrating the fecundation of the Earth by the Waters, and that the king was above all "he who brings forth rain". Economic order and symbolic order are in fact closely bound up together and it is not possible to make any prejudgment about which came first.

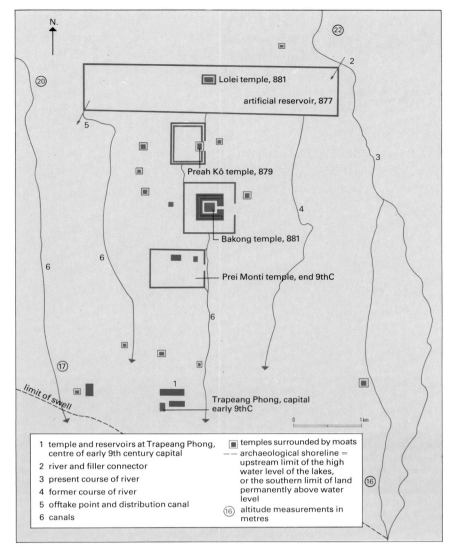

**Plan of Hariharālaya (Roluos),
the first hydraulic city, created by Indravarman, 877–89**

Key:
1 temple and reservoirs at Trapeang Phong, centre of early 9th century capital
2 river and filler connector
3 present course of river
4 former course of river
5 offtake point and distribution canal
6 canals

☐ temples surrounded by moats
— archaeological shoreline = upstream limit of the high water level of the lakes, or the southern limit of land permanently above water level
⑯ altitude measurements in metres

Hariharālaya, Angkor

The way in which the first hydraulic city of Angkor worked can be seen from the diagram above. An aerial view shows the system, from the storage of water taken upstream from the river, to its return to the lake farther downstream after use. The area of scrubland (dark), which is now a reserve formed by the conservation authority, marks the ancient settlement. In the surrounding area the present-day paddy fields still benefit partly from the water that used to be channelled.

Tâ Prohm of Bati, Takeo, Cambodia

East of the sanctuaries that cannot be seen on this picture, the reservoir lies between dykes. The monsoons reach their peak in September and the waters of the Bassac rise. The water enters through breaches on the NE of the ditch, the NW of the reservoir. These gaps have only to be plugged for the water to be held, and the final rains supplement it still further. In the dry season these reserves are used by the villages and for livestock, and for watering the rice seedlings before they are planted out. And finally food crops can be grown on the bed of the reservoir which remains damp and is enriched with sediment. Modern settlement sites are protected from high water on the ancient dikes. Paddy fields have now been laid out on the bed of the former reservoir. This is the prototype of "automatic" irrigation, the functioning of which relies on the correct positioning of the reservoir which is filled by the river in spate.

China: the archaeological background

China, where archaeological research goes back to the 11th century AD,
has the longest recorded continuity of any living civilization, from the
Neolithic to the present day. It continues to produce sensational
archaeological finds, such as the army of terracotta warriors in the
Mausoleum of Qin Shi Huangdi found in 1974.

The venerable origin of archaeology in China is invariably ascribed to that country's early awareness of history and its respect for the past, maintained since antiquity. However, there may be a more prosaic explanation. China is certainly a nation that has taken more care than most over the burial of the dead, and has consigned to the grave the richest of funerary offerings. But it is also a country where the tradition of violating and looting graves, although officially condemned and repressed, has been, if not the oldest, at least among the most lasting and deep-rooted of any.

A taste for archaeology and collecting was born, at least in part, from the objects that returned to the world clandestinely and confirmed scholars in their nostalgia for a golden age of antiquity. This phenomenon, gigantic in view of the extent of Chinese territory and history, was not without consequences for modern archaeology, which remains, more than elsewhere and in spite of current tendencies, an archaeology based on tombs and, what is more, frequently on violated tombs. Fortunately, the latter were sufficiently richly equipped to provide material both for ancient Chinese robbers and modern archaeologists.

In the 11th century, important finds on the site of the last Shang (17th–11th century BC) capital at Xiaotun, near Anyang (Henan province), excited tremendous interest in court circles. The excavated bronzes enriched the imperial collection and stimulated the production of imitations, and led to the first archaeological studies in the form of illustrated catalogues of objects.

The first of these catalogues, the *Kaogu tu*, (Illustrations for the Study of Antiquity, preface dated 1092), lists some 224 bronze and jade pieces from the palace and private collections, and gives for each piece the place of origin (when known), the dimensions, weight and a detailed drawing of the object and its inscription.

Other catalogues following the model for the *Kaogu tu* were soon drawn up, together with repertories of inscriptions. But this considerable work of listing and documentation, carried out by the Sung scholars at the instigation of emperors such as Huizong (1101–1125), was not followed up and researches conducted between the 14th and 15th centuries were determined more by the interests of collectors than by scientific considerations. The revival of interest in archaeology shown in the 18th century was almost exclusively concerned with epigraphy (the study of inscriptions), and all attempts at dating and chronology continued to be based on inscriptions until the beginning of the 20th century.

Western influence

The works of Chinese historians, and also the tastes of amateur collectors and the collections of antiquaries, prepared the ground, but scientific archaeology was born through contact with the West. The stimulus came from European missions of exploration; from vast engineering works such as the Zhengzhou-Luoyang-Xi'an railway, which cut its way through the immense cemetery of what from the 10th century BC to the 10th century AD had been the metropolitan zone; and from the discovery beginning in 1899 of thousands of prophetic and divinatory texts going back to the Shang dynasty.

The deciphering of these oracular inscriptions on bones and tortoise shells (*jiaguwen*), the oldest Chinese texts that have come down to us, gave birth to a new discipline noted from the beginning for the work of such eminent scholars as Luo Zhenyu (1866–1940), Wang Guowei (1877–1927) and Dong Zuobin (1895–1963). The fragments of shells and bones came from Xiaotun, near Anyang in Henan, the site which had yielded bronze ritual vessels since the

11th century. The importance of these texts led to the systematic excavation of the site of the last Shang capital. Excavations began in 1928 under the aegis of the recently founded Academia Sinica—Institute of History and Philology.

The site, known equally as Xiaotun and as Anyang, has no equal except for the major sites of the ancient Near East, and its study was to be the fundamental task of Chinese archaeology from 1928 to 1937. The Academia Sinica, under the direction of Li Chi (1896–1979), carried out 15 fieldwork operations there and formed a brilliant team of young researchers who were to become the masters of post-war Chinese archaeology. The work included the collection of numerous new inscriptions, and the exploration of the Shang town and the royal cemetery (unfortunately already looted). In 1937, on the declaration of the Sino-Japanese War, the archaeological team of the Academia Sinica withdrew to South China with the material dug up at Xiaotun. At the end of the war, this material was evacuated to Taiwan.

Prehistoric archaeology developed in parallel from 1920 with the Neolithic discoveries of J.G. Andersson (1874–1960) in Henan and then at Gansu, and the Paleolithic finds of E. Licent, P. Teilhard de Chardin and Pei Wenzhong (1904–1982). During the same period, the first attempts at interpretation and classification were made, with studies of ancient society by Guo Moruo (1892–1978) and researches by B. Karlgren (1889–1978) into the stylistic development of archaic bronzes. From 1937 to 1949, the interruption of excavations enabled a full report on the Anyang research to be written, and also the preparation of works of synthesis and the drawing up of future programmes.

Three periods can be distinguished in contemporary Chinese archaeology: the first from 1949 to 1965, the second from 1966 to 1976 and the third from 1976 to 1983. From 1950, the Institute of Archaeology of the Academy of Sciences took over from the Academia Sinica, which had emigrated to Taiwan, and reopened the Anyang site. During the 1950s and 1960s, the main task was to clarify the stratigraphy* of the site and work out a typology of the ceramics which would permit a chronology of future discoveries, itself linked to the results of studies of the oracular inscriptions.

In 1952, a second major site of the Shang dynasty was discovered at Zhengzhou (Henan). Considered by Chinese archaeologists as a capital exterior to Anyang, the town, encircled by a wall with foundations dated to c.1600BC, may not have been abandoned in favour of Anyang; it could have maintained an existence complementary to the more formal role of Anyang. Erlitou, another important centre from the Shang period or earlier, has been the scene of fieldwork since 1959.

Thus since the 1950s the emphasis has been on the first Chinese dynasties, not only on the Shang, but also on their predecessors, the Xia, whose remains are to be found both in the cultures from the end of the Neolithic and (for some scholars) at Erlitou, and finally on the Chou (11th–3rd century BC), where the research is mainly directed to the early phase and origins of the Chou culture.

Fieldwork from 1949 to 1965

This interest in the Bronze Age should not be thought to overshadow the other fields tackled by the archaeologists of the youthful People's Republic, for since 1950 sites have been opened up all over the country. These digs are basically salvage operations, dictated by the economic reconstruction of the country, but even if they exhibit the faults of this type of fieldwork, their

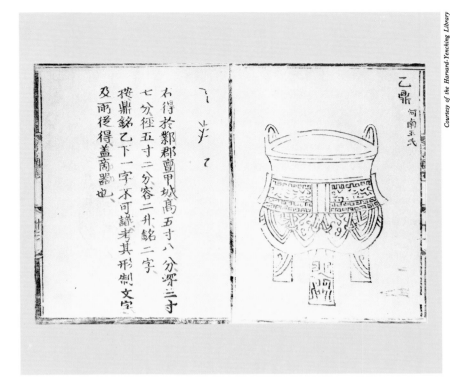

Ritual vase *(Yi ding)*

This illustration of a bronze vase is taken from a 1299 edition of *Kaogu tu* by Lü Dalin (originally published *c*.1092). The text accompanying the illustration specifies that the vase comes from Xiaotun (Anyang) and attributes it to the Shang period. Dimensions of the vase: overall height *5 cun 8 fen* (approximately 18cm or 7.2in); depth *3 cun 7 fen* (approximately 11.5cm or 4.6in); diameter *5 cun 2 fen* (approximately 16cm or 6.4in). Capacity: 2 *sheng*, that is 1.328 litres. Harvard Yenching Library.

results are rapidly published in specialized reviews: *Kaogu xuebao* (Archaeological Journal) as from 1951, *Kaogu tongxun* (Archaeological News) from 1955 (retitled *Kaogu* in 1959) and *Wenwu cankao ziliao*, from 1950, retitled *Wenwu* (Cultural Traces) from 1959. Provincial and municipal museums have been established and commissions for the preservation of ancient monuments have been set up in every province and village.

Literally thousands of sites have been surveyed or excavated. Major discoveries include the Neolithic village of Banpo in Shaanxi, the tombs of the kingdom of Chu (5th–3rd century BC), the tombs of the kingdom of Dian at Shizhaishan in Yunnan (2nd–1st century BC), and the ruins of the Han and Tang capitals at Xi'an (Shaanxi). Several positive developments of long-term importance stand out in this period from 1949 to 1965. Accurately dated tombs have been excavated in large numbers, making possible the establishment of an evolution of types and a precise chronology of grave goods, in particular for the period from the Han to the Tang (3rd century BC to 10th century AD). And the industrial work undertaken in South China, together with the discoveries that attended it, has begun to define the extraordinary regional diversity of prehistoric and historic cultures on Chinese territory.

The Cultural Revolution

From 1966 to 1976, China was shaken by ten years of disturbance, dark years for scientific research. The publication of archaeological reviews was suspended from 1966 to 1972; the training of future professionals was put in abeyance; intense ideological pressure led to dubious choices, as well as analyses and interpretations frequently falsified or forced. At the same time, under the effect of certain slogans and more generally a certain relaxation at the local level, destruction and depredation of the national heritage multiplied, while the old demon of grave robbing reared its head again.

Nevertheless, work in the field continued intensively, although often badly controlled at the scientific level. This period is marked by exceptional discoveries, which count among the most important of the last 30 years. Here we can mention only a few of them.

From the Neolithic, the discovery of the Hemudu culture in the lower basin of the Yangzi (Yangtze), contemporary with the Yangshao in North China and the cultures of Peiligang (Henan) and Cishan (Hebei), prior to the Yangshao and the Dawenkou culture (Shandong), enables archaeologists to propose a much more complex picture of the development and interactions of different Chinese Neolithic centres.

From the historical period, apart from the salvage excavations of part of the 14th-century Dadu capital Pekin (Peking), the main find has been that of the princely tombs which have yielded grave goods of extraordinary richness, such as the tomb of Fu Hao and Xiaotun, the first discovery of an unlooted royal Shang sepulchre, and the two Han tombs of Mancheng in Hebei. In addition, texts on bamboo strips and documents on silk paper of considerable importance (Yunmeng in Hubei, Mawangdui in Hunan, Astana in Xinjiang) have been recovered from some of these tombs. Other tombs were found decorated with mural paintings, such as Helingeer in Inner Mongolia from the Han dynasty, or the princely mausoleums of the T'ang at Xi'an. There have also been occasional important finds of caches, such as those of the Western Chou bronzes in Shaanxi, or Tang treasures of Hejiacun at Xi'an. Finally, there is the sensational discovery of the funeral pits containing warriors near the Mausoleum of Qin Shi Huangdi, which have been excavated since 1974.

This hasty enumeration gives only a brief and incomplete idea of the incredible mass of material brought to light during these difficult years, the scientific study of which will take several decades and will profoundly transform our vision of ancient China. The exceptional discoveries continued from 1977 to 1983 with the excavation of several tombs from the period of the Warring States, in particular the great tomb of Marquis Yi of Zeng at Suixian in Hubei and tombs of the ancient kingdom of Zhongshan in Hebei.

At the same time, a great deal of effort has been devoted to the improvement and diffusion of scientific methods and laboratory techniques. New reviews have multiplied, as have efforts to achieve better coordination between institutions, wider circulation of information and the promotion of planned archaeology. Numerous national and (since 1981) international conferences have been organized. The law of 19 November 1982 on the protection of cultural assets clearly shows the intentions of modern Chinese archaeology and its present direction. It also shows an awareness of its heritage, whose safety it must ensure. Thus a real policy for the promotion of ancient culture has been established; it is accompanied by a more enlightened attitude to the problems of studying and preserving the national heritage such as the campaign against tomb robbing, clandestine sale of items, destruction of ancient ceramic kilns, and so on.

Chinese archaeology today

Chinese archaeology remains an archaeology based on the object. It concentrates on typologies (the correspondence between different types), on technological analyses and classification by periods, but it deals only incidentally with the ways in which changes took place within ancient societies. Nor is man often studied in the context of his environment. There are no excavations of habitations in the historical period; studies of natural regions and the connections involved in cultural developments remain on a modest scale. A more serious omission, perhaps, is the comparative silence of Chinese archaeologists when it comes to placing Chinese history in its Asiatic context. This somewhat closed attitude weighs heavily on archaeological research and delays the solution and even study of many crucial problems.

Nevertheless, as regards the interior of the national territory there have been recent changes in the way of tackling problems. Starting with the excavations of the last 30 years, the importance of regional variations has made itself felt, especially with regard to the Neolithic, but also with regard to the Bronze Age. The primacy traditionally given to the basin of the Yellow River as the unique centre from which civilization issued is gradually being erased by the acceptance of cultural zones with a mutual effect on each other.

Rather than presenting a few major discoveries which are readily available in recent syntheses and exhibition catalogues, we have chosen in the following pages to clarify a certain number of themes and problems in the fields of the history of science and technology, of art, of religion and of material culture. We have also attempted to deal with certain aspects of the relations between China and the outside world as they have been revealed in excavations conducted recently in and outside China.

North and south in the Chinese Neolithic

The tremendous increase in archaeological work in China since 1947 has brought new insights into how Chinese civilization originated and developed in Neolithic times.

Until very recently, it seemed to be accepted that the cradle of Chinese civilization was in the basin of the Huanghe (Huang Ho) river. The rest of China, supposedly less advanced, must have received from this favoured region the people and techniques which finally enabled it, in the Bronze Age and under the Chou dynasty, to present a relatively homogeneous cultural aspect. The discovery of numerous Paleolithic remains in various regions, consisting of 89 sites (36 in the south of the country) and the study of more than 6,000 Neolithic sites, indicates that things were not so simple. In spite of its importance, the region of the Huanghe or Yellow River is only one zone among others in a country where the centres of Neolithic activity correspond exactly to the zones which are most densely populated to this day.

The major questions now under discussion concern the emergence of agriculture—millet in the north, rice in the south—and the evolution of Neolithic societies to the stage when the state could emerge. Although the oldest Neolithic remains go back to the 10th millennium, at Zengypiyan, Guangxi (Kwangsi) 9360BC ± 180, some regions still lived in a Neolithic context until the 2nd millennium, when others had already entered the Bronze Age.

In spite of the still fragmentary nature of the information available, we can distinguish two large archaeological areas of equal importance during this long period, whose different traditions were to fertilize Chinese civilization as a whole: the north with the basin of the Huanghe or Yellow River, occupied by the Hua Xia ethnic group, and the south with the basin of the Yangzi (Yangtze) or Blue River, where the ethnic groups of the Miao Man were active. Between the two, the eastern coastal strip was occupied by the Dong Yi tribes, whose cultures were associated sometimes with one great region, sometimes with the other.

The most ancient Neolithic cultures so far recognized in north China date to the 6th millennium. The sites of Laoguantai (Huaxian, Shaanxi), Beiligang (Henan), and Cishan (Hebei), have yielded traces of millet, stone tools and the bones of dogs, pigs, cattle and sheep. The crude red pottery is decorated with corded and combed motifs and already includes tripods.

Yangshao, Dawenkou and Longshan

The Yangshao culture, dated from the end of the 6th to the beginning of the 2nd millennium, seems to be a direct descendant of these cultures. On the evidence of about 100 sites scattered in the basin of the Huanghe from Gansu and Qinghai to western Shandong (Shantung) it is characterized by unfortified villages with specialized quarters occupied periodically by partly settled farmers. The millet harvest was stored in pits or granary jars and hunting played an important part in the diet, in spite of some domestication of dogs, pigs, sheep and cows. Crafts seem to have been well developed. They included the weaving of hemp and silk, and in particular the production of fine red pottery hand-cast but finished on the wheel, with dark, very carefully painted decoration. Some pieces bear engraved marks which could be the ancestors of Chinese characters. The Yangshao culture underwent several regional variations, sometimes staged at different times, and was diffused westward to Gansu and Qinghai until the 2nd millennium.

At the time when the Huanghe basin saw the development of the activities of the Yangshao farmers, present-day Shandong province, in the neighbourhood of Taishan, saw the Dawenkou culture prosper from c.5000BC to about 2300BC. Its precursors can be found in the Early Neolithic of the Yangzhou (Wangyin) and Beixin (Xixian), at Beiligang and beyond that in the Paleolithic cultures of the region. It was to spread southwards as far as Jiangsu.

Famous for its cemeteries of individual tombs indicating marked social differences, the Dawenkou culture consisted of farmers who worked with stone, bone and deer-tooth tools and practised the same type of stockbreeding as their Yangshao contemporaries. The red pottery, grey and black in the final phase, sometimes bears incised marks. The most characteristic form is the *gui* tripod ewer with hollow legs in the form of lobes, as found at Longshan.

In effect Dawenkou is the direct ancestor, and the immediate predecessor, of the Longshan culture of Shandong and was long considered the sole point of departure for the Longshan culture as a whole (3rd millennium), identified for the first time at Chengziyai and Liangchenzhe in 1928.

The villages are surrounded by walls of rammed earth, and the strange and sometimes hasty burials, with bodies packed into abandoned granary pits, suggest raids or deadly combats unknown at Yangshao. Beyond its regional grouping of Shaanxi, Henan, and Shandong, the Longshan culture, like the Yangshao culture with which it coexisted for a time on certain sites before replacing it, was based on millet farming. Totally settled, the people also grew wheat and barley. They improved their conditions and their diet by hunting with spears and fishing with harpoons, and perfected stockbreeding with the domestication of the buffalo. Their finely polished stone tools are sometimes incised with an animal mask motif comparable to that of the first Shang bronzes. The high-quality red, grey and white pottery continued, but it is the very thin black pottery, with a sober decoration of strips in relief or incised lines (raised on the wheel in 50 percent of cases) that remains the characteristic feature of Longshan. Such pieces were undoubtedly ritual vessels.

Important social stratification and the practice of scapulomancy (divination using "oracle bones") indicate that the transition to the Bronze Age was approaching, and the conditions for this came together in the Longshan of Henan, the immediate predecessor of the Shang culture.

Daxi and Qujialing cultures

In the south of China, from the 4th millennium, the first phase of the Neolithic of the middle Yangzi (Yangtze) is represented by the Daxi culture, on both banks of the great river, from Wushan in eastern Sichuan to Jiangling and Gong'an in Hubei and Lixian in Hunan, and southward as far as Lake Dongting. Characterized by its finely polished stone tools and red pottery with red slip, and black, brown or red painted decoration, this culture is illustrated by a whole series of remains, including those from the eponymous site of Daxi. The most typical pottery shapes are cylindrical vases unknown elsewhere, cups with rounded curves (for hunting, it has been surmised), balls and animal statuettes. Burial methods, with body kneeling and limbs flexed, differ from the Yangshao practices, although mutual contacts existed in the northern band of the Daxi cultural area.

In the 3rd millennium, the second phase of the Neolithic of the middle Yangzi, that of the rice-growing culture of Qujialing (*c.*2750–2650BC), is characterized by beautiful, small, polished stone tools and by a delicate pottery which began to be raised on the wheel. Its decoration, sometimes painted, sometimes of basketwork, is applied to various shapes, the most typical being the cup with a broken profile on a tall circular foot.

The third phase of the Neolithic of the middle Yangzi corresponds to the end of the Yangshao culture and to the Longshan culture of Henan in the Huanghe region. Contacts between the cultures multiplied. The number of painted ceramics decreased, basketwork or checked decoration was applied to the greyish-white wares, and forms were mostly raised on the wheel. The *gui* ewer with hollow feet, common in the Dawenkou and Longshan cultures, now made its appearance, but with more conical feet. This indicates a mixed culture still based on the Qujialing culture, but enriched by contributions from the Longshan of the middle Huanghe.

In 1973, the site of Hemudu, the oldest layer of which goes back more than 7,000 years, was discovered at Zhejiang to the south of the Bay of Hangzhou (lower Yangzi). Living in wooden houses of complicated mortice and tenon manufacture, undoubtedly on piles and, according to Chinese archaeologists, in a matriarchal society, the inhabitants of Hemudu cultivated rice in water-fed paddies, using bone hoes mounted on wooden handles. These elaborate tools, found in large numbers on the site, were not used until much later in the Huanghe basin, where the stone shovel long continued in use. The black, simply made pottery, rich in carbon, consists of receptacles and supports with forms and decorations very different from those found in the Yangshao culture.

The region of Nankin, southern Jiangsu, and the environs of Shanghai, Changzhou and Wuxian have already yielded many Neolithic sites from the Majiabin culture, going back to about 4000BC, in particular villages with rectangular houses of hardened earth. Their inhabitants cultivated rice in flooded paddies and harvested the water chestnut; they practised stockbreeding (oxen, buffalo), as well as hunting (deer, wild boar, fox) and fishing (fish and turtle). The cemeteries with individual tombs in which the dead were laid out face downwards, accompanied by pottery and sometimes by finely polished jade ornaments, were situated far from the dwellings. The sandy or fine red hand-cast pottery was often covered with slip. *Ding* tripods, characteristic of northern cultures, are rare and have broad and flat feet. No painted pottery has been found. The most characteristic tools are still flat axes with a central perforation. To some authors, the Majiabin culture represents the southern aspect of a culture from the coastal strip separating the lower basin of the Huanghe from the basin of the Yangzi.

The eastern coastal strip also developed an important culture in the Neolithic period. This was contemporary with the Yangshao culture, a fact that poses so many problems that certain archaeologists propose two distinct cultures, one connected with the northern millet-growing area, the other with the southern rice-growing area, instead of two local groupings of a single culture. Discovered in 1951 in the north of Jiangsu, the Qingliangang culture (4800–3600BC), revealed in numerous sites at Jiangsu, Anhui and Zhejiang, seems to have been diffused from the south to the north, where it became confused with the final phase of the Dawenkou culture. Characterized by a fine or sandy red hand-cast pottery, with decoration painted on the slip, the Qingliangang culture is one of farmers, stockbreeders and fishers who lived in houses of cob (clay and chopped straw) and buried their dead laid out in individual graves with few grave goods. They used many good-quality polished stone tools such as perforated axes, knives, scissors, perforated hoes, occasional adzes with removable heads, and heavy-duty axes.

The Liangzhu culture, discovered on the boundaries of Jiangsu and Zhejiang in 1936, succeeded the Qingliangang–Majiabin between 3600 and 2400BC. The rice farmers of Liangzhu used stone tools in the Qingliangang tradition and had developed the crafts of basket-making and textiles (hemp and silk). The pottery is mainly black, delicate, and made on the wheel with little or no decoration; it is reminiscent of Longshan ceramics, but sometimes bears incised marks that differ from those of the northern culture. A typical form is that of the animal-form ewer that is also found in Shandong.

Overlapping cultures

The boundary between the Neolithic and the Bronze Age does not emerge clearly. This was a time when the whole of the area covered by present-day China contained a multitude of different cultures, and many networks of villages that maintained relations and engaged in various forms of exchange. It is not impossible that a more socially developed group, the Xia, heirs of the Yangshao culture, according to some authors, or the Shang heirs of the Longshan culture in Henan, according to others, found themselves in a position to impose a certain political and religious supremacy, probably as flexible as it was fluctuating, on human groups in the north of China who had stayed in the Neolithic stage. From elementary knowledge of metalworking (attested by several Yangshao and Longshan sites), this group reached a stage of mastery of bronze metallurgy, on which it based its internal and external power, and its legitimacy. Exchanges with other cultures continued; the Shang borrowed from the coast the use of tortoiseshell and jade work, and perhaps from the south the manufacture of an early kind of porcelain, and the other cultures gradually absorbed new techniques and consequently new values. It seems quite possible that the Shang civilization spread widely beyond the limits of the strictly political domain of the dynasty.

The Neolithic of the southeast of China is thus beginning to be better known. Today the sites of Xianrendong (Jiangxi), Fugotun (Fujian) and Zengpiyan (Guangxi) seem inseparable from the Hoabinhian and Bacsonian of Vietnam. The influence of these cultures on the more northerly ones of the rest of the country, and indirectly on the Bronze Age civilization, remains to be decided.

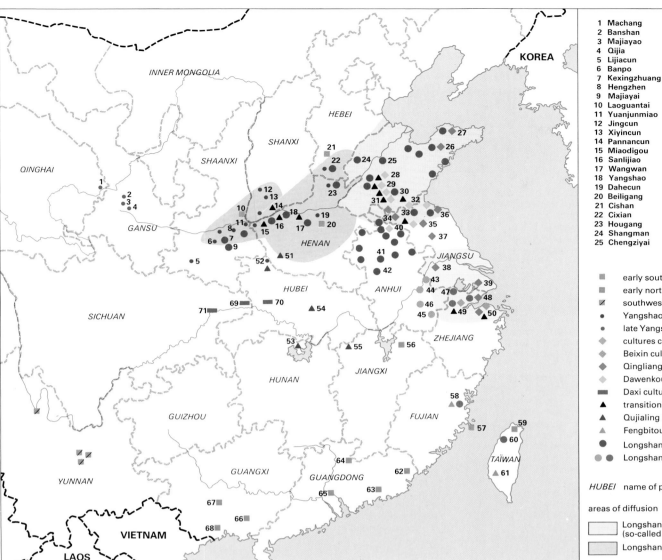

1 Machang	26 Jingzhizhen	51 Xiawanggang
2 Banshan	27 Zijinshan	52 Dasi
3 Majiayao	28 Dawenkou	53 Mengxi
4 Qijia	29 Xixiahou	54 Qujialing
5 Lijiacun	30 Yedian	55 Paomaling
6 Banpo	31 Kangshan	56 Xianrendong
7 Kexingzhuang	32 Dafeizhuang	57 Fuguotun
8 Hengzhen	33 Dadunzi	58 Tanshishan
9 Majiayai	34 Liulin	59 Dapenkeng
10 Laoguantai	35 Huating	60 Yingpu
11 Yuanjunmiao	36 Lianyungang	61 Fengbitou
12 Jingcun	37 Qingliangang	62 Chao'an
13 Xiyincun	38 Beiyingyangyin	63 Haifeng
14 Pannancun	39 Sunze	64 Wengyuan
15 Miaodigou	40 Xiaoxian	65 Xijiaoshan
16 Sanlijiao	41 Shouxian	66 Lingshan
17 Wangwan	42 Huoqiu	67 Nanning
18 Yangshao	43 Dangtu	68 Dongxing
19 Dahecun	44 Wuhu	69 Daxi
20 Beiligang	45 Jiqi	70 Xilingxia
21 Cishan	46 Jingde	71 Zhongxian
22 Cixian	47 Qianshanyang	
23 Hougang	48 Majiabin	
24 Shangman	49 Liangzhu	
25 Chengziyai	50 Hemudu	

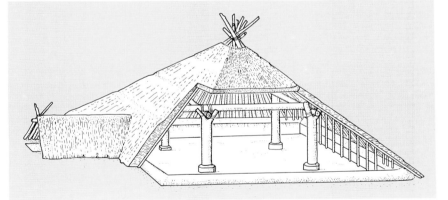

- ■ early southern Neolithic, cultures allied to Dapenkeng
- ■ early northern Neolithic (pre-Yangshao)
- ▨ southwestern Neolithic
- • Yangshao
- • late Yangshao
- ◆ cultures contemporary with Yangshao
- ◆ Beixin culture
- ◆ Qingliangang and allied cultures
- ◆ Dawenkou culture
- ▬ Daxi culture
- ▲ transitional Yangshao-Longshan (ex: Miaodigou II)
- ▲ Qujialing culture
- ▲ Fengbitou culture
- ● Longshan
- ●● Longshanoid

HUBEI name of province

areas of diffusion

- Longshan of Shandong (so-called classical)
- Longshan of Henan
- Longshan of Shaanxi
- Southern Longshan (Liangzhu)

The principal Chinese Neolithic sites

Rich in archaeological sites, long looked on as the cradle of the country, the basin of the Huanghe or Yellow River, where political activity was concentrated throughout Chinese history, is today considered one of the three great Chinese cultural areas, in addition to the basin of the Yangzi or Blue River and the eastern coastal strip. Still little known, but comparable to the Neolithic of Southeast Asia, the southern Neolithic undoubtedly played an important part in the formation of Chinese civilization.

House at Banpo (Shaanxi), Yangshao culture. 5th–4th millennium BC

Built in the centre of the village, measuring 11 × 10m (36 × 33ft), the house shown here was the largest building in the village and probably served as a communal house. In spite of the roof descending to ground level, the fundamental principal of Chinese architecture already stands out. The columns on a stone base are supporters. Walls are made of clay and straw. After Chang Kwangchih, *The Archaeology of Ancient China*.

Ceramic basin with painted black decor. Banpo (Shaanxi), Yangshao culture. 5th–4th millennium

Present in both classical Yangshao and classical Gansu, this type of deep bowl may have had a totemic and propitiatory significance, and may have been connected with fishing. At all events, the stylized figures on either side of the face represent fish.

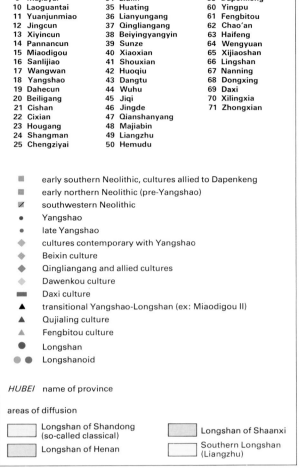

Jade plaque engraved in low relief

This beautifully fashioned plaque comes from the coastal zone where the Liangzhu culture soon became distinguished for its exquisite jade work. Freer Gallery of Art, Washington.

White ceramic *gui* tripod pot, Weifong (Shandong). Late 3rd–early 2nd millennium

Characteristic of eastern Longshan, the *gui* ewer, with its body divided into three lobes and fashioned by hand, is decorated here with lozenges in relief resembling the rivets on a metal model. This form disappeared in the Bronze Age.

Bronze, iron and steel

Chinese archaeologists have recently been able to show how the Chinese Bronze Age was quite distinct from Bronze Age cultures in the West. Indeed, steelmaking technology was to develop in China far in advance of Western cultures.

It is not possible to give an accurate date for the appearance of metal in China. It probably did not occur in any single point in time, because this vast territory already possessed in the Neolithic period many cultures at widely different technological levels.

The oldest copper object is a knife 12.6cm (5in) long, with a convex back and hammered handle, recovered from a site of the Majiayao culture in Gansu (c.3000BC). The oldest bronze objects come from the same region and were found on sites of the Machang culture (c.2300–2000BC) and the Qiji culture (c.2000BC). These are genuine bronze pieces, made of copper and tin. Others appeared on sites of the Longshan culture in Shandong (Shantung) with an estimated C^{14}* dating of 4100BC ± 90, and in Hebei (Hopei). It is generally thought that China entered the Bronze Age at the end of the Xia dynasty (21st–16th century BC) or at the beginning of the Shang dynasty (16th–12th century BC), according to whether the sites of the Erlitou culture are attributed to one or the other dynasty. These sites confirmed the transition from the Longshan Neolithic to the Erligang Bronze Age (early Shang phase). The diffusionist theory which proposes a western origin for Chinese metallurgy has been abandoned today by most archaeologists, who support the theory of a native or indigenous emergence of the art of bronze working.

Associated with the aristocracy, on whom it conferred political power, bronze metallurgy in China includes several original features. As elsewhere in the world, the possession of bronze weapons permitted a restricted elite to enjoy power over other levels of society and, by means of wars fought abroad, to acquire material goods and wealth. In addition, however, the manufacture and use of ritual vessels had a special relevance. These were devoted to the cult of royal ancestors, and constituted both a sign of authority and a guarantee of legitimacy. The other original feature (leaving aside the possibility of cold-metal working, for which there is at present no convincing proof) relates to the complicated casting method used by the Chinese. This derived from their long familiarity with pottery kilns, which even in Neolithic times produced pieces fired at high temperatures. The foundries were established near the palaces, and were also very close to the potters' kilns.

Installed in the basin of the Huanghe (Huang Ho), the Xia and the Shang had at their disposal reasonably abundant tin ore and very abundant copper ore within a radius of 300km (186 miles) around Zhengzhou, Erlitou and Yanshi. The centre and south of Shanxi and to a lesser extent the region of the middle Yangzi and the Huai were supply centres to be protected or conquered by force. This ore never had a very high metal content and so produced a great deal of slag. When slag is absent from foundry sites, this indicates that refining was done at the mine and that the ingots of purified metal were transported from there to the foundry.

Archaeologists have discovered an old copper mine at Tonglushan, Hebei, which goes back to the Chunqiu period, and was exploited for several centuries. These show how vertical shafts were dug to the base of the deposit, and then narrow galleries, propped up by wooden posts, followed the vein upwards to the surface.

The sites of several Shang foundries have been excavated, and those in the environs of Zhengzhou have yielded the remains of bronze and ceramic moulds. The immense foundry of Yinxu, with an area of 5000 sq m (54,000 sq ft) and dated to the end of the Shang dynasty, produced enormous quantities of ritual vessels, many examples of which have been found nearby. Later, the Houma factory, in the industrial quarter of the capital of the Jin principality (6th–5th century) to the southwest of Shanxi, was divided into workshops specializing in the production of a particular type of object, including ritual vessels, bells, equipment for chariots and cavalry, and mirrors.

Bronze casting techniques

From Phase III of the Erlitou culture, casting methods had already become established and very elaborate. Undamaged objects from the levels of the palace and its annexes include weapons, such as halberds, axes and arrowheads, as well as bells and ritual vessels, some with very thin sides. These already exhibit the special Chinese techniques and qualities which encouraged the success of Anyang bronzes. Bronze alloys varied from 92 percent copper and 8 percent tin in an Erlitou *jue* tripod, to about 71–75 percent copper, 10–11 percent tin and 10–16 percent lead in objects from the end of the dynasty. The pieces were cast in ceramic crucibles inside furnaces capable of withstanding the 1150°C (2102°F) required for a smooth flow of the alloy. The fuel for this continued to be wood charcoal for several centuries. It was only under the eastern Chou that coal began to be used concurrently. The low melting point of tin and lead ensured fineness of detail in the decoration.

For weapons, hinged ceramic moulds were used, or in some rare cases moulds of porous sandstone. For ritual vessels, the procedure of casting in sectional moulds, a feature peculiar to China, was the only method used by founders until the 6th century BC.

A model of the receptacle was first made of very high quality clay, on which all the decoration was incised. A mould of this was then made by applying to it a layer of clay about 1.5cm (0.5in) thick. To ensure the correct placing of the decoration, the mould was then divided into several sections. After scraping the model, small bronze wedges were inserted between the latter, now a core, and the outside mould, to give the object a uniform thickness. When the molten metal was poured in, air escaped through vent holes. After cooling, the mould was opened and the vase was retouched, filed or polished if necessary.

The founder generally carried this out in a single operation, but in certain cases, especially from the Chunqiu period, the handles and the bases, which often still contained their core, were cast in advance and then arranged in the mould for the main flow of metal.

To this complicated procedure, which allowed great accuracy in the decoration, and owed a great deal to the skill and experience of the potter, was added, from the Chunqiu period, the *cire perdue* (lost wax*) technique. Thus the luxuriant openwork decoration on certain vases discovered in the tomb of the Marquis of Zeng at Suixian, Hubei, could not have been executed with a sectioned mould.

Iron casting techniques

In the same period, founders were at work on the composition of alloys, whose viscosity they sought to improve. Metallurgical techniques were now completely mastered, but bronze remained an expensive metal, and although it continued to be used for arms for several centuries, iron began to replace it towards the 6th century BC for the manufacture of tools and a variety of agricultural implements.

The first objects containing iron date to the Shang or early Chou. These were bronze axes with cutting edges of meteoric iron. Two were discovered at Gaocheng, Hebei, and two others at Xunxian, Henan. However, the Iron Age did not really begin until the 6th century.

After a phase when hammered iron was probably used, the employment of cast iron for tools and everyday objects spread very quickly. The first mention of a cast iron object goes back to 513BC and it shows clearly that the casting of white metal had been mastered and was in general use. Iron ore was available everywhere and in much greater abundance than copper ore, especially in Shanxi and Shaanxi, the traditional zone of activity of the first dynasties.

Thanks to the profusion of clay ideally suited for the building of kilns and the manufacture of crucibles, Chinese craftsmen were able to smelt the ore completely and eliminate the slag. Refining was done with coal at a fairly low temperature of 800–1000°C (1472–1832°F) and produced spongy pig iron, rich in carbon. The melting point of this was less than that needed for pure iron, and could fall to 1130°C (2060°F) for a carbon content of 4.3 percent—only 80°C (176°F) more than that of bronze.

These high temperatures were obtained with different types of fuel, used in larger quantities than in the West: wood and charcoal to begin with, and then coal at the end of the Eastern Chou period. Coal replaced charcoal from the end of the 1st millennium AD.

From the Han period, many foundries have been discovered. Some furnaces built of large refractory clay bricks were of sufficient size and volume to enable a production of half a tonne to one tonne a day. Under the Western Han (206BC–AD8), a double-action piston bellows capable of producing a continuous blast, was operated by labourers, but from about the beginning of our era, in the time of Wang Mang, hydraulic power took the place of human effort, owing to the invention of a vertical wheel activated by the current of a river.

The foundry of Tieshenggou, Gongxian, Henan, was in operation from the middle of the Western Han dynasty to the period of Wang Mang, and some 2000 sq m (21,527 sq ft) of this site has been excavated, revealing an area for the preparation of ore, 18 furnaces, a crucible furnace and a forge, as well as pudding basins and sunken warehouses. Some of the furnaces reduced the ore at a relatively low temperature and produced ingots of spongy iron, while others produced cast iron at a high temperature, and yet others steel.

Early steel production

In fact, besides the technique of casting iron, which was already considerably in advance of contemporary Europe, the Chinese were from the 2nd century AD capable of making steel by a variety of empirical methods. One consisted in introducing carbon into the metal in the solid state—the iron was heated in coal for at least 20 hours at more than 900°C (1652°F)—or continuing to heat the metal during forging.

Another technique, inaugurated in the middle of the Western Han dynasty, is that of the decarburation of the cast iron in its solid state. At the end of the dynasty, steel was produced from semi-liquid cast iron agitated in an oxidizing atmosphere (often under cold blast). Partial decarburation produced steel, and complete decarburation wrought iron.

The well-known technique called the "thousand refinings" could be operated either by puddling cast iron with wrought iron by introducing carbon and forging the metal to the stage of steel, or by puddling the cast iron until, once the right carbon content had been achieved, the metal could be forged and eventually transformed into steel.

The abundance of ore and the availability of large quantities of cast iron were far greater in China than in medieval Europe. This, together with the needs of the rapidly expanding Han economy and the expertise of the craftsmen, are all factors which explain the industrial nature of Chinese iron and steel metallurgy at the beginning of our era. The technique of moulding was improved for mass production. Stacks of ceramic moulds, still hot from being fired or specially reheated, received the molten metal which stayed fluid enough to fill every corner of each mould in the pile. The piles were smeared with a mixture of chopped straw and clay which solidified while drying and facilitated handling. Reconstruction experiments have been carried out by Chinese archaeologists on the site of the foundry of Wenxian, Henan, which was in operation under the early Han: these show that the ideal temperature for the moulds during firing was 600°C (1112°F), a temperature which had to be maintained for several hours before it could be reduced to the 300°C (572°F) favourable for the molten metal.

Belt buckles and items of harness were mass-produced at Wenxian, where certain multiple moulds enabled the manufacture of up to six models of objects in piles of fourteen layers. For objects with simple shapes, individual cast iron moulds with thick walls replaced ceramic moulds. Because of the speed with which they could be manipulated, these brought about an increase in productivity and a considerable saving in cost. When the government nationalized the metal industry in 111BC, the number of iron commissioners to be established was no fewer than 49.

Originally used for tool manufacture, ferrous metals later found a place in sculpture, with numerous Buddhist statues of the 6th century AD, as well as in architecture, with the suspension bridges of south China where wrought-iron chains replaced bamboo cables from the 6th century. Some religious buildings from the Tang dynasty contained pillars or other supporting elements of cast iron. Several cast iron pagodas, one built in Hebei in 1061, have survived to this day.

Although China's technological advance over Europe is old and undeniable, it should not be forgotten that the empirical procedures so successful in different technical fields were based on the common sense and habits of observation of the ancient Chinese, and were not the product of scientific thought. In this regard, Joseph Needham has very rightly pointed out that the idea of natural law was unknown in China.

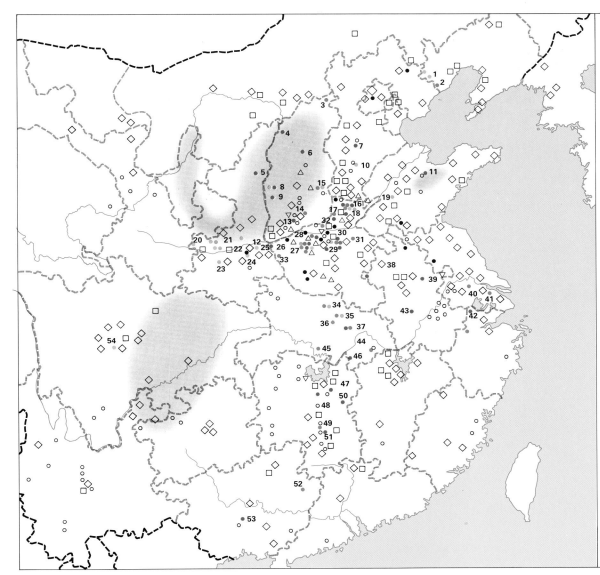

1 Kezu	15 Changzhi	29 Dengfeng	43 Feixi
2 Tangshan	16 Anyang	30 Zhengzhou	44 Tonglüshan
3 Liyu	17 Huixian	31 Xinzhang	45 Jiangling
4 Baode	18 Xunxian	32 Wenxian	46 Chongyang
5 Suide	19 Feicheng	33 Shangcunling	47 Changsha
6 Xinxian	20 Baoji	34 Suixian	48 Ningxiang
7 Gaocheng	21 Qishan	35 Jingshan	49 Hengshan
8 Shilou	22 Fufeng	36 Tianmen	50 Liling
9 Yonghe	23 Meixian	37 Panlongcheng	51 Changning
10 Xingtai	24 Chang'an	38 Funan	52 Gongcheng
11 Yidu	25 Lintong	39 Jiashan	53 Wuming
12 Lingtai	26 Lingbao	40 Yandushan	54 Pengxian
13 Xiaxian	27 Luoyang	41 Wujin	
14 Houma	28 Erlitou	42 Changxing	

- archaeological sites of the Erlitou culture (Xia or early Shang). First use of bronze, 19th-16thC BC
- sites of the Erligang culture (Shang), 16th-14thC BC
- regional cultures using bronze under the Shang, 15th-11thC BC
- sites of the Anyang culture (Shang), 13th-11thC BC
- Xi Zhou sites, 11th-10thC BC
- Late Xi Zhou sites, 10th-8thC BC
- Chunqiu period sites, 770-476BC
- ○ copper ore
- △ tin ore
- ▽ principal sites of the Chunqiu period which have yielded iron objects
- □ principal sites of the Zhanguo period which have yielded iron objects
- ◇ sites of the Han period which have yielded iron objects
- ● sites of iron foundries from the Zhanguo and Han period

coal mining zones

Sites yielding metal objects

Once metallurgical techniques were mastered, bronze first, then iron some 10 centuries later, they spread throughout the country, reaching isolated areas after some delay. A great number of sites have yielded bronze and iron artifacts, but the sites where the objects were manufactured are much less numerous. Generally situated in regions close to mining zones, as at Houma (Shanxi), Tieshenggou and Wenxian (Henan), the foundries have been excavated for some 20 years.

Jue ritual vessel (for alcohol), Erlitou (Henan), First half of 2nd millennium BC

Cast in a mould with three segments, this vase, made in a single operation, has a fold at the edge of the opening which has led certain authorities to propose that a phase of cold-working bronze by hammering could have preceded the casting process.

Zun ritual vessel (for alcohol), Minxyiang (Hunan). 14th–11th century BC

Cast in several stages (the small dragons' heads, the horns and ears of rams were incorporated with the principal casting), this vessel shows that, from the time of the Anyang craftsmen, the southern workshops had metallurgists capable of strong realism and technical masterpieces.

Bimetallic qi axe. Shang period 16th–12th century BC

This classical bronze axe is distinguished from other Shang pieces by the presence of iron of meteoric origin on its cutting edge. The iron blade, previously pierced with three holes, was adapted to a mould specially made so that the bronze melt poured in easily. Freer Gallery of Art, Washington.

Iron furnace; Reconstruction of the furnace at Wenxian, Henan. Han period

The combustion of wood piled up near the door of the furnace produced gases passing uniformly between the piles of moulds, thus ensuring regular firing. Above the furnace, the production chain normally included an open crucible where the pigs to feed the moulds were cast.

Burial practices of the Chu kingdom

At the time of the heyday of classical Greece in the 5th century BC, a splendid civilization existed not only in China proper but also among her so-called "barbarian" neighbours, such as the Chu.

For a long time the Chinese believed that the plain of the Yangzi (Yangtze) river did not have its own culture; the people of the Chu Kingdom were called barbarians or "Manyi". Archaeological discoveries in the Changsha region, begun in the 1930s, covered the whole territory under Chu influence at its zenith, and have made that belief out of date. They have also revealed a civilization of the 5th and 6th centuries BC that rivalled the splendour of all the princely courts of China.

Ancient texts referring to the country of Chu tell us little about the precise extent of its territory or about its religion and customs. But archaeologists have the evidence of approximately 3,500 excavated tombs from the period, with funerary rites and grave goods attesting both to the extent that the inhabitants of Chu absorbed Chinese speech and customs, and to the singular character of their culture. The majority of these tombs date from the middle and end of the period of the Warring States (c.481–221BC). With the exception of Tomb No 2 from Xiaxi in Henan, dated to about the middle of the 6th century BC, and far removed from the political centre of Chu, there is no large-scale burial prior to this period. This is all the more surprising because excavations have revealed two large 5th century tombs, which although not Chu, demonstrate close links with its culture: the tombs of the Lord of Cai, at Shouxian, Anhui, from perhaps the early 5th century, and that of Marquis of Zeng at Leigudun, Hubei, from the end of the 5th century. Some of the tombs, including the largest, contain ceramic vessels associated with bronze ritual vases, whose shapes they imitate. A number of small or medium-sized tombs contain only ceramics in place of bronzes, or even small-scale mingqi* ("spirit utensil") copies.

The unique nature of Chu culture does not derive from the existence of such imitations, since they had appeared elsewhere in China and earlier (9th century), but on the spread of this custom and on the remarkable quality of the pieces. As a symbol of all that is most original in the Chu culture, we may single out the sculpture of a monster with antler-crowned head, which is often placed at the head of the coffin. This position suggests that the fantastic animal may have protected the deceased, or symbolized a shaman and his power. In its sculptured form, this gradually disappears from tombs during the 3rd century, but increasing numbers of wooden figurines were placed in compartments next to the coffin, and the treatment of their faces and clothes became increasingly individualized.

These different characteristics, like the iconographic repertory of images peculiar to the Chu, reveal the existence of a cult that differs from those of the northern principalities in being not exclusively devoted to ancestors. Musical instruments and, even more, weapons, are found in considerable numbers, both in medium-sized and large tombs. In addition to these pieces, lacquerware consisting of crockery, boxes, and toilet cases has been recovered, increasing in quantity in the 3rd century BC. The nature of these grave offerings indicates the funerary practices of the period of the Western Han, which consisted in providing the dead with objects needed for their life in the hereafter. But in the Chu period, the ritual function of the grave goods still seems to predominate.

Even more than their grave goods, it was the structure of the tombs which attracted the excavators' attention. There seemed to be a rule or code that prescribed a type of tomb for each individual, depending on his rank. Nevertheless, if this code really did exist, it still has to be deciphered, not forgetting that it may have altered with the passage of time. This research is just beginning and has encountered many difficulties. The large or medium-sized tombs with a wooden protective structure or external coffin are too few (about 15) compared with the small tombs of the same type and the countless tombs without wooden protection or even any coffin. Moreover, many tombs are no longer in their original state, owing to looting (fortunately often partial) or because they have not resisted the ravages of time, even though the methods used to preserve them in the Chu world were far more advanced than in the rest of China. Finally, the dating of most of the examples available is far from satisfactory.

Distinctive Chu features

With these reservations, the arrangement of the various Chu tombs shows many common features which differentiate them clearly from those of the rest of China; they form a relatively homogeneous whole, apparently organized in a hierarchy. The types of tomb are limited to four categories: they may have one or two external caskets and an internal casket, only one casket, or no casket at all. Of large or medium size, with an opening in the ground longer than 4.5m (14ft), they are marked by a tumulus with height of 6–7m (19–22ft) and a diameter of as much as 100m (330ft). Thus, some 800 hillocks of various sizes cover the countryside around Jiangling. Some are even surrounded by secondary

tumuli, and these may be royal tombs. The ground is generally dug out in the shape of an inverted pyramid, the sides of which are cut into steps, from 3 to 15 in number, down to the level of the external coffin, surrounded by vertical partition walls with a total depth of 5–12m (16–38ft). A passage of varying length and width usually led to it. At the bottom of the pit, two or more beams were placed at ground level to support the external coffin built with thick planks. Thus, unlike many northern tombs, the funerary chamber proper was not hollowed out of one side of the pit, and no stone was used in its construction. Its protection was ensured by "white" (actually often grey) clay of very fine quality which enveloped it and is typical of Chu tombs.

The largest of the tombs contain, in the space between a central funeral chamber with several fitted coffins and the area of the outside coffin, a number of compartments containing the grave goods—up to 6 at Changtaiguan and Tianxingguan. There may be a correspondence between the number of fitted coffins and the status of the deceased, but we lack the data to confirm the precise details. Many Chinese archaeologists interpret the layout of these tombs as symbolizing an earthly dwelling or residence, but this interpretation neglects the deeply religious nature, emphasized in ancient texts, of the inhabitants of Chu. Nevertheless, it is probably not without foundation, because finds have included sculptures or engravings on the walls of tombs from the Warring States period and, later, depictions of doors and windows. But these may merely by symbolic openings to suggest the passage of the deceased's soul. The windows painted on the sides of coffins in the tomb of Leigudun seem to support this interpretation.

The smaller tombs are built on the same model, but the pit is shallower or non-existent, with no steps or access passage, and the outside compartment is reduced to one funerary chamber, sometimes flanked by a lateral compartment and a compartment at the head. In the simplest tombs, the grave goods are placed at the head of the coffin, protected by a simple covering of planks.

At the end of the period of the Warring States there seems to have been a greater care in preserving the body. We see this in particular in the massive size and more compact plan of Qin and Han tombs, the replacement of rounded by squared-off coffins which fit perfectly in their wooden casings, the use of nails rather than pegs, and a framework of ropes fixed with wedges to seal them in hermetically; and, lastly, in the generalized use of white clay around the outside coffin.

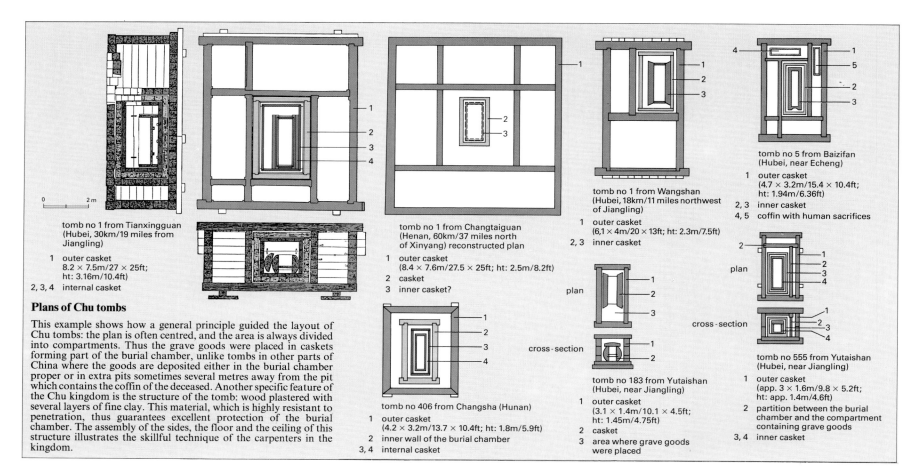

Plans of Chu tombs

tomb no 1 from Tianxingguan (Hubei, 30km/19 miles from Jiangling)
1 outer casket 8.2 × 7.5m/27 × 25ft; ht: 3.16m/10.4ft)
2, 3, 4 internal casket

This example shows how a general principle guided the layout of Chu tombs: the plan is often centred, and the area is always divided into compartments. Thus the grave goods were placed in caskets forming part of the burial chamber, unlike tombs in other parts of China where the goods are deposited either in the burial chamber proper or in extra pits sometimes several metres away from the pit which contains the coffin of the deceased. Another specific feature of the Chu kingdom is the structure of the tomb: wood plastered with several layers of fine clay. This material, which is highly resistant to penetration, thus guarantees excellent protection of the burial chamber. The assembly of the sides, the floor and the ceiling of this structure illustrates the skillful technique of the carpenters in the kingdom.

tomb no 1 from Changtaiguan (Henan, 60km/37 miles north of Xinyang) reconstructed plan
1 outer casket (8.4 × 7.6m/27.5 × 25ft; ht: 2.5m/8.2ft)
2 casket
3 inner casket?

tomb no 406 from Changsha (Hunan)
1 outer casket (4.2 × 3.2m/13.7 × 10.4ft; ht: 1.8m/5.9ft)
2 inner wall of the burial chamber
3, 4 internal casket

tomb no 183 from Yutaishan (Hubei, near Jiangling)
1 outer casket (3.1 × 1.4m/10.1 × 4.5ft; ht: 1.45m/4.75ft)
2 casket
3 area where grave goods were placed

tomb no 1 from Wangshan (Hubei, 18km/11 miles northwest of Jiangling)
1 outer casket (6,1 × 4m/20 × 13ft; ht: 2.3m/7.5ft)
2, 3 inner casket

tomb no 5 from Baizifan (Hubei, near Echeng)
1 outer casket (4.7 × 3.2m/15.4 × 10.4ft; ht: 1.94m/6.36ft)
2, 3 inner casket
4, 5 coffin with human sacrifices

tomb no 555 from Yutaishan (Hubei, near Jiangling)
1 outer casket (app. 3 × 1.6m/9.8 × 5.2ft; ht: app. 1.4m/4.6ft)
2 partition between the burial chamber and the compartment containing grave goods
3, 4 inner casket

plan

cross-section

cross-section

plan

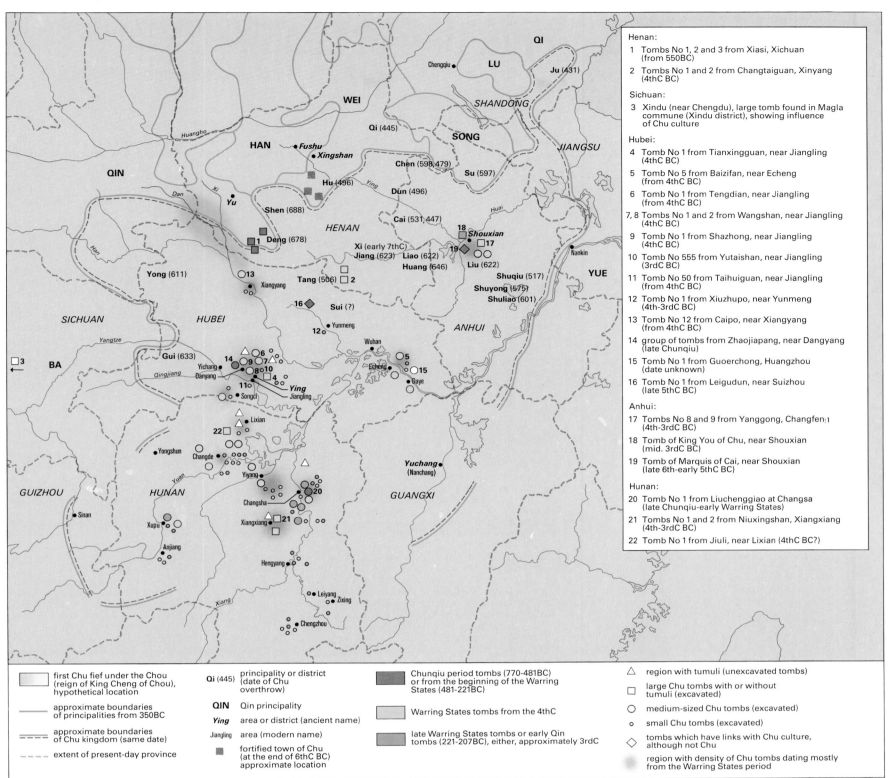

Henan:

1 Tombs No 1, 2 and 3 from Xiasi, Xichuan
   (from 550BC)
2 Tombs No 1 and 2 from Changtaiguan, Xinyang
   (4thC BC)

Sichuan:

3 Xindu (near Chengdu), large tomb found in Magla
   commune (Xindu district), showing influence
   of Chu culture

Hubei:

4 Tomb No 1 from Tianxingguan, near Jiangling
   (4thC BC)
5 Tomb No 5 from Baizifan, near Echeng
   (from 4thC BC)
6 Tomb No 1 from Tengdian, near Jiangling
   (from 4thC BC)
7, 8 Tombs No 1 and 2 from Wangshan, near Jiangling
   (4thC BC)
9 Tomb No 1 from Shazhong, near Jiangling
   (4thC BC)
10 Tomb No 555 from Yutaishan, near Jiangling
   (3rdC BC)
11 Tomb No 50 from Taihuiguan, near Jiangling
   (from 4thC BC)
12 Tomb No 1 from Xiuzhupo, near Yunmeng
   (4thC-3rdC BC)
13 Tomb No 12 from Caipo, near Xiangyang
   (from 4thC BC)
14 group of tombs from Zhaojiapang, near Dangyang
   (late Chunqiu)
15 Tomb No 1 from Guoerchong, Huangzhou
   (date unknown)
16 Tomb No 1 from Leigudun, near Suizhou
   (late 5thC BC)

Anhui:

17 Tombs No 8 and 9 from Yanggong, Changfen₁1
   (4th-3rdC BC)
18 Tomb of King You of Chu, near Shouxian
   (mid. 3rdC BC)
19 Tomb of Marquis of Cai, near Shouxian
   (late 6th-early 5thC BC)

Hunan:

20 Tomb No 1 from Liuchenggiao at Changsa
   (late Chunqiu-early Warring States)
21 Tombs No 1 and 2 from Niuxingshan, Xiangxiang
   (4th-3rdC BC)
22 Tomb No 1 from Jiuli, near Lixian (4thC BC?)

	first Chu fief under the Chou (reign of King Cheng of Chou), hypothetical location

Qi (445)	principality or district (date of Chu overthrow)
QIN	Qin principality
Ying	area or district (ancient name)
Jiangling	area (modern name)
■	fortified town of Chu (at the end of 6thC BC) approximate location

approximate boundaries of principalities from 350BC

approximate boundaries of Chu kingdom (same date)

extent of present-day province

Chunqiu period tombs (770-481BC) or from the beginning of the Warring States (481-221BC)

Warring States tombs from the 4thC

late Warring States tombs or early Qin tombs (221-207BC), either, approximately 3rdC

△ region with tumuli (unexcavated tombs)

▢ large Chu tombs with or without tumuli (excavated)

○ medium-sized Chu tombs (excavated)

o small Chu tombs (excavated)

◇ tombs which have links with Chu culture, although not Chu

region with density of Chu tombs dating mostly from the Warring States period

Tombs of the Chu kingdom

This map is based on two sources: first, ancient texts (*Chunqiu, Zuozhuan, Shiji*) and their commentaries establishing the boundaries of the Chu kingdom, together with locations and ancient countries, and secondly information from excavations.

The location of the first site occupied by the Chu people, that of the principalities destroyed by the Chu, and the boundaries of the kingdom *c.*350BC remain approximate and sometimes hypothetical. Comparison of the written sources with the results obtained by archaeology brings out a major contradiction. The area of the regions with characteristic Chu tombs is five or six times smaller than the total area of the kingdom *c.*350BC.

The Chu's military control of annexed territories was probably not accompanied by a cultural domination on the same scale. Tomb No 1 at Leigudun, situated in the heart of the kingdom, illustrates the size of the problem. By its irregular plan, its unique layout and its grave goods, this tomb exhibits both Chu influences and profoundly original features. Nevertheless, its proprietor, the Marquis Yi of Zeng, maintained close relations with the Chu royal court.

Carved wooden plank with openwork decoration and lacquering, from tomb No 26 at Yangjianhu in Changsha, province of Hunan

The body rested on this plank, which lined the bottom of the coffin. This burial custom, which was peculiar to the Chu and of unknown origin, seems to have developed late, towards the 4th–3rd centuries BC, and not to have been practised systematically. Some tombs at Jiangling, and many more at Changsha, attest its usage.

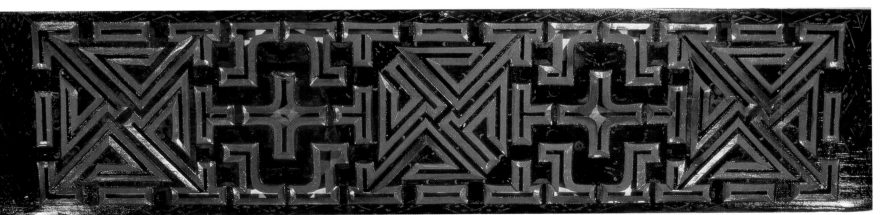

Kodansha et Cultural Relics Publishing House

The origins and production of lacquer

The technique of using lacquer is now thought to have originated in the Far East in Neolithic times, both as a preservative and as a means of making decorative objects more brilliant.

As a result of archaeological discoveries, the history of lacquer in China has been revised several times in the course of this century. The sites of Lolang in Korea (1st century BC to 1st century AD), and Changsha in Hunan province, excavated since the 1930s, have pushed back the origin of lacquer first to the Han period (206BC–AD220) and then to the period of the Warring States (c.481–221BC). Today the map of discoveries covers the whole of eastern China and includes far older sites. Moreover, the parallel existence of different, possibly regional styles can be identified. Archaeologists have found inscriptions engraved or branded on lacquerware of c.3rd century BC which certainly appear to indicate their place of manufacture, and confirm the development of a trade that, in view of the discovery of stylistically similar pieces in widely scattered sites, probably went on in the 5th and 4th centuries BC. Despite the abundant finds, some questions remain unsolved, but it has nevertheless been possible, using certain fixed reference points, to outline a historical development of the art and techniques of lacquer.

Lacquer, the secretion of a tree which grows only in the Far East, *Rhus verniciflua*, must have been used very early because of its unique properties: once dry it renders impermeable the objects it covers; its resistance to the effects of time means that often the lacquer on an object in a 3,000-year-old tomb may disintegrate, but the thin film that it leaves indicates the original shape and decoration; finally, its fluidity and brilliant appearance make it an ideal material for the decoration of everyday objects as well as grave goods.

The quality of the lacquers attributed by some archaeologists to several Neolithic remains is dubious in the absence of scientific analysis. A bowl, discovered in 1973 during excavation of the lower level (4) of the site of Hemudu, in Zhejiang province, which can be dated to about 5000BC, would be the oldest example known in China, if it really is lacquerware. However, lacquer may well have been used in China at that period because, 5,000 or 6,000 years ago it was used in Japan to protect and decorate wooden objects, as seen in the discovery of Torihama, Fukui district, with C[14]* dating.

From the Shang period (c17th–11th century BC), only a few fragments of lacquer have survived, but they are sufficient to attest to a very refined art. Initially, some red traces found in the earth were controversially interpreted, shortly after their discovery near Anyang, Henan province, in the 1930s, as being the remains of a lacquer where the bases had disintegrated. Since then,

other more obvious remains have shown that lacquer from this period was applied to wood, ceramics and even bronze. Its decoration is identical to that of certain bronzes, with such borrowed motifs as the *taotie** (monster mask), *kui** (one-legged dragon), *leiwen** ("thunder-pattern") or grasshoppers, as well as the techniques of light relief and inlay, and the skilful contrasting of colours.

Hardly more numerous, but less attractive in appearance, are the lacquer pieces from the Western Chou period (11th century to 770BC), mostly discovered in metropolitan China*. These exhibit the same features: their fragile bases have disappeared, leaving a very thin layer of lacquer, generally inlaid with circular shells. However, no important discovery foretells the spread of an art that suddenly appeared in all its inventive fertility at the end of the 6th century BC. The discoveries of Fenshuiling (Shanxi, tombs No 269 and 270) are the first known examples. These large lacquer fragments display sumptuous interlaced dragons, their bodies enhanced by stippled motifs and triangular spirals, indicating a continuing reference to the art of bronze, but in modified form, visible in the fluid rendering of the body.

Base materials

Indeed, the large number of lacquered objects after the 6th century BC owes much to the diversification of grave goods and also to the growing prosperity of the land of Chu. Here the inventiveness of the craftsmen is shown in the solutions used to make the lacquer adhere better to its base. The site of Qingchuan in Sichuan, dated to the late 4th century BC, offers a large sample, illustrating particularly the *jiazhu* technique which consists in using a shaped cloth as a base and coating it with lacquer. Light and manageable, the object thus obtained is subject to breakage but impervious to age, and does not lose its shape. This technique is probably derived from another rather more common method in which the wood base is covered with cloth before being lacquered. These two methods have persisted down to our own day.

With the progress of tool-making, towards the 3rd century BC, wood was not only carved or hollowed out, but also turned or, after being cut into thin leaves, rolled into a cylindrical shape, fixed to a circular base and reinforced with bronze supports. The joints assembling the two ends of the leaf were hidden beneath the lacquer. This technique, used in *lian** toilet cases and *zhi* goblets, kept the lacquer pieces in a perfect state of preservation

wherever they came from (Qingchuan in Sichuan, Yunmeng in Hubei, Changsha). Wood remained by far the commonest base material, but leather was preferred for armour, wickerwork for some containers, and even ceramics (as at Shanxi in Hubei) and bronze (a lamp from tomb No 5 at Shangcunling, Henan, discovered in 1975) received a lacquer finish.

The variety of base materials was matched by an equal variety of forms. Decoration reflecting the object's usage led to the lacquering of arms, musical instruments, coffins and crockery.

Certain tombs (No 1 at Leigudun and No 1 at Tianxingguan in Hubei, both discovered in 1978), or groups of tombs (tombs No 1 and No 2 at Wangshan and No 1 at Shazhog in Hubei; the site of Chuihudi, Yungmeng district; the site of Qingchuan; discovered in 1965, 1975 and 1979 respectively), contain more than 200 pieces of lacquer, the commonest being cups with handles, boxes and, at the end of the period, the *lian*. Some even rarer pieces are the *mingqi**, or "spirit utensils", such as the funerary statuettes discovered in tomb No 2 at Changtaiguan, with their formalized appearance showing two clasped hands emerging from starched sleeves. More numerous but no less remarkable are the *zhenmushou** which count among the first examples of Chinese sculpture. At Leigudun, archaeologists recovered a box and at Yutaishan (the site in Hubei comprising 554 tombs, excavated in 1975), a cup with a *dou* foot in the shape of a waterbird with a body covered with vermilion, yellow and gold motifs on a black lacquer ground. Other pieces display animal motifs—52 have been counted on one screen—sculpted as openwork and then lacquered, a speciality in Chu decorative art.

The decoration of lacquer objects, from the period of the Warring States is best expressed in geometrical motifs with curvilinear outlines, the composition of which is controlled by diagonals, but also in the rarer figurative representations where hybrid creatures with a man's head and a snake's body are part of a complicated bestiary. The coffin of Leigudun, dated to the end of the 5th century BC, is one of the oldest and richest examples, but its exact sense still remains to be clarified. Similarly, debate surrounds the figures which ornament a *se* zither from tomb No 1 at Changtaiguan, discovered in 1956 and probably dating to the 4th century. These were painted on a black lacquer ground in a dozen colours, including gold and silver, and probably fixed by some other binder than lacquer, without which most pigments would have changed colour.

Lacquered wood dish from tomb No II at Yunmeng, Hubei, excavated 1975. End of 3rd century BC

Left: interior of the dish; below, left: profile of dish and illustration of the motifs painted on the inside and outside rim; below, right: inscriptions incised in the lacquer or engraved in the wooden base with a branding iron. From the 4th century, in the region of south central China (i.e. Hubei, Hunan and Anhui) and Sichuan, the grave goods placed in tombs include an increasingly large number of lacquered objects, generally containers. Their motifs, executed in black on a vermilion ground (or vice versa), probably have a symbolic character, but also show a certain invention and decorative sense.

This piece, found in the tomb of an official of the Qin, the principality which progressively annexed all the territories of China before uniting them in 221BC, may have come from Xianyang, the capital of Qin, situated more than 700km (434 miles) from Yunmeng. The branded inscriptions seem to indicate this place of origin. The partially legible engraved inscriptions probably give the name of the craftsman responsible for making the dish.

A group of laws and decrees in force in Qin was found in the same tomb. Some of these deal with the work of lacquer craftsmen, revealing an extremely hierarchical organization.

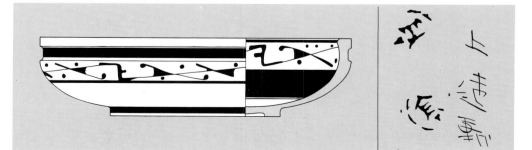

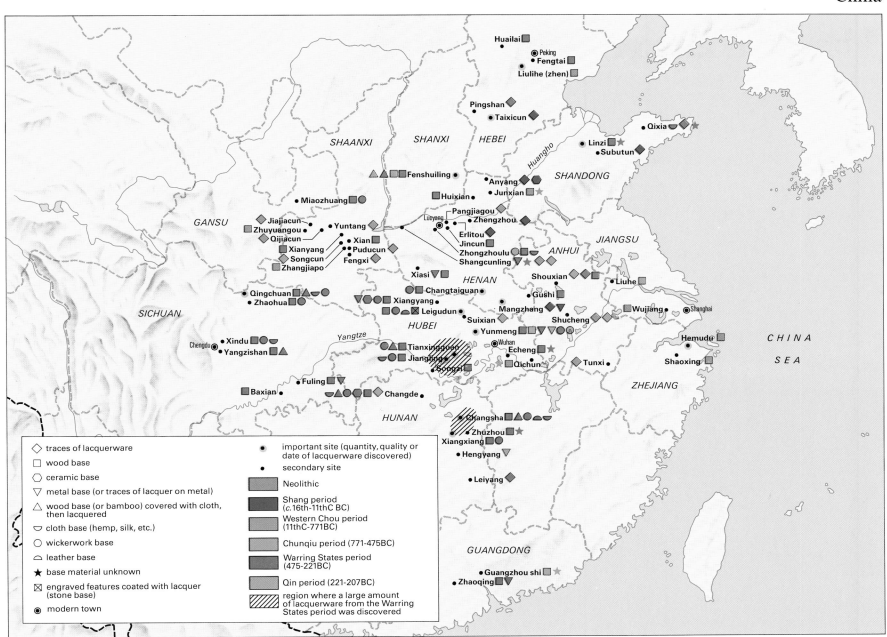

traces of lacquerware
wood base
ceramic base
metal base (or traces of lacquer on metal)
wood base (or bamboo) covered with cloth, then lacquered
cloth base (hemp, silk, etc.)
wickerwork base
leather base
★ base material unknown
⊠ engraved features coated with lacquer (stone base)
◉ modern town

⊙ important site (quantity, quality or date of lacquerware discovered)
• secondary site
Neolithic
Shang period (c.16th-11thC BC)
Western Chou period (11thC-771BC)
Chunqiu period (771-475BC)
Warring States period (475-221BC)
Qin period (221-207BC)
region where a large amount of lacquerware from the Warring States period was discovered

Lacquered wood buckler from tomb No 406 of Wulipai, at Changsha, Hunan. Period of the Warring States

All kinds of objects were lacquered: weapons, armour, wooden musical instruments, coffins and artifacts in everyday use; for this material possessed many special qualities. Its value was not only decorative but also preservative, for it becomes hard and waterproof on drying and has powerful adhesive qualities. Height, 64.5cm (25in); width, 45.5cm (18in); thickness, 0.7cm (0.3in).

Kodansha et Cultural Relics Publishing House

Provenance of lacquerware dating from the Neolithic to the foundation of the Empire (221BC)

These sites consist mostly of tombs, and cover a large part of present-day Chinese territory; but their distribution proves very uneven in terms of dating. Apart from the Neolithic lacquer artifacts, which are few in number and must be treated with caution, these pieces appear in appreciable quantities relating to a specific period in regions which at the time represented an established power: Anyang and the central region for the Shang period, the region of Xian for the period of the Western Chou (c.11th century–770BC).

As from the 7th century BC, the dispersal of sites containing lacquerware increased, and, around the 4th century, indicates the general application of this craft, some tombs holding as many as 200 pieces. Simultaneously, techniques were diversified: all kinds of bases were used and the range of colours amplified. Then the central region of the Chu kingdom and eastern Sichuan stood out, both for the number of discoveries and the quality of the pieces, indicating the probable existence of large workshops in those regions. Nevertheless, the problem of the location of the workshops remains, because it is necessary to take into account not only the increase in commercial exchanges, but also the fact that the much better protected Chu tombs have preserved down to our own day pieces which elsewhere would reach us only in an extremely fragmentary condition.

Impressions left by fragments of lacquer(?)

Traces of decoration from a Shang period tomb at Xibeigang, near Houjiazhuang, district of Anyang, Henan. The wooden base of this decoration has disintegrated, leaving in the earth fragments of a material identified as lacquer and containing shell inlays. Thus the motif of a dragon seen in profile can be made out. Other more recent discoveries show that the use of lacquer was in fact widespread in the Shang period.

Kodansha et Cultural Relics Publishing House

Music in ancient China

As it has done in Mesopotamia and Egypt, archaeology in China has extended the history of music far beyond the period of surviving texts: instruments have been recovered from as far back as the Neolithic period, and recent finds include a set of Bronze Age bells.

The study of ancient Chinese music has long been dependent on texts and on certain decorations engraved on bronze vessels. But during the last 30 years, this field has considerably expanded through the discovery in tombs of many instruments, sometimes in an excellent state of preservation. We also have ample information about the musical notation, mostly taken from inscriptions in tomb No 1 at Leigudin, Hubei, dated to the end of the 5th century BC. Moreover, figurative scenes on engraved or inlaid bronzes, vessels and lacquerware reflect the musical context before the Han period.

The oldest known instruments appear in the Neolithic (Yangshao culture). They are terracotta whistles (ocarinas), spherical or ovoid in shape, and in their primitive form possess only one hole. As they became more elaborate, they had one hole for blowing and three holes for fingering, as in the example from Gansu, Yumen district. Together they produced the sounds of a heptatonic scale (seven notes), but we cannot be sure that their makers had sufficient technical mastery to have deliberately arranged this. However, from the Shang period (about 17th–11th century BC) their technical quality improved. At least two such instruments, recovered at Liulige in the Huixen district of Henan, were capable of sounding eight consecutive semitones. It is possible that a pentatonic scale (five notes), mentioned by later texts, was known by then, as appears the case with another instrument much more important in the history of Chinese music, the bronze bell.

Bell types and shapes

In 1976, a group of five bells, identical in form but decreasing in size, and therefore producing different sounds, was taken from the tomb of Fuhao, one of the wives of King Wuding (Anyang, Henan province, dated to the late 14th–early 12th century BC). Until then, finds in the north of China had been restricted to series composed at the most of three pieces. These *nao* bells lack clappers and have a short truncated cone handle at their base and two convex sides enlarging progressively to an upward turned opening. They are small, the largest being 20cm (8in), in comparison with many isolated bells discovered in southern China, the oldest of which would be contemporary with them. To sound them, the player probably held these *nao* bells fixed to the end of a wooden stick, as their often hollow handles suggest. On the other hand, the handle of the southern bells, sometimes 80cm (31in) high, was embedded in a block up to its base and surrounded by a ring which stabilized the whole, a feature not found on the *nao* recovered in the north.

Another type of bell with decoration akin to the bronze bells of southern China, and contemporary with them, is the *bozhong* bell, which has a fixed suspension ring and a straight-sided rather than in-curving opening.

They are an immediate extension of the little bells attached to horses' harnesses and dogs' necks, but are distinguished from them by the absence of clappers and by their sharply incised outlines. Although they continued until the period of the Warring States, they are rare, probably because their use was reserved for high dignitaries, whereas the *niuzhong* ringed bells (which have no incised decoration and keep an in-turned shape) are more common and often form peals or carillons.

Towards the middle of the Western Chou (around 11th century to 770BC), a new form appears in southern China, combining the two preceding types. This was the *yongzhong* bell with a handle like the *nao* bells and a ring forming part of the handle at its base. Three to twelve or thirteen bells, cast in a series of decreasing size, made up the carillons, the most celebrated example of which was recovered at Leigudun. This numbered 64 pieces divided into a series of bells with a handle or a ring. Its discovery is essential to the history of music on more than one count, for it was definitely responsible for numerous innovations among the peoples of south central China. Using one of the wooden mallets found in the tomb, each bell could be struck at two places, marked by the name of the appropriate note, in order to produce two sounds, ranging in interval from a major second to a minor third. The oval section of each bell entailed the existence of two fundamental areas of vibration, and thus made it possible to produce this double sound.

As the Leigudun carillon does not seem to have suffered serious damage, we have for the first time direct information on the musical notation, as well as valuable indications of how it was played. The degrees of the pentatonic scale were marked there, and combinations of characters reveal the existence of modified sounds, enabling the use of scales with 6 and 7 notes to be worked out after this period. Also, by enlarging the peal of 12 bells to one of 64, the new series had a potential range of 128 notes, with a register, far exceeding the minimal five-octave range. Nor did it only give the pitch, but also formed an integral part of an orchestra, which suggests an accompaniment of drums, a set of lithophones (musically pitched stones) and various wind and stringed instruments. It also suggests a remarkable technical mastery, the size and structure of each bell being in close relation to the two sounds it produced.

Other musical instruments

Bronze bells may have been the most important of all ancient instruments, so much so that some tombs which lacked them contained pottery substitutes instead, but other instruments were also important, for example the lithophones, or musically pitched stones, which appear in crude form from the Neolithic period. In the Shang period these took on an approximately trapezoidal shape, with the hole for hanging them situated not far

from the upper angle. The form then became fixed and did not change until modern times, when it became a plaque with two sides of unequal length set at an obtuse angle. The most complete example was discovered in 1970 near Jiangling, Hubei, from the period of the Warring States, and consisted of 25 pieces, the register of which exceeded three octaves. Other instruments of rarer production apparently did not undergo subsequent development, at least in the form in which they have reached us. Examples include a bronze drum recovered in 1977 in the district of Chongyang in the south of Hubei, and a curious pair of instruments cast in bronze from Dunxi district, Anhwei, during the period of Western Chou. Both of these consisted of five pipes 20cm (8in) high on a hollow base, each pipe giving a different sound, with a resonance that varied depending on the area struck.

It seems that percussion instruments predominated in both number and variety until towards the 6th century BC, but it is quite possible that fragile instruments could have disappeared without leaving traces. Nevertheless, this preponderance does tally with the depictions on some bronze objects, that show performers striking bells or chimes while other performers beat drums.

The oldest wood or bamboo instruments appeared in many tombs from the land of Chu from the 5th century. These were mostly zithers or drums. The Leigudun finds provide the biggest sample of instruments from the pre-Han period, comprising, in addition to carillons, 4 drums, 12 zithers, 5 mouth-organs, 2 panpipes, 2 straight flutes and 2 unidentified stringed instruments. The two panpipes, which have similarities with a 6th century stone flute found in tomb No 1 at Xiasi, Henan province, are identical in shape but quite different in size, and consist of 13 bamboo pipes of decreasing length. These would each have produced distinct sounds. The two unidentified instruments have been wrongly considered to be *qin* zithers, an oblong instrument, flat and without a handle, having seven strings in later examples. Both are clearly characterized. The first is very long and narrow, 115 × 7cm (45 × 3in) at its largest dimensions and has five strings held by one peg and covering both the sound box and the handle. The second is larger, but offers the performer only a narrow playing range. Neither is easy to classify in musical terms; perhaps they are ancestors of the *qin* zither which so excited the imagination of the poets of antiquity, but remains strangely absent from pre-Han tombs.

The technical development and variety of these instruments imply that there existed in south central China, from before the Han period, musical theories, evidence of which was later lost. The pre-Han texts however, tend to emphasize the supposed relation between the quality of a type of music and the moral doctrine which inspired it.

 *Avec l'aimable autorisation de Cultural Relics Bureau, Beijing, et du Metropolitan Museum of Art, New York*

Detail of a bronze *hu* vase with inlaid copper decoration

This vase (6th–5th century BC) was discovered at Chengdu in Sichuan in 1965. Like other bronzes with similar decoration, it is ornamented in one area with a scene of a ritual ceremony in which music plays an important part: four performers are striking bells and lithophones (chime stones) with small mallets, and a musician beats a big drum. Three people sitting on their heels are playing mouth organs and a fourth plays the panpipes. The discovery in 1978 of tomb No 1 at Leigudun, Hubei (end of 5th century BC) was to confirm the accuracy of this ornamental scene, because it yielded the same instruments in a perfect state of preservation, plus 14 stringed instruments, 2 straight flutes and 3 small drums.

Two instruments of lacquered wood from tomb No 1 at Leigudun, district of Suixian in Hubei (end of 5th century BC)

Top left: *se* zither (L.169cm/65in, W.1.43cm/0.55in, H.11cm/4in) with 25 strings. Twelve examples of the same type and size were found in the tomb. The performer played it sitting on his heels. The traces left by the strings have made it possible to reconstruct the way in which they were attached. Fastened to one end of the instrument, they passed over moveable bridges (not visible in the photograph), then penetrated the other end of the zither, re-emerging and rolled round 4 pegs that were used to regulate their tension (detail left). Zhongguo Wenwu No 2.

Top right: mouth organ made out of a gourd and several tubes of varying length some of which still retain their bamboo reed. Cultural Relics Publishing House, Beijing

Lithophone discovered in 1950 in the great royal tomb of Wuguancun near Anyang, Henan

One of the rare pieces to be found in a good state of preservation after recovery from this much-looted tomb, this lithophone may have belonged to a carillon made up of several pieces with different lengths, and therefore giving out different sounds. Shang period (*c*.16th–11th century BC). L.84cm (33in), W.1.42cm (.55in).

Bronze drum, discovered in 1977 in southern Hubei, district of Chongyang

Like the example in the Sumitomo collection at Kyoto (Japan), recovered earlier, this piece resembles a model with a wooden frame and two snakeskin (?) membranes, both fastened by three rows of small nails or pegs. The exact purpose of the upper part of the drum is not known. Total height 75.5cm (29in), diam. 39.5cm (15in), W.38cm (15in), Shang period. Zhongguo Wenwu No 3.

Bronze *yongzhong* bell with handle from tomb No 1 at Leigudun, Hubei

This piece formed part of a carillon of 64 bells. Because of its oval middle section, it emitted two sounds of different intervals when it was struck in the central area of its lower part, or on the side. It appears that (possibly) from the Shang period, but more certainly under the Western Chou, this particular shape was purposely conceived to extract two sounds. To correct imperfect sonority, the inside surface of the bell was trimmed. Height 68cm (26in), weight 24.7kg (54lb). 5th century BC. Zhongguo Wenwu No 2.

269

Food and diet in the Han period

Tombs of the Han period (206BC–AD220) were abundantly stocked with food to sustain the departed; they provide archaeologists with an extraordinarily detailed knowledge of a cuisine 2,000 years old.

Excavations carried out in China during the last 30 years have yielded an impressive number of remains illuminating many aspects of the material culture of the country, especially in the Han period (206BC–AD220). Nearly all these objects come from the tombs of the ruling classes, tombs conceived in that period as replicas to replace the earthly dwelling in the next life. In the 1st century BC and even more in the period of the later Han, the underground chambers were decorated with scenes stamped or painted on brick and painted or engraved on stone, and evoking, among other themes, the worldly goods and pleasures it was hoped the deceased would rediscover in the hereafter.

At the same time, the tomb contained grave goods – real objects or terracotta models – intended to accompany the deceased. In some tombs an inventory on slips of bamboo or wooden tablets provided the name and function of the objects interred. Food, cookery and the art of the table are especially well evoked in the tombs, because there are no burials without offerings of food to the deceased, even if they simply take the form of various containers.

Thus a number of food products, as well as cooked dishes have been discovered. The richest tombs in this respect are those of Mawangdui at Changsha in Hunan, especially tomb 1, burial of the Lady of Dai (d. shortly after 168BC), and that of her son (tomb 3) (d. 168BC). The two tombs, excavated in 1972–73, preserved a unique collection of provisions and prepared dishes placed in different lacquer, ceramic and bamboo containers, but also bamboo inventory slips giving the composition of the dishes.

The study of these buried foods, the inventory slips, the labels attached to the containers (giving the name of the products) and ancient texts gives a better idea of the broad outlines of the Han diet.

Han staples and delicacies

The basic sustenance consisted of cereals: different varieties of millet and rice, glutinous or otherwise, wheat and barley. Naturally consumption depended on the region; millet, barley and wheat predominated in northern China, whereas rice was the cereal most cultivated in the centre and south.

The grains were eaten more or less finely hulled, then steamed or boiled. As from the 1st century BC, preparations based on wheaten flour, especially in the form of noodles, spread gradually, at first in northern China and the urban environment.

The basic food was complemented by accompanying foods: pulses and seeds (hempseed, haricot beans, mustard), vegetables, meat and fish, condiments and fruit. The chief of these side dishes, found in most kitchens, rich and poor, was *geng*. *Geng* was a sort of thick soup or meat broth, a food for rich or for special banquets, but it could also be a soup of cereals, meat and vegetables; or, for the poor, it could be a vegetable soup.

Like the cereals, the types of meat consumed varied according to the region. Apart from poultry, which certainly provided the most accessible form of meat (and eggs were also eaten), they included beef, mutton, horse, dog, pork, venison, wild boar, hare and other kinds of game. The inventory slips of Mawangdui and the labels attached to the containers give precise information about how the side dishes were prepared and about the cuts of meat which were cooked. Meat and fish were boiled to make *geng*, but meat could also be roasted on a spit or wrapped in clay and roasted. Or it could be braised or fried in a little animal fat. Fish could be steamed. To preserve them, meat and fish were dried in the sun, or marinated in salt and spices to make sauces. Finally, some meats (mutton, venison) and fish were sometimes cut in strips and eaten raw, like the Japanese *sashimi*. Condiments included salt, vinegar, soya sauces, sugar, honey, ginger, garlic, onion, cinnamon, and galingale.

The commonest vegetables were lotus roots, bamboo shoots, gourds, soya sprouts, mallows, yams, leeks and radishes. The vegetables were often macerated, like the meat, in salt, vinegar or soya sauce. Fruits were plentiful in the centre and south, including melons, watermelons, plums, arbutus berries, oranges, mandarins, peaches, pears, apricots, persimmons, water chestnuts, etc; whereas in the north they were far fewer with the jujube as the commonest fruit.

Most sweetmeats were made of glutinous rice and millet, flavoured with sugar, honey, jujubes and often water chestnuts.

Han drinks included pure water, the water in which cereals were cooked, sour drinks made from fruit (peaches and plums) or milk (fermented mare's milk), sweet drinks (sugar-cane juice) and alcoholic drinks, which were in fact beers, made from different cereals, mainly millet, rice and wheat. There was a distinction between sweet, cloudy beers with a short fermentation period (1 to 4 days) and clarified stronger beers with a longer fermentation (3 to 4 months), often repeated several times. Distillation was still unknown.

The Han kitchen

Kitchen scenes formed one of the favourite themes of the painted and engraved decoration in burial chambers in the time of the later Han. Kitchens were generally installed near wells. The essential feature was the rectangular oven with a fire vent in front and a smoke vent at the other end. In the top were several holes for cooking, one of them large and reserved for the double saucepan (*fu* + *zeng*) used for steaming. These two items (*fu* and *zeng*) clearly reflect the fundamental combination of the Han meal: cereal and *geng* soup.

Cooking utensils were often made of terracotta, but cast iron was increasingly used for saucepans. Another important feature of the kitchens was the reserve stock of fish and meat. The various pieces were put out to dry, hanging from metal hooks attached to a framework.

In the Han house, where life went on at ground level, meals were taken from platters brought from the kitchen already garnished and placed before the mat or low couch which acted as the seat. These individual platters were rectangular or circular, and generally rested on low legs. At certain banquets, instead of the platter a long low table was set before the personage to be honoured. This table carried round plates with very short legs or none at all.

The platters, like the crockery, were of terracotta, wood or bamboo among the poorer classes; among the rich they were of lacquered wood, red on top and black underneath, sometimes decorated with themes painted in several colours. Corners and legs were sometimes plated with gilded bronze.

The table services of rich families were usually lacquered. Cereals were served in bowls or cylindrical covered boxes, the more substantial side dishes in plates and the *geng* and the sauces in two-handled cups: Chopsticks and spoons were used for serving and eating. No friendly gathering or banquet was complete without beer. It was brought in in various bronze or lacquer vases which were placed near the plate. A ladle was used to transfer it to oval two-handled cups like those used for the *geng*.

This lacquer service, enhanced with painted motifs, incised or inlaid with sheet metal, was very expensive. Easy to look after, waterproof and durable, it could be handed down for several generations, like the outstandingly beautiful bronze vases. Like them, it was often inscribed with the name of its proprietor, the date and place of its manufacture, and the name of the craftsmen who worked on it.

A special meal with musicians and entertainers

On the right there are dancers and jugglers; at the top on the left, the two guests; below, two musicians playing pan-pipes. On the ground there are trays and two *zun* vases for beer. This brick, 42cm (16in) high and 46cm (18in) wide, has a light-relief decoration similar to that adorning the walls of a tomb. Chengtu, 2nd c. AD. Szechwan Provincial Museum, Chengtu.

Banqueting scene

The host is sitting on a couch enclosed by a draught screen in front of a low table laden with drinking cups. Some guests are sitting on mats, while others are arriving, greeted by servants. Above the scene are the curtains of a daïs. Engraved stone slab, embellishing one of the chambers in Tomb 1 at Mixian, Honan. 2nd century AD. Width 1.53m (4.8ft), height 1.14m (3.6ft).

Avec l'aimable autorisation de Cultural Relics Publishing House, J.-L. Princelle

Avec l'aimable autorisation de Cultural Relics Publishing House, J.-L. Princelle

Vessel for warming beer (wenjiu zun)

Found with other bronze items at Yuyu, in the north of Shansi, this carries a relief decoration of animals in a mountain landscape. The inscription round the edge of the mouth reads: "bronze *zun* vessel for heating beer, weighing 24 *jin*, made in the third year of Heping [26BC] by Hu Fu of Zhongling [present-day Yuyu]." Vessels of this shape are often seen on pictures of drinking parties on the walls of tombs of the later Han dynasty. But was it really used for heating beer? The inscription can also be taken to mean "bronze *zun* vessel for *yun* beer . . . " (*yun*: a kind of beer that was fermented several times).
Bronze gilt, height 24.5cm (9.6in); diameter 23.4cm (9.1in). Date 26BC.

Platter with a meal served on it, as found when the northern side compartment of the tomb of the Lady of Dai was excavated, at Mawangdui (Tomb 1), Changsha, Hunan Province

The platter and the dishes are made of lacquer; there are small plates for meats and vegetables, goblets and a cup with handles for the beer. The sides of the compartment where it was found imitate the walls of a house and have silk hangings. The dead person, a woman to judge by the presence of a dress, is thought to have been seated in front of the tray. Shortly after 168BC.

Hu container for beer

The scrolls form an inscription in decorative *niaozhuan* script extolling the beauty of the receptacle and the pleasures of beer, and wishing the user a long life. The receptacle was found in the tomb of Liu Sheng, king of Zhongshan, who died in 113BC. Bronze inlaid with gold and silver. Height 44.2cm (17.3in); diameter at widest part 28.5cm (11.2in).

Cooking scene incised on a stone slab from a 2nd century AD tomb at Liangtai, Zhucheng, Shantung Province

Wells, stoves, a foodstore, a pile of trays for the meals, animals being slaughtered, food being skewered and spit-roasted, doughs being prepared, and liquids being filtered and fermented: all this is conveyed in this scene. Height 1.52m (4.8ft), width 76cm (2.4ft).

New perspectives in philosophy and religion

Recently Chinese archaeology has afforded new evidence not merely of the practice of ancient Chinese religion, but also of the texts themselves, including, in 1973, the oldest version of one of the central Taoist texts – Lao Tze's *Tao Te Ching*

For a long time Chinese religions were studied mainly by philologists who approached the subject cautiously, because so many of the texts were apocryphal. Art history and archaeology have recently complemented and sometimes challenged traditionally accepted information. From the beginning of the 20th century, the paintings and sculptures, and manuscripts of all kinds found at Dun huang, a Buddhist rock site in Gansu, have provided several generations of scholars with an inexhaustible field of study.

Comparable in scope are the many manuscripts written on wood, bamboo, silk and paper recovered from tombs: for example divinatory texts from the period of the Western Han (206BC–AD8) found at Yinqueshan near Linyi (Shandong), and Taoist talismans from Astana near Turfan (Xinjiang). The most unusual complex is the one housing the three tombs of the family of the Marquis of Dai (d.186BC) at Mawangdui near Changsha (Hunan). The third, that of the son, dating to 168BC and excavated in 1973, contained manuscripts on silk of incalculable value. Most of these texts, comprising more than 120,000 characters, were folded and stored in lacquered wood caskets. In the whole history of ancient Chinese manuscripts, this discovery is one of the most significant and makes a unique contribution to our knowledge of history, geography, medicine, astronomy and philosophy, and especially Taoism. It has yielded us the oldest version of Lao Tze (*Tao Te Ching*) known to date. The text appears here in two forms: the first (A) from before 206BC, the second (B) dating to the reign of the Emperor Gaozu (206–195BC). The two sections of version B, entitled respectively *Te* (Virtue) and *Tao* (Way), upset the traditional order of the work. Should this be seen as the influence of legists*, in view of the importance given to the Te section (devoted to human and political problems) over the Tao section (dealing with cosmological and ontological questions)? Or was the usual order the result of an earlier reversal made in order to emphasize the metaphysical content? In fact, the original form remains uncertain; the two traditions could have co-existed from antiquity. Another new feature, the absence of chapters, frees us from a sometimes arbitrary division and permits a better understanding of obscure passages. These manuscripts have also brought to light texts which were believed to have disappeared: four well-preserved works preceding version B of Lao Tze, entitled respectively *Jingfa* (Invariable Law), *Shidajing* (the Ten Great Writings), *Cheng* (Weighing) and *Taoyuan* (Tao: the Origin). These texts could be the lost works supposedly influenced by Huangdi, the Yellow Emperor, a mythical sovereign looked on as the patron of esoteric Taoism, the *Huangdi*

sijing (the Four Writings of the Yellow Emperor) mentioned in the bibliographical chapter of the Annals of the Western Han. This Taoist school, which merged with that of Lao Tze, the father of mystical Taoism*, to become the sect of Huanglao, was in favour under the Han. It was weakened by the prominence of Confucian ideology under the reign of the Emperor Wu (140–85BC), and completely effaced by the pre-eminence of Lao Tze. This explains the scarcity of literature on the subject. These four texts may help to illuminate a philosophical trend, some of whose features persisted in religious Taoism. Although its content is recognized as being somewhere between Taoist thought and the ideas of the legists, its identification still excites controversy. The other manuscripts include the *Yiying*, an ancient work of divination, two texts on Yin-Yang and the Five Elements, a treatise on astrology, and a silk fragment with some 40 illustrations of physical exercises with explanatory notes. Some of these are gymnastic exercises based on animal movements, others demonstrate specialized breathing techniques. A short passage is perhaps a treatise on a diet without cereals and the control of the breath. This kind of text accompanying the burial of the dead proves that the Taoist techniques employed in the quest for immortality (gymnastics, diet, drug taking, embryonic respiration, meditation, etc.), one of the major concerns of the Han period, were already in favour at that time.

The iconography of Taoism

The way in which the majority of the tombs of this period were decorated and the grave goods they contained certainly evoked immortality. Nevertheless, this concern for life in the hereafter was not associated with a wish to avoid death. The first aspect prevails in several iconographic forms which reflect the development of Chinese thinking about death: the ascension of the deceased's soul to immortality (banners of Chenjiadashan, Zidanku, and tombs Nos 1 and 3 at Mawangdui); mythical lands of paradise such as Mount Kunlun, one of the Five Sacred Peaks, as places of sojourn in the world beyond after ascension (banner of Jinquashan); immortality personified in the features of the immortals decked in plumes or those of Xiwangmu, the Mother Queen of the West, who controls the cosmos and gives birth to immortality (painting on the ceiling of the tomb of Bu Quianqiu). The abundance and detail of both literary and figurative documents supplied by recent excavations considerably enrich the field of investigation of the study of Taoism. By comparing traditional or recently discovered texts with the works themselves, it has been possible to establish or revise the iconography, dating and development of certain themes. Thus, the

hybrid beings of the famous Chu manuscript (Sackler collection, Metropolitan Museum of Art, New York) from the end of the 5th century BC and the fantastic animal guides to the other world on the banners of Mawangdui could be a legacy from the mythological universe of the ancient kingdom of Chu, with its undercurrent of shamanism. This is also expressed in works such as the *Shanhaijing*, a book on mythical geography (the oldest parts of which date to the 4th century BC) or the *Chuai*, an anthology of Chu poetry containing the ecstatic chants in tribute to Qu Yuan (340–278BC). The first portrayals in art of the lands of the immortals (Mount Kunlun, the Island of Penglai, etc.) have been pushed back by a few centuries. Some scholars now even date them to the tracery decorations of tomb No 1 at Mawangdui. The iconography of Xiwangmu, the subject of a popular cult at the origin of the first sotereological* movement (a movement believing in the doctrine of salvation) in China, is found from the first known representation in the tomb of Bu Quianqiu (d.49BC) to the numerous engraved bricks and slabs of the Eastern Han (AD25–220).

Buddhism also comes within the scope of recent archaeological research in China. The known rock sites (Dunhuang, Binglingsi, Yungang, Longmen, etc) have been greatly restored, and many excavations have been made of the temples and pagodas so often destroyed during persecutions (for example the ruins of the Changlesi temple at Gushan near Handan, Hebei, excavated in 1982). Carved cliffs, forgotten beneath the sand for almost 2,000 years, are being rediscovered. One of the first and most spectacular examples was found in 1980 in the Kongwang Mountains near Lianyungang (Jiangsu). Here, some 100 figures combine Taoist themes (bearers of offerings in Chinese dress, masked dancers, etc.) similar to those found in the Han tombs, and Buddhist subjects (the Buddha standing, seated and leaving this world surrounded by his disciples). This confirms the interpenetration of the two religions in the Han period, a symbiosis which is reflected in both the terminology of the first translations of the sacred texts and their artistic expression. For a long time it was thought that Buddhism first entered China by the land route of Central Asia, but this major discovery could provide support for the theory that the sea route preceded it. Texts confirm the existence from AD65 of the first official Buddhist community at Pengcheng in the region of Jiangsu. Nevertheless, the two routes could have coexisted from remotest antiquity. The dating and identification of the subjects carved on this cliff, which must have been a place of pilgrimage and intense devotion for several centuries, are still the subject of fierce controversy.

Ascension to immortality, painting on brick, tomb of Bu Quianqiu (86–49BC) and his wife. Luoyang, Henan

This tomb excavated in 1976, has a remarkable group of paintings illustrating Taoist themes. On the ceiling of the main chamber, 20 rectangular bricks form a horizontal frieze representing a scene of ascension to immortality (drawing below, to be read from right to left). Fu Xi and Nu Gua, two mythical demiurges, creators of the universe, preside almost symmetrically to right and left. Fu Xi, with a human head and bust, and a serpent's tail, wears a red robe covered with a violet shawl. His hands are joined inside his sleeves (brick no. 3 and detail opposite right). He faces a red sun containing a three-legged black crow, symbol of the *yang* essence (2). Nu Gua, with the same attributes as Fu Xi (19) is turned towards the white moon, symbol of the *yin* essence, in which are the mythical mulberry tree of the Levant, connected with the legend of Yi the archer, and the frog, metamorphosis of Yi's spouse after she had stolen the potions conferring immortality (18). Framed by this cosmogenic summary, the funeral procession unfolds. The woman, standing on a three-headed bird, wearing a long robe and holding a black bird, and the man standing on a snake and holding a bow (4) are doubtless portraits of the deceased couple, as on the central part of the banner from tomb No 1 at Mawangdui. The fox with nine tails and the frog which accompany them, and the hare which holds the herbs of immortality, form here, for the first time, the attributes of the Mother Queen of the West. She, seated on a cloud and wearing a two-pointed cap, welcomes the deceased (5). A tiger, a hybrid bird (9–10), two unicorns (11–13) and two dragons (13–16) form a powerful display between the enlaced clouds. Lastly, a winged immortal, clothed in plumes and holding the insignia of heavenly messengers (17), leads this posthumous procession towards immortality.

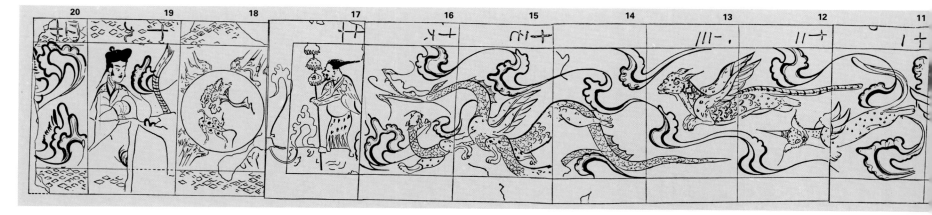

Buddhist-Taoist rock sculptures. Eastern Han (AD25–220) to the beginning of the Six Dynasties (AD220–598). Kongwan shan, Lianyungang, Jiangsu

Above left three groups can be distinguished among the sculptures on the cliff. A. Buddhist themes with an Indian iconography: standing appeasing Buddha (1 and detail opposite), the Buddha seated in meditation (2) and preaching? (3); episode in the life of the Buddha: death/liberation (*parinirvana*) in the presence of his disciples (4); illustrations of the Buddha's earlier lives: giving his body to the starving tigress (5). B. The Buddhist-Taoist themes with a Chinese aesthetic: beings destined for enlightenment (*bodhisattva*) clothed like Taoist dignitaries or divinities of the place? (6–7); narrative scenes: conversation with Vimalakīrti or banquet? (8). C. Themes from the cultural and religious repertory of the Han period: acrobats and dancers (9), bearer of offerings (10), exorcist (11). Right, detail of figure no. 1: standing Buddha with cranial protuberance, making the gesture of giving and appeasing.

Left: Fragments of the manuscript of Lao Tze, version B (tomb No. 3 at Mawangdui, Changsha, Hunan)

Inscribed in ink on silk in *lishu* style characters current in the Han period (221BC–AD220), this version is preserved better than version A. The replacement of the forbidden imperial character *bang*, which represents The Emperor Gaozu, known as Liu Bang, by the character *guo*, and the retention of the characters *ying* and *heng* composing the names of the emperors who followed him suggest that this manuscript should be dated to the reign of Gaozu (206–195BC). The text contains 5,467 characters, i.e. 467 more than the traditional version.

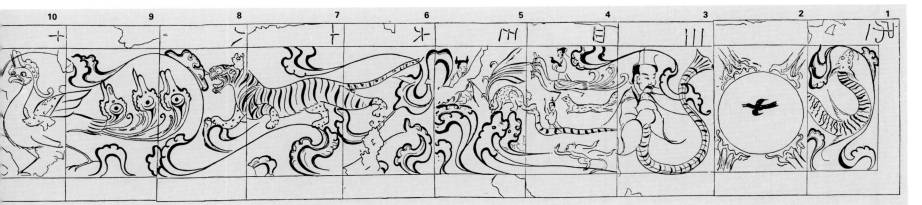

273

Tang burial paintings: views of a courtly society

Dramatic recent discoveries in Chinese archaeology include wonderfully preserved wall paintings from tombs of the Tang period (7th–10th century AD). These throw new light on artistic techniques of the time.

Nothing has advanced our knowledge of ancient China during the last 20 years so much as archaeology. In the field of painting, periods long known only from the few literary sources have been illuminated by discoveries showing the continuity of creative activity from the period of the Warring States (475–221BC). The coffin and lacquer goods from Leigudun (c.433BC), the banners and scrolls from Mawangdui (c.168BC) and mural paintings from burials throughout the 2nd century are the main landmarks, although they are widely scattered in time and place. Certain periods (early Han) and certain geographical areas (the Chu kingdom) have provided exceptional discoveries. Nevertheless, they give only a patchy picture of the development of Chinese painting as a whole.

From the Tang period, however, we have a large body of tombs decorated with murals which furnish valuable information about Chinese society from the 7th to the 10th centuries. There are about 30 of these tombs, 24 of which are situated in the territory of ancient Chang-an. Three of them are extraordinarily rich princely tombs, now well known from publications and the exhibitions mounted in Europe since 1973. Chinese archaeological reviews of the others supply the specialist with documentation and iconography which are unfortunately of lesser value. Nevertheless, the first-hand material made available by archaeology does exist and enables us for the first time to grasp the nature and development of Chinese painting during the three centuries of the Tang dynasty, a period for which we previously had only written sources and, except for the rock site of Dunhuang, works of doubtful authenticity. One question arises: was Tang painting confined to funerary murals? The texts emphasize the preponderance of mural paintings under the Tang and associate all the celebrated painters with the practice, but nothing remains of these religious and palace paintings, because of Buddhist prohibitions and the ephemeral nature of Chinese architecture. Chinese funerary paintings were not signed and were looked on as the work of craftsmen. Nevertheless, because of their nearness to the capital, their conception as underground palaces and their magnificent decoration, Tang tombs are undoubtedly a direct reflection of painting at the court of Chang-an.

Through the long epitaphs engraved on square stone slabs, these tombs can be dated and their owners identified: they are members of the imperial family or high officials. All the tombs have the same structure, which is more or less elaborate depending on the rank of the deceased. Orientated from north to south, they are divided into two sections. The first, on an inclined plane, leads to a stone door with engraved decoration. The second, built on a horizontal plane, is the residence of the deceased. In the most important tombs the painted decoration may occupy the entire surface of walls and ceilings. Unfortunately, these have nearly all been looted and have not preserved the whole of their painting scheme, because the openings left by thieves let in the air.

Innovation and iconography

It is not so much the originality of the themes as their new treatment which strikes us in the iconographic work of Tang funerary groups. The celestial representations familiar since the Han are often found on the vaulted ceilings of the chambers, while the animals of the four cardinal points continue to line the near end of the entrance of the access ramp. Decorative motifs (floral friezes, whirls of clouds with birds) sometimes appear on the ceilings or the upper edge of walls. Nevertheless, the schemes are primarily naturalistic and represent the various activities of the nobility and everyday life in the residence of the deceased. The main innovation was the perfect integration of the painting into the structure of the tomb: guards, servants, teams of horses and buildings had been depicted on the walls of tombs from the Han period, but now for the first time they were subordinated to an overall composition. This new formula represented a progression from the outside to the inside of a palace, an idea further emphasized by the continuous architectonic framework and the life-size human figures. These schemes had a unity which is particularly well achieved in the tombs of the princes Zhanghuai and Yide, and Princess Yongtai. The first committed suicide in 684, the other two, brother and sister, were killed in 701 on the orders of Empress Wu Zetian and were not given an imperial mausoleum until the accession of the Emperor Zhongzong. The three tombs date from 706. The tomb of Zhanghuai was reopened and its painted decoration partially refurbished for the interment of his wife in 711. The first section of the tombs is devoted to open-air scenes; polo and setting out hunting (Zhanghuai), view of a citadel and an impressive army (Yide); next come pictures of servants, officials and guards right to the palace enclosure flanked by racks bristling with halberds (axe-headed spears), their number indicating the rank of the master of the household. In another princely tomb (Wei Jiong, 708), the majesty of the palace entrance is portrayed, with a pavilion with two storeys and five bays, an important item of information about Tang wooden architecture. Beyond the stone door, manservants and maidservants holding everyday objects and ladies from the women's quarters surprised at their pastimes appear behind a wooden gallery opening on to a garden.

This very narrative type of decoration is the mark of Tang mural painting at its zenith in the early 8th century, but between the tomb of Li Shou (630), the oldest excavated to date and the tombs of the late 9th century, an iconographic development is obvious. The themes of rural and domestic economy predominating under the Han and the Six Dynasties continue in the scenes of tillage and cooking in the tomb of Li Shou. In later tombs, the somewhat confused verve of the early 7th century gives way to well articulated compositions drawing their inspiration from the cosmopolitanism of Tang society. There are many foreign human types and panthers, camels, etc., replace beasts of burden.

A new theme appeared c.745 in the framework of much smaller painting schemes: men and women are depicted, in each case in front of a tree within panels framed by a thick line like the wings of a screen. Flower and bird motifs multiply until they make up most of the decoration of later tombs (844, 847, 864), announcing a genre of painting characteristic of the later court.

Mural painting in China was executed on a dry ground. The wall was prepared with layers of clay mixed with straw and, later, hemp. The final dressing, lime plus an absorbent binder, received the drawing in ink and mineral pigments. The painter made a sketch, inside which he laid out the colours in flat tints. Then he used ink to convey facial features, folds in clothing, etc. Because it is applied to a thin film, the representational layer is fragile and its preservation depends on the dressings' adherence to the wall. The mineral pigments, however, have been sheltered from light and have preserved their freshness. The artists' flair for colour should not hide the graphic quality of their work. An ink outline of even thickness defines the forms without hesitation or florid embellishment, inscribing them clearly in a neutral space, animating them by the simple play of attitudes, the exchange of looks and the relative proportions. The engraved decoration of the stone doors and coffins is linked to the painting scheme: its themes are identical and it is the same essentially graphic art. The importance of landscape increases, but it is still treated elliptically: rocks, tufts of grass and elongated trees with sparse foliage serve as a background for human activities, although their main purpose is to create depth in the composition.

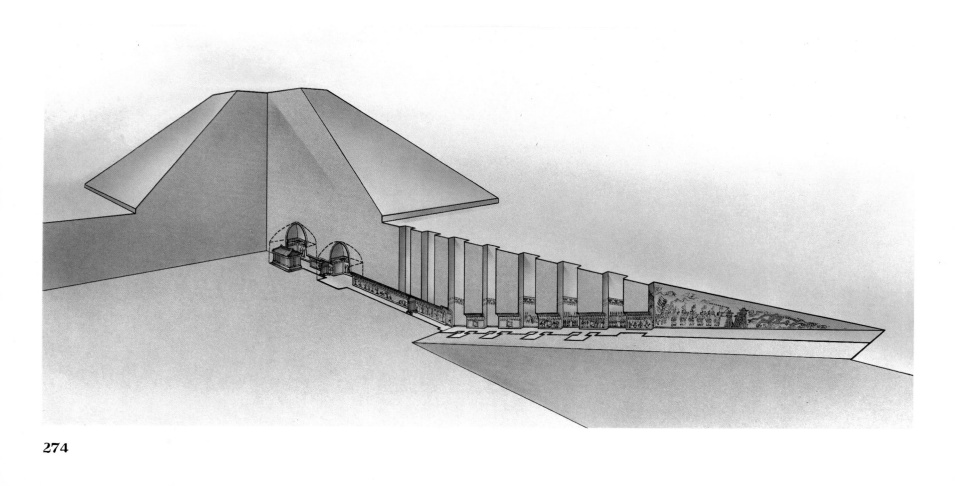

The harnessed horses of Princess Yongtai

Led by a young man and an old groom, these horses in harness decorate the east wall of the causeway leading to Princess Yongtai's tomb. The scene combines an acute sense of detail (in the harness) and an elliptical drawing style, a feeling for realism and a tendency to caricaturize (physiognomy of the groom), apparently contradictory qualities which make up the richness of Tang mural painting.

Decoration of the coffin of Princess Yongtai, Shaanxi, (8th century). Detail of the north wall

This rubbing of a detail of the engraved stone coffin of Princess Yongtai illustrates the perfect iconographic and stylistic unity achieved in the decoration of Tang princely tombs. This scene, which is typical of 8th century courtly art, is depicted with great graphic virtuosity.

"Flying gallop" of a Tang horse

The horse, with a heavy body and delicate legs, takes off above the great void of the undecorated wall; the rider clinging to its mane seems to be one with his steed. The liveliness of the red, the different tones of ochre in the animal's cover married to a nervous ink line, all contribute to a remarkable expression of the speed and power of the horse in this detail from the decoration of the tomb of Prince Zhanghuai, Shaanxi.

Three painted panels from the tomb of Su Sizhu at Xi'an, Shaanxi (745)

As yet, no mausoleum comparable to the three princely tombs from the beginning of the Tang period has been brought to light for the subsequent period (745–864), which is exemplified by the tombs of officials with decoration confined to the burial chamber. The portrait of the deceased repeated in a series of adjoining panels forms the principal theme of the schemes.

Evidence of 8th century military architecture

The axonometric projection of the tomb of Prince Yide, Shaanxi, clearly shows the relation between interior and exterior on which the conception of the decoration of the Tang princely tombs was based. The powerful watch towers of a citadel stand beside a green dragon, emblem of the east. Solid masses of masonry surmounted by a corbelled wooden structure supporting a projecting tiled roof (see detail, opposite, right), these towers mark the access to the prince's domain, at the beginning of the inclined way leading to the door of the burial chambers.

Bourgeois life: Sung, Liao and Chin dynasties

Elaborate family mausolea of the 10–13th centuries AD, recently excavated, furnish fascinating details of the life of the "middle class" in Chinese society – palace officials, wealthy businessmen, landowners, and their clans.

The hitherto unknown pictorial art of the barbarian Liao (947–1125) and Chin (1115–1234) kingdoms is gradually being revealed by archaeological discoveries. The comparison of increasingly rich material reveals the existence across a vast territory running from Inner Mongolia to Sichuan of a funerary art which has an undeniable kinship in spite of geopolitical and cultural frontiers. It is an iconographic and stylistic kinship which confirms the relations maintained by the barbarian kingdoms with the Chinese Sung Dynasty (960–1279) from the 10th to the 13th century.

The body was placed on a catafalque inside the funeral chamber, buried in a stone or wood coffin, cremated and the ashes dispersed or preserved in a bier or urn – the methods of burial are extremely varied under the Sung, Liao and Chin Dynasties, as is the structure of the tombs, most frequently a single chamber, but sometimes multiple (two, three or even four chambers), on a square, rectangular, polygonal or circular plan. The extremely rich decoration is usually confined to the walls and vaulted ceiling of the sepulchral chamber, sometimes including the outside of the door, which may be ornamented with floral and good-luck motifs and flanked by guardian gods. In the richest tombs the pictorial scheme extends to the corridor (*mudao*) and perhaps to the ventilation shaft (*tianjing*).

These mausoleums are mainly family tombs: tombs of married couples sometimes side by side with other clan tombs (Sung tombs at Baisna and Henan, Chin tombs of the Dong brothers at Houma, Shanxi, etc.). Except for some members of the Kitan nobility (Liao), the masters of the Sung, Liao and Chin tombs excavated so far seem to be mostly officials of intermediate rank, wealthy businessmen and landowners – archaeological confirmation of the advent of a middle class in China during this period.

The oldest Liao tombs illustrate the basis of the Kitan culture by representing nomadic life. One of the most complete examples decorates the inside walls of the stone coffin from tomb I at Keqi Erbadi (Liaoning): a flight of wild geese in a landscape with three felt tents, herds of oxen and horses, shepherds with their flocks of sheep, wild horses – all themes of Kitan nomadism which were soon to disappear. The decoration of the rich mausoleum of Yemaotai which dates from the beginning of the Liao Dynasty, as we can see from its complex structure and its grave goods, shows that the tribal heritage has already been abandoned: the only reminders of it are the ink drawing of a hunt in which

two horsemen followed by an unsaddled horse pursue a wild beast pierced with arrows and, in the principal scheme, a few servants with clothes and headgear in the Kitan mode painted in a style evoking Tang mural work. The hunting scene is depicted on a window sill of the miniature house sheltering the carved stone coffin. This complete and very well preserved construction offers an early example of miniature architecture and painted and engraved decoration from the *Ying Tsao Fa Shi*, the celebrated Chinese architectural treatise presented to the Sung throne in 1100 by a Sung official. In addition, within the tomb, two silk paintings were hung on either side of the coffin: a scroll showing rabbits frisking in a clump of bamboos and a landscape in the purest style elaborated under the Five Dynasties (907–960) and the early Sung. The iconography and treatment of the carved decoration of the coffin also reflect the profound Chinese influence exerted from the beginning of the dynasty upon their powerful neighbour, the Liao. The Kitan, like their successors the Jürchen Chin, were rapidly "Sinocized". The iconography of the tombs from the middle and end of the Liao dynasty provide excellent information about this assimilation. In the vast tomb I of Kulunqi (Jilin) dated to *c*.1080 the painted decoration of the ventilation shaft contains representations of Kitan servants of both sexes, and rocks, foliage, friezes of clouds, cranes, bamboos, and lotus pools in a typically Chinese style. In the same way in its principal painting, depicting the departure on and return from a journey by the master – the crowd is a mixture of Kitan and Chinese. The last tomb, dated to 1116 by the epitaph of its owner, a Liao official, owes its fame to the very accurate star map painted on the vault of the main chamber. By the realism of the scenes evoking the everyday life of the household with its sentries, its servants, its orchestra and its dancer all in Han costume, the painting of Xuanhua marks the culmination of the process of Sinocization at the end of the Liao dynasty. Under the Chin hardly any of the individual traits of the culture of the steppes were to remain in funerary paintings.

Simulated architecture

The structure and composition of the paintings, the architectonic element, acquired a hitherto unknown importance from the 10th century onwards. The painted peristyles which framed the scenes of Tang mural paintings gave way to extremely realistic simulated architecture, brick copies of the console systems of

Chinese frameworks running along the tops of walls, sometimes resting on pilasters which separate the painted scenes and supporting the tiled porch roofs which ornament the entrance doors of most burial chambers. To complete the illusion, the artists painted these dummy frameworks red and decorated them, sometimes even drawing wood graining on them.

Painters and sculptors suggested three dimensions by tricks of perspective and *trompe-l'oeil*. They painted screens, lattice-work windows and fake half-open doors with people framed in or disappearing through them. These devices, which were rare and somewhat clumsily done under the Liao (Wohuwan, Shanxi), were more widely applied from the 12th century on (Xuanhua: 1116; Baisha: 1099; Chin tomb of Guotang in Shandong, 1197) and showed a new virtuosity in the handling of space. A frequent theme of mural paintings from the Han and a favourite subject of Liao decorative ensembles, which derived from the iconography of the Tang style, the evocation of daily life was transformed in the Sung and Chin tombs into an illustration of middle-class values, the ostentatious presentation of the family background and a conventional portrait of the masters of the tomb. Husband and wife pose for eternity, full face, surrounded by their most precious possessions: books, luxury pottery, landscape paintings, and flanked by servants and ceremonial objects (Sung tombs at Houma and Baisha; Chin at Macun and Houma, Shanxi, etc.).

Music and the dramatic arts were the favourite pastimes of the middle classes. The Chinese theatre, which acquired its present-day form at that period, is evoked for the first time in Sung and Chin tombs. Its characters – clown, juggler, young scholar – appear either in consort on a real stage (carved decoration of the Chin tomb of Houma), or isolated on painted (Sung: Houma) or carved panels (Sung: Yanshi, Baisha; Chin: Houma, Jiaozuo).

The theatre infects the representation of life itself: open curtains or raised blinds almost inevitably frame figurative scenes. In the tomb of Zhaitang near Pekin (late Liao), the landscape itself is shown between the folds of a tapestry.

The theatre representing life, and the life represented as if it were theatre are two strands which interweave in the decoration of the tombs from the end of the Sung and Chin dynasties.

Funeral procession of an important Liao dignitary

The centre of the painted scheme of tomb I at Kulunqi, Jilin (*c*.1080) represents the master departing on (*mudao*, north wall) and returning from (south wall) a tour. This group shows the ethnic mixture of Liao society: Kitan guards and servants are shown side by side with Han soldiers and scholars. This painting provides valuable information about the costumes, hair styles, harness and vehicles used in the 11th century in the barbarian fringes of China.

A burgeoning bourgeoisie

In the tomb of Zhao Daweng at Baisha, Henan, the modelled and painted decoration is combined with sculpture to illustrate the wealth of the household of the masters of the tomb. The use of *trompe l'oeil* and the framing of each composition within curtains irresistably evoke the idea of a theatre set.

Landscape

Landscape as a separate pictorial genre appeared in China in the 10th century, but works from that period are extremely rare. The scroll painted in ink and colours on silk discovered in the Liao tomb at Yemaotai, Liaoning (10th century) is an inestimable work for both its quality and its value as a historic landmark. By the architecture on different levels, its composition suggests the idea of spaces situated opening out beyond each other which was to be a constant preoccupation of landscape painting in China.

Eleven musicians and a dancer in Chinese costume

Direct and transverse flutes, mouth organ, Pan pipes, *pipa* (pear-shaped lute) and large and small drums, all the categories of instruments accompanied by the indispensable metrical tablet which marks the rhythm of Chinese melody, make up the orchestra depicted in the Liao tomb of Xuanhua, Hebei. Chinese music, Han musicians, yet another proof of the rapid Sinocization of the Liao.

The little world of the great cities of northern China

Thanks to the discovery of inscriptions from the Jin period, the dates of the Yanshan temple, Shanxi, have just been recalculated. The west wall of the southern hall relates the life of the Buddha in a panoramic composition shaped by the architecture of an immense palace. The details showing the wine pavilion and the minor trades of the city illustrate the documentary and artistic value of this vast complex of mural painting dated 1167.

The emergence of agriculture

The latest archaeological discoveries show that in China agriculture was born spontaneously, different regions developing different foods, and was not the result of a diffusion of stimuli from neighbouring countries.

Archaeological discoveries made since 1949 have given us a much more accurate idea than before of the development of Chinese agriculture. As from 1965, thanks to the dating of organic samples by radiocarbon* and by calibrating the results with the help of the data of dendrochronology, we can appreciate the antiquity of this agriculture in an absolute manner and not by comparative stratigraphy* alone. Excavations carried out at widely separated points on present-day Chinese territory have shown that agricultural techniques originated spontaneously in several different regions. The results of pollen studies made in Taiwan by Tsukada Matsuo and published in 1967 have revealed that there occurred, c.10,000BC, an important change in the local vegetation, marked by an increase in shrubs and a higher rate of charcoal in the composition of lakeside deposits. This phenomenon has been attributed to the clearance of forests to make way for fields. However, the oldest sites of the Neolithic period in continental China, according to dates ascribed by the archaeologist Xia Nai (1977), only go back to c.5000BC at Shuangmiaogou (district of Dengfen, Henan) and Hemudu (district of Yuyao, Zhejiang).

In northern China, agriculture appeared at the confluence of the Huanghe and its tributaries, the Fen and the Wei, a transitional region between the high wooded plateaus to the west and the low marshy lands to the east. This was a centre where two types of millet originated: *Setaria italica* (foxtail millet) and *Panicum miliaceum* (little millet), cereals with large ears containing small grains and particularly resistant to aridity. At Banpo, near Xi'an (Shanxi), grains of *Setaria italica* have been found in large quantities at the bottom of wells, in storage receptacles and in granaries where the earth had been dug out to preserve them. Bampo was the site of the Yangshao culture (c.5000–3000BC), which has been the most closely studied culture until today. Grains were found there that date to the 5th millennium and indicate the predominance of millet at this period, as well as seeds of *Brassica sinensis* or Chinese cabbage, the oldest vegetable known and cultivated in northern China.

The imprints of cords or fabrics on pottery attest the importance of hemp, cultivated or not. Pollen studies have shown that this region was semi-arid in those days. However, the nature of the soil, a very fine loess, made it easy to till with digging sticks. The stone tool kit is exemplified by finds of perforated weights which were fitted onto the sticks, hoes, spades, polished axes and knives, such as the tools found at Anyang (Henan). Dogs, pigs and chickens were already domesticated there.

Central and Southern China

In central China, the Dawenkou culture (c.4300–1900BC), which takes its name from the site discovered in Shandong in 1959, developed in that region and to the north of Jiangsu. It has a rather elaborate tool kit of bone and animal horns, which seems to be intermediary between the tools of the Yangshao and Lungshan cultures in Shandong (c.2900–2200BC).

In southern China, from 1960, excavations of Neolithic sites in the valley of the Yangtze and southeast coastal regions have shown that agriculture and the domestication of animals were known just as early as in the north, but in different geographical conditions and a different cultural context. In 1973, the discovery of the site of Hemudu (district of Yuyao, Zhejiang) revealed an agricultural economy of a richness comparable to that of the Huanghe region between 5000 and 3700BC. Excavations have yielded tools made of wood, bone (shoulder-blade shovels), antler and horn, and polished stone (axes and scissors). But the most interesting dicovery is still *xian* rice (*Oryza sativa indica*), which was therefore not introduced into China from India, Southeast Asia or even Japan, as had been maintained. In addition to rice, another cereal, *Zizania*, a kind of gramineous *Oryza*, has been found in China, as have water chestnuts, the grains and rhizomes (stems) of water lilies and certain vegetables. Dogs, pigs and buffalo were already domesticated. In 1961 excavations of the toponym site of Qing-liangang, in Jiangsu (c.4800–3600BC), revealed the existence, in a hotter and damper climate than today, of a culture showing such affinities with the Hemudu culture as rice, polished stone tools, and domestication of the same animals.

Among the cultures of south China, we should mention the oldest one known today in Taiwan, the Dapenkeng culture, remarkable for its duration (4000–2500BC and even 1000BC in some places). It was characterized by a meticulously polished stone tool kit, in particular rectangular shouldered adzes, and a corded pottery recalling that found at Fujian for the same period. It mainly developed an agriculture based on small tubers. The culture of the toponym site of Liangzhu, near Hangzhou, is the first Lungshan-type culture found south of the Yangtze. It is dated 3450–2000BC. The remains of *xian* and *keng* rice (*Oryza sativa japonica*) have been found at Qianshanyang, near Wuxing (Zhejiang), as have certain species of peaches, water chestnuts, melons and groundnuts (*Arachis hypogea*, well known in ancient America). The agricultural tools include flat and perforated spades, crescent-shaped and rectangular knives pierced with holes. Some

wood tools have been preserved in addition to the stone and bone tools. The discovery in 1958 of a bamboo basket containing silk thread, ribbons and gauze is of great interest. It is the oldest evidence of silk manufacture in China. Indeed, according to Xia Nai, the famous half cocoon found at Xiyincun in Shanxi in a level of the Yangshao culture is an isolated specimen too well preserved to be contemporary with its place of discovery; it must have been introduced there at a later date. The oldest bamboo remains known in China were also found at Qiang-shanyang. They consisted of cords of bamboo fibres dated to c.2627BC. So it seems as if this plant was originally used for its haulms.

Bronze Age agriculture

The Bronze Age began c.1850BC in Henan in the basin of the Huanghe with the Shang civilization, which was to last until the 11th century BC. It had a script and its agriculture was more advanced. Wheat and barley were cultivated in addition to millet and rice. Soya needs a lot more water than millet and it could not have been domesticated until the very end of the Shang. Its antiquity is attested on a Shang bronze by the character *shu* which designates it, the lower part of the character apparently representing the nodules formed on the plant's roots. Tilling implements show little improvement in comparison with preceding periods, and the successors of the Shang, the Chou, still used stone hoes, bone shovels, wood spades and knives made out of shells. Even though the use of cast iron can be shown to go back to 513BC in Shansi, the archaeological discoveries of recent decades have shown that use of iron agricultural tools did not really begin to spread until the 4th century BC in north China and the basin of the Yangtze. It was under the Han (206BC–AD220), with progress in the manufacture of wrought iron objects that a more efficient tool kit for clearing and tilling the soil began to spread. It was in the same period that the first great irrigation networks were built, especially in Sichuan where the works of the hydraulic expert Li Ping (306–215BC) were developed. Since 1949 more than 100 swing-boards and ploughs of this period have been found, their shares comprising an increasingly elongated triangular or sometimes trapezoid iron cutting edge. The discovery in 1956 of miniature terracotta granaries in the tombs of Loyang (Henan) suggests that the principal plants cultivated were little millet, foxtail millet, a kind of haricot bean, hemp and wheat. Some grave goods from Chengdu (Sichuan) are models of fields connected to a basin or irrigated by channels. The growing of rice on terraces was already practised at this period.

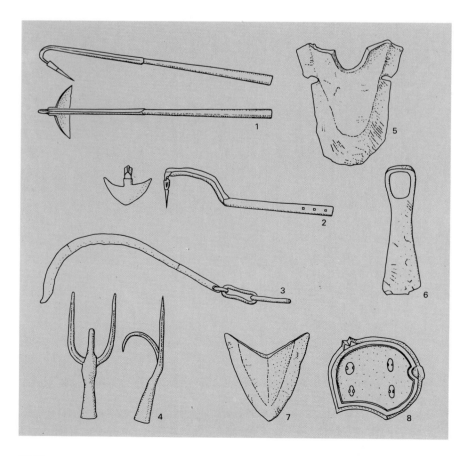

Agricultural tools from Hebei

Since 1949 archaeologists have found numerous agricultural tools buried in the ground of the suburbs of Peking, and dating from the end of the Tang period to the Yuan (10th–13th centuries), a period during which agricultural output was developed in conjunction with an improvement in tools. Nonetheless, some of these tools, such as the reaping hook, can be seen as early as on prints of the Han period (206BC–AD220). All these items are similar to those shown by Wang Chen in his *Manual of agriculture* (Nongshu), 1313. This small tool kit was to persist throughout China from the 14th to the 20th century, virtually unchanged.

Iron tools 1. *Mattock*. The handle is 75cm (30in) long; the head is 22cm (8.8in) high and 13cm (5.2in) long. 2. *Hoe*. The handle, which is 85cm (34in) long, has three holes through one end so that it could be fixed to a wooden support and drawn along by a man or animal. 3. *Reaping hook*. Two rings attached to an iron chain are linked to its end through a hole. Length 53cm (21.2in). 4. *Fork*. Length 25cm (10in). 5. *Spade*. This had a removable blade that could be changed. Length 24cm (9.6in), width 21cm (8.4in). 6. *Large hoe*. From Kaogu, No. 3, 1963. Length 25cm (10in), width 8cm (3.2in). 7. *Ploughshare*. It is triangular in shape and can be fitted onto a ploughstock. Length 14cm (5.6in). 8. "*Plough mirror*". Width 32cm (12.8in). This item was attached to the framework of the plough; on its back were four studs, each with two holes, through which a cord could be threaded.

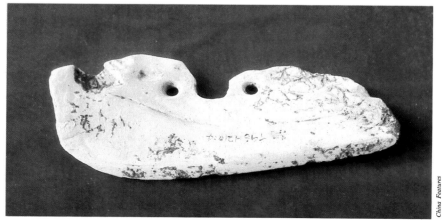

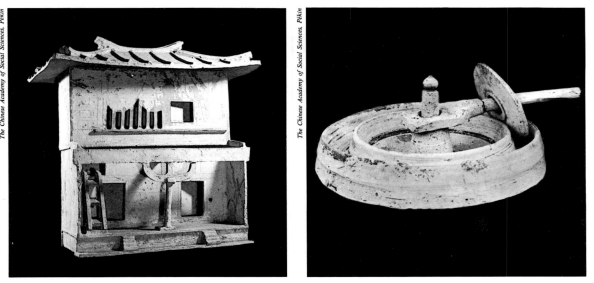

Grave goods in clay, representing rural life

The well, left, dates from the beginning of the Han dynasty (*c*.200BC) and is from the Chengtu area (Szechwan), a province that pioneered irrigation methods with the use of reservoirs, canals or wells. Under the Han dynasty every cultivated area of any size had its own well; canals were built in Shaanxi which between them supplied wells which were never far apart.

A great number of models of pigsties (above) have been found; this one is from the Chengtu area. The sties were often built beneath latrines; they were connected by pipes to a cesspool to provide manure.

The model of a millstone (above right) with a handle is from the Sui period (581–618) and was found at Anyang (Honan).

Preparation of cereals during the Han dynasty

Right, impressed on a Han brick from Pengshan (Szechwan), the scene shows, on the right, winnowing taking place in front of a granary standing on piles. A winnower is holding in his hands a rectangular fan made of plaited bamboo leaves, mounted on two vertical stakes; he is moving it to and fro while a helper is slowly pouring the grain onto it. This fan remained in use until the 20th century in South China. On the left, the husks are being removed by means of foot-operated rocking pestles. This process is not mentioned in Europe prior to the 16th century. Szechwan Provincial Museum

Below, a clay model found in a Han tomb at Jiyuan (Honan) in 1969. At the rear a winnower with rotating sails is being operated by a handle. This machine, known in the Han period, is the earliest example of the use of a crank handle, occurring five centuries earlier than the first crank handle for which there is evidence in Europe. In the foreground there is a rocking pestle. Michèle Pirazzoli-t'Serstevens, *La Chine des Han, Histoire et Civilisation*.

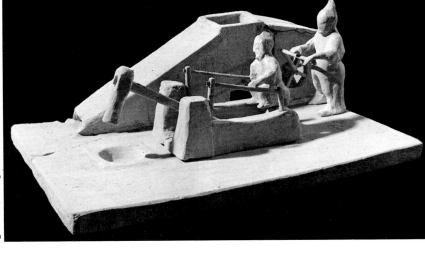

Opposite: Knife from Hsia dynasty

This knife, which dates from 2000BC, is certainly the earliest Chinese agricultural tool known to us today. It was found in 1977 near Gaocheng (Honan), believed to be the site of the former capital of the Hsia dynasty (21st to 16th centuries BC). Reaping knives made of stone, shell or pottery have been found throughout China on sites from the Neolithic, Shang and Chou periods. These were used by the first growers of millet or rice, and could be handled easily by means of a cord passing through the two holes in them, whereas knives with only one hole were hafted.

Ploughing scene from the Tang dynasty

Recently discovered wall paintings representing wooden agricultural implements include this ploughing scene, a funerary painting discovered in 1973 at Lingxian (Shaanxi) and dating from AD630 (beginning of the Tang dynasty). As in the earliest pictures of ploughing, the implement is here drawn by animals. It was at the period of the Warring States (475–221BC) at the latest that ploughshares with iron cutters made their appearance. The Han plough had a long, straight beam, while that of the Tang period had a shorter, curved beam which was better suited to ploughing heavy soil. Lu Guimeng in his famous *Leisi jing (Classic of the Plough)*, 880, describes the latter. It is more complex than the implement illustrated here and enabled the ploughshare to be fixed higher or lower, so varying the depth of the furrow ploughed.

Chinese astronomy

All ancient societies concern themselves with astronomy; like the Babylonians the Chinese specialized in it early, and recent archaeological finds demonstrate the originality of their contribution.

Since about 1970 a number of important archaeological discoveries have given us a better understanding of Chinese astronomy. Although it was subject to foreign influences (Babylonian, Indian, Arabic and occidental) down the centuries, there can be no doubt that Chinese astronomy was always an autonomous science. However, it is difficult to date its beginnings. The presence of cyclic characters indicating the days on oracle bones of the Shang dynasty (c.1766–c.1155BC) suggest the existence of cycles of 60 days, but that does not necessarily imply the existence of a calendar. The first names of stars such as Zhujiao (in Hydra) and Huoxing (in Scorpio) appear on engraved bones in the reign of Wuding (c.1339–c.1281BC), but we have to wait until the 9th or 8th century BC to find the names of eight constellations appearing in a famous anthology of poetry, the *Shijing*.

Specialists consider that one of the most important systems of Chinese astronomy, the 28 *xiu* or houses, originated around the 6th century BC. According to H. Maspero, the *xiu* are sidereal guiding points representing spindles of variable extent measured on the (celestial) equator but converging towards the Pole. Each house bears the name of the constellation found in it. By means of this system, astronomers can follow the progress of the stars in the sky, but the houses also have an astrological function; each *xiu* has a corresponding terrestrial territory to which the predictions based on phenomena observed in the sky are applied. When we realize this, the treatise on predictions associated with the appearance of comets, haloes, clouds, etc., discovered in tomb No 3 at Mawangdui in 1973, acquires a political dimension. It was meant to guide the actions of the governors of the states associated with the houses where those phenomena were observed.

The *xiu* were also used as decorative motifs. A box lid from the period of the Warring States (475–221BC) on which the names of the 28 houses figure prove that the system was already known throughout the Chinese world, because the tomb in which this lid was found was in Hubei, comparatively far from the administrative centre of the period.

Along with the creation of the *xiu* system, 24 guiding stars were chosen by which the position of the other stars in the sky could be determined. In this, Chinese astronomy differs greatly from Greek heliacal astronomy, which is based on the observation of the rising and setting of stars just before dawn and just after dusk. In China, where the celestial Pole symbolized the Emperor, astronomers studied the circumpolar movements of the constellations around the Pole. The Great Bear (Ursa Major) was one of the constellations which was closely studied. Its function as a celestial clock was noted very early; the tail is turned to the east in spring; to the south in summer, etc. But much more remarkable was the discovery under the early Han (206–8BC) of Mizar, the most visible of the double stars in the Great Bear. It was not until 1650 that this phenomenon was observed in Europe by Riccioli. Thus from the Han period we find

representations of the Great Bear with eight stars in China, as well as more traditional models with seven stars.

The movements of the planets were also studied, as is proved by an extraordinary document found in tomb No 3 at Mawangdui. This contains a record of the hours of the setting and rising of the planets covering 70 years, from 246 to 177BC. These notations enabled astronomers of the period to calculate the cycles of Venus, Saturn and Jupiter with such accuracy (to 0.48 of a day for the Venusian cycle, 1.09 of a day for the Saturnian cycle and 3.44 days for the Jupiterian cycle) that modern experts think that precise measuring instruments must have been used. So far no instrument from this period has been found, but specialists postulate the use of the armillary sphere (a model of the celestial sphere), the invention of which probably dates to c.350BC. This primitive sphere is thought to have consisted of four elements: a graduated fixed circle indicating the axis of the sky into which two moveable graduated rings were inserted, probably representing the equator and the ecliptic, and a viewing tube for isolating the part of the sky to be observed. A sphere of this kind would have allowed the adepts of the theory of the Huntian, one of the cosmological theories established around the 4th and 3rd centuries BC, to give a concrete expression to their conception of the world. Moreover, it was the Huntian which later gave its name to the armillary sphere, the *hunyi*, which means "instrument of Hun".

Conceptions of sky and earth

According to the theory of the Huntian, the sky is a globe in the centre of which is the earth, "like an egg yolk in a shell", as the ancient texts say. The sky turns from left to right and the sun revolves vertically around the earth. The alternation of day and night is brought about by the Sun's passing above and below the earth. The theory of the Huntian remained in vogue until it was amalgamated with modern science as introduced to China by the Jesuits in the 16th century.

Another theory, the Tiankai, only survived to the 6th century AD. It conceived the sky and the earth as two domes nested one inside the other. The circumference edge of the sky was round, but that of the earth was square to take into account the four cardinal points. Some authors, including J. Needham, think that this conception of the world is of Babylonian origin. In the Tiankai, the hemisphere of the sky turns from left to right, while the sun, moon and constellations turn much more slowly in the opposite direction; they do not disappear, but remain permanently visible on the horizon. The sun moving away and coming closer produces day and night. It may be that among the 250 documents and astronomical maps discovered at Mawangdui, but not yet published, are sky maps drawn according to the theories of the Tiankai school. Meanwhile, there is no shortage of later planispheres enabling scholars to follow the development of astronomical knowledge. Thus, the number of stars on the Lingan

chart (900BC), one of the oldest known, is smaller than that on the more recent chart of Xuanhua.

To give concrete form to the conception of the world they offer, the cosmological systems adopt a series of accurate but theoretical measurements: the diameter of the celestial sphere is fixed at 357,000 *li* (a *li* equals about 414m). The distance between heaven and earth at the winter solstice is 80,000 *li*, etc. These abstract measurements hindered the observation of real phenomena, falsified the correct calculation of the solstices and equinoxes, and made it difficult to establish a calendar. The astronomers' task was further complicated by the combined lunar and solar nature of the calendar, the Chinese apparently being the only people to adopt this version. To reconcile the tropical solar year of 365.242 days with the lunar year of 12 synodic months of 29.531 days, astronomers resorted to intercalary months. One formula, adopted in 104BC, remained in force, with only a few minor changes, until the adoption of the Gregorian Calendar in 1912. To palliate the inconveniences of the lunar calendar (in which the beginning of the year and the beginning of the seasons are uncertain) 7 months were interpolated, spread over 19 years, so that the winter solstice always fell in the 11th month, the spring equinox in the 2nd, the summer solstice in the 6th, and the autumn equinox in the 8th month.

This formula still did not permit the accurate prediction of eclipses, a serious problem in a country where these phenomena were looked on as extremely ominous. The Jesuits' skill in this field was one of the factors which encouraged the adoption of western science in China, but the originality of Chinese astronomy, which is being increasingly demonstrated by fresh archaeological discoveries, was still remarkable.

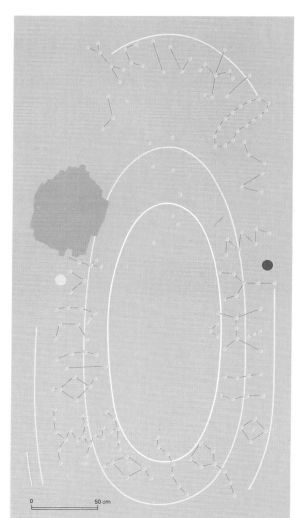

The oldest Chinese astronomical object

Lid of a black lacquer box incised with red motifs discovered in the tomb of the Marquis Yi of Zeng (d.433BC) at Leigudun in Hubei. Water leaking into the tomb long ago destroyed the box to which the lid belonged. Right, the "green dragon", symbolizing the east; left, the "white tiger", symbolizing the west. In the centre, the names of the 28 houses form an irregular circle around the character *dou*, Chinese name for the Great Bear.

Map of the celestial sphere from the end of the Tang period

Planisphere incised on the ceiling of a funerary chamber completed in AD900 at Lingan in Zhejiang and discovered before 1979. Originally, this map had 183 stars, but 13 of them were destroyed when a hole was made in the ceiling by grave robbers (patch on the left of the drawing). With the exception of the 8 stars of the Great Bear, all the stars are connected by lines to form 28 constellations. Three ellipses and the fragment of a fourth represent the celestial latitudes. Two small circles to right and left symbolize the sun and the moon. The map was coloured by filling the incised trace of the drawing with a mixture of clay and colouring matter.

Map of the heavens, Liao dynasty (947–1125)

Planisphere from the year 1116 decorating the ceiling of a tomb at Xuanhua in Hubei. This map has a diameter of 2.17m (7.1ft) and gathers up elements from three different civilizations: Babylonian, Indian and Chinese. In the centre is a lotus with nine petals, of Indian inspiration, around which are grouped 29 constellations containing a total of 186 stars. The shapes of the constellations, especially of the first and third constellations to the left of the Great Bear, often differ from those in planispheres from the end of the Tang period. Between the lotus blossom and the constellations are 9 small circles, 8 of which represent unidentified stars; the 9th, inside which is a crow, an ancient Chinese solar symbol, situated to the east, symbolizes the sun. Around the constellations, 12 drawings encircled in black represent the attributes of the 12 palaces of the sun, of Babylonian origin. Some elements of the drawings, such as the clothing of the personages depicted, have been Sinocized. A bronze mirror, in the centre of the lotus, indicates the summit of the heavens.

Double star

Engraved stone from the offering chamber of the Wu family (Wuliang ci), district of Jiaxiang, Shandong, c.AD150. It shows the Emperor surrounded by courtesans and fabulous animals in the chariot of the Great Bear. To the right, a figure points to the double star Mizar.

Constellations and legend

Engraved stone slab decorating a Han tomb from the district of Nanyang in Henan. It represents five constellations and the animals or personages associated with them. To the right, a cowherd and his ox, symbols of the constellation of the ploughman. In the centre, a tiger, symbol of the constellation Wei; top left, a hare, symbol of the constellation Fang. The kneeling woman, left, symbolizes the constellation of the weaver. According to legend, the ploughman and the weaver were too much in love with each other and neglected their respective occupations, so they were condemned to live on opposite banks of the Milky Way, that celestial river which is the prolongation of the Yellow River. Nevertheless, once a year, on the 7th day of the 7th moon, they were allowed to meet again. So they crossed the river by a bridge made by all the earth's magpies, who flew up to heaven for this purpose.

Book of portents

Detail of the *Tianwen qixiang zazhan* (mixture of astronomical and meteorological prognostics) discovered in 1973 in tomb No. 3, sealed in 168BC, at Mawangdui near Changsha in the Hunan. This book, in several sections, is written on a piece of silk 150cm long by 48cm wide (59 × 14in). The section on the comets, represented here, contains drawings executed in black and red ink. The vegetal aspect of certain comets explains the names of the plants which were attributed to them. The texts under the pictures indicate the portents connected with the comets in question. This document represents one of the first attempts to classify the comets by the length of their tails.

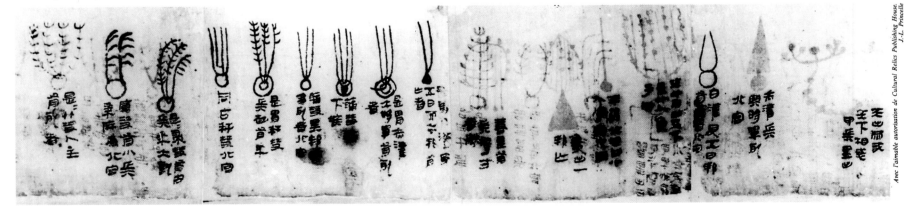

Vietnam:
the archaeological background

Archaeologists of the colonial period, investigating the prehistory and protohistory of Vietnam, produced fascinating discoveries but their conclusions were not always based on sufficient knowledge; since 1975 Vietnamese specialists have developed a dramatically clearer picture of the region's indigenous archaeology.

When, in 1896, Paul Daumer founded the Indochina Archaeological Mission under the scientific control of the Academy of Inscriptions and Fine Art, the French colonial administration realized the necessity to understand, study and safeguard the cultural history of the country. A library and museum were to be founded and a publication launched. Soon experienced researchers and promising students and officials were working within the ranks of the new institution. By January 1900 the Mission had already become the hub of intense linguistic, ethnological and archaeological activity and was reorganized under the name of Ecole Francaise d'Extrême-Orient (EFEO). Geographically, and even culturally during prehistory and protohistory, Vietnam, like its neighbour southern China, belongs to Southeast Asia; however, it is usually studied together with the Far East for purely historical reasons, and this convention is observed here.

Archaeologically speaking, one of the main roles of the EFEO was the conservation and recording of buidings and important monuments as well as of movable items. All reports of excavations and discoveries made had to be circulated at all levels. A report on amateur excavations, published in 1902, while acknowledging the goodwill of the researchers, deplored the fact that incomplete results had been obtained because of "the lack of a properly thought out method, rigorously applied". It also recommended circumspection and careful attention to detail, as well as a healthy respect for the sites. EFEO was also the driving inspiration behind the first Congress of Far-Eastern Studies held in Hanoi in December 1902.

The attaché to the Geological Service of Indochina, Henry Mansuy , possessed a remarkable knowledge of fossils and soil formation and was naturally interested in prehistory. In 1906 he discovered the Neolithic Bacsonian culture in the cave or Pho Binh Gia (Bac Son, Bac Thai), with its stone and pottery implements. Stratigraphy* not having been invented, the only way to follow the evolution of the items was to study their morphology, or comparison of forms, and this Mansuy did with particular care. In 1910 the EFEO museum was founded in Hanoi and he was put in charge of the classification of the "cut stones" in the prehistory room.

Bronze drums

In 1908, three bronze drums, whose "decoration and scope are still an enigma for archaeologists", were added to the museum's collections. It was thought they had originated among the non-Han populations of southern China. In 1913 EFEO acquired part of the prehistorical and archaeological collections gathered by André d'Argence; these objects included pediform (foot-shaped) axes, a hatchet with an exaggerated curved cutting edge and lance heads from Son Tay, whose style is definitely not Chinese. The first representation from prehistory to be found in Indochina appeared on a bronze axe fragment acquired by the museum in 1915: it depicts a dug-out canoe with two oarsmen and two animals with antlers. However, nothing had yet been discovered which could throw light on pre-Chinese Vietnam, which was at the time only known from isolated objects, outside the archaeological context.

In 1918, Henri Parmentier, an architect and member of EFEO who had already excavated several ancient Chinese burial sites, published an article entitled "Ancient Bronze Drums" entirely devoted to these instruments and their importance in Vietnamese protohistory. He also increased the number of objects discovered to 188; 166 had been mentioned in 1902 by F. Heger. Further scholarly interest was aroused by the discovery of enigmatic bronze objects, weapons and clothes or ornamental accessories, or "elephant" bells

with decorative motifs similar to those of the drums and dating from the Metal Ages of the east of the peninsula. The same period also saw the rapid expansion of historical archaeology. By 1910, the study of the Tonkin (north Vietnam) monuments was well and truly launched, and restoration had begun on a number of temples and pagodas, among them the famous Temple of Literature in Hanoi. The architectural earthenware found in and around Hanoi and the pottery from Bat Trang, Tho Ha and Phu Lang were added to the museum's collections.

In the 1920s H. Mansuy continued with his prehistorical research and excavated the cave of Keo Phay (Lang Son), while Etienne Patte, of the Geological Service, unearthed the *kjökkenmodding** (shell mound) of Bau Tro (Binh Tri Thiên). Struck by the fact that men using roughly hewn stone were also capable of polishing it, Patte concluded that the coexistence on the same sites of both kinds of tool probably indicated that the latter technique had been introduced by a foreign ethnic group, perhaps one with a western origin. This theory has now been invalidated.

Hoa Binh culture

In 1926 Madeleine Colani discovered the Hoa Binh culture (named after the town) which she first attributed to the Paleolithic, then to the Neolithic age. In the space of four years she excavated some 50 sites in the centre and the north of the country. However, nothing from the Paleolithic period was found, and it was thought not impossible that Indochina and the Far East did not experience this phase of human development. According to Mansuy, the Neolithic suddenly followed a Paleolithic period with extremely primitive features. Furthermore, problems surrounding the Neolithic period were still far from being solved, and the theory gained ground that its more recent phase coincided with the first use of bronze.

Knowledge of protohistory, on the other hand, was definitely progressing. Following a fortuitous discovery of bronzes and pots by the inhabitants of the Dong Son countryside (Thanh Hoa), the banks of the Song Ma at Dong Son were excavated in the years 1924–30. For the first time, objects were found still in place in their context, making their discovery all the more important. All the pieces brought to light—weapons, drums and other bronzes—were sent to the EFEO museum, which, in 1927, also acquired the second half of the Argence collection.

Further south, the necropolis of Iron Age jars of Sa Huynh (Quang Ngai, central Vietnam), discovered at the beginning of the century and widely pillaged in the meantime, was studied again by H. Parmentier, as was the one found in the nearby village of Phu Kuong. Research into prehistory continued on an intensive scale throughout the 1930s. Excavations and research were undertaken of the kjökkenmodding of Da But (Thanh Hoa), which were thought of as Bacsonian, and the Neolithic remains of the Along Bay with its numerous open-air settlements; a programme of surveys and digs was carried out in the south as a result of which the importance, so far unsuspected, of the deposits and of the prehistory of Cochin-China was finally recognized. Several papers on the prehistory and protohistory of Vietnam were presented to the Congress of Prehistorians of the Far East (Hanoi 1932, Manila 1935, Singapore 1938) and to the twelfth session of the French Prehistorical Congress (Toulouse-Foix 1936). The excavations of Thanh Hoa were followed by those of Dong Son (from 1935 to 1939) and Dan Ne, where, in 1936, were discovered tombs of a Dongsonian type which contained a certain number of weapons and iron tools mixed with the usual bronze objects. These

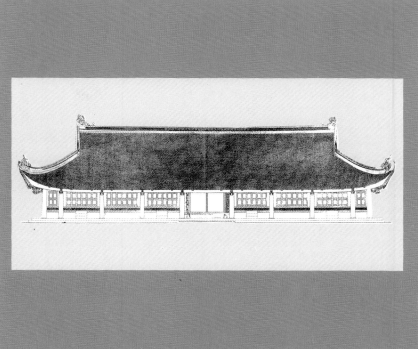

Façade of the *dinh* communal house in the village of Dinh Bang (Bac Ninh)

A direct descendant of protohistoric architecture and a symbol of village autonomy in the context of centralized power, the *dinh* communal house is the only building constructed on pilework (invisible from outside) among all the secular or religious constructions built at ground level, in the Chinese style. The house of Dinh Bang, built in the 18th century, is one of the most beautiful monuments of Vietnamese art. In Louis Bezacier, *Relevé des monuments anciens du Viêtnam*, French School of the Far East, Paris 1959, pl.LXIII.

tombs are thought to represent the end of the local Bronze Age. The bronze drums, which form such a large part of the museum's collections were dated to the beginning of the Christian era, some of 250 found in Southeast Asia (with the exception of Java) and more particularly in northeast Indochina.

The overall picture of Vietnamese protohistory is still confused with many gaps. Foremost is the problem of the Bronze Age. The prolonged coexistence of stone and metal tools is one of the main sources of the question marks which surround the cultures which existed before Chinese colonization. Scientific dating methods only allow us to reach relative chronologies.

As far as historical archaeology is concerned, research, preservation and restoration work continued without interruption. The proximity of Khmer and Cham relics did not prevent scholars such as Charles Batteur from harbouring strong feelings about Annamite art, ignored or regarded as a pathetic copy of Chinese art, while, to Batteur, it represented a totally original approach only broadly based on Chinese influences. As a result of the general interest in archaeology, a museum was founded in Thanh Hoa in 1939, and in the same year the first flights of aerial archaeological reconnaissance took place. Science and art, however, were not cut off from the real world, and both World War II and the fight for Vietnamese national independence have had their effect on the country's archaeology.

In 1945, President Ho Chi Minh founded the Institute of Archaeology and, with his decree no. 65, showed that the young Democratic Republic of Vietnam, nine years before independence, already attached great importance to the relics of its past. After the return of peace in 1954, most of the archaeological discoveries took place in the north of the country, where excavations have been carried out by the Institute of Archaeology, the Museum of Vietnamese History and Hanoi University. Notwithstanding the work of many foreigners and a reliance upon Chinese and East German laboratories for C^{14}* datings, Vietnamese archaeology is now the domain of specialist Vietnamese scholars.

Discoveries since 1960

In 1960 a very important discovery was made when traces of a Lower Paleolithic site were first found in the open-air settlement of Mount Do (Thanh Hoa) represented by utensils belonging to various traditions. A second great discovery was made in 1968 by the team of Hanoi's Faculty of History under Professor Ha Van Tan. The Son Vi culture (Vinh Phu) filled the gap between the Lower Paleolithic and the Hoabinian periods, regarded today as Mesolithic although no microlithic remains have been found. Still within the context of prehistory, the Mieng Ho (Bac Thai) culture, important to the study of the industrial traditions of Southeast Asia, presents more problems than it solves, as is the case of the Paleolithic tools of Xuan Loc in the south of the country.

A third important discovery shed light on the Phyng Nguyen (Vinh Phy, 1959) culture, which bridges the gap between the end of the Neolithic period and the beginning of the Bronze Age in the Red River delta.

During this period, surveys and excavations were carried out along all the river basins and the coastal plains. Dongsonian sites were systematically explored: Viet Khe (Hai Phong) in 1961, Chau Can (Ha Son Hinh) in 1971, Lang Vac (Nghe Tinh) in 1972, Lang Ca (at the confluence of the Hong and the Claire rivers) in 1976–77. The existence of a Dong Son phase, predating the ancient phase of the site, has been recognized in several Thanh Hoa sites as well as in the one at Ru Tran (Nghe Tinh) which includes dwellings and a

burial ground. In 1975, Nguyen Van Huyen and Hoang Vinh focused on the problem of the drums in a volume published by the Vietnamese History Museum, and protohistory was usefully discussed at the national congresses held in 1968, 1969, 1970 and 1971.

The reunification of the country in 1975 allowed archaeologists to resume their work in the south. The necropolis of Sa Huynh was again excavated on several occasions, and the discovery of sites containing both dwellings and tombs of the same culture helped in placing it within the regional context, as well as leading to interesting comparisons. While Vietnamese prehistory and protohistory were, during the colonial period, still blurred and too often judged in comparison with Chinese examples, successive and often spectacular discoveries, coupled with the study of objects within their context, a new approach to existing problems and modern, multi-disciplinary methods have enabled archaeologists to compile a clearer picture of the indigenous societies which preceded the Chinese invasion, and to establish a more detailed chronology of the Metal Ages. However, it has not always been easy to distinguish between the regional features and the chronological stages of the various cultures.

Recent discoveries and their interpretations have shown quite clearly that Vietnam entered the Bronze Age at an early date and quite independently from northern China, where a contemporary but very different elitist culture developed within the context of the city-palace. During the first part of the Bronze Age, until the 8th or 7th centuries BC, a civilization based on a network of villages produced simple, small bronze objects and cleared for cultivation what is now central Vietnam. As agriculture improved, particularly the culture of rice, and as the population increased, societies became more complex and peoples moved down to conquer the lowlands. Towards the 7th century BC—and this is what distinguishes Vietnam from neighbouring Thailand—economic and social changes led to a differentiation of the social classes and the formation of an elite with temporal and spiritual powers, who owned such splendid ritual objects as the bronze drums, the large jars and the situlae . These changes must have brought about the formation of a state, the nature of which is still little known. The details of this process of economic and social transformation are not yet clear. The relations which existed between the various cultural centres of Southeast Asia before the introduction by China of different values, peoples and techniques (2nd century BC), deserve, as does their ancient agricultural system, to be the object of much more research. Vietnamese archaeologists, well aware of their country's importance to the study of protohistorical civilizations, have a keen interest in the work carried out in other countries, and there is no doubt that the results of their own activities will greatly enrich our knowledge of protohistorical, non-Chinese Asia in years to come.

The pebble tools of the Hoabinhian culture

Just as the first clues in European prehistoric research came from examination of flint tools, so in Southeast Asia the examination of artificially shaped pebbles and their decoration has led to understanding of the Paleolithic people of this region.

The different techniques used by Paleolithic peoples in the manufacture of tools in Vietnam have become clearer recently, both with the re-examination of material from the excavations carried out by Madeleine Colani in 1929 and its comparison with material from recent digs, and also with the results of recent experiments in shaping pebbles. Two main groups of tool industries emerge: those made from blocks of clastic material (composed of fragments of pre-existing rock) with sharp edges, and those made from river pebbles with a coarser texture. The first is generally considered as forming part of the Lower Paleolithic; the second comprises two industries from the Upper Paleolithic: the so-called "Sonviian" and "Hoabinhian" cultures, which form the objects of our study.

Analysis of the levels in the cave of Con Moong (1976) made it possible to establish the chronological succession between the Sonviian and the Hoabinhian (see opposite, top right). The Sonviian was a pebble culture using fairly thick quartzite river pebbles which were turned into choppers by removing large oblique flakes, working in one direction. The working edge, however, was not very sharp. Together with the remains of the unworked faces, it usually formed a point or a sort of pick, probably used to dig up food. In the most ancient groupings of the Hoabinhian culture, such tools may be found mixed with typical Hoabinhian material.

So-called "Sumatraliths", "short axes" or unifacial tools (i.e. those worked on one side only) have long been considered as the characteristics of the Hoabinhian industry. The most striking feature of its tools is in fact the extreme economy of means required for their manufacture, achieved by making the fullest use of the shape of the pebble. Indeed the pebble is frequently used in its natural state. Often the judicious removal of just a few flakes is enough to make it thinner and create a working edge between two slight shoulderings, not unlike a keeled scraper.

The making of the tools shows regularity and symmetry that suggest a preoccupation with efficiency and functional beauty absent in the industries of Sonvi or the Lower Paleolithic. The gripping area often remains unworked or is formed by a clear 90° fracture of the rock. Use of the natural shape of pebbles is also apparent on the triangular pieces, where a few simple retouches emphasize the working edge or a butt to be used for fixing onto a handle. Nevertheless, these pieces are fairly late, stemming from the Late Hoabinhian or even the still later so-called "Bacsonian". Thus, in spite of great typological diversity, the Hoabinhian industry is mainly characterized by steady adherence to its own technology.

The tools have been given various names that presuppose their use: "axes", "short axes", "end-scrapers", "side-scrapers", and so on. But although the shape of the tool may give a clue as to use, the most definite evidence of a particular kind of utilization comes from the signs of wear left on various parts of the pebbles: pitting, pecking, splintering, scratches, signs of rubbing, or shininess due to use.

The signs must be interpreted with the greatest caution, but several observations are relevant. The majority of Hoabinhian tools are pebbles of volcanic origin (porphyrites, rhyolites), the edges of which are naturally blunted. This handicap is often compensated for by the weight of the pieces. Even when not sharp, pebbles weighing from 200 to 300gr and up to 2kg (7 to 10oz up to 4lb) or more were heavy enough to strip bark from trees or cut branches and hollow-stemmed bamboos. It is sometimes difficult to distinguish between very slight traces of polishing on the working edge of pebbles resulting from contact with hard solids, and those traces left by the first stage of deliberate polishing. The existence of a blade removed from a pebble and fashioned into a small tenon axe, suitable for sophisticated cutting, emphasizes the fact that the end of the Hoabinhian culture marks the junction of two complementary techniques.

Tools, diet and habitations

Significantly, there seems to be no direct connection between the functions of these tools and the food-acquiring activities of the people, as revealed by other archaeological remains. Numerous deep piles of shells witness to a thorough and widespread activity in the gathering of molluscs and snails, both freshwater and land-based. The remains of fossilized, sometimes carbonized bones are evidence of hunting that did not exclude big game such as elephants, rhinoceroses and large herbivores, yet none of the Hoabinhian tools so far discovered appear to apply directly to these activities. On the other hand, the hammering tools with their numerous pock-marks were no doubt used in the manufacture of stone tools, which were employed in their turn in the fashioning of bone, antler, wood and bamboo implements, or in the preparation of fibres, leather, etc. It was the rubbing of pebbles thus prepared against these materials that caused the signs of wear observable on certain pieces.

Moreover, the preparatory flakes and the hammer tools found with the rest of the implements prove that the shaping of pebbles took place in the cave or habitation itself. Other handicrafts could well have been practised in the same place. The shape and texture of some pebbles makes them suitable for grinding or polishing hard, as yet unidentified objects. Although no vegetable traces remain (apart from certain pollens recently discovered, but hard to interpret), wooden and bamboo implements may reasonably be assumed to have existed, prepared with the help of stone tools and pointed and hardened by fire. Prepared pebbles could also have served to split bamboo, to make laths and thin plates for cutting, dismembering, binding, plaiting, and a variety of other uses.

It is obvious that other excavations with more definite stratigraphies*, datings and records will enable us to define the activities of the Hoabinhians more accurately. These excavations are all the more necessary because in Vietnam aspects of the Hoabinhian culture show a wider concern than the mere quest for a daily living. For example, there appear to be several Hoabinhian graves among the piles of shells. Artistic preoccupations are also indicated: in the rock shelter of Lang Vanh numerous balls of ochre were discovered, with bowl-shaped pebbles, as well as bone fragments probably used as palettes. Many shaped pebbles were heavily covered with ochre; one ball-shaped pebble shows the removal of thin exterior flakes without any obvious utilitarian purpose. Was this simply a "found object" brought home by prehistoric man because of its singularity? The canine teeth of foxes, pierced at the base and used as ornaments, as well as the shells of *Cypraea* and *Arca*, buried in the midst of kitchen debris at the same time as the Hoabinhian pebbles, are further evidence of concerns other than practical.

Although they were not the first grinders of grain, or even early cultivators, as has been over-hastily asserted, the Hoabinhian people were able to make the best use of unpromising material. From the pebbles, they manufactured tools for many different uses with outlines revealing a latent aesthetic feeling. Admittedly, there are still many mysteries about the Hoabinhian caves which served as shelter, workshop, kitchen and burial place, but one thing is certain: the men who lived there were more than mere pebble dressers.

DINH Trong Hieu

Worked pebbles and signs of use

In the case of flat pebbles, the flakes have been removed around the circumference, leaving the faces almost entirely blank (a). These flakes may be unifacial (i.e. taken from one side only) (b, d, f), or bifacial (c, e, i); they are generally cut towards the centre. Note the long shallow retouches on the working edge (c, d).
Signs of use include traces of grinding, marks left by hammering and slight "pecking" on the faces and edges of natural pebbles (g, h), as well as pecking caused by hammering or crushing on the edges and faces of pebbles (f, i, j), and pecking on the working edge caused by wear (b, c, e).
The pieces in the drawings come from the Musée de l'Homme, Paris; the pebble in the photograph is in the Historical Museum of Vietnam, Hanoi.

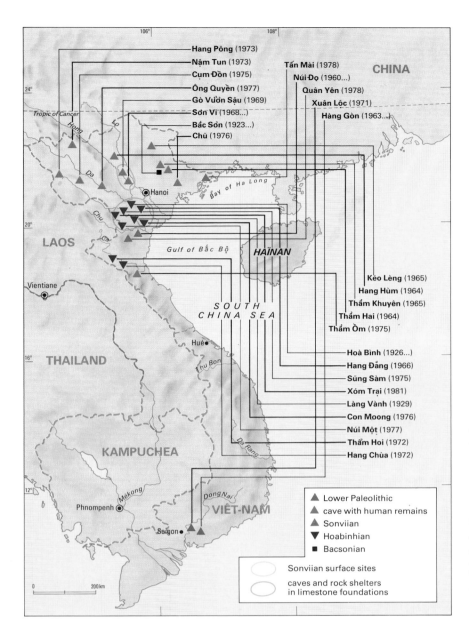

Representative section of the cave of Con Moong

Level 1, the Sonviian industry, provides three C14 datings: 9140BC, 9805BC and 9890BC: level II, the Hoabinhian industry, provides one C14 dating: 7955BC. Level III, which is both Hoabinhian and Bacsonian, has not been dated.

Prehistoric sites in Vietnam

The geographical distribution of sites in the Lower Paleolithic is widely divergent because the industry has no genuinely common characteristics and it has not been possible to give any accurate datings. On the other hand, the concentration of Sonviian surface sites (hills in the central region of North Vietnam) and of Hoabinhian sites (caves and rock shelters in limestone formations) are noteworthy.

The date given next to each site shows the long continuity in the discovery of sites from the Hoabinhian culture, which incidentally is widely represented in Southeast Asia, as well as the increased attention that has recently been paid to the oldest industries.

The working and shaping of pebbles

Sonviian quartzite pebbles with flakes removed in one direction (a, b). Levallois "tortoise back" flakes, with no retouches or traces of use, from the preparation of the pebble core (c, e). Example of a naturally flat pebble (f) of sub-triangular shape with some signs of dressing on the smaller side. It was probably the rough first stage of a tool, before the cutting edge was given a final polish. Blade removed from a pebble, with shouldering, partially polished on both sides so that it could be transformed into a tenon axe (d): Archaeological Institute of Vietnam, Hanoi (a, b): Historical Museum of Vietnam, Hanoi (c, e).

Examples of the use of ochre

(a) Piece of bone used as a palette for ochre with numerous traces of scraping. (b) Natural pebbles, shaped like bowls and stained with ochre. (c) Small flat pebble with fine scratches. Examination under a magnifying glass shows a series of double parallel grooves traced by unknown tools. (d) Hoabinhian pebble, dressed and heavily stained with ochre. (e) Example of an ochre ball. (f) Pebble with flake marks possibly caused by heating that may have been a "found object" collected by prehistoric man. (g) Ochre-grinder with heavily stained crushing face.

Bronze drums of Southeast Asia

Ownership of these vividly decorated objects from Vietnamese protohistory probably indicated spiritual and political power for their possessors, "the masters of the drums", as Chinese texts call them.

Bronze drums appear constantly from protohistory to the first half of the 20th century over a huge area spreading from southern China to eastern Indonesia, including Burma, Laos, Thailand and Malaysia. Handed down from generation to generation in the families of mountain tribal chiefs; religiously guarded in the temples or sometimes buried with the dead, bronze drums are particularly numerous in Vietnam. These drums were mentioned in ancient Chinese texts on the region, and by the end of the 19th and beginning of the 20th century had aroused the interest of European scholars, who quickly realized their importance in Vietnamese protohistory, even before the discovery of the site at Dong Son gave them access to excavated relics. Several archaeological finds since 1954 have contributed considerably to the study of the subject and enabled more exact dating of the relics to be made.

Well before falling under Chinese occupation in the 2nd century BC, Vietnam entered the Bronze Age with the final phase of the Phung Nguyen culture during the 15th or 14th century BC. This culture was replaced in the 14th century by the Dong Dau, during which the first bronze hatchets appeared, and which lasted until the 11th century. The Go Mun culture then took over, characterized by pottery decorated with rectangular, meandering motifs which would later appear often on the bronze drums of the Dong Son culture (from the 7th century BC to the beginning of our era).

The first drums to be brought to light by archaeological excavations were found at the Dong Son site (Thanh Hoa), excavated in the 1930s. They are characteristic of a classic phase of that culture (2nd half of the 1st millennium) and are usually found in tombs together with decorated bronze *situlae** (vessels), foot-shaped hatchets with a rounded heel, and daggers with a bulging pommel or an anthropomorphic handle.

The "masters of the drums", referred to as Lac Viet or Luo Yue in the Chinese texts, were rice growers living in the river valleys and coastal plains of northern and central Vietnam; they were also sailors and fishermen as well as master metallurgists.

F. Heger, in a study published in 1902, divided the bronze drums into four large groups according to their shape, a classification which, although contested in China, is still in use in Vietnam and in Europe. The manufacture of the drums required a perfect control over the techniques of metal manufacture. The oldest, with which we are particularly concerned here, belong to group I; they consist of three distinct parts, a globular core supporting the cover, a cylindrical body and a foot in the shape of a flattened cone. Over the centuries their shape would be greatly simplified: the last to be made, in the 20th century, have wide tops on a body resembling in profile a flattened S, almost cylindrical.

On the finest specimens the geometric motifs of curves, spirals, circles and triangles, are combined with figurative designs which are one of our best sources of information on the Dong Son culture. Houses on stilts, processions of plumed dancers, figures grinding rice, aquatic birds in flight or at rest, and grazing animals are among the remarkable themes to be found on the cover of the splendid drum of Ngoc Lu. One of the most frequent images to appear on the core is that of boats loaded with warriors or oarsmen.

The meaning of the drums

The scenes appearing on the covers are believed to represent either the inauguration ceremony of the drum or a funerary festival similar to the Tiwah of the Dayak of Borneo, or even a resumé of everyday life in Dong Son. In the first instance, the boats on the core might be carrying guests to the ceremony, in the second they might be transporting the souls of deceased warriors to the other world. Neither interpretation is certain, especially since on some drums the people in the boats are warriors and on others they are oarsmen who may well be competing in a canoe race, as they used to do in southern China and Indochina. Quite apart from any archaeological context, the dating of the drums also poses difficult problems. Gradually the decoration became more simplified, often even undergoing a process of degeneration; geometrical motifs became more numerous and relief representations of frogs began to appear on the cover. Whatever their decoration might mean, the drums played a complex but fundamental role in protohistoric cultures. They symbolized political power and were used during religious and social ceremonies or agricultural rites (particularly to invoke rain). They were also buried with their wealthy and powerful owner, guaranteeing his continuing status in the other world.

In Vietnam at least, there are no problems as to the geographical origin of the drums; it is simply their morphological origin which is under discussion. According to one theory, they would have developed from the mortars used to grind rice, turned upside down and beaten rhythmically on solemn occasions. According to another, an inverted bronze cooking pot could be the origin of the drums of group I. An earthenware prototype of a drum was apparently discovered a few years ago in the area of the Red river.

Technically speaking, the bronze most frequently used by the people of Dong Son for their tools as well as for their drums was an alloy of copper, tin and lead, easy to heat and melt, solid and supple, and of better quality than the alloy of copper and lead or that of copper, lead and zinc, which is too soft. There is no doubt that the drums were manufactured locally, since mineral ores are to be found not far from the archaeological sites. There were three manufacturing methods in use: casting by means of a sectioned mould, without wax, around a ceramic or wooden model; the lost wax* method; or a mixture of the two. As far as we know, no mould or fragment of mould has yet been found.

Unsolved problems apart, the bronze drums of Vietnam represent not only a first-class source of information but also remarkable proof of the technical and artistic development of Southeast Asia during the protohistoric period. This section of the continent witnessed a cultural and social development quite different from that which took place in northern China during the Bronze Age. There the privileged classes set themselves apart from the rest of society by manufacturing and using bronze ritual vessels as part of the cult of royal ancestors. It is possible that the drums, and perhaps the large *situlae*, played a similar role, although not an identical one, according to the customs of the region, over a vast area and within a totally original cultural, climatic and physical context. The comparison between Vietnamese and Chinese archaeological remains (from Yunnan and Guangxi), concerning the drums and the Bronze Age in general, should stimulate the study of a period marked by the transition between village or tribal communities and the first manifestations of a state.

The drum of Ngoc Lu

A perfect example of Heger's type I, the drum of Ngoc Lu is one of the oldest in Vietnam. Similar pieces discovered by archaeologists confirm the importance of these objects, the property of chiefs, and their social and religious significance. The problem of the prototype is still unsolved: this type of drum is the end product of a long technical and aesthetic tradition. Hanoi Museum.

Large bronze jar of Dao-Thinh (Yen Bai)

Like the drums and the similarly decorated *situlae* (bronze vessels), these large *thap* jars (only a few of which have been found), were probably invested with an important ritual function. On the cover of the jar, the theme of mating couples is probably linked with a fertility rite. The manufacture of such a piece demanded a large amount of ore and a sure technical ability. Height 81cm (32.4in), diameter 75cm (30in). Hanoi Museum.

Bronze drums of type I found in Southeast Asia

The region containing drums of type I extends over a wide area. Not all of them are equally old and they were used by different peoples. Ethnology alone is not sufficient to explain the meaning of these drums in protohistory, for exchanges between peoples took place according to various patterns and could entail a change in values. An original cultural area may therefore be determined on the eve of the Chinese conquest (*c*.100BC).

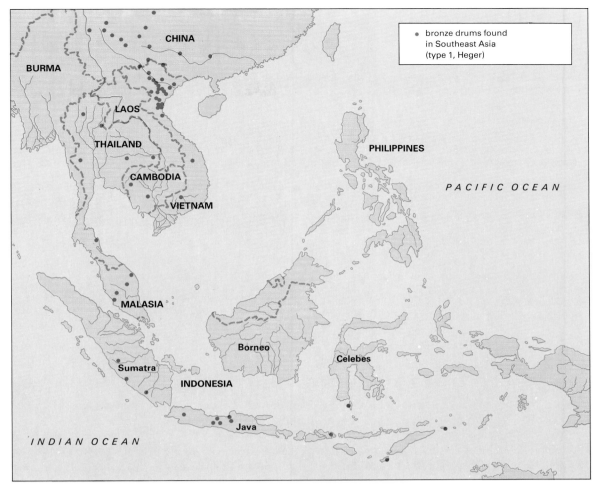

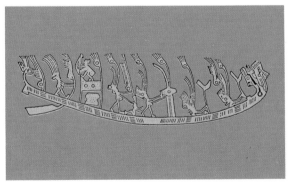

Houses of Dong Son (shown on the surface of the drum of Ngoc Lu)

The Dong Son house was built on piles and had a roof with a central spine curved upwards at the two extremities. Similar to present-day dwellings of the Batak of Sumatra, it has survived in the form of the communal Vietnamese house, the *dinh*, of the historical period.

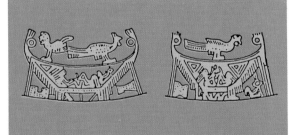

Cover of the drum of Ngoc Lu

The size itself of this drum, with its height of 63cm (25.2in) and diameter of 79cm (31.6in), and the problems which its smelting must have caused, are proof of the complexity of the society capable of producing it. Sometimes regarded as an agricultural calendar or an anthology of the major events in the social and religious life of the Dong Son community, this drum is a source of valuable information on these rice-growers, whose ruling classes seem to have been endowed with a military and religious power based on economical wealth—a wealth probably brought about by the control of surplus production and of commerce.

A barge depicted on the side of the drum of Ngoc Lu

The barge is crowded with plumed warriors. Subject till recently to different interpretations, the barges depicted on drums are today considered to be regatta or festival vessels.

Typology of the bronze drums

F. Heger's typology, rejected by some but still used in Vietnam and Europe, distinguishes four groups of drums; type I is the oldest, while the drums of type III were still manufactured in Burma at the beginning of the 20th century. After L. Bezacier, *Le Vietnam*, Picard, 1972.

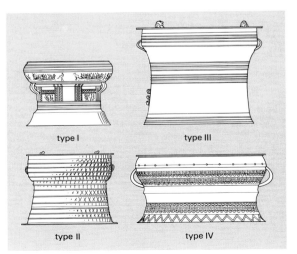

Korea and Japan:
the archaeological background

Although their prehistory has long been culturally and even physically connected, Japan and Korea have been separated by geophysical and, later, by political upheavals that have made the work of modern archaeologists very difficult. More recently, Japanese archaeologists have done much to reveal the independent artistic and technological nature of Japanese island tradition, despite the influence of China.

The Japanese began to develop an interest in their past during the Tokugawa period (1603–1867) under the influence of neo-Confucianism and of the writings of Chinese men of letters. At the end of the 17th century Arai Hakuseki realized that the jade *magatama** (claw-shaped ornaments) and the obsidian arrowheads, which until then had been regarded as supernatural objects, had actually been carved by human hands. While travelling in the Fukuoka region, Ito Togai noticed some human effigies in roughly hewn stone near a tumulus and compared them with the Chinese *mingqi** and with the *haniwa* (clay cylinders) of Yamato great burials (*kofun**). A team of amateurs then collected the *magatama* and produced catalogues and sketches. The *daimyo* (territorial magnate) of Chikuzen (Fukuoka and Karatsu) was also interested in the ancient remains of a region rich in the relics of the past.

This new interest in antiquity was supported by the followers of Shinto, such as Motoori Norinaga, who were opposed to neo-Confucianism and who drafted the first Japanese annals (*Kojiki*, 712, *Nihongi*, 720) relating the creation of the world to the advantage of the imperial lineage. The study of ancient texts formed the cornerstone for the Meiji revolution (1868) and the birth of a passionate nationalism which would characterize the Japanese mentality for many years to come.

A new impetus was imparted to Japanese archaeology when the country opened its doors to foreigners. In 1877, the American zoologist E.S. Morse, while travelling by rail from Yokohama to Tokyo, noticed near the siding a heap of shells which he believed to be a *kjökkenmodding** (shell-mound). A few weeks later, excavations revealed human fossils together with pots with corded string-like decorations. His detailed report represented the very first publication of the Faculty of Natural History of Tokyo University. *Shell-mound of Omori* was soon translated in Japanese and stimulated the creation of a whole new vocabulary: *kaizuka*, (shell-mound); *jōmon* (string decoration). Thus Japan learnt of the existence of a Neolithic age during which an original ceramic art had developed; this discovery was all the more surprising since it was not till 1920 that the Chinese farmers of the Neolithic period were identified by C.S. Anderson. At the same time, the German engineer Heinrich von Siebold, while investigating the mineral resources of Tonoku, brought to light the more elaborate pieces of Kamegaoka (the Hill of Jars) in the province of Aomori. He attributed these to the Ainus, who, according to him, had been the first inhabitants of Japan, and had been driven from the country to take refuge at Hokkaido. The theory aroused a great deal of controversy among Japanese academics and contributed to the development of the study of anthropology at Tokyo University.

At Kanto, Morse's students continued to excavate the *kaizuka* as far as the Gumma mountains and discovered half-subterranean habitats (*tate-ana*) which formed increasingly developed villages; here they also found tools made of stone, bone and horn (arrow heads, harpoons, fish-hooks), pointing to the existence of hunting and fishing populations who also lived as gatherers. The classification of the various styles of Jōmon pottery found at Kanto constituted the basic source of reference for the extremely varied artifacts discovered throughout the archipelago (proto, middle and late Jōmon), as well as providing guidelines for the definition of what was later to be called the Jōmon culture.

The Faculty of Archaeology had in the meantime been founded at Tokyo University and the relics found during excavations had been collected by Miyake Yonekichi (1860–1929) and displayed in the Imperial Museum. Kyoto, however, had not been inactive. Its archaeology faculty was led by

Hamada Kosaku* (1881–1938) who had taken it over after a period spent in London (1912–16) during which he had greatly admired Sir Flinders Petrie. His work and his methodological writings show him to be the real father of Japanese archaeology. Important scholars such as Umehura Sueji, Kobayashi Yukio and Mizuno Seiichi (1901–58) were trained at his school.

After the end of the Meiji period, political circumstances opened new investigative grounds to Japanese archaeologists in Korea and Manchuria. The results of excavations of the Lelang tombs (a Chinese colony dating from 108BC to AD 313) were published in the 1930s and revealed to the public the Han artifacts, still little known. The tombs of Koguryo and Paekche were studied by the architectural historian Sekino Takaashi and were accepted as having been the models for the more damaged ones of northern and central Kyushu. A new method of studying architectural remains, particularly the Buddhist monasteries, was based on the examination of the terraces of packed earth where the marks left by columns are preserved and show their number and frequency (*ken*); the plan of various buildings and even their shape and roof span have been reconstructed.

The Yayoi period

The Japanese had mainly concentrated on the Neolithic period and on the historical period of the *kofun* which they had proved to have started in the kingdom of Silla (southern Korea) but which in Yamato were characterized by the first appearance of locks and by the row of *haniwa* supporting the accumulated earth of the tumuli. The gap was filled by protohistory, *Yayoi jidai*, running from the 3rd century BC to the 3rd century of our era. Hamada had excavated the kaizuka of Ko, at Osaka, and had found two superimposed strata, the lower one containing jomon pottery and the upper one pots of a much closer texture similar to the fragments found in 1884 in a *kaizuka* of the Yayoi quarter near Tokyo University. The pots still carried the marks left by grains of rice, a sign of agricultural activity. Yamano Sugao, on the other hand, discovered traces of irrigated ricefields in the Fukuoka and Karatsu regions, in northern Kyushu, as well as several funerary jars (*kame-kan*) containing human bones, Korean mirrors, and Chinese weapons and mirrors. The Yayoi potteries, prototypes of which had been found in a *kaizuka* of Kimnae, near Pusan, spread, together with rice culture, to the island of Honshu, off the coast of the Inner Sea. A first attempt at classifying this pottery was published in 1939.

The Yayoi period is characterized by the use of bronze. Lacking any knowledge of alloy techniques, these farmers melted down imported pieces to manufacture long, lance-shaped halberds with no cutting edge which, in Kyushu, they buried in vast numbers on the hillsides; in Kinai, the ornaments of Korean horses became *dotaku*, elongated bells covered with a wavy decoration or decorated with animals or domestic scenes. Did all these objects represent the various needs of one agricultural cult unifying several districts, a cult mentioned in Chinese texts, or do they indicate imports from different routes? This is a problem which deserves further investigation. In the 1940s, the excavations of Karako at Yamato and of Toro near Shizuoka yielded a series of tools made of wood which seem to have been cut with an iron object. Toro has revealed not only the *tate-ana* but also a granary on stilts obviously built as a storeroom for the crops. The origin of these granaries (*kura*), inspired by the first Shinto sanctuaries, had at first been traced to the islands of the south Pacific. We now know that they already existed in the 4th

Musées nationaux

Anthropomorphic figurine (*Dogu*)

This terracotta figurine, 12cm (4.7in) appears to be a female representation. Both sides are decorated with incised bands, the eyes are round, the mouth set and surrounded by an engraved motif (a tattoo?). The flat face is extended to the back by a perforated hairstyle; the same perforations can be seen under the chin and around the face. The short arms, indicated in relief, have fingers only hinted at by incisions; the legs have disappeared. It is thought that such *dogus* may be cult objects. They are mainly found in the Kanto and in the northern region of Honshu. This work is thought to date from the end of the Jōmon period, 1st millenium BC. Don Hosokawa Moritatsu, 1955. Musée Guimet, Paris.

millennium BC in the Hemudu culture, in Zhejiang, and that they had spread to southern China.

At the end of World War II, Japanese researchers abandoned their activities in Korea, Manchuria and northern China, where their work yielded considerable results: the discovery of the bronzes of Ordos (Egami Fujio), the locating of the Ding kilns at Hebei by Koyama Fujio, the research into Liao art (Kitan) (936–1125) initiated in Peking and Dadong (the Yungang caves had been explored by Mizuno and Naganiro), the excavation of the painted tombs in Manchuria, and the study of the metalwork and ceramics at Jenol and in Manchuria. An account of the tombs of the late Han at Liaoyang, the painted decoration of which resembles that of the Koguryo Tong'gou tombs in southern Manchuria, has been published by Umenara Sueji.

The presence of early man

In Japan itself, archaeological research had long been carried out in a rather haphazard way, but in the 1950s it was reorganized under the leadership of Bunkasai (Commission for the Protection of Cultural Heritage, founded in 1894), a branch of which was set up in each province. By studying Himalayan glaciations, geophysicists have traced the geomorphological history of the islands stretching from the Aleutians to Taiwan and the Philippines and have demonstrated that the Japanese archipelago was, in certain periods, linked with the Asiatic continent to the north (Siberia) and south (China). Both $C^{14}*$ and palynology* have led to the discovery of a Paleolithic stage in central Honshu and along the Pacific, and Akashi man being contemporary with Peking man. The presence of humanoids is further confirmed by marks in the primitive clay (loam) buried under strata of lava. Human beings survived in Japan notwithstanding frequent natural catastrophes. In the Fukui cave, near Nagasaki, several strata have revealed the existence of a Mesolithic period; some of these contained the fragments of pots decorated with lines in relief which have been dated from the Upper Paleolithic period, and similar fragments have been found further north near Niigata.

It is impossible to list here the achievements of Japanese archaeologists, whose work promises to break through the barriers of too rigid a chronology. But we must at least mention the following: Nara and Dazaifu, the place of Yamato and especially that of Heijo-kyuat Nara, monasteries, the pottery kilns which have brought to light the ceramics of the Heian and Kamakura periods (Sanage, Atsumi, Tokoname in the Nagoya region), the study of Chinese pottery imports, the examination of several kilns at Karatsu (Korean influence) and of those of the Arita region (porcelain). In Japan, archaeology is concerned with even the most recent periods, as shown by the museums of rural and urban architecture at Toyama and the Tokyo museum of Meiji relics.

The Institute for Cultural Heritage

The Koreans, liberated from Japanese occupation in 1945, resumed their archaeological research in the late 1940s; but this was abruptly interrupted by the war between North and South which exhausted the country's resources. In 1961, the University of Seoul instituted a faculty of archaeology under the direction of Dr Kim Won-Yong, a graduate from Harvard. Other institutions initiated archaeological digs, but experience was lacking and research suffered from being too dispersed. The Institute for Cultural Heritage was founded in 1975 to take charge of the Government's archaeological projects

and to look after historical monuments and Dr Kim was appointed director. The formation of the Institute put an end to the so-far erratic character of archaeological research and allowed foreign scientists to begin to work with local researchers in properly integrated teams. In 1974 a C^{14} laboratory had been founded so that more accurate dating could be obtained. Through these changes the work of the archaeological teams has been rewarded by important results, such as the discovery of several Paleolithic sites both in the North and in the South; here, it seems that the populations, during the period of warmer climate in between two glaciations, followed to the north the animals they depended upon for their diet. The absence of Mesolithic remains seems to indicate that the peninsula remained uninhabited until the 5th millennium BC, when it was again settled by Paleo-Asiatic peoples from the north. According to the hypothesis of Korean archaeologists and American specialists, the earthenware found at Tongam-dong (Pusan), with its flat or rounded base and a decoration of lines and dots scraped off the surface, was probably a local creation and preceded by 1,000 years the "Combed" pots of Siberian origin which Japanese archaeologists had regarded as the first to be produced in Korea. The latter type of ware was probably imported down the west coast and along the Taedong river as far as the Han river. Both in the North and in the South, local variations are apparent but have not yet been dated by stratigraphy*. A definitive dating of the contents or the various strata of a given site is hampered by the lack of geological and geomorphological research. We know that in North Korea, the herringbone patterns on the pottery became curving lines contemporaneously with the appearance of agricultural activities derived from northern China. Around the 3rd millennium, at Tongsam-dong, the herringbone motifs are drawn with thick and very deep lines and resemble certain Jōmon pieces from Kyushu, thus pointing to contacts between the peninsula and the nearby archipelago via Tsushima.

The Bronze Age coincided with the arrival from the north of the Tongus Yemaek, an Altaic people believed to have learnt the bronze-working techniques from the peoples of the steppes (Siberian-Ordos art) who produced daggers without handles and button-studded mirrors, found in Liaoning, along with bronzes similar to the Chinese ones of the 9th and 8th centuries BC. This particular technique should then be dated to c.700BC together with the first signs in South Korea of rice culture and of polished earthenware. Several attempts have been made to classify and date the megaliths which first appeared at about the same time and which are at present attributed either to indigenous art or to influences from Southeast Asia. The chronologies and classifications established by scientists in the North of the peninsula are different from those in the South, which makes it rather difficult to reach any form of synthesis; a situation further complicated by the fact that relations between the People's Republic of China and South Korea are rather strained and do not encourage the visiting of the sites and study of recent discoveries. However, the Koreans are aided by Japanese archaeologists, who are at the moment welcome in the country and whose work is highly appreciated. The solution of the archaeologists' problems—and they are many—is further delayed by the conflict between China and Vietnam.

The emergence of the Paleolithic

The turbulent geology of Japan has obliterated much of its Paleolithic past; archaeology shows how these rock upheavals are reflected in the Stone Age tool kits made throughout the Japanese Paleolithic period.

The discovery in about 1945 of Paleolithic-type artifacts in Japan raised many questions. Where did the first men who populated the land we now call Japan come from? Was it already an archipelago or was it rather, as geographical studies suggest, connected to the north Asian continent, at least by its two extremities Hokkaido in the north and Kyushu in the south?

Geographically, Japan has certainly changed a great deal, even since the late Paleolithic period. The glaciers covering the principal summits represent both the cause and effect of a climate that was much colder than it is today. It is well known that in the late phase of the Pleistocene* glaciation the total land area of the globe was 30 percent greater than it is today, the freeze having caused a general lowering of ocean levels. At this time the large Japanese islands (Kyushu, Shikoku, Honshu) formed a single block connected with Korea.

Our great difficulty, when trying to form an understanding of the human dimension of these phenomena, remains the extreme scarcity in Japan of bone remains dating back to that dawn of humanity. The geological upheavals which occurred later and which brought about the present-day appearance of the country as an archipelago doubtless account for this. Whole settlements sank, slowly or suddenly, into the sea as the result of the fracturing of the land and the inroads made by the sea. Many people must have perished or disappeared beneath tides of burning lava during these geophysical changes. All that has been found of these original inhabitants today are a few teeth or fossil fragments in such famous sites as Akashi (Hyogo area), Ushikawa (Aichi area), Mikkabi (Shizuoka area) and Hamakita (Shizuoka area). The southern coast of Honshu with its well-protected creeks seems to be the area that best preserved the remains of the first "people" to live there, from *Homo erectus** to *Homo sapiens**, not to mention the Neanderthalians*.

Thus the Paleolithic remains of Japan are almost exclusively confined to finds of rudimentary tool kits, the first identifiable examples of which were discovered at Iwajuku (Gunma area) in 1949. Thirty-five years later such relics abound. More than 30 fully representative sites distributed throughout the archipelago hint at some aspects of the precarious life of the period. Two important deposits, Minatogawa, on the southern coast of Okinawa, and Yamashita, dated to 18,000 and 30,000 years ago respectively (C^{14}* analysis), evoke the people

of those times: a *Homo sapiens* who trapped bears, snakes, frogs and deer, animals which played a large part in his diet. And we also know that *c*.18,000 BC navigation was already sufficiently developed and trade existed on a large enough scale for tools to have been transported from Kozushima, an islet situated off the Izu peninsula, to Tokyo Bay (at Suzuki). The tools are identifiable as they are made from a highly vitrified obsidian which is found only at Kozushima.

Paleolithic remains

The most complete excavations carried out to date are on the plain of Kanto. The materials discovered there serve as a point of reference for the establishment of a possible evolution for the Japanese Paleolithic period.

The centre of the Kanto Paleolithic remains is the plateau of Musashino formed during the Pleistocene age. It extends to the northwest of Tokyo and beneath the present-day town. It comprises four great archaeological levels, dated (C^{14}) between 30,000 and 8,000 BC, and itself made up of 12 different geological levels, contains traces of industry, mostly small items 5–7 cm (2–3in) in size. This stratum is situated beneath a layer of dark humus containing all the human material from the Mesolithic period to our own time. The 20,000 stone tools from the centre of Musashino alone, which correspond to the period long named "period before pottery" (*sendoki jidai*), or "period without pottery" (*mudoki jidai*), enable us to define four phases.

Phase I, the oldest, is represented by simple pebbles and flakes, unifacial and bifacial choppers* and chopping-tools*.

Phase II, the richest of all, suggests a flowering of life in this period. Tools from a core* which was prepared and reworked until it was exhausted, seem to have been highly diversified. Carefully dressed blades tend to replace the crude flakes which formed most of the repertoire of tools in the preceding period.

Phase III is characterized by a comparatively large production of microliths*, often taken from cores which were microlithic themselves and the large flakes of the earlier period lose their importance, but geometric microliths, such as segments or circles, are rare.

Lastly, Phase IV probably represents a transitional period between the last phase of the Pleistocene age and the first Jōmon industries of an epi-Paleolithic period

known as the Holocene* or Postglacial period, during which ceramics were also produced.

Thus Japanese archaeologists think they have evidence of a typological chain of Japanese Paleolithic industries whose raw materials clearly illustrate the geological transformations that were taking place: quartzite, sandstone, basalt, conglomerate, andesite, obsidian, schist. However, they accept the existence of important regional variations, notably the stronger influences from Southeast Asia in the cultures of Kyushu, at Sozudai (Oita area). Lastly they emphasize the difficulty of forming a chronological system when it comes to assessing the cultures of the neighbouring countries of China and Korea. Nevertheless, in the present state of research they think it tenable to suggest that the first dressed pebbles appeared *c*.30,000 BC. The use of microliths must have spread *c*.8000 BC. The making of microliths was undoubtedly imported from northern China, the undeniable influence of which, at the end of the Japanese Paleolithic period, is fully accepted by Japanese archaeologists.

The discovery of a Korean Paleolithic level is recent, going back only to 1962 when A. Mohr and L. Sample located a few stone flakes at Sokchang-ni near Kongju in the southwest of the country. Excavations followed two years later. Other Paleolithic sites are gradually being uncovered, for example Turubong (1976–78), while the bones of Neanderthaloid types and *Homo sapiens sapiens* have been found at Tokch'on (1962) in North Korea.

The opening in South Korea of a laboratory for C^{14} analysis, which followed the establishment of an archaeological section at the National University of Seoul, now permits new research to be done. This is still in its early stages, but looks full of promise. Thus the site of Sokchang-ni has been dated to between 30,000 and 20,000 BC. The lower layers contained unifacial and bifacial tools which geologists, in the absence of any animal remains, attribute to the Middle Pleistocene age. On the other hand the caves of Turubon (excavated in 1976) contained a large quantity of animal bones, many of which came from warm regions and were doubtless from the interglacial Riss-Würm period. The complex suggests that it may have been a seasonal camp used by hunters who lived there during the hunting season and made tools from long broken bones.

The site of Sokchangni, Korea

Paleolithic discoveries in Korea are on the increase, making it possible to identify a number of cultures: Kulpori, in the northeast; Chommal, near Turubong in central Korea, rich in animal fossils, which is unusual for this period (the lack of fauna is an enigma to be studied in relation to the glaciations); Chongokni, buried under an enormous layer of basalt (the product of a volcanic eruption 270,000 years ago) and on which life only gradually renewed itself. On the north bank of the River Kumgang, excavations begun in 1964 have revealed an important stratigraphic complex. The first C^{14} datings suggest an average occupation date of 30,600 ± 3,000 years BP. But the lower layers contain bifaces which Korean archaeologists compared to the Choukoutien industries in China and which would therefore be much older, although this Choukoutien level is not yet confirmed.

Korea and Japan in the Paleolithic and Neolithic

The great mountain-building movements of the Quaternary gradually shaped the physical aspect of Japan and Korea. On the fringes of a continent, the shores of which were hollowed out by deep marine trenches, these countries during the time of the Middle Pleistocene and the Upper Pleistocene were attached to Eurasia only by their extremities. In the north, Japan was joined to Sakhalin. In the south it was attached to Korea. The respective states of archipelago and peninsula as we now know them only go as far back as the Holocene. The influence of this very ancient past was to prove a lasting one. Throughout Japanese history, the transmission of culture took place mainly along old terrestrial routes. Thus the Siberian current in the north was joined by the Sino-Korean current, perceptible from the end of the Chinese Paleolithic. Then the current of central and southern China became influential, beginning in the Neolithic. It is largely in relation to the development of rice-growing in the Yangtze basin that scholars now try to explain the implantation of this type of culture in Japan.

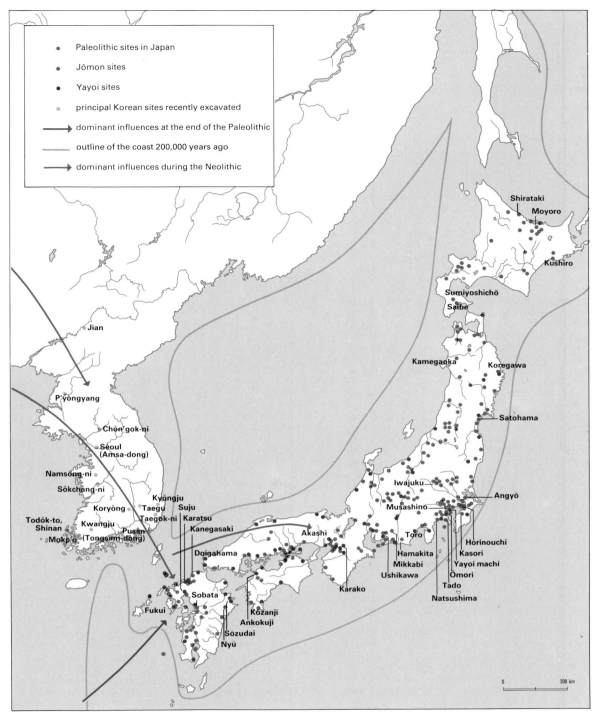

Legend:
- Paleolithic sites in Japan
- Jōmon sites
- Yayoi sites
- principal Korean sites recently excavated
- → dominant influences at the end of the Paleolithic
- outline of the coast 200,000 years ago
- → dominant influences during the Neolithic

Map labels: Shirataki, Moyoro, Kushiro, Sumiyoshichō, Saibe, Jian, P'yŏngyang, Kamegaoka, Koregawa, Chŏn'gok-ni, Satohama, Séoul (Amsa-dong), Namsŏng-ni, Sŏkchang-ni, Koryŏng, Taegu, Kyŏngju, Suju, Iwajuku, Angyō, Musashino, Taegŏk-ni, Karatsu, Todŏk-to, Shinan, Kwangju, Pusan (Tongsam-dong), Kanegasaki, Akashi, Toro, Horinouchi, Mokp'o, Kasori, Hamakita, Yayoi machi, Mikkabi, Ōmori, Ushikawa, Tado, Natsushima, Doigahama, Kārako, Fukui, Sobata, Kōzanji, Ankokuji, Sōzudai, Nyū

0 — 200 km

A core and its flakes

This core was partially reconstructed from six effective blades and 15 flakes which all fitted together. It provides us with a better idea of the method of knapping and the striking of angles. The initial core of the schist was quite small (overall height: 10cm), and all the tools obtained were microliths. They were mostly used as a series, mounted on a base, and forming complex tools with a cutting edge notched like a saw.

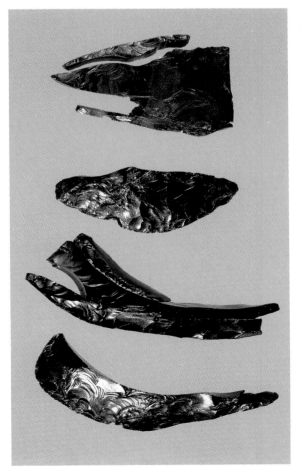

Hearth

Like all those hitherto discovered in Japan, this hearth belongs to phase IV of the Paleolithic cultures defined in relation to the site of Musashino. They belong to the epi-Paleolithic period. Here the stones show the marks of fire which leave no doubt about their usage.

The knapping of obsidian

This obsidian tool (second from above) is leaf-shaped and of a translucent material suggesting lightness. It was obtained from a triangular flake identical to those shown below and then carefully retouched. Obsidian, a volcanic vitreous material, occurs in all kinds of subtle shades in Japan, from bluish-grey to deep black. It is found throughout the archipelago.

295

Rice cultivation

Rice-growing came to Japan comparatively late in the Neolithic, probably because natural resources provided abundant food; once installed, the new agriculture gave rise to ingenious developments.

Japan's entry into a new technological age occurred slowly: the relative plentifulness of food on these islands where conditions were favourable for the spread of life is undoubtedly one of the main factors in this delay. In Japan the polishing of stone and the creation of pottery did not go hand in hand with the immediate development of agriculture: rather they are found in conjunction with a long period when the rich natural produce of the land was systematically collected, in particular shellfish which were to be found in great abundance in the fruitful seas around this country. That is the reason why the people and cultures that take their name from the hand-shaped "Corded Pottery" (*jōmon doki*), and who fed themselves by hunting, fishing and gathering, go back to the Mesolithic period, as was also the case for a long period in the south China area. It was only towards the end of the period that agriculture began gradually to appear, in the growing of certain cereals on ground cleared by fire, but the origins of this method are not yet known. The grain found, as at Itazuke or Ukikunden (in northern Kyūshū) is not in itself sufficient evidence: some traces of fields would also have to be discovered, whatever method of cultivation was used. Everything seems to indicate that in Japan people continued to live within the framework of a semi-nomadic hunting and fishing economy for a very long time, and came late to an acceptance of an organized, settled, agrarian economy, the model for which was taken from the mainland. And so Japan started on her destined path, an archipelago cut off through outside influences, a country of long-surviving tradition and of sudden change.

Climatic fluctuations with periods of alternating temperature, successive variations in sea level, and a well-favoured latitude must together go a long way towards explaining the sequence of steps taken by a civilization which in the end based its development on rice-growing. Two methods of rice cultivation were employed, always in conjunction with one another: cultivation in dry fields as it was practised in north China and cultivation in flooded fields, in accordance with the formula worked out in south China. It thus becomes necessary to conceive of penetration from the mainland by two routes, according to a process which is fully demonstrated for the earlier stages, as for the following stages of the Bronze and Iron Ages: one route from north China, the other from south China.

It was with the coming of metal in the 3rd century BC, as if it formed part of the same cultural package, that rice-growing really came into its own. The nature of the terrain was certainly favourable to rice becoming established as a crop: marshland, converging rivers and the estuaries which are so abundant in Japan must have made a considerable contribution to the adoption of a method which, to be fully effective, required a certain number of artifacts: these were the pride of the men of the Bronze Age, known in Japan as the Yayoi period, from the name of a suburb of Tokyo where pottery typical of this period was first found.

Two particularly explicit witnesses to this new organization of agriculture are the villages of Toro (in the Shizuoka district) and Karako (in the Nara district). For two millennia a protective covering of mud preserved a priceless group of village settlements, corn granaries standing on piles, dikes constructed with fascines (bundles of long sticks) making it possible to move between the flooded paddy fields, and a great variety of stone and wooden tools of the kind required for every operation from sowing the rice to harvesting it (though not for planting out, a practice that was not then in use). These discoveries, along with the Shinto worship of the fox, a mysterious messenger of the god of rice whose mythological existence seems to go back much farther than the historic period, prove, if proof were needed, the role played by rice in Japan as in China from Neolithic times. Thus the information derived from studies of ancient agriculture is gradually adding further illumination to that provided by the traditional study of artifacts alone.

In Japan where long static periods seem to have been suddenly followed by the very rapid acquisition of new skills, the Neolithic and the Chalcolithic periods seemed for a long time to have been telescoped. For many years the first Japanese typological tables took account only of pieces of bronze and even more of pottery, of which there were abundant examples everywhere. Thus very elaborate typological tables were worked out for every area of Japan, as they were for the Corded ware of the Mesolithic period. All point to three main phases, (Proto, Middle and Late) covering the complete output of this red or reddish yellow, thin-walled ware which was thrown on the wheel, and which tended to imitate bronze in both its shape and its decoration. It was not until the end of the 3rd century BC that grey pottery appeared on the scene, related to Chinese Bronze Age pottery, as the precursor of a new stage in technology: the use of iron, which, as it favoured the warrior class, markedly upset the old balance of the agrarian societies.

In these technological and social revolutions, the methods of acquiring food changed little. But it may be of interest to establish exactly what slow transformations were gradually accepted, changing in an apparently modest, but in fact inevitable way the bases of survival and thereby of society itself.

New climates and new populations

In Korea, the move from the Paleolithic to the Neolithic culture is just as complex, though for different reasons. The most difficult problem is still to explain the waves of human migration which seem to have occurred over Korea possibly at a faster pace than elsewhere. Thus it seems we have to conceive of the peninsula as being relatively empty between late Paleolithic and Neolithic times, for which there is evidence in the 5th millennium BC. It may be that the Paleolithic communities disappeared at the same time as the animals they fed on, following the wild animals native to cold areas which were driven farther north by the increasing warmth of the climate. So far no Mesolithic level has been found to fill this vacuum; but it is still too soon to draw any firm conclusions and much is expected from the immense amount of work which remains to be completed.

Two phenomena effectively marked the start of the Korean Neolithic culture: the spread of pine trees, largely replacing the deciduous trees which had themselves taken over from sub-Arctic trees with needles; and the arrival of a new Paleo-Siberian or Paleo-Asiatic population from the mainland.

Little is known about the development of agriculture, the economic foundation of future societies, apart from a discovery (1957) at Chit'apni in the northwest of the country which revealed traces of charred millet; and the presence of rice c.1500 BC at Naju in the southwest of the peninsula is indicated only by palynological* studies. As in Japan, more or less, we have to wait until the 8th century BC to find rice in the form of grains, when it occurred both in the centre of the country (at Hunamni) and in the southwest, at Puyo. Meanwhile on the mainland the final period of the Bronze Age had already been reached, with the expansion of an Altaic people, the Yemaek Tungus, who seem then to have advanced into Korea and gradually assimilated the Neolithic population of Paleo-Asiatic origin. Perhaps their arrival should be associated with the spread of rice-growing.

Korean archaeology, which is in its early stages but developing fast, does not enable us as yet to put forward views with certainty—rather we should consider lines of research. For a long time it was based solely on the study of typologies provided by ceramic artifacts, and it is only just getting to grips with some recent disciplines which are becoming daily more influential.

Pottery with Corded decoration

Japanese Corded (*Jōmon*) Pottery, unpainted and made without a potter's wheel, is divided into five typological sequences corresponding to the same number of cultural levels: pottery with a conical base (I), then with a flat base (II); vases with necks, decorated with many additions (III) which disappeared later as the shapes became complicated and multiplied (IV); finally, pieces copied from bronzes (V).

Yayoi vases

Yayoi pottery, which was thrown on the wheel and often polished and painted, acts as a chronological and typological reference, like that of Jōmon. Three levels can be established, following the complexity of the forms, the homogeneity of the clay, the fineness of the walls and the quality of the lustre. Generally speaking, Yayoi pottery is recognizable by the obvious influence of the metal items which it reflects. Kyoto University.

Rice paddy embankment

Although the origins of rice-growing in Japan are still the subject of argument, mastery of growing the cereal as from the middle of the Yayoi period has long been attested. This embankment in the village of Toro (prefecture of Shizuoka) is retained by brushwood faggots. The wood, preserved in the damp soil, keeps for thousands of years. This system is still used today to retain the water in the flooded paddies.

Remains of habitations at Toro

The Neolithic villages of the Yayoi were generally situated on a natural terrace or a slight hill close to the low-lying land where rice was cultivated. They were often surrounded by a protective ditch, as in China. The round or square habitations were half-buried in the ground. Four wooden pillars supported a fibre roof which was pierced in the centre to allow the smoke from the hearth to escape.

Wooden mortar, Toro

Decoration on certain bronze bells (*dōtaku*) of the Yayoi period show this type of mortar in front of a figure pounding the rice with a pestle.

Agricultural implement

The richness of the Toro site, now supported by other discoveries, notably in the region of northern Kyūshū, rests mainly on its amazing complex of establishments and rice paddies, but also on the presence of a range of wooden tools, the complete equipment of the cultivator. It includes a hoe, suitable for working the muddy soil of the rice paddies before they were submerged.

Pins and ornaments

These pins, hooks, pendants and other ornaments are made of bone and antler. They belong to the final Jōmon. Their rhythmic decoration of curves and protuberances recalls that of pottery made at the same period, but the "claw" forms prefigure the *magatama* (pendants in the form of claws) which appear from the early Bronze Age (3rd century BC) to the end of the Iron Age (6th century). The skill of Jōmon bone carvers goes back to a very old tradition, already noticeable in the manufacture of harpoons with barbs, from which developed the improved form of harpoons with movable heads in the Middle Jōmon. Tohoku University.

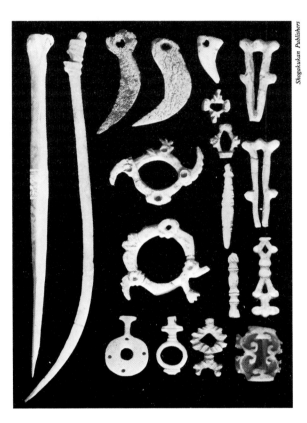

Needles and fish-hooks, Korea

These bone implements, indispensable to hunters and fishermen, come from level 3 of the site of Tongsamdong: a shell mound situated on an island in the Bay of Pusan and forming evidence of the oldest Neolithic culture in Korea. Uncovered in 1963, it comprises four levels. These artifacts belong to the third level, which must have been occupied c.3000BC. The culture is characterized by pottery with a comb decoration, an extensive tool kit of bone and horn, and the presence of certain cult objects (masks made of shells).

Pottery with comb decoration, Korea

This vase with a conical base comes from the site of Amsadong at Seoul. A comb was used to decorate it with a zigzag motif of the kind found in the oldest level at Tongsamdong, now serving as a point of reference. By analogy and also by reference to the related site of Todoriki in Japan (Kyūshū), it is possible to propose a date of c.4000BC

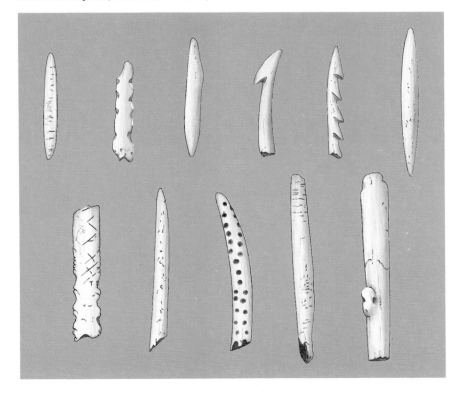

Death and burial in the Three Kingdoms period

The splendour of Korean and Japanese funerary art, with its spectacular treasures of gold and precious stones, reveals links with an ancient shamanistic tradition found in South Russia and Siberia.

The large tombs which are characteristic of this period, so-called because Korea was then divided into the three autonomous states of Koguryŏ, Paekche and Silla, did not appear until around the 4th century AD, when the authority of the rulers and the governing class began to be firmly established. To mark the high rank of the dead buried there, rich funerary furnishings were placed in the vaults. Some objects assumed a magic or religious significance, but the only role of most of them was to vouch by their luxury for the prestige of the nobles. Thus archaeologists are uncovering items with a high decorative value and showing skilled craftsmanship. In comparison with the humble objects found in the dolmens or funerary jars of the Bronze Age, a remarkable technical progress had taken place, which can be explained by the arrival of Han craftsmanship imported into Lolang and Daifang—Chinese colonies grafted onto the northwest of the peninsula. However, despite the Chinese contribution, the objects found in Korean tombs are either original or subject to other influences. The Chinese contribution is mainly on the technical level: metalworking, lacquer, fine basketwork, etc.

The tombs of Koguryŏ and Paekche

Three types of tombs exist in Koguryŏ: piles of rough stones, monuments of carefully dressed stone, and earth tumuli covering a stone structure. The first type is the earliest; the second appears after the switch of the capital from Huanren to Tonggou where Changgunch'ong is situated—a majestic granite mausoleum rising in tiers which dates from the 5th century. The earth mounds date mainly from the time after the capital had been moved to P'yŏngyang, in AD427. Usually the interior consists of a chamber preceded by an antechamber; about 40 of these monuments have mural paintings which are derived from the funerary decoration of the Han period and of the (Chinese) Three Kingdoms period (AD220–265). Tomb No. 3 at Anak dating from 357 contains the earliest funerary paintings in Koguryŏ: more than 250 horesemen, infantrymen and musicians throng round General Tongsu and his wife for whom the tomb was constructed. From the 5th century on, domestic, hunting, and war scenes predominate, but the decoration becomes even richer, including lotus flowers and celestial creatures (Buddhist motifs), constellations of stars on the ceilings and, on the four walls, the divine animals. These, according to Taoist belief, reign at the cardinal points and protect the cosmos as well as its microcosms, the domains of the living and the dead: the Green Dragon in the East, the Red Phoenix in the South, the White Tiger in the West and the Black Warrior (a tortoise entwined by a snake) in the North. Then in the 6th and 7th centuries the four cardinal divinities were to become the main theme, framed by ample undulations and elegant arabesques on the walls of the chambers of the dead.

The tombs in Koguryŏ have almost all been emptied by looters. However, the gilded bronze fretwork ornament, overlooked by the intruders in tomb no. 1 at Chinp'ari (7th century), is a marvellous example of the work carried out in precious metals in northern Korea. A three-legged crow, a Chinese symbol for the sun, stands amidst winding cloud-shaped scrolls. In the openwork on the band edging the base of the object the speckled wing-sheaths of the coleopteron, or "jewel-insect", appear. This type of decoration was also used in Silla and in Japan around the same period.

In Paekche as in Koguryŏ there were three successive capitals: Hansŏng (3rd century–475), Ungjin (475–538) and Sapi (538–660). The tombs of the first period are strongly influenced by Koguryŏ, which drew its inspiration from north China. But after the capital had moved to Ungjin, Paekche developed direct trading links by sea with southern China, links which had marked repercussions in the field of culture. Inside the tomb of King Muryŏng (526), built at Songsanni near Kongju (Ungjin), the floor is of embossed bricks very similar to those found in the Nanking area, going back to the Liang period. Moreover, among the 2,500 items removed from the monument there are pieces of porcelain from south China. The other items include ornaments and weapons made of gold and silver, bronze mirrors and pieces of lacquer, among other objects. The tomb of Nŭngsanni (7th century) near Puyŏ (Sapi) dates from the following period and is one of the few burial places in Paekche to be decorated with paintings. The four cardinal animals embellishing the walls, and the motifs of the lotus flower and of clouds which decorate the ceiling, are reminiscent of some late works in Koguryŏ, such as tomb No. 1 at Chinp'ari.

Treasures of the tombs of Silla

Most of the funeral monuments in Koguryŏ and Paekche have been violated; those in Silla, on the other hand, have been left intact, for they are so closely constructed as to deter robbers. The tumuli of this southeastern Korean kingdom are strongholds stuffed full of gold treasure, the most outstanding items of which are the royal crowns. Several of these headdresses have been brought to light; one of the finest is the piece dug up in the northern mound of the great tomb of Hwangnam (5th–6th century), near the capital Kyŏngju. These crowns consist of a diadem with various figurative decorations riveted onto them—stylized representations of a tree in the shape of a cross, a stag's antlers and a pair of bird's wings. The whole is decorated with jade and beryl pendants which Japanese archaeologists call *magatama**. It is known that these adornments ensured magic protection to the dead.

There can be hardly any doubt that the symbolism of these headdresses originated in southern Russia and Siberia. A Scythian burial place at Novotcherkassk not far from the Sea of Azov was found to contain a crown decorated with stags and trees, while the headdresses worn by the Siberian shamans have real reindeer antlers on them, the reindeer being an animal which enables the sorcerer to travel at great speed. And in a number of areas, shamans dress up as birds so as to fly through the air. Finally, the tree is the emblem of ritual ascent, and again enables the shaman to rise up into the sky.

The tumuli in Silla do not contain funerary chambers, so no mural decoration was possible. However, we have some evidence of the pictorial art of this period, in particular the image of a winged horse painted on birch bark which was found in Ch'ŏnma-ch'ong tomb (5th–6th century) at Kyŏngju. This Far Eastern version of the Greek Pegasus is also found on a 7th-century silver ewer now in Japan. But this is not the mount of a hero: the "celestial horse" of the Orient is rather related to the flying chargers of the Walkyries and enables the shaman to reach the sky and to transport the deceased into the world beyond.

We should not conclude this review of the dwellings of the dead in ancient Korea without mentioning, albeit briefly, the funerary pottery of Silla. Though the humble material from which it is made, of a dreary, greyish colour, cannot rival the sparkling gold of the sumptuous ornaments chiselled by the master craftsmen of Korean toreutics (ornamental reliefs in metal), yet we cannot remain unaffected by the variety of forms it assumed. The most amazing pieces are skilfully naïve representations of knights, wheeled vehicles, birds, boats and fabulous animals, not to mention those earthenware rhytons (horn-shaped drinking vessels) illustrative of the farflung travels of a form that conquered almost the whole of Eurasia.

Left: the "Black Warrior"

Painting on the north wall of the vault of Sasin-ch'ong tomb, Tonggou, Hian (Jilin). 6th–7th C.

Right: the "Red Phoenix"

Painting on the right side of the entrance piercing the south wall of the vault of the middle tomb at Uhyŏnni, Gangsě-gun, P'yŏngan-nam-do. 6th–7th C.

The tombs containing these paintings are reduced models of the universe: the animal divinities symbolize the four cardinal points, and on the ceilings there were often drawings of the constellations that are evocative of the canopy of heaven. Another Taoist theme is that of hermits who possess the secret of immortality. Taoism was introduced into Koguryŏ in AD624, but the tomb paintings seem to prove that the sacred imagery was there before the body of ideas. What is more, Buddhist elements are also to be found in the tombs.

Interior of King Muryŏng's tomb, Kyŏngju, Korea AD526

The mausoleum of the ruler Muryŏng is in the district capital of Paekche and was opened by archaeologists in 1971. The finds enabled researchers to confirm that cultural relations between the southwest kingdom of Korea and southern China had existed. Lotus flower motifs decorate many of the bricks.

Pottery figurine of an imaginary animal, from tomb No. 3, district *C*, Michuwang-nŭng, Kyŏngju, Korea 6th C.

These figurative pieces of pottery are among the finest products of Korean ceramic art. The morphology of this one, dug up in 1973, is hard to identify. Some researchers believe this is a tortoise, but the head is like that of a dragon; it is also possible to see in it the shape of a phoenix. Height, 14cm (5.4in). Kyŏngju National Museum.

Gold crown from the north tumulus of the great tomb of Hwangnam, Kyŏngju, Korea, 5th–6th C.

Up to the present time five pieces of this type, all dating from the same period, have been recovered from the tombs around Kyŏngju, the capital of the Korean kingdom of Silla. The Hwangnam crown was found during a series of digs, conducted from 1973 to 1975 in a sector with a good number of early burial places. Height, 27.5cm (9in) (excluding pendant pieces).

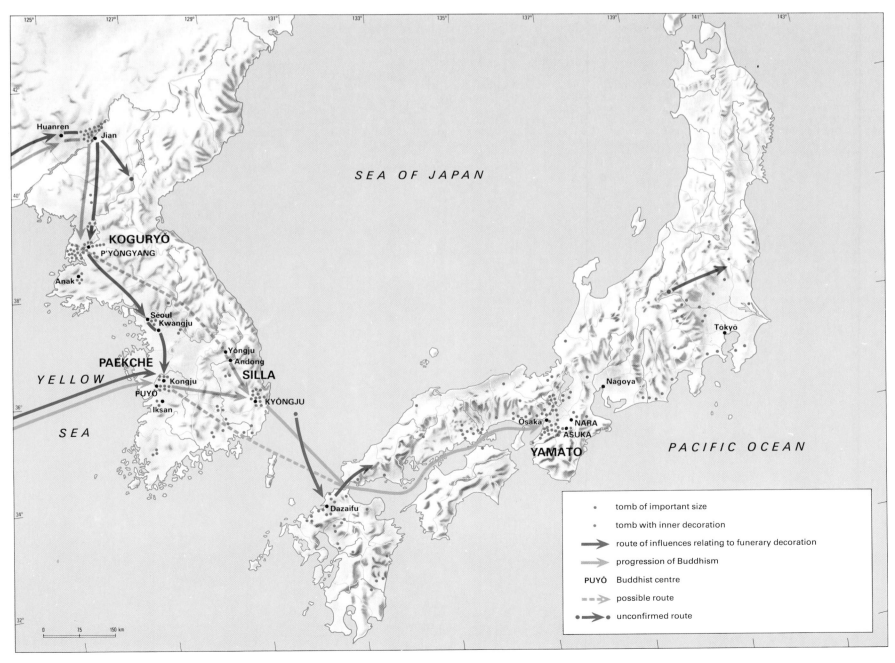

Legend:
- • tomb of important size
- • tomb with inner decoration
- → route of influences relating to funerary decoration
- → progression of Buddhism
- PUYŎ Buddhist centre
- ⇢ possible route
- •→• unconfirmed route

The funerary world of the Old Tomb period

The Old Tomb period of Japan saw the beginning of Japanese unification. Study of the elaborate burials of the time has revealed fascinating links with Korea and the Chinese mainland, in terms of beliefs and practices.

In the 3rd century AD Japan came to an important turning point. A Chinese text dating from this period informs us that a queen called Himiko—the "Sun Priestess"—gathered together some 30 small kingdoms, thus making a start on the unification of the country. The same document relates that the emperor of China presented Himiko with 100 bronze mirrors—the chronicler further tells us that these articles were much prized by the Japanese of the day. We can infer from this information that the Chthonian (earth) cult of the previous period—the Bronze Age—illustrated by little bronze bells that were ritually buried, had given way to a Uranian (sky) cult: the mirror is the attribute of the sun goddess, Amaterasu. However that may be, towards the end of the 3rd century, or the beginning of the 4th century, a new period began which Japanese archaeologists have called the Old Tomb period.

This mainly protohistorical period, corresponding approximately to the Iron Age, did not really come to a close until the end of the 7th century, although Buddhism was introduced into Japan in AD538, thus bringing the archipelago onto the historical stage. For about a century and a half two fundamentally different, though not opposing, cultures coexisted.

The Old Tomb period saw the building up of the Japanese empire, started by Himiko. Countless tombs were built at that time, the most spectacular of which are the so-called "keyhole" tombs because of their very strange construction: the usual circular tumulus has a vast trapezium-shaped projection, and the whole structure is enclosed by trenches. These tombs, which were intended for emperors, princes and the most powerful clan chiefs, are very imposing monuments. The most impressive is that of Emperor Nintoku near present-day Osaka, dating from the 5th century. It extends over almost half a kilometre (600yds) and rises to a height of about 30m (100ft). It is one of the grandest funeral monuments in existence.

These giant mausoleums are today overgrown by luxuriant vegetation; but they used to be surrounded by thousands of haniwa ("clay cylinders") some of which represented various objects, human beings or animals. The haniwa showing human beings and animals are generally on the projecting part of the tomb, forming sculptural groupings: according to some early texts this had to do with the enthronement ceremony of a new emperor or clan chief—a ritual suggested on top of the mounds by symbolic objects, but recorded realistically on the projecting part. It may be conjectured, moreover, that these rites actually took place on the tombs: there are some remains that would lend credence to such a theory. In that case the haniwa would have been intended to perpetuate these ceremonies throughout the succeeding centuries.

The haniwa stood in the open and could therefore be seen by everyone. The vaults of some tombs, on the other hand, are decorated with paintings and drawings that nobody—except a desecrator of the tomb—could see. It is a strange thing that most of the monuments which conceal such interior decoration are at Kyushu in the southwest of the archipelago, and in the northeast of Honshu, the main island. Whereas the burial chambers of the huge tombs, which are so numerous in the centre of the country, have no paintings, the humble provincial tombs provided the first expressions of Japanese pictorial art. It is also odd that while there are obvious links between the decorated tombs of the southwest and those of the northeast, the heart of the archipelago does not reveal any connection between them. This gap is one of the mysteries of the Old Tomb period.

In the 4th century funerary ornamentation made its appearance on the sarcophagi, and consisted only of geometric motifs cut into the stone. Then it spread onto the walls and was enhanced by colour. Built at the beginning of the 6th century, the Hinooka tomb (Fukuoka district) affords the earliest example of decoration consisting only of painting. The engraved and/or painted motifs of these primitive monuments are combinations of segments of straight lines and curves (chokkomon), circular figures, quivers and shields. The first of these motifs, which belongs to protohistorical Japan, seems to have developed from the stylized representation of a shell which had some apotropaic (evil-averting) power. The circles must have symbolized the sun. The quivers and the shields probably fulfilled the same protective function as did the haniwa representing them.

It was from the middle of the 6th century that this art came into full flower. The decorative vocabulary became richer. The Mezurashizuka tomb (Fukuoka district) offers the first example of coherent composition; a human in silhouette rows a boat at the front of which a bird is standing, and then ventures into a place of danger, protecting himself with his shield. This probably represents the deceased sailing towards the next world, and cautiously setting foot upon it. The "boat of the dead" is frequently found as a funerary vehicle in shamanic beliefs, while the pilot bird as a guide for the souls of the departed is reaffirmed in Korea as early as the 3rd century. In the Benkei-ga-ana tomb (Kumamoto district, 6th century) it is no longer a bird but a horse that stands in the boat of the dead. The horse—a psychopompal (soul-escorting) animal—bears the corpse away to the kingdom of shadows. Thus the bird and the horse are synonymous in the symbolic language of protohistorical Japan. This equivalence can also be observed at the Three Kingdoms period in Korea, a land imbued with shamanism.

The Korean connection

The funerary furnishings in the Korean state of Silla and those in Japan at the same period are closely related. The pottery dedicated to the dead which abounds in the tombs of the southeast Korean kingdom can be found in almost identical form in the burial chambers of ancient Japan. The only notable difference is in the greater simplicity of the Japanese pieces. Headdresses in gilded bronze, unquestionably inspired by the rich gold crowns of Silla, have been dug up in Japan. What is more, magatama*—ornaments in delicate stone which were highly prized in Korea, and were used in particular to embellish the crowns of the kings of Silla—are found in large quantities in the tombs of the Japanese archipelago and are even linked to an 8th century Buddhist ornament.

Mention should also be made of the similarities in harness objects: the two saddle cantles of carved and gilded bronze, found in a tomb related to that of Emperor Ojin (5th century) in the Osaka area, are practically identical with the almost contemporary item found near Koryŏng, in Silla. Many other examples could be adduced, proving the extent to which Silla and Yamato (Japan) were in contact at this period, just prior to their emergence into the historical period under the guiding star of Buddhism.

The vaults of the great tombs in the centre of the Japanese archipelago are for the most part devoid of paintings, but there is one exception in the area, though late: a small tumulus excavated in 1972, probably dating from the very early 8th century. On the walls of the funeral chamber of Takamatsuzuka are paintings of the four cardinal (or compass-point) animals which are found in the tombs of North Korea, and of four groups of people who are connected with the processions depicted in the tombs of the Tang period.

The unique status of this monument in Japan puzzled archaeologists for more than 10 years. But in 1983 an endoscopic probe into Kitora tomb—a small mound near Takamatsuka—showed that the north wall of the vault bore a painted portrayal of the so-called "Black Warrior". So it is likely that when it is opened the tumulus will reveal the presence of the three other divine animals. Since this discovery was made, the Takamatsuzuka tomb has emerged from the solitude to which it was confined. It can be assumed that new finds will lead to a wider and deeper knowledge of Japan in ancient times.

Typology of tombs from the 4th to 7th centuries

In the course of almost 400 years there was hardly any change in the form of the great burials; most had a "keyhole" design. But they differed in size gradually becoming bigger until they reached their maximum size in the 5th century. They then decreased in size, finally shrinking back to that of the earliest times. The construction of the funerary chambers also changed: pits on the top of mounds were followed, towards the second half of the 5th century, by dolmen-like vaults.

A small ornamental plaque in gilded bronze

The horses of the chiefs were richly harnessed. Among the most typical ornaments are small plaques which were hung on the horse's croup. These pieces can be traced directly to the metalworking art of Silla and provide eloquent proof of the close links that existed between the southeastern Korean kingdom and the Japanese archipelago. 6th–7th century. Width: 9.5cm (3.7in) Munakata-jinja, Fukuoka department.

Munakata-taisha

Clay statuette of a deer, Hirodokoro, Shimane, Japan

This recently discovered statuette depicts one of the most highly prized game animals in ancient Japan; alternatively, it may be a local version of the shamanic reindeer on which the sorcerers of Siberia travelled on their astral flights. Ht. 91cm (35.7in) 6th century. Shimane departmental Education Committee.

Painting decorating the Mezurashizuka tomb, Fukuoka department

This is the first deliberately arranged picture in Japanese pictorial art. In the scene depicted a dead person is travelling by boat out of this world and into the world beyond. A bird is acting as the dead man's pilot. In other tombs it is a horse that acts as the animal guide to the other world. Whether they are crossing the sea or flying through the air, the bird and the horse are fulfilling the same funerary mission. Late 6th century.

The so-called *chokko-mon* motif of the Idera tomb, Kumamoto department

The "motif of straight lines and curves" that was first of all engraved on sarcophagi spread onto the walls of the vaults and was picked out in colour. It was elaborated in Japan from the 4th century, and reached its peak in the 5th century, dying out in the following century. As the *chokko-mon* appears on *haniwa* representing weapons, it is thought that it was believed to fulfil a protective function. Late 5th century.

Decoration on the back wall of the Torazuka tomb, Ibaraki department

This tomb, investigated in 1973, contains one of the few funerary paintings known in the northeastern part of the Japanese archipelago. Geometric patterns—triangles and circles—are above schematic drawings of sabres, quivers and pieces of armour. Though later than the Kyūshū tombs, those of Honshū are more crude. First half of 7th century.

Green Dragon on the wall of the Takamatsuzuka tomb, Nara department

Both in theme and in technique there is a gulf between this grave and those of the Iron Age. Here Korean and Chinese influences can be clearly seen. But in the final analysis the paintings decorating the funerary chamber are original in the way that they harmoniously unite mainland elements of various origins and periods. It is a good example of Japanese art's capacity for synthesis. Late 7th or early 8th century.

Monasteries and palaces

Archaeologists have found links between religious and secular architecture in early Buddhist Japan, and also an interesting continuity from the earlier Old Tombs era.

Buddhism brought a highly developed culture to Korea which was introduced into Koguryŏ in AD372 and into Paekche in 384. It did not officially reach Silla until about 528, and Japan until 538. The previous article shows how similar were the funerary furnishings of Silla and Yamato, and it should be stressed that these two countries adopted the religion of the mainland at roughly the same time, and much later than Koguryŏ and Paekche. This leads us to reconsider the traditional breakdown of the Korean-Japanese area: while historians see the Three Kingdoms period and the Old Tombs period as distinct, it would seem more correct to consider this geographical area as consisting of two cultural zones: on the one hand, the north and southwest of the peninsula where Buddhism arrived from the end of the 4th century; on the other, Silla and Yamato, lands which for mainly geographical reasons remained isolated longer from Sino-Buddhism. Thus it would be better within the context of Korea and Japan at that period to recognize the unity in spite of their armed conflicts, of Koguryŏ and Paekche, and the strong relationship, despite their own violent clashes, between Silla and Yamato.

Buddhism may have been established early in Koguryŏ and Paekche, but hardly any tangible traces from that early period are to be found. According to texts, the monasteries of Ch'omunsa and Ipulnansa were built in the first days of Buddhism in the north of the country; then in the reign of King Kwangkaet'o-wang (391–412), a fervent Buddhist, nine Buddhist establishments were constructed. But it has been possible to investigate only a few sites at P'yŏngyang, one in particular being that of the monastery sited at Ch'ŏngamni—which is believed to date from the end of the 5th century. The results of these excavations are very illuminating when Korean Buddhist archaeology is compared with that of Japan.

In Paekche Buddhism did not really get going until the capital was moved to Puyŏ, in 538. It is on the site of that city, whose sovereign Sŏngmyŏng-wang conveyed the Sino-Indian religion to Japan, that archaeologists have found important Buddhist ruins, including those of the Kŭmgangsa monastery, the plan of which was followed by the architects who built Shitennōji at Naniwa (Japan), probably in the early 7th century.

Silla, which was late and cautious in its reception of the new religion, learnt Buddhist arts from its two neighbours. In the field of architecture, the master builders of Paekche took part in constructing Hwangryongsa (6th–7th century), one of the grandest religious monuments on the Korean peninsula.

The first Buddhist monastery in Japan was Asukadera, or Hokoji (late 6th–early 7th century). When excavations were carried out, two surprises awaited archaeologists. For one thing, the layout of the buildings which were constructed under the direction of foremen from Paekche is not the so-called "Shitennoji" type that predominates in the southwestern Korean kingdom; on the contrary, it is related to the plan of the Ch'ŏngamni remains in North Korea. It seems that Asukadera, founded by the chief of the very powerful Soga clan, was altered by the prince regent, Shotoku-taishi, who for primarily political reasons accepted the primacy of northern Buddhism which identified the Emperor with the Buddha. Thus, in order to affirm the supremacy of the sovereign over the clan chiefs, the man who was the *de facto* ruler of Japan at that time seems to have transformed Asukadera into a kind of state monastery. The second surprise was caused by the exploration of the foundations of the tower: this secret and holy place, which ought in theory to conceal Buddhist relics, yielded *magatama** and other objects usually forming part of the funerary furnishings of the Old Tombs era. Thus the tower was resting not on an orthodox Buddhist reliquary, but on some kind of cenotaph from the proto-historic period. This occurrence reflects the confusion—or the cohesion—prevalent in these times when a foreign religion had just reached Japan, without however extinguishing indigenous beliefs.

These wooden buildings which, though stoutly constructed were vulnerable to fire, have almost all disappeared; all that survives is the stone foundations and some tiles, few in number. Nonetheless, Horyuji monastery, founded at the beginning of the 7th century, struck by lightning in 670, but rebuilt from its ruins in the following decades, is the oldest surviving wooden Buddhist monument in the Far East. If the layout of the buildings is original, the hybrid nature of the architectural and ornamental components shows that the late 7th century Japanese builders had not yet managed to create a specifically Japanese style and were still the pupils of their masters from the mainland.

In the 8th century Japan turned away from Korea and followed Chinese fashion. This explains the paradox that Tang architecture is to be found more in Nara, the Japanese capital of that period, than on the mainland. But in the 9th century, Japan, feeling that it had learnt enough from its neighbours, gradually turned in upon itself to regain its own identity.

Palaces, royal residences and a great capital

Palaces are also a fruitful source of information. In Korea, the excavations carried out at Kyŏngju, Silla's only capital and one of the main urban centres of the peninsula, have been the most rewarding. The remains of the royal palace of Wŏlsŏng are surrounded by an earth rampart about 20m (65ft) high and more than 1km (0.62 miles) long, and lie beside a river. Inside the enclosure foundation stones and many tiles are scattered. A little to the north of the palace lie the ruins of the royal residence of Imhae-jŏn, which was built near the Anapji pond. Thousands of tiles and embossed paving stones have been collected on this site, as well as a number of wooden and metal objects: in all, more than 15,000 items. Many of these are of a utilitarian nature, and thus enable archaeologists to gain a better understanding of the everyday life of the rulers of Silla. Not far from the residence are the remains of the Posŏk-jŏng pavilion where an artificial stream with many bends has been uncovered that was used for the "entertainment of the winding waters"; this consisted of floating down cups filled with alcohol, which could only be grabbed as they went by once the participant had composed and recited a short poem.

Nara, the first great capital of Japan, was founded in 710 and was modelled on the Chinese city of Changan, built about a century before in a strict grid design. The imperial palace of Heijō was in the centre of the northern part of the town, occupying an area of 121 hectares (300 acres). The grounds were enclosed by a wall, with a break to the south for the main gate, which opened onto the Avenue of the Red Phoenix, the north-south axis of the city. A large number of buildings were laid out in a symmetrical fashion, but only one survives, and it has been transformed into one of the main monasteries of Nara: the Tōshōdaiji (8th century). This is the only example of Japanese imperial architecture of this period, doubly precious as it proves that these two kinds of sacred space, Buddhist monasteries and imperial palaces, barely differed from one another. Moreover, one of the Horyuji monuments dating from the same century comes from the residence of a prince. This is evidence of the close links between religious and secular architecture. Occurring over a period of time there are other cases showing that a human being might bequeath his place of residence to the Buddha. We will mention only one cases here: the Phoenix Pavilion of Byodoin—the country house of the minister Fujiwara no Yorimichi, near Kyoto, which was transformed into a sanctuary in 1052; and in Kyoto itself, the Golden Pavilion of Rokuonji (1398), lived in by the *shogun* Ashikaga Yoshimitsu and then dedicated by him to Amida Buddha; and the Silver Pavilion of Jishoji (1489), which Ashikaga Yoshimasa, Yoshimitsu's grandson, in turn converted into a place of worship.

Plans of the remains (below left) of the monastery at Ch'ŏngamni (2nd half of 6th century) near P'yŏngyang, Korea, and (below right) of the Asukadera monastery (late 6th-early 7th century), Nara, Japan

The results of the archaeological investigations undertaken on the site of Asukadera took experts by surprise. While they were expecting an overall plan similar to that of Shitennoji monastery with its south-north alignment of the main buildings, it was realized that two side sanctuaries had been added to the central shrine. This formula comes from northern Korea.

Tile from Sach'ŏnwangsa monastery (c. mid-6th century) at Puyŏ, Korea (bottom), and tile from Asukadera monastery, Japan (top)

Architects and skilled tradesmen came from Paekche to Japan to take part in building Asukadera monastery, and the team included tilers. Information provided by old texts is corroborated by the similarity between tiles from Sach'ŏnwangsa and Asukadera.

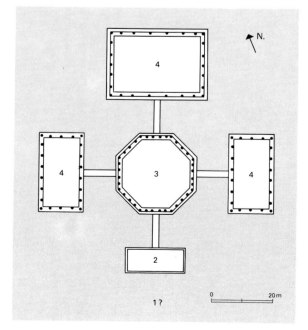

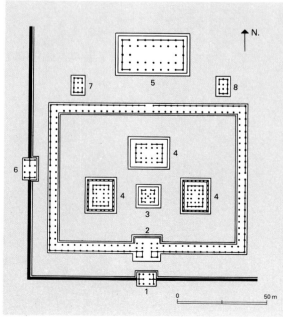

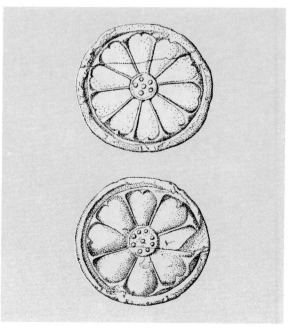

Iwanami Shoten Publishers

Aerial view of Horyuji monastery, Nara, Japan

Horyuji was built at the beginning of the 7th century, but was burnt down in 670; rebuilding continued thereafter until 711. The plan of the original monastery was of the Shitennōji type, but in the second version the sanctuary and the tower were placed on an east-west axis. This arrangement, which is not found on the mainland, indicates that Japanese architects at the end of the 7th century were beginning to move away from Sino-Korean models. The style does nonetheless show a strong influence from the continental mainland.

Agency of Cultural Affairs, Nara

A monumental stone representing Mount Sumeru

This small monument consisting of three superimposed parts is a carved image of Sumeru—a sacred mountain which, according to the Hindu and Buddhist concept of the cosmos, stands in the centre of the universe. Ducts cut out of the stone suggest that this was a fountain used to ornament a garden. If so, this would be the earliest known evidence of garden art in Japan. Height 2.3m (7.5ft) 7th century.

Reconstruction model of the imperial palace of Heyjō-kyō (Nara, Japan), built in the 8th century

Lying at the heart of the capital, the imperial palace combined the roles of royal residence, seat of government, and sacred ground where national ceremonies were celebrated. Its main buildings were the Abode of the Emperor and the Throne Room, which opened southwards onto a huge esplanade. Included in the complex were buildings intended for the main governing organs of the state, as well as numerous sentry posts.

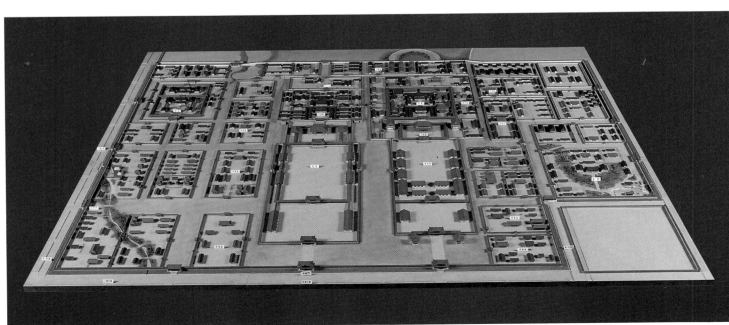

Agency of Cultural Affairs, Nara

Medieval Japanese ceramics

From the Neolithic Age to the medieval period, Japanese ceramics have characterized the technical development and cultural independence of Japan.

The discovery of Japanese pottery from the Neolithic Age, known as Jōmon, and from the Bronze Age, known as Yayoi, dates back to the end of the last century. However, the scientific study of these types of pottery began only during the 1920s, using stratigraphic* methods. It was not until the middle of the 20th century that dating by C14* was applied to them.

At all events, serious gaps remained in the history of Japanese ceramics, especially between the protohistoric period (the Old Tomb period: 3rd–6th centuries AD) and the period of the creation of objects intended for use in the tea ceremony (14th century). Recent excavations have thrown new light on the activity in the kilns during the Nara and Heian periods (7th–12th centuries). A reddish terracotta (hajiki), derived from Yayoi ware and manufactured from the 4th century, and a hard, grey stoneware (sueki) which appeared in the Suemura kilns near Ōsaka in the second half of the 5th century, were produced throughout Japan. But under the influence of the Chinese "Three Colours" (sancai) of the Tang period, lead glazes were used by Japanese craftsmen. The nationwide production of these wares was recognized when pieces from Shōsō-in were studied, and confirmed by the excavations at the palace of Nara, monasteries and provincial seats of government. The most outstanding event between the 6th and 14th centuries was the creation of a hard pottery (shirishi) with a whitish body and a wood-ash glaze, natural at first, then applied rapidly to each piece with a brush.

Excavations carried out on the sites of kilns in the Sanage area (Nagoya, Aichi district) have made it possible to complete the study of these periods and to find the missing link in the history of the development of Japanese ceramics. Of the 438 Sanage kilns in use between the second half of the 8th century and the 12th century, kiln No. 32 at Narumi, dating from about AD760, is the first in which shirishi ware was fired. Production and development remained confined to the Tōkai area (around Nagoya) which in the medieval period was to become the centre for the manufacture of ceramics with an applied glaze, in the kilns at Seto and Mino.

Kilns and their output in medieval Japan

Historically speaking, the Japanese Middle Ages cover the Kamakura and Muromachi periods (late 12th–16th centuries). However, the history of the production of medieval ceramics starts from the end of the Heian period, at the beginning of the 12th century, and continues until the end of the 16th century. In fact elements peculiar to medieval output appear very early. Three characteristic shapes were used for basic utilitarian items: the tsubo (a narrow-necked jar) and the kame (a jar with a wide opening) are sturdy in appearance; the suribachi (a bowl with a pouring lip used as a mortar) answered the needs of a new diet associated with the introduction of Zen Buddhism.

The discovery some 10 years ago of more than 40 sites with remains of medieval kilns situated in areas ranging from the north-east of Honshū down to the island of Kyūshū has given archaeologists a more accurate appreciation of the intense activity of that period. It also corrects the earlier theory, developed after World War II with the find of the Echizen kilns, of "six ancient kilns" existing in medieval Japan (Shigaraki, Bizen, Tokoname, Tamba, Echizen, Seto). From now on we must assume there were areas of production as large as those in the Mino region, which has yielded the remains of more than 500 kilns, and in the Atsumi peninsula, with the remains of more than 400 kilns.

At the same time, study of the output of the medieval kilns has made considerable progress through the excavations carried out on the sites of tombs, kyozuka*, towns, castles or ports such as Ashidagawa, Fushō-ji, Tosaminato and Tomitajō. These digs have yielded material which makes it possible to establish a chronology from the basis of dated items. Thus the fact that the Tokoname kilns were in use before the middle of the 12th century is proved by a tsubo decorated with three engraved lines and dated 1125, found in the Shinto Imamiya shrine in Kyoto. The same is true of the Atsumi kilns where a vessel for a sūtra reliquary (kyōzutsu) was produced, dated 1114, discovered in Ōku-no-in on Mount Kôya (Wakayama district). A kame and a suribachi dated 1167 and produced in the Suzu kilns were dug up in a kyōzuka behind the temple of Nisseki-ji (Toyoma district). These excavations have also enabled archaeologists to attribute pieces to particular kilns, for example the receptacle for a sūtra reliquary made in the Iizaka kilns, dated 1171, and found in the kyōzuka of the temple of Yoneyama-ji (Fukushima district).

Archaeologists have been confronted with a very diversified medieval output, as shown by excavations of the harbour town found in the Ashida river bed (Fukuyama, Hiroshima district). This yielded a small quantity of imported Chinese or Korean ware and pottery with an applied glaze from Seto, and also a large amount (45 per cent) of earthenware bowls and plates of the hajiki type and tsubo and kame from Bizen, Tokoname and Kameyama. The large quantities of material available have led researchers to establish a new classification. Professor Shōichi Narazaki has recognized three main categories of output, derived from earlier periods. In fact, thanks to better knowledge of the Nara and Heian periods, it has been possible to prove that, far from being a sudden movement, medieval production is partly based on what was being made before, and shows the persistence of old techniques.

Three types of medieval ware

Hajiki ware (first type, see table) was dominant for the production of everyday utensils throughout medieval Japan. But some forms, such as kettles (kama), were made of iron, for its hard-wearing qualities, from the end of the Kamakura period.

The second tradition, which carried on right through the Middle Ages, was that of the sueki. In eastern Japan Suzu seems to have been the kiln that best represented this style, and it appears to have been its main source. Digs carried out by the Archaeological Society of Ishikawa have enabled us to establish the groundwork for a chronology of this site, through research done on the Saihō-ji kilns (1963) and the Hōjū-ji kilns (1972). Suzu's five phases of production place the beginning of use of the kilns in the 12th century. Suzu seems to have fallen into disuse around the end of the Muromachi period (early 16th century) with the development of the Echizen kilns which captured the ceramics market in the northern part of Hokuriku. Co-existing with kilns given over to the sueki tradition like Suzu, there were other sites with a more original output, such as Bizen.

The third type of ware produced in medieval times is a hard pottery (jiki, see table). The kilns at Seto and Mino are representative of this. As well as kilns that followed the shirashi tradition of the Heian period, producing coarsely moulded bowls with no glaze (yamajawan), 203 kilns producing pieces with an applied glaze known as Ko-Seto (old Seto) have been located at Seto, and nine at Mino. The varied forms and the original glazes based on wood-ash or iron oxides reflect the influence of Chinese Song and Yuan pottery (four-handled jars, meipin* bottles, perfume pans, flower vases). The kilns producing jiki-style pottery at Atsumi, Tokoname, Sanage and Echizen all had an output that included tsubo, kame and cylindrical receptacles made to be buried in the kyōzuka. The existence of kilns at Kaga was confirmed recently in 1969, and research carried out by Komatsu municipal museum has uncovered 12 kilns, the oldest of which, Okudani No. 1, dates from the second half of the 12th century. Of the early pieces found, jars decorated with three engraved lines are similar to pieces produced at Tokoname or Echizen. However, the most characteristic motif of Kaga is that of a lattice intertwined with chrysanthemums.

The production of medieval ceramics ended when a new type of kiln appeared in the Seto area: the ôgama. As far as we know at present, the Mukashida kiln at Seto, which seems to have started up at the beginning of the 16th century, is the earliest ôgama in the Seto and Mino area. It was in use from the Tembun (1532–55) to the Momoyama (1573–1603) periods. Though items produced there still used the forms that existed in the previous period (bowls, cha-ire*, bowls of the temmoku* type, bottles, perfume pans), there were also plates decorated with cobalt (gosu-e) in imitation of the blue-decorated porcelain of Ming China, which was imported into Japan and highly prized. The ôgama kilns, which were also built on other sites where there were medieval kilns, are a reflection of the transformation of the medieval into the modern output.

Atsumi: kiln of the anagama type (Sôsaku No 14)

There were about 20 kilns in the Sôsaku group, found between 1973 and 1975. The Atsumi kilns are 15–18m long (49–59ft), and of the anagama type. The marked slope of the floor between the entrance and the column dividing the flame is a characteristic feature.

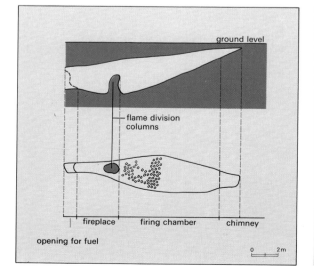

Seto: kiln of the anagama type (Konagaso), 15th century

From the end of the Kamakura period, the kilns of the Seto region began to develop, the centre of manufacture being the Akatsu district. The upper part of the firing chamber was narrowed, and a separating wall built in the middle of it so as to increase the effectiveness of combustion and obtain a better quality glaze.

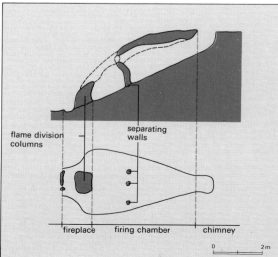

Mino: kiln of the ôgama type (Myôdo), early 16th century

Problems remain about the date when anagama kilns were replaced by the ôgama type at Mino and at Seto, where they originated. These kilns were no longer dug out of a slope, but were built on the slope itself. Columns supported the vault and there was a side access to the chamber. The floor of the main chamber was slightly raised in relation to that of the combustion chamber. The ôgama kilns herald the end of medieval manufacture.

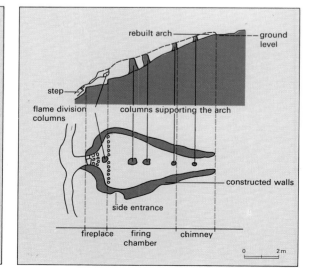

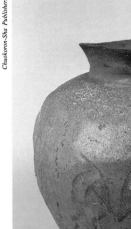

Chuokoron-Sha Publishers

A jar (*tsubo*) from Kaga, 13th century

Found in a medieval tomb at Karumi-machi, Komatsu-shi, Ishikawa, this *tsubo* is identical in form to jars decorated with three horizontally engraved lines, manufactured in the Echizen kilns. The body consists of yellowish clay with small stones mixed into it. These have come up to the surface during firing, forming little cavities. Traces of the bamboo knife (*hera*) used to correct the shape can be seen on the body. Wood-ash has run down to form long greenish stains on the neck and body of the *tsubo*. Jars of this type were used as funerary urns in the medieval period. Height 23.8cm (9.5in), diameter 19.4cm (7.8in). Private collection.

Komatsu Municipal Museum and Shogakukan Publishers

A jar (*tsubo*) from Suzu, 14th century

This famous piece was discovered in 1972 at Jike, in the town of Suzu. On the body, which is built up from rolls of clay, there is a decoration covering all four sides. Autumn grasses have been incised using a knife (*hera*), a process that was widespread in the Suzu kilns. The dark bodies of the Suzu pieces can be recognized by their decoration of waves or incised parallel lines, sometimes covering the entire piece. Motifs from nature are less usual. Height 27.3cm (10.9in), diameter 26cm (10.4in). Private collection.

Right: a jar (*tsubo*) from Atsumi, 12th century

This big-bellied jar with an open lip was built up from rolls of clay in three parts. The lower part of the body shows traces of the bat used. A decorative pattern of lotus petals and parallel lines has been drawn on the shoulder and can be seen under a yellow wood-ash glaze. This jar which was found in a *kyôsuka* at Kakegawa (Shizuoka), was used as a receptacle for a reliquary containing a sutra. Height 43.5cm (17.4in), diameter 41cm (16.4in). Private collection.

Chuokoron-Sha Publishers

Chuokoron-Sha Publishers

Far right: a jar (*kame*) from Kaga, 13th century

Found at Hiyoshi-machi, Tsurugi-machi (Ishikawa), this wide-shouldered *kame* with a narrow band running round the opening is decorated with printed floral patterns. The manufacture of jars as large as this was common in the Tokoname and Echizen kilns. Height 62.3cm (24.9in), diameter 65cm (26in). Komatsu Municipal Museum, Ishikawa.

ceramic group	type	principal production	particular characteristics	principal kilns and geographic distribution
hajiki tradition, terracotta	1	bowls, plates, kettles, cooking pots: hajiki type	firing and oxidation reddish colour/body	all of Japan
	2	bowls, small bowls, small plates: gaki type	firing and reduction black body	Japan west of Kinai and north of Kyūshū
sueki tradition, stoneware	1 ●	tsubo, round and elongated body, kame, suribachi	firing and oxidation brown body	Bizen, probably Iga, Shigaraki, Tamba
	2 ●	tsubo, round and elongated body, kame, suribachi	firing and reduction grey-black body differences exist between eastern Japan (Suzu and Suzu tradition kilns) and western Japan	all of Japan Suzu, Kameyama Iizaka
jiki tradition, stoneware	1 ●	varied shapes, numerous influences from northern Song, southern Song and Yuan (China)	ceramic form derived from earlier ceramics with a wood-ash glaze (shirashi, Heian period) pieces with a wood-ash or iron-base glaze	Seto, Mino
	2 ●	bowls, plates, dishes	ceramic form derived from earlier ceramic with a wood-ash glaze	Sanage, Tōkai region
	3 ●	tsubo, kame, suribachi	ceramic form derived from earlier ceramics with a wood-ash glaze and a coarse ceramic without glaze	Atsumi Tokoname Kojōzan Nakatsugawa
	4 ●	tsubo, kame, suribachi	mainly coarse ceramic without glaze produced in the regions which had no earlier tradition of wood-ash ceramics and which have imported the shirashi techniques from the regions of Tōkai in the Middle Ages	Echizen Kaga Sasagami Tōkita Kumakari Shinanoura

(After Shōichi Narasaki "The Production of Ceramics in Medieval Society" in Sekai Tōji Zenshū, Vol. III, Shogakukan, 1977.)

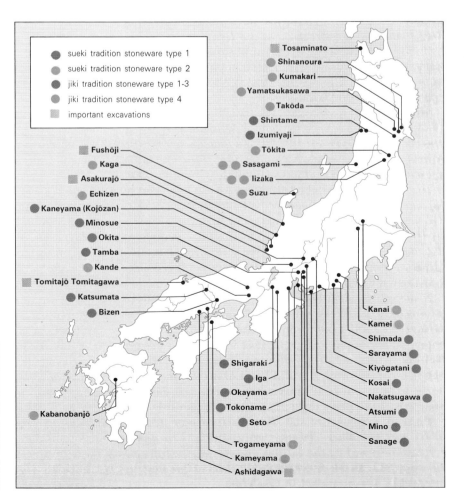

- ● sueki tradition stoneware type 1
- ● sueki tradition stoneware type 2
- ● jiki tradition stoneware type 1-3
- ● jiki tradition stoneware type 4
- ■ important excavations

Tosaminato
Shinanoura
Kumakari
Yamatsukasawa
Takōda
Shintame
Izumiyaji
Tōkita
Fushōji
Kaga
Asakurajō
Echizen
Kaneyama (Kojōzan)
Minosue
Okita
Tamba
Kande
Tomitajō Tomitagawa
Katsumata
Bizen
Sasagami
Iizaka
Suzu
Shigaraki
Iga
Okayama
Tokoname
Seto
Kabanobanjō
Togameyama
Kameyama
Ashidagawa
Kanai
Kamei
Shimada
Sarayama
Kiyōgatani
Kosai
Nakatsugawa
Atsumi
Mino
Sanage

Africa:
the archaeological background

Africa has the oldest prehistory in the world, the most complete series of traces left by man at all stages of evolution. Because of European colonization – intellectual and material – this discovery is one of the more recent and significant achievements of archaeology.

In Africa, archaeological research devoted to the cultures of the Mediterranean has a long history, but until recently the situation was different south of the Tropic of Cancer, with the exception of Ethiopia. A continent "without a history" because it was "without writing", Africa was also – and this became a dogma – "without archaeological remains". Before World War I a few officers and administrators excavated sites from all periods, some of them taking more care than others. Africans, in the role of uninterested spectators or an ignorant labour force, took very little part in these preliminary investigations. There were few periodicals which would accept articles about them. *Man* in England and *L'Anthropologie* in France first began to draw their readers' attention to the "exotic" discoveries.

World War I, its consequences for Europe, and the economic, political and cultural disturbances which followed it, put a stop to these early efforts. Publications between 1914 and 1938 were virtually non-existent. A few English, Belgian, German and French pioneers restarted the "machine to discover the past". The Africans were still limited to the same roles. Large-scale investigatory activity was directed from Dakar by the IFAN team (l'Institut Français d'Afrique Noire), from Lagos, London, Algiers and some other centres. Ground reconnaissance, the collecting of information, and excavations were carried out with little material and technical help. From 1938 to 1960 discoveries followed in rapid succession. They involved all periods in the life of the continent, though not in sequence, and scholars began to suspect that Africa might well have a long history. Surprising evidence of hominization (the emergence of the *Homo* species) was found in the south from 1921 and in the east of the continent from 1932. In 1936 L. S. B. Leakey* began to publish results which left more than one specialist sceptical. It took more than 10 years before his propositions were taken into serious consideration world-wide.

Meanwhile, archaeological reviews grew more frequent. At Dakar, from 1942 to 1984, *Notes Africaines* published texts of very unequal value, especially from 1949 to 1958, and the *Bulletin de l'Institut Français d'Afrique Noire* printed intensive studies after 1951. New specialized publications also appeared in Nigeria and in the modern state of Ghana.

However the essential information was still covered by *Man* and *L'Anthropologie*, which were joined by the *Bulletin du Comité d'Etudes Historiques et Scientifiques de l'AOF*, the *Journal des Africanistes, the Journal of the Royal African Society* and, in Belgium, by the *Bulletin de la Société Royale Belge d'Anthropologie et d'Histoire*. Characteristically for this period, the wide dispersal of all these various publications made comparisons and syntheses extremely difficult.

A succession of further discoveries raised such serious questions about the origins of man and the antiquity of his presence in Africa that "prehistory" became the focal point for impassioned discussions and the development of improved techniques. After the 1947 Pan-African Congress on Prehistory at Nairobi, where the proposition was finally accepted that Africa had "the oldest prehistory in the world" and above all the most complete series of traces left by man at all stages of his evolution, Pan-African congresses on prehistory took place regularly from 1952 onwards.

To read Volume I of the *General History of Africa* (UNESCO), which might well be called "Twenty years after", is to understand the absolute revolution caused by the various discoveries, the full consequences of which have not yet been felt. Since the publication of this work in 1975 the rhythm of discoveries has continued to accelerate.

Necessary confrontations

There have been violent theoretical and ideological confrontations between frequently incredulous or hostile professional historians and those experts who are trying to mark out the incredible field of research which has just opened up to them in Africa. The works of Sheikh Anta Diop* are a remarkable illustration of these necessary and inevitable confrontations, which have also involved chronology, because many investigators feel that the stages of African prehistory could not have been the same as the rest of the world's. Hard-fought discussion of this point is still in progress.

The most remarkable consequence of the progress made by prehistoric archaeology in Africa is probably the evolution of the actual conception of "prehistory". Is it reasonable on this continent where man's history is measured in millions of years to reduce the chronological field of *history* – according to ancient conventions – to written or oral sources? For 40 years archaeology in Africa has proved that it and it alone can provide complete reconstruction of the continent's past. Our knowledge of the last 10,000 years has advanced so fast that today we can reconstruct cultures and societies in large areas of the continent. With every year the need to put archaeological discoveries in historical perspective (Sutton, 1974, Phillipson, 1977, Devisse, 1982) pushes the limits of our knowledge further back.

However there are still a few shadows in the picture. The desire to use archaeology for the rapid construction of large-scale syntheses, for example in the field of migrations, has led to many spectacular and hasty conclusions, which must be reconsidered today from the point of view of more attentive and more patient research. The example of "Bantu migrations" will probably remain a landmark in the history of African archaeology, showing the danger involved in drawing overhasty conclusions from incomplete investigations.

Haunted by the example of the Rosetta Stone, many research workers have long thought that in tropical Africa it was necessary to proceed from the known to the unknown to establish the patterns of archaeological inquiry or frameworks for interpreting the African past. Such was the reasoning of N. Chittick who, in the course of his enthusiastic work in east coast cities, was sometimes side-tracked by features that in fact came from elsewhere. This was also the case with successive investigators who worked at Zimbabwe. Hence an urban archaeology arose at the points of contact between several cultures, that was supposed to supply accurate information about the "obscure" period between the 7th and 12th centuries. Now it has been strikingly demonstrated (Shaw, 1970, McIntosh, 1980) that the same methods of work, applied to "monocultural" sites without a "Rosetta Stone", can supply results that are extremely important for the reconstruction of Africa's past. Volume III of the *General History of Africa* (UNESCO) sums up 20 years of progress in this field.

On the whole, methodological progress has been considerable. African archaeology has now found its preferred areas, its lines of research and its objectives. In cases where efforts have not yet been vigorous enough, programming syntheses show how to set-up research (Van Noten, 1982). The following pages show some (and only some) of the very diverse aspects of this discipline. The organization of space in the past, relations with the environment, food remains, material traces of all kinds, pollens, vestiges of ancient animal and plant life, all these are material for reflection and research by the archaeologist who works in Africa and has the legitimate ambition of restoring its past to a continent labelled as having "no history". The new, long, complex and costly research programmes place archaeology at a

Terracotta from Nok (Nigeria), between 500BC and AD200

.o the discoverer, this represents a museum piece, admirable of
.s kind, or a valuable collector's item. To the archaeologist, it
has no value unless the place and stratigraphical context of its
discovery are known. Anthropological and socio-cultural
analysis, and study of the composition of its paste and
modelling techniques, have made this piece a historical indicator with many different meanings.
To an archeometrist, thermoluminescence will bracket it
chronologically. Analysis of the paste will show whether it was
made in the place where it was found or elsewhere.
Measurement of the firing temperature will show if that took
place in a kiln or in the open air. The archeometrist sees the
piece as a chronological and technical indicator. National
Museum, Lagos.

crossroads in research which is of necessity multi-disciplinary. It has acquired
its autonomy vis-à-vis "traditional" (i.e. European) history; it has even come
close to the working methods of prehistorians in recent periods, without
neglecting the approaches of economic anthropology and sociology. A new
and original discipline, it is constantly upsetting preconceived ideas.

African history is more encumbered by myths than the history of any other
country. As time passes, all the myths added by foreign cultures are
superimposed on the myths which the African peoples have themselves
created. The ancient production of metal in Africa is a good example of
"mythological accretion". For decades discussions have centred on what
direction to give arrows illustrating one diffusionist theory or another. When
archaeologists began to work according to their own methods, these myths
were exploded. For some years the investigation of metals has become a
serious preoccupation. It immediately resulted in calling on the services of
archeometry.* Research on metals is going on in Mali, Niger, Senegal, at
Burkina Faso, on the Ivory Coast, in Benin, Nigeria, Ghana, Cameroon, in
Zaire, the Congo, Angola, at Rwanda, Burundi, and in Madagascar; and for
the first time it is largely being conducted by African or Malagasy researchers.
This is one of the greatest transformations experienced by this archaeology
for 10 years, and highly qualified African investigators are playing a large part
in it. But this has by no means led to the exclusion of foreign research workers.
For example, a French archaeologist has demonstrated the antiquity,
c.9000BP (before present) of ceramic production in Aïr, and also a Belgian
archaeologist, P. de Maret, has revealed the existence of coherent cultures in
Cameroon (c.7500BP), after carrying out detailed excavations at Shaba. This
is the logical consequence of work undertaken during the preceding decades.
However, Africans and Malagasy are now directly responsible for large-scale
works and they work out their own programme of research without undue
influence from directors of research. Long-term research programmes which
include important archaeological sections are beginning in Mauretania,
Senegal, Mali, Niger, Burkina Faso, Benin, Nigeria, Cameroon, Congo,
Gabon, Angola, Burundi, Kenya, Tanzania, Madagascar and Mozambique.

It became a matter of urgency to make public the progress accomplished.
Although all the problems involved in the publication of studies are not yet
resolved, indeed far from it, specialized reviews began after 1960 to take a
wholehearted or partial interest in archaeological research carried out in
Africa. Each foreign organization, each European review has on the whole
pursued its previous policy. Gradually the editorial spectrum has also been
complemented by the *Journal of African History*, from 1960, the *West African
Journal of Archaeology*, from 1971, *Azania*, from 1965, *World Archaeology*,
and *Niame Akuma* since 1972 in North America.

New dating methods

The increase and improvement in methods of dating* have helped to
construct the chronological framework which was lacking for the African
past. Today the guidelines for the last 10,000 years of the life of the continent,
including its northern parts, are securely based and numerous. They must
include the contribution of laboratory work to the study of pottery, copper,
iron, gold, and the coins struck from them, as well as some other fields in the
course of expansion. The dating of pottery by thermoluminescence* adds to
the basic elements of our knowledge in the most spectacular fashion. It has
just enabled archaeologists to establish the paramount place in African
history of the large-scale manufacture of terracotta statues, hitherto hard to

date. These products, attested from Mauretania to Cameroon (at the present
state of research), stretch over the last three millennia.

The chemical analysis of pastes helps to establish with increasing accuracy
the reasons for technological choices of fabrication and firing, to identify the
place where the objects were manufactured and hence the possible range of
their distribution. Research on iron has not yet produced such spectacular
results. However, we can already see that the study of basic metallurgy
(production of metal) is becoming an area of great importance for the years to
come. As for copper, analyses are multiplying. They reveal the spectrum of
alloys (bronzes made with lead greatly intrigue the specialists), the art of
soldering and the antiquity of the use of lost-wax* moulds.

Nor should one omit the importance of the analysis of African gold and the
promising palynological* studies of soils and construction materials. Here it
is more useful to point out that hematology is becoming important for the
archaeologist. The study of blood samples is opening up the study of diseases.
In this field too "archeometry" is going to enrich the history of Africa.

Within a very short time archeometry has given archaeologists working in
Africa the means to define brand new fields of research. Unfortunately, it only
makes them more dependent on those who, providing the financial resources
indispensable to the success of such research, are still in a position to direct its
course as they wish and in fact to oppose the effective disclosure of the past
which sleeps in the soil of Africa. To some extent archaeology is an interesting
and significant example of current confrontations between an imperious self-
confident north and a south which does not always formulate its projects,
wishes and policy clearly enough.

The origin of man and his first habitats

Two million years ago our earliest ancestors were shaping tools, constructing temporary camps and sharing their food—all characteristically human activities identified by archaeologists in the last two decades.

Eastern Africa, cut through by the Great Rift Valley linking Lake Tanganyika to the Jordan Valley, appears to be, at least on the basis of our present state of knowledge, the part of the world where the most significant event in terms of our development took place: the quiet and gradual emergence of the *Homo* genus. Yet Raymond Dart's discovery in 1924 in the cave at Taung, of australopithecines, creatures which are no longer apes but are not yet men, had created an expectation that southern Africa would prove to be the cradle of humankind. Then, in 1960, L.S.B. Leakey* found in the Olduvai Gorge, Tanzania, among shaped stone tools of the type called Oldowan*, a skull differing from that of the "ape-man" *Australopithecus boisei*￼ which came from the same level, Bed I. This he named *Homo habilis*￼ (handy man) to make it clear that this creature must have been the creator of the stone tools — 1,800,000 years ago! New finds at Koobi-Fora, Shungura in the Omo valley and especially in Ethiopian Afar have led paleontologists to revise the date for the emergence of the *Homo* genus to more than 3,000,000 years ago. And finally the discovery of a 40 percent "complete" skeleton by the international team in Afar has been the paleontological event of recent years: D. Johanson and T. White place *Australopithecus afarensis*￼ (Lucy) 3,500,000BP (before the present) on the tree of our common ancestors. The contemporary footprints amazingly preserved in the solidified volcanic ash at Laetoli in Tanzania are a remarkable and moving witness to the bipedal locomotion of these hominids. It was not until later, *c.*2,500,000BP, that the australopithecines were to branch out from the *Homo* line of descent, though *Australopithecus robustus*￼ persisted till *c.*1,000,000BP. P. Tobias believes in a fairly similar genealogical tree. Y. Coppens on the other hand thinks that "Lucy" might be more of a distant cousin, with the roots of the development of the *Homo* genus going much farther back. Finally, R. Leakey considers the branch of the australopithecines as completely separate from that of the humans for these periods.

The development of man is linked not only to an upright stance and increase in the volume of the brain, but also to the consequences brought about by these changes, such as the freeing of the front limbs: the availability of the hand meant that it was possible to hold a tool or a weapon while moving. For the prehistorian the true criterion for the emergence of man is usually judged to be the presence of worked tools. Stone objects could be used directly for cutting, crushing scratching, or indirectly for contriving wooden tools or weapons.

The use of manufactured objects must have resulted in the relative stability of a human group. Camps may have been set up on a provisional, mobile basis, as stopping-places for nomadic eaters of fruit or molluscs, or hunters who would stay long enough to prepare a weapon, to break the fruit or seeds collected, or skin the animal. There are only fleeting vestiges left as evidence for these unstructured camps, but oddly enough it is in fact these which provide evidence of the earliest hominid settlements, as if the temporary camp was hierarchically speaking an intermediate stage between the overnight stopping place of the large primates and Paleolithic man's base camp. It is very probable that the earliest evidence of worked objects goes back to 3,000,000BC in the lower Omo valley in Ethiopia; but the earliest tools found in stratigraphy* are believed to date from 2,600,000BP, and come from Ethiopian Afar; and the oldest camp was found in the Omo Valley at Shungura, on the shores of the ancient Lake Turkana. In Omo site 71, a quartz pebble chopper* was found together with fragments of mammal and fish bones. In Omo site 123 (2,000,000BP), on a silt-laden bank that had been buried, tipped over and raised up again, hominids have left traces of their brief stay: there are fragments of quartz pebbles, broken off by percussion, small chips or flakes resulting from making a chopper or broken off from a core*, sometimes used as they were, seldom worked on any further. These particular kind of tools, known as Shungurian*, are earlier than the Oldowan tools of eastern Africa. The hominids who lived at the time of these camps were *Australopithecus africanus*￼ and *Australopithecus robustus* .

Evidence of social life

The base camp was a permanent site to which man kept returning; an organized habitat, some of its outlines are known to us, either from indications of the positioning of the structures (huts or branch shelters) or from the artificial accumulation of stones, tools and remains of animals. What do these mean? They are the first evidence of social life, of the group being a fixed entity, generally settling near a source of water and shores which provided them with pebbles for manufacturing tools. The presence of broken bones is also the first concrete evidence that man was a meat-eater, and so a hunter: he probably robbed the big predators of the wounded or dead animals that were their prey, thus acting as a scavenger, and he would quite easily have been able to hunt small game or even to use his cunning to capture large mammals using spears or other wooden or bone weapons, made with stone implements.

In the Olduvai camps at Melka-Kunture and Koobi Fora there are a good many choppers, but there is a surprising variety of shape, size and weight, indicating different functions. We also find polyhedra*, as well as notched* tools, scrapers*, planes* and burins*, all made from pebbles. Items made from flakes are used, and were to increase considerably in number and quality from the Early Acheulian* to the Middle Paleolithic periods. As the size of tools made from flakes gradually decreased, humans of the post-Acheulian period eventually achieved mobility and independence from natural surroundings, for the lighter tools became easier to transport, together with small cores from which tools were made. Often broken bones would be roughly worked into shape and used as tools (Makapansgat in South Africa); there must also have been wooden weapons, but these have not been preserved. The camp must also have been a place of rest and security. The sites can be detected on the ground by an accumulation of stones and objects, more or less circular in shape, as at Olduvai (1,800,000BP), or by an absence of objects in certain areas suggesting some obstacle such as a bush or some other barrier, as at Melka Kunture (1,600,000BP and 1,000,000BP). Some animals build improvised shelters, but the conjunction of a shelter and worked tools is truly characteristic of man. Throughout the Oldowan period two lines of descent existing contemporaneously can be observed: that of the australopithecines, *Australopithecus robustus*, and *Australopithecus boisei* (Olduvai), and that of *Homo, Homo habilis* (Olduvai) or an archaic *Homo erectus*￼ (Melka Kunture). The Oldowan is found both in the south of Africa and in the north African Maghreb (Sidi-Abderrahman, Aïn Hanech).

The first bifacial tools

The first signs of the Acheulian can be seen in Tanzania at Olduvai around 1,400,000BP. The first true bifacial* tools would seem to date from the same time as the presence of burnt clay, apparently evidence of fire already being used for domestic purposes, observed in the Chesowanja layer in Kenya and in a site in the mid-Awash valley in Ethiopia. The Acheulian makes a gradual appearance at Melka Kunture about 1,000,000BP. But first signs of it are later in other areas. However, around 700,000 years ago, *Homo erectus* left evidence of his passing throughout most of Africa, with a large number of bifacial tools, some small axes and the first bolas* (throwing stones), along with small flake tools which are amazingly varied in shape and type.

Okobambi hut and the earliest habitat

At the Olduvai Gorge, Tanzania, base of Bed I dating from 1,800,000 years ago, M. Leakey discovered a site rich in bones and stone tools, a circular structure, and a sort of protuberance partly made from large fallen stones. It suggests a shelter made of branches, covered with grass and wedged at the base by large upright stones like this present-day hut of the Okobambi, a people of Southwest Africa. After a photograph by MacCalman and Grobbelaar in *Olduvai Gorge*, vol. 3, M.D. Leakey, Cambridge University Press.

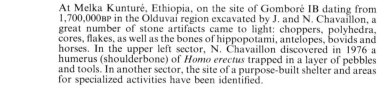

***Homo erectus* in the pre-Acheulean site of Gomboré**

At Melka Kunturé, Ethiopia, on the site of Gomboré IB dating from 1,700,000BP in the Olduvai region excavated by J. and N. Chavaillon, a great number of stone artifacts came to light: choppers, polyhedra, cores, flakes, as well as the bones of hippopotami, antelopes, bovids and horses. In the upper left sector, N. Chavaillon discovered in 1976 a humerus (shoulderbone) of *Homo erectus* trapped in a layer of pebbles and tools. In another sector, the site of a purpose-built shelter and areas for specialized activities have been identified.

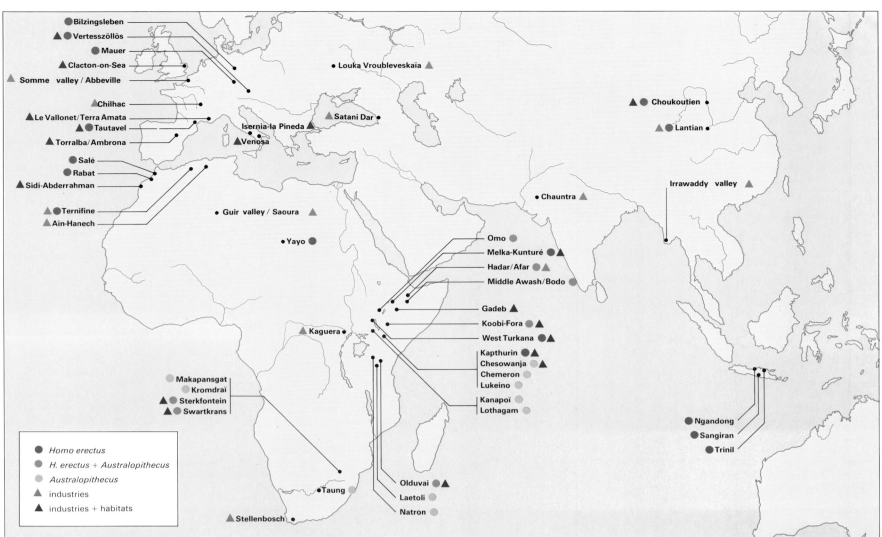

Legend (map)

- ● Homo erectus
- ◑ H. erectus + Australopithecus
- ○ Australopithecus
- ▲ industries
- ▲ industries + habitats

Map labels:
Bilzingsleben, Vertesszöllös, Mauer, Clacton-on-Sea, Somme valley / Abbeville, Chilhac, Le Vallonet/Terra Amata, Tautavel, Torralba/Ambrona, Isernia-la Pineda, Satani Dar, Venosa, Salé, Rabat, Sidi-Abderrahman, Ternifine, Aïn-Hanech, Guir valley / Saoura, Yayo, Louka Vroubleveskaïa, Choukoutien, Lantian, Irrawaddy valley, Chauntra, Omo, Melka-Kunturé, Hadar/Afar, Middle Awash/Bodo, Gadeb, Koobi-Fora, West Turkana, Kapthurin, Chesowanja, Chemeron, Lukeino, Kanapoi, Lothagam, Kaguera, Makapansgat, Kromdrai, Sterkfontein, Swartkrans, Taung, Stellenbosch, Olduvai, Laetoli, Natron, Ngandong, Sangiran, Trinil

Archaeological deposits and sites of hominids of the Pleiocene and Early Pleistocene periods

The main discoveries dating from 3,500,000 to 700,000BP are shown on this map of the ancient world. The oldest of the high-density zones is east Africa, then come South Africa and lastly the shores of the Mediterranean. The deposits in the USSR, India, Indonesia and China are more dispersed. But all affirm that migrations could have taken place as from 2,000,000BP, with East Africa as their starting-point.

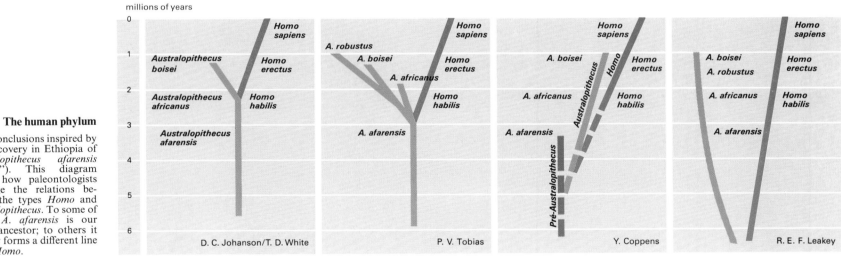

millions of years

The human phylum

Four conclusions inspired by the discovery in Ethiopia of *Australopithecus afarensis* ("Lucy"). This diagram shows how paleontologists envisage the relations between the types *Homo* and *Australopithecus*. To some of them, *A. afarensis* is our direct ancestor; to others it already forms a different line from *Homo*.

Diagram 1 (D. C. Johanson/T. D. White): Homo sapiens, Homo erectus, Homo habilis; Australopithecus boisei, Australopithecus africanus, Australopithecus afarensis

Diagram 2 (P. V. Tobias): Homo sapiens, Homo erectus, Homo habilis; A. robustus, A. boisei, A. africanus, A. afarensis

Diagram 3 (Y. Coppens): Homo sapiens, Homo erectus, Homo habilis; A. boisei, A. africanus, A. afarensis; Australopithecus, Homo, Pré-Australopithecus

Diagram 4 (R. E. F. Leakey): Homo sapiens, Homo erectus, Homo habilis; A. boisei, A. robustus, A. africanus, A. afarensis

J. Chavaillon

Ground of pre-Acheulean habitat

Excavations by G. and M. Piperno at Melka Kunturé, Ethiopia, Garba IV, evolved Olduwan period, dating from 1,400,000–1,300,000BP. In the centre we see a fragment of a long large bone; it has been split to extract the marrow by a heavy chopper like that placed beside it.

The oldest encampments of hominids

The Omo Valley, Ethiopia, Shungura: 2,000,000BP site at Omo 123, excavated by the International Omo mission. This is the site of one of the excavations by J. Chavaillon. In the mud of the River Omo deposited between two eruptions of volcanic ash were found the remains of provisional encampments used by hominids.

J. Chavaillon

The evolution of the environment and archaeology

In the last 10,000 years Africa has undergone extraordinary climatic fluctuations; the archaeology of the Sahara has revealed the remains of fishing villages in today's waterless desert.

The development of climate in Africa is marked from the Quaternary by alternating wet and dry phases. These various oscillations, as archaeology shows, have caused profound changes in the environment in which man has lived, and by the same token have forced him to adapt his way of life to the demands of biotopes* or ecosystems undergoing radical change.

From the Holocene* (c.10,000 years ago), which saw the last great humid phase, archaeologists can clearly follow man's adaptation to his surroundings. The Saharan and Sahelian areas offer a rich field for the study of Stone Age environment. These areas, now desert and completely inhospitable to life, contain a large number of sites of human occupation testifying to the profound change in climate. The environment 10,000 years ago was better supplied with water; sites of permanent and seasonal settlements are found near former lakes, which can themselves be recognized by the blocks of travertine (a type of porous rock) left as they dried out. The inhabitants of these areas lived off fishing, as witnessed by the large number of bone harpoons and the traces of a plentiful freshwater wildlife: fish, molluscs, crocodiles, turtles etc. This "aquatic civilization" varied and supplemented its diet by hunting, gathering and to some extent by cattle-rearing. The remains of what is described as "Ethiopian" fauna (elephants, hippopotamuses, giraffes, buffalo, rhinoceroses, etc.) are evidence of the existence of adequate vegetation cover. Purely descriptive pollen inventories had led many writers to affirm the existence of a tropical vegetation with essentially Mediterranean flora, but recent research and new methods in palynology* suggest that this picture of the Saharan landscape is no longer tenable. What is more readily accepted today is that in the Holocene the vegetation found in the modern Sahel area extended farther northwards into the Sahara by some three or four degrees of latitude. As is still the case in Sahel today, where water was available there was a greater density of human settlements.

Carbon 14* datings suggest that settled communities remained in the central Sahara until about 4000BP (before present). Then the drying up of the land forced them to disperse to be nearer permanent or temporary water sources in more southern areas, or to the mountains where the altitude tempered the extremes of climate: striking examples for the Neolithic period are at Tichitt on the shores of Lake Aouker (Mauritania) and at Karikarichinkat in the Tilemsi Valley (Mali). In the Egyptian desert the inhabitants had recourse to the terraces of the Nile, far from the seasonal flood areas, where they simultaneously exploited river resources and those still provided by the desert.

The effects of desiccation

From the 5th millennium BC, the last lakes and rivers of the southern Sahara failed in their turn. Rain levels fell sharply to reach the current averages. Human habitation was considerably reduced. Small groups with a strong capacity for adaptation remained in the Sahara, but mainly there were nomadic tribes travelling over the desert and leaving only graves as evidence of their passing. The 5th millennium is the starting point of a general process in which fertile land became desert, a process which is still continuing in an inexorable curve today. However, it is accepted by many writers that within this process of "desertification", minor upward turns towards humidity have occurred, namely in the 7th, 14th and 17th centuries AD, making possible a temporary recolonization of areas that had become inhospitable to life. Such a rise in humidity—probably that of the 7th century—may have led to the emergence and development of the medieval fortified towns on the southern fringes of the Sahara. Excavations of the site of Tegdaoust in the Noudache cirque in Mauritania show that the town of Aoudaghost was founded in a climatic context remote from the present-day aridity of the area. There was of course no longer any question of its being a lakeside environment, but water was plentiful, due to a deep underground water table, and there was sufficient plant life to maintain herds of cattle. It was in a biotope or ecosystem such as this that Aoudaghost was developed to its maximum economic success. From the 13th century there was a marked deterioration in the biotope: the water level dropped, the plant cover deteriorated in quality, and in the course of the years these processes accelerated. In the 14th century water became so scarce that urban life in Aoudaghost ceased to be possible.

The tendency towards increasing aridity indicated by archaeological data over nearly 3,000 years reflects a profound change in climate. But though this climatic change explains the dryness, it does not in itself account for the spread of the desert. Human factors such as overgrazing and deforestation have played a considerable role, at least locally, in speeding up the process of ecological degradation. This was the conclusion reached by Jean Devisse at Aoudaghost, and it was also used by Randi Häland to explain, in part, the deterioration of the environment in Mema (Mali). This Sahelian area where few people live today still afforded extremely favourable conditions for humans in the 11th century. This is proved by the large number of toguere (banks of earth showing human occupation) lying along the dead Delta of the Niger. The population fished, cultivated land and reared sheep and goats, but first and foremost they were very active in the manufacture of metal goods which required the use of a great deal of wood. By using up the wood and exploiting grazing land beyond a point where species could be regenerated, man undoubtedly contributed towards the acceleration of the process of environmental impoverishment which climatic factors made inevitable.

In equatorial regions pollen studies of the various sites, complemented by geomorphological observations, show that the men of the Upper Pleistocene* lived in a semi-arid environment, hunting such big game as the savannah offered. In the Holocene, a resurgence of the flora suited to wet, warm conditions can be observed, following a swing towards a more humid climate. It is generally considered that this humid period, contemporary with that observed in Saharan regions, lasted until the 6th millennium BC.

The various changes in the environment forced man, while it was still possible to do so, to work out a strategy to ensure his own survival. The method of studying variations in the environment during the most recent millennia, based on archaeological observation, has enabled us to open up a whole chapter in the history of mankind in Africa.

Millstone and grinder

In the now desolate regions of the Sahara, careful observation can still reveal made objects indicating intensive occupation during the prehistoric period.

Harpoons and fishhooks

Numerous sites with bone implements indicate that the prehistoric peoples of the Sahara practised fishing at a time when the desert had not yet reached its present degree of hyperaridity. Collection I.F.A.N., Dakar.

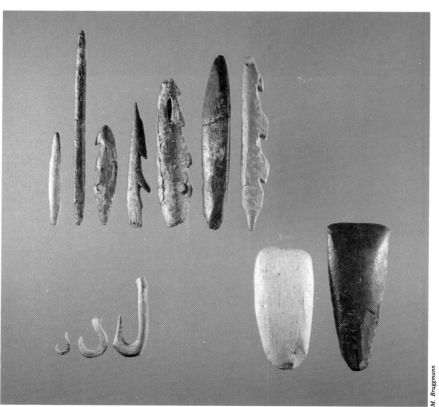

Basic map of the Sahara in the Quaternary

At the time of the last phase of humidity in the Sahara a certain number of lakes reappeared. Their geological traces still exist in what are today desert landscapes. After H.J. Hugot, 1974.

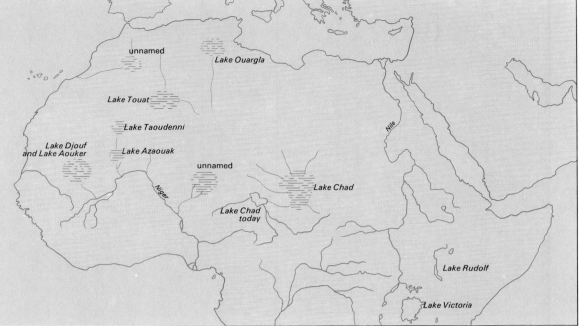

Sites yielding fishing implements

Semi-permanent and permanent habitats where the main activity was fishing have been revealed on the shores of most of the ancient lakes and watercourses in the Sahara and East Africa. Phillipson: *The Later Prehistory of Eastern and Southern Africa*, London, 1977.

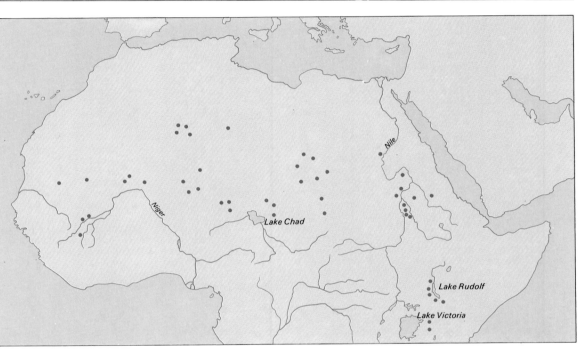

Northwest Sudan

This Landsat photograph of northwest Sudan is a remarkable illustration of the ancient hydrographical system of the Sahara. Beneath 6m (20ft) of sand, the satellite image reveals (upper dark area) a valley as large as the Nile's. Dark lines in the lower part also indicate river systems.

Traces of hominids at Laetoli, Tanzania

This deposit dating to nearly 4 million years ago has preserved, due to exceptional circumstances, the imprints of a hominid and animals of various kinds, such as the prints of a three-toed horse (*Hipparion*), seen in the lower right-hand area. This has enabled archaeologists to reconstruct the environment of the ancestor of man.

Archaeology and the history of art

From 10,000-year-old rock paintings to 17th century terracottas, African art is a fertile field for art historians; but it can be misleading for archaeological interpretation.

Early African art was a peculiar, but perfectly serviceable, instrument of communication. In every society art is a privileged reflection of the integration of economic and religious factors. It is archaeology's job to reconstitute the situations in which these works were produced in order to explain them. Enormous damage is done when the contexts in which they were found are destroyed and when these works are stolen. Taking them by stealth from the place where they are buried, thus preventing them from ever being accurately dated, selling them illegally and scattering them overseas deprives Africa of its heritage irrevocably.

Until recently researchers contented themselves with analysing early cultural products from Africa according to historical criteria; the findings often served to verify assertions made in oral or written sources. Each period was encapsulated by a fixed description and provided with a kind of standard analysis. Interpretation was no more than providing an ethnic label and assessing the diffusion of cultural exchanges between societies that were basically static. Even now early African works of art seen within the context of an overall perception of the development of "art" are often assigned to a "primitive" stage. This point of view provides little real illumination of the subject under study.

A classic case of artistic material being put to use in this way is that of the cartographical reconstitution of the routes followed by trans-Saharan wagons. Herodotus speaks of Libyan Garamantes on wagons harnessed with horses pursuing cave-dwelling, supposedly black Ethiopians. So a search was instituted for paintings and drawings of wagons, and today more than 600 are known. Based on the places where they were found, some scholars have put forward the idea that there were at least two regular trading routes across the Sahara: from Tripolitania to Gao via Abalessa and Tademekka, and from around Oran to the inland delta of the Niger at Goundam. This theory is being questioned today. The "routes" coincide with nothing but the pictures, some of which are in inaccessible places; the wagons shown are too light to have been used as a means of transport for bartered goods. Nonetheless, some scholars have suggested that the pictures mark out the lines of penetration of the Sahara by the Paleo-Berbers; others that the wagons acted as prestige symbols for the aristocrats of the Sahara. The debate is still going on, but it seems to be inconclusive and of limited interest.

Any chance of throwing light on the social relations obtaining in the Sahara has unfortunately been limited by giving pride of place to chronology, with stultifying effects. Around the 10th to the 7th millennium BC is thought to be the period of the large grassland animals: the "era of the ancient bubal"; from possibly the 7th to the 6th millennium there are symbolic representations from the "era of the round heads"; from 6000 to 1200BC, the period of the herdsmen, with extremely naturalistic representations of large herds of domesticated animals, scenes from everyday life, and inter-community fights; the "era of the horse" and of the wagons came next, then that of the dromedary, from 300AD.

Several writers explain the transition from one phase to the next by a migration. But this approach is not capable of explaining why some of the themes are absent from some areas in the Sahara; for example, it is rare to find anything to do with herding in the Aïr massif, while excavations at Adrar Bous have shown that cattle were domesticated between 4310 and 3310BC. Some areas have their own sequences: in the Dra and Atlas areas, for example there is great stress on the spheroid ram during the "bubal period", and cattle do not count for much in late naturalistic art. A preoccupation with dividing everything into phases has imprisoned "cave painting". In investigating this subject, few expeditions have conducted stratigraphic excavations on nearby sites. The "Neolithic" deposits at Tassili, Ennedi, Jebel Uweinat and Aaggar date from the 6th–5th millennia; are they or are they not contemporary with the "herding phase"? Radiocarbon datings are few and far between. A hearth associated with remnants of a painted wall from the "herding phase" at Uan Muhuggiag (Acacus) is dated at between 3090 and 2470BC; these paintings may have been made in the late herding era; a charcoal residue, dating from the 5th millennium, was attached to a painted wall from the recent "round heads" period at Uan Telocat; silhouettes of animals on pebbles or ostrich eggshells have been found at Taforalt near Oran—the media on which they are drawn date from the 9th millennium BC—and at Tarfaya—where they date from the beginning of the 1st millennium BC. Very laboriously we can garner from these data a few pieces of information about the culture and the environment of the hunter-gatherers of the Sahara prior to the 8th millennium BC, about the reasons for the emergence of ceramics, about the change in methods of working stone at the period known as the Neolithic of the Sahara-Sudanese tradition, and about the origins of animal husbandry. There have been recent cautious attempts to link some of the scenes represented with the Berbers' rain ceremonies, the Peul people's initiation rites, and the mythological motifs of the Tuareg people.

Rock paintings in southern Africa

While the Sahara has suffered from an excessive categorization of objects according to periods, southern Africa on the other hand benefits from a lack of precision: for the 8,000 years covered by the Wilton* and Smithfield* "industries", rock paintings can be linked to either one or the other culture; many scholars attribute the 150,000 rock drawings known in this area to the immediate ancestors of the San (Bushman) people. The dating of the amino-acids surviving in the paintings, and that of the archaeological remains, invalidate theories of the recent nature of most of the pictures: four "tombstones" from the southern Cape area have been given radiocarbon* datings of the 1st millennium BC and the 1st millennium AD; we have post-AD datings for layers taken from rock paintings at Glen Elliott Shelter (Cape) and Sehonghong (Drakensberg). Datings at other sites reveal long continuity and conservative attitudes in the choice of subject matter. Engraved and painted pebbles have been found in deposits relating to the 5th and 4th millennia BC (Boomphaas and Matjes river shelter); fragments of painted and engraved rock have been brought back from Wonderweek (northern Cape Province) and various caves in Zimbabwe. The dating of seven stone slabs decorated with human and animal themes from the Apollo 11 site (near Brandberg), dated between 26,900/26,000BC and 24,750/23,950BC, raises far more problems.

Ethnologists who study the peoples of this area tell us that their culture has continued unbroken throughout a long period of time, and this encourages interpretations linking their life to their environment. The Spatial Unit for Archaeological Research (Cape) is integrating its thorough research on the sites at Elands Bay to other work relating to more than 1,000 sites with rock paintings in the interior of the continent; from this it is inferring models of seasonal movements to make use of the resources available; these movements seem to have led to the concentration and dispersal of communities and the localization of specific activities. But other scholars prefer a symbolic interpretation; in their eyes art is used to communicate social values, the coherence of the people's culture, along with the specific rites depicted. Yet others see the art as a public expression of extraordinary private experiences, or ceremonies such as a state of trance. These new explanations have all eclipsed the argument of "art for art's sake", and that of sympathetic magic, dear to Frazer. Only 29 of the 3,909 scenes recorded at Ndedema Gorge are hunting scenes; the most frequently portrayed hunted animal, the eland, is depicted only four times.

Generally speaking the study of rock paintings is very neglected: yet the great naturalist tradition of central Tanzania and the herding pictures of Ethiopia and Somalia have the same potential importance for an understanding of Africa's past. In western Angola, samples dated by radiocarbon to between the 9th and 6th millennia BC are probably from engraved or painted schematic representations of human beings.

Terracotta figures and their meaning

More recent sites have yielded terracotta statuettes; these are indicators of the emergence of herarchical societies and are linked to the development of towns and long-distance trading. Hundreds have been illegally exported from the inland delta of the Niger (Mali); the only study that can be made of them now is descriptive and typological, superficial at best. However we do have four statuettes and a good many heads which have been found in their stratigraphic position at Jenné-Jeno (Mali), dating from between the 9th and 13th century. These figures shed light on the bases of social relationships at Jenné-Jeno, and in other developing hierarchical societies: for example, those that created the 700 hillocks in the Chad region, or the Kareygourou-Birniwol site in Niger—two areas where an elaborate tradition of terracotta images is to be found during the 1st and 2nd millennia AD. The growing number of groups of people with a special function in the life of these communities—classes of producers, specialists, different ethnic groups—created a more complex pattern of inter-dependency and a greater need for objects symbolizing membership of the community.

Some authorities propose that art provides a key to the constellation of signs from which in the past a unifying discourse was born. But we must expect a disconcerting variety in the decorative motifs and the way they were used, especially in the inland delta of the Niger. It was possible for terracotta figures to have a specific function: among the Agan-Agni people in the Ivory Coast and Ghana commemorative figurines dating from the early 17th century are clearly connected with the funerals of the élite. But in the absence of any scientific excavation, we can only postulate theories as to the purpose of the terracotta figures of the Bassari people, the stone statuettes of the Kissi (Guinea), and the stone representations of the Nomoli* in Sierra Leone, among the Esie and at Cross River (Nigeria).

Of more than 200 terracotta figures found around Nok in an area 160 by 480km (99 × 297 miles), only four come from properly conducted excavations: at Samon Dukiya, Targa, and Katsina Ala. However, there can be no doubt that the Nok culture lies between the 8th century BC and the 2nd century AD. Its iconography and the diversity of places with vestiges of settlement and ironworking have resulted in the need to consider a great variety of objects: amulets, ornaments for thatched roofs, altars to the fruitfulness of the earth, and symbols relating to the upper level of a social hierarchy. But we do not know much about how this stretch of country came to adopt shared forms of expression at the very time when there is first evidence of a hierarchical structure in Nigerian society.

Artistic themes indicating the emergence of complex political communities can be seen right across the continent. Meroe's synthesizing art links Nubian naturalism and more formal elements originating from Egypt. Metalworking and terracotta production in the forests of present day Nigeria are a more recent discovery; many scholars were at first reluctant to accept the 9th century datings given by radiocarbon methods for excavations carried out at the Igbo Ukwu site, where insignia of power made of bronze, lead, or tin were found in a prepared depository and in a hole in which they had been deliberately placed. A grave containing a person of high rank and his servants yielded copper, bronze, cornelian beads, (probably from the Sahara), and 100,000 glass beads from the Mediterranean. It is now generally accepted that goods were imported to Igbo Ukwu from the north across the Sahara—no doubt the same was true of Jenné-Jeno centuries earlier—well before the large-scale trade across it relating to gold.

From the middle of the 1st millennium AD Ife grew rich through trade with the north based on cola products, ivory and slaves; before 1400 it became the religious centre of the Yoruba country. From 1150 to 1450 Ife produced a huge quantity of realistic portraits in terracotta, copper and bronze alloyed with lead. We have 25 radiocarbon datings for 7 carefully excavated localities; at Ita Yemoo and Lafogido Obalara works were found in their original settings. These objects fulfilled a multiplicity of functions: tomb decorations, memorials for second funerals, substitutes for sacrifices. Even though no site containing ancient works of art has yet been found in early Benin, dates ascribed to busts and plaques confirm the date traditionally given—*c.*1100—for the development of the power of the Oba* (Yoruba chief). The Oba kept "state artists" totally dependent on him; their output, which was standardized and very regimented, glorifies the gods and the Oba's ancestors; there is a very marked contrast with the development of art that was independent of authority, as at Jenné-Jeno for example.

In the forests of central Africa few examples of statues have been found so far, except for an 18th century terracotta head (Group X) at Kingabwa-Kinshasa and anthropomorphic pottery items from the classic Kisalian period (10th–14th century) in the Upemba basin; once again the appearance of the latter coincides with the emergence of the earliest known social stratification. The earliest item of carved wood known at present came from Liavela (Lunda in Angola); it dates from the 8th century.

We are only beginning to know ancient African art thanks to the archaeological and scientific study of its cultural contexts and to the development and broadening of the hypotheses for interpreting it. We can consider rock art as an open window through which we can observe ritual acts and beliefs. Another form of artistic output may give information about groups which shared the same iconography and ideology to the point of forming vast provinces with a common means of expression, as in the inland delta of the Niger, at Nok, around Lake Chad, among the Akan people, in the Upemba area, and the area between the Limpopo and the Zambezi; this output coincided with the emergence of hierarchical societies.

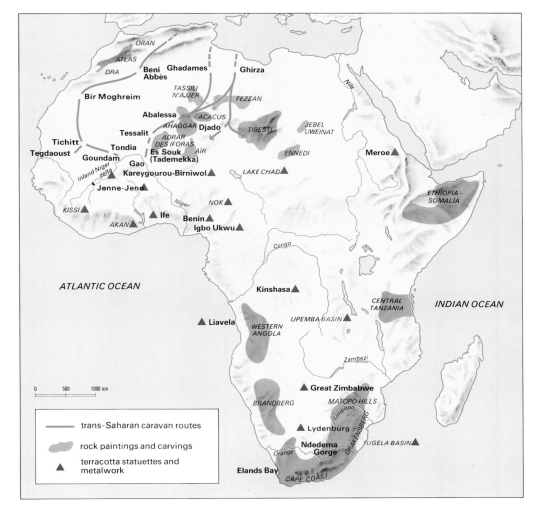

Terracotta head found at Ndaloa (Ivory Coast), 17th century AD

This head, found with two others on the shore of the Aby lagoon, belongs to the Eotile culture. The archaeological context of the ethnological and historical research suggests these heads were ritual portraits executed when high-ranking chiefs died. Institute of Art, Archaeology and History, Abidjan.

Androgynous Jenné-Jeno figurine (Mali) 12th–13th century AD

One of the finest terracotta pieces found in a stratigraphical context, this statuette nevertheless lay in a deposit of minor importance. It was buried in a sector which had already been abandoned as the rest of the city was experiencing the last moments of its evolution. In view of the other proofs of the rising influence of Islam on the city's commercial elite, this statue, and the set of African beliefs contained in its remarkable iconography, were sacrificed to the now universal religion. Jenné-Jeno itself was a victim; at the end of the 13th or in the 14th century, the city was transferred to Djenné, 3km (2 miles) away, perhaps to avoid ground "polluted" by ancient pagan practices.

Cave of Sebaaieni, valley of Ndedema, (South Africa, 16th–17th century BC)

This scene, which superimposes depictions of elands, symbols of power, on other human and animal representations, has been the subject of various interpretations discussed in the text. The people are assembled for a ritual ceremony, with a medium in a trance. This religious theme appears in many aspects: figures wearing masks representing elands' heads and the death of elands. In other representations, the trance is symbolized by a nasal haemorrhage, by arms flung backwards or by death-dealing winged creatures.

Archaeology and trade

African archaeology today is shifting its interest away from trans-continental trade in "luxury goods" to that of ordinary objects which reveal the movement of peoples and techniques through the continent.

Until a short time ago archaeology was merely required to supply the proof and follow the tracks of the large-scale trade which, especially after the 9th century, linked Africa more or less strongly to outside world economies. For this reason too much weight was probably attached to the importation into some towns of the Sahel or on the eastern coast of fine ceramic ware and glass from the Moslem world. Study of these in the laboratory today does at least supply conclusive proof of their origin and the long distances they travelled; but despite the abundance of the material, these items, like the Chinese celadon ware found in eastern Africa and Madagascar, were of interest only to a very limited market, socially and geographically; they were not part of significant large-scale trade with the interior of the continent.

Trade in precious stones, pearls and shells for adornment, which was once a subject of great interest to archaeologists, also seems to have lost some of its importance. More of these items were produced within the continent than was thought even recently, but there was a limited number of customers for such things, even allowing for the vagaries of taste. "Luxury goods" certainly provided non-African merchants with the means of exerting pressure; but generally speaking they had no very great economic significance, as the volume or continuity of output of these objects was not of any great size.

On the other hand, archaeology has highlighted the originality of the material cultures of Africa, and this is providing an increasingly coherent framework for the history of African societies. The importance of trade of every kind, evidence of the movement of people, goods and techniques within the continent, and the ways in which imported techniques and products were selectively adopted, are coming to be ever better known. Gradually archaeology is also helping us to understand how the products basic to the diet of early peoples were chosen, grown and traded. The discovery of grains of cultivated African rice, *Oryza glaberrima*, at Jenné-Jeno in Mali, helps archaeologists to formulate how, at the beginning of the first millenium AD, rice producers traded this commodity in areas where iron was manufactured. Several millennia ago in Cameroon the oil palm was already supplying seeds, carbonized remains of which have been found; cabbages and lentils were cultivated at Niani in Guinea in the 9th century. When we have been able to establish the routes and the chronology by which sorghum*, millet and yams* travelled from Africa to the rest of the world, and by which bananas, mangoes and date palms came into Africa from outside, we will be much better informed. The stages and methods by which peasant communities adopted plants from America after 1500, and the study of the ensuing revolution in diet, form part of the field of archaeological research. A related area is the study of

the spread of cattle of the sanga or zebu* type over the past two millennia. The earliest indications of the techniques for drying and smoking fish in the western coastal areas and in Mali suggest that even before our era Africa was involved in trading this precious food commodity over considerable distances. Through the evidence of food refuse, the study of human and animal excreta, and pollens, we will soon be able to follow the stages of dietary evolution on the continent and of the methods used to store protein. The forms that trade took and the way societies were organized may become clear if we can follow this lead.

As the basic diet changed, salt from all sources was ever more necessary to man's survival, and much study has been devoted to this during the last 20 years. Salt can be obtained from the evaporation of seawater, by leaching the soil in brackish lagoons as at the Bight of Benin, by washing the ash produced by halophytic* (salt-storing) plants as at Burundi or Tanzania, by collecting efflorescences (Senegal), by treating water rich in sodium carbonate (Niger, Tanzania) or by extracting slabs of rock salt (Western Sahara, Ethiopia, Namibia); salt can be transported, or animals can be taken to restorative salt waters. Much research has been done, but so far nobody has put these studies together to examine the movement and economic significance of this major trading commodity in the course of the last two millennia.

Gold, metals and other currency systems

Archaeology has as yet given us little information about goods exported by Africa. Even if, as at Tegdaoust in Mauritania for example, interesting evidence of gold-smithing has been found, archaeological knowledge of gold production and working is still inadequate. The present state of research does not give us access to information about the export, mentioned in written sources, of a considerable quantity of treated hides, of cloth dyed with indigo*, or of ivory. The study of the way in which techniques travelled is likewise vague as yet, and very poorly supported by finds. We have a few chronological points of reference as regards iron, copper and copper alloys, soldering methods, casting by the lost wax* method, cotton-weaving, woodworking and work in ivory, but these do not yet enable archaeologists to fill in the general outline which can already be discerned in the case of foodstuffs.

Africa did not adopt a system of metal coinage minted by the rulers, nor did it follow Mediterranean societies in attaching value to coins and the wealth that they could mobilize. This does not mean that Africa did not have any means of exchange, and archaeology is gradually unveiling the importance and antiquity of these. Lengths of woven cotton are still in use today as a medium of exchange and this custom goes back to the 11th century at least; but they leave few traces. Nor do

the raffia loincloths and materials made from beaten bark, used as currency reserves for dowries and trade in Central Africa, and the same is true of iron artifacts, which also do not keep well. This is not the case with the many small items made of copper and copper alloys which are to be found from the Sahel to Zambia from the 7th century on, which served as both weights and currency. The well-known cowrie shells are also found in a good state of preservation; these came from the Indian Ocean and were used for eight centuries to facilitate and betoken the exchange of goods, until their exchange value was disorganized after 1500AD when the Europeans eagerly imported great quantities of them by the boatload, and then introduced European monetary systems. The economic system of the old land of Kongo was "regulated" by the use of shellfish which were caught under a royal monopoly near Luanda. All these "currencies" which are known to us through the findings of archaeologists have still to be studied from the economic point of view.

Local trading would entail the establishment of reserved sites in the markets, and these cannot easily be identified by excavation. Middle and long-distance trading leaves more traces. Firstly, there is the presence in houses and tombs of products that are unusual in the place in which they are discovered, and which could only come from elsewhere. There is a varied range of such goods: wood, glass, textiles, ceramics, articles of adornment, various metals, fruit kernels, seeds and pollens—the remains of food obtained by hunting or fishing can also come into this category. These items enable us, in view of the number of examples found of each type and the dating of the strata where they have been preserved, to build up a picture as to the nature and scale of the trade. Temporary or permanent dwellings, and workshops and warehouses connected with production and trading activities, also leave traces behind. With a little training all archaeologists can recognize places lived in by subsistence farmers consuming their own produce, the habitats of hunter-gatherers and fishermen, and also places where merchants and craftsmen lived and worked. It is also possible to identify the groups of buildings, set apart from, for example, the sites of a royal residence where, as written sources tell us, foreign merchants lived as a community. Such groups of buildings have been identified at Kumbi Saleh (Mauritania), Niani (Guinea) and Soba (Sudan). For the present it is harder to detect whether, in places where those specializing in trade lived among the population, they frequented their own special districts as in Moslem towns. Whatever the case may be, trading exchanges created at various levels a variety of arrangements of space which those involved in a dig can identify.

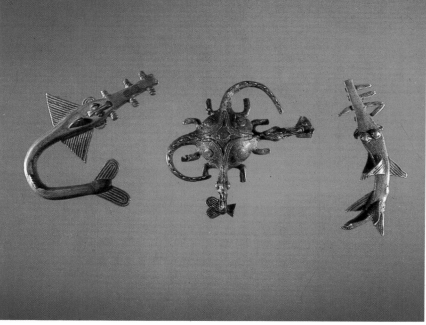

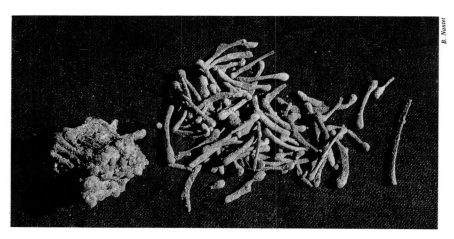

Bundle of copper wires, Mauritania

A bundle of small copper wires, found in an excavation at Kumbi Saleh, probably represents a store of valuta in units of account.

Ashanti weights, Ghana

The beauty of their form should not obscure the practical value of these standard weights. Their multiplicity made it possible to pass from one system of weighing to another, for example from Moslem to European systems.

Landscape of the Ethiopian Dalol

Salt is not as rare in Africa as was thought 20 years ago. The landscape of the Dalol (right) has spectacular salt formations in the region of Danakil. Before being transported, the salt is cut into bars (left).

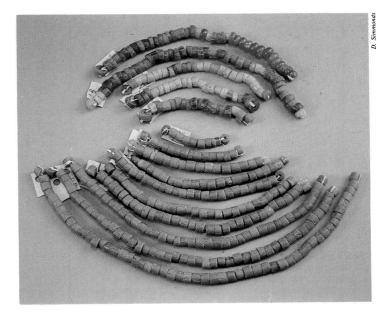

Cornelian and stone beads

Beads and stones are still traded in Africa. It was long thought that they came from afar: for example, in the case of red cornelians*. But now it is increasingly being discovered that Africa also produced these objects, sometimes in the very places where they were exchanged, very probably for high prices.

Cowries

There are several types of cowry shell. Indian Ocean shells, like those shown here, were particularly coveted. Private collection.

Copper crosses from the Upemba

The two smallest crosses date to the 17th–18th century, the largest were made around the 14th–15th century. At Copperbelt, Zambia, identical, though larger, crosses, probably date to the 8th–10th centuries. Archaeologists believe that these crosses constituted a genuine form of coinage.

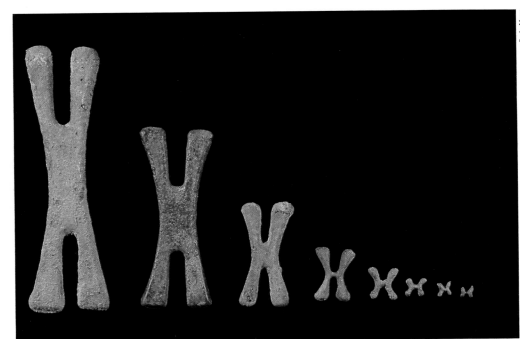

Gold and iron in western Africa

West African gold was worked long before the trans-Saharan trade with Islam in the 9th century; iron-working too is now known to go back earlier than the 5th century BC.

Gold is to be found in the soil of Africa in many forms. The deep seams that are exploited today were inaccessible to periods preceding the 19th century because they lay under water. Smaller seams lying in quartz, of irregular shape and unequal grade, were exploited by means of shafts and galleries; gold was extracted from the seam and then brought to the surface, crushed and washed. It was easier to obtain gold from eluvial strata on slopes, formed from detritus, or alluvial deposits from rivers.

Alluvial and eluvial prospecting was based on chance finds; after each rainy season grains of gold showed up in the sand and mud; trees uprooted by tornadoes uncovered accumulations of gold. Prospecting for small seams was harder. There were the so-called "gold seers" who employed magic methods about which little is known as yet, as well as iron rods which they sank into the ground; certain plants were also thought to act as reliable indicators of the presence of gold. Early exploitation was mainly based on eluvia and alluvia, eluvia being extracted by means of a great many shafts sunk to the bedrock, while alluvia were exploited by removing the dross, then washing the gold-bearing sand and gravel in a trough. It was probably these forms of extraction , which tend to be scattered and to produce a very low yield per cubic metre, that led to the fantastical descriptions of Arab authors from the 9th century on. One named Ibn al-Faqîh wrote:

Plantations of gold are made in the sand, the same way as carrots are planted. It is harvested at daybreak.

while Mad'udi explained:

There are two gold-producing plants . . . You dig a hole and find gold roots shaped like stones . . . The gold begins to grow in the month [of August], at the time when the Nile begins to rise and swell.

In western Africa gold-bearing areas lie between longitudes 9° and 15°W and latitudes 2° to 16°N. They are found in basins that were exploited to a lesser or greater extent in earlier times in most modern countries in the region, particularly along the upper reaches of the Senegal and Niger rivers and in the pre-forest and forest zone of Sierra Leone, Guinea, the Ivory Coast, Upper Volta and Ghana. Research which has been in progress for some years leads us to think that all of these basins were producing gold for the trans-Saharan trade with the Moslems from the 9th or 10th century; but the exploitation of gold was certainly much more ancient, answering local needs and perhaps extending in some cases towards the Mediterranean.

Attempts are being made to find out what quantities were produced by the hundreds of thousands of "gold-hunters" involved, at least for some months of the year, in this very scattered exploitation. Researchers' opinions differ. It seems reasonable at present to estimate the annual production of exportable gold at four to five metric tonnes for the whole of West Africa—very little in terms of present-day requirements even for coinage. Much of the gold produced, which was organized by black traders and controlled at the point of sale by the African rulers, was distributed through the large regional markets, which varied from one period to another: Ghana, Gao, Djenné and Timbuktu were among them; but a lot of other towns also served as distribution points. There was a regular trade in gold across the Sahara between the 10th and 16th centuries for the few tonnes transported and this kept up until the colonial period. It was mainly as a result of the disorganization of African societies by the slave trade that this ancient output slowed down and dried up. Today it is possible by means of laboratory analysis to recognize in coins struck north of the Sahara gold from western Africa because of its particular composition: there is a characteristic percentage of copper and traces of silver and platinum.

Mining for iron ore

Evidence of early iron production has been found in western Africa; and ores with a high iron content are present in the lateritic crust of the earth in this area of the continent. From early times they were extracted by a great variety of techniques and methods, as different archaeological research projects have revealed. Everything nowadays seems to indicate that diffusionist theories, according to which iron metallurgy came to this region from the east via Egypt, the Sudan, Lake Chad and the loop in the River Niger, or from the north (the Sahara notwithstanding) should be abandoned.

The extremely fragmented nature of early iron metallurgy in West Africa suggests spontaneous local discoveries and archaeological research now taking place appears to offer some verification for this hypothesis. C[14]* datings indicate the great age of certain sites in which iron was produced or used. Five sites have given us dates prior to 500BC, and 34 other dates between 500BC and 550AD.

Lodes of iron were located in such a way that finding it was fairly similar to prospecting for gold. Once discovered, these lodes were exploited by one village or several working together. The ironworkers extracted the metal by means of vertical shafts of varying depth, open quarries or underground galleries.

The ore, which was transported sometimes for 10 or more kilometres (6 miles) to the furnaces, was then prepared for smelting. Wood or charcoal was used to heat the furnaces, specific types of wood being used, usually acacia. Furnaces varied greatly in size, shape and capacity. At present it is hard to establish an exact typology: but we can make a broad distinction on the basis of structure between low-hearth furnaces and furnaces proper. The low-hearth furnace was small: the bottom half, about 30cm (12in) in depth, was dug into the ground, its walls lined with clay, and the bottom carpeted with ash or straw. The superstructure, which was formed by an upward continuation from the inside of the sides, was also made of clay. At ground level a clay nozzle led into the furnace, and was linked to a pair of bellows which could be worked by one person. Under the nozzle a hole was made for removal of the cinders and slag. Inside the furnace charcoal was placed next to the nozzle. The ore was stacked between the charcoal and the opposite wall. The low-hearth furnace technique would seem to be the most ancient in western Africa. Similar furnaces dating from the 1st millennium AD have been found in central Europe (Radwan, 1962). In western Africa they sometimes continued in use until the colonial period, being used simultaneously with furnaces proper.

The word "furnace" includes a great variety of types which have still not been completely recorded. The group is subdivided into nozzle furnaces and bellows furnaces, but it would be risky at present to put forward a chronology for these two systems, which interpenetrate one another geographically. Nozzle furnaces generally stand over 2m (6.5ft) high. The system works by natural air draught induced by sets of nozzles arranged at the base of the furnace. Bellows furnaces are lower than 2m (6.5ft) in height, and are equipped with a set of bellows which ironworkers work in relays, sometimes throughout the day. Both systems are loaded in the same way, with the fuel and the ore in alternating layers.

Few research workers have attempted to estimate the amount of iron produced in pre-colonial Africa. At the end of last century, Yatenga, a metalworking centre in the north of Burkina Faso, had 150 furnaces producing 539 metric tonnes of iron (Captain Noire, 1904). But for the area as a whole no figure can yet be suggested for annual output.

Though geologists today are usually pessimistic concerning the exploitable mining resources of western Africa, the large scale of the remains of early metalworking is truly extraordinary. The thousands of shafts, trenches and collapsed galleries bear eloquent witness to the ingenuity with which generations of miners searched for ore, and the furnaces that have been found provide evidence of the skill ironworkers had in methods of smelting iron.

Nanano, Burkina Faso

Shaft sunk to find eluvial gold, excavated by J.-B. Kiethega. The notches in the side walls for descent and ascent are still intact in the upper part of the shaft. Lower down, underground water has undermined the old walls.

Women gold-washers in the region of Kemiba, Mali

Gold-washing in Africa is a mainly female activity.

**Ground traces of ancient furnaces,
north bank of the Senegal, Mauretania**

In recent years, thousands of old furnace bases have been found on the Mauritanian side of the Senegal river. The inventory was made by the Mauritanian Institute for Scientific Research. Preliminary soundings have made it possible to date these furnaces to a period between the 9th and 15th centuries. When their study has been completed, in some 12 years or so, we shall know the exact output of iron production in this region.

Blast-pipe furnace, Yuba, Burkina Faso

These large furnaces exist in several countries of the Sahel. They seem to have produced good quality iron. Around the now disintegrating furnace can be seen evidence of the metallurgy practised there, especially dark-grey slag.

Kougri, Burkina Faso

Archaeologists have recently discovered immense numbers of hearth furnaces for the smelting of iron ore at Burkina Faso. Identical furnaces were used in Poland in the 1st millennium. The date of the Kougri furnaces is still unknown.

Remains of a furnace, Kiene, Burkina Faso

Probably not of the same standard as the Yuba furnace (top illustration), the method of construction of this furnace is obvious. It was made of bits of slag left after manufacturing iron mixed with clay. Similar small-sized furnaces are generally linked with a limited local production of iron.

317

African ceramics

Far from being introduced from Egypt and the Near East, as was once believed, the African arts of pottery have been traced back by archaeologists to an indigenous origin and a very early date.

Archaeological researches in eastern Africa and, since 1982, the southern areas of the Sahara, contradict the theory that ceramics came to Egypt and then to the whole of Africa from the Near East. African ceramics would seem to have been invented within the context of a culture of fishing communities living around numerous lakes, from Hodh in Mauritania across to Lake Victoria and Lake Nakuru in Kenya, between the 9th and 3rd millennia BC. In the Sahara, charcoal associated with ceramics and located in stratigraphy* have made possible radiocarbon* datings indicating that the move towards a Neolithic culture could have started almost 10,000 years ago. At that time very favourable climatic conditions led to important changes in the way of life: the exploitation of new fishing resources and wild cereal crops occurred then, and the invention of ceramics met new requirements with regard to the preservation and cooking of food.

The fishers of the Sahara preceded by at least one millennium the populations of the Sudanese valley of the Nile and the Rift Valley in the production of pottery, decorated with wavy lines, which was to survive alongside the pottery coated with red slip and with black rims from Nubia; the latter is akin to the later manufacture of Upper and Middle Egypt, where it is associated with wares with an incised and stippled decoration, indented lines and painted patterns, white on a red background or brown on a pink background. There then appeared in Lower Egypt a monochrome burnished or polished ware, either red, brown or black, sometimes with a base, indicating a cultural unity for the Nile Valley between Memphis and the northwest of the Delta; pre-dynastic Lower and Upper Egypt was to experience a shared culture around 3000BC. To the northwest of the Sahara, pottery appears at the beginning of the 7th millennium in the Saoura valley, apparently imported from Tilemsi. The Ibero-Maurusian* civilization, present from the 6th millennium in the Mediterranean and Atlantic coastal areas, slowly progressed southwards where its pottery, described as crude for North Africa, is on the contrary very varied in its forms and decoration. In the humid coastal areas, Neolithic ceramics of the so-called Capsian tradition became important c.4500BC, and a migration towards the western Sahara extended its distribution into the interior of Mauritania.

Towards the middle of the 3rd millennium, the expansion of Saharan aridity broke the former unity of the African continent. In the north, the Libyan-Berber peoples forgot their links with areas to the south, and

thenceforth formed part of the civilizations of the Mediterranean: the nomads did not know how to make pottery, but the settled communities used a modelled ware that has been preserved in their tombs. In the 6th century BC Phoenician colonies established themselves along the coast and imported their own standard pottery and a variety of products from Greece and Italy. The destruction of Carthage in 146BC marked the beginning of Roman occupation, and workshops were set up where pottery for everyday use was turned, while Italian and Gallic wares were imported at the same time. To the south, migratory movements introduced ceramics into western Africa: ecological frontiers determined a division according to areas where the pottery may be found together with other elements of everyday life: microlithic* tools and a variety of bone implements with harpoons and fish-hooks in Sahel; polished axes and microliths in the savanna; polished axes in the forest regions; bone implements in conjunction with huge shell-mounds along the coasts. Little is known of the ancient pottery of Central Africa, where the Neolithic seems to have lingered on into the historic period: ceramics dating from the first two centuries AD have been found in Gabon and Lower Zaïre; the tool kits of the Uele area, in which polished stone is associated with incised and patterned wares with flat bottoms, are not thought to be earlier than the 4th century AD.

To the east of the desert, the countries of the Nile remained a link between the Mediterranean and the African interior. Exchanges between these areas brought together jars from Dynastic Egypt and Nubian pottery with a black interior (Type A), as well as bowls with engraved patterns picked out in white (Type C).

The Bantu expansion

In the Kush empire a sequence of styles included fine polished ware, turned on the wheel and coloured red with black rims, vases of animal form or decorated in a naturalistic way (Kerma); and modelled ware for everyday use made by women, together with turned pottery made by men, often with a painted decoration depicting men or animals (Meroe). Nubian influences have been detected in Ennedi and Tibesti. In pre-Axumite and Axumite* Ethiopia, the influence of Meroe is discernible in the pottery made from a mica paste, with geometric patterns either incised or painted in red and white, while terracotta statuettes and devotional objects have been affected by a southern Arabic influence. Kushite and Axumite influences are

also apparent among the agricultural and pastoral peoples of the Upper Nile and highland regions.

Bantu expansion to the south of a line linking Cameroon to Malindi on the east coast introduced a pottery with a shallow indentation on the base (to ensure that the receptacle would balance) such as the Urewe ware with base indentations; this is found at and to the west of Lake Victoria, while Kwale pottery reached northern Tanzania and southeastern Kenya, and fluted pottery farther to the south; the Bantu expansion also brought ceramics into the southern savannas along with metalworking in iron and the forging of tools.

In West Africa a modelled ware is found over a long period, decorated either by means of an impression made as the object was turned, or by the use of a potter's comb*. The mound civilization in the North of Nigeria, and that of the Sao people of Chad and North Cameroon, are well known, both being characterized by animal and human terracotta figurines. These precede the remarkable Nok portraits, which date from the first Iron Age (c.500BC).

The break persisting between north and south was accentuated from the 7th century AD; the contrast grew between Maghrebi countries, benefiting from the Moslem introduction of workshops where potters turned glazed wares on the wheel, and the immense territory below the Sahara where, up until our own day, women continued to fashion pottery by simply modelling the clay. The most widespread method was that of modelling the base and building up the sides by means of clay rolls. This technique was in use from the Neolithic and still survives, with special practices associated with different periods; the use of a slip along with polishing was mainly found in the period corresponding to the European Middle Ages, while the technique of smoking* is still in use in a large part of eastern and central Africa. In the countries round the Bight of Benin, decoration was often in relief; in the Zaïre area pottery was often based on the human form. In the regions to the south of Lake Victoria, earthenware pottery began at the top and ended at the base. Terracotta figurines were modelled from early times in the inland delta of the River Niger, in Ghana, in Benin and in Nigeria. Modern Mali and the southern areas around Lake Chad also practised the custom of burial in jars.

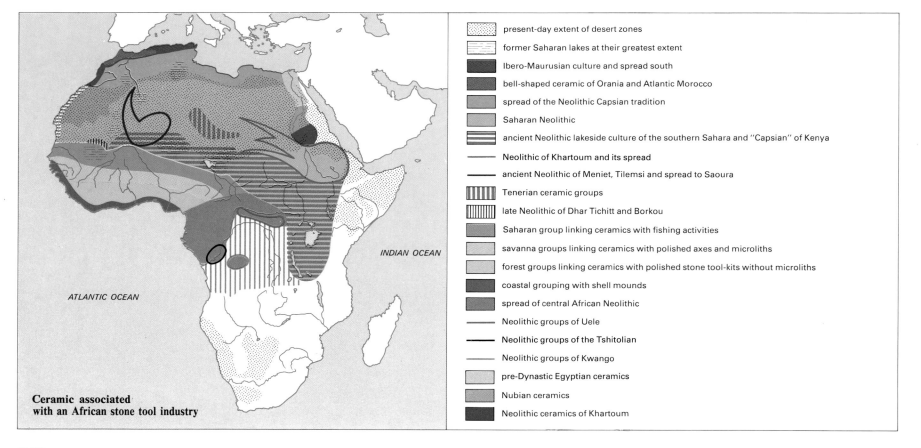

Ceramic associated with an African stone tool industry

present-day extent of desert zones

former Saharan lakes at their greatest extent

Ibero-Maurusian culture and spread south

bell-shaped ceramic of Orania and Atlantic Morocco

spread of the Neolithic Capsian tradition

Saharan Neolithic

ancient Neolithic lakeside culture of the southern Sahara and "Capsian" of Kenya

Neolithic of Khartoum and its spread

ancient Neolithic of Meniet, Tilemsi and spread to Saoura

Tenerian ceramic groups

late Neolithic of Dhar Tichitt and Borkou

Saharan group linking ceramics with fishing activities

savanna groups linking ceramics with polished axes and microliths

forest groups linking ceramics with polished stone tool-kits without microliths

coastal grouping with shell mounds

spread of central African Neolithic

Neolithic groups of Uele

Neolithic groups of the Tshitolian

Neolithic groups of Kwango

pre-Dynastic Egyptian ceramics

Nubian ceramics

Neolithic ceramics of Khartoum

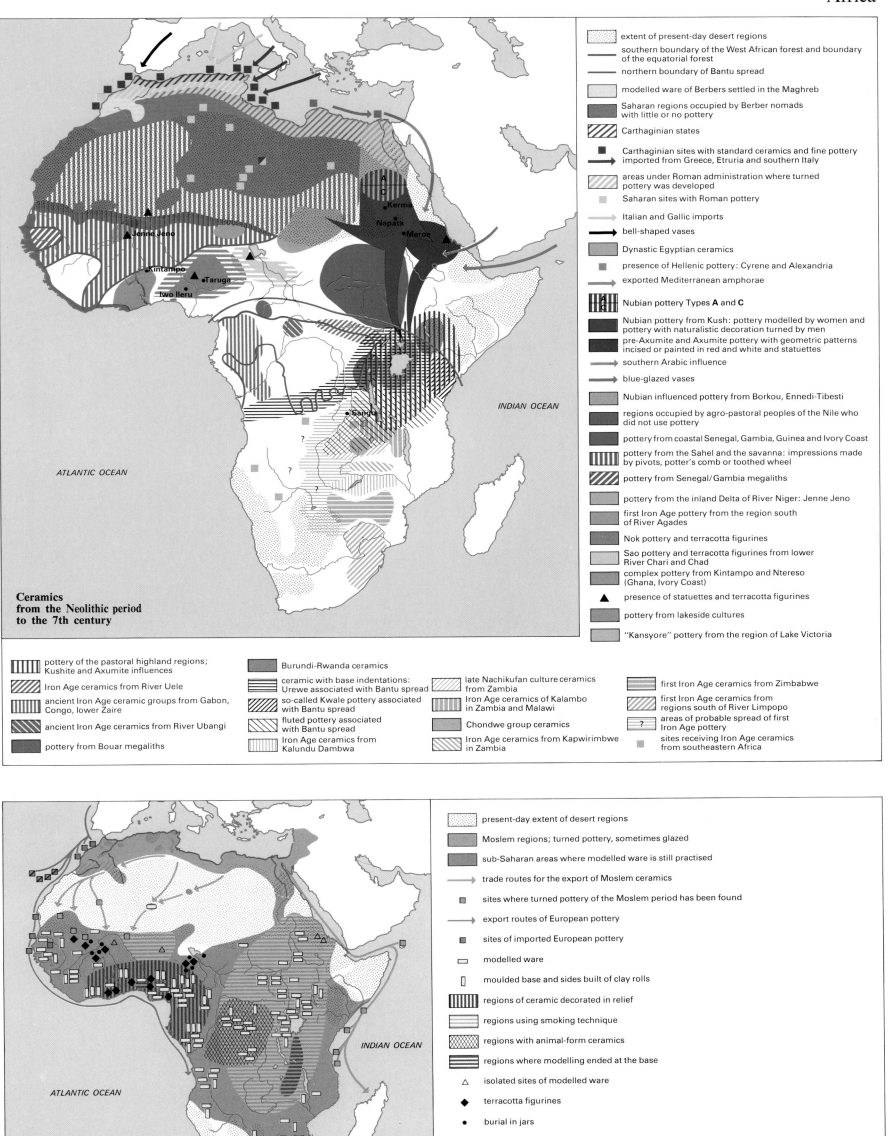

**Ceramics
from the Neolithic period
to the 7th century**

extent of present-day desert regions

southern boundary of the West African forest and boundary of the equatorial forest

northern boundary of Bantu spread

modelled ware of Berbers settled in the Maghreb

Saharan regions occupied by Berber nomads with little or no pottery

Carthaginian states

Carthaginian sites with standard ceramics and fine pottery imported from Greece, Etruria and southern Italy

areas under Roman administration where turned pottery was developed

Saharan sites with Roman pottery

Italian and Gallic imports

bell-shaped vases

Dynastic Egyptian ceramics

presence of Hellenic pottery: Cyrene and Alexandria

exported Mediterranean amphorae

Nubian pottery Types **A** and **C**

Nubian pottery from Kush: pottery modelled by women and pottery with naturalistic decoration turned by men

pre-Axumite and Axumite pottery with geometric patterns incised or painted in red and white and statuettes

southern Arabic influence

blue-glazed vases

Nubian influenced pottery from Borkou, Ennedi-Tibesti

regions occupied by agro-pastoral peoples of the Nile who did not use pottery

pottery from coastal Senegal, Gambia, Guinea and Ivory Coast

pottery from the Sahel and the savanna: impressions made by pivots, potter's comb or toothed wheel

pottery from Senegal/Gambia megaliths

pottery from the inland Delta of River Niger: Jenne Jeno

first Iron Age pottery from the region south of River Agades

Nok pottery and terracotta figurines

Sao pottery and terracotta figurines from lower River Chari and Chad

complex pottery from Kintampo and Ntereso (Ghana, Ivory Coast)

presence of statuettes and terracotta figurines

pottery from lakeside cultures

"Kansyore" pottery from the region of Lake Victoria

pottery of the pastoral highland regions; Kushite and Axumite influences

Iron Age ceramics from River Uele

ancient Iron Age ceramic groups from Gabon, Congo, lower Zaire

ancient Iron Age ceramics from River Ubangi

pottery from Bouar megaliths

Burundi-Rwanda ceramics

ceramic with base indentations: Urewe associated with Bantu spread

so-called Kwale pottery associated with Bantu spread

fluted pottery associated with Bantu spread

Iron Age ceramics from Kalundu Dambwa

late Nachikufan culture ceramics from Zambia

Iron Age ceramics of Kalambo in Zambia and Malawi

Chondwe group ceramics

Iron Age ceramics from Kapwirimbwe in Zambia

first Iron Age ceramics from Zimbabwe

first Iron Age ceramics from regions south of River Limpopo

areas of probable spread of first Iron Age pottery

sites receiving Iron Age ceramics from southeastern Africa

**Ceramics
after the 7th century**

present-day extent of desert regions

Moslem regions; turned pottery, sometimes glazed

sub-Saharan areas where modelled ware is still practised

trade routes for the export of Moslem ceramics

sites where turned pottery of the Moslem period has been found

export routes of European pottery

sites of imported European pottery

modelled ware

moulded base and sides built of clay rolls

regions of ceramic decorated in relief

regions using smoking technique

regions with animal-form ceramics

regions where modelling ended at the base

isolated sites of modelled ware

terracotta figurines

burial in jars

Archaeology and Apartheid

Archaeology challenges the common Apartheid argument that southern Africa was virtually uninhabited before the 17th century; iron-using, cattle-rearing black communities had been living there for centuries.

It has frequently happened since World War II that a state has tried to demonstrate through archaeological investigation its supposed historic rights to a territory; two famous examples of this are Poland and Israel. Archaeology may also help to answer one of the arguments most constantly advanced by hardline partisans of Apartheid. The black population of southern Africa, according to this view, came from countries farther to the north, emigrating towards what is now the Republic of South Africa at about the same time as the Europeans were settling in the south of the continent. On 24 October 1974 the South African prime minister, speaking at the United Nations, declared that towards the middle of the 17th century "the white and black peoples of southern Africa converged towards what was then a virtually uninhabited part of the continent". It may be asked whether southern Africa really was empty of inhabitants, as was cited 20 years ago to justify separate black and white communities.

We will take only a brief look at the paleontological and archaeological investigations relating to the millenia prior to the Christian era. There has never been any argument about the fact that they reveal the presence of Australopithecines* in southern Africa between three and one million years ago, that of hominids up to *Homo sapiens sapiens**, that of stone-cutting people, and that of hunter-gatherers living in rock shelters and caves between 8000BC and the beginning of the AD period. We know of no trace up to now of a Neolithic* phase and of real development of agriculture between the Zambezi and the Cape: the hunter-gatherer economy remained in existence for a long time, especially among the San Bushmen, who have today withdrawn to the Kalahari. Southern Africa down to its south coast took a long time to develop, and there is complete agreement about its evolution, although incompletely studied and inadequately investigated.

In recent years the later periods have been intensely studied in Zambia, Namibia, on the Zambezi, in Botswana, Swaziland and Lesotho. And these studies enable us today to trace clearly the lines of development, even if many divergences of interpretation still sometimes exist between one scholar and another.

First, we now know as a total certainty that iron and copper production south of the Zambezi and the Limpopo rivers, and even in present-day Lesotho, dates back a long way. We are very far from having sorted out all that ensues from this virtual reversal of information, in comparison with what was accepted 20 years ago. Investigation is still being pursued; but it does confirm that iron was produced as early as between 500 and 1000AD, except in the south between the Orange river and the coast. But in that area sheep-rearing people were living in the 1st millennium (from the first centuries AD), and (after 400) cattle-rearers, beside the hunter-gatherers. We still have only a very hazy idea of whether the production of iron corresponded with agricultural development, which undoubtedly took place among Bantu-speaking peoples, who may have come there in the 6th century, and whether iron was produced in small or large quantities. At Tsodilo it is found in association with the work of cattle farmers, in eastern Botswana in conjunction with sheep-rearing, while between the Zambezi and Blackburn it is associated with the production of sorghum*. Copper was also being produced at that time in what are now northern Zambia and Zaïre, and this has left traces of copper working at Messina and Phalabaorwa. It no longer seems surprising that, much later, in the 16th century, the Portuguese should have named the Limpopo "the copper river".

Socio-economic development and agriculture

A second certainty, for which massive evidence has been found, especially over the past ten years, results from the systematic study of the droppings of domestic cattle in the pens into which they were herded at the centres of permanent settlements, sometimes in the hands of increasingly powerful accumulators of capital. At Schroda near Zhiso, for example, "dung archaeology" has provided information which is today leading to firm reconstructions of history. Especially between the Limpopo and Shashi rivers, where it is likely that an increase in population density was upsetting the old socio-economic conditions of existence, peoples related to the present-day Sothos developed increasingly elaborate methods of cattle-rearing. Traces of the bones of domestic cattle have been found in Lesotho (4th–5th century) and in the Transvaal (5th century); but it is still very difficult to try to pinpoint where this systematic animal husbandry, involving animals which had probably come from the north, began. From the 8th century, archaeological traces of animal rearing become more numerous and the area in which they are found becomes larger. In many areas the people gradually abandoned hunting and gathering as a means of feeding themselves, though these means were still supplying 40 percent of the diet on certain sites in Zambia in the 7th century; we begin to find sorghum (Kalundu, Zhiso, Zambia, eastern Botswana and Blackburn), *pennisetum* millet (Inyanga) and vegetables, beside milk and meat. After 900AD a new type of dietary, economic, political and social organization developed. It also led to an increasingly settled existence in areas suitable for this mixed economy based mainly on animal husbandry complemented by agriculture; included in this animal husbandry were sheep and goats, found in very varying numbers and proportions, not equally distributed. Men took on an increasingly important role in the organization of the family, inheritance and political life; the accumulation of livestock signified for a man a right to an increased number of wives. This model spread geographically into areas neighbouring the areas where it first developed.

However it seems very probable that the African cultivated plants limited the possibility of expansion towards the southwest down to the coast: ecological conditions may not have been so favourable there; neither could these tribes of herdsmen have had enough room for demographic expansion between present-day Lesotho and the Zambezi without attempting to claim the western Kalahari and the area south of the Orange river from the Khoi and San peoples. The way in which land was organized changed from the 8th to the 11th centuries with the development of a more dynamic economy. Urban groupings became larger, living accommodation better built; political power was gained by the rich and is shown by archaeological research in the abundance of livestock: a hierarchic society was being created, at both Blackburn and Zhiso and undoubtedly in many other places. Finds made at Lydenburg probably represent a foretaste of many other discoveries, yet to be made, with regard to the artistic expression of these peoples.

Ceramic traditions and language

On all that has been said so far scholars are agreed. Their paths diverge as soon as it comes to a question of how this transformation came about. In the opinion of D.W. Philipson, Bantu-speaking peoples came from the north between the 5th and 7th centuries, bringing with them south of the Zambezi a type of pottery, iron and agriculture; he does not have much to say about animal husbandry, being more concerned with the way in which they migrated, supposedly travelling 2,000km (1,240 miles) from north to south in two centuries: 10km (6 miles) a year. On the other hand, T.N. Huffman believes that the development of an original herding civilization was achieved by a single people formerly dwelling between the Shashi and Limpopo rivers, where they found ivory from large quantities of elephants and possibly alluvial gold as well; certainly in this "island" between the two rivers and south of the Limpopo a great many traces of occupation going back to the different stone ages have been found. Huffman thinks that this people, which had had a continuous output of a stable type of pottery from the 5th to the 11th centuries, gradually moved northwards, eventually crossing the Zambezi, over a period of time. The patrilineal culture of these Bantu-speaking peoples became quite widespread after 1000AD throughout the southern part of the continent. The two writers, though at odds when it comes to the crux of the matter, are in broad agreement, albeit with shades of difference, in thinking that cattle rearing gained ground through contact with certain neighbouring peoples to the west around the present Kalahari and to the south down to the coast, but that these neighbours did not know how to make iron or how to grow crops. Thus the Khoikhoi are thought to have adopted a way of life original to them, different from that of the San people, and to have long maintained their own ceramic traditions and preserved their own language. We are poorly informed as to the chronology of the movement of cattle and as to the species involved; all we know at present is that remains belonging to the Sanga people have been found in the northwest of Botswana, dating from the end of the 1st millennium BC. The presence of cattle on the south coast between 50BC and 450AD is demonstrated by C^{14} dating, but it is difficult to draw conclusions on the basis of what is still very piecemeal information.

Bantu, San and Khoikhoi

We are still inclined to think in terms of three different "peoples" being associated with three differing ways of life. The Bantu-speaking people who had immigrated at some period from the north to present-day Lesotho are thought to be characterized by the use of iron, the practice of agriculture, intensive cattle-rearing and a settled way of life; the San—referred to formerly in old texts as Bushmen—are seen as the survivors of the hunter-gatherers from the south; and the Khoikhoi, a connecting link between the other two groups, are thought to have added sheep and cattle rearing to the old dietary customs of the San, and to have had characteristic types of pottery, distinct in both shape and the methods by which it was produced. Nowadays, these proposals are being called into question; perhaps we are too quick to confuse a people with a group of techniques, or for that matter a language, forgetting that different techniques, inventions and vocabularies travel, respecting only environmental frontiers, far more quickly than, and in a different way from, organized human groupings. In spite of great progress recently, much work has still to be done before we can understand clearly and fully what movements took place in every kind of field south of the Zambezi between the 4th and 19th centuries. At least we are now fully aware that the area in question was densely and coherently occupied by various African cultures. When research in South Africa, Angola, Namibia and Mozambique is further advanced the historic development of this area of the world will probably be seen in the fullness of scientific knowledge as very far removed from the formulas to which people have wanted to reduce it.

Trade in gold and ivory, glass and shells

One final and far from insignificant factor brought about new changes in the life of the area from the 9th century on, or possibly even earlier. In sites dating from the 7th and 8th century, at Inyanga, Mabwani near Zhiso, Schroda and various sites in southern Zambia, cowries from the eastern coast, as well as imported glass beads and shells have been found; it seems likely that ivory was the first commodity traded for these objects from afar, and possibly iron too. It seems almost certain that gold was traded. A text by al-Mas'udi dating from the mid-10th century, which is very well known but very inadequately translated, gives the impression that the whole Sofala area was at that period already exporting gold. A little further south, at Chibuene and Manikweni, recent finds made by the University of Maputo dating from the 9th–10th centuries justify us in thinking that trading posts there were the first to do business with the interior. A working hypothesis can be put forward that some poorly organized trading existed from the 7th century on, involving ivory and perhaps a little gold exported in exchange for beads, shells and perhaps cloth. In the 10th century gold was already being exported, but more to the north; al-Mas'udi explicitly says that the inhabitants of the area burned cow dung as their sole means of melting down the gold. Gold working must have developed with a view to export from the 9th century on in Zimbabwe; it became organized in the 10th and 11th centuries. Astute chiefs at Mapungubwe and then at Zimbabwe took over its exploitation on a commercial basis, probably in the 10–11th century. Around them a wealthy economy based on barter came into being, detracting from the use of livestock as capital, and enhancing the accumulation of gold with a view to selling it. The transformation of the area in and around the town at Mapungubwe and Zimbabwe and the surrounding areas came next. Those wielding power, in charge of international trading, now dwelt apart from their dependants; the cattle pens were built away from the "palace". Stone buildings began to appear, though as yet there is no consensus of opinion as regards their dating, and important buildings were to be built in stone from the Indian Ocean to the Atlantic until at least the 17th century. Social differences left their mark in the distribution of dwellings; in the 12th century at Mapungubwe a gold-plated emblem of power was placed in a tomb and local ceramic production became more refined to meet the requirements of the rich. Representations of animals, hundreds of which have been found dating from the 11th–13th centuries, as well as anthropomorphic terracottas, were replaced in 14th–15th century Zimbabwe by true insignia of power, particularly plinths supporting bird effigies in steatite. The 14th–15th centuries also saw an increase in imported goods. The herdsmen had now entered into a period of dependence on the Moslem world economy. The area of power and influence extended from the Zambezi to the Limpopo, and slightly further south.

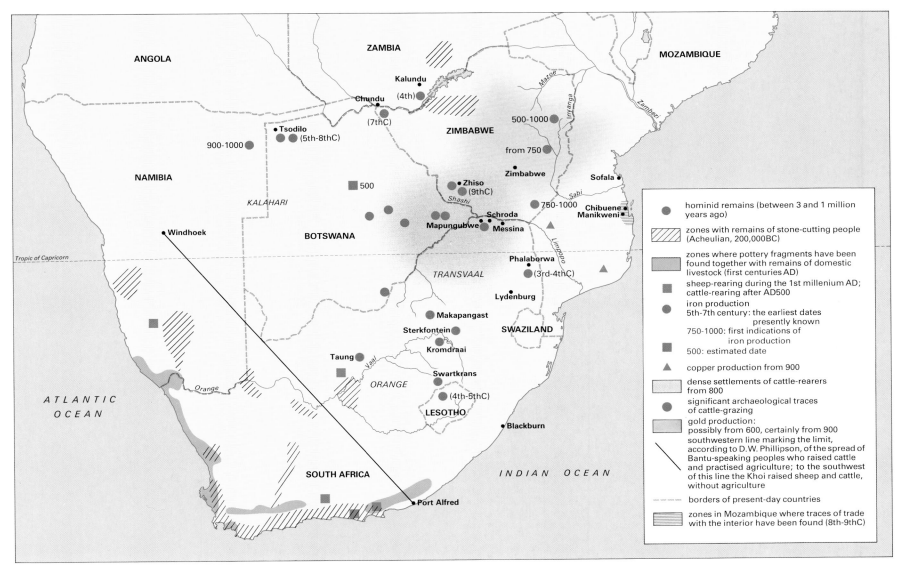

African occupation of the south of the continent during the last two millennia

Map legend:

- ● hominid remains (between 3 and 1 million years ago)
- ▨ zones with remains of stone-cutting people (Acheulian, 200,000BC)
- ▨ zones where pottery fragments have been found together with remains of domestic livestock (first centuries AD)
- ■ sheep-rearing during the 1st millenium AD; cattle-rearing after AD500
- ● iron production
  5th-7th century: the earliest dates presently known
  750-1000: first indications of iron production
- ■ 500: estimated date
- ▲ copper production from 900
- ▨ dense settlements of cattle-rearers from 800
- ● significant archaeological traces of cattle-grazing
- ▨ gold production: possibly from 600, certainly from 900
- ╱ southwestern line marking the limit, according to D.W. Phillipson, of the spread of Bantu-speaking peoples who raised cattle and practised agriculture; to the southwest of this line the Khoi raised sheep and cattle, without agriculture
- ‒ ‒ borders of present-day countries
- ▤ zones in Mozambique where traces of trade with the interior have been found (8th-9thC)

Map labels: ANGOLA, ZAMBIA, MOZAMBIQUE, NAMIBIA, ZIMBABWE, Kalundu (4th), Chundu (7thC), Tsodilo (5th-8thC), 900-1000, KALAHARI, 500, Zhiso (9thC), 500-1000, from 750, Zimbabwe, Sofala, 750-1000, Chibuene, Manikweni, Schroda, Mapungubwe, Messina, BOTSWANA, Windhoek, Tropic of Capricorn, Shashi, Sabi, Mazoe, Inyanga, Zambezi, TRANSVAAL, Phalaborwa (3rd-4thC), Limpopo, Lydenburg, Makapangast, Sterkfontein, Kromdraai, Swartkrans (4th-5thC), SWAZILAND, Taung, Vaal, ORANGE, LESOTHO, Blackburn, Orange, ATLANTIC OCEAN, SOUTH AFRICA, INDIAN OCEAN, Port Alfred

A site comparable to Great Zimbabwe discovered in Mozambique

At Manikweni, Mozambique, archaeologists have discovered a large stone enclosure very much like that at Great Zimbabwe. Their dating of the overall site to the 9th and 10th centuries probably does not apply to the actual remains. The site is almost certainly related to commercial activity in the region during those centuries.

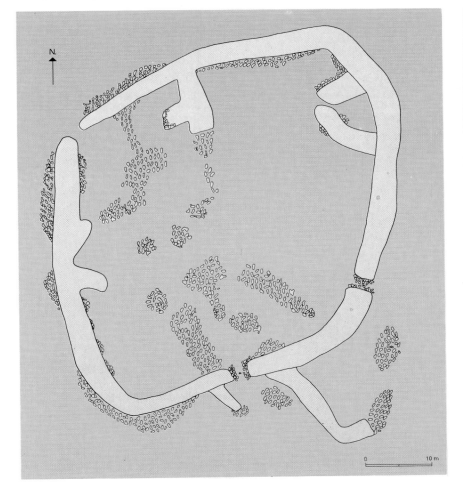

Terracotta head found at Lydenburg, Transvaal

This artifact, reconstructed from fragments discovered during excavation next to beads and parts of an ivory bracelet, is dated to approximately 500AD. It belongs to an important series of anthropomorphic terracotta artifacts found in fragments from Natal to the Transvaal. Much elaborated by incision and applied paste, the decoration was probably finished off with areas of white paint. This object obviously had a ritual significance. It was surmounted by an animal representation.

A. Byron, South African Museum

321

Pre-colonial plant systems of defence

Durable, fire-resistant fortresses, created from different kinds of purpose-grown vegetation, testify to pre-colonial African people's skilful use of their resources—a skill now being rediscovered by archaeologists.

Military reports or accounts of "police operations" at the beginning of the colonial period in Africa mention difficulties encountered in approaching many settlements surrounded with thickets of thorns and euphorbias. These plant vegetation fortifications were man-made, and the colonial powers often demanded that they should be dismantled in token of submission. Thus they disappeared rapidly in the colonial period, being destroyed, abandoned or adapted by communities with livestock into hedges protecting their fields. Borders alongside the paths which made it possible to pen in the stock were preserved, while the defensive lines were eliminated. Many of these natural vegetation structures can still be detected in the landscape, where there are successive lines of tree-type growth. Their unexpectedly frequent occurrence cannot be explained simply by the necessity of keeping livestock to certain tracks, any more than the curtains of thorny bushes on the foothills can be attributed solely to action against erosion. Moreover the existing earthworks and dry stones are so obviously ineffective as defences on their own that their true purpose becomes clear, namely to act as a framework for vegetation structures formed of thorns or euphorbias, the vestiges of which are still attached to these walls. These plant defences are widespread over large areas, revealing true refinement in their various combinations. To reconstitute and understand them represents a real undertaking in archaeological terms. Here we will describe some examples of vegetation fortifications put up in Cameroon, some of which were still in use when colonial penetration occurred.

Defensive systems based on plants are to be found throughout Africa, both on grassland and in the forests. However, in the Sudan-Sahel area a certain number of conditions favoured the elaboration of these "fortifications". They did not exist in centralized states such as the kingdoms of Bornu (near Lake Chad) or Baguirmi (part of modern Chad), where only the capital had the right to be fortified. In the cities of the Hausa (Nigeria) area, on the other hand, plant defences reinforced fortified walls. These plant constructions tended to be built up particularly in areas where there was too great a population density for a simple no-man's-land area of forest to act as a barrier ensuring protection. They were also essential to groups who were frequently besieged or under constant threat. Some especially vulnerable areas had several lines of defence in the population corridors resulting from the continual pushing back of peoples from the great empires, or in regions directly exposed to the activities of these empires with their periodic raids. The vegetation in many cases rounded off natural refuges, hills and rocky massifs thrusting out into the low-lying plain.

The plants used

Protection could be provided by a single species, but more often several species were used together to build up a succession of lines made up of different varieties. Plants which grew easily were used to support other creepers or thorns, forming advanced lines and creating high screens. In forward positions species resistant to fire were used, or those that were difficult or even dangerous (like the highly toxic latex plants) to cut down. The last line was made up of plants that grew to form hermetic "walls". There was a wide range of combinations available, but the particular method of defence chosen was, in its complexity, representative of the ethnic group or sub-group which had brought it into being, and it was reproduced indefinitely.

The Guiziga, an ethnic group from North Cameroon in the Maroua area, made their habitat at the foot of rocky outcrops. As part of their land was in great need of protection, plant walls followed the line of the foothills between 20 or 30 to several hundred metres from the first scree. The Guiziga propagated *Commiphora africana*, with a fair space between each plant. *Acacia ataxacantha* was sown parallel to it by means of a hollow millet cane, filled with seeds that rolled out through the end as it was drawn along a groove in the soil. As the plant fortification grew, *Acacia ataxacantha*, which is a thorny bush, mingled with the *Commiphora africana* to form a barrier 3 to 4m (10 to 13ft) high. A second line based on the densest and highest variety of *Euphorbia unispina* grew a few metres behind the first. Finally *Commiphora africana*, a shrub with a twisted outline whose branches are a mass of spines, was planted out to form a row of cross-defences at the rear.

Complementing these first general lines of defence, the entrances of little valleys were barred by drystone walls forming an environment conducive to the growth of *Euphorbiaceae* or *Acacia ataxacantha*. These low dry stone walls that cut across the valleys, nowadays uncovered, did not just serve to break cavalry attacks mounted by neighbouring kingdoms; they as often as not formed a durable framework for complex systems of plant defence.

The plentifulness of one species, *Commiphora africana*, on the ranges to the west of Maroua, or of *Acacia ataxacantha* along river banks, allowed defences to be established quickly—one rainy season was enough—and hundreds of metres of hedging could be renewed frequently. These defensive curtains were constantly evolving, pushing forward into the plain, or withdrawing nearer the loose heaps of stones, at first partially surrounding the massifs and then completely girdling them, according to the fluctuations of popula-

tion density on the range. Latex plants such as *Adenium obaesum, Euphorbia unispina* and especially *Euphorbia desmondi*, on the other hand, tended to be imported from other areas, and they were propagated from existing stocks. These acted as a mechanical barrier, and one strain was kept in reserve and was used along with *Strophantus** solely as a source of poison for arrows.

In and around forested areas, plant ramparts could grow to impressive sizes, as in the Yambassa country to the north of Yaounde. Here the defensive skeleton was provided by a tree, the kapok (*Ceiba pentandra*), which can grow to a height of 30 to 40m (98 to 131ft). The Yambassa propagated "living walls" of kapok trees several miles long. Spurs at the base of the tree trunks overlapped one another, forming a true defensive wall 3 to 4m (10 to 13ft) high, affording a hermetic shield with only a few gaps to be guarded. However, these walls of huge trees had other functions. Not only did they mark the boundary and defend the space of a village community; they also created the workable land of the Yambassa. Planted in grassland, their lines encircled high positions and acted as firebreaks. Behind them the community could tend tree-covered ranges where the dominant species was the oil palm.

For the archaeologist, reconstructing these plant fortifications provides information about the diffusion of certain species and the art of building defences. Above all they provide evidence about the way in which the African civilizations controlled their territory. Seen in this light, it would be most interesting to draw up, using oral traditions, a typology of defensive systems for the whole of Africa.

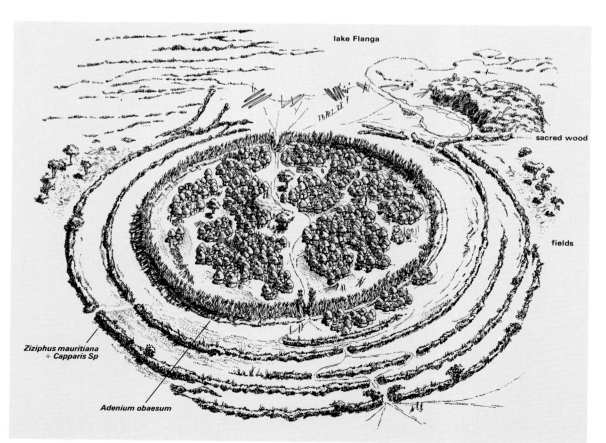

Fortifications on the shores of Lake Fianga

On the approaches of the Logone and Lake Fianga, earth fortresses, rarely more than 100m (330ft) in diameter, were reinforced with plant defences. Some were reduced to a simple bank of earth which facilitated the growth of *Adenium obaesum*. In front of it, a maze of approximately concentric hedges of clipped *Ziziphus* supported *Capparis*, forming bushes and creepers with double axillary spines.

Labels in image: lake Fianga; sacred wood; fields; Ziziphus mauritiana + Capparis Sp; Adenium obaesum

Example of the defensive system of the Guiziga Kaliaw

The line of *Acacia ataxacantha* mixed with *Commiphora africana* was followed by a line of *Euphorbia unispina*. Then a line of *Commiphora africana*, the branches of which were arranged in a criss-cross manner. Behind, *Euphorbia kamerunica* acted as an occult protection and a poisonous plant.

Acacia ataxacantha   Euphorbia unispina   Commiphora africana   Euphorbia kamerunica

Defensive system used by the Guiziga Midjiving

Acacia ataxacantha preceded a closely packed line of *Commiphora africana* which flanked a double row of *Adenium obaesum*, forming a raised path. From this double forward line ran paths lined with *Adenium obaesum* which, by partitioning off the foothills, provided protection from surprise attacks.

Acacia ataxacantha   Commiphora africana   Adenium obaesum   Acacia ataxacantha

Map of plant defence areas

An area of defensive systems dominated by *Euphorbia desmondi* and *Euphorbia kamerunica* was used by herding societies situated on the highlands and raising bulls.

Plant fortifications based on *Commiphora africana* were widespread in the foothills of the northern Mandara mountains, often limited to small defensive woods (region of Pulka in Nigeria). Whereas *Adenium obaesum* and *Euphorbia unispina* were used in the more localized defensive systems, *Acacia ataxacantha* is not represented, so generalized was its use.

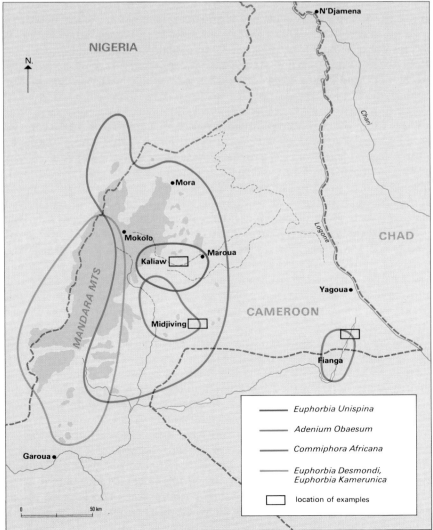

Village of Djagaral (Guiziga Midjiving): defensive path

These paths were usually raised above the fields. Hedges of *Adenium obaesum*, like those of other plant defence lines, acted to prevent erosion.

323

North America:
the archaeological background

Cultural imperialism and genocide conditioned the first phase of
European relations with the Amerindians. Only now, as the fight is on to save
the remnants of the original cultures, is their true antiquity being understood.

Archaeology in North America has developed within a cultural and political context very different from that of Europe. In the latter, prehistory is clearly distinguished from history, which gradually crystallized with the advent of writing and the establishment of states. By contrast, during the colonization of the New World there was a blending of European history with the still continuing prehistory of the Amerindians. Furthermore, in North America archaeology and prehistory were confused until recent years; but today the shallow deposit caused by a few centuries of European presence is beginning to justify the existence of a colonial or Euro-American archaeology.

At first North American archaeology was basically a tool for the investigation of the recent past of the indigenous peoples. As in Europe, a literal interpretation of the biblical Genesis formed an obstacle to the perception of the prehistoric depth of the Amerindian past. At first ethnocentric prejudices attributed the impressive Amerindian constructions, such as the mound cities of the Mississippian civilizations, to European or Mediterranean influence. Nevertheless, the origin of the monuments and tribes of America intrigued archaeologists. Finally, even when archaeological facts began to prevail over biblical literalism, the majority of American archaeologists were rather reluctant to accept that the Amerindians had occupied America a long time before the Europeans. However, a few individualistic or unorthodox archaeologists tried to establish that man appeared in the New World at the same time as in Europe, if not before.

At the end of the 1960s, a few American archaeologists accepted dates before 13,000 BC for the first Amerindians. In the early 1980s the insistence of certain archaeologists on dates that sometimes went back more than 100,000 years, but were based on poorly established data, inspired prudence in the majority of specialists, who are now willing to accept an antiquity of 16,000 or 17,000 years. Some go as far back as 27,000–30,000 years, very few beyond 40,000. Gordon Willey and Jeremy Sabloff have divided the history of American archaeology into four major periods, each marked by a dominant way of thinking which still left room for the marginal tendencies announcing the next period.

The development of archaeology

The first period began with the conquest in 1492 and developed until 1840 before its gradual decline and final disappearance by 1960. It was characterized by all the speculations and conjectures, often irrational, arising from the strangeness of a world unforeseen in the Bible and difficult to understand in European terms of reference. Theological and biblical attitudes prevailed, as seen in references to the "lost tribes of Israel" to explain the origin of the Amerindians. Publications took the form of travel accounts by naturalists or literary men. North America, less rich in impressive monuments than Central America or Peru, was comparatively neglected at this period. But some workers anticipated a more historical approach, notably Thomas Jefferson, future president of the United States, who undertook the meticulous and precociously stratigraphic* excavation of a burial mound in Virginia in order to understand its origin (European or Amerindian?) and purpose. Far in advance of his time, he was unfortunately an isolated case.

During the centuries of European conquest, missionaries, explorers and adventurers left accounts of their travels that often contained details of the customs of Amerindian populations. These documents assume a capital importance for the prehistory of the New World because they describe Amerindian cultures before their acculturation became too rapid, and while they still retained a continuity with the most recent prehistoric occupations. The question then was just how far to develop inferences from archaeological remains and ethnographical observations.

The second period began in 1840, when publications first appeared abandoning speculation for organized description, cartographical survey of sites and the earliest attempts to classify archaeological data. Following the European model, museums, universities and learned societies appeared in the principal towns of North America. The great antiquity of man and the evolution of forms of life, clearly formulated by Darwin, also influenced America when European scholars went to work there. The great Ohio and Mississippi mounds still fascinated archaeologists, some asserting that these constructions were erected on the American continent by a "lost race", others that they were the work of the ancestors of certain Amerindian groups. This period saw the appearance of the fundamental concepts of North American archaeology, such as "culture", "style", "horizon" and "cultural period", concepts strongly influenced by ethnology. As from the end of the 19th century, archaeology was to concern itself increasingly with the study of material culture, which was progressively abandoned by ethnography. But American anthropology, dominated by the school of Franz Boas, became anti-evolutionist, and archaeological attitudes remained static and without a wider perspective, scarcely aware of a chronology going beyond the origin of the historical tribes, for lack of stratigraphical excavations and analyses. Nevertheless, the excavation of the shell middens that had accumulated along the Atlantic and Pacific coasts of North America indicated a certain interest in chronology.

The third period, on the other hand, was dominated by the chronological classification of events and archaeological cultures as a result of the development of stratigraphical excavation after 1914. By relating objects to stratigraphical levels and sites, archaeologists were able to integrate types of object into a context of time and space, leading to the first regional syntheses. The generalization of stratigraphical excavation stimulated the improvement of methods. Side by side with stratigraphy the Americans introduced in 1930 another tool for chronological measurement, the technique of seriation*. This consists in evaluating the relative proportions of each of the types or styles of objects (pottery, stone, etc.) represented on different archaeological sites. Used at first to classify surface sites chronologically in relation to each other, this technique was later given another function: estimating the speed and importance of cultural change. This was the first tool elaborated for the quantitative interpretation of archaeological data, and it spread very widely throughout America.

In its concepts and interpretations North American archaeology remained an extension of ethnology, but it began to emerge as a specific discipline through its concern with the relations between cultures and their physical environment. Indeed, while American ethnology was developing the concept of cultural ecology, archaeologists were trying to apply it in their own discipline by examining methods of establishment and settlement.

Between 1940 and 1960 archaeologists began to produce syntheses, showing a certain diachronic* sense of the development of a phenomenon through time stimulated by the appearance of radiocarbon* dating. Freed, at least partly, from an obsession with the chronological arrangement of sites and cultures by the methods of absolute dating*, American archaeologists could ask questions about the objectives of archaeology and develop the notions of the "cultural area", "archaeological culture" and "cultural

"Panorama of the Monumental Grandeur of the Mississippi Valley" (detail)

This illustration from an early 19th century work depicts the excavation of an Amerindian burial mound in the Mississippi valley. The origin of these large manmade structures was the cause of lively discussion among American archaeologists. Some scholars attributed them to transatlantic peoples, others to the ancestors of Amerindians.

history". Chronology as an end in itself now gave way to a desire to reconstruct the past; but how was this to be done? In North America during the 1950s and 1960s, this questions crystallized around the problem of how much could be known. Some archaeologists considered that the classification of remains created artificial categories having little if any connection with actual prehistoric behaviour. Others believed that the classes and types established by archaeology took into account a very large part of prehistoric reality. Although this debate is still going on, today it represents nothing more than a part of the reflection on the capacity of archaeologists to rediscover and interpret the past.

New Archaeology

The fourth and last period began in 1960 and is still going on. The notions of evolution and cultural systems combined to direct North American archaeology towards a reasoned explanation of the past, integrating in a dynamic way the data accumulated and classified during earlier periods. Fascinated by the spectacular growth of the natural sciences, physics and chemistry, and by the potential of computers, the supporters of the New Archaeology, symbolized by Lewis Binford, were also attracted by the concept of the ecosystem, and are now discovering affinities with disciplines other than anthropology. However the archaeologists of this new tendency are still intimately linked to that discipline, since they are specialists in material culture, which they are sometimes ready to study even in the milieu in which they live, as is shown by Rathje's work on the trashcans of a town in Arizona. The New Archaeology was also prepared to borrow the notion of evolution, understood as an adaptive process, from the cultural ecology developed in ethnology. So archaeology will no longer simply demonstrate the fact of cultural change, but also explain how that change took place.

The travel narratives collected during the centuries of conquest, and the ethnographical observations accumulated from about the mid-19th century, supply a frame of reference from which archaeological remains can be interpreted. However, the New Archaeology stresses the fact that analogies drawn from ethnographical information can only give an incomplete or even biased account of prehistoric reality. First it has to be shown that prehistoric and ethnographic cultures both developed in the same conditions. This can often only be done rather unsatisfactorily, given the large gaps in prehistoric objects and often too the inadequacy of ethnographical data for archaeological interpretation, because archaeology is concerned with the field of material culture, often neglected by ethnography.

In this context archaeologists began to develop ethno-archaeology* which seeks to define the role of material culture in living societies as a basis for analogy with archaeological data; and experimental archaeology* which aims to reproduce, with the physical and intellectual means available today, various products of vanished societies (dwellings, tools, building works, etc.) but cannot verify, unlike the exact sciences, the validity of the experiment. By linking the study of man to that of his environment, North American archaeology tends to become "systemic". It seeks to take into account a growing number of cultural and ecological data as well as their interactions. The treatment of this growing amount of data is made possible by the development of computers.

Armed with statistics and the computer, and supported by the natural and exact sciences, the New Archaeology is still involved in a great movement of theoretical reflection about the nature of the discipline. In the early 1960s in particular, it was asserted that the fundamental objective of archaeology was to contribute to research into the general laws governing cultural systems. The hypothetical and deductive reasoning borrowed from the experimental sciences suggested that the New Archaeology might have discovered the ideal tool for revealing those laws. Since then, many archaeologists have become disillusioned. A new concept was then proposed, the "middle range theory", which in essence sought to provide an immediately usable tool for the understanding and interpretation of archaeological remains, seen as the outcome of human behaviour. This led archaeologists to envisage the "archaeological site" as a group of remains of all kinds, the original arrangement of which was disturbed by a succession of natural and cultural phenomena. It was argued that, as these phenomena have a regular character, they could be understood, and the original organization of the prehistoric site could be reconstructed. But will this lead, as some scholars think, to the elaboration of a general theory of human behaviour? The profusion of reflections on concepts, methods and techniques leaves a picture of extreme tension between the protagonists of the different trends in North American archaeology between 1970 and 1980. Quite recently disagreements are apparently being resolved in favour of a sort of combination between the New Archaeology and the more traditional tendencies.

The first peopling of North America

Most archaeologists agree that the first Americans came to the continent from Siberia by way of a land bridge that emerged when Ice Age conditions "locked up" water as ice, and thus substantially lowered sea levels. But the date of the first migrations remains controversial.

Prehistorians are still divided over the question of the first peopling of America. Not only are the best established archaeological data interpreted in different ways, but evidence relating to the earliest periods is the rarest and least trustworthy. Moreover the subject can be tackled by a variety of disciplines such as linguistics, genetics, biology and paleology, and when the data from these different disciplines are compared they are found to generate conflicting views.

It was certainly before the appearance of the very first hominids that continental drift separated America from the other continents, and everything leads us to believe that the emergence of the human species occurred only in the Old World. The relative homogeneity of present-day Amerindians in comparison with the rest of humanity, as well as their many Asiatic characteristics, suggest a relatively recent population of the Americas by people of a single dominant origin situated in Asia, which does not exclude the possibility of occasional and very secondary influxes by other peoples.

The most widely accepted theory is that this peopling could only have been carried out by way of the Beringian region, which implies the movement of man across northern Asia and his adaptation to an Arctic environment. This seems to have taken place in the Upper Paleolithic period during the last Ice Age, from Würm in Europe to Wisconsin in America, which lasted approximately from 100,000 to 8000BC. The population of *Homo sapiens sapiens** which appeared during the middle of this period grew appreciably and showed an ever-increasing aptitude for exploiting different environments.

In eastern Siberia the oldest traces of human occupation at present hardly go back more than 30,000 to 35,000 years. The reduction of wooded territories following on the Ice Age had already led peoples of the northern regions to replace wood with bone, ivory and antlers for the manufacture of many objects, and to use bones as fuel. The eyed needle which appeared at about this time enabled sewn garments to be made that were warmer because they fitted better. The Siberian hunters of the Upper Paleolithic mainly sought out herbivorous mammals living in herds inland. They are represented *inter alia* by the Diuktai culture*, first identified in the basin of the Lena, especially on the Aldan (cave of Diuktai, site of Bal'kachi) and Kamchatka (Lake Uhski). This corresponds to what is sometimes called, though the term is not clearly defined, the Siberian Paleo-Arctic tradition*.

The development of the Bering isthmus

During the last Ice Age, the considerable growth of glaciers forced down the sea level on several occasions to below the level of the continental platforms surrounding Alaska, Siberia and Southeast Asia. Thus Indonesia, Japan, continental Asia and America were connected, and mankind could expand into regions unoccupied by glaciers. As the mean depth of the sea bed around the Bering area was 50m (164ft) lower than the present-day sea level, the strait must have been replaced by an isthmus which may have been 1,000km (621 miles) wide during the three periods of maximum glaciation. The most recent estimates put these at between 100,000 and 93,000BC, 74,000 and 62,000BC, and 28,000 and 15,000BC. This isthmus and the regions situated on either side of it made up Beringia, which extended from the Lena to the Mackenzie and had a special ecosystem which probably disappeared about 12,500 years ago. The steppe/tundra where the large herbivores grazed was the dominant and original landscape. However, opinions differ about other geographical and climatic peculiarities of central Beringia, which fluctuated considerably, and the advantages it might offer to man and the animals he hunted.

During these three periods the migrations between Siberia and America of Pleistocene musk ox, woolly bison, caribou and horse could have entailed the migration of the peoples hunting them. Unfortunately, a large part of the territory which may conceal material evidence of their presence is submerged today. Nevertheless the Bering isthmus is not indispensable to explain man's arrival in America. Recent information suggests a first peopling of Australia 40,000 years ago, involving the crossing of a sea channel equivalent to the existing Bering Strait, so the latter was not an impassable obstacle.

The oldest remains attributed to man in the American part of Beringia come from the Yukon. These are the bones of large mammals that have been splintered or broken, sometimes by twisting. According to their discoverers they are evidence of tool making in bone which was practised at least 50,000 and some say more than 100,000 years ago. However, only at the Bluefish caves, dated to a far more recent period (18,000 years) has any bone artifact been found in an undisturbed archaeological context. The chronological estimations are generally based on the immediate geological environment. The only universally accepted tool from this ancient period is an implement for scraping hair from skins. Made of a caribou's tibia and found in 1966, it is similar to those of the ancient Amerindians. A radiocarbon* dating using apatite has given 27,000BC. Experiments have shown that the bone could not have been fashioned in that way unless it was in its original state, which would eliminate the possibility of the modern reutilization of a fossil bone. The validity of this date and the human origin of the fractures or marks made in the cutting up of animal flesh are questioned by many archaeologists who do not accept a first population of America before 10,000 or 13,000BC.

A pre-projectile period in America

However, to the south of the region occupied by the glaciers of Wisconsin, there are more and more sites for which a date prior to 10,000 is proposed in North America, Mexico and South America, for example Dutton, Selby, Lamb Spring, Calico Hills, and Louisville. On the whole no manmade projectile points have been found, hence the name "pre-projectile" attributed to this poorly defined period. Finds include split pebbles and flakes, and indications of an often very crude industry, but one or more of the following features needed to convince the sceptics is nearly always missing: a clear stratigraphy*, reliable and multiple radiocarbon datings and a well-established geological and paleological context. Among the sites discovered recently and excavated by modern methods, several have been given apparently certain dates going back 18,000 years in the United States (Meadowcroft shelter in Pennsylvania) and back as far as 30,000BC in Brazil (see "Prehistoric rock art", page 358). The great number of sites attributed to the pre-projectile period and of dates prior to 10,000BC tend to confirm the reality if not the extent of this period. Nevertheless if a human occupation going back more than 35,000 years were confirmed in America, we should have to inquire into the place of origin of those first occupants of whom there is almost no trace in eastern Siberia (admittedly still little excavated) and ask whether the oldest inhabitants could not have been Neanderthaloids. So far no other paleontological evidence supports the hypothesis of a presence prior to *Homo sapiens sapiens* in America. Nevertheless, the announcement in 1984 by the Russians that the archaeologist Mochanov had discovered, south of Irkutsk near the Lena, a stone tool industry contemporary with a cold climate and geologically dated to 2,000,000 years ago would overturn, if it were ever confirmed, the prehistorians' view about the possibility of a population of America earlier than *Homo sapiens sapiens* and of the antiquity of man's adaptation to cold regions.

The Beringian Upper Paleolithic tradition

In Alaska several archaeological formations bear the mark of the Upper Paleolithic and are associated with a rather poorly defined American Paleo-Arctic tradition, known as the Beringian tradition* or Beringian Upper Paleolithic. The fact remains that in this first American territory traversed by peoples of the Siberian Upper Paleolithic after crossing the Bering isthmus, there are hardly any sites prior to 10,000BC whose dating has been conclusively established. Indeed, there are more finds from 10,000–8000BC than from the following periods, although they are often small and not rich in artifacts. This density may be the mark of a population that suddenly increased in size. But after 5000BC the sites that still bear the mark of the Upper Paleolithic, such as those of the Denalian culture*, disappear completely; they nearly all occur inland where big game could be hunted. The Aleutian site of Anangula is one of the rare exceptions which gives evidence for the beginning of adaptation to coastal resources perhaps 10,000 years ago among the groups located in the south of Beringia.

It cannot yet be established whether the Paleo-Arctic hunters merely passed through the Beringian isthmus or whether they exploited it intensively as a region rich in game and favourable to their demographic expansion, before it was covered by the sea. In the first hypothesis, compatible with the idea of an inhospitable environment, the sites of the American Paleo-Arctic period would simply be evidence of the arrival of populations coming directly from Siberia without lingering in the isthmus. The second hypothesis implies that the Beringian isthmus was rich in prairies hospitable to the large mammals and their hunters; in this case the oldest sites in Alaska would have sheltered the "survivors" of the submerged part of Beringia, who would have progressively sought refuge in the high valleys.

Archaeologists find it difficult to link the Paleo-Arctic to the later cultures of Alaska and even to those contemporary with it in the rest of America. A large part of Alaska and the Yukon was spared by the glaciers which extended from the Pacific to the Atlantic in two ice sheets, one centred on the Laurentian shield, the other on the Rocky Mountains. The most recent geological data suggest that at the time of their maximum extent, these ice sheets approached each other and, if they did not actually fuse, probably left no more than a very narrow and inhospitable corridor on three occasions, namely *c.*68,000, 33,000 and 18,000 to 13,000BC. Outside these periods, it is no longer thought that the ice cap of the Rockies developed enough to stop groups of hunters advancing southwards. One may even ask whether the Pacific coast did not sometimes offer a transit route partly practicable by boat. However, as the oldest Alaskan sites previously mentioned go back to 10,000BC at most, some archaeologists do not believe that the more southerly regions could have been populated before that date.

Big game hunters

To the south of the territory formerly covered by glaciers, the oldest sites considered as Paleo-Indian, and with datings accepted by most archaeologists, appeared *c.*10,000BC. The Paleo-Indians were big game hunters, and used bifacial* projectile points comparable to those of the Siberian Upper Paleolithic. These points, which vary in form according to time and place, characterize the various Paleo-Indian formations. The oldest and most numerous Paleo-Indian remains have been found in the plains of the Middle West of the United States. The asymmetrical Sandia points prepared the way for the first channelled points. This channelling, obtained by the removal of a long flake from the base of the point on one or both of its faces, was made so that the shaft could be attached more efficiently. This appears to have been a genuinely American invention, because until now channelled points have not been found outside America. Variants of these points of the Clovis (*c.*9000BC) and Folsom type (*c.*8000BC) make up what is often called the Llano horizon. The few channelled points found in Alaska and the Yukon or to the north of the former ice sheets are interpreted rather as an indication of an advance northwards by a few Paleo-Indian bands from the Prairies. The Plano horizon, which succeeded the Llano, is characterized by a very great variety of channelled points (for example the Agate Basin, Plainview and Cody types). The Paleo-Indian period is also represented by numerous sites used as bases for the intensive hunting of large mammals and encampments where stone and wood were worked. It is possible that the over-exploitation of this large Pleistocene fauna by the first Paleo-Indian hunters who spread in large numbers as far as the extreme south of America, precipitated rather than caused the extinction of several species of large herbivores such as the mammoth and the prehistoric horse. This would be the first example of ecological upset caused by man. It has been calculated that 1,500 years would have sufficed for groups of people to traverse America from north to south, moving from one hunting ground to another.

The anthropometric, biological, genetic and linguistic data concerning the populations of Asia and America all agree with the hypothesis of an Asiatic origin for the Amerindians, Eskimos and Aleutians. Starting from a common Mongoloid stock, those groups who were to become Amerindians on the one hand and the Eskimos and Aleutians on the other, began to differentiate themselves from each other in Siberia a little less than 20,000 years ago. Those who were to become the Amerindians presumably penetrated America through the interior of Beringia, perhaps in two distinct movements. The Eskimos and Aleutians diverged only 9,000 years ago after having frequented the south coast of Beringia. They exploited coastal resources more intensively, which would have encouraged their demographic development.

It is likely that research still in progress will provide more details of the pre-projectile period prior to the Paleo-Indian. For the moment, however, it is difficult to connect this period with the data concerning Alaska and eastern Siberia provided by archaeology and other disciplines.

Clovis points found with mammoth bones, site of Lehner, Arizona

Clovis points, like Folsom points, were used by the Paleo-Indians who hunted large mammals, especially mammoths. They resemble certain Siberian/Paleo-Arctic points, but the channellings of various lengths running from the base, which characterize them and are unknown in the Old World, ensured that their attachment to the spear was more stable.

Bone tool industry of Old Crow Basin, Yukon

The Old Crow sites have yielded more than 100 bones of large animals which seem to have been splintered deliberately or, as with these examples, to have been worked like a stone core. Are they evidence of a bone industry more than 15,000 years old or the deliberate removal and consumption of marrow, or are they the result of natural causes? Splintered bones have been found on many sites in Colorado. They, too, are pre-Clovis and their range of stone tools is scanty. Ottowa museum.

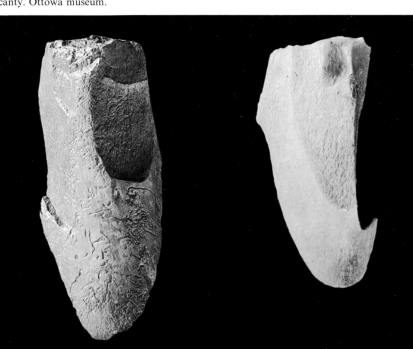

Skin scraper made from a caribou's tibia, _c_.27,000 years before present

Identical with scrapers used by Amerindians in historic times, this skin scraper found in the Yukon is believed to be one of the oldest tools in America, but its age has been queried. The method of dating was experimental and the date obtained may be that of the bone, which was perhaps not made into a tool until long afterwards. Nevertheless, experiments have shown that to be easily worked bone must be fresh. Ottowa museum.

Skeleton of mammoth in the process of being uncovered on a Paleo-Indian site in Arizona

The animal's teeth can be seen in the foreground. Sometimes whole mammoths have been found on American sites, specially in Alaska and the western states. In spite of its size, the mammoth was fairly easy to hunt. It disappeared, like the mastodon, the prehistoric horse, the camelids and other large Pleistocene mammals, some time after 8000BC, perhaps as the combined results of hunting and the ecological changes following the post-glacial rise in temperature.

Hunters of the Arctic

The first Americans came over the land bridge of Beringia, a region which in Ice Age times connected Alaska with Siberia. But the permanent occupation of the true Arctic, the most inhospitable region on earth, occurred considerably later and produced a number of resourceful cultures.

The hunters of the Arctic are partly descended from the first peoples of America crossing the now submerged land bridge of Beringia. In the Holocene*, waves of exchanges, influences and people between Asia and Alaska also left their mark on the formation of the American Arctic cultures. Although recent archaeological information does not yet enable us to follow clearly the routes by which cultures travelled from Siberia to Alaska, it is nevertheless possible to retrace the different phases of the Mongoloid hunters' adaptation to the marine resources available to them from the end of the Pleistocene*, and the movement of their expansion from the Bering Sea to Greenland.

The first known American site supplying evidence of this maritime adaptation is that of Anangula on the Aleutian Islands, which may go back more than 10,000 years. Among the microlithic tool industries, probably deriving from the Paleo-Arctic* tradition, which appeared in the northwest of America, the Arctic microlithic tradition provided the basis of the Paleo-Eskimo and Eskimo cultures. It became apparent at the end of the 3rd millennium BC in the northwest of Alaska (the sites at Denbigh and Onion Portage, for example).

The most ancient sites of the Arctic microlithic tradition indicate a form of subsistence relying mainly on hunting the caribou, with seal-hunting as a secondary activity. It has not yet been clearly established whether these hunters evolved from Paleo-Arctic Alaskan peoples or came from Siberia. However, that may be, the Arctic microlithic tradition spread very rapidly, in the course of two or three centuries, from the south of the Bering Sea across to Labrador and even as far as the northeastern tip of Greenland (Independence Fjord). While it is possible to follow its development in the central and eastern Arctic until about AD1500, the tradition seems to disappear in Alaska from about 1000BC. The hunters belonging to this tradition were to become progressively more specialized in exploiting the Arctic environment, in particular its coastal resources. This is called the Paleo-Eskimo period. The development of the Paleo-Eskimo cultures is different in the central and eastern Arctic (Canada and Greenland) from its evolution in the western Arctic (Alaska).

Cultures of the Far North

The Paleo-Eskimos were the first inhabitants of the central and eastern Arctic, and go back to at least 2000BC. This was towards the end of the hypsithermal, the period of maximum warmth which followed the last glaciation. Some dates in the region of 3000BC have even been put forward recently for the site at Old Nugdlit in the Thule area in the north of Greenland, but these are still very much open to question. It is generally thought that the Paleo-Eskimos emigrated from Alaska, following the herds of musk ox and caribou.

A distinction is usually made between two early archaeological formations: the Independence* culture, first identified in Independence Fjord and Ellesmere Island, then in other parts of the Arctic, especially northern areas; and the Pre-Dorset* culture, more often called Sarqaquian in Greenland, which was identified in Foxe Basin and Baffin Island, then throughout the Canadian Arctic. Pre-Dorset seems to be slightly later than Independence I, which disappeared c.1700BC and re-emerged in the same areas c.1100BC in the form of Independence II (which shows some similarities with late Pre-Dorset, and has some features equivalent to those of the Dorset culture). Between 1500 and 700BC, a slightly warmer period, the Pre-Dorset peoples spread into the inland of the Barren Grounds where they hunted caribou. Between 800 and 500BC a new archaeological formation emerged, becoming increasingly distinct from the previous, Dorset culture.

The material culture of the Dorset people displayed new technical features whose origin it has not been possible to establish. It indicated a very clever exploitation of coastal resources. There is hardly any further evidence of the bow; perforations, especially the eye of a needle, were no longer drilled with a drill-bow – they were achieved by incisions or the use of a burin. Stone polishing was developed, lamps were made from steatite, dwellings became more complex and sometimes very large. Another distinctive characteristic of the Dorset culture, especially in its final phase, was a very rich artistic expression in the form of small human and animal figurines. Traces of the Dorset tradition disappear between AD1350 and 1500, depending on the area – at the same time that the Thule Neo-Eskimos, who had been coming from Alaska from the 11th century, were present in the same territories.

In Alaska, an area where very different cultures met, the development of the Arctic microlithic tradition is harder to follow. In the south, from 3000BC, two other regional traditions are apparent: that of the Aleutian Islands and that of Kodiak Island, the latter being characterized by the use of polished slate prior to 1000BC. Elsewhere the Arctic microlithic tradition, though it came in shortly before 2000BC, ceases to be clearly in evidence from 1000BC. Shortly afterwards, first the Choris and then the Norton cultures in the north seem to preserve some elements of it, manufacturing a type of pottery that was Siberian in origin, as well as stone lamps and polished slate objects. There were also developments in the use of the coastal resources. The sites associated with these cultures correspond to large coastal villages where archaeologists have sometimes found several hundred semi-underground dwellings. A similar evolution occurs in the strange culture of the Near-Ipiutak and Ipiutak, regarded as special forms of the Norton culture despite the obvious differences (the absence of pottery and polished slate at Ipiutak, whale-hunting at Near-Ipiutak), and a very original form of artistic expression, revealed in a great diversity of objects, the purpose of which is sometimes inexplicable. The Choris, Norton and Ipiutak cultures, more or less derived from the Arctic microlithic tradition, correspond to the eastern Paleo-Eskimo. They are sometimes regrouped under the name of the "Norton tradition". This latter did not disappear in the north until the end of the 1st millennium AD when the Neo-Eskimo culture was already beginning to appear.

In the south of Alaska and on the shores of the Bering Sea we can also follow the development of the Norton and of other Siberian coastal cultures. This convergence of Siberian and Alaskan influences in the Bering area is at the origin of the development, during the 1st millennium AD and based on the Norton tradition, of a northern maritime tradition which is also known as Thule. This incorporates the Old Beringian (the Old Bering Sea culture) and the Okvik, Punuk and Birnik cultures in the north of Alaska, from which the Thule culture was to emerge shortly before the end of the 1st millennium AD. Whaling, of which there is intermittent evidence in the Paleo-Eskimo period, benefited from the technical developments achieved in hunting other marine mammals on open water: kayaks, oumiaks (a kind of animal-skin whaleboat), harpoons with baited floats, and rocking harpoon heads were used. On St Lawrence Island whales were regularly hunted by the people of Panuk from AD500. At Point Barrow special ecological conditions favoured whaling during the animals' seasonal migrations. It may have been these that attracted the peoples of the Thule culture, who dominated the North Pacific in both Siberia and Alaska towards the central and eastern Arctic from the beginning of the second millennium AD at a period when the climate underwent a rise in temperature.

"Multiface" from the Dorset tradition found on Bathurst Island, Canada

Coming from the eastern Arctic and from Greenland, these objects, generally made from Caribou antlers, were perhaps carved by shamans. Each one has dozens of faces, expressions and diverse forms, all overlapping each other. National Museum of Mankind, Ottawa.

Miniature wooden mask found at the Dorset site of "Nanook" in Baffin Island, Canada

Animal and human representations in Dorset art are generally in miniature form. Full-sized masks also existed, but very few have been found. Similar faces were also carved in the steatite quarries of Arctic Quebec. The mask depicted here measures 61mm (2.2in). National Museum of Mankind, Ottawa.

Ivory harpoon from Independence Island originating from Port Refuge, Canada

The oldest Paleo-Eskimo harpoon heads were bone or ivory without a stone sheathing. The style of harpoon head is a good chronological and cultural guide for Arctic prehistorians. The perforation allows a tassel made from the skin of an aquatic mammal to be inserted. National Museum of Mankind, Ottawa. Length: 63mm (2.3in).

Microlithic tools from Independence I originating from Port Refuge, Canada

The point with a stem, on the left, was probably used as a lance, and has denticulated edges characteristic of the Independence period. The burins on the right, from 2 to 3cm in length (0.7 to 1.1in) with a support modelled sometimes on both faces, were abundant in the old Paleo-Eskimo period. They were used for working on bone and ivory, and became rare from the Dorset era onwards. The heads of the burins, although very small, show signs of use. National Museum of Mankind, Ottawa.

Site of a long house of the Dorset culture on Ungura, Arctic Quebec

The people of the Dorset culture built large communal dwelling places, covered by skins. The families of a regional group were able to reunite there, probably in autumn, before separating again for the winter. Size 40 × 6m (128 × 19ft). Laboratory of Archaeology at the University of Quebec at Montreal.

Composite ivory funeral mask, found at Ipiutak in Alaska

The pieces were joined by means of thin strips of material through the perforations. American Museum of Natural History, New York.

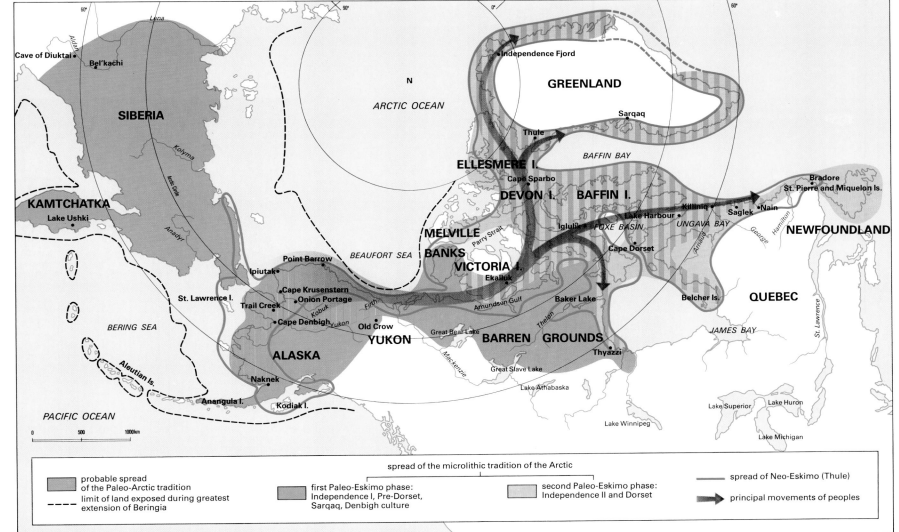

probable spread of the Paleo-Arctic tradition

limit of land exposed during greatest extension of Beringia

spread of the microlithic tradition of the Arctic

first Paleo-Eskimo phase: Independence I, Pre-Dorset, Sarqaq, Denbigh culture

second Paleo-Eskimo phase: Independence II and Dorset

spread of Neo-Eskimo (Thule)

principal movements of peoples

Hunters of the eastern forests

Ingenious and versatile adaptation by humans to the forest resources of eastern North America, beginning 7,000 years ago, was so successful that it continued until the arrival of Europeans in the 16th century.

Eighteen thousand years ago the northeast of North America was nothing but a huge field of ice. A human desert extended over the part of the territory east of the Mississippi which was covered by the continental glacier at the period of the widest extent of the last Ice Age, the Wisconsin glaciation, corresponding to the Würm glaciation in Europe. The ice cap began to shrink shortly after this, and about 12,000 years ago was at the latitude of the Great Lakes and the St Lawrence River. The effects of glaciation on the environment became less marked from about 6000BC, but between that date and the beginning of the glacial decline a series of bio-geographical adjustments created a succession of vegetation zones from cold desert to dense forest, with tundra and taiga as intermediate stages. The landscape that became established during the 5th millennium BC over the whole of this area was identical to that seen by the first Europeans in the 16th and 17th centuries AD. The forest extended as far as the eye could see, but the type of tree cover varied according to latitude. Hickory, oak, walnut and maple predominated in the southern forests; maple, aspen, birch and pine in the central forests; and the northern forests were mainly composed of spruce. As vegetation was specific to certain latitudes, so also were types of wildlife; there was a wealth of animal species in the southern areas, gradually lessening to the north. Archaeologists must keep these fluctuations in mind to understand regional adaptions.

However, the forest cover of this area was quite recent in date, and the first Americans who came in pursuit of large game east of the Mississippi during the 10th millennium found no trees; they encountered instead a landscape of lichens on which browsed the last herds of mammoths and mastodons, members of large species of mammals of the Pleistocene*. The disappearance of the "megafauna" and the gradual establishment of forest transformed the conditions available for exploitation by the first inhabitants, known as Paleo-Indians. The new afforested landscapes resulted in major adjustments, and the human communities adopted a new way of living, that characteristic of the Archaic period which, according to area, spread over the period from 6000 to 1000BC. These five millennia saw the conquest of an entire territory, heavily wooded and intersected by numerous fast-running rivers. This was a new country

that man had to tame, and in order to do it he had to master a major new element of the landscape: the vegetation cover.

The peoples of the Archaic period retained many characteristics of their forerunners: a similar but much less carefully executed technology of worked stone, a similar nomadic way of life associated with the pursuit of animals, the same type of socio-economic organization consisting of small autonomous groups made up of several families. Subsistence still relied on hunting, but seasonal variations in resources compelled the groups to diversify their activities. According to the time of year, they were hunters, fishermen or gatherers, but hunting was still the most productive and prestigious pursuit, undertaken by groups of men using a variety of techniques. Hunting proper was used to catch large and medium-sized animals such as moose, wapiti, roe deer, caribou, bear and beaver, while techniques such as trapping were employed for small game like muskrat and hare. Javelins were equipped with tips of shaped stone, and cunning traps were placed on animal trails. The everyday diet consisted mainly of meat, but this was supplemented by fish and wild berries. Fishing continued throughout the year, even under the ice, but the summer period was the most productive. Edible plants were gathered, mainly by the women, throughout the summer and into the autumn.

The relative abundance of resources during the summer led the many small groups to assemble each year to deal with collective business and to reinforce the sense of belonging to a larger group, or band. The end of the summer and the autumn were a crucial period in which preparations were made for winter. After the gatherings and festivities of summer, during the autumn there was a dispersal and disintegration of the band so that resources could be exploited to the best possible advantage. Food was gathered, and fishing and hunting were pursued to stock up for winter, and at the same time the groups moved towards the best places in which to face up to the cold season ahead without too much privation. A sub-group would have required a hunting and trapping area of at least 1,000sq km (386sq m) to be able to withstand the rigours of winter. Exploitation of the land had to be regulated according to the season. Respect for the annual cycle of activities essential for

subsistence guaranteed the survival of human groups.

Hunters' tools and their circulation

In order to reconstruct man's activity at that far-off period, we can by analogy base our assumptions on the descriptions of hunting groups made by Europeans upon their arrival in this part of North America in the 16th century. Archaeological information very often consists only of the stone tool kit. Following a line of reasoning based on analogy, we can take it that articles were made from wood and other materials, remains of which are not usually to be found on archaeological sites. The Amerindians used such materials to make means of transport (boats, snow shoes, toboggans, sledges, etc.), dwellings, snares and traps, firewood, receptacles, utensils, weapons (bows, arrows and javelin shafts), fishing nets, medicines, and so on. Likewise they used bone to manufacture pointed implements, fish hooks, harpoons, awls, scissors and needles.

In the course of the five millennia that covered the duration of the Archaic period, human adaptation to the environment developed and became increasingly effective. Regional differences resulting from adaptation to varying local resources appeared over the vast area involved, but at the same time the circulation of objects between groups was considerable. Thus, during the 3rd millennium BC, some groups in the vicinity of Lake Superior specialized in the manufacture of tools of local copper. These artifacts, lance tips, bracelets and rings, were exported throughout the east by means of a large network of exchange. The various groups were always open to outside contacts in spite of the isolation caused by the winter.

Despite the hostility of the environment, the hunters of the eastern forests of North America developed a widespread network of communication. Their way of life enabled them to adapt to a vast territory and this special system of adaptation endured in the northern groups until the arrival of the Europeans. For example, the use of pottery receptacles only came at a late date, and half-heartedly. The way of life pursued by the forest hunters to the east of North America did not give rise to a very elaborate socio-economic organization, but it did enable them to master and successfully exploit a difficult environment for thousands of years.

Habitations and dwelling places (above and right)

The prehistoric peoples of the east of North America lived in small groups often consisting of two or three nuclear families. Each family unit had its own habitation composed of a framework of interwoven poles covered with the skins of deer. A hearth occupied the centre of the area. Recent archaeological research has revealed at Quebec (right) the plan of a house more than 30m long × 6m wide (98 × 20ft) built by groups whose subsistence came mainly from hunting and fishing. It was the dwelling place for small groups who assembled in the summer for exchange and social reorganization. This discovery challenges the theory that such habitations were used exclusively by smallholders and emphasizes the social organization of these groups.

A land of ice

The forests of the east of North America did not exist 18,000 years ago. Hunting groups had certainly not crossed the Mississippi at this period. The land was then under more than a kilometre of ice and we have no irrefutable proof of the presence of man to the south of the glacial front. The regression of the ice sheet first allowed a tundra to be established and it was not until around the 7th millennium BC that deciduous and coniferous forests progressively invaded this vast territory and gave it its definitive character. After V.K. Prest, "The Geology of the quaternary in Canada", in R.J.W. Douglas, L.P. Tremblay ed. *Geology and Mineral Resources in Canada*, 1975, Ottawa.

maximum expansion of glacier 16,000BC

extent of glacier 10,000BC

expansion of Lake Champlain 10,000BC

extent of glacier 6,000BC

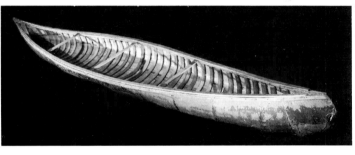

Paleo-Indian period (10,000–6000BC)

Archaic period (6000–1000BC)

continuing Archaic lifestyle (recent Prehistoric period: 1000–1750AD)

Hamilton Inlet
L'Anse Amour
Port-aux-Choix
site of Longue-Maison
Washadimi
site of Minto river
Rivière-au-Bouleau
Sainte-Anne-des-Monts
Tadoussac
Bic
Debert
Saint-Augustin
Cow Point
Allumettes and Morisson Is.
Pointe-du-Buisson
Vail
Reagen
Sheguiandah
Neville
Whipple
Bull Brook
Fisher
Inverhuron
Brewerton
Renier
Potts
West Athens Hill
Holcombe
Parkhill
Dutchess Quarry Cave
Lamoka
Plenge
Meadowcroft Rockskelter
Koster
Williamson

The people of the forest

Around 9000BC, the first groups had adapted themselves to the fluctuations of the environment and are found on nearly all the territory freed from the ice. These Paleo-Indians lived essentially by hunting big game; they may sometimes have encountered mammoths and mastodons, but archaeological research has not yet proved that these animals were hunted in the east, whereas plenty of evidence of this activity exists in the west of North America. The groups of the Archaic period adapted so successfully to the northern forests that although archaeologists fix the end of the Archaic at 1000BC, a way of life based on hunting continued in the coldest latitudes down to the historical period.

Projectile points, site of Pointe-du-Buisson

The great dependence of populations on food acquired by hunting contributed much to North American mythology. Nevertheless, the adaptation of hunting groups to their environment encouraged them not to concentrate on a single activity. They preferred hunting, but they also regularly practised fishing and gathering. Archaeologists have identified hunting activities by the presence of projectile points, but the bow and arrow did not appear at the same time. It is accepted that the bow was not used before the beginning of our era. As for the projectile points which armed a spear, they were undoubtedly propelled by an *atlatl* (throwing stick).

The means of transport

The recession of the ice caused a surplus of water, making the use of waterborne craft a matter of primary importance in the conquest of this new land. Bark canoes and dug-outs made from single tree trunks represent a basic element of adaptation to the environment. With the help of snowshoes and toboggans, the ingenuity of the hunters transformed winter into a period when nomadism was practised on the largest scale.

Adaptation to the cold

The conquest of the northern latitudes necessitated adaptation to the cold. The use of fire, well-insulated dwellings, clothing made of skins and techniques of winning food, have been identified by archaeologists, but they rarely tackle the psychological aspect of this adaptation. The Naskapis of Quebec-Labrador still sew caribou skins together to make clothes, just as the Archaic groups must have done. The complicated decoration of the coat shown here confirms that adaptation to the cold did not entail cultural impoverishment. Unfortunately, archaeologists are rarely able to discover this lavish artistic display, because the ground excavated only preserves organic materials in exceptional cases. Royal Ontario Museum, Toronto.

Burial practices

Archaeological evidence for the cosmologies of hunting groups is somewhat rare. It is confined to burials where the dead, either dismembered or burnt, were placed in a foetal position. In order to undertake the journey to the beyond, everyday objects were placed near the dead person. The existence of an elaborate ritual may be assumed, and the discovery of a tumulus at Anse-Amour on the coast of Labrador revealed complicated burial practices carried out by the forest hunters. In this grave, which goes back more than 7,000 years, blocks were piled up over a ditch which contained the body of an adolescent and artifacts, some of which probably had a religious function.

331

The development of agriculture

Unlike the Near East, where the "agricultural revolution" marked a decisive advance in human development, North America at first saw agriculture as complementing rather than replacing existing ways of life.

Hundreds of sites have yielded information about the emergence of agriculture in North America, enabling us to establish the chronology of the introduction of the various plants grown, and to evaluate their importance in the economy and their effects on the organization of human groups. In this research archaeology has benefited from information provided by ethno-history. The appearance of agriculture marked a considerable change in the quality of life for the American groups that became dependent on it, but we now know that this change was much less sudden than was thought around 20 years ago. It was believed then that agriculture represented a real advance, that the life of the hunter-gatherer was marked by economic insecurity and that the use of cultigens* must have resulted in the rapid, welcome and desirable development of agriculture. Ethnologists have now shown that the hunting life was not as insecure as had been thought, that agricultural populations were subject to various natural disasters (too dry or too wet a climate, plagues of insects, etc) that a way of life based on the production of cultivated plants often involved a heavier work load, the imposition of a mixed economy, an acceleration in population growth, and restricted territories and resources. It is becoming increasingly apparent that the adoption of a way of life dependent on agriculture was the costly answer to a crisis situation brought about by relative overpopulation and the deterioration of natural resources in areas that can already be seen to have quite distinct boundaries. Moreover, adoption of this lifestyle as often as not followed upon a period during which the traditional hunting was supplemented by the use of hitherto neglected resources: intensive fishing, shellfish gathering, large-scale gathering of plant foods, etc. It also tended to follow a cycle of exploitation of resources that had included various forms of seasonal settlement. Indeed, it sometimes happened, as on the Pacific coast in the northwest, that this form of adaptation was in itself enough to satisfy new needs, and did not necessarily lead to agriculture.

It is now known, from ethno-historical sources, that in some areas agriculture was to be found in the form of small gardens where plants were grown to supplement the diet, and which were relatively insignificant to the economy; this was still true of some Algonquin groups in the 17th century living in the vicinity of the Ottawa River (a tributary of the St Lawrence). Cultigens were often known and appreciated, but not grown as crops; and often any surplus of these wild resources was bartered in exchange for agricultural produce. This was a general phenomenon in North America.

Economic changes through agriculture

When it was practised intensively, agriculture is usually found to have been accompanied by a complex, sometimes rapid process of deterioration in the economic relationship between a given population and the territory it exploited, but in some cases it existed for centuries at a time simply as a secondary, complementary phenomenon. In North America where the prehistoric population was never large, agricultural exploitation of the land developed late, and did not bring about such complex changes as occurred in the smaller areas available in mid-America or on the western fringe of the Andean belt.

When the Europeans arrived in the 16th century, the horticultural populations of North America were occupying a considerable area. But at the beginning of the AD era, while agriculture had already been moulding a dominant and widespread way of life in Mexico for a long time, in more northern areas attempts at horticulture were little developed and were always associated with a mixed economy in which hunting was always important and usually dominant. Nonetheless the most important cultigens, maize, haricot beans and cucurbitaceous plants (gourds and the like), had crossed what is now the northern frontier of modern Mexico long before the AD period. Maize actually made its appearance on the low, semi-arid mountain areas of the American southwest during the 3rd millennium BC and haricot beans and cucurbits were certainly present c.1000BC; however, they appear to have been no more than seasonal supplements to the diet, and it is hardly appropriate to talk of a horticultural way of life before 300BC. In the course of the following centuries (300BC–500AD) there was quite a sizeable regional diffusion of cultigens, as well as more general development of pottery, and we see an increasingly settled way of life, an increase in village life, in irrigation in some places, and ever more complex forms of social organization, marked both by a more noticeable division into cultural provinces (Anasazi, Mogollon, Hohokam, Patayan) and the building of sizeable villages. Yet despite the existence of various and sometimes close links between the southwest of America and the cultural groups in Mexico, different cultural forms developed in these two areas.

In eastern North America we find a very similar picture; cultigens which had spread from more southern latitudes appeared relatively early on but for a long time provided only seasonal supplements. The same species (maize, haricot beans and cucurbitaceous plants) were the staple diet of village groups. The first significant experiments in horticulture along certain stretches on the banks of the Mississippi date back to the 1st millennium BC, but the first development of agriculture during that millennium was tardy and restricted. There can be no doubt that at that period mixed economies were prevalent, and hunting, fishing and gathering played a very important part in them. Nonetheless, the practice of horticulture gradually spread, and was adopted by groups living on the prairie and on the Great Lakes, and along the banks of the St Lawrence, and by various peoples on the Atlantic coast and the Gulf of Mexico. Cultigens moved across cultural and linguistic frontiers, being adopted by different regions with greater or less speed. Thus certain prehistoric groups which settled along certain tributaries of the Mississippi or along the mid-St Lawrence region did not introduce cultigens until AD 1000.

The less prosperous north

In comparison with the peoples of Central America, the northern populations seem to have been less prosperous—or it would perhaps be more correct to say that they have left less spectacular evidence of their existence. They often organized themselves into small-scale, egalitarian villages, and much more seldom created towns with a hierarchical, administratively complex structure like Cahokia in Illinois (a site in the St Louis area which M. Fowler has been excavating for the past 20 years). They did not produce a complex, lasting state structure, nor develop monumental stone art, writing or metallurgy as was the case in Central America.

The peoples of North America adopted cultigens only in certain parts of their territory after long experimental periods during which cultivated plants played a purely complementary role. The use of crops did not become a predominant feature until a relatively recent period, often forming the basis of autonomous, semi-permanent societies, bound together by inter-tribal alliances and divided by endemic guerrilla attacks. Complex power structures and authoritarian social hierarchies, social systems involving the maintenance of specialists or states based on kingship—these made only brief, isolated appearances.

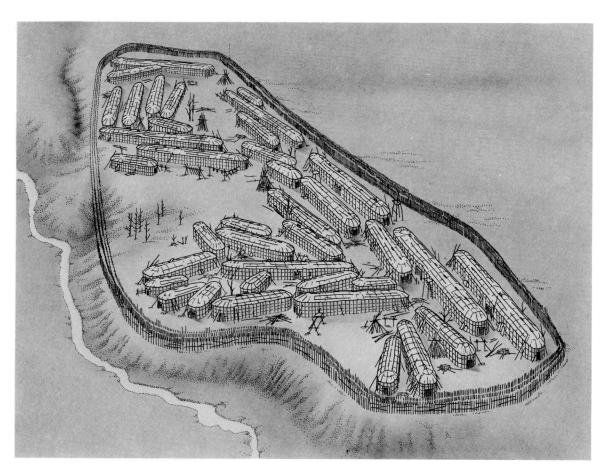

The Iroquois village of Draper, Ontario

The agricultural communities of northeastern America were divided into several linguistic groups and separate cultures. The Iroquois numbered more than 100,000, and were scattered over a territory that was larger than modern Greece, consisting of several culturally distinct provinces, sometimes hostile towards one another, but with many things in common. After beginning to use pottery (1000–500BC), making several marginal attempts at horticulture (650–1000BC) and developing seasonal fishing grounds which required a semi-settled existence, they all developed agriculture along the same lines (maize, haricot beans, *Cucurbitaceae*) in about 1000AD, adopted the same type of multi-family dwelling and the same extremely adaptable model of village organization, which very rarely exceeded 2,000 inhabitants. From Ivan Kocsis, Museum of Indian Archaeology, an Affiliate of the University of Western Ontario, London, Canada.

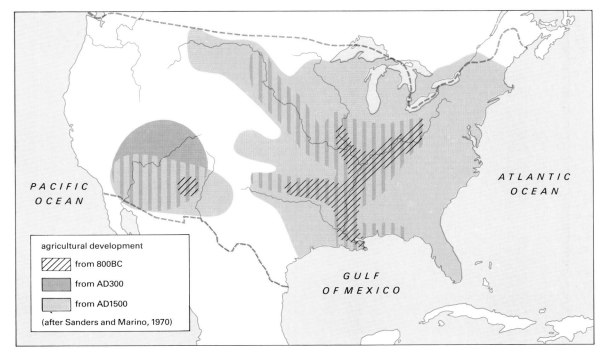

agricultural development

▨ from 800BC

▨ from AD300

▨ from AD1500

(after Sanders and Marino, 1970)

PACIFIC OCEAN

ATLANTIC OCEAN

GULF OF MEXICO

Bibliothèque nationale, Paris

Illustration taken from *Brevis narratio Floridae* by Théodore de Bry, 1591

The peoples of North America had nothing to help them prepare the fields cleared from the forest and sow their seed except digging sticks, hoes, crude rakes and winnowing baskets. There was little irrigation and it was more common to leave ground to lie fallow. The transformation of basic cultigens into food was effected with very simple implements (for picking, fumigating, storing and cooking) which varied according to region.

Illustration taken from the *Codex Canadiensis*

Inhaling the smoke fumes from dried, crushed plants was a widespread practice in North America. It became general with the cultivation of *Nicotiana*, but was not confined to horticultural communities or to that plant. It was already known during the 1st millennium BC, especially among several groups of nomadic hunters. The descriptions given of this custom in the 17th century show us that tobacco had considerable ritual significance, and that it was often smoked in special circumstances, especially on the occasion of political councils. Thomas Gilcrease, Institute of American History and Art, Tulsa.

The village of Pueblo Bonito, New Mexico

The settled, horticultural peoples of the American Southwest had contacts with communities in Mexico, and seem to have been more influenced by them than were peoples living to the east. They did, however, have their own original culture, distinguished by a communal way of life in villages perched on hillsides (cliff-dwellings) or in huge adjacent complexes of dwellings. Illustrations taken from *Prehistory of North America* by Jesse D. Jennings.

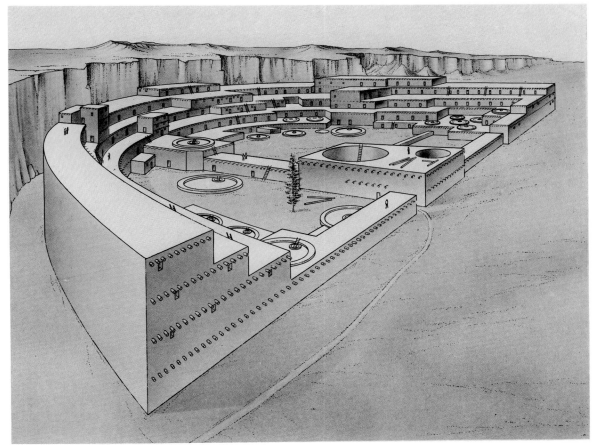

Thomas Gilcrease Institute of American History and Art, Tulsa

From hunter-gatherers to cave-dwellers

In the arid Southwest of America, natural conditions have preserved many vestiges of a resourceful and creative people, ancestors of the modern Hopi Indians, enabling archaeologists to reconstruct their lives in fine detail over more than 1,000 years

Isolated in the middle of the Colorado desert, Mesa Verde owes its name to the deep green of the conifers which cover its great table-like reliefs and its deep narrow canyons. To archaeology's great good fortune, the majority of biological remains are well preserved there through desiccation due to the low humidity of the air, which is constantly swept by the winds of the plateau, and to the excellent ventilation of the sandstone and sand which made up the essential components of the geological environment. So, through a meticulous study of material collected from tombs, we can describe in detail the inhabitants of the Mesa, their clothing, their everyday artifacts made from animal and vegetable fibres, and their food. These hunter-gatherers, who probably came from Utah shortly before the beginning of our era, have been given the name of Basketmakers. During this first period, called Basketmaker I in the comparative chronology of the American Southwest, these hunter-gatherers roamed the summits of the Mesa and sometimes used the great natural shelters of its canyons. The only structural remains they left behind were underground stone coffers, or cists. Between the seasonal migrations they variously stored wild grasses or a little cultivated maize. Sometimes they even buried their dead in them. So we know that the Basketmakers had light brown skin, smooth black hair and an average height of 1.63m (5.3ft) for men and 1.52m (4.9ft) for women. The men wore their hair very long and separated into three parts, with the ends tied into knots over the ears and on the neck. Apart from a few pendants and bracelets made of shells, their only article of clothing was a pair of sandals with double soles of finely plaited string, essential footwear for traversing rocky regions full of thorn bushes. The women had their hair cut short, and used it to make the string for tying on the indispensable sandals worn by every member of the group. They wore beautifully worked belts and small "G-strings".

The daily life of the Basketmakers

The women's everyday activities were divided between gathering, preparing food, making baskets and other objects of vegetable and animal fibres, and looking after the children. During the first year, the babies were carried by their mothers in a sort of basketwork backpack made of branches carefully joined together by fine cords and covered with rabbit skin. The men, for their part, made snares, nets and other traps used for hunting. Their only projectiles were a curved stick with a linear trajectory, a kind of non-returning American boomerang, and the Mesoamerican *atlatl* (a sort of spear and thrower). The furs of the rodents killed with this weapon were prepared by the women, cut into strips and rolled round thin cords. With these the women wove long capes used as a protection against the cold in winter and as a covering at night.

A transition from the nomadic life appears among the Basketmakers increasingly during the second period (AD1–500). Possibly developing from the cists, curious semi-subterranean structures (pit-houses) made their appearance. Maize, which was now increasingly cultivated, created surpluses which led to a gradual reduction in the nomadic way of life. At first the Basketmakers lived in small hamlets, but these rapidly developed to form genuine villages during the ensuing period, Basketmaker III (AD500–700). Technical innovations borrowed from Mesoamerica appear to have encouraged these changes: the cultivation of the haricot bean, the manufacture of pottery and the bow and arrow. The haricot bean contributed vegetable protein to balance the carbohydrates of maize and the vitamins of squash, and this was the decisive step towards an agricultural economy. The women consolidated this stage by making pottery, a skill probably transmitted by the neighbouring Hohokam who were in contact with Mesoamerica. But instead of modelling, they used a fine spiral of clay which was compressed by means of a bone point, just as they did when making their vegetable fibre baskets. The men took longer to abandon the spear and spearthrower for the bow and arrow, which were much more convenient and could be adapted to a greater variety of game. But they did adopt them in the end and they were to be found in all the small villages which gradually invaded the summits of the Mesa. There the people lived off the surrounding areas by growing maize in the rainy season.

A golden age

Benefiting from these new possibilities, the following period, Pueblo I (AD700 to 900) was to constitute a major stage in the economic, political and social transformation of the Mesa Verde human groups whom their modern descendants, including the Hopi, call the Anasazi (the ancient ones). Their *pueblos*, or villages, consisted of masonry houses, but as a link with their earlier traditions the Anasazi retained the semi-underground house (*kiva*) as the ceremonial place where the men organized communal life and religious rites. The women were not admitted to these *kivas*. However, if we are to believe ethnological studies of the present-day descendants of the Anasazi, women played an essential part in society, because they owned the matrimonial home and the fields. A matrilocal and matrilinear system dominated the communal life of this and the ensuing period (Pueblo II, AD900–1100), rightly called the golden age of the Great Southwest. Then came the discovery of cotton, and its advantages for bodily decoration to which the people attached growing importance.

But the Anasazi began to experience great difficulties towards the end of this period. The bonds of mutual aid formed with the villages of neighbouring regions, especially with Chaco Canyon, led Mesa Verde to shelter whole tribes which had abandoned their territories. According to some authors (Gladwin, 1957, Grant, 1978), this phenomenon can be explained (Lamb, 1958, using archeolinguistic data) by an intensification of the raids by Athapascan and Shoshone predators on these peaceful farmers' villages. Others claim it was due to the population explosion at Chaco (the fortified village of Pueblo Bonito alone contained 800 rooms and 32 *kivas*) or to the ecological changes caused by the collecting of surface water by means of dams across temporary watercourses.

However that may be, Mesa Verde very soon (Pueblo III period, AD1100 to 1300) assembled the largest group of Anasazi in the whole Great Southwest. The cave-dweller villages, which mark a step backwards in the building of habitats, nevertheless show the considerable efforts that were made in construction and adaptation to a particularly constricting environment. Far from the cultivated fields which remained on the flat summits, these refuges were difficult and even dangerous to reach. The long dry period from 1276 to 1299, as revealed by dendrochronology* had little effect (according to Gladwin, 1950) on the agriculture of the Mesa Verde, which depended on seasonal rains. Nevertheless at the end of the 13th century the whole area was abandoned, as Chaco Canyon had been in 1130 and as the whole region of Kayenta was to be soon afterwards. The Fremont of Utah, the Hohokam of Illinois and the Mogollon of New Mexico dispersed in search of new territories. Ecological catastrophes, population explosions and harassment by hostile groups may have all combined to cause this great exodus of the Anasazi.

Cliffs at Mesa Verde

Towards AD1100, caves which had been abandoned for more than a millennium were reoccupied and made into cliff-dweller villages. In these inaccessible fortresses, the Anasazi were sheltered from bad weather and possible predators.

A cliff-dwelling habitat at Mesa Verde (restoration)

"Cliff Palace" contains 200 habitable structures, some of which are 4 storeys high, and 23 *kivas*. Its restoration has been reduced to a minimum so as to preserve the appearance it offered to its first discoverers. Protected for more than eight centuries by the gigantic natural vault which shelters it, this remarkable construction has retained all its character.

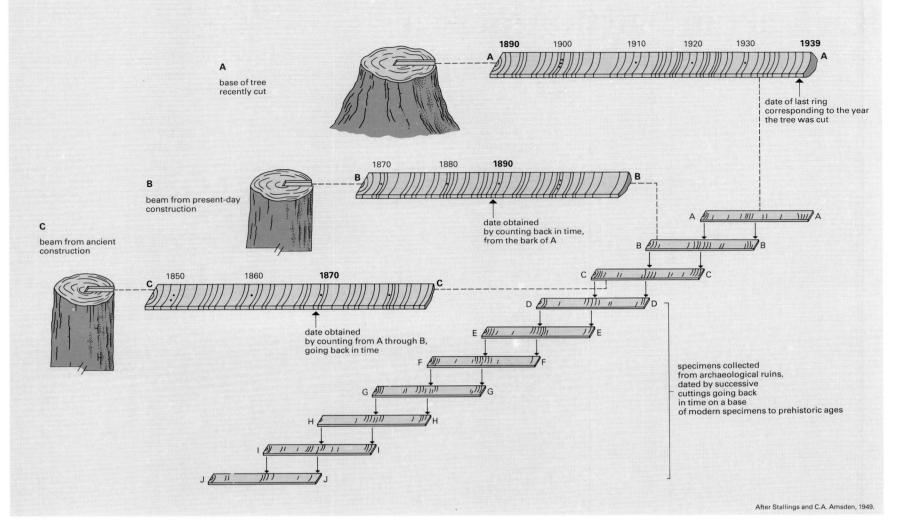

A
base of tree
recently cut

B
beam from present-day
construction

C
beam from ancient
construction

date of last ring
corresponding to the year
the tree was cut

date obtained
by counting back in time,
from the bark of A

date obtained
by counting from A through B,
going back in time

specimens collected
from archaeological ruins,
dated by successive
cuttings going back
in time on a base
of modern specimens to prehistoric ages

After Stallings and C.A. Amsden, 1949.

Dendrochronology

The first studies of dendrochronology (dating by the annual growth rings of trees) are the indirect result of A.E. Douglass's work in 1901 on sun spots and their effect on climates. This theory was that the trees of semi-arid Southwest America might provide good evidence of the amount of rain which had affected their development. It was gradually realized that they did in fact record climatic fluctuations in the form of their annual growth rings. By comparing some of these highly characteristic rings, observed on existing trees, with those of older trees used as beams in construction, very clear cross-checks could be made. Given the cyclic nature of their formation, it was thus conceivable that they could be used as a sort of calendar, enabling time spans to be traced back. The reliability of the method was soon demonstrated: for material found at the same stratigraphic levels, the succession of dates obtained by dendrochronology from the remains of beams tallied closely with the dating system based on stylistic differences of ceramic sequences worked out by archaeologists. However, the technique is only applicable in regions where biological remains remain in a good state of preservation. In the case of the Anasazi cultures, it has supplied the closest sequence possible in the absence of written material.

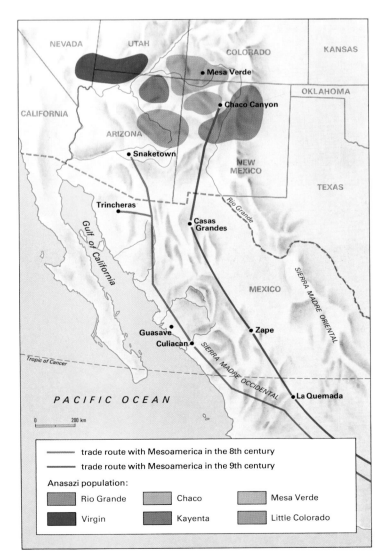

trade route with Mesoamerica in the 8th century
trade route with Mesoamerica in the 9th century
Anasazi population:
Rio Grande
Chaco
Mesa Verde
Virgin
Kayenta
Little Colorado

Situation of Mesa Verde

Compared with other Anasazi regions, Mesa Verde is particularly remote from the agricultural Mesoamerican civilizations. The technical advances of these civilizations reached Mesa Verde through the intermediary of populations situated further south, who carried on with it a trade in "luxury" articles, supplying turquoises in particular.

Basketmakers use of bow and arrow

The bows used from the Basketmaker III period were about 1m (3.3ft) long, with a semi-circular transverse section that gave them a considerable draw of the order of 40 pounds, according to present-day estimates. Unlike the spear and spearthrower, they enabled hunters to attack their prey from a considerable distance, 60m (200ft) according to Grant (1978). This painted decoration inside a pot depicts hunters following the trail of a stag. After Stewart Peckham.

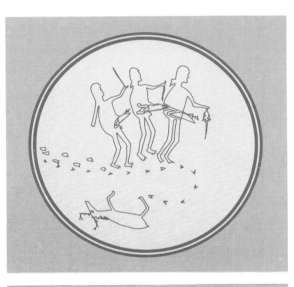

Hunting with snares among the Basketmakers

Hunting with snares and nets was widespread among the Basketmakers. Snares were mainly used to catch birds, attracted by decoys, as shown on the interior decoration of this vase. Nets were sometimes stretched across a canyon in which the tribe assembled to head back the game. One of these nets, found in excellent condition at White Dog Cave, was 63.34m long × 1.25m (201 × 4ft) wide. Cylindrical nets placed over the entrance to burrows were also used. After Stewart Peckham, Museum of New Mexico Press.

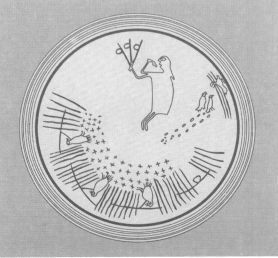

Rock art in North America

Found throughout the continent, Amerindian rock art is not only visually superb; it is also a rich record of spiritual beliefs, actual events and everyday life, from prehistory to modern times.

Rock art is widespread throughout North America. Wherever rocky outcrops provided a suitable base, Amerindians from prehistoric times until the 19th century produced figurative works of art. Here we will be discussing work from both periods, prehistoric and historical. The South West of the United States and Calfornia are particularly rich in rock art, but this inequality of distribution may result simply from the particularly favourable conditions for preservation brought about by the climate and the isolation of these regions; an inventory drawn up by Campbell Grant in 1967 (*Rock Art of the American Indians*) demonstrates the size of this disparity.

The techniques of American rock art are linked with the possibilities afforded by the rock on which it was carried out. In places where the rock is very hard (granite or schist) there are mainly paintings. Where the rock is relatively soft (sandstone, limestone or soapstone), representations are incised. The amount of "leisure" available to the artists and their level of technological development played a role in determining how the work was done. In the northern forests, the finger was used to draw rather crude forms in red ochre. The Eskimoes or their ancestors produced geometric faces reminiscent of masks (Hudson Strait), or marine animals (Alaska). The Indians in the South West, on the other hand, produced compositions with a truly extraordinary wealth of colours and forms, both realistic (especially the animals they hunted) and abstract (subjects from mythology and related themes). In the South West brushes were generally used to apply the various mineral pigments which were easy to obtain. Some examples of these instruments have been found on the spot in decorated caves or rock shelters. Petroglyphs or carvings were achieved by means of incising, making dot marks or scraping, according to the type of rock. The use of stone as a medium for artistic expression was only one among many forms found among the Amerindians. They recorded the important events of their existence on many other materials, such as birch bark, carved wood, animal skins and the human body, which was painted or tattooed, also a very widespread practice. But most of these have disappeared, while rock art still survives today.

Communication with the Beyond

The subjects depicted represent the preoccupations of the groups that produced them, but it seems on the basis of ethnographical evidence that painted or incised rocks were often invested with supernatural significance. Rock art would have been seen as a means of communicating with the world beyond, with all that lay outside the world of simple appearances. Dreams were also a favoured means of communicating with the super-

natural, and this only added to the variety of subjects depicted. Motifs that occur most frequently include, according to Grant: hands, bear tracks, serpents with feathers or horns, thunderbirds and various game animals such as the mountain sheep. However, the problem of interpreting these works is not an easy one.

With certain exceptions, contemporary Amerindian witnesses, still alive, whose traditions are rooted in the distant past are not of great help as far as studying the meaning of this art is concerned. Many refuse to speak about it at all, either through ignorance or out of respect for the sacred character of the works; others may answer from a desire to satisfy the enquirer or to get rid of the inquisitive. However, comparative studies, the analysis of Amerindian myths and some early testimony enable us to put forward some possible explanations. The subjects depicted can be grouped into a certain number of themes, with the proviso that no theme should be thought of as "pure": quite the opposite is true, and certain pictures can belong to several genres at the same time, concerning the ritual, the recording of "history" as an aid to memory, clan or heraldic symbols, or graffiti.

The ritual interpretation draws both on what we know of the Amerindians' beliefs and concept of the world, as described by ethnographers, and on the accounts of missionaries and chroniclers. Puberty rites and rites of passage, in particular, were sometimes conveyed by means of rock pictures. Thus among the Salish tribes of British Columbia, a young boy had to spend several days alone in the hills fasting and praying until he saw in his dreams the supernatural being that would be his guardian spirit or totem. The vision would of course bear some relationship to the young man's aspirations: the sun, a bear or an eagle if he dreamt of becoming a great warrior, a fish or a boat if his mind was bent on fishing. Then the young man would go and draw his vision on a rock, as if to give it some permanence. Where a girl was concerned, representations tend to be connected with her talents in performing domestic tasks, which would mean that she would be a good wife: basket-making, weaving, and so on. Girls' rock drawings appear more abstract, consisting of crisscross lines and superimposed zigzag lines. In agricultural areas we find pictures of supernatural beings associated with ceremonies intended to bring rain or to make it stop. For example, the Katchina dolls of the Hopi ceremonies had their counterparts, stylized to a greater or lesser degree, painted on the rocks. Other portrayals were aimed at ensuring the salmons' ascent from the sea to the rivers, hunting success or even the fertility of a couple wishing to have a child.

There are also a great many pictures of a memorial nature. Just as the Dakota Indians' "winter-counts", where each year was noted by a bison-skin drawing of

some image recalling an outstanding event (the year of the epidemic, the year of the famine, etc.), so the rock pictures are sometimes historical in nature. For example, hands performed the function of a signature; or a person might have drawn the symbol of his clan to mark each occasion on which he passed by a place. One remarkable example is provided by the picture story which Henry Schoolcraft obtained in 1852 from an Ojibwe chief, which tells of a warring expedition that had taken place about 1800, involving crossing Lake Superior in bark boats (something quite out of the common run). In 1958 Selwyn Dewdney (*Indian Rock Paintings of the Great Lakes*) found this story again, painted on a cliff at the northeast of the lake. All the details were there: the boats with the animal symbols of the chiefs drawn below them, the four suns indicating the length of the journey, and even the "Michipichou", the Great Lynx, a mythical spirit whose protection had ensured the success of the crossing.

Other pictures are harder to interpret. For example, there is widespread use of the bear or the eagle, and their roles could vary according to the tribes involved or the circumstances. The thunderbird is a very frequent symbol. In many legends of the Amerindian peoples, thunder is represented by a large eagle whose eyes shoot lightning and the rustle of whose wings can be heard from afar. This assimilation is based on observation of bird behaviour: when autumn comes and the birds fly south, thunder is no longer heard.

Problems of dating

Dating these pictures is a task fraught with hazards, especially on sites exposed to the weather. Dating has to be by various signs of relative age, such as patina, lichen growth, sedimentary cover, or the superimposing of works of different styles. The subjects depicted (the presence of a gun, for example) are also useful indicators. Moreover, the microscopic study of red ochre paintings in Mauricie National Park (Quebec province) shows not only how the paintings were preserved but also how they might eventually be dated: these granite rocks, which have been polished by glaciers, acquire a patina formed by a thin transparent film that is deposited by the evaporation of runoff water. The latter is acid and gradually dissolves the rock containing it. If the rate at which the patina accumulates can be worked out, we will know the approximate age of the painting.

Canoe and solar figure

The Peterborough petroglyphs, near Stony Lake, Ontario: right, canoe surmounted by a solar emblem and an unidentified object; right, figure with a long neck surmounted by a sun instead of a head: height 1.43m (4.6ft). These two figures were picked out of a horizontal rock, surrounded by hundreds of other motifs: animals, animal tracks, signs, human representations and fantastic forms. The vertical lines on the canoe represent the crew, whereas the central figure is a solar mast—or perhaps even a personage with a solar head, like the figure on the left. These two representations can be connected with a solar cult, or they may recall the dream of a shaman making a fantastic journey, or again they may show the shaman invested with the power of the sun.

Eskimo mask

Mask incised in a steatite quarry on the island of Qikertaaluk, Ungava, near the Hudson Strait. These outcrops of soft rock were once much sought after as raw material for making lamps and cooking pots. The numerous engraved masks on this island are attributed to the Dorset culture (c.800BC) because of their style. The human face depicted here seems to have the wolf's ears characteristic of small ivory Dorset sculptures, but this may be a way of representing a clothing detail, the raised collar seen on certain statuettes in the round.

Michipichou

Painting from the site of Agawa, an impressive cliff to the northeast of Lake Superior, representing Michipichou, the "Great Lynx" of Algonquin mythology, spirit of the underworld whose power is evoked by its horns and a spiny back. This painting was executed by the chief of a group of Ojibwa warriors who had crossed Lake Superior in four days at the time of the Anglo-American War of 1812, an exploit undoubtedly attributed to the clemency of Michipichou, because the "gentle sea" remained calm. The rest of the panel carries depictions of canoes, the emblems of captains, four suns (days) surmounting two crescents (the two shores) and the chief on horseback (this animal can only have been known by hearsay, because it looks more like a moose). The story of this band was recorded on a bark roll and told to H. Schoolcraft in 1851. A century later, S. Dewdney discovered it on the rock of Agawa.

Combat scene

Drawing incised on a rock at Castle Butte, Montana, representing a combat between two warriors, one armed with a musket and the other with a spear. The scene takes place during the protohistoric period at the time when the arrival of the horse, introduced by the Spaniards, and bartered objects profoundly changed the lifestyle of the prairie Amerindians. Within a few generations, the latter became mounted hunters of bison. K. Wellmann, *A Survey of North Indian Rock Art*, Akademische Druck- u. Verlagsanstalt, Graz (Austria), 1979.

Navaho divinities

The Navahos of New Mexico interbred with Pueblo Indians at the end of the 17th century and borrowed several cultural traits from them. Thus the *"yéis"* of the Navahos are supernatural beings like the *"katchinas"* of the Pueblos. On the left is Ganaskidi, the humpbacked divinity of harvests, abundance and mist, and guardian of sheep. The head is ornamented with two sheep's horns, whereas the humpback which contains seeds and mist is represented beneath a covering of feathers. The divinity holds what is probably a digging stick. The central figure with a pointed hat recalls Dsahadaldza, a divinity honoured in modern Navaho ceremonies and represented in sand paintings. The right-hand figure is a female divinity recognizable by her rectangular head. Painting from Delgadito Canyon, New Mexico Rock, Arizona. Klaus Wellmann, *A Survey of North Indian Rock Art*, Akademische Druck- u. Verlagsansatalt, Graz (Austria), 1979.

Geometric figures and fantastic beings

Rock drawings in the National Park of the Petrified Forest in Arizona are characteristic of the Anasazi culture inherited by the contemporary Hopi Indians. Picked out of the rock, the figures stand out against the patina. The hand prints, "lizard-men", snake, and cougar with moufflon horns in the centre of the panel are familiar themes in this culture. It is probable that several of these drawings are clan symbols used as "signatures". Nevertheless, the stepped pyramid motif (which traditionally represents clouds) and the solar disc evoke rain-making ceremonies.

Mesoamerica: the archaeological background

Archaeologists and historians now recognize the extraordinary originality of ancient Mesoamerican civilization; its separateness is no longer a historiographical problem. Archaeology alone has been able to give an outline of a "history" which stretches back many millennia before the advent of the Europeans.

As a discipline concerned with the study of past societies, archaeology has only recently developed to any extent in that part of the American continent which is known to archaeologists as Mesoamerica. The first steps towards scientific archaeology in Mexico and Central America date from the end of the 19th century; but the most important historiographical study on Mexican archaeology was published only in 1980. Its author, Ignacio Bernal, is a member of the generation which is the first, in Mexico, to be able to acquire professional training. The concept of Mesoamerica, so familiar to modern scholars, was only coined and defined in 1943 by the anthropologist Paul Kirchhoff: the name covers that region of Central America which includes half of modern Mexico, Guatemala, Belize, El Salvador and part of Honduras and Nicaragua, and in this area, before the arrival of the Spaniards, complex societies thrived and differentiated themselves, to varying degrees, from the ethnological groups surrounding them. Archaeology plays as important a role in Mesoamerica as it does anywhere else in the American continent; while it is true that a few indigenous texts predating the Conquest have been found from the central Mexican plateau to the Maya area, it is still acceptable to use the term prehistoric, as North American scholars like to do, of the period which preceded contact with the European world. This means that history only really begins in Mesoamerica in 1519 and archaeology is thus the only means of studying anything from before the beginning of the 16th century.

The collecting of ancient objects, of "antiquities", has often been a prelude to archaeological activities proper; this method of preserving old records is generally motivated by curiosity towards the past, and such a curiosity existed in Mesoamerica even before the Spanish Conquest. This is demonstrated by the recent excavations of the main pyramid of Mexico-Tenochtitlán, where thousands of objects were found forming several different groups of offerings;

some of these objects were obviously much older than the Aztec period, exceptional among them being a stone mask in Olmec style which, at the time it was buried with the ritual offerings inside this pyramid, must have been at least 2,000 years old. Again, we also know that the Aztecs regarded as specially sacred the ruins of Teotihuacán which their cosmogonic mythology considered to be the place where the sun and the moon were created.

Old World conquerors

Links with the past were brutally broken by the Conquest. Although Europe began to question the origins of the American societies and various theories were formulated, most of them based on the hypothesis of a transoceanic migration from the Old World to the New, there was never any attempt to look for solid foundations for these theories. Very early on, the military and spiritual conquerors came into contact with existing ruins, not to mention those they caused themselves, but until the 18th century any search for antiquities was rare – except for the looting of treasures. What is more, all material traces of indigenous cultures were regarded with some suspicion. Fr. Diego de Landa, who in 1566 wrote a report on Yucatán which included a description of Chichén Itzá, and who, with amazing intuition, attributed its construction to the ancestors of contemporary Mayas, was himself responsible for a gigantic *auto-da-fé* in which almost all Mayan manuscripts were destroyed. And the priest Duran went as far as to sanction the demolition of Mexico City Cathedral, soon after it was built, on the simple pretext that the materials used included fragments of pagan temples.

The pre-Columbian past of Mesoamerica remained more or less voluntarily ignored until the beginning of the 19th century. However, a few positive elements can be salvaged from this long period of intellectual poverty. First of all, there are the many chronicles and descriptions which soon became a speciality of the missionaries. The most famous of these, for the wealth of its information and the modernity of the research methods employed by its author, is that of the Franciscan Bernardino de Sahagun. Thanks to him we know much about Aztec society at the time of the Conquest. However, these early works, with the exception of a few concentrating on the Maya area, shed no light on the relics of more ancient times: Chichén Itzá, Uxmal, Copán, Mitla, Teotihuacán are among the few archaeological sites to be described in the course of over 150 years. On the other hand, the ethnohistorical work of the first generations of missionaries stimulated an interest which led to the collecting of indigenous documents and later of archaeological finds, which was still fraught with risks at the beginning of the 18th century: the nobleman Boturini was arrested and expelled in 1743, and his collection confiscated.

A few isolated examples of premature archaeology date from this period. One thinks of what seems to have been the first excavation ever to take place on the American continent when, around 1680, Carlos de Sigüenza y

Les Ateliers M.S.

The Temple of the Cross, Palenque

This lithograph after an original drawing by Count Waldeck is one of the illustrations in the book *Ancient Monuments of Mexico. Palenque and other ruins of the ancient Mexican civilization*, published in 1866 by C.E. Brasseur de Bourbourg. Waldeck's caption reads: "A picturesque view of the Temple of the Cross seen from the entrance gate to the Palace; at the foot of the pyramid is the dwelling I built myself." During the first 80 years of the 19th century Paris was at the centre of the spate of publications devoted to the antiquities of Mesoamerica.

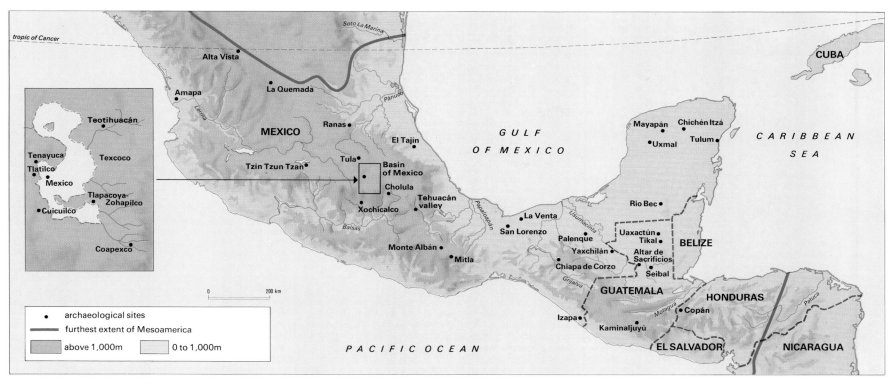

Góngora opened up a shaft in the Pyramid of the Moon at Teotihuacán to assess whether such buildings were hollow or not. Later, the Jesuit Father Alzate was the first to devote a whole monograph (*Antigüedades de Xochicalco*) to one archaeological site. His work was almost contemporary with a series of official expeditions to the Palenque site; the last of these, led by Captain Antonio del Río, caused a great stir and the publication of his report attracted new researchers. These events were followed by the fortuitous discovery in the centre of Mexico City of two spectacular, sculpted Aztec monoliths: the Sun Stone and the statue of the earth goddess Coatlicue. However, at the end of the 18th century, conditions were not yet ripe for proper research and study of the relics of the past: the statue of Coatlicue was re-buried at least twice after it was first discovered.

Exploration and re-evaluation

Tribute has often been paid to the influence of the philosophy of the Enlightenment on the progressive change of attitudes towards pre-Columbian sites and objects. In reality, several illustrious characters of 18th-century Europe were reactionary in their attitudes: among them, Buffon, who virtually considered the Amerindians to be simple primates. Nevertheless, between the end of the 18th century and that of the 19th, the understanding of pre-Spanish Mesoamerica entered a new phase, which could be defined as pre-archaeological. There was increasingly frequent exploration accompanied by the formation of important collections of indigenous documents and the rediscovery of Spanish chronicles, and the first efforts were made to preserve and show to the public what was increasingly being regarded as a cultural heritage. By the end of this period the first contingents of archaeologists in the modern sense of the word came in from the United States, and took up the work begun by the Europeans. But the first systematic exploration of Mexican ruins was sponsored by Spain: the three expeditions led by Dupaix between 1805 and 1807, in which the draughtsman Castañeda took part. The results of their work were published in Paris in 1848, as was the monumental work of Baron von Humboldt, who, however, during the year he spent in Mexico seems to have visited only one site and was never very receptive towards pre-Columbian antiquities! Many are the explorers who followed in the footsteps of these pioneers. Among them were the Count Waldeck, who gave his name to one of the buildings at Palenque; the American Stephens and his draughtsman colleague Catherwood, whose two books of travel are amongst the most beautiful works on Maya civilization; the priest Brasseur de Bourbourg who compiled the *Popol Vuh*, the great mythical text of the Maya Highlands, re-discoverer of Landa and a member of the scientific mission to Mexico; and Désiré Charnay, the first traveller to use photography.

At the same time, Lord Kingsborough in England and Joseph-Marie-Alexis Aubin in France gathered together the richest ever collection of Mexican manuscripts. In 1864 a site was designated in Mexico City for a national museum, and in 1897, for the first time, a law was passed declaring all antiquities to be the property of the state. By the end of the 19th century and the beginning of the 20th there developed a properly scientific attitude based on positivism on the one hand and the first manifestations of an anthropological approach on the other. The personality of the great German scholar Eduard Seler, who dominated these first years of scientific research, should not make us forget the contribution made by the United States to Mesoamerican archaeology.

The years from 1910 to the present have seen the development of archaeology as a science, the evolution of its methods and objectives, and with its material and intellectual development there has been a rapid increase in the results obtained. In their history of American archaeology, already a classic, G.R. Willey and J.A. Sabloff distinguish three main phases within these past 75 years. Until about 1940 archaeological research was based on chronological and historical considerations. At the beginning of this period, stratigraphy* was first applied to the archaeology of the Mexican Basin. The Mexican Manuel Gamio first classified the archaeological material originating from this area into three main periods, which, from the most recent to the oldest, were called Aztec, Teotihuacán and Archaic. The progress achieved can today be measured by consulting the chronological map of this sector, which could however still be improved: all relics later than 1500 BC are now dated to periods which rarely extend beyond two centuries, sometimes less. One important contributor to the extraordinary improvements made in chronological knowledge has been Vaillant, a specialist on the Mexican Basin and a pioneer of Maya chronology. Two great Mexican scholars are Noguera and Caso.

However, the excessively historico-chronological approach of these pioneers and the attention devoted exclusively to the main sites to the detriment of the rest of the country resulted, in the 1940s, in a new assessment of archaeological objectives and a partial reorientation of research towards themes until then little explored: among them, regional studies concentrating on the structure of the habitat, an effort to understand the links between the various cultures and their natural environment, and similar questions of a more functional type.

At about this time, archaeology was strengthened by other disciplines, and a multi-disciplinary organization of research programmes was born from the merging of new objectives and new means. Evolution, however, does not stop here. It is too early to assess the extent of the impact of the so-called "new archaeology" on Mesoamerican research, but it is undoubtedly important, negatively or positively. Another new important element is the formation of national policies, particularly in Mexico, for the study and protection of its prehistoric heritage. Until a few years ago, a resumé of Mexican archaeology disclosed in a completely arbitrary fashion the existence of 11,000 archaeological sites on Mexican territory – a figure which will no doubt be increased by the inventory to be made by the ambitious archaeological programme which the Government has planned for the years after 1985. But the real importance of such a programme lies in the fact that it is an incontestable sign of a new understanding on the part of the policy-makers of the value of the cultures of the past.

Towards the Neolithic

Entirely cut off from the influence of the Neolithic and Bronze Age civilizations of the Old World, how did prehistoric societies of Central America develop from nomadic to settled communities?

Some 10,000 years ago an irreversible phenomenon took place in the history of ancient communities: the change to a style of life mainly based on the production of food. The term *Archaic* stage or period, corresponding to the Mesolithic period of the Old World, covers all the changes that took place between the Paleolithic and the Neolithic periods in the technological economy of the American hunting nomads, as they adjusted to an environment affected by the bioclimatic fluctuations that followed the Pleistocene*. For about 5,000 years, during the Holocene*, a selective process of adjustment to changed ecological situations began to take shape in the evolution of small groups of hunter-gatherers and fishers. With the disappearance of the large animals of the Quaternary, these groups began to incorporate new areas into their basic territories. This process is sometimes known as "neolithization". Some of these archaic, pre-village communities retained the elements of their ancient traditions, particularly in the composition of their stone equipment: remains of chipped stone instruments have often been found near polished stone objects associated with plant culture and preparation.

The stratified levels of prehistoric deposits excavated in the arid highlands of Mesoamerica, as well as in low-lying tropical areas and the humid coasts, have yielded collections of stone tools with new shapes, and also utensils made of bone or vegetal matter. Such tools tend to replace the remains from the earlier Paleo-Indian levels, indicating, with their relatively uniform shapes, the blurred outlines of Paleolithic habitation. Finds include large bifacial* tools, heavy scrapers, large pointed tools with fluted or divided bases, others with lateral notches, stone axes, adzes, hoes, and a large quantity of grinders, mortars, millstones and cutting wheels. The slow emergence of a Neolithic lifestyle (still perceptible in certain cultural practices of the present indigenous populations) is indicated in the appearance of the first processes linking the various areas to be occupied by pre-village communities as they developed into settlements. Their subsistence activities produced a network of economic and cultural interaction between the maritime areas and the highlands of the interior. This interaction was relatively weak, but marks the origin of the traditions* that can be dated, and form part of the fascinating mosaic of the transformed landscape of regionalized Mesoamerica.

The beginnings of traditions

The origins of these traditions can be discerned in communal initiatives and developments of long standing (not including cattle-rearing) which led to the higher civilizations of the 2nd millennium BC. Here we find the traits which characterize that complex techno-cultural phenomenon called Neolithic, a term invented in 1865 by the English archaeologist J. Lubbock and now somewhat contested. On the whole, gathering, hunting, trapping and fishing became seasonal activities from the 9th millennium. Control of natural resources, provided by various and often complementary ecological systems, was adapted to the customs of an emergent agriculture, certain forms of food stocking, and settled life in rock shelters, or settlements near the sea, rivers or lake. By the 5th millennium, the cultivation of maize, squashes and beans was common; baked clay objects began to be manufactured around 2300BC. Metal objects came much later and were confined to precious ornaments (7th century AD). Residential stability, indicative of the process of Neolithization, is still difficult to assess in its forms of archaic territorial groupings, for nomadic populations such as the Chichimecs survived in sub-desert northern Mesoamerica until the 18th century.

In the southeast fringe a maritime tradition existed between 7000 and 5000BC, illustrated by the complexes at Concheros in Veracruz state, and at Sand Hill in Belize, where large flint blades were found, probably used to carve wood, or even to make small boats. Not only the waterland resources were exploited, but also those of various inland ecologies. The discovery of millstones indicates the practice of grinding grains, and is attested in the high plateaus of Chiapas (Santa Marta cave), and in the Oaxaca region (the Jicaras complex) where the trapping of small animals complemented a diet based on the cultivation of squashes and beans. Further to the north, the El Riego tradition, represented in the Tehuacan valley, in the Texcal cave (Puebla state), in the Tecolote cave (Hidalgo state) and in the Valley of Mexico (Playa I), shows a typical hunter-gatherer lifestyle. Here, large or small groups exploited the various environments according to a seasonal calendar and an established territorial base, ceremonially buried their dead, and cultivated avocados, peppers and courgettes. To the northeast, in the Tamaulipas, the Infier-

nillo tradition produced not only characteristic stone utensils but also nets and baskets; the latter are also typical of the Cochise tradition of the northwest, which saw the development of a "Desert Culture" typified by the variety of its grinding stones.

Plant remains, fossilized excrements, mortars, pestles and various grinders dated between 5000 and 3000BC, enable archaeologists to reconstruct partially the diet of the populations in the northwest (Chiricahua phase). Those of the northeast, with their characteristic tools such as gouges, small round scrapers and small points (Repelo tradition, Ocampo, La Perra and Nogales phases) seem to have been closer to the central Mexican plateau. Various forms of social contact between inhabited territories allowed the spread of agricultural practices and produce such as maize, squashes, amaranth, sapodillas, and peppers. On the other hand, the stone tools of the south-eastern Belize tradition, on the Atlantic side of the humid tropics, show no trace of agricultural activity; no examples of this tradition have been found on the Pacific coast. At Nayarit and Guerrero a few isolated finds indicate a settled life but lacking any agriculture, as at Matanchen, dated to 4000BC, and Ostiones, dated to 5000. There the shell middens are similar to those of the Chiapas coast (Chantuto) and include a few stone tools.

On the Atlantic coast, the discovery of pre-pottery remains at Veracruz ("Palo Hueco") and, in the Gulf of Belize, the complexes of Melinda and Progreso, reveal exploitation of marine resources and the practice of horticulture on flooded river banks. It is believed, although it has not been proved, that cassava was used in the extreme south-east of Mesoamerica.

The transition to the establishment of agricultural villages using pottery and growing cereals and hybrid maize has been dated to between 3500 and 2300BC. These were mainly sited on the dry valleys of Tehuacan (Abejas tradition), Oaxaca (Martinez tradition) and perhaps in the basin of the Mexico river. Generally speaking, it is now agreed that the Neolithization process is at the root of the organization of rural societies, whether or not centrally controlled.

Occupation areas and activities at zone VIII, cave of Coxcatlan

In the rock shelter of Coxcatlan (valley of Tehuacan, Mexico), stratigraphical investigation has revealed 28 successive occupation levels, covering almost 10,000 years. The diagram shows, in simplified form, one of the habitation levels from the late pre-pottery period (zone VIII), dated by Carbon 14* to 3000BC. The distribution and nature of the remains, collected on the site, then analysed and classified, indicate four areas of complex activity occurring at particular seasons: one relates to winter (A), the others (B, C, D) to autumn and spring.In B, a structure for fire-making is apparent. After R.S. MacNeish and A. Nelken-Terner, 1973.

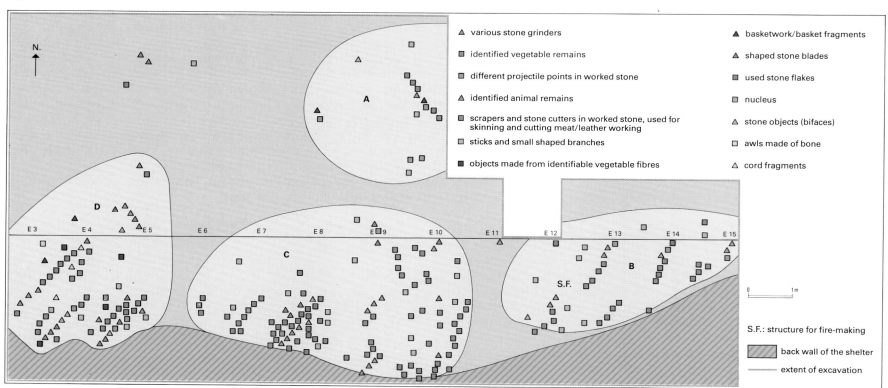

△ various stone grinders
◻ identified vegetable remains
◻ different projectile points in worked stone
△ identified animal remains
◻ scrapers and stone cutters in worked stone, used for skinning and cutting meat/leather working
◻ sticks and small shaped branches
◼ objects made from identifiable vegetable fibres
▲ basketwork/basket fragments
△ shaped stone blades
◻ used stone flakes
◻ nucleus
△ stone objects (bifaces)
◻ awls made of bone
△ cord fragments

S.F.: structure for fire-making

▨ back wall of the shelter
— extent of excavation

Scrapers and large flake-blades

The Sand Hill culture and technology, situated in the north of Belize and dating back more than 5,000 years, included in its stone tool kit big pedunculate "scrapers" (with "stalks") and large flake-blades. The latter seem to link up with the exploitation of banks of flint nodules, which also supplied the raw material.

Landscape of Belize

Work undertaken at Belize since 1980 by an international team (Belize Archaeological Archaic Research) has revealed an ancient pre-Maya occupation of the Caribbean front of the Yucatán peninsula. An intricate network of waterways and marshlands, and a complicated arrangement of coastal islets, lagoons and cayes, give a special character to the survey of these humid tropical lands.

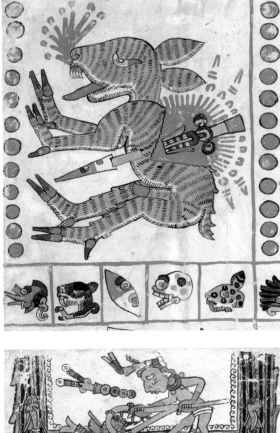

Illustrations from the *Codex Borgia*

Vividly coloured images from the *Codex Borgia* (14th century), reflect, in sublimated form, the ritual of subsistence activities: grinding, fishing (above), hunting (top) and making fire, an ageless routine articulating the development of a bygone evolutionary system. Biblioteca Apostolica Vaticana.

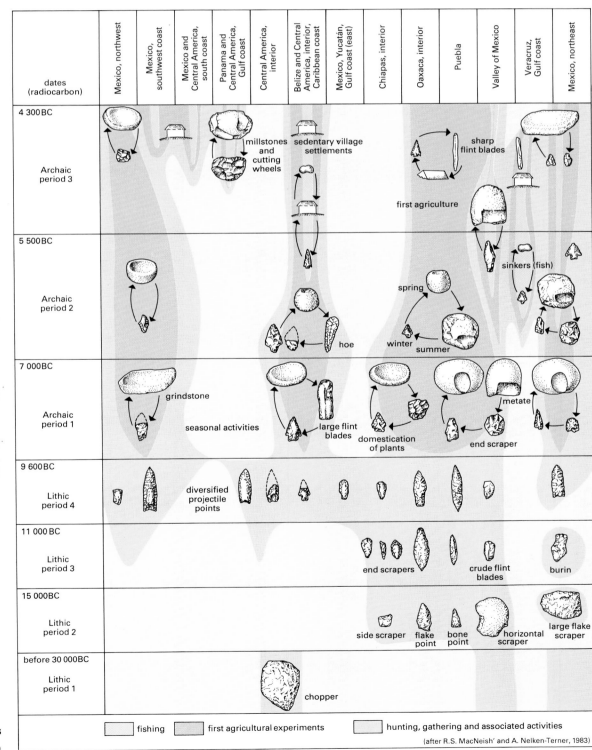

The main Mesoamerican archaeological regions

(after R.S. MacNeish and A. Nelken-Turner, 1983)

Early settlements and environments

How did agriculture develop in what is now Mexico and the southern United States? Archaeologists now can trace an extraordinary continuity between the hunters of 10,000 years ago and the life led by 19th century American Indians—in particular, their profound knowledge of the annual natural cycle.

Between North and Central America lies a vast territory of about 2,200,000sq km (84,920sq miles), covered mainly by the present country of Mexico, where climate, geography and plant life are all remarkably different. Within the totality of climatic, biological and soil variables that characterizes this complex geographical space, certain factors are particularly significant from the point of view of prehistory and human ecology. Overall, 50 percent of the territory of Middle America has less than 700mm of annual rainfall. Below this level is a semi-arid zone within which all "pluvial" or rainwater agriculture (i.e. not relying on irrigation) is somewhat risky, and gradually becomes unprofitable or impossible as the average rainfall diminishes.

Paradoxically, the largest group of material evidence collected on the development of agriculture in general, and on the cultivation of maize in particular, comes from a semi-arid area of the plateau of Mesoamerica: the valley of Tehuacán. The dryness of the valley has enabled several archaeological remains of organic origin to survive, and these indicate that Tehuacán must be considered as one of those regions receptive to the development of agricultural techniques that crystallized elsewhere. Two paleoeconomists from Cambridge University, E.S. Higgs and M.R. Jarman, rightly pointed out in 1972 that our knowledge of the way that peoples developed a Neolithic culture of settled agriculture (neolithization) throughout the world has been distorted because discoveries tend to be confined to very limited areas of America and the Middle East. Today, several excavations in many areas provide us with enough data to modify or qualify our knowledge of the beginnings of agricultural and settled life in Mesoamerica between 6000BC and 2000BC. This wider range of study emphasizes the diversity of cultural developments which, in Mesoamerica, divided the semi-arid regions from the coastal and temperate mountain lakeside ones.

Environments demanding flexibility

The semi-arid environment of the high plateaus of central and northern Mexico, as well as of the Great Basin of southwest America, varied little during the Holocene*. Rainfall averaged less than 500mm a year and vegetation was characterized by a scattered plant life adapted to dry surroundings, and comprising mainly thorny plants, cacti and seasonally fertile *leguminosae* (pod-producing plants). Following J. Jennings' work, several studies of the area have underlined the extraordinary archaeological and ethnological continuity of its ways of life. The methods of occupation and exploitation of the territory, developed as long as 10,000 years

ago, survived until the 19th century among the Païute Indian tribes of Utah and Nevada. Such methods and techniques imply a profound knowledge of the annual cycle of even the smallest woodland natural resource, and a great mobility of populations in the exploitation of widely dispersed environments. This mobility, together with a well planned exploitation of various ecosystems, characterizes the prehistoric populations who lived in the semi-arid Tehuacán valley from 7000BC to 1800BC. This implies, according to the interpretation of R. MacNeish, the formation during the dry season of small isolated groups who subsisted by hunting and gathering in different natural environments; and, during the rainy season, the merging of such groups into larger ones who practised an intensive cropping of grasses and legumes within temporarily fertile natural areas. The pioneering paleobotanic work of C.E. Smith, P. Mangelsdorf, W. Galinat, L. Kaplan, H. Cutler and T.W. Whitaker has shown that, during the 6th and 5th millennia BC, various plants in the process of being domesticated—such as peppers, squashes, avocados, beans, sapodilla and maize—appeared in the archaeological strata of Tehuacán.

Strangely enough, however, the relative development of agriculture did not, over the next four millennia, affect the ancestral pattern of exploiting and occupying the territory on a semi-nomadic basis. Agricultural experiments did take place, but the hazards of "pluvial" cultivation in a semi-arid area induced the hunter-gatherers of Tehuacán to retain their traditional mobility, upon which their very security was based, until the adoption of the Mesoamerican irrigation practices in the first millennium BC.

Stable ancient settlements

In the richer areas of Mesoamerica, the post-Pleistocene development was clearly quite different. The first archaeological studies carried out by M. Coe and K. Flannery along the marine estuaries of the Ocos, where the Mesoamerican civilization possessed very ancient roots, have revealed not only the wealth and variety but also the contrast between the various natural environments that could be exploited. The natural resources of the ocean, the estuaries, the mangroves, the internal lagoons, the forests and the savannas (particularly mammals, aquatic birds, reptiles, amphibians, molluscs, crustaceans and fish) could be exploited from a settled location. The excavations carried out by B. Voorhies at Chantuto, on the Pacific coast, and by J. Wilkerson at Santa Luisa on the Atlantic coast, have shown that in certain maritime areas settled occupation occurred early, either before or at the very start of agriculture.

In the temperate mountainous area, the southern part of the ancient lake Basin of Mexico set the scene, c.6000BC, for another example of early settlement. The perfectly preserved fossilized pollen found on the Tlapacoya-Zohapilco site shows that this region reached its bioclimatic peak around 5500BC. The pollen count indicates the presence of pines, oaks, elms and sweetgum, and reveals a temperate climate, more humid and slightly warmer than at present. Within a relatively small area, the prehistoric communities enjoyed three natural environments, all of them exploitable: the forest and its mammals; the alluvial areas of the rivers, suitable for the first agricultural experiments including the amaranth, certain *cucurbitaceae* (cucumber-type plants), tomatoes and the genus *Zea* (maize); the lakes, which allowed the exploitation of all-year resources such as white fish and waterfowl, summer resources such as edible reptiles and amphibians (turtles and *axolotl**), and, in winter, the important birdlife of migratory ducks and geese.

Thus two situations confronted the prehistoric and pre- or proto-agricultural populations of Mesoamerica. In the first instance, the environment offered only limited or temporary resources, so that critical periods occurred during the year when the resident populations had to move in search of other exploitable habitats. The ancient communities of Oaxaca and Tehuacán fall into this group. In the second, the wealth and the excellent distribution over the year of natural resources encouraged a settled occupation of the territory. Examples of this can be found in certain areas along the coast and in the mountain lake site of Tlapacoya-Zohapilco, where strata dating to c.6000BC preserve the traces of multiseasonal activities around central zones. An early settling process implies several consequences: a systematic organization of the inhabited area; a keener sense of territorial rights; a significant increase in population; a more complex socio-political organization; a tighter relationship between men and plants, the seasonality of which accelerates the development of agricultural practices.

Middle America contains many different ecological areas whose populations developed, very early on, symbiotic relationships with each other. However, there is no doubt that it was in the regions favourable to ancient settlement, which are particularly of interest to modern prehistoric research, that the economic, social and cultural foundations of the Mesoamerican civilization took form, and made possible the emergence of the Mesoamerican civilization itself towards 1500BC.

Models of territorial occupation in Mesoamerica between 7000 and 1000BC

altitude and environment	geographic zones		phases or archaeological sites							
above sea level; tropical estuary zones	1	Pacific coast					Puerto Marques San Blas			
							Chantuto			
	2	Atlantic coast					Santa Luisa			
semi-arid zones altitude 900–1900m	3	Tamaulipas	Infiernillo		Nogales Ocampo		La Perra	Almagre		
	4	Tehuacán	El Riego		Coxcatlan		Abejas			
	5	Oaxaca	Guila-Naquitz B2		Gheo-Shih		Cueva Blanca D			
temperate mountain lakeside zones over 2000m	6	Basin of Mexico		Playa I	Playa II		*	Zohapilco		
			7000	6000	5000	4000	3000	2000	1000 BC	

seasonal migrations { large settled groups in the rainy season / small isolated semi-nomad groups in the dry season

permanent occupation based on exploitation of year-round resources available in nearby forests

Mesoamerican model of occupation organized around a central base: agrarian village communities attached to a regional capital; fully developed ceramic industry

no data

*lakes resulting from deposits of volcanic ash on study sites

sources:
1 C. F. Brush, 1965
   J. B. Mountjoy, 1972
   B. L. Stark and
   B. Voorhies, 1978
2 J. K. Wilkerson, 1975
3 R. S. MacNeish, 1972
4 R. S. MacNeish et al., 1967
5 K. V. Flannery and
   J. Marcus, 1983
6 C. Niederberger, 1979

Lacustrine sites in the Mexico Basin

View of the residual lakeside extensions of Mixquic (right), and excavations on the lacustrine fossil basins of Tlapacoya-Zehapilco (far right). Fieldwork by C. Niederberger Betton.

Landscape of the Tehuacán valley

The semi-arid landscape features tropical balsams (*Bursera*) and candelabra cactus (*Lemaireocereus*). This difficult biogeographical environment provided a setting for the oldest occupation of the territory, implying seasonal migrations to exploit in succession a series of temporarily fertile ecological niches (MacNeish and Byers 1967).

Pacific coast of Nayarit at San Blas

The ecology of maritime estuary zones varied little during the Holocene. The concentration and abundance of natural resources encouraged early permanent settlement, but the prehistory of these regions is still not well known.

Food resources from Tlapacoya-Zehapilco, Mexico Basin

A temperate lacustrine zone of mountains, the Mexico Basin constitutes, for archaeologists studying the emergence and development of Neolithic characteristics ("neolithization"), an example of precociously early settlement in a pre- or proto-agrarian context. This permanent territorial establishment was due in particular to the excellent distribution and variety of woodland resources throughout the annual cycle.

	Basin of Mexico site of Zohapilco-Tlapacoya food fragments gathered from archaeological levels at Playa (5000BC)	monthly availability ● maximum availability ○ minimum availability											
		dry season					rainy season						
		Nov.	Dec.	Jan.	Feb.	Mar.	April	May	June	July	Aug.	Sept.	Oct.
ducks	*Aythya* spp. (sea or bay ducks)	●	●	●	●	●							
	Spatula clypeata (shoveller)	●	●	●	●	●							
	Anas acuta (pintail)	●	●	●	●	●							
	Anas platyrhynchos (mallard)	●	●	●	●	●							
	Querquedula sp. (Old World Garganey)	●	●	●	●	●							
	Anas diazi (Mexican duck)	●	●	●	●	●	●	●	●	●	●	●	●
grebes	*Podiceps caspicus* (crested grebes)	●	●	●	●	●							
	Podilymbus podiceps (pied-billed grebe)	●	●	●	●	●	○	○	○	○	○	○	○
	Aechmophorus sp. (eastern grebe)	●	●	●	●	●	○	○	○	○	○	○	○
geese	*Branta* spp. (geese)	●	●	●	●	●							
coots	*Fulica americana* (coot)	●	●	●	●	●	○	○	○	○	○	○	○
amphibians, tortoises and snakes	*Ambystoma* (axolotl*)						●	●	●	●	●	●	●
	Kinosternon (lake tortoise)						●	●	●	●	●	●	●
	Thamnophis (garter snake)						●	●	●	●	●	●	●
fish	*Chirostoma* spp. (atherines)	●	●	●	●	●	●	●	●	●	●	●	●
	Girardinichthys sp. (goodeides)	●	●	●	●	●	●	●	●	●	●	●	●
	cyprinid	●	●	●	●	●	●	●	●	●	●	●	●
mammals	*Odocoileus virginianus* (white-tailed stag)	●	●	●	●	●	○	○	○	○	●	○	○
	Sylvilagus cunicularius (Mexican rabbit)	●	●	●	●	●	●	●	●	●	●	●	●
	canidae	●	●	●	●	●	●	●	●	●	●	●	●
	rodents						●	●	●	●	●	●	●
plants of alluvial soil	*Zea* (corn-teosinte)	●										●	●
	Amaranthus (amaranth)	●										●	●
	Cucurbita (cucurbit)	●							●	●	○	○	●
	Physalis (green tomato)											●	●
	Portulaca (portulaca)	○	○				●	●	●	●	●	●	●

C. Niederberger Betton

The Olmec civilization

The brilliant civilization of Mesoamerica with its remarkable planned cities emerged at the time of the end of the Bronze Age in the ancient Near East—towards 1200BC. Its original genius and distinctiveness continue to impress and perplex archaeologists.

"The Mesoamerican civilization, strictly speaking, began around 1200BC with a culture which, for want of a better name, we call Olmec." These words are from an article by the poet and essayist Octavio Paz, that emphasizes not only the originality and isolation, but also the quality of *otherness* characteristic of the Mesoamerican world. In 1926 Blom and La Farge, and later Stirling, made the first discoveries in the marshy, overgrown and humid Mexican states of Tabasco and Veracruz on the Gulf coast. The archaeological sites of Tres Zapotes, La Venta and San Lorenzo, with their monumental sculptures of volcanic rock and their delicate engravings on jadeite, were classified without further thought by a term already proposed by Saville: Olmec. The word actually describes a historical ethnic group, the Huixtotin Olmecs or inhabitants of the land of Caoutchouc, who lived along the Gulf coast shortly before the arrival of the Spaniards, and had no clear relations with the archaeological culture that had been discovered. Nevertheless, the usage became conventional and the word Olmec has since acquired inappropriate overtones of meaning. A sort of linguistic determinism has led to a belief in the existence of a chosen archaeological race, originating in the Gulf coast but quickly expanding to migrate and conquer, by force or faith, the neighbouring populations. These, by the mere fact of being unknown, seemed passive and less developed. However, modern research has not come up with any data to support such a theory. Consequently, the conventional word Olmec will only be used here in two respects: as a style, and as a civilization affecting in some sense the whole of Mesoamerica.

The facts are that, shortly after 1300BC, and at about the same time, a number of important cities or regional capitals, the bases of firmly established political and religious power, appeared in several parts of Mesoamerica. Surviving architecture shows that such cities were built according to a strict plan, at the heart of which was a sacred enclosure where meetings and rites periodically took place. This new kind of spatial organization round a centre emphasizes the development of social hierarchies. Archaeological evidence suggests the emergence of powerful political figures and of a class of dignitaries characterized by particular costumes and insignia, and concerned with directing sacred affairs. Seats of power and centres for the transmission of knowledge, these cities also saw the development of a complex imagery, remains of which can be seen in the stone sculptures and ceramics. The masterly modelling of the figurines, masks and votive jadeite axes, and the precisely cut and highly polished mirrors of magnetite, indicate the importance, within the communities, of an organized class of craftsmen.

Finally, the presence of commodities originating in distant regions and ecosystems emphasizes that these cities of emergent Mesoamerica participated in an already solidly structured network of interregional commerce.

Olmec architecture

Our best sources of information on the layout and organization of a city of this time come from the pioneering excavations carried out at La Venta by P. Drucker, R. Heizer and R. Squier, and from the more recent ones by M. Coe and R. Diehl at San Lorenzo. La Venta consists of three groups of civil and ceremonial architecture, called Complexes A, B and C. Complex A, with two courts defined by symmetrical earth mounds and rows of basalt columns, has yielded a series of votive masks and massive underground offerings consisting mainly of jewels, figurines, votive axes and blocks of jadeite and of serpentine. Complex B is less well known, and comprises several elongated earthen mounds and a large platform known as Stirling Acropolis. Complex C contains the most famous architectural element of the whole site: a monumental earthen structure, 30m (99ft) high and 130m (416ft) in diameter, shaped like a cone with fluted sides. The probable existence of a ball court, a typical feature of Mesoamerican life, has also been suggested. The custom of colouring the surface of the inhabited territory was followed to its extreme at La Venta: layers of soil have been discovered which are in turn bright red, white, olive green, blue, purple-brown, siena and pink. Within the city, imposing monoliths appeared at intervals: colossal heads weighing some 18 tonnes, and massive blocks and slabs carved in low relief, depicting political events, such as portraits of dynastic chiefs or meetings between notables, or mythological scenes.

Away from the Gulf coast, archaeologists long remained ignorant of these ancient archaeological levels. Nevertheless, numerous objects of Olmec design have been found in Guatemala, El Salvador and the Mexican states of Chiapas, Oaxaca, Guerrero, Puebla, Morelos and the Basin of Mexico, which was first excavated in 1942 at Tlatilco. More recently, important remains of Olmec architecture have also been found away from the Gulf, including a ceremonial platform and public buildings at Oaxaca (studied by K. Flannery, J. Marcus and R. Drennan); pyramidal structures on mound 20 at San Isidro and on mound 30A at Izapa, in the Chiapas (described by T. Lee and S. Eckholm); and on the vast site of Tlacozotitlan in Guerrero, discovered in 1983, where G. Martinez Donjuan's team is currently unearthing a rich collection of remains, including the thick stone wall of an enclosure, a complex system of drains made of hollowed slabs, and some powerful monoliths representing anthropomorphic jaguars.

Sacred themes

Over the whole of Mesoamerica, the list of rock carvings, stone slabs and sculpture is contantly growing. These include themes already known from the Gulf coast: the dynastic presentation of children, feline masks, kneeling prisoners or vassals, dignitaries dressed in capes or holding, in a very Mesoamerican gesture, symbolic wand of power, caves where soothsayers or rain-makers officiated. But it is perhaps the art of ceramics that illustrates best the multiregional dynamism of Olmec unity. The finest examples of this undoubtedly came from the Olmec capitals of Tlapacoya, Tlatilco and Las Bocas, as shown by the publications of M. Coe, D. Grove, C. Niederberger, R. Piña Chan, P. Tolstoy and L. Paradis.

The themes include one of the main divinities of the Olmec world, the anthropomorphic jaguar, together with notations of abstract symbols and several hybrid creatures of animal form with human, bird, feline or reptile features; these are the sacred symbols of natural phenomena relating to the earth, caves, celestial bodies, lightning and springs. D. Joralemon has clearly demonstrated the extraordinary power of abstraction and dissociation of the various graphic elements, a single one of which can evoke, on the strength of the principle of *pars pro toto* (the part standing for the whole), a sacred entity or even a whole mythical cycle. Moreover, it is now generally agreed that certain elements of the classical Mesoamerican script and calendar already existed in latent form in the Olmec world. Four Maya astronomical symbols derived, according to M. Coe, from a prototype in the Olmec iconography: the glyph in the shape of a widened U, symbol of the moon; the glyph *lamat*, or lozenge, corresponding to the planet Venus; the celestial motif of the crossed bars; and the glyph *kin*, or the four-petalled flower, symbol of the sun. All these elements are frequently found in the Olmec symbolic language of the high plateau of about 1000BC; the motif of the segmented bird-snake is also found, and recalls an ancient form of the classical number system based on circles and triangles.

However, large gaps still remain in the archaeological data relating to the origin of the Olmec world. But numerous finds already indicate that this first expression of Mesoamerican civilization flowed from a long period of cultural maturation, with a forceful and varied contribution coming from numerous regions of the ancient agricultural world of Mesoamerica, regions by their nature favourable to the evolution of complex societies.

Pottery with Olmec decoration

Tlapacoya, in the Basin of Mexico, is one of the principal capitals of the Olmec world in the central altiplano. This site possesses a remarkable amount of pottery with very pure and particularly elaborate Olmec iconography. Thus this vessel bearing the effigy of the mythical dragon has human and feline connotations. The vigorous, stylized facial features emphasize the eyes, the eyebrows "on fire" and the dual symbolism of mouth and cavern: cave, subterranean water, agrarian fertility and semi-darkness suitable for initiatory rites. National Anthropological Museum of Mexico.

Head of terracotta figurine

The important contribution of the state of Guerrero to the birth of the Mesoamerican civilization *c.*1200BC has long been sensed by archaeologists. The recent discovery of the Olmec capital of Tlacozotitlan confirms it. Near the ceremonial centre of the capital, with its aqueduct and monoliths displaying the effigy of the anthropomorphic jaguar, C. Niederberger-Betton has brought to light the remains of domestic dwellings. In addition to the evidence connected with everyday life (dietary customs and specialized craftwork in onyx, obsidian, jadeite and seashells), it was possible, in this context, to collect many fragments of terracotta figurines. These fragments of hollow figurines, covered with white slip* and traces of cinnabar*, illustrate the stylistic canons and fashions reigning *c.*1000BC, such as voluntary strabismus (squinting), a prerequisite for elegance which is found again later in the Maya world. Height 4cm (1.5in). Excavations: C. Niederberger-Betton.

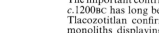

C. Niederberger Betton

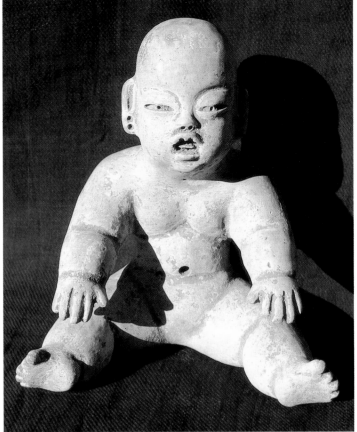

Terracotta figurine

This asexual, obese, hollow terracotta figurine, originally from Guerrero, corresponds to a group characteristic of Olmec art: that of chubby-cheeked babies. On this example, 22cm (8.4in) high, deliberate skull deformation can be seen as well as the three-dimensional modelling of the silhouette with plump, dimpled limbs and the excellent gloss of white slip. Numerous Olmec bas-reliefs emphasize the magic power and sacred nature of these representations of infants, sometimes with half-human, half-feline features.

Monolith of La Venta

La Venta, an important Olmec capital, constitutes one of the first known and systematically studied examples of a ceremonial centre in Mesoamerica in which public monuments, caches and offerings, stelae and monoliths are distributed according to a rigorous spatial plan. This monolith represents a dignitary, sitting cross-legged, emerging from a niche dominated by the mask of a humanized jaguar. He holds a cord which links him to the secondary figures. This scene may express a creation myth or depict an act of vassalage or the capture of prisoners.

1. **Complex Olmec engraving of five faces seen in profile. Jadeite plaque.**
2. **Sculpture no. 52 from San Lorenzo bearing the effigy of the anthropomorphic jaguar Basalt.**
3. **Votive axe ornamented with the incised motif of an Olmec divinity. Jadeite.** After Joralemon.

Principal sides of the Mesoamerican Olmec

Pre-urban settlements

Recent work by archaeologists has shown that the great "classic" urban phase of Mesoamerica had its roots in a precociously early development, prefiguring many aspects of city life. Modern research is also beginning to reveal the role of the village.

During the 1,500 years before the present era, and particularly between 600 and 100BC, several innovations took place in the Mesoamerican world affecting the religious domain, the concept of individual and collective space, and the technical and economic spheres. This period is essential to our understanding of the birth of the powerful urban conglomerations of classic Mesoamerica, yet was for a long time practically unknown. Faced with a lack of data, or with incomplete or contradictory information, some authorities placed the majority of sites dating from this period (with the exception of a few along the Gulf coast) at an archaic political and socio-economic level, namely that of primitive villages. This view has been substantially modified by recent archaeological discoveries. Several authorities now firmly support a theory of a precocious urban evolution occurring in many areas of Mesoamerica during the 1st millennium BC.

It is now necessary to give a theoretical definition to the particular grouping that we call a city. Several of the criteria which are considered necessary to the definition of an urban centre in terms of Euro-Asiatic archaeology (writing linked with commerce, for instance, or metallurgy) are not directly applicable in the case of Mesoamerica. However, it is possible to argue that the Mesoamerican conglomerations did achieve the identities of towns through such criteria as, in particular, the coexistence of political and religious institutions with clear hierarchical structures, planned monumental public architecture, a highly specialized class of craftsmen, markets linked with an interregional commercial network, and complex intellectual achievements such as precise astronomical observations or an iconographical method of keeping permanent records. If these criteria are accepted, then one must admit that the Mesoamerican city was already in full evolution during the 1st millennium BC. Let us then follow the example of W. Bray and recognize that neither a qualitative leap nor a sudden change separates the regional capital (*caput*) of 1000BC from the first large urban conglomerations (*urbs*), with their high architectural and demographical density, which flourished at the beginning of our era: for instance, Tikal in the Mayan areas, Monte Albán in the Zapotec area, or Teotihuacán in the Mexico Basin. What we are faced with is a quantitative process and an intensification of existing phenomena.

Regional capitals, towns and villages

The regional capital of the 1st millennium BC, which we have defined as *caput* rather than *urbs*, is the core of the Mesoamerican centralized conception of a territory, according to which the town, the centre of political and religious power, ruled over a whole constellation of nearby villages. Of the two parts of this symbiotic relationship, the village has long been the least known, until the excavations carried out by K. Flannery and M. Winter in the valley of Oaxaca supplied us with the missing information. Between 1300 and 800BC, the rural, rectangular Oaxaca house was built of organic materials (wooden posts and reeds); the walls were covered in clay, often smoothed and occasionally whitewashed. These walls sometimes rested on low stone bases. A domestic unit of about 300 sq m (3,229 sq ft) included the house itself and its surrounding yard, where several family activities took place, such as the cooking of certain foods, the grinding of cereals and the manufacture of pots.

This external domestic enclosure also contained the domesticated animals (dogs and parrots), family graves and the bell-shaped pits whose first function was to hold cereal stocks. Around 900BC the village of Tierras Largas spread over 2 hectares (5 acres) and contained five domestic units. Its regional capital, at San José Mogote, covered some 20 hectares (49 acres) and included from 80 to 120 domestic units and several public buildings erected on large adobe and stone platforms and provided with staircases. Around 500BC the site had grown to 40 hectares (99 acres). Some of the architectural structures in the regional capitals studied by P. Tolstoy and S.K. Fish may have been covered with a vivid coat of red pigments made from a haematite (iron ore) base. While most of the villages of *c.*900BC hardly ever spread over more than 2 hectares (5 acres), the town of San Lorenzo in Veracruz covered 53 hectares (130 acres) and it is estimated that Tlapacoya, in the Basin of Mexico, reached 35 hectares (86 acres).

The basic economy of these groups of towns and villages relied on the cultivation of the amaranth, maize, squash, peppers, tomatoes, beans, and, in the southern tropical forests, tuberous plants. Agricultural techniques were by now well advanced from the simple methods of nomadic slash-and-burn farming. The excavations carried out by N. Hammond on the site of Cuello in Belize have revealed the existence of a complex hydraulic system and of a horticulture practised on raised beds surrounded by irrigation channels. Beside lake Tlapacoya, in the Basin of Mexico, blocks of bat droppings, a manure commonly used on the *chinampas* in the Aztec period, demonstrate how intensive cultivation methods developed around 800BC. The most important products of hunting and fishing everywhere were deer, rabbits, peccary and freshwater turtle.

Domesticated dogs were also part of the diet. There were abundant sources of high quality protein in the lakeland areas of the temperate mountains. Traces of cannibalism, as found in the Basin of Mexico, are thus not linked to food deficiency but to ritual practices.

Long-distance trade and religion

The network of interregional commerce covers the whole of the Mesoamerican area: trade exchanges were based on bitumen, salt, obsidian, jadeite, serpentine, magnetite, the feathers of certain birds, pots, cotton and sea shells. Life in the town was enlivened by markets, rites and public games, depicted in the terracotta figures of dancers, musicians and acrobats which have been found. It was also in the town that the iconographical expression of beliefs took shape and was transmitted. This iconography evolved, during the first millennium BC, from a common basis, that of the Olmec world, and gave rise, around 500BC, to vigorous regional styles. The symbolic sacred representations of the protohistoric period, illustrated in the works of J. Soustelle and H. Nicholson, were rooted in this iconography: the five-pointed motif, a mark of civilizing heroes; the plumed serpent; the closed eyelid, symbol of death; and the early forms of hybrid creatures, incarnations of rain or wind.

The study of graves has provided us with precise information on the hierarchical structures and social divisions of the time. The burials of Tlatilco, studied by R. Pina Chan, A. Romano and M. Porter, or the later ones of El Arbolillo and Zacatenco, known through the pioneering work of G. Vaillant, represent a wide spectrum of status and functions: simple plebeians without grave offerings; young women buried with their grinding instruments or pots; craftsmen sent to the other world with their awls and scrapers; divines with their polished amulets; noblewomen wrapped in cloaks of feathers; high dignitaries, their skulls intentionally deformed and their teeth encrusted with rare gems, accompanied by rich, exotic foodstuffs. Two thousand years before Tezozomoc, the Tepanec king, skeleton 141 of El Arbolillo was buried with a jade bead in his mouth, and represents one of many examples of the antiquity and the continuity of certain Mesoamerican traditions. Towards 300BC, some of the regional capitals, such as Cuicuilco in the Gulf of Mexico, enjoyed a considerable expansion, a prelude to that process which was to give rise to the powerful large cities of the first centuries AD.

Musée national d'anthropologie de Mexico

Terracotta figurine

One of the delicate terracotta figurines common in central Mexico at the beginning of the 1st millennium BC. Often painted, tattooed or adorned with jewels, these figurines represent various scenes of everyday life: dances, family life (the rocking of a child, for instance) or, as here, playing with a small domestic dog.

Excavations in the village of Terremote, Mexico Basin

Before the emergence of the great metropolis of Teotihuacan *c.*200BC, several villages connected with a main centre (*caput* not *urbs*) flourished in the Mexico Basin. This view shows one aspect of the excavations at the pre-Teotihuacán village of Terremote, situated on an island in the ancient freshwater lake of Chalco-Xochimilco. This rural community lived on horticulture and craft products manufactured from willow and reeds. Excavations by M.C. Serra P. and Y. Sugiura, 1979.

C. Niederberger Betton

Domestic unit in the Oaxaca valley

The archeological material discovered by K. Flannery and M. Winter (1976) helps us in understanding how a village house in the valley of Oaxaca was arranged *c*.900BC, together with its outbuildings. Outside was an area for family burials, open air ovens, grain silos and domestic activities; inside were, areas reserved for male activities, such as stone carving, or female tasks, like spinning and weaving.

Burials and offerings at Tlatilco

This famous archaeological site can be regarded as one of the regional capitals of the Mexico Basin during the 1st millennium BC. For a long time the site was considered to be a cemetery since its burials and related offerings had formed the main object of study. In reality, these tombs are linked with the remains of dwellings. Markets, ceremonies and games, in which acrobatic contests were highly valued, punctuated the life of the bustling regional capital.

Varieties of urban architecture

Our popular image of the Mesoamerican city tends to be governed by the temple and ritual areas, but what was life like for the ordinary people?

The relationship which Precolumbian communities, possessing only basic techniques, developed with their environment, is revealed over a period of about 3,000 years (the Formative period) by the monumental relics of large architectural complexes. A rural lifestyle which had slowly established itself over the preceding Archaic periods provided a common base from which emerged unrelated types of built-up areas – hamlets, marsh villages or fortified settlements – indicating an urban land use whose definition is still a matter of controversy. We still know very little about the various factors which led to the formation, in the Mexico Basin, the Oaxaca valley, and the lowlands of the Mayas, of what are perceived as degrees of urban complexity. Were these the result of population increase combined with the development of food resources within the framework of a growing social organization, or were they a symbiosis of regional groups through the multiplication of commercial systems? But it should be noted that Mesoamerican civilizations, like those of the rest of the continent, were not necessarily achieved within a framework of urbanization.

The study of the development of this complex phenomenon, in its demographical, spatial and economic aspects, has been tackled over the past decade with the help of methods drawn from anthropology, urban sociology and sometimes economic geography. Such methods are complementary to normal archaeological work as carried out by the interdisciplinary teams of Milton, Sanders, Coe, MacNeish and Flannery among others; they also allow researchers to evaluate the various types of human concentration within a given area. The nature of such settlements is indicated by the expansion of built-up areas (a datable phenomenon) and by the density of the structures. During the 5th century AD, for instance, in the north-eastern part of the Mexico Basin which dominated the development of the classic Mesoamerican civilizations, Teotihuacán concentrated a population of 200,000 within 20 sq km (7.7 sq miles).

The specific texture of urban entities is naturally linked with the levels of organization of the human groups that originated it. It reveals, besides the innovations of the Formative period, the Classic plans of the 1st millennium AD and the achievements of the Postclassic period in the persistence of several architectural styles. These include pyramidal or conical structures with superimposed parts, plastering of the walls, and polychromic treatment of surfaces, and share a continuity with the main principles of spatial organization, such as the orientation of axes, monumental buildings, space available for subsidiary services, enclosures for ritual ball games and markets, districts reserved for the activities of specialized craftsmen, hierarchical treatment of residential sectors, and technical control of water resources. Archaeologists may be able to define a typology of Mesoamerican urban settlements on the basis of recurring and recorded features, but it would be dangerous to claim an understanding of the functional evolution of the urbanized areas and their relationship with basic agricultural activities and their derivatives.

The rural metropolis

In the Olmec area along the coast of the Gulf, the site of San Lorenzo (1500BC) and that of La Venta (700 years later) do not conform, despite their unequalled technical and artistic achievements, to the definition of urban centres as applied to Teotihuacán, Tenochtitlán, Monte Albán or Tikal. Should they be given the title of "rural metropolis"? Their communal buildings differ markedly from domestic units, and the two complexes seem to have acted as religious, administrative and commercial centres for a large hinterland with a dispersed population. A similar dispersed population is found in the territory of the neighbouring Maya civilization, both in its central area (El Mirador) and in the south (Izapa).

The character of "city", as applied to the large centres of Guatemala and Honduras (Tikal, Kaminaljuyú, Copán, etc.), is perhaps related to the presence, from the end of the Formative period and up to the city states of the Classical period, of various prestigious structures: ceremonial complexes several times reinforced and enlarged, sometimes connected by paved lanes (*sacbés*), temples, and "palaces" (so called since the 16th century) serving an urban population of low residential density (6th–8th century Tikal and its area only contained some 50,000 inhabitants over 180 sq km/69 sq miles). Indications of social stratification and of a mixed ethnic origin for the occupants emerge from a detailed study of the foundations and locations of the houses, and the variety of pottery types, burials and votive offerings. Objects found in association with the large buildings – carved stones and inscribed panels – provide not only dynastic information and the elements of a hierarchical arrangement for the monumental Maya centres, but also very elaborate astronomical and calendrical data. Terraces for agricultural purposes, constructed in stone, have recently been discovered in the centre of the Yucatán peninsula (Rio Bec region), in the northeast (southern Quintana Roo) and the southeast (Maya mountains of Belize). Taken in conjunction with the *chinampas* (long and narrow artificial fields more often found in the semi-arid areas of the high central plateau), these terraces testify to prehistoric agricultural practices and the management of a regional economic area which, seen on a large scale, provide a new image of the urban characteristics of the Maya centres.

The tendency to separate prestige buildings, domestic areas and districts reserved for the activities of craftsmen is particularly clear at Teotihuacán, but can also be observed at Monte Albán, founded around 500BC. The more restricted dimensions of the latter and its smaller population which, at the end of the Classical period, amounted to less than 30,000 people, give a special character to this political entity. After the decline of the Classical cities during the 8th century AD, the regional centres became the main landmarks in Mesoamerica (Xochicalco, Cholula, El Tajín) before the hegemony of Tula in the north of the Mexico Basin imposed its own architectural style upon the urban settlements of the Post-classic period. From the 11th century, in northern Yucatán, after the fall of the Maya-Toltec centre of Chichén Itzá and of some of its competing city-states, new concerns reveal themselves in the choice of naturally protected sites surrounded by defensive walls, such as Tulum on the Caribbean coast, and Mayapán in the interior, the seat of a confederation which during the 13th century numbered 12,000 inhabitants in 2,000 domestic units. The peninsular region of the Maya territory witnessed the formation of a network of alliances between invading Toltecs and the indigenous Putun populations of Campeche and Tabasco, which lacked any noteworthy urban settlements; but mixed nomadic groups from the northwest of the country, the Mexica, settled in the lakeland area of the Mexico Basin at the end of the 14th century and formed a new built-up area. A concerted plan of urban construction, spread over less than two centuries, emerged from the founding of the twin island town of Mexico-Tenochtitlán, linked to the mainland by carefully built and maintained roads. Within the "marvellous organization" of the Aztec capital, as described by the Spanish conquerors and recently confirmed by the excavations of the "Templo Mayor" project, the hydraulic works had pride of place with aqueducts, canals and locks – circulation by boat was particularly important in the absence of pack animals. Over an area of 12 sq km (4.6 sq miles), more than 100,000 people lived in a series of districts whose buildings were aligned in decreasing size in relation to the ceremonial enclosure of the "great temple". Divided by its four major roads, at the intersection of the ways that ran through the Mesoamerican territory, this pre-colonial urban centre was to retain its status as capital town even after the Spanish conquest.

Buildings on the site of Lubaantun, Belize

Archaeologists can determine architectural complexes by evaluating their respective heights and volumes, thus enabling them to classify the edifices of the site of Lubaantun in the Maya lowlands in four groups. After N. Hammond, 1972.

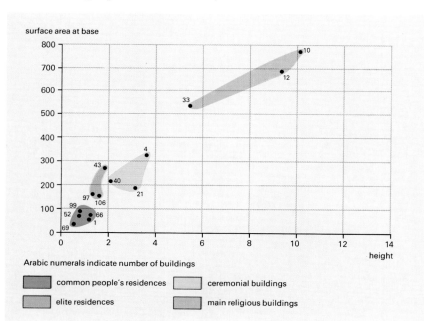

Town squares of Lubaantun, Belize

This diagram illustrates the degree of connection between the principal squares of the Lubaantun site. Ideas of accessibility and centralization seem to have guided the organization of this site between the 8th and 10th centuries in a region where trade polarized the activity of a large but scattered population.

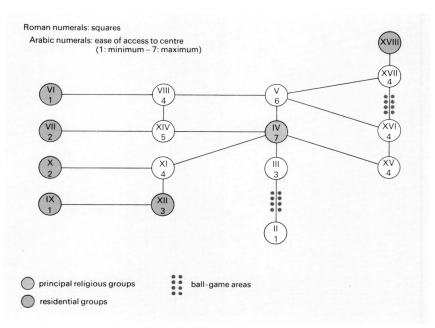

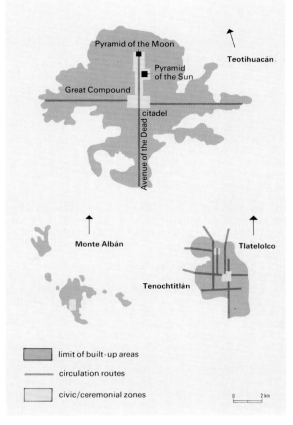

M. del Carmen Nissley

Diagram of four built-up areas

Over a period of more than 4,000 years, the structure of the habitat assumed different aspects in Mesoamerica. Nevertheless, the inventory of archaeological remains and the reconstruction of their successive outlines within major built-up complexes reveal the existence of an overall plan. In different natural (albeit organized) environments, urban areas in the highlands, ceremonial centres, and "rural metropolises" in the lowlands conform to a various but organized use of space.

Teotihuacán

Aerial view of Teotihuacán taken from its south-south-west corner. In the foreground, the Market and the Citadel, in the centre, the Avenue of the Dead.

F. Wagner

Monte Albán

The great square seen from the south-south-east.

V. Lagarde

Tenochtitlán-Tlatelolco

Reconstruction of the Aztec capital shortly before the Spanish conquest. Frieze by L. Covarrubias in the National Anthropological Museum of Mexico.

349

The Maya city of Copán

The architectural wonders of the Maya people, built when Europe was in the Dark Ages, embellished their impressive cities, among which Copán was an outstanding example.

"The sight of this unexpected sculpture once and for all dispelled from our minds all doubt on the character of American antiquities and confirmed us in our conviction that the objects we were looking for were worthy of interest not only as relics of an unknown people but also as works of art proving, as a newly discovered historical text might have done, that the peoples who once occupied the American continent were no savages."

These lines, which the American explorer John L. Stephens was prompted to write after the discovery of a stele (stone slab) at Copán, form the introduction to a description of the site and its sculptures. The text, beautifully enhanced by the drawings of the English architect F. Catherwood, has ensured for Copán a first-class reputation among all the ruins of Central America ever since the mid 19th century. It has since been established that Copán, at its height, was one of the three or four main centres of the Classic Maya civilization. Almost a century of scientific research—begun in 1891 and still continuing to this day—have made the site one of the most intensively worked in the Maya world (probably next to Tikal and its area), as well as one of those about which many publications exist.

The Main Group at Copán

The first subject of interest, both the first to be researched and of prime importance in the monumentality and wealth of its relics, is an architectural group of about 12 hectares known as the Main Group. This comprises, to the north, a large square with several connecting structures and a remarkable concentration of independent sculptures, particularly of stelae sculpted in relief. To the south is an imposing artificial acropolis (citadel) covered with terraces and pyramidal buildings. This group has been intensively researched right up to very recent times. It was the object of the first excavating expedition organized in Maya territory, by the Peabody Museum, Harvard University, and is also the area upon which the Carnegie Institution archaeologists concentrated their efforts in the course of nine long campaigns of excavation, conservation and restoration between 1935 and 1946. As an example of the measures taken in the field of conservation we must cite the diverting of the river Copán, which was affecting the eastern borders of the acropolis and in 50 years had caused the destruction of at least three important structures. Apart from this kind of operation, several excavations had revealed, for instance, three successive stages in the construction of the ball game stadium, the presence of rich ritualistic relics in the chambers built underneath the stelae of the large square, and an ancient staircase, covered in hieroglyphs, that had lain hidden under structure 11.

Meanwhile, the study of the ceramics found in several stratified deposits, particularly on the southern edge of the acropolis, had led to the elaboration of a chronological sequence stretching from the last centuries BC to the collapse of the town in the 9th century AD. We also know of the existence there of a ceramic ware which is of an earlier date than that of the main group in the area; and a few burials intruding into Classical buildings indicate a limited re-occupation of the site after it had been abandoned. The period of peak development of the main group has been pinpointed and can be dated to the so-called Late Classic Period, that is, c.AD700–850.

The stelae inscriptions have also been the subject of research at Copán right from the beginning. The important work published by S.G. Morley* in 1920 records the main inscriptions then known and dates them precisely. However, the development of epigraphy from the 1960s onwards and the discovery of the historico-dynastic content of an important proportion of Maya texts, have paved the way, at Copán and elsewhere, to new interpretations. One of the main objectives of archaeological research at present being conducted at Copán, which began in 1977 under the directorship of C. Baudez, consists in the reconstruction of the dynastic history of the site and the attempt to relate the latter with the history of the architectural development of the main group. In contrast to Tikal, the Copán acropolis has never been subjected to extensive and thorough excavation, which means that our recently acquired knowledge of the site is rather limited, albeit very important. The large square, on the other hand, has been extensively excavated, using the technique of electrical resistivity as applied to geophysical survey*, a technique which reveals any anomalies in the excavated layers.

The information gathered over the past few years has not yet been completely interpreted, particularly as it reflects the beginnings of Copán's dynastic history, comprising 16 kings in all. This history becomes clearer after the 13th king, known as "18-Rabbit". Obviously, several architectural pieces belonging to the main group pre-date the beginning of his reign in the early 8th century. For instance, several buildings beside the great square have been built or altered since the Late Classic Period (AD100–400), at the end of which time Copán seems to have maintained some links with the most dynamic area of the Maya lowlands, the northeast of Petan. The construction of the acropolis probably took place more recently and was more concentrated: the main part would date from the 150 years of the height of Copán's importance, and there are good grounds for maintaining that the present-day layout is due mainly to the last great king there, "Rising Sun". Among all the temples which he had built, building no. 18, to the extreme southeast of the acropolis, is probably also his burial place.

Surrounding sites and their enigmas

But Copán does not consist only of the main group, and the history of this group could not itself be understood without reference to the other sites around it. Only in 1941 was the first regional study undertaken, and a very imperfect archaeological map, covering 18 sq. km (7 sq. miles) drawn up. The most recent research programme is based on a concept which had already begun to be put into operation shortly before, and attempts to establish the role played by Copán in its entirety, at the level of the valley within which the main ruins are found. On the basis of what we know today, it seems that the history of human occupation began here around the year 1000BC. The first thousand years, however, are represented by only few remains, a fact which, at least for the last few centuries of the millennium, is regarded as a mystery. Everywhere else in the Maya lowlands the period between the years 400BC and AD100 seems to have been one of intensive demographical development and innovations in various fields. In the Copán valley, human occupation became more intensive only gradually from AD100 and reached its zenith during the Late Classic Period. In those years, apparently, over 4000 structures stood in the valley, and, besides the main group, at least two other sectors were particularly highly populated. In one of them, named Sepultura, excavations have revealed the existence of several residential buildings, which should enable us better to understand Copán society at its peak. They have already shown that prestigious artistic creations particularly sculptures, were not the monopoly of the Main Group.

The fall of Copán was sudden. It came immediately after the death, in AD800, of "Rising Sun", and is still little understood. This is one of the still mysterious aspects of the history of the site which even a century of research has only partly been able to illuminate.

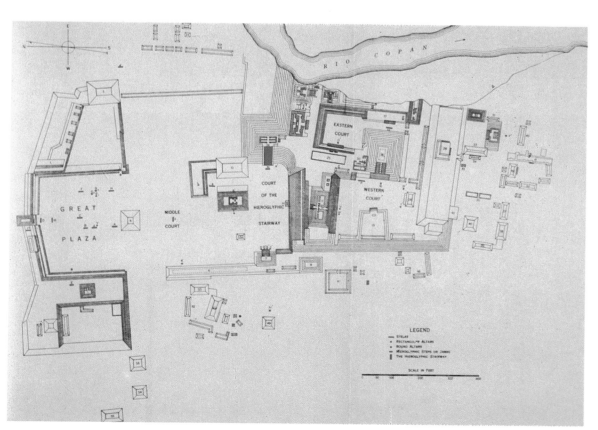

The Main Group at Copán

This plan of Copán's Main Group was published in 1920 together with a study of the inscriptions found on the site by S.G. Morley; it is part of a long cartographical tradition culminating in the publication, in 1981, of the work of the architects Hohmann and Vogrin. Archaeological research carried out at Copán since 1977 has considerably widened our field of knowledge by drawing up a precise map of Copán's valley, covering some 24 sq. km (9.6 sq. miles).

Carving: emblem of Copán

In 1958 the epigraphist H. Berlin identified for the first time a type of carving, with regular attachments, that seemed to have the function of emblem for certain sites. The carved emblem of Copán has a bat's head as its specific element, surrounded to the left and above with fixed features.

Stele B, Copán

Front face of Stele B dating from AD731, drawn by F. Catherwood in 1839 and photographed in 1975. The stele was erected during the reign of the great king "18-Rabbit", who, defeated by the king of Quirigua in 737, was captured and killed. This style of high relief sculpture has made Copán famous.

Ceramic cylinder with polychrome decoration

Cylinder of the Polychrome Copador type discovered in a tomb during the excavations carried out by the Carnegie Institution in 1938. Polychrome Copador is a type of painted ceramic very specific to the valley of Copán, and produced mainly during the 8th century.

Temple of structure 18, Main Group of Copán

The excavation of structure 18, to the southeast of the acropolis, was carried out in 1979 and has yielded important data. "The discovery of the sculpted door jambs in the first room and of the masks decorating the stepped seat between the two rooms of the temple, prompted us to continue with our exploration of the structure . . . we were rewarded when we found the tomb, albeit robbed, and further sculptures . . . Structure 18 is the first example of a funerary temple at Copán." After C.F. Baudez, 1983.

Main residence of the site CV36 in the "Sepultura" sector, Copán

The sector called "Sepultura", to the northeast of the large square of the Main Group, consists of several residential buildings. Among these, site CV36 includes several important buildings arranged around square A. To the south, the more elaborate residence was decorated with sculptures on the façade and, inside the central room, there was a seat decorated with bas-reliefs. One of the hieroglyphs on this seat represents "Rising Sun", the last great king of Copán.

The collapse of the Classic Maya civilization

What brought about the brutally sudden demise of the magnificent Classic Maya civilization and the decimation of its people in the 9th century AD? Archaeologists propose a variety of causes.

Between the end of the 8th and the beginning of the 10th century AD, the Classic Maya civilization which had flourished from Palenque to Copán, and from Calakmul to Seibal, came to an end in the lowlands on the south of the Yucatán peninsula. Unlike the disintegration of other Mesoamerican cultures and societies, such as those of Teotihuacán or Monte Albán, the collapse of the Maya has been the object of much research and many dissertations and written studies. Scientists have looked far and wide in their search for an explanation. A seminar held in 1970, the findings of which were published under the title *The Classic Maya Collapse*, seemed to offer one of the most convincing surveys of the subject. However, a careful appraisal of the facts so far known shows that even this work does not completely solve the problem. Three aspects of the phenomenon are still to be explained: establishment of the facts, reconstruction of the situation, and identification of the causes.

An irreversible cultural decline

One of the peculiarities of the fall of the Classic Maya civilization is that it affected a large area—not only several hundred sites but also many centres of power. Notwithstanding the fact that the phenomenon was dispersed in terms of space and, up to a point, of time, we can see that it was essentially one event.

The final collapse itself is revealed above all by three factors. The first, which began to emerge several decades ago, is the termination of all cultural manifestations connected with the elite classes. Ever since we have been able to transpose into our own calendar the dates of the Maya monuments and sculptures covered by the Long Count* system, it has been clear that this system ceased to be used throughout the whole of the Maya area within little more than the space of a century. But the break was not limited to the abandonment of a calendar; almost simultaneously, the Maya ceased to sculpt, to build their temples and pyramids, and to manufacture luxurious objects such as polychrome ceramics. All this leads one to assume that there was a disintegration of the ruling classes, promoters of such activities. More recent studies have shown that the collapse did not involve only the ruling classes; it now seems that several centres and their surroundings became suddenly and substantially depopulated at about the same time. Therefore, and this is the second aspect, the disappearance of Classic Maya civilization was also marked by an important demographical decline in the southern lowlands, through either extinction or migration. Finally, the third key aspect of this phenomenon is its rapidity (over one century) and its irreversible nature.

Even at the level of these general, well-documented factors there are points which are still not as rigorously established as one would wish. While the completeness and suddenness of the collapse cannot be contested, the chronology of events is more difficult to establish. If one takes as a chronological departure point the last dated inscription of all the sites where any are to be found, one would obtain a first sequence ranging from AD795 (last inscription at Piedras Negras) to AD909 (last inscription at Tonina). But the interruption in monumental building and the changes in ceramic production supply quite different clues. It must also be admitted that the second notable element of the phenomenon, the drop in population, although clearly revealed on a site like Tikal (where 200 groups of occupied dwellings of the Imix phase dropped to only 14 during the following Eznab phase) still has to be confirmed in the case of many other Mayan sites.

If we leave to one side for the moment the general trends and examine the particular facts about the various sites affected by the collapse, we have to face the question of the overall unity or diversity. For instance, the data gathered at Tikal show that its decline took place during the second half of the 9th century, but there is no real trace of violence nor of any interruption altogether in human occupation, which merely suffered a spectacular diminution. At Tonina, on the other hand, the lapse of time between the erection of the two last sculptures, dated 837 and 909, is characterized by the appearance of new elements, probably foreign, particularly in the manufacture of ceramics. The site was then abandoned and later only sporadically reoccupied. Statues appear to have been wilfully mutilated, whether by an uprising or an invasion is not known. Some archaeologists favour the hypothesis of an invasion. Other cases could be mentioned which would reveal different peculiarities. However, the reconstruction of a general picture, true of the whole area, is not to be ruled out, on condition, of course, that it should take into consideration all the variants, whether already known or still to be revealed.

Multi-causal reasons for the Mayan collapse

As to the causes of the collapse of the Classic Maya civilization, it would seem that one of the most important results of the 1970 conference mentioned above was the suggestion of a multi-causal explanation in contrast with the single-cause accounts which had so far been advanced. These accounts differ widely, most of them supposing some fault or weakness inherent in Maya society or in its type of ecological adaptation. In 1921, for instance, O.F. Cook emphasized the risk of soil impoverishment when the fallow period is shortened in order to cope with the needs of an increasing population. Other conjectures based on a disruption of ecological balance have been proposed; what they have in common is the fact that they blame long-term agricultural problems for the Maya collapse. Even the theory of a climatic change, all too often advanced to explain cultural disruptions, has recently been put forward in connection with this episode of Maya history. However unsatisfactory they may appear today, all these explanations have been supported, up to a point, by the analysis of the remains of human bones dating from the end of the Classic Maya period, an analysis which has shown an increase in dietary deficiencies. Whatever the case, these explanations seem to be more solidly founded than the suggestions of certain scholars who stress the propensity of the area to natural disasters (earthquakes or cyclones), or the opinion, never really accepted, according to which the enigma is not so much the collapse as the development of a civilization within the tropical forests. Alongside the ecological or multi-causal explanations, the hypothesis of a social collapse within the Maya world has been supported by J.E.S. Thompson. One should also reconsider the various indicators which point to an invasion of various sites. The conclusion reached by the 1970 conference was based on a summary of the facts (albeit incomplete) and on the systematic analysis of Maya civilization before its decline, stressing some of the factors contributing to an imbalance: agricultural problems, the increase in population and malnutrition, the role of the élites who may have worsened the "crisis" by increasing their extravagant outlay on propitiatory rites, the widening of the social gap between these élites and the people of the countryside, competition between the cities, the dependence of the area on commercially obtained goods. Eventually a general qualitative scheme has been constructed which incorporates all these elements.

But even the propounders of this conclusion recognize that it still does not explain all the known facts. The 1970 conference has not put an end to the debate, since at least seven new contributions have since been published. Some of these reiterate specific factors already mentioned (such as the peasants' revolt) or explore new explanations (the fatalistic view of adherents of the cyclic vision of history). A few others try to achieve a formal and quantified presentation of a multi-causal theory. Whatever the interest inherent in individual efforts, it is now necessary to take another look at the facts.

J. P. Courau

Peak and collapse of the Maya civilization

Within about one century, the sites of the Maya lowlands in the south were abandoned and the tropical forest began to claim them back. At Tikal, all important architectural activity practically ceased in AD830. At about the same time, the population also sharply fell.

Last date of the Long Count at Tonina

Monument 101 of Tonina carries, on its reverse side, the last date of the Long Count calendar so far known within the Maya area: 10.4.0.0.0.12 Ahau 3Uo (AD909). After 837 Tonina produced no dated sculpture, and in the years 837–909 foreign influences can be detected on the site. The status of the person represented on the front (the last king of Tonina?) is not clear: certain features suggest the possibility of a captivity. After Becquelin and C.F. Baudez, 1982.

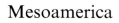

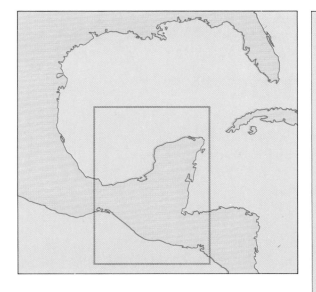

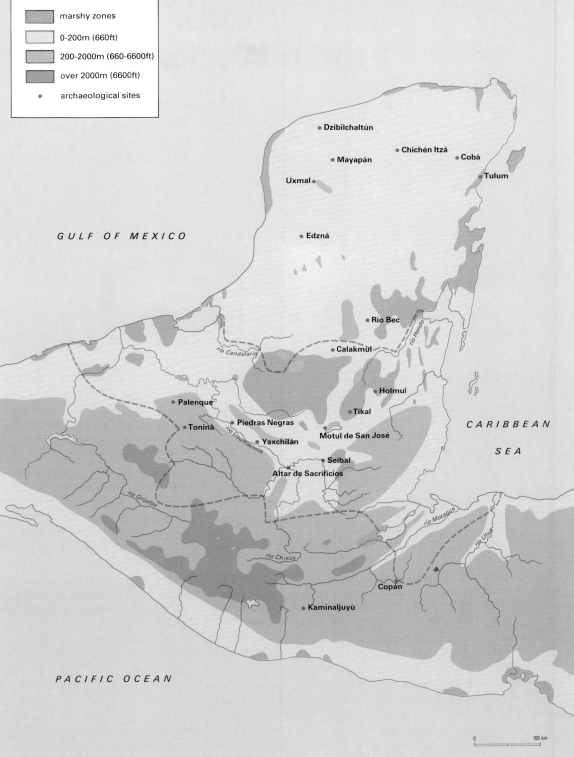

General map of the Maya region

The collapse of the Classic civilization affected above all the central part of the region or lowlands to the south of the Yucatán peninsula. The political organization of this sector before the collapse is still unknown in its details, but there are good reasons to believe that several sites constituted city states hierarchically organized around capitals. According to J. Marcus (1976), in AD849 there were four capitals: Calakmul, Tikal, Motul de San José and Seibal.

Detail of Stele 8 of Seibal

The features of the person here depicted differ from the canons of Classic Maya aesthetics, and could be the portrait of a Maya-Putun chief (an ethnic group occupying the site in the early 9th century, and responsible for keeping Seibal active until about 928).

Diagram illustrating possible causal chains

A diagram showing the causes for the collapse of the Classical Maya civilization marks a stage in the explanation of the phenomenon by a simulation process. The plus sign indicates a proportional relationship between two elements, the minus sign indicates an inversely proportional relationship. After D. Hosler, J.A. Sabloff and D. Runge, 1977.

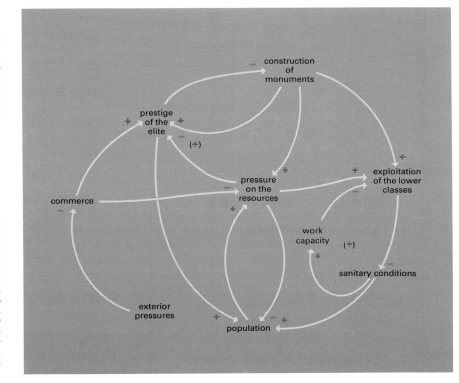

South America: the historical background

The wholesale destruction of the pre-Columbian antiquities of South America by the European conquerors, and the suppression of native cultures over the succeeding centuries, have retarded the discovery of the true antiquity of the South American cultures.

South America is a "young" continent, and its archaeology is even younger. Admittedly, important finds were made there from the middle of the 19th century, but scholars were not ready to admit the idea of prehistoric man in America when the notion had only just been accepted in Europe. At the beginning of the 20th century, it was still thought that the American past could not go back more than a few millennia, and the totality of excavated remains were all catalogued together as "pre-Columbian antiquities", a sort of catch-all where shaped stone tools some 10,000 years old were alongside pottery at the most a few hundred years old. In the Andean area, monuments and works of art were still indiscriminately attributed to the Incas, who came late into a history more than 20,000 years old.

However, curiosity about this world first grew when the Conquest revealed the existence of beings to amazed Europeans who wondered whether they were human beings at all. In 1537, Pope Paul III confirmed that the "Indians" really were men. Then it was necessary to explain where they came from and how they reached America. As A. Laming-Emperaire* wrote, "the list of hypotheses is impressively long and includes Phoenicians, Assyrians, Egyptians, Canaanites, Israelites, Trojans, Greeks, Etruscans, the Romans and Scythians". All these have been called in to explain the high civilizations of the American Indians, and as for the origin of the others, the "savage" cultures, this is hardly ever the subject of research. Only one man of that time combined practical observation with theoretical ideas, the Jesuit priest J. de Acosta. In his *Histoire naturelle et morale des Indes* (1590), he explained that "the human lineage" must have spread gradually and in a natural way from countries near to or connected with the New World in some way, and that the first men to reach America were undoubtedly "wild men and hunters". He rejected the theories of his contemporaries on the supposed Jewish or Atlantean origin of the Amerindians, and thus showed remarkable foreknowledge, with a theory that, although advanced centuries ago, links up with the current view of a first wave of populations bringing a Paleolithic culture over the Bering Strait.

Conquistadors and chroniclers

Along with these basic questions, attention focused in a more or less disinterested way on various aspects of the newly discovered cultures. In a sense, the first archaeologists of the pre-Columbian past were the Spanish and Portuguese chroniclers of the 16th and 17th centuries: priests, soldiers and officials whose works are filled with descriptions of native monuments and objects. Their accounts are not without value, for the oldest of them record living cultures and buildings still in all their splendour at the time they were written. Among those writers was Cieza de León, who came to Peru in 1547 as a soldier, but in his free time visited and described the monuments he encountered on the way – Chavín, Pachacámac, Tiahuanaco and many others. His work is one of the most important sources for the study of ancient Peruvian art. Garcilaso de Vega, whose father was Spanish and whose mother was a niece of the Inca chief Huayna Cápac, published *Comentarios reales* as from 1609. His descriptions of the temples and palaces of Cuzco, and the manners and customs of the Inca, which he must have learnt from his mother, are irreplaceable documents despite an evident partiality in favour of the Inca. Another important work is the *Histoire du Nouveau Monde* by the Jesuit B. Cobo who described from a different perspective the pagan temples he had visited: Pachacámac, the temples on the islands of Lake Titicaca, and the Temple of the Sun at Cuzco.

In other countries less richly endowed with the remains of monuments, the Spaniards also described and observed the natives and their customs, at the same time as they looted and massacred. G. Jimenez de Quesada and S. de Belalcázar tirelessly sought for El Dorado in the region that was to become Colombia, and found the Muisca peoples (1536–59). In Chile, A. de Ercilla wrote the excellent heroic poem *La Araucana* (1569). A little later, when all the regions had been conquered, envoys of the Spanish crown charged with "extirpating idolatry" such as F. de Avila, J. de Arriaga and others made observations, interrogations and descriptions that effectively achieved a kind of archaeological survey long before its time. In order to accumulate even more gold and silver, they excavated the walls and floors of the *huacas* (holy places) and fortresses, according to methods scrupulously controlled by edicts of the viceroy Toledo. These included issue of a permit, inspection, written records of discoveries, and a compulsory bi-monthly report – all practices which foreshadowed modern archaeological methods.

As from the 17th century, too, fine objects from various regions were collected to enrich the rulers' "cabinets of curiosities", but the colonial authorities took care not to encourage the study of old aboriginal cultures which might encourage "nationalist" tendencies that were then emerging.

Later European expeditions

During the Age of Enlightenment, research took another course under the influence of ideas coming from Europe, and from France in particular. Metaphysical speculations were abandoned in favour of rationalist explanations, and the disorganized acquisitions of disparate objects gave way to systematic collection. South America was a favourite field for European expeditions, which were as much political and commercial as scientific. Scholars such as I. de Feuillée and J. Dombey travelled through Peru excavating ruins, native cemeteries and shell mounds. Dombey returned to the court of Louis XVI with more than 400 pieces of pottery, later to be housed in the Musée de l'Homme in Paris and the Madrid Museum. Even more important was B.J. Martinez de Compañon, who took an interest in ancient monuments when he was Bishop of Trujillo in Peru in 1779. He left nine volumes illustrated with 1,411 drawings, maps, plans of buildings and reproductions of all kinds of objects, and he is rightly regarded as the founder of Andean archaeology.

The early 19th century was marked by the revolts of various colonies liberating themselves from Spanish or Portuguese rule. Europeans and North Americans found in the new nations a fresh field for exploration (and profit). Wealthy travellers, businessmen and diplomats traversed South America in every direction, taking notes and collecting archaeological objects. Those objects were to enrich the museums of their own countries, although most South American countries had also founded museums and drawn up laws protecting their national heritage.

In Brazil towards 1840 a discovery took place which created quite a stir. The Danish botanist P.W. Lund*, who had spent years investigating the numerous caves of the Lagoa Santa region (Minas Gerais) and collecting the bones of fossil animals, found in the cave of Sumidouro human remains mixed with those of animals. These human remains were in his opinion contemporary with the great animals that were now extinct. However, the public was not ready to accept that humanity could be so ancient, and Lund, alarmed by the controversy that attended his work, halted his investigations and took refuge in silence. Nevertheless, he had intuitively grasped, some years in advance, what Darwin was to propose in his *Origin of Species* in 1859.

Museum für Völkerkunde, Staatliche Museen Preussischer Kulturbesitz, Berlin-Ouest

A tomb from the burial ground of Ancón, *c*.1880

Immense pre-Inca burial grounds, subjected to constant looting for centuries, existed in the coastal desert of Peru. In the 19th century, the first archaeologists worthy of the name naturally carried out their first excavations in these cemeteries, using methods which clearly did not pay too much attention to accuracy. Without squaring off the site or making stratigraphical observations they dug, or rather watched the workmen dig, in expectation of the discovery of some richly ornamented funerary *fardo**, fine fragment of pottery, or even the ever-present possibility of a gold item.

In the same period, and also in Brazil, another Dane, J.A. Worsaae, intrigued by the presence on the coast of enormous piles of shells almost identical with those of his own country, advanced the hypothesis that both were artificial heaps placed there by man. At the end of the 19th century, several missions went to the coast encouraged by King Pedro II, a keen anthropologist, to collect the objects buried in these *sambaquis* , used then (as they still are) as chalk quarries. A dispute arose (and continued till 1940) between those who supported a natural origin, suggesting that the heaps were deposited by the sea, and those who supported a man-made origin.

Amateur archaeologists in the Andes

It was naturally the Andean regions, with their rich vestiges of the "high cultures" that attracted the greatest number of amateur travellers. Following the naturalists, some devoted themselves exclusively to the study of the pre-Hispanic past. *Peruvian Antiquities* by E. de Rivero and J.J. von Tschudi, the first general work dealing with Peruvian archaeology, appeared in 1851. In 1856 Angrand's *Letter on the Antiquities of Tiahuanaco and the Presumed Origin of this Ancient Civilization of Upper Peru* was published in Paris, setting out the theory of the Toltec origin of Tiahuanaco. Finally, in 1880 the work of C. Wiener, *Peru and Bolivia*, offered the reader a copious, though often fanciful, archaeological iconography.

From the end of the 19th to the beginning of the 20th century the explorations multiplied, generally led by Europeans and North Americans such as C.R. Markham, E.G. Squier, E. Middendorf and A. Bandelier, who combined scientific curiosity with a spirit of adventure and a good deal of romanticism. This led to a certain lack of accuracy, apart from descriptions by Squier and, particularly, by W. Reiss and A. Stübel (*Das Todtenfeld von Ancón*, 1886–1887) which represent the first genuine reports of excavations. These years also saw the appearance of the first ethnological syntheses compiled by Latin American scholars such as L. Netto in Brazil (*Investigação sobre a archeologia brasileira*, 1885) or J.T. Medina (*Los aborigenes de Chile*, 1882) and R. Latcham in Chile.

Despite these promising beginnings, some strange theories were put forward: in 1880 the Argentine F. Ameghino launched a celebrated hypothesis which proposed a human origin in the Argentine pampa, where a small animal, *Homunculus patagonicus*, was supposed to have emerged in the middle of the Tertiary era. Although rapidly refuted, Ameghino's thesis did much to discredit the idea of ancient American man.

Nevertheless, at the start of the 20th century South American archaeology had a solid base. The field was ready for a methodical and fully scientific approach practised by professionals, as seen in the fieldwork of the German M. Uhle* in Peru (1896–97) and then in Chile.

In 1903 Uhle published *Pachacámac*, a work which contained the first description based on stratigraphical (vertical section) research, and the first classification in series of Peruvian ceramics. Uhle was also the first to discover the existence, along the coasts of Peru and Chile, of pre-pottery traces which he attributed to "primitive fishers". However, he thought that the more recent cultures of Peru, such as Mochica and Nazca, or of Esmaraldas in Ecuador, derived from Mesoamerican cultures. Thus he embodied the diffusionist point of view, which he carried to its extreme limit by postulating that all the higher American cultures had their origin in Chinese civilizations.

The great theoretical and ideological conflict between the evolutionist and diffusionist schools, born in Europe and North America, extended to South America. Uhle was opposed in Chile by Latcham and in Peru by J. Tello*, whose spectacular discoveries were from 1919 to shake diffusionist theories: the ruins of Chavín in 1919, Paracas in 1925, Kotosh in 1935, and Cerro Sechin in 1937. These suggested that the origin of the great Peruvian cultures was to be found in Peru itself and not in Mexico, and that the Amazonian forest in 1000BC (the date proposed by Tello) gave rise to the cultural elements peculiar to the Chavín culture. This theory found immediate acceptance in the country. Archaeology, to Tello and his disciples, formed part of the social sciences as a whole. It was connected with the "Indian problem", the problem of land, and was a weapon in the social struggle. This explains the passionate, vibrant and often biased point of view of Tello, who tried to show that the true creator of Andean civilization, this world which made the Europeans so rich, was the despised Indian.

After a marked slowing down during World War II, research was resumed in 1945. Tello died in 1947 and a few years later the discovery of C^{14}* confirmed the great antiquity of Chavín. Nevertheless, it was the American J. Bird* who in 1946 revealed the existence of a still older "pre-pottery" phase at Huaca Pireta, dated to 2500BC. A growing preoccupation with method, and the establishment of sequences that were as complete as possible, led the North Americans to organize the "Virú valley project" in Peru, the most important programme then initiated in South America, and also the first example of an inter-disciplinary study. The post-war period was also marked by a new interest, stimulated by the discoveries of Bird in Chile and Peru, in the most ancient human settlements, and the same period saw discoveries that have gradually pushed back the dates of the South American past. Finally, since the 1970s, research has been strongly influenced by the new archaeology of the English-speaking nations, which draws on the model of the exact sciences such as physics, and seeks to apply theoretical principles to discoveries made in the field. Whatever its actual novelty, an approach like this, which although an approach firmly based on paleo-ethnology*, or the study of ancient races and peoples, imposes a renewed vision of archaeological remains which can no longer be examined independently of their natural environment.

The oldest human settlements

During the last 15 years, archaeologists have pushed back the human record in South America by 15,000 years; modern emphasis on culture and evolution has given the prehistory of the region a new human dimension.

Since 1970 there has been increased research into the arrival of humans in South America, and our knowledge of the first settlements has made considerable progress. Nevertheless, research into human origins in the area has not been without heated controversy, because to many Latin American countries the discovery of their past is far more than a simple scientific exercise.

There are two opposing views: the bolder proposes that man could have arrived in South America as early as 30,000BC, whereas the more cautious dates the event to around 12,000BC. Recent discoveries apparently favour the first hypothesis.

The earliest evidence of human presence comes from two regions with contrasting geographic and climatic conditions: the northeast of Brazil and the Andes. In Brazil, excavations led by N. Guidon have revealed remains apparently going back to before 25,000BC in a rock shelter situated in the heart of the "arid polygon" in the state of Piaui. The deep levels of Toca do Boqueirão da Pedra Furada have supplied a series of dates ranging from 30,000 to 25,000BC. The remains of a hearth and some 15 worked stone tools indicate the presence of a small group of hunters. Other caves in the same region (Toca do Caldeirão do Rodriguez 1, Toco do Meio) were occupied later, around 16,000BC. Further south, the work of A. Laming-Emperaire* since 1974 has revealed a stratigraphic sequence running from about 23,000 to 9,000BC in the Great Shelter of Lapa Vermelha (Minas Gerais). The remains, though scanty, are enough to show a human presence some 15,000 years ago in the form of fires and abandoned stone tools. The deepest level contained charcoal (possibly the remains of a natural conflagration), but no cultural traces. Still in Brazil, in the deposit on the terrace of Alice Boer (São Paulo) excavated by M.C. Beltrão, a level dated to about 12,000BC covered a deeper and older (albeit undated) level containing primitive stone tools, worked pebbles and massive flakes. However, this material was deposited on the terrace by a river in flood, and some specialists even doubt if these tools were made by man.

In the heart of the Andean Cordillera, excavations conducted by R. MacNeish have provided evidence of early human occupation in the cave of Pikimachay (basin of Ayacucho). The site was occupied by man towards 12,000BC (Ayacucho phase), and even, according to its discoverers, from 18,000BC (Pacaicasa phase). However, several archaeologists deny the existence of the last-named phase. The dating in this case was not based on charcoal (the level did not contain any), but on the bone of a Scelidotherium, a kind of giant sloth which undoubtedly occupied the cave long before man. Furthermore, nearly all the "tools" from the "Pacaicasa" levels (69 out of 73) are from the same rock as the cave walls, a sort of tufa particularly unsuitable for working, and look extremely worn, if not altogether without shape. Yet MacNeish believes that small bands of hunters tracked down the giant sloths in their lairs before cutting up and eating them. If scrupulous scholarship and caution require us to accept only the Ayacucho phase, in which a more abundant stone tool kit was certainly produced from stones that had come from elsewhere, caves and shelters in the Andean region were definitely used by hunters from 12,000BC.

New discoveries

These early occupations, which as we have seen yield few remains, have two characteristics: hunted animals consist mainly of species belonging to the now extinct Quaternary varieties (mastodon, horse, giant sloth, etc.); and the hunters apparently used neither bifacial* stone points, nor delicately fashioned tools in general. So the deposits correspond to what A. Krieger called in 1964 the "pre-projectile phase", characterized by the absence of bifacial points. The idea was greatly criticized at the time, because of the unreliability of the deposits adduced in evidence, whether they were groups of crude tools found on the surface and not dated (Garzón, Exacto, Guatchi) or associations of tools and animal remains dated solely by geological correlation, as at Manzanillo and Camare, Taima-Taima, and at Muaco, where stone tools were found with Quaternary animals, but also with bits of broken glass that were definitely recent; or, lastly, objects to which a human origin can only dubiously be attributed (Chuqui).

In the light of recent discoveries, it seems most likely that the first South American hunters, who were very few in number, did not manufacture bifacial tools and had not mastered the technique of pressure flaking (known in the Old World since the Solutrean culture*, c.19,000BC).

The number of known deposits from later than 12,000BC is larger, both on the plateaus of east Brazil and in the Andes. The levels contain mainly Pleistocene* animals, soon to disappear and be replaced by existing species, deer and camelids in particular. The tool kit increased in range. In some places it was still exclusively made up of flakes retouched to a varying degree (El Abra in Ecuador, Guitarrero I in Peru, Santana do Riacho in Brazil, Los Toldos 11 and El Ceibo in the Argentine); others contain handsome bifacial points, suggesting that their absence elsewhere may simply reflect excavation on too small a scale or specialization in the areas excavated (the food-gathering activities may not have needed points).

A spectacular discovery has recently been made in Chile by T. Dillehay and a Chilean team: the remains of an encampment of mastodon hunters hitherto unknown in South America and dated to c.12,000BC have been uncovered at Monte Verde, preserved in a peat bog. This comprised 14 dwellings of wood and skin which could have housed about 56 people for several successive seasons. Apparently the occupants did not use worked points, but shaped pebbles and flakes, and they also possessed weapons and tools of wood. In addition, they used stone balls (the oldest bolas* in America) as missiles. The high degree of organization of all the remains transforms the rather simplified image of the "primitive" South American hunters that is sometimes put forward.

The period which follows (about 10,000 to 8000BC) is represented by many deposits scattered all over the continent, with the exception of the tropical forest, which is as hostile to modern archaeologists as it must once have been to prehistoric man. So it is hardly surprising to find man installed in the southern tip of the continent, in Patagonia (Fell and Palli-Aike caves) from 10,000BC and even in Tierra del Fuego (shelter of Marassi) around 8000BC. In some deposits (El Inga, Fell, Palli-Aike), the presence of "fishtail" bifacial points, the origin of which may go back to the Clovis and Folsom points of North America, undoubtedly demonstrates the arrival of a differentiated tool kit well suited to hunting. It is difficult to trace the route followed, but the distribution of tools and weapons (found in stratigraphical* levels and on the surface) suggests an advance along the Andean chain, probably by way of the eastern foothills, which had less vegetation cover in those times.

This period also marks the beginning of the occupation of the Andean highlands at a level above 4,000m (13,200ft), after the withdrawal of the Quaternary ice. From then on, the whole continent was populated by humans well adapted to a variety of natural environments, all of whose resources were exploited.

Cave of Pikimachay

Pikimachay (Quechua for "cave of the fleas") is situated in the temperate basin of the Ayacucho, Peru, at an altitude of 2,850m (9,400ft). It is the oldest known deposit occupied by prehistoric man in the Andean area.

The shelter of Marassi

A large erratic boulder left behind by glaciers near the shore of Bahia Inutil (Tierra del Fuego) afforded temporary shelter, 10,000 years ago, for a group of hunters. There they left some fine worked stone tools, two bolas and the bones of small mammals. The shelter was discovered in 1964 by A. Laming-Emperaire and excavated from 1964 to 1967.

Reconstruction of a mylodon

Animals taken by the first hunters included giant sloths (*Edentata*). Remains of one type, the mylodon, have been found in various Patagonian deposits dated to *c*.9000BC. However, some specialists dispute that they were contemporaneous with man, claiming that the species had already disappeared before the first waves of population had reached the far south. By kind permission of J. Schobinger, *Prehistoria de Sudamérica*, Editorial Labor S.A., Barcelona.

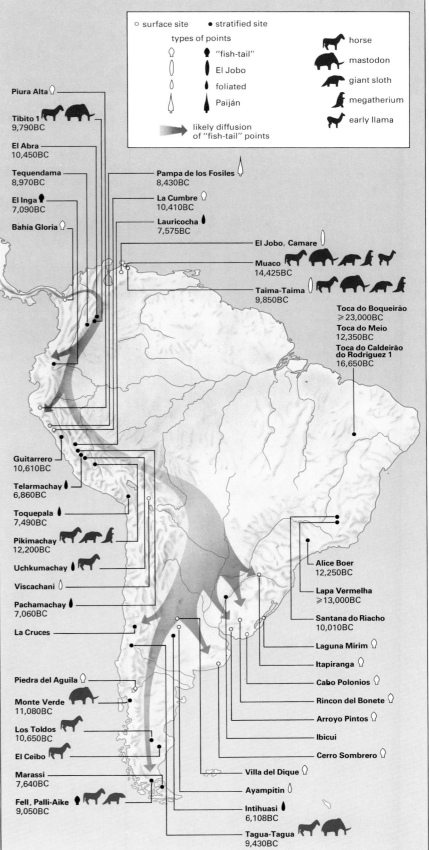

Earliest sites of human activity in South America

The map shows a relative concentration of sites along the Andes, and a fairly regular distribution on the edge of the Atlantic, contrasted with an absolute void in the tropical centre. The number of "fishtail" points found in the Parana basin and some stratified Andean sites convinced archaeologists such as J. Schobinger that the diffusion ran from north to south (line marked with arrows). However, other authorities maintain that this could have been a local "invention" in the south with diffusion occurring in the opposite direction, on the grounds that South American points bear little resemblance to the channelled points of the United States.

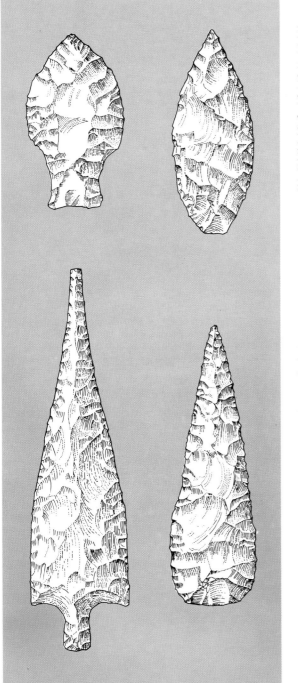

Principal types of bifacial points

Top left, "fishtail" Fell point, *c*.10,000–7000BC (after R. Humbert); top right, El Jobo point, *c*.8000–7000BC (after R. Humbert); bottom left, pedunculate Paijan point, *c*.9000–6000BC (after P. Laurent); bottom right, foliate Ayampitin-Lauricocha point *c*.8000–4000BC (after R. Humbert).

Toca do Boqueirão de Pedra Furada, Brasil

The oldest known human traces in South America were found in this cave of the Caatinga, at the foot of immense red sandstone cliffs. The rock walls also display magnificent paintings which go back some 15,000 years.

N. Guidon, laboratoire d'anthropologie préhistorique d'Amérique, E.H.E.S.S., Paris

Prehistoric rock art

A rich and diverse rock art, going back at least 20,000 years, is found the length of South America from Argentina to the Guyanas.

Prehistoric rock art in South America requires appropriate techniques for its classification, and should be interpreted according to a definite method that places it within a precise cultural context. On-site research at present involves the following stages: drawing plans and cross-sections of the site, copying the images onto transparent plastic film, marking the position of the images on topographical records, and, finally, photographing and filming the paintings. Once in the laboratory, the panels on plastic film must be photographed and reduced. The various details are then assembled to reproduce the works of art on a smaller scale. The result is then copied exactly. The reproduction permits observers on the site to verify that the images have been correctly placed. Each image is then carefully studied from the point of view of technique and colour, and all superimpositions are analysed under a microscope. Quite often this examination reveals new figures. All corrections are then reproduced onto the original, which is again checked before being published.

Rock art in South America seems to be local in character, although it is geographically widespread and covers a considerable chronological period. There is, however, very little chronological information which might allow us to date it with any certainty. In 1957, for instance, O.A. Menghin suggested a stylistic classification of Argentine art which was subsequently proved to be premature.

The art of the Holocene hunters
South American rock art can be dated to three successive periods: that of the first hunters, the Holocene* hunters, and the farming communities. The earliest examples of the art of the first hunters were discovered on the site at Toca do Boqueirão da Pedra Furada (in the state of Piaui, northeastern Brazil). The finds are few but certain. In 1983 an archaeological layer between 26,000–22,000 years old (C^{14}* dating) was uncovered, yielding part of a collapsed wall showing traces of red paint. This layer also contained the remains of mineral pigments as well as red and yellow ochre. The small size and poor condition of the pieces of painted wall precluded identification of the images.

The Neolithic industry corresponding to this art of the first hunters consists of choppers* and chopping tools, pointed shingles showing traces of usage, unworked splinters, and a single scraper.

The remnants of the art of the Holocene hunters, which have been discovered on many sites throughout the São Raimundo Nonato region (Piaui state, Brazil),

have led to the identification of different traditions and different artistic styles dated variously between 10,000 and 3000BC: in the Mato Grosso (Brazil), certain engravings go back to c.10,000BC; in Patagonia (southern Argentina), finds have been dated 9000–7000BC; and at Minas Gerais (Brazil), there are rock paintings 6,000 years old.

The art of this period can be divided into two categories: on the one hand, a figurative art showing human beings, a number of signs, and above all animals (deer-type animals, armadillos, nandus, felines, lizards, birds, fish, snakes, rodents and, in Andean sites and Patagonia, camelids); on the other, a non-figurative art with a preponderance of geometrical figures and symbols. The figurative art traditions of the Holocene hunters can be defined according to their themes, but the same method does not work in the case of non-figurative art. Here it is sometimes impossible to determine the scope of the motifs, and any interpretation of theme would be without foundation.

All representations of art from the figurative tradition are painted; red is the dominant colour, but yellow is also found, as well as black, white, grey and brown. Green and blue were used later, and can only be found in the Andean and Patagonian sites. The Northeastern tradition includes several styles and is the oldest yet known. Characterized by human figures, animals and plants, as well as objects and some signs, it prevailed in northeastern Brazil between 10,000 and 5,000 years ago. This tradition has left us representations of hunting scenes, fights, sexual encounters, births and dances.

At the extreme south of the continent, shelters beneath rocky overhangs display silhouettes of hands and groups of camelids surrounded or pursued by human figures. According to Mengin, two different styles may be represented here, that of the "hand negatives" being the older (7,000 years). This particular style of art may be defined as the "Patagonian tradition". In central Brazil, in the states of Minas Gerais, Goias and Mato Grosso, certain sites have revealed paintings in the so-called Planalto tradition, where animals and human figures predominate and the signs are less numerous.

The art style or tradition called "Rustic" developed some 5,000 years ago from northeastern Brazil to north of Minas Gerais. It is characterized by the predominance of large human figures, together with drawings of hands, feet and some animals depicted in a very crude style. Here, too, the signs are less numerous.

In north-western Argentina, in the river basins of the

Loa and the Salado, as well as in Chile and southern Peru, sites have been found which go back to the Andean tradition, the main theme of which is a large representation of a camelid. These undated paintings seem to be recent and could be the work of groups of hunters. Isolated sites in the equatorial forests of Columbia, Brazil, Venezuela and Guyana, as well as in southern Brazil, show examples of figurative painting.

Non-figurative traditions
Over the whole of Amazonia and the Guyanas, from the states of Mato Grosso and Randonia to the eastern coast of Brazil, at Bahia, Goias, Minas Gerais and southern Brazil, in Uruguay, Argentina and Chile, sites displaying incised signs and geometrical figures attest to an extremely ancient non-figurative tradition. This is the tradition of Icoatiaras, which seems to have originated in the high basin of the Rio Guaporé (Brazil), where a date of 10,000BC has been obtained.

The so-called "geometrical" tradition includes a certain number of regional groups characterized by paintings of geometrical figures and, occasionally, human and animal images whose outlines reveal stylization of a geometric tendency. The dominant colour is red, but in certain areas two colours and three colours (red, yellow, black) are also widely employed. Sete Cidades in northeastern Brazil, the region of the Sierras Centrales, and northern Patagonian are all very rich in such sites. The datings obtained at Piaui place this tradition at about 2,000BC, but in central Brazil and the south of the continent the work seems more recent and could even be by agricultural peoples.

Along the whole of the Andean range, a number of sites have yielded examples of the art of agricultural settlements between 1000BC (C^{14}* dating) and the European conquest in the 16th century. Paintings and etchings have been found there representing domestic camelids (llamas), condors, felines, dogs, human beings and occasionally even horses. In the Januaria region (Minas Gerais, Brazil), paintings in black represent maize plantations.

The prehistoric art of South America has had a very long lifespan and a very slow evolution; the same themes have occasionally been preserved for thousands of years. Such art can supply valuable information on the origins of South American ethnic groups and their migratory routes.

Boqueirão do Sitio da Pedra Furada. São Raimundo Nonato, Piaui, Brazil

More than 200 overhang shelters with paintings have so far been identified in the southeast of the Piaui state. The paintings in this shelter belong to the Northeastern tradition, with figures painted in red, white, grey, yellow and black. All the niches in the wall have been used, and superimpositions are frequent. Cervids, jaguars, armadillos, nandus, lizards and humans are represented together with geometrical motifs. Hunting, sexual and ceremonial scenes follow each other. In the niche shown here, a series of red sticks have been embellished with white stripes (three at the top and three at the bottom), which can, with certainty, be interpreted as human figures. At Pedra Furada excavations have been carried out to a depth of three metres and the wall thus discovered has shown traces of red paintings. This shelter had been used uninterruptedly from 28,000 to 2,000BC.

Toca da Extrema. São Raimundo Nonato, Piaui, Brazil

In the Sierra Branca region, the superimposed figures belonging to different traditions (Northeastern, Rustic, Geometrical) show that several human groups followed one another over the centuries on these sites. The Rustic tradition is well represented with large anthropomorphic figures, shown in stilted and isolated form, and roughly outlined animals are superimposed on scenes typical of the Northeastern tradition. During the latter, dated to about 3,000BC, the colour red predominates.

Caldeirão dos Rodriguez. São Raimundo Nonato, Piaui, Brazil

These paintings in red, white, yellow and grey belong to the Northeastern tradition. The elaborate panels include cervids (deer), nandus, capybaras, humans and a few geometric figures. The humans are probably participating in religious ceremonies, as indicated by individuals with ornamental headdress or carrying objects. Other scenes have been thought to represent sexual encounters or family relations. Rows of men and animals are depicted, and in this example indicate an understanding of perspective.

N. Guidon, Mission française du Piaui

d. r.

Cueva de las Manos. Rio Pinturas, Patagonia, Argentina

This is one of the best known sites in South America. Rock art finds on Patagonian sites provided the basis for Menghin's first classification of the styles of prehistoric Argentinian art. According to him, the oldest style, the so-called "Paleolithic" tradition, is represented by negative depictions of hands. Hundreds of hands in red, black, white, green and blue cover the walls of these sites. The hand motif was often associated with that of camelids and human figures, as well as with certain geometrical motifs.

Montalvania, Minas Gerais, Brazil

In the basin of the Rio São Francisco, to the north of the Minas Gerais state and south of Bahia state, the Montalvania region has revealed several sites with polychrome geometrical figures. Predominant themes include fairly elaborate geometrical motifs, representations of objects rather than animals, and human beings shown in a very schematic style. The representation of aligned anthropomorphic figures is characteristic of the art of Montalvania. The predominant colour is red, but figures in red and yellow abound in certain sites, and the colour range is completed with black and white. This style belongs to the important group comprising the geometrical tradition, and is a regional variation known as the São Francisco tradition. According to some archaeologists, this art could be the product of agricultural communities.

Boqueirão do Sitio da Pedra Furada. São Raimundo Nonato, Piaui, Brazil

One of many examples showing the superimposition of figures. Red human figures with rounded bodies and elongated limbs, their heads emerging from their body or trunk (they have no neck), are frequent in the Northeastern tradition. Over these figures, two men have been painted in grey with erect phalli and hair arranged in a particular style. The inclined position of the body and legs, and the relation between the straight abdomen and the wide chest, suggest a twisted perspective, partly full face and partly in profile.

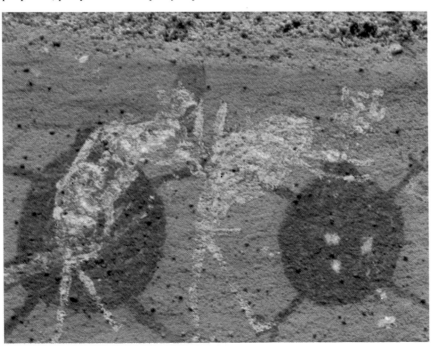

N. Guidon, Mission française du Piaui

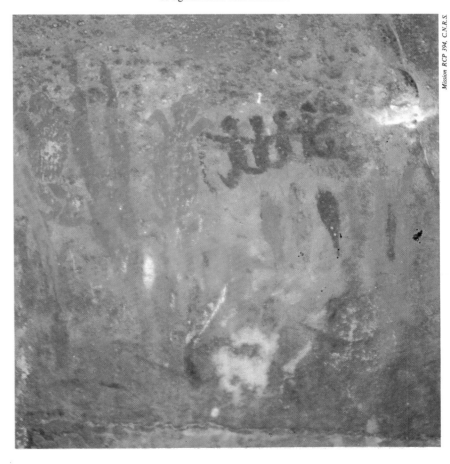

Mission RCP 394 C.N.R.S.

Cultivation and settlement in the Andean region

Andean "civilization" preceded the introduction of agriculture, which may have been brought to the earliest villages by settlers from the tropical lowlands.

Man's mastery of natural resources through animal domestication and plant cultivation was not a unique and exceptional phenomenon, still less a "revolution", as V. Gordon Childe thought in 1951, but a long process of evolution that began at different times in different parts of the world. One of the primary areas was tropical America, where two centres of this process of "neolithization" are distinguished: the Mesoamerican area, and the Andean region extended to include the Amazonian foothills. These two regions were to give the western world some of its commonest food plants. Several of these were cultivated independently from wild stocks in both regions (cotton, maize, beans, pumpkin, chili pepper), whereas others seem to be exclusively South American (potato, quinoa, ground nut, manioc).

Contrasting with this profusion of vegetables, domesticated animal species in America are rare. Nearly all are native to the Andes, where the llama, the alpaca and the guinea pig were essential to economic development. The breeding of camelids began on the Andean altiplano (the llamas of South America, for example, live on the heights), whereas the camels of the Old World are animals of the plain well adapted to deserts. The shelter at Telarmachay (Peru) at an altitude of 4,420m (14,500ft) has supplied evidence of the transition from specialized hunting to the domestication of the llama as from 4000BC.

From 5000BC the guinea pig (*Cavia porcellus*) formed a substantial part of man's diet in the Colombia deposits of El Abra and Tequendama. Possibly domesticated early in this region, it is not found acclimatized in Peru until 3000BC, in the basin of Ayacucho. However, this extremely prolific little animal rapidly became part of the Andean farmers' household. From 2000BC it is found in abundance in the Cordillera and on the coast. Finally, the dog (*Canis familiaris*), which apparently reached America already domesticated at the same time as the first population wave crossed the Bering Strait, very soon became the companion and help of the Andean hunter. However, dog remains are very rare and do not go back beyond 5000BC, as at the shelters of Uchkumachay and Telarmachay, Peru.

Agriculture is even older than stockbreeding, and the question of its origin and diffusion assumes particular importance in South America. Its emergence as a "dominant" economy is closely linked with that of the higher cultures which developed in the Andean regions from the 2nd millennium. Its origins are even more remote, and throughout the Andean territory agriculture and stockbreeding precede the appearance of pottery. Highly complicated processes are involved and

their development is still only partially understood, in spite of progress recently made through archaeological discoveries, analyses of ancient animal life and the introduction of new techniques (palynology*, flotation*, the analysis of coproliths* and phytoliths*), and lastly through the contributions of genetics.

Some facts suggest that Andean agriculture was first "invented" on land lying at altitudes between 2,000 and 3,000m (6,560–9,840ft). Two species of cultivated bean are present in the cave of Guitarrero (Peru), occupied at the time by hunters, *Phaseolus lunatus* between 6800 and 6200BC and *Phaseolus vulgaris* around 5720BC. Cultivated squash (*Cucurbita* species) and gourds (*Lagenaria* species) appear in the cave at the same period and in the basin of Ayacucho between 5500 and 4300BC. Finally, remains of maize (*Zea mays*) are reported at Ayacucho dating between 4300 and 2500BC and at Guitarrero between 5500 and 4000BC (which would make it the oldest cultivated maize in America).

However, other specialists have put forward a different scenario. Basing his theory on the fact that the majority of plants once cultivated were native to the tropical lowlands, D. Lathrap has proposed that the first attempts at domestication were made in the east of the Andes, at a period when the vegetation cover, less dense than it is today (during a relatively cool and dry climatic phase at the beginning of the Holocene* period), allowed humans to settle in what was then a savanna. Subsequently a warmer climate, an increase in rainfall and the growth of the forest cover forced men to seek different lands. Travelling upstream to the sources of the great rivers, they reached the Cordillera and the coast, and introduced agriculture to both regions. This would explain the presence of cultivated maize at Las Vegas in Ecuador from 4500BC and in the region of Valdivia from 3000BC, where the settlers rediscovered natural conditions like those in the Amazonian countries from which they came.

Agriculture and social change

Both these theories presuppose a long period, for the process of hybridization which originates cultigens* (plants produced by cultivation) takes several generations. At all events, it seems certain that agriculture did not begin in the coastal regions: in Peru it appeared later than in the interior of the country. The bean is reported at Chilca c.3250BC, but does not become common until 2500BC. Squash and gourds, as well as cotton (*Gossypium barbadense*) are present in the majority of coastal sites as from 3000BC and maize was cultivated almost as early at Los Gavilanes. Here the occupants

stored the ears in pits dug in the ground, which would already imply intensive culture, then at Aspero and Culebras between 2500 and 1800BC. On the coast, less important food plants were also cultivated between 3000 and 2000BC: the chili pepper (*Capsicum* species), the avocado (*Persea americana*), the groundnut (*Arachis hypogaea*) and the sweet potato (*Ipomoea batatas*). Manioc or cassava (*Manihot esculenta*) did not appear until the first millennium BC, and was apparently linked to the diffusion of the Chavin culture. In addition to the chronological gap between the coast and the Cordillera, it is significant that the first species cultivated on the coast were not food crops, but cotton and gourds.

In fact, inhabitants of these regions were leading a settled existence before they had learnt the art of cultivation. Permanent establishments installed along the shore existed from 3500BC. Modest groups of rush huts, as at Chilca, these villages based their economy almost exclusively on the exploitation of marine resources, complemented by gathering and a little hunting. It was not until 2500BC that agriculture became predominant with the introduction of new horticultural techniques and the appearance of new cultigens. The villages, now larger in size and more numerous, henceforth based their subsistence on three crops—maize, squash and beans.

At the same time, the first public buildings were erected in the largest centres (Real Alto in Ecuador, Aspero, Rio Seco, El Paraiso in Peru), their construction implying the existence of a highly organized society. A powerful, probably theocratic, authority governed the production and distribution of resources and was able to mobilize large work forces, because of the existence of food surpluses. A parallel development took place between 2000 and 1500BC in the highlands, where centres such as Kotosh (Peru) were based on an agricultural economy complemented by stockbreeding.

Thus Andean "civilization" had begun to evolve on a non-agricultural foundation, and we may well ask why communities abandoned a system of stable subsistence based on the highly organized exploitation of natural resources to bind themselves to the constraints imposed by agriculture. It may be that the move to give agriculture priority and to exploit the most productive species arose in order to support a larger population on the same location. In other words, it was not tactical adaptation to economic or demographic pressure, but a deliberate strategy.

D. Graf, Museum für Völkerkunde, Staatliche Museen Preussischer Kulturbesitz

The sacred plant of the Inca

This ear of maize with silvered grains and gilded husks dates to the Inca period (13th–15th centuries). The Spanish chroniclers relate that in the capital, Cuzco, there was a "Garden of the Sun" where all the plants and animals in the empire were reproduced lifesize in precious metal. Maize, whose grains were believed to share the colour of the god, held a place of honour.

The potato harvest

To unearth the potatoes, Inca farmers and their predecessors used the *taclla*, a large digging stick with a handle and sometimes a copper or bronze point. The harvest, which took place in June, was solemnly inaugurated by the Inca sovereign; surrounded by the nobility, he personally extracted the first potatoes from a sacred field. After Guaman Poma de Ayala.

The first Andean herdsmen

In the shelter of Telarmachay on the Andean altiplano, 5,000 years ago, herds of alpacas and llamas died at birth in such large numbers as a result of cold or diseases (from which their guardians could not protect them) that it was impossible to eat them all. A dozen almost complete carcasses were buried in a pit dug near a hearth and carefully closed by a slab.

A great delicacy

This ceramic guinea pig belongs to the Chancay culture (12th–15th centuries). At the time, every house contained dozens of guinea pigs which provided meat for festive meals and which also kept the houses clean by consuming all the edible debris. Reproductions of these animals were often placed in tombs. Museo nacional de antropologia y arqueologia, Lima.

The llama, toy or talisman?

In the tombs of the Chancay culture, doll-like models are sometimes found of plants or animals made of strands of coloured wool wrapped round a wood or reed core. These "toys" may have had symbolic meaning and were often found in the tombs of children. Private collection.

The alpaca, symbol of prosperity

Llamas and alpacas also played a great part in the agrarian rituals of ancient Peru, and the Inca made amulets of them in carved polished stone, called *conopa*. These had a cavity in the back in which coca leaves mixed with fat were placed. They were then buried in the fields to guarantee the prosperity and fertility of the herd. Private collection.

Dogs for hunting and herding

All the peoples of ancient Peru had dogs. In the Mochica period (3rd–6th centuries AD), hunting was primarily a sport reserved for the nobility. Small short-haired spotted dogs helped to drive the animal into a net where it was then killed. Many centuries earlier, in the 9th century BC, the llama herdsmen who occupied the shelter of Telarmachay buried at the foot of a low wall, probably as an offering, the body of a young dog wrapped in a leather sack (below).

The appearance of pottery

The potter's wheel remained unknown in the Americas until the European advent in 1492. Handmade pottery, however, made its appearance in the 4th millennium BC.

Between 3500 and 3000BC there appeared in various parts of the northern Andean region the first traces of the earliest known ceramic industry on the American continent. These dates are later than those for the appearance of ceramics on other continents, but scholars are now quite sure that American peoples were the source of the ancient traditions found on the coast of Ecuador and the Caribbean coast of Colombia.

The new invention of pottery was first applied to the manufacture of receptacles for preparing or storing food, a purely functional concern that later yielded to the production of various forms with incised, modelled or painted decorations. Finally came the anthropomorphic (human-form), zoomorphic (animal-form) and phytomorphic (plant-form) vases and statuettes that were prized by nearly all pre-Columbian civilizations.

This pre-Columbian pottery was made of various clays plastic enough to allow the potter either to make the receptacles directly from lumps of clay, or to fashion a vase gradually by rolling out clay "sausages" in spirals or concentric circles, or, some time later, to mould them onto standarized forms. The potter's wheel, which speeds up the process, was unknown to the Amerindian peoples and was not introduced to the continent until after the Spanish conquest.

In Ecuador, the archaeologists Emilio Estrada, Clifford Evans and Betty Meggers discovered an important ceramic tradition dating to c.3100BC on the site of Valdivia. For a long time this pottery was regarded as the oldest on the continent, and at first its resemblance to the pottery of the fishing people of Japan's Jomon culture led some archaeologists to propose the theory of a migration from Asia bringing the technique of pottery to the American continent. Subsequently, a careful examination of the chronological evidence, and the unlikely possibility of such a crossing being made at that period, cast doubt on the theory, especially when new archaeological sites corresponding to the Valdivian culture were found in the same region and yielded pottery which left no doubt as to its origin.

Valdivian pottery is thus certainly the work of Amerindian groups who lived in this coastal region of Ecuador. Archaeological research during recent years has also revealed the importance of Valdivian culture

and the chronological succession of cultural phases, in the course of which it developed to become the first great civilization of pre-Columbian Ecuador (between 3100 and 1600BC). It was at this time that the first examples of plastic art in the Andean region appeared in the form of female figures, at first carved out of soft stone and then modelled in clay; from this emerged a virtually continuous tradition of anthropomorphic ceramic figures. The Valdivian people had an economy that was already diversified: some groups may have relied mainly for their subsistence on hunting, fishing and gathering wild vegetable products, but others already practised an agriculture that included the production of maize. Finally, the excavation of Real Alto revealed that this site was one of the very first ceremonial centres on the continent.

However, the Valdivian is not the only ancient pottery tradition in Ecuador. The archaeologists Henning Bischoff and José Viteri have discovered another that was even slightly earlier, and which they attributed to a phase named the San Pedro. This pottery, which was very different from Valdivian ceramics, does not seem to have lasted for very long nor to have originated an evolutionary process comparable to that of Valdivia. San Pedro wares have been found elsewhere in Ecuador, but in insignificant quantities compared to Valdivian.

Other ancient ceramic sites

In Colombia, the low-lying alluvial plain which lines the Caribbean coast contained the sites where the oldest pottery was discovered, and this is quite unlike the Ecuadorian ceramics. At Puerto Hormiga, around 3200BC, the inhabitants of this site were already making pottery receptacles of a globe shape. The archaeologist Gerardo Reichel Dolmatoff, who discovered this site, established that fragments of vegetable fibres had been deliberately incorporated into the clay; this, he suggested, was characteristic of a technology in its early stages, although the pottery appeared to be too elaborate to represent a genuinely initial phase. Beside this pottery, occupants of the site made a ware using a sand grease-remover, representing a later stage of occupation. This Puerto Hormiga pottery is sometimes decorated with incised curving lines, patterns of dots obtained by

stamping, or decorations modelled in light relief. These first occupants of Puerto Hormiga did not yet practise agriculture but took their food from wild plants and fruits, as well as the flesh of molluscs and small animals.

The site of Puerto Hormiga is not an isolated case. At Bucarelia, Dolmatoff found similar pottery, representing the ware of a fishing people located on a beach on the lower reaches of the River Magdalena.

In the Monsu region, not far from the Puerto Hormiga site, Dolmatoff discovered yet another, quite distinct, ceramic tradition characterized by decoration of deep incisions. This ware was dated to the beginning of the second half of the 4th millennium BC, and is at the time of writing the oldest known pottery on the whole American continent. Even so, in the opinion of Reichel Dolmatoff this may not represent any more than the Puerto Hormiga site, the period of invention of the pottery. All the archaeologists involved in the discovery of these very old pottery traditions share the view that fragments of pottery they have exhumed do not, despite their apparent simplicity, correspond to the very first period when pottery was invented and made.

So there still remain to be discovered, no doubt in the vicinity of the sites mentioned above, new archaeological deposits which might supply the prototypes of these very ancient ceramic complexes. The abundance of different stylistic traditions, as well as the great differences between them, makes it doubtful that pottery was invented at a single point on the continent and subsequently diffused. It seems more likely that, during the second half of the 4th millennium, groups that were separated geographically and organized on different social and economic systems had the idea of shaping clay and then baking it to make receptacles. These would have been more efficient than the easily damaged vessels they could obtain from organic matter, for example goatskin bottles and gourds dried and emptied of their pulp. This convergence of inventions, which runs counter to diffusionist theories, is in any case not unique, for it has also been observed in connection with the appearance of buildings and agriculture in both the New and the Old World.

Fragments of ceramics from Monsu (north coast of Colombia)

Monsu is probably the oldest site in the New World to yield ceramics. The five fragments shown are decorated on their external faces with broad deep incisions made before firing, when the clay was still moist and retained some plasticity. According to G. Reichel Dolmatoff, who discovered the site, Monsu corresponds to a ceramic tradition distinct from, and older than, Puerto Hormiga pottery (below centre and right), long considered as the site where pottery first appeared, if not in the New World, at least in the extreme north of South America. By kind permission of G. Reichel Dolmatoff.

Two types of pottery, Puerto Hormiga

The upper fragment corresponds to a type of pottery considered by G. Reichel Dolmatoff to be the oldest at Puerto Hormiga. It contains a grease-remover of vegetable fibres which appear on the face of the fragment in the form of grooved lines. The use of these vegetable fibres is assumed to indicate that this pottery is older than the other type of pottery found at Puerto Hormiga (lower fragment) which uses a sand grease-remover. By kind permission of G. Reichel Dolmatoff.

Sherds from Puerto Hormiga

These four sherds represent three distinct types of decoration: sherds decorated with incised motifs in the form of dots and circles (a); sherds decorated with motifs incised by a stiletto-type implement, the desired motif being obtained by keeping the point of the stiletto embedded in the clay (b, c); sherd with notched decoration achieved by stamping (d). G. Reichel Dolmatoff, who discovered and excavated the site of Puerto Hormiga, classified the pottery according to the various decorative techniques and the form of the motifs.

Fragment of a receptacle with anthropomorphic decoration, Valdivia

Some of the pottery receptacles of the Valdivia tradition have a figurative element in the midst of geometric motifs. Here a human head is recognizable, traced by a broad incised line. This head resembles some of the faces of the small female figurines (see right) which were produced in abundance by the potters of the Valdivian tradition. If we exclude the rock paintings by the hunting groups of the New World, these are the first representations in the round or low relief of the human face. Archaeological Museum of the Central Bank of Ecuador, Quito.

Valdivian figurines

The Valdivian ceramic tradition marks the appearance of New World plastic art depicting the female form. Some of these figurines, probably the oldest according to certain investigators, are simply carved in soft rock. Nevertheless, the majority are modelled in clay and fired. These representations are generally 8–10cm (3.2–4in) high, but a few larger examples are known. They very probably played an important part in the cultural world of the populations embraced by the Valdivian tradition, and are probably representations of a female divinity or the expression of a fertility cult. Archaeological Museum of the Central Bank of Ecuador, Quito.

Valdivian receptacles

Among the oldest pottery traditions in the New World, the Valdivian tradition also contains vessels with the greatest variety of forms. From left to right: two open receptacles, the upper diameter of which coincides with, or is almost equal to, the maximum diameter, and two closed vessels with an upper diameter less than the maximum diameter. The upper part of the two receptacles on the left is covered with incised geometric decoration. This decoration was executed before firing when the clay was still slightly pliable. It is often difficult to establish the function of these vessels, whether they were for storing, cooking or consuming food, or were decorative, votive or funerary receptacles. Banco del Pacífico, Guayaquil, Ecuador.

Principal sites in Andean America containing finds of the earliest pottery

Archaeological sites containing the oldest pottery traditions of the New World divide into two regions, the Caribbean coast of northern Colombia and the coastal region of central Ecuador. In each region, archaeologists have looked for sites with the same pottery as that of the reference sites (Valdivia in Ecuador and Puerto Hormiga in Colombia). In Ecuador, investigation has resulted in the discovery of numerous sites, making it possible to demarcate an area of diffusion inside which variations in time and space are observed. In Colombia, the area of diffusion is more restricted and the recent discovery of a new site, Monsu, shows that several traditions succeeded each other in a limited territory. Differences identified by specialists between San Pedro pottery in the Valdivian tradition in Ecuador, and Puerto Hormiga and Monsu pottery in Colombia show that each was invented separately without any contact between the two regions. It is not until a later period that we can assume, on the basis of scanty and inconclusive evidence, that the two regions had continuous relations which, however, do not seem to have appreciably modified the cultural development of either region.

Sherds from the San Pedro phase

These sherds were found in a region where deposits corresponding to the Valdivian tradition were known. Careful analysis suggests that they should be attributed to another, different tradition. They are an important argument in favour of a multiplicity of centres where pottery was invented in the New World. The fact that no other important archaeological deposit of the San Pedro phase has been discovered seems to indicate that this tradition was short-lived. In the present state of archaeological knowledge of this part of Ecuador, we can only confirm its presence side by side with the Valdivian tradition, which did give birth to a lasting cultural development. Reiss Museum, Mannheim.

Origin and expansion of the Chavín culture

The Chavín culture, thought by some archaeologists to be the precursor of all subsequent ancient Peruvian civilizations, was not identified until this century, but its origins are still surrounded by controversy.

Chavín is a ceremonial centre, the impressive ruins of which were "discovered" in 1919 by J. Tello* on the eastern slope of the Cordillera Blanca in Peru. From the 16th century onwards they had been described by many travellers, but their importance was not fully recognized until Tello had made and interpreted his explorations. According to him, the site was the cradle of the ancestral culture from which all the cultures of ancient Peru emerged, this association being reflected in the diffusion throughout the country and during all its pre-Hispanic history of the cult of a god with feline features.

Chavín has a magico-religious art with an essentially curvilinear style in which human elements such as the head, limbs and hands are joined with animal elements such as muzzle, fangs, claws and tail in a combination of curves, volutes or, more rarely, straight lines. The theme of a half-human, half-feline creature is omnipresent, alone or accompanied by secondary figures such as the jaguar, the bird of prey, the snake or the fish. In the architecture of Chavín we find buildings with a U-shaped plan composed of truncated pyramids with external facings of dressed stone and traversed by obscure internal galleries communicating by ramps and stairways. The pottery associated with these buildings is black, grey or brown monochrome, with incised, champlevé or low relief decoration using similar motifs to those found in stoneworking art. These stylistic features recur in many parts of Peru, but especially in the centre and the north. With variations linked with the geographical context—stone architecture and engraving in the highlands, adobe (or sun-dried brick) on the coast—the Chavín style seems to represent a cultural "horizon" characterized by the motif of the feline and its numerous physical manifestations.

The age and central importance of the Chavín culture were generally recognized by the archaeologists who came after Tello, but opinions differed as to its origin and the mechanism of its diffusion. Whereas Tello had located its origin in the Amazonian forest and R. Larco Hoyle on the north coast, but in both cases in Peru, others (M. Coe, F. Kauffman) saw in it a Mesoamerican and even (R. Heine-Geldern) a Chinese contribution. The studies and excavations carried out over some 20 years in Peru (works of J. Rowe, L. Lumbreras) and on the coast of Ecuador have enabled us to make a better definition of the true nature of the Chavín phenomenon. They have also enabled us to reconstruct the architectonic history of the site itself, even if there are differences in assessments of its chronology. The first monuments erected were those making up the Ancient Temple, dating from 1300BC according to Lumbreras, and not before 850BC according to R. Burger. This consists of an architectural complex in the shape of a U open to the east, at the heart of which is the *Lanzón*, a stone idol of ferocious aspect engraved with half-human half-feline features. Around it radiates a complicated network of underground passages extending beyond the limits of the edifice and which may have served, according to Lumbreras, as channels for water taken from the nearby river. The mysterious noise this caused near the idol would have served to create a feeling of awe. The complex must have been altered on many occasions before it was abandoned and partially covered by new structures around the 9th or 6th century BC.

Even larger, but with an identical plan, the New Temple called *El Castillo* is a stepped pyramid, the east side of which has a monumental portico giving access to the upper part and in front of which spreads an enormous square surrounded by secondary buildings. Great differences in the stonework which ornaments the two complexes, and also in the ceramic styles associated with them (*Ofrendas, Mosna*, then *Rocas*), demonstrate fundamental changes in their symbolic content. The god of the *Lanzón* is apparently replaced by a new entity, represented on the "Raimondi Stone" by a figure holding a long sceptre in each hand. Like his predecessor, this "Staff God" has demoniacal attributes (fangs, claws and a snake headdress) and reigns over a terrifying supernatural world. About 800BC according to Lumbrera, or 500BC according to Burger, Chavín de Huantar was a major religious centre, if not the capital of a kind of theocratic state, which through interregional exchanges imposed the cult of its gods from the far north of Peru to Ayacucho and Ica in the south. About 400 or 200BC the Temple of Chavín was partly destroyed and apparently abandoned for some unknown reason. Throughout the territory subject to its influence, there followed a process of stylistic decadence which probably reflects the disintegration of religious power. "Chavín-like" features gradually disappear, while specific regional traits reappear, later giving birth to the independent political units of the classical period.

Origin of the culture

Such is the history of the Chavín temples as reconstructed for us by the most recent excavations. Nevertheless, it does not explain the origin of the complicated and already highly elaborated image of the god of the *Lanzón* which has no known antecedents. For D. Lathrap, who takes up Tello's theory, the origin of Chavín and even of central Andean civilization as a whole is to be sought in the forests to the east of the Andes. The presence on the engraved stones and columns of Chavín of a variety of animals typical of the great forest, as well as the forest origin of most of the plants cultivated in the Andean area, suggests that all the elements composing the civilization came from the low-lying tropical lands. By following the course of the great rivers, these would first have reached the coast of Ecuador where the Machalilla culture* flourished (1500–1100BC); then they would have been diffused in various directions along with the trade in shells which the peoples of Ecuadorian coastal areas gathered and redistributed throughout the Andean world. This would explain the undeniable similarities between Chavín art and the Olmec art of Mexico, and also between Chavín art and the art of Chorrera, demonstrating not some chance affiliation, but a single dominating influence coming from Ecuador.

This audacious theory is not accepted unreservedly, and some specialists think that on the contrary the Chavín civilization must have had its roots in Peru. Here the difference between the dates advanced by Lumbreras and Burger (which are both based on C^{14}*), if it is of comparative importance for retracing the stages in the construction and the vicissitudes of the Chavín site, acquires special weight. Indeed, according to the earlier chronology, Chavín is really at the origin of the culture of the same name. At its height (*c.*800BC), the great ceremonial centres already in existence, such as Pacopampa and Kuntur Wasi, must have adopted its religious ideology, allowing its stylistic canons to replace local forms, while new centres closely linked with Chavín were built elsewhere, for example Cerro Blanco, Punkiri, Moxeque and Garagay on the coast. But according to the later chronology, the opposite happened: it was the great city centres which gave birth to Chavín, the architecture of which (in particular the adoption of the U-shaped plan) was inspired by older coastal examples.

The controversy has not abated, for as we know, the use of dates obtained by C^{14}* rarely results in coherent and universally valid results. It is probable that the origin of Chavín art was not single, but multiple, the site of Chavín representing the point of convergence and the integration of various cultural trends arriving from both coast and forest. It is also clear that the emergence of Chavín marks not a beginning, but the culmination of a lengthy process. Begun many millennia earlier, it was here that the first communities settled and built the first ceremonial complexes, in which a priestly élite governed production and social relations through an increasingly repressive and heavy-handed religious system.

Mortar in jaguar form

The feline motif is omnipresent at Chavín, but rarely in the form of the animal alone. This mortar is one of the few known pieces carved in the round and one of the finest examples of the Classic Chavín style. The symbols representing the fur are the same as those ornamenting the jaguars engraved on the cornice of the New Temple at Chavín de Huantar. University Museum, Philadelphia.

The "Pickman conch"

Long before Chavín, the conch and the *Spondylus* shell were used in Ecuador from 3000BC onwards for utilitarian or ritual purposes. The symbolism connected with these two shells appears in Peru *c.*1100BC, itself connected with the Chavín cult. The conch motif is engraved on the stelae of the temple and the actual shells, undoubtedly brought from the warm northern seas, are ornamented with motifs typical of the Chavín style. Brooklyn Museum.

General view of the Temple of Chavín de Huantar

Situated in Peru in the Callejon de Huaylas at the confluence of two valleys 3,180m (10,500ft) high, the architectural complex of Chavín is the most important ceremonial centre of this culture. According to some specialists, the place was chosen and the overall plan oriented so that the movement of the stars could be observed, thus making this temple an observatory with liturgical functions.

Painted cloth of the Chavín period

A cotton hanging found near Paracas, Peru, depicts a type of feline monster similar to the "Staff God" incised on the Raimondi Stone at Chavín, indicating the close relations maintained by the peoples of the coast in the Middle Chavín period with the great ceremonial centre of the northern cordillera. Dumbarton Oaks Collection.

The eagle motif from Chorrera to Chavín

These illustrations, one painted on a Chorrera ceramic cup (top) from the Ecuadorian coast (1500–500BC), the other engraved on a lintel of the New Temple at Chavín, clearly indicate, with their identical theme of the harpy eagle, a unity between the two cultures in terms of stylistic and probably religious relations (connected through the trade in *Spondylus* shells). The American Museum of Natural History.

Contacts and exchanges in the Andes

The sea shell known as *Spondylus* was so highly prized from Mesoamerica to Peru that it provided the basis for an astonishing international trade, carried out by merchant seamen who were also sometimes priests. The *Spondylus*, they believed, was the food of the gods.

From the beginning of the Andean civilization and the appearance of the first Neolithic societies, ideas, cultural traits and products travelled, sometimes over very long distances. This permanent interaction, constantly confirmed by new discoveries, outdates the controversy between the diffusionists and the supporters of an indigenous origin for Andean cultures. It now seems to be proved that the creative capacity of each people, and the elements introduced by the multiple and historically undeniable processes of diffusion, combined according to an inner dynamic to give birth to cultures which, although completely original, were never isolated.

We shall mention only a few examples of these exchanges among those most recently studied, whether they take place in a single cultural area or between different areas. One of the most spectacular is undoubtedly the traffic in *Spondylus*, a large mollusc from the tropical waters of the Pacific with a brilliant red shell, which was the cause of multiple contacts from Mesoamerica to Peru. From the 2nd millennium large quantities of these shells, which apparently played an essential economic and ritual role, are found in all the archaeological deposits of the southern Andean area (southern Colombia, Ecuador and northern Peru), both on the coast and in the highlands. They are found in the central Andes at Kotosh from the Waira-Jirca phase (*c*.1800BC) and the shell is engraved on the Tello obelisk at Chavín. From the beginning of our era, the use of the *Spondylus* (*mullu* in Quechua) spread as far as the high plateaus of southern Peru.

The *mullu* was the favourite food of the gods; it brought the rain and millions of Andean farmers offered it to the tutelary divinities of the harvests, whole, in fragments or powdered. The species used, *Spondylus princeps princeps*, lives at a depth of more than 35m (117ft), from the Gulf of California to off-shore Ecuador. It seems impossible that the millions of shells distributed throughout the Andean territory came from the Ecuadorean littoral alone. So there must have been a network of maritime trade extending as far as the shores of Mesoamerica.

The island of La Plata

Since 1978, the excavations of J. Marcos and P. Norton on the little island of La Plata, off the province of Manabi in Ecuador, have revealed the existence of a commercial site devoted exclusively to traffic in *Spondylus*, which operated from the Valdivia III phase (*c*.2500BC) to the arrival of the Spaniards. In one place the ground was covered with hundreds of carefully cleaned shells. According to the discoverers, these had been brought by sea from the coasts of Central America before being dressed on the island (only the red part of the shell was valued) and then redistributed. This would explain most of the stylistic borrowings observed among all peoples who exchanged or used the *Spondylus*, for example the presence of Mesoamerican decorative elements in the classical cultures of Ecuador, such as the Mexican "old god of fire" omnipresent at La Tolita, or the Tlaloc elements common at Jama Coaque. In the reverse direction, influences of the Bahia style appeared in the Gulf of Mexico, where Mayan traders probably met navigators from Ecuador. Finally, other styles from Ecuador show striking similarities to Costa Rican and Guatemalan styles.

The island of La Plata was also a great sanctuary, where hundreds of offerings were recovered, among them decapitated terracotta figurines. One single offering even included figurines in different styles (Bahia, Tolita, Jama Coaque, *c*.300BC), proving that people from various provinces met there for a ceremony or to exchange goods. At a later period, pottery brought from the north coast of Peru, but also from the Inca capital of Cuzco in the southern Andes, is evidence of the far-ranging trade in *mullu*. The transport of shells from the places of origin to the island, and from there to various points on the coast, was carried out by means of reed or wood vessels about which we have no details.

In the last centuries before the Spanish conquest, traders undoubtedly used large rafts with sails like the one which the Spanish pilot Bartholomé Ruiz encountered off Tumbés in 1525. It was manned by a crew of 20 and carried "gold and silver ingots, helmets and armour, pectorals, tongs, necklaces, mirrors ornamented with silver, wool and cotton coverings, shirts and robes" (Relación Sámano-Xerez). They transported all those goods to exchange them "for those shells from which they make beads the colour of coral . . ." On land, the shells were probably transported by human carriers or, further south, by caravans of llamas. From the 10th century BC, the people of Cerro Narrio, in the Andes south of Ecuador, had a virtual monopoly of the redistribution of *mullu*, which was sent to Peru by the valley of the Marañon river on the eastern slopes of the Andes.

Merchant priests and navigators

At first, the traffic in *Spondylus* was probably in the hands of local chiefs or priests (the two were often confused). However, at the time of the Conquest, there was a confederation of merchant sailors on the Ecuadorian coast, who were both priests and traders (in the real sense of the word) and practised human sacrifice and headhunting to ensure the success of their farflung enterprises. They were certainly not the only ones, because in a document of 1570 published by M. Rostworoski, mention is made of a group of 6,000 merchants established in the rich coastal oasis of Chincha in Peru. They "went from Chincha to Cuzco . . . and others went to Quito and Puerto Viejo (more than 2,000km away), whence they brought back gold and emeralds." The *Spondylus* is not mentioned by the narrator, doubtless influenced by the European obsession with gold, but it is more than likely that it formed part of the traders' cargoes.

Thus long-distant trade, which could be called international, was complemented by a smaller exchange network, responsible for distributing valuable products brought from afar to the various regions, but also for bartering in common consumer products. From the coast of Peru, cotton cloth, salt fish, chili peppers and gourds left for the interior; from the cordillera (mountain ridge) came wool fabrics, dried meat, gold, silver and especially copper. In connection with this metal, the same document makes an astonishing statement: "They [the merchants of Chincha] were the only ones in the kingdom to use money, because they bought and sold what food and clothing they possessed for copper." Admittedly, the document is post-Conquest and its author may have misinterpreted the facts. Nevertheless, this allusion to primitive money forms a disturbing parallel to the celebrated money-axes of Ecuador studied by O. Holm. These objects of very pure copper, generally fashioned by hammering, came from various late cultural contexts (between AD800 and AD1500). They were shaped like an axe blade, their weight varying from a few grammes to more than 20 kilos (44lbs) and they were often tied in bundles of 20, which suggests units of payment or barter using a vicenary system (based on 20). Another coincidence: evidence of the use of axe-money also occurs at the same period in Mexico, in the region of Oaxaca in particular.

It appears that nearly all the exchanges that took place in the Andes, or between the Andes and Mesoamerica, for more than three millennia, were connected in some way with the traffic in *Spondylus*, itself associated with a fertility cult that appeared on the Ecuadorian coast as from the Valdivia period. The expansion of this cult into the interior of the country, and then to the whole of the Andean area, gradually created an ever-increasing demand for the shells. Collected from far away, then treated and redistributed from Ecuadorian centres, these conferred a key role on the northern Andes, and made a simple shell with no practical or intrinsic value a means of cultural diffusion of the first importance.

Deposit of Spondyli at La Plata

This detail of the archaeological site floor shows shells still in their rough state, although they have been cleaned or already half-dressed. More than 600 examples were found over some 20 sq m (200 sq ft) mixed with potsherds of Ecuadorian and Peruvian design and manufacture.

J. G. Marcos, Escuela superior politécnica del litoral, Guayaquil

J. G. Marcos, Escuela superior politécnica del litoral, Guayaquil

Spondylus

This beautiful specimen of *Spondylus princeps princeps* was recently taken in the waters of the island of La Plata, 23km (14 miles) off the coast of Ecuador. The exterior growths and red fringe of the shell were the parts mainly used. Escuela superior politécnica del litoral, Guayaquil.

The raft seen by Bartolomé Ruiz

Rafts made of balsa trunks (light and virtually proof against rot) were used to transport heavy cargoes. Some were big enough to support a hut with a roof of palm branches, and the crew were even able to cook on board, using a fire lit in the after section. J. Juan y A. de Ulloa, *Relación histórica del viaje a la America meridional*, 1748.

Real academia de la historia, Madrid

12th-century Peruvian vessels

This Chancay-type ceramic represents a fisherman on his raft made of two bundles of reeds attached to each other. Larger rafts of the same type were used along the whole of the Pacific coast to transport small quantities of goods. Museo nacional de antropologia y arqueologia, Lima.

The "little sea-horses" of Huanchaco

These light reed craft, whose spindle shape has not varied for more than 1,000 years, are still used in this fishing village on the north coast of Peru. The fishermen venture several miles out to sea and on their return haul up their *caballitos* to dry on the beach. In the past vessels made of inflated seal skins were also used.

Peruvian scales of the 8th century

We do not know what measures were used in the Andean area in Pre-Columbian times, but we do know that small scales with a beam of carved bone or wood supporting two nets of braided cord were used to weigh gold.

The axe money of Ecuador

Apparently barter was still the predominant system of exchange in the pre-Hispanic period. Nevertheless, many thousands of axe coins have been found in Ecuadorian sites of the Integration period, mainly those of the Manteño and Milagro-Quevedo cultures (AD800–1500). This Manteño vase in the form of a head contained several hundred.

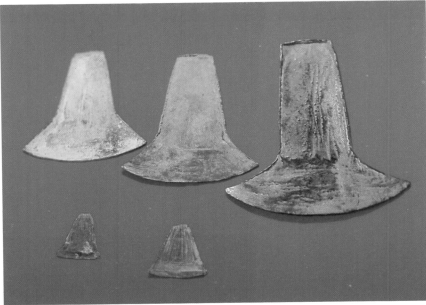

Birth of the great cities of the Andes

The holy cities of the Andes, with their temples, sanctuaries and treasuries, were pilgrimage centres for many centuries before the Spanish conquest – New World equivalents of Mecca or the Vatican.

Whether the great ceremonial centres of the Andes, together with their secular annexes, are looked on as towns or as the ancestors of towns, they mark a stage in the development of societies with a political organization based on the existence of sovereign kingdoms. The most celebrated examples are Pampa Grande and the complex of the two *Huacas* of the Sun and Moon on the north coast of Peru, Maranga on the central coast, and Cahuachi on the south coast. Pukara and Tiahuanaco represent the same phenomenon on the high plateau of the south. The characteristic shared by these centres is that most of their buildings are devoted to ceremonial or ritual functions. Genuinely "planned" cities did not appear in the Andes until the state was consolidated. They differ from these ceremonial centres in the predominance of civil over monumental architecture and in the multi-purpose complexity of their structures. The only cities whose plans we really know are Chan Chan and El Purgatorio on the north coast of Peru, and Cuzco and Huanuco Viejo on the Altiplano (plateau).

We are attempting to study here the origins not of urban forms (which go back to the beginning of settlement), but of the first genuine towns where a dense population was assembled within an organized system so as to ensure the workings of the political and economic functions of the state. Two broad types may be distinguished during the period that corresponds roughly to the last phase of the Middle Horizon and Late Intermediary on the coast (AD1100–1480) to the Late Intermediary and Late Horizon, or Inca period, in the Altiplano (AD1400–1530). In both regions, primitive forms of urbanization appeared during the Middle Horizon (AD800–1100).

The well-known urban areas of Pachacamac, Pacatnamú and Batán Grande are no more representative of real towns than are the ceremonial cities of the Vatican, Mecca or Angkor Wat for the Old World. Many great ceremonial centres—a type of complex most common during the Early Intermediary (AD200–800) both on the coast and in the Cordillera—disappeared during the Middle Horizon, retaining purely residual functions as sacred funerary areas (for example the *Huacas* or Pyramids of the Sun and Moon at Moche). Yet, even so, the towns around them continued to grow and became holy cities which were to remain independent centres of pilgrimage until the Spanish conquest. The complexes of the Island of the Sun on Lake Titicaca and Coropuna near Arequipa are probably Andean examples of such sacred cities, where the model of the ancient ceremonial centres was simply enlarged to include sanctuaries, lodging for the pilgrims and places for depositing offerings. Buildings for housing the priestly administration were rare and permanent residential complexes were altogether nonexistent.

Residential areas for the élite

Towards the end of the Early Intermediary, the overall increase in the Andean population inaugurated a stage when considerable progress was made, especially in agriculture and technology. This is reflected in the composition of the primarily theocratic élites, which now began to form a sort of governing bureaucracy with a main function of controlling the distribution of water. On the north coast the largest establishments were generally installed in places where the valley narrowed and the distribution of water could be controlled along a whole river bank. They represent the forerunners of the great coastal cities that came later.

This transformation of residential centres, though at first spontaneous, seems to have been imposed on the population during the Middle Horizon, suggesting that large labour forces were deliberately mobilized to build public works and urban complexes which included their own sleeping quarters. Both the towns on the coastal slopes and the first towns in the Altiplano such as Huari, Pikillakta and Wiracochapampa incorporated an area reserved for the housing of the lower social strata. This clearly seems to indicate that genuine urbanization and the formation of residential concentrations were based on the mobilization of forced labour.

At Huari there were residential areas for the élite too. The original function of this élite was to direct ceremonies and subsequently to control resources and administer surpluses. The design of these residences for the élite, rectangular in shape and enclosed by walls, seems to have been the model for the first element of town planning employed in the Altiplano, which not only encompassed the multi-functional sectors, but also shaped the new city as a whole in relation to the natural slope of the hillside. Incidentally, this model is less evident in the plan of Huari itself than in the provincial capitals of Pikillakta and Wiracochapampa, where the design is obviously imposed, and ill-adapted to the topography of the location.

The population of the largest coastal towns in the Middle Horizon can be estimated at about 10,000 inhabitants, distributed in residential quarters built at intervals over several kilometres. Such a distribution was necessary both to build the new town itself, which required a massive work force to level the ground, clean out dried-up riverbeds and cultivate the surrounding land, and to ensure various storage and redistribution services. It is probable that some of the population returned periodically to their original community and that the residential sectors reserved for the poorer classes were occupied in turn by other groups in the work force. Finally, the towns included administrative sectors which were both residences for the élite and "offices" for the use of high-ranking figures whom the

Spaniards were later to call *caciques* or *principales*.

The living area of the poor classes on the coast in the Late Intermediary was less concentrated, except in the large towns of El Purgatorio and Chan Chan. Certain provincial centres reserved for the élite, such as Pueblo Moxeque in the valley of Casma, clearly illustrate a situation in which the élite of half the population of a valley was concentrated, along with its servants, in an urban unit. If this example represents the residence of a high-ranking chief and his entourage, larger urban concentrations ought to be looked on as the combination of several such centres of limited size. The absence of housing for the workers possibly indicates that the builders of the town, who also contributed to its upkeep, lived in now vanished hamlets of wood and thatch huts built in other parts of the valley close to the ground under cultivation.

The principles governing the planning of towns in the Altiplano have not yet been discovered. As from the Middle Horizon, the main object in urban development consisted in housing a dense population and using that manpower to produce and redistribute essential products in order to ensure the subsistence of a large administrative élite. However, the development which led from urban agglomerations like Huari to the planned city of Cuzco requires further explanation.

The principles of division into four and into two, found in Inca cities, appeared after urbanization of the Huari type. The *Kancha*, a number of houses grouped around a court, was the Inca model which replaced the rectangular model. The provincial Inca capitals reproduced the quadripartite division of Cuzco. Such planning elements, including that of functional symmetry, reflect a return to considerations of a ceremonial nature rather than a pragmatic attempt to solve problems posed by the density of the population. In reality, the Incas sought rather to limit urban growth, as is shown by their regulations covering foreigners in the towns and the creation of large rural estates for the élite.

When the Spaniards arrived, major preindustrial metropolises were only just on the point of appearing in the Andes. The most developed example may be Chan Chan, although the architect J. Hordoy writes, "At Chan Chan we see the dawn of an urban form in a culture restrained by technological limitations." According to him, Cuzco was even less a town. To J. Rowe, it was primarily a great ceremonial centre, in spite of its extent. Were the Inca planners influenced by Chan Chan? A unique quotation taken from a lost manuscript alludes to this: "When Yupanqui entered Chan Chan as a conqueror, he was stupefied to see the richness and beauty of the coastal city, built to a vast plan with its straight aligned roads . . . far superior to the crude semi-barbarous constructions of Cuzco."

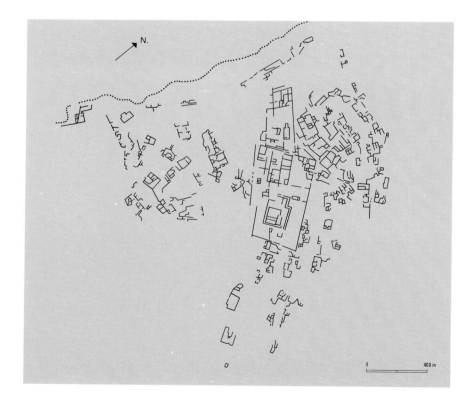

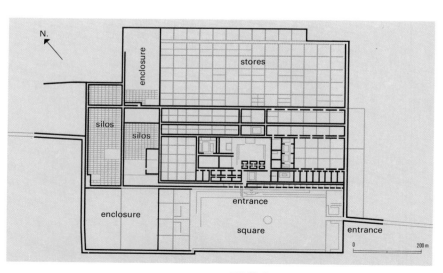

Pikillakta, region of Cuzco, AD800–1000

This planned urban complex was built during the Middle Horizon; it is characterized by the existence of sectors with different functions (dwellings, but also stores and warehouses). The complex covers more than 50 hectares (125 acres). After E. Harth-Terré "Pikillacta, ciudad de depositos y bastimentos", *Revista del Museo de Cuzco*, no. 18, Cuzco, 1950.

Pampa Grande, valley of the Lambayeque, AD650–700

Example of a ceremonial and residential centre for the élite. Sectors reserved for the cult, craftsmen and stores have been identified next to the main square. The complex could have housed as many as 10,000 people, but there is no proof of any planning of the civic sector.

Tschudi citadel, Chan Chan, valley of the Moche

Partial view of the sector of the *audiencias*, buildings used as "offices" where the assessment and distribution of state property was made.

El Purgatorio, valley of La Leche

Photograph taken *c.*1910 from the northwest shoulder of the hill showing the main citadel (400m long) and adjacent to it, in the foregound, large open spaces surrounded by walls.

Milagro de San José, valley of the Moche, AD1100–1200

Urban administrative centre situated to the north of Chan Chan, possibly capital of a chieftainry incorporated later into the Chimú "citadels" where tribute from the northern regions was collected and stored.

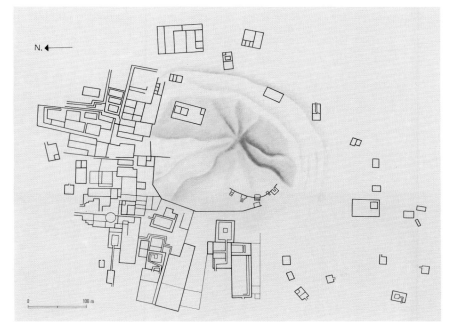

El Purgatorio, AD1100–1300

Capital city of the Lambayeque people, it later came under Chimú domination. "Citadels" with multiple compartments are grouped around a natural eminence surrounded by a defensive wall. The dwellings reserved for the people, the cemetery and the stores are on the hill's south flank.

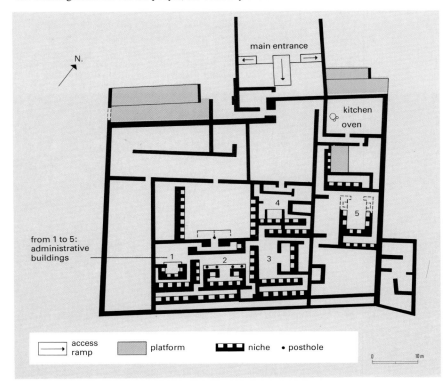

main entrance

kitchen
oven

from 1 to 5:
administrative
buildings

access ramp
platform
niche • posthole

Huánuco Viejo, AD1490–1540

Plan of the most important of the provincial capitals built by the Inca. After E. Harth-Terré "El Pueblo de Huanuco Viejo", *El Arquitecto Peruano*, nos. 320–321, Lima, undated.

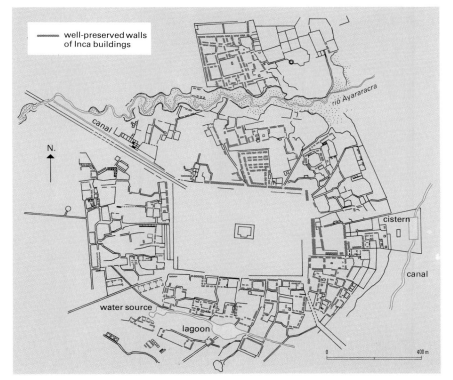

well-preserved walls of Inca buildings

rió Ayararacra

canal

water source

lagoon

cistern

canal

The archaeology of the Caribbean

The first New World peoples encountered by Columbus did not long survive the impact of the Europeans. They vanished, but today archaeologists can recreate the lost pre-Columbian cultures of the Caribbean in some detail.

The earliest people to live in the Caribbean definitely go back to the beginning of the 5th millennium BC, although there are no radiocarbon* datings prior to 3000BC. Bands of hunter-gatherers who have left nothing behind but stone tools were then living in the caves and rock shelters of Cuba and Hispaniola. Their ability to make tools developed rapidly at the beginning of the 2nd millennium, heralding the Archaic age, which was marked by the presence of a stone tool industry with large flakes retouched into daggers, as well as tools made of bone, shell and polished stone. The way of life of these bands was thereafter concentrated around very localized marine produce (for example shellfish and fish from coral reefs), and consequently archaeologists have found sites associated with heaps of shells on the coasts, and extending to Puerto Rico, Antigua and even Trinidad. The other islands in the Lesser Antilles, by contrast, do not seem to have been used as a migratory route. These archaic peoples already practised a rudimentary form of art, and decorated their ritual objects and ornaments with a few incised lines.

The colonization of the West Indies by groups familiar with agriculture and pottery goes back to the beginning of the present age. The Saladoid culture, which originated on the lower reaches of the Orinoco (where it was present from the end of the 3rd millennium BC) suddenly spread towards the islands, starting from Trinidad and the nearby coasts of the Guyanas and reaching Puerto Rico by the beginning of the 2nd century AD. The staple diet of these groups of simple cultivators was manioc cassava (bread), as indicated by the large earthenware plates or platters which have been found. These people were not very different from the tribal societies of the tropical forests of South America from which they had emerged; but remains that have been found, mainly pottery and some ornaments, do demonstrate unusual refinement.

The bell-shaped vases that they manufactured are almost always decorated, and often embellished with small modelled human or animal heads; the thin whitish paste used to make their best ceramics is sometimes almost reminiscent of porcelain. The stylized decoration of their pottery consists of fine criss-crossed incisions or white paint on a red base, which is characteristic of this group. The composition follows strict rules, and the principal themes include batrachians or reptiles such as the frog or the tortoise. Some deposits have revealed a great many ornaments, pendants or beads from necklaces, in mother-of-pearl and semi-precious stones.

These Saladoid groups represent the culture from which West Indian prehistory emerged, for no trace of subsequent migration is to be found in the archaeological sequence of the islands. However, between the 7th and 9th centuries AD, internal ethnic changes gave rise to regional cultural groups, especially in the Greater and in the Lesser Antilles. The colonization of the Greater Antilles by groups familiar with agriculture continued, extending to all the islands, including the Bahamas, except for the western part of Cuba, where archaic Ciboney peoples, with no knowledge of agriculture or pottery, survived until the arrival of the Spanish.

In the Lesser Antilles these changes resulted in the short-lived Troumassoid culture, during which there was a decline in the technical skill of pottery-making which continued until the emergence of the Suazoid culture towards the beginning of the 12th century. The main pottery output consisted of bowls and cooking pots in simple geometric shapes, but there were also a few pieces that were better finished and decorated with incised motifs, or painted with lines forming scrolls and parallelograms. Though the presence of manioc is indicated by huge platters, now made with three feet, heaps of shells consisting of conches (*Strombus*) and mangrove oysters are evidence of the increased importance of sea and shoreline food resources. The Suazoids have often been taken to be the same peoples as the Caribs whom the Europeans found; however, the differences in material culture, especially with regard to pottery, indicate that they were different populations.

Island chieftains

In the Greater Antilles, on the other hand, we find a phenomenon that was unusual in American prehistory: the local evolution of a hierarchical society or chieftaincy system which was not influenced by the civilizations of Central America or the Andes. The population increase that accompanied this led, as a result of the more intensive practice of agriculture, to the populating of the inland areas of the islands. Examples of this effect are the Ostionoid and Meillacoid cultures, one marked by a sturdier, less decorated style of pottery, the other by a novel style which seems to have taken over the incised geometric decoration used by the archaic peoples that had preceded them. These two regional cultures contributed to the formation from the beginning of the 12th century of the Chicoid culture which represented the peak of this development, as seen in their descendants, the Tainos, whom Columbus found.

This group of powerful chiefs, who between them ruled over large areas of Hispaniola and Puerto Rico, left traces which reflect their development. Pottery was now sculptural, with anthropomorphic vases, breast-shaped containers and two-handled urns, but it was in stone that Taino art expressed itself best: three-pointed carved stones representing their gods or "zemis", masks, monolithic axes, idols whose heads were surmounted by shelf structures that may have been used during the inhalation of *cohoba* (a narcotic substance derived from a plant) and lastly stone rings which must be connected in some way with their ball game. We have very few objects in wood which seems to have been a highly developed skill among the Tainos: a few statuettes, but the principal survivals are the duhos* or ceremonial seats, which are decorated with gold or mother-of-pearl. There are many large sites belonging to this culture, but they contain few remains of an architectural nature. The only remains of a relatively monumental character are the bateys*or ceremonial ball games, long courts edged with upright stones and connected with each other by paved avenues.

Objects characteristic of the Haïtian Cowrie culture in the Archaic period in the Greater Antilles

Top left, double-edged axe made of polished stone; right, polisher made of polished stone. Second row, centre, incised bead from a necklace, made of polished stone; right, ball of polished stone. Third row, left: fragment of a bowl made of incised polished stone; right: fragment of an arrowhead made of worked bone. Bottom row, from left to right: *gladiolito* made of polished stone; pendant made of carved, incised stone; large flint blade retouched to make a knife; large flint blade retouched to make a "dagger". The Peabody Museum of Natural History, Yale.

Vase shaped like a boat or a bell, painted white on red, characteristic of the Saladoid culture of the West Indies

Decoration of geometrical appearance depicts on a plane surface a highly stylized motif of animals such as tortoises and frogs. The Peabody Museum of Natural History, Yale.

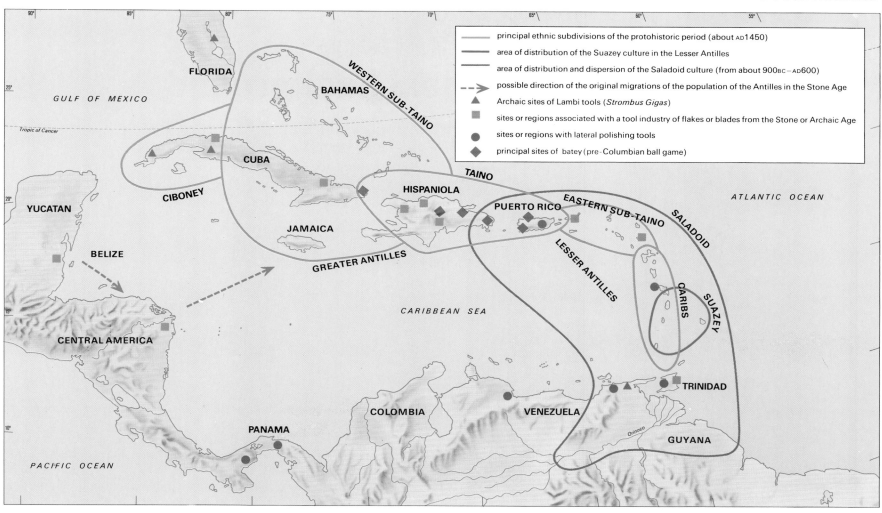

Stages of development in the prehistory of the Caribbean

This map illustrates in simplified fashion the main stages of West Indian prehistory, from its origins to the beginning of the historical period. The arrows pointing from the coast of Belize and Central America suggest, though this is only a hypothesis, the probable source of the population of the Greater Antilles, based on a more or less identical flint tool kit, though its relative age on the mainland has not been established. The distribution of certain types of tools belonging to the Archaic period (flint blades, shell gouges and lateral polishers) shows geographical breaks which seem to be the result of successive chance drifts occurring in various points in the Caribbean basin. By contrast, the rapid expansion of peoples belonging to the Saladoid culture, manufacturing pottery and practising agriculture, from the 1st century AD, quite definitely

followed the islands arc of the Lesser Antilles. The high point of cultural development in the Antilles, which was at its peak when the Europeans arrived, occurred in the Taino area of influence with its chieftaincies, its works of art and its ceremonial centres with ball games.

The adjacent areas, less developed but derived from this culture, form the Sub-Taino area extending to the Bahamas, and the same title can also be applied to the Leeward Islands in the Lesser Antilles. The whole western part of Cuba was to remain marginal, i.e. without agriculture and pottery, until the arrival of the Spaniards. The main part of the Lesser Antilles, the Windward Islands, at that period was the home of the island Caribs, but the archaeological culture immediately prior to them, the Suazoid culture, covered a smaller area.

Large boat-shaped vessel from the Ostionoid culture of the Greater Antilles

These undecorated containers have as their distinguishing feature a keel-like outline with an inward-turning edge and large ribbon-shaped handles rising above the level of the vase. The Peabody Museum of Natural History, Yale.

Ball game area at the ceremonial centre of Tibes, Puerto Rico

This ceremonial centre consists of four areas for ball games. The "courts" are marked out by rows of upright stones, and are linked by paved ways. They are the only structural remains left by the Taino chieftaincies.

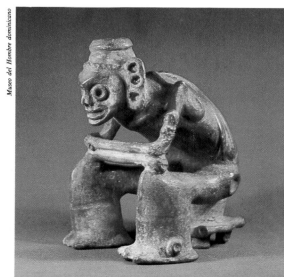

Anthropomorphic vase from the proto-historic Taino culture of Santo Domingo

This type of container with an opening at the back of the head shows a seated person. It may well relate to the desiccated remains of a chief, shown in the characteristic burial position.

Items in polished or carved stone from the Taino culture, Greater Antilles

Top left: bowl in polished stone; right, ball made of incised stone. Below, from left to right: stone statuette representing a seated person; stone with three points, or "trigonolith", of a snake's head; stone pestle with a bird's head.

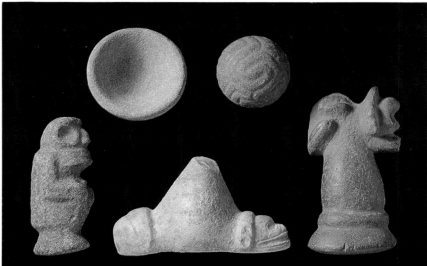

Oceania:
the archaeological background

Though artefacts from Oceania were widely studied in 18th century
Europe, there was virtually no archaeological excavation in some areas,
like Polynesia, until the 1950s: here, it has been said, "the glories of the
Stone Age" survived into our own time.

Oceania consists of two different prehistorical and historical groups: the
Australasian group and the islands of Oceania. Australia and the two islands
closely linked with it, New Guinea and Tasmania (which were connected with
the mainland by land bridges during the coldest periods of the Quaternary),
were settled by man some 40,000 years ago. Apart from New Guinea,
agriculture and cattle-rearing were still unknown in the region when the first
Europeans began to explore it in the 16th century. The second group consists
of the islands and archipelagoes scattered over the vast expanses of the Pacific
Ocean. Man arrived here much later, about 2000BC, first landing in the
western islands and only reaching the remotest ones by about 800AD. The
peoples of Oceania must have been expert in deep-sea navigation, for they
could not otherwise have coped with such distances. They were also familiar
with agriculture, animal rearing and pot-making, but did not know the wheel,
weaving, writing and metallurgy.

Insular Oceania remained untouched by Europeans for much longer than
the rest of the area. Magellan had crossed the Pacific from east to west in 1520,
but he met not a living soul until he reached the western islands of Micronesia.
His Spanish successors were no luckier in their regular travels from Callao in
Peru or Acapulco in Mexico to Manila in the Philippines. Mandana alone
succeeded in discovering the Marquesas archipelago in 1595, and he was
sailing to the south of the usual routes. During the 17th century, a few Dutch
sailors ventured into the South Pacific, but not until the great scientific
expeditions organized by England and France at the end of the 18th century
did Europeans become fully aware of this insular world, particularly
Polynesia. By then, the coasts of New Guinea, Australia and Tasmania had
long been known and explored.

In 1788, England had established a penal colony in New South Wales and
later deported the more intractable of the convicts to Tasmania. Soon, free
colonists followed, both to southern Australia and to Tasmania. Apart from a
few people of enquiring minds, such as the governor Phillip and R. Etheridge,
no one was interested in the native aboriginal peoples of these areas, who were
hunted like animals until a law protecting them was passed in 1842. Insular
Oceania was colonized later, and greater care was taken for the continued
existence of the native population, particularly in Polynesia, where the
physical appearance of the people conformed more closely to the European
ideal of beauty and therefore earned them a more favourable treatment. The
presence of people on islands which were at this time completely cut off from
any continental land puzzled scholars, who immediately began to look for
solutions to the mystery. But this problem did not apply to the inhabitants of
Melanesia, whose physical appearance and customs were regarded as much
more primitive and who could have reached their islands, which lay close to
the Australian continent, without great technical difficulty, and even perhaps
by crossing on foot.

Interpreting oral traditions

From the 18th century onwards, growing European interest in the problem of
the origin of the Polynesians was complicated by the absence of prehistoric
archaeology, which had not even been thought of then. It was supposed that
the history of these peoples could be retraced through their oral traditions,
since writing was unknown to them, particularly in the Society Islands and
New Zealand, where they were best known. Here the Maoris referred to
several large migrations of peoples who had left central Polynesia, particularly Tahiti, in their pirogues (dug-out canoes). According to them, their

Tahitian ancestors had originated in a land situated in the direction of the
setting sun and called *Hawaiki*, a name also found on Samoa under its form
Sava'i, and which could have been that of Raiatea, in the Society Islands,
before being given to an island in an archipelago far to the north of Tahiti
which is still called Hawaii.

During the 19th century, the efforts to interpret these oral traditions were
further boosted when it was discovered that their study could help the
archaeologists in their reconstruction of Oceanian history, as happened on
Vanuatu. But the pre-condition for the success of this approach was that these
traditions should still be necessary to the cohesion of the social groups. This
was no longer the case with the Polynesians, who for dozens of years had been
exposed to a foreign culture. Things would have been different if the first
European discoverers had carried out some research, but their knowledge of
local tongues was then insufficient, and their scientific interest turned to the
study of the natural habitat. Nevertheless, by comparing linguistic, racial and
cultural data, however uncertain, the conclusion was rapidly reached that the
Polynesians had originated from Asia or America, or even Polynesia itself.
The latter hypothesis was proposed, surprisingly, at a time when the dogma of
the church was not to be contradicted, particularly where the creation of Man
was concerned. The theory, nonetheless, was formulated by one of Cook's
companions, J.R. Forster, in 1777. Dumont d'Urville and others also
considered it, but its most ardent supporter was J.A. Moerenhout, who
devoted several chapters to it in his work, *Voyages aux Iles du Grand Ocean*
(Journeys to the Islands of the Great Ocean, 1837). He based his argument on
linguistic, cultural, botanical, zoological, geographical and geological considerations, and tried to show that the Polynesians' origin could not have been
an Asiatic or Amerindian one. A large continent must have existed in the
middle of the Pacific, a continent which disappeared under the waves as a
result of a cataclysm so that only its highest summits survived—the ten
islands of today. Modern Polynesians must be the survivors of this
catastrophe, which marked the beginning of their decline. What little was left
of their religion and their political customs pointed to their ancient
civilization. The myth of a primeval golden age also reappeared in his book,
together with the concept of a hierarchy among races, with white peoples
being pre-eminent. Hence, in the same work, Moerenhout contrasted the
Polynesians with the negroid peoples of Melanesia who "represent the lowest
link between mankind and the animals". This naïve form of racism could be
easily dismissed were it not for the fact that the same concepts influenced,
much more recently, certain scientific preconceptions concerning the "proto-
Polynesian" culture.

We know today from studies of the bottom of the Pacific that no continent
ever existed there. But the theory of an Amerindian origin for the Polynesians
was also formulated very early on, particularly by W. Ellis in his *Polynesian
Researches* (1829). This notion was constantly revived, even up to the 1950s,
with the Kon Tiki adventure and Thor Heyerdahl's publications. However,
the theory of an Asiatic origin for the Polynesians, which is as old as the other
two and has received widespread favour, has now been confirmed by
archaeological results.

Very few archaeological excavations had been carried out in Polynesia
before 1950. Genealogical calculations had led to the belief that the islands
had only been populated for a few centuries, so it seemed pointless to search
the soil for what could be found on the surface or observed in the
ethnographical collections already in existence. The objects that were

Bibliothèque nationale, Paris

The first archaeological records of Easter Island

On 1 August 1785, Jean François de Galaup, Count of Pérouse, sailed on a journey of scientific exploration accompanied by scientists and artists. Louis XVI himself had instigated the venture, which had been meticulously organized. On 9 April 1786 Galaup landed on Easter Island, where the geographer Bernizet drew up detailed records of the many monuments. This example shows a *moai* 5m (16ft) tall, one of the gigantic statues which so surprised the Europeans. The facial features are less stylized than in reality, and the plane which cuts the bust at shoulder height is a unique phenomenon in local sculpture. The aesthetic taste of the time manifests itself quite clearly in the way the islanders are depicted, their physique being closer to the Greeks than the Polynesians. The contemporary Romantic belief of the "noble savage" also appears in the way they are shown committing petty theft in all innocence. Drawing by Duche de Vancy, one of the illustrations for the *Voyage de la Perouse autour de monde (1785–1788)*, Paris, Imprimerie de la Republique, year V.

discovered differed so greatly from one another that the old concept of a homogeneous population had to be abandoned in favour of theories postulating various ethnic components, and at least three successive migrations. This concurred with what was already known of the ancient social order based on three main classes: the common people, the landowners and the nobility. The first group, which was undoubtedly the oldest, fell under the rule of the second, and this in turn, under that of the third. From this emerged the formulation of new theories, an even greater confusion in the understanding of the islands' original settlement, and a few mistakes in the interpretation of the first archaeological finds. For instance, in the years 1925–30, the inventory of the religious monuments of central Polynesia (the *marae*) were divided into a three-fold spatial and chronological classification: those found in the interior of the islands (the oldest, belonging to the people), those of the noble chieftains along the coasts (the more recent), and the so-called "intermediate" *marae*. Archaeologists now know that these monuments are all relatively recent and that their classification is much more complex, and that the social hierarchy varied considerably in different parts of Polynesia.

Conclusive evidence

The year 1950 was an important one in the history of Polynesian archaeology. It was then that the new method of radiocarbon* (C[14]) dating was applied for the first time (in Hawaii), and the dates which were thus obtained gradually provided the basic landmarks of Pacific prehistory and confirmed that the migrations had taken place from west to east. The other significant advance occurred with the publication of Roger Duff*'s work, *The Moa-Hunter period of Maori Culture*. The moa, a large flightless bird of the genus *Dinornis*, was thought to belong to the mythical world of the Maori until the discovery, first, of a few fossilized bones, and then, in 1947, of some eggs pierced by human hand and associated with a splintered, unpolished tool. Further discoveries followed, leading to many a controversy. According to some scholars, the moa had disappeared well before the arrival of the Polynesians, in the days of a much older Paleolithic population; others maintained that Melanesian hunters had caused its extinction before being themselves wiped out by the Polynesians (the Maoris); and others still, that the Maoris were these very hunters, the first to settle in New Zealand.

These controversies are interesting in that they led to earlier archaeological excavations than elsewhere. These gradually grew in number and became increasingly scientific. Duff confirmed the Polynesian origin of the first settlements, dating from the year 900AD, and identified an archaic period, that of the so-called "moa hunters", followed four centuries later (and only in North Island) by a classical or "Maori" period, resulting from an internal evolution rather than external influences. It now looks as though this applied to the whole of the western Pacific, the centre of which was settled by a culturally homogeneous population at the beginning of our era. These peoples later migrated towards the farthest islands: Hawaii, New Zealand and Easter Island, where this culture developed along different lines in order to adapt to a new ecosystem in relative isolation.

Stages of migration

Having recognized the Asiatic origin of the Polynesians, archaeologists still had to determine the various stages of their migration across the western Pacific. The route through Micronesia seemed the most likely, even though it

had not been confirmed archaeologically. It was also difficult to explain how they could have spent any length of time in Melanesia without their physical appearance being altered by the inevitable cross-breeding. The presence in Melanesia of Polynesian groups might be explained by later migrations, some returning from west to east, according to the theory proposed by Peter Buck* in 1938. The discovery, in Melanesia, of a ceramic ware considered too refined to be Melanesian (the Lapita ceramic), reopened the discussions after World War II, and stimulated several archaeological excavations in the area. Since 1964, our understanding of the settling process in the Pacific has been greatly improved by the study of the stylistic varieties of Lapita ceramics, of the objects found at the same sites and in association with them, and of their distribution in space and time. Nevertheless, the problems concerning the first relations between Melanesians and Polynesians remain unsolved and probably ill-formulated.

It is perhaps surprising that archaeological research in Melanesia should have started so recently, and that it should have been motivated, at least at the beginning, by a desire to discover the origins of the Polynesians. But apart from the special attention, already mentioned, which the latter have enjoyed from Europeans, their ocean-going enterprise was enough to attract attention, being apparently unique in the history of so-called primitive mankind. The past of the Melanesians appeared to be much less interesting, but their cultures, disregarded and consequently much less infiltrated by the Europeans, attracted the attention of ethnologists.

In the 19th century, prehistorians were particularly interested in Australia, as they believed here they could observe in the people a living example of the ancient evolutionary stages of the European Paleolithic man. Ethnography was at first the main discipline to be applied, stratigraphic* research being undertaken seriously only in 1929, when the cave of Devon Downs, in South Australia, was studied. Here, and later elsewhere, researchers found what they were looking for: a succession of cultural sequences comparable to those of Europe but much shorter. It was initially thought that the first settling of Australia could only have taken place in the recent past, since it required a nautical knowledge acquired by contact with Neolithic populations. However, since 1962, C[14] dating has gradually pushed back the limits of Australian prehistory, and the discovery of new sites, such as that of Mungo in 1968, led archaeologists to abandon their overly European conception of such a prehistory.

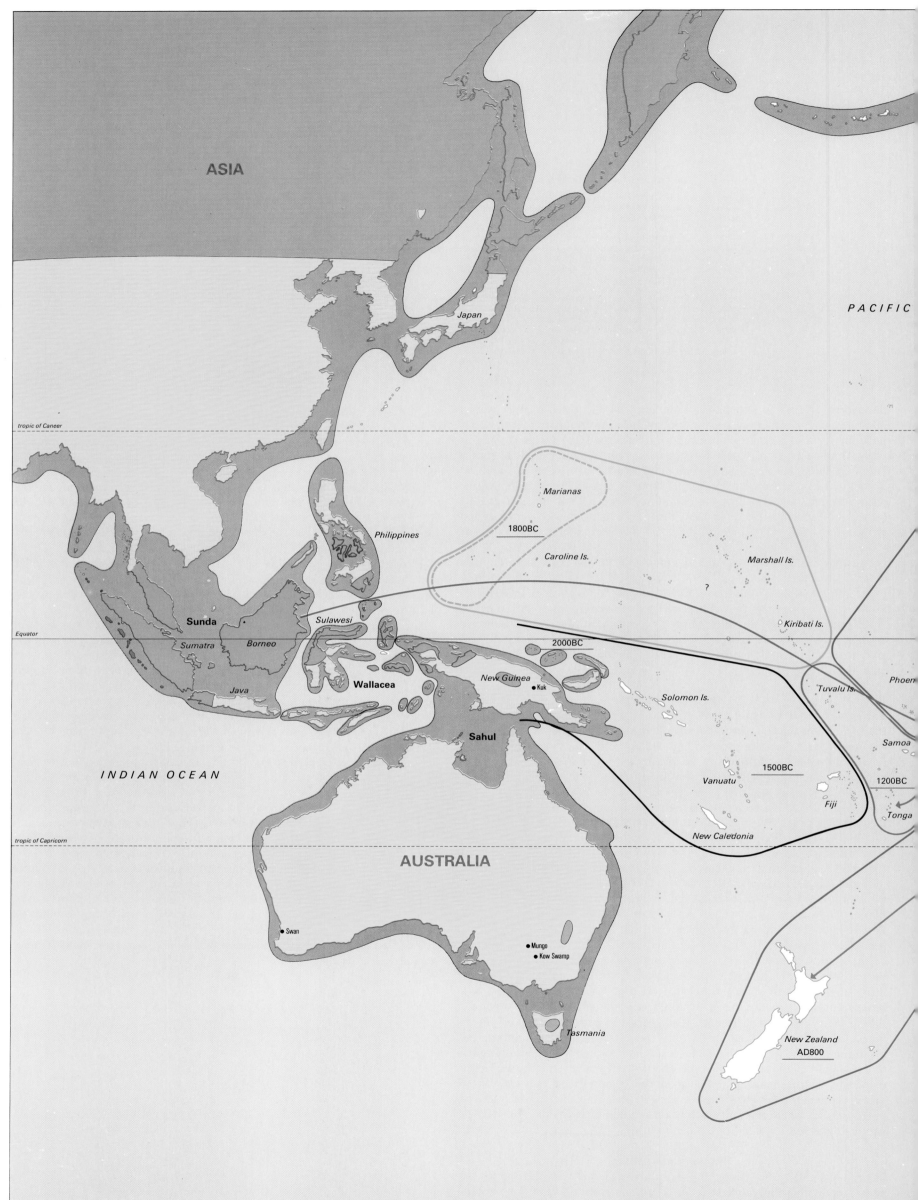

ASIA

PACIFIC

tropic of Cancer

Japan

Marianas

1800BC

Philippines

Caroline Is.

Marshall Is.

?

Sunda

Sulawesi

Kiribati Is.

Equator

Sumatra

Borneo

2000BC

Tuvalu Is.

Phoen

Java

Wallacea

New Guinea

• *Kuk*

Solomon Is.

Samoa

INDIAN OCEAN

Sahul

1500BC

1200BC

Vanuatu

Fiji

tropic of Capricorn

Tonga

New Caledonia

AUSTRALIA

• *Swan*

• *Mungo*
• *Kow Swamp*

Tasmania

New Zealand
AD800

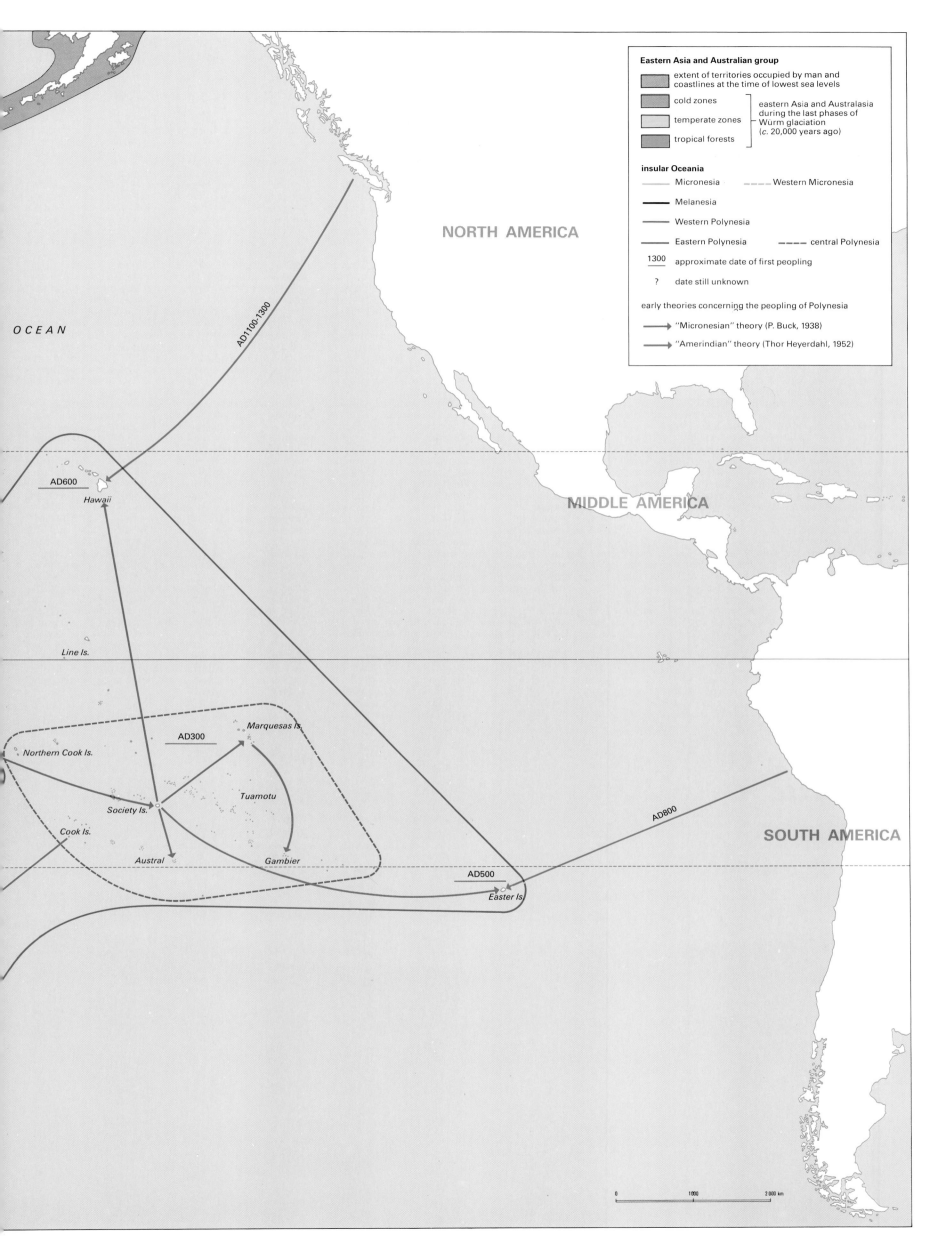

Eastern Asia and Australian group

extent of territories occupied by man and
coastlines at the time of lowest sea levels

cold zones

temperate zones

tropical forests

eastern Asia and Australasia
during the last phases of
Würm glaciation
(c. 20,000 years ago)

insular Oceania

Micronesia

Western Micronesia

Melanesia

Western Polynesia

Eastern Polynesia

central Polynesia

1300   approximate date of first peopling

?   date still unknown

early theories concerning the peopling of Polynesia

"Micronesian" theory (P. Buck, 1938)

"Amerindian" theory (Thor Heyerdahl, 1952)

NORTH AMERICA

MIDDLE AMERICA

SOUTH AMERICA

OCEAN

AD1100-1300

AD600

Hawaii

Line Is.

Marquesas Is.

AD300

Northern Cook Is.

Tuamotu

Society Is.

Cook Is.

Austral

Gambier

AD800

AD500

Easter Is.

0   1000   2 000 km

The peopling of Australasia

The first inhabitants of Australia arrived by sea at least 40,000 years ago. This is by far the earliest deep-sea voyage known to archaeologists.

During the glaciations of the Quaternary era, the level of the seas dropped and huge land bridges appeared between New Guinea, Australia and Tasmania; the three formed a continent today called Sahul Land. For the same reason, most of the islands of Southeast Asia were then connected with the Asian mainland and formed the subcontinent called Sunda Land. A small archipelago, Wallacea, still exists between Sahul and Sunda: its islands, such as Sulawesi, Timor and the Moluccas, were larger than they are today but were nevertheless separated by very deep and wide sounds, some of them up to 100km (62 miles). The first Sahulian immigrants, therefore, arrived not on foot, as was once thought, but by sea, and this, as we now know, was a very long time ago. The radiocarbon* datings which have been obtained since 1955 have gradually pushed back the date of these peoples' arrival in southern Australia. The discovery in 1969 of the site of Mungo in New South Wales pointed to a date some 33,000 years ago. This site is still of major importance to our knowledge of mankind and his environment during the Pleistocene* in southeastern Australia. A site discovered in 1981 in the valley of the Swan (on the southwestern point of Australia) has been dated to some 39,500 years ago. While its paleo-ethnological* value cannot compete with that of Mungo, its dating seems to confirm the theory that the peopling of Australia took place all along the western coast of Sahul. One could also reasonably surmise that the last sound separating Wallacea from Sahul had been crossed a few thousand years earlier, probably some 45,000 years ago or more. This maritime adventure of the Pleistocene is by far the oldest known in the history of humanity.

Mungo is the name of an ancient lake which dried up some 10,000 years ago and was part of a series of depressions periodically fed with fresh water when the climate of the Pleistocene became colder and wetter. In the same period, on the eastern plains alongside these depressions, the wind built a group of crescent-shaped dunes whose stratigraphy* has been revealed by recent erosion. The nature of the layers thus deposited varies according to the paleoclimates. Three main phases of wind-borne deposits have been identified, separated by ancient soils: Golgol, predating the year 70,000BP (i.e. before the present); Mungo, between 70,000 and 19,000BP; and Zanci, from 14,000 to 11,000BP.

The Mungo deposits belong to a period when the lake had again been filled with fresh water, and yielded the most ancient relics of human activity: hearths, utensils made of stone (large, hardly worked splinters, rounded scrapers), food scraps (bird and fish bones, shells). Several C14* datings place this earliest occupation at about 33,000BP. Three burials were also found in slightly more recent levels, and they were arranged in a way that suggests a preoccupation with the future of the dead. Anatomically, these Mungo hominids were hardly different from present-day Aborigines, unlike another population living on the site of Kow Swamp, 300km (190 miles) to the south of Mungo, between 13,000 and 9,500BP. Over 40 individuals have been found at Kow Swamp, all more recent than those of Mungo but characterized by morphologically more ancient skulls, and facial and jaw bones. Other similar but isolated fossils have been found in southern Australia. Various hypotheses have been put forward to explain the chronological anomaly and the origin of these groups, which reached an apparently different evolutionary stage. The problem is still unsolved. Whatever the answer to this paleontological mystery, the stone relics of their material culture hardly vary from one group to the other, both across the whole of Australia and throughout the Pleistocene—with the exception of a few regional variations caused by differences in the raw materials available. One remarkable innovation is the technique of polishing the cutting edge of large tools resembling adze blades. This technique first appeared in northern Australia a few thousand years before the end of the Pleistocene. All over the rest of the world it appeared considerably later, and was contemporary with the first tentative agricultural activities involving cutting and chopping.

The last post-glacial warmer period caused the level of the sea to rise. By 12,000BC, large coastal areas of Sahul Land began to disappear: by 8000BC the Bass Strait was formed and isolated Tasmania from Australia; the isthmus which connected New Guinea with Cape York disappeared around 4000BC. At the same time, all the ecosystems changed in some degree, as did lifestyles: less in Tasmania, but considerably in Australia and New Guinea, and in different ways. The reason for this dissimilarity of evolution is still unclear.

Links with the Australian Aborigines

When the Europeans arrived in Australia, the Australian Aborigines were using tools made with flakes rather than splinters, finely worked, widely diversified and generally supplied with handles. We now know that these tools were the end product of techniques profoundly different from the very primitive ones of the ancient inhabitants of Sahul Land, and that they dated back several thousands of years, but we still know nothing about their origin: were they imported from outside or the product of internal evolution? One also wonders why such populations had remained hunter-gatherers up to the arrival of the Europeans, even though they had for a long time been in contact with Melanesian and Indonesian horticultural peoples. It is easier to see how the Tasmanians would have preserved the techniques of the Pleistocene: they could not maintain links with their neighbours in Australia who, like them, were not seafarers and had no means of crossing the Bass Strait. The dingo was unknown to them (it is still a mystery how this dog reached Australia during the Holocene period), as were the spear-thrower* and the boomerang, widely used on the Australian mainland. Perhaps it was simply that, having long adapted to ecological conditions which had changed less here than elsewhere during the Holocene period, they had no use for technological innovations developed by other cultures.

The prehistory of the last of the Sahul territories, New Guinea, is still little known. The interior of the Irian Jaya is still unexplored, and the heart of Papua New Guinea has been visited by Europeans only since 1933. The most important archaeological discoveries have taken place in its highlands since the 1960s. Apart from a site on the northeastern coast which has recently been dated to 40,000 years ago, no site has yet been discovered in the lowlands which might be older than 3,000BC. Several sites under rocks or in the open have been excavated in the central mountain range. The most ancient levels are some 30,000 years old and are characterized by a production of rough splinters and modified shingle. Large blades with lateral identations appear after 18,000BP: they are also known from Australian sites of the Pleistocene and probably had handles. But the most amazing discovery was at the Kuk site: a swampy area which was drained by man at least 9,000 years ago. This may well have represented a first, pre-agricultural effort to encourage the growth of native edible plants, such as the yam, the taro (sweet potato), sugar cane, and the pandanus* for making mats. This interference with the natural habitat had, by 3,000BC at the latest, become horticultural activity proper, involving the complete management of the area with draining ditches and irrigation.

The former beach of Lake Mungo uncovered by wind erosion

Here lived the first Aborigines who colonized this region of southern Australia 33,000 years ago, when the climate was much wetter than today. The black patches visible on the ground are cores, tools or waste flakes. The bright patches are freshwater molluscs (*Unionidae*) gathered by the inhabitants of the site from the fresh water of the lake, which has been dry since the Holocene period.

Lake Mungo's "Great Wall of China"

This is the name given by the Australians to the crescent-shaped dune which borders the eastern shore of Lake Mungo. The nature of the sediments thus stratified by the west wind reflects the fluctuations of the environment during the Quaternary era. The same applies to all the dunes lining the ancient lakes of the region, drained by the network of tributaries of the Murray river during the cold periods of the Pleistocene.

376

Knives for cutting up meat

The Australian tool kit, very simple during the Pleistocene, as it was everywhere else on the continent of Sahul Land, became very diversified during the last ten millennia. These saw-toothed knives are made of small flakes without retouch, fixed to the handle by resin. Only the stone parts would have remained if they had been found during the excavation of a somewhat older level and interpretation of their function would been a very haphazard affair, if indeed they had been recognized at all as evidence of human industry. Musée de l'Homme, Paris.

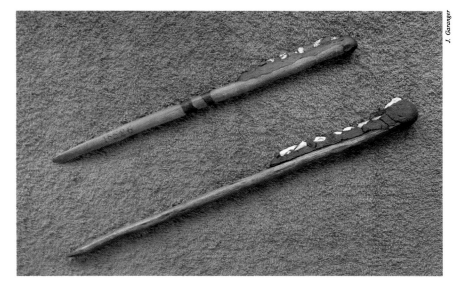

Recent Australian tools

Two finely retouched and notched points, one porcelain, the other glass. Driven into regions often lacking the kind of stone needed to fashion their traditional tool kit, the Aborigines made use of substitutes unwittingly supplied by the newcomers; a porcelain insulator from a telegraph pole and glass from bottles.

Tasmanian rock art

Rock carvings from Sandown Creek on the northwest coast of Tasmania, believed by some researchers to be astronomical symbols, though this is unlikely. The same style and the same technique (picking) are found in many Australian Pleistocene sites where rock art developed during the Holocene period, although Tasmania was completely cut off from any mainland influence.

First excavation of the prehistoric site of Kuk, New Guinea

The complex of zones of grey clay surrounded by darker sediments dates back 6,000 years. It corresponds to a system that combined the culture of food plants in a dry environment (drainage) and also in a wet one (irrigation). The remains of rectilinear ditches are more recent. Further excavations have revealed the existence of similar arrangements dated to 9,000 years ago, but these could have been to facilitate the natural growth of plants rather than representing genuine horticulture.

Navigation in southern Tasmania at the time of the visit by Nicolas Baudin, 1802

These frail skiffs, made of three bundles of reeds tied together, enabled the Aborigines to sail out of the estuaries and reach the nearest islands, but not to navigate over more than 6 or 7km (4 miles), which was also the limit for their eucalyptus-bark rafts. This explains the isolation of the Aborigines after the formation of the Bass Strait which separated Tasmania from Australia, and the depopulation of the islands too remote from Tasmania, such as King and Furneaux Islands. (Plate No. XIV from the *Atlas* of Lesueur and Petit, 1812.)

Lapita culture and the Polynesians

Who were the ancestors of the Polynesians, the intrepid colonists of the world's remotest islands? Modern archaeology is questioning traditional answers to this age-old enigma.

When the Europeans first discovered them, the Polynesians knew nothing of ceramic art. In the eastern Pacific, no archaeological excavation has recovered any pottery, apart from a few sherds in the most ancient levels of two Marquesas sites (3rd century AD). On the other hand, potteries were still working in several Melanesian villages. Excavations have shown that this technique was already practised and widespread in prehistory, indeed more so than today. In general, these products are of very simple shape, decorated with geometric incisions and applied reliefs which are related, as we now know, to a ceramic tradition called "Mangaasi" after a site on the island of Efate in Vanuatu, dating from the beginning of the 6th century BC. Another ceramic tradition, known as "Lapita", has been discovered which has no apparent equivalent in the preceding tradition, whether historical or prehistorical. The Lapita tradition shows very different, often composite shapes, with flared and flat bases; the wares are decorated with dots produced with a comb on red slip and arranged in various motifs, including a spiral and a castellated border pattern. They first appeared in the western Pacific during the 2nd millennium BC and disappeared, practically everywhere, at the beginning of our era. Soon after it was discovered, the Lapita ceramic was attributed, not without some prejudice, to the ancestors of the Polynesians.

Lapita pottery owes its name to a site on New Caledonia where the American archaeologist E.W. Gifford found sherds in 1952. A few years earlier he had found others in several Fijian sites. However, the first discoveries had been made during the first half of the 20th century by amateurs. In 1947 this pottery was again found on Pine Island, to the south of New Caledonia, and its resemblance to the wares of Watom (New Britain, discovered in 1908 by Otto Meyer) was remarked upon. The more cautious authorities placed its origin in Neolithic Asia, but later it was attributed to the ancestors of the Polynesians who had set forth to occupy the Pacific islands. In the past 20 years, archaeological excavations have become more numerous in the western Pacific and have uncovered an increasing number of Lapita sites from one end of Melanesia to the other, as well as within western Polynesia: Tonga, Samoa, Wallis and Futuna. Today archaeologists prefer to talk of a "Lapita cultural complex" rather than of Lapita pottery, in view of all the other remains which have been found associated with it on the sites, and in the belief that the latter are evidence of the ancestral culture of the Polynesians and mark the stages of their migration through Melanesia. The details, the means, and the process itself of this population spread are a matter of discussion, but a general agreement has been reached on the overall scheme of development.

Some 4,000 years ago, according to this view, the ancestors of the Polynesians, Mongoloids speaking an Austronesian language, left southeast Asia and ventured towards the islands of the western Pacific, already inhabited by the Melanesians, who were physically and culturally different. Originally not very numerous, they settled on the coasts and on the small neighbouring islands, leaving the interior to the agricultural and land-based Melanesians. The Polynesians were essentially a people of the sea, but were well versed in the art of ceramics, since they produced the Lapita pottery. They quickly spread to the north and south of Melanesia but maintained a network of communications with the original settlements. Thus, for instance, the obsidian exported from the extreme north of Melanesia can be found all over the Lapita sites and as far as Pine Island. They might have established commercial exchanges with the Melanesians, but apparently on a very small scale, because the Lapita sites maintain their originality through time and space. They might however have learned from them, or perfected, their own horticultural and breeding techniques, and in return have taught the technique of making pots. Thus the Melanesians, a few centuries later, began to manufacture pottery in the Mangaasi tradition. Whatever the case may be, these contacts, confirmed by the evolution of the languages, did not lead to a proper cross-miscegenation: the ancestors of the Polynesians therefore must have been endogamous*.

Continuing with their eastward-bound exploration, they discovered islands further away and not yet inhabited – the Fiji islands and present-day western Polynesia, where remains of Lapita culture have been found. In their ancient habitat in the west, they gradually disappeared, exterminated or assimilated by the Melanesians. In the east, on the other hand, they prospered for a long time, subsisting on maritime resources as well as on agriculture and animal rearing, without competition on these new island homelands. Thus, throughout a whole millennium, Polynesian culture slowly evolved from an ancestral culture born in eastern Asia, hardly altered by the centuries in Melanesia. Gradually the Polynesian world discovered by the Europeans in the 18th century took shape, remaining different from the Melanesian one.

Towards 500BC a group of Melanesians settled on Fiji, as shown by the physical appearance of modern inhabitants, and above all by the remains of their material culture, particularly the pottery, which have been discovered in the course of archaeological excavations. This, combined with the increased pressure of population expansion in the whole area, forced the western Polynesians into a new exodus at a time when, for unknown reasons, they no longer manufactured any ceramics. Towards the beginning of our era, some of them reached central Polynesia, the Marquesas Islands and Society Islands, and, a few centuries later, the farthest edge of eastern Polynesia.

There is a variant to this proposed scheme. In 1974 the anthropologist W.W. Howells returned to the old theory, advanced by Peter Buck* in particular, according to which the Polynesians could have journeyed from Asia to western Polynesia by way of Micronesia rather than Melanesia. This would explain more easily their failure to interbreed with the Melanesians. When Howells was writing his work the oldest Lapita sites had been found on Fiji and Tonga, and the more recent ones in Melanesia, so a few Lapita groups might have ventured at a later stage through that part of Melanesia which had remained unknown to them. However, it must be asked how the Polynesians could have invented, or rediscovered, the pottery techniques necessary to manufacture Lapita wares on Fiji and Tonga after having spent centuries in the Micronesian atolls which are naturally without clay. The study of the variations in the ocean levels also shows that 3,000 years ago, at the time of this hypothetical migration through Micronesia, these atolls were barely above the sea. Since then, several older Lapita sites have been discovered in Melanesia.

A myth of two peoples?

This hypothesis, like the more recent one of endogamy being practised by Lapita populations, was designed to explain the differences between the physical appearance of the Polynesians and the Melanesians. Such differences have often been exaggerated by taking into account only the most extreme of anatomical characteristics, while neglecting the role played by the environment in physical modification and the evolution of phenotypes* during over three millennia of Oceanic wandering. Racial distinctions of genuine relevance should be rather sought outside the Pacific and in much more ancient times then those of its settlement. This seems to be confirmed by recent studies of historical linguistics. So-called "Proto-Austronesian" would actually have formed in eastern Asia some 7,000 years ago, if not earlier. It is at the origin of all the Oceanic languages (over 400), apart from the "Papuan" languages, which are older and of a different origin. One might also ask whether the intensity with which, in the western Pacific, the Lapita sites have been studied has not left in the shadows a much more complex prehistorical reality. This seems to be confirmed in the light of new results.

The hypothesis that Melanesia might have been peopled even before the arrival of the "Lapita" (which would explain why the latter settled by the sea shores) has never been demonstrated, except for the islands closer to New Guinea which were much more easily accessible during the retreat of the sea in the Pleistocene*, due to water being locked up as ice. Elsewhere, such ancient migrations from pre-Holocenic* Australia are highly improbable: the distances to be covered were always far too great. Thus a Melanesian presence in the western Pacific, Austronesian but pre-Lapita, is pure conjecture: given the present state of our knowledge, the Lapita sites are everywhere the oldest. The fact that they are to be found along the coastline is probably misleading: such sites are more easily identified by archaeologists, unlike those in the interior which are fossilized beneath a thick alluvial layer. Besides, ancient Melanesian, or Mangaasi, sites have been discovered along the coasts, and, by contrast, some Lapita sites have been found in the interior of the islands where alluvial deposits are thinner and the vegetation cover less dense.

Another recent discovery concerns the remains of cultivation and animal-raising activities found in very old Lapita sites. The hypothesis that the later Mangaasi pottery was the result of a period of apprenticeship on the part of settled Melanesians, who had come into contact with the Lapita, appears increasingly unfounded. Many sites throughout Melanesia are known where the upper level (Mangaasi) and the lower (Lapita) are divided by a third level where both types of pottery appear. This has been attributed to a disturbed stratigraphy*. But it could be concluded that these intermediate levels testify to a transitional cultural phase, and that the Lapita and Mangaasi traditions cannot in reality be attributed to two different peoples. Finally, Mangaasi pottery has been found not only in central and southern Melanesia, but also as far away as islands off the coast of New Guinea and on the edges of Micronesia. This shows that the Lapita people and the Melanesians relied on the same system of inter-island contacts. This is confirmed, on the sites, by other examples of material culture, and was still in operation when the Europeans arrived.

Melanesian colonists

The distinction between an ancient Melanesian population, on the one hand, based on the land and living on cultivation and animal husbandry, and a sea-going people, (the Lapita) on the other—travellers, pottery-makers, and direct ancestors of the Polynesians—appears increasingly to be an artificial one. The mere presence of Lapita pottery in western Polynesia does not imply that the latter was colonized by a distinctive population, but quite simply by one of the groups coming from the Melanesian area and practising such techniques. Others, non-potters, might have accompanied them. Apart from their mobility, one of the characteristics of Oceanic societies is the tendency to specialize in certain techniques, the products of which were then circulated between the various groups. Pottery was part of this system, without being of prime importance as kitchen and tableware. Pottery disappeared in Polynesia at the same time as it did in Melanesia, but was not followed by other ceramic products. This was probably due to a weakening of the network of contacts with the west in favour of neighbouring archipelagoes, where lifestyles and exchanges were of necessity different. These populations, having become aceramic and "Polynesian", later spread towards the eastern Pacific.

Archaeologists have in vain looked for 'traces, in southeast Asia, of a pottery in the Lapita tradition. It now seems that this might have originated in northern Melanesia, at least as far as the style is concerned, if not the technique itself, which originated elsewhere, like other elements of the material culture of the first inhabitants of Oceania. Eastern Asia alone could possibly have been the cradle of such an ancestral culture, and certain facts can throw some light on the process by which it emerged. During the Pleistocene different populations lived in eastern Asia: black-skinned people to the south and, along the Chinese coast and in Japan, Mongoloid and Paleo-Siberian populations. In the Holocene , the populations living in southeast Asia first began to cultivate plants, and all the varieties grown in Oceania have their origin here. The populations of the coastal plains of China and Japan, on the contrary, only came to agriculture much later (in the 3rd century BC in Japan). They lived as hunter-gatherers and above all on maritime resources, having learnt the art of navigation. The coastal and island regions of all this part of eastern Asia were considerably affected by increases in sea level which took place at the beginning of the Holocene. The sea gradually covered 40 percent of the land, with obvious consequences for the populations concerned, Neolithic or pre-Neolithic. In their search for new territories, some might have been encouraged, in the course of time, to intensify their relationships with other people, thus enlarging the Austronesian language and founding that Oceanic world that is at once so unique and so multifarious. It seems therefore, that it would be reasonable to abandon the hypothesis of the successive arrival on the Pacific islands of two populations culturally alien to each other.

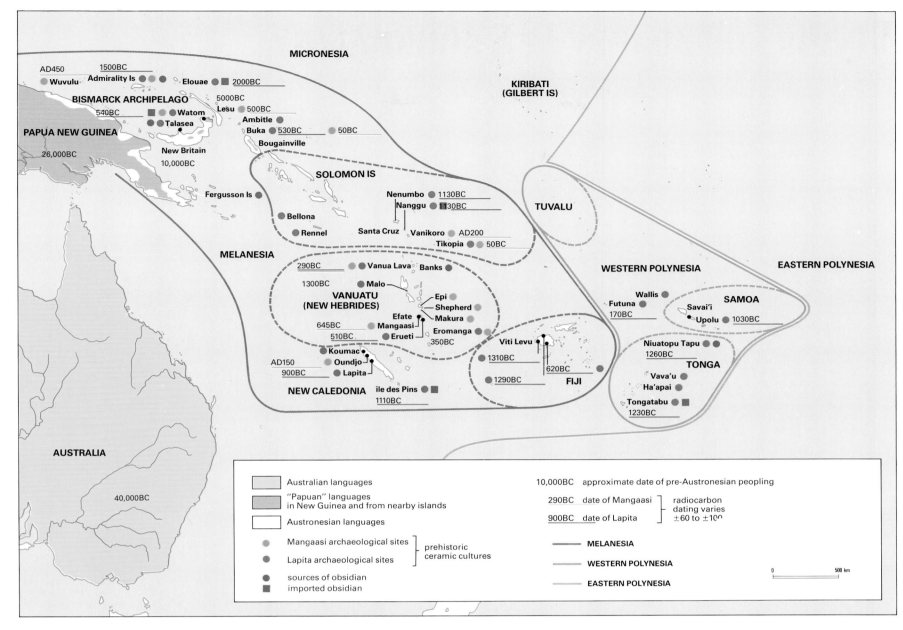

Map legend:

Australian languages	10,000BC	approximate date of pre-Austronesian peopling
"Papuan" languages in New Guinea and from nearby islands	290BC	date of Mangaasi
Austronesian languages	900BC	date of Lapita

radiocarbon dating varies ±60 to ±100

- Mangaasi archaeological sites ⎫ prehistoric
- Lapita archaeological sites ⎭ ceramic cultures
- sources of obsidian
- imported obsidian

MELANESIA
WESTERN POLYNESIA
EASTERN POLYNESIA

0   500 km

Pottery in the Lapita tradition

Lapita pottery differs from other ceramic traditions, and in particular from the Mangaasi tradition, because of its composite shapes and its stippled decoration, made with a comb. A red slip is often used. Site of Watom, New Britain, 6th century BC. Musée de l'homme, Paris.

Pottery in the Mangaasi tradition

This pottery tradition is characterized by incised patterns and applied reliefs. Like all pottery in prehistoric Oceania, it is not associated with burials. Consequently the sherds are very scattered over the sites, and no complete object has been recovered. Nonetheless it is certain that Mangaasi earthenware was simple in shape, generally spheroidal. Central Vanuatu, 7th–6th century BC. Private collection.

Mangaasi on the north coast of Efate, Vanuatu

This site has given its name to one of the two great ceramic traditions of the western Pacific. It was also said to be the place where the hero Roy Mata lived in the 13th century AD. The graves that have been uncovered here are more recent (17th century). Study of the site has enabled archaeologists to follow the development of Mangaasi pottery from its earliest level (645 ± 95 BC).

Myths and history at Vanuatu

Study of one particular group of Polynesian myths and their possible historical content has given results of far wider significance to historians and anthropologists.

During the 19th century, Europeans tried to discover the past of the Polynesians through their oral traditions. They met with little success, here and elsewhere, and thus concluded that societies without a form of writing were societies without history, and that the study of mythologies, these being the product of the collective unconscious, could only be fruitful if used comparatively and within the perspectives of a structural analysis. Archaeological research carried out in the 1960s at Vanuatu (formerly New Hebrides) revealed that some of the information supplied by Oceanian mythology could nevertheless have had historical foundations, particularly in the case of two closely connected myths: the myth of *Kuwae* and that of *Roy Mata*.

Kuwae was a legendary island destroyed by a cataclysm, the only remaining traces of which were the Shepherd islands (so called by Cook when he discovered them in 1774). In the late 19th century, the first missionary to settle on this small archipelago, the Rev. Oscar Michelsen heard the history of the cataclysm from the natives themselves: "A young man called Tombuk was cheated by some people who, without his knowing it, led him to sleep with his mother. Having realized, too late, what had happened, and distraught by his incestuous act, he decided to kill himself and, at the same time, those responsible for his sin. His uncle supplied him with the means for his revenge in the shape of a lizard, transmitter of volcanic power. The youth then organized a feast which lasted six days. Each day, a pig was sacrificed and its inflated bladder was attached to an iron tree, under which the lizard had been hidden. At the end of the six days, Tombuk burst the first four bladders in succession, thus generating an earthquake of increasing intensity. Kuwae rocked and then burst into pieces at the same time as the fifth bladder. When Tombuk burst the sixth, a volcano rose in place of the iron tree under which the lizard had been hidden. All present were killed. . . ."

The tradition went on to say that several chiefs of Kuwae, natives of Efate, had returned there in their pirogues (dugout canoes) at the first signs of the cataclysm. A youth, Asingmet, and a girl also survived by taking shelter from the volcanic eruption. They were rescued by the inhabitants of a nearby island, Makura, and after a few years Asingmet noticed some vegetation on Tongoa, one of the islands left after the destruction of Kuwae. He was then renamed *Ti Tongoa Liseiriki* and

organized the colonization of the new archipelago by appealing mainly to the chiefs who had taken refuge on Efate. When he died, he was buried on Tongoa with his wives and with one of the men of his entourage, as was the custom. When the Rev. Michelsen studied the genealogy of all the chiefs who had succeeded one another after these events, he estimated that the catastrophe of Kuwae could have taken place around the year AD1540.

The tomb of Roy Mata

Roy Mata is one of the most important heroes of Vanuatu mythology, much more famous than Ti Tongoa Liseiriki. It is said that in ancient times he landed on Maniura, to the south of Efate, with a group of pirogues coming from a great distance. He rapidly rose to rule over the whole of the inner archipelago, sending his companions across the waters (particularly to Kuwae), creating new outposts and organizing a system of hierarchical, inter-island relations which still exists today. Gradually he transformed the social structures of the area, which, under his rule, enjoyed a period of peace and prosperity. He had asked to be buried on Retoka, a small island near the coast of Efate. A large crowd was present at his funeral. He was buried at the foot of two large vertical stone slabs together with some members of his entourage. Individuals and couples representing the various clans who owed him their allegiance were also buried there, having volunteered to accompany him to the underwater land of the dead. Certain other people were sacrificed in addition. After a long funeral ceremony, the survivors withdrew and the island was declared tabu. All this happened long before the Kuwae catastrophe.

Archaeological interest in excavation at Vanuatu was motivated not only by these questions of oral tradition, but also by the problems of its distant prehistory, which was then totally unknown, but remained an essential subject of research for an understanding of the settling of the western Pacific, where Vanuatu occupies a central position. Thus it was at Efate that the "Mangaasi" type of pottery, which is now known throughout Melanesia, was first identified. It was present there from 645BC ± 95 years, in association with stone utensils which were very common in ancient Melanesia; it disappeared, like all ceramic wares, in about AD1200 to be replaced by very varied shell tools in a Micronesian style. Research

carried out on Tongoa has enabled scholars to follow the evolution of this "Mangaasi culture" on sites covered by a thick layer of volcanic deposits which Carbon 14* has dated to AD1460 ± 37 years. Geological observations have revealed not only a very violent volcanic explosion but also a volcano-tectonic "cataclysm" with fault lines and collapses, linked with the creation of a vast caldera* situated immediately to the east of the Shepherd islands. Geologists have also been able to reconstruct the ancient profile of the island before its destruction. There is no doubt that this was the legendary Kuwae. This was definitively proved by the discovery of the tomb of Ti Tongoa Liseiriki, dated to AD1475 ± 37 years. Both the date and the arrangement of the tomb conform with the oral tradition.

The tomb of Roy Mata was also discovered on Retoka: it is a vast collective burial, the exceptional importance of which links it with that of the hero; almost 50 people, including 11 embracing couples, have been recovered. By studying the spatial organization of the remains, archaeologists have been able to retrace the progress of the funeral ceremonies, which closely resembles that described by oral tradition. The tomb can be dated to AD1265 ± 140 years, thus confirming the story according to which "Roy Mata had lived long before the Kuwae cataclysm".

This cooperation between ethnology and archaeology has thus produced excellent results in Vanuatu, where oral traditions have guided archaeological research, and archaeology has conferred historical dimension upon the contemporary, social and cultural facts observed by the ethnologists. However, this was only possible because the survival of traditions guaranteed that of the social structures, assuming the role which elsewhere was played by written documentation and history. In this case, cooperation has led further back than the memorized events. Indeed, oral traditions do not recall the sharp transformations affecting material culture, which have been observed by prehistorians and dated from the 13th century. They thus appear to be contemporary with, and even a consequence of, the arrival of Roy Mata and his people on Vanuatu, and they even indicate where these people came from, Micronesia, as well as throwing new light on the prehistory of the western Pacific.

J. Garanger

The island of Tongoa and the Kuwae disaster

The coast by the village of Mangarisu. Andesitic lava in the foreground forms the base rock of the island while, above, several layers represent eruptions prior to man's arrival. Above them is a layer of dark brown sediment in which several layers of human occupation are stratified, consisting of hearths, pottery, etc, and dating from AD600 to 1300. A layer of pumice 1m (3.3ft) thick, left by the last volcanic eruption in the Kuwae disaster, covers the whole.

The collective grave of the hero Roy Mata on Retoka, 13th century

The disposition of the burials and their date conform with information handed down by oral tradition. The study of the spatial distribution of the material has enabled archaeologists to follow the stages of the ceremony, from the placing of Roy Mata in his deep grave (no. 13) to the final sacrifices, those of couples, no. 7, 2, 3, 4, and 5. The grave was then completely filled in; dressed stones were set up to indicate the principal figures; then various marine conch shells were laid on the ground after the singing of a final hymn declaring Retoka to be a tabu island. Oral tradition has preserved to this day the music and words of the hymn.

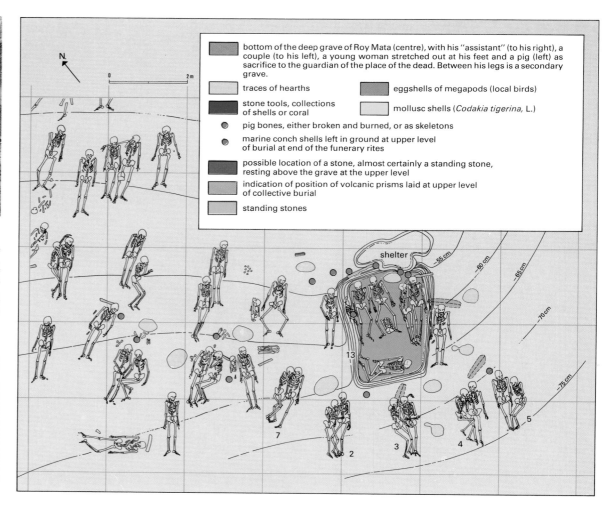

bottom of the deep grave of Roy Mata (centre), with his "assistant" (to his right), a couple (to his left), a young woman stretched out at his feet and a pig (left) as sacrifice to the guardian of the place of the dead. Between his legs is a secondary grave.

traces of hearths

eggshells of megapods (local birds)

stone tools, collections of shells or coral

mollusc shells (*Codakia tigerina*, L.)

pig bones, either broken and burned, or as skeletons

marine conch shells left in ground at upper level of burial at end of the funerary rites

possible location of a stone, almost certainly a standing stone, resting above the grave at the upper level

indication of position of volcanic prisms laid at upper level of collective burial

standing stones

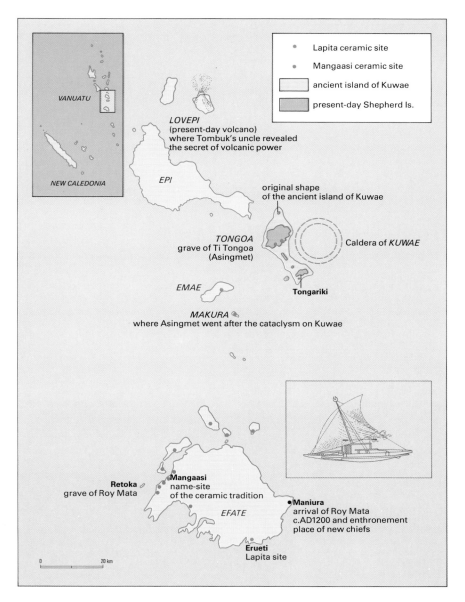

Start of excavations on the collective tomb of Roy Mata

In the foreground, removal of the topsoil covering the tomb reveals several slabs of stone, which were originally dressed, but are now broken or leaning over. At the back, on the left, two large stones rest on their edges at the site of the deep grave, with the marine conch shells that were placed there. In the background, on the right, the excavations have reached the second level of the collective grave and reveal a single person and three entwined couples.

One of the couples in the collective tomb of Roy Mata

The woman, huddled against her companion, is holding his right arm with both of her hands. He is stretched out on his back in an attitude of repose. The men were drugged with a heavy dose of *kawa* before they were sacrificed, but the women were not. Both wear many necklaces and bracelets; on the woman's shoulder there is an ornament made of perforated shells that rang like bells during dances.

Detail from the collective tomb of Roy Mata

The hero is in the centre, richly adorned: necklaces with pendants made of whale teeth and shells, three bracelets of artificially curved boar's tusks, armbands embroidered with beads shaped from the cones of shellfish. All these ornaments had a symbolic value. He is also wearing two ornaments associated with dancing made of perforated seashells.

Central area of the collective tomb of Roy Mata

In the foreground, two couples from the second level of the burial. In the background, in front of the two large upright stones, the deep grave where the hero lay; a folded skeleton has been placed between his legs; a young woman lies stretched out at his feet; on his left there is a couple, on his right a single man: his *avati*, an official charged with keeping the peace around his master, both on earth and in the land of the dead.

Easter Island: a microcosm

The extraordinary statues of Easter Island have fascinated westerners ever since the 18th century. Today they are confirmed as the product of a lonely and isolated Polynesian community, cut off from the rest of the world.

Easter Island owes its name to the Dutch navigator Jacob Roggeveen, who discovered it on Easter Sunday in 1722. Lost in the immensity of the Pacific, 4,000km (2,500 miles) from the coast of Chile and 1,900km (1,190 miles) from the nearest Polynesian island, it has always amazed visitors with the number and size of its monuments. These contrast sharply with the austerity of its volcanic landscape, its small dimensions of 160 sq km (64 sq miles) and its scarce and destitute population. Many westerners thought that these works could not possibly have been produced by the islanders, and the most extravagant hypotheses have sometimes been put forward to explain their origin. More serious students have long stressed the futility of such theories. Archaeology has since confirmed the simple human reality of the prehistory of the Easter Islanders.

There are no longer any doubts as to the Polynesian rather than Amerindian origin of the first inhabitants of Easter Island. They were probably Puamotu of Marquesan origin who first established themselves, around the year AD500, on what was then a deserted island. Here they found conditions which were less favourable than those in the tropics: a cooler and windier climate impeded the cultivation of the food-providing plants they had taken along in their pirogues (dug-out canoes), as all Polynesians did when setting off to discover new lands. The breadfruit plant and the coconut palm, for instance, could not bear fruit on the island; but they succeeded in acclimatizing the banana palm, the yam, the taro and other useful tropical plants by devoting particular care and attention to them. The island was then wooded, as shown by recent pollen analyses, but when Roggeveen arrived only a few trees were left, and shortly afterwards only a few stunted shrubs. Man had exploited these resources more quickly than nature could replace them. This decline of the habitat explains that of the island's people during the last years of its prehistory. A mystery has therefore been cleared up: there was no shortage of wood for the transport and erection of gigantic statues, nor were the tough bark ropes lacking which would have made the operation easier.

These famous statues, the *moai*, are giant images without lower limbs, sculpted out of the tufa of the volcano Rano Raraku. Three hundred of them have been left unfinished, their faces to the sky, and only partially separated from the underlying rock. Seventy other completed statues stand at the foot of the volcano and inside its crater. Most of these were meant to be transported across the island and placed on the platform of a ceremonial centre, or *ahu*. The *moai* would then receive their finishing touches on the spot in order to represent an ancestor: sockets would be hollowed for the eyes, cut out of white coral and with a moveable iris of red tufa; the body would be incised to indicate a belt or tattoos, and sometimes red and white paint would be added. The head often bore a headdress, a huge cylinder weighing several tons, cut from the reddish-brown tufa of another volcano, the Puna Pau. The platforms of some hundred *ahu*, generally built on the shore, thus contained one or several statues in a row (up to 15), their backs to the sea and their faces towards the court of the sanctuary. Their average height is between 4 and 5m (13–16ft), the smallest being some 2m (6.6ft) high, the largest 9.80m (32.3ft), or 11.50m (38ft) with the cylindrical headdress. The smallest of these *moai* are also the oldest, dating back to the beginning of the 10th century AD. Other, isolated statues of a different style that somewhat resembles a type found elsewhere in eastern Polynesia, are probably even older, and some of these may date from the first days of the island's colonization. This also applies to some *ahu* without *moai*; their function has remained the same as that of other Polynesian monuments such as the *marae* of the Society Islands, the Marquesan *Tohua*, the *heiau* of Hawaii. Each social group erected its own monuments as a link with ancestors and an indication of their genealogy.

The architecture of the Easter Island *ahu*, and their statuary, developed their gigantic size through a process caused by cultural isolation. Indeed, it seems that Easter Island society as a whole developed without the influence of important external contributions. For example, certain technical innovations, such as the various types of adze found in eastern Polynesia, never reached Easter Island. Such isolation can be explained by the island's geographical position, as well as by the fact that the inhabitants found it impossible to maintain, as elsewhere in the Pacific, inter-island contacts with the rest of Polynesia. The first Europeans did not find any ocean-going pirogues on the island, but only a few frail vessels consisting of small planks expertly joined; wood for boat-building was lacking, as it was for the construction of dwellings. The Europeans did not find solidly built houses, but simple huts made of branches. The more elaborate were long and narrow, with a stone foundation consisting of square blocks aligned end to end, and with a perforation to hold frail hoops for the roofing. Other shelters were built exclusively of stone, and the numerous caves on the island had been adapted to be used as dwellings.

Cult of the bird-man
At the end of the 17th century, the sculptors of Rano Raraku ceased work and the peoples of the island began a long period of internal warfare. The *moai* were cast off their pedestals one after the other, and in a way that broke them in the fall. When Cook sailed past the island in 1774 the spectacle was already so amazing that Forster, the naturalist of the expedition, assumed it was the consequence of a volcanic cataclysm. In 1866 not one statue was left standing on the *ahu*, which were also partly in ruins. During these decades of tribal warfare, the cult of the bird-man developed in the ceremonial village of Orongo, built on the clay of the crater of Rano Kau, on top of a cliff which plunges into the sea more than 200m (660ft) below. The village consists of an *ahu* surmounted by one *moai*, 47 stone huts with turf-covered corbelled roofs, and a remarkable series of rock carvings depicting the great god Makemake and the bird-man. Opposite the site are three small islands where terns come to nest in the early spring. A large crowd would then gather at Orongo. The main warlords would send one of their servants to the largest of the islands to watch, sometimes for weeks on end, for the arrival of the birds and the beginning of the breeding. The first to bring back one of these eggs, symbols of fertility, would earn his master the title of bird-man of the island for a year. The religious, political and economic powers attached to the title did not stop the continuation of the wars or the disintegration of the island's society. The islanders did not succeed in maintaining the balance between the resources of the environment and their demographical expansion, a balance which many Polynesians managed to attain in order to survive. Cut off within their island with its unfavourable climate, and no longer capable of leaving it, they reached a stage of overpopulation which led to two centuries of famine and war after more than 1,000 years of relative prosperity and of technical and artistic achievements unparalleled elsewhere.

Te Pito Te Kura *ahu* in La Pérouse Bay

This ruined monument was still intact when visited by sailors in 1786. Paro, as its *moai* was called, was deliberately thrown off its pedestal during one of the many tribal wars that shook the island for over a century. It broke as it fell, and the headdress of red tufa (in the foreground) was hurled forward a few metres.

Some of the 70 statues standing on the slopes of Rano Raraku volcano

Some of these statues were waiting to be finished on site before being moved to one of the island's *ahu*, where they represented ancestors. Others may have been intended to remain beside the quarry; excavations have shown that their bases were resting on paved platforms. All have gradually been fossilized by sediments issuing from the sloping side of the volcano. Only the upper part stands above ground, measuring 5 to 6m (16–19ft) here, and representing barely half the total height. The largest of these *moai*, which had not been finished, is nearly 20m (66ft) tall and, once completed, would have weighed some 300 tonnes . . . It would probably have remained on site!

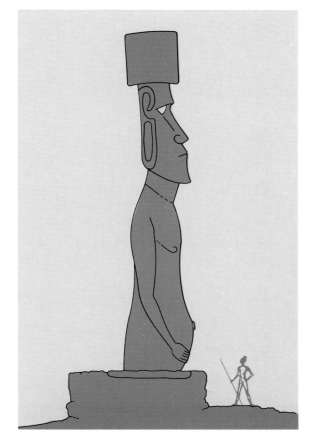

Te Pito Te Kura *moai*

The Te Pito Te Kura *moai* (see opposite page, right), as reconstructed in a drawing by the archaeologist C.S. Smith. It is 9m 80cm (32.3ft) high and its estimated weight is 80 tonnes. With a headdress of 2m 40cm (7.9ft) diameter and 1m 80cm (5.9ft) high, it is the largest *moai* to have been erected on an *ahu*.

Nau Nau *ahu* in the course of study and restoration 1978

The *ahu* was built in Anakena Bay where, according to tradition, chief Hotu Matua, the first to colonize the island, disembarked. Six *moai* with their backs turned to the sea stand on the *ahu*, one of which could not be completely restored. Four have red tufa headdresses of various shapes. Two ramps, regularly paved with large cobblestones and edged with a line of carefully squared stones, lead up to the central platform. The whole group overlooks a huge area where people gathered for communal, social and religious activities.

Akivi *ahu* and its seven *moai*

One of the very few *ahu* built in the interior of the island, 2km (1.2) miles from the west coast, this was studied and restored in 1961. Seven very eroded *moai* stand on a platform, which is extended by two side wings. The length of the whole structure is 80m (263ft). A paved ramp leads to it, with a small court in front and an earth bank. Unlike many other *moai*, they do not appear ever to have had red tufa headdresses.

The eye of the Nau Nau *moai* at Anakena

In 1978 during work on the Nau Nau *ahu*, archaeologists uncovered the debris of what proved to be an eye. The sclera, or white of the eye, is made of white coral, and the iris consists of a disk of red tufa. The iris was placed in a slit cut at the back of the sclera, but did not move. The whole eye was inserted into a socket that had been hollowed out for this purpose when the statue was being finished. Further discoveries showed that most of the *moai* standing on all *ahu* were provided with eyes.

The ceremonial village of Orongo

Of basically oval design, similar to ordinary houses on the island, the buildings at Orongo are made of slabs of lava, with an earth-covered corbelled roof. The entrances are low and narrow and the inside height is less than 1m 50cm (5ft). These buildings were in use for the several weeks of the festival devoted to the cult of the bird-man. The inside surfaces of the slabs used as foundations were decorated with drawings and paintings, many of which have since disappeared, including birds, ritual objects (such as canoe paddles) and even European boats.

The three islets and rock carvings on the Orongo site

The foreground shows one of the many portrayals of the bird-man incised on the rocks of the ceremonial village of Orongo, at the place called Mata Na Rau. The site overlooks three tiny islands, and on the largest, Motu Nui, a watch was kept in spring for the start of the terns' egg-laying season. Whoever gained possession of the first egg enabled his master to become bird-man, and the foremost chief on the island for a whole year.

Modern period:
the archaeological background

The "archaeology of the present" may seem a contradiction in terms:
but the techniques used by archaeologists can be applied
to the buildings, artifacts and rituals of our own culture with illuminating
results. Ultimately the science tells us about ourselves.

Can the research methods developed for the study of older times be applied to the modern and contemporary period? The development of industrial archaeology, and the recent appearance of a "modern archaeology" conceived as a systematic study of "pieces of work" manufactured in the 19th and 20th centuries, would seem to provide the answer. Never has there been so much talk of modern, or more accurately contemporary, archaeology, if we accept the terminology of the historians according to which "modern times" (16th–18th century) precede the "contemporary" period.

But in both cases is it still archaeology we are talking about? The success of these new expressions, due largely to their paradoxical nature, may make us forget that there are other kinds of research, undeniably archaeological, which are much less talked about. Any consideration of modern and contemporary archaeology leads to an examination into the nature of archaeology, for the definition of that science becomes increasingly problematical as our own time approaches.

Archaeological research has two facets. It deals with material remains (objects or buildings), which distinguishes it from research in archives or libraries using written or illustrated sources. Its aim is to discover such remains and make them "legible" by restoring them to their original state, establishing their date and place of origin, and fitting them into an overall group and a series. By so doing it contributes new and specific elements of information to history and the history of art.

Understood as a method of research dealing with the material products of human activity, either buried or still visible, archaeology has its place in the study of the modern and contemporary world, but its importance in the formation of historical knowledge is necessarily less, because information obtained from written or illustrated documentation carries far more weight than what is learnt from the direct study of objects and buildings. The industrial techniques of antiquity, for example, are known through archaeology; in the Middle Ages and modern period they are known through

a combination of illustrated representations, texts and archaeological data; in the industrial age, they are basically known through technical descriptions. There is no need to dismantle an electricity generator from the 1880s, or even to see it, in order to understand it. There are books which explain how it was constructed and how it worked.

Industrial architecture

The last observation forces us to reconsider the notion of industrial archaeology as it is understood today. Archaeological research, while applicable to machines made by craftsmen, cannot concern itself with machines built through the application of scientific knowledge, all the elements of which are known from books and assembly diagrams. Nor is it valid for the study of factories when their buildings are easily legible and their history well documented by the archives. So research dealing with industrial architecture and the instruments of production is only partly archaeological. It should not be carried on under a misleading label, the principal merit of which was undoubtedly to legitimize a new field of study by an implicit reference to antiquity.

The modern (actually contemporary) archaeology conceived by Philippe Bruneau, a specialist in Greek civilization who later took an interest in the contemporary world, has a much wider objective, because its field of study covers everything manufactured in the 19th and 20th centuries. The idea is to apply the methods of archaeology to these works, which historians tend to disregard and ethnologists neglect because they are mainly concerned with traditional societies. This field of research is new and exciting, but is it always archaeology? An inquiry into the current cult of St Anthony by the observation of statues standing in the churches of Paris has an archaeological nature, because it implies an inventory made on the spot and the careful observation of material objects. A study of posters for the electoral campaign of 1981, dealing with published documents, would seem to be a historical

Archaeology and architectural history: excavations at the Louvre, Paris, in 1964

The walls discovered in front of the east façade of the Louvre during the digging of the ditch have revealed a very abrupt change of plan between 1661 and 1673. The base apparent in the foreground belongs to the façade planned by Le Vau, begun in 1661 and abandoned in 1664. In 1667 work began on the present façade without pause to demolish the old base. A ditch was anticipated then, because this new façade also consisted of a matched base. Hardly was the colonnade finished (1673) than the work was abandoned, the king then being concerned entirely with Versailles, and it was decided to cut any losses by covering the bases with earth, and discarding the ditch which was not dug until three centuries later.

Should these walls have been preserved, constituting as they do valuable evidence of the doubts of Colbert and the youthful Louis XIV? Or should they have been destroyed to carry out the 1667 plan, and so give full meaning to the colonnade, a monarchic monument, and masterpiece of architecture in the French style? Not without reason, André Malraux decided that in this case the requirements of monumental architecture should prevail over archaeological interests.

Detail of the château of Chambord

Linkage of one tower of the keep (right) with the west gallery built some 15 years later. Archaeological research has shown that the addition of a floor of the gallery was anticipated from the start, since the first stage of the wall was built at the same time as the keep (the capital to the right of the window is alone similar to those of the keep). On the other hand, the second floor was not envisaged in this form, for the cornice and the roof abut on a capital that was already carved.

exercise, using a pattern of specialized reading, of an iconographical type (both subjects are discussed in the second number of the French journal, *Revue d'archéologie moderne et générale*). So the problem becomes one of definition. Bruneau calls the examination of posters archaeological because he looks on archaeology as an autonomous discipline, having as its aim the study of all "works" including images (but why not books, too, which are also manufactured?), whereas many others look on it as a method of research fundamentally different from documentary research, although always associated with it, in the process of building up historical knowledge.

The example of the bathroom, an excellent subject for "modern archaeology", helps to illuminate this point. To study the recent development of this room, and thereby the changing image of the body in present-day civilization, will experts proceed, as with classical baths, by studying remains or collecting bathtubs? The observation of some examples preserved on the site will doubtless be useful, but the inquiry will mainly concentrate on documentary evidence – manufacturers' catalogues and magazine advertising – which tell us all about the material used and its symbolic value. Thus, in most cases, contemporary inquiry will be documentary; it will not concentrate on things, but on their representation. The role of archaeology can only decrease in a civilization of the written word and the image where everything ultimately tends to find a place in the archives. In these circumstances, what place should we reserve for archaeology in the study of the modern and contemporary world?

Architecture offers one of the first such fields of application. Archaeological analysis is required when a building is not well known through written and illustrated documentation – a common phenomenon, especially in the 16th and 17th centuries. To explain the transformation of a building, restore its original appearance and discover the original plan, it is necessary to observe the thickness of the walls, the joints of the masonry, the assembly of timberwork, the moulding of doors and windows, and to distinguish the often barely visible traces of the successive stages of construction. New methods (dendrochronology*, thermoluminescence*), still little used due to lack of specialized laboratories, may now help the investigator by indicating the date of the wood and bricks used in a building. But we must not expect miracles from these techniques, for "objective" data are never conclusive in themselves (re-used materials, for example, may be older than the building). Analogous to a police inquiry or a medical diagnosis, because like them it is founded on the observation of signs, architectural analysis is the most common form of modern archaeology – and the least talked about. To recall its importance in the study of monuments, as well as in the study of the most commonplace dwelling, we have somewhat provocatively placed at the head of these pages the photograph of a building which seems exclusively to come within the province of the history of art. The château of Chambord in France has a complicated history which can only be reconstructed by archaeological observation, because the stages of construction and the changes in method discernible in the stone are not mentioned in any text. In order to understand this monument and proceed subsequently to a stylistic analysis, the architectural historian must first be an archaeologist.

Recovering destroyed buildings

Another more recent type of modern archaeology is excavation aimed at recovering a building that has been destroyed. This kind of research is highly developed in England, where many of the great 16th century castles have disappeared, and in Hungary where the Turkish invasion wiped out nearly all the Renaissance monuments. In certain cases, partial reconstructions using fragments found in the ground can even give an exact idea of the destroyed building. Such discoveries make it possible to renew the history of architecture, especially when they reveal major edifices like Nonsuch (England) or Višegrad (Hungary). So far this does not seem to have been understood in France, where the first "modern" monumental excavation – of Saint-Leger, one of Henri II's châteaux built by Philibert Delorme – was carried out amid general indifference.

Fortunately, the situation with regard to urban archaeology seems more favourable. The excavation of the soil in towns has in fact led to an increase in the excavation of sites where "modern" remains are not the least numerous. The methodical excavation of the Cour Napoléon of the Louvre, Paris, will thus contribute to a better knowledge of the objects used by Parisians in their daily life from the Middle Ages to the 19th century. Nevertheless, it will be noted that this urban archaeology remains essentially an archaeology of the terrain, whereas it could be given a wider scope and include the study of buildings – all the more necessary as the old districts change very quickly. Archaeological analysis should precede "restorations" which often efface every trace of the original internal layout. But houses, for the moment, only interest historians of architecture, who are looked on as art historians. At all events, archaeology of the terrain will never play a very important part in the most recent periods, because a good part of the "works" made by man still exist. Also the investigation of buildings or objects that are new or little known often assumes the form of an inventory which we look on as a sort of "above-ground" excavation.

Drawing up a catalogue of the altar screens or windmills in a region, researching tools or headgear, studying a canton systematically, as the *Inventaire général* does in France, are activities of an archaeological kind because they always involve discovering and analysing material remains in order to write history afterwards. Of course, no one dreams of designating as archaeologists those historians, ethnologists and art historians who call on archaeological inquiry for new information, whereas we do call the historian or art historian who works on an ancient site an archaeologist; but the imprecision of the vocabulary only proves that it is impossible to identify a type of research with a body of researchers.

So modern and contemporary archaeology exhibit specific characteristics. The large amount of evidence preserved diminishes the importance of excavation, and the abundance of written or illustrated documentation makes the study of "things" less necessary. Nevertheless, it does not differ basically from ancient or medieval archaeology, for like them it is concerned with existing or destroyed buildings, with visible or buried objects. Much confusion and many spurious problems would doubtless be avoided if people stopped equating archaeology with excavation, or confusing it with historical works based on the study of material remains. These two antithetical errors are in danger of making us forget the unity of a discipline which employs widely differing methods, but always aims at the same goal – finding "works" and making them legible for history.

Castles of the 16th century

The castle was a key image of the European feudal age; its later role in the 16th century has proved a challenge for archaeologists due to widespread destruction of the main evidence—the buildings themselves.

For many, if not most, Renaissance castles, archaeological research is the only way to acquire and extend information on this difficult branch of architectural history. The 16th century castle very often had a short life: 30 years for the residences of King Matthias Corvinus before destruction by the Turks in 1541, 130 years for the royal castles of Nonsuch, England, and Saint-Léger-en-Yvelines, France. Careful descriptions or detailed plans of these and many others no longer exist. And the destruction, when it came, tended to be thorough. Many Renaissance castles have literally disappeared.

In France, at Verger and Limours, the buildings have vanished without trace. In Hungary, at Buda and Višegrad, the so-called Turkish town has absorbed a group of admirable buildings. The siting of these edifices is often uncertain, if not forgotten: it would be difficult to decide now on the exact location of the grotto pavilion of Montceaux castle, built by Philibert Delorme in 1557. And, once erased from the countryside, the 16th century castle is difficult to reconstruct from the usual documents: pictorial representations are vague or false, written descriptions are ambiguous, archives are either fragmentary or compiled in such a way as to be utterly inadequate for the purposes of reconstruction. Moreover, castles that have been preserved seldom survive through the centuries without undergoing modifications that considerably alter their original character.

Until recently, this situation was accepted with resignation, and even experts assumed that a vanished castle was one about which nothing could be learnt. As for surviving buildings, only their present appearance was assessed, without any attempt to discover the stages of transformation, or the modification of the original design. This attitude persisted in spite of important discoveries, such as that of the staircase of the oval court at Fontainebleau in 1930, which provided new information on the original spatial organization of what was once the heart of the palace of François I.

However, these discoveries were chance affairs that could not be regarded as a development of archaeology; on the contrary, their infrequent occurrence demonstrates how little even the experts concerned themselves with this approach. But after 1955 the situation radically changed, with limited but carefully controlled fieldwork showing how valuable archaeological excavations could be to the history of architecture. Historians now no longer wait for chance to reveal useful fragments, but initiate discoveries themselves, organizing research programmes in which archaeology is essential.

In the countries concerned, namely those of central and western Europe, the problems, methods and results vary. In Hungary, considerable progress has been made since the chance discoveries of the 1930s. These included the villa of King Matthias at Nyèk in the suburbs of Budapest, the royal palace at Višegrad on the Danube, and the archbishop's palace and the murals in the chapel at Esztergom, north of the capital. These finds suddenly revealed to the people a side of their history that had been lost. After 1950, multidisciplinary groups grew up, inspired by the exceptional interest of the pre-war finds. These groups set out to explore systematically the locations which, before the Turkish invasion, had been the sites of royal and princely residences.

The lost palaces of King Henry VIII

In England, an analogous project is under way. In 1955 the authors of the monumental *History of the King's Works* ran into the difficult question of the residences of Henry VIII. The most famous of these, Nonsuch, was destroyed at the end of the 17th century, and only survives in inadequate general views. The need to examine new sources such as the sites of vanished castles emerged from questions raised by historians; and between 1969 and 1975 eight areas were marked out for fieldwork, including some in towns (for instance Bridewell Palace, London). These were established with exemplary speed because all the preliminary questions had been precisely drawn up, and the work was prepared with care and entrusted to teams of proven ability. Archaeology of the historic period is a recognized discipline in England with its own specialists, readers and publications, such as the *Journal of Post-Medieval Archaeology*. This research programme has delivered results beyond all expectations: palaces that were almost unknown are now familiar in terms of detailed layouts, construction materials, decoration of interior walls and floors, and even the plumbing systems and foundation-laying methods (which are of course hidden in preserved buildings).

In France the situation is quite different. Archaeological research in this field is still at a very early stage, limited, disorganized and hampered by general indifference. Sixteenth century castles are not included in the official guidelines for excavations, and there are many obstacles to opening proper working sites and organizing research in a systematic way. For instance, the discovery of the site of Saint-Léger castle built by Philibert Delorme, one of the most famous architects of the 16th century, has met with little enthusiasm. Work was restricted to preliminary probing, and all hopes of bringing to light the precious fragments of mouldings had to be abandoned.

Fieldwork is very rarely organized on the sites of Renaissance castles; when it is, voluntary workers have few means and less experience. There are no combined projects, no overall organization for an excavation programme to fill in the worst gaps and make up for the disappearance of key buildings such as the castles of Verger, Bury, Verneuil and Charleval.

Italy and Great Britain have dealt with the problem differently and with more success. In these countries information gathered on the site is regarded as essential, so that the archaeology of buildings complements that of the soil. In Italy, contemporary sources relating to the north facade of the Palazzo del Té, Mantua, revealed after careful study the existence of a small building, a country retreat designed by Giulio Romano to Federico Gonzaga's commission, and later incorporated when still hardly finished into a new project for a large palace. Under the 18th century plastering, researchers uncovered the original bosses, which were three times as thick than the dubiously reconstructed covering. The characteristics of Romano's style thus emerged through scholarly deduction, from the inaccurate restoration.

Archaeological revelations

Architectural analysis of this kind relies on traditional archaeological procedures. Recently, highly technical methods, such as thermoluminescence*, have also been applied. The structures of four Palladian villas have been examined by these means and their history has consequently been rewritten. The timetable of the fieldwork, as well as the siting and dating of pre-existing buildings incorporated in new structures, and also later transformations and additions, are by now clearly established. Archeometry* has speeded up the transformation of the history of architecture by replacing the traditional dating methods based on stylistic differences. The detailed analysis of structures (or tectography, to use the neologism coined by M. Kubelik and J. Tuttle) provides new guidelines for the work of both restorer and historian. The original state of the building can then be seen, and also the conditions that prevailed when the architect began work—usually a task of modernizing an earlier structure rather than starting from the beginning. Thus the historian often needs archaeological research if he is to rid himself of his preconceived ideas about grand projects springing, fully realized, from the architect's imagination.

Hungarian archaeology and the castles of the First Renaissance

Archaeology has contributed to the national history of Hungary by enabling the restoration of buildings with the pieces that have been found. Thus at Višegrad, the summer residence of King Matthias Corvinus (left), the square arcaded courtyard surrounding the fountain of Hercules (1484) has been reassembled. The mixture of Gothic and Renaissance styles is characteristic. The red marble basin of the fountain is a product of the studio of the Italian sculptor, Giovanni Dalmata. Balusters (right) from Nyèk (1488–90) are attributed to the same artist and draw on a pattern used by Brunelleschi. Thus excavations have revealed the role played by Italian artists who were employed in large numbers on royal building sites in Hungary. Budapesti Történeti Museum.

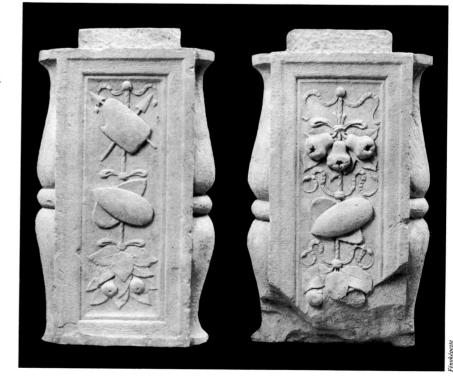

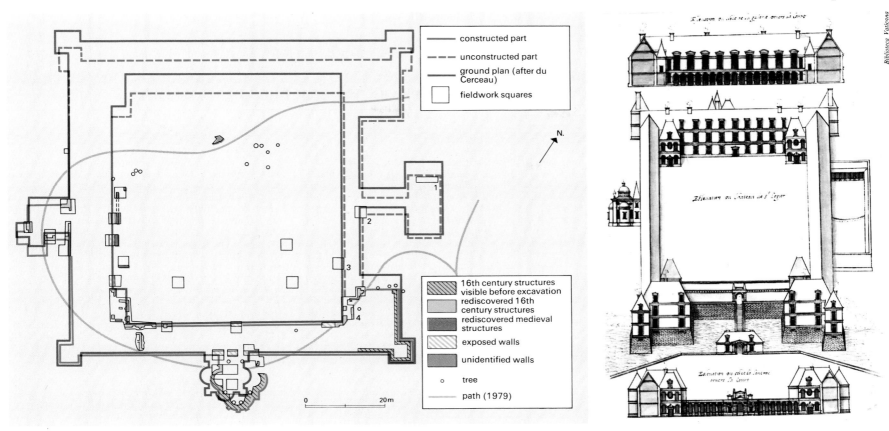

Biblioteca Vaticana

The royal castle of Saint-Léger-en-Yvelines

The French King Henri II's castle, built by Philibert Delorme (1548–59) and demolished in 1668, used to be entirely unknown until drawings rediscovered in 1956 revealed its aspect. In 1978 an analysis of early maps enabled the site to be located, and excavations became possible. Of the four wings which were drawn up, only the west and south wings were built. The construction of the east wing was planned (see hole stones, no. 4), but the work was not carried out (see probes, nos. 1, 2 and 3). The castle was built of brick and stone, as demonstrated by the remains. Excavations have enabled an accurate reconstruction to be made of the gallery wing and of the corner pavilions, which were of a skilful design creating a remarkable organization of space in the interior. These discoveries represent an original contribution to our knowledge of Delorme's work and enable us to make a detailed assessment of the drawings of Jacques Androuet du Cerceau (above, right), which are broadly correct, but with mistakes of detail; Biblioteca Apostolica Vaticana, Barberini manuscript, folio 5. Excavations supervised by J. Blécon and F. Boudon.

The royal palace of Nonsuch, Surrey

Nonsuch, begun in 1538 on the 13th anniversary of Henry VIII's reign, was a building without parallel, or "none such", as indicated in the watercolour drawing by Joris Hoefnagel, 1568 (private collection): a huge palace, flanked by domed polygonal towers, it carried a decoration of sculptured panels running right round it. This remarkable building seems to have quickly fallen into ruin, and was demolished in 1682. Excavations (1959–60) have shown the accuracy of this illustration; they have also supplied the exact plan of the palace (below, right), which was arranged round two ceremonial courtyards; the kitchen courtyard was equipped with a remarkable network of pipes. The 100,000 fragments collected from it have enabled archaeologists to reconstitute the structure of the external decoration, which covered an area of 2,044 sq m (22,001 sq ft). Above the ground floor, which was built of masonry, the walls consisted of a timber frame covered with panels of stucco with high relief moulding, 136 × 89cm (54 × 35in), set in frames of engraved, gilded slates. The decorative scheme featured mythological subjects; but very few panels could be restored. They are the work of Nicholas Bellin of Modena, and show the influence of Rosso and the Fontainebleau School. By kind permission of Martin Biddle.

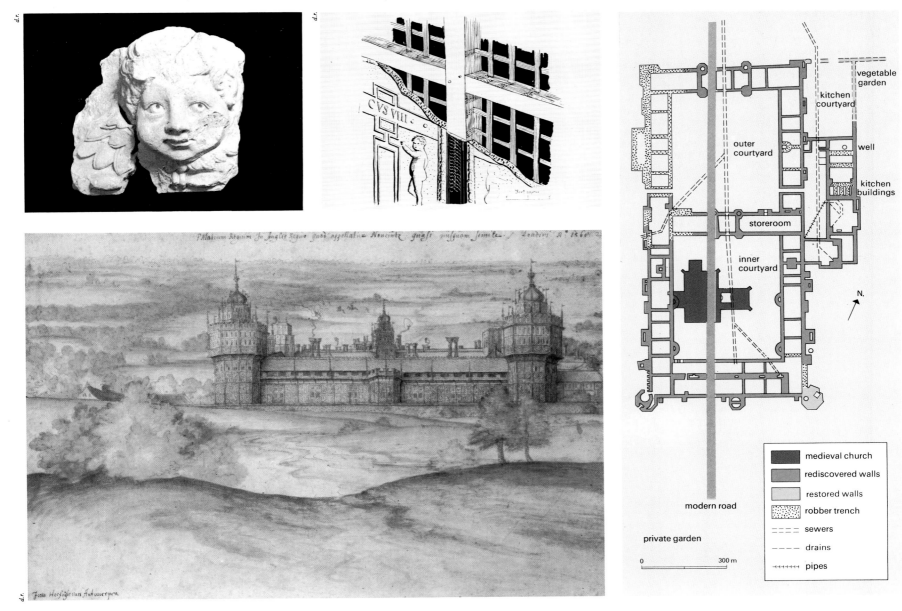

387

Archaeology and East-West exchange

Spices, tea, textiles, porcelain, ceramics and works of art from the East; precision instruments, clocks, forts and firearms from the West: the post-Renaissance material interchange between Europe and the Orient is a fertile area for modern archaeologists.

Seen as a means of revealing history by uncovering its remains, archaeology seems to apply solely to remote and enigmatic civilizations, so much so that many people associate it exclusively with prehistory. Yet its methods can also throw light on more recent historical events, and even when a great deal is known about these from literary sources it can lead to their reconsideration. Such is the case with trade between Europe and Asia since the Renaissance.

Material traces of Asian exports to the West are hard to find, for Europe mainly bought luxury consumer goods. Moreover, the multiplicity of intermediaries makes the study of trade difficult, as we see from three examples illustrating this complexity: gunpowder, the compass and paper. The Chinese origin of all three is well known, but it has not been possible to reconstruct chronologically their exact migration. However far back we go, spices were always the most sought-after products (and the most costly) from the Far East. But we have only the classical texts from which to guess at the scope of this trade, because pepper and cardamom have not survived, nor was it possible to transplant them. There was no cessation of the trade after the fall of Rome; and it persisted throughout the Middle Ages, especially in the case of pepper. The reduction or suppression of the spice trade as a consequence of the conquest of Constantinople by the Turks (1453), and the Venetian monopoly, drove the Portuguese, then the Dutch, and finally the British, to sail round Africa and found their own Asiatic warehouses. Unfortunately, here again, apart from the texts (and the influence of the spice trade on vocabulary), no trace of this impressive flow of imports remains, except for the indirect effects it had on the techniques of navigation and commerce.

Eastern textiles were imported on an equally large scale, but the material evidence of the trade is just as difficult to grasp, except for a few shreds of Chinese and Indian fabrics uncovered in the Near East, and from the imitation of motifs. Silk reached Constantinople, where it was adapted to local conditions and became the object of a European industry. The same was the case with Indian textiles, which aroused tremendous interest in Europe. There was much enthusiasm in the 17th century for the use of painted linen as a substitute for tapestry, and cashmere became a mark of social status at the same time. Like silk, these cloths were imitated—cloth was printed in Indian style—and eventually European industries went to Asia to compete with the craftsmen who had originated the designs, and often caused their ruin. The same thing also happened with Chinese decorative paper, which was first copied and then eliminated.

Pottery has survived, and it is this, especially Chinese porcelain, which has constituted the prime example of Euro-Asian exchanges. Indeed, the European market had such an effect that the term celadon, used to designate enamelled stoneware decorated with the green ribbons of the French shepherd hero of D'Urfé's *Astrée*, was to be adopted by the Chinese themselves. From the mid-16th century Chinese "blue and white" ware was to enjoy a great success in Europe. During the first phase of this trade, Europe had forms and designs to its own liking made in China, and the popularity of this pottery (an economical substitute for silverware) was such that it was constantly imitated, from Delft to Augsburg, from Dresden to Sèvres. The history of the stages of development from soft pastes to genuine porcelain, once kaolin had been identified, are well known; but the Europeanization of Chinese pottery could still be better documented, for example through the analysis of forms. It seems possible that certain Chinese models were adopted by the West, for example cups with attached saucers, tea-pots, and baluster-stem vases.

Oriental inspiration in European art

The imitation of eastern techniques, materials, forms and designs is an important chapter in the history of European art over a long period. Rembrandt himself copied Mogul miniatures. In architecture and furniture there was a strongly marked taste for Chinoiserie. From the 17th century, japanned panels were imported to decorate furniture, and their success led to the invention of a substitute—Martin's varnish. But beyond this exoticism, we can see the influence of Chinese painting in lacquered panels, and of cabinet-making in subtler treatment of volume in furniture. We know that Chippendale deliberately imitated Chinese pieces, and it is also likely that the colour schemes of certain paintings were inspired by colour schemes in Indian fabrics. In the *Deux Soeurs* by Chassériau or *Mme de Senonnes* by Ingres, it is obvious that the sitters' Indian cashmere garments determined the chromatic scheme of the painting. Finally, of course, we can see the effect of the discovery of Japanese engraving on the Impressionists and the School of Pont-Aven. An archaeological approach could usefully show that Eastern influence was more important than it once seemed in the fields of technique and aesthetics, just as it was significant in the field of ideas as Orientalism grew.

It is generally believed that Europe's material influence on Asia was infinitely greater than Asia's on Europe. But this is wholly true only from the end of the 18th century. When the Europeans first sailed into the Asian seas, they were at about the same technical level as India and China, and in any case the cultures remained completely distinct. Commercially speaking, their influence was barely perceptible; they were customers for natural or everyday manufactured products, and they paid for them with precious metals. For a long time, this resulted in a very adverse balance of trade for the Europeans. Politically, their commercial stations and even their first conquests were, in Eastern eyes, no more than insignificant episodes in the long history of invasions that had shaped the fate of India and China for 2,000 years. And, despite their zeal, the missionaries too had a miniscule effect in comparison with the tremendous success of Buddhism and, later, Islam.

Nevertheless, a closer look at the material evidence of the European contribution reveals the outlines of a definite evolution. One of the key contributions to this was the gradual spread of applied mathematics to the measurement of time and space, through the use of precision instruments. Both India and China had developed excellent systems of astronomy which were effective so far as they went. But Europe introduced the telescope, instruments for measuring arcs, clocks and sighting apparatus which made it possible to include time and space in a logical reference system. The development of calculation methods, the production of good maps, and the accuracy of navigation had a marked effect on knowledge and administration of territory and the relations between states. Very remarkable monuments to this Western penetration still exist, which deserve the study of comparative archaeology. They are the great observatories built on the advice of Europeans, from the astronomical office of Peking, reformed by Matteo Ricci from 1601, to the observatory of Jaipur built in 1728. For two centuries, the watch and the clock fascinated and were much coveted by the whole of Asia.

Westerners in Eastern art

Western influence on Asian arts has been studied in detail, especially in China where it began very early and took hold in particular through the contribution of Father Castiglione (who translated Andrea Pozzo's *Perspective*, 1729, into Chinese). This was also true in India where Western art had an effect on miniaturists both in portraiture and landscape, influences which decisively affected the subsequent development of figurative art. Asia partially adapted its court art to Western fashions, but it did not adopt European techniques, forms or decorative design for its furniture, utensils or objects of everyday life, even though it made such objects for export. Meanwhile, the religious arts systematically represented Europeans as "temple guardians"—the latter being traditionally depicted as repulsive and hideous figures. Incidentally, Eastern artists liked painting the invaders, but only because of their exoticism, as if they were some strange kind of animal. So Asia depicted the West with the curiosity of the ethnographer, but kept it at a distance, whereas Europe made increasing use of Chinese inspiration, even in its most banal objects, though it was used in a caricatural way and absolutely without realism.

European models made a deep impression on Asia in one field, that of architecture—or more accurately in the new cities which became seats of power. Of course, China, India and the kingdoms of Southeast Asia had, for centuries, developed enormous fortified cities, centres of power and religion ensuring the stability of the universe and the favour of the gods, but the Europeans were to create a new type of city, better defended, more effective and above all economic, and regulated by different social groups. The first of these were ports, and until this time not one of the great historical capitals of Asia had been built by the sea.

Malacca is an excellent example with its fort built by Albuquerque in 1511, and its Church of St Francis Xavier, the fortress of the Dutch, who governed the town from 1614 to 1795, and the city of bungalows of the British who finally took over. The canals and streets of Malacca were lined with narrow Dutch-gabled houses, decorated with Chinese faience tiles imitating those of Delft (themselves copied from China!), with a shop on the ground floor, storerooms around the court and the women's quarters above. They represent fascinating models, variations of which can be seen to follow throughout Asia. From former Batavia, Jakarta still has its canals and massive Dutch houses. In 1570 Manila was a Spanish town. In the Philippines (a unique case), a religious art developed, which was inspired by Spain and Italy but used local materials and designs; for instance, the village churches had bamboo organs. India offers the greatest variety of towns influenced by the Europeans, from the Portuguese cities of Goa and Damian to Tranquebar, reconstructed by the Danes in 1777. Pondicherry was rebuilt from 1785 in post-Louis XV colonial style, and Madras and Calcutta were laid out at the end of the century following superb neoclassical plans. Here even before colonial power was fully established, the architectural settings for that power had been constructed.

European military techniques too had great succss. Firearms and fortifications had already reached the Indies with the Turks who had developed them while fighting against the Franks. Forts in the manner of Vauban predominated. One of the most remarkable but little-known complexes was built in Vietnam by the French, who helped Gia Long to reconquer his throne at the end of the 18th century. All over the East mercenaries fired cannon, organized arsenals and instructed armies. An archaeological study of firearms in Asia would be fascinating, especially of the cannons copied from European models, with their inscriptions and coats of arms included. Engineers in the service of local potentates began to design factories, bridges, ports, silos and irrigation systems which initiated the technical transformation of the country's methods of production.

The buildings of the new masters, partly based on the old palaces, and using local skills, retained their best features. But they were no longer the residences of hereditary chiefs supported by religion. They were the edifices of secular civilian masters who were connected with the army, together with clerks, lawyers, manufacturers and money-lenders, a group native in composition but summoned to play a new role and henceforth to be in close communication with the foreign world. Next, previously unknown building types appeared: assembly halls for the new bourgeoisie, law courts, clerical offices, schools, barracks, hospitals and, finally, banks and industrial complexes.

More detailed knowledge of material exchanges between Europe and Asia up to the end of the 18th century would establish a comparison full of contrasts. On the one hand, Europe was profoundly but almost unconsciously influenced by Asia. Spices left their mark on its dietary habits, and some other customs developed as a result, for example Europeans began to drink tea. Crockery, silk, printed cloths and paper were heavily in demand in the West, which led at first to a drain on monetary resources and then to big industries. These objects introduced an "Orientalizing" tendency into Europe design, directly or by imitation. Nevertheless, neither ideas nor aesthetics were deeply marked by these fashions, and scientific contributions from the East were non-existent. Knowledge of Asia remained the province of a few aesthetes and orientalists. In some ways Asia got more out of the exchanges, especially in fields such as the organization of the state, trade, industry and the applied sciences, although there was no change in its diet, clothing, furniture or even the aesthetics of its everyday objects, and none in its philosophies and religions. Before it was opened up by Perry in 1853, Japan was the outstanding example of this resistance. However, Asia had received such a vigorous graft from the West, even if she was unconscious of it, that it was to change the continent completely, even before (or without) colonial domination.

"Europeans dining on a terrace", Indian painting in the Mogul style

European influence (probably from engravings) is obvious in the arrangement, the perspective and the costumes. But there are some mistakes: note the treatment of the feminine breasts. The landscape, the balustrade of openwork marble, the furniture, the tableware and the way of eating, as well as certain elements of the maid's costume, are native. The fusion of the two aesthetics is flexible and successful, and the result most attractive. Painting on canvas. British Museum, London.

Louix XV cabinet with Chinese panels

An exceptional example of the integration of a foreign art. The Chinese oblique lines are filled out by the curves of a French piece of furniture. The plant motifs of the side panel extend into the interlacings of the bronze fittings. The gold and black harmony of the panels recurs in the gold of the bronze and the black lacquered wood. From the Château de Valençay. The Louvre, Paris.

Chinese earthenware dish in the form of a buffalo's head

The head is decorated with a romantic scene after drawings sent from Europe for this so-called "East India Company" porcelain. To Western eyes, the dish may seem to express its usual contents by its form, but represented in an "exotic" fashion. The romantic scene must have seemed out of place, but all the more amusing for that—Chien Lung porcelain, 1736–95. Private collection, Lisbon.

Street in Malacca, Malaysia

The houses of the 18th century and beginning of the 19th imitated Dutch types: narrow façades (the ground was expensive), shops at ground level, dwellings on the first storey protected from the climate by loggias, and facings of Chinese faience tiles imitating Delft tiles. The houses extended to the rear with courts containing storerooms. A canal fronted the street. Thus the Chinese adopted, adapted and improved the Dutch commercial city.

"Gola" granary, Patna, Bihar, India

Built by John Garstin (1752–1820) in 1784 to combat famine, the silo was filled by grain poured in from the top. Two spiral staircases enabled a continuous ascent and descent by the bearers. This was the only silo built and it was to remain unused, the first example of a technical approach to the problems of underdevelopment.

The European colonization of North America

American archaeologists have not only expanded our knowledge of the European colonizations of America; they have also developed admirably clear presentations of the material for a growing public.

The European presence in North America is a comparatively recent phenomenon. During the 16th century whalers or cod fishermen frequented Newfoundland and the St Lawrence, but it was not until the beginning of the 17th century that permanent settlements related to summer fishing were established, followed by a population, first of French and then of British. In 1604 Samuel Champlain wintered at St Croix in present-day Maine and in the following year he established present-day Annapolis (Nova Scotia) at Port Royal on the other side of the Bay of Fundy. In 1608 he sailed up the St Lawrence and founded Quebec, and from then on the French population of Acadia and the St Lawrence was to grow.

The English began to settle on the Atlantic coast from 1607 with the foundation of Jamestown in Virginia. Further north, various establishments which were to become large towns, such as Plymouth (1620) and Boston (1630), were created in Massachusetts. A number of other settlements gradually established themselves around Boston in the north and Virginia in the south, as well as points in between.

During the 17th century a marked imbalance appeared between the French and the British colonies, which were established along the Atlantic over a comparatively small area but with a much larger population. This situation and the consequences of the confrontation between France and England in Europe saw the beginning, in the late 17th century, of a struggle between the two mother countries in North America that lasted almost 100 years. It was not until the Treaty of Versailles, which put an end to the American War of Independence in 1783, that clashes between the two countries ceased on American soil. In the 18th century forts and fortified towns were established in the sectors where confrontation traditionally occurred: the mouth of the St Lawrence and Acadia, the valley of the St Lawrence, the river Richelieu south of New France towards Boston and New York, and the zone of the Great Lakes and the valleys of Ohio and Mississippi.

Archaeology of colonization

The archaeology of colonial sites in North America to a large extent consists of research into the history of colonization in the 16th and especially the 17th centuries, and study of the principal and earliest sites from those periods. It is also an archaeology which is often associated with the restoration and presentation to the public of the sites where England and France confronted each other in the 17th and particularly the 18th century. These two research areas predominated in both the United States and Canada until the 1960s, but for some years the subject of study has been enlarged, and North American archaeology now deals with aspects which sometimes have no equivalent in Europe. Recently, by tackling the 19th century, North American investigators have begun to develop a sub-contemporary archaeology which is completely original and most uncommon in Europe.

The first North American researches were associated with the study and reconstruction of major sites dating back to the origins of colonization, such as Jamestown and Williamsburg in Virginia (United States) and Louisburg in Nova Scotia (Canada). Attention has also been devoted to tracing the ancestry of colonization. These include soundings in 1958 and 1959 to rediscover the two first encampments of Jacques Cartier in Quebec, and the excavation in 1950 of Champlain's first overwintering in North America in St Croix, an excavation resumed on a larger scale in 1968–69. In the region of the Great Lakes, similar efforts have been made to study the missions of Sainte-Marie (Ontario) between 1940 and 1954, and of Marquette at St Ignace (Illinois). In both cases they were the first European establishments in the region, the first dating to between 1639 and 1649, the second founded in 1671.

The forts marking Anglo-French confrontations have similarly been restored and excavated. From Fort Beauséjour (New Brunswick) built by the French in 1751, to that of Michilimackinac (Michigan), an important French trading post established on Lake Huron in 1715, as well as those on the River Richelieu, important studies have been devoted to wood and stone fortifications, one of the most remarkable examples certainly being Louisburg (Nova Scotia).

But apart from these early concerns, the archaeology of the North American colonial period since the 1970s has developed new ground with the archaeology of towns built from the 17th to the 19th century, handicraft and industrial sites, and methods of transport by sea and river. The archaeology of towns is a very recent development in North America, for example at Quebec and Montreal. The origins of Quebec are now well known through the excavation in 1976 of Champlain's second residence, which was built of stone in 1624. In the same way, research currently in progress at Strawberry Bank (New Hampshire) has revealed the first stages of this port, founded in 1620.

Research into fishing stations and wrecks is essential if we are to learn more about 16th century maritime activities. Excavations in progress at Red Bay, Labrador, of a whaling station, and a ship sunk in 1565, are among the most original and illuminating archaeological projects in the whole of North America. There, for the first time, we can see what the 16th century European ships used for fishing and trade in the Atlantic actually looked like. Other programmes have investigated the wrecks of European maritime and river ships from the 16th to the 19th century in the United States and Canada. The Seneca Lake project in the State of New York has researched wrecks in lakes and canals in a sector essential to the 19th century regional economy, and the excavation at Restigouche, Quebec, of a frigate provisioning French troops in Canada which sank in 1760, has yielded remarkable results.

Everywhere there is a constant concern to present the results of research to the public. In Virginia, the Yorktown Shipwreck Archaeological project now in progress clearly illustrates these new concerns. It is involved both in studying an English provisioning ship that sank on 19 October 1781 during the Battle of Yorktown (sealing the fate of the British armies in North America) and in presenting it on the site in a watertight enclosure filled with clear filtered water.

The study of industrial and handicraft activities is an essential element of recent research in the United States and Canada. The principal activities, glass-blowing, pottery, metallurgy, etc., have been the object of excavations in both countries. These include the forges of St Maurice, established in Quebec in 1730 and active until 1883, and, in the United States, the forge of Saugus in a settlement site founded near Boston in 1630.

North American archaeologists have developed a type of research based on propositions comparable to those of the medievalists, but for more recent periods. Their preoccupations now extend to the 19th century; for example, work is now in progress in California to study some of the 21 missions established in that state as far as the River Sonora at the end of the 18th century during the Spanish period. Nineteenth-century cemeteries are now being excavated, for example the cemetery of Monroeville, Glenn County (California), in use between 1851 and 1910, or at Philadelphia (Pennsylvania) the first American Baptist Church cemetery, where 80 burials were made between 1820 and 1840; 50 of these were studied in 1983.

Such research may seem of secondary interest but, in North America as in Europe, many aspects of human history are little known or quite obscure in these and older periods, in spite of abundant written and photographic documentation. On the other hand, the need to salvage monuments and above all to present them to the public means that it is often essential to carry out excavations before the complete disappearance of sites or archaeological levels. These projects clearly show that excavation is the only documentary source capable of producing certain data, and even more of casting light on certain problems. The archaeology of the colonial period in North America is not simply the study of the transatlantic prolongation of European history; the work of North American archaeologists also gives us information about Western societies that we did not possess before, and confirms the importance of developing an archaeology of post-medieval periods in the Old World.

Louisburg port and fortress (1719-1760),
Nova Scotia, Canada

1	King's bastion	13	Lime Kiln
2	Barracks	14	Curtain Wall
3	Guardhouse	15	Powder Magazine
4	Rampart	16	Dauphin gate
5	Postern	17	Dauphin bastion
6	Icehouse	18	Spur
7	King's garden	19	Wharf
8	Royal square	20	Dauphin dock
9	Royal avenue	21	Frederic gate
10	Armoury forge	22	Toulouse dock
11	Bakery	23	Marine House
12	Artillery forge	24	Port square

Rediscovery of an 18th century French stronghold, Louisburg, Nova Scotia, Canada

The Treaty of Utrecht in 1713 deprived France of most of her possessions at the mouth of the St Lawrence, Newfoundland and Acadia. To protect the entrance to the river and the fishing, in 1719–20 France undertook the construction of Louisburg, a port, fortress and town. Captured by English troops in 1745 and again in 1758, the fortress was destroyed in the following years. At its height Louisburg comprised a garrison of 1,000–4,000 men, a population of about 2,000, and important harbour and fishing activities, making it the second port in North America after Boston. A bastioned perimeter contained all the elements necessary for a garrison, a whole range of dwellings and work places, especially those related to cod fishing. Studied by archaeologists for some 20 years, they have been progressively reconstructed as a result of information from the excavations and from numerous texts and graphic documents preserved in the French archives. The scope of the excavations have made Louisburg one of the major sites in North America from the colonial period.

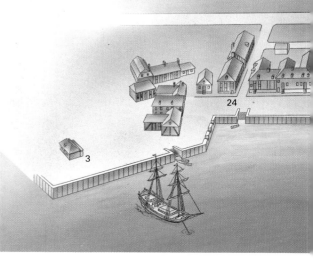

Wreck of a Basque whaler, Red Bay, Labrador

From the beginning of the 16th century, European fishermen, mostly Basques, came to hunt whales off the coasts of Labrador and Quebec. This activity was highly developed, especially between 1540 and 1590. In 1974, following written sources that showed Red Bay in Labrador to have been much frequented by these fishermen, the site became the scene of important excavations. The land area, particularly a small cemetery and establishments for rendering down whale blubber, are still being studied. Under water, in the bay, one of the largest excavations of wrecks ever organized is also under way. Several so-called "galleons" (the largest fishing vessels of the period) and various other items have been identified. One of the galleons, perhaps the *San Juan*, sunk in Red Bay in 1565, is the subject of careful attention every year.

Pottery workshop, Goshen, Connecticut

The existence of a pottery workshop founded by Hervey Brooks and active 1818–1864, was known from the texts and from collector's pieces such as that shown at the top, engraved with the initials of the maker and the date of its execution, 1858. (Property of the Litchfield Historical Society.) The excavation of the Brooks workshop led to the discovery of numerous potsherds and even a dish (above).

The Mission of San Juan Capistrano, California

In California, several missions characteristic of the early days of the Spanish occupation have been or are being excavated. The Mission of San Juan Capistrano was founded seven years after a Spanish expedition had reconnoitred the site in 1769. A church consecrated in 1806, and destroyed by an earthquake in 1812, was the focus of various buildings, notably a ceramics factory. As is typical of North American archaeology, the overriding concern here is for a clear presentation of the results and the development of the site: the church and the two wings (reproduced here) of the cloister. By kind permission of Nicholas M. Magalousis, director of the excavations.

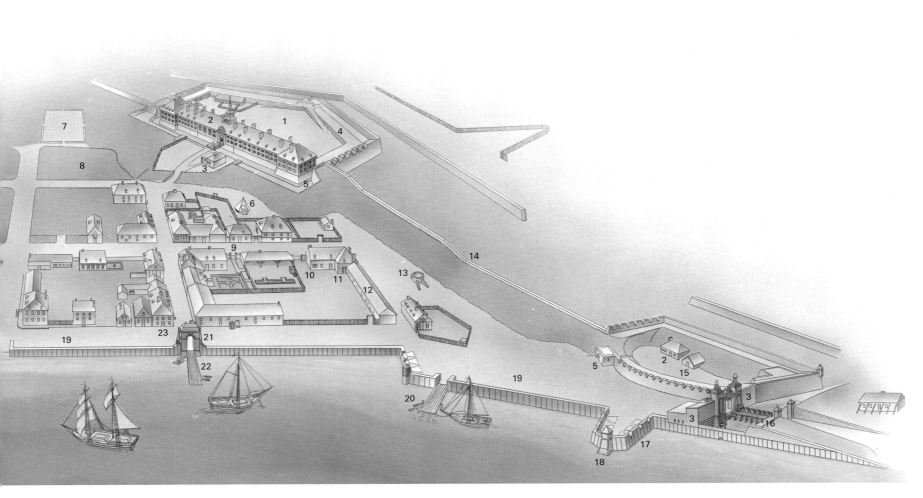

Industrial archaeology

Industrialization, the most important phenomenon since ancient times, has received surprisingly little attention from many archaeologists. Rather belatedly, intensive efforts are now being made to preserve and record it.

Of all the human sciences, industrial archaeology is probably among the most controversial, for this subject has existed for less than 30 years, and arouses lively controversy among scholars, lying as it does at the meeting-point of several traditional disciplines. Archaeologists, social historians, historians of technology and art historians tend to regard the same object with a different eye; and while they are perfectly aware that the richness of their material is a fundamental reason for this variety of interest, they are nonetheless constantly affected by differences in training, culture and methods.

With all due respect to R.A. Buchanan, the founder of industrial archaeology in England, it is really the *second* industrial revolution which underlies the development of a shift in historians' attitudes: technological change is a basic fact of our culture, which profoundly affects our awareness and responses. At the technological level, the development of electronics has completely transformed and continues to transform the nature and production of manufactured objects—which until this development was purely mechanical. Functions as simple as memory storage, remote control or automatic filing belonged until recently to the realms of fantasy; "mechanical" conceptualization, on the other hand, if one may so describe it, has a concrete character which means that it is accessible to everybody. By breaking the connection between what can be seen and what is happening, micro-technology has seriously disturbed the mechanistic culture of the first industrial age.

The first countries to become industrialized, and which have consequently been the most seriously upset by the technological changes of the present era, were also the first to become aware of the existence of an industrial heritage and the need to preserve it. This interest crystallized round a monument dating from the beginning of industrial art, Euston Station in London. In Germany or Poland the ravages of World War II gave rise to similar movements: under the title "history of material culture" a movement developed which had as its aim the gathering of knowledge about, and the preservation of, a whole sector of modern history. Old Europe is by and large the area most directly concerned: it is surprising to discover that over the past two centuries little scholarly attention has been paid to the most important phenomenon to have occurred since ancient times—industrialization. Rather belatedly efforts are being made to preserve our records of it. However, these records will differ according to the discipline in which the student is trained. The history of technology may hereafter occupy a more prominent position. Bridges, machines and manufactured articles, which had long been part of the field of art, but became separated from it after the end of the 18th century, may now be making a notable return.

Meanwhile, recent industrial change is having a marked effect on town planning and social organization: the locating of industrial sites outside built-up areas, the re-use of sites previously occupied by industry for speculative building, and the effects arising from the resultant change in the social composition of these districts, constitute a chain of transformation with an impact that can hardly be ignored: sociologists and architects need to study the working life of these districts and the changes in their buildings. The studies resulting from this are of course inspired partly by nostalgia. Moreover, in some of them there is a degree of confusion between industrial architecture and the use of metal in architecture (turning a branch of the history of contemporary art into one of the aspects of industrial archaeology). Finally, the radical changes in industrial activity throughout the world, the movement of factories to the Middle East or Far East, have given rise to "industrial wastelands" in European towns and cities that would have been unthinkable 25 years ago. When industry ceases to exist in a given area, leaving behind traces of its operation both on the landscape and in people's minds, the importance of the changes it has brought about suddenly becomes apparent, together with the need to preserve its memory.

The latest arrivals in this field may be the art historians who have discovered from movements in the art market that industrial output—manufactured articles, machines, architecture or landscape—could be appreciated from the point of view of the object, if not of the culture. The idea of an industrial heritage was late to emerge—raising problems concerning the classification and preservation of this whole range of objects on top of the already huge corpus of works of art (educated, popular or craft) accumulated by earlier generations.

The roots of industrial societies

As the field of history widens, it now appears that industrialization is a very old cultural phenomenon that came into its own during and after the Middle Ages, at least according to some experts on the history of technology. J.F. Finó's work on the *Fortresses of Medieval France*, 1967, suggests that archaeology and art history can be enriched through contact with the history of science, and by implication has opened the way for a new approach to industrial archaeology. On a purely theoretical level an "archaeology" of the modern world that considers archaeology not as a discipline for gaining knowledge of the past, but as a methodology for describing and analysing material objects, may be an interesting area. However, this approach tends to overlook the methodological potential of history, and it also overlooks an interesting aspect of contemporary archaeology, which does not hesitate whenever possible to turn to an analysis of written sources: namely, the fact

that it needs to be in a position of cultural disjunction from the object it is considering. Archaeology is a science of the past, even though it may be at times the very recent past, as Buchanan pointed out in stating that the first generation of computers was passing into the field of industrial archaeology. Its confrontation with the past draws from archaeology its most stimulating results, casting an indirect and reflected light on the characteristics of the present—as present-day history understands very well. But unfortunately this definition of archaeology may well be eventually confused with the definition of history. It is useful to remember that a fundamental trait is shared by art history and archaeology: they alone of human sciences are interested in *material* objects—and from this point of view the definition of industrial archaeology current in East European countries is much to be preferred.

What distinguishes art history from archaeology is its way of looking at an object, whether or not from an aesthetic point of view. The two disciplines may concern themselves with the same objects without drawing the same conclusions from them: for example, a Monet painting may be seen as indicative of techniques used in producing a painting in the 19th century, or as a work of art among other works of art. Understood in this way, industrial archaeology forms one of the branches of archaeology in general—but in that case it is not in any way multi-disciplinary. Would it not be better to refer to the "industrial heritage", rather than to industrial archaeology? This concept, together with that of preservation, has contemporary relevance, and at the very least indicates an area of desirable intervention. Archaeological method, on the other hand, can be applied to the study of industrial products with original and stimulating results: perhaps a history of industrial art should be developed, in which the industrial product, factory or construction should be considered in the same light as a piece of furniture or architectural feature, objects which have long been recognized as having an artistic dimension. In future perhaps we will use the term "history of material culture", as they do in Eastern Europe, and that the beguiling but misleading "industrial archaeology" will be reserved for archaeology proper, namely the study of the object itself, whether or not discovered in the course of excavation (which is a distinction of secondary importance). Then industrial archaeology will be able to take its proper place among the various historical disciplines—social history, technological history, history of economics, history of art and so on—which contribute to our knowledge of industrial civilization.

Houses of the Eleven Apostles, Chexmsko, Lower Silesia, Poland

This group of houses, dating from the first half of the 17th century, contained the lodging and workshops of textile operatives. There were once many such groups of buildings in Poland, housing craftsmen and their workplaces, but only two have survived, Chexmsko being the largest. Poland has for many years sought to preserve and display to advantage the remains of its "material civilization", to use the expression current in Central Europe to describe the industrial heritage. F.H.

Forges at Cornwall, Pennsylvania, USA

In the 18th century Pennsylvania was the main supplier of iron for the colony of America. The Cornwall furnace, built in 1742, used charcoal and was operated by hydraulic power. In 1856 the blast furnace was rebuilt and the wheel was replaced by a steam engine. The forges went out of use in 1883. The site became the property of the State of Pennsylvania in 1932 and has been turned into a museum. F.H.

Coalport ceramic kilns, Ironbridge, Shropshire, Great Britain

These kilns, built near the river Severn, produced porcelain of Chinese type from the middle of the 18th century, remaining in use until 1926. They are now part of the Ironbridge Gorge Museum complex.

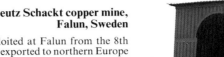

Pithead of Creutz Schackt copper mine, Falun, Sweden

Copper was exploited at Falun from the 8th century, and was exported to northern Europe from the 13th century, with maximum output achieved in the 17th century (3,000 tonnes were extracted in 1650). In 1687 the three shafts collapsed, thereafter forming a single one called Stora Stöten. The old wooden buildings have largely disappeared, but their surviving elements constitute essential vestiges of the Swedish industrial heritage. The Creutz Schackt pithead dates to 1836. F.H.

Tile works at Malbrans, Doubs, France

The use of tiles had become general in the 19th century, and the Malbrans tile works were set up in 1839–64. The chimney of the kiln and the drying chamber with a large roof ventilated by means of a lantern aperture were typical of this kind of industrial plant in a rural setting. F.H.

Dannes cement works, Pas-de-Calais, France

Range of chimney stacks from the cement works set up at the end of the 19th century, and now no longer in use. F.H.

The Lingotto Fiat factory, Turin

A factory with an integrated assembly line, designed by the Turin architect, Giacomo Matte Truco, during World War I (on the model of the Ford factory at Highland Park) was built between 1922 and 1925. A test track with a spiral access ramp was set up on the roof of the building (there was a similar scheme for the Citroën factories at Javel, Paris). The Lingotto factory, which has been given up in favour of a more modern plant, clearly exemplifies the problem of the re-use of large industrial buildings of a high architectural quality. F.H.

393

Bibliography

Introduction, René Ginouvès **11**

The following list of publications, many of which are recent, is combined with more detailed bibliographies provided for each section in order to present an overview of the theory and practices of archaeology.

History of archaeology:
BINFORD, L.R., *An Archaeological Perspective*, London, 1972
DANIEL, G. *A Short History of Archaeology*, London, 1981

General works on particular topics:
CLARKE, D.L., *Analytical Archaeology*, London, 1968
CLARKE, D.L., *Models in Archaeology*, London, 1972
CLEERE, H. (ed.), *Approaches to the Archaeological Heritage*, Cambridge University Press, 1984
MOBERG, C.A., *Introduction à l'archéologie*, Paris, 1976

Aerial and land surveys:
AGACHE, R., "Detection aérienne de vertiges protohistorique, gallo-romains et médiévaux", special issue of the *Bulletin de la Société de Préhistorie du Nord*, 7, Amiens Museum, 1970
CLARK, A., "Archaeological Prospecting: A Progress Report", *Journal of Archaeological Science*, 2, 1975
DASSIÉ, J., *Manuel d'archéologie aérienne*, Paris, 1978
PALMER, R. "Aerial Archaeology and Sampling" in J.F. Cherry, C.S. Gamble and S.J. Shennan (eds.), *Sampling in Contemporary British Archaeology*, Oxford, 1978

Excavations, and underwater excavations:
GIANFROTTA, P.A. and P. Poiney, *Archeologia subaquae*, Milan, 1981
HOSTER, T.R., R.F. Heitzer, and J.A. Graham, *Field Methods in Archaeology*, 6th ed., Palo Alto 1975
JOUKOWSKY, M., *A Complete Manual of Field Archaeology*, New York, 1980
MUCKELROY, K., *Maritime Archaeology*, Cambridge, 1978
UNESCO, *L'archéologie subaquatique, une discipline naissante*, Paris, 1973
WHEELER, M., *Archaeology from the Earth*, Oxford, 1954

Experimental archaeology:
COLES, J., *Archaeology by Experiment*, London, 1973

Physical techniques, especially methods of dating:
AITKEN, M.J., *Physics and Archaeology*, Oxford, 1974
FLEMING, S., *Thermoluminescence Techniques in Archaeology*, Oxford, 1979
Dating in Archaeology, New York, 1977
TITE, M.S., *Methods of Physical Examination in Archaeology*, London-New York, 1972

Mathematical techniques:
DORAN, J.E. and F.R. Hodson, *Mathematics and Computers in Archaeology*, Edinburgh, 1975
BORILLO, M. (ed.), *Archéologie et calcul*, Paris, 1978
LAGRANGE, M.S. and M. Renaud, "Simulation d'un raisonnement archéologique. Description de l'application d'un système expert: the système SNARK", in *Panorama 1983 des traitements de données en archéologie*, H. Ducasse (ed.), Valbonne 1983, pp. 31–64

Landscape and environmental archaeology:
BRADFORD, J., *Ancient Landscapes*, Portway–Bath, 1974
BUTZER, K.W., *Environment and Archaeology*, 2nd ed., London, 1972
CLARKE, D.L. (ed.), *Spatial Archaeology*, London, 1977
JANKUHN, H., *Einführung in die Siedlungsarchäologie*, Berlin–New York, 1977
VITA FINZI, L., *Archaeological Sites in their Setting*, London, 1978

Archaeology and cultural systems:
GOULD, R.A. (ed.), *Explorations in Ethnoarchaeology*, New Mexico, 1978
RENFREW, A.C., *Approaches to Social Archaeology*, Edinburgh, 1984
RENFREW, A.C. (ed.), *The Explanation of Culture Change: Models in Prehistory*, 1973

PREHISTORIC EUROPE

Paleolithic Europe

The archaeological background, Michèle Julien **20**
BINFORD, L.R., *In Pursuit of the Past. Decoding the Archaeological Record*, London, 1983
BORDES, F., *A Tale of Two Caves*, New York, 1972
DANIEL, G., *150 Years of Archaeology*, London, 1978 (1st ed. 1952)
DANIEL, G., (ed.), *Towards a History of Archaeology*, London, 1981
LAMING-EMPERAIRE, A., *Origines de l'archéologie préhistorique en France*, Paris, 1964
WAECHTER, D. d'A., *Man before History*, Oxford, 1976

The first inhabitants of Europe, Michèle Julien and Catherine Farizy **22**
BONIFAY, E., "Les traces des premiers hominidés en France", in *La Recherche*, 128, Paris, Dec. 1981
BUTZER, K.W., and G. Isaac (eds.), *After the Australopithecines*, The Hague, 1975
HUBLIN, J.J., "Les origines de l'homme de type moderne en Europe" in *Pour la Science*, 64, Paris, Feb. 1983
DE LUMLEY, H., "Cultural Evolution in France in its Paleoecological Setting", in K.W. Butzer and G. Isaac, *op. cit.*
Origine et évolution de l'Homme, Laboratoire de Prehistoire du musée de l'Homme, Muséum d'Histoire Naturelle, Paris, 1982
The Origins of Man, Museum catalogue, Musée de l'Homme, Paris, 1976
Les premiers habitants de l'Europe (1500 000–100 000 ans), Laboratoire de Préhistoire du Musée de l'Homme. Museum d'Histoire Naturelle, Paris, 1981

The Middle Paleolithic cultures in Europe, Catherine Farizy **24**
BORDES, F., *The Old Stone Age*, New York, 1968
CLARK, J.D., and F.C. Howell (eds.), *Recent Studies in Paleoanthropology, American Anthropologist* Special Publication, 68, 1966
FARIZY, C. and J. Leclerc, "Les grandes chasses de Mauran", *La Recherche*, 127, Paris, 1981
GABORI, M., *Les civilisations de Paleolithique moyen entre les Alpes et l'Oural*, Budapest, 1976
HARDING, D.W., *Prehistoric Europe*, Oxford, 1976
KEELEY, L.H., "The Functions of Paleolithic Flint Tools," *Scientific American* 237, 1977
DE LUMLEY, H., "Les civilisations du Paléolithic moyen", in *La Préhistoire Française*, 1, C.N.R.S., Paris, 1976

From Neanderthal man to *Homo sapiens sapiens*, Arlette Leroi-Gourhan **26**
HOWELLS, W.W., *Education of the genus Homo*, London, 1973
LEROI-GOURHAN, A., "Chronologie des grottes d'Arcy-sur-Cure", *Gallia-Préhistorie*, Vol. VII, Paris, 1965
LEROI-GOURHAN, A., Le neandertalien IV de Shanidar." *Bulletin de la Société Préhistorique Française*, Vol. 65, C.R.S.M. 3, Paris, 1968
LEROI-GOURHAN, A., "La place du Néandertalien de Saint-Césaire dans la chronologie würmienne", *Bull. Soc. Préh. Franc.*, Vol. 81, 7, Paris, 1984
LEROYER, C. and A. Leroi-Gourhan, "Problemes de chronologie: le Castelperronien et l'Aurignacian". *Bull. Soc. Préh. Franc.*, Vol. 80, 2, Paris, 1983
LEVEQUE, F. and B. Vandermeersch, "Décourverte de restes humains dans un niveau castelperronien à Saint-Césaire (Charente-Maritime)", *Comptes-rendus de l'Académie des Sciences*, t. 291, No. 2 série 0, Paris, 1980
PILBEAN, D.R., *The Ascent of Man*, New York, 1972

Burial in the Paleolithic, Michèle Julien **28**
KLEIN, R., *Ice Age Hunters of the Ukraine*, Chicago, 1973
LEROI-GOURHAN, A., *Les religions de la Préhistoire*, "Mythes et religions", PUF, Paris, 1964 (2nd ed. 1971)
QUECHON, G., "Vers une préhistoire de la Mort", in *La vie préhistorique*, special edition of *Sciences et Avenir*, Paris, 1971
VANDERMEERSCH, B., "Les premières sépultures" in *La Mort dans la Préhistoire*, Histoire et Archéologie Dossiers, 66, Paris, Sept. 1982

Woman in the Paleolithic Age, Michèle Julien **30**
BAFFIER, D., M. Julien, C. Karlin, "La femme dans la Préhistoire", *Pénélope*, 4, Les Femmes et la Science, Paris, 1981
DELPORTE, H., *L'image de la Femme dans l'art préhistorique*, Picard, Paris 1979
FISHER, H.E., *The Sex Contract: The Evolution of Human Behaviour*, Granada, 1981
NOUGIER, L.R., "La femme préhistorique" in *Histoire mondiale de la Femme*, Vol. 1, *Préhistoire et Antiquité*, Nouvelle Librairie de France, Paris, 1965
MAKEPEACE TANNER, N., *On Becoming Human*, Cambridge, 1981

Everyday life 12,000 years ago, Michèle Julien **32**
KEELEY, L.H., *Experimental Determination of Stone-Tool Uses: a Microwear Analysis*, Chicago, 1980
DE SAINT-BLANQUAT, H., "La vie quotidienne il y a treize mille ans", *Sciences et Avenir*, 435, May 1983
VAUGHAN., P. "The Function of Prehistoric Tools", *La Recherche*, 148, Oct. 1983

Paleolithic rock art and its meaning, Dominique Baffier **34**
BREUIL, H., *Four Hundred Centuries of Cave Art*, Montignac, 1952
GIEDION, S., *The Eternal Present: The Beginning of Art*, New York and London, 1962
GRAZIOZI, P., *Paleolithic Art*, translated from Italian to English, London, 1960
LAMING-EMPERAIRE, A., *La signification de l'art rupestre paleolithique*, Paris, 1962
LEROI-GOURHAN, A., *Les religions de la préhistoire*, Paris, 1971
LEROI-GOURHAN, A., *Préhistoire de l'art occidental*, Paris, 1971 (2nd ed.)
PERICOT, L., A. Lommel and J. Galloway, *Prehistoric and Primitive Art*, London, 1969
UCKO, P.J. and A. Rosenfeld, *Paleolithic Cave Art*, London, 1967

The first bowmen of the European forests, Michel Orliac **36**
La fin des temps glaciaires en Europe, Vol. 2, Colloque international du C.N.R.S., 271, C.N.R.S., Paris, 1979
The Mesolithic in Europe, International Archaeological Symposium, Warsaw, 1973
La Préhistoire française, Vol. 3, C.N.R.S., Paris, 1976

Neolithic Europe

The archaeological background, Jean Guilaine **38**
BERNABO, BREA L., *Gli scavi nella caverna delle Arene Candide*, Instituto di Studi Liguri, Bordighera, Vol. 1, 1946; Vol. 2, 1956
BOHM J. and S. De Laet (ed.), *L'Europe à la fin de l'Age de la pierre*, l'Académie Tchécoslovaque des Sciences, Prague 1961
CHILDE, G., *The Dawn of European Civilization*, London, 1935
HIGGS, E., *Palaeoeconomy*, Cambridge, 1975
PIGGOTT, S., *Ancient Europe*, Edinburgh, 1965
RENFREW, A.C., *Before Civilisation*, London, 1973
RENFREW, A.C., *The Emergence of Civilisation, the Cyclades and the Aegean in the Third Millennium BC London*, 1972
SCHWABEDISSEN, H., *Fundamenta. Die Anfänge des Neolithikums vom Orient bis Europa*, Cologne, Vol. 8, 1973

The triumph of agriculture, Jean Guilaine **40**
GEDDES, D., *De la chasse au troupeau en Méditerranée occidentale*, Archives d'Ecologie Préhistorique, 5, Toulouse, 1980
GUILAINE, J., *Premiers bergers et paysans de l'Occident méditerranéan*, Paris-La Haye, 1976
MURRAY, J., *The First European Agriculture*, Edinburgh, 1970
RENFREW, J., *Paleoethnobotany, the Prehistoric Food Plants of the Near East and Europe*, London, 1973
TRINGHAM, R. *Hunters, Fishers and Farmers of Eastern Europe*, London, 1971

Neolithic dwellings, Jean Guilaine **42**
BARKER, G. and D. Webley, "Causewayed Camps and Early Neolithic Economies in Central Southern England", *Proceedings of the Prehistoric Society*, 44, London, 1978
CLARK, J.G.D., *World Prehistory in a New Perspective*, 3rd ed., Cambridge, 1977
PÉTREQUIN, P., *Gens de l'eau, gens de la terre*, Paris, 1984
SOUDSKY, B., "Study of the Neolithic house", *Slovenska Archeologia*, XVII, Bratislava, 1969
THEOCHARIS, D., *Neolithic Greece*, Athens, 1973

The farmer's tools, Jean Guilaine **44**
CLARK, J.G., *World Prehistory in New Perspective*, 3rd ed., Cambridge, 1977
MULLER, BECK H.J., *Holzgeräte und Holzbearbeitung, Seeberg-Burgäschissee-Süd*, Acta Bernensia, II. Berne, 1965
PIGGOTT, S., *The Earliest Wheeled Transport from the Atlantic Coast to the Caspian Sea*, London, 1983
RENFREW, A.C., *The Emergence of Civilization*, London, 1972
SIGAUT, F., *L'agriculture et le feu*, Paris, 1975
WAILES, B., "The origins of settled farming in temperate Europe", in *Indo-European and Indo-Europeans*, (ed. G. Cardona, H.M. Hoenigswald and A. Senn), Philadelphia, 1970

Megaliths, Jean-Pierre Mohen, Jean Guilaine **46**

Northern and Western Europe:
EVANS, J.D., B. Cunliffe, A.C. Renfrew (ed.), *Antiquity and Man*, London, 1981
L'HELGOUACH, J., *Les sépultures mégalithiques en Armorique*, Travaux du laboratoire d'Anthropologie préhistorique de la faculté des Sciences, Rennes, 1965
JOUSSAUME, R., *Des dolmens pour les morts*, Paris, 1985
SHEE TWOHIG, E., *The Megalithic Art of Western Europe*, Oxford, 1981

Mediterranean Europe:
CAMPS, G., *Aux origines de la Berberie: monuments et rites protohistoriques*, Paris, 1961
LEISNER, V. and G., *Die Megalithgräber der Iberischen Halbinsel*, Madrider Forschungen, I: *Der Suden*, Berlin 1943; II: *Der Westen*, Berlin 1956–59; *Der Osten*, Berlin 1965
LILLIU, G., *La civiltà Nuragica*, Sassari, 1982
PERICOT, L. *Los Sepulcros Megaliticos catalanes y la cultura pirenaica*, Instituto de Estudios Pirenaicos, Barcelona, 1950
STEKELIS, M., *Les Monuments mégalithiques de Palestine*, Mémoires de l'institut de Paléontologie Humaine, 15, Paris, 1935

Religious cults and concepts, Jean Guilaine **48**
EVANS, J.D., *The Prehistoric Antiquities of the Maltese Islands*, London, 1971
GIMBUTAS, M., *The Gods and Goddesses of Old Europe, 7000 to 3500BC*, London, 1974
KALICZ, N., *Dieux d'argile*, Budapest, 1980
MELLAART, J., *Catal Huyuk, a Neolithic Town in Anatolia*, London, 1967
SOUDSKY, B. and I. Pavlu, "Interprétation historique de l'ornementation linéaire," *Pamatky Archeologicke*, Prague, 1966

Protohistory in Europe

The archaeological background, Jean-Pierre Mohen **50**
BLEGEN, C.W., *Troy and the Trojans*, London, 1963
CLARK, J.G.D., *World Prehistory in a New Perspective*, 3rd ed., Cambridge, 1977
COLES, J.M., A.F. Harding, *The Bronze Age in Europe*, London, 1979
FILIP, J., *Manuel encyclopédique de Préhistoire et Protohistoire européennes*, Vol. 2, Prague, 1966 and 1969
GIMBUTAS, M., *Bronze Age Cultures in Central and Eastern Europe*, The Hague, 1965

JENSEN, J., *The Prehistory of Denmark*, London, 1982
KASTELIC, J., *Situlenkunst*, Vienna and Munich, 1964
MOHEN, J.P., *L'Age de fer en Aquitaine*, Mem. Société Préhistorique française, 14, Paris, 1980
MULLER-KARPE, H., *Handbuch der Vor-und Frühgeschichte*, Munich, III, 1974, IV, 1980
PIGGOTT, S., *Ancient Europe*, Edinburgh, 1965
POWELL, T., *The Celts*, London, 1967
RENFREW, A.C., *The Emergence of Civilization, the Cyclades and the Aegean in the Third Millenium BC*, London, 1972
WARREN, P., *The Aegean Civilizations*, Oxford, 1975

The metal ages, Jean-Pierre Mohen **52**
ELUÈRE, C., "Les ors préhistoriques", *l'Age du Bronze en France*, 2 Paris, 1982
MUHLY, J.D., "Copper and Tin", *Transactions*, Connecticut Academy of Arts and Sciences, New Haven, 1973
PLEINER, R., *Frühes Eisen in Europa*, Schaffhausen, 1981
ROTHENBERG, B. and A. Blanco-Freijeiro, *Studies in Ancient Mining and Metallurgy in South West Spain*, London, 1981
TYLECOTE, R.F., *Metallurgy in Archaeology*, London, 1962

Burial customs, Jean-Pierre Mohen **54**
BERG, S., R, Rolle, H. Seemann, *Der Archäologue und der Tod*, Bucher Report, Munich-Lucerne, 1981
BITTEL, K., W. Kimmig, S. Schiek, *Die Kelten in Baden-Württemberg*, Stuttgart, 1981
BRIARD, J., "Les tumulus d'Armorique", *l'Age de bronze en France*, 3, Paris, 1984
CHAPMAN, R., I. Kinnes, K. Randsborg, ed., *The Archaeology of Death, New Directions in Archaeology*, Cambridge, 1981
GLOB, P.V., *The Bog People*, London, 1977

Trade routes, Jean-Pierre Mohen **56**
BANDI, G., V. Csermenyi, ed., *Nord-Süd-Beziehungen, Savaria*, 16, Szombathely, 1983
BECK, C.W., M. Gerving, E. Wilbur, "The provenence of archaeological amber artefacts", in *Art and Archaeology Technical Abstracts*, 1966, 1967
VON MERHART, G., *Hallstatt und Italien*, Römisch-Germanisches Zentralmuseum zu Mainz, 1969
RITTATORE VONWILLER, F., "La diffusione dell'ambra in Europa e in Italia durante la protostoria", in *Studie richerche sulla problematica dell'ambra*, Rome, 1975
THRANE, H., *Europaeiske forbindelser*, Nationalmuseet, Kobenhaun, 1975

Wine and horses: symbols of prestige, **58**
Jean-Pierre Mohen
BENOIT, F., *Recherches sur l'hellénisation du midi de la Gaule Ophrys*, Aix-en-Provence, 1965
JOFFROY, R., *Vix et ses trésors*, Paris, 1979
KOSSACK, G., *Gräberfelder der Hallstattzeit am Main und Fränkisher Saale*, Kallmünz, 1970
PIGGOTT, S., *The Earliest Wheeled Transport from the Atlantic Coast to the Caspian Sea*, London, 1983
ROSS, A., *Everyday Life of the Pagan Celts*, London, 1970
SCHÜLE, W., *Die Meseta-Kulturen der Iberischen Halbinsel, Mediterrane und eurasische Element in früheisenzeitlichen Kulturen Südwesteuropas*, Madrider Forschungen, 3, Berlin 1969

Protohistorical settlements, Jean-Pierre Mohen **60**
Ausgrabungen in Deutschland, 1950–1975, Catalogue of the Mainz exhibition, Römish-germanisches Zentralmuseum, 4 Vol., 1975
BÜCHSENSCHUTZ, O. (ed.), *Les structures d'habitat a l'âge du fer en Europe tempérée*, Maison des Sciences de l'Homme, Paris, 1981
CUNLIFFE, B., *Iron Age Communities in Britain*, London, 1975
PETREQUIN, P., *Gens de l'eau, gens de la terre*, Paris, 1984
SANGMEISTER, E. and H. Schubart, *Zambujal*, Madrider Beiträge, 5, Mainz, 1981

The protohistorical peoples of Europe, Jean-Pierre Mohen **62**
BIANCHI BANDINELLI, R. and A. Giuliano, *Les Étrusques et l'Italie avant Rome*, L'Univers des Formes, Paris, 1973
CHADWICK, N.K., *The Celts*, Penguin, 1971
DUVAL, P.M., *Les Celtes*, L'Univers des Formes, Paris, 1977
HODINOTT, R., *The Thracians*, London, 1981
MENENDEZ PIDAL, R. (ed.), *Historia de España*, Vol. III, Madrid, 1963
ROLLE, R., *Die Welt der Skythen*, C.J. Bucher, Lucerne-Francfurt-sur-le Main, 1980
WENEDIKOW, I. and I. Marasow, *Gold der Thraker*, Mainz, 1979

THE CLASSICAL WORLD

The archaeological background, Bernard Holtzmann **64**
BIANCHI BANDINELLI, R., *Introduzione all' archeologia*, Rome, 1976
BINTLIFF, J.L., "Natural environment and human settlement in Prehistoric Greece", *British Archaeological Report*, Oxford, 1977
British Archaeological Report Supplementary Series
COOK, R.M., *Greek Painted Pottery*, 2nd ed., London, 1972
COURBIN, P., *Qu'est-ce que l'archéologie?*, Paris, 1982
GINOUVÈS, R., "L'archéologie gréco-romaine", *Que sais-je?*, P.U.F., 2nd ed., 1982
GOTEBURG, P.A.F., *Studies in Mediterranean Archaeology*, Oxford
HAUSMANN, U., C.H. Beck (ed.), *Allgemeine Grundlagen der Archäologie*, Munich, 1969
HOPE-SIMPSON, R., *Mycenaean Greece*, Park Ridge, New Jersey, 1981
LING, R., *The Greek World*, Oxford, 1976
MOMIGLIANO, A.D., *Essays on Ancient and Modern Historiography*, Oxford, 1977
MOMIGLIANO, A.D., *Studies in Historiography*, London, 1966
PFEIFFER, R., *History of Classical Scholarship*, Oxford, 1968
RENFREW, A.C. and M. Wagstaff (ed.), *An Island Polity*, 1982
SANDYS, J.E., *A History of Classical Scholarship*, Cambridge, 1908 (reprint, New York, 1958)
SCHNAPP, A., *Archéologie et tradition académique en Europe aux XVIIIe et XIXe siècles*, Paris, 1982
WEISS, R., *The Renaissance Discovery of Classical Antiquity*, Oxford, 1969

Neolithic figurines: idols or toys?, René Treuil **66**
DELPORTE, H., *L'image de la femme dans l'art préhistorique*, Paris, 1979
FRENCH, E., *Sanctuaries and Cults in the Aegean Bronze Age*, R. Hägg, N. Marinatos, (ed.). Stockholm, 1981
GIMBUTAS, M., *The Gods and Goddesses of Old Europe 7000 to 3500BC*, London, 1974
HÖCKMANN, O., *Die menschengestaltige Figuralplastik der südost-europäischen Jungsteinzeit und Steinkupferzeit*, Hildesheim, 1968
LE BRUN, A., "La notion de style dans les figurines anthropomorphes néolithiques du Proche-Orient et de l'Europe du Sud-Est, Thèse de IIIème cycle", Paris I, Paris 1975
TREUIL, R., *Le Néolithique et le Bronze Ancien égéens*, Paris, 1983
UCKO, P., *Anthropomorphic Figurines of Predynastic Egypt and Neolithic Crete*, London, 1968

The end of the Minoan civilization, *René Treuil* **68**
Acta of the 1st International Scientific Congress on the Volcano of Thera, Archaeological Services of Greece, Athens, 1971
DOUMAS, C. (ed.), *Thera and the Aegean World*, London, 1978 and 1980
DOUMAS, C., *Thera, Pompeii of the Ancient Aegean*, London, 1983
HALLAGER, E., *The Mycenaean Palace at Knossos, Evidence for Final Destruction in the III B Period*, Museum Memoirs 1, Medelhavsmuseet, Stockholm 1977
HIGGINS, R., *Minoan and Mycenaean Art*, London and New York, 1967
PAGE, D., *The Santorini Volcano and the Destruction of Minoan Crete*, The Society for the Promotion of Hellenic Studies, London, 1970
WARREN, P., "Knossos: Stratigraphical Museum Excavations 1978–80, Part I", in *Archaeological Reports*, for 1980–1, published by The British School of Athens
WIEMEIER, W-D., "Mycenean Knossos and The Age of Linear B", *Studii Micenei* XXII 1982, p. 219–87

Princely burials, Bernard Holtzmann **70**
ANDRONIKOS, M., *Finds from the Royal Tombs of Vergina*, A. Reckitt Archaeology lectures, British Academy, 1981
ANDRONIKOS, M., "Totenkult" in *Archaeologia Homerica 3*, Göttingen, 1968
BERARD, C., "L'Héroon à la porte de l'Ouest", in *Eretria III*, Berne, 1970
GNOLO, G., J.-P. Vernant (ed.), *Death and Dying in Ancient Societies*, Paris, 1982
KARAGEORGHIS, V., *Salamis in Cyprus*, London, 1969
KURTZ, D.C., J. Boardman, *Greek Burial Customs*, London, 1971
MYLONAS, G., *Golden Mycenae*, Athens, 1983

Scripts and writing in the Aegean world, **72**
Jean-Pierre Olivier
CADOGAN, G., *Palaces of Minoan Crete*, London, 1976
CHADWICK, J., *The Decipherment of Linear B*, Cambridge, 1971
CHADWICK, J., *The Mycenean World*, 1976
HEUBECK, A., *Archeaologia Homerica*, Vol. III, Göttingen, 1979
PALMER, L., *The Greek Language*, London, 1980
RENFREW, A.C., "Problems in the general correlation of archaeological and linguistic strata in prehistoric Greece: the model of authochthonous origin" in *Bronze Age Migrations in The Aegean*, R.A. Crossland and A. Birchall (ed.), 1984
VANDENABEELE, F. and J.-P. Olivier, *Les idéogrammes archéologiques du linéaire B*, Paris, 1979
VENTRIS, M., and J. Chadwick, *Documents in Mycenaean Greek*, (2nd ed.), Cambridge, 1973

Greek expansion in the Mediterranean, **74**
Bernard Holtzmann
BOARDMAN, J., *The Greek Overseas*, London (2nd ed.), 1980
COLDSTREAM, N.J., *Geometric Greece*, London 1977
COOK, J.M., *The Greeks: Ionia and the East*, London, 1962
DUNBABIN T.J., *The Greeks and their Eastern Neighbours*, London, 1979
JOHNSON, A., *The Emergence of Greece*, Oxford, 1976
MARTIN, R., *L'urbanisme dans la Grèce antique*, A. and J. Picard, Paris (2nd ed.), 1976
MOMIGLIANO, A.D., *Alien Wisdom Limits of Hellenization*, Cambridge, 1975
MOREL, J.-P., "L'expansion phocéenne en Occident", in *Bulletin de Correspondance Hellenique*, 99, 1975
SNODGRASS, A.M., *The Dark Age of Greece*, Edinburgh, 1971
TSCHERIKOWER, V., "Die hellenistischen Stadtegrundungen", *Philologus*, Suppl. XIX, 1, Leipzig, 1927
WOODHEAD, A.G., *The Greeks: The West*, London, 1962

Commercial routes and amphorae, Jean-Yves Empereur **76**
EMPEREUR, J.-Y., A. Hesnard, "Les amphores hellénistiques" in *Céramiques hellénistiques et romaines*, Vol. 2, Centre de Recherche d'Histoire Ancienne, Besançon, 1985
GARLAN, Y., "Greek Amphorae and Trade" in P. Garnsey, K. Hopkins, C.R. Whittaker (ed.), *Trade in the Ancient Economy*, London, 1983
GRACE, V., *Amphoras and the Ancient Wine Trade*, American School of Classical Studies at Athens, Princeton (2nd ed.), 1979
GRACE, V. and J.-Y. Empereur, "Un groupe d'amphores ptolémaïques estampillées", in *Bulletin de l'Institut Français d'Archéologie Orientale*, 81, 1981

Monetary treasures, Olivier Picard **78**
KRAAY, C., O. Mørkholm, M. Thompson, *Inventory of Greek Coin Hoards*, American Numismatic Society, New York, 1973
NEWELL, E.T., *Alexander's Hoards II, Demanhur Hoard*, American Numismatic Society, 1923
PICARD, O., "Monnayage thasien du Ve siècle av. J.-C.", *Comptes-rendus de l'Académie des Inscriptions et Belles Lettres*, Paris, 1982
PRICE, M. and N. Waggoner, *Archaic Greek Coinage, the "Asyut" Hoard*, London, 1975

Manuscripts and inscriptions, Bernard Holtzmann **80**
BATAILLE, A., "La Papyrologie", in *L'histoire et ses methodes, Encyclopédie de la Pléiade*, Paris, 1961
COURCELLE, P., *Late Latin writers and their Greek sources*, Harvard University Press, 1969
DAIN, A., *Les manuscrits*, (2nd ed.) Paris, 1964
KLAFFENBACH, G., *Griechische Epigraphik*, (2nd ed.), Göttingen, 1966
LESKY, A., *A History of Greek Literature*, London, 1966
LOWE, E.A. *Codices Latini Antiquiores*, 11 Vols. and supplement, Oxford, 1934–71
PFEIFFER, R., *History of Classical Scholarship*, Oxford, 1968
REYNOLDS, L.D. and N.G. Wilson, *Scribes and Scholars*, Clarendon Press, 1974
TURNER, E.G., *Athenian books in the Fifth and Fourth Centuries BC*, London, 1952
TURNER, E.G., *Greek Manuscripts of the Ancient World*, Oxford, 1971
TURNER, E.G., *Greek Papyri, An Introduction*, Oxford, 1968

Rome and the development of the city in Latium, **82**
Agnès Rouveret
COARELLI, F., *Il Foro Romano*, I: *Periodo arcaico*, Rome, 1983
D'AGOSTINO, B., "L'ideologia funeraria nell'età del ferro in Campania: Pontecagnano. Nascita di in potere di funzione stabile", in *La mort, les morts dans les sociétés anciennes*, G. Gnoli, and J.P. Vernant (ed.), Cambridge–Paris, 1982
Enea nel Lazio, Archeologia e Mito, (exhibition catalogue), Palazzo dei Concervatori, Rome, Sept–Dec, 1981, Rome, 1981
GJERSTAD, E., *Early Rome*, Lund, 1956–63
"La Formazione della Citta nel Lazio fra X e VI sec. a.C.", in *Dialoghi di Archeologia*, 2, Rome, 1980 (see especially the analyses by C. Ampolo, and A.M. Bietti-Sestieri,)
Naissance de Rome, (exhibition cataloque), Petit-Palais, March–May 1977, Paris, 1977
SEULLARD, H.H., *The Etruscan Cities and Rome*, London, 1967
ROSTORTZEFF, M.I., *Social and Economic History of the Roman Empire*, 2nd ed., Oxford, 1957
TORELLI, M., *Storia degli Etruschi*, Laterza Rome-Bari, 1981
WARD-PERKINS, J.B., *Cities of Ancient Greece and Italy*, New York, 1974

The past of a capital city: Republican Rome, **84**
Agnès Rouveret
BALSDON, J.P.V.D., *Life and Leisure in Ancient Rome*, New York, 1969
COARELLI, F., *Roma*, Guide archeologiche Laterza, Bari, 1980
CRAWFORD, M.H., *The Roman Republic*, London, 1978
GROS, P., *Aurea Templa. Recherches sur l'architecture religieuse de Rome à l'époque d'Auguste*, Ecole Française de Rome, Rome, 1976
LAFON, X. and G. Sauron, (ed.), *L'art décoratif à Rome à la fin de la République et au début du principat, ibid.*, Rome, 1981
NICOLET, C., *Le métier de citoyen dans la Rome républicaine*, Paris, 1976
STRONG, D. E., *Roman Art*, London, 1976
TORELLI, M., *Typology and Structure of Roman Historical Reliefs*, Ann Arbor, 1982
VICKERS, M., *The Roman World*, Oxford, 1976
ZANKER, P. (ed.), *Hellenismus in Mittelitalien*, Kolloquium in Göttingen, 5–9 June 1974, Abhandlungen der Akademie der Wissenschaften in Göttingen, Göttingen, 1976

Mediterranean markets and trade, Jean Andreau **86**
GARNSEY, P., K. Hopkins, and C.R. Whittaker (ed.), *Trade in the Ancient Economy*, London, 1983
GIARDINA, A. and A. Schiavone (ed.), *Società romana e produzione schiavistica*, Vol. 2; *Merci, mercati e scambio nel Mediterraneo*, Bari, 1981
Memoirs of the American Academy in Rome, 36, The Seaborne Commerce in Ancient Rome: Studies in Archaeology and History, 1980
Recherches sur les amphores romaines, taken from a colloquium in 1971 organized by l'Ecole Française de Rome, Rome, 1972

TCHERNIA, A., *Le vin de l'Italie romaine, essai d'historie économique d'après les amphores*, Rome

Agriculture and rural life, Jean Andreau **88**
AGACHE, R., *La Somme préromaine et romaine*, Société de antiquaires de Picardie, Amiens, 1978
KOLENDO, J., *L'agricoltura nell'Italia romana*, Rome, 1980
PERCIVAL, J., *The Roman Villa: A Historical Introduction*, London, 1976
WHITE, K.D., *Roman Farming*, London, 1970

Pompeii, the archives of domestic decoration **90**
Agnès Rouveret
ANDREAE, B. and H. Kyrielis (ed.), *Neue Forschungen in Pompeji und den anderen vom Vesuvausbruch 79 n. Chr. verschütteten Städten*, Recklinghausen, 1975
BRAGANTINI, I., M. de Vos and F. Parise Badoni, *Pitture e pavimenti di Pompei I. Regioni 1,2,3*, Ministero per i Beni Culturali e Ambientali. Instituto Centrale per il Catalogo e la Documentazione, Rome, 1981
BRAGANTINI, I. and M. de Vos, *Le decorazioni della Villa Romana della Farnesina*, Rome, 1982
CARETTONI, G., *Das Haus des Augustus auf dem Palatin*, Mainz, 1983
Pompei 1748–80. I tempi della documentazione, (exhibition catalogue). Roman Forum, July–Sept 1981 and Pompei (Antiquarium), Oct. 1981, Rome, 1981
SAURON, G., "Nature et signification de la mégalographie dionysiaque de Pompéi", in *Comptes rendus de l'Académie des Inscriptions et Belles-Lettres*, Paris, 1984

The necropolis at Isola Sacra, Ida Baldassare **92**
BALDASSARRE, I., "La necropoli dell'Isola Sacra," in *Un decennio di ricerche archeologiche, Quaderni de la ricerca scientifica*, 100, Rome, 1978
BALDASSARRE, I., "Una necropoli imperiale romana: proposte di lettura", in *Annali dell'Instituto Universitaris Oriental Archeologia e Storia antica*, VI, 1984
CALZA, G., *La necropoli del Porto di Roma all'Isola Sacra*, Poligrafico delle Stato, Rome, 1940
MEIGGS, R., *Roman Ostia*, Oxford 1973

Town and country in the Roman west, Philippe Leveau **94**
BROWN, P., *Religion and Society in the Age of St. Augustine*, London, 1972
BROWN, P., *The World of Late Antiquity*, London, 1971
CASEY, P.J., *The End of Roman Britain*, British Archaeological Report 71, Oxford, 1979
FINBERG, H.P.R., "Roman and Saxon in Worthington: a study in continuity", *Lucerna*, 1964, p. 21–65
GIARDINA, A. and A. Schiavone (ed.), *Societa romana e produzione schiavistica*, Vol. 1, *L'Italia: insediamenti e forme economiche*, Bari, Rome, 1981
LEVEAU, P., "La ville antique et l'organisation de l'espace rural", *Annales E.S.C.* 4, 1983, p.920–42
RIVET, A.L., *The Roman Villa in Britain*, London, 1969
THOMAS, A.C. (ed.), *Rural Settlement in Roman Britain*, London, 1966
THOMAS, C., *Christianity in Roman Britain to 500AD*, London, 1981
WACHER, J., The Towns of Roman Britain, London, 1975

The frontiers of the Roman Empire, **96**
Eliane and Maurice Lenoir
BALSDON, J.P.V.D., *Rome, the Story of an Empire*, London, 1977
BREEZE, D.J., *The Northern Frontiers of Roman Britain*, London, 1982
JOHNSON, D.E. (ed.), *The Saxon Shore*, CBA Research Report 18, 1977
PETRIKOVITS, H., *Die Innenbauten römischer Legionslager während der Prinzipatzeit*, Opladen, 1975
POIDEBARD, A., *La trace de Rome dans le désert de Syrie. Le limes de Trajan à la conquête arabe. Recherches aeriennes (1925–1932)*.
REBUFFAT, R., "Au-delà des camps romains d'Afrique mineure: renseignement, contrôle, pénétration" in H. Temporini, and W. Haase, (ed.) *Aufstieg und Niedergang der romischen Welt*, II, 10, 2, Berlin–New York, 1982
WEBSTER, G., *The Roman Imperial Army of the First and Second Centuries AD*, London, 1969

THE EARLY MIDDLE AGES

The archaeological background Patrick Périn **98**
AHRENS, C., *Frühe Helzkirchen im nördlichen Europa*, Museum catalogue, Helms-Museum, Hamburg, 1981–2
Ausgrabungen in Deutschland (1950–75), Museum catalogue, Römisch-Germanisches Zentralmuseum, Mainz, 1975
BORLEY, M.W. (ed.), *European Towns: their Archaeology and Early History*, London, 1977
HEITZ, C., *L'architecture religieuse carolingienne*, Paris, 1980
HUBERT, J., J. Porcher and W.-F. Volbach, *L'Europe des invasions*, L'Univers des Formes, Paris, 1967
LOVE, E.A., *Codices Latinum Antiquares*, 11 Vols. and supplements 1934–70
PÉRIN, P., *La Datation des tombes merovingiennes. Historique, methodes, applications*, Geneva, 1980
Sachsen und Angelsachsen, Museum catalogue, Helms Museum, Hamburg, 1978–9
SALIN, E., *La civilisation merovingienne d'apres les sepultures, les textes et le laboratoire*, 4 Vols., Paris, 1950–59
TALBOT RICE, D. (ed.), *The Dark Ages*, London, 1965
TODD, M., *The Northern Barbarians*, London, 1975
WALLACE, J.M., *The Barbarian West*, 3rd ed., London, 1967
WALLACE, J.M., *Early Germanic Kingship in England and on the Continent*, Oxford, 1971
WALLACE, J.M., *Early Medieval History*, Oxford, 1975
WILSON, D.M. (ed.), *The Northern World*, London, 1980

The great invasions and archaeology, Patrick Périn **100**
ADDYMAN, P., "The Anglo-Saxon Village at Chatton, Hertfordshire", *Medieval Archaeology* XIVII, p. 1–25
ALCOCK, L., *Arthur's Britain*, London, 1973
AMENT, H., "Franken und Romanen im Merowingerreich als archäologisches Forschungsproblem" in *Bonner Jahrbücher*, Vol. 178, Cologne, 1978, p. 377–94
BUCHET, L. (ed), *Le phénomène des "Grandes invasions", realité ethnique ou échanges culturels: l'anthropologie au secours de l'Histoire*, Centre de Recherches archeologiques, Valbonne, 1983
HARDEN, D. (ed.), *Dark Age Britain: Studies Presented to E.T. Leeds*, Oxford, 1956
HILLS, C., "The Archaeology of Anglo-Saxon England of the Pagan Period: a Review," in *Anglo-Saxon England*, 8, 1979, p. 279–329
JAMES, E., "Cemeteries and the Problem of Frankish Settlement in Gaul", in Sawyer, P.-H. (ed.) *Names, Words and Graves: Early Medieval Settlement*, Leeds, 1979, p.55–89
JONES, M.U., "Saxon Mucking" in *Anglo-Saxon Studies* I, (ed.) S.C. Hawkes *et al*, p. 21–37
LEEDS, E.T., *Early Anglo-Saxon Art and Archaeology*, Oxford, 1936
LORREN, C, "Des Saxons en Basse-Normandie", in *Studien zur Sachsenforschung*, Vol. 2, 1980, p. 231–59
LOSCOR BRADLEY, S., "The Anglo-Saxon Settlement in Catholme, Staffs." *Trent Valley Archaeological Research Committee*, report no. 8, 1974, p. 3–34
MYRES, J.N.L., *Anglo-Saxon Pottery and the Settlement of England*, Oxford, 1936
PERIN, P., "A propos de publications recentes concernant le peuplement en Gaule a l'epoque merovingienne: la question franque", in *Archéologie médiévale*, Vol. XI, Caen, 1981, p. 125–45
PILET, C., *The Necropolis of Frenouville (Calvados)*, British Archaeological Reports, International series, Vol. 83, Oxford, 1980
ROWLEY, T. (ed.), *Anglo-Saxon Settlement and Landscape*, British Report 6, Oxford, 1974
WELCH, M.G., "Late Romans and Saxons in Sussex", in *Britannia* 2, 1971
WERNER, J., "Zur Entstehung der Reihengräberzivilisation, in *Archaeologia geographica*" Hamburg, 1950, p. 23–32

New towns and antique cities, Patrick Périn **102**
BARLEY, M.-W. (ed.), *European Towns, Their Archaeology and Early History*, London, 1977
BIDDLE, M. and D. Hudson, *The Future of London's Past, a Survey of the Archaeological Implications of Planning and Development in the Nation's Capital*, Hertford, 1973
BIDDLE, M., "Winchester", *Studies* I, 1976
BONNET, C., "Saint-Pierre de Genève, récentes découvertes archéologiques", in *Archéologie suisse*, 4, Basle, 1980, p. 174–91; "Les origines du groupe épiscopal de Genève", in *Comptes rendus de l'Académie des Inscriptions et Belles-Lettres*, July–Oct 1981, Paris, 1982, p. 414–33
GALINIÉ, H. and B. Randouin, *Les archives du sol à Tours, survie et avenir de l'archéologie de la ville*, Societé archéologique de Touraine, Tours, 1979
HASLAM, J. (ed.), *Anglo-Saxon Towns*, London, 1984
HILL, D., *Archaeological Atlas of Anglo-Saxon England*, Blackwell, 1981
RALEIGH-RADFORD, C.A., "The pre-conquest boroughs of England", *Proceedings of The British Academy* LXVV 1978, p. 131–53
SAWYER, P., "Kings and Merchants", in P. Sawyer and I. Wood, *Early Medieval Kingship*, Leeds, 1977
SAWYER, P.H., *From Roman Britain to Norman England*, London, 1978
VANS ES, W.A. and W.J.H. Verwers, *Excavations at Dorestad 1. The Harbour: Hoogstraat I*, Nederlandse Ouheden, 9, 2 Vol., Amersfoort, 1980
WILSON, D.M., *Archaeology of Anglo-Saxon England*, London, 1976

The making of the medieval countryside, **104**
Patrick Périn
BAKER, A.R. and R.A. Butlin, *Studies of Field Systems in the British Isles*, Cambridge, 1973
CHAPRELOT, J. and R. Fossier, *Le village et la maison au Moyen Age*, Paris, 1980
DARBY, A.C. (ed.), *A New Historical Geography of England Before 1600*, Cambridge, 1976
FLORIN, B., *L'habitat du Haut Moyen Âge en milieu rural dans le Nord – Pas-de-Calais. État de la question*, Centre culturel, Amis du Cambrésis, Cambrai, 1983
JONES, G.R.J., "Settlement Patterns in Anglo-Saxon England", *Antiquity* 35, 1961
LORREN, C., "Le village de Saint-Martin de Mondeville, Calvados (1e–12e siècles. Premiers résultats des fouilles (1978–80)", in A. Van Doorselaer (ed.) *De Merevingische Beschaving in de Scheldevallei*, Courtrai, 1981
PORTE, P., *L'habitat mérovingien de Larina à Hières-sur-Amby (Isère)*, Grenoble, 1980
SAWYER, P.H., *English Medieval Settlement*, 1979
SAWYER, P.H. (ed.), *Medieval Settlement*, 1974
TAYLOR, C., *Fields in the English Landscape*, Dent, 1982

New directions in funerary archaeology, Patrick Périn **106**
BRUCE-MITFORD, R. (ed.), *The Sutton Hoo Ship Burial*, British Museum, 3 Vol., London 1975, 1978 and 1981
DOPPELFELD, O. and R. Pirling, *Fränkische Fürsten im Rheinland. Die Gräber aus de Kölner Dom, von Krefeld-Gellep und Mor-Ken*, Düsseldorf, 1966
ERISON, V., "The body in the ship at Sutton Hoo", *Anglo-Saxon Studies I*, 1979, S.C. Hawkes et al, p. 121–38
MERTENS, J., "Tombes mérovingiennes et églises chrétiennes", in *Archaeologia belgica*, 187, Brussels, 1976
PÉTREQUIN, A.-M. and P. et al, "Le site funéraire de Soyria à Clair-vaux-les-Lacs (Jura), II.- Le cimetière mérovingien", in *Revue archéologique de l'Est et du Centre-Est*, no. 121–2, Dijon, July–Dec. 1980, p. 157–230
PRIVATI, B., *La Nécropole de Sézegnin (IVe-VIIIe siècle)*, Société d'Histoire et d'Archéologie de Genève, Geneva, 1983
YOUNG, B.-K. "Four Merovingian cemeteries in Eastern France: Lavoye, Dieue-sur-Meuse, Mézières-Manchester and Mazerny. A quantitative and qualitative study of funerary practices", *British Archaeological Reports*, International Series, 208, Oxford, 1984

Artisan production, Patrick Périn **108**
DECAENS, J., *Un nouveau cimetière du Haut Moyen Age en Normandie, Hérouvillette (Calvados)*, from Archéologie médiévale, 1971, pp. 1–126
PARRY, M.L., *Climatic Change, Agriculture and Settlement*, Folkestone, 1978
PLATT, C., *Medieval England: A Social History and Archaeology from the Conquest to AD1600*, London, 1978
SALIN, E., *La civilisation mérovingienne . . . , III. Les techniques*, Paris, 1957
WERNER, J., "Zur Verbreitung frühgeschichtlicher Metallarbeiten. Werkstatt, Wandernhandwerk, Handel, Familienverbindung", from *Antikvarist (Early Medieval Studies)*, Stockholm, Vol. 38, 1970, pp. 65–81

Trade and commerce, Patrick Périn **110**
CLARKE, H., and A. Carter, *Excavations in King's Lynn, 1963–70*, London, 1977
DUBY, G., *The Early Growth of the European Economy*, London, 1974
HUBERT, J., "Les grandes voies de circulation à l'intérieur de la Gaule mérovingienne d'après l'archéologie", in *Arts et vie sociale de la fin du monde antique au Moyen Age*, Geneva, 1977, pp. 317–24
JEZEGOU, M.-P., "L'épave byzantino-mérovingienne de Fos-sur-Mer (Bouches-du-Rhone)", in *Bulletin de liaison de l'Association française d'Archeologie merovingienne 2*, Paris, 1980, pp. 93–102
LAFAURIE, J., "Les routes commerciales indiquées par les trésors et trouvailles monetaires mérovingiens", in *Moneta e scambi nell' Alto Medioevo, Settimane di Studio del Centro italiano di Studi sull'Alto Medioevo*, (Spolete 1960), Spolete, 1961, pp. 231–78
WERNER, J., "Fernhandel und Naturalwirtschaft im östlichen Merowingereich nach archäologischen und numismatishen Zeugnissen", in *Moneta e scambi nell'Alto Medioevo, Settimane di Studio del Centro Italiano di Studi sull'Alto Medioevo* (Spolete, 1960), Spolete, 1961, pp. 557–618
WERNER. J., "Waage und Geld in der Merowingerzeit", in *Sitzungsberichte der Bayerischen Akademie der Wissenschaften*, Ph.-Hist, 1, Munich, 1954,

The archaeology of everyday life, Patrick Périn **112**
BUCHET, L., "La nécropole gallo-romaine et mérovingienne de Frénouville (Calvados). Etude anthropologique", in *Archéologie médiévale*, VIII, Paris, 1978
CHRISTLEIN, R., "Besitzabstufungen zur Merowingerzeit im Spiegel reicher Grabfunde aus – und Süddeutschland", in *Jahrbuch des Römisch-Germanisches Zentralmuseum Mainz*, 20 Jhrg., Mainz, 1973, pp. 147–80
DEMOLON, P., *Le village Mérovingien de Brébières (Pas-de-Calais)*, VIe–VIIe siecles, Historic Monuments Department, Pas-de-Calais, XIV, Arras, 1972
DOCKE, P. *Medieval Slavery and Liberation*, Chicago, 1982
KOENIG, G.G., "Schamane und Schmied, Medicus und Monch: ein Uberblick zur Archäologie der merowingerzeitlichen Medizin im südlichen Mitteleuropa", in *Helvetia Archaeologia*, 13, Basel, 1982, 51 and 52, pp. 75–154
MARTIN, M., *Das fränkische Gräberfeld von Basel-Bernerring*, Basler Beinträge zur Ur-und Frühgeschichte, I, Mainz and Basel, 1976
PÉRIN, P. and P. Forni, *La vie privée des hommes au temps des royaumes barbares*, Paris, 1984
PILET, C., "The necropolis at Frenouville (Calvados)", *British Archaeological Reports*, International Series, 83, 3 Vols., Oxford, 1980
WALLACE-HADRILL, J.M., *Early Medieval History*, Oxford, 1975
WERNER, J. et al, *Die Ausgrabungen in St. Ulrich und Afra in Augsburg*, (1961–66), Munchner Beitrage zur Vor- und Frungeschichte, 23, 2 vol., Munich, 1976

Barbarian cultures in the north and east, **114**
Michel Kazanski, Nicole Périn

Eastern Europe:
DUBROVIĆ, N., *Urbanizam krov vekove*, Vol. 1: Jugoslavija (Belgrade, 1950); B. Krekić, *Dubrovnik in the 14th and 15th Centuries*, Norman, 1972
GODLOWSKI, K., *Z badán nad zagadnieniem rozprzestrzenienia Slowian w V–VII w.n.e.* (Study of the spread of the Slavs in the 5th and 6th centuries), Institut Archeologii Universitetu Jagellonskiego, Cracow, 1979
RUSANOVA, I.P., *Slavjanskie drevnosti VI–VII vv* (Slav objects of the 6th and 7th centuries), Nauka, Moscow, 1976
SEDOV, V.V., *Vostočnye slavjane v VI–XIII vv.* (Oriental Slavs of the 6th and 8th centuries), Nauka, Moscow, 1982
TRET'JAKOV, P.N., *Finno-ugry, balty i slavjane na Dnepre i Volge*, (The Finno-Ugrians, Balts and Slavs in the Dnieper and Volga Valley), Nauka, Moscow, 1966
VÁNA, Z., *Le monde slave ancien*, Paris, 1983

Northern Europe:
FOOTE, P.G. and D.M. Wilson, *The Viking Achievement*, 3rd ed., 1978
OXENSTIERNA, E.G., *Die Nordgermanen*, Stuttgart, 1957
STENBERGER, M., *Vorgeschichte Schwedens*, Berlin, 1977
TODD, M., *The Northern Barbarians, 100BC–AD300*, London, 1975

THE MIDDLE AGES

The archaeological background, Jean Chapelot **116**
BOUÄRD, M. de, "Où en est l'archéologie médiévale?", *Revue historique*, 489, Paris, 1969
DUBY, G., *The Early Growth of the European Economy: Warriors and Peasants from the Seventh to the Twelfth Century*, London, 1974
PLATT, C., *Medieval England: A Social History and Archaeology from the Conquest to AD 1600*, London, 1978
SAMARAN, C. (ed.), *Encyclopedie de la Pléiade*, Paris, 1961
VAUFREY, R., "L'organisation des recherches et des études préhistoriques en France", *Revue scientifiques*, 10, Paris, 1941, pp. 438–518

Articles illustrating the main problems of medieval archaeology:
BARKER, P., *The Techniques of Archaeological Excavations*, London, 1977
BOUÄRD, M. de, *Manuel d'archéology medievale*, Paris, 1975
CHAPELOT, J. and G.D. d'Archimbaud, "Dix ans d'archéologie médiévale en France (1970–80)", in *Archeologia Medievale*, X, Genoa, 1983, pp. 297–316

Periodicals:
Anglo-Saxon England, Cambridge, from 1972
Archeologia Medievale, Genoa, since 1974
Medieval Archaeology, London, from 1957
Zeistchrift fur Archaologie des Mittelalters, Cologne, from 1973

Monumental archaeology, Marcel Durliat **118**
PRESSOUYRE, L., "Le cloître de Notre-Dame-en-Vauz à Châlons-sur-Marne", in *Congrès archéologique, Champagne, 1977*, Paris, 1980, pp. 298–206
PRESSOUYRE, S., *Images d'un cloître disparu. Le cloître de Name-Dame-En-Vaux à Châlons-sur-Marne*, Joël Cuénot S.I., 1976
RAVAUX, J.-P., "Les campagnes de construction de la cathédrale de Reims au XIIIe siècle", dans *Bulletin monumental*, CXXXVII, 1979, pp. 7–66
TALBOT-RICE, D., *English Art 871–1100*, 1952
TAYLOR, H.M. and J., *Anglo-Saxon Architecture*, 3 vols., 1966
VALLERY-RADOT, J., "L'Ancienne Prieurale Notre-Dame à la Charité-sur-Loire in *Congrès archéologique de France, Nivernais*, CXXV, 1967, pp. 43–83

Villages and houses, Jean Chapelot **120**
D'ARCHIMBAUD, G.D., *Les Fouilles de Rougiers, Contributions à l'archéologie de l'habitat rural médiéval en pays méditerranéen*, Paris, 1980
BERESFORD, G., *Clay Land Village: Excavations at Goltho and Berton Blount*, Society for Medieval Archaeology, Monograph Series, London, 1975
BERESFORD, M. and J. Hurst, *Deserted Medieval Villages*, London, 1971
BERESFORD, M., *The Lost Villages of England*, 1983 ed.
CHAPELOT, J., and R. Fossier, *Le village et la maison au Moyen Âge*, Paris, 1980; English translation, London, 1985
DYER, C., *Lords and Peasants: a changing society*, Cambridge, 1980
HURST, J.G. (ed.), *Wharram: Study of Settlement on the Yorkshire Wolds*, Society for Medieval Archaeology, Monograph Series, London, 1979
POSTAN, M., *The Medieval Economy and Society*, Pelican, 1975
ROWLEY, T., *Villages: the Landscape*, London, 1978

Fortifications, Jean Chapelot **122**
ABERG, F.A. (ed.), *Medieval Moated Sites*, London, 1978
BIDDLE, M. and D.H. Hill, "Anglo-Saxon planned towns", *Antiquaria Journal*, 51, 1971, pp.70–85
BOUÄRD, M. de, *Manuel d'archéologie médiéval. De la fouille a l'historie*, SEDES, Paris, 1975
DAVISON, B.K., "The origins of the castle: England", in *The Archaeological Journal*, CXXXIV, 1967, pp. 202–11
FINO, J.-F., *Forteresses de la France médiéval*, 1st ed., Paris, 1967
HALSLAM, J. (ed.), *Anglo-Saxon Towns*, 1984
RADFORD, C.A.R., "The later pre-conquest boroughs and their defences", *Medieval Archaeology*, 14, 1970, pp. 83–103
RITTER, R., *L'architecture militaire du Moyen Age*, Paris, 1974

Religious buildings in the early Romanesque, **124**
Jean-François Reynaud
ADDYMAN, P., and R. Morris, *The Archaeological Study of Churches*, research report no. 13, Council for British Archaeology, London, 1976
BARGELLINI, P., G. Morozzi, and G. Batini, *Looking Back to Santa Reparata; a cathedral within the cathedral*, Florence, 1971
BONNET, C., "Saint-Pierre de Genève. Récentes découvertes archéologiques", *Archeologie Suisse*, 4, 1980, pp. 174–91
MALONE, C., "Les fouilles de Saint-Benigne de Dijon (1976–78) et le problème de l'église de l'an mil". in *Bulletin Monumentale*, III, 1980, pp. 253–92
RENIMEL, S., "L'établissement clunisien primitif de la Charité-sur-Loire: bilan préliminaire de découvertes archéologiques de 1975", in *Bulletin Monumentale*, III, 1976, pp. 169–230
REYNAUD, J.F., "L'église Saint-Etienne du groupe episcopal de Lyon", *Revue de l'Art*, 47, 1980
SAINT-JEAN, R., "La Tribune monastique de Cruas," in *Les cahiers de Saint-Michel de Cuxa*, 1975
SAPIN, C., "L'ancienne église de Saint-Pierre l'Estrier à Autun", *Archéologie Médiévale*, XII, 1982, pp. 51–106
THOMAS, C., *Britain and Ireland in Early Christian Times*, London, 1971
THOMAS, C., *Christianity in Roman Britain*, Batsford, 1981
THOMAS, C. *The Early Christian Archaeology of North Britain*, Oxford, 1971

The medieval town, Jean Chapelot, **126**
Archeologie urbaine. Actes du colloque international, Tours, 17–20 Nov 1980, Association pour les fouilles archéologiques nationales, Paris, 1982; see special issue of *Monuments Historiques*, "Archéologie et project urbain" 136, Dec 1984–Jan 1985
DUBY, G., (ed.), *Histoire de la France urbaine*, Paris 1980–83
HALL, R.A. (ed.), *The Viking Age in York and the North*, London, 1975
HASLAM, J. (ed.), *Anglo-Saxon Towns*, Oxford, 1984
HEIGHWAY, C., *The Erosion of History*, Council for British Archaeology, London, 1972

Industry and everyday life, Jean Chapelot **128**
DODWELL, C.R., *Anglo-Saxon Art: Manchester, a new perspective*, 1982
HEWETT, C., "Anglo-Saxon Carpentry", *Archaeological Society of England*, vol. 7, 1978, pp. 205–29
HURST, J.G., "Anglo-Saxon pottery: a symposium", *Medieval Archaeology*, iii, 1959, pp. 1–78
WILSON, D.M., "Craft and Industry", in *The Archaeology of Anglo-Saxon England*, 1976, pp. 253–81

Two French museum catalogues cover daily life in the Middle Ages:
Aujoud'hui le moyen Âge: archéologie et vie quotidienne en France meridionale, Laboratory for Medieval Mediterranean Archaeology, University of Provence, Aix-en-Provence, 1981
Des Burgondes à Bayard: mille ans de Moyen Âge. Recherches archéologiques et historiques, Centre for historical archaeology for the museums of Grenoble and Isère, Grenobles, 1981

From Viking ship to three-master, Éric Rieth **130**
BASS, G.F., F.H. Van Doorninck *Yassi Ada I, A seventh-century Byzantine Shipwreck*, College Station, 1982
GREENHILL, B., *Archaeology of the Boat*, London, 1976
McGRAIL, S. (ed.), "Sources and techniques in boat archaeology", *British Archaeological Report*, s.29, Oxford, 1977

The Byzantine World

The archaeological background, Jean-Pierre Sodini **132**
Antioch-on-the Orontes, the Excavations. Publications of the Committee for the Excavations of Antioch and its Vicinity: I: ELDERKIN, G.W., *The Excavations of 1932*, Princeton, 1934; II: STILLWELL, R., *The Excavations of 1933–36*, Princeton, 1938; III: STILLWELL, R., *The Excavations of 1937–39*, Princeton, 1941; IV, 1: WAAGE, F.O., *Ceramics and Islamic coins*, Princeton, 1948; IV, 2: WAAGE, D.B., *Greek, Roman, Byzantine and Crusader Coins*, Princeton, 1952; V: LASSUS, J., *The Porticoes of Antioch*, Princeton, 1972
BECKWORTH, J., *The Art of Constantinople*, London, 1961
BELL, G.L., "Churches and monasteries of Tür Abdin and neighbouring districts", re-issued by A.A. Mango, London, 1982
BROWNING, R., *The Byzantine Empire*, 1980
DOWNEY, G., *Constantinople in the Age of Justinian*, London, 1964
GYLLES, P., *De Bosporo Thracio libri tres*, Lyon 1561 and *De Topographia Constantinopoleos et de illius Antiquitatibus libri quatuor*, Lyon 1561. These two essays are taken up again in: *Imperium Oriental sive Antiquitates Constantinopolitanae*, by A. Banduri, Paris 1711, pp. 264–428
HUMPHREY, J.H. (ed.), *Excavations at Carthage Conducted by the University of Michigan*, Vol. I-VII, Kelsey Museum, Ann Arbor, 1976–82
JONES, A.H.M., *The Later Roman Empire*, 3 vols., Oxford, 1970
LIEBESCHUETZ, J.H.W.G., *Antioch*, Oxford, 1972
MATTHEW, G., *Byzantine Aesthetics*, 1973
OSTROGORSKY, G., *History of the Byzantine State*, 1958
SEGAL, J.B., *Edessa, the Blessed City*, Oxford, 1970
TALBOT-RICE, D. *Byzantine Art*, 2nd ed., 1968
TEXIER, C. and R.P. Pullan, *Byzantine Architecture*, London, 1864
TOYNBEE, A. *Constantine Porhpyrogenitus and his World*, London, 1973
WELLESZ, E., *A History of Byzantine Music*, Oxford 1971
WHITTING, P., *Byzantium: an Introduction*, Oxford, 1971

Towns of the early Byzantine period, Jean-Pierre Sodini **134**
BALTY, J.C., *Guide d'Apamée*, Centre Belge de Recherches Archéologiques à Apamée de Syrie, Brussels, 1981
FOSS, C., *Byzantine and Turkish Sardis*, Cambridge-London, 1976
FOSS, C., *Ephesus after Antiquity: a late Antique, Byzantine and Turkish City*, Cambridge-London, 1979
JONES, A.H.M., *The Later Roman Empire*, Oxford, 1964
KONDIC, V. and V. Popovic, *Caričin Grad*, Galerie de l'Académie Serbe des Sciences et des Arts, Belgrade, 1977
KRAELING, C.H., *Gerasa, City of the Decapolis*, American Schools of Oriental Research, New Haven, 1938

Rural life at the end of antiquity, **136**
Jean-Pierre Sodini
Lyceum:
HARRISON, R.M., "Nouvelles découvertes romaines tardives et paléobyzantines en Lycie", *Comptes Rendus de l'Académie des Inscriptionset Belles Lettres*, Paris 1979, pp. 222–39

Cilicia:
EYICE, S., "Einige byzantinische Kleinstädte im Rauhen Kilikien", 150 Jahre, *Deutsches Archäologisches Institut 1829–1979*, Mainz 1982, pp. 204–09

Syria:
BUTLER, H.C., *Syria. Publications of the Princeton University Archaeological Expeditions to Syria in 1904–1905 and 1909. Architecture.* Section A: *Southern Syria*, Leiden, 1913; Section B: *Northern Syria*, Leiden, 1920
SODINI, J.-P., G. Tate B. and S. Bavant, J.-L. Biscop and D. Orssaud, "Déhès (Syrie du Nord), Campagnes I–III (1976–78)", in *Syria*, 57 Paris 1980, pp.1–306
TCHALENKO, G., *Villages Antiques de la Syrie du Nord*, I–III, Paris, 1953–58

Material culture, trade and exchange, **138**
Jean-Pierre Sodini
BASS, G.F., and F.H. van Doorninck, Jr., *Yassi Ada, A Seventh-Century Byzantine Shipwreck*, vol. 1, Texas A and M University Press, 1982
CRUIKSHANK DODD, E., *Byzantine Silver Stamps*, Dumbarton Oaks Studies, 7, Washington D.C., 1961
DEICHMANN, F.W., *Ravenna, Hauptstadt des spätantiken Abendlandes*, Wiesbaden: I: *Geshichte und Monumente*, 1969; II: *Kommentar*, 1, 1974, 2, 1976; II: (1976) *Plananhang*; III: *Frühchristlichen Bauten und Mosaiken von Ravenna*, 1968
HAYES, J.W., *Late Roman Pottery*, The British School at Rome, London, 1972
RILEY, J.A., "Coarse Pottery", *Excavations at Sidi Khrebish Benghazi (Berenice)*, vol. II, suppl. to *Libya Antiqua V*, vol. II, Tripoli, 1982
ROSS, M.C., *Catalogue of the Byzantine and Early Medieval Antiquities in the Dumbarton Oaks Collection*, Dumbarton Oaks Research Library and Collection, Washington, D.C.; vol. I: *Metalwork, Ceramics, Glass, Glyptics, Painting*, 1962; vol. II: *Jewelry, Enamels and Art of the Migration Period*, 1965
WALDBAUM, J.C., *Metalwork from Sardis: the finds through 1974*, Harvard University Press, 1983
WERNER, J., "Byzantinische Gürtelschnallen des. 6 und 7. Jahrhunderts aus Sammlung Diergardt", *Kölner Jahrbuch für Vor-und Frügheschichte*, Berlin, 1, 1955, pp.36–48

Invasions and collapse: the dark centuries, **140**
Michel Kazanski, Cécile Morrisson, Jean-Pierre Sodini
CHEETHAN, N., *Medieval Greece*, Yale and London, 1981
FOSS, C., "Archaeology and the "Twenty Cities" of Byzantine Asia", *American Journal of Archaeology*, 81, Cincinnati 1977, pp. 469–86
HADIDI, A. (ed.), *Studies in the History and Archaeology of Jordan I*, Department of Antiquities, Amman 1982. *See especially*:
McNICOLL, A. and A. Walmsley, "Pella/Fahl in Jordan during the Early Islamic Period", pp. 339–345
PICCIRILLO, M., "Forty years of archaeological work at Mount Nebo-Siyagha in Late Roman-Byzantine Jordan", pp. 291–300
SAUER, J.A., "The pottery of Jordan in the Early Islamic Period", pp. 329–36
TELL, S.K., "Early Islamic architecture in Jordan", pp. 323–28
HUSSEY, J.M., *Church-learning in the Byzantine Empire, 867–1185*, Oxford, 1937
JENKINS, R., *Byzantium, the Imperial Centuries, AD600–1071*, London, 1966
KURNATOWSKA, Z., *Słowiňaszczyzna poldniowa*, Warsaw-Krakow-Gdansk, 1977
LEMERLE, P., *Les plus anciens recueils de miracles de saint Démétrius*, 2 vols., CNRS, Paris, 1979–81
METCALF, D.M., "Corinth in the ninth century: the numismatic evidence", *Hesperia*, 42, Baltimore 1973, pp. 180–251
OBOLENSKY, D., "The empire and its northern neighbours", *Cambridge Medieval History IV*, I, Cambridge, 1966
POPOVIC, V., "La descente des Kourigours, des Slaves et des Avars vers la mer Egée: le témoninage de l'archéologie", *Comptes-rendus, Académie des Inscr. et Belles-Lettres*, 1978, pp. 596–648; "Aux origines de la slavisation des Balkans: la constitution des premières sklavinies macédoniennes vers la fin du VIe siècle", *Comptes rendus, A.I.B.L.*, 1980, pp. 230–57
POPOVIC, V., "Les temoins archéologiques des invasions avaro-slaves dans l'Illyrium byzantin", *Mélanges de l'Ecole Française de Rome, Antiquité*, 87, 1975, pp. 445–504
PREDA, C., "Circulatsia monedelar bizantine in regiunea carpato-dunareana", *Studi si cercetari de istorie veche*, 23, 1972, pp. 375–415
STRATOS, A.H., *Byzantium in the Seventh Century*, vols. 1–3, 1968–75
TOYNBEE, A., *Constantine Porphygenitus and his World*, London, 1973

Expansion and crisis: the end of Byzantium, **142**
Jacques Lefort, Cécile Morrisson, Jean-Pierre Sodini
BOURAS, C., "City and village: urban design and architecture", *Jahrbuch der Osterreichischen Akadenie Byzantin-*

istick, 31 vol., Wien, 1981, pp. 611–53; "Houses in Byzantium", in *Deltion tis Christianikis Archaiologikis Heterias*, I, II, 1982–83, Athens, 1983, pp. 1–26
CHEETHAN, N., *Medieval Greece*, Yale University Press, 1981
LEFORT, J., "En Macedoine Orientale au Xe seicle: habitat rural, communes et domaines", in *Occident et Orient au Xe siecle*, Actes du IXe Congrès de la Société des Historiens Médiévistes de l'Enseignement Supérieur Public (Dijon, 2–4 June 1978), Les Belles Lettres, Paris, 1979, pp. 251–72
LEFORT, J., *Villages de Macedoine 1, La Chalcidique occidentale*, Paris, 1982
LEMERLE, P., *Archives de l'Athos*, 12 vol., Paris since 1937
LEMERLE, P. *The Agrarian History of Byzantium from the Origins to the Twelfth Century*, Galway, 1979
MANGO, C., *Storia dell'Arte, La Civilta Bizantina dal IX al XV secolo, Corsi di Studi II, 1977*, Universita degli Studi di Bari, Bari, 1978, pp. 241–323
MILLER, W., *The Latins in the Levant: a History of Frankish Greece, 1204–1566*, London, 1908
NICOL, D.M., *Church and Society in the Last Centuries of Byzantium*, Cambridge, 1979
NICOL, D.M., *The End of the Byzantine Empire*, London, 1979
NICOL, D.M., *The Last Centuries of Byzantium, 1261–1459*, London, 1972
RUNCIMAN, Sir. S., *History of the Crusades*; Vol. 1: *The First Crusade*, Cambridge University Press, 1951; Vol. 3: *The Kingdom of Acre*, Cambridge University Press, 1954
RUNCIMAN, SIR. S., *Mistra: Byzantine capital of the Peloponnese*, Thames and Hudson, 1980
SCRANTON, R.L., *Corinth XVI, Medieval Architecture in the Central Area of Corinth*, The American School of Classical Studies in Athens, Princeton, 1957
ZEKOS, N., "Preliminary findings in Rodolibos and the surrounding region", (in Greek), *Orphéas*, 8–9, 1983, pp. 3–31

Ceramics: a new approach, Jean-Michel Spieser **144**
MEGAW, A., "An early thirteenth-century Aegean glazed ware", *Studies in Memory of D. Talbot-Rice*, Edinburgh University Press, 1975, pp. 34–45
MEGAW, A., "Zeuxippus Ware", *Annual of the British School at Athens*, 63, 1968, pp. 67–88
MORGAN, C.T., *Corinth*, vol. XI: *The Byzantine Pottery*, Cambridge, 1968
PESCHLOW, U., "Byzantinische Keramik aus Istanbul", *Istanbular Mitteilungen*, 27/28, Istanbul, 1977–8
TALBOT-RICE, D., *Byzantine Glazed Pottery*, Oxford, 1930

ISLAM

The archaeological background, Michel Terrasse **146**
ARTS COUNCIL OF GREAT BRITAIN, *The Arts of Islam*, London, 1976
CRESWELL, K.A.C., *A Bibliography of Architecture, Arts and Crafts of Islam*, Cairo, 1961
KHALDUN, I., *Histoires des Berberes*, 4 vols., Algiers, 1852–6
KHALDUN, I., "The Mugaddimah: an introduction to history", *Bollinger Series*, XLIII, 3 vols., New York, 1958
LACOSTE, Y., *Ibn Khaldun: The Birth of History and the Past of the Third World*, London, 1948
POPE, A.U., *A Survey of Persian Art*, London, 1939
TERRASSE, H., *L'art hispano-mauresque des origines a XIIIe siècle*, Paris, 1932

The Islamic town, Michel Terrasse **148**
BALBAS, L.T., *Ciudades hispano-musulmanas*, Instituto hispano-arabe de culture, Madrid, 1971
GOITEIRI, S.D., *A Mediterranean Society*, 4 vols., California, 1983
HOURANI, A.H. and S.M. Stern, *The Islamic City*, Oxford, 1970
SOURDEL, D. and J., *La Civilisation de l'Islam classique*, Paris, 1962

"Rediscovery" of the mosque, Michel Terrasse **150**
CRESWELL, K.A.C., *Early Muslim Architecture*, Oxford, 1969
GABRIEL, A., *Monuments turcs d'Anatolie*, Paris, 1931–4
GALDIERI, E., *Isfahan, Masjid i-Juma*, Rome, 1972
TERRASSE, H., *La mosquée al-Qarawiyin a Fès*, Paris, 1968

Regional traditions and domestic architecture, Michel Terrasse **152**
ARTS COUNCIL OF GREAT BRITAIN, *The Arts of Islam*, London, 1976
ASLANAPA, O., *Turkish art and architecture*, London, 1971
CRESWELL, K.A.C., *Muslim architecture of Egypt*, Oxford, 1952–9
GRABAR, O., et al., *City in the Desert, Qasr al-Hayr East*, Cambridge, 1978
HAMILTON, R. W., *Khirbat al-Mafjar: an Arabian Mansion in the Jordan Valley*, Oxford, 1959
MITCHELL, G., *Architecture of the Islamic World*, London, 1978
SCLUMBERGER, D. and J. Sourdel, *Lashkari Bazar ...*, Paris, 1978
TERRASSE, H., *Islam d'Espagne*, Paris, 1957

Trade routes, Michel Terrasse **154**
BRANDEL, F., *The Mediterranean*, 2 vols., Collins, 1972
CHALMETA, P., *El señor del zocco*, Instituto hispano-arabe de cultura, Madrid, 1973
Città portuali del Mediterraneo, collected works of the Faculty of Architecture, Genoa, 1985
GARZON PAREJA, M., *La industria sedera en España*, Granada, 1972
RICHARDS, D.S., *Islam and the Trade of Asia*, Oxford, 1970
ROSELLO BORDOY, G., *Ensayo do Systematización de la ceramica arabe en Mallorca*, Diputación Provincial, Palma de Mallorca, 1978

Hydraulic techniques, Michel Terrasse **156**
GRABAR, O., et al, *City in the Desert, Qasr al-Hayr East*, Cambridge, 1978
SOLIGNAC, M., *Recherches sur les installations hydrauliques de Kairouan et des steppes tunisiennes*, Algiers 1952

Fortifications and fortified sites, Michel Terrasse **158**
BASSET, H., and H. Terrasse, *Sanctuaires et forteresses almohades*, Paris, 1932
Encyclopédie de l'Islam, Brill, 2nd ed., since 1954, especially sections on Burdj and Hisn
TERRASSE, M., *La fortification omeiyade de Castilla*, Instituto de estudios islamicos, Madrid, 1968
TORRES BALBAS, L., *Ciudades hispano musulmanas*, Instituto hispano-arabe de Cultura, Madrid, 1971

Archaeology and the Islamic garden, Michel Terrasse **160**
ASLANAPA, O., *Turkish Art and Architecture*, London, 1971
CRESWELL, K.A.C., *Muslim Architecture of Egypt*, Oxford, 1952–9
GRABAR, O. et al, *City in the Desert, Qasr al-Hayr East*, Cambridge, 1978
HAMILTON, R.W., *Khirbat al-Mafjar: an Arabian Mansion in the Jordon Valley*, Oxford, 1959
SCHLUMBERGER, D. and J. Sourdel, *Lashkari Bazar*, Paris, 1978
TERRASSE, H., *Islam d'Espagne*, Paris, 1957

THE NEAR EAST

The Prehistoric Near East

The archaeological background, Francis Hours **162**
CAUVIN, J., and P. Sanlaville, (ed.), *Préhistoire du Levant*, International CNRS, Colloquium 598, Lyon, 10–14 June 1980, Paris, 1981
GARROD, D. and D. Bate, *The Stone Age of Mount Carmel I*, Oxford 1932
HOURS, F., L. Copeland and O. Aurenche, "Les industries paléolithiques du Proche-Orient, essai de corrélations", in *L'Anthropologie* 77, Paris, 1973, pp. 229–80 and 437–96
LLOYD, S., *The Archaeology of Mesopotamia*, London, 1978
MARKS, A. (ed.), *Prehistory and Paleoenvironments in the Central Negev, Israel*, 3 vol., Dallas, 1976–83
NEUVILLE, R., *Le Paléolithique et le Mésolithique du désert de Judée*, Paris, 1951
OPPENHEIM, A.L., *Ancient Mesopotamia*, Chicago, 1964
RUST, A., *Die Höhlenfunde von Jabrud (Syrien)*, Neumunster, 1950
WENDORF, F. and A. Marks (ed.) *Problems in Prehistory, North Africa and the Levant*, Dallas, 1975

Occupation of the Near East in the Paleolithic, Francis Hours **164**
CAUVIN, J. and P. Sanlaville (ed.), *Préhistoire du Levant*, International CNRS, Colloquium 598, Lyon, 10–14 June 1980, Paris, 1981
HOURS, F., L. Copeland and O. Aurenche, "Les industries paleolithiques du Proche-Orient, essai de corrélation", in *L'Anthropologie*, 77, Paris, 1973, PP. 229–80 and 437–96
WENDORF, F. and A. Marks (ed.), *Problems in Prehistory, North Africa and the Levant*, Dallas, 1975

The birth of agriculture, Jacques Cauvin **166**
CAUVIN, J., *Les Premiers villages de Syrie-Palestine du IXe au VIIe millénaire avant J.-C.*, Lyon, 1978
CAUVIN, J. and P. Sanlaville (ed.), *Préhistoire du Levant*, International Colloquium CNRS, 598, Paris, 1981
DANIEL, G., *The First Civilizations*, London, 1968
MELLAART, J., *The Neolithic of the Near East*, London, 1975
REDMAN, C.L., *The Rise of Civilization: from Early Farmers to Urban Society in the Ancient Near East*, San Francisco, 1978
REED, C.A. (ed.), *The Origins of Agriculture*, The Hague, 1977
UCKO, P.J., R. Tringham, G.W. Dimbleby (ed.), *Man, Settlement and Urbanism*, London, 1972

From village to town, Olivier Aurenche **168**
AURENCHE, O., *La maison orientale: l'architecture du Proche Orient ancien des origines au milieu de IVe millénaire*, Bibliothèque archéologique et historique 109, Paris, 1981
AURENCHE, O., "L'architecture mésopotamienne du VIIe au IVe millénaires", in *Paléorient*, 7 (2), 1981, pp. 43–55
AURENCHE, O., "Les premières maisons et les premiers villages, in *La Recherche*, 135, July–Aug 1982, pp. 880–9
BURNEY, C., *From Village to Empire*, Oxford, 1977
KENYON, K., "Ancient Jericho", in C.C. Lamberg-Karlovsky (ed.) *Old World Archaeology*, San Francisco, 1972
KRAMER, S.K., *The Sumerians*, Chicago, 1963

The expansion of the arts of fire, Marie le Mière and Claudine Maréchal **170**
BRAIDWOOD, R.J. and L. Braidwood, *Excavations in the Plain of Antioch. The Earlier Assemblages Phases A-J*, Oriental Institute Publications 61, The Oriental Institute of the University of Chicago, Chicago, 1960
GOURDIN, W.H. and W.D. Kingery, "The Beginnings of Pyrotechnology: Neolithic and Egyptian Lime Plaster", *Journal of Field Archaeology*, 2, Boston, 1975, pp. 133–50
LE MIÈRE M. "La céramique préhistorique de Tell Assouad, Djezireh, Syrie", in *Cahiers de l'Euphrate*, 2, Paris, 1979, pp. 4–76
MARÉCHAL, C., "Vaisselles blanches du Proche-Orient: El Kowm (Syrie) et l'usage du plâtre au Néolithique", in *Cahiers de l'Euphrate*, 3, Paris, 1982, pp. 217–51
MELDGAARD, J., P. Mortensen and H. Thrane, "Excavations at Tepe Guran, Luristan: a preliminary report of the Danish archaeological expedition to Iran", *Acta Archaeologica*, 34, Copenhagen, 1963, pp. 97–133

Neolithic art and ideology, Jacques Cauvin **172**
CAUVIN, J., *Religions néolithiques de Syro-Palestine*, Paris, 1972
MELLAART, J., *Catal Hüyük: A neolithic town in Anatolia*, London, 1967

Ancient Near East

The archaeological background, Jean-Louis Huot **176**
AMIET, P., *L'Art antique du Proche-Orient*, Paris, 1977
BURNEY, C., *From Village to Empire, an Introduction to Near Eastern Archaeology*, Oxford, 1977
CHARLES-PICARD, G., *L'archéologie, découverte des civilisations disparues*, Paris, 1969
DESHAYES, J., *Les civilisations de l'Orient ancien*, Paris, 1969
MALLOWAN, M.E.L., *Early Mesopotamia and Iran*, London, 1965
PARROT, A., *Archéologie Mésopotamienne, les étapes*, Paris, 1946
SETON-LLOYD, *Early Anatolia*, Penguin, 1956
SETON-LLOYD, *Foundations in the Dust*, 1947 and later editions

The colonization of Lower Mesopotamia, Jean-Louis Huot **176**
ADAMS, R. McC., *Heartland of Cities, Surveys of Ancient Settlement and Land Use on the Central Floodplan of the Euphrates*, Chicago and London, 1981
ADAMS, R. McC. and H.J. Nissen, *The Uruk Countryside, the Natural Setting of Urban Societies*, Chicago and London, 1972
HUOT, J.L., et al, *Larsa et 'Oueili, travaux de 1978–1981*, Paris, 1983
REDMAN, C.L., *The Rise of Civilization, from Early Farmers to Urban Society in the Ancient Near East*, San Francisco

The invention of writing, Daniel Arnand **178**
DRIVER, G.R., *Semitic Writing*, London, 1954
KRAMER, S.N., *History Begins at Summer*, London, 1958
KRAMER, S.N., *The Sumerians*, Chicago, 1963
"The Invention of Writing", in M.E.L. Mallowan's *Early Mesopotamia and Iran*, London, 1965
Naissance de l'ecriture. Cuneiformes et hieroglyphes, Museum catalogue from the Grand-Palais exhibition, Paris, 7 May–9 August 1982

Burial practices and society, Jean-Daniel Forest **180**
BINFORD, L., "Mortuary practices: their study and their potential", in *Approaches to the Social Dimensions of Mortuary Practices*, Memoirs of the Society for American Archaeology, 25, Washington D.C., 1971, pp. 6–290
FOREST, D., *Les pratiques funéraires en Mésopotamie du cinquième millénaire au début du troisième*, in Recherche sur les civilisations, ADPF (Association pour la diffusions de la pensée francaise), Paris, 1983
WOOLLEY, C.L., *The Royal Cemetery. Ur Excavations*, vol. II, British Museum, London, 1934
WOOLLEY, L., *Ur of the Chaldees*, first published 1919; revised ed. 1950

The emergence of Syria, Jean-Claude Margueron **182**
GELB, I.J., "Thoughts about Ebla: A Preliminary Evaluation", *Syro-Mesopotamia Studies*, 1977
MARGUERON, J.C., (ed.) *Le Moyen Euphrate, zone de contacts et d'échanges*, Strasburg Colloquium of 10–12 March 1977, Leiden, 1980
MATTHIAE, P., *Ebla, un Impero ritravato*, Turin, 1977
STROMMENGER, E., *Habuba Kabira, ein Stadt vor 5000 Jahren*, Mainz, 1980

Towns of the Iranian plateau in the 3rd millennium, Serge Cleuziou **184**
AMIET, P., "En Iran central, la civilisation du désert de Lut", in *Archéologia*, July 1973, pp. 21–7
GHIRSCHMAN, R., *Iran, Parthians and Sassanians*, London, 1962
LAMBERG-KARLOVSKY, C. and M. Tosi, "Shahr-i-Sokhta and Tepe Yahya, Tracks on the Earliest History of the Iranian Plateau", in *East and West*, 23, Rome, 1973, pp. 21–58
SCHMIDT, E.F., *Excavations at Tepe Hissar (Damghan)*, Philadelphia, 1937
TUCCI, G., (ed.), *La Citta 'brucciata del Deserto Salato*, Venice, 1977

The prehistory of the Gulf region, Serge Cleuziou **186**
BIBBY, G., *Looking for Dilmun*, New York, 1970
CLEUZIOU, S. and L. Constantini, "À l'origine des oasis", in *La Recherche*, 137, 1982, pp. 1180–2
FRIFELT, K., "On the Prehistoric Settlement and Chronology of the Oman Peninsula", in *East and West* 25, pp. 329–423
LARSEN, C.E., *Life and Land Use in the Bahrain Islands*, Chicago, 1984
OATES, J., "Prehistory in Northeastern Arabia", in *Antiquity*, vol. L, 197, London, 1976, pp. 20–31

Copper metallurgy in the 4th and 3rd Millennium BC, Thierry Berthoud **188**
BERTHOUD, T., S. Cleuziou, et al, "Cuivres et alliages en Iran, Afghanistan et Oman aux IVe et IIIe millenaires", *Paleorient*, Paris, 1982
HERMANN, G., *The Iranian Revival*, Oxford, 1977
LIMET, H., *Le travail du métal au pays de Sumer au temps de la IIIe dynastie d'Ur*, Paris, 1960
MUHLY, J.D., "Copper and Tin", in *Transactions*, 43, The Connecticut Academy of Arts and Sciences, New Haven, 1973; "Supplement to Copper and Tin", *ibid.*, 46, New Haven, 1976, pp. 77–136
SINGER, et al, *A History of Technology*, Oxford, vol. 1
WERTIME, T.A. and J.D. Muhly (ed.), *The Coming of the Age of Iron*, New Haven, 1980

Hittite seals, Dominique Beyer **190**
BERAN, T., *Die hethitische Glyptik von Boğazkoy*, I, 76. Wissenschaftliche Veröffentlichungen der deutschen Orient-Gesellschaft, Berlin, 1967
BITTEL, K., *Hattusha, the Capital of the Hittites*, London, 1970
BOEHMER, R.M., "Kleinasiatische Glyptik", in *Der Alte Orient, Propyläen Kunstgeschichte*, 14, Berlin, 1975
GURNEY, O., *The Hittites*, Harmondsworth, revised edition 1981
GÜTERBOCK, H.G., *Siegel aus Boğazköy I et II*, Archiv für Orientforschung, Beiheft 5 and 7, Berlin, 1940 and 1942
LAROCHE, E., "Documents hittites et hourrites" and D. Beyer, "Le Empreintes de sceaux", *Meskéné-Emar, dix ans de travaux, 1972–1982, à l'occasion d'une exposition*, Recherche sur les civilisations, Paris, 1982, pp. 53–60 and 61–8
LAROCHE, E. *Les Hiéroglypes hittites*, I, Paris, 1960

Syria and the Temple of Solomon, Jean-Claude Margueron **192**
BUSINK, T.A., *Der Tempel von Jerusalem von Salomo bis Herodes*, Leiden, 1970
MARGUERON, J., "À propos des temples de Syrie du Nord" in *Sanctuaires et clergés*, publication by Centre d'Histoire des Religions de l'Université in Strasburg, P. Geuthner
DE VAUX, R., "Note sur le temple de Salomon", *Bible et Orient*, Paris, 1967, pp. 203–16

The Phoenicians in Phoenicia, Jean-Louis Huot **194**
BRIEND, J. and J.B. Humbert, et al, *Tell Keisan (1971–1976), une cité phénicienne en Galilée*, Paris, 1980
CULICEN, W., *The First Merchant Venturers*, London, 1966
HARDEN, D.B., *The Phoenicians*, London, 1962
HITTI, P., *A History of Lebanon*, London, 1957
MOSCATI, S., *The Phoenicians*, London, 1970
PRITCHARD, J.B., *Recovering Sarepta, A Phoenician City*, Princeton, 1978

EGYPT AND SUDAN

The archaeological background, Jean Leclant **196**
ADAMS, W.Y., *Nubia: Corridor to Africa*, Princeton, 1977
ALDRID, C., *The Egyptians*, London, 1961
DAVID, A.R., *The Egyptian Kingdoms*, Oxford, 1975
DAWSON, W.R., and E.P. Uphill, *Who was who in Egyptology?* (2nd ed.) Oxford, 1972
EMERY, W.B., *Archaic Egypt*, Harmondsworth, 1961
GARDINER, A., *Egypt of the Pharaohs*, Oxford, 1961
HAYES, W.C., *The Scepter of Egypt*, (2 vols.) New York, 1953–9
MONTET, P., *Isis ou à la recherche de l'Egypte ensevelie*, Paris, 1956
SCHIFF GIORGINI, M., J. Leclant and C. Robichon, *Soleb*, I, Sansoni, Florence, 1965
SMITH, W.S., *The Art and Architecture of Ancient Egypt*, Baltimore, 1958

Egypt and the desert: rock carvings and oases, Jean Leclant **198**
DE CENIVAL, J.-L., *L'Égypte avant les Pyramides*, Museum catalogue, Reunion des Musées Nationaux, Paris, 1973
EMERY, W.B., *Archaic Egypt*, Harmondsworth, 1961
HUARD, P. and J. Leclant, *La culture des Chasseurs de Nil et du Sahara*, Memoires du CRAPE (Centre de Recherches Anthropologiques, Prehistoriques et Ethnographiques), 2 vols., Algiers, 1980

Necropolis of a capital: Memphis and Saqqara, Jean Leclant **200**
CAPART, J., *Memphis, à l'ombre des pyramides*, Brussels, 1930
EMERY, W., *Great Tombs of the First Dynasty*, 3 vols., i, Cairo, 1949; ii, London, 1954; iii, London, 1958
FRANKFORT, H., *Kingship and the Gods*, Chicago, 1948
GOYON, G., *Le secret des batisseurs des grandes pyramides*, Paris, 1977
LABROUSSE, A., J.-P. Lauer, and J. Leclant, *Le temple haut de complexe funéraire du roi Ounas*, Cairo, 1977
LAUER, J.-P., *Le mystère des pyramides*, Paris, 1974
LAUER, J.-P., *Saqqarah, le nécropole royale de Memphis*, Paris, 1977

Karnak: a dynastic sanctuary, Jean Leclant **202**
BARGUET, P., *Le temple d'Amon-Rè à Karnak*, Cairo, 1962
GARDINER, Sir A., *Egypt of the Pharaohs*, Oxford, 1961
KITCHENER, K.A., *Pharaoh Triumphant: The life and times of Rameses II, King of Egypt*, Warminster, 1982
LAUFFRAY, J., *Karnak d'Egypte*, domaine du divin, Paris, 1979
LEGRAIN, G., *Les temples de Karnak*, Brussels, 1929
SCHWALLER DE LUBICZ, R.A., *Les temples de Karnak*, Paris, 1982
SMITH, W.S., *The Art and Architecture of Ancient Egypt*, Baltimore, 1958

The Theban necropolis, Jean Leclant **204**
BELLOD, A., J.-C. Golvin and C. Traunecker, *Du ciel de Thèbes*, Paris, 1983
LECLANT, J., *Recherches sur les monuments thébains de la XXVe dynastie dite éthiopienne*, Cairo, 1965
NIMS, C., *La Thèbes des Pharaons*, Paris, 1965
WINLOCK, H.E., *The Rise and Fall of the Middle Kingdom in Thebes*, New York, 1947

Abu Simbel and Nubia, Jean Leclant **206**
ADAMS, W.Y., *Nubia, Corridor to Africa*, Princeton, 1977
CHRISTOPHE, L.A., *Abou Simbel et l'épopée de sa découverte*, Brussels, 1965
DESROCHES-NOBLECOURT, C. and C. Kuentz, *Le petit temple d'Abou Simbel*, Centre de Documentation, Cairo, 1968
GERSTER, G., *Nubien, Goldland am Nil*, Zurich, 1964

Kerma and Meroe, the first African empires, Jean Leclant **208**
BUDGE, E.A.W., *The Egyptian Sudan*, 2 vol., London, 1907
GRATIEN, B., *Les cultures Kerma, essai de classification*, Lille, 1978
HINTZE, F. and U., *Les Civilisations du Soudan antique*, Paris, 1967
SHINNIE, P.L., *Meroe, a civilization of the Sudan*, New York, 1967
ZABKAR, L.V., *Apedemak, Lion God of Meroe*, Warminster, 1975

SCYTHIA AND THE STEPPES

The archaeological background, Veronique Schiltz **210**
BRAŠINSKIJ, I.B., *V poiskax skifskix sokrovišč* (the quest for Scythian treasure), Nauka, Leningrad, 1979
DYSON-HUDSON, N., and W. Irons (eds.), *Perspectives on Nomadism*, Leiden, 1972
HERODOTUS, *Histories*, Book IV, Harmondsworth, 1968
JETTMAR, K.M., *Art of the Steppes*, London, 1967
MONGAIT, A., *L'archéologie en URSS*, Moscow, 1959
TOLSTOI, I.I., and N.S. Kondakov, *Russkie drevnosti v pamjatnikax iskusstva* (Russian antiquities in works of art), St Petersburg, 1890
RUDENKO, S.I., *Frozen Tombs of Siberia*, London, 1970
SULIMIRSKI, T., *Prehistoric Russia*, London, 1970
VADEČKAJA, E.V., *Skazy o drevnix kurganax* (collection of ancient kurgans), Nauka, Novosibirsk, 1981
WITSEN, N. *Noord-en-Oost Tartarye*, Amsterdam, 1785

The archaeology of a nomadic world, Veronique Schlitz **214**
EKVALL, R.B., *Fields on the Hoof*, New York, 1968
MASSON, V.M., and V.I. Sandriani, *Central Asia*, London, 1972

The Scythians and Asia, Veronique Schiltz **216**
BURNEY, C., *From Village to Empire*, London, 1977
PIOTROVSKY, B.B., *Urartu*, Geneva, 1969

Animals in art and religion, Veronique Schlitz **218**
ARTAMONOV, M., *Les tresors d'art des Scythes*, Cercle d'art, Paris, 1971
BESSONOVA, S.S., *Religioznye predstavlenija Skifov* (Religious concepts of the Scythians), Naukova dumka, Kiev, 1983
JETTMAR, K.M., *Art of the Steppes*, London, 1967
Scythian Gold, Museum catalogue of exhibition, British Museum, 1975
TALBOT-RICE, T., *The Scythians*, London, 1958
XAZANOV, A.M., *Zoloto skifov* (Scythian gold). Sovetskij xudoznik, Moscow, 1975

Burial practices: Tolstaia Mogila, Veronique Schiltz **220**
MOZOLEVSKIJ, B.M., *Tolstaia Mogila*, Naukova Jumka, Kiev, 1979

The art of the Steppes, 5th to 3rd centuries BC, Veronique Schlitz **222**
GRYAZNOV, M.X., *Southern Siberia*, Geneva, 1969
RUDENKO, S.I., *Frozen Tombs of Siberia*, London, 1970
RUDENKO, S.I., *Kul'tura naselenija central'nogo Altaja v skifskoe vremja* (Culture of the central Altai people in the Scythian period), Moscow-Leningrad, 1960

The Scythians and the Greek world, Veronique Schiltz **224**
MINNS, E.H., *Scythians and Greeks*, Cambridge, 1913
ONAIKO, N.A., *Anticnyi import v Pridneprov'e i Pobuz'e v IV–IIIvv do n.e.* (Ancient trading in the Dniepr and Bug regions in the 4th to 3rd centuries BC), S.A.I., Nauka, Moscow, 1970
ROSTOVTZEFF, M.I., *Iranians and Greeks in South Russia*, Oxford, 1922

CENTRAL ASIA

The archaeological background, Jean-Claude Gardin **226**
BALL, W., *Archaeological Gazetteer of Afghanistan*, 2 vol., Editions Recherche sur les Civilisations, Paris, 1982
BARTHOLD, V.V., *La découverte de l'Asie: historie de l'orientalisme en Europe et en Russie*, Paris, 1947
FRUMKIN, G., *Archaeology in Soviet Central Asia*, Leiden, 1970
HARMATTA, J. (ed.), *Prolegomena to the sources on the history of pre-islamic Central Asia*, Budapest, 1979
HOPKIRK, P., *Boudhas et rôdeurs sur la route de la soie*, Paris, 1981
LUNIN, B.V., *Srednjaja Azija v nauchnom nasledii otechestvennogo vostokovedenija*, Central Asia in the scientific heritage of the east, FAN Uzbekskoj SSR, Tashkent, 1979
MASSON, V.M. and V.I. Sandriani, *Central Asia*, London, 1972
SULIMIRSKI, T., *The Sarmatians*, London, 1970
VON GABAIN, A., *Einführung in der Zentralasienkunde*, Wissenschaftliche Buchgesellschaft, Darmstadt, 1979

Towns in the Bronze Age, Henri-Paul Francfort **228**
CASAL, J.-M., *Fouilles de Mudigak (Records of the Délégation Archéologique Française en Afghanistan, XVII)*, Klincksieck, Paris, 1961
DESHAYES, J., *Le plateau iranien et l'Asie centrale des origines à la conquête islamique*, Colloqium, Paris, 1977
KOHL, P.L., *Central Asia: Palaeolithic Beginnings to the Iron Age*, Recherches sur les Civilisations, no. 14, Paris, 1984
KOHL, P.L., *The Bronze Age Civilization of Central Asia*, New York, 1981
MASSON, V.M. and V.I. Sarianidi, *Central Asia: Turkmenia before the Achaemenids*, London, 1972
TALBOT-RICE, T., *The Arts of Central Asia*, London, 1958

Early irrigation: a model for archaeologists, Jean-Claude Gardin **230**
BILALOV, A.I., *Iz istorii irrigacii Ustrushany*, (history of irrigation in Ustrushan), Donish, Dushanbe, 1980
GARDIN, J.-C., "L'archéologie du paysage bactrien", in *Comptes rendus de l'Académie des Inscriptions et Belles-Lettres*, 1980, Paris, 1981, pp. 480–501
GARDIN, J.-C. and P. Gentelle, "L'exploration du sol en Bactriane antique", *Bulletin de l'Ecole Française d'Extrême-Orient*, LXVI, Paris, 1979, pp. 1–29
GARDIN, J.-C. and B. Lyonnet, "La prospection archéologique de la Bactriane orientale (1974–78): premiers résultats", in *Mesopotamia*, XIII-XIV (1978–79), Florence, 1980, pp. 99–154
GENTELLE, P., *Etude géographique de la plaine d'Aï-Khanoum et de son irrigation depuis les temps antiques*, Report of the URA 10, C.N.R.S., Paris, 1978
GULJAMOV, J.G., *Istorija oroshenija Khorezma e drevnejshikh vremen do nashikh dnej* (history of irrigation in Khwarezm from ancient times until the present), Tashkent, 1957
LISICYNA, G.N., "The history of irrigation agriculture in Southern Turkmenia", in P. Kohl (ed.) *The Bronze Age Civilization of Central Asia*, New York, 1981, pp. 350–58

The Hellenistic towns of Central Asia, Pierre Leriche **232**
BERNARD, P., "Ai Khanoum on the Oxus", *Proceedings of the British Academy*, 53 (1968)
MARTIN, R., *L'urbanisme dans la Grèce Antique*, Paris, 1982
ROSTOVTZEFF, M.I., *Caravan Cities*, Oxford, 1932
SCHLUMBERGER, D., *L'Orient hellénisé*, Paris, 1970
STAVISKII, *La Bactriane kouchane*, CNRS, Valbonne, 1985
WYCHERLEY, R.E., *How the Greeks Built Cities*, London, 1962

The last days of the Sogdian civilization, Frantz Grenet **234**
AZARPAY, G., *Sogdian Painting* (with contributions by A.M. Belenitsky, B.I. Marshak and M.J. Dresden), Berkeley–Los Angeles–London, 1981
BELENITSKY, A., *Asie centrale*, Paris-Geneva-Munich, 1968
BELENITSKY, A.M. and B.I. Marshak, "L'art de Piendjikent à la lumière des dernières fouilles (1958–68)", in *Arts Asiatiques*, XXIII, Paris, 1971, p. 3
BELENITSKY, A., *Mittelasien. Kunst der Sogden*, Leipzig, 1980

Funerary practices in pre-Islamic Central Asia, Frantz Grenet **236**
AZARPAY, G., "Iranian divinities in Sogdian painting", *Acta Iranica* 4, Tehran, 1975, pp. 19–29
BOYCE, M., *Zoroastrians: Their Religious Beliefs and Practices*, London, 1979
DROWER, E.S., "Death and rites for the souls of the dead", in *The Mandaeans of Iraq and Iran*, Oxford, 1937
FRUMKIN, G., *Archaeology in Soviet Central Asia*, Handbuch der Orientalistik (VII. Abt., III. Bd., 1. Abschn.), Leiden-Cologne, 1970
GRENET, F., *Les practiques funéraires dans l'Asie centrale sedentaire de la conquête grecque a l'islamisation*, CNRS, Paris, 1984
RUDOLPH, K., *Mandaeism*, Leiden, 1978

THE INDIAN WORLD

The archaeological background, Jean-François Jarrige **238**
ALLCHIN, B., and R. Allchin, *The Rise of Civilization in India and Pakistan*, Cambridge, 1982
ALLCHIN, B., and R. Allchin, *The Birth of Indian Civilization*, Harmondsworth, 1968
ALLCHIN, F.R. and D.K. Chakrabarti (eds.), *A Source Book of Indian Archaeology*, Delhi, 1979
FAIRSERVIS, W.A., *The Roots of Ancient India*, Chicago, 1975
LAL, B.B., and S.P. Gupta (eds.), *Frontiers of the Indus Civilization*, New Delhi, 1984
SANKALIA, H.D., *Prehistory of India*, New Delhi, 1977
WHEELER, Sir M., *The Indus Civilisation*, Cambridge, 1968

Agricultural origins in the Indian subcontinent, Jean-François Jarrige **240**
COSTANTINI, L., "The beginning of agriculture in the Kachi Plain: the evidence of Mehrgarh", in *South Asian Archaeology 1981*, Cambridge, 1984

JARRIGE, J.F., "Chronology of the earlier periods of the Greater Indus as seen from Mehrgarh", in *South Asian Archaeology 1981*, Cambridge, 1984
LECHEVALLIER, M., and G. Quivron, "The Neolithic in Baluchistan: new evidence from Mehrgarh", in *South Asian Archaeology 1979*, Berlin, 1981
MEADOW, R.H., "Prehistoric animal exploitation in the Greater Indus Valley: notes on the afaunal remains from Mehrgarh, Pakistan, with a focus on cattle (Bos.)", in *South Asian Archaeology 1981*, Cambridge, 1984
MEADOW, R.H., "Animal domestication in the Middle East: a view from the eastern margin", In *Animals and Archaeology, vol. 3: Early Herders and their Flocks*, J. Clutton-Brock and C. Grigson (eds.), British Archaeological Reports International Series 202, 1984, pp. 309–37

Baluchistan villages and Indus cities, 242
Jean-François Jarrige
CASAL, J.M., *La civilisation de l'Indus et ses enigmes*, Paris, 1969
JARRIGE, J.F., "Economy and society in the early Chalcolithic Bronze Age of Baluchistan: new perspectives from recent excavations at Mehrgarh", in *South Asian Archaeology* 1979, H. Härtel (ed.), Berlin, 1981
SHAFFER, J.G., *Prehistoric Baluchistan*, Indian Society for Prehistoric and Quarternary Studies, Delhi, 1978
WHEELER, M., *The Indus Civilisation*, 3rd ed., Cambridge, 1968

The second agricultural revolution, Jean-François Jarrige **244**
COSTANTINI, L., "Paleoethnobotany at Pirak: a contribution to the 2nd millennium BC agriculture of the Sibi-Kacchi Plain, Pakistan", in *South Asian Archaeology 1979*, H. Hartel (ed.) Berlin, 1981, pp. 271–7
DHAVALIKAR, M.K., "Early farming cultures of the Deccan", D.P. Agrawal and D.K. Chakrabarti (eds.) *Essays in Indian Protohistory*, Indian Society for Prehistoric and Quaternary Studies, Delhi, 1979
JARRIGE, J.F., M. Santorini and J.F. Enault, *Fouilles de Pirak*, Paris, 1979
JOSHI, J.P. et al, "The Indus civilization: a reconsideration on the basis of distribution maps", *Frontiers of the Indus Civilization*, B.B. Lal and S.P. Gupta (eds.), Indian Archaeological Society, New Delhi, 1984

The Ganges valley at the dawn of history, 246
Jean-Francois Jarrige
BANERJEE, N.R., *The Iron Age in India*, Delhi, 1965
GHOSH, A., *The City in Early Historical India*, Indian Institute for Advanced Study, Simla, 1973
SILVI ANTONONI, C. and G. Stacul, *The Proto-historic Graveyards of Swat*, Rome, 1972

SOUTHEAST ASIA

The archaeological background, Bernard Philippe Groslier **248**
GROSLIER, B.P. (ed.), "Cinquante ans d'Orientalisme", in Bull. Soc. Etudes Indoch., XXVI, 4, Saigon 1951; "Cinquante ans d'Orientalisme en France", special edition, *Journal Asiatique*, 1973, CCLXI, 1–4
FILLIOZAT, J. (ed.), *Travaux et perspectives de l'École française d'Extrême-Orient ... 75*[e] anniversaire, Ecole française d'Extreme-Orient, Paris, 1976
SMITH, R.B., and W. Watson (eds.), *Early South East Asia*, Oxford, 1979

The prehistory of Thailand, Per Sørensen **250**
GORMAN, C., "Excavations at Spirit Cave, North Thailand", *Asian Perspectives*, 13, Honolulu, 1972
HEEKEREN, H.R. van, and Count E. Knuth, "Sai Yok: Stone Age settlements in the Kanchanaburi province", Archaeological Excavations in Thailand, 1 Copenhagen, 1967
SØRENSEN, P., "Further notes on the Early Paleolithic of Northern Thailand", *Annual Newsletter of Scandinavian Institute of Asian Studies*, 15, Copenhagen, 1982
SØRENSEN, P., "Preliminary note on the relative and absolute chronology of two Early Paleolithic sites from Northern Thailand", *Union Internationale des sciences prehistoriques et protohistoriques*, Coll. 7, Nice, 1976
VERSTAPPEN, H.T., "On palaeoclimates and landform development in Melasia", *Modern Quaternary Research in Southeast Asia*, 1, Rotterdam, 1975

Agricultural civilizations, Per Sørensen **252**
BAYARD, D.T., "Excavations at Non Nok Tha, Northeastern Thailand, 1968: an interim report", *Asian Perspectives*, 13, Honolulu, 1972
GORMAN, C. and P. Chareonwongsar, "Ban Chiang: a mosaic of impressions from the first two years", *Expedition*, 18, No. 4, Philadelphia, 1976
HIGHAM, C.F.W., "The Ban Chiang culture in wider perspective", *Sir Mortimer Wheeler Archaeological lecture*, London, 1983
WHITE, J.C., "The Ban Chiang tradition: innovators and artists in prehistoric Northeast Thailand", in *Discovery of a lost Bronze Age: Ban Chiang*, Philadelphia, 1982

The "Indianization" of Southeast Asia, 254
Bernard Philippe Groslier
CASAL, J.M., *Fouilles de Virampatnam-Arikamedu*, PUF, Paris, 1949
COEDES, G., *The Indianized States of Southeast Asia*, Honolulu, 1968
FILLIOZAT, J., "La Valeur des connaissances gréco-romaines sur l'Inde," *Journal des Savants*, April–June 1981, Paris, pp. 97–136
MALLERET, L., *Archéologie du delta du Mékong*, Ecole francaise d'Extrême-Orient, 4 vol. Paris, 1959–62
SCHLUMBERGER, D., *L'Orient hellénisé; L'Art dans le Monde*, P.A. Michel, 1970 (pocket edition 1984)
WARMINGTON, E.H., *The Commerce between the Roman Empire and India*, Cambridge, 1928
WHEELER, Sir Mortimer., *Rome beyond the Imperial Frontier*, London, 1954

Angkor: the archaeology of an agricultural empire, 256
Bernard Philippe Groslier
GROSLIER, B.P., "Agriculture et Religion dans l'Empire angkorien", in *Etudes rurales*, 53–6, Paris, 1974, pp. 95–117
GROSLIER, B.P., *Angkor et le Cambodge au XVI*[e] ..., PUF, Paris, 1958
GROSLIER, B.P., "La Cité hydraulique angkorienne ...", in *Bull. École française d'Extrême-Orient*, LXV, Paris, 1978, pp. 161–202
GROSLIER, B.P., "Pour une géographie historique du Cambodge", in *Cahiers d'Outre-Mer*, Bordeaux, 1973, 104, pp. 337–79
SMITH, R.B., and W. Watson (eds.), *Early South East Asia*, 1979

CHINA

The archaeological background, 258
Michèle Pirazzoli-t'Serstevens
CHANG KWANG-CHIH, *The Archaeology of Ancient China*, New Haven and London, 1977
ELISSEEFF, D. and V., *Nouvelles découvertes en Chine, l'histoire revue par l'archéologie*, Office du Livre, Fribourg, 1983
HUGHES-STANTON, P., and R. Kerr, *Kiln Sites in Ancient China, Recent Finds in pottery and porcelain*, Oriental Ceramic Society, London, 1981
KEIGHTLEY, D.N. (ed.), *The Origins of Chinese Civilization*, Berkeley, 1983
LOEWE, M., *Records of the Han Administration*, Cambridge, 1967
NEEDHAM, J., *Science and Civilisation in China*, Cambridge, 1954
WANG SHONGSHU, *Han Civilization*, New Haven and London, 1982
WATSON, W., *China*, London, 1961
WATSON, W., *The Genius of China*, London, 1973
WEN FONG (ed.), *The Great Bronze Age of China*, Metropolitan Museum of Art, New York, 1980

North and south in the Chinese Neolithic, 260
Maud Girard-Geslan
CHANG KWANG-SHIH, *The Archaeology of Ancient China*, New Haven and London, 1977
DU YAOXI, Li Jiafang, *Song Zhaolin, Zhonguo yuanshe shehuishi* (a history of primitive Chinese society), Peking, 1983
HO PING-TI, *The Cradle of the East*, Chicago, 1975
KEIGHTLEY, D.N. (ed.), *The Origins of Chinese Civilization*, Berkeley, 1983
SU BINGQI and Yin Weizhang, "Guanyu kaoguxue wenhuade quxi leixing wenti" (the differentiation of cultures in archaeology) *Wenwu*, Peking, 1981–5
YIN DA, *Xin shiqi shidai* (the Neolithic) 2nd ed., Peking 1979

Bronze, iron and steel, Maud Girard-Geslan **262**
BARNARD, N., *Bronze Casting and Bronze Alloys in Ancient China*, Canberra, 1961
BARNARD, N., and Satō Tamotsu, *Metallurgical Remains in Ancient China*, Tokyo, 1975
BARNARD, N., "Further Evidence to Support the Hypothesis of Indigenous Origins of Metallurgy in Ancient China", in D.N. Keightley (ed.), *The Origins of Chinese Civilization*, Berkeley, 1983
FRANKLIN, U.M., "On Bronzes and Other Metals in Early China", in *The Origins of Chinese Civilization*, Berkeley, 1983
NEEDHAM, J., *Science and Civilisation in China*, Cambridge, 1954
WATSON, W.X., *Ancient Chinese Bronzes*, London, 1962

Burial practices of the Chu kingdom, Alain Thote **264**
BARNARD, N. (ed.), *Early Chinese Art and its Possible Influence in the Pacific Basin*, New York, 1972
JULIANO, A.L., "Three Large Chu graves recently excavated in the Chiangling district of Hupei province," in *Artibus Asiae*, 34, 1, Ascona, 1980
MAJOR, J.S. "Research Priorities in the Study of Ch'u Religion", in M. Eliade and J.M. Kitagawa (eds.) *History of Religions*, vol. 17, Chicago, 1978
RAWSON, J., *Ancient China, Art and Archaeology*, London, 1980

Specific sites mentioned in the text are further discussed in these Chinese publications (site listed in parentheses):
Wenwu 1979/7/ (Leigudun); *Wenwu* 1980/10 (Xiasi); *Kaogu Xuebao* 1982/1 (Tianxingguan)

The origins and production of lacquer, Alain Thote **266**
GARNER, H., *Chinese Lacquer*, London, 1979
LAWTON, T., *Chinese Art of the Warring States Period*, Washington D.C., 1982
MEDLEY, M., *A Handbook of Chinese Art for Collectors and Students*, London, 1964

Specific sites mentioned in the text are further discussed in these Chinese publications (site listed in parentheses):
Henan Xinyang, 1959 (Changtaiguan); *Kaogu* 1980/5 (Yutaishan); *Kaogu Xuebao* 1974/2 (Fenshuiling), 1982/1 (Tianxingguan); *Wenwu* 1965/5 (Wangshan), 1974/8 (Taixicun), 1976/3 (Shangcunling), 1979/7 (Leigudun), 1981/1 (Qingchuan).

Music in ancient China, Alain Thote **268**
HIGUCHI, T., *Gakki*, Benrido, 1982
KANE, V., "The Independent Bronze Industries in the South of China Contemporary with the Shang and Western Chou Dynasties", included in *Archives of Asian Art*, 28, Kansas, 1974–5
MA HIAO TS'IUN, "La Musique chinoise", in N. Dufourcq, *La Musique des origines à nos jours*, Paris, 1946
WATSON, W., *The Genius of China*, London, 1973
WOSKIN, K.J. de, *A Song for One or Two: Music and the Concept of Art in Early China*, Michigan Papers in Chinese Studies, 42, Michigan, 1982

Food and diet in the Han period, 270
Michèle Pirazzoli-t'Serstevens
Changsha Mawangdui yihao Han mu (Han tomb No. 1 at Mawangdui in Changsha), 2 vols., Wenwu chubanshe, Peking, 1973
HAYASHI, M., *Kandai no bumbutsu* (Civilization in the Han period), Research Institute for Humanistic Studies, Kyoto, 1976
LOEWE, M., *Everyday Life in Early Imperial China during the Han Period*, London, 1968
PIRAZZOLI-T'SERSTEVENS, M., *La Chine des Han*, Paris, 1982

New perspectives in philosophy and religion, 272
Evelyne Mesnil
"A Report on Stone Statues discovered in Mt Kongwangshan", in *Wenwu*, 1, Peking, 1981 (Chinese text with many illustrations)
HENRICKS, R.G., "Examining the Ma-wang-tui Silk Texts of Lao-tzu", in *T'oung Pao*, 65, Leiden, 1979
JAN, Y.-H., "The Silk Manuscripts on Taoism", *T'oung Pao*, 63, Leiden, 1977
LOEWE, M., *Ways to Paradise: The Chinese Quest for Immortality*, London, 1979
TU, W.-M., "The Thought of Huang-Lao: a reflection on the Lao Tzu and Huang Ti Texts in the Silk Manuscripts of Ma-wang-tui", in *Journal of Asian Studies*, 39, U. of Washington, 1979

Tang burial paintings: views of a courtly society, 274
Caroline Gyss-Vermande
FONG, M., "Four Royal Chinese Tombs of the Early 8th Century", in *Artibus Asiae*, XXXV, 4, Ascona, 1973
FONG, M., "T'ang Tomb Wall Paintings of the Early 8th Century", in *Oriental Art*, XXIV, 2, London, 1978
QIN WEN, "Deux Galeries souterraines de peintures murales de la dynastie de Tang", in *Nouvelles Découvertes archéologiques en Chine*, II, Peking, 1980
SULLIVAN, M., *Chinese Landscape Painting in the Sui and T'ang Dynasties*, Berkeley, 1980

Bourgeois life: Sung, Liao and Chin Dynasties, 276
Caroline Gyss-Vermande
KARETZKY, P.E., "The Recently Discovered Chin Dynasty Murals illustrating the Life of the Buddha at Yen-shang ssu, Shansi", in *Artibus Asiae*, XLII, 4, Ascona, 1980
MAEDA, R.J., "Some Sung, Chin and Yüan representations of actors", in *Artibus Asiae*, XLI, 2–3, Ascona, 1979
"Peintures murales d'une tombe de la dynastie des Liao a Kulun", in *Nouvelles Découvertes archéologiques en Chine*, II, Peking, 1980
SU BAI, *Baisha Songmu* (Tombs from the Sung Period at Baisha) Peking, 1957

The emergence of agriculture, Colette Diény **278**
Ancient China's Technology and Science, compiled by the Institute of the History of Natural Sciences, Chinese Academy of Science, Peking, 1983
CHANG KWANG-CHIH, *The Archaeology of Ancient China*, 3rd ed., New Haven, 1977
HO PING-TI, *The Cradle of the East*, Hong Kong, 1975
HSU CHO-YUN, *Han Agriculture*, Seattle, 1980
KEIGHTLEY, D.N., *The Origins of Chinese Civilization*, Berkeley, 1983
LIU XIANZHOU, *Zhongguo gudai nongye jixie faming shi* (History of the discovery of agricultural instruments in ancient China), Peking, 1963

Chinese astronomy, Carole Morgan **280**
MASPERO, H., "L'Astronomie chinoise avant les Han", in *T'oung Pao*, XVI, Leiden, 1929
MASPERO, H., "Les Instruments astrologiques des Han", in *Mélanges chinois et bouddhiques*, Vi, Brussels, 1939
NEEDHAM, J., *Science and Civilisation in China*, III, Cambridge, 1957

(For archaeological discoveries mentioned in the text, see *Wenwu* 9 (1972), 8 (1975), 2 (1978); *Kao gu* 1 (1975)

Iran and China: importation and influences, 282
Michèle Pirazzoli-t'Serstevens
FONTIEN, J., and Tung Wu, *Unearthing China's Past*, Boston, 1973
RAWSON, J., *The Ornament on Chinese Silver of the Tang Dynasty (AD618–906)*, occasional Paper no. 40, British Museum, London, 1982
Wenhua dageming qijan chutu wenwu (Cultural remains discovered during the cultural revolution), Wenwu chubanshe, Peking, 1972

The ceramic route, Michèle Pirazzoli-t'Serstevens **284**
GROSLIER, B.P., "La Ceramique chinoise en Asie du Sud-Est, quelques points de methode", in *Archipel*, 21, Paris, 1981
GYLLENSVARD, B., "Recent finds of Chinese ceramics at Fostat", in *Bulletin of the Museum of Far Eastern Antiquities*, I–II, 45, Stockholm, 1975
LOCSIN, L and C., *Oriental Ceramics Discovered in the Philippines*, Tokyo, 1967
McKINNON, E.E., "Oriental Ceramics excavated in North Sumatra", in *Transactions of the Oriental Ceramic Society*, London, 1975–77
SALMON, C., and D. Lombard, "Un vaisseau du XIII[e] siecle retrouve avec sa cargaison dans la rade de Zaitun", in *Archipel*, 18, Paris, 1979
Special Exhibition of Cultural relics found off Sinan Coast, National Museum of Korea, Seoul, 1977
TREGEAR, M., *La Ceramique Song*, Fribourg, 1982
WHITEHOUSE, D., "Maritime Trade in the Arabian Sea", in M. Taddei (ed.) *South Asian Archaeology*, Naples, 1979

VIETNAM

The archaeological background, Maud Girard-Geslan **286**
BEZACIER, L., *L'Asie du Sud-Est* (vol. 2): *Le Vietnam*, Paris, 1972
Bulletin de l'Ecole française d'Extrême-Orient, Hanoi, Paris
DAVIDSON, J., "Archaeology in Northern Viet-Nam since 1954", in *Early South-East Asia*, Oxford, 1979
DAVIDSON, J., "Archaeology in Southern Viet-Nam since 1954", *ibid.*, Oxford, 1979
HA VAN TÂN, "Nouvelles Recherches prehistoriques et protohistoriques au Vietname", in *Bulletin de l'Ecole française d'Extreme-Orient*, 1980
Kao cô hoc (Archaeological Review), Hanoi
NGUYEN PHUC LONG, "Les Nouvelles recherches archéologiques au Vietnam", in *Arts Asiatiques*, XXXI, Paris, 1975

The pebble tools of the Hoabinhian culture, **288**
Dinh Trong Hieu
BORISKOVKII, P.I., "Vietnam in Primeval Times", *Soviet Anthropology and Archaeology*, VII–IX, New York, 1968–71
COLANI, M., "L'Age de la pierre dans la province de Hoa-Binh (Tonkin)", *Memoire* du Service geologique de l'Indochine, XIV, Hanoi, 1929
DINH TRONG HIEU, "Remarques apres quelques travaux en archéologie prehistorique effectues sur le terrain et en laboratoire au Vietnam", *Cahiers d'Etudes Vietnammiennes*, 4, Paris, 1980
GLOVER, L.C., "The Hoabinhian: Hunter-Gatherers or Early Agriculturists in South-East Asia?", in J.V.S. Megaw (ed.), *Hunters, Gatherers and First Farmers beyond Europe*, Leicester, 1977
HA VAN TÂN, "Le Hoabinhien dans le contexte du Viet Nam", in *Donnees archéologiques*, vol. 1, *Etudes Vietnammiennes*, No. 46, Hanoi, 1976
MATTHEWS, J.M., *The Hoabinhian in South East Asia and Elsewhere*, Canberra, 1964

Bronze drums of Southeast Asia, Maud Girard-Geslan **290**
GOLOUBEW, V., "L'Age du bronze au Tonkin et dans le Nord-Annam", *Bulletin de l'Ecole française d'Extreme-Orient*, vol. XXIX, Hanoi, 1929
HEGER, F., *Alte Metalltrommeln aus Sudost Asien*, Leipzig, 1902
NGUYEN DUY HINH, "Vê quan diêm cua môt sô hôc gia Trung quôc nghiên cú'u trông dông ngu'ò'i Viêt", Khao co hoc, no. 4, Hanoi, 1979
PIRAZZOLI-T'SERSTEVENS, M., "The Bronze Drums of Shizhaishan, their Social and Ritual Significance", in R.B. Smith and W. Watson (eds.), *Early South-East Asia*, Oxford, 1979

KOREA AND JAPAN

The archaeological background, **292**
Madeleine Paul-David

Japan
(The bibliography of Japanese archaeology is extensive, with universities and museums publishing numerous reports. The two oldest and most respected are *Shigaku zasshi* [Historical journal] and *Kokogaku zasshi* [Archaeological journal]. The evolution of Japanese archaeology has been covered by Saito Tadashi, *Nihon Kokogaku Shi*, Tokyo, 1974. *Nihon no bijutsu*, published by the national museums of Tokyo, Kyoto and Nara, covers subjects from the Paleolithic [Kyuseki jidai] to the Yayoi era, nos. 188–92.)
BERTHIER, F., *Extreme-Orient (Japon: art et archéologie)*, Paris, 1984
CHARD, C.S., *Northeast Asia in prehistory*, Madison, Wisconsin, 1974
ELISSEEFF, V., "Le Paleolithique de l'Asie nord-orientale et le Neolithique de l'Asie nord-orientale", in A. Varagnac (ed.), *L'Home avant l'ecriture*, Paris, 1968
Sekai kokogaku jiten (world dictionary of archaeology), Tokyo, 1979

Korea
(A very full bibliography can be found in the *Korea Review*, a publication of the national Korean commission on behalf of UNESCO, vol. XIII, no. 4, winter 1981 (Korean studies today). See also Kim Won-Yong, "Korean Archaeology Today", pp. 56–96).
DAVID, M.-P., *Corée (arts)*, Paris, 1984
DAVID, M.-P., *Extrême-Orient (Coree: prehistorie, archéologie et art), ibid.*
GARDINER, K.H.J., *The Early History of Korea*, Canberra, 1969
GOEPPER, R., and R. Whitfield, *Five Thousand Years of Korean Art*, catalogue of exhibition organized by the National Museum of Korea presented internationally in Britain and the United States, 1979–81
GOEPPER, R., and R. Whitfield, *Treasures from Korea*, Trustees of the British Museum, London, 1984

The emergence of the Paleolithic, **294**
Danielle and Vadime Elisseeff
AKAZAWA, T., S. Oda and I. Yamanaka, *The Japanese Palaeolithic: a Techno-Typological Study*, Tokyo, 1980
GAMI, E., N. Seriawa, H. Otsuka and K. Mori, *Image and Life: 50,000 Years of Japanese Prehistory*, museum exhibition catalogue, Ann Arbor, Michigan, 1978
PEARSON, R., "Paleoenvironment and human settlement in Japan and Korea", *Science*, Washington D.C., 1977

Rice cultivation, Danielle and Vadime Elisseeff **296**
ELISSEEFF, V., *Japon*, Archaeologia Mundi collection, Geneva, 1974
Five thousand years of Korean Art, museum catalogue of exhibition organized by the National Museum of Korea for museums in the United States, Asian Art Museum, San Francisco, 1979
ISHIDA, E., and S. Izumi, *Shimpojyumu. Nihon noko bunka no kigen*, Symposium on the origin of the Japanese agrarian civilization, Tokyo, 1966
NEGI, O., "The Significance of Wooden Agricultural Tools", in *Kokogaku kenkyu*, 52, 4, Tokyo, 1976
OKAMOTO, T., T. Doi and H. Kanfko, *Jōmon jidai*, coll. Nihon no bijutsu, 188, 189, 190, Tokyo, 1982

Death and burial in the Three Kingdoms period, **298**
François Berthier
BERTHIER, F., *Arts du Japon – les temps avant l'histoire*, Paris, 1984
ELISSEEFF, V., *Japon*, Archaeologia Mundi collection, Geneva, 1974
KIDDER, J.E., *Ancient Japan*, Oxford, 1977

The funerary world of the Old Tomb period, **300**
François Berthier
KIM CHE-WON and Kim Won-Yong, *Corée: 2,000 ans de création artistique*, Office du livre, Fribourg, 1966

Monasteries and palaces, François Berthier **302**
BERTHIER, F., *Genèse de la sculpture bouddhique japonaise*, Publications orientalistes de France, Paris, 1979
MASUDA, T., *Japon*, Architecture universelle collection, Office du livre, Fribourg, 1965

Medieval Japanese ceramics, Christine Shimizu **304**
NARAZAKI, S., *Recent Studies on Ancient and Medieval Ceramics of Japan*, International symposium, Seattle, 1972
NARAZAKI, S., *Mino no kotō* (ancient ceramics of Mino), Kyoto, 1976
NARAZAKI, S., "Seto and Mino Ceramics of the Medieval Age", *Chanoyu Quarterly*, 29, Kyoto, 1981
NARAZAKI, S., and P. Zauho, *Ceramic Art of the World, Japanese Medieval Period*, vol. 3, Tokyo, 1977
SHIMIZU, C., "Musée Guimet: quelques pièces de céramique médiévale", *Revue du Louvre*, 5–6, Paris, 1984

AFRICA

The archaeological background, Jean Devisse **306**
CHAVANE, B., *Villages anciens du Tekrour*, Paris, 1985
CLARK, J.D., *The Prehistory of Africa*, London, 1970
DEVISSE, J., "L'Apport de l'archéologie à l'histoire de l'Afrique entre le Vme et le XIIme siècle", *Comptes rendus de l'Acad. des inscriptions et de belles lettres*, Paris, 1982
DAVIDSON, B., *Africa: History of a Continent*, London, 1966
DAVIDSON, B., *The Story of Africa*, London, 1983
ECHARD, N. (ed.), *Métallurgies africaines*, Paris, 1983
GARLAKE, P.S., *The Kingdoms of Africa*, Oxford, 1978
GRUNNE, B. DE, *Terres cuites anciennes de l'Ouest africain*, Louvain-la-Neuve, 1980
KIETHEGA, J.B., *L'Or de la Volta noire*, Paris, 1984
McINTOSH, S., and R., "Prehistoric Investigations at Jenne, Mali: A Study in the Development of Urbanism in the Sahel", *British Archaeological Review*, London, 1980
PHILLIPSON, D.W., *The Later Prehistory of Eastern and South Africa*, London, 1977
SCHMIDT, P.R., *Historical Archaeology: A Structural Approach in an African Culture*, Westport, London, 1978
SHAW, T., *Igbo-Ukwu: An Account of Archaeological Discoveries in Eastern Nigeria*, 2 vols., London, 1970
SHAW, T., *Nigeria: Its Archaeology and Early History*, London, 1978
VAN NOTEN, T., and others, *The Archaeology of Central Africa*, Graz, 1982

The origin of man and his first habitats, **308**
Jean Chavaillon
BALOUT, L., *Préhistoire de l'Afrique du Nord*, Paris, 1955
CHAVAILLON, J., N. Chavaillon, F. Hours and M. Piperno, "From the Oldowan to the Middle Stone Age at Melka-Kunturé (Ethiopia): Understanding Cultural Changes", *Quarternaria*, XXXI, Rome, 1979
COPPENS, Y., F. Clark Howell, G.Ll. Issac and R.E.F. Leakey (eds.), *Earliest Man and Environments in the Lake Rudolf Basin*, Chicago, 1976
ISAAC, G. Ll. and E.R. McCown (eds.), *Human Origins: Louis Leakey and the East African Evidence*, Menlo Park, California, 1976
LEAKEY, M.D., *Olduvai Gorge: Excavations in Bed I and II, 1960–1963*, vol. 3, Cambridge, 1971
WALKER, A., and R.E.F. Leakey, "The Hominids of East Turkana", *Scientific American*, 239, 1978

The evolution of the environment and archaeology, **310**
Samuel Sidibé
SUTTON, J.E.G., "The Aquatic Civilization of Middle Africa", *Journal of African History*, 15, 1974
UNESCO, *A General History of Africa*, vol. 1, 1st ed., revised ed. 1984

Archaeology and the history of art, **312**
Susan Keech and Roderick James McIntosh
CAMPS, G. and M. Gast (eds.), *Les Chars Préhistoriques du Sahara*, Aix-en-Provence, 1982
DAVIS, W., "Representation and Knowledge in the Prehistoric Rock Art of Africa", *African Archaeological Review*, No. 2, 1984
EYO, E., *Two Thousand Years of Nigerian Art*, Lagos, 1974
GARLAKE, P., *Great Zimbabwe*, London, 1973
LEWIS-WILLIAMS, J.D., *Believing and Seeing: Symbolic Meanings in Southern San Rock Paintings*, London, 1981
ROSET, J.-P., "Les Peintures préhistoriques du Sahara", *La Recherche*, 151, 1984
SHAW, T., *Nigeria: Its Archaeology and Early History*, London, 1978

Archaeology and trade, Jean Devisse **314**
For additional information and bibliography, see UNESCO, *A General History of Africa*, volumes of which are now in course of publication

Gold and iron in western Africa, **316**
Jean-Baptiste Kiethega
AJAYI, J.F.A., and M. Crowder, *History of West Africa*, 2 vols. London, 1971–4
DEVISEE, J., "Une enquête à développer: le problème de la propriété des mines en Afrique de l'Ouest du VIIIe au XVIe siècle", *Bull. de l'Institut belge de Rome*, XLIV, 1972
DIOP, L.M., "La Métallurgie traditionelle et l'Age du fer en Afrique", *Bull. de l'I.F.A.N.*, series B, vol. XXX, Dakar, 1968
HOLL, A., "La Question de l'Age de fer ancien de l'Afrique occidentale: essai de méthode", *Colloque sur l'histoire de la metallurgie*, Paris, 1983
MAUNY, R., *Tableau géographique de l'Ouest africain au Moyen âge*, I.F.A.N., Dakar, 1961

African ceramics, Denise Robert-Chaleix **318**
CAMPS-FABER, H., *Matière et art mobilier dans la préhistoire nord-africaine et saharienne*, Paris, 1966
DROST, D., "Töpferei in Afrika: Ökonomie und Soziologie", *Jahrbuch Museum Volkerkunde*, 25, Leipzig, 1968
ROSET, J.-P., "Nouvelles Données sur le problème de la néolithisation du Sahara méridional: Air et Ténéréau Niger", *Cahiers ORSTOM*, Geology series, vol. XIII, no. 2, Paris, 1983
UNESCO, *A General History of Africa*, vols. I and II, rev. ed., 1984

Archaeology and Apartheid, Jean Devisse **320**
CORNEVIN, M., *L'Afrique du Sud en sursis*, Paris, 1977
DENBOW, J.R., *Iron Age Economics: Herding, Wealth and Politics along the Fringes of the Kalahari Desert during the Early Iron Age*, (Ph.D. dissertation), Indiana University, 1983
DENBOW, J.R., "Prehistoric Herders and Foragers at the Kalahari: the Evidence for 1500 Years of Interaction", in C. Schrire (ed.), *Past and Present in Hunter Gatherer Studies*, New York, 1984
FOUCHE, L., *Mapungubwe, Ancient Bantu Civilization on the Limpopo*, Cambridge, 1937
HUFFMAN, T.N., "Archaeology and Ethnohistory of the African Iron Age", *Annual Review of Anthropology*, XI, 1982
HUFFMAN, T.N., "Leopards Kopje and the Nature of the Iron Age in Bantu Africa", Zimbabweana, I, no. 1, 1984
HUFFMAN, T.N., "Southern Africa to the South of the Zambezi: Known Centres of Cultural Activity", in UNESCO *General History of Africa*. vol. III, ch.24, to be published 1986
PHILLIPSON, D.W., *African Archaeology*, Cambridge World Archaeology, London–New York, 1985

Precolonial plant systems of defence, **322**
Christian Seignobos
PORTERES, R., "Le Caractère magique originel des haies vives et de leurs constituants (Europe et Afrique Occidentale)", *Journal d'agronomie tropicale et de botanique*, nos. 6,7,8, Paris, 1965
SEIGNOBOS, C., "Les Systèmes de défense végétaux précoloniaux", *Annales de l'Université du Tchad*, N'Djamena, 1978
SEIGNOBOS, C., "Stratégies de survie dans les économies de raziés", *ibid.*,1979
SEIGNOBOS, C., "Des fortifications végétales dans la zone soudano-sahélienne (Tchad et Nord-Cameroun)", Cahiers ORSTOM, vol. XVII, nos. 3,4, Paris, 1980
SEIGNOBOS, C., "Matières grasses, parcs et civilisations agraires (Tchad et Nord-Cameroun)", in *Cahiers d'outre-mer*, no. 139, Bordeaux, 1982
SEIGNOBOS, C., "Végétations anthropiques dans la zone soudano-sahelienne: la problematique des parcs", Revue de géographie du Cameroun, vol. III, no. 1, Yaounde, 1982

NORTH AMERICA

The archaeological background, Patrick Plumet and Jean-François Moreau **324**

COURBIN, P., *Qu'est-ce que l'archeologie?*, Paris, 1982

FITTING, J.E., *The Development of North American Archaeology*, New York, 1983

FLANNERY, K.V. "Archaeology with a capital S", in C.L. Redman, *Research and Theory in Current Archaeology*, New York, 1973, pp. 57–58

"The Golden Marshalltown: a parable for the archaeology of the 1980s", in *American Anthropologist*, vol. 84, no. 2, 1982, pp. 265–78

LAMING-EMPERAIRE, *Le Probleme des origines Americaines*, Lille, 1980

LUBBOCK, J., *Pre-historic Times*, London, 1865

MORLOT, A., "General Views on Archaeology", in *Annual Report of the Smithsonian* Institution for the Year 1860, 1861, pp. 284–343

TRIGGER, B.G., "Archaeology and the Image of the American Indian", in *American Antiquity*, vol. 45, no. 4, 1980, pp. 663–76

WILLEY, R.G. and J.A. Sabloff, *A History of American Archaeology*, 2nd ed., San Francisco, 1980

The first peopling of North America, Patrick Plumet **326**

BRYAN, A.L., *Early Man in America from a Circum-Pacific Perspective*, Occasional Papers No. 1, Department of Anthropology, University of Alberta, Calgary, 1978

HOPKINS, D.M., J.V. Matthews, C.E. Schweger and S.B. Yound, *Paleo-ecology of Beringia*, New York, 1982

LAMING-EMPERAIRE, A., *Le Probleme des orgines americaines*, Paris, 1980

LAUGHLIN, W.S., *Aleuts: Survivors of the Bering Land Bridge*, New York, 1980

LAUGHLIN, W.S. and A.B. Harper, *The First Americans: Origins, Affinities and Adaptations*, New York-Stuttgart, 1979

SHUTLER, R., *Early Man in the New World*, Beverly Hills–London–New Dehli, 1983

WEST, F.H., *The Archaeology of Beringia*, New York 1981

The hunters of the Arctic, Patrick Plumet **328**

BANDI, H.G., *Eskimo Prehistory*, 3rd ed., University of Alaska Press, 1972

DUMOND, D.E., *The Eskimos and Aleuts*, London, 1977

GESSAIN, R., *Ovibos, la grande aventure des hommes et des boeufs musques*, Paris, 1981

GIDDINGS, J.L., *10,000 ans d'histoire arctique*, Paris, 1973

LAUGHLIN, W.S., *Aleuts, Survivors of the Bering Land Bridge*, New York, 1980

PLUMET, P., "L'Origine des Esquimaux", in *La Recherche*, no. 146, Paris, Jul–Aug 1983

The hunters of the eastern forests, Claude Chapdelaine **330**

CHAPDELAINE, C., "Images de la prehistoire du Quebec", in *Recherches amerindiennes au Quebec*, Montreal, 1978

TRIGGER, B.G., "Northeast", in *Handbook of North American Indians*, Smithsonian Institution, Washington, 1978

The review *Recherches amerindiennes au Quebec* (Montreal) has published a number of articles on the subject since 1971

The development of agriculture, Norman Clermont **332**

MENGELSDORF, P.C., *Corn Origin, Evolution and Improvement*, Cambridge, 1974

NOBLE, C.W., "Corn and the development of village life in Southern Ontario", in *Ontario Archaeology*, 1975, pp. 37–47

STRUEVER, S., *Prehistoric Agriculture*, Garden City, New York, 1971

STURTEVANT, W.C., *Handbook of North American Indians*, 20 vols., Smithsonian Institution, Washington D.C., 1978

YARNELL, R.A., "Early Plant Husbandry in Eastern North America", in C.E. Cleland, *Cultural Change and Continuity, Essays in Honor of James Bennett Griffin*, New York, 1976, pp. 265–73

From hunter-gatherers to cave-dwellers, François Rodriguez Loubet **334**

AMSDEN, *Prehistoric Southwesterners, from Basketmakers to Pueblos*, Southwest Museum of Los Angeles, 1949

CATTANACH, G.S., "Long House, Mesa Verde National Park, Colorado", in *National Park Service Publications in Archaeology*, no. 7, Washington, 1980

DEAN, J.S., "Tree ring dating in archaeology", in *Anthropological Papers*, Salt Lake City, 1978

JETT, S.C., "Pueblo Indian migrations: an evaluation of the possible physical and cultural determinants", in *American Antiquity*, 29, 3, Washington D.C., 1964, pp. 281–300

WATERS, F., *The Book of the Hopi*, New York, 1963

Rock art, Gilles Tassé **336**

DEWDNEY, S. and K.E. Kidd, *Indian Rock Paintings of the Great Lakes*, Toronto, 1967

GRANT, C., *Rock Art of the American Indian*, New York, 1967

MALLERY, G., *Picture-Writing of the American Indian*, 2 vols., Dover–New York, 1972

TASSE, G. and S. Dewdney, *Releves et travaux recents sur l'art rupestre amerindien*, Montreal, 1977

VASTOKAS, J.M. and R.K., *Sacred Art of the Algonkians*, Peterborough (Ontario), 1973

MESOAMERICA

The archaeological background, Dominique Michelet **338**

BERNAL, I., *A History of Mexican Archaeology, the Vanished civilizations of Middle America*, London, 1980

BRUNHOUSE, R.L., *In Search of the Maya*, Albuquerque, 1973

BRUNHOUSE, R.L., *Pursuit of the Ancient Maya, some Archaeologists of Yesterday*, Albuquerque, 1975

MICHELET, D., *Amérique précolombienne: tendances actuelles de la recherche*, Paris, 1984

PORTER WEAVER, M., *The Aztecs, Maya and their Predecessors: Archaeology of Mesoamerica*, New York, 1981

WAUCHOPE, R., *They Found the Buried Cities. Exploration and Excavation in the American Tropics*, Chicago, 1965

WILLEY, G.R. and J.A. Sabloff, *A History of American Archaeology*, San Francisco, 1980

Towards the Neolithic, Antoinette Nelken-Terner **340**

FLANNERY, K., *The Early American Village*, New York, 1976

MACNEISH, R.S., *et al.*, *Prehistory in the Tehuacan Valley*, Austin, 1967–72

NELKEN-TURNER, A., *Les Instruments de la mouture préhispanique: essai methodologique*, 1968

TURNER, B.L., *Once Beneath the Forest. Prehistoric Terracing in the Rio Bec Region of the Maya Low Lands*, Boulder, 1983

WILLEY, G.R. and J.A. Sabloff, *A History of American Archaeology*, San Francisco, 1980

Early settlements and environments, Christine Niederberger Betton **342**

BATAILLON, C., "Regions geographiques au Mexique", in *Travaux et memoires de l'Institut des hautes etudes de l'Amerique latine*, Paris, 1968

COE, M.D. and K.V. Flannery, *Early Cultures and Human Ecology in South Coastal Guatemala*, Washington, 1967

MACNEISH, R.S., D.S. Byers *et al.*, The Prehistory of the Technacan Valley, in D.S. Byers, vol. I: *Environment and Subsistence*, Austin, 1967

NIEDERBERGER BETTON, C., "Early sedentary economy in the Basin of Mexico", in *Science*, vol. 203, Washington, 1979

STARK, B. and B. Voorhies,*Prehistoric Coastal Adaptations*, New York, 1978

The Olmec civilization, Christine Niederberger Betton **344**

COE, M.D. and R.A. Diehl, *In the Land of the Olmec. The Archaeology of San Lorenzo Tenochtitlan:* I; *The People of the River:* II; Austin, 1980

FLANNERY KENT, V. and J. Marcus, *The Cloud People*, New York, 1983

GROVE, D., "The Olmec Paintings of Oxtotitlan, Guerrero, Mexico", in *Studies in Pre-Columbian Art and Archaeology*, no. 6, Washington D.C., 1970

JORALEMON, D. "The Olmec Dragon: A Study in Pre-Columbian Iconography", in H.B. Nicholson, *Origins of Religious Art and Iconography in Preclassic Mesoamerica*, vol. 31, Los Angeles, 1976

NIEDERBERGER BETTON, C., *Zohapilco. Cinco Milenios de Ocupación Humana en un Sitio Lacustre de la Cuenca de Mexico*, Mexico, 1976

Pre-urban settlements, Christine Niederberger Betton **346**

FLANNERY, K.V. *et al.*, *The Early Mesoamerican Village*, New York, 1976

GRAHAM, J.A., *Ancient Mesoamerica*, Palo Alto, 1981

NIEDERBERGER BETTON, C., *Paléopaysages et archéologie préurbaine du bassin de Mesico*, Mexico, 1985

SOUSTELLE, J., *La Pensée cosmologique des anciens Mexicains*, Paris, 1940

TOLSTOY, P., "Western Mesoamerica before AD900", in R.E. Taylor and C.W. Meighan, *Chronologies in New World Archaeology*, New York, 1978

Varieties of urban architecture, Antoinette Nelken-Terner **348**

BATALLION, C. (ed.), *Etat, Pouvoir et Espance dans le Tiers-Monde*, Paris, 1977

BLANTON, R.E., S. A. Kowalewoski, G. Feinman and J. Appel, *Ancient Mesoamerica. A comparison of change in three regions*, New Studies in Archaeology, Cambridge, 1981

HARDOY, E. and R.P. Schaedel, (ed.) *Las cuidades de America Latina y sus areas de influencia a traves de la historia*, Buenos Aires, 1975

MARGOLIES, L. and R.H. Lavanda, (ed.) *Urban Anthropology*, vol. 8, no. 3 and 4, 1979

MILLON, R., "Teotihuacan: City, State and Civilization", J. Sabloff, (ed.), *Supplement to the Handbook of Middle American Indians*, Austin, 1981, pp. 198–243

The Maya city of Copán, Dominique Michelet **350**

BAUDEZ, C.F. (ed.), *Introducción a la arqueologia de Copán, Honduras*, Proyecto aquelológico Copán, Secretaria de Estudo en el Despacho de Cultura y Turismo, Tegucigalpa, 1983

GORDON, G.B., "Prehistoric ruins of Copan, Honduras", *Memoirs of the Peabody Museum, Harvard University*, vol. 1, no. 1, Cambridge, 1896

LONGYEAR, J.M. III, *Copan Ceramics. A Study of Southeastern Maya Pottery*, Washington D.C., 1952

MORLEY, S.G., The Inscriptions at Copan, Washington D.C., 1920

STRÖMSVIK, G., *Guide book to the ruins of Copan*, Washington D.C., 1947

WEBSTER, D. and E.M. Abrams, "An elite compound at Copan, Honduras", *Journal of Field Archaeology*, vol. 10, no. 3, Boston, 1983

The collapse of the classical Maya civilization, Dominique Michelet **352**

ADAMS, R.E.W. and N. Hammond, "Maya archaeology, 1976–80: a review of major publications", in *Journal of Field Archaeology*, vol. 9, no. 4, Boston, 1982

BAUDEZ, C.F. and P. Becquelin, *Les Mayas*, Paris, 1984

CULBERT, T.P., *The Classic Maya Collapse*, Albuquerque, 1973

RENFREW, C., M.J. Rowlands and B. Abbott Segraves, *Theory and Explanation in Archaeology: the Southampton Conference*, New York, 1982

RENFREW, C. and K.L. Cooke, *Transformations: Mathematical Approaches to Culture Change*, London, 1979

THOMPSON, J.E.S., *The Rise and Fall of Maya Civilization*, Norman, Oklahoma, 1954

SOUTH AMERICA

The archaeological background, Danièle Lavallée **354**

BONAVIA, D. and R. Ravines, *Arquelogia peruana: precursores*, Lima, 1970

BROWMAN, D., *Advances in Andean Archaeology*, La Haye, 1978

LAMING-EMPERAIRE, A., *Le Probleme des origines americaines*, Lille, 1980

LANNING, E., *Peru before the Incas*, Englewood Cliffs, 1967

LUMBERAS, L., *Arqueologia de la America andina*, Lima, 1981

PROUS, A., "Historia da pesquisa e da bibliografic arqueologica do Brasil", in *Arquivos do museu de Historia natural*, vol. IV-V, Belo Horizonte, 1982

RAVINES, R., *100 Años de arqueologia en el Perú*, Lima, 1970; *Panorama de la arqueologia andina*, Lima, 1982

SACO, M.L., *Fuentes para el estudio del arte peruano precolombino*, Lima, 1978

WILLEY, G., *An Introduction to American Archaeology*, vol. II: *South America*, Prentice Hall, 1971

The oldest human settlements, Danièle Lavallée **356**

CARDICH, A. and L.A. and A. Hajduk, "Secuencia arqueológica y cronologiá radiocarbónica de la cueva 3 de Los Toldos (Santa Cruz, Argentina)", in *Relaciones*, Buenos Aires, 1973

DILLEHAY, T., "Monte Verde: radiocarbon dates from an early man site in south-central Chile", in *Journal of Field Archaeology, vol. IX, Boston, 1982*

GUIDON, N., "Les Premières Occupations humaines de l'aire archaeologique de São Raimundo Nonato", in L'Anthropologie, Paris

LYNCH, T., "The Paleo-Indians", in J. Jennings and W.F. Freeman, *Ancient South Americans*, San Francisco, 1983

MACNEISH, R. *et al.*, *Prehistory of the Ayacucho Basin*, 3 vols., Ann Arbor, 1980–83

Prehistoric rock art, Niède Guidon **358**

GONZALEZ, A.R., *El Arte precolombino de la Argentina. Introducción a su historia cultural*, Buenos Aires, 1977

GRADIN, C.J., "Algunos Aspectos de la metadologiá y el desarrollo del arte rupestre de Pampa-Patagonia", in *Actas. Primeras jornados de arte rupestre de la provincia de San Luis (1978)*, San Luis, 1980

GUIDON, N., "Peintures rupestres de Varzea Grande, Piaui, Brésil", in *Cahiers d'archéologie d'Amerique du Sud*, no. 3, 1975

MENGHIN, O.F.A., "Estilos del arte rupestre de Patagonia", in *Acta prehistorica*, Buenos Aires, 1957

Cultivation and settlement in the Andean region, Danièle Lavallée **360**

BONAVIA, D., *Los Gavilanes*, Lima, 1982

LYNCH, T.F., *Guitarrero Cave*, Studies in Archaeology, New York, 1980

PEARSALL, D.M., "Phytolith Analysis: applications of a new Paleoethnobotanical technique in archaeology", in *American Anthropologist*, Washington D.C., 1982

PICKERSGILL, B. and C.B. Heiser, "Origins and distribution of plants domesticated in the New World tropics", in E. Benson, *Advances in Andean Archaeology*, La Laye, 1978

WHEELER, J.C., "Camelid domestication and early development of camelid pastoralism in the Andes", in *Animals and Archaeology*, British Archaeological Reports, Oxford, 1983

WING, E.S., "Domestication and use of animals in the Americas", in L. Peel and D. E. Tribe, *Domestication, Conservation and Use of Animal Resources*, Amsterdam, 1983

The appearance of pottery, Jean-François Bouchard **362**

BISHOP, H. and J. Viteri, "Pre-Valdivia occupations on the Southwest coast of Ecuador", in *American Antiquity*, Austin, 1972

LATHRAP, D., D. Collier and H. Chandra, *Ancient Ecuador: Culture, Clay and Creativity (3000–300BC)*, Field Museum of Natural History, Chicago, 1975

MEGGERS, B., C. Evans and E. Estrada, "The early formative period of coastal Ecuador: the Valdivia and Machalilla phases", in *Smithsonian Contributions to Anthropology*, Washington D.C., 1965

REICHEL DOLMATOFF, G., "Excavaciones arqueologicas en Puerto Hormiga (departamento de Bolivar)", in *Antropologia*, no. 2, Bogotá, 1965

REICHEL DOLMATOFF, G., *La Ceramique de Monsu*, Bogotá

Origin and expansion of the Chavín culture, Danièle Lavallée **364**

BENSON, E.P., *Dumbarton Oaks Conference on Chavín*, Washington D.C., 1971

BURGER, R.L., "The radiocarbon evidence for the temporal priority of Chavín de Huantar", in *American Antiquity*, vol. 46, no. 3, Austin, 1981

LUMBRERAS, L. "Los Estudios sobre Chavín", in *Revista del Museo nacional*, Lima, 1973
ROWE, J.H., *Chavin: an Inquiry Into Its Form and Meaning*, Museum of Primitive Art, New York, 1962
TELLO, J.C., *Chavín, culture matriz de la civilisacion andina*, Lima, 1960

Contacts and exchanges in the Andes, Danièle Lavallée   366
HOLM, O., "Hachas monedas del Ecuador", in *III Congresso peruano sobre el hombre y la cultura andina*, Lima, 1972
MARCOS, J. and P. Norton, "Interpretación sobre la arqueologia de la Isla de La Plata", in *Miscelánea antropológica ecuatoriana*, vol. I, Guayacuil, 1981
MURRA, J.V., "El Tráfico del *mullu* en la costa del Pacifico (1971)", in *Formaciones económicas y politicas del mundo andino*, Lima, 1975
PAULSEN, A.C., "The thorny oyster and the voice of God: *Spondylus* and *Strombus* in Andean Prehistory", in *American Antiquity*, vol. 39, no. 4
ROSTWOROWSKI DE DIEZ CANSELO, M., "Mercaderes del valle de Chincha en la época prehispánica: un documento y unos comentarios", in *Revista española de antropologia americana*, vol. V, Madrid, 1970

Birth of the great cities of the Andes,   368
Richard P. Schaedel
HARDOY, J.E., *Urban Planning in Pre-Columbian America*, New York, 1968
ISABELL, W.H., *The Rural Foundation for Urbanism: Economic and Stylistic Interaction Between Rural and Urban Communities in Eighth-Century Peru*, Urbana, 1977
ROWE, J.H., "Urban growth and ekistics on the Peruvian coast", in *Actas y Memorias del 39° Congres o internacional de americanistas*, 1970, vol. II, Lima, 1972
SHIMADA, I., "Economy of a prehistoric urban context: commodity and labor flow at Moche V Pampa Grande", in *American Antiquity*, vol. 43, no. 4, 1978

The archaeology of the Caribbean, Louis Allaire   370
ALEGRIA, R.E., *Ball Courts and Ceremonial Plazas in the West Indies*, New Haven, 1983
KOZLOWSKI, J.K., *Preceramic Cultures in the Caribbean*, Warsaw, 1974
MAGGIOLO, M.V., *Las Sociedades arcaicas de Santo Domingo*, Saint-Dominique, 1980
ROUSE, I., "Prehistory of the West Indies", in *Science*, vol. 144, Washington D.C., 1964
ROUSE, I and L. Allaire, "Caribbean", in R.E. Taylor and C.W. Meighan, *Chronologies in New World Archaeology*, New York, 1978

OCEANIA

The archaeological background, José Garanger   372
BELLWOOD, P., *Man's Conquest of the Pacific*, Auckland, 1978
BUCK, P., *Vikings of the Sunrise,* New York, 1938
DUFF, R., *The Moa-Hunter Period of Maori Culture*, Wellington, 1950
GARANGER, J., "Petite histoire d'une prehistoire", *Journal de la Société des Océanistes*, no. 74–5, Paris, 1973
MOERENHOUT, J.A., *Voyages aux files du Grand Océan*, A. Bertrand, Paris, 1867

The peopling of Australasia, José Garanger   376
ALLEN, J., J. Golson and R. Jones, *Sunda and Sahul, Prehistoric Studies in Southeast Asia, Melanesia and Australia*, London, 1977
MULVANEY, D.J., *The Prehistory of Australia*, London, 1968
MULVANEY, D.J. and J. Golson, *Aboriginal Man and Environment in Australia*, Canberra, 1971
WHITE, J.P. and J.F. O'Connel, *A Prehistory of Australia, New Guinea and Sahul*, North Ryde (Australia), 1982

Lapita culture and the Polynesians,   378
José Garanger
BELLWOOD, P., *Les Polynésiens, Archéologie et Histoire,* Papeete-Tahiti, 1983
GARANGER, J., "La poterie Lapita et les Polynesiens", *Journal de la Société des Océanistes*, no. 42–43, Paris, 1974
GARANGER, J., "Les recherches prehistoriques dans l'arc insulindien: une base pour la compréhension du peuplement du Pacifique", *Bulletin de la Société des Etudes Océaniennes*, Papeete-Tahiti, 1984
GREEN, R.C., "Lapita", *The Prehistory of Polynesia*, Cambridge, 1979
GROUBE, L.M., "Tonga, Pottery and Polynesian Origins", *The Journal of the Polynesian Society,* vol. 80, no. 3, Wellington, 1971.
HOWELLS, W.W., *The Pacific Islanders*, New York, 1973
KIRCH, P.V., "Advances in Polynesian prehistory: three decades in review", in F. Wendorf and A.E. Close, *Advances in World Archaeology*, New York, 1982
SPRIGGS, M., *The Lapita Cultural Complex: Origins, Distribution, Contemporaries and Successors*, Hawaii, 1984
TYRON, D.J., "Le peuplement du Pacifique: une evaluation linguistique", *Bulletin de la Société des Etudes Océaniennes*, no. 227, Papeete-Tahiti, 1984

Myths and history at Vanuatu, José Garanger   380
ESPIRAT, J.J., J. Guiart *et al.,Système de titres dans les Nouvelles-Hébrides centrales, d'Efate aux îles Shepherd*, Paris, 1973
GARANGER, J., *Archéologie des Nouvelles-Hébrides, contribution à la connaissances des îles du centre*, Paris, 1972
GARANGER, J., "Traditions orales et pré histoire en Océanie", *Cahiers ORSTOM Sciences humaines*, Paris, 1976

Easter Island: a microcosm, José Garanger   382
HEYERDAHL, T. and E.N. Ferdon, *Report of the Norwegian Archaeological Expedition to Easter Island and the East Pacific, vol. I,* School of American Research Museum, Sante Fe, 1961
McCOY, P.C., "Easter Island", in J.D. Jennings, *The Prehistory of Polynesia*, Cambridge–London, 1979
METRAUX, A., *L'Île de Pâques*, Paris, 1941

MODERN PERIOD

The archaeological background, Jean Guillaume   384

There are two specialized publications on this topic: *Post Medieval Archaeology* in Great Britain and *Historical Archaeology* in the United States. In Canada, numerous studies can be found in *Lieux historiques canadiens* and in the periodical *Histoire et archéologie* (monographs on history, ethnology, archaeology, and so on). Both of these publications are edited by Parcs Canada. Further reading includes *Cahiers . . .* and *Dossiers du partrimoine*, edited by the Ministry of Cultural Affairs in Quebec. Many of the studies published are fundamental, especially those on the materials of archaeology, such as glassware, metalwork and above all, pottery.

A large number of general interest works are available, more often concentrating on industrial archaeology. See, for example:

BUCHANAN, R.A., *Industrial Archaeology in Britain*, 1972
DAUMAS, M., *L'Archéologie industrielle en France*, Paris, 1980

Works dealing with 19th and 20th century archaeology are somewhat more difficult to find. These include:

HUME, I.N., *Here Lies Virginia: an archaeologist's view of colonial life and history*, New York, 1963
HUME, I.N., *Historical Archaeology*, New York, 1969
HUME, I.N., *Martin's Hundred: the discovery of a lost colonial Virginia settlement*, New York, 1979

Several recent works discuss methodology:

DICKENS, R.S. Jr. (ed.), *Archaeology of Urban America: the search for pattern and process*, New York, 1982

Periodicals:
The Journal of Industrial Archaeology, London, quarterly, 1964 to 1974
Industrial Archaeology Review, National Association for Industrial Archaeology, London, quarterly, since 1976
L'Archéologie industrielle en France, C.I.L.A.C., Paris, irregularly since 1977

Castles of the 16th century, Françoise Boudon   386
France
BOUDON, F., J. Blécon and L. Saulnier, *Philibert Delorme et le château royal de Saint-Léger-en-Yvelines*, Paris

Great Britain
BIDDLE, M., "The stuccoes of Nonsuch", in *The Burlington Magazine*, London, July 1984
DENT, J., *The Quest for Nonsuch*, London, 1962
GADD, D. and T. Dyson, "Bridewell Palace. Excavations at 9–11 Bridewell Place and 1–3 Tudor Street, City of London, 1978", in *Post Medieval Archaeology/The Journal of the Society for Post Medieval Archaeology*, vol. 15, London, 1981

Hungary
BALOGH, J., *Die Anfänge der Renaissance in Ungarn. Matthias Corinus und die Kunst*, vol. 18, Graz, 1975

Italy
FORSTER, W. and R.J. Tuttle, "The Palazzo del Te", in *Journal of the Society of Architectural Historians*, vol. 30, no. 4, New York, 1971

Archaeology and east-west exchange,   388
Bernard Philippe Groslier
BEURDELEY, C. and M., *Castiglione, peintre jésuite à la Cour de Chine*, Office du Livre, Fribourg, 1971
EDWARDES, M., *Asia in the European Age*, London, 1961
JARRY, M., *Chinoiseries*, Office du Livre, Fribourg, 1981
LACH, D., *Asia in the Making of Europe*, Chicago, 1970
MORRIS, J., *Stones of the Empire*, Oxford 1983
NILSSON, S., *European Architecture in India*, London, 1968
REICHWEIN, A., *China and Europe*, London, 1968
DE THOMAZ DE BOSSIÈRE, Y., *F.X. Dentrecolles et l'apport de la Chine*, Les Belles-Lettres, Paris, 1982

European colonization of North America, Jean Chapelot   390
HUME, I.N., *Historical Archaeology*, New York, 1975
HUME, I.N., *Martin's Hundred: the discovery of a lost colonial Virginia settlement*, New York, 1979
PICARD, F., *Les Traces du passé*, Quebec, 1979

Periodicals and reviews:
"Le Canada depuis ses origines", special edition of *Dossiers de l'archéologie*, Dijon, March–April, 1978. Contains several articles on the important excavations in Canada.
Historical Archaeology, Journal of the Society for Historical Archaeology, published yearly by the Institute of Archaeology and Anthropology, University of South Carolina, Columbia

Industrial archaeology, François Loyer   392
BORSI, F., *Introduzzione alla archeologia industriale*, Rome, 1978
DAUMAS, M., *L'archéologie industrielle en France*, Paris, 1980
HOSKINS, W.G., *The Making of the English Landscape*, 1955
HUDSON, K., *Industrial Archaeology. A New Introduction*, London, 1963–1976
SANDE, T.A., *Industrial Archaeology, a New Look at the American Heritage*, New York, 1976

Glossary

Glossary entries are marked in the text by an asterisk* on their first appearance in each article or feature.

ACHAEMENIDS. Iranian dynasty, originating from present-day Fars (southern Iran), which included Cyrus the Great, founder of the Persian empire (*c*.550BC). This empire united for the first time all the peoples of the east – from Thrace and Egypt to the Aral Sea and the Indus Valley – and had as its capitals Pasargadae, Susa and Persepolis. In spite of its size and diversity, the empire lasted for more than three centuries thanks to efficient administration and a policy of religious tolerance. Its last ruler, Darius III Codamannus, was conquered by Alexander who proclaimed himself his heir (330BC) and attempted unsuccessfully to pursue a policy of amalgamation between the Greeks and the Persians.

ACHEULIAN. Prehistoric culture, taking its name from the site of Saint-Acheul, a suburb of Amiens, where a tool assembly from the Lower Paleolithic was found, characterized by the biface (shaped on both surfaces). This culture appeared in France *c*.700,000 years ago, but in eastern Africa the Acheulian seems to start *c*.1,400,000BP, the earlier phases equating with a previous European stage. The biface is everywhere its more representative tool, and with it are associated a large cutting implement, the handaxe, and numerous varied small flake tools. The culture of biface, the principle tool of *Homo erectus*, is found from the north to the south of Africa, and from western Europe to China.

ACROTER (acroterion). Pedestal on the side of a pediment, on which a statue is placed.

ADOBE. Unbaked clay building material, hand-moulded and sun-dried, still used today by the peasants of Central America for construction purposes.

AD SANCTOS (tombs). From the time of Constantine's Edict of Milan in 313, which granted tolerance to Christians, *memoriae* were erected over the tombs of martyrs; the sites of these tombs were still known through the secret veneration of earlier Christians. Some of these miniature wooden or stone temples were the starting-point for the funerary basilicas which became increasingly numerous in the burial grounds adjacent to towns from the 4th century on. At this time it was believed that burial near to the tombs or relics of the saints would guarantee their protection in the next world and this gave rise to the custom of arranging to be buried in or just beside churches, whence the expression *ad sanctos* tombs (near the saints).

AGRI DECUMATES. Name given to the territories lying to the north and east of the upper reaches of the Danube and the Rhine (the Black Forest, the Swabian Jura, and the Taunus). The frontier, established along the rivers, formed a strategically dangerous bulge which the Roman emperors of the 1st century tried to reduce by establishing garrisons and building roads. Domitian built the first line of fortifications there (ditches and palisades) north of the rivers Main and Neckar, and Antoninus pushed it still further eastwards, strengthening it at the same time.

ALEXANDRIA. Greek city founded by Alexander in 332BC on the Mediterranean coast of Egypt. Capital of the Greek dynasty of the Ptolemys, who ruled over Egypt until 30BC, the city very rapidly became the most important centre of trade and culture in the eastern Mediterranean. Its large and cosmopolitan population – Greek, Egyptian and Hebrew – proved hard to govern. Its monuments include the Pharos (lighthouse), the great jetty of Heptastadion, the royal palaces with their original development of architecture and art, and the Museion, an institution for scientific and philological research with a library that represented the memory of the Greek civilization. Alexandria was thus the capital of the Hellenistic world and, later on, the eastern counterweight to Rome.

ANALYTICAL ARCHAEOLOGY. The tendency to formalize the archaeological process, which appeared in the 1960s became more marked through the work of L.R. Binford (USA), D.L. Clarke (Great Britain) and J.-C. Gardin (France). Computer science and mathematics are used to elaborate the means for transforming simple descriptions of archaeological data into economic, social and cultural reconstructions of earlier societies. The development of this research is aimed at providing archaeology with a strict theoretical framework based on scientific method.

ANDERSSON, Johan Gunnar (1874–1960). Swedish geologist who worked in China as a mining research consultant and stayed there 1914–24, and became an expert on Chinese prehistory. In 1920 he discovered the Neolithic site of Yangshao, a name applied today to a group of sites belonging to a culture dated between 5000 and 3000BC. He also investigated a large number of important Neolithic sites, especially in Gansu. On his return to Sweden he created the Museum of Far Eastern Antiquities, buying for it major items from all periods. Although the Neolithic village of Yangshao is now thought to belong to the final phase of the culture that bears its name, and to be much earlier in date than J.G. Anderson initially thought, its discovery is still crucial in that it was the first of the prehistoric sites discovered in China.

ARAMBOURG, Camille (1885–1969). Professor at the Museum d'Histoire Naturelle in Paris, Arambourg started off as an agronomic engineer in Algeria. Working in the field, he carried out many paleontological surveys in Africa, first in the Maghreb; to him are due, in particular, the excavation of the pre-Acheulian bed at Ain Hanech, and of the Acheulian site at Ternifine where he discovered a *Homo erectus* which he named Altanthropus. He was then active in Ethiopia and Kenya where he carried out several missions: Omo-Turkana in 1932–33 and the Omo Valley in 1967–69, with the discovery of the jawbone of so-called *Para-australopithecus aethiopicus*.

ARCHEOGRAPHY. Descriptions of archaeological objects made without any specially archaeological end in view by travellers, pilgrims, traders or official envoys, who were often in a position to see sites and monuments in a much better state of preservation than that in which they are in today, and who gave an account of them either in writing or in drawings.

ARCHEOMAGNETISM. The sum of the magnetic properties of a material resulting from a physical change which has taken place in the past. Such a change fixes in the material the parameters of the magnetic field of the place where it was situated at the time when the change occurred. As this form of change is associated with a rise in temperature, archeomagnetism is observed both in baked clay and in volcanic rocks. As the earth's magnetic field has varied in dip and declination in the course of the millennia, an archeomagnetic material can be dated if it has not been moved and if the curves of variation of the magnetic field are known for the time and place in question.

ARCHEOMETRY. Application to archaeology of scientific knowledge and methods from physics, chemistry, geology, natural sciences, human sciences, etc.

ARCOSOLIUM. Type of tomb in antiquity found inside both pagan and Christian burial places, consisting of a recess with a vaulted ceiling.

ARMILLARY SPHERE. Instrument for astronomical measurement consisting of graduated rings corresponding to the latitudes and longitudes of the sky; essential in determining a celestial position.

ARTAMONOV, Mikhail I. (1898–1972). Russian archaeologist and author of works on Scythian art. Director of the Hermitage Museum, 1951–64.

ASH TUFF or tufa. Rock formed from solidified volcanic ash, which has often been re-formed after the eruption and deposited elsewhere by runoff water carrying it into the bottom of lakes or rivers. It serves as an excellent stratigraphic indicator and, because of the presence of very small crystals, is used to obtain potassium-argon (K-A) datings. Ash tuffs are found in volcanic areas, in parts of Europe and in eastern Africa.

ASSYRIAN (language). One of the two main dialects of ancient Mesopotamia, used in the north of the country. A Semitic language very close to Babylonian, from which it is thought to have diverged at the end of the 2nd millennium, Assyrian probably disappeared with the destruction of Assyria in the 7th century BC.

ATRIDES. Dynasty that may have reigned at Mycenae at the end of the 2nd millennium BC, exercising some pre-eminence over the other Greek principalities: in Homer's *Iliad* it was the king of Mycenae, Agamemnon, who led the Greek's expedition against Troy. The murder of Agamemnon by his wife Clytemnestra, and the tribulations of their children, Orestes, Electra and Iphigenia, are among the favourite themes of Greek tragedy.

AURIGNACIAN. Cultural grouping of the European Upper Paleolithic period, named after the type-site of Aurignac (France), which was first excavated in 1868 by E. Lartet. It covers the period from approximately 30,000 to 27,000 BC. People of the Aurignacian culture are the earliest *Homo sapiens sapiens* in western Europe. Their tool kits are characterized by long blades with retouched edges, "keeled" scrapers and burins. Industry based on bone, the first ever to produce such a varied output, included pierced sticks and spears with split bases, followed by lozenge-shaped spears. The first examples of Paleolithic art appear at this period.

AUSTRALOPITHECINES. First discovered in South Africa, australopithecines were also present in large numbers in eastern Africa. Their brain volume was about 400 to 500cc (that of *Homo sapiens sapiens* being on average 1400cc). *Australopithecus afarensis* is known to have existed *c*.3,500,000 years ago. *A. africanus*, also called *A. gracilis* was about 1.25m (4.1ft) tall and was more advanced in certain characteristics than *A. robustus* or *A. boisiei* (or *Zinjanthropus boisiei* from Olduvai in Tanzania), still extant 1,000,000 years ago. The latter was strongly built and 1.5m (4.5ft) in height, and tended to a vegetarian diet. One of the australopithecine species was the starting-point of the human stock, but all the australopithecines survived, sometimes with very different characteristics, until about 1,000,000 years ago, and were thus for a very long time contemporary with species of the *Homo* genus.

AUSTRALOPITHECUS AFARENSIS. Discovered in Wollo, Ethiopia, by the international Afar expedition, *Australopithecus afarensis* is remarkable for its extreme age and the large number of remains (52 skeleton bones) found in a single place in the same sedimentary layer, dating from 3,000,000 to 3,500,000 years BP (before present). Better known as Lucy, it is the fossil of a small biped, a little more than 1m (3.3ft) tall. D. Johanson and T. White believe that it represents the common ancestor of the other australopithecines and of the *Homo* genus. Other paleontologists (Y. Coppens) see it as belonging to a line of descent distinct from that of man.

AXOLOTL. Aztec word meaning "water toy", used to refer to an amphibian creature (*Ambystoma* spp.) found in the Mexico Basin and much prized as a food by the pre-Hispanic people.

AXUM. Kingdom formed in the 1st century AD in southwestern Ethiopia. During succeeding centuries it developed into an empire which included northern Ethiopia, Sudan and southern Arabia. Its culture incorporated elements from the pre-Axumite cultural heritage, especially Ge'ez writing, which came into being in the 2nd century and was derived from South Arabic writing. Axum was the first state in eastern Africa to strike gold, silver and copper coins, evidence of economic prosperity resulting from international trade. The rulers and people of Axum adopted Christianity in the 4th century.

AYMONIER, Etienne (1844–1929). Indo-China specialist. In 1870 he became an inspector of native affairs, then Resident in Cambodia (Kampuchea) and later the first director of the Paris Colonial School. A deep knowledge of the country and its monuments, and the study of Old Khmer enabled him to produce a Khmer history. *Le Cambodge* (Paris, 1900–03, 3 vols.) was the first synthesis of the country's archaeology and history.

AZILIAN. Epi-Paleolithic (late Paleolithic) culture uncovered by E. Piette in 1889 in the Mas d'Azil cave. This grouping follows directly upon the final phase of the Magdalenian culture in many French and Spanish sites, and corresponds to the first postglacial periods. It is dated to *c*.8000BC, and is characterized by Azilian points, short blades with a convex retouched edge, small clawlike scrapers, and flat harpoons made from deer's antlers.

BABYLONIAN (language). Semitic language first spoken and written in southern Mesopotamia, where there is evidence of it from the 3rd millennium, and where it replaced Sumerian. From the 2nd millennium it became the literary and diplomatic language of the whole Near East, including Egypt and Cyprus. During the 1st millennium it slowly but inexorably declined in favour of Aramaic, also a Semitic language but written using the Phoenician alphabet. Nevertheless it did not finally disappear until the 1st century AD.

BACSONIAN. From Băc Són, a limestone massif in North Vietnam; the Bacsonian is a Neolithic culture discovered by H. Mansuy in 1924, characterized by worked pebbles polished on the cutting edge, by "Bacsonian marks" and by pottery. The Bacsonian marks are the parallel grooves formed in polishing, observed by H. Mansuy on Bacsonian pebbles and reproduced in experiments by S.A. Semenov in 1966.

BACTRIA. Ancient region in the northern plain of Afghanistan, surrounding the Balkh oasis (Balkh-Ab delta). The name of the province, which goes back at least to the Achaemenid period in Persia (6th–4th century BC), has been handed down to us by early Greek writers. Bactria was an important satrapy (administrative district) in the eastern part of the Achaemenid empire. After being conquered by Alexander it lay at the centre of a Graeco-Bactrian kingdom that extended from the Syr Darya river to northwestern India. Archaeological investigations undertaken since the early 1970s have demonstrated that the Bronze Age culture of Bactria extended on both sides of the Amu Darya (Oxus) river.

BAKRI, AL- (1040–94). Arab geographer from an illustrious Andalusian family (his grandfather had tried to create a kingdom in the Huelva area). He lived and died in Cordoba where his father had taken refuge. His *Kitāb al-Masālik wa'l-Mamālik*, a work of great learning, is valuable for archaeological research because it describes the Islamic world just before the Sunnite reaction.

BARROW. Long barrows are earthen mounds covering a grave, characteristic of the Neolithic period. They usually covered a structure containing multiple burials. *Round barrows* are more comon and usually cover single burials, mostly dating from the Bronze Age.

BATEYS. Native name for the grounds used for ball games and as ceremonial areas by the Taino Indians in the Greater Antilles (West Indies).

BERBOTINE. Technique of applying incrustations of thick slip to a ceramic surface for decorative effect.

BERINGIAN tradition. Term suggested and used by H. West to cover various Alaskan and Siberian archaeological formations which had developed from the Siberian Upper Paleolithic period, found in the territory between Siberia and Alaska, now largely submerged. Chronologically these formations lie between the middle of the Holocene period, i.e. from *c.*35,000 to 9/10,000 BP (before present) depending on the area. West's categorization is not completely accepted, as it is too general. It includes the Bel'kachi, Diuktai and Lake Ushki cultures in Siberia, the Denalian culture and the American Paleo-Arctic formations in Alaska and the Yukon.

BIFACE. Stone implement shaped on both surfaces. The basic material can be a lump of stone, a flint nodule, a pebble or a large flake. The biface may be oval, triangular or almond-shaped in form and is characterized by axial symmetry, even if the marks made by use are more plentiful on one face or on one edge: the cutting edge could be straight, but could equally well be very jagged. It is the classic tool of the Acheulian cultures and the main tool of *Homo erectus*. Depending on their size, shape or weight, bifaces could act as picks, knives, scrapers or even weapons, sometimes mounted on a handle, sometimes not.

BIGA. Chariot drawn by two horses.

BIOTOPE. Restricted geographical area constituting the habitat of a specific plant and animal grouping.

BIRD, Junius B. (1907–82). North American anthropologist and curator of the American Museum of Natural History in New York. After several missions to the Arctic, from 1931 he concentrated his research on South America, the Pacific Coast and the Andes. His excavations in the Fell and Palli-Aike caves (Chilean Patagonia) made it possible to establish a cultural sequence for prehistory in these southern areas. His pioneering work on the pre-ceramic period in Chile and Peru (*Preceramic cultures in Chicama and Virú* and *Excavations in northern Chile*, 1948) are still excellent examples of methodology and have lost none of their scientific value.

BOAS, Franz, (1858–1942). American anthropologist of German origin who studied the Eskimos and, in particular, the North American Indians. Reacting against the evolutionist tendencies of the late 19th century, he showed by example the value of detailed work based on observations in the field and the analysis of traditional societies, in contrast to the broad syntheses of ethnology. With him, ethnology left the classroom to confront reality in the field. He was a linguist, folklorist and a physical anthropologist.

BOLAS. The surfaces and ridges of rounded, facetted stones were chipped away to a smooth surface, giving them something of the shape of a sphere of the type used in bowls games. They have been called bolas because of their resemblance to the throwing weapon, consisting of stone or ivory balls attached to a net and used in South America to capture game on the savannah. Bolas are found in Africa in the Middle and Upper Acheulian strata. They may have been used for hunting or for domestic activities.

BORDES, François (1919–81). French prehistorian. By training a geologist, Bordes had a superb understanding of the techniques of stone working. He directed several large Paleolithic excavations in Périgord, and frequently worked abroad, especially in the United States and Australia. He was responsible for a new approach to the analysis of prehistoric tools, using both statistical methods and technological observation. Bordes' many works include *Les Limons quaternaires du Bassin de la Seine* (1951), *Typologie du Paléolithique ancien et moyen* (1961), and *Le Paléolithique dans le Monde* (1968).

BOTTA, Paul-Emile (1802–70). Born in Turin, Botta lived in Egypt and Yemen, and was selected by the French government to be the consular representative at Mosul in 1842. He was attracted by the tells (mounds developing on a settlement over a long period of time) of Nineveh where according to tradition the ancient capital of Assyria had stood. He first undertook excavations at Kuyunjik, continuing on to Khorsabad, 15km (9.5 miles) from the town, where he began the work of undercovering the capital city of Sargon II (721–705BC). The first large relief carvings found on that site arrived at the Louvre in 1847, and two volumes of descriptions were published. Botta had to leave Mosul after 1848. His work marks the beginning of field archaeology in the Near East.

BOUÄRD, Michel de, b.1909. Medieval archaeologist. He collaborated with medieval English and Dutch medieval archaeologists, and in 1954 set up the Centre de Recherches Archéologiques Médiévales at Caen University, the first specialized research unit in France. Much of his work has been devoted to the study of earthworks as fortifications, but he has also worked on ceramics and various other aspects of medieval material culture. He has developed archaeology in the laboratory on the basis of various sciences: chemistry, physics, pollen analysis and physical anthropology.

BOUCHER DE CREVECOEUR DE PERTHES, Jacques (1788–1868). French prehistorian, customs official, and one of the great pioneers of prehistory. He was an enthusiastic collector of cut and polished stones, and in 1837 he found in the alluvial deposits of the Somme river worked pieces of flint at the same level as bones from large extinct mammals. It was partly through his work that scientific opinion became convinced that man had existed before the Flood.

BRASSEUR DE BOURBOURG, Charles-Etienne (1814–74). French traveller and writer. His first contact with Mesoamerica was in 1848, and this marked the beginning of a fruitful but uneven career. His excavation took place in libraries, archives, and bookshops, which led to his discovering the *Popol-Vuh*, the *Memorial de Solola*, the *Relación de las Costas de Yucatán* and part of one of the three Maya codices to have survived the Spanish Conquest.

BREUIL, Abbé Henri (1877–1961). French prehistorian responsible for working out the chronologies of the French Upper and Middle Paleolithic periods. He devoted the greater part of his energies to studying and recording Paleolithic cave painting in France and Spain, and in 1952 published *400 Siècles d'art pariétal*, the first comprehensive work on prehistoric Franco-Cantabrian art. Excavations in China with Teilhard de Chardin, and study trips to South Africa, eastern Europe and the Spanish Levant brought him an international reputation.

BUBASTEION. Name of the sanctuaries dedicated to the Egyptian cat goddess Bastet, the presiding deity of Bubastis (the modern town of Zagazig on the Nile Delta). Her special place of worship was on the edge of the Saqqara cliff, in a temple whose superstructure has completely disappeared; however, its huge subterranean galleries have survived, in which thousands of mummified cats were piled up, presented to the goddess as votive offerings.

BUCK, Sir Peter H. (1880–1951). New Zealand ethnologist. He also used the name Te Rangi Hiroa because of his Maori descent. He specialized in Polynesian cultures, and was director of the B.P. Bishop Museum in Honolulu from 1936 until his death.

CAATINGA. Type of vegetation (dry, thorny, deciduous forest) typical of northeastern Brazil.

CALAMUS. Implement used by a scribe working on clay. Calami were usually made from reeds in Mesopotamia where reeds were very abundant in the south of the country, but also from wood, with the point sharpened to form a triangle. The pressure of the calamus on the clay produced wedge-shaped signs (whence the so-called cuneiform script). By pressing the calamus lightly or firmly into the clay, longer or shorter lines were obtained.

CALCULI. Small stones or pebbles used in antiquity for purposes of calculation.

CALDERA. Huge circular depression caused by intense volcanic activity, leading to the expulsion of a large quantity of internal magma. It is surrounded by faults with instabilities that can bring about a renewal of volcanic activity.

CALIBRATION. Chronology based on radiocarbon dating results which does not correspond exactly to "real" time, in the historian's sense. Disparities are caused by variations in the proportion of carbon in the atmosphere throughout the ages. To obtain the most accurate dating, the results have to be "calibrated". Calibration is a process whereby radiocarbon dates can be converted into "real" dates through dendrochronological (tree-ring) correction. The study of tree rings, especially those on very old trees, using successive cross-checkings with fossil trees, has helped establish a new chronology which is closer to reality.

CANNIBALISM. The strongest argument for the existence of cannibalism in Paleolithic cultures is the lengthwise splitting of long bones so as to extract marrow from them. This is known to have taken place from the Middle Paleolithic at Krapina (Yugoslavia) and L'Hortus (France), though there is no way of being certain whether the cannibalism practised was ritual in origin. In Mesoamerica there is evidence of cannibalism among the hunter-gatherers at the start of the Holocene to *c.*7000BC. The custom persisted throughout the 1st millennium BC in farming villages where isolated human bones have been found among cooking refuse, bearing the marks of cutting implements. Finally there are many written documents concerning cannibalism among the Aztecs in the 15th century AD. Some experts believe that a shortage of flesh and protein, caused by the absence of herbivorous domestic animals led the pre-Hispanic peoples to cannibalism based on necessity. Others deny the existence of chronic dietary deficiencies in Mesoamerica and uphold a theory of ritual cannibalism allied to a system of beliefs. Among the Aztecs in particular, it is thought that after being sacrificed and offered to the gods the human being became a sacred food.

CARBON^{14} (see Dating, Radiochronometry).

CARIČIN GRAD. Site in southern Serbia where the ruins were discovered of a town which appears to have existed from the mid-6th to the early 7th century AD. Its destruction can be linked with the Slav and Avar invasions. It should perhaps be identified as Justiniana Prima, a town founded by the Emperor Justinian near his native village.

CARVEL BUILT. Method of boatbuilding in which the planks forming the skin of the hull are laid flush, edge to edge.

CASO, Alfonso (1896–1970). Mexican archaeologist. Caso's work was associated mainly with the Oaxaca area. In the 1930s a long series of investigations at Monte Albán enabled him to establish one of the longest cultural sequences known at the time, from 500BC until the Spanish conquest.

CATHOLICON. Main church of a Byzantine monastery.

CAUMONT, Arcisse de (1801–73). French medievalist. He travelled widely in France and a large part of Europe, and his interests embraced not only the major monuments but also secondary buildings, such as barns for whose preservation he was often responsible, as well as the whole field of military fortifications. For decades his work influenced the course of medieval archaeology as it concerned buildings, particularly churches and castles.

CAUSEWAYED CAMP. Enclosure typical of the Neolithic in south Britain, it usually consists of a hilltop enclosed by concentric ditches with internal banks. Some archaeologists believe that causewayed camps were ceremonial meeting places for populations over a wide area.

CAYO or KEY. Name given in the Caribbean to islets of coral sand lying "under the lee", standing out from underwater shelves.

CENTURIATION. In antiquity, the process of registering the land. It involved the marking out of the ground with reference to perpendicular east-west axes (*decumani*) and north-south axes (*cardines*) into rectangular or square units edged with ditches or paths. Centuriation was in some cases linked with the redistribution of land and the creation of a new city. In other cases it seems to have been used when clearing land taken from the local inhabitants. It was necessary for establishing tax levels, and made a lasting contribution to the shaping of the rural landscape. Laboratory study of aerial photographs has enabled us to reconstitute these units over large areas.

CENTURION. Under-officer in a Roman legion, in command of the legion's basic unit, the century (80 men). Junior members of the equestrian order started their career as centurions, but most centurions were former legionaries who had risen from the ranks. They tended to be the most experienced and best officers in the army. Their promotion followed strict rules: they were promoted from century to century and from cohort to cohort (the cohort consisted of 6 centuries) in inverse numerical order. The centurion of the first century of the first cohort, the *primipilus*, was an important figure; after being sent to Rome and being *primipilus* for a second time, he could attain equestrian rank.

CHA-IRE. Japanese word which appeared during the Momoyama period (final quarter of the 16th century). It literally means "tea receptacle" and describes the small pottery jar intended for dry tea leaves in the tea ceremony. The *cha-ire* was the main item in the tea ceremony from the Muromachi period until the Edo period. The first *cha-ire* were made to hold medicine or cosmetics and were manufactured inChina. Their introduction to Japan is usually attributed to the Zen monk, Eisai, in 1191. Their use in the tea ceremony began to spread in the period of Shôgun Ashikaga, Yoshimasa (1436–90).

CHAMPOLLION, Jean-François (1790–1832). Having learnt Latin, Greek, Hebrew and Arabic, Champollion was fascinated by the Egypt of the Pharaohs whose hieroglyphic writing he believed could be approached through Coptic, the language of Christian Egyptians. He was responsible for work on the Rosetta Stone which carried an inscription in three scripts – Egyptian hieroglyphs, Egyptian demotic (common speech) and Greek – and received from Nubia tablets bearing royal names which gave him the key to the hieroglyphs; in September 1822 he published his work of decipherment in the *Lettre à M. Dacier relative à l'alphabet des hiéroglyphes phonétiques* and in 1824 in the *Précis du système hiéroglyphique*. While travelling in Italy he had the opportunity to study certain papyri, in particular the Royal Papyrus of Turin. He was keeper of the Egyptian collection at the Louvre and a Chair was created for him at the Collège de France.

CHÂTELPERRONIAN. Cultural grouping that marked the beginning of the European Upper Paleolithic period, named after the type-site of Châtelperron, France, which was excavated in 1867 and covers a period from 35,000 to 30,000BC. Recent discoveries have shown that the people of this culture were Neanderthalians. Their industry, which still has many of the characteristics of the advanced Mousterian tradition, is typified by the Châtelperron knife, a cutting blade with a convex back and a straight retouched edge, and by the development of an industry based on bone (spears made of reindeer antlers or ivory, bone "pick-axes", etc).

CHIFLET, Jean-Jacques (1588–1673). Surgeon to Philip IV of Spain and the Low Countries, he was entrusted with studying and reporting on the objects found in the tomb of Childeric I (AD481/482), Clovis's father, discovered by chance at Tournai in 1653. *Anastasis Childerici I*, which appeared in Antwerp in 1655, can perhaps be regarded as the earliest scientific archaeological publication. It was to prove all the more precious as part of Childeric's "treasure", (stolen in November 1831).

CHILDE, Vere Gordon (1892–1957). Born in Sydney, Australia, Childe became Professor of Prehistoric Archaeology at the Universities of Edinburgh (1927) and London (1946). His many books include *The Dawn of European Civilization* (1925), *The Most Ancient East* (1928), *The Danube in Prehistory* (1929) and *The Bronze Age* (1930) in which he devoted attention to the problems relating to the emergence of the earliest Neolithic cultures in certain areas in the Near East and to the diffusion of the new economy across Europe. Later he wrote several books dealing with more general questions relating to the evolution of societies: *Man Makes Himself* (1936); *What Happened in History* (1942); *Social Evolution* (1951); *Piecing together the Past* (1956); *Society and Knowledge* (1956).

CHINAMPAS. Artificial islets made by the accumulation of silt and aquatic vegetation in the shallow freshwater lagoons of the Mexico Basin. They were used as areas of intensive cultivation of various plants.

CHOPPER AND CHOPPING-TOOL. Tools with a curved or straight cutting edge, worked from pebbles or pieces of stone. Some writers prefer to reserve the term chopper for items which have been worked on one face only and to call chopping-tools those which have been prepared bifacially. Other prehistorians are more concerned with the shape: lateral choppers, terminal choppers, pointed choppers, etc. These were multi-purpose tools, often more effective for breaking than for cutting. They are found at the earliest levels of the Oldowan industries. Although they persisted until the Neolithic period, they are generally characteristic of the pre-Acheulian industries of the Old World.

CHRONOLOGY. Collection of dates or successive datings establishing the position in time of a series of phenomena such as the phases of a civilization or the events of the history of a state. A chronology is called relative (or "floating") when only the order of a succession of facts is known, but not their dates, and absolute when the opposite is true (see Dating).

CIMMERIANS. People based to the north of the Black Sea, in Crimea in particular, who crossed the Caucasus Mountains in the 8th century BC, making deep inroads into southwestern Asia and causing much destruction which can be detected archaeologically at many sites. They continued to form a severe threat, as Assyrian source material shows, until they eventually merged into the local populations.

CINNABAR. Natural mercuric sulphide, red in colour, used by the Olmecs for painting sculptures, pieces of pottery and figurines.

CIST *or kist*. Burial in the form of a casement enclosed on four sides by stone slabs standing upright, and closed with a lid. Cists were intended for one or several burials; unlike megalithic burial chambers they could be totally or partially buried, and were of restricted size.

CLAY ROLLS. These were formed by the potter rolling the clay between the palms of the hands, and used to make moulded pottery. They were either laid in rings one on top of the other, or coiled in spirals, and were smoothed internally and externally to remove any trace of the joins.

CLEAVER. Tool worked on a flake, generally large in size, with a sharp transverse cutting edge, almost always notched by use but never sharpened. The cleaver, which was made for cutting, could be hafted and used as an adze. Along with bifacial tools it was one of the main instruments of *Homo erectus*. Found mainly in Africa, it is very widespread in Acheulian sites, and particularly so in those of the Upper Acheulian.

CLINKER-BUILT. Boatbuilding method in which the planks (forming the covering of the hull) are assembled by a partial overlapping like slates on a roof.

COCHET, Jean Benoit Désiré (1812–75). Medieval archaeologist. Cochet concentrated mainly on cemeteries from the Merovingian period. Following the example of English antiquaries, he studied funeral practices and laid the foundations for a typology and chronology of the archaeological object. He kept a careful journal during his excavations and made a study of bones or had chemical analyses carried out, showing early awareness of their importance.

COEDÈS, Georges (1886–1969). French philologist. Curator of the National Library of Siam, he mastered Khmer and Thai epigraphy (as well as Sanskrit, Cham and Malay epigraphy), and wrote on the inscriptions of Indo-China. His book, *Les Etats hindouisés d'Indochine et d'Indonésie* (1944, 3rd ed. 1964; revised English transl. 1968), has become a basic source book. The contributions he made to the religious and symbolic interpretations of the monuments of Angkor, and the history of the religions and literatures of Indo-China are equally outstanding.

COLANI, Madeleine (1866–1943). Doctor of science, known for her work on prehistory and comparative ethnography. The first to identify the Hoabinh industry (from Hoà Bînh, a province in North Vietnam), she excavated 54 Hoabinh sites, possibly over-hastily; study of the material has not yet been completed. We are indebted to her for many publications relating to the prehistory of Indochina. She was a corresponding member of the Ecole Française d'Extrême-Orient, and took part in its first congress on Far Eastern prehistory (1932).

CONSTANTINOPLE, Great Palace. Built by the Emperor Constantine (r.306–337), but enlarged and altered on many occasions, the Great Palace was the principal residence of the Byzantine emperors until about the end of the 11th century AD. All that has been found of it is an important group of mosaics.

COPROLITE. Fossilized dung of animal or human origin. By studying coprolites through a microscope and analysing their constituent elements archaeologists can identify the kind of food eaten. In particular, they can locate plant remains and determine the species to which they belong. The study of coprolites thus provides valuable information about the date at which cultivated species appeared.

CORBELING. A stone roofing method whereby successive layers, each stepped outward from the previous layer, form a progressively narrowing aperture.

CORE (nucleus). Lump of stone from which flakes or blades have been removed. Although often a mere by-product of tool-making, a core may also be shaped to serve as an implement on its own.

CORNELIAN. Pinkish red quartz. When found in Africa, it was thought to have come from India. But in fact there are large amounts of it in the Nile Valley.

CROIX, Camille de la (1831–1911). Jesuit priest whose research proved vital to our knowledge of the religious monuments of the Merovingian period. In 1879 he discovered the famous Dunes *hypogeum-martyrium* in Poitiers, a chapel mausoleum built in the 7th century; this is one of the most remarkable surviving pieces of Merovingian architecture in Gaul. In 1885 de la Croix transformed the baptistry of St Jean at Poitiers into an attractive lapidary museum.

CROSS RIVER. Valley in Nigeria where more than 300 anthropomorphic monoliths of huge size were found, probably dating from the 16th century AD.

CULTIGEN. Term used to describe a plant species which, after a series of cumulative changes brought about by human selection (intentional or otherwise) has acquired certain characteristics which make it better suited to being cultivated and/or productive. An example is cultivated wheat, the grains of which, unlike those of wild wheat, do not scatter once they have reached maturity, but remain attached to the ear.

CUMULATIVE DIAGRAM. Technique of graphic representation which makes it possible to assess the degree of similarity between collections of tools or groups of sites. Along the horizontal x-coordinate are arranged the tools or characteristics in question, in accordance with a defined order corresponding to the "type list" of the collections or sites; on the vertical y-coordinate, their relative frequency is plotted. The diagram appears as a "staircase", each "step" of which conveys the relative numerical importance of each tool or characteristic, added to the relative frequence of the elements which precede it in the type list.

CUNEIFORM (writing). This term is used today to describe three writing systems which in fact have nothing in common but their appearance: signs built up from a more or less complicated combination of *cunei* (wedges), impressed into clay, engraved on hard materials and even tattooed onto human skin. The first cuneiform script spread from southern Mesopotamia at the end of the 4th millennium throughout the Levant. It was based on both ideograms and syllables. The second was a consonantal alphabet, developed at Ugarit, which vanished with the town at the beginning of the 12th century BC. The third was a syllabary script, used solely by the Achaemenid Persians to transcribe their language; the latter script was used only for monumental inscriptions and was short-lived, lasting from the 6th to the 4th century BC, but it was from this third script that cuneiform began to be deciphered in the 19th century.

CUNNINGHAM, Sir Alexander (1814–83). British general and archaeologist. Upon leaving the army in 1861, Cunningham became the first director-general of the Archaeological Survey of India. He published a report annually for 20 years which listed and described for the first time the principal monuments of ancient India.

CUPELLATION. Process in metallurgy which consisted in melting down metal in a crucible (cupel) in order to extract its principal element. The method was used to obtain silver by separating it from the lead with which it is naturally associated in argentiferous lead ores, or to obtain gold from the naturally occurring alloy of argentiferous gold (electrum).

DANEVIRKE. Defensive system consisting of an earth bank about 10m high and 2m wide (33ft x 6.6ft), a wooden palisade and a ditch, which protected the Hedeby area from Germanic raids. Medieval legend linked these fortifications to the 10th century, but dendrochronological (tree-ring) studies carried out after recent excavations indicate that the first building goes back to AD737, and was altered later. In the 10th century the fortifications were nearly 14km (9 miles) long.

DATING. Whereas a date is a more or less precise, but objective, moment in time, dating is the process whereby the archaeologist or historian attempts, by means of a hypothesis, to situate a given historical phenomenon in time. To do this various methods can be used: stratigraphic (study of the sequence of layers), historical (comparisons with chronologies that have already been established, comparitive deductions, etc.), physics (C^{14} or radiocarbon, potassium-argon, thermoluminescence, retentive magnetism, etc), chemical, etc. If only the sequence of these phenomena can be established, without a date, this is said to represent a *relative* dating. The aim obviously is to arrive at an *absolute* dating, that is, a proposition formulated in calendrical terms: but the reasoning which leads to the conclusion is the main element on which the value of the conclusion depends.

DÉCHELETTE, Joseph (1861–1914). French archaeologist. Author of monographs on Mont Beuvray (Bibracte) and decorated pottery vases of Roman Gaul, Déchelette was also the author of the *Manuel d'Archéologie préhistorique, celtique et gallo-romaine*, published in Paris in 4 volumes from 1908 to 1914. For 50 years this work had a great influence on protohistoric studies in France.

DEFFUFA. Local name given to two huge mudbrick structures which dominate the Kerma plain in northern Sudan. One suggestion is that these mark the site of the palace of the princes of Kerma, who would then have dominated the surrounding area from the top of an artificial hill; another is that they were funeral sanctuaries, since they stand in the middle of a huge necropolis. A third very interesting interpretation, recently proposed by the archaeological mission of Geneva University, suggests that the *deffufa* lying to the west could be the groundplan of an Egyptian temple introduced into Sudan.

DEICHMANN, Friedrich Wilhelm, b.1909. German archaeologist who has contributed greatly to our knowledge of Early Christian architecture throughout the Mediterranean basin, through his detailed study of its specific features and the convergence in it of different styles. He was the first to demonstrate the importance within this architecture of Constantinople (plans, materials and architectural sculpture). Apart from his monumental work on Ravenna, his main works include *Corpus der Kapitelle der Kirche von S. Marco zu Venedig* (Wiesbaden, 1981), and *Rom, Ravenna, Konstantinopel* (collected writings, Wiesbaden, 1981).

DENALIAN culture. Culture defined by the archaeologist H. West in 1967, based on the sites of the Tangle Lakes in Alaska. It is characterized by worked stone cores of the "Gobi Desert" type, which are wedge-shaped and finely worked, and include burins on flakes, bifacial tools, scrapers on flakes, microblades and large blades. This tool kit is similar to that of the Siberian Diuktai culture. There is evidence of the Denalian culture between 10,000 and 6,000BC.

DENDROCHRONOLOGY (tree-ring dating). The width of tree trunks increases annually, revealed in section as a series of rings. These rings vary, showing climatic fluctuations that provide a recognizable pattern which can be cross-referenced to older trees, giving a sequence covering thousands of years. A piece of timber can thus be assigned its place in the sequence.

DIACHRONIC. The study of the development of a phenomenon through time.

DIOP, Sheikh Anta, b.1923. Senegalese scholar whose ideas have provoked a great deal of controversy over the past 30 years. They relate to the Black African origin of mankind, on which point agreement is now general; the idea that Egypt was at its earliest periods populated only by black peoples is still treated more cautiously. But the notion that African cultures go back a very long way in time is no longer disputed. He is the author of many essays, including *Nations nègres et culture*, published in 1955.

DIUKTAI culture. The Diuktai Cave, at the confluence of the Diuktai and Aldan rivers (two tributaries of the Lena in Siberia) has given its name to a culture of the Siberian Upper Paleolithic period characterized by bifacial tools of various shapes, burins on flakes and on blades, blades and micro-blades. This industry is found in conjunction with mammoth, bison and horse bones, and is similar to the Denalian tradition in Alaska. The Diuktai Cave has yielded the earliest traces of occupation in eastern Siberia, from 33,000BC. There is no further evidence of the Diuktai culture after 10,500BC.

DOLMEN. Originally used to describe megalithic tombs lacking their covering mounds, the word now usually defines closed megalithic chambers.

DONG ZUOBIN (1895–1963). Chinese archaeologist and expert on oracle bone inscriptions from the Yin phase of the Shang dynasty (about 1400–1100 or 1027BC). He first attempted to reconstruct the context in which they had been found and looked for criteria which would enable fakes to be detected. According to his estimates, made by adding together the number of pieces found clandestinely and of those dug up during the site excavations from 1928 to 1937, they amounted to almost 10,000 complete or fragmentary items (this number has risen only slightly since).

DRACHMA. In many monetary systems in ancient Greece, in particular those of fifth-century Athens, of Alexander the Great and of Thasos from 395BC, the monetary unit was the drachma weighing, both in Athens and in Alexander's empire, 4.3 grammes. But the most usual currency was in multiples of the drachma, normally a tetradrachma (four-drachma) for silver, and a didrachma (two-drachma) for gold. Experiments with heavier coins, such as the decadrachma (43 grammes), lasted for only short periods.

DUFF, Roger Shepherd (1912–78). One of the pioneers of Polynesian archaeology, he carried out several important excavations, proving the Polynesian origin of the first inhabitants of New Zealand. We are indebted to him for many works which are vitally important to our knowledge of the prehistory of Oceania.

DUHOS. Large concave ceremonial seats used by the Taino Indians of the Greater Antilles (West Indies). They are made of carved wood, often with insets of gold or mother of pearl.

ECOSYSTEM. Area having the same microclimate and topographic, geochemical and biotic characteristics; the interacting organisms within such an area.

EDAPHIC. From the Greek *edaphos*, soil. The word is applied to ecological factors associated with the properties of the soil and the underlying rock which, along with climate, determine the characteristics of the surrounding plant and animal life.

EMIREAN. Term which covers a complex situation marking the beginnings of the Upper Paleolithic period in the Levantine Near East. The level of the Emireh cave (excavated by Garrod, 1951) from which the name is derived yielded tools of types belonging to the Middle and Upper Paleolithic periods, and also a triangular arrowhead with a base tapered by means of bifacial retouches. In the Lebanon and the Negev areas different characteristics cast doubt on the unity of this "culture".

ENDOGAMY. From the greek *gamos* (marriage) and *endon* (within): a kinship rule which obliges people to choose their spouse from within their own social and/or territorial group—sometimes, but more rarely, from among their own relations.

EPI-ACHEULIAN. Term used to describe stone industries from the early phase of the Middle Paleolithic period which combine some very rare Acheulian-type bifaces with an already well-developed tool kit based on flakes.

EPI-PALEOLITHIC. Term originally used to designate cultures using a tool kit consisting mainly of microliths which emerged after the last glaciation, preceding the Neolithic. Present usage of the term, especially in relation to the Near East, tends to describe any predominantly microlithic industry dating from the end of the Upper Paleolithic, even if it occurs before the end of last glacial period (8300BC).

EPONYM. Magistrate who, in the Greek city states, gave his name to the year. At Athens this was one of the ten Archons; at Rhodes, the Sun Priest; at Cnidus, the Demiurge, etc. In Rome the function of eponym was fulfilled by the two consuls.

EQUESTRIAN ORDER. Second class in Roman society, created and organized by Augustus. Its members, who had to provide proof that they had a fortune amounting to 400,000 sesterces, had the right to wear a gold ring and a toga with a narrow band of purple; generally they came from the provincial middle classes. After spending some time in the army they followed a civilian career which could take them to the highest state offices.

ESIE. Site in Nigeria where steatite statuettes have been found representing men and women with musical instruments. They probably date from the 18th and 19th centuries AD.

ETHNIC. Attribution indicating the relationship of a person, text or object to a particular city or city state. Knidion, for instance, a term frequently appearing on seals of amphorae (literally, belonging to the Cnidians) indicates a product of the city state of Cnidos.

ETHNOARCHAEOLOGY. A discipline still lacking clear definition and principles, ethnoarchaeology aims to improve understanding of lost societies through the study of those which still survive. It should not be confused with the comparative ethnography practised at the end of the 19th century.

EVANS, Arthur John (1851–1941). Curator of the Ashmolean Museum, Oxford, his interest in early Cretan scripts took him to Crete in 1894 to collect and study Cretan hieroglyphic seals. He bought the site of Knossos and excavated it from 1900 to 1932, which enabled him to uncover – as well as a palace covering more than 20,000 sq m and the most significant remains of the Minoan civilization – 3,500 clay tablets written in an unknown script which he named Linear B (to be deciphered by his fellow-countryman, Michael Ventris, 50 years later). His name will remain linked to the determination of the various chronological sequences of Minoan civilization.

EXPERIMENTAL ARCHAEOLOGY. Study of the methods of fabrication and manufacture of objects has led archaeologists to verify their hypotheses by making the objects themselves: prehistorians shape flints, protohistorians cast bronze. More elaborate techniques, such as traction of megaliths or reconstruction of agrarian activity, enable them to test the behaviour of a human group in its natural setting. The case of the Iron-Age village reconstructed at Butser in England is a prime example of this, but it also demonstrates the limits of experimental archaeology which can grasp only the material aspects of life and not the totality of a past, which has disappeared for ever.

FARDO. Term applied in the archaeology of Peru to the "package" formed by a human mummy wrapped together with various funerary offerings (amulets or small objects), usually in several yards of material. Often a false head made of wood or straw or a metal mask was fixed to the top of the *fardo*.

FAYUM. To the west of the Nile in Middle Egypt, linked to the Nile Valley by a former branch of the river, the deep depression of Fayum was mainly marshland surrounding Lake Qarun, fish from which were regarded as a delicacy by Egyptians throughout the ages; crocodiles abounded in the area and always had a dominant position among local deities. In the Middle Empire (c.2000BC) the Pharaohs (principally Amenemhet III) engaged in huge irrigation and drainage schemes to bring the area under cultivation. Ringed round by sandy, stony desert, Fayum became an oasis, rich and fertile, with varied scenery, famed for its orchards and gardens. After a period of relative decline, the Ptolemies in turn took an interest in Fayum, establishing numerous small towns there, the papyrus archives of which have survived in large quantity and in an excellent state of preservation. The Fayum masks, wax paintings on wood, which were placed on sarcophagi at that period have provided us with an amazing portrait gallery.

FLOOR RIDER. Lower part of a rib (part of the cross-timbering of a boat), the centre of which is placed above the keel.

FLOTATION PROCESS. Process enabling the separating out of organic remains, especially grains and plant refuse, from the earth containing them. The soil sample is placed in a receptacle containing water and gently shaken. Mineral matter, being heavier, falls to the bottom while vegetable remains or scraps of bone rise to the surface where they can be collected.

FOLLIS. Bronze coin struck during the Byzantine Empire from AD498 to 1092. It was originally inscribed with its value (40 nummi), and was worth between 1/180 and 1/360 of the solidus. From the 6th to the 8th centuries, the follis and fractions of the follis (½, ¼, ⅛), which were used as change, were in circulation. Silver coins appeared as a medium of currency in the 7th century and more particularly from the 8th to the 11th centuries.

FREEBOARD. Type of assembly in which the planks of a vessel's ribbing are arranged edge to edge, as opposed to overlapping.

FURNACE. Term generally used to describe any installation for producing iron by direct methods. There is as yet no precise typology of furnaces.

GAMIO. Manuel (1893–1960). Mexican archaeologist. One of the first modern archaeologists to concentrate on the study of Mesoamerica, Gamio is associated with the first stratigraphic excavations carried out in Mexico, but his most important work is a monumental study on the populations of the Teotihuacan valley.

GEOMETRIC (period). First period (1100–700BC) in Greek history after the fall of the Mycenaean civilization, marking the transition from the Bronze to the Iron Age. The name comes from the geometric patterns used on ceramics, the new style being developed at Athens. The first phase, known as Protogeometric (1100–900), corresponds to the "dark ages" when the Greek culture was inward looking and very poor. Its final phase, Late Geometric (770–700), coincided with the resumption of relations with the Asian cultures and the beginning of the colonization of the northern, southern and western shores of the Mediterranean.

GHIRSHMAN, Roman (1985–1979). Born in Kharkov, Ghirshman emigrated to France after the Russian Revolution. In 1931 he led a rescue mission in Iranian Luristan and carried out excavations at Tepe Sialk near Kashan (1933–37), a site which was for a long time one of the basic reference points of Iranian archaeology. After World War II, Ghirshman was appointed to head important excavations at Susa, in south-western Iran.

GLADIOLITOS. Spanish word meaning "little swords", used to refer to the objects made of polished stone, more or less phallic in shape, which characterize the Archaic cultures of Cuba and Hispaniola.

GLAZE. Term applied to the coating of a ceramic combining the functions of decoration and protection. The method was known in Ancient Egypt where a mixture of fine sand, quartz or crystal dust was used with an alkaline base (soda, potash). This glaze did not adhere well to clay. In the Hellenistic period lead glaze was invented, in which lead monoxide replaced the soda or potash. This gave much better adherence to the clay. This kind of glaze was usually used in the Middle Ages.

GLYPTICS. Art of engraving precious stones. In the archaeology of the ancient East, the term describes the engraving of seals, which achieved such heights in those areas that it can be considered as a major art. The more precise term sigillography is seldom used.

GRAVETTIAN. This cultural grouping of the Upper Paleolithic period, named after the type-site of La Gravette (Dordogne), is also known as Upper Perigordian. Dating from 27,000 to 20,000BC, the culture's stone industry is characterized by typical points, refined blades with one edge squared by a sharp retouch, various types of burins, and bone or ivory spears; in eastern Europe it includes numerous other bone tools incised with an elaborate geometric pattern. The famous carved "Venus" figurines, whose exaggerated shapes observe a precise aesthetic canon and are found from France to the Urals, date from this period.

GREAT KING. The Greeks accorded to the Persian King of Kings, all-powerful master of a monarchy founded by the divine will, the title of *Basileus*, used in Greece to designate Homeric kings, and then in the classical period to describe the holders of various offices, hereditary or otherwise, very different from the Persian monarchy; modern historians have taken to translating *Basileus* used in this context as Great King.

GROTESQUES. Name given in the Renaissance to the paintings found in the "grottoes" formed in Rome by the remains of Nero's Golden House, and derivatively used to describe the fantastical motifs inspired from antiquity created by Italian artists, in particular Raphael.

GRYAZNOV. Mikhaïl P. (*b.* 1902). Russian archaeologist, responsible for initiating the excavations of Scythian remains at Pazyryk from 1929. He led several expeditions in Siberia and in particular excavated the princely kurgan (burial mound) of Arzhan between 1971 and 1974.

GUN PORT. Opening cut out of the ship's hull, usually square in shape, at deck-level so that a cannon can be installed in firing position.

GUO MORUO. (1892–1978). An outstanding figure in Chinese archaeology, his passionately Marxist interpretation of history influenced all his work. He was one of the leading authorities on Shang bone inscriptions, and on bronze from the Chou period, using these first written texts as a basis for his study of Chinese society. His research work on bronzes from the Chou period, carried out at the same time as B. Karlgren's, followed similar lines: it consisted of making a chronological classification of the bronzes based on their inscriptions, disregarding their typology, then, as a second procedure, begun only after completing the first, of studying their form and decoration. In this way he managed to reconstruct the development of these bronzes and to define the base on which research being carried out today still rests.

HADRIAN'S WALL. The result of a decision by the emperor Hadrian himself, the wall was constructed between AD122 and 127 along a line 117km (73 miles) long running from the Solway to the Tyne. It consisted of advanced observation camps; a ditch averaging 8m wide and 1m70 deep (26ft × 5.6ft); the wall itself, 12m to 15m wide (40ft to 50ft) built of stones with towers and small forts built into it at 1.5km (1 mile) intervals; a strategic road running parallel to it; and lastly a ditch lying 80m (265ft) behind the wall, to protect it from attack from the rear. Antoninus built a second wall about 100km (62 miles) to the north, along the line between the rivers Forth and Clyde (Scotland); this wall was 60km (37.5 miles) long, and was built of turf on a stone foundation; it was 4m (13ft) wide, and had a ditch in front of it. This second line of fortifications existed for only a brief period (*c.* AD145–160).

HALAFIAN (culture). Named after the site of Tell Halaf on the upper reaches of the Khabur, this culture dates from the end of the 6th millennium BC and beginning of the 5th, and was centred around the upper part of Al Jazirah where present-day Turkey, Syria and Iraq meet. In the villages, where the typical dwelling was a round house with a vaulted dome (*tholos*) a remarkable painted ware was produced, often having streamlined shapes and with a polished geometric or naturalistic pattern. This pottery was widely distributed and imitated locally as far as the Syrian coastline and into lower Mesopotamia.

HALOPHYTIC (plants). Plants which can tolerate the absorption of a certain amount of mineral salts present in the soil in which they grow. These salts impregnate the plant tissues.

HAMADA KOSAKU (1881–1938). Born in Osaka, Japan, Hamada played a distinguished part in the development of archaeology in Japan, undertaking excavations in Kansai. Realizing the importance of the links between the Japanese archipelago and the main continent (Korea and China), he created a chair of Far Eastern archaeology at his university. In 1925 he founded the Society of Far Eastern Archaeology with Harada Yoshito (1885–1974), who undertook several excavations in Korea and Kiaoning (north-east China) and was in overall charge of excavations in the Korean peninsula.

HARAPPA (civilization). Named after the first Indus Valley site to be discovered, the Harappa civilization corresponds to the urbanization period of the area between 2400 and 1800BC. It is characterized by the development of large towns, Mohenjo-Daro and Harappa in particular, which are remarkable for the standard of their town planning and their public and private systems of hygiene and sanitation.

HASSUNA (culture). Neolithic culture from Upper Mesopotamia which in the 6th millennium occupied the area now known as Al Jazirah and the Mosul area. Consisting of small villages with rectangular or round buildings, the culture grew crops without irrigation, and reared goats or sheep. Its domestic art is characterized by simple pottery with rounded shapes, decorated with incised linear patterns (sometimes painted in its final phase).

HAYES, John W. Curator of the Graeco-Roman department of the Royal Ontario Museum, Hayes is a specialist in ceramics with a very wide-ranging expertise. His crucial contribution has been to unify the classification systems currently in use for Roman seals from the east and west (2nd–7th c.) and adding to them a great deal of hitherto unpublished material. His main work is *Late Roman Pottery* (London, British School at Rome, 1972), a supplement to which appeared in 1980. His contributions on the recent excavations of Carthage and his catalogues for the Royal Ontario Museum are regarded as authoritative.

HEDEBY and BIRKA. These Scandinavian *emporia* or trading stations marked the development of urban life, probably encouraged by Frisian merchants. Recent excavations of the settlement and harbour at Hedeby, which was strategically located on the isthmus linking Denmark to Saxony, provide proof of the existence of a flourishing trade and craft activity from the 8th century AD. Hedeby was protected by impressive fortifications. At Birka, which was on an island in Lake Mälar, excavations have revealed a statue of Buddha and jewels from the British Isles; outside the fortified settlement were tombs with rich funerary furnishing (weapons, jewels, dishes and even a horse) and burials in wooden chambers under tumuli. Birka was at its height in the 9th century, at which time (*c.* 830–53) Ansgar established a Christian church in this cosmopolitan trading post.

HELLENISTIC period. Final phase of Greek history, the Hellenistic period started in 323BC with the death of Alexander and the emergence of the kingdoms that sprang from his empire (Macedonia, Egypt, the Seleucid empire and Pergamum). It ended in 30BC when these states were finally conquered by Rome or the Parthians. During these three centuries, Greek culture crossed many political frontiers and spread from the Atlantic to India through many cities founded at that time, especially the new capital cities of Alexandria, Antioch and Pergamum, lively centres of intense creativity. At that period a common civilization became established throughout the known world for the first time, one which integrated the cultural heritage of each region and subsequently left a deep impression on the institutions, thought, religions and art of the Roman, Parthian and Kushan empires.

HELLENISTIC (urbanism). Hellenistic town planning was characterized by two basic principles: choice of a site whose natural defences could be used to advantage (by a strong perimeter wall suited to the terrain and with a citadel overlooking it), and concerted organization of the interior space. In the 4th century BC cities were divided according to a grid plan which was based on island blocks of habitations into which the monuments were fitted. This rigid plan tended to ignore the natural topography and was not linked to defence. From the 3rd century, however, care was taken with regard to the terrain, especially with a view to displaying monuments to advantage: in Pergamum, the town climbs up on a series of terraces, linked by a main road, so that it would appear almost like an urban stage set.

HEROIZATION. Ritual process whereby the Greeks invested a dead man with divine qualities of intelligence and strength which made him worthy of being honoured by a cult. The founders of city states (such as Theseus at Athens) were often heroized. Heracles is the most famous Panhellenic hero.

HERÖON. Space or building dedicated to the cult of a hero, often built around his tomb or a cenotaph.

HISPANIOLA. Island in the Greater Antilles (West Indies) which since the 17th century has been divided between Häiti and the Dominican Republic.

HITTITE (language). The discovery of the Hittite language was the major advance this century in the field of Indo-European languages, of which Hittite is the earliest form yet recorded. The mass of main texts come from the site at Boğazköy, 200km east of Ankara in the centre of Turkey where from 1906 German archaeologists have been uncovering the remains of the Hittite capital Hattusa. The archives of the city have yielded thousands of tablets in many languages, best known being Hittite from the 17th to 13th centuries BC; they are mainly in a cuneiform script borrowed from Mesopotamia, though some use Hittite "hieroglyphic" script. The great period of the Hittite empire was 14th–13th century BC when a vast amount of material was recorded – some in the important sister Anatolan languages of Palaic (Paphlagonia) and Luvian (west and south Anatolia). The latter survived into the classical period in Lycia. Hattusa itself was destroyed around 1180BC though "neo-Hittite" slates survived in Syria.

HOABINHIAN (culture). Named after Hoà Bình, a limestone massif in North Vietnam; the Hoabinhian is an industry and a culture defined by M. Colani in 1927, characterized by pebbles fashioned into tools found in piles of shells. Colani placed it as belonging to the Mesolithic, but in 1976 it was redefined by Ha Van Tan as belonging to the Upper Paleolithic.

HOLOCENE. Transitional period between the Pleistocene and the present day, starting 10,000 years ago with the end of the last glaciation (Würm-Wisconsin) which was followed by a progressive rise in temperature. During the Holocene, *Homo sapiens* diversified his tool technology, organized his habitat more efficiently, adapted his way of communal life, first of all during the Epi-Paleolithic (the final period of chipped stone, represented in France by the Azilian, the Sauveterrian and the Tardenoisian cultures) then right through the Neolithic periods, and finally during the great metalworking civilizations.

HOMO ERECTUS. Also known as *Pithecanthropus*, *Sinanthropus* and *Altanthropus*. The transition from *Homo habilis* to *Homo erectus* occurred gradually. Characterized by very thick cranial bones, prominent eyebrow ridges and a brain volume of about 1000 cc, *Homo erectus* remains are in evidence from *c.* 1,600,000BP (before present), indicating an omnivorous and nomadic hunter. The type is generally associated with the Acheulian industries in the Old World especially the so-called handaxes, and the discovery of fire-making. The transition to *Homo sapiens*, *c.* 300,000 to 200,000 years ago, is the subject of controversy.

HOMO HABILIS. Member of the *Homo* genus, the first traces of which were found in 1960 by Louis Leakey in Bed I at Olduvai in Tanzania. It was at first named Pre-Zinjanthropus because of its stratigraphical and chronological position, prior to that of the australopithecine, *Zinjanthropus boisiei*, and its brain volume was between 500 and 700 cc. It is found in conjunction with the Oldowan industries and is believed to have lived in eastern Africa before *Homo erectus*, from 2,200,000 to 1,700,000 years ago.

HOMO SAPIENS. Species constituting the final evolutionary phase of the *Homo* genus. Two lines of descent evolved more or less at the same time from an ancient stock derived from *Homo erectus* (Archanthropic): *Homo sapiens neandertalensis* (Paleanthropic) and *Homo sapiens sapiens* (Neanthropic). From this evolutionary process, which lasted several hundred thousand years, we find fossils possessing in varying degrees the earlier structural characteristics and more modern characteristics foreshadowing the two *sapiens* sub-species. They are often referred to as "pre-Neanderthal" and "pre-sapiens" types.

HOMO SAPIENS NEANDERTALENIS. First appearing in "classic" form between 100,000 and 75,000BC in western Europe, Neanderthal man died out with no direct line of descent around 35,000–30,000BC. This sub-species of *Homo sapiens* is characterized by a strong frame, a jutting face with thick brow ridges and a flattened skull with receding forehead. It is found in Europe, the Near East and Central Asia, and was contemporary with the Middle Paleolithic period. Human remains which have some Neanderthal characteristics but do not conform to the classic type are referred to as Neanderthaloid.

HOMO SAPIENS SAPIENS. This direct ancestor of present-day man appears in Europe in forms that were already varied around 35,000BC, but archaic forms must undoubtedly have been present before that. Compared with *Homo sapiens neandertalensis*, the face is smaller and the forehead straighter, with smaller brow ridges, and slighter in build. The brain volume varies from 1100 to 1200 cc and reveals a complex system of meningeal irrigation.

HOUSE OF THE DEAD. Wooden buildings above a tomb, or connected to a grave, widespread in Denmark and Germany, but also found in other areas of northern Europe during the Neolithic period. They could have been places of meditation as were some mortuary chapels in historic time.

HUMAN SACRIFICE. Although human sacrifice is often mentioned in ancient biblical, Greek or Mexican texts, it is hard to find archaeological proof of this religious practice. The traces indicating probable cannibalism (see Cannibalism) or left by violent man-inflicted death found in the Paleolithic and the Mesolithic periods given no definite proof of human sacrifice. However, this was very probably the case with regard to the servants of the royal burials at Ur (end of 4th millenium BC); there are indications that Roy Mata's subjects in Vanuatu were the object of human sacrifice; and this may also be the case for the men from the Iron Age found strangled in the Scandinavian peat bogs. The Gallic severed heads and the piles of human bones found at Ribémont (France) may result from massacres during war.

HURRIAN (language). Hurrian is not related to any known linguistic group, but is close to the Urartu (Armenian) language. There is evidence of its existence from the end of the 3rd millennium in upper Mesopotamia, and the area in which it was used subsequently spread to extend from the Zagros to the Mediterranean during the following millennium. Hurrian is a form of agglutinative language, with a series of suffixes being added to nouns or verbs to express grammatical inflexions. It seems to have disappeared at the beginning of the 1st millennium BC.

HURRIANS. The Hurrians are one of the most mysterious peoples of the ancient Near East. They were established in the northern areas of Syria and Iraq and in south-eastern Anatolia from at least the end of the 3rd millennium BC. It would seem that the Hurri, together with Semites and Indo-Aryans, played an important role in the Mitannian empire in the 2nd millennium. We know from written evidence that they exerted considerable cultural and religious influence over their Hittite neighbours. However, we are not at all clear at present about the characteristics of their material culture.

IBERO-MAURUSIAN (culture). Culture of the Mechta-el-Arbi, related to the Cro-Magnon people, living along the Mediterranean coast from Tunisia to Morocco; the Mechta-el-Arbi entered upon a Neolithic phase there and spread southwards along the Atlantic shoreline. Their way of life was linked to the presence of the sea: on the shores of southern Morocco, the western Sahara and Mauritania their food refuse can be found in the form of sometimes imposing shell mounds of mussels, oysters and arca (*Anadara senilis*). Associated with these are pottery and a limited stone-tool industry, in conjunction with hearths, sometimes still marked by supporting stones.

ICONOCLASM. Religious crisis that shook the foundations of the Byzantine Empire between 726 (when the emperor had an image of Christ destroyed in the Chalkoprateia or metalsmiths' area in Constantinople) and 843, the date of the official restoration of the images which marked the victory of the iconodules (servants of the images). The crisis was about whether the worshipped image was imbued with the divine or was merely a commemorative sign of it. The iconoclastic emperors were not the uncouth troopers depicted by the icon-loving tradition. There can be no doubt that they were impelled to adopt this "heresy" out of fear that the peoples of Asia Minor, who were already largely converted to these ideas which brought them closer to Islamic faith (which was then gaining ground), would defect from the Empire. Thus iconoclasm could be seen as a politically astute concession to the religious mentality of the Asiatic East.

IDEOGRAM. In Cretan scripts from the 2nd millennium BC, a sign symbolizing, by means of a drawing that could be either to some extent realistic or entirely abstract, a living being (man, animal), a produce (wheat, wine) a natural object (tree), or a product (vase); the term "logogram" (sign of word) would be more precise.

IGNAMES. Succulent tubers, originally from Africa, that in several millennia reached Asia and America. These plants held a leading place in the social and religious life of some African societies.

IMPRESSED WARE. Early Neolithic pottery found in the western Mediterranean, *c.*5000–3000BC. It may have originated in Asia Minor, or even in Yugoslavia (Starcevo culture). The pottery forms are simple, but display impressed decoration including cardium shells.

INCUSE-SQUARE. Greek coins consist of a lozenge of metal (gold, silver or bronze) known as a blank, on which are hammered the impressions of two images engraved onto dies or stamps: the die on the reverse, or anvil, side is that onto which the blank is placed, while the obverse die on the top of the blank is the one which directly receives the hammer blow.

In most dies the engraving was etched into the surface, producing a relief image on the coin; but in a few archaic workshops, the reverse die, which was square or rectangular in shape, bears an irregular design engraved in relief: when the coin is struck, the image produced is a sunken one, or an incuse-square.

INDEPENDENCIAN. Independence Fjord in northeast Greenland is the site that has lent its name to two Paleo-Eskimo formations, Independencian I and Independencian II. The first seems to be the earliest manifestation of the Arctic microlithic (miniature stone) tradition in the eastern Arctic. The Independencian is distinguished by the fairly standardized and precise shapes of the tools, a fine saw edge on bifacial artifacts, and the absence of polished stone and of any adze blades. About 40% of known dwellings are arranged axially in a very characteristic way with slabs of stone placed vertically round a central hearth, and spaces on each side where food could be stored. Possibly the pursuit of musk ox herds may have led the hunters of the Independencian to the far north of Greenland. They also hunted the caribou and the seal, according to season.

INDIGO. Dye plant used in Africa where it has been cultivated for a long time; it can be prepared to produce a very dark blue which is still today characteristic of many African materials.

INDO-ARYAN. Philological investigations have established that groups speaking languages of the Indo-European family settled in eastern Iran and Afghanistan, probably in the 3rd millennium BC. Some of these groups, which referred to themselves as Aryans, seem to have gradually worked their way into the Indian world. In the 1st millennium BC these groups of Indo-Aryans seem to have been responsible for the diffusion of the Vedic culture and of Sanskrit throughout northern India.

ISOHYET. Line on a map linking places with the same average rainfall.

JABRUDIAN. Stone-tool industry first identified at Yabrud in Syria, and transcribed in German as Jabrudian by its discoverer (A. Rust 1950). It marks one of the ways in which the transition from the Lower Paleolithic to the Middle Paleolithic cultures occurred in the Levant, about 150,000BC. It is distinguished by thick scrapers, often together with bifaces, and by a flaking technique which is different from the Levallois technique.

JENNINGS, J.D. (*b.* 1909). American anthropologist and archaeologist who has undertaken the most thorough research into the archaic civilizations, the "desert cultures", occupying the semi-arid western areas of North America during the past 10,000 years. His work at Danger Cave in Utah, the deepest levels of which date from 9000BC, confirms the persistent survival of the earliest ways of life in the American West until historic times.

JERMANOVICIAN. Industry dating from the beginning of the Upper Paleolithic period, the early phase of which relates to industries with foliated (leaf-shaped) points of the Middle Paleolithic period. Stone-working techniques seem to have freed themselves more quickly here from Mousterian characteristics than was the case for the contemporary Szeletian industry. The type site is the Nietoperzowa cave at Jermanovice near Cracow in Poland.

JOHN LEO THE AFRICAN (1495–*c.* 1555). Al-Hasan ibn Muhammad al-Wazzān al-Zaiyāti or al-Fasi is known by the Latin name Johannes Leo Africanus. He was born in Granada in 1495, brought up at Fez, and lived at the court of the Banu Wattas. On his way back from a journey to Mecca and Istanbul he was captured by Christian pirates who put him ashore in Naples, and gave him to Pope Leo X. In Rome he wrote his *Description of Africa* which provides a great deal of information relating to the geography, history and archaeology of that continent. He died at Tunis.

JOUANNET, François-Benit Vatar de (1785–1845). Known as the "grandfather of prehistory" he toured the Paleolithic caves of central France in search of fossil remains, 1815–34. He anticipated Boucher de Perthes with his discovery that worked stone tools were earlier than polished stone tools.

KARLGREN, Bernhard (1889–1978). Swedish archaeologist. The first person to reconstruct the phonology of Chinese characters in use around AD600 and then in earlier periods, he next undertook the study of numerous fundamental texts of the pre-Han period and succeeded in assessing their authenticity and in translating them (into English), and providing commentaries of outstanding value. In the field of early bronzes, he laid the foundations for an analytical method, the principles of which are still valid today.

KEBARIAN. Stone-tool industry identified by D. Garrod in 1937 from Bed C of the Kebareh cave (Mount Carmel, Israel). It is characterized by microliths which are not geometric in the early phases. The difference in the proportions of the tools according to area has led some archaeologists to give different names to industries that were contemporary, but slightly dissimilar.

KEEL. That part of the ship's hull which is under water when it is loaded, also referred to as the quick works or vitals. The job of repairing or completely overhauling the part of the vessel described as the keel is known as careening.

KERN, Hendrik (1833–1917). Dutch philologist specializing in Indo-European languages, from 1871 he made a study of the Sanskrit inscriptions of Southeast Asia and initiated study of old Javanese. He realized the potential interest of medieval Javanese literary texts and of the local versions of Indian epics. In his study of the dialects of the Fiji Islands, he inaugurated research into Malayo-Polynesian languages.

KJÖKKENMÖDDING. From the Danish *Kjökken*, a kitchen, and *mödding*, a midden. In 1847 Danish archaeologists applied this term to the kitchen refuse piled up amidst coarse pottery and wooden and horn tools found in the peat bogs of northern Europe. In Japanese the term is translated *Kaizuka*, a heap of shells.

KOENIGSWALD, Gustav Heinrich Ralph von (1902–82). Born in Berlin, his main achievement was the discovery of the famous *Pithecanthropus* remains in Sangiran, Java, which he was able to assign to the *Homo* genus. His last discovery in Java in 1950 was that of *Meganthropus palaeojavanicus*.

KOFUN. In Japan the great tumuli of the Kansai area were called *ryō* (imperial burials) in the 18th century. Other smaller ones were referred to at the end of the 19th century by the term *Kofun* (old tombs). In the division of Japanese history into periods, the term Old Tomb Period has been adopted to describe the period extending from the 4th to the 7th century AD.

KOLDEWEY, Robert (1855–1925). Trained as an architect, Koldewey was appointed by the Royal Prussian Museums in 1896 to undertake excavations at the prestigious site of Babylon. Work started in 1899 and continued uninterrupted until 1917. This excavation site, where most German archaeologists of the early 20th century were trained, revealed not the destroyed capital of Hammurabi, but the capital of the neo-Babylonian empire (7th–6th century BC) and remains from the Seleucid-Parthian and Sassanian periods. This work marked the beginning of scientific archaeology in the Near East in that, being directed by a trained architect, it concentrated as much on surveying the architectural remains as on recovering items that could be displayed in museums.

KROEBER, Alfred L. (1876–1960). North American anthropologist. He was the author of many monographs on Peruvian archaeology, and of several general studies in which he sketched out a chronology for Pre-Columbian cultures, much wider in scope than those outlined by M. Uhle and then J. Tello. He was responsible for creating the present school of North American archaeology.

KROM, Nicolaas J. (1883–1945). Dutch historian and archaeologist, he was a member of the Commission of Javanese Antiquities in 1910, and initiated the Archaeological Service of which he was director from 1913 to 1915. With Van Erp he published a monograph on Borobudur, and his *Inleidig tot de Hindoe-Javaansche Kunst* (1921, revised 1923) provides the basis of the history of Indonesian art.

KUI. Chinese term denoting a dragon motif, shown in profile and with only one leg, often depicted on Shan and Chou bronzes.

KYÔZUKA. Japanese word meaning "*sûtra mound*". The practice of burying Buddhist texts (*sûtra* in Sanskrit, *kyô* in Japanese) in underground hiding places (sometimes resembling cairns) became widespread in Japan with the belief in *mappo*, the third of the Buddhist cycles which was to bring confusion and a disappearance of the faith. This custom was common in the Heian, Kamakura and Muromachi periods. Calligraphic scrolls were placed in a reliquary (*kyôzutsu*), usually made of metal (bronze) and this was placed inside a ceramic receptacle. For this jars (*tsubo*) fired in the Japanese kilns at Tokoname, Atsumi or Seto were used, or sometimes Chinese celadons of the Sung period and blue and white painted porcelain pieces of the Yuan period. Archaeological excavations have resulted in the discovery of whole "fields" of *kyôzuka*, for instance at Mount Hôrai-ji (Aichi-ken).

LAMINA. Sample of clay which has been cut in section and placed between two plates of glass, enabling a petrographic analyst to read and determine, through a microscope, the constituent ingredients of a piece of ceramic.

LAMING-EMPERAIRE, Annette (1917–77). French prehistorian specializing in the study of prehistoric rock art. From 1951, with her husband José Emperaire, she undertook archaeological investigations in Brazil and then in Chilean Patagonia. They were responsible for finding and studying various prehistoric sites in southern Chile—Englefield, Ponsonby, Munición—and in Brazil—José Vieira and several sambaquis (shell middens or heaps). After her husband's death, she carried on their work, excavating Marassi (Tierra del Fuego—1965–1967), and Lapa Vermehla (Brazil—1971), as well as analysing many sites of rock art in the Lagoa Santa area in Brazil.

LAPICIDE. In antiquity, workman specializing in the incising of inscriptions on stone.

LA QUINA. French site from which the Mousterian of the Quina type is named. The stone tool industry produced numerous thick scrapers with a very curved cutting edge and stepped, splintered retouches. Another industry with many thin scrapers, produced by the Levallois technique and called Mousterian of Ferrassie type, is linked with the Quina type because of the predominance of scrapers or *racloirs* in both industries and the large number of identified sites in northern Périgord; together they have been called Mousterian of the Charentes type.

LARTET, Edouard (1801–71). French paleontologist and prehistorian. In 1860 he excavated the Aurignac cave (Haute-Garonne, France) where he found prehistoric levels of occupation. From 1863 until his death he explored the Eyzies area in Périgord, whose prehistoric riches were then unknown, with his friend and patron, the English banker, H. Christy. Together they discovered most of the great Paleolithic sites of that area. He was responsible for one of the first classifications of the Paleolithic period, and *Reliquiae Aquitanicae*, a work credited jointly to Lartet and Christy, and published posthumously, describes all the sites he had excavated in Périgord.

LATEEN SAIL. The lateen sail, which is typical of the Mediterranean, is triangular in shape and fixed onto a short mast and a long lateen yard; there is evidence of its use in the Mediterranean basin from the early Middle Ages only.

LATIFUNDIA. The Latin word *latifundia* which is still in use today (e.g. in South America) refers to very large estates in antiquity. Nowadays it is used only when these estates are run in an archaic fashion. *Latifundia* are typified by extensive (as opposed to intensive) agriculture, the absence of investment in the estate, low productivity, and often by absentee landlords.

LEAF-SHAPED (foliated) Term used to describe tools which have been retouched on both faces to produce a flattish effect. Many Upper Paleolithic tools are named after leaves (the Solutrean laurel leaf being the best known). Some Middle Paleolithic industries are characterized by the presence of bifaces, others by the presence of leaf-shaped objects. The Mousterian industries producing leaf-shaped items are mainly in central and eastern Europe.

LEAKEY, Louis Seymour Bazett (1903–72). Leakey was born in Nairobi and spent almost his whole life in eastern Africa, especially in Kenya. As a geologist and a paleontologist he clarified the paleo-climatic scale of the Pleistocene. But the main part of his work relates to paleo-primatology and paleoanthropology: *Proconsul*, *Kenyapithecus*, *Zinjanthropus boisiei*, *Homo habilis* etc. Accompanied by his wife Mary and often by his children, especially his son Richard, he explored many sites in Kenya and Tanzania, including the celebrated Olduvai Gorge site.

LEGISM. This movement, of great importance in China of the 4th–3rd centuries BC, appears in the *Hanfeizi* as a reflection on the conduct and organization of the states, whereby political and social institutions were for the first time rigorously submitted to the supremacy of law. Further developed in the feudal period of the Warring States (475–221BC), legism became the basis of the centralized state of Shih Huang Ti (221–210BC), founder of the empire, and from then on was a constant source of inspiration in Chinese political thought.

LEIWEN. Chinese term denoting the "thunder" motif, represented by a spiral of square or rectangular form. It often appears in very low relief to decorate the bodies of fabulous animals or as the background against which a pattern in higher relief stands out.

LEPSIUS, Karl-Richard (1810–74). Born in Naumburg-an-der-Saale, Lepsius was from 1842 to 1845 entrusted by the King of Prussia with responsibility for a large expedition to Egypt and the Sudan, from which he brought back the material published in *Denkmäler* as well as numerous antiquities; on his return a chair—the first in Germany—was created for him at the University of Berlin; he was elected a member of the Berlin Academy (1850) and was made responsible for the Egyptology collection at the Berlin Museum; in 1873 he also became Conservator of the Berlin Library. Having virtually recreated Egyptology as a subject after the premature death of Champollion, he had a decisive influence in this field.

LEVALLOIS technique. Technological process of flint flaking which ensures that a flake of a predetermined shape is produced from a core which has previously been subjected to a preparatory process of varying complexity; named after the site at Levallois-Perret, near Paris. A Levallois flake or blade bears the scars of the preparatory work on the core and the residual core very often still has faceted marks left by small retouches of the preparatory plan. The Levallois technique was known from the Acheulian period and flourished during the Middle Paleolithic, remaining in use until the Neolithic. From 1931 to 1953 the adjective "Levalloisian" was used to describe a tool industry in which Levallois flakes were abundant: but it is now regarded as one of the aspects of the Mousterian culture.

LIAN. Chinese term generally used to describe a lacquered wooden box in which toilet necessities are kept. In some cases it may refer to a food box probably containing cooked cereals.

LI CHI (1896–1979). Chinese archaeologist responsible for supervising the great series of excavations carried out at Anyang between 1928 and 1937 (while Dong Zuobin saw to the study of incriptions). The information acquired on site enabled him to identify the features distinguishing the Shang civilization from earlier Neolithic cultures. His achievement included the making of a typology of bronzes based on their shapes, replacing traditionally applied names; the unearthing at Xiaotun near Anyang of nearly 250,000 ceramic shards and more than 1500 complete or nearly complete pieces; and his studies of small items such as bone hairpins, which the tomb-robbers at Anyand had ignored so that they were present in sufficient number to enable the remains to be dated stratigraphically.

LINDENSCHMIT, Ludwig (1809–93). The brothers Ludwig and Wilhelm (1806–48) Lindenschmit deserve the credit for having attributed the burials that they excavated at Selzen, near Mainz, from 1844 to 1846 to the period of the Great Invasions and the Franks. Until then similar burials discovered in Germany had been thought to be Celtic or Roman. As well as using comparative methods (the tomb of Childeric I, found at Tournai in 1653), they made proper use of the *terminus post quem* provided in the case of two burials by the dates on which two silver coins from the reign of Justinian I (527–565) had been struck.

LONG COUNT SYSTEM. Of the various forms of recording time used in Mesoamerica, the Long Count system is the only one to refer to an initial fixed date, which was perhaps the equivalent of 3113BC. The passage of time is recorded in decreasing units equalling × times 144,000 days, × times 72,000 days, × times 360 days, × times 20 days, and × times 1 day. In the Maya lowlands to the south, the Long

Count system was used between c. AD300 and 900, but the Mayas are not thought to have invented this system of calculation.

LOST WAX (casting process). Casting process which uses either a wax model or a clay model covered in wax; this is then coated with sand or plaster. When the wax is melted it leaves room for the liquid metal. An object manufactured in this way can thus be solid or hollow. This method, widespread in its use, except in China under the Shang dynasty which developed its own techniques, enables very complicated shapes to be cast, in fretwork for example, which could not be achieved in any other way.

LUCE, Gordon Hannington (1889–1979). Appointed Professor of English at Rangoon in 1912, he translated Burmese chronicles with his brother-in-law Pe Maung Tin. Realizing the inadequacy of these sources, he concentrated on the study of inscriptions in Mon, Pyu and Burmese, and assembled information on Burma from Chinese literature. His studies on the iconography and symbolism of Burmese monuments are of fundamental importance. Expelled in 1964, he continued his work in England. *Old Burma, Early Pagan* (1969–70, 3 vols.) provides a synthesis of his research.

LUND, Peter W. (1801–80). Danish naturalist. A pupil of Cuvier's, he settled in Brazil in 1834 in the Lagoa Santa area and excavated more than 800 caves there. His many finds of fossilized animals were used by Darwin in his research into evolution. The discovery of human bones in association with animal remains from the Pleistocene led him to suggest in 1844 that these animals might have been contemporary with an "antediluvian" man.

LUVIAN OR LUWIAN (language). This Indo-European language, a sister tongue to Hittite, was spoken in the 2nd millennium BC in western and southern Asia Minor, especially in the important Late Bronze Age power of Arzawa: indeed it was probably the language of the Trojans at the time of the Trojan War. This huge area was loosely known as Luwiya—the area where Luvian was spoken and the language survived in Lycia in south-west Turkey until the Roman period, where it has been found in inscriptions at the main sites, such as Xanthus. As yet it remains only partially deciphered.

MACHALILLA CULTURE. Prehistoric culture from eastern Ecuador known chiefly through its ceramics.

MAGATAMA. Japanese word meaning "curved jewel". *Magatama* are small ornaments in the shape of a comma and made of precious stones, crystal or gold. Apart from their decorative function, *magatama* had magic properties: *tama* can mean not only "jewel" but also "soul". These ornaments are peculiar to Silla (Korea) and Yamato (Japan).

MAGDALENIAN. The most recent grouping of the Upper Paleolithic, named after the type-site cave of La Madeleine (Dordogne), excavated from 1863 by E. Lartet who attributed this culture to the "Age of the Reindeer". The period extends from 15,000 to 8,000BC, with a stone industry consisting of many small blades with a steep retouched edge, burins, scrapers and awls; but the Magdalenian is characterized above all by a productive bone industry, with spear-throwers, spears of various types (depending on the phase of the culture), harpoons with one or two rows of barbs, and numerous portable works of art, engraved or carved. Its early phase is known only in France, but in its late phase this culture extended to northern

and eastern Europe (England, Belgium, Germany, Czechoslovakia).

MAGLEMOSIAN. Mesolithic culture characterized by stone axes, triangular flint heads and a varied, abundant, often decorated tool kit in bone and deer antler. It extended over northern and north-western European countries, during the period from 7600 to 5800BC.

MAGNETOMETER (or Proton magnetometer). A piece of equipment which makes possible the detection of the irregularities of the earth's magnetic field. When an element is brought to a temperature of over 600°C, the magnetic particles are disturbed; once cooling down has taken place they fall into position according to the local alignment on that day. Thus what has been baked and rebaked—a kiln or piece of ceramic—will present anomalies when compared with the environment which has not been subjected to such heat.

MANSUY, Henri (1857–1937). French geologist and prehistorian. After entering the Geological Service of Indo-China at the age of 45, he carried out many geological missions. In 1909 he discovered the Bacsonian culture at Pho Binh Gia and worked on animal paleontology. In the 1920s, after excavations at Samrong Sen (Cambodia), he pursued his study of the Bacsonian on new sites.

MARGIANA. Ancient province lying on the plains of southern Soviet Turkmenistan, around the Murgab delta. The Achaemenid satrapy (administrative district) of Margiana was chiefly known for its rebellion against Darius I. Subsequently its history tended to be confused with that of Bactria as we know from investigations carried out since 1975 in ruins situated in the fringe areas of Kara Kum, north of the zones now under cultivation.

MARIETTE, Auguste (1821–81). Sent by the Louvre to Egypt in 1850 to acquire Coptic manuscripts, he used his position to excavate Saqqara, where he gained access to the Serapeum. There he found the burials of the Apis bulls and the jewels belonging to Rameses II. After being appointed a curator at the Louvre, he returned to Egypt, where in 1857 Said Pasha entrusted him with setting up the Service of Antiquities and organizing the Egyptian Museum in Cairo. His activity was phenomenal: he uncovered sites at Saqqara, Giza, Abydos, Thebes, Edfu, Elephantine and in the Delta, sometimes employing more than 2,000 workers at a time. As well as this, he worked on the book and costumes for Verdi's Aida. He died in Egypt and was buried in a sarcophagus in front of Cairo Museum.

MARSHALL, Sir John (1876–1959). British archaeologist. Director-General of the Archaeological Survey of India from 1904 to 1934. He had been educated as a Hellenist, and was at first interested in Alexander's campaigns and in Graeco-Buddhist monuments; then from 1920 on he coordinated the important prehistoric excavation sites of Harappa and Mohenjo-Daro. He also excavated the Buddhist site of Sanchi and the town of Taxila.

MASPERO, Gaston (1846–1916). French archaeologist of Milanese origin. In 1880 he was made responsible for creating the Archaeological Mission which was later to become the Institut Français d'Archéologie Orientale, and upon the sudden death of Mariette was appointed Director of Antiquities. At Deir el Bahari he came upon a fabulous collection of royal mummies, organized the inventory of the huge collection and the museum to house them, and ensured the

publication of an account of the Nubian monuments threatened by the construction of the first Aswan Dam. Author of a distinguished series of publications, he was appointed Secretary for life of the Academy of Inscriptions in 1914.

MASTABA. In Arabic, a "little bench"; the name given by the workmen employed by Mariette to the private tombs of the Old Kingdom which they were uncovering, the lightly banked silhouette of which was reminiscent of a bench seat. Mastabas comprised an underground vault walled up after the burial and linked by a shaft to a cult chapel, and were often grouped round a monument to the pharoah himself, whether pyramid or funerary temple. The decoration of the chapel walls was often inspired by scenes from everyday life, full of simple and charming details.

MEDIAN WARS. In the course of its rapid expansion, the Persian empire, which between 549 and 525BC extended from Afghanistan to Egypt and Turkey, had subjugated the Greek cities of Ionia (on the coast of Asia Minor). These revolted in 499, with the aid of Athens and another Greek city state, and in revenge the great King Darius declared war in 490 (first Median War); this punitive expedition was defeated by Athens at Marathon. Ten years later, his son Xerxes mounted a huge expedition to conquer Greece, by land and sea, which ended in disaster after the defeat of the fleet at Salamis (480) and of the army at Plataea (479). The two Median Wars, described by Herodotus, were at the origin of a lively monetary activity, attested by numerous Greek treasure hoards buried during these years in the Persian empire, notably the treasure of Assiyut.

MEIPIN. Japanese name (*Meiping* in Chinese) for a type of bottle with a narrow neck, high shoulders and a pinched-in base. The *Meipin* was originally a Chinese creation; it was very popular in the Sung, Yuan and Ming periods and at the beginning of the Tsing period, and the shape spread to Korea (Kŏryŏ celadons, for example) and to Japan. In Japan, under Chinese influence, the Seto kilns took up and transposed this type of bottle.

MERCATI, Michael (1541–93). Italian scholar and naturalist responsible for the Pope's gardens, who during the course of his life formed a collection of fossils and curiosities. In his inventory of these objects, he was the first to propose that "thunder stones" were tools made by man at a period when metal-working was unknown. His work was not published until 1717, by which time the ideas he had put forward were beginning to be current in the scientific world.

METROPOLITAN CHINA. Term used to describe that part of China lying along the middle reaches of the Yellow River and in immediately adjacent areas, namely northern Honan, southern Shansi and the eastern part of Shensi. This region is regarded as the cradle of Chinese civilization.

MICROBURIN technique. Procedure whereby a strong head with a sharp point could be obtained by breaking up flint blades after making a notch in them; the part left is the "microburin". This technique, seldom used in the Upper Paleolithic period, became widespread in the Mesolithic as a means of manufacturing arrowheads.

MICROLITH. A very small stone tool which may be less than one centimetre in length. The word microlith is often reserved for tools of

geometric shape, such as a triangle, rectangle, trapezium, or a segment of a circle (also called geometric microliths). Though these are found in the industries of the Upper Paleolithic, they are really plentiful more in the epi-Paleolithic levels. These tiny pieces could be used as the tips of arrows or, placed together and held in a groove, they could be useful in the manufacture of harpoons or sickles.

MICROTOPONYMY. The extension of toponymy (place-name research) to small areas such as the streets of a town, or the woods, hills and streams of a stretch of countryside.

MINGQI. Chinese term used to describe objects, sometimes very small, imitating objects of daily life, or buildings, which were placed in tombs as offerings. They seem to have been of fairly early origin, as is demonstrated by some pieces from the Shang period, but relatively little is yet known about them.

MINOAN (civilization). Given this name by Arthur Evans from the name of the legendary Cretan king Minos; according to Greek tradition of the 1st millenium BC, Minos reigned over Crete and, through his fleet, extended his power over the Aegean as well as trading throughout the eastern Mediterranean. The Minoan civilization was at its height between 1900 and 1450BC: its palaces and towns (with their records) are evidence of its spiritual strength; its architecture, metallurgy, jewellery, sculpture and painting indicate a very high level of technology and art; and its forms of writing show its genius.

MITANNI. Large empire in upper Mesopotamia and northern Syria formed in the middle of the 2nd millennium BC by a combination of Hurrian and Indo-Aryan peoples. The latter may have constituted a military-style governing aristocracy, though the official language was Hurrian. About 1360BC the Mitanni's political power was broken by the Hittite king Suppiluliuma I. Artistically, the Mitannian style is associated with works (such as the Mitanni seals) belonging to the northern parts of Syria and Iraq from the 16th to the 14th centuries BC, and even later, for the style survived after the fall of the Mitanni empire. During the latter centuries of the 2nd millennium, objects in the Mitanni style were widely distributed throughout the Near East.

MORELEY, Sylvanus G. (1883–1948). American archaeologist noted for his work on the Mayan civilization. His fieldwork extended over half a century, but his major contribution relates to carved Mayan inscriptions, which he catalogued, reproduced and partly translated. *The Ancient Maya*, which he published at the end of his life, is the first great modern attempt to take an overall look at the civilization of that part of Mesoamerica.

MORSE, Edward Sylvester (1838–1925). American zoologist and geologist whose excavations along the American coastline uncovered numerous Kjökkenmödding (food debris and shell mounds). In 1877 he was invited by the University of Tokyo to lecture on zoology and the theory of evolution. His chance discovery of the Omori *kaizuka* (shell mounds) and his publication of the report on the excavations he undertook there make him a key figure in the modern archaeology of Japan.

MORTILLET, Gabriel de (1821–9). French prehistorian. In 1864 he founded the first French prehistorical journal, *Matériaux pour l'histoire positive et philosophique de l'homme*. Between 1869 and 1872 he established a chronological framework for the phases of the Paleolithic period which for a long time served as the reference for study of this period: Chellean, Acheulian, Mousterian, Aurignacian, Magdalenian, etc.

MOUSTERIAN. Cultural grouping of the Middle Paleolithic named after the stone tools – scrapers and points – found in Moustier Cave (Dordogne) in 1865. Mousterian artifacts are present throughout Europe during the first half of the last great glaciation (Würm), and are particularly associated with Neanderthal peoples.

MURUS GALLICUS. Timber framework used to strengthen a stone or earth rampart. Often employed at the great Iron Age hillforts of Europe during the prehistorical period.

MYCENAEAN (civilization). Named after the town in the Argolis that was the main fortress of the Greek dynasty ruling in Hellas from the 16th to the 12th century BC. Mycenae was at its most powerful between 1450 and 1200BC. It had very early contact with the Minoan civilization and borrowed some technical skills from the Minoans, including writing. Some time around 1450 a Mycenaean dynasty was established at Knossos; the palace there was destroyed *c.* 1375BC, but a mixed Mino-Mycenaean civilization continued in existence until the Dorian "invasion" (12th century BC). On mainland Greece most of the Mycenaean palaces, with their archive tablets written in Linear B, were destroyed towards the end of the 13th century BC.

NATUFIAN CULTURE. Epi-Paleolithic Levantine culture, between 10,000 and 8300BC, first identified on the Wadi an-Natuf (Palestine), characterized by its tool kit of geometric microliths with segments of the circle predominating. These people were hunters of small herbivorous animals (especially gazelles), gatherers of wild cereals, and fishers, occupying all the semi-arid part of the Levant from northern Syria to the Nile Delta. They built the first permanent village settlements, in pre-agricultural times, in Palestine (Mallaha) and on the middle Euphrates in Syria (Mureybet and Abu Hureyra).

NEOLITHIZATION. Group of cultural processes marking the transition from an economy based on hunting and gathering to an agricultural economy. These processes are linked with the development of village life, and the beginning of firing techniques and the production of artifacts (such as pottery) connected with them.

NESTORIAN CHRISTIANITY. Doctrine professed by Nestorius, a bishop of Constantinople who placed the bond between God and Christ on a moral plane, denying the divine nature of Christ. Nestorius was condemned as a heretic by the Council of Ephesus in 431, but his doctrine was adopted by the Christian communities of Iran, which organized themselves into a national church under the leadership of the patriarch of Seleucia-Ctesiphon. Alternately protected and persecuted by the Sassanian kings, Nestorian Christianity spread along the great trade routes and reached India, Central Asia and China (where a stone slab was found at Chang'an commemorating its introduction in 631). In the Middle Ages its existence among the Turks and Mongols of Upper Asia gave rise in the West to the legend of "Prester John".

NEUTRON ACTIVATION ANALYSIS. Method of analysis that consists of irradiating the ceramic specimen with a neutron beam; some of the atoms in the specimen then become radioactive and emit various gamma rays, the wavelength and intensity of which make possible a qualitative analysis (nature of atoms present) and a quantitative analysis (number of atoms present).

NILE. Arab writers used the word Nile to denote the River Niger or the River Senegal when they were describing West Africa.

NOME. Greek term used to designate the territorial divisions of the administration in ancient Egypt; their number varied in the course of the centuries. At their head were the Nomarchs, who were appointed as delegates of the central power of the Pharoah, and tended to become virtually autonomous chieftains in troubled periods.

NOMOLI. Figures carved in steatite originating from Sierra Leone. They have always been found without excavation, on the surface of the ground, and for this reason cannot be dated.

NUCLEUS OR CORE. Block of primary material from which flakes have been removed by percussion for use as tools. The nucleus is what is left after the stone has been worked on, and it often bears characteristic signs of the method used to fashion the pieces required.

NUMERI. Bodies of troops recruited from the barbarian tribes living on the margins of the Roman Empire. They preserved their own language, weaponry and traditional fighting methods, but their leaders were always made subject to the authority of a Roman officer. We know nothing of the strength and internal organization of these corps, which must have contributed to "barbarizing" the army. They developed mainly from the time of Trajan and Hadrian.

OBA. Ruler of ancient Benin (present-day Nigeria).

OCHRE. Red pigment containing iron used by men since the Lower Paleolithic. Until the end of the Middle Paleolithic, it is mainly found in the form of small blocks worn away by rubbing or scraping. From the Upper Paleolithic on, the ground on which some dwellings stood and the sediment in many burial places were impregnanted with ochre. As crayons or powder it was used from the Aurignacian period to make paintings on the walls of caves or on bone or stone artifacts. Recent examination has revealed the presence of ochre inside the flint micro-fissures of certain tools, such as scrapers. This suggests that beside its aesthetic and perhaps magic and religious uses, ochre could be employed in technical operations, especially in treating skins.

OLDOWAN. Adjective formed from Olduvai (Olduvai Gorge, Tanzania – an important Paleolithic site), and applied to the pebble tool industries of south and east Africa.

OPPIDUM. Term used by Julius Caesar in the 1st century BC to describe a provincial Celtic fortified town. The most spectacular parts of these towns, found both in hill country and on the plain, continue to this day to be the ramparts and the *vallum* (entrenchment). Some are very large, such as the *oppidum* of Grabenstetten near Stuttgart in Germany which covers an area of 1600 hectares. Excavations at some *oppida*, such as Mont Beuvray (Bibracte) in France, Manching in Germany or the Hradischt Stradonice in Czechoslovakia, have yielded the remains of various craft, trading and religious activities.

OSSUARY. Receptacle used or specially manufactured for holding the bones, normally of one person only, after they have been picked clean by animals (according to Zoroastrian rites) or made bare by natural decomposition.

OSTIA. Roman colony founded in the 4th century BC at the mouth of the Tiber, Ostia became increasingly important as the port of Rome at the end of the Republic and during the early Empire, to such an extent that large brick apartment blocks were built there in the 1st and 2nd century AD. To make it easier to keep the capital supplied, Claudius (AD41–54) and Trajan (98–117) had two harbours built at Portus, immediately north of Ostia.

PALEO-ARCTIC TRADITION. Somewhat disparate tradition grouping together industries developed in America (American Paleo-Arctic tradition) and sometimes in Siberia (Siberian Paleo-Arctic tradition) which are derived from the Siberian Upper Paleolithic. The common features of these industries are blades and microblades, small wedge-shaped cores of the "campus" type, various kinds of bifaces which are in varying degrees foliated, end scrapers, side scrapers and often burins (pointed tools) made out of thick flakes.

PALEODEMOGRAPHY. Discipline that aims to reconstruct the demography of ancient populations on the basis of archaeological evidence using bone remains and the traces left by occupation. The reconstruction of the population of a site or of a region is based on the area covered by settlements and on the housing density. However, a wide margin of uncertainty remains, due to our ignorance of the real output of the land during the period in question, in terms of agriculture, hunting, animal husbandry, etc. Moreover, within a settlement, the population density is very hard to assess, despite the contribution of ethnographical studies and historical sources. Estimates of early populations lie within very wide margins, and are useful only in yielding *relative* estimates, comparing the density, say, of hearths or silos on a particular site at two successive periods, or the density of sites in the same region at two different periods. However, studies of paleopathology (signs of rheumatism, dental wear and decay, etc.), estimates of life expectancy (about 35 in the Bronze Age in Central Asia), and evaluations of infant mortality, male deaths (war) and female deaths (childbirth) are more firmly grounded. Sometimes burial grounds which have been used over a long period enable the demographic development of a population to be traced; in other cases a full burial ground near a correctly defined site enables us to arrive at a good approximation of the population.

PALETHNOLOGY. Term created in 1865 referring to the study of the behaviour of vanished peoples. Evolutionary theories of the time led to an erroneous search for universal principles in the behaviour of "primitive" peoples. Today palethnology (also called *paleoethnology*) is the ethnological study of prehistoric peoples, based solely on archaeological evidence.

PALEOMETALLURGY. Science which studies ancient metallurgy in its widest sense from its beginnings up to the industrial age. It examines and interprets the remains of old metal-working equipment and sites: the areas where metal was extracted and where the ore was treated, the workshops of goldsmiths and silversmiths, bronze and iron-workers. It uses metallographic methods to analyse the metal objects themselves. It collects together any written sources, such as the texts of Pliny or Agricola, which provide information about certain aspects of ancient technology. Sometimes experiments that attempt to rediscover the different phases of metallurgical manufacture are used to test out various theories.

PALLADIUM. Wooden idol of Pallas Athene whose presence was believed to ensure the protection of the city of Troy. A group of sanctuaries dedicated to the god of war, Menthu, built to act as a magic line of defence all round the Egyptian capital, was designated the "sacred Palladium of Thebes"; it included the temples of Medamud, North Karnak, Tod and Ermant.

PALYNOLOGY. Pollen analysis. Study of the pollens, male elements of flowering plants, and spores of lichens and mosses. The range of their morphology provides botanical information, and the effectiveness of their protective envelopes ensures their preservation from the earliest times. Geologists, geographers and prehistorians make use of the sequence of past flora to establish chronological scales. Human environments, primary materials and foods can thus be revealed to archaeologists.

PANDANUS. Tree of Indo-Malay origin with many varieties. The kernels of its composite fruit and the tips of its aerial roots are edible, and were eaten in great quantities during the prehistoric period in New Guinea. They are rarely eaten now, except on the Pacific atolls where horticulture cannot supply what is needed, but the pandanus is still highly prized for the materials it supplies: wood and leaves, the latter being used to make roofs and mats and for basketwork.

PAPYRUS. Writing material manufactured from the fibres of a water plant that flourished in the Nile valley and delta. The contiguous lamellae were placed in two perpendicular layers pressed into sheets, then stuck to each other to form a roll of variable length; only the inner surface was used for writing. Light but fragile, it was produced only in Egypt; nonetheless papyrus was the preferred medium for writing throughout classical antiquity. Unlike clay tablets, which were engraved, papyrus allowed a light and cursive script, thus encouraging the spread of a technique that was originally very restricted and specialized.

PARCHMENT. Writing material made from animal skin (calf, sheep or goat) which gradually replaced papyrus during the late Roman empire, resulting in the book (codex) replacing the scroll. The discovery of this writing material is credited to Pergamum because of the word's etymology (*pergamenum*). It is less fragile, and could also be reused after the original text had been erased by scraping; such parchments are called palimpsests. Paper took over from the 14th century.

PARTHIANS. Dynasty arising from an Iranian tribe originating somewhere between the Caspian and the Aral Sea. In the 3rd century BC they seized the Seleucid province of Parthyene and founded the kingdom of Parthia, with Nisa as its capital. For a long time they had to defend themselves against the Bactrian Greeks and the Seleucids, but the kingdom expanded rapidly from the 2nd century BC and the reign of Mithridates I. Iran, lower and middle Mesopotamia and then Armenia were all conquered and a new capital was founded at Ctesiphon on the Tigris. To the east, the Parthians played their part in eliminating the kingdom of Bactria and took up residence in India. The Parthian empire lasted five centuries and was replaced by the Sassanian empire (222AD).

PEBBLE. Stone shaped by the action of waves, torrents or rivers, and marked by splintering, or rounded through rubbing. Tools such as the chopper and polyhedra (with several sides) were fashioned from pebbles gathered on sea beaches or on the banks of rivers. They could also be fashioned from unrounded stones with sharp sides.

PEBBLE CULTURE. The stone industries which preceded the Acheulian were based on pebbles which provided a cutting edge (a chopper) or a faceted sphere (a polyhedron) formed by the removal of one or several pieces or flakes. These tools, found in conjunction with flakes, are characteristic of the civilizations of the *Pebble culture* from southern Africa to Peking. Today a more regional terminology is preferred: one of the best known is the Oldowan (1,800,000–1,600,000 years ago) the type-site of which is the Olduvai gorge in Tanzania. Vestiges of this culture have been found in other sites in eastern Africa.

PEBBLE TOOLS. Plane and scraper tools made of chipped stone from a rock or a pebble, which have one flat or slightly concave surface, occurring naturally or artificially contrived, from which a number of pieces have been sharply chipped, in a more or less regular way, with the chipped-off areas adjoining one another, so as to achieve a vertical front (a plane) or a sloping one (a scraper). They were intended for scraping animal skins and stripping bark, and are present in large numbers on Oldowan and even Acheulian sites. The plane persisted, often smaller in size, into the industries of the European Upper Paleolithic, and even into the Neolithic periods. Together with choppers, polyhedra and planes, we find on the Oldowan and pre-Acheulian sites of Africa tools made from pebbles that were often flat which had been prepared with the object of achieving a narrow chamfered edge (burin) or edges that were intended for scraping or stripping bark (notched and serrated). These same types of tool are to be found from the Oldowan period based no longer on pebbles but on flakes, and by the end of the Acheulian era flake tools had replaced pebble tools.

PEI WEN CHUNG (1904–82). Chinese paleontologist who discovered at Choukoutien, and then made a study of the many fossil remains of "Sinanthropus", also known as "Peking man" (*Homo erectus*). Before World War II he worked in collaboration with Pierre Teilhard de Chardin.

PELLIOT, Paul (1878–1945). The best known of French Sinologists, Pelliot began his career in 1905 at the French School of the Far East, and continued it in Central Asia (1906–08), bringing back a wealth of archaeological and philological material that has still not been fully assessed and exploited.

PELOPONNESIAN WAR. Athens profited from the great prestige resulting from her role in the Persian Wars to organize a maritime alliance, theoretically intended to prevent any return attack by the Persians. However, this was soon transformed into a kind of empire. Concerned at the rise of Athenian power, in 431BC Corinth urged Sparta to mobilize its allies in the Peloponnese (hence the name of the war) and elsewhere. The first phase (431–21BC) proved inconclusive, but the war broke out again because of Athens' foolhardy attempt to conquer Sicily (415BC), and Persian involvement on the side of Sparta brought about the capitulation of their enemy (404BC).

The success of the Athenian alliance made Piraeus the foremost port in the Mediterranean, and the Athenian tetradrachma (the so-called Owl) the international currency of the period.

PERGAMUM. Capital of the kingdom of the same name, in Asia Minor. Thanks to the kings of the Attalid dynasty (241–133BC), this small town became one of the capitals of Hellenistic culture: both in architecture (monumental planning and design of the middle and upper town) and in sculpture (the baroque style culminating in the frieze of the altar of Zeus), Pergamene creativity signalled the last great moment of Greek civilization. In 133BC, Attalus III bequeathed his kingdom to Rome, who made it the province of Asia.

PERIPHERAL CHOPPER. Pebble tool, worked on both faces and often irregular in shape. The cutting edge can go the whole way round the periphery or there may be a break in it, and it can be plano-convex in section. This tool differs from the biface in that it is frequently not axially symmetric and in the undifferentiated position of the cutting edge, the part of the chopper that is used. It is characteristic of the Oldowan and advanced Oldowan industries, and is found in some Acheulian sites.

PERNETTE. Small terracotta tripod used to stack vases in the kiln so as to prevent them sticking to one another during firing.

PERSIAN WARS (MEDIAN WARS). In the course of its rapid expansion the Persian empire, which between 549 and 525BC extended from Afghanistan to Egypt and Turkey, brought into subjection the Greek cities of Ionia (on the west coast of Asia Minor). These rebelled in 499BC, aided by Athens and another Greek city state, and it was to exact vengeance for this that the Great King Darius launched the first Persian war (490BC), a punitive naval expedition, against Athens at Marathon.

Ten years later Darius' son Xerxes mounted a huge expedition by sea and land with the aim of conquering Greece, which ended in catastrophe after the defeat of the fleet at Salamis (480BC) and of the army at Plataea (479BC). The two Persian wars, which are known to us through the writings of Herodotus, were the cause of very lively currency activity, as witnessed by the many hoards of Greek coins buried during these years in the Persian empire: among them was the Assiyut treasure.

PETRIE, Sir William M. Flinders (1853–1942). English archaeologist, self-taught, who in 1880 went to Egypt to draw up plans and take measurements of the Pyramids; after various digs (Tanis, Naucratis, Daphnae, Hawara, Kahun, Meidum, El Amarna), he became the first English Professor of Egyptology at University College, London (1892–1933). He then worked at Nagada, Abydos, Memphis, Sedment and Qau. Gifted with a fine sense of the terrain, he proposed for the protodynastic period a system of sequence-dating (a chronology based on pottery sequences) that included all the material discovered, even the most humble of objects. He published more than 1000 books, articles and reports. Towards the end of his life he also worked in Palestine.

PEYRONY, Denis (1869–1954). French prehistorian. A primary schoolteacher at Eyzies at the end of the 19th century, Peyrony was the first to conduct truly scientific excavations; by this means he defined several cultures of the Upper and Middle Paleolithic periods. His stratigraphical observations are still today essential references for prehistory in Périgord.

PHENOTYPE. Totality of an individual's apparent characteristics, resulting from the interaction of genetic heritage ("genotype") and living environment. Individuals of different genotypes can thus manifest similar phenotypical characteristics. Modern awareness of the complexity of the genetic heritage and of the effects of environment mean that today the old "racial" classifications of the human species are no longer relevant.

PHOENICIAN (alphabet and language). At the end of the 2nd millennium BC at Byblos, the Phoenician alphabet took over the principles employed by the Ugaritic alphabet (a single sign for each consonantal sound, and conversely a single consonantal sound for each sign), but the principles were adapted to the writing materials of Egyptian scribes who used ink and had a supple surface to work on. This system is the direct ancestor of all alphabets that have added vowels, placed either beside the consonants as in Greek and Latin, or above or below them as in Aramaic, Hebrew and Arabic. The Phoenician language belongs to the northern group of western Semitic languages along with Ugaritic, Hebrew and Aramaic, while Arabic is representative of the southern group.

PHOTO-INTERPRETATION. Aerial photographs have contributed a considerable body of documentary evidence to archaeological knowledge concerning structures that cannot be seen from the ground. There are two techniques which should not be confused. One makes laboratory use of vertical aerial views taken during missions undertaken to establish maps; pictures taken at various scales are subjected to increasingly complex manipulations intended to show up "fossil" units of land division. The other is a viewing method of archaeological exploration, carried out by plane, in which photographing oblique views is intended to make a record of the picture of a structure that has appeared fleetingly thanks to the climatic (rain, frost, etc.) or botanical (plant growth, etc) circumstances of the moment.

PHYLUM. A group of living beings in the animal or plant kingdom that follow one another in a direct line of descent from the same stock: the human phylum, for example, can be compared to a genealogical tree covering several million years, with modern man as its end product.

PHYTOLITHS. Worked stone tools used to cut the stems of silica-rich plants (e.g. cereals) sometimes preserve, encrusted on their cutting edge, tiny particles of plant silica, or phytoliths. These can be detected by an electronic scanning microscope, and their presence makes it possible to identify the plant that has been cut or worked on.

PIETTE, Edmond (1827–1906). French prehistorian. Piette excavated many caves in the Pyrenees at the end of the 19th century and was the first to recognize the Azilian culture, which came immediately after the cultures of the Upper Paleolithic, in the postglacial period. Unlike many prehistorians of his time, he made a precise record of the prehistoric strata containing remains of human origin, and his stratigraphical descriptions can still be used today.

PIOTROVSKY, Boris B., *b.* 1908. Russian archaeologist. He excavated the Urartu (Armenia) citadel of Karmir-Blur (ancient Teishebaini), and published his results. He has written widely on the Scythians in the Caucasus and Transcaucasia. Director of the Hermitage Museum in Leningrad since 1964.

PLEISTOCENE. The Quaternary has two subdivisions, the Pleistocene and the Holocene. One of the distinguishing characteristics of the period, apart from the onset of an increasingly cold climate (glaciation) is the presence of man, but it is now known that man was already in existence in the Tertiary, and the boundary between the (Tertiary) Pliocene and the (Quaternary) Pleistocene is now fixed at about 1,800,000BP, as it is no longer linked with the first fossils of hominids and the first tools, but more with climatic, geological and paleomagnetic phenomena and changes in animal and plant species and families. The boundary between Early and Middle Pleistocene is *c.* 1,000,000BC.

PLIOCENE. The most recent of the subdivisions of the Tertiary era, from 5,500,000 to 1,800,000BP. During this long period of time, a crucial event occurred: the separation of the *Homo* genus and the *Australopithecus* genus, both derived from one ancestral stock. In the Upper Pliocene the first worked tools appear, as do the very first camps, though these are organized in an improvised fashion and were no doubt occupied on a temporary basis.

POLYHEDRON. Pebble or a piece of stone which has been totally or partly reshaped by chipping of the surface in a number of directions; in appearance they often resemble a ball. These objects are common in pre-Acheulian and Acheulian sites, indeed even in sites of the Middle Paleolithic period. Polyhedra would have been used as percussion tools, throwing weapons and perhaps also as nuclei for flakes.

POMPEIIAN STYLES. Typology of the styles used to decorate houses in Pompeii, established by A. Mau in 1882 and continually refined in terms of definition and chronology. The first style, Greek in origin, is an imitation, using stucco and painting, of the exteriors of the ashlar walls used in civic and religious architecture, transposed into the interior decoration of houses (used at Pompeii between the 2nd century BC and 80BC). The second style depicts *trompe-l'oeil* buildings, inspired from the scene paintings of the Hellenistic period (used till 40–30BC, when Augustus came to power). With the third style, the wall is no longer seen as an architectural imitation, but as a flat surface to be decorated. Fantastic motifs, already to be found in the second style, proliferated, and the centre of the wall was often decorated with a painting depicting a mythological scene or a landscape. This fashion continued until Claudius' reign (mid-1st century AD). The fourth style (Nero's reign) combined the baroque vein present in the final phase of the third style with the architectural *trompe-l'oeil* typical of the first two styles.

PORPHYRITE. Volcanic rock, finer-grained than quartzite, and a constituent element in the river pebbles used in the Hoabinhian industry.

POTASSIUM-ARGON dating. Method of dating which can be used on certain minerals and enables us to establish the age at which the rocks concerned were formed. It is based on the radio-active decomposition of potassium 40 (K^{40}) into argon (A^{40}), the half-life of the K^{40} isotope being 1300 million years. Potassium is found in rocks in its natural state. The principle behind the dating presupposes that the K^{40}/A^{40} ratio has not been adversely affected by chemical or physical changes in the course of time, and this necessitates a thorough geochemical study of the position and the assessment of the minerals in question. The time-scale which can be estimated stretches from 100,000 years to several million years. Potassium-argon dating is used to date the surroundings in which the earliest hominids are buried.

POTTER'S COMB. Implement with a serrated edge capable of producing an impressed decoration on pottery. The teeth of the comb may be on the front or side edge, and it may be made of stone, bone, shell or wood. Threaded combs are made by winding a piece of string round a rigid or flexible support; others are made from braids with a varying number of strands. These combs are held in the palm of the hand and rolled over the surface of the pottery while it is damp; sometimes the decoration is achieved by simple pressure.

PRAETORIAN COHORTS. The Roman emperor's guard (10 cohorts of 480 infantrymen and 120 cavalry) recruited from Italians and stationed in Rome. Its commander, the prefect of the praetorium, was the second-ranking officer in the state. The praetorian guards were well paid (their pay was one and a half to two times that of a legionary) and well equipped, and they were liable for a shorter period of service (16 years against 20 for legionaries). They accompanied the emperor on his campaigns outside Rome and were regarded as the elite of the army. The role they played in the crises of the Empire is well described by Latin historians.

PRE-AXUMITE PERIOD (5th century BC to 1st century AD). In the 5th century BC in the northern part of the Ethiopian plateau, south Arabian elements were assimilated, through the influence exerted by the kingdom of Sheba, into a local culture which had developed from the Neolithic. Archaeology has uncovered contributions in the fields of architecture and statuary which demonstrate a religious and linguistic impact, with texts engraved on stone using south Arabian script. There are also influences from Meroe, showing that even at that period Ethiopia was a crossroads for trade, traffic and cultural influences.

PRE-DORSET. Term used after 1925 firstly to designate the archaeological formations of the Canadian Arctic which came before the Dorset culture, the connection between the two not yet being understood. Since 1968, excavations carried out in the Arctic in the extreme northwest of Quebec have shown that the Dorset culture developed from a regional form of the pre-Dorset and that no outside influence seemed necessary to explain this evolution. Subsequently the term pre-Dorset has been used to describe just one of the eastern Paleo-Eskimo formations which came before the Dorset, and is most frequently found in the Canadian Arctic between c.1700 and 600BC. Pre-Dorset tools belong to the microlithic tradition of the Arctic. Unlike people of the Dorset tradition, those of the pre-Dorset habitually used a bow, and exploited inland resources (caribou, freshwater fish) fairly intensively.

PRE-POTTERY NEOLITHIC A (PPNA). Palestinian village-based culture dating from the 8th millennium, first defined at Jericho. It is derived from the Natufian culture, making use of and developing Natufian architecture with its round houses, and provides evidence of the first attempts at agriculture in the near East, though still in a hunting context.

PRE-POTTERY NEOLITHIC B (PPNB). Levantine culture pre-dating the use of pottery, lasting from 7500 to 6000BC, and first defined at Jericho. It originated in Syria and is characterized by rectangular builings with lime-coated or plastered floors, by the cultivation of cereal crops and by the beginnings of small-animal husbandry. Its final phase (Late PPNB: 6500–6000BC) saw the first expansion of agriculture and the spread of Neolithic culture beyond its semi-arid zone of origin towards the

temperate coastal regions of Syria (Ras Shamra) and the desert oases, and the sporadic appearance of the first pottery ware.

PUNIC WARS. Term used to describe the three wars between Rome and Carthage, a city state in North Africa founded by Phoenicians from Tyre (in Latin, the Carthaginians were called *Poeni*). If it had not conquered Carthage, Rome would not subsequently have been able to subdue all the shores of the Mediterranean. The first Punic War (264–241BC) enabled Rome to conquer Sicily, Sardinia and Corsica. After years of dreadful fighting against the Carthaginian general Hannibal Rome finally also won the second (218–201BC); that victory was partly responsible for bringing about a profound change in Roman society (an increasingly wealthy aristocracy, an increase in the number of slaves, etc). The third war (149–146BC) ended in the annihilation of Carthage and the setting up of the Roman province of Africa.

QUARTZITE. Metamorphic rock based on sandstone, a constituent element in the pebbles used in the Sonviian industry.

RABAD. In Islamic towns, a district outside the walls where craftsmen and merchants tended to concentrate; it could in turn be fortified and develop into a new town centre.

RADIOCHRONOMETRY (see also Dating). Dating technique based on the fact that radioactive isotopes disintegrate with the passage of time. The isotopes used in archaeology have a half-life (the time necessary for the amount of the isotope in question to be reduced by half) of from several thousand years to more than one million. The best known, Carbon 14 (C^{14}), has a half-life of 5,730 years, while that of Potassium is 1,400,000 years (potassium-argon or K-A method). C^{14} is acquired from the atmosphere when the organic material being dated forms part of a living organism, and decays thereafter, losing half its original amount in a period of 5,730 years, so that the amount of radioactivity still remaining will establish the time elapsed since the death of the object being dated. However, the rate of production of C^{14} has not always been uniform, as seen in comparisons with dates based on, say, tree-ring dating (dendrochronology). Nevertheless, the method (first proposed in 1946 by W.F. Libby) has enabled a solid chronological framework to be formed in numerous cases, thus playing an important part in the so-called archaeological revolution.

REINECKE, Paul (1872–1958). German archaeologist. In a book published in 1965, Reinecke defined a four part chronological system for the Bronze Age (from A to D), the first Iron Age or the Hallstatt period (from A to D) and the second Iron Age or La Tene period (from A to D). Today much work is based on this chronology.

REISNER, George Andrew (1867–1942). After studying law in the United States Reisner devoted himself to Semitic studies and then, in Berlin, to Egyptology, with K. Sethe; as the director of the Hearst excavating mission from the University of California to Egypt (1899–1905), he worked at Deir el Ballas, Naga ed Deir and Giza; he then took part in the survey of Nubia organized by the Egyptian government; he carried out excavations at Samaria in Palestine (1909–1910), then both at Giza (tomb of Queen Hetepheres, and many mastabas) and in Sudan (Kerma, Meroe, Gebel Barkal).

REMEDELLIAN. Copper Age culture c.2000BC,

named from the type-site of Remedello in the Po valley, Italy. Finds include crouched skeletons, flat axes, triangular daggers, copper halberds and flint arowheads.

RESISTIVITY. Method used to identify underlying deposits without excavation. Different materials offer varying resistance to electrical currents, depending on the amount of water present.

RHYOLITE. Volcanic rock, a constituent element in Hoabinhian pebble tools.

RIBS (nautical). Transverse stiffening timbers or joists forming the frame of a ship's hull.

RUDENKO, Sergei I. (1885–1969). Russian archaeologist and ethnographer, an expert on the peoples of Siberia and the Volga area. He excavated the frozen tombs at Pazyryk.

RUNES. Writing system (also called *futhark* after the first six symbols) which appeared in Denmark in the 3rd century and spread widely within the Germanic world. The early alphabet, with 24 letters divided into three groups of eight, was mainly used for short commemorative or magic protective formulae engraved on weapons, jewels and other valuable objects such as the horn of Gallehus (and no doubt on pieces of wood that have not been preserved). A simplified alphabet of 16 characters was developed in Scandinavia from the 9th century, and this was used for more elaborate inscriptions, such as those on the Gotland stones, continuing for a long period in the Middle Ages. The etymology of the word (*rûna* in Gothic, *rûn* in Norse) has the meaning secret, mystery, counsel and charm.

SAKAS. Iranian steppe people from central Asia organized into a confederacy which, like that of the Scythians (to whom they were related), brought together tribes of agriculturists and of nomadic herdsmen. They took part in the great movement of peoples which swept away the Greek kingdom of Bactria in the mid-2nd century BC. After being repulsed by the Parthians, the Sakas settled in Drangiana (Seistan) and in the Indus Valley.

SALIN, Edouard (1889–1970). Industrialist and medieval archaeologist. Salin has made an important contribution to Merovingian cemetaries in eastern France, and applying his laboratory skills to the study and restoration of metal objects excavated. He carried out the first scientific excavations in the crypt of the basilica of St-Denis (Gallo-Roman tombs and royal Merovingian necropolis), and has published numerous important books.

SAMARRA CULTURE. Neolithic culture from upper Mesopotamia remarkable for its elaborate painted pottery with geometric or naturalistic patterns. It existed at the end of the 6th millennium on the semi-desert banks of the Mid-Tigris and farther east in the Mandali area. It is characterized by large villages with complex, many-roomed buildings, and the introduction of irrigated agriculture and cattle rearing.

SANGA. Cattle found in eastern Africa (from the Nile Valley down) recognizable by their brown hides and long horns. They are probably earlier in origin than zebus; remains of sangas have recently been found by archaeologists in the depths of the Kalahari, dating from about 1000AD.

SANKALIA, H.D. (*b.* 1908). Indian archaeologist. His field work since 1929 has played a considerable role in the development of Indian

archaeology. A director of Deccan College in Poona he trained generations of Indian archaeologists, and has published comprehensive surveys and research papers, the most important of which relate to the prehistory of the Deccan.

SARMATIANS. The Sarmatians emerged from the union of the Sauromatian tribes living as nomads between the Urals and the Caspian Sea. The Sarmatians moved westwards in the 3rd century BC, driving back the Scythians and settling in their stead to the north of the Black Sea. At the beginning of our era they constituted a political and cultural force whose influence extended into central Asia and Transcaucasia, as well as into western Europe where the Sarmatians challenged the Romans before themselves being driven back by the Huns.

SATRAPY. Administrative division of the Persian Achaemenid empire, the name has been passed down to us by Greek writers. The satrap, a kind of Persian proconsul, held his power from the sovereign. Sometimes a satrapy became an apanage of the royal princes. The Greeks described the Iranian Plateau and Central Asia as the "high satrapies".

The satrapy, which was a collection of ethnic groups rather than a piece of land with precise boundaries, had to make payments (tribute) to the empire and provide military contingents. The bas-relief sculptures of the *apadana* (state throne room) at Persepolis show the procession of tributaries of the empire, from Egypt to India. A Greek text (Herodotus) tells us the amount (in talents) of the tributes exacted from the various satrapies: the most heavily taxed, because they were the richest, were Egypt and Babylon: India too had to provide a sizeable tribute in the form of gold dust.

SAUVETERRIAN. Mesolithic culture characterized by arrowheads which are triangular or needle-shaped, often less than 2 cm long; trapezoid shapes were added to these forms in the later stages. Sauveterrian relates to the period from 8000 to 4500BC, and the southern half of France.

SCAPULOMANCY. Divination method used in ancient China, consisting of the burning of shoulder blades of domesticated animals and interpretation of the cracks caused by the fire.

SCHLIEMANN, Heinrich (1822–90). Wealthy German businessman and self-taught Homer enthusiast, he wished to demonstrate the historical truth of Homer's epics. In 1870 on the site of Hissarlik near the Dardanelles he discovered, below a Roman city and a Greek colony of the 8th century BC, a small Bronze Age citadel which had existed from the late 4th millenium BC. One level of this(VI or VIIa) may be the "Troy" of Homer's *Iliad* composed in 700BC. The jewels known as the treasure of Priam which he found there disappeared in 1945 during the capture of Berlin. In 1876 at Mycenae he discovered tombs arranged within an enclosure ("Circle A") which he identified as those of Agammemnon and his family, although in fact they predate Agammemnon by 400 years. Despite his mistakes of interpretation, he must be regarded as the initiator of proto-historic archaeology in the Aegean.

SELER, Edouard (1849–1922). German scientist, philologist and Mesoamerican expert. Although he was not involved in fieldwork, his annotated editions of the Borgia, Vaticanus B and Féjérváry-Mayer codices have not yet been superseded and reveal whole aspects of the pre-Columbian ways of thinking. His great knowledge of Mesoamerica convinced him very early on that this part of the New World had been a single cultural entity.

SELEUCIDS. Dynasty founded after the death of Alexander by one of his generals, Seleucus Soter, who in 312BC inherited the greater part of his empire (Asia Minor, the Near East, Mesopotamia, Iran and Central Asia). This kingdom enjoyed a century of power and its two capitals, Antioch and Seleucia, were active in elaborating and diffusing Hellenistic civilization. However, from 250BC, Asia Minor, Bactria and Parthia gradually broke away from it. In the 2nd century BC the Parthians took possession of all that part of the empire lying to the east of the Euphrates. Reduced to Syria only and torn by internal conflicts, the kingdom was finally annexed by Armenia (83BC) and then by Rome (64BC) which reduced it to the status of a province.

SENATORIAL ORDER. The highest class in Roman society, developed from the republican senatorial order as reorganized by Augustus. Senators had to provide proof that their fortune amounted to 1,000,000 sesterces, and had the right to wear a toga with a wide band of purple. Senators' posts were more honorific than those reserved for the equestrian order, but they were less influential.

SERIATION. Method of classification by time-scale and culture type based on a theoretical "evolutionary" principle whereby cultural characteristics emerge, reach a zenith, and then disappear. By expressing in terms of their relative frequency (%) the importance of the various categories of archaeological evidence found on a site or belonging to a culture, it becomes possible to classify (by relating them to one another) many sites and cultures for which there is no other chronological point of reference.

SHAHRESTAN. In the Islamic towns of Iran and Central Asia, the old, fortified part of the lower town, distinct from both the citadel and the outer districts (see *Rabad*).

SHUNGURIAN. In Ethiopia the Shungura region in the lower Omo valley north of Lake Turkana is known for its remains of animals and hominids. Several archaeological deposits have been discovered on the site, dating back two million years, with an industry based on very small quartz flakes (2–4 cm), derived from a nucleus or from the accidental shattering of pebbles used as percussion tools. They have rarely been retouched, and have been used only occasionally. The Shungurian industry is different from the Oldowan.

SIGUENZA Y GONGORA, Carlos de (1645–1700). Born in Mexico to Spanish parents, Sigüenza was for a time a member of the Society of Jesus, and seems to have been the first to carry out excavations at Teotihuacan, more than a century before Thomas Jefferson's much vaunted expoloration of the mounds of Virginia. Sigüenza was also the greatest collector of manuscripts and curios of his time.

SITULA. Taken from Latin, this term is used to describe the deep, cylindrical bronze receptacles from the Vietnamese proto-historical period (*tho* is the Vietnamese name), by analogy with western Bronze Age *situlae*.

SLAVE. The existence of slaves (who have no rights and are the property of their master) is known in a great many societies; but they did not always play much part in production. According to M.I. Finley, Ancient Greece and Rome, the Confederate States of America and Brazil are probably the only "true" slave societies to have existed, since in these societies production actually depended on the slave system. In ancient Italy the number of slaves seems to have increased greatly between the 3rd and 1st centuries BC. From then on (until the 2nd or 3rd centuries AD) they were often used in agriculture. Other slaves were servants, workmen or craftsmen; yet others, especially during the Empire, worked in the administration. It was not unusual for slaves to be freed.

SLIP. Term used in ceramics, to describe a surface coating of homogeneous texture which may be the base onto which decoration is applied or may itself form the decoration. In the first case it is applied as a thin layer to give the surface of a vase or any other earthenware item a more uniform appearance, masking the colour of the clay and serving as a base for the glaze. It is usually made of clays and may go white after being fired. In some cases it may be a coat of whitewash. But for a great many varieties of early pottery archaeologists have still not carried out the analyses necessary to gain information about the composition of the slip. Used as a decoration, it is applied fairly thickly to form white or tinted patterns. This technique is described by the term "slip-painted".

SMITH, Charles Roach (1807–90). Founder in 1843 of the British Archaeological Association, Smith gave the British Museum 5,000 items from his collection and presented the remainder to a private museum at Strood in Kent. He published seven volumes of the *Collectanea Antiqua* (1848–1880), in which he was the first to tackle the problems of subdividing Anglo-Saxon antiquities chronologically and by style.

SMITHFIELD. Stone Age industry of southern Africa virtually contemporary with the Wilton, but technologically different from it.

SMOKING. Process used at the end of the firing of pottery whereby materials which produce a thick smoke are burnt in the kiln or hearth. Smoking alters the appearance of the pottery, colouring it deep black, and makes receptacles less porous.

SOLIDUS. Gold coin (*nomisma* in Greek) struck in the Eastern Roman empire of Constantine I in the mid-4th century AD, and continuing through the Byzantine period. It weighed 1/72 of a pound (= 4.5 gr) and was extremely pure (99.9% Au), but was debased in the 11th century. After being restored to 20 carats (80% Au) by Alexius Comnenus in 1092, it once again declined after 1204, falling to 12 carats (50% Au) by 1300.

SOLUTREAN. Cultural grouping of the Upper Paleolithic, named after the type-site of Solutré (France), and excavated from 1866 onwards. It dates from approximately 20,000 to 15,000BC, and has an industry characterized mainly by points which have been shaped by glancing retouches, the most famous of which are the "laurel leaves" typical of the Middle Solutrean, and the longer and narrower "willow leaves from the final stages of the Solutrean. The bone needle with an eye was invented in this period.

SONVIIAN. Named after the Son Vi hills in North Vietnam, Sonviian is a pebble tool industry of the Upper Paleolithic defined by Ha Van Tan in 1968.

SORGHUM. Cereal, several varieties of which were selected in Africa and the near East, probably at the period where increasing dryness began to affect the already numerous human groups, after 7000BP. This plant with its fine ears of grain needs 500 to 600 mm of water a year. We could speak of a "sorghum-belt" in Africa, rather like the corn-belt in the United States.

SOTERIOLOGICAL MOVEMENT. Towards the end of the reign of the Western Han (206BC–AD8) a climate of uncertainty prevailed in China, with political instability, an agricultural crisis, epidemics and the passing of a comet; and this led in 3BC to a popular messianic movement. Its adherents, travelling through the empire provided with talismans, proclaimed the coming of the divinity known as the Queen Mother of the West, who could dispense immortality. Although it did not last long, this movement started the tradition of politico-religious uprisings which were to become endemic, and undermined Chinese power.

SOUDSKY, Bohumil (1922–76). Teacher at the University of Prague (1948), who became a research worker at the Archaeological Institute of the Czechoslovak Academy of Science (1957), and finally an associate Professor at the University of Paris (1971). He specialized in studying the problems associated with cultures of the Danubian area. His excavations at the Neolithic site of Bylany in particular and the computer analysis of his findings enabled him to propose an economic and social model of Bandkeramik culture.

SPEAR-THROWER. Launching device for thrown weapons, consisting of a stick or small plank with an attachment at one end into which the butt of the spear shaft was fitted. This implement was held in the hand and considerably increased the thrust given when weapons were propelled, making it possible to attack animals at some distance. Spear-throwers ending in a carved hook made of reindeer antlers are found from the middle of the Magdalenian period in Europe. This system was also used in pre-Columbian America (Peru, Mexico) and until recently in the Arctic and Australia.

STATER. Word normally used in ancient Greece to describe the heaviest coin in a monetary system, except in Athens and in mints where the Attic standard of weights and measures was used, such as those of Alexander. In Central Greece, following Aegina's example, the stater was a didrachma. Elsewhere, notably in Asia Minor and Thasos, the stater was subdivided into three *tritēs*.

STEIN, Aurel (1862–1943). British archaeologist and explorer. His expeditions to Baluchistan in eastern Iran and into Central Asia during the first half of the 20th century revealed the existence of a great many sites in areas considered to be inaccessible. His published work still forms the basis for study of those areas which he was first to visit.

STEIN-CALLENFELS, Paul Van (1883–1938). Disappointed by his career as a civil administrator in Java, he became a coffee planter with a great enthusiasm for shadow theatre, from which starting point he identified certain Indonesian bas-reliefs. His surveys and excavations are the basis of the prehistory of Indonesia, which, through the knowledge he had acquired in his travels, he was able to integrate into the context of Southeast Asia as a whole. His extraordinary personality resulted in his being worshipped as a local spirit on several sites in Java that he excavated: he is thus the only known example of an archaeologist to have been deified.

STERN, Philippe (1895–1979). When curator of the Musée Guimet, 1930, he noticed that the chronology of the Khmer items, based on extrapolating from inscriptions, was partly incorrect. He set about rectifying this, using a strict, stylistic method of analysis. On a mission to Angkor in 1936 he undertook excavations which enabled him to find proof for his hypotheses. He was the founder of the history of Khmer art and of the art of Champa; he also made a notable contribution to the history of the art of ancient India.

STERN POST. Vertical or sloping structure in the line of a boat forming the rear end of the hull. In some cases it can be used as a rudder stand, in which case it is called the rudder post; these appeared in the boats of north and north-west Europe at the end of the 12th century.

STRAKE. Line of planking extending from one end to the other of a ship's hull.

STRATIGRAPHY. Study of the way in which sediments in a given bed or site have settled in superimposed layers, or, in other words, of their stratification. As in geology, the main interest of this study is that it enables us to make a classification of the remains from the earliest (at the bottom) to the most recent (on the top). In fact the details of stratification are often complex, and a number of factors may have intervened to affect the original disposition of the layers. The nature of the materials used in building, the type of sedimentation and the kinds of erosion also play an important role. During a dig, the stratigraphic method consists of removing the sediments layer after layer, taking great care to distinguish between them.

STRONG, William D. (1899–1962). North American anthropologist who analysed the archaeological collections brought back from Peru by M. Uhle. The books listing and describing this material—*The Uhle Pottery Collections from Ica, . . . Chincha, . . . Ancon* (1924–26) are still regarded as authoritative. From 1941 he worked in Peru, especially at Pachacamac, and in 1946 took part in the Viru valley project as the representative of the University of Columbia: this was the first multi-disciplinary research project of an area carried out in Peru (*Cultural stratigraphy in the Viru valley: the Formative and Florescent Epochs*, 1952). In 1952–53, he carried out excavations on the south coast and defined the stylistic relationships between the various pre-Inca cultures of the Ica area.

STROPHANTUS SARMENTOSUS. Small tree growing in Africa, with seeds which were a sought-after trading commodity as they could be used to make poison. For a long time it was thought that *strophantus* was used only to make poison for arrows. However, in the Lake Chad basin it was used as a poison on other projectiles, javelins for instance, and it had an especially important role in the systems of plant defences.

STUTTERHEIM, Willem Frederik (1892–1942). Appointed in 1918 to the Indonesian Civil Service, Stutterheim traced the transition from the Indianized art of central Java to the art of eastern Java. His interpretation of the *Ramayana* in the bas-reliefs was definitive. He became the Director of the Archaeological Service in 1936.

SUDAN. Arab writers used to refer to the areas corresponding to modern West Africa as Biladwes-Sudan, or land of the blacks.

SUMATRALITH. Used to describe unifacially worked pebbles found in 1920 in north Sumatra, this term was later extended to Hoabinhian unifacial tools.

SUMERIAN (language). Sumerian appears to be the language written on the earliest tablets in southern Mesopotamia at the end of the 4th millenium BC. It has invariable bisyllabic or monosyllabic roots, around which prefixes or suffixes, likewise invariable, were arranged to express grammatical inflexions. The structure of the language must have made it easier to invent writing, and in a second period the use of syllabic characters. Sumerian was overtaken by Babylonian and ceased to be spoken at the beginning of the 2nd millennium BC, but it then became a language used for cultural purposes and retained that function until cuneiform writing itself disappeared in the 1st century AD.

SUPPILULIUMA I. Great Hittite king who first subdued almost the whole of Asia Minor and then took advantage of the weakness of Armarna Egypt to establish Hittite rule in northern Syria, overcoming the Mitanni. He placed his sons, based in Aleppo and Carchemish, in authority over the Syrian territories.

SURVEYING. Surveying is a means of acquiring archaeological information which does not destroy remains; it enables us to study them through a wide variety of techniques of observation and analysis without excavation. Techniques are based sometimes on long-distance detection by means of aerial surveys. These are then studied on a stereoscope which reconstitutes relief, or corrected by ortho-photography, or reconstituted using photogrammetry. Surveying often uses geophysical methods, including measurements of electric resistivity and measurements of variations in the earth's magnetism ("magnetic surveys"). This approach, which brings together qualitative and quantitative criteria, is much less costly than traditional methods of research when dealing with the same reference area; surveying, unlike traditional methods, makes it possible to conduct a rapid study of fairly extensive areas.

SUSA CULTURE. Typified by fine quality ceramic ware with geometric motifs painted in dark colours onto a light background, the Susa culture came into being at the end of the 6th millennium in the eastern part of lower Mesopotamia, around Susa, the type-site. It then spread over the Iranian plateau, following directly upon the Neolithic Zagros cultures, and like the Ubaid culture was a precursor of the urban phenomenon. The development of the Susa and Ubaid cultures in similar geographical zones (the alluvial plain) was parallel.

SYLLABOGRAM. In Cretan scripts of the 2nd millennium BC, a sign denoting by means of an arbitrary drawing an open syllable, generally of the type "consonant + vowel" or "single vowel".

SZELETIAN. This term is usually applied to the industries with bifacial foliated (leaf-shaped) points of the early Upper Paleolithic period in the Danube basin, but it has often been applied also to the industries with foliated points which mark the transition from the Middle Paleolithic to the Upper Paleolithic periods throughout the eastern part of Central Europe. The site from which the name is taken is the Szeleta cave in the Bükk Mountains in Hungary.

TALATATE. Small blocks of sandstone, always the same size (approximately 55 cm × 25 cm × 20 cm, or 22 × 10 × 8 in), generally with a carved and painted decoration on at least one face. They were easy to handle and were used by Akhenaten at Karnak in building the very large number of monuments dedicated by this heretic pharoah to the sun disc, Aten. After a return to the orthodox worship of Amen, these monuments were dismantled and their components were then used by Akhenaten's successors as rubble hardcore in later buildings.

TAOISM (esoteric). Together with the school of mystical Taoism as it is expressed in the *Huainanzi* (late 2nd century BC) and the political thoughts of Huanglao, there flourished in the China of the Han dynasty (206BC–AD220) a tradition of esoteric practices inherited from the old guilds of smiths and potters. It was the fusion of these that esoteric Taoism developed under the Han. Its patron came to be regarded as the Yellow Emperor, the first mythical ruler to bring civilization, who supposedly had had revealed to him secret formulae for longevity.

TAOISM (mystical). The Taoism of the China of the Warring States (475–221BC) is better described as mysticism rather than as philosophy, for it is characterized less by intellectual consideration of first causes than by a life style that is in harmony with the universe and techniques for inducing trance states. Incorporating earlier concepts (*dao*, *yin-yang*), three works sum up the *Zhuangzi* and the *Liezi*. Its ideal figure is the wise man living in retirement, cultivating the vital principle and following the spontaneous rhythm of nature.

T'AO T'IEH. Chinese term for the motif of the glutton in the decorative repertory of Shang and Chou bronzes. It shows a zoomorphic mask seen full face with a gaping mouth and no lower jaw, the eyes, ears and horns placed symmetrically on either side of a vertical frontal line. It often consists of two *kui* (dragons facing each other, also placed symmetrically, with the body seen in profile, winding tail and a clawed foot). Their two heads together form the glutton's mask.

TARDENOISIAN. Mesolithic culture characterized by triangular arrowheads in the early stages and by trapezoid ones in the late stages; these are generally less than 2.5 cm (1 in) in size. The Tardenoisian lasted from 7000 to 4000BC, and extended over the Parisian Basin and central France.

TARO. Polynesian name for *Colocasia* (*Araceae*), plants which came from Southeast Asia where they were cultivated from very early times for the nutritional value of their tubers. They are the most important of all the food-giving plants in Oceania.

TAWANANNA. Generic name given to the Hittite queen who played an important part in the monarchy. Her title was transferred independently of the king's, so that the widow of a king remained titular queen. She had both political and religious responsibilities.

TCHALENKO, Georges, Bauhaus-trained architect who has devoted his life to the study of northern Syria. He was able to provide a historical interpretation of the 2nd–7th century AD settlements (remarkably well preserved in that area) in an influential book, *Villages antiques de la Syrie du Nord* (1953–1958). Another work, *Églises de villages de la Syrie du Nord* is being prepared for publication.

TELL. Word of Arabic origin describing mounds that have formed through the accumulation of urban remains and subsequent levelling, over many generations. Some may be over 100ft high and cover several millennia.

TELLO, Julio C. (1880–1947). Peruvian archaeologist. After studying medicine, he turned his attention to the archaeology of his country and in the course of 35 years of reseach he discovered, and studied, some of the most important sites in Peru: Chavín de Huantar in 1919 (*Chavín, cultura matriz de la civilización andina*, 1960); the necropolises of Paracas in 1925 (*Paracas*, 1959); the temples of Cerro Blanco and Punkuri in 1933, Kotosh in 1935 and Cerro Sechin in 1937 (*Arqueologia del valle de Casma*, 1956). His work reveals the high level of development of the pre-Inca cultures; unlike M. Uhle, Tello ascribed an Amazonian origin to these (*Antiguo Perú*, 1929, and *Origen y desarollo de las civilizaciones prehistóricas andinas*, 1942).

TEMMOKU. Stoneware bowl with an iron or manganese black or brown glaze. This Japanese term was applied to Chinese bowls used in the tea ceremony, referring to the pieces which Zen Buddhist monks had brought to Japan at the Kamakura period, and which came originally from Mount Tianmushan (Chekiang province). However, no kiln producing *temmoku* has been found at Tianmushan, though we know that *temmoku* bowls were fired in the Sung period in the Jian kilns (Fukien), not far from that mountain. In the Kamakura period Japanese kilns at Seto copied China and began to turn out work with a glaze like that of the *temmoku*. However, some Japanese bowls are called *temmoku* solely on account of their similarity of shape, and do not have the glaze: for example white *temmoku* (*shirotemmoku*). These bowls were highly valued when the tea ceremony first started (15th century), and were classified according to seven types of glazing decoration.

TERRASSE, Henri (1895–1971). French archaeologist. Through his work on Hispano-moorish art from its beginnings to the 13th century he is known as the discoverer of the Hispano-Maghreb world and was one of the generation of archaeologists who developed systematic research.

THERMOLUMINESCENCE (dating). Thermo-luminescence is a physical phenomenon enabling us to date certain materials, such as pottery, flint and glass, provided they have been subjected to heat. Affected by radioactivity in the atmosphere, these materials undergo a change in the disposition of the electrons within the crystalline network of some of their component elements (quartz, zircon). On being heated in the laboratory they emit light whose intensity varies according to the amount of radioactivity to which they have been exposed since they were last heated. If the materials have never been subjected to heat, thermoluminescence measures their geological age, which is of little interest to the archaeologist. This method is widely used for dating ceramics and burnt pieces of flint.

THULE (culture). Culture of the ancestors of the Inuit peoples defined by the archaeologist Mathiassen in 1927. It appeared at the very end of the 1st millennium AD in the Bering Strait and spread rapidly across the whole American Arctic and to Greenland. It is characterized by an adaptation to the mainly marine resources of the Arctic, including whales. The tools of the Thule culture are mainly made of bone, ivory and polished slate rather than chipped stone. A series of coastal cultures in Alaska and Siberia that precede the Thule culture (Old Bering Sea, Okvik, Punuk, Birnik), as well as the Greenland Inugsuk culture, are today sometimes grouped together under the overall description of the "Thule tradition".

TRACEOLOGY. The study of the traces left by use on the cutting edges of stone tools. In about 1930 the Russian S.A. Semenov first had the idea of looking at the traces of use on prehistoric and experimental tools under the microscope. His work was not taken up again until about 1975 when several groups of research workers studied the worn edges of prehistoric and experimental tools in various enlargements.

TRADITION. Term used frequently in American archaeology (while in Europe it is little, or no longer, used) to embrace a set of distinct cultural groups (or the sites which represent them), all of which, however, have one or several common characteristics, such as: the use of a certain type of tool kit (for example, the tradition of fishtail heads in South America), a certain subsistence pattern (for example, tradition of the big game hunters), a certain way of life adapted to a particular environment (for example, the desert tradition, in North America).

TRIGONOLITH or **THREE-CORNERED STONE.** Triangular or breast-shaped stone object, with or without decoration, usually representing a *zemi* (q.v.). Small pottery or shell examples can also be found. They occur only in the West Indies.

TYRANNY. In the Greek city states, a form of dictatorship generally established following serious social tensions. In the Archaic period (700–480BC), tyranny covered the transition from the feudal regimes of the Geometric period (1100–700BC) to the representative and more or less democratic regimes of the classical period (480–338BC). The tyrants with the support of their personal guard often carried out a policy of major public works and of stimulating cultural and trading activity, showing similarities with the type of enlightened despotism practised by Napoleon Bonaparte. Thus in a number of great cities (Corinth, Athens, Samos) tyranny went hand in hand with crisis of growth. Outmoded in metropolitan Greece as a form of government from the end of the 6th century BC, tyranny continued in some overseas cities, especially in Sicily, until the Roman conquest.

UBAID culture. The Ubaid culture which is characterized by pottery with geometric patterns painted in black on a greenish base, came into being at the end of the 6th millennium BC in the low alluvial plain of Mesopotamia. It had a great drive towards expansion, and between 4500 and 3700BC it influenced almost the entire Near East, from the coasts of Syria to the Iranian plateau and the Arabian Gulf. As well as its pottery, it also disseminated a new model of society which directly foreshadowed the "urban revolution"; this is demonstrated in monumental architecture ("temples") and burial grounds which were from that time on set apart from the dwelling houses.

UGARITIC (language). Language spoken from at least the middle of the 2nd millennium at Ugarit and in the surrounding plain: it belonged to the so-called "western" group of Semitic languages (like Arabic and Hebrew) and was conveyed alphabetically, the alphabet being the earliest of which we have a complete record. When the region was laid waste at the beginning of the 12th century BC (Ugarit fell *c.* 1180BC), all written documents ceased, but Ugaritic itself must have continued in use and no date can be suggested for its disappearance.

UHLE, Max (1856–1944). German anthropologist, and author of many studies relating to various archaeological sites in Argentina, Bolivia (*Die Ruinenstaette von Tiahuanaco*, 1892), Chile, and, first and foremost, Peru. *Pachacámac*, published in 1898, describes the first stratigraphical study carried out in America. Uhle was the first to establish a chronological sequence for the cultures of Peru based on stratigraphy, and he suggests that these cultures originated in Mesoamerica. He published more than 130 books, and is regarded as the "father of Peruvian archaeology".

UMCHARA, Sueji (1893–1982). Born near Osaka, Japan, he played a part in cataloguing the archaeological collections of Kyōto University in 1914. In 1921 he was made responsible for excavations by the general government of Korea. From 1925–29 he travelled in Europe and the United States. He was awarded a doctorate in 1939 by the University of Kyōto for his study of the Bronze Age in China, on which he was one of the foremost experts.

URARTU. Kingdom which arose in the 9th century BC against the background of the Hurrian communities of eastern Anatolia and centred at first around Lake Van. In the 8th century it expanded northwards until it reached the River Aras and the southern Caucasus Mountains. It then formed the strongest power in western Asia, rivalled by Assyria which nevertheless exercised great cultural ascendancy over it. Though politically it became weaker in the 7th century BC it then developed intensely from the artistic point of view, with particularly brilliant achievements in the field of bronze work. The kingdom disappeared at the beginning of the 6th century BC with the rise of the newly formed Medic state.

URARTUAN (language). Urartuan is mainly known from rock-face inscriptions dating from the 8th century BC in the eastern part of Asia Minor. In its grammatical structure and its vocabulary it is close to Hurrian, though not directly descended from it.

URBAN COHORTS. Police force (4 cohorts of 480 men) responsible for security and public order in Rome, under the command of the City prefect. Carthage and Lyons also had an urban cohort.

URUK. One of the great Sumerian city states, developing on from the Ubaid period. It probably enjoyed a life of some 4,000 years, and was the site of numerous innovations, the most important of all being the invention of writing. In dynastic terms it was a religious and political centre. It lost its importance with the rise of Ur, *c.*2100BC, but remained occupied till the Parthian period.

VAILLANT, George C. (1901–45). The life of this great North American expert, known mainly for his work on the High Plateau of central Mexico, is fundamentally bound up with the radical movement of our knowledge of Mesoamerican chronology. He was the first to investigate systematically the remains predating the time when the Classical civilizations were at their height. His passion for chronology was also used to great effect in the Maya area.

VENTRIS, Michael (1922–56). English architect who for more than 15 years, using a systematic, coherent method of investigation, studied the Linear B script discovered by Arthur Evans at Knossos at the beginning of the century. By 1 June 1952 he was able to entitle a memo sent to ten or so scholars interested in Cretan scripts: *Are the Knossos and Pylos tablets written in Greek?* The evidence produced by his method was difficult to refute, and rapidly convinced international scientific opinion.

VESELOVSKY, Nikolai I (1848–1918). Russian archaeologist and Orientalist, he excavated the kurgan at Maikop in the Caucasus and a number of Scythian kurgans in the Kuban area (Kostromskaya, Kelermes, Ulskii–ayul) and on the Dneior (Solokha).

VEXILLATIO (Latin), pl. *VEXILLATIONES*. Detachment of soldiers commandeered from various corps and placed together under the command of a prefect. Through Latin inscriptions we know of *vexillationes* of auxiliaries and of legionaries. These detachments were mobile and flexible and were formed for specific operations, such as building a road or a fort or quelling a rebellion. They could on occasion operate far away from their usual quarters.

WELDING. Technique employed in protohistoric iron metallurgy whereby the blacksmith hammers together several bars which have been carburized to a greater or lesser extent (to form steel) so as to combine the different qualities of malleability or hardness of these metals. This method was used in Europe at the end of the Iron Age to produce formidably effective sword blades. During the early Middle Ages, welding was used extensively in the output of the great "barbarian" workshops.

WERNER, Joachim (*b.*1909). German archaeologist and the foremost expert on archaeological problems from the period of the migrations, Werner has concentrated on defining the chronology (by means of numismatics) and the typology of objects of the period (especially *fibulae* and buckle-plates), basing his work on the study of the topographical distribution of tombs and their grave goods. His research is fundamental to the study of Merovingian Gaul, the reign of Attila (*Beiträge zur Archäologie des Attila-Reiches*; Munich, 1956), the Lombards (*Die Langobarden in Pannonien*, Munich 1962), the Slavs and the Bulgarians (*Der Grabfund von Malaja Perescepina und Kuvrat, Kagan der Bulgaren*, Munich, 1984).

WHEELER, Sir Mortimer (1890–1976). After a career as an archaeologist in Great Britain, became director-general of the Archaeological Survey of India in 1944. He completely reorganized Indian archaeology, introducing new methods of excavation, in particular stratigraphical excavation. Before he left in 1947, he trained those who would be responsible for archaeology in India and Pakistan in the future in various key sites (Brahmagiri, Harappa).

WILTON. Stone-Age period subsequent to 15,000 BP in southern Africa. The name comes from a cave in the western part of Cape province.

WINCKELMANN, Johann Joachim (1717–68). A shoemaker's son, he took up residence in Rome in 1755. As a protégé of Cardinal Albani, in 1764 he was appointed the Pope's prefect for antiquities. His *History of the Art of Antiquity* (1764) prefigured a coherent system of critical analysis based on the primacy of Greek classical art, regarded as the absolute reference point. This setting of aesthetic norms made a lasting impression, especially in Germany, where Winckelmann is regarded as the founder and patron of classical archaeology.

WITSEN, Nicolas (1641–1717). Became burgomaster of Amsterdam after accompanying the Dutch ambassador to Moscow in 1664–1665, and kept in touch with a network of correspondents who sent him news from Russia, and pieces of ancient Siberian gold and silver work. In 1692 he published *Noord-en-Oost Tartarye*, with new editions in 1705 and 1785, illustrated with plates showing the items in his collection, which no longer exists today. He was a friend of Peter the Great who stayed with him in Amsterdam in 1697, and was instrumental in arousing his interest in Siberian antiquities.

X-RAY FLUORESCENCE SPECTROMETRY. Method of analysis that consists of subjecting the ceramic specimen to be analysed to an X-ray beam. The atoms in the specimen then re-emit a so-called fluorescence X-ray, the wavelength of which depends on the nature of the atoms present (qualitative analysis) and the intensity of which depends on the number of atoms present (quantitative analysis).

YAMS. These succulent tubers which came originally from Africa, have, in the course of a few thousand years, become much cultivated in Asia and America too. The plants occupy a vital place in the social and religious life of some African societies.

ZARZIAN. Name given to the epi-Paleolithic culture of Iraq and Iran, from the material found in the Zarzi cave in Iraqi Kurdistan (by D. Garrod 1931). The Zarzian industry was based on microliths, has almost no identifying features and is not widely known; towards the end of the period there were many geometric shapes. The application of the term from the Caspian Sea to the Zagros Mountains is somewhat contentious.

ZEBU. Race of cattle widespread in Africa and Madagascar: their characteristic feature is a fatty hump.

ZEMIS. Supernatural beings or divinities worshipped by the Taino Indians on the Greater Antilles (West Indies), often depicted on ceramic decorations or represented in stone or wooden sculpture.

ZEUXIPPOS WARE. Type of Byzantine pottery so named because it was first identified in excavations carried out at Instanbul near the old baths of Zeuxippos. It dates from the late 12th and early 13th century and is characterized by, among other things, a high quality of clay and firing.

ZHENMUSHOU. Modern Chinese term applied to a figure sculpted in natural or lacquered wood representing a divinity or a monster with stylized forms, the head of which usually has antlers standing out from it. Its eyes are globular and a disproportionately large tongue protrudes from the mouth. This carved figure, found on a great number of tombs in the Chu kingdom, has a magical power of protection against evil influences.

ZIGGURAT. Rectangular temple tower or tiered mound erected by the Sumerians. Akkadians and Babylonians in Mesopotamia in honour of their gods. The Tower of Babel is thought to be one of these.

ZOROASTRIANISM. Religion preached by Zoroaster in Central Asia some centuries before that area was integrated into the Persian Achaemenid empire around 540BC. Its doctrine is contained in the holy books of the *Avesta*, first handed down orally and then written down during the Sassanid dynasty (3rd–7th centuries AD): the Gathas, hymns attributed to Zoroaster himself, preach a strict dualism opposing Ahriman, the principle of evil, with the god Ahuramazda who is invested with every moral quality; the so-called "recent" *Avesta* reintroduces the cult of divinities which predated Zoroaster's message, the main ones being Mithra and Anahita. Zoroastrianism became the national religion of Iran under the Achaemenids, and was organized as a hierarchical state church under the Sassanians, while at the same time it had an independent life of its own in Central Asia. It still has about 130,000 followers, mainly in India (the Parsees) and in Iran.

Index

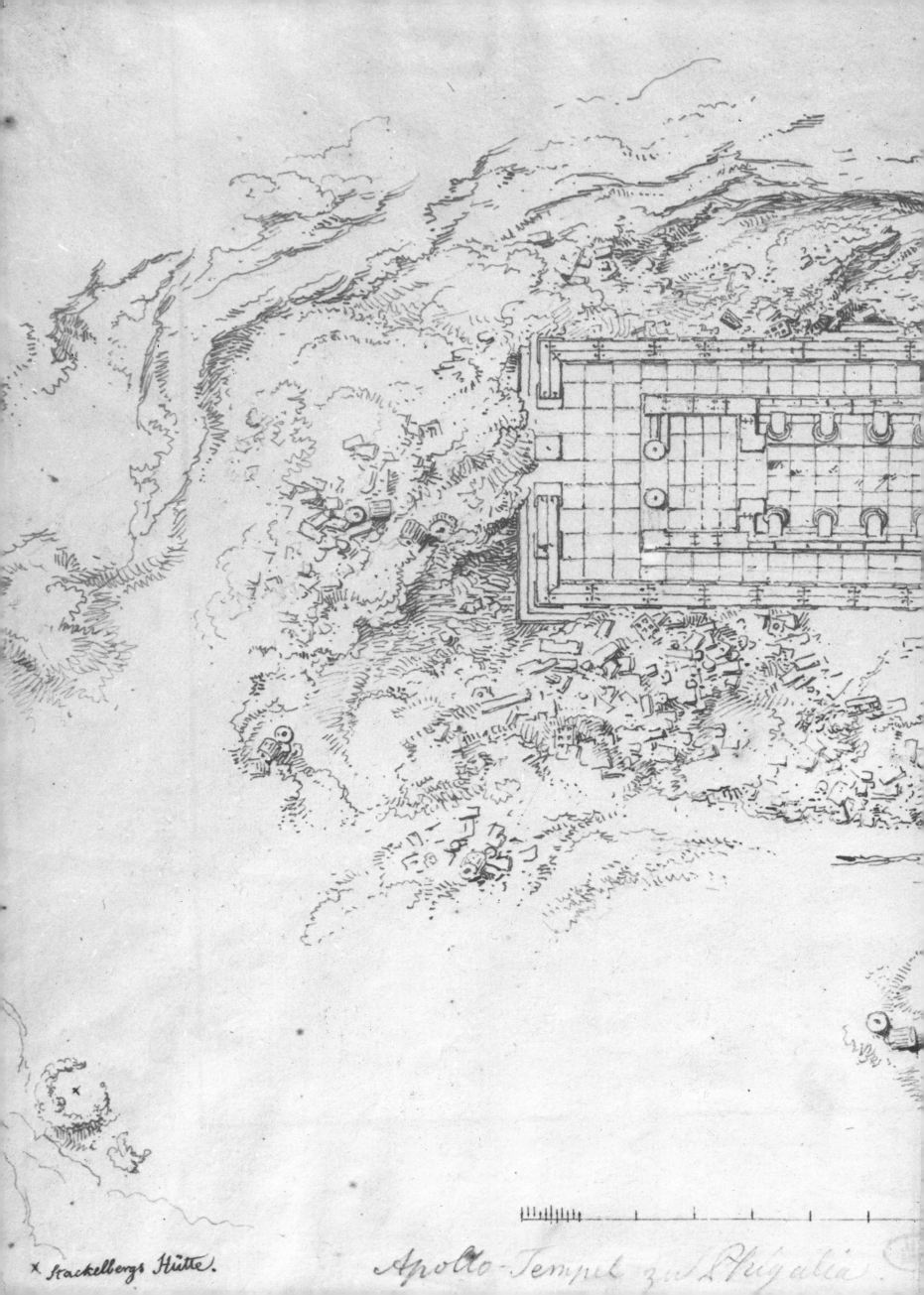

× Stackelbergs Hütte.　　　　　Apollo-Tempel zu Phigalia